ENCYCLOPEDIA OF WORLD BIOGRAPHY

7

ENCYCLOPEDIA OF WORLD BIOGRAPHY

SECOND EDITION

Grimke
Howells **7**

GALE

DETROIT • NEW YORK • TORONTO • LONDON

Staff

Senior Editor: Paula K. Byers
Project Editor: Suzanne M. Bourgoin
Managing Editor: Neil E. Walker

Editorial Staff: Luann Brennan, Frank V. Castronova, Laura S. Hightower, Karen E. Lemerand, Stacy A. McConnell, Jennifer Mossman, Maria L. Munoz, Katherine H. Nemeh, Terrie M. Rooney, Geri Speace

Permissions Manager: Susan M. Tosky
Permissions Specialist: Maria L. Franklin
Permissions Associate: Michele M. Lonoconus
Image Cataloger: Mary K. Grimes

Production Director: Mary Beth Trimper
Production Manager: Evi Seoud
Production Associate: Shanna Heilveil
Product Design Manager: Cynthia Baldwin
Senior Art Director: Mary Claire Krzewinski

Research Manager: Victoria B. Cariappa
Research Specialists: Michele P. LaMeau, Andrew Guy Malonis, Barbara McNeil, Gary J. Oudersluys
Research Associates: Julia C. Daniel, Tamara C. Nott, Norma Sawaya, Cheryl L. Warnock
Research Assistant: Talitha A. Jean

Graphic Services Supervisor: Barbara Yarrow
Image Database Supervisor: Randy Bassett
Imaging Specialist: Mike Lugosz

Manager of Data Entry Services: Eleanor M. Allison
Data Entry Coordinator: Kenneth D. Benson

Manager of Technology Support Services: Theresa A. Rocklin
Programmers/Analysts: Mira Bossowska, Jeffrey Muhr, Christopher Ward

Copyright © 1998
Gale Research
835 Penobscot Bldg.
Detroit, MI 48226-4094

ISBN 0-7876-2221-4 (Set)
ISBN 0-7876-2547-7 (Volume 7)

Library of Congress Cataloging-in-Publication Data

Encyclopedia of world biography / [edited by Suzanne Michele Bourgoin and Paula Kay Byers].
      p. cm.
    Includes bibliographical references and index.
    Summary: Presents brief biographical sketches which provide vital statistics as well as information on the importance of the person listed.
    ISBN 0-7876-2221-4 (set : alk. paper)
    1. Biography—Dictionaries—Juvenile literature. [1. Biography.]
I. Bourgoin, Suzanne Michele, 1968- . II. Byers, Paula K. (Paula Kay), 1954- .
CT 103.E56 1997
920′ .003—dc21
                                    97-42327
                                      CIP
                                      AC

Printed in the United States of America
10 9 8 7 6 5 4 3

ENCYCLOPEDIA OF
WORLD BIOGRAPHY

7

G

Archibald Henry Grimké

Archibald Henry Grimké (1849-1930), American lawyer, author, and diplomat, was an ardent champion of equal rights for black people.

Archibald Grimké was born on Aug. 17, 1849, near Charleston, S.C., of Nancy Weston, a slave by birth, and Henry Grimké, a prosperous white planter with liberal tendencies. Grimké entered Lincoln University, Pa., earning his bachelor of arts degree (1870) and master of arts degree (1872). Aided by his white aunts, Sarah and Angelina Grimké, and Angelina's husband, Theodore Weld, he completed Harvard Law School (1874). Grimké entered law practice in Boston with an established firm and met many former abolitionists and reformers. In 1879 he married Sarah E. Stanley and began his career as a civil rights spokesman and author.

From 1883 to 1885 Grimké edited the *Hub,* a Boston newspaper devoted to the welfare of African Americans. At the invitation of a leading publishing firm he wrote biographies of two antislavery leaders: *William Lloyd Garrison, the Abolitionist* (1891) and *The Life of Charles Sumner, the Scholar in Politics* (1892). Meanwhile he was a special columnist for several newspapers and contributed to the *Atlantic Monthly.*

From 1894 to 1898 Grimké served as U.S. consul to Santo Domingo. Returning to the United States, he lived in Washington, D.C., where he continued to champion civil rights and combat prejudice. In 1899, representing the Colored National League, he wrote an open letter to President William McKinley on behalf of black voters. He became a member of the American Negro Academy almost from its inception in 1897, serving as president from 1903 to 1916.

Throughout this period Grimké published articles and pamphlets concerning black life and history. These included "Right on the Scaffold, or the Martyrs of 1822" (1901), a life of Denmark Vesey, leader of a slave revolt; "Why Disfranchisement Is Bad" (1904), showing the harmful effect of disfranchisement on African Americans, the South, and the nation; "The Ballotless Victim of One Party Governments" (1913), attacking disfranchisement; "The Sex Question and Race Segregation" (1915), a protest against the double standard; "The Ultimate Criminal" (1915), demonstrating the causal relationship between discrimination and crimes committed by African Americans; and "The Shame of America, or the Negro's Case against the Republic" (1924). These are all in the *Occasional Papers of the American Negro Academy,* reprinted in 1969.

In 1913 Grimké wrote President Woodrow Wilson, protesting segregation of government employees, and in 1916, as national director of the National Association for the Advancement of Colored People (NAACP), he testified against segregation before the House Committee on Reform in the Civil Service. In 1919 the NAACP awarded him the Spingarn Medal.

Grimké was president of the Frederick Douglass Memorial and Historical Association and a member of both the Authors' Club of London and the United States and of the American Social Science Association. He died on Feb. 25, 1930.

Further Reading

Aspects of Grimké's career are discussed in Anna Julia Cooper, *Life and Writings of the Grimké Family* (2 vols. in 1, 1951), and Gerda Lerner, *The Grimké Sisters from South Carolina:*

1

Rebels against Slavery (1967). Biographical sketches of Grimké are in Richard Bardolph, *The Negro Vanguard* (1959), and Wilhelmena S. Robinson, *Historical Negro Biographies* (1967; 2d ed. 1968). His writings are discussed in Vernon Loggins, *The Negro Author: His Development in America to 1900* (1931).

Additional Sources

Bruce, Dickson D., *Archibald Grimké: portrait of a black independent,* Baton Rouge: Louisiana State University Press, 1993. ☐

Sarah Moore and Angelina Emily Grimké

Sarah Moore (1792-1873) and Angelina Emily (1805-1879) Grimké were antislavery leaders and early agitators for woman's rights.

Sarah Grimké

Sarah Grimké was born on Nov. 29, 1792, and Angelina Grimké was born on Feb. 20, 1805; their father was a distinguished South Carolina jurist. Partly through the influence of their older brother Thomas, who was prominent in temperance and pacifist reforms, and partly from their own religious beliefs, the sisters early opposed slavery, although the family owned several slaves.

On a trip to Philadelphia in 1819 Sarah was converted to Quakerism and later so was Angelina Grimké. They settled in Philadelphia in the 1820s. The Quakers' passivity failed to satisfy energetic Angelina. After reading William Lloyd Garrison's abolitionist newspaper, the *Liberator,* she wrote to him and then wrote a pamphlet, which the abolitionist press eagerly published. Her *An Appeal to the Christian Women of the South* (1836) urged her Southern sisters to "overthrow this horrible system of oppression and cruelty, licentiousness and wrong." That this was written by a Southern woman made it unusually valuable to the antislavery cause and aroused such disapproval in South Carolina that authorities threatened to prosecute Angelina if she returned.

Sarah Grimké, shyer than her sister, wrote *An Epistle to the Clergy of the Southern States* (1836), urging churches to oppose slavery on religious grounds. The sisters freed the slaves they had inherited and offered their services to the Northern abolitionists. "As I left my native state," wrote Angelina, "to escape the sound of the driver's lash and the shrieks of tortured victims, I would gladly bury in oblivion the recollections of those scenes. But it may not, it cannot be."

The Grimké sisters were highly effective in speaking to and organizing women. The American Antislavery Society appointed them lecturers (after much discussion of the propriety of sponsoring women to speak in public), and in 1836-1837 "Carolina's high-souled daughters," as John Greenleaf Whittier named them, toured New York and New England. The prevailing prejudice against women appearing publicly before "promiscuous assemblies," however, led to many objections and brought up the question of women's rights. Sarah's *Letters on the Equality of the Sexes* (1838) and Angelina's *Appeal to the Women of the Nominally Free States* (1837) firmly linked the rights of slaves to the rights of women and helped introduce the divisive "woman question" into the abolitionist movement. Garrison urged them to continue speaking. But Theodore Weld counseled Angelina not to "push your *women's* rights until *human* rights have gone ahead."

After Weld and Angelina Grimké were married on May 14, 1838 (they had one son, Charles Stuart), the sisters spent most of their time assisting Weld with his writing and his political work in Washington. When Weld, in poor health, retired from the abolitionist movement in 1843, Sarah accompanied the couple to New York and later helped conduct Weld's interracial school in New Jersey. Sarah died on Dec. 23, 1873, and Angelina on Oct. 26, 1879.

Further Reading

Catherine H. Birney, *The Grimké Sisters: Sarah and Angelina Grimké, the First American Advocates of Abolition and Women's Rights* (1885), adulatory and old-fashioned, is still useful. The best modern study is Gerda Lerner, *The Grimké Sisters from South Carolina: Rebels against Slavery* (1967). Gilbert H. Barnes and Dwight L. Dumond, eds., *The Letters of Theodore Dwight Weld, Angelina Grimké and Sarah Grimké*

(2 vols., 1934), remains the major source of biographical information. □

Jakob and Wilhelm Karl Grimm

The brothers Jakob Karl (1785-1863) and Wilhelm Karl (1786-1859) Grimm were German scholars, known for their "Fairy Tales" and for their work in comparative linguistics, which included the formulation of "Grimm's law."

Wilhelm (left) and Jakob Grimm

The romantic movement in Germany awakened the Germans' interest in the past of their own country, especially its cultural origins, early language, and folklore. Although some work in the rediscovery and edition of medieval German literature had already been undertaken in the 18th century, it was the first generation of romantic poets and theorists about the beginning of the next century, especially Ludwig Tieck, Novalis, and the Schlegel brothers, who first focused national attention on the origins of German culture and literature. While most of the poets viewed medieval literature chiefly as an inspiration for their own writings, others turned their attention to the methodical investigation of the past. The Grimm brothers were the most important of these romantic historians of early medieval language and folklore.

Jakob Grimm was born on Jan. 4, 1785, in Hanau. His brother, Wilhelm, was born on February 24 of the following year. As small children, they were inseparable and, aside from a brief period of living apart, they were to remain together for the rest of their lives. Their eventempered dispositions assured cooperation on all the projects they undertook together. The main difference in their personalities seems to be that Jakob, the more robust of the two, had more taste for grueling research work, and it was he who worked out most of their grammatical and linguistic theories. Wilhelm was physically weaker but had a somewhat warmer temperament and more taste for music and literature. His literary talent was responsible for the pleasant style of their collection of fairy tales.

The brothers first attended school in Kassel, then began legal studies at the University of Marburg. While there, however, the inspiration of Friedrich von Savigny awakened in them an interest in past cultures. In 1808 Jakob was named court librarian to the King of Westphalia in Wilhelmshöhe, and in 1816 he became librarian in Kassel, where Wilhelm had been employed since 1814. They were to remain there until 1830, when they obtained positions at the University of Göttingen.

"Grimm's Fairy Tales"

For some years the brothers had been in contact with the romantic poets Clemens Brentano and Achim von Arnim, who in Heidelberg were preparing a collection of German folk songs. Following their own interests in folklore and legends, the brothers brought out their first collection of tales, *Kinder-und Hausmärchen* (*Tales of Children and the Home*), in 1812. These tales were collected by recording stories told by peasants and villagers. Wilhelm put them into literary form and gave them a pleasant, childlike style. The brothers added many scholarly footnotes on the tales' sources and analogs.

In addition, the Grimms worked on editing remnants of other folklore and primitive literature. Between 1816 and 1818 they published two volumes of *Deutsche Sagen* (*German Legends*), and about the same time they published a volume of studies in early literary history, *Altdeutsche Wälder* (*Old German Forests*).

Linguistic Research

In later years their interest in older literature led the Grimm brothers increasingly to a study of older languages and their relationship to modern German. Jakob, especially, began to specialize in the history and structure of the German language. The first edition of his *Deutsche Grammatik* (*German Grammar*) was published in 1819. Later editions show increasing development of a scientific method in linguistics.

The brothers, and especially Jakob, were also working to codify the relationship between similar words of related languages, such as English *apple* and German *Apfel*. Their formulation of the rules for such relationships became known as "Grimm's law." It was later elaborated to account for all word relationships in the Indo-European group of languages. The Grimm brothers were not the first to take note of such similarities, but they can be credited with amassing the bulk of linguistic data and working out the details of the rules.

Later Years

In 1830 the brothers moved to the University of Göttingen, where Jakob was named professor and head librarian and Wilhelm was appointed assistant librarian. As professor, Jakob held lectures on linguistics and cultural history. Wilhelm also attained the rank of professor in 1835. Both were dismissed in 1835 for political reasons: they had joined in signing a protest against the King's decision to abolish the Hanover constitution. They first moved back to Kassel but later obtained professorships at Berlin, where they were to remain until their deaths.

Their last years were spent in preparing the definitive dictionary of the German language, tracing the etymological derivation of every word. The first volume, published in 1854, has 1,824 pages and gets only as far as the word *Biermolke.* Four pages are devoted to the letter A alone, which is termed "the most noble and primeval of all sounds." The Grimms' dictionary was carried on by generations of scholars after the brothers' deaths, and it was finished in 1960. Its completed form consists of 16 weighty volumes.

Wilhelm died in Berlin on Dec. 16, 1859. Jakob continued the work on the dictionary and related projects until his death in Berlin on Sept. 20, 1863.

Further Reading

A good biographical study of the Grimm brothers is Murray B. Peppard, *Paths through the Forest: A Biography of the Brothers Grimm* (1971). Informative brief discussions of their lives and works can be found in more general studies of the German romantic movement. Perhaps the best is Ralph Tymms, *German Romantic Literature* (1955), which discusses the romantics' attitudes toward folklore and legends. A brief treatment of the brothers, chiefly as editors of the *Tales,* is also in L. A. Willoughby, *The Romantic Movement in Germany* (1966). Further helpful discussions, with literary background material, may be found in Oskar Walzel, *German Romanticism* (trans. 1932). □

Hans Jakob Christoffel von Grimmelshausen

The German author Hans Jakob Christoffel von Grimmelshausen (1621?-1676) is best known for his picaresque romance, "Simplicissimus," the greatest 17th-century German prose work.

There is little accurate information about Jakob von Grimmelshausen. Some of his ancestors were Protestants and became wine growers, innkeepers, and bakers. Grimmelshausen was born in Gelnhausen, Hesse. The description of the early life of Simplicissimus in the Thirty Years War is to some degree autobiographical. Grimmelshausen spent some years as soldier's boy and wagoner in the imperial forces; he served as musketeer and later as secretary in the Schauenburg regiment. A year after the Peace of Westphalia (1648) he married Catharina Henninger, the 21-year-old daughter of a lieutenant in Schauenburg's army. Later, in the service of Lt. Col. Schauenburg, Grimmelshausen was a bailiff—an office which he held until ca. 1659. He then became an innkeeper. Finally, from 1667 he was a magistrate who collected taxes and administrated the law in Renchen.

It was not until Grimmelshausen was over 40 years old that he published *Schwarz and Weiss oder der satirische Pilgram* (1666), a book inspired by and modeled on H. M. Moscherosch's *Wunderliche and wahrhaftige Geschichte Philanders von Sittewald* (1642). About that time he also wrote fashionable love stories, but his world fame justly rests with *Der abenteuerliche Simplicissimus Teutsch* (ca. 1668). This extraordinary literary success led him to write more Simplicissimus stories, which he considered parts of his great novel: *Trutz-Simplex; oder ausführliche und wunderseltzame Lebensbeschreibung der Ertzbetrügerin und Landstörtzerin Courasche* (1670), *Der seltzame Springinsfeld* (1670), and *Das wunderbarliche Vogel-Nest* (1672). Bertolt Brecht's *Mutter Courage* obviously borrowed its title from the above, and Brecht may also, at least to some extent, have modeled Courage's character on Simplicissimus's cast-off mistress. Grimmelshausen, moreover, wrote gallant heroic romances such as *Dietwald und Amelinde* (1670). He published all his works anonymously; that is, he assigned them to fictitious writers whose names he liked to invent partly out of letters of his own name.

Simplicissimus is, after Wolfram von Eschenbach's *Parzival* and before Goethe's *Faust,* one of the greatest original and artistic documents in German literature, in which the struggle between good and evil, purity of heart and lustful greed, is presented with vivid immediacy. This novel transcends the horizon of a merely bawdy, picaresque story; it is much more than an entertaining tale full of coarse descriptions of bestial adventures and human follies. It clearly leads the reader through godless unrest and sinfulness into an existence of inwardness and a recognition of the individual's responsibility toward society: being a creature of this earth man must recognize and accept his limitations; only through God's grace can man ever transcend himself.

When, in 1674, Louis XIV plundered Alsace and the neighboring regions, Renchen was endangered. Grimmelshausen did military service for the imperial army, but at the same time he remained a magistrate in his little town, where on Aug. 17, 1676, he died.

Further Reading

There is no biography of Grimmelshausen in English. A valuable background study is Roy Pascal, *German Literature in the Sixteenth and Seventeenth Centuries,* vol. 2: *Renaissance, Reformation, Baroque* (1968), in the Introductions to German Literature Series. □

Juan Gris

The Spanish painter Juan Gris (1887-1927) is one of the major cubist painters. His work is distinguished by its lucidity and austerity.

Juan Gris, whose real name was José Victoriano Gonzalez, was born in Madrid on March 23, 1887. He studied engineering at Madrid's School of Arts and Sciences. He also took painting lessons with the minor academic artist José Maria Carbonero and sold humorous drawings to local newspapers.

Gris arrived in Paris in 1906 and remained in France the rest of his life. He had skipped military service, so he could not return to Spain. He settled in the Bateau Lavoir, a tenement that housed many painters, critics, and poets, and there he met Pablo Picasso, Georges Braque, Guillaume Apollinaire, Max Jacob, and Maurice Raynal. Gris produced his first cubist paintings in 1911-1912; they were in the analytical cubist vein of Braque and Picasso but characterized by a metalliclike sheen, as in the *Guitar and Flowers* (1912) and the *Portrait of Picasso* (1912), in which Picasso's Napoleonic attitude is cleverly caught. The year 1913 marks the beginning of Gris's synthetic cubism, a cubist approach in which the object was no longer faceted into smaller parts but was recombined with other objects or parts of objects to form a new esthetic totality.

Gris and his wife spent the summer of 1913 with Picasso at Ceret, and that year Gris began to use collage consistently in his work. Gris's early collages are frequently richer in detail and bolder in color than contemporary collages of Picasso and Braque, as in the *Guitar, Glasses, and Bottle* (1914).

In 1914 Gris spent time with Henri Matisse at Collioure. Gris returned to Paris in 1915, and he suffered bleak poverty during World War I. In late 1916 his paintings became more stately and architectonic, and forms became larger and flatter as multiple viewpoints were to an extent abandoned, as in the *Violin* (1916). Gris referred to these paintings as "flat, colored architecture." In 1917 he executed his only sculpture, a painted plaster *Harlequin,* which was close to what Jacques Lipchitz was doing at the time.

Between 1917 and 1920 Gris introduced a new complexity in his art. He set up interplays between objects and their shadows and reintroduced complicated planar intersections and sumptuous colors and textures, as in the *Fruit Bowl on Checkered Cloth* (1917). In 1920 he participated in the Salon des Indépendants at the last exhibition of the united cubist group. That year he fell ill with pleurisy and wintered at Bandol, where he discussed with the ballet impresario Sergei Diaghilev plans for décors for ballets. Some of these commissions were canceled through intrigues, but others, like *Les Tentations de la Bergère,* were executed in 1922 and 1923.

Daniel Henry Kahnweiler, who became Gris's dealer in 1920, wrote the first monograph on the painter in 1929. Kahnweiler praised the works of the artist's last period, but many subsequent critics found them empty compared to his previous output. It was as though Gris were producing parodies of himself: in single works there is an uncertain wavering between austerity and decorative complexities, as in the *Two Pierrots* (1922). Gris's health continued to deteriorate in his last years.

In 1924 and 1925 Gris spent much of his time writing and lecturing on his views on painting. In 1924 he delivered a paper at the Sorbonne, *Les Possibilités de la peinture (On the Possibilities of Painting),* which was later translated and widely published. He died in Paris on May 11, 1927.

One of Gris's most famous pronouncements was made in 1921: "I consider that the architectural element is mathematics, the abstract side; I want to humanize it. Cézanne turns a bottle into a cylinder, but I begin with a cylinder and create an individual out of a special type: I make a bottle—a particular bottle—out of a cylinder." Recent investigations have shown that precise measurements, some incorporating a golden mean, were used in a few of Gris's paintings.

Further Reading

An intimate view of Gris is in *Letters of Juan Gris, 1913-1927,* collected by Daniel Henry Kahnweiler and translated and edited by Douglas Cooper (1956). The best study of Gris is Kahnweiler's *Juan Gris: His Life and Work,* translated by Cooper (1947; rev. ed. 1969), which is a moving tribute by the artist's loyal friend and dealer and a penetrating analysis of Gris's character and work. The book also includes most of Gris's published writings in English translation. James Thrall Soby, *Juan Gris* (1958), is a useful guide to the artist's development. □

John Grisham

Popular novelist John Grisham (born 1955) is the author of several thrillers that have been made into blockbuster films. His works, which center around the legal profession, include *A Time to Kill, The Firm, The Client,* and *The Pelican Brief.*

I t is no understatement that John Grisham, author of the legal thrillers *A Time to Kill, The Firm, The Pelican Brief,* and *The Client,* has achieved the status of what *Entertainment Weekly* called "a genuine pop-culture demigod." His have shared unprecedented weeks—and months—on best-seller lists, have numbered more than 60 million in print across the world, and have been translated into 31 languages. Dubbed "grab-it-at-the-airport" novels, they have also made their author a multimillionaire; Grisham's income for the 1992-93 fiscal year alone was $25 million. Along with author Scott Turow, also a former practicing attorney, Grisham has been credited with mastering a genre: the fast-paced, plot-driven legal thriller that thrusts an unwitting, sympathetic hero or heroine in the middle of a corrupt conspiracy and provides them with the means to extricate themselves. Despite his seemingly untouchable success, Grisham still wants each novel he writes to improve upon the last. "[Right now] I could crank out anything, and it would sell," he told the same source. "But I want the next to be better than the first five. That keeps me awake at night."

Drawn to Courtroom Drama

Born in Arkansas in 1955, Grisham spent much of his childhood traveling with his family throughout the South, settling for short periods in places where his father, a construction worker, managed to find work. When Grisham was 12, he moved with his parents and four siblings to Southaven, Mississippi. "We didn't have a lot of money," he remembered in *People,* "but we didn't know it. We were well fed and loved and scrubbed." Though not a stellar student in high school, he excelled in sports—baseball, in particular—and was captivated by the novels of John Steinbeck. Grisham later attended Mississippi State University, where he received his B.S. degree in accounting and decided on a career as a tax attorney. His first course on tax law at the University of Mississippi dampened his interest,

however, and he switched to criminal-defense law instead, discovering that he was drawn to courtroom drama and had the ability to think well under pressure.

After graduating from law school and passing the bar exam in 1981, Grisham married Renee Jones, a childhood friend from Southaven, and the couple returned to their home town where Grisham became a litigator. In recalling his first murder trial, he told *People,* "I defended a guy who shot another guy in self-defense, but I had to explain why he shot him in the head six times at three-inch range. It was a pretty gruesome case, but I won." When he shifted his focus to more lucrative civil cases, his practice began to thrive, and he is credited with one of the largest damage settlements in De Soto County, which he won on behalf of a child who sustained extensive burns when a water heater exploded. In 1983 Grisham was elected to the Mississippi state legislature, where he served as a Democrat for seven years, hoping to increase spending for education. However, he resigned from his position before the end of his second term, because, as he told the same source, "I realized it was impossible to make changes."

Inspired by Real-Life Trial

The incident that inspired Grisham's first novel, *A Time to Kill,* occurred years before it was actually written, when he was still practicing law in Southaven in 1984. One day he went to the local courthouse to observe a trial and heard a ten-year-old girl testify against a man who had raped her, leaving her for dead. "I never felt such emotion and human drama in my life," Grisham remembered in *People.* "I became obsessed wondering what it would be like if the girl's father killed that rapist and was put on trial. I had to write it down.'' Despite the 70 hours a week he was putting in at his own firm, he was able to complete *A Time to Kill* by waking up at 5:00 each morning to write, a schedule that he adhered to for three years. Then, in 1987, after the manuscript had been rejected by several publishers, New York agent Jay Garon offered to represent Grisham. Garon made a deal with Wynwood Press for $15,000, and two years later, 5,000 copies of *A Time to Kill* were published, one thousand of which Grisham bought himself. Of all his novels, it's the only one that he will not sell to Hollywood for a movie version, because, as he remarked in *Entertainment Weekly,* ''it would be very, very easy to botch if it's not done with a great deal of delicateness and feeling. It's very dear and very special to me.''

The *Firm* was also rejected by numerous publishers and might have suffered a similar fate as *A Time to Kill* if a bootleg copy of the manuscript hadn't started a bidding war in Hollywood. Early in 1990 Renee Grisham called her husband out of church to inform him that Paramount had offered him $600,000 for the movie rights to his book, and Grisham soon signed a contract with Doubleday, one of the publishers who had rejected *A Time to Kill* two years earlier. *The Firm* is the story of Harvard Law School graduate Mitchell McDeere, who signs on with a prestigious Memphis law firm offering him an irresistible package: an excellent salary and such perks as a new BMW car, a low-interest mortgage, and membership in a posh country club. Yet just as Mitchell and his wife, Abby, are settling into their new upscale lifestyle, two of the firm's lawyers die mysteriously, and FBI investigators start pressuring the young lawyer for inside information. When he learns that the Mafia has set up the firm to launder money, Mitch faces the decision of whether to cooperate with the FBI and risk his life, or be implicated with the other firm members and spend time in prison. For Grisham, completing *The Firm* signalled a turning point: he decided to close his law practice and write full time.

Best-Seller for 47 Weeks

People magazine called *The Firm* a ''thriller of the first order, powered to pulse-racing perfection by the realism of its malevolent barristers,'' and *Library Journal* noted that Grisham ''set a daringly high standard, one that his readers will hope he can reach again and again.'' A *New York Times* best-seller for 47 weeks—and the longest-running paperback on *Publishers Weekly* best-seller list—*The Firm* was made into a the 1992 film directed by Sidney Pollack, starring Tom Cruise, Gene Hackman, Jeanne Tripplehorn, and Holly Hunter, among others.

Grisham's next effort to be adapted for the big screen 1993's *The Pelican Brief,* featuring Julia Roberts and Denzel Washington. Although Grisham usually disassociates himself from the movie versions of his novels, he was apparently pleased with this one, which he and wife Renee first watched with President and Mrs. Clinton at the White House. Not only was it rated PG-13, meaning that his children could see it, but it was, as he told *Entertainment*

Weekly, ''a wonderful adaptation of the novel. [Director] Alan Pakula's vision was very similar to mine.''

In this story, Darby Shaw, a Tulane University law student, prepares a legal brief that becomes a crucial puzzle piece in an FBI investigation of a suspected conspiracy behind the murders of two Supreme Court justices. Like Mitch in *The Firm,* Darby spends much of her time narrowly escaping the evil forces around her, though here Grisham targets other bureaucratic agencies—the CIA and White House, in addition to the FBI—as demoralized and corrupt. This novel, however, did not fare as well with reviewers: *Time* claimed that it ''is as close to its predecessor as you can get without running *The Firm* through the office copier''; *Publishers Weekly* complained that the ''hairbreadth escapes . . . are too many and too frequent, and the menace wears thin, partly because the characters lack the humanity of those in Grisham's earlier novels.'' Nevertheless Grisham remained stoic about the criticism, telling Michelle Bearden of *Publishers Weekly:* ''It's the American way. As a rookie, people were really pulling for me with *The Firm,* but the second time around, those same people were secretly wishing I would fail so they could rip me to shreds.''

Ordinary People, Heroic Deeds

Grisham has gotten into the habit of beginning his next novel the morning after he has sent a completed manuscript to agent Garon in New York. In shaping a story he adheres to what he considers three basic principles: an opening that grips readers and makes them want to continue reading, a middle that sustains the narrative tension, and an ending that brings the action to an edge-of-your-seat climax. As in *The Firm* and *The Pelican Brief,* his protagonists are often ordinary people who find themselves caught in the middle of a conspiracy and must perform heroic feats to save their own and others' lives. ''And always, there's something dark, shadowy and sinister lurking in the background,'' the author told Bearden. While he seems to have hit on a surefire formula for his novels, Grisham credits Renee, who offers him particular advice on his women characters, for her role as an editor and a critic. His manuscripts must meet with her approval before publishers even see them. ''She makes those [editors] in New York look like children,'' he was quoted as saying in *Publishers Weekly.*

In reflecting on what appears to be a trend—popular books being written by attorneys-turned-writers—Grisham confided to Bearden that ''most lawyers I know would rather be doing something else.'' Yet he admits, according to *People,* that much of the fiction churned out by these professionals is ''dreadful,'' and that to be a ''master'' of the genre—a category in which he places only himself and authors Scott Turow and Steve Martini—a writer must be able to convey the legal aspects of a story without overwhelming or alienating the reader. *Publishers Weekly* commended Grisham on this very point in its review of *The Firm:* ''[The author] lucidly describes law procedures at the highest levels, smoothly meshing them with the criminal events of the narrative.'' Still Grisham acknowledges that in some respects, his writing process still needs fine-tuning. In particular, he wishes that he had dedicated more time to

The Pelican Brief and *The Client,* which he wrote in three months and six months, respectively. He has also endeavored to address past criticism that his novels contain shallow characters by slowing down the narrative pace in his most recent books and adding more depth and dimension to the personalities he creates.

Developed Characters in *The Client*

The Client, which is not a true mystery because the crime, motive, and criminal are all revealed within the first chapter of the book, reflects Grisham's growing interest in character development. Mark Sway, a streetwise 11-year-old who has grown up too fast due to an absent father and little money, becomes the unwitting witness to a suicide; yet before he kills himself, lawyer Jerome Clifford tells Mark where the body of a U.S. senator has been buried and who the killer is. Once word spreads to the Mafia and FBI that Mark has this information, his life is in danger, and he retains the legal services of Reggie Love, a middle-aged female attorney whose life has been even more difficult than his own. Grisham not only put their relationship at the emotional center of *The Client* but also invented more complex and well-rounded minor characters than in past books, and his efforts did not go unnoticed among reviewers: *Publishers Weekly* commended his creation of "two singular protagonists sure to elicit readers' empathy," and *People* found the character of Reggie Love to be "a truly memorable heroine . . . well worth a return visit."

With his novel *The Chamber,* Grisham put in more time—it took more than nine months to write—*and* wrote it out longhand, which he had not done since he'd penned his first effort, *A Time to Kill. The Chamber* features Sam Cayhall, an aging former Ku Klux Klan member who has been convicted of bombing the office of a Jewish civil rights lawyer and killing the man's two young sons. In trying to prevent Cayhall's execution after he has received the death penalty, a shrewd lawyer named Adam—who turns out to be Cayhall's grandson—not only faces bureaucratic agencies that seem as debased as the criminal himself but, finally, he confronts his own conscience. *Time* applauded Grisham for his struggle to show the complexities of capital punishment as an ethical issue: "[The Chamber] is a work produced by painful writhing over a terrible paradox; vengeance may be justified, but killing is a shameful, demeaning response to evil." Grisham was also pleased with the outcome of this novel and particularly proud of its characters. "It's much more about the people," he told *Entertainment Weekly.* "It will appeal to different kinds of readers. I have no doubts about it."

Returned to the Courtroom

For Grisham, the 1980s meant hard work and, at times, going without. While *A Time to Kill* has since joined the ranks of his other novels in best-sellerdom, it was not very long ago that he couldn't give copies away for free. "We'd give them as Christmas gifts," his friend and fellow state legislator Bobby Moak recalled in *Entertainment Weekly.* "A truckload got wet and mildewed, so we just took 'em to the dump. It was hell gettin' rid of those dadgum things."

That was a far cry from Grisham's success in the 1990s. He was paid a $3.75 million advance for the *The Chamber,* and his 1995 book, *The Rainmaker,* shot to the top of the best-seller lists. In *The Rainmaker,* a poor young lawyer fights a corrupt insurance company. *Entertainment Weekly* commented, "*The Rainmaker* seems very tapped into America's current skepticism about lawyers and the legal system."

Continuing his focus on the legal system and current topics, Grisham in 1996 released *The Runaway Jury.* The story centers around a trial in which a woman, Celeste Wood, is suing a cigarette company for the death of her husband, Jacob. There is much intrigue and inside dealings with the jury, especially the secretive juror Nicholas Easter. Christopher Lehmann-Haupt in the *New York Times* commented, "The story's suspense builds like that of a lengthening cigarette ash that refuses to drop off," and praised the plot as "entertainingly unpredictable."

In addition to his writing career, in 1995 Grisham announced he was returning to the courtroom. He had not practiced law for seven years, but agreed to represent the estate of an employee of the Illinois Central Railroad who was killed on the job. He had accepted the case in 1991. *USA Today* reported that Grisham "came across as a nice guy: well-prepared, deferential, sincere-sounding and self-effacing."

Continuing to craft best-selling novels, Grisham saw the publication of *The Partner* in 1997. In this story, a lawyer steals $90 million from his firm and its wealthiest client, fakes his own death, and flees to Brazil. "For lawyers, the main dream of escape is to get out of the profession," Grisham told the *New York Times.* "They dream about a big settlement, a home run, so that they can use the money to do something else." Grisham himself has taken the money and run, all the way to Hollywood, which routinely turns his novels into movies.

In the wake of his success, Grisham continues to rely on friends and family to help him stay grounded. He and Renee have used part of their windfall to build a Victorian-style home on 20 acres of land in Oxford, Mississippi, and he spends as much time as he can with his children—attending his daughter Shea's soccer matches and coaching his son Ty in Little League. Grisham, who never loses sight of the fact that his success may be transient, remains positive about those blessings in his life that cannot be measured by book sales. "Ten years from now I plan to be sitting here, looking out over my land," he told *People.* "I hope I'll be writing books, but if not, I'll be on my pond fishing with my kids. I feel like the luckiest guy I know."

Further Reading

Entertainment Weekly, April 1, 1994; May 5, 1995.
Library Journal, January 1991.
New York Times, May 23, 1996, p. B5; March 31, 1997, p. C11.
People, April 8, 1991; March 16, 1992; March 15, 1993.
Publishers Weekly, January 11, 1991; January 20, 1992; February l, 1993; February 22, 1993.
Time, March 9, 1992; June 20, 1994. □

Andrei Andreevich Gromyko

Andrei Andreevich Gromyko (1909–1989) represented the Soviet Union for many years in major international conferences after World War II, first as minister of foreign affairs and then as president of the USSR.

ndrei Gromyko was born on July 18, 1909, in a village in Belorussia, then a province in the western region of the Russian Empire. His parents were peasant farmers. After the Revolution of 1917 the Communist state helped young people from working families to obtain a higher education and encouraged them to join the Communist Party. Gromyko took advantage of these opportunities.

Despite the hardships which the collectivization of agriculture imposed on the peasant population, he became a loyal supporter of Stalin's regime. He joined the Communist Party in 1931 and attended an agricultural technical school in his province, graduating in 1936. He then went to Moscow to work in the Institute of Economics of the Soviet Academy of Sciences, where he completed his doctoral thesis on the mechanization of agriculture in the United States. For several years he occupied the position of senior researcher in the institute, where he specialized in the American economy.

A Career in Diplomacy

He began a new career in 1939 in the Soviet Diplomatic Service. Many older diplomats had disappeared during the late 1930s in Stalin's police terror. The new recruits who took their place received quick promotion to important diplomatic positions. Gromyko had the necessary qualifications for advancement. Son of working peasants, well educated, and a member of the party since the beginning of the Stalin take-over, he belonged to the new generation of Stalinists. He had no experience or previous training in international relations. He learned his leadership skills on the job. Until 1985 his entire career was devoted to Soviet foreign affairs.

Gromyko began his work at the Soviet embassy in Washington, D.C., one of the Soviet Union's most important diplomatic posts. In 1943 at age 34 he was made Soviet ambassador to the United States. While serving in Washington he learned to speak fluent English. In World War II the Soviet Union and the United States were allies against Nazi Germany and Japan. Gromyko attended the major Allied conferences at Yalta and Potsdam in 1945, assisting Stalin in his negotiations with US leaders. The Soviet Union that year joined in the founding of the United Nations. Gromyko participated in the writing of the U.N. Charter, which made the Soviet Union a member of the Security Council with the right to veto any U.N. policy. In 1946 he became the permanent representative from the USSR to the Security Council.

In the two years that followed, the beginning of the Cold War produced serious diplomatic conflicts in the United Nations between the Soviet Union and the West. Gromyko faithfully carried out the new Soviet policy, casting 26 vetoes to prevent the United Nations from adopting resolutions of which Stalin disapproved. His unsmiling public appearances earned him the title among Western diplomats of "Old Stone Face." His work satisfied Stalin and Molotov, minister of foreign affairs, and in 1949 he was promoted to first deputy minister, becoming Molotov's direct assistant. In ten years he had risen from the position of research scholar in agriculture to one of the most important posts in Soviet foreign relations.

After Stalin's death in 1953 Gromyko continued to serve the new leaders competently and loyally. When Khrushchev came to power in 1955 he introduced a policy of "peaceful coexistence" to improve relations with the West. New conferences were held between East and West. Gromyko collaborated in these meetings. His influence grew when in 1956 he was appointed a member of the Central Committee of the Communist Party. His career advanced again in 1957 when the minister of foreign affairs joined a group of other leading Communists opposing Khrushchev's policies in an attempt to remove him from power. They failed and were themselves removed from their leadership positions (Molotov left Moscow to become Soviet ambassador to the Mongolian People's Republic). Gromyko's reward for loyal service and for taking no part in the plot to depose Khrushchev was promotion to minister of foreign affairs.

Minister of Foreign Affairs

In his years as minister he distinguished himself by his ability to implement effectively the policies of the Soviet leadership. He was adept at accommodating every Soviet leader from Stalin to Gorbachev, and in dealing with nine US presidents during his career. He participated actively in all international meetings and negotiated with leaders of important countries. In 1962 Khrushchev secretly ordered the installation of Soviet intermediate-range nuclear missiles in Cuba. Gromyko went to Washington at that time to talk with President Kennedy, who warned him of the danger of a US-Soviet war if the Soviet missiles were actually placed in Cuba. Gromyko never admitted that his country was involved in this dangerous action; later he claimed that he had not concealed the move since the US president had never put the question of the missiles directly to him.

In the mid-1960s the Soviet Union began major industrial projects with the aid of Western corporations, including the Fiat automobile company in Italy. In 1966 Gromyko led the Soviet delegation to Rome to conclude the Fiat agreement. There he asked for and received an audience with the Pope. He was the first Soviet statesman publicly to recognize the importance of the Papacy. He appeared to have felt a deep satisfaction at the growing power and influence of his country in world affairs, asserting in 1971 that "today there is no question of any significance (in international relations) which can be resolved without the Soviet Union or in opposition to her."

Gromyko belonged to the Soviet political elite who enjoyed special comforts and privileges. He took personal pleasure in fine clothes, having his business suits specially made by Western tailors. He was probably instrumental in the successful career of his son, who became director of the Institute of African Affairs and wrote many authoritative articles on Soviet foreign policy (one consisting of a rare interview with his father discussing the Cuban missile crisis).

A Power in the Politburo

In the early 1970s the Soviet Union concluded with the United States an important treaty for the limitation of nuclear armaments, the Strategic Arms Limitation Treaty (SALT). Gromyko helped to negotiate the final agreement. He acquired extensive knowledge of ballistic missiles and nuclear weapons. When negotiating, noted one observer, Gromyko "never took a note, never looked at a folder or turned to his assistants for advice." His service in these negotiations and support for the Soviet leader, Brezhnev, earned him in 1973 a position in the Communist Party's ruling committee, the Politburo. In addition, he received during his years as foreign minister many honors, including the Order of Lenin and Hero of Socialist Labor.

Relations with the United States gradually worsened during the 1970s. Gromyko sought in international meetings to strengthen the global influence of the Soviet Union. He promoted close ties with African states regardless of their

type of government or economic system, declaring that "we do not consider ideological differences in social systems." When in the early 1980s Brezhnev became ill and could not make major foreign policy statements, Gromyko took his place. In the campaign to prevent the United States from placing new nuclear missiles in Europe, he declared in 1982 in the United Nations that the Soviet Union, "the world's foremost peace loving nation," promised never to be the first state in any international conflict to use nuclear weapons. This "no first use" pledge did not represent a new policy, for the Soviet Union had built its nuclear weapons arsenal to match that of the United States and to prevent a nuclear attack. In making the speech Gromyko established that he had begun to play a major part in decisions on Soviet foreign policy. His decades of experience in international relations had by then earned him a new title—"Dean of World Diplomacy."

The Rise of Gorbachev and the Demise of Gromyko

After Brezhnev's death in late 1982 Gromyko became one of the small circle of Soviet Communists in the Politburo to choose the new Soviet leader. Two successors died soon after their appointments. In 1985 the Politburo picked their youngest member, Mikhail Gorbachev, to be general secretary. Gromyko made the formal announcement of this choice. He occupied by then the informal position among his colleagues as senior member of the Politburo. Gorbachev elevated Gromyko's position to that of President, (the official title being Chairman of the Presidium of the Supreme Soviet, thus replacing Chernenko, who had died in March, 1985. This position, though prestigious, lacked an effective degree of power, and essentially brought Gromyko's political career to an end after 28 years. Gromyko was replaced as Minister of Foreign Affairs by Eduard Shevardnadze, former party boss of the Soviet Republic of Georgia. In 1989, the Politburo voted Gromyko out as president. He was hospitalized for vascular problems shortly thereafter, and died in July 1989, at the age of 80. Only one Politburo member attended his funeral.

Gromyko's autobiography *Memoirs* was begun in 1979, published in the Moscow in 1988 and in the US in 1990. There are countless discrepancies between events, not only in the nine years it took Gromyko to write the book, but also in the later English translation. In his autobiography, Gromyko recounts meetings with everyone from Marilyn Monroe to Yasar Arafat to Pope John Paul II. Although he reveals little, Gromyko remained a loyal Stalinist to the end. Despite recent reassessment of Stalin's career and methodologies, Gromyko stubbornly defends him. With regard to the Cold War, Gromyko blames the US and holds Stalin himself blameless.

Further Reading

Summary biographies are included in *Who's Who in the Soviet Union* (1984) and in *The International Who's Who 1984-85* (1984); brief biographical accounts of his life are provided in "A Diplomat for All Seasons," *TIME* (June 25, 1984); "Winds of Kremlin Change," *TIME* (July 15, 1985); in various book reviews of *Memories:* see *New Republic* (May 14, 1990); and

National Review (April 30, 1990); and in "An Enduring Russian Face," *New York Times* (July 3, 1985); scattered references to his activity as minister of foreign affairs are found in Robin Edmunds, *Soviet Foreign Policy: The Brezhnev Years* (1983); Gromyko's memoirs, titled *Memories,* were published in 1990. □

Red Grooms

Red Grooms (born 1937) was an American artist best known for his large scale, intensely colored, environmental sculptural pieces made of wire, acrylic, and fabric. These scenes typically capture figures engaged in places and activities characteristic of the United States, presenting a humorous and/or satirical view of contemporary life.

Red Grooms was born in Nashville, Tennessee, in June 1937. He attended Peabody College in Nashville, the New School for Social Research in New York City, the Art Institute in Chicago, Illinois, and the Hans Hoffmann School. In 1961 he married Mimi Gross, who worked in close collaboration with him. Grooms began exhibiting at the Sun Gallery in Provincetown, Massachusetts, in 1958. He also performed public pieces which came to be known as "happenings" there. As the creator of one of the first "happenings", Grooms turned away from Abstract Expressionism formerly in favor and forged the way for the Pop Art movement. Like a number of other artists in the late 1950s—George Segal, for example—he was drawn to art forms that maximized the experience of three dimensions and was clearly representational in striking contrast to the one and even two-dimensional similarities of most abstract art of the time.

Among his earliest public works in 1958-1959 were several "happenings"—*Play Called Fire, The Walking Man,* and *Burning Building*—and he was loosely tied to the group in New York in the 1950s that was developing that form of dramatic art, including Allan Kaprow, Jim Dine, and Claes Oldenburg. His work displays a sophisticated knowledge of the history of art and incorporates some stylistic approaches of the abstract expressionists in the shaping and coloring of figures. Some of his females seem like mundane cousins of the demonic women of De Kooning's paintings. His major works for specific installations were produced by a collaborative team.

Using sculpture wire, vinyl, elastic, fabric, wood, and any other apt materials needed, he constructed large-scale environments peopled by various human figures. These "sculpto-picto-ramas" were sometimes based very directly on a particular setting. His characteristic work took shape in the 1960s, culminating in *The City of Chicago* (1968). *Ruckus Manhattan* (1976), which recreates many features of lower Manhattan from the Statue of Liberty uptown to Rockefeller Center, is based on a series of drawings and sequences of photographs of selected features which achieve a convincing level of accuracy in the representation of the city. The familiarity of the selected images creates a carnival-like amusement, but closer examination often reveals a less humorous, satiric, or even penetrating view of society and its denizens. Buildings that are clearly identified with specific activities or are landmarks of the urban environment (such as the Brooklyn Bridge, the New York Stock Exchange, and the World Trade Center), tourists, a subway car, the sleazy environment of 42nd Street in the 1960s—all are brought to life in these large-scale scenes.

Grooms' view of our historical past was given form in another major work, *Philadelphia Cornucopia* (1982), created as a commission for the Institute of Contemporary Art in Philadelphia to celebrate that city's tricentennial. Forty-foot-long canvas flats with vignettes of Philadelphia history and a "ship of state" with the United States' founding fathers—George Washington, Thomas Jefferson, and Benjamin Franklin—were part of this work, which occupied 2,500 square feet.

Grooms' examination of the history of art is often clever and insightful. *Nighthawks Revisited* (1980) is a colored drawing based on a well-known painting by Edward Hopper, a major American artist. Unlike Hopper's brooding work, Grooms's version shows Hopper in the scene looking lonely and out-of-place in the very ordinary environment. The viewer realizes how much Hopper reshaped the environment in his paintings when he sees the scene through Grooms's eyes.

Red's Roxy (1985) is a work produced in a multiple edition. It is an actual movie theater consisting of a plexiglass box into which are inserted color lithographed figures. An external crank operates a tiny movie made up of scenes drawn by the artist on mylar. Like his larger works, the viewer can actively participate in this small-scale piece. Movement, change, and elements of this society—such as its video culture—are all incorporated.

Grooms chronicled the American scene with insight, wit, and humor. Yet at times his vision aroused controversy. *Shoot-out* (1983), a 26-foot-long painted aluminum sculpture showing a cowboy and an American Indian shooting at each other, brought about intense criticism in Denver, Colorado, where it was commissioned for a public site. Now in the Denver Art Museum, the sculpture was criticized for the artist's insensitivity to Indian history and its inaccurate view of the history of Indian-white settler conflict. Yet Grooms's vision of society was generally an optimistic one, and the general public responded with enthusiasm to his work.

In 1985, Grooms's first major retrospective showing 29 years of his work opened at the Pennsylvania Academy of Fine Arts in Philadelphia. The 170 objects and works in the show consisted of paintings, sculptures, prints, drawings and enormous "sculpto-pictoramas" from *The City of Chicago* to the Woolworth Building in *Ruckus Manhattan*. The retrospective ended in Nashville, Groom's hometown, at the Tennessee State Museum on October 26, 1986. Grooms also illustrated a children's book *Rembrandt Takes a Walk* written by M. Strand and published in 1986.

One of Groom's most exciting "sculpto-pictoramas" was designed in Chicago in 1995. Neel Keller, the artistic director of the Remains Theatre in Chicago, brought together new creations by playwright John Guare and Grooms in a production called, aptly enough, *Moon Under Miami collides with Chicago! Seer predicts audiences stunned! Outraged! Delighted!* For the production, Guare wrote a depressing but mildly satirical account of money and politics, while Grooms designed a backdrop inspired by "Miami's tropical lushness, its third world sleaze, its trailer-park hoke and salsa glamour," as Penelope Mesic described it in her review of *Moon Shot* in *Chicago*. The backdrop is also a mobile home with its lights on, and sitting outside it, the three-dimensional figures of an older couple sitting down to enjoy Guare's play, which concerns congressmen on the money trail looking for funding for campaign TV commercials. The mix of delight, parody, and current affectations among politicians is typical of both Guare's and Groom's styles. The pairing of these two was excellent and effective. Guare had previously written the prize-winning plays *House of Blue Leaves* and *Six Degrees of Separation*, the latter having recently been made into a successful full-length movie.

Further Reading

Red Grooms and Ruckus Manhattan by Judd Tully (1977) is a book-length source on Grooms's work; Judith Stein has written *Red Grooms: A Retrospective, 1956-1984* (1986); frequent reviews of his work can be found in the periodicals *Art News* and *Art in America;* other articles can be found through the bibliographic source *The Art Index;* Grooms's work may also be seen in the children's book *Rembrandt Takes a Walk*, illustrated by Grooms and written by M. Strand (1986). □

Gerard Groote

The Dutch evangelical preacher Gerard Groote (1340-1384) is considered the founder of the Brethren of the Common Life and of the Devotio Moderna, a religious movement which contributed to the Protestant Reformation.

Born of wealthy parents at Deventer, Gerard Groote received extensive education in law, medicine, and theology at Aachen, Cologne, Paris, and Prague. But about 1375 his life changed dramatically when he experienced a spiritual conversion. Influenced by his friend Jan Van Ruysbroeck, he gave up his wealth and possessions and entered a Carthusian monastery. After 2 years there he wanted to preach, was ordained a deacon (but never a priest), and left the monastery. He began to preach in the diocese of Utrecht and attracted large, enthusiastic audiences.

Groote's popularity was the result of his preaching in the vernacular (unlike the Latin services of the Church) and his appeal to the spiritual ideals of the times. Popular religious feeling centered on the imitation of Christ, the idea that all Christians should practice his virtues. Groote preached this message, and although never heretical, he angered the Church by his criticism of the clergy's wealth and power. For this reason, in 1384 the bishop of Utrecht ordered Groote to stop preaching. Groote obeyed, but he appealed to the Pope. Before the Pope could reply, Groote died at the age of 44, on Aug. 20, 1384.

Although his career was cut short, Gerard Groote is tremendously important for his influence on others. His followers formed the Brethren of the Common Life, whose aim was to teach the common people and thus develop their moral and spiritual qualities: the practical result of this movement was greatly improved education in the Netherlands. Groote's disciple Florent Radewyns founded the Windesheim Congregation of Canons Regular, which was copied in the Netherlands, Germany, and Switzerland. A member of this order was Thomas à Kempis, probable author of *The Imitation of Christ*. The Brethren of the Common Life and the Windesheim Congregation, in turn, gave rise to the Devotio Moderna (New Devotion), a religious reform movement of the Low Countries and the Rhineland which influenced Renaissance humanists and figures of the Reformation. Thus Gerard Groote has a double significance: he is the culmination of popular religious feeling in the Middle Ages, the search for a more meaningful faith; and he is one of the spiritual forerunners of the Protestant Reformation.

Further Reading

The definitive work on Gerard Groote in English is Albert Hyma, *The Brethren of the Common Life* (1950), which includes a biography of Groote. Groote's influence is further considered in Hyma's *The Christian Renaissance: A History of the "Devotio Moderna"* (1924; 2d ed. 1965). Another biography is by T. P. Van Zijl: *Gerard Groote, Ascetic and Reformer* (1969). □

Walter Gropius

The German-American architect, educator, and designer Walter Gropius (1883-1969) was director of the famed Bauhaus in Germany from 1919 to 1928 and occupied the chair of architecture at the Harvard University Graduate School of Design from 1938 to 1952.

Walter Gropius was born in Berlin on May 18, 1883. Although he studied architecture in Berlin and Munich (1903-1907), he received no degree. He then went to work in Berlin for Peter Behrens, one of several German architects who was influenced by the British Arts and Crafts movement and who attempted to go further by adapting good design to machine production.

In 1910 Gropius set up practice with Adolf Meyer. They designed the Fagus Works in Alfeld an der Leine (1911) and the office building at the Werkbund Exhibition in Cologne (1914), using a combination of masonry and steel construction, from which, in some areas, the external glass sheathing was hung. The plan of the Cologne building was axially designed in the Beaux-Arts tradition, but the major influence was predominantly that of Frank Lloyd Wright, whose "prairie houses" were widely known in Europe through the 1910 and 1911 publications of Ernst Wasmuth in Berlin. Gropius and Meyer were influenced by Wright's style especially in the horizontality and the wide overhanging eaves, but also in the symmetry, the corner pavilions, and the whole spirit of Wright's concept. World War I interrupted their architectural practice, and thereafter they designed only one project prior to Meyer's death in 1924: the unsuccessful entry for the Chicago Tribune Tower competition of 1922.

The Bauhaus

During the war Gropius was invited to become the director of the Grand Ducal Saxon School of Applied Arts and the Saxon Academy of Fine Arts in Weimar, and he took up his duties at war's end. He combined the two schools into the Staatliches Bauhaus (State Building House) in 1919. The aim of the Bauhaus was a "unity of art and technology" to give artistic direction to industry, which was as lacking in 1919 as in the mid-19th century, when the Arts and Crafts movement began. The greatness of Gropius as an educator was that he did not put forward any dogmatic policies, but rather he acted as a balance between the rational, representative, and physical on the one hand and the spiritual, esthetic, and humanitarian on the other. An artistic community of prima donnas is difficult to coordinate, but Gropius acted as choreographer and exacted the best from his fac-

Walter Gropius (bottom, left)

ulty, from the mysticism of Johannes Itten to the Marxist socialism of Hannes Meyer.

When right-wing criticism forced the Bauhaus to leave Weimar in 1925, Gropius designed the structure for the new Bauhaus in Dessau, one of his finest works, which embodied a new concept of architectural space. When criticism mounted there against him as director in 1928, he resigned rather than allow the criticism to spread from him as leader to the whole institution. (Nazism and the Bauhaus stood for diametrically opposing viewpoints, and in 1933 under Ludwig Mies van der Rohe the school, which had moved to Berlin, was forced to close.)

Gropius practiced in Berlin from 1928 to 1934, experimenting with prefabricated housing in his Toerten housing development in Dessau (1926) and dwellings at the Werkbund Exhibition (1927). He went to England in 1934, where he worked with E. Maxwell Fry until 1937, designing mainly individual houses, but also Impington College, Cambridgeshire. This structure partially influenced the post–World War II school design program in Britain.

Works in America

When Gropius went to the United States in 1937, he collaborated with Marcel Breuer, a former pupil, on individual and group housing, including a house for himself at Lincoln, Mass. (1937). Gropius held the chair of architecture at Harvard from 1938 to 1952, a period of his life from the age of 55 to 69, when most architects would have been designing their major works. This was due to his intense commitment to the educational process. "I have been 'nobody's baby' during just those years of middle life which normally bring a man to the apex of his career," Gropius admitted, when he received the American Institute of Architects' Gold Medal in 1959.

Gropius had, however, established The Architects' Collaborative (TAC), a group-oriented practice, in 1946, and he retired from Harvard in 1952 to devote his full attention to the practice of architecture. TAC and Gropius designed the Harvard University Graduate Center (1949-1950); executed a project for the Boston Back Bay Center (1953), which was not carried out; and designed the U.S. Embassy in Athens (1960) and Baghdad University in Iraq (begun 1962 but incomplete as of 1971).

Gropius also designed locomotives and railroad sleeping cars (1913-1914), the Adler automobile (1930), and a host of everyday products. He believed in "the common citizenship of all creative work."

Further Reading

Works on Gropius include Sigfried Giedion, *Walter Gropius: Work and Teamwork* (1954); Gilbert Herbert, *The Synthetic Vision of Walter Gropius* (1959); and J. M. Fitch, Walter Gropius (1960). Studies of the Bauhaus are L. Hirshfeld-Mack, *The Bauhaus* (1963), and Hans M. Wingler, *Bauhaus* (1969), which is the most detailed and comprehensive study. For bibliographies of Gropius's works see American Association of Architectural Bibliographers, *Walter Gropius: A Bibliography,* prepared by Caroline Shillaber (1965), and William B. O'Neal, *Walter Gropius* (1966).

Additional Sources

Isaacs, Reginald R., *Gropius: an illustrated biography of the creator of the Bauhaus,* Boston: Little, Brown, 1991. □

Baron Gros

Antoine Jean Baron Gros (1771-1835), was one of the first French romantic painters. He is best known for his depictions of Napoleon's military campaigns and heroic deeds.

The son of a painter, Antoine Jean Gros was born in Paris on March 16, 1771. At the age of 14 he entered the studio of Jacques Louis David, the acknowledged leader of the classical revival. Although his own work became radically different from David's, he maintained a lifelong respect for his teacher and envisioned himself as the upholder of the Davidian tradition.

In 1787 Gros entered the Académie de Peinture, and when the Académie dissolved in 1793 (a result of the French Revolution) he went to Italy. He met Josephine Bonaparte in Genoa in 1796, and she introduced him to Napoleonic society. Gros entered Napoleon's immediate entourage and accompanied him on several north Italian campaigns. Gros

also became involved with Napoleon's program of confiscating Italian art for removal to France.

Gros returned to Paris in 1800 and began to show his Napoleonic paintings in the annual Salons. The most famous of these are the *Pesthouse at Jaffa* (1804) and *Napoleon at Eylau* (1808). These works served to deify Napoleon, showing him engaged in acts of heroism and mercy. Stylistically, the paintings were revolutionary: their exotic settings, rich color, agitated space, and general penchant for showing the gruesome specifics of war and suffering differed radically from the cool generalizations of Davidian classicism that Gros had learned as a student. The presentation of contemporary historical events was also new, a harbinger of the realism that developed steadily during the first half of the 19th century in French, American, and English painting. Finally, the emphatic emotionalism of Gros's art established the foundation of romantic painting that Théodore Géricault and Eugène Delacroix developed after him.

Unlike that of some of his countrymen (David is a case in point), Gros's position did not suffer after the fall of Napoleon. Gros painted for the restored monarchy, for instance, *Louis XVIII Leaving the Tuileries* (1817), and he decorated the dome of the Panthéon in Paris with scenes of French history (1814-1824). For this Charles X made him a baron in 1824. But these works lack the zest and commitment of Gros's Napoleonic period, perhaps because they were not based on the immediate kinds of historical experiences that had inspired the earlier paintings.

Although marked by considerable public success, Gros's later career was in many ways acutely troubled. Basically, he could not resolve his personal esthetic theories with his own painting or with the work of his younger contemporaries. To the end Gros wished to propagate the classicism of David, and he took over David's studio when the master was exiled in 1816. By the 1820s, however, the revolutionary romanticism of Géricault and Delacroix, among others, had clearly begun to eclipse classicism, and Gros found himself fighting a lonely and losing battle for conservatism. Ironically, he was fighting a trend that his own best work had helped to originate. As he persisted, moreover, his own painting began to show a diffident mixture of classic and romantic attitudes. Thus, while he was inherently a romantic, he tragically came to doubt himself. Gros died on June 26, 1835, apparently a suicide.

Further Reading

The most thorough and penetrating analysis of Gros's art in relation to the complexities of romanticism and classicism is in Walter F. Friedlaender, *David to Delacroix* (trans. 1952). □

Robert Grosseteste

The English churchman and statesman Robert Grosseteste (1175-1253) played an important role in the politics of his time. He was also a major English medieval writer and thinker.

Robert Grosseteste was born at Stradbrooke, Suffolk, of humble parents. Educated at Oxford, where he became magister, or master, in 1199, he then studied at Paris. He was back in England by 1215, where he is believed to have been at the meeting of King John and the barons at Runnymede, where the King accepted the Magna Carta.

Since he was the first English scholar who knew both Greek and Hebrew, Grosseteste soon rose within the Church. In 1224 he was made the first rector of the Franciscans at Oxford, and the next years saw him going through a series of Church positions: archdeacon of Wiltshire, then Northampton and Leicester, prebend of Lincoln, and chancellor of Oxford.

Grosseteste was one of the few medieval churchmen to be sympathetic to the Jews. Tradition has it that he first came in contact with the Jews of England through learning Hebrew from a rabbi in Oxford, and by 1231 he was writing such works as *De cessatione legalium* to try and gain converts. In 1232 he gave up many of his posts so that he could remain at Oxford, but in 1235 he was elevated to the bishopric of Lincoln, one of England's largest sees.

For the next years Grosseteste was active in the administration of his cathedral and from 1239 to 1245 carried out a dispute with the chapter over his rights of visitation, which he finally won after visiting the Pope in Lyons to gain his support.

Grosseteste was active in support of the papacy in England and supported the papal claims against the barons at the Council of Merton, but he was also to stand out against the papacy in matters of practical abuses, such as papal attempts to find presentations in England for Italians. In 1253 he refused to place the Pope's nephew in the canonry of Lincoln due to his lack of knowledge of English. In addition, he often stood against the King. In 1244 Grosseteste prevented the granting of a subsidy to the King, was appointed a clerical representative to discuss the financial needs of the Crown, and was one of the 12 appointed to regulate the conduct of the King and his ministers. In 1252 he opposed Henry III's demand for a tenth of the Church's revenues, nominally granted for a crusade, even though it had papal support.

A friend and adviser to Simon de Montfort, Grosseteste played an important part in the politics of his age, but his most long-lasting influence was in his writings and his fame as a scholar. Roger Bacon was one of his pupils, and Grosseteste appeared in his own time as a universal genius as his long list of publications indicates. He produced works on law, philosophy, French poems, physics, and agriculture, as well as theology, and he produced translations and commentaries on such works as Aristotle's *Physics* and *Ethics* and on the *Testament of the Twelve Patriarchs* and the *Ignatian Epistles*. His work on optics was the basis of some of his rebuilding of Lincoln Cathedral.

Taken ill during the summer of 1253 while at Buckden, Grosseteste died on October 9 and was buried in the south transept of Lincoln Cathedral. Miracles were soon reported at his tomb, but repeated attempts for his canonization failed as his public career had been spent in opposition to papal authority, and he was to be canonized informally by the people of northern England. He has been described as an example of the best influences in the public life of the 13th century.

Further Reading

There are many biographies of Grosseteste, including Samuel Pegge, *The Life of Robert Grosseteste: The Celebrated Bishop of Lincoln* (1793), and the classic study by Francis S. Stevenson, *Robert Grosseteste, Bishop of Lincoln: A Contribution to the Religious, Political and Intellectual History of the Thirteenth Century* (1899; repr. 1969). His role in English life is discussed in C. R. Cheney, *English Bishops' Chanceries, 1100-1250* (1950). See also A. C. Crombie, *Robert Grosseteste and the Origins of Experimental Science* (1953), and D. A. Callus, ed., *Robert Grosseteste, Scholar and Bishop: Essays in Commemoration of the Seventh Centenary of His Death* (1955). S. Harrison Thomson, *The Writings of Robert Grosseteste: Bishop of Lincoln, 1235-1253* (1940), is a scholarly bibliography. □

Jennie Grossinger

American hotel executive and philanthropist Jennie Grossinger (1892-1972) brought worldwide promi-

nence to her family's 800-acre resort in New York State's Catskill Mountains.

Jennie Grossinger, the oldest of three children of Asher Selig and Malke Grumet Grossinger, was born June 16, 1892, in Baligrod, a town in the Bieszczady region of southeast Poland, part of the former Austro-Hungarian empire. The family, devout members of the Jewish religion, spoke Polish and Yiddish. To secure a better future for his family, Selig, an estate overseer, came to America in 1897. Malke, Jennie, and younger daughter Lottie joined him three years later.

A tenement in New York City's Lower East Side was their new home. Selig, who was in poor health, pressed coats in a factory and made several unsuccessful attempts to open a business. At this time a son, Harry, was born. A fever made the infant unable to hear or speak, and Malke sought medical advice in Europe. A cure was not available, but separations and illness resulted in a loyal and united family.

To help her parents, Jennie, then 13, sewed buttonholes in a factory and continued her education at night school. On May 25, 1912, she married her first cousin, Harry Grossinger; they rented a flat next to her parents. In 1913 Selig and Malke opened a small restaurant and Jennie joined them. Although the venture failed, it gave Jennie experience in the hospitality business.

In 1914 Selig decided to try farming for a living. A successful relative suggested the Catskill Mountain region

northwest of New York City. Selig made a $450 down payment on a 35 acre farm in Sullivan County near Ferndale, a town with a small Jewish community. Jennie and her husband contributed $200, and Jennie moved with her parents while Harry kept his job in New York. Selig's health returned. However, the scenic rolling hills and valleys did not sustain profitable farming. Nearby farm families took in summer boarders and advised the Grossingers to do the same.

Peaceful surroundings and the Kosher food prepared by Malke, the daughter of an innkeeper, attracted their first boarders. Each guest was treated as a valued friend. Harry arranged for more guests, and the summer's profit convinced Selig to expand. Soon Harry was active in the business full time.

Although the seven-room farm house had no indoor plumbing or electricity, guests were pleased with the food and service. Word-of-mouth advertising brought more guests and further expansion. In 1919 the family purchased a large, modern facility on a hilltop near the town of Liberty. Grossinger's Terrace Hill House, widely known as Grossinger's, continued to expand. Jennie's close contact with the guests led to many improvements. By 1931 the resort had tennis courts, an 18-hole golf course, a dining room for 400 guests, a theater, a social director, and an athletic director. These attractions plus the plentiful food, landscaped grounds, and lake brought increasing numbers of guests. It began to operate as a winter resort in a limited way.

The 1930s saw Grossinger's good reputation expand beyond its loyal Jewish clientele. Milton Blackstone, a former guest and tutor to Jennie's son Paul, opened an advertising agency in New York in the early 1930s. He used many promotions to attract guests to Grossinger's during the Great Depression years. Noted sports writers came to the resort when Barney Ross, the world's lightweight boxing champion, had his training camp there. Their syndicated columns included praise of the resort and family. After Ross's 1934 victory as the world's welter-weight champion, Broadway and Hollywood celebrities arrived and kept returning. Show business columnists followed, and the resort's fame spread; its facilities continued to expand also.

The family's business philosophy, however, remained unchanged. Jennie, who managed the resort with her husband, believed, "A resort isn't buildings and kitchens and lakes or nightclubs. The real hotel is the people who work here." Hard work, family loyalty, and an astute ability to satisfy guests led to Grossinger's continued success.

Gratitude for opportunities they found in America was expressed through gifts to local charities and needy families by Selig, who died in 1931, and by Malke, who died in 1952. Malke taught Jennie that "a life without sharing is barren."

Over 100 awards, citations, certificates, and keys to cities honored Jennie, who had become a naturalized citizen in 1919. Fund raising for disease research and contributions to hospitals and nonsectarian institutions such as the City of Hope in Duarte, California, were among her interests. Medical facilities in Tel Aviv and Zefat (Safed), Israel, are named for her. Concern for servicemen and the disabled extended beyond World War II. By 1958 over 3,500 five-day all-expense-paid vacations had been given to members of the Armed Forces. Over $10 million worth of war bonds were sold at Grossinger's during the war.

Education was a major interest of Jennie Grossinger. She was named a fellow of Brandeis University in 1958; in 1959 Wilberforce University in Ohio awarded her an honorary Doctor of Humanities degree, and in 1966 New England College in New Hampshire awarded her an honorary Doctor of Humane Letters degree. Her personality and belief in the brotherhood of man won the hotel executive friends from all walks of life and from all faiths and races. In 1954 she was featured on the television program "This Is Your Life." Over several decades the most prominent names in all fields came to Grossinger's and met Jennie. Impressed with her activities and accomplishments, Gov. Nelson A. Rockefeller proclaimed June 16, 1968, as Jennie Grossinger Day in New York State. He wrote that she "exemplified the American Dream of success from humble beginnings and a lifetime of humanitarian achievement for others rarely equalled in the annals of the United States."

When her husband died in 1964, Jennie became the sole owner of Grossinger Hotel and Country Club. Paul Grossinger, her son, and Elaine Grossinger Etess, her daughter, who were active in the resort's management for many years, became the owners after Jennie's death from a stroke on November 20, 1972. Her children and grand-children continued to manage the resort until it was sold to outside investors in late 1985.

Further Reading

Jennie Grossinger is included in *Who's Who in America* and *Notable American Women: The Modern Period* (1980). The only detailed and accurate biography is Joel Pomerantz, *Jennie and The Story of Grossinger's* (1970). Noteworthy articles about her and the resort include: Quentin Reynolds, "Jennie," *Look* (July 13, 1965); Morris Freedman, "The Green Pastures of Grossinger's," *Commentary* (July and August 1954); and Al Hine, "Grossinger's," *Holiday* (August 1949). Her obituary is in the *New York Times* (November 21, 1972). Awards, photographs, and numerous articles documenting her career can be found at the resort in Grossinger, New York. □

George Grosz

The German painter and graphic artist George Grosz (1893-1959) was the most outstanding caricaturist and political satirist of the period after World War I.

George Grosz was born on July 26, 1893, in Berlin. He studied at the art academies of Dresden (1909) and Berlin (1911) and visited Paris (1913). He started his career as a cartoonist for humoristic reviews such as *Ulk* and *Lustige Blätter;* his concern for the actualities of the day was even then predominant.

During World War I Grosz was an infantryman in the German army. About 1916 he began to portray with biting

satire the militarism and ruthlessness of the ruling classes. In Berlin in 1917 he joined the Dada movement, which was essentially a protest against war and exploitation and a call for a new humanism. By 1918 he was acknowledged as Germany's leading social critic in the field of the visual arts, whose pity for the underdog and hatred of capitalism penetrated deep into the consciousness of the postwar mentality in a Germany riddled by misery, inflation, and political failure.

Grosz's lithographic series in particular made him internationally known. His style was quite novel in the history of modern draftsmanship. His most famous series are *Das Gesicht der herrschenden Klasse* (1919), *Abrechnung folgt* and *Ecce Homo* (both 1922), *Spiesser Spiegel* (1924), and *Das neue Gesicht der herrschenden Klasse* and *Die Gezeichneten* (both 1930). Only the work of the German painter Otto Dix could compare with the acidity, the fantastic aggressiveness, and the determination of Grosz to unmask the social lie, the cruelty of war, and the depraved moral code.

In 1920 Grosz visited Italy, and in 1922 he spent 6 months in Russia. About 1925 he approached in his paintings a style that was utterly realistic; it was called the Neue Sachlichkeit (New Objectivity), and it was a reaction to the expressionist trends of the era. This is exemplified in his portrait of Max Hermann Neisse (1927).

In 1932 Grosz accepted an invitation by the Art Students League of New York City to teach there. The following year he opened an art school, which he conducted until

1937. That year he was included in the German exhibition of "degenerate" art; a year later he was deprived of his German citizenship and became an American citizen. Grosz taught at the School of Fine Arts, Columbia University (1941-1942). For a short time he painted landscapes and figural compositions with nudes, but he soon returned to works in a social realist mode. He died in Berlin on July 6, 1959.

Further Reading

Grosz's *A Little Yes and a Big No* (1946) is his autobiography. Herbert Bittner, ed., *George Grosz* (1961), includes an essay by the artist, "On My Drawings." John I. H. Baur, *George Grosz* (1954), is a study of the artist's work deepened by psychological insight. The artistic climate in which Grosz worked is described in Franz Roh, *German Art in the 20th Century* (1968). Reproductions of his work are in Arts Council of Great Britain, *George Grosz, 1893-1959* (1963).

Additional Sources

Flavell, M. Kay (Mary Kay), *George Grosz, a biography,* New Haven: Yale University Press, 1988.
George Grosz: his life and work, New York: Universe Books, 1979.
Grosz, George, *The autobiography of George Grosz: a small yes and a big no,* London; New York: Allison & Busby, 1982.
Grosz, George, *George Grosz, an autobiography,* New York: Macmillan, 1983. □

Hugo Grotius

The Dutch jurist, statesman, and historian Hugo Grotius (1583-1645) founded the modern school of international law.

Born in Delft on April 10, 1583, Huig de Groot is known by the Latinized form of his name Hugo Grotius. As a boy, he excelled his father, a learned patrician of Delft, Johan Hugo de Groot, by becoming a marvel of scholarly precocity. He wrote Latin poems at the age of 8 and attended Leiden University from 1594 to 1597. He took his doctorate in law at Orléans in 1599, during a stay in France as a member of a diplomatic mission led by Johan van Oldenbarnevelt, Land's Advocate of Holland, his political sponsor for the next 2 decades. He entered the private practice of law in The Hague at the age of 16 and 8 years later was named state's attorney (advocate fiscal) of the Court of Holland. In 1608 he married Maria van Reigersberch, a Zeelander who stiffened his rather soft personality with her own determination and resourcefulness.

In 1604 Grotius wrote a treatise, *The Law of Prizes,* for the East India Company, which was not published until its discovery in 1864; however, one chapter, which defended Dutch trading and sailing rights, was published in 1609 under the title *Mare liberum* (The Free Sea). In 1610, in *De antiquitate reipublicae Batavae* (The Antiquity of the Batavian State), he argued that the province of Holland had been sovereign and independent since the time of the Romans. In

1613, at Oldenbarnevelt's suggestion, Grotius accompanied a delegation sent by the Dutch East India Company to London as juridical counselor to plead its case in a dispute with the English East India Company. Although favoring free trade in Europe, he argued for the monopoly of the Dutch company in the East Indies, as granted by the native princes for the sake of its protection.

When Grotius was named pensionary (legal officer and political representative) of Rotterdam in 1613, he entered the higher ranks of Dutch politics. He represented Rotterdam in the States of Holland and supported the strongly Remonstrant (moderate Calvinist) position of Oldenbarnevelt against the increasing hostility of Prince Maurice of Nassau, the stadholder and captain general. In that same year Grotius published a treatise defending Holland's right to intervene in church affairs, and various theological treatises from his pen appeared from 1613 to 1618 defending the Remonstrant position. He became Oldenbarnevelt's right hand and was arrested with him on Aug. 29, 1618, when Maurice decided to cut short the measures taken by the States of Holland against his military authority. He was sentenced to life imprisonment on May 18, 1619; Oldenbarnevelt received the death penalty. After almost 2 years of imprisonment in Loevestein Castle, Grotius escaped in a book chest brought in by his wife and servant and went to France.

Grotius continued his scholarly publications in Paris. The most notable was his masterpiece, *De iure belli ac pacis* (1625; The Law of War and Peace), in which he argued for a system of law in the relations between sovereign states, with

emphasis upon the notion of "just war." He built his arguments upon the idea of "natural law," derived from ancient, medieval, and recent (especially Jesuit) authors, as a principle of right deriving from the nature of things rather than from the commandments of either God or lay rulers.

In 1631 Grotius published *Introduction to the Jurisprudence of Holland,* which profoundly influenced legists in the Netherlands and abroad and continues to be considered part of the constitutional law of South Africa. His religious ideas evolved into a broad ecumenicism, whereby he favored reconciliation between Protestants and Catholics. He lost his certitude that the Protestant revolt against Rome had been justified—without, however, gaining confidence in Rome's infallibility. His *De veritate religionis Christianae* (1627; The Truth of the Christian Religion) was an attempt with the weapons of legal scholarship to prove the unity of Christendom; it was widely read in his own time and long afterward.

Incurring Cardinal Richelieu's hostility, Grotius returned to Holland in October 1631 and lived quietly; but he would not request pardon and fled in April 1632 to avoid arrest. Taking refuge in Germany, he came into contact with the Swedish authorities and returned to Paris in 1634 as Swedish ambassador. He proved a better scholar than diplomat and was recalled in 1644. On his return from Stockholm, Grotius suffered shipwreck at Rostock, Germany; he was rescued but died 2 days later, on Aug. 28, 1645, from exhaustion. When his identity was discovered, his body was brought home to Delft for burial.

Further Reading

The standard life of Grotius is William S. M. Knight, *The Life and Works of Hugo Grotius* (1925). Robert W. Lee, *Hugo Grotius* (1931), is a collection of essays.

Additional Sources

Vreeland, Hamilton, *Hugo Grotius: the father of the modern science of international law,* Little, Colo.: F.B. Rothman, 1986, 1917. □

Jerzy Grotowski

Jerzy Grotowski (born 1933) was the founder of the Laboratory Theatre in Wroclaw, Poland, an experimental theater in which attention is focused almost exclusively on the actor and his/her message, rather than on such props as costumes, music, and makeup, which were eliminated.

Jerzy Grotowski was born August 11, 1933, in Rzeszow, Poland. His father, Marion Grotowski, was a painter and sculptor; his mother, Emilia, a teacher. Jerzy attended school in Rzeszow, but he spent a year seriously ill in a hospital when he was 16. During his stay Grotowski read, studied, and pondered carefully what he would do with his life. He decided to devote his life to art. Upon leaving the hospital he lived with his family in Krakow and finished school there. Subsequently he entered the Advanced School of Dramatic Art in 1951 at the age of 18 to become a director. When not at the School of Dramatic Art he found time for some travels which helped shape his concept of directing. In 1955 he visited Moscow to attend the Academy of Stage Craft. Later he traveled on a fellowship to Central Asia, where he was introduced to Oriental philosophy. In 1962 he visited China, where he became interested in the ancient art of Chinese opera. In 1965 he settled in Wroclaw and opened the Laboratory Theatre. Since 1985, he has been working in Pontedera, Italy with a small group of actors and actresses.

The theater is aptly named, for it is not a place where one goes for dramatic entertainment; rather, it is a place of research where the acting troupe explores the potentialities in any given text. The group does not attempt to perform a wide variety of works, but concentrates instead upon a limited number of dramatic pieces and constantly reinterprets and rediscovers them. In doing so they try to get at the mythic archetypes in the work, rather than its literal meaning.

According to Grotowski, when theater was still a part of religion it liberated the spiritual energy of the tribe by incorporating myth and then by profaning and transcending it. The spectator had a renewed awareness of his personal truth in the truth of the myth, "and through fright and a sense of the sacred he came to catharsis." Today, however, social groups are not defined by religion; mythic forms have al-

tered and are disappearing and reappearing in new forms. Thus it is more difficult to elicit the shock needed to pierce the so-called "life mask" and get to the psychic truths that lie behind that mask. What is possible is to "confront" archetypes, and, in so doing, perceive the relationship between human problems and their connection to myth.

The actor is vitally important because, according to Grotowski, the myth is incarnate in him, and through his actions, speech, wails, and gestures he stimulates the audience to confront the truth of the myth for themselves. Grotowski believed that theater could exist without makeup, costumes, and scenery, but that it could not exist without the actor-spectator relationship of perceptual, direct, and "live" communion.

He differentiated between what he called the "Rich theatre" and the "Poor theatre." The "Rich" is one that is rich in faults. It draws upon other disciplines but fails to produce a work of art that has integrity. The Rich theater, in its attempt to compete with film and television, uses mechanical devices that are more appropriate for film and television. Grotowski proposed poverty in the theater, one in which a new space is designed for actors and spectators for each new work. He eliminated costumes, lighting, makeup, and music from his theater and insisted that the actors' physical flexibility is infinitely more interesting than costumes or makeup. Direct lighting and shadows can be utilized effectively without the need for elaborate lighting schemes and mechanisms. The actor can make his own music with his voice.

Grotowski's radical departure from the usual theatrical approach resulted in highly disciplined and rigorously demanding performances. Best known among the Laboratory Theatre's efforts were Wyspianski's *Akropolis,* Byron's *Cain,* Caldoron's *The Constant Prince,* Shakespeare's *Hamlet,* Marlowe's *Doctor Faustus,* and an original piece, *Apocalypis cum Figuris.* All of the plays are about human suffering and treat that suffering so painfully that great demands are put upon the actor and spectator.

Grotowski's methods, which put great emphasis on preparation, exercise, and physical conditioning and discipline, were questioned by some, praised by others. There can be little doubt, however, that he had considerable impact upon contemporary theater.

In 1991, Grotowski and his work were the subjects of a documentary entitled *Art as Vehicle.* In it, Mercedes Gregory documents a performance of Grotowski's in which he draws upon the power and the passion (now defunct, he believes) of the traditional Catholic liturgy to release the individual from self. Drawing from a myriad of cultural sources—Greek, Egyptian, African, West Indian and Christian—Grotowski incorporates chant, minimal dialogue and ritualistic motions such as rocking, swaying and reeling about to enable his "doers" (his term for actors and actresses) to achieve a freedom from self-consciousness, from acting, and from the performance itself. The performance was enacted solely for the benefit of the "doers," and the documentary was not to be shown unless Grotowski was present to interpret its contents for a select group of viewers. In making his "liturgy" rational and comprehensible by

drawing upon a universal human consciousness, Grotowski "doers" have attempted to live (via acting) the very essence of life itself.

Further Reading

Grotowski presented his ideas in his essay "Towards a Poor Theatre" (1965); Oscar G. Brockett discussed his accomplishments in *History of the Theatre,* 4th edition (1968); Margaret Croyden analyzed his work in *Lunatics, Lovers and Poets: The Contemporary Experimental Theatre* (1978); a critical biography of Grotowski is by Raymonde Temkine, *Grotowski,* translated by Alex Sxogyi (1972); Also see *Grotowski and His Laboratory* by Kazimierz Brawm (1986) and *Grotowski's Laboratory Theatre: Dissolution and Diaspora* by Robert Findlay and Halina Filipowicz (1986); *At Work with Grotowski on Physical Actions,* written by Thomas Richards and Jerzy Grotowski in 1995 is an excellent source. The important aspects of the biography include Thomas's apprenticeship to Grotowski, the similarities between Grotowski and Stanislavski and the experience of being involved with Grotwoski's Workcenter in Italy. The author(s) show that Grotowski's work is a continuance of Stanislasvki's Method, and not its opposite. □

Frederick Philip Grove

Frederick Philip Grove (ca. 1871-1948), Canadian novelist and essayist of European birth and mysterious background, is best known for his realistic novels of pioneer life in western Canada.

S erious doubt has been cast by D. O. Spettigue (1969) on the facts of Frederick Philip Grove's autobiography. One thing is reasonably certain—our knowledge of his life in Canada is accurate. Having taken this *caveat* into account, we can say that Grove was born in northern Europe, probably in Germany, emigrated to North America in his youth, and spent the years of his early adulthood in the United States, where he may have taught school in Kentucky and traveled as a harvest hand in the Middle West. This itinerant experience, which may have taken up as much as 2 years of his life, appears to have had a profound effect on his writing.

In 1912 Grove appeared in Haskett, Manitoba, where he became a teacher in a small rural school. In 1915 he married Catherine Weins, a fellow teacher, and settled down to a 9-year career at various levels of primary and intermediate education. He began to write and studied for an extramural degree from the University of Manitoba. The Groves were outstanding teachers, and he was noted in particular for his enthusiasm and enlightened and progressive views.

Grove's first book was *over Prairie Trails* (1922); it was followed by another collection of essays based on his Manitoba experiences, *The Turn of the Year* (1923). These books are distinguished by a freedom of style and a control of language admirably suited to the evocation of the climate, the scenery, and the variable moods of the Manitoba prairie.

A third collection of essays, *It Needs To Be Said* (1929), is a distillation of his speeches and thought on culture and society.

Grove is best known for his novels, which are frequently divided into the "prairie novels" and the "Ontario novels." Two of the prairie novels—*Our Daily Bread* (1928) and *Fruits of the Earth* (1933)—can be described with one of the Ontario novels, *Two Generations* (1939), as being novels of the soil. In them Grove presents a self-centered and single-minded protagonist who labors unremittingly at taming the soil in order to found the basis of "a new world which might serve as the breeding-place of a civilization to come." In *Settlers of the Marsh* (1925) and *The Yoke of Life* (1930) Grove again uses a pioneer prairie setting, but he explores human relationships and the psychological elements that underlie them. He holds that man acts not out of reason but as a result of passion. Human passion drives man to irrational and tragic conflict within himself, and man is fated to defeat and destruction by forces which are beyond his control and which he neither understands nor recognizes.

In *The Master of the Mill* (1944), Grove's most ambitious and complex work, he tells the story of a family whose growth to power and wealth parallels in nearallegorical terms the development of Canada as a confederated nation. The major themes are the rise of modern capitalism, generational conflict, and the rise and fall of family fortunes as these are linked with the drive to materialistic power, the realization of creative ideals, and the decay of mind and vision.

Grove's autobiographical work, now questioned as to factual reliability, comprises *A Search for America* (1927) and *In Search of Myself* (1946). In the latter he states that the tragic quality of man's existence is heightened in the North American experience. He believes that American civilization is characterized by mass production which destroys the artist and by a standardization of life which erodes individuality. He gave himself to fantasy-satire in his last published work, *Consider Her Ways* (1947), an unrecognized but unusually clever, successful, and prophetic "study" of an expedition of ants engaged on a research project on man.

In the latter part of his life Grove was well known as a public lecturer. He lived briefly in Ottawa, where he was a director of the Graphic Press, and then moved to a farm outside Simcoe, Ontario, where he worked as a dairy farmer and struggled with his writing. In 1934 the Royal Society of Canada awarded him the Lorne Pierce Medal.

Further Reading

The first book-length study of Grove was Desmond Pacey, *Frederick Philip Grove* (1945). In terms of contemporary and readily accessible appraisals, D. O. Spettigue's intriguing investigation, *Frederick Philip Grove* (1969), is recommended. There is, as well, a more traditional approach to Grove in Ronald Sutherland, *Frederick Philip Grove* (1969). For a useful and handy cross section of critical opinion see Desmond Pacey's *Frederick Philip Grove* (1970) in the McGraw-Hill series "Critical Views on Canadian Writers."

Additional Sources

Hind-Smith, Joan., *Three voices: the lives of Margaret Laurence, Gabrielle Roy, Frederick Philip Grove,* Toronto: Clarke, Irwin, 1975. □

Leslie Groves

Leslie Groves (1896-1970) was the officer in the United States Army Corps of Engineers who directed the Manhattan Project (atom bomb) during World War II.

L eslie Richard Groves was born in Albany, New York, on August 17, 1896, the son of Leslie Richard Groves, a chaplain in the United States Army, and Gwen Griffith Groves. Given his father's army career, Groves could call no one place home. He entered the University of Washington in 1913 while his father was stationed at a post in Seattle, transferred to the Massachusetts Institute of Technology the following year, and in 1916 gained an appointment to the U.S. Military Academy. In November 1918 Groves graduated, fourth in his class, under an accelerated program instituted during World War I. Commissioned too late to see combat in France, Groves joined the Army Corps of Engineers as a second lieutenant and completed the basic and civil engineering courses at the Engineer School at Camp Humphreys (later renamed Fort Belvoir), Virginia. In 1922 he married Grace Wilson; the couple had two children.

Between 1921 and 1925 Groves served at various posts, including Fort Worden in Washington, the Presidio in San Francisco, and Schofield Barracks in Honolulu. Afterward he became assistant to the district engineer in Galveston, Texas, and directed the opening of the siltedup harbor at Port Isabel in Texas. Duty in Nicaragua surveying possible sites for a new canal was followed by four years in Washington, D.C. (1931-1935), where Groves was attached to the Military Supply Division, the army agency that developed new equipment, from jackhammers to searchlights. He was promoted to captain in 1934 and made chief of the division.

Over the next five years Groves, who was known as Richard or Dick to acquaintances, had a tour with the Missouri River Division of the Corps of Engineers (1936-1938) and studied at both the Command and General Staff School (1935-1936) and the Army War College (1938-1939). Assigned in 1939 to the general staff, Groves was promoted to major in July 1940 and four months later to lieutenant colonel (temporary). With a military defense buildup well underway by 1941, the Army's construction expenditures were averaging in excess of $500 million monthly. Groves was named deputy chief of construction with a mandate to complete dozens of new camps and other army facilities throughout the United States. Supervising the building of the Pentagon was one of his many responsibilities.

Creation of the Manhattan District

By the time the United States entered World War II, important research on various aspects of nuclear fission had been ongoing at several major universities and other locations for more than a year. Enough was known by 1942 for authorities to believe that a nuclear weapon might be developed before the end of 1944. Since much of the nuclear program would involve immense construction tasks, some calling for unprecedented technical sophistication, the Army was given overall responsibility for it. To direct the program a new office, named the Manhattan Engineering District (later called the Manhattan Project), was established in Washington, D.C. Colonel James Marshall, the first head of the Manhattan District, began the search for sites for the various new facilities that would be needed. Once it became evident that the Army's task would be far larger than anticipated, Groves was given authority over the Manhattan District in September 1942 and promoted to brigadier general.

Groves soon put the stamp of his forceful, albeit abrasive, personality on the project. For instance, as there was still considerable doubt over which of several enrichment technologies might be best suited for the task of making available uranium of sufficient quality for nuclear weaponry, Groves decided to pursue several promising options, including both gaseous diffusion and electromagnetic separation methods as well as thermal diffusion. He also ordered the construction of giant nuclear reactors where plutonium would be produced. "When in doubt, act," he reasoned. Unlike the cautious Colonel Marshall, he did not hesitate in purchasing gigantic tracts of land at Oak Ridge, Tennessee, and Hanford, Washington, for the construction of these facilities and for townsites that would house the thousands of civilians and military personnel required to build and operate them. Services such as schools for the children of residents would also have to be provided. To do the work, Groves contracted with hundreds of firms, including such giants as du Pont, Union Carbide, and Eastman Kodak. Eventually over 125,000 people would work under the aegis of the Manhattan Engineering District.

Another of the Manhattan District's new facilities was the bomb laboratory at Los Alamos, New Mexico. This would be the site of the arduous work of designing and assembling the world's first nuclear bombs. Several key scientists resented Groves' hard-driving methods and emphasis on security, but the collaboration between Groves and J. Robert Oppenheimer, the brilliant theoretical physicist Groves chose to direct the laboratory, proved fruitful. Groves secured for Oppenheimer the personnel, equipment, and materials he needed while the scientist ably guided work at the laboratory. Although some formidable problems about the final design of the two types of atom bombs under development remained to be solved as 1945 began, by the spring enormous progress had been made, especially on the more complicated but more promising implosion bomb. Planning for the use of the atom bomb began. Both Oppenheimer and Groves agreed the gadget—the name given to the atom bomb by project insiders—should be employed in combat. Groves, as chair of the target committee, had a major voice in determining the timing and circumstances of the A-bomb's use against Japan. Not until the first bomb had actually been dropped on Hiroshima on August 6, 1945, could the secrecy that had previously cloaked the Manhattan Project begin to be lifted; Groves inevitably became the center of a flurry of media attention.

Cold War Warrior

After the end of World War II, Groves, virtually the prototype of a Cold War warrior, advocated the buildup of a stockpile of nuclear weapons ready to use should war develop between the United States and the Soviet Union. He remained head of the Manhattan Project until the end of 1946 when authority over the nuclear program was transferred to the newly created Atomic Energy Commission. Groves retired from the Army in 1948 and became vice president of research and development at Remington Rand. There he had responsibility for developing the commercial potential of the UNIVAC computer. Groves retired in 1961. He died in Washington, D.C., on July 14, 1970.

Despite his accomplishments in the Army prior to 1942 and in business after his retirement from the Army, Groves will be remembered for his direction of the Manhattan Project during World War II. His style of leadership provoked controversy, but his ability to see to the heart of matters and to make difficult decisions at the risk of jeopardizing his own reputation were vital to the success of the program. He was, in the words of Los Alamos scientist Robert Bacher, "a genius at getting things done under very adverse circumstances."

Further Reading

The papers of Leslie Groves are at both the National Archives in Washington, D.C. (where they are accessioned as the Office of the Commanding General File), and at the Hoover Institution in Stanford, California. William Lawren, *The General and the Bomb* (1988), is a helpful biography. Of the many books on the Manhattan Project, three of the most useful are Leslie Groves, *Now It Can Be Told* (1962); Vincent Jones, *Manhattan: The Army and the Atomic Bomb* (1985); and Stephane Groueff, *Manhattan Project* (1967). An overall view of the theory of nuclear fission and its application to the atom bomb is provided by Richard Rhodes, *The Making of the Atom Bomb* (1986). The best works on the Manhattan District's key facilities are James Kunetka, *City of Fire* (rev. ed. 1979); Charles W. Johnson and Charles O. Jackson, *City Behind a Fence* (1981); and Michele Stenehjem Gerber, *On the Home Front: The Cold War Legacy of the Hanford Nuclear Site* (1992). Major Allen C. Estes, "General Leslie Groves and the Atomic Bomb," *Military Review* (August 1992), assesses Groves' leadership style. Issues relating to the atom bomb and the early Cold War are discussed in Gregg Herken, *The Winning Weapon: The Atomic Bomb in the Cold War, 1945-1950* (1981). Also of interest is *The Beginning or the End* (1947), a film about the Manhattan Project containing some fact and considerable fiction. The role of Groves is played by Brian Donlevy. □

Matthias Grünewald

The painter Matthias Grünewald (ca. 1475-1528), the greatest German colorist of the Renaissance, represented the highest achievement of German artistic development not directly affected by the Italian style.

The real name of Matthias Grünewald was Mathis Neithart Gothart. Grünewald was the name given to "Mathis, painter of Aschaffenburg" by the German art historiographer Joachim von Sandrart in 1675. At that time he wrote, "not a single man could be found who might be able to give account of Grünewald's activities even in a scanty memorandum or by word of mouth." The memory of the artist had indeed become so vague that only in the late 19th and 20th centuries was his historical existence reconstructed, although in a fragmentary and hypothetical manner.

It used to be thought that Grünewald was born in Würzburg between 1450 and 1480 and that he settled in Seligenstadt, where he bought a house in 1501. But it has since been shown that the artist by the name of Mathis who was active at Seligenstadt was a sculptor, and there is no record that Grünewald made sculptures. Furthermore, Mathis the sculptor was still active at Seligenstadt in 1529, a year after Grünewald's death. It is now held that Grünewald was born about 1475, since his style presupposes a knowl-

edge of Italian Renaissance art, and he was probably of the same generation as Albrecht Dürer. Grünewald's first datable picture is the *Mocking of Christ* (probably 1503).

Beginning in 1509 Grünewald was active as a painter for Archbishop Ulrich von Gemmingen at Aschaffenburg, as well as architect and superintendent of building activity at the Aschaffenburg castle. From 1510/1512 to 1516 Grünewald executed his masterpiece, the *Isenheim Altarpiece:* a large folding altar for the church of the Anthonites at Isenheim in Alsace. He painted few other works, and some of these have disappeared. From 1516 on he was court painter to Cardinal Albrecht of Brandenburg. The most important work Grünewald executed for him was the altarpiece for the new monastic church of Saints Moritz and Mary Magdalen at Halle on the Saale, the *Meeting of Saints Erasmus and Maurice,* painted before 1525, in which Cardinal Albrecht is represented as St. Erasmus.

In 1525 the Peasants' War disrupted the feudal order in the Mainz area. After the insurrection was put down, the Lutherans and those who sympathized with the reformers had to leave the area. Grünewald must have been strongly involved in the movement, for after his death Lutheran books were found among his possessions. Dismissed from his post of court painter after the Peasants' War, he settled in the Protestant community of Halle, where he worked as a hydraulic engineer. He died there in August 1528.

Isenheim Altarpiece

Altogether, only about 10 works of painting (some composed of several panels) and about 40 drawings by Grünewald are known. Attempts to ascribe other works to him have been made, but these attributions have not been generally accepted. The *Isenheim Altarpiece* (now in Colmar, France) is by far his most important work, and it is the largest and most individual painted ensemble of the German Renaissance.

The central shrine of the *Isenheim Altarpiece* is composed of carved wood figures of the enthroned St. Anthony flanked by Saints Augustine and Jerome; it was carved about 1503 by Nikolaus von Hagenau on the order of the preceptor of the Anthonites, Jean d'Orliac. His successor, Guido Guersi, commissioned Grünewald to execute the paintings, and the artist was probably the author of their iconographic program.

The altar was so conceived as to fulfill various liturgical functions. According to the occasion, it can remain closed; the Crucifixion is then seen, with the figures of Saints Anthony and Sebastian on the fixed wings and the Lamentation over Christ on the predella. When the first pair of wings is opened, the Angel Concert and Nativity are seen, depicted according to the vision of St. Bridget as described in her *Revelations,* with the Annunciation and the Resurrection on the wings. When the second pair of wings is opened, the sculptures of the central shrine are visible, and on the painted wings appear, to the left, Saints Paul and Anthony in the wilderness, fed by the raven, and, on the right, the Temptation of St. Anthony.

A Christological and Passion content dominates in the first opening, suitable for Lent and normal weekdays. The second opening, Mariological in content, is appropriate for Easter, Christmas, the feasts of triumphant Christ, and Sundays. The third opening, devoted to St. Anthony, the patron saint of the order for which the altar was executed, is suitable for his feast days.

The paintings of the *Isenheim Altarpiece* are exceptional in style and expression. In contrast to the then current German and Netherlandish custom of dividing the surface of altarpieces into separate panels, Grünewald composed large images, filling the entire area of the closed wings, as in the Crucifixion and the Angel Concert and Nativity. He reached a stage in his development similar to Italian artists in his ability to correctly represent three-dimensional objects rendered in perspective. But he wholly disregarded Italian ideals of harmony and beauty, which Dürer accepted and sought to introduce into German art.

For Grünewald, ugliness and deformity were fully justified artistic means to achieve his end: to move the spectator by the dramatic expressionism of the work. His main artistic preoccupation was not so much drawing as color. In contrast to almost all his German contemporaries, Grünewald had no interest in the graphic arts. He was not a linear-minded artist but first of all a painter. His importance as an innovator lies above all in his masterly, free, and individual use of color, with which he achieved not decorative but expressive effects. Of all his known drawings, only one is done in pen and ink; all the others are painterly drawings which the artist executed in soft chalk.

The only really outstanding picture executed by Grünewald outside of the *Isenheim Altarpiece* is the *Meeting of Saints Erasmus and Maurice* (now in Munich), which is equally individual in concept. Here he shows his mastery in contrasting various kinds of materials: the glittering apparel of Bishop Erasmus and the light-reflecting armor of the black saintly knight.

Grünewald was a unique artist. Guido Schoenberger (1948) states: "He never had a school, he never had a real pupil; it even seems that he never had an assistant." Outside of his immediate vicinity, in the Mainz region and the Middle and Upper Rhine, he had no influence whatsoever and his name was soon forgotten. Early in the 20th century the expressionists rediscovered his work; they were able to accept an art not intent upon esthetic beauty, and they valued his mysticism. Not only the expressionist painters were inspired by his work: the opera *Mathis der Maler* (1934) by Paul Hindemith deals with Grünewald's life, and he also wrote a symphony from three extracts of the opera whose movements have descriptive titles from the *Isenheim Altarpiece.*

Further Reading

The most dependable book in English on Grünewald is Nikolaus Pevsner and Michael Meier, *Grünewald* (1958). Arthur Burkhard, *Matthias Grünewald: Personality and Accomplishment* (1936), is a good monograph, but it was published before the definitive book by W. K. Zülch (in German) appeared in 1938. A very fine and useful catalog of Grünewald's drawings is Guido Schoenberger, ed., *The Drawings of Mathis Gothart Nithart, called Grünewald* (1948). Charles D. Cuttler, *Northern Painting* (1968), devotes a chapter to Grünewald and

discusses the *Isenheim Altarpiece* in detail. For background material see Otto Benesch, *The Art of the Renaissance in Northern Europe* (1945; rev. ed. 1965). □

Francesco Guardi

The Italian painter Francesco Guardi (1712-1793) is famed for his oil sketches of Venice and its lagoons, loosely painted with open, clearly visible brushstrokes and a sense of the sparkle of light.

The records of his parish in Venice show that Francesco Guardi was baptized on Oct. 5, 1712. His father, Domenico, who died when Francesco was 4, had a workshop. Francesco and his elder brother, Gian Antonio, worked in a small studio, carrying out such orders as they could get for almost anything the client wanted: mythological pictures, genre, flower pieces, battle scenes, altarpieces, and even, on rare occasions, frescoes. They did not hesitate to copy compositions by other artists, but what they borrowed they always transformed into something more capricious, less stable, more fragmentary in the refraction of light.

Francesco did not emerge as an independent personality until 1760, when his brother died. Then, 48 years old, he married, established his own studio, and devoted himself chiefly to painting views of Venice. For the most part he worked in obscurity, ignored by his contemporaries. He was not even admitted to the Venetian Academy until he was 72 years old.

Guardi and Canaletto have always been compared to one another because the buildings they chose to paint were often the same. But the way each artist painted them is very different. Canaletto's world is constructed out of line. It provides solid, carefully drawn, three-dimensional objects that exist within logically constructed three-dimensional space. Guardi's world is constructed out of color and light. The objects in it become weightless in the light's shimmer and dissolve in a welter of brushstrokes; the space, like the forms in space, is suggested rather than described. Canaletto belonged essentially to the Renaissance tradition that began with Giotto and, as it grew progressively tighter and more controlled, pointed the way to neoclassicism. Guardi belonged to the new baroque tradition that grew out of the late style of Titian and, as it became progressively looser and freer, pointed the way toward impressionism.

Such differences appear even in Guardi's early view paintings, where he was obviously trying to copy Canaletto, such as the *Basin of San Marco*. The famous buildings are there, but they are far in the background, insubstantial, seeming to float. In front is a fleet of fishing boats, their curving spars seeming to dance across the surface of the canvas. What is important for Guardi is not perspective but the changing clouds and the way the light falls on the lagoon.

Guardi became increasingly fascinated by the water that surrounds Venice. In late works, such as the famous *Lagoon with Gondola,* buildings and people have been stripped away until there is nothing but the suggestion of a thin line of distant wharfs, a few strokes to indicate one man on a gondola, a long unbroken stretch of still water, and a cloudless sky.

Guardi also painted the festivals that so delighted visitors to the city, such as the *Marriage of Venice to the Sea.* This was a symbolic ceremony in which the doge, in the great gilded galley of the head of state, surrounded by a thousand gondolas, appeared before all Venice, in Goethe's image, "raised up like the Host in a monstrance."

Of all Guardi's paintings the most evocative are his caprices, the landscapes born out of his imagination though suggested by the ruined buildings on the lonely islands of the Venetian lagoon. A gentle melancholy clings to such scenes. They had a special appeal to connoisseurs of the late 18th century, like Denis Diderot, who, on seeing a painting of ruins and thinking perhaps of the lengthening shadow that was falling across his own era, wrote, "All things are destroyed, all things perish, all things pass away." Guardi died on Jan. 1, 1793, 4 years after the outbreak of the French Revolution and as many before the end of the 1,000-year-long history of the Venetian Republic.

Further Reading

Rodolfo Palluchini, *Francesco Guardi* (1966), has a brief, good text in English and numerous color plates. J. Byam Shaw, *The Drawings of Francesco Guardi* (1951), is the fundamental study of Guardi's work in pen and wash. See also Vittorio Moschini, *Francesco Guardi* (trans. 1956). ☐

Guarino Guarini

Guarino Guarini (1624-1683) was an Italian architect, priest, and philosopher, whose mathematical studies enabled him to create the most fantastic of all baroque churches.

Guarino Guarini was born in Modena on Jan. 17, 1624. He joined the austere new Theatine order in 1639 and went to Rome for his novitiate. This was during the period when the architect Francesco Borromini was most active. Guarini studied philosophy and theology—and apparently also architecture—before returning to Modena in 1647, where he was ordained, began to work as an architect, and taught in the Theatine house until a disagreement with the ruling Este family in 1655 forced him to leave.

Guarini was in Messina, Sicily, in 1660; his works there were destroyed in the 1908 earthquake. He was back in Modena by 1662, and soon afterward he went to Paris, where he taught, wrote on philosophy and mathematics, and designed Ste-Anne-la-Royale. This church is now known only from engravings, but it must have seemed an extraordinary fantasy among the soberly classical buildings of contemporary Paris. Building was suspended soon after it was begun and was not resumed until 1714.

In 1666 Guarini went to Turin, where his last years were spent and where he created his masterpieces: the Chapel of the Holy Shroud (Sta Sindone), S. Lorenzo, and the Palazzo Carignano. His reputation is attested to by his designs for a church in Prague (but his plans were not followed) and another in Lisbon, destroyed in the 1755 earthquake. In fact, all central European baroque churches owe much to Guarini's example, but few, if any, of the architects who designed them were able to imitate his extraordinarily daring feats of construction. His buildings could have been designed only by an expert in solid geometry (for example, the dome of the Chapel of the Holy Shroud), and there is reason to believe that Guarini was aware of the work of such contemporary mathematicians as Gérard Desargues in projective geometry.

The Chapel of the Holy Shroud is a large circular chapel added to the east end of the Cathedral and intended to contain the Holy Shroud, recently brought by the Savoy ruling family from France. Work on the chapel had commenced before Guarini's arrival, but his design of 1667 is remarkable for the treatment of the upper stages, which consist of a series of latticed arches forming a whole sequence of skeleton domes, so that the eye sees through one into the next in a manner that had never been attempted previously. It is almost impossible to describe these structures except in mathematical terms, but they make even Borromini's most daring inventions, such as the dome of S. Ivo alla Sapienza in Rome, seem almost earthbound, so great is the illusion of light, fragile forms floating in space created by Guarini.

The nearby church of S. Lorenzo, begun in 1668, is perhaps slightly less virtuoso in its handling of the dome structures, but it is more complicated in plan and overall effect, since here Guarini was responsible for the whole work and was not taking over from another architect. The church was not finished until 1687, after Guarini's death, but it was sufficiently far advanced in his lifetime for him to be able to celebrate the first Mass said in it.

The Palazzo Carignano, begun in 1679, is slightly less daring in its treatment of the plan, although it does have a deeply curved facade, inspired by Borromini's Oratory of the Filippini in Rome. The texture of the palace is very rich and is notable for being in carved brick, not stone.

During these years Guarini continued to write on theology, philosophy, and mathematics, and while visiting his publisher in Milan, he died on March 6, 1683. His drawings, which are the source of our knowledge of many of his lost works, were published in 1686, and in 1737 the architect Bernardo Vittone published the text Guarini had intended to accompany them.

Further Reading

The best account of Guarini in English is in Rudolf Wittkower, *Art and Architecture in Italy, 1600-1750* (1958; 2d ed. 1965). Guarini is discussed in relation to his contemporaries in Henry A. Millon, *Baroque and Rococo Architecture* (1961).

Germain Bazin, *The Baroque* (1968), contains an analysis of Guarini and reproductions of his work. □

Bob Guccione Jr.

Bob Guccione Jr. (born ca. 1956) publisher of *Spin* a music magazine for Generation X, becoming profitable when the music it endorsed finally started rising to the top of the charts.

In 1985 Bob Guccione Jr. introduced a new magazine to the American public. While it was centered around popular music, *Spin* gained greater attention for its irreverent take on American culture. In this respect it was more similar to edgy, youth-oriented 1980s magazines such as *Spy* than to its direct competitor, *Rolling Stone.* "Let the Baby Boomers read *Rolling Stone ,*" Guccione seemed to be saying; "this is a magazine for Generation X."

You Can't Keep Me in Your Penthouse

The son of the publisher of *Penthouse* and *Omni,* Guccione came into magazine publishing naturally. His parents separated in 1965, and he lived with his mother in her native England until they moved to New Jersey when he was fifteen. A high-school dropout, Guccione worked in magazine circulation and marketing before launching *Spin* under the *Penthouse* aegis with $500,000 from his father. It was a bold venture: in sharp contrast to *Rolling Stone,* the magazine covered unknown performers and criticized major names in the music business. At first it failed to attract enough subscribers and advertisers to turn a profit, and Guccione Sr. announced in 1987 that the magazine would cease publication. But Guccione Jr. decided to separate *Spin* from *Penthouse* and publish it with support from independent investors—a move that created a rift between father and son.

Success

Spin would remain unprofitable until 1992. It was able to hang on because young music fans found its irreverence appealing, and because the alternative rock it championed went to the top of the charts in the early 1990s. *Spin* was more current than many magazines of the late 1980s: for instance, it featured a monthly column on AIDS long before the mainstream media devoted much attention to the disease. It also featured offbeat journalism and satire.

Further Reading

Eric Konigsberg, " 'Dad Always Liked You Best!,' " *GQ,* 65 (June 1995): 101-106.
Patrick Reilly, " 'Spin' Whirls with Guccione Jr.," *Advertising Age,* 59 (13 June 1988): 57.
"The 'Spin' Doctor," *Forbes,* 156 (17 July 1995): 98. □

Martín Güemes

Martín Güemes (1785-1821) was one of the major figures in the Argentine struggle for independence against Spain. His particular contribution was as leader of the crucial Gaucho War in northwestern Argentina from 1814 to 1821.

Martín Güemes was born in Salta. There he attended school until the age of 20, when he was transferred as a military cadet to Buenos Aires. Until 1814 his military career, while successful, was somewhat commonplace. In that year he was assigned by Gen. José de San Martín to take charge of the irregular resistance to the Spanish in Upper Peru (modern Bolivia). The base of his subsequent career was again the city of Salta. It was from this command that Güemes acquired real historical importance.

Gaucho War

Prior to the arrival of Güemes in 1814, resistance to Spanish invasions had become a part of the existence of the ordinary citizen of the province and city of Salta. When Güemes arrived, he took general command of the groups of gauchos. Güemes's first task was to organize these groups and to coordinate their efforts. His next was to defeat the royalist army of Joaquin Pezuela, which was currently occupying the city of Salta with over 3,000 Spanish troops. If this force had been permitted to push on, there would have been no effective force of patriots between Salta and Buenos Aires. Thus began the Gaucho War.

The basic stratagem of Güemes and his gaucho followers was to cut the Spanish forces off from any supply of cattle and horses. All herds were driven south of the city into territory controlled by the gauchos, and any Spanish attempt to obtain them was greeted with wild cavalry charges by the gauchos, repeated as often as 12 times an hour. The inevitable result was the return of the Spanish empty-handed to an army already short of supplies. So successful were these tactics that Pezuela evacuated the city in June 1814 and retreated to Upper Peru. After a short interlude with an Argentine invasion of Upper Peru, Güemes returned to Salta. He was elected governor of the province and assumed political as well as military responsibility.

Between 1815 and 1821 Güemes and the people of Salta defeated four more Spanish invasions. Their courage gained them the title "Bulwark of the North" and made Argentina's fragile independence secure from the Spanish in Peru. On June 7, 1821, however, a royalist column penetrated the city, and Güemes was killed, but his death did not prevent the Salteños from again repelling the invader.

Güemes and the people of Salta had accomplished a great deal against the Spanish. They had provided a shield behind which San Martín could build and train the Army of the Andes, eventual conquerors of the Spanish in Peru. They had closed to the Spanish the vital gateway into the Argentine heartland, making all Spanish attempts to reconquer the

Platine region dependent on a maritime power that Spain did not possess.

Further Reading

The standard works on Güemes are in Spanish. In English see Roger M. Haigh, *Martín Güemes: Tyrant or Tool?* (1968). ☐

Guercino

The Italian painter Guercino (1591-1666) was probably the first Italian artist to create works that can be called fully baroque in the stylistic sense of the term.

Giovanni Francesco Barbieri, called Guercino because of his squint, was born early in February 1591 in Cento, a little town near Bologna. He went to Rome during the reign (1621-1623) of Pope Gregory XV, who was from Bologna; when the Pope died, Guercino returned to Cento. There he stayed until 1642, when he moved to Bologna, where he spent the rest of his life. He died on Dec. 22, 1666.

There had never been any important artists in Cento, and Guercino apparently taught himself, working largely from engravings and such paintings as were available locally. He said that the picture that influenced him most was Ludovico Carracci's *Madonna with St. Francis* in a local church. From it Guercino learned about deep, rich colors, applied loosely in the Venetian way, and about the new, more intimate manner of interpreting religious themes.

The protobaroque style that Guercino took in part from Carracci he carried much further in his own early works. *Elijah Fed by Ravens* (1620), for example, is filled with movement and excitement. The seated prophet, clad in loose, voluminous draperies, turns sharply so that lines of force seem to radiate outward in all directions, like a star. Everything seems unstable, in flux. Light and dark flicker over the surface, breaking up form, reducing clarity. Deep shadows swallow up details, and where light strikes, the surface gleams.

Guercino's *Purification of the Virgin* (1654) shows how very different his late work was. The mood is now one of calm and withdrawal. The figures are arranged like building blocks in planes parallel to the surface of the painting. A soft, even light fills the interior space, creating transparent shadows that do not obscure the forms they overlay. The emphasis is on dignity and maximum clarity.

This change in style, which began during the early 1620s, was a result of pressure on Guercino both from the art critics he encountered in Rome, who were strongly classical in their orientation, and from the people who bought his paintings, who were often conditioned in their likes and dislikes by the critics. Francesco Scannelli, who knew Guercino well, wrote in 1657: "More than once [Guercino] had heard complaints from those who had paintings that were done in his first manner that . . . parts of the body were hidden because of too much darkness. For that reason they

considered that some parts were unfinished. They asserted that often they could not make out the face, and sometimes even the specific action, of the figures. And thus to satisfy as best he could most of the people, especially those who asked for paintings and had the money to pay for them, he had made paintings in the lighter [that is, less baroque and more classical] style.''

Further Reading

The best analysis of Guercino is in Denis Mahon, *Studies in Seicento Art and Theory* (1947). A good, brief essay on him is in E. K. Waterhouse, *Italian Baroque Painting* (1962; 2d rev. ed. 1969). ☐

Otto Von Guericke

The German physicist Otto von Guericke (1602-1686), known for his invention of the vacuum pump, also investigated the properties of air and the atmosphere.

Otto von Guericke was born on Nov. 20, 1602, in Magdeburg (then in Prussian Saxony and now Germany). At the age of 15 he entered the University of Leipzig, where he studied jurisprudence, and continued his study of law at Jena and Helmstedt. In 1623 he went on to the University of Leiden, where he pursued mathematics, mechanics, and military engineering.

After traveling in France and England, Guericke returned to Magdeburg, where he married the daughter of a prominent local politician in 1626. He became active in politics and was elected to the city council in 1627. In 1631 the city was sacked and burned by the invading imperial armies; Guericke and his family barely escaped with their lives. Upon Magdeburg's liberation the following year Guericke returned as a military engineer and once again became actively involved in politics. He was reelected to the city council. In 1646 he became one of the four burgomasters of Magdeburg and served in that capacity for the next 35 years. He retired to Hamburg and there died on May 11, 1686.

Scientific Investigations

In spite of his active political life Guericke managed to pursue his scientific interests as well. He had become increasingly interested in the current debates concerning the possible existence of a vacuum and set out to experimentally investigate the problem. When he actually invented his vacuum pump is uncertain, though it was apparently about 1650. He had begun his experimental researches much earlier, and the instrument underwent a gradual evolution, having begun simply as a modified water pump. Attempting to create a vacuum by pumping out the contents of a sealed container, Guericke sealed a wooden barrel, filled it with water, and then, using a pump, withdrew the water, believing that as the water was removed from below, a vacuum would be produced above it. As the water was withdrawn, however, air could be heard rushing into the barrel through the pores in the wood.

After several failures and modifications Guericke succeeded in evacuating a large, specially constructed sphere made of metal and connected with carefully fitted parts to a pump. Utilizing his first vacuum pump Guericke was able to obtain fairly high vacuums in the metal spheres. His most dramatic demonstration of the effects of this vacuum took place before Emperor Ferdinand III and the assembled Reichstag in Regensburg in May 1654. Two bronze hemispheres—known ever since as the Magdeburg hemispheres—were carefully fitted edge to edge and evacuated. Two teams of eight horses each were attached to this globe, one to each side, but they were unable to separate the hemispheres. When the air was allowed to reenter, however, the two hemispheres fell apart of their own accord.

Guericke has traditionally been credited with important contributions to electricity and is generally cited as having constructed the first frictional electrical machine. This device consisted of a large globe of sulfur mounted on an axis in such a manner that it could be rotated rapidly. When Guericke rubbed the rotating globe with a dry hand, he observed the attraction and repulsion of feathers near it, as well as other effects which are today recognized as electrical in origin. It should be emphasized, however, that Guericke's sulfur globe was not devised to investigate the properties of electricity but to illustrate what he saw as certain innate virtues (such as attraction) which existed in all matter. Nowhere does he refer to the effects of his globe as electrical, and not until the following century was their electrical nature recognized.

Most of Guericke's researches were described and published for the first time in his *New Magdeburg Experiments on Empty Space* (1672), a Latin work devoted largely to cosmology. However, he had completed his researches much earlier, and his experiments with the vacuum pump were described in 1657 in an appendix to a work by Kaspar Schott, a professor of physics and mathematics at Würzburg.

Further Reading

There is no major work on Guericke in English and no English translation of the *New Magdeburg Experiments*. Information on Guericke is in Ernst Mach, *The Science of Mechanics: A Critical and Historical Account of Its Development* (trans. 1893; 5th ed. 1942), which includes a discussion of Guericke's experiments, and Lynn Thorndike, *A History of Magic and Experimental Science*, vols. 6 and 7 (1958). □

Vicente Guerrero

Vicente Guerrero (1783-1831) was a hero of the Mexican fight for independence from Spain. The second president of the Mexican Republic, he was an ardent defender of Indian rights and a harsh oppon-

ent of social and economic inequalities in his country.

Vicente Guerrero lived during a crucial period of Mexican history. In the early 19th century the Spanish colony of New Spain was convulsed by Joseph Bonaparte's usurpation of the Spanish throne. Deep-seated rivalries between Spaniards and Creoles suddenly increased. Mobs of Indians led by Fathers Miguel Hidalgo and José María Morelos roamed through the countryside killing, looting, calling for independence, and demanding a place in a society dominated by a Spanish aristocracy. The role of the wealthy Church came under attack as did Spain's economic and political policies toward the colony.

Guerrero was born on Aug. 10, 1783, in the village of Tixtla. His parents were humble peasants, and under the caste system the mestizo Guerrero did not receive a formal education. He was forced to earn a living by working as a muleteer.

When the revolutionary movement led by Father Hidalgo broke out in 1810, Guerrero joined it. He soon achieved the rank of captain, showing superior tactical ability and outstanding courage. It was, however, under the leadership of Hidalgo's successor, Father Morelos, that Guerrero proved his military qualities. Morelos entrusted him to carry on the revolution in the south. With weapons and supplies captured from royalist forces Guerrero began to build his army. Despite some initial setbacks, he staged several successful attacks against Spanish forces, and Morelos rewarded his victories by raising him to the rank of colonel. From a ragged band of less than 100, his army grew into a militant force of over 1,000 men.

Guerrilla Leader

By 1815, however, the revolutionary tide had begun to turn. Morelos was captured and executed by the Spaniards. Other insurgent leaders were also captured, scattered, or pardoned. Guerrero's army in the south suffered the brunt of the Spanish onslaught. Yet he managed to continue the fight. Deserted by some of his men, persecuted by royalist troops, for several years he carried on guerrilla warfare. In 1818 the Spanish viceroy even used Guerrero's elderly father to try to induce him to surrender. But Guerrero refused and, gathering his soldiers, explained to them that his father had come to offer him positions and rewards. "I have always respected my father," he said, "but my country comes first."

Imbued with Morelos's ideas, Guerrero believed in what he was fighting for. Like Morelos, he despised the existing social distinctions based on race as well as the monopoly exerted by the Spaniards over most of the important government jobs. He advocated land distribution and favored the abolition of the Church's special privileges. A staunch Catholic, he nevertheless favored civil registration of marriages, births, and deaths, and public education not controlled by the Church. He supported the proposition that only Catholicism should be allowed in Mexico. His greatest contribution, however, was in his determination to expel the Spaniards from his homeland. More than any other insurgent leader, he kept alive the independence cause at a very difficult time.

War of Independence

The 1814 restoration of conservative Ferdinand VII to the throne of Spain dealt a heavy blow to liberalism. However, the 1820 Riego revolt among troops destined for South America forced Ferdinand to change his antiliberal position and to restore the 1812 Constitution. The victory of liberalism in Spain alarmed Mexican conservatives and reactionaries. They feared that a liberal Spain would not protect their properties and privileges and would side with Mexican liberals. The only solution, they reasoned, would be independence from Spain. To achieve this, they secured the services of an ambitious officer in the Spanish army, Col. Agustin de Iturbide, who soon marched against Guerrero.

Unable to defeat him, Iturbide invited Guerrero to join him. The two met at Iguala, where Iturbide convinced the simpleminded patriot to join in issuing the Plan of Iguala. The plan called for independence, equal treatment for Spaniards and Creoles, and supremacy of the Catholic religion. These three principles were to be guaranteed by the army. Envisioning the fulfillment of his long struggle, Guerrero supported Iturbide, and on Sept. 27, 1821, the two marched into Mexico City proclaiming the independence of Mexico.

Troubled Independence

Iturbide, however, was less interested in Mexico's problems than in furthering his own personal ambitions. In May 1822 he crowned himself Agustin I, Emperor of Mexico, and moved to extend his empire into Central America. Guerrero soon realized that the policies of the newly established regime resembled only faintly the ideals of the Hidalgo-Morelos movement. Guerrero together with other insurgent leaders, aided by Antonio López de Santa Ana, commander of the port of Veracruz and future dictator of Mexico, forced Iturbide's abdication in 1823.

Following the collapse of the empire, a federalist republic was established with insurgent leader Guadalupe Victoria as Mexico's first president. In the presidential elections of 1828 Guerrero ran against conservative Gen. Manuel Gómez Pedraza, a former officer in the royalist army and Victoria's minister of war. As a hero of the independence movement, Guerrero was perhaps the more popular candidate. But Pedraza used the army to apply pressure on the state legislature and to win the election. Unhappy with the electoral result, Guerrero, together with Santa Ana, staged a rebellion forcing Pedraza into exile.

On April 1, 1829, Guerrero assumed the presidency. He soon found out that to govern was more difficult than to fight. He was generous with his opponents, pardoning many of them. But at a time when Mexico needed strong leadership, he was vacillating and timid. Appeals to patriotism failed to convince the states that they should contribute to the national treasury or to reconcile the Mexican aristocracy to the fact that they were being ruled by a mestizo. Guerrero's presidency marked the assertion of Mexican *indi-*

anismo. It frightened Creoles and conservatives and led to their reaction.

Opposition increased and became bitter. Early in 1830 the army, led by conservative Vice President Anastasio Bustamante, staged a revolt. Guerrero fled southward into the mountains, where for 4 years he had fought for Mexican independence. With some of his old comrades he now resisted Bustamante for a year. But early in 1831 he was enticed on board an Italian ship at Acapulco and betrayed by the captain, who turned him over to the government allegedly for 50,000 pesos. Guerrero was declared mentally incapable and was afterward convicted of treason and sentenced to death. Despite many efforts to save his life, he was executed in Cuilapan on Feb. 14, 1831. The Mexican state of Guerrero was named in honor of his memory.

Further Reading

The best available study in English on Guerrero's revolutionary career is William Forrest Sprague, *Vicente Guerrero, Mexican Liberator: A Study in Patriotism* (1939). Information can also be found in William Spence Robertson, *Rise of the Spanish-American Republics, as Told in the Lives of Their Liberators* (1918). □

Ernesto Guevara

Ernesto Guevara (1928-1967) was an Argentine revolutionary, guerrilla theoretician, and the trusted adviser of Cuban premier Fidel Castro.

Ernesto Guevara was born on June 14, 1928, in Rosario. Of Spanish and Irish descent, he suffered from asthma, spending his childhood in a mountain town near Rosario. At an early age he read history and sociology books and was particularly influenced by the writings of the Chilean Communist poet Pablo Neruda. At 19 Guevara entered the medical school of the University of Buenos Aires.

In 1952 "Che" Guevara ("Che" is an Argentine equivalent of "pal") broke off his studies in order to set out with a friend on a transcontinental trip which included motorcycling to Chile, riding a raft on the Amazon, and taking a plane to Florida. He returned to Argentina to resume his studies, graduating with a degree of doctor of medicine and surgery in 1953.

Late in 1953 Guevara left Argentina, this time for good. He moved to Guatemala, where he had his first experience of a country at war. He supported the JacoboArbenz regime, and when it was overthrown in 1954 Guevara sought asylum in the Argentine embassy, remaining there until he could travel to Mexico.

It was here that Guevara met the Castro brothers. At the time Fidel Castro was planning an expedition against Cuban dictator Fulgencio Batista, and Guevara agreed to go along as a doctor. On Dec. 2, 1956, the expeditionaries landed in eastern Cuba, becoming the nucleus of a guerrilla force which operated in the Sierra Maestra Mountains. The guerrillas contributed to the crumbling of the Batista regime on Dec. 31, 1958.

In January 1959 Guevara was one of the first rebel commanders to enter Havana and take control of the capital. He held several posts in the Castro government: commander of La Cabaña fortress, president of the National Bank, and minister of industries. But always, most important of all, he was one of Castro's most influential advisers. Guevara visited Communist countries in the fall of 1960 to build up trade relations with the Soviet bloc and criticized United States policy toward Cuba. He also directed an unsuccessful plan to bring rapid industrialization to Cuba and advocated the supremacy of moral over material incentives to increase production. Guevara also masterminded Cuba's subversive program in Latin America and wrote extensively on this subject. In his first book, *Guerrilla Warfare* (1960), he provided basic instructions on this type of conflict.

Guevara's official tasks did not cure him of his restlessness. He continued to travel. In December 1964 he addressed the United Nations General Assembly and then set out on a long journey to Europe, Africa, and Asia. After his return to Havana he surprisingly disappeared from public view. His wanderings took him to Africa to lead a guerrilla movement which failed. He returned to Cuba, preparing a team of Cuban army officers who would accompany him to his next fighting area, Bolivia.

Guevara expected that a spreading guerrilla operation in Bolivia would force United States intervention, thus creating "two, three, or many Vietnams." Instead the Bolivian army tracked down and annihilated the guerrillas and captured Guevara on Oct. 8, 1967. The next day Guevara was executed.

Further Reading

Jay Mallin, ed., *Che Guevara on Revolution* (1969), contains Guevara's most important writings on guerrilla warfare as well as a valuable introduction. Daniel James, *Che Guevara* (1968), is the most complete biography. Two works on Guevara's activities in Bolivia are Luis J. Gonzales and Gustavo A. Sanchez Salazar, *Che Guevara in Bolivia,* translated by Helen Lane (1969), a study of Guevara's last months in Bolivia, and Richard Harris, *Death of a Revolutionary: Che Guevara's Last Mission* (1970), a fair-minded account of his guerrilla campaign in Bolivia and its long-range implications. Written with a left-wing point of view, Jean Larteguy, *The Guerrillas* (trans. 1970), is an analysis of the South American revolutionary tradition which attempts to link Guevara to Bolívar. Martin Ebon, *Che: The Making of a Legend* (1969), provides valuable insights into Guevara's personality and activities. ☐

Lamine Gueye

Lamine Gueye (1891-1968) was a Senegalese statesman. One of the major political leaders of French-speaking West Africa, he attacked the autocratic and discriminatory aspects of colonial rule—never colonial rule itself.

L amine Gueye was born on Sept. 20, 1891, in Médine in what is today Mali. Completing his education in France, he graduated as a lawyer in 1921. He returned home to found one of Africa's first political parties and in 1924 became mayor of Saint-Louis. In 1937 he became the leader of the Senegalese branch of the French Socialist party (SFIO) and with Léopold Senghor was elected deputy for Senegal to the French National Assembly in 1945. In 1946 he again won the seat of deputy and also the mayoralty of Dakar. In 1948, however, Senghor left Gueye to form his own party, causing Gueye to lose his seat in the 1951 elections. In 1958 Gueye rejoined Senghor in a movement of national reconciliation and in 1959 was elected president of the Senegalese National Assembly, a position that he held until his death in June 1968.

In a career spanning half a century, as the doyen of French African politicians, Lamine Gueye rejected political independence as a solution for the problems of underdeveloped African states: he demanded only that the laws of France be applied equally to all, at home or overseas.

His two books, *Étapes et perspectives de l'Union Française* (1955; Stages and Perspectives of the French Union) and *Itinéraire africain* (1966; African Journey), as well as his doctoral dissertation, were efforts to demonstrate the compatibility of French citizenship and African civil status. Two laws passed by the French National Assembly were named after him. The law of May 7, 1946, declared that all the inhabitants of the overseas territories had the rights of citizenship as French nationals. The law of 1950 stipulated that French and African civil servants were entitled to equality of treatment.

Gueye was more than simply the "grand old man" of African politics. He worked hard for his constituency of a mainly urban bourgeoisie, proudly accepting at their face value France's most heroically proclaimed ideals, and acted as a bridge to the period of mass nationalism.

Further Reading

Ruth Schacter Morgenthau does a fine job of placing Gueye in the proper historical context in her *Political Parties in French-speaking West Africa* (1964). Gueye is also discussed in Ronald Segal, *Political Africa: A Who's Who of Personalities and Parties* (1961). For a consideration of Gueye's role in the development of modern French African politics see Irving Leonard Markovitz, *Leopold Sédar Senghor and the Politics of Negritude* (1969). ☐

Meyer Guggenheim

Meyer Guggenheim (1828-1905), Swiss-born American industrialist, and his seven sons created a mining empire that eventually stretched halfway around the world.

orn on Feb. 1, 1828, in the ghetto of Lengnau, Switzerland, Meyer Guggenheim and his family emigrated to Philadelphia in 1847. The family was desperately poor, and Meyer peddled household goods in the coal towns of northeast Pennsylvania. Eventually he began to manufacture a stove polish. Aware of the profits to be made in manufacturing, Guggenheim, acting in partnership arrangements, began to produce and sell lye and a synthetic coffee. He also built a prosperous wholesale business in household merchandise.

When the first machine-made lace was woven in Switzerland,. Guggenheim sent two sons there to establish factories and made a modest fortune importing and selling the lace in the United States. In 1881 Guggenheim accepted a half interest in two Colorado silver mines in payment of a debt. After he had reluctantly invested $20,000 more to get the mines into operation, they suddenly proved to be two of the richest in the area.

Guggenheim felt victimized by the smelting companies. Aware that in the long run the processing of ore would be a good hedge to the high risks involved in mining it, he built a large smelter in Colorado in 1889. In 1895, in order to evade tariff restrictions on Mexican ore, the Guggenheims built a second smelter in Mexico. They also made heavy investments in mines in Mexico and the United States and built a copper refinery in New Jersey.

In 1889 many of the Colorado smelting companies were combined into the American Smelting and Refining Company, and the Guggenheims were asked to join. They refused, and by way of defense against the new giant they formed the Guggenheim Exploration Company. When, due to overcapitalization and a damaging strike, American Smelting began to founder, the Guggenheims joined it on their own terms and took control of the $100 million corporation as well.

Meyer Guggenheim retired in 1895 and died in Palm Beach, Fla., on March 15, 1905. He maintained nominal ties with his orthodox Jewish faith although he apparently had few religious commitments. His business success was due to vision and an ability to combine prudence with a willingness to take big risks when conditions warranted. He also owed much to his seven sons, whom he trained to become one of the best management teams in the nation.

Further Reading

The most complete coverage of Guggenheim's career is Harvey O'Connor, *The Guggenheims: The Making of an American Dynasty* (1937). Other material is in Karl Schriftgiesser, *Families* (1940), and Isaac F. Marcosson, *Metal Magic: The Story of the American Smelting and Refining Company* (1949). Stewart H. Holbrook presents an excellent sketch of the Guggenheim empire in *The Age of the Moguls* (1953). □

Francesco Guicciardini

The Italian historian and statesman Francesco Guicciardini (1483-1540) is best known for his history of Italy, which covers the period from 1492 to 1532.

rancesco Guicciardini was born in Florence into a prominent mercantile family. After graduating in civil law from the University of Pisa, he began a successful practice with clients drawn from the leading Florentine families, merchant organizations, and monastic orders. In 1508 he married Maria Salviati, who bore him seven daughters. His first political appointment, the important one of ambassador to Spain, came to him at the early age of 28. After the return to power of the Medici in Florence and the elevation to the papacy of Cardinal Giovanni de' Medici as Leo X, Guicciardini insisted upon being recalled, arriving home in January 1514. Two years later he was appointed governor of Modena, beginning a career of Church service that endured until the triumph of imperial forces in Italy and the occupation of Rome by troops of Charles V in 1527.

Under Pope Clement VII, his close friend, Guicciardini's power in Romagna was extended. An able governor, he resolutely established order and instituted fiscal reforms and a program of public works. He played a key role in the formation of the anti-imperial League of Cognac in 1526. The third and last Florentine Republic condemned him in absentia on trumped-up charges in 1530, shortly before it fell. When Guicciardini opposed absolute power for the reinstated Medici regime, Clement VII sent him away to be governor of Bologna. When Cosimo I de' Medici reached an accord with Charles V, Guicciardini, still an anti-imperialist, lost favor and retired to his villa of Santa Margherita in Montici. Like his friend Niccolò Machiavelli, he wrote his most important works during a period of political disgrace.

Guicciardini's masterpiece, the *Storia d'Italia* (History of Italy), was written from 1537 to 1540. Published in 1561, the work met with great success, spreading throughout Europe in translation. The *Storia d'Italia* was a history not just of Italy but of Europe. Guicciardini's skill at interrelating political movements in many states, his objectivity even in analyzing events in which he directly participated, his combination of broad perspective with shrewd psychological insights into the contemporary makers of history are truly remarkable. Among the famous passages, sometimes anthologized for their literary verve, are his delineation of conditions in Italy upon the death of Lorenzo de' Medici in 1492 and his portrait of Clement VII.

His other works include *Storia fiorentina* (1509), *Relazione di Spagna* (ca. 1514; Report on Spain), *Dialogo del reggimento di Firenze* (1525; Dialogue on the Government of Florence), *Ricordi politici e civili* (1529; Political and Civil Memoirs), and *Considerazioni sui Discorsi del Machiavelli* (1529; Considerations on Machiavelli's *Discourses*). Of these works the last two are the most important. Guicciardini's *Ricordi* fails to make the clear distinction between public and private morality made by Machiavelli, but it combines shrewd personal observation with fragmentary political analysis.

Further Reading

Guicciardini's *Selected Writings* (1965) has an introduction by the editor, Cecil Grayson. A biography is Roberto Ridolfi, *The Life of Francesco Guicciardini* (1960; trans. 1967). See also Vincent Luciani, *Francesco Guicciardini and His European Reputation* (1936), and Felix Gilbert, *Machiavelli and Guicciardini: Politics and History in Sixteenth-century Florence* (1965). ☐

Guido d'Arezzo

Guido d'Arezzo (ca. 995-ca. 1050) was an Italian music theorist and pedagogue who developed the hexachord system and the musical staff.

Guido d'Arezzo was probably born in Italy, although it has been conjectured that he may have come to Italy from France at an early age. He studied at the Benedictine Abbey of Pomposa and then taught singing there. He left the abbey about 1025 because his ideas did not meet with understanding. The bishop of Arezzo invited him to teach music at his cathedral school and became a great admirer of Guido's new pedagogic devices. These were incorporated in Guido's famous textbook, *Micrologus,* written about 1030.

At Pomposa, Guido had developed a new way of writing Gregorian chant, adopting a four-line staff and clefs. He explained his new methods in the foreword to his antiphonal, a volume of chants that he rewrote in his new way during the 1020s and presented to Pope John XIX, who was greatly impressed. This system of notation is the direct ancestor of all subsequent musical notation.

Educator that he was, Guido developed this idea further in a complete system of ear training and sight singing, which he explained in a letter written from Arezzo to the monk Michael at Pomposa. This system, known as solmization, became the basis of modern solfeggio. For a well-known 8th-century hymn for the feast of St. John the Baptist, Guido created a melody, the first notes of whose first six lines form a scale of two whole tones, a half tone, and two whole tones. This symmetric series of six notes, called a hexachord and sung to the Latin syllables that begin the six lines, *ut-re-mi-fa-sol-la,* became his central tool for ear training and sight singing. By shifting this hexachord to various pitch levels, the singer could always determine where the crucial half-tone interval must be sung.

Guido or one of his disciples also invented a memory aid for learning the names of all the notes in his musical system, which extends over a range of 20 white keys on the piano: the so-called Guidonian hand. Here the note names of the system were written on the various portions of the left hand and fingers, so that they could be read off by the pupil.

Guido's fame was great, and his ideas had a lasting influence on musical notation, music teaching, and musicianship. In these fields he was one of the most outstanding men in all of Western music.

Further Reading

The best account of Guido d'Arezzo is in Donald J. Grout, *A History of Western Music* (1960). See also the fuller treatment of him in Gustave Reese, *Music in the Middle Ages* (1940). ☐

Guillaume de Lorris

The French poet Guillaume de Lorris (ca. 1210-ca. 1237) was the author of the first part of the "Romance of the Rose," the most popular work in medieval French literature.

The only place in the *Romance of the Rose* in which the name of Guillaume de Lorris appears is in the continuation of Jean de Meun, which indicates that Guillaume died some 40 years earlier. Since Guillaume refers to a dream in his twentieth year 5 or 6 years earlier, the date of his birth can be assumed to be about 1210. He was probably born in Lorris, a small town some 30 miles east of Orléans. Just as death prevented Chrestien de Troyes from completing the *Perceval,* so Guillaume died before he finished the *Romance of the Rose;* he stops at line 4,058 (4,028 in Lecoy's edition). Nothing more is known of Guillaume.

The age of the Arthurian romance, with its pageantry, adventures, and thrills, was passing. Hence Guillaume turned to the moral and psychological aspects, represented symbolically in an elaborate allegory. He is not interested in the plot but rather in an exquisitely delicate analysis of young love. Indeed, he says that his poem sets forth the art of love.

In a dream the author sees himself wandering. He comes upon an idyllic formal garden enclosed in a wall bearing hideous paintings of Hatred, Wickedness, Baseness, Covetousness, Avarice, Envy, Sadness, Old Age, Hypocrisy, and Poverty. Gracious Idleness bids the dreamer enter the garden of Amusement, where he meets fair company. The dreamer, henceforth called the lover, is captivated by a rose and immediately the god of Love pierces him with five arrows and instructs the lover in the 10 commandments of love, a veritable abstract of the courtly love code. His quest to pick the rose is long, helped by such as Hope and especially by Fair Welcome but frustrated by Danger, Slander, Shame, Fear, and Jealousy. After the lover succeeds in kissing the rose, Jealousy has the rose shut up in a donjon along with Fair Welcome, and the lover laments his lot as Guillaume's poem ends.

Guillaume's themes were not new; Ovid, Chrestien de Troyes, the troubadours, and Andreas Capellanus furnished him with much, but the freshness of Guillaume's imagination and the delicacy and elegance of his treatment made the work persistently successful, to which the preservation of some 300 manuscripts attests. The influence is manifest in Geoffrey Chaucer's translation, Clément Marot's edition, and Madeleine de Scudéry's Map of Love, and echoes continue to appear down to the works of Marcel Proust and Antoine de Saint-Exupéry.

Further Reading

The best monographs on Guillaume de Lorris are in French. In English, Clive S. Lewis, *The Allegory of Love: A Study in Medieval Tradition* (1936), and Charles Muscatine, *Chaucer and the French Tradition: A Study in Style and Meaning* (1957), are useful. □

Nicolás Guillén

The Cuban author Nicolás Guillén (1902-1989) was one of the most famous writers in Latin America. His poetry showed that he was one of the greatest innovators in Latin American verse. Guillén introduced the Hispanic world to Afro-Cuban folk and musical forms.

Nicolás Guillén was born on July 10, 1902, in Camagüey, Cuba. He was one of six children of mulatto parents. Guillén received his early education in his native Camagüey. His father, who was involved in provincial politics, was murdered when Nicolás was 17. After his father's death he helped support his family by working as a typesetter. He completed his secondary schooling in just two years and began publishing poetry which reflected the prevailing influence of Modernism in the journal *Camagüey Gráfico*.

In 1920 Guillén went to Havana to study law but was forced by economic restraints to return home. In 1921 he returned to Havana and managed to complete one year of formal study at law school. During this period he became actively interested in writing through his association with the literary circles of the capital. He returned to Camagüey in 1922 where, with the help of his brother, he founded the literary journal *Lis* and worked as the editor of a local newspaper from 1922 to 1926.

Early Work

In 1926 Guillén again returned to Havana, where he worked as a typist. In the late 1920s he began writing for a special Sunday newspaper section—"Ideales de una Raza"—of the *Diario de la Marina* devoted to aspects of Black life. It was in this Sunday supplement that he launched his literary career with the publication on April 20, 1930, of *Son Motifs*. Guillén's slim collection of eight poems describing the lives of Blacks in Cuba's urban slums had an electrifying effect on both whites and Blacks who saw in it the genesis of an authentic Cuban art form. The poems were based on the *son,* an Afro-Cuban dance which was popular at the time and symbolized the dual ethnic/ racial makeup of the island. Although these poems explored a variety of urban situations among poor Blacks—the search for money, tension between Blacks and mulattoes, "passing"—they presented these themes from a festive, musical perspective. The poems in *Son Motifs* were soon set to music by composers such as Eliseo Grenet and Silestre Revueltas.

Guillén's next book, *Sóngoro Cosongo* (1931), was longer (it contained 15 poems) and represented a step toward artistic maturity. Although he continued to develop the themes and styles of his first book, the folkloric and picturesque elements were subordinated to capture more authentically the violence and cynicism of ghetto life. In many ways this book is reminiscent of the themes introduced by Langston Hughes in the United States with his *Fine Clothes to the Jew* (1927). In this second book Guillén focused slightly more attention on problems of general national concern. This was noted in the subtitle "Mulatto poems," which clearly indicated Guillén's concern with what was properly the national essence.

Change in Style

The collection of poems *West Indies Ltd* (1934) marked a turning point both in Guillén's poetic techniques and in his political ideology. Here Guillén universalized his concern for the common man by expanding his vision to include all the marginated peoples of the Caribbean. For example, the poem, which gives title to the collection enumerates a long list of evils which plague the Caribbean, many of which are attributed to U.S. economic imperialism.

During the 1930s Guillén worked as a journalist for the liberal newspaper *Meiodía* and became increasingly involved in politics. He joined the Communist Party in 1937, the same year he made his first trip out of Cuba to attend a congress of writers and artists in Mexico. In 1937 he also traveled to Spain to attend the Second International Writers Congress for the Defense of Culture, where he met writers such as Octavio Paz, Pablo Neruda, Langston Hughes, and Ernest Hemingway, among others. In 1937 he published two books: *Songs for Soldiers and Songs for Tourists* and *Spain: Poem in Four Anguishes and One Hope*. In these collections, Guillén increasingly turned to more universal themes and motifs and abandoned temporarily his exploration of Afro-Cuban life. Thus in *Spain* he decried the evils of fascism and poetically called upon the soldiers of Cortés and Pizarro to return and fight the evils of the modern era. Similarly *Song for Soldiers* is a moving indictment of militarism.

In 1947 Guillén published *The Entire Son,* a book which marked the integration of his earlier stages into a universalist apprehension of man's social dilemma. This was followed by *The Dove of Popular Flight—Elegies* (1958), a collection of poems written in exile from Cuba which focuses directly on social issues of the 1950s. Here Guillén treated contemporary political material in an explicit and forceful way. Typical of his political bent are poems such as "Elegy for Emmett Till" and "Little Rock" (both U.S. racial confrontations), whereas "My Last Name" is a mythological search for his African heritage. Published in 1964, *I Have* represented the culmination for the poet of the revolutionary process and evinced a sense of satisfaction. Later collections such as *The Big Zoo* (1967), *The Serrated Wheel* (1972), and particularly *The Daily Diary* (1972) show that Guillén continued to mature and was capable of producing verse which is ironic, humorous, and yet ever faithful to his artistic vision which embraced the condition of the common man.

Apart from the poetry already mentioned, Guillén wrote hundreds of essays for newspapers, many of which dealt with racial problems in Cuba. An anthology of these articles was published in 1975 under the title *Hurried Prose*. In 1953 he was awarded the Stalin Prize in Moscow. After the Cuban revolution in 1959, he served in a variety of diplomatic and cultural missions. In 1961 he was named National Poet of Cuba and became president of the Union of Cuban Writers and Artists.

Robert Marquez and David McMurray edited *Man-making Words: Selected Poems of Nicolas Guillén's* in 1972. *Man-making Words* was a collection of the Afro-Cuban poet's works ranging from his early experimental political poetry to his mature descriptions of the socio-historical and everyday life of his beloved Cuba. Broadening the significance of Guillén's poetry, Ian Isidore Smart wrote *Nicolás Guillén, Popular Poet of the Caribbean* (1990), protraying the breath and richness of the artistic ability of the poet.

Further Reading

Dennis Sardinha's *The Poetry of Nicolás Guillén* (1976) offers a good general introduction to his work and contains considerable information about his life; Frederick Stimson's *The New Schools of Spanish American Poetry* (1970) has a full chapter dedicated to Guillén in addition to a good bibliography; The introduction to Robert Márquez and David Arthur McMurray's *Man Making Words* (1972) also offers a good biographic overview of his life and works with a good discussion of his poetry of social protest; An excellent study of Guillén in relation to the poets of *Negritude* is found in Martha Cobb's *Harlem, Haiti, and Havana: A Comparative Critical Study of Langston Hughes, Jacques Roumain and Nicolás Guillén* (1979); Wilfred Cartey's *Black Images* (1970) has a chapter related to the poetry of Guillén which deals with the Black experience; Lorna V. William's *Self and Society in the Poetry of Nicolás Guillén* (1982) defines Guillén's racial identity and evaluates his sociopolitical views as they are expressed in his poetry; Keith Ellis' *Cuba's Nicolás Guillén: Poetry and Ideology* (1983) is the most comprehensive literary study of the totality of the poet's work to date. It contains an extensive bibliography. Also see *Twentieth-century Latin American poetry: a bilingual anthology,* edited by Stephen Tapscott (Univ of Texas Press, 1996). □

Jorge Guillén y Alvarez

The Spanish poet Jorge Guillén y Alvarez (1893-1984) is best known for his work *Cantico,* which contains radiant lyrics of impeccable form affirming the joy of living. He was one of the older members of the Generation of 1927.

Jorge Guillén was born on Jan. 18, 1893, in the medieval imperial town of Valladolid in Old Castile and received his early schooling there. He later received a solid classical education in schools in Switzerland, Madrid, Granada, and Germany. In 1917 he became a lecturer in Spanish at the Sorbonne, beginning a distinguished and varied career as a professor.

A somewhat shy person, Guillén was a mature man before he began to write poetry in 1918. In 1921 he married Germaine Cahen in Paris. Their daughter, Teresa, was born in 1922; their son, Claudio, in 1924. As adults, Teresa married Harvard professor Stephen Gilman, and Claudio became a professor. Guillén continued his career with a series of professorships in various schools: Murcia, Oxford, Middlebury, McGill, and especially Wellesley, where he remained for almost 20 years. He retired from Wellesley as Professor Emeritus in 1957.

In 1928, during a very fruitful period for Spanish poetry, Guillén published a first edition of *Cántico,* containing 75 poems. As he continued to create poems, he chose to expand the book from within, increasing the number of lyrics but retaining the original order. (This was Walt Whitman's procedure in *Leaves of Grass.*) A second edition appeared in 1936, a third in 1945; in 1950 Guillén published the completed edition, containing 334 poems, in

Buenos Aires, noting that he began it in Brittany in 1919 and finished it in Wellesley in 1950.

In an epoch generally given to negativism and disillusion, Guillén's *Cántico* (Song of Praise) is an affirmation of the simple act of being, without transcendental overtones. Guillén shows a strong influence of Juan Ramón Jiménez but rejects his persistent tendency toward sublimation of human emotions into transcendental or symbolic values. Not a poet of memory (like Antonio Machado), Guillén prefers to exalt the vital moment, the now; his is a delicate and radiant poetry of the senses. His poems often spring from the simple moments of life; for example, he wrote fine lyrics extolling a glass of water and a favorite armchair. As a poet of the vital, lived moment, Guillén concentrated often on the expression of human love, as in the poem *Salvación de la primavera*.

Guillén employed the whole range of traditional forms, usually preferring short meters, such as the artistic heptasyllable, often with the subtle music of Spanish assonance. He masterfully used the *décima*, a tightly rhyming stanza of 10 lines. But he also demonstrated astonishing ability with the sonnet form. Guillén was therefore a traditionalist in form, but within these forms he continued to demonstrate a surprising originality. He was an exponent of "pure poetry," that is, poetry stripped of anecdote and extraneous elements. Guillén's phrasing and images often show an intellectual tone and are frequently quite difficult, but his poetry is never common and always bears his personal stamp.

With *Cántico* completed, Guillén began a second major book called *Clamor,* obviously indicating the darker side of existence, published in three parts: *Maremágnum* (1951), *Que van a dar en la mar* (1960), and *A la altura de las circunstancias* (1963). These books are more "historical" than *Cántico;* that is, they reflect more normally the vicissitudes of existence. However, Guillén's particular forte is still the elegant and radiant expression of a vital faith in living. In 1967 he published *Homenaje,* an extensive collection of laudatory poems. Later works include books of poetry, such as *Y Ostros Poemas* (1973) and *Final* (1981), and the essay collection *El Argumento de la Obra* (1969).

In his later years Guillén continued his career as a scholar and lecturer, receiving many prizes and honors. In 1955, he received the Award of Merit from the American Academy of Arts and Letters; he was also the recipient of San Luca Prize, Florence (1964), Cervantes Prize (1976), Alfonso Reyes Prize, Mexico (1978), and Ollin Yolitzli Prize, Mexico (1982). After his first wife died in 1947, Guillén married Irene Mochi Sisimondi in 1961. His permanent residence was in Italy, but he spent much time in the United States. Guillén died of pneumonia, February 6, 1984.

Further Reading

The most important study in English of Guillén's poetry is Frances Pleak, *The Poetry of Jorge Guillén* (1942). Another work on Guillén, also in English, is Ivar Ivask and Juan Marichal, eds., *Luminous Reality* (1969). □

Guido Guinizzelli

The Italian poet Guido Guinizzelli (c.1230-1276) is considered a precursor of Dante and the originator of the so-called dolce stil novo, or sweet new style.

The son of Guinizzello da Magnano and Guglielmina di Ugolini Ghisilieri, Guido Guinizzelli was born in Bologna between 1230 and 1240, probably toward the end of the decade. He was a judge and married to Beatrice della Fratta; they had one son, Guiduccio. In 1274 he was banished from Bologna together with members of his family and other partisans of the Ghibelline faction of the Lambertazzi. They spent their time of exile in Monselice, where he died before Nov. 14, 1276.

The chronology of Guinizzelli's collection of canzoni and sonnets cannot be established, but his early poetry tends to be under the influence of Guittone d'Arezzo. Guittone's elaborate virtuosity of style is reflected in a sonnet which Guinizzelli wrote to him, addressing him as his "dear father" and respectfully submitting to Guittone—as to a "master"—a canzone, with the request that he should correct and polish it.

Guinizzelli's poetry reflects a background in scholastic philosophy and above all a thorough knowledge of the Provençal and Sicilian tradition of lyric poetry. Within this tradition, however, Guinizzelli was an innovator, and he was recognized as such by his contemporaries. Bonagiunta da Lucca, a Tuscan poet of the Sicilian tradition, wrote a sonnet to Guinizzelli accusing him of having changed the style of elegant love poetry, of speaking obscurely and composing poetry by dint of learning. Guinizzelli answered, also in a sonnet, that the wise man does not reveal his thought before he is sure of the truth. The sonnet shows Guinizzelli's concern with the thought which underlies the poetic expression. Dante, who was almost 30 years younger and belonged to a new generation of poets, acknowledges his debt to Guinizzelli in *Purgatory,* XXVI. He calls him "my father and the father of all my betters who ever composed sweet and graceful verses of love."

While the older Bonagiunta da Lucca criticizes Guinizzelli for his intellectual approach, the younger Dante praises him for his harmonious style. Guinizzelli's poetry does in fact contain both these elements. His "new manner" is characterized by musical equilibrium and acute psychological analysis that is often expressed in terms of vivid concrete imagery drawn from the natural world. In the similes and comparisons that he invents, Guinizzelli's creativity is particularly evident. His poetry of praise translates the woman's beauty into images of light and splendor.

Guinizzelli's intellectual bent is prominent in his most famous canzone, *Al cor gentil rempaira sempre amore.* This theoretical poem equates love with virtue in the noble heart. Nobility is defined as a natural, not a hereditary, disposition toward virtue. The woman's beauty brings the potential for virtue into actuality. Finally, there is a daring theological comparison derived from Thomistic philosophy: just as God causes the heavens to fulfill their nature by revolving in obedience, so the woman should arouse in the noble man a desire to obey her. There is an apparent reconciliation between earthly and divine love, but the final stanza constitutes a lighthearted, epigrammatic recantation. This road from an earthly to a divine love would not be traveled again in literature until Dante wrote his *Divine Comedy*.

Further Reading

For material on Guinizzelli consult Frederick Ozanam, *The Franciscan Poets of the Thirteenth Century* (1852; trans. 1914); Oscar Kuhns, *The Great Poets of Italy* (1903; repr. 1969); Vincent Luciani, *A Brief History of Italian Literature* (1967); and Eugenio Donadoni, *A History of Italian Literature* (2 vols., trans. 1969). □

Alec Guinness

The British actor Sir Alec Guinness (born 1914) was noted for his versatility and disguise. In his career, which spanned more than half a century, he performed in a wide range of roles on stage, in films, and for television.

The birth certificate registers Alec Guinness de Cuffe as born on April 2, 1914. Speculation as to Guinness' paternity levels the responsibility at a banker named Andrew Geddes, who paid for young Alec's board and schooling. When Guinness was five years old, his mother married a Scot named David Stiven and for a time Stiven became the boy's surname.

Guinness developed an early love for the variety show and, later, the legitimate theater. When he was six, it was as the guest of a kindly elderly Russian lady that he was first taken to the Coliseum. There he was mesmerized by Nellie Wallace's act. His benefactress allowed him to purchase a small bouquet for Miss Wallace, which was delivered to her backstage.

As a teenager, Guinness posted a letter to Sybil Thorndike. He had just seen her in *The Squall* and was curious as to how to create thunder onstage for his school play. Miss Thorndike brought him backstage after a matinee performance of *Ghosts* (to which she also provided the youth a seat) and gave him a first-hand viewing of the storm mechanisms.

With his schooling complete, Guinness began employment as a copywriter at a London advertising agency. But he was determined to break into the theater. He decided to audition for the coveted Leverhulme scholarship at the Royal Academy of Dramatic Art. The Royal Academy, however, offered no such scholarship that year, and learning this on the very day of the alleged audition, Guinness walked into another audition, for the Fay Compton Studio of Dramatic Art. He was accepted. The studio offered a full scholarship but no stipend, so after seven months, in 1934, Guinness was forced to seek employment again—this time as an actor.

His first role was as a non-speaking junior counselor in *Libel!,* followed by three small parts—a Chinese cook, a French pirate, and a British sailor—in *Queer Cargo.* These were the inauspicious beginnings of a long career filled with a vast array of character roles.

Big Break

Guinness' "big break," as he saw it and as it is recounted by others, came in November of 1934 when John Gielgud cast him as the Third Player and, later, as Osric in *Hamlet.*

From the inception of his career Guinness had the good fortune of performing with Britain's most notable actors—among them John Gielgud, Laurence Oliver, Peggy Ashcroft, and Edith Evans. He was directed by such world class figures as Gielgud, Tyrone Guthrie, Theodore Komisargevsky, Peter Brook, and, in film, David Lean.

Guinness played in Gielgud's 1935 revival of *Romeo and Juliet;* acted in the 1936-1937 all-Shakespeare season at the Old Vic, understudying Laurence Olivier in the title role for Guthrie's production of *Hamlet.* However, Guinness was not able to shake his image of Gielgud's Hamlet when the next year he was cast in the role by Guthrie for his famous modern-dress, uncut version. Although he was praised for giving a sincere portrayal, the ever self-critical Guinness was disappointed in his Hamlet. Years later he wrote, "I was over-familiar with Gielgud's manner and timing. If only Tony had said to me, 'Forget about John . . . ,' I might have come up with something truer to myself."

Guinness' stage career was interrupted by World War II, during which he served in the British navy. The war had a profound effect on him, but, in his characteristic way, Guinness viewed the experience with humor. When asked what he considered to have been his best performance, Guinness often replied, ''That of a very inefficient, undistinguished, junior officer in the Royal Navy Volunteer Reserve. It also proved to be the longest-running show I have ever been in.''

Guinness' postwar roles became increasingly more diverse. At the Edinburgh Festival in 1949 he originated the role of Sir Henry Harcourt-Reilly in T. S. Eliot's *The Cocktail Party.* He performed at the inauguration of Canada's Shakespearean Festival in Stratford in 1953 in the title role of *Richard III* and as the King of France in *All's Well That Ends Well.* The 1960s brought major roles in Rattigan's *Ross,* Ionesco's *Exit the King* and *Dylan,* and Miller's *Incident at Vichy.* He received a Tony award for his portrayal of the title role in *Dylan* (1964).

More Time to Films

Meanwhile Guinness devoted more and more of his time to film. He had made his debut in *Evensong* (1934) as an extra, and next appeared onscreen as Herbert Pocket in *Great Expectations* (1947), but it was *Kind Hearts and Coronets* in 1949 that established him as a film actor of note. In that film he adroitly impersonated eight family members. Perhaps his most famous screen role was that of Colonel Nicholson in *The Bridge Over the River Kwai* (1957), for which he won an Oscar for best actor. Another unforgettable Guinness performance was that of the butler, Bensonnum, in Neil Simon's *Murder by Death* (1976). In a greatly different role he played Ben (Obi-Wan) Kenobi in *Star Wars* (1977), a role which earned him a best supporting actor Oscar nomination. Because of the hype surrounding the re-release of *Star Wars,* Guinness declined to attend the London premiere in 1997.

Guinness also adapted novels to the stage (*Great Expectations,* 1939, and *The Brothers Karamazov,* 1946) and directed (*Hamlet,* 1951). In the 1980s he also made television appearances, such as that of George Smiley in *Tinker, Tailor, Soldier, Spy* (1980).

Guinness was characterized as ''excruciatingly shy'' and was quoted as saying he possessed ''an unfortunate chameleon quality'' that held him in good stead as an actor ''but not as a person.'' He was knighted in 1959, and in 1990 he lived modestly with his wife, Merula (Salaman) at their country home in Hampshire. He has grown ever more reclusive in his later years.

Further Reading

Guinness credits are cited in *Contemporary Theatre, Film, and Television* (Vol. 1); There are Guinness entries in *Who's Who in Theatre* and in *The Oxford Companion to the Theatre;* John Clifford Mortimer devotes several pages to the actor's work in his 1988 *Character Parts;* Kenneth Von Grunden's *Alec Guinness: The Films* offers the most comprehensive study of Guinness's film career, coupled with his biography; Guinness's own *Blessings in Disguise* (1985) reveals a man of great intellect, wit, and honesty. □

Ricardo Güiráldez

The Argentine poet and novelist Ricardo Güiráldez (1886-1927) is most widely known for his evocative novel *Don Segundo Sombra,* about the passing away of the gaucho's style of life.

Ricardo Güiráldez was born in Buenos Aires on Feb. 13, 1886, into a distinguished Argentine family. As an infant, he was taken to Paris, where he learned French before Spanish. He was a world traveler from his earliest years and, in a sense, adopted Paris as his spiritual home. Yet he always maintained a deep love for the Argentine pampa and, especially, for the family ranch, La Porteña, at San Antonio de Areco. His university education was spotty, as he shifted from architecture to law, finishing neither.

However, a genuine passion for literature was awakened in Güiráldez through the intensive but informal reading he did during these student years. The modernist author Rubén Dario and the influential Argentine poet and writer Leopoldo Lugones had a strong influence on Güiráldez's esthetic formation. But later exposure to European literature, especially that of French writers Gustave Flaubert, Charles Baudelaire, and Stéphane Mallarmé, accounted for much of his stylistic grace and elegance.

Travels and Early Work

Güiráldez left Argentina in 1910 for Paris on what proved to be a long sojourn throughout Europe and Asia. He returned to Buenos Aires in 1912 and, in 1913, married Adelina del Carril, who became his intimate intellectual companion until his death in 1927.

Güiráldez was now sure he wanted to be a writer. In 1915 his first two books appeared: *El cencerro de cristal,* a collection of his apprentice poetry not too favorably received by reviewers; and a volume of short stories, *Cuentos de muerte y de sangre,* which, revealing some of the same stylistic shortcomings, suffered a similar fate.

In 1917 Güiráldez published *Raucho,* his first novel, begun in Paris and finished in Argentina in 1916. It is a seemingly autobiographical work, full of nostalgia and a sense of two places—the ''outer world'' of Paris and other exotic cities and the lovingly evoked pampa.

During the last decade of his life Güiráldez combined travel (three more trips to Europe) with energetic collaboration on a number of influential but short-lived literary magazines that appeared in Buenos Aires. Some of his collaborators were Jorge Luis Borges, Norah Lange, Oliverio Girondo, and Macedonio Fernández.

Crowning Success

In 1920 Güiráldez had completed in Paris the first 10 chapters of a novel to be called *Don Segundo Sombra,* inspired by the character and experiences of an old peon who worked at the family ranch. But he did not finish it then. In 1922 he published a slight, sentimental novel entitled *Rosaura.* And in 1923 he completed *Xaimaca,* another romantic tale, written in diary form, that had a tropical cruise as its setting.

However, fame did not come to the author until 1926, when he published *Don Segundo Sombra,* but then it was immediate and overwhelming. Perhaps no novel has ever appeared in Argentina to the accompaniment of so much acclaim. Güiráldez was able to catch on these pages the essence of a way of life, as seen through the eyes of a ranch boy, and, by means of a highly sensitive prose style, infuse that special type of existence—the disappearing way of the gaucho—with a near-mythical quality.

This was the culmination of Güiráldez's life. Shortly after the publication of *Don Segundo Sombra,* the author discovered he was afflicted with Hodgkin's disease. In March 1927 he left for the last time for Paris, in vain search for a cure. On October 8 of that year he died in Paris.

Further Reading

The principal study of Güiráldez in English is Giovanni Previtali, *Ricardo Güiráldez and Don Segundo Sombra: Life and Works* (1963). See also Enrique AndersonImbert, *Spanish-American Literature: A History* (1954; trans. 1963; 2d ed., 2 vols., 1969).

□

Robert Guiscard

The Norman adventurer Robert Guiscard, Count and Duke of Apulia (1016-1085), was the most famous of the Norman brothers, members of the Hauteville family, who entered the wars of southern Italy and carved out important principalities for themselves.

Of the early life in Normandy of Robert Guiscard, very little is known. In the 1030s his older brothers William, Drogo, and Humphrey went to southern Italy to serve as mercenary captains in the numerous wars between Lombards and Byzantine Greeks. Within 2 decades they had begun to establish themselves in castles and to carry great weight in the affairs of their adopted homeland. In 1046 Robert came to Italy to join them. Robert received no immediate benefits, and he, like other Norman knights ambitious for land and wealth in southern Italy, had to occupy himself in the many military campaigns and small battles that filled its 11th-century history. In 1049 Robert's brother Drogo offered him a castle in Calabria, and for the next 4 years Robert lived a life of brigandage and robbery, earning for himself the nickname Guiscard, the "Crafty One," which he was to retain throughout his life.

Robert came out of Calabria in 1053, when a papal army, backed by the forces of the German emperor, threatened the Norman possessions in the south. In the battle of Civitate in that year, the forces of Norman-controlled Apulia crushed the armies of Pope Leo IX and won papal recognition for their conquests in the south. Robert spent the next 2 years completing the conquest of the last Byzantine lands in

Italy. In 1057 Robert's brother Humphrey, Count of Apulia, died, and Robert, by now the most renowned leader of the Normans, succeeded him. To his younger brother Roger, Robert gave the task of driving the Arabs out of Sicily and adding the island to his possessions.

In 1059 Pope Nicholas II formally confirmed Robert's titles: Duke of Apulia and Calabria and Duke of Sicily, although the island had not yet been conquered. Robert, in his turn, swore an oath of loyalty to the Pope and agreed to pay tribute. In the brief space of 6 years the Norman-papal relations had been reversed. Instead of thieves and usurpers, the Normans were now loyal and faithful papal vassals, servants and allies of the Church. By 1060 Robert and Roger had expelled the Greeks from all of southern Italy except Bari, and they now concentrated upon the conquest of Sicily. This task took 30 years, years that Robert spent in suppressing revolts in Apulia and Calabria and in pressing the remaining Byzantine stronghold at Bari. In 1071 Bari fell to Robert, and the last Byzantine enclave in the West was lost. In the same year Norman forces finally captured Palermo, the capital of Sicily, and in 1072 Robert entered his new domains in triumph.

After dealing with yet another rebellion and surviving a protracted illness, Robert renewed his attempts to crush pockets of resistance to his rule. In 1077 he conquered Salerno, and in 1080, after years of disputes, wrangling over rights, and personal insults, Robert renewed his oath of loyalty to the papacy in the person of Pope Gregory VII and was in return confirmed in the possession of his lands. From 1080 on, Robert began to form another plan, this time to attack the Byzantine Empire itself, across Greece and the northern Aegean Sea to the very capital city of Constantinople. Throughout 1081 Robert assembled a massive fleet and army at the ports of Brindisi and Bari. In May 1081 Robert's fleet crossed the Adriatic. In a furious battle at Durazzo, Robert defeated the army of the Byzantine emperor Alexius I Comnenus and forced him to retreat. Alexius, however, had instigated a revolt in Apulia, and this revolt, along with an appeal from Pope Gregory VII for aid against the army of the German emperor, Henry IV, recalled Robert to the Italian mainland, where he spent 1082 and 1083 in suppressing the revolt in Apulia and preparing an assault on Rome to rescue the embattled Pope Gregory.

In 1084 Robert attacked the city of Rome, the German defenders fled, and the Normans entered the city and sacked and burned it, taking Pope Gregory with them. Gregory was installed in a palace at Salerno, where he died in May 1085. Several months earlier Robert had returned to the campaign in Greece. He resumed the campaign, which had faltered during his absence, and captured the island of Corfu. After wintering on Corfu, the Norman army was suddenly struck by a ravaging epidemic, possibly typhoid fever, and on July 17, 1085, Robert himself succumbed to it. He was buried at Venosa in Apulia.

Further Reading

There is no better introduction to Robert Guiscard's life than John Julius Norwich, *The Normans in the South, 1016-1130* (1967), an excellent popular history of Norman expansion in southern Italy. See also David C. Douglas, *The Norman Achievement* (1969), the best survey of Norman activity in France, England, and southern Italy, and Denis Mack Smith, *Medieval Sicily* (1970). □

François Pierre Guillaume Guizot

The French statesman and historian François Pierre Guillaume Guizot (1787-1874) was a cold and clever politician whose refusal to grant electoral reforms precipitated the February Revolution of 1848. His scholarly publications, however, have been widely praised.

Though born at Nîmes on Oct. 4, 1787, François Guizot was educated in Geneva, where his mother had emigrated after his father's execution in 1794. Returning to Paris in 1805, Guizot studied law but soon forsook it for a literary career. The publication of a critical edition of Edward Gibbon's *Decline and Fall of the Roman Empire* established his reputation as a historian and secured his appointment (1812) to the chair of modern history in the University of Paris. There he became a disciple of the moderate royalist philosopher Pierre Paul Royer-Collard.

Guizot took no active part in politics under the Empire, but during the first Bourbon restoration he held the post of secretary general of the Ministry of the Interior. After the Hundred Days he twice held office: secretary general of the Ministry of Justice (1815-1816) and director in the Ministry of the Interior (1819-1820). But the assassination of the Duke of Berry in February 1820 produced a reactionary backlash that swept Guizot and the moderates from office.

Out of office for most of the next decade, Guizot concentrated on historical research and writing. From his productive pen came the *History of the Origin of Representative Government* (2 vols., 1821-1822); *History of the English Revolution from Charles I to Charles II* (2 vols., 1826-1827); *General History of Civilization in Europe* (3 vols., 1828); and *Histoire de la civilisation en France* (4 vols., 1830). Guizot's histories have been justly praised for their excellent scholarship, lucid and succinct style, judicious analysis, and impartiality.

Returning to active politics in January 1830, Guizot entered the Chamber as a deputy for Lisieux and immediately joined the opposition to the Polignac ministry. Since 1815 Guizot had shared with Royer-Collard the leadership of the Doctrinaires, who considered the Charter of 1814 the epitome of political wisdom since it established a balance between the power of the Crown, the nobility, and the upper middle classes. As right-wing liberals, they supported the restoration monarchy so long as it governed according to the Charter, but when Charles X attempted to rule by decree, they turned from the Bourbon to the Orleanist dynasty. During the July Revolution of 1830, they helped to elevate Louis Philippe, Duke of Orléans, to the throne.

In August 1830 Guizot became minister of the interior. For the next 2 years he gradually became more conservative as a series of Paris disorders instilled in him a fear of anarchy. But his conservatism had deeper roots. A devout Calvinist, he identified the sanctified elect with the political elite, who, he believed, had a divine mission to govern the masses.

By October 1832, when he became minister of public instruction, Guizot had assumed leadership of the right-center. His one great legislative act was the law of June 28, 1833—the charter of France's elementary school system—which required every commune to maintain a public primary school. Always the champion of the academic community, he reestablished the Académie des Sciences Morales et Politiques, which Napoleon had suppressed, founded the Société de l'Histoire de France, and published at state expense huge collections of medieval documents and diplomatic dispatches.

In February 1840 Guizot went to London as ambassador, but in October he became foreign minister and the dominant personality in the Soult ministry. The tenets of his foreign policy were nonintervention, friendship with Britain, and cooperation with Austria. In 1847 Guizot became premier. But overthrown by the February Revolution of 1848, he went into exile in England. After a year in London, devoted primarily to research in the British archives, he retired to his estate at Val Richer near Lisieux in Normandy.

Though Guizot survived the Orleanist monarchy by 26 years, he never reentered the political arena but focused his energy on academic activities and writing historical works. Between 1854 and his death on Sept. 12, 1874, he published the *Histoire de la république d'Angleterre et de Cromwell* (2 vols., 1854); *Histoire du protectorat de Cromwell et du rétablissement des Stuarts* (2 vols., 1856); *Mémoires pour servir à l'histoire de mon temps* (9 vols., 1858-1868); and the *Histoire parlementaire de la France* (5 vols., 1863), which included his speeches.

Further Reading

The best biography of Guizot in English is Douglas Johnson, *Guizot: Aspects of French History—1787-1874* (1963). Though mindful of the statesman's faults, Johnson attempts to rehabilitate him by emphasizing his "sound intellect" and "historical consciousness" and by showing that his foreign policy was "always reasonable and usually realistic." Elizabeth Parnham Brush, *Guizot in the Early Years of the Orleanist Monarchy* (1929), is an excellent special study. A good general account of Guizot's political career is J. Lucas-Dubreton, *The Restoration and the July Monarchy* (trans. 1929), which also analyzes the social and intellectual currents of the period. □

Ludwig Gumplowicz

The Polish-Austrian sociologist and political theorist Ludwig Gumplowicz (1838-1909) is considered one of the more significant "conflict" theorists in sociology.

Ludwig Gumplowicz was born on March 9, 1838, the son of prominent Polish Jews living in Cracow. His early career was as a journalist, but in 1875 he began his university career as a teacher of law at Graz, where he remained until shortly before his death.

Gumplowicz viewed sociology as the study of groups in conflict. Sociology was dominated by the social Darwinists, who crudely applied Charles Darwin's theories of "the survival of the fittest" and "the struggle for existence" to the development of human societies. Gumplowicz and others refined the application of these theories to society into a sociological system known as conflict theory. The theory, now considered to be somewhat dated, exercised an extraordinary influence in political, social, and legal studies, an influence which continues to this day.

Gumplowicz's theories played a major role in reorienting American political science away from the study of public law and the structure of government and toward the process of politics by focusing on interest groups.

Gumplowicz minimized the importance of the autonomous individual, viewing him in a Marxist deterministic manner. The individual never functions as individual but only as a member of a group, the influence of which determines his behavior. Thus social change and the development of history are entirely the products of social groups,

their conflicts being analogous to the biological struggle for existence, with the result being growth. Human history, however, does not develop linearly but—as in all nature—cyclically, from birth, to growth, to maturation, to decline, to death, and then begins a new cycle.

According to Gumplowicz, the state originates in the conflict among races, which in turn are simply primitive groups. At the outset of his *Outlines of Sociology* he describes the foundation of the state: "Every political organization and hence every developing organization, begins when one group permanently subjects another. Subjection of some to the others is the source of political organization, is the condition essential to social growth." According to Lester Ward, this principle constitutes the cornerstone of Gumplowicz's theory.

Gumplowicz argued that there are no natural rights antecedent to the state, all rights being of the civil type only, that is, existing to the extent that they happen to be guaranteed by a particular state. The history of every nation is one of class conflict in which the fittest necessarily survive and dominate the less fit. Each group strives to become the controlling group within the state, the only motive being self-interest.

The same principles are applied to the behavior of states as to groups. Their most natural tendency is incessant increase of power, and territorial expansion is the expression of the very being of a state and is so inevitable that rulers and people are powerless to resist it. Gumplowicz also gave currency to the terms "syngenism" and "ethnocentrism."

Ironically, since Gumplowicz was Jewish, his work *Race Struggle* (1883) is regarded by some scholars as having been an important influence on the development of Nazi theories. Early in 1909 Gumplowicz left the University of Graz, and shortly thereafter he and his wife committed suicide.

Further Reading

Gumplowicz's influence on racism is discussed in William M. McGovern, *From Luther to Hitler* (1941). His contributions to the development of sociology are assessed in Lester F. Ward, *Outlines of Sociology* (1898), and Harry Elmer Barnes, *Historical Sociology: Its Origins and Development* (1948). A recent evaluation of Gumplowicz's significance is in the second English-language edition of his *Outlines of Sociology* (1963), edited and with an introduction and notes by Irving Horowitz. □

Ignaz Günther

Ignaz Günther (1725-1775) was the foremost German rococo sculptor. His elongated forms and pastel polychromy combine Viennese sophistication and the gaiety of Bavarian folk art.

gnaz Günther was born in Altmannstein near Ingolstadt on Nov. 22, 1725, the son of a cabinetmaker and sometime sculptor, who was also his first teacher. Günther was sent to Munich in 1743 and apprenticed to the sculptor Johann Baptist Straub, who had a large workshop and trained many artists. In 1750 Günther set out as a journeyman, going first to Salzburg and then to Mannheim, where he worked with Paul Egell, whose dramatic style he admired greatly, until Egell's death in 1752. Günther then enrolled at the academy in Vienna in early 1753, with Mathias Donner, brother of the great Georg Raphael Donner, among his teachers, and in November he won a first prize.

Günther returned to Munich to work on his own, but few of his early works remain. His first major commission was the high altar in Rott am Inn (1760-1762), where he produced some of his masterworks: notably the *Holy Trinity* above the high altar, the supremely elegant figures *Emperor Heinrich* and *Empress Kunigunde* in white and gold flanking it, and the realistic *St. Peter Damian* and *St. Notburga* in vivid color on the side altars. These were followed by his major works in Weyarn, a small parish church not far from Munich, where his famous *Annunciation* (1764) is to be seen; one of the chief examples of European rococo sculpture, its gracefully curving forms are made doubly thrilling by the beauty of the polychromy and the elegance of the faces and gestures of the Madonna and the archangel Gabriel. The highly emotional *Pietà* at Weyarn (1764), also in polychromed wood, is a dramatic version of the subject, not without its naive touches. Other works at Weyarn are an *Immaculata*, a *Mater Dolorosa,* some statues of saints, and the figures decorating several of the altars, notably the cherubs and cherub heads, with their fat cheeks and pensive expressions.

Günther's polychrome *Guardian Angel* (1763) for the Bürgersaal in Munich is probably his greatest, and certainly his most famous, work. The angel reveals a debt to Georg Raphael Donner's revival of mannerist canons of form, derived from the study of late Renaissance sculpture, which Günther had absorbed during his student days at the academy in Vienna. Its elongated and supernatural elegance is heightened by the contrast with the charmingly realistic little Bavarian child it leads by the hand.

Günther also produced models for the ducal porcelain works of Nymphenburg (1771), as well as other works in Munich, such as altars in the church of St. Peter and five portals for the Cathedral, the Frauenkirche. In 1773 he was appointed court sculptor. In 1774 he produced the *Pietà* at Nenningen, one of the most moving works of art of the rococo period—an era not usually characterized by depth of feeling. A comparison with the Weyarn *Pietà* reveals how much Günther's art had deepened in emotional feeling and how subtly he was able to suggest profound tragedy without recourse to theatrical gestures or expressions. He died in Munich on June 26, 1775.

Further Reading

The best work on Günther is the monograph, in German, by A. Schönberger, *Ignaz Günther* (1954), with excellent photographs. Satisfactory discussions in English are in John Bourke, *Baroque Churches of Central Europe* (1958; 2d rev. ed. 1962); Nicholas Powell, *From Baroque to Rococo: An Introduction to Austrian and German Architecture from 1580 to 1790* (1959); and Eberhard Hempel, *Baroque Art and Architecture in Central Europe* (1965). □

Gustavus I

Gustavus I Eriksson (1496-1560), first king of modern Sweden, reigned from 1523 to 1560. He led Sweden from chaos to a position as a minor European power.

Gustavus Vasa was born at his mother's estate at Lindholm on Ascension Day, 1496. The Vasas had played an active role in Swedish politics during the 15th century, but usually in the Union party rather than the Nationalist. His father, however, was in the party of Sten Sture, Regent of Sweden, who led the peasantry and some nobles against the Danish Union. In 1516 Gustavus was sent to Denmark as a hostage and was imprisoned in the island fortress of Kalö. He escaped to Lübeck in September 1519 and returned as a fugitive in May 1520 to Kalmar in Sweden.

In January of that year Sten Sture had died and left the forces of the Swedish peasantry leaderless. In March, Christian II had been proclaimed king by the Union aristocracy. On November 8 between one and four o'clock Christian carried out the "bloodbath" of Stockholm, in which no less than 82 persons were beheaded; others fell victim the next day. Among them were Gustavus's father, brother-in-law, and other relatives, and most of the Sture party. Gustavus was hunting near Lake Mälaren when he heard of this event, which overnight made him leader of the Nationalists.

His estates confiscated, a price on his head, Gustavus appealed to the peasants and miners of Dalarna, as had other antiunionists since the days of Engelbrekt. Already bled white by struggle, they first refused him, but when news came that Christian planned to spread fire and sword to Dalarna, ski runners were dispatched to recall the fugitive bound for Norway. They overtook him, and at Mora Church in January 1521 they proclaimed him their leader.

Aided by Lübeck's navy, the courage of the peasants and miners, and the leadership of patriotic nobles, the forces of Gustavus Vasa drove Christian's troops out of the country. A revolt at home deprived Christian of his throne, and in May 1523 the Swedish Riksdag (Diet) met at Strängnäs. On June 6 it elected Gustavus Vasa king.

Gustavus inherited a divided kingdom. Much of the leadership of the nobles had been liquidated in the bloodbath, and Gustavus was hard put to find competent administrators. He owed a tremendous financial debt to the Lübeckers. Moreover, the independent men of Dalarna felt that they had won the crown for Gustavus and expected political and economic compensations. They made at least four serious attempts to limit the Crown. An open revolt in

1531, when they refused to give every second church bell to pay off the debt due Lübeck, led to the arrest and execution of many of the King's old friends and comrades in arms. By intervening in the Count's War in Denmark (1534-1536), he helped place Christian III on the Danish throne and freed himself of Lübeck's economic restrictions.

The Swedish Church possessed great wealth and political power, and the archbishop of Stockholm, Gustavus Trolle, not only had backed the Danish kings but had been a catalyst in the Stockholm bloodbath. Needing money and faced with a revolt in Dalarna by the peasants, and elsewhere by some of the high ecclesiastics, Gustavus in June 1527 called a Riksdag at Västerås and threatened to resign as king if his ecclesiastical policy was not approved. In an agreement known as the Recess of Västerås, the King had his way. A break took place with Rome; church courts and discipline came under the Crown. Thus began the drift of Sweden toward Lutheranism, a movement primarily political and economic. In no country was church property so despoiled as in Sweden, the majority of it going to the Crown. Still, the transition was gradual and claimed few victims.

During his lifetime Gustavus was highly controversial, but time has usually weighed the scales heavily in his favor. Although he was greedy, lustful for power, overbearing, and at times cruel, he gave Sweden a strength and unity that it had heretofore lacked. He had an extraordinary memory, and often his writing and oratorical skills bordered on the theatrical. He had three wives and many children and was

survived by a daughter, Cecilia, and four sons, Erik, John, Magnus, and Charles.

Gustavus's achievements in advancing his country culturally, economically, and politically survived his death on Sept. 29, 1560, at the Royal Palace in Stockholm. As his grandson Gustavus II Adolphus said of him, "This king was the instrument by which God again raised up our fatherland to prosperity."

Further Reading

Perhaps the best account of Gustavus I in English is in Michael Roberts, *The Early Vasas: A History of Sweden, 1523-1611* (1968). Extended accounts of him appear in Carl Hallendorf and Adolf Schück, *A History of Sweden* (1929; rev. ed. 1938), and Andrew A. Stomberg, *A History of Sweden* (1931). □

Gustavus II

Gustavus II (1594-1632) was king of Sweden from 1611 to 1632. He did much to make Sweden a major European power, and his military exploits were highly important in the history of Russia, Germany, Poland, and the Baltic Provinces.

The eldest son of Charles IX of Sweden and Christina of Holstein-Gottorp, Gustavus II was born on Dec. 9, 1594. Although his parents had Calvinist leanings, Gustavus received heavy doses of Lutheranism. History, government, warfare, and engineering were among the subjects he pursued, with special emphasis on language. Count Axel Oxenstierna, his most trusted adviser, said of his sovereign, "In his youth he obtained a thorough knowledge and perfect command of many foreign tongues, so that he spoke Latin, German, Dutch, French, and Italian like a native, understood Spanish, English, and Scotch, and had besides some notion of Polish and Russian." At 9 Gustavus was introduced into public life, and at 13 he was receiving petitions. At 15 he began to administer his duchy of Västmanland and opened the Riksdag at Örebro in his father's absence. On Aug. 15, 1609, he made his first speech to the Estates when he dismissed them after a stormy session, for his father was incapacitated by a stroke from which he never completely recovered. He henceforth was coregent until his father's death in October 1611.

His Character

A Dutchman described the new king as being "of lofty stature, of finely proportioned build, with a fair complexion, long face, blond hair, and pointed beard of an almost golden hue." As the years passed, the hair became more golden and the beard reddish, and in spite of his strenuous life, the King became corpulent and his features heavier. An engraving of 1616 confirms the rather elongated face, the large eyes, and the nose that gave him the nickname Gösta, or Hooknose. He suffered one serious physical defect: he was nearsighted, which hampered him on the battlefield and was a factor in his death.

Of an ardent and passionate nature as his relations with Ebba Brahe and the Dutch woman Margareta Slots would indicate, Gustavus was simple in his clothing and eating habits, often inspiring his troops by sharing their hardships. He was temperate in his drinking, not by inclination as his daughter Christina relates, but "of reasons of state." On the other hand, he delighted in the pageantry of ceremonial occasions. He was quick-tempered, impatient, intolerant, and strict and sometimes used wrath for a purpose.

Gustavus Adolphus believed strongly in honor, work, duty, and destiny. Knowing his own imperfections, he put his trust in God. He blended caution and constancy of purpose with a love of spontaneous action that attains its goal because of its unexpectedness. Active, energetic, and impervious to danger, he still had time to show interest in theology and was "a lover of all arts and sciences."

Such was the young king who took over a country at war with Russia, Poland, and Denmark. Kalmar had already fallen to the Danes, and soon Älvsborg capitulated. The newly built Göteborg (Gothenburg) was burned to the ground. Yet Stockholm held, and the armies of Christian IV encountered unexpected resistance from the Swedish people. Consequently a peace was signed at Knäred in January 1613 whereby Sweden agreed to pay Denmark one million riksdaler within 6 years and give up all claims to certain disputed Arctic regions. Älvsborg fort and the surrounding region were to be occupied by the Danes as pledge for payment. All other boundaries were to remain the same. Sweden did, however, retain exemption from the tolls at the Sound.

The struggle with Russia was aided by succession problems in the Muscovite state known as the "Time of Troubles." Playing off various succession candidates, Gustavus was able to conclude on Feb. 27, 1617, at Stolbova a favorable peace which excluded Russia from the Baltic. In autumn of that year Gustavus's long-delayed coronation took place in the Cathedral of Uppsala. On Nov. 25, 1620, he married Maria Eleanora of Brandenburg and thereby achieved "his first victory on German soil," whose political rewards were obvious. Not so obvious was the Queen's emotional unbalance which made the King's domestic life difficult and which was passed on to their daughter Christina.

Less than 2 years before his death Gustavus wrote Oxenstierna: "If anything happens to me, my family will merit your pity, not for my sake only, but for many other reasons. They are womenfolk, the mother lacking in common sense, the daughter a minor—hopeless, if they rule, and dangerous, if others come to rule over them."

Domestic Affairs

Gustavus inherited the throne by the Pact of Succession of 1604 and at the Estates of Nyköping in December 1611 was recognized king despite his youth. On the other hand, he was forced to concede certain powers to the Council and the Estates. Some of these concessions aided the Crown because Swedish administration was extremely complex.

The Charter of 1617 sanctioned all former privileges of the nobility and stipulated that all important crown offices be reserved to the nobility. No commoner could be employed in the central administration or serve as a judge or diplomat. By the Statutes of the Nobility of 1626 grades in the nobility were defined, and it became the right and the duty of the upper class to enlist in the civil service of the country. The nobility, however, was not a closed caste and was constantly recruited from below. Commoners with conspicuous abilities as soldiers and administrators were given the title commensurate with their positions. As time passed, a cleavage developed between the new aristocracy of service and the aristocracy of land and family. Furthermore, Gustavus gave the Estates considerable power and balanced the lower estates against the upper. The meetings of the Estates gradually were transformed into orderly discussions as opposed to the stormy and highly dramatic meetings held by earlier sovereigns. There were complaints over taxes, but the successful foreign policy of the King usually kept the Estates loyal.

Gustavus and his able chancellor Oxenstierna worked tirelessly to create a central organization to meet the country's administrative needs. Their efforts reached fruition in the 1634 Års Regeringsform (Constitution). A central office, or college, was established for each of the chief administrative departments: war, justice, and so on. Over each college was an official with a seat on the Council, which most of the year sat permanently in Stockholm instead of meeting at the command of the King. On the local level, the country was divided into provinces with a crown official residing in the castle of the most important city of the province. It was this machinery that made it possible for government to function during the long absences of Gustavus and during the minority of Christina. Sweden was also fortunate in the number of able leaders it had to fill posts provided under the new arrangements.

Economic Measures

The payment of the Älvsborg ransom, enlarged political responsibilities, and the heavy expenses of almost constant war put a strain on Sweden's finances that could not be maintained without adequately utilizing the natural resources of the country. An elaborate mercantilist system was erected which not only specialized arts and crafts within various cities but specialized cities themselves. Some cities were newly built or resurrected, but the only really successful one was Göteborg. Government policies were highly successful in the mining industries. Dutch capital, traders, and industrialists such as Louis de Geer established large new ironworks and reorganized old ones. Large numbers of Flemings and Walloons came into the country, and Calvinists mingled with the native Lutherans. Many characteristics of Low Country origin may be discerned in the areas in which they settled. Soon Sweden had sufficient ordnance for its army and navy plus some for export. Shipyards were busy building naval and merchant ships, and a Swedish colony in the New World was planned but not actually attempted until 6 years after the death of Gustavus. Although the results of the economic policy did not always reach government hopes and expectations, they must be regarded as fairly satisfactory because they enabled Sweden to carry successfully the heavy burdens imposed from the outside.

War and Diplomacy

For Gustavus Adolphus war and diplomacy intermingled. It has been said that he was the first man in modern times to reduce war to a system and to secure brilliant results by strict application of that system. He was skilled in military engineering and cartography and was a student of the scientific side of war. Some of his officers were trained by Maurice of Orange, and Gustavus took the tactics of the brilliant Dutchman and gave them his own twist by combining them with the best of the Spanish school. Consequently there developed through his efforts a general European system of fighting—formation in line.

Gustavus developed naval superiority since campaigns across the Baltic were impossible without it. The backbone of his army was Swedish and Finnish regiments drafted from each province, but a number of Germans and Scots served under him. His armies were usually outnumbered, but he substituted maneuverability for size. His highly mobile army was supplied with light up-to-date equipment with large stores of supplies kept in readiness for their needs. His artillery was capable of rapid fire, and his units coordinated the various arms into an organic whole possessing superior striking power. Gustavus paid close attention to detail and to instructing his officers personally. Consequently he developed a school of generals which included Swedes, Germans, and Scots.

Sigismund of Poland refused to recognize Gustavus's right to the throne partly because of his own claims and partly as an element of the Catholic offensive in Europe militarily underway since the outbreak of the Thirty Years War in 1618. In 1621 Gustavus captured Riga and soon the rest of Livonia. From 1626 to 1629 he continued military operations against Poland. In these he built his military skills and trained his forces. He could not obtain sufficient guarantees to help Christian IV against the Catholics, and after the defeat of Christian in Germany by the Catholic general A. E. W. von Wallenstein, the Swedes were beaten at Struhm on June 29, 1629, by the Poles led by Stanislaus Koniecpolski aided by 10,000 mercenaries of Gen. Wallenstein. This battle led to the Peace of Altmark, which left Gustavus free to cope with the German situation. Wallenstein meanwhile threatened Pomerania, and Gustavus sent aid to the besieged city of Stralsund. After much soul-searching, Gustavus decided to espouse the Protestant cause, motivated by religion highly mixed with a concern for Sweden's well-being.

On May 19, 1630, Gustavus formally took leave of the Estates, realizing he might never return to Sweden. On June 24 he landed at Rügen. He cleared Mecklenburg of imperial troops, and Pomerania soon followed. In the spring of 1631, strengthened by a definite alliance with France, the Treaty of Bärwalde, and aided by the dismissal of Wallenstein, Gustavus decided to relieve the city of Magdeburg, which was under siege by the imperial general the Count of Tilly. Brandenburg and Saxony refused his troops passage so

Gustavus remained in Pomerania while Magdeburg was sacked. Tilly found Gustavus's fortifications at Verden too strong to attack so he moved into Saxony to compel its elector, John George I, to disband his army. This leader of the neutral princes in Germany appealed for aid, and Gustavus joined his troops to those of the Saxons, and on Sept. 7, 1631, at Breitenfeld battle was joined. Although the Saxon wing was shattered, the Swedes held firm and turned defeat into victory. This was the turning point in the war because never again did the imperial forces gain complete ascendancy.

Wallenstein was recalled to action, and Gustavus mobilized the whole of northern Germany to meet him. In 1632, when he received news that Wallenstein was threatening Protestant Nuremberg, Gustavus began a successful invasion of Bavaria. He was repulsed in his attempts to relieve that city and turned his troops toward Austria, hoping to draw off Wallenstein. In this he was successful. He then made a series of rapid marches, hoping to return to his base, but found Wallenstein entrenched in Saxony. On Nov. 6, 1632, the two met at Lützen. The Swedish troops won the battle but lost their king. Gustavus fought without armor because it irritated old wounds and was uncomfortable because of his weight. Somehow in the mists, the near-sighted king became detached from his troops and was slain. There was no one to take his place, and henceforth neither Catholics nor Protestants were able to gain a complete mastery over the other.

Gustavus's life was cut short when he stood at the height of his success. He has been called everything from a selfish Swedish nationalist who ruined Germany to a dreamer for a united Scandinavian-German empire. He has been hated and revered by posterity as he was in his own lifetime. There can be no doubt that he set his stamp on his age and that he is one of the outstanding examples of the importance of the personal factor in history.

Further Reading

Two excellent works in English on Gustavus are Nils Ahnlund, *Gustav Adolf the Great* (trans. 1940), and Michael Roberts, *Gustavus Adolphus: A History of Sweden, 1611-1632* (2 vols., 1953-1958). Considerable accounts of Gustavus appear in Carl Hallendorf and Adolf Schück, *A History of Sweden* (1929; rev. ed. 1938), and Andrew A. Stomberg, *A History of Sweden* (1931). □

Gustavus III

Gustavus III (1746-1792) was king of Sweden from 1771 to 1792. He was an enlightened despot and a *philosophe*.

Born on Jan. 24, 1746, Gustavus III was the eldest son of Adolphus Frederick, an ineffectual king of Sweden, and Louisa Ulrika, the sister of Frederick the Great of Prussia. He was educated by Carl Gustav Tessin and Karl Scheffer, two of Sweden's more eminent statesmen, and by Olof von Dalin, poet and historian. On Nov. 4, 1776, he joined Sophia Magdelena of Denmark in what proved to be an unhappy marriage.

Throughout most of the 18th century Sweden was at the mercy of two selfish factions, the Hats and the Caps, which had made effective government almost impossible. The former wanted revenge on Russia and were subsidized by France, and the latter were subsidized by Russia, whose empress, Catherine the Great, used bribery, corruption, and diplomatic pressure to prevent any reform of the Swedish constitution.

After a trip to France and Prussia in early 1771, Gustavus III attempted mediation between the factions. The Caps, who held power, wanted to limit the monarchy and make Sweden a pawn in the Russian system. Between Aug. 17 and 21, 1772, Gustavus by a coup took over the government. The Riksdag (Diet) was dissolved and a new constitution adopted which curbed the power of the Estates but did not do away with them. In 1778 the Estates enthusiastically backed his administrative reforms, but in 1786 they opposed him. In 1788, while Sweden was at war with Russia and Denmark, certain members of the nobility were working and intriguing with the Russians. Gustavus appealed in person to the peasants of Dalarna, and on Feb. 17, 1789, by the Act of Unity and Security he was able to override the opposition of the nobility and, with the approbation of the three lower estates, to establish a constitution in which royal power was predominant except for the power of the purse. Because of events, Gustavus, a more ardent friend of the

nobility than any other Swedish king, was forced to undermine the nobles' power and favor the lower estates.

Gustavus strengthened Sweden's naval and military forces. Although these moves were not directed against any single country, Gustavus had much to fear from Russia, who resented a nonsubservient Sweden. He entered the League of Armed Neutrality against Great Britain and through preparedness and luck was able to ward off attacks from both Russia and Denmark. On July 9-10, 1790, the Swedes won a resounding naval victory at Svensksund and the next month were able to sign at Värätä a peace with Russia in which Sweden was spared many humiliating concessions. Gustavus then tried to form a league against the French Jacobins.

Ever since the turbulent days of 1789, the Swedish nobility had been bitter. This was especially true among the younger aristocrats, who, fired by hatred and the battle cries of the French Revolution, imagined that they were fighting for justice and liberty against the King. Joined by hotheads and other malcontents, they plotted against the "Swedish tyrant." At the Stockholm Opera House, which he had done so much to foster, Gustavus attended a masquerade on March 16, 1792, and was shot in the back. He died on March 29.

Gustavus III, enlightened despot and *philosophe,* modeled his court on Versailles. He promoted the liberty of the press and was hurt when it attacked him. His court was highly ceremonial and at times reflected a theatrical king who not only could act but with his own hand created some of the best dramas of the Swedish theater. He wrote exquisitely, and his court became a meeting place for most of Sweden's great writers. The Swedish Academy was founded in 1786, and Gustavus made generous gifts to the advancement of science and to the University of Uppsala. He amended the poor law, proclaimed absolute religious liberty, and reformed the judicial system. No longer was torture used in legal investigations. There can be little doubt that he spent too lavishly for a poor country, that he surrounded himself with frivolous and adventurous flatterers, and that he welcomed every opportunity for pleasure and display. Still he was patriotic and saw an identity between the welfare of his subjects and the enhancement of his own glory. When compared with his immediate predecessors and his successors up to Charles XIV, his reign was refreshing and enlightened.

Further Reading

R. N. Bain, *Gustavus III and His Contemporaries, 1746-1792: An Overlooked Chapter of Eighteenth Century History* (2 vols., 1894), although dated, is a useful work in English. Detailed accounts of Gustavus III appear in Carl Hallendorf and Adolf Schück, *A History of Sweden* (1929; rev. ed. 1938), and Andrew A. Stomberg, *A History of Sweden* (1931). □

Philip Guston

American painter Philip Guston (1913-1980) was a key member of the New York School with a strongly urban point of view. The unique aspect of his career is that he moved from being a successful figurative artist to pure abstraction and then, late in life, returned to figurative art.

Philip Guston was born in 1913 in Montreal, Canada. The youngest of seven children, Philip moved with his family to Los Angeles in 1919. Plagued by financial difficulties and personal conflict, his father committed suicide soon after.

Guston attended Manual Arts High School in Los Angeles and was a classmate of Jackson Pollock. The two became firm friends. In 1930 Guston briefly studied at Otis Art Institute, but soon dropped out. He was largely a self-taught artist.

Between 1934 and 1935 Guston travelled with a friend to Mexico, where he served briefly as an assistant to Mexican mural artist David Siqueiros. He later returned to Los Angeles to work on a mural project before following Pollock to New York in 1935. He joined the Federal Art Project of the Work Projects Administration, executing murals for the 1939 World's Fair and for the Queensbridge Housing Project on Long Island.

From 1941 to 1945 Guston held a teaching position at the State University of Iowa. Between 1945 and 1947 he taught at Washington University in St. Louis. In 1947 he settled in Woodstock, New York, and during the 1950s he taught painting at both New York University and Pratt Institute.

Guston's work has been widely exhibited. He had his first New York show in 1945. In 1956 some of his paintings were included in the Museum of Modern Art's "Twelve Americans" show. In 1960 the Guggenheim mounted a major retrospective exhibition, and in 1966 the Jewish Museum in New York did a show of his "gray paintings." In 1980, the year of his death, the San Francisco Museum of Modern Art put together a travelling exhibition which was later shown in Chicago, Denver, New York, and Washington, D.C.

Guston always approached painting as a means of self-discovery. He was preoccupied with paradox, especially personal paradox, and his work was the result of a constant dialogue with himself. His artistic development was shaped by his need to synthesize two antagonistic modes of working: naturalism and abstraction. His way of painting reflected this. He sketched his subject rather literally, and then attempted to "erase" most of the representational elements.

Deeply steeped in the past, Guston was inspired by many artists. Paintings by de Chirico and Picasso impressed him while still in high school. He was also preoccupied for nearly a decade with the study of Renaissance art, responding particularly to the architectural sense of structure inherent in paintings by Mantegna, Masaccio, Piero, and Uccello.

Guston always viewed the history of art as having two over-riding themes—paintings based on pleasure and beauty and paintings based on care and pain. His own work reveals a constant struggle to unify these two trends, yet the painful side always seemed to dominate.

Stylistically, Guston's evolution from figurative art to Abstract Expressionism was gradual. His mural art of the 1930s was concerned with solving spatial problems, synchronizing voids and solids in controlled depth. Never a realist, Guston moved closer to a Cubistic approach as he began working with flat planes instead of volumes.

His work of the early 1940s reveals Renaissance structure and order being fused with Cubist simplification. The 1940s were a decade of transition for Guston. His work became more abstract as he turned to form and color as equivalents for feelings and emotions. Recurring themes of childhood culminated in 1945 with his painting *If This Be Not I* (Washington University, St. Louis). His first truly painterly work, it depicts costumed children with Ensorlike masks against an urban backdrop. The painting is strange and unsettling, but not frightening.

This period was turbulent for Guston. He grew frustrated at his inability to resolve his emotional feelings within the framework of his chosen forms. His first non-objective painting dates from 1947-1948. Finally, in 1948, he stopped painting entirely.

An opportunity to travel in Europe on a Guggenheim Fellowship and a Prix de Rome provided him with new directions. During this time (1948-1949) he drew a lot, but did not paint. He also discovered a new interest in painterly artists from the past, particularly Titian. When Guston began to paint again in 1949 he had banished all vestiges of Cubism from his style. The process of painting had become very important and resulted in a freer mode of working with new emphasis on surface.

During the early 1950s Guston's style was dubbed "Abstract Impressionism" due to his soft, pastel palette, atmospheric approach, painterly brushwork, and shimmering surfaces. Midway through the decade his style changed again, this time becoming more vital, aggressive, and impulsive. He began working on a larger scale, emphasizing vibrant colors and black. The work of this period seems to totally reject Renaissance order. A sense of conflict between form and chaos underlies the ambiguous shapes and expressive brushwork. The years 1957-1958 found Guston as close as he ever came to Action Painting. His usual approach was by no means spontaneous. He worked by layering paint, scraping and revising as he went.

In the 1960s his work softened. A deliberate muddying of tones and a move towards grays and half-tones resulted in a mood of reverie and introspection. Then, in a 1970 exhibition which shook the art establishment, Philip Guston suddenly returned to literal subject matter painted in a primitive, cartoon-like manner with forms recalling those of Léger. The first of these paintings (such as *The Studio,* 1969) include hooded and masked Ku Klux Klan figures which hark back to similar themes explored by the artist in the 1930s and 1940s. This time, however, the brushwork is harsh, the colors garish, and the shapes simplified and outlined.

Later themes include interiors, landscapes, cars, light bulbs, cigarettes, paint brushes, and shoes—sometimes attached to numberless, intertwined legs, sometimes alone. Many of Guston's contemporaries were horrified by his move back to humanistic content. Yet, like his early mural work, this change in style allowed the artist to once again engage in narrative works of art.

Guston once said, "I'm puzzled all the time by representation or not, the literal image and the nonobjective. There's no such thing as nonobjective art. Everything has an object, has a figure. The question is what kind?" This statement helps viewers to bridge the seeming gap between Guston's non-objective works of the 1950s and 1960s and the paintings of his last years.

In 1937 he married Musa McKim, and in 1943 their daughter, Musa Jane, was born. Guston received two Guggenheim Fellowships (1947, 1967) and an honorary doctorate from Boston University (1970).

Further Reading

Dore Ashton's monograph, *Philip Guston* (1960) is a standard work and provides useful information about Guston's first 45 years. The catalogue issued by the San Francisco Museum of Modern Art, entitled *Philip Guston* (1980) provides the best information about his late work and contains a chronology and a very extensive bibliography of articles and reviews. Among the many discussions of Guston's work in magazines, the following are especially useful: Thomas B. Hess, "Inside Nature," *Art News* (February 1958); Irving Sandler, "Guston: A Long Voyage Home," *Art News* (December 1959); and Sam Hunter, "Philip Guston," *Art International* (May 1962).

Additional Sources

Mayer, Musa, *Night studio: a memoir of Philip Guston,* New York, N.Y., U.S.A.: Penguin Books, 1990.
Storr, Robert, *Philip Guston,* New York: Abbeville Press, 1986. □

Johann Gutenberg

The German inventor and printer Johann Gutenberg (ca. 1398-1468) was the inventor of movable-type mechanical printing in Europe.

Johann Gutenberg was born Johann Gensfleisch zur Laden, in Mainz. He was the third child of Freile zum Gensfleisch and his second wife, Else Wirick zum Gutenberg, whose name Johann adopted. Nothing is known of Gutenberg's studies or apprenticeship except that he learned the trade of a goldsmith while living in Mainz. About 1428 his family was exiled as a result of a revolt of the craftsmen against the noble class ruling the town, and in 1430 Gutenberg established himself in Strassburg, where he remained until 1444.

Gutenberg's experiments in printing began during his years in Strassburg. He was already familiar with the techniques of xylography, the process used to make books and other printed matter in Europe since the 14th century, and in the Far East much earlier. Then came the transition from xylography to typography, infinitely more practical for text printing since, instead of reproduction by means of wood carving, a small separate block (type) was used for each sign or character. The idea of movable type may have occurred to many people independently; Gutenberg may have worked in this field about 1436.

Business of Printing

There is no record of Gutenberg's whereabouts after 1444, but he appears again in Mainz according to a document dated October 1448. By 1450 he is known to have had a printing plant, for which he borrowed 800 guilders from the rich financier Johann Fust to enable him to manufacture certain tools and equipment. In December 1452 Gutenberg had to pay off his debt. Being unable to do so, he and Fust concluded a new agreement, under which Gutenberg received another similar loan and the financier became a partner in the enterprise. At that time Gutenberg already printed with movable type, thus making the idea conceived in Strassburg a reality in Mainz. A very valuable assistant to Gutenberg was his young employee and disciple Peter Schoeffer, who joined the firm in 1452. In spite of their successes, the relationship between Gutenberg and Fust

took a bad turn, Fust sued Gutenberg for 2,000 guilders, and in 1455 the partnership was dissolved. Fust won the court action and thereby acquired Gutenberg's materials and tools and went into partnership with Schoeffer.

Provenance of printed works of this period is therefore difficult, especially since there are no printed works surviving with Gutenberg's name on them. From that period dates the monumental and extremely beautiful 42-Line Bible, also called the Gutenberg Bible and Mazarin Bible, a work in big folio which is the crowning of many years of collaboration by the Gutenberg-Fust-Schoeffer team. However, when the first finished copies were turned out in early 1456, Gutenberg, undoubtedly the main creator of the work, no longer belonged to the partnership. Fust continued printing successfully with Gutenberg's equipment and also with machinery improved by Schoeffer. In the meantime Gutenberg, not at all favored by fortune in his various undertakings, had to start all over again. It is believed that the fruit of his work in these years is the 36-Line Bible and the famous *Catholicon,* a kind of encyclopedia. Again, as Gutenberg never put his name on any of his works, all ascriptions are hypothetical.

Later Years

In 1462 Mainz was sacked by the troops of Adolph II. Fust's printing office was set on fire and Gutenberg suffered losses as well, the same as other craftsmen. In consequence of this disaster many typographers left Mainz, and through their dispersion they also scattered their until now so jealously protected know-how. Gutenberg remained in Mainz,

but he was again reduced to poverty, and he requested the archiepiscopal court for a sinecure, which he obtained on Jan. 17, 1465, including salary and privileges "for services rendered . . . and to be rendered in the future." Gutenberg's post at the court allowed him some economic relief, but nevertheless he carried on with his printing activities. The works from this final period in his life are unknown because of lack of identification.

Reportedly, Gutenberg became blind in the last months of his life, living partly in Mainz and partly in the neighboring village of Eltville. He died in St. Victor's parish in Mainz on Feb. 3, 1468, and was buried in the church of the Franciscan convent in that town. His physical appearance is unknown, though there are many imaginary depictions of his face and figure, including statues erected in Mainz and Strassburg. In 1900 the Gutenberg Museum was founded in Mainz with a library annexed to it to which all the objects and documents related to the invention of typography were entrusted.

Further Reading

Gutenberg's original documents are in Karl Schorbach, ed., *The Gutenberg Documents,* translated by Douglas C. McMurtrie (1941). There are many biographies of Gutenberg, but most of them contain inaccuracies. Those that are reliable include Laurence E. Tomlinson, *Gutenberg and the Invention of Printing* (1938); Pierce Butler, *The Origin of Printing in Europe* (1940), which is perhaps excessively critical; and Victor Scholderer, *Johann Gutenberg: The Inventor of Printing* (1963), probably the most accurate. Douglas C. McMurtrie, *The Invention of Printing: A Bibliography* (1942), is a guide to the literature on Gutenberg and on printing. □

Edwin Ray Guthrie

Edwin Ray Guthrie (1886-1959) was an American psychologist. Although he wrote on philosophy and in different areas of psychology, Guthrie was primarily noted for his work in evolving a single simple theory of learning.

Edwin Guthrie, born Jan. 9, 1886, in Lincoln, Nebr., was one of five children. His mother was a schoolteacher, and his father a store manager. He graduated and received a master's degree from the University of Nebraska, specializing in mathematics, philosophy, and psychology. He entered the University of Pennsylvania as a Harrison fellow, receiving his doctorate in 1912. His educational training and background reflect his analytical frame of reference in his psychological writings.

Guthrie taught high school mathematics for 5 years in Lincoln and Philadelphia. In 1914 he joined the University of Washington as an instructor in the department of philosophy, changing to the department of psychology 5 years later. During his rise to full professor in 1928, he developed his learning theory in association with Stevenson Smith, who was then department chairman of psychology at Washington.

Guthrie married Helen MacDonald of Berkeley, Calif., in June 1920. They traveled widely, and in France Guthrie met Pierre Janet, whose *Principles of Psychotherapy* he translated with his wife. Janet's writing had a great influence on Guthrie's thinking. To Janet's descriptive psychology and physiological concepts as sources of action, Guthrie added an objective theory of learning.

In the latter part of the 1920s Guthrie concerned himself with such topics as fusion on nonmusical intervals, measurement of introversion and extroversion, and purpose and mechanism in psychology. He seemed more inclined toward the exploration of learning in the 1930s and thereafter.

Much honored, Guthrie was elected president of the American Psychological Association. During World War II he was a lieutenant in the U.S. Army, serving as a consultant to the overseas branch of the general staff of the War Department and Office of War Information. He was made dean of the graduate school at the University of Washington in 1943.

Guthrie was considered a behaviorist. Behaviorism was a school of psychology which felt that psychology as a science must be predicated on a study of what is observable. Behaviorists excluded self-observation as a scientific method of investigation and preferred experimentation. They examined the concept of association and its limits in explaining how learning takes place. Guthrie's interpretations in his writings are based on the theory of learning: "A combination of stimuli which has accompanied a movement will on its recurrence tend to be followed by that movement."

In his theory Guthrie avoids mention of drives, successive repetitions, rewards, or punishment. He refers to stimuli and movement in combination. There is one type of learning; the same principle which applies for learning in one instance also applies for learning in all instances. The difference seen in learning does not arise from there being different kinds of learning but rather from different kinds of situations.

Further Reading

Most of the literature on Guthrie is concerned with his theory of learning. A recent, sophisticated analysis of his theory is in Ernest R. Hilgard, *Theories of Learning* (1948; 3d ed. 1966). For a shorter analysis see Bergen Richard Bugelski, *The Psychology of Learning* (1956). □

Tyrone Guthrie

Tyrone Guthrie (1900-1971) was an English theater director, largely responsible for the founding of the Shakespeare Festival Theatre, Stratford, Ontario, and of the Guthrie Theatre, Minneapolis.

Born in Tunbridge Wells, Kent, Tyrone Guthrie was the great-grandson of the Irish actor Tyrone Power. As a schoolboy Guthrie soon showed an interest in the theater, music, and writing. At Oxford University he studied history and was an active member of the Dramatic Society. In 1923 he joined the newly-founded Oxford Playhouse. However, the company's director, James B. Fagan, developed little confidence in Guthrie's acting abilities and did not re-hire him the following season.

Guthrie then accepted a job as a broadcaster for the British Broadcasting Company (BBC) in Belfast and soon began to produce plays over the air. His success as a radio director led him back to the theater and to a directing position with the Scottish National Players in Glasgow (1926). In 1928 the BBC produced two of Guthrie's radio plays, *Squirrel's Cage* and *Matrimonial News,* and employed him as a script editor in London.

Guthrie soon left the BBC to become artistic director of the Anmer Hall Company at the Festival Theatre, Cambridge. With this new company Guthrie's directing repertoire could shift away from the somewhat parochial national plays favored by the Scottish Players. He directed Euripides, Shakespeare, Ibsen, Chekhov, and Pirandello. It was here at the Festival Theatre that Guthrie also began to develop his gift for staging innovative, animated crowd scenes, eventually one of his directorial trademarks. In late 1929 another of Guthrie's radio plays, *The Flowers Are Not For You To Pick,* was successfully produced by the BBC. Despite Guthrie's primary involvement with the theater, his reputation as a radio writer and personality continued to grow. Accord-

ingly, he was engaged to produce in Montreal a radio series of dramatized popular history, "The Romance of Canada" (1930-1931).

Upon returning to the Anmer Hall Company Guthrie directed James Bridie's *The Anatomist* (1931). The play opened the company's second home at Westminster Theatre and was Guthrie's first London production. He had his first West End directing success with *Dangerous Corner,* J. B. Priestley's first play (1932). That same year Guthrie published the first of his many books, *Theatre Prospect,* and his Westminster production of *Love's Labours Lost* brought him to the attention of Lilian Baylis. As administrator of the esteemed Old Vic, Baylis was in search of a new resident director for the company. She offered Guthrie the position for the 1933-1934 season.

Guthrie brought Charles Laughton to the Old Vic and directed him in several leading roles, most notably as Angelo in *Measure for Measure* (1933). However, Guthrie received mixed reviews for his year's work and subsequently concentrated on tallying up a number of West End and Broadway successes. Having proven himself in the commercial theater, Guthrie rejoined the Old Vic in 1936. As resident director, he staged a number of important, if not always entirely successful, productions: Wycherly's *The Country Wife* (1936), with Edith Evans and Ruth Gordon; *A Midsummer Night's Dream* (1937, 1938) with Mendelssohn's music; a modern dress *Hamlet* (1938) with Alec Guiness; and Ibsen's *An Enemy of the People* (1939). Two of his productions, *Hamlet* (1937) and *Othello* (1938), became famous for their Freudian interpretations, with Laurence Olivier playing major parts in both. During World War II Guthrie struggled to keep the Old Vic organization afloat in the provinces. One of his finest productions of this period was Ibsen's *Peer Gynt* (1944) with Ralph Richardson in the title role.

From 1945 to 1951 Guthrie worked as a freelance director. Among his many productions during these years were Rostand's *Cyrano de Bergerac* (1946), again with Richardson in the lead role, and *Oedipus Rex* in Israel, New York, and Finland (1947, 1948). He also directed several operas and presented plays at the annual Edinburgh Festival. Guthrie returned to the Old Vic as interim artistic director for the 1951-1952 season, but his focus then moved to a new project in Canada.

The project was the Shakespeare Festival Theatre in Stratford, Ontario. It was founded in 1953 and originally housed in a huge tent. Guthrie's impulse to become involved with this venture was threefold: to help to develop a national theater tradition in Canada; to work with a resident ensemble, for Guthrie was a strong advocate of theater done by a *community* of artists; and to stage Shakespeare in a spatial configuration true to the Elizabethan spirit. After years of experience with Shakespeare's plays, Guthrie felt that an amphitheater setting with a large thrust stage better served the Bard's theatrical vision than the more common proscenium stage. Guthrie was the festival's artistic director for its first two summer seasons and directed plays for the company until 1957.

In 1958 Guthrie began plans to expand the ideas he had realized in Canada and to transfer them to America. His goal was to establish a fully professional classical repertory company free from commercial pressure. His efforts came to fruition with the 1963 opening of the Minneapolis Theatre, designed somewhat on the lines of the Stratford theater. For the opening season Guthrie directed his second modern dress *Hamlet* and Chekhov's *The Three Sisters.* His later productions in Minneapolis included *Henry V* and Jonson's *Volpone* in 1964; Chekhov's *The Cherry Orchard* and *Richard III,* with Hume Cronyn in the title role, in 1965; *The House of Atreus,* an adaptation and monumental staging of Aeschylus's *The Orestia,* in 1967; and Chekhov's *Uncle Vanya* in 1969. In 1971 the theater was renamed in honor of Guthrie. He was knighted in 1961.

Further Reading

Besides *Theatre Prospect* (1932), Guthrie's own books on the theater include *A Life in the Theatre* (1959), his autobiography; *A New Theatre* (1964), which chronicles the development of the Minneapolis Guthrie Theatre; and *In Various Directions* (1965), a collection of essays. He also co-authored three volumes on the Shakespeare Festival Theatre, Stratford, Ontario: *Known at Stratford,* with Robertson Davies and Grant MacDonald (1953); *Twice Have the Trumpets Sounded,* with Davies and MacDonald (1954); and *Thrice The Brinded Cat Hath Mew'd,* with Davies (1955). An informative biography is James Forsyth, *Tyrone Guthrie* (1976). Interviews with numerous actors and designers about their work with Guthrie are collected in Alfred Rossi, *Astonish Us in the Morning: Tyrone Guthrie Remembered* (1977). □

Woodrow Wilson Guthrie

Writer and performer of folk songs, Woodrow Wilson Guthrie (1912-1967) composed "This Land Is Your Land," an unofficial national anthem.

Guthrie was born July 14, 1912, in Okemah, Oklahoma. He had little formal education, for which he compensated to a degree with intensive reading. Guthrie led one of the most tragic lives of any notable American. His father was a failure in both politics and business and died on skid row. His mother killed his only sister in an insane rage before dying of Huntington's chorea, which she passed on to Guthrie. In later years Guthrie lost his own infant daughter in a fire. Virtually orphaned at the age of 14 when his family broke up, Guthrie developed an itinerant way of life that he never entirely abandoned until his final hospitalization.

In the course of his travels Guthrie learned to perform folk songs, first those of others but later increasingly his own. In 1937 he obtained through a cousin the first of many, usually short-lived, radio jobs, singing and playing on a Los Angeles station. He also acquired permanent ties to the Communist Party. In 1940 he arrived in New York and was discovered by Alan Lomax, assistant director of the Archive of Folk Songs of the Library of Congress. Lomax recorded many of Guthrie's songs for the library and promoted his career in other ways, such as by inducing Victor Records to produce a two album, 12 record set of Guthrie's "Dust Bowl Ballads." Though they did not sell, the ballads were to have lasting influence.

In 1941 Guthrie joined the Almanac Singers, a left-wing folk music group that included Pete Seeger, ultimately, with Guthrie, its best known member. On February 14, 1942, the Almanacs achieved their greatest exposure by performing on a program called "This Is War" that was aired by all four networks. But newspaper stories about the group's Communist affiliations prevented the Almanacs from achieving commercial success, and they dissolved within a year. Most of the members of the Almanacs were ardently anti-Nazi and went into the military. Guthrie too supported the war. "This Machine Kills Fascists" was inscribed on his guitar. But he hoped to accomplish his goal at a distance, trying vainly to be exempted from the draft. To avoid induction he served in the merchant marine. That was a dangerous strategy: two of the three ships he served on were lost. In addition, he was drafted anyway. Upon his discharge from the army in 1946 he joined People's Songs, another radical music association. It too failed because of the Communist connection, which gave even more offense during the Cold War than earlier.

Pete Seeger organized a folk-singing group called The Weavers in 1948, and for several years it produced one hit record after another. Though Guthrie was not a Weaver, their success helped his music. His "So Long, It's Been Good to Know You" became one of their most popular

numbers. But The Weavers were soon blacklisted, and the vogue for popularized folk music disappeared with them. By this time Guthrie was visibly failing, and in 1952 Huntington's chorea, a gradual but invariably fatal disease of the nervous system, was diagnosed. He died of it on October 3, 1967.

Though a poor musician and erratic performer, Guthrie wrote an estimated 1,000 songs which have earned him a secure place in musical history. When he was discovered, folk music had few fans except radicals and a handful of admirers and musicologists. Guthrie and The Weavers were responsible for its brief popularity in the late 1940s and early 1950s and influenced the greater following it developed ten years later. Though folk music became less popular, it continued to exist, and Guthrie's legacy is very much a part of it.

Guthrie's legend is harder to assess. He was famous among leftists in the 1940s, and by the 1960s, though hospitalized and unable to speak, he had become a mythic figure. Bob Dylan, before he himself became famous as the leading composer of political songs, made a pilgrimage to Guthrie's bedside. Guthrie's reputation was based on his authentic folk origins and hobo inclinations, his remarkable talents as a writer and composer, and a romantic appreciation of his politics. This last was especially misplaced. Guthrie's political instincts were populist, nourished by the indigenous American socialism that flourished briefly in Oklahoma before and during World War I. He was influenced too by the Industrial Workers of the World, the fabled Wobblies, some of whom he met in his travels. But he early became associated with the Communist Party and, though never subject to party discipline (or any other kind), faithfully followed the Communist line during its worst phases from the 1930s through the Korean War.

Further Reading

An honest though politically unsophisticated biography is Joe Klein, *Woody Guthrie: A Life* (1980). Guthrie's own memoir, *Bound for Glory* (1943), bears only a poetic relation to the truth and ends before he had gained any reputation. His miscellaneous writings, all edited by other people, include *Born To Win* (1965), *Seeds of Man* (1976), and *The Woody Guthrie Songbook* (1976). □

Gustavo Gutiérrez

The Peruvian theologian Gustavo Gutiérrez (born 1928) was known as the father of liberation theology.

Gustavo Gutiérrez was born in the Monserrat barrio of Lima, Peru, on June 8, 1928. He was a *mestizo,* part Hispanic and part Quechuan Indian. He had polio as a boy and spent most of his teenage years in bed. This experience motivated him to begin training for a career in medicine, but along the way he decided instead to become a Roman Catholic priest. Because of his outstanding work in theology, the church sent him to do graduate work in Europe, at Louvain (Belgium), Lyons (France), and the Gregorian (Italy).

On his return to Lima to begin work as a priest and teacher, he discovered that the "classical" formation he had received in Europe had not equipped him to deal with the needs of the poor and oppressed in Latin America. Three discoveries in particular were important. First, instead of seeing poverty as a "virtue," or at least something to be accepted by Christians, he came to see poverty as something destructive that must always be opposed. Second, instead of seeing poverty as the result of laziness or bad luck, he came to see it not as accidental but structural, something that society conspires to ensure, so that there will always be enough poor people to keep wages down. Third, instead of accepting poverty as inevitable, he came to see that the poor were a social class and could organize to bring about change.

Re-reading the Bible in the course of making these discoveries, he realized that the God of the Bible makes "a preferential option for the poor," rather than (as the institutional church so often implied) for the rich. God loves all persons, but has a special concern for the victims, and sides with them in their struggle for justice. The true concern of both the Bible and the Christian tradition, Gutiérrez came to feel, is the promise of liberation, a three-fold liberation from unjust social structures, from a sense of fate, and from personal sin and guilt.

These concerns received his powerful expression in what became the most influential theological work in the 1970s and 1980s, A Theology of Liberation (1971; reissued with a new introduction in 1988). The prominence of this book led many to describe Gutiérrez as "the father of liberation theology," a description he disavowed because, as he insisted, a theology of liberation is not the work of the experts but of "the people," meaning the poor people for whom he was simply the one to write a book about what he had learned from them.

The main themes of liberation theology are congruent with the themes of the Christian tradition, save that they are always seen "from the underside of history," namely, from the perspective of the poor and oppressed. There has been "an irruption of the poor" challenging the unjust structures of society and the church when either becomes a defender of the status quo rather than the champion of its victims. God is the God of the poor, Jesus Christ is "God become poor" in a Galilean carpenter, and the Holy Spirit is the power of God on the side of transformation. All this is particularly evident in the "base communities," small groups within the church who combine Bible study with involvement for change. Over a hundred thousand base communities sprang up in Latin America in the 1970s and 1980s.

Because liberation theology means, among other things, a challenge to the authorities, there was heavy opposition from those same authorities. Those holding power killed thousands of priests and lay people for siding with the poor and seeking to improve their lives. Gutiérrez himself was attacked from within the church by those who did not want the church to be on the side of change. A familiar charge in the 1970s was that he and liberation theologians like him were Marxist, seeking to transform Christianity into nothing but left-wing politics. The charge was unpersuasive to any who had actually read his writings or examined his life, and by 1990 this criticism was receding from the scene.

Gutiérrez was essentially a parish priest in Rimac, a slum area of Lima near where he grew up. But his writings made him a world figure, and he occasionally visited the United States and Europe to speak and teach. The fullness of the faith he thus communicated was further evident in such later works as We Drink From Our Own Wells (1984), in which he described a "spirituality of liberation" and argued that the two terms could not be understood apart from each other. His book On Job: God-Talk and the Suffering of the Innocent (1987) distinguishes two types of "God-talk," prophetic language about God that stressed the need for justice in human affairs, and mystical or contemplative language addressed to God, a language of praise and relationship. He contended that the two forms of speech were essentially one.

While his later writings were less overtly "political" than his earlier ones, they nevertheless served to make the basis for political involvement increasingly firm. They mined the resources of scripture and tradition for fuller understanding of the God of the Hebrew prophets and of Jesus Christ, a God who, rather than being remote and uninvolved, is found "in the midst" of the world and the suffering of God's people. Thus, Gutiérrez affirmed that human effort for social justice contributes to laying of the groundwork for the Kingdom of God, which is ultimately God's gift rather than a human achievement.

Gutiérrez spent 20 years writing Las Casas: In Search of the Poor of Jesus Christ, the story of the early Spanish missionary Bartolome de Las Casas, which was released in the mid-1990s. During this time he also alienated some Peruvian feminists by saying that feminism was alien to Latin America. Critics argued that this showed he was losing touch and dividing communities.

Further Reading

Although a professional theologian, Gutiérrez wrote in a style that can be understood by lay people. His book The Truth Shall Make You Free (1990) is an irenic account of his faith, in response to the many charges made against him by the Vatican. We Drink From Our Own Wells draws deeply on the Catholic tradition of spirituality, and On Job is a careful excursion through one of the bestknown books of the Hebrew Scriptures. Part 4 of A Theology of Liberation is still the best and most detailed setting-forth of his thought. Robert McAfee Brown, Gustavo Gutiérrez: An Introduction to Liberation Theology (1990) is a full interpretation in English, and Arthur McGovern, Liberation Theology and Its Critics (1989) positions Gutiérrez clearly within the broad spectrum of liberation concerns.

Book reviews of Las Casas: In Search of the Poor of Jesus Christ appeared in America (August 27, 1994) and The Christian Century (July 13, 1994). Also see National Catholic Reporter (October 18, 1996) for additional information on Gutiérrez. □

Guy de Chauliac

The French surgeon Guy de Chauliac (ca. 1295-1368), also known as Guido de Cauliaco, was the most famous surgical writer of the Middle Ages. His major work remained the principal didactic text on surgery until the 18th century.

Guy de Chauliac was born, very likely, at Chauliac, a village near the southern border of Auvergne. He was probably of peasant stock. The little that is known of his childhood and early training stems from brief, but frequent, autobiographical comments in his writings.

Because Guy cited the views of one of his Toulousian teachers, he is believed to have begun his medical and surgical studies in that city. At the University of Montpellier, whose medical faculty was renowned throughout the medieval world, he fulfilled the requirements for the degree of master of medicine. Subsequently, that title accompanied his name in most official documents, even though he had previously taken holy orders.

Sometime after 1326 Chauliac attended the anatomical lectures of Nicolò Bertuccio, the student of and successor to the important medieval anatomist Mondino da Luzzi at the University of Bologna. The next trace of Chauliac is in Paris, where during the late 13th century great surgeons such as Lanfranc and Henri de Mondeville had taught and practiced. The courses that their followers offered may have piqued but did not hold Chauliac's interest, for unlike many students, he did not linger in Paris but seems to have drifted slowly southward, perhaps performing surgical procedures to earn his way.

After having practiced surgery in or near Lyons for a decade or more, Chauliac moved to Avignon, where he accepted the post of private physician to Pope Clement VI. The date of his appointment to his office can be fixed between the Pope's election in 1342 and the onset of the bubonic plague epidemic at Avignon in 1348, which Chauliac described as a resident physician in that city. He also served Clement's successors at Avignon, Innocent VI and Urban V. In 1363 Chauliac, who had become papal first physician, composed his most important work, *The Inventory of Medicine,* or as it is known in Latin, *Chirurgia magna.*

This book, though not the earliest medieval surgical text, is remarkable in several respects. It begins with a historical account of the development of medicine and incorporates Chauliac's evaluation of the medical sources available in the mid-14th century. He reveals that he prized the Galenic texts recently rendered from Greek to Latin but scorned John of Gaddesden's medical encyclopedia, *Rosa Anglica.*

Of more interest today, however, are the personal experiences that Chauliac sprinkled throughout his text. These findings, together with his efforts to reconcile them with authoritative statements, contributed to the enormous success of his book; the *Chirurgia magna* was translated into many languages and passed through innumerable editions and abridgments. Five years after completing it, probably during the month of July, in 1368, Chauliac died.

Further Reading

There is a chapter on Chauliac in Leo M. Zimmerman and Ilza Veith, *Great Ideas in the History of Surgery* (1961). See also Fielding H. Garrison, *An Introduction to the History of Medicine* (1913; 4th ed. 1929); Arturo Castiglioni, *A History of Medicine* (1927; 2d ed. 1947); and W. J. Bishop, *The Early History of Surgery* (1960). □

H

George Habash

George Habash (born 1926) was a founder of the Arab Nationalists' Movement in 1952 and of the Popular Front for the Liberation of Palestine (PFLP) in 1967.

George Habash was born in Lydda (now Lod) in 1926 to a family of Christian Palestinian merchants. When Arab-Jewish fighting broke out in Palestine in 1948, he was a medical student at the American University of Beirut in Lebanon. He returned home to Lydda to try to help his community, but was forcibly expelled from Lydda by the advancing Jewish forces.

Like others in Palestine and the Arab states, Habash was embittered by the Arabs' defeat in 1948 and sought a way to redeem Arab honor. In 1950, back at his classes in Beirut, he joined with other students from many different Arab countries to form the Arab Nationalists' Movement (ANM). The ANM preached that only the unified actions of all the Arab people could liberate the Arab world, including Palestine. Because the movement rejected the Islamic fundamentalism then rife in the Arab world, it attracted much support from the minority of Arabs who were Christians. It also rejected such socially divisive ideologies as socialism and communism, as well as the splitting up of the Arab world into separate states.

During the 1950s Habash had criticized Yasser (or Yasir) Arafat's Fateh (also transliterated as Fatah) organization and other Palestinians who were guilty of what the ANM considered to be "Palestinian separatism" from the pan-Arab cause. It was not until 1964 that the ANM started doing systematic political work in the Palestinian community.

Many of the ANM's ideas and aims were shared by Gamal Abdel-Nasser, who came to power in Egypt in 1952. From 1954 through 1967, the ANM worked closely with Nasser, pursuing their joint aims throughout the Arab world. In 1967, however, Nasser was humiliated by his country's defeat in the Six Day War with Israel, so Habash and his colleagues started rethinking their alliance with him.

The shock of the 1967 defeat caused the ANM's leaders to rethink some of their other ideas, too. In December 1967 the ANM decided to found its own Palestinian organization, which it called the Popular Front for the Liberation of Palestine (PFLP). Habash became its general secretary.

The PFLP was always smaller than Fateh. At the beginning the PFLP's leaders considered that the only way they could compete with Fateh for popular attention was to stage large-scale terrorist operations against Israeli and pro-Israeli targets. The most spectacular of these was the hijacking of four Western airliners to a desert airstrip in Jordan in September 1970. This action gave the Jordanian government the opportunity to crack down on the Palestinian guerrillas who then moved to Syria.

Shortly thereafter the PFLP sought inclusion in the Fateh-dominated Palestinian Liberation Organization (PLO). At some stage in the early 1970s Habash's official PFLP leadership disavowed the terrorist operations that were still being carried out by PFLP extremists. But the PFLP maintained its hard-line political stance. In 1974 it vehemently opposed the PLO mainstream's shift toward calling for the establishment of a Palestinian state in just part of historic Palestine and formed a new alliance of PLO oppositionists called the "Rejection Front."

55

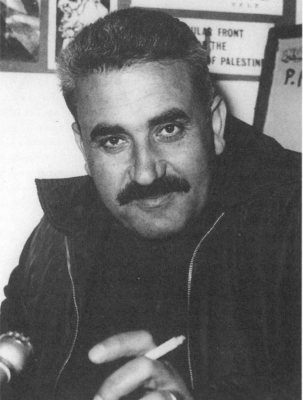

ence within the PFLP and on Arab politics in general. The silver-haired Habash, however, still posed a threat to peace in the Middle East. In the mid-1990s, he travelled to Libya to confer with Muammar Qadhefi, while Naef Hawatmeh, leader of the DFLP, flew to Iraq for a meeting with Saddam Hussein. Both national leaders alledgedly support and finance terrorism, including high-tech weaponry and terrorist training camps. As the political climate in Syria changes, Habash could be planning to move the PFLP headquarters to Iraq.

Further Reading

An account of PFLP and ANM politics can be found in Walid Kazziha, *Revolutionary Transformation in the Arab World* (1975); Leila Khaled's *My People Shall Live: the Autobiography of a Revolutionary* (1973) is the account of a close Habash colleague who herself participated in many PFLP hijacks; The political development of the PFLP is recounted in Helena Cobban, *The Palestinian Liberation Organization: People, Power and Politics* (1984).

Additional Sources

U.S. News and World Report, March 25, 1996, p. 44
Washington Post, March 13, 1997, p. A26.
Biographies of Habash can be found in Yaacov Shimoni's *Biographical Dictionary of the Middle East* (1991); and *The Cold War, 1945-1991*, Volume 2 (Gale Research, 1992). □

In 1978 the Rejection Front was dissolved, as Palestinian nationalists united their ranks in opposition to the Egyptian-Israeli peace process. Five years later, however, it was the PLO's Fateh-based leadership which was seeking a peaceful settlement with Israel, and once again the PFLP moved to the opposition. In 1984 the PFLP and the Democratic Front for the Liberation of Palestine (DFLP) formed the backbone of a new coalition of Palestinian hardliners called the Democratic Alliance.

Since his rejection of Arafat's (PLO) plan for peace with Israel and the establishment of a Palestinian Arab State, Habash moved his headquarters to Damascus, Syria, where his PFLP was tolerated by Syrian leader, Hafes Assad. Habash continued to deny Arafat's leadership and opposed peaceful co-existence with Israel—although he agreed to accept the Palestine National Council's decisions.

Habash was known to Palestinians as *al-hakim* (the Doctor). Possessed of a high degree of charisma, he kept the PFLP intact through many internal schisms and failed alliances. In the late 1960s he had announced his conversion from pure nationalism to Marxism, and he maintained some relations with the Soviets after the early 1970s. He was married and had two daughters. In 1980 he suffered a stroke, which left him partially paralyzed. While he was undergoing treatment for the stroke, the PFLP suffered massive internal faction-fights, but his return to the helm apparently restored some stability.

The partial paralysis resulting from his 1980 stroke moderated Habash's political fervor and limited his influ-

Fritz Haber

Fritz Haber (1868-1934) won the Nobel Prize in 1918 for developing the Haber process, which produced ammonia. Haber directed Germany's chemical warfare during World War II.

One the foremost chemists of his generation, Fritz Haber's legacy did not end with his considerable achievements of both theoretical and practical value in the fields of physical chemistry, organic chemistry, physics, and engineering. Perhaps of even greater importance were his tireless attempts to promote communication and understanding between scientific communities across the globe. The Kaiser Wilhelm Institute for Chemistry, under his direction, became famous in the years after World War I as a leading center of research whose seminars attracted scientists from all nations. In his most outstanding contribution to chemistry—for which he won the 1918 Nobel Prize in Chemistry—Haber found an inexpensive method for synthesizing large quantities of ammonia from its constituent elements nitrogen and hydrogen. A steady supply of ammonia made possible the industrial production of fertilizer and explosives.

Haber was born on December 9, 1868, in Breslau (now known as Wroclaw, Poland), the only child of first cousins Siegfried Haber and Paula Haber. Haber's mother died in childbirth. In 1877, his father, a prosperous importer of dyes and pigments, married Hedwig Hamburger, who bore him three daughters. Haber and his father had a distant relationship, but his stepmother treated him kindly. From a local grade school, Haber went to the St. Elizabeth Gymnasium (high school) in Breslau. There he developed an abiding love of literature, particularly the voluminous writings of Goethe, which inspired him to write verse. Haber also enjoyed acting, considering it as a profession early on before settling on chemistry.

After entering the University of Berlin in 1886 to study chemistry, Haber transferred after a semester to the University of Heidelberg. There, under the supervision of Robert Bunsen (who gave his name to the burner used in laboratories everywhere), Haber delved into physical chemistry, physics, and mathematics. Getting his Ph.D. in 1891, Haber tried working as an industrial laboratory chemist but found its rigid routines too intellectually confining. He decided instead to enter the Federal Institute of Technology in Zurich, Switzerland, in crder to learn about the most advanced chemical engineering techniques of his time, studying under Georg Lunge.

Haber then tried, without success, to work in his father's business, opting after six months to return to academia. In 1894, after a brief stint at the University of Jena, he took an assistant teaching position with Hans Bunte, professor of chemical technology at the Karlsruhe Technische Hochschule in Baden. Haber enjoyed Karlsruhe's emphasis on preparing its students for technical positions, stressing the connections between science and industry. His studies led him to investigate the breakdown at high temperatures of organic compounds known as hydrocarbons, an area

pioneered by the French chemist Marcelin Berthelot. After correcting and systematizing Berthelot's findings, Haber's results, published in 1896 as a book entitled *Experimental Studies on the Decomposition and Combustion of Hydrocarbons,* led to his appointment that year as lecturer, a step below associate professor.

Haber married another chemist, Clara Immerwahr, in 1901. They had a son, Hermann, born in June, 1902. While a lecturer, Haber moved his experimental focus from organic chemistry to physical chemistry. Although he lacked a formal education in this area, with the help of a colleague, Hans Luggin, he began to research the effect of electrical currents on fuel cells and the loss of efficiency in steam engines through heat. Haber also devised electrical instruments to measure the loss of oxygen in burning organic compounds, outlining this subject in a book published in 1898, *Outline of Technical Electrochemistry on a Theoretical Basis,* which earned him a promotion to associate professor. Haber's exceptional abilities as a researcher, which included his precision as a mathematician and writer, induced a leading German science group to send him in 1902 to survey America's approach to chemistry in industry and education.

Haber published a third book, *Thermodynamics of Technical Gas Reactions,* in 1905. In the volume he applied thermodynamic theory on the behavior of gases to establish industrial requirements for creating reactions. His clear exposition gave him an international reputation as an expert in adapting science to technology. That same year, Haber began his groundbreaking work on the synthesis of ammonia. Europe's growing population had created a demand for an increase in agricultural production. Nitrates, used in industrial fertilizer, required ammonia for their manufacture. Thus, Haber's goal to find new ways to fabricate ammonia grew out of a very pressing need. Other scientists had been synthesizing ammonia from nitrogen and hydrogen but at temperatures of one thousand degrees centigrade, which were not practical for industrial production. Haber was able to get the same reaction but at manageable temperatures of three hundred degrees centigrade.

The chemist Walther Nernst had obtained the synthesis of ammonia with gases at very high pressures. He also had disputed Haber's results for his high-temperature reaction. Goaded by Nernst's skepticism, Haber executed high-pressure experiments and confirmed his earlier calculations. He then combined Nernst's technique with his own to greatly increase the efficiency of the process. To augment the yield even further, Haber found a superior catalyst for the reaction and redirected the heat it produced back into the system to save on the expenditure of energy.

The final step of bringing Haber's work into the factory fell to the engineer Karl Bosch, whose company, Badische Anilin- und Sodafabrik (BASF), had supported Haber's research. After Bosch solved some key problems such as designing containers that could withstand a corrosive process over a period of time, full-scale industrial output began in 1910. Today the Haber-Bosch process is an industry standard for the mass production of ammonia.

In 1912 Haber was appointed director of the newly formed Kaiser Wilhelm Institute for Physical Chemistry and Electrochemistry at Dahlheim, just outside of Berlin; Richard Willstätter and Ernst Beckmann joined as codirectors. With the outbreak of World War I in 1914, Haber volunteered his laboratory and his expertise to help Germany. At first, he developed alternate sources of antifreeze. Then, the German War Office consulted both Nernst and Haber about developing a chemical weapon that would drive the enemy out of their trenches in order to resume open warfare. In January, 1915, the German Army began production of a chlorine gas that Haber's team had invented. On April 11, 1915, in the first chemical offensive ever, five thousand cylinders of chlorine gas blanketed 3.5 miles of enemy territory near Ypres, Belgium, resulting in 150,000 deaths.

Haber hated the war but hoped that in developing the gases he would help to bring it to a speedy end by breaking the deadlock of trench warfare. His wife, however, denounced his work as a perversion of science. After a violent argument with Haber in 1915, she committed suicide. Haber was married again in 1917 to Charlotte Nathan, who bore him a son and a daughter. Their marriage ended in divorce in 1927.

In 1916 Haber was appointed chief of the Chemical Warfare Service, overseeing every detail in that department. His process for developing nitrates from ammonia became incorporated into Germany's manufacture of explosives. Because of his duties as supervisor of chemical warfare, American, French, and British scientists vehemently contested his 1918 Nobel Prize in Chemistry. Although many of the Allied scientists had also contributed to the war effort, they charged that Haber was a war criminal for developing chemical weapons.

Since the 1918 prize had been reserved for until after the war ended, Haber accepted his Nobel Prize in November, 1919. Unquestionably, Haber had invented, in the words of the prize's presenter, A. G. Ekstrand of the Royal Swedish Academy of Sciences, "an exceedingly important means of improving the standards of agriculture and the well-being of mankind." Yet the controversy over his award, on top of Germany's defeat, his first wife's suicide, and his developing diabetes, depressed Haber greatly.

Nevertheless, Haber continued to turn his technical acumen to patriotic ends. In 1920, to help Germany pay off the onerous war reparations that the Versailles Treaty had imposed, Haber headed a doomed attempt to recover gold from seawater. Unfortunately, he had based his project on unverified nineteenth-century mineral analyses that had grossly overestimated the quantities for gold. It turned out after several abortive sea voyages that there was simply not enough gold present in seawater to make refining profitable. However, Haber did perfect a very precise method for measuring concentrations of gold.

Haber had much greater success as continuing director of the Kaiser Wilhelm Institute. His proven leadership ability attracted some of the best talent in the world to his laboratory in Karlsruhe and to the Institute, where in 1929 fully half of the members were foreigners from a dozen countries.

In 1919 he began the Haber Colloquium, an ongoing seminar that during the postwar years brought together the best minds in chemistry and physics, among them Niels Bohr, Peter Debye, Otto Meyerhof, and Otto Warburg. Haber's sharp wit, critical intelligence and broad knowledge of science were greatly appreciated at the seminars. When he ceased attending regularly, they became markedly less popular. Haber traveled widely to foster greater cooperation between nations. As an example, he helped establish the Japan Institute in that nation to foster shared cultural interests with other countries. From 1929 to 1933 he occupied Germany's seat on the Union Internationale de Chimie.

When the Nazis came to power in 1933, the Kaiser Institute fell on hard times. After receiving a demand from the minister of art, science, and popular education to dismiss all Jewish workers at the institute, Haber—a Jew himself—resigned on April 30, 1933. He wrote in his letter of resignation that having always selected his collaborators on the basis of their intelligence and character, he could not conceive of having to change so successful a method.

Haber fled Germany for England, accepting the invitation of his colleague William J. Pope to work in Cambridge, where he stayed for four months. Chaim Weitzmann, a chemist who would become the first president of Israel, offered Haber the position of director in the physical chemistry department of the Daniel Sieff Research Institute at Rehovot, in what is now Israel. Despite ill health, Haber accepted and in January, 1934, after recovering from a heart attack, began the trip. Resting on the way in Basel, Switzerland, he died on January 29, 1934. His friend and colleague Willstätter gave the memorial speech at his funeral. On the first anniversary of his death, over five hundred men and women from cultural societies across Germany converged on the institute—despite Nazi attempts at intimidation—to pay homage to Haber.

Further Reading

Dictionary of Scientific Biography, Volume 5, Scribner, 1972, pp. 620–623.
Farber, Eduard, *Nobel Prize Winners in Chemistry, 1901–1961,* Abelard-Schuman, 1953, revised 1963, pp. 71–75.
Wasson, Tyler, editor, *Nobel Prize Winners,* H. W. Wilson, 1987, pp. 402–404. □

Jürgen Habermas

The German philosopher and sociologist Jürgen Habermas (born 1929) challenged social science by suggesting that despite appearances to the contrary, human beings are capable of rationality and under some conditions are able to communicate with one another successfully; the barriers preventing the exercise of reason and mutual understanding can be identified, comprehended, and reduced.

ürgen Habermas was born in Düsseldorf, Germany, on June 18, 1929. He grew up in nearby Gummersbach, where his father was director of the local seminary. He was 16 when World War II ended. At that time he experienced a sense of revulsion with the Germans' "collectively realized inhumanity," which characterized, he believed, their lack of response to the revelations in the Nürenberg trials about the Nazi death machine. His own very different reaction, one of shock and horror, constituted what he described as "that first rupture, which still gapes."

He entered the University of Bonn in 1946. Here he began to speculate about the meaning of such concepts as reason, freedom, and justice, in part by reading such German philosophers as Hegel and Marx, as well as 20th-century Marxists, particularly the Hungarian Georg Lukács.

The Frankfurt School

Habermas obtained his Ph.D. in 1954 with a dissertation on the philosopher Friedrick von Schelling. Shortly thereafter he moved to the University of Frankfurt where, until 1959, he served as assistant to Professor Theodor Adorno, who was associated with the Institute for Social Research. The Frankfurt Institute, originally established in the 1920s, had resumed its activities there several years earlier after moving to the United States during the Nazi period. The Frankfurt School became famous as a movement of philosophical and social thought. It breached traditional boundaries that separate literary criticism, philosophy, psychoanalysis, and social science and attempted to understand critically the various elements comprising modern society. In time Habermas would become the successor to the tradition of the Frankfurt School.

Even before he came to Frankfurt, Habermas had begun publishing criticism and social commentary which ranged over a variety of areas, from analyses of Konrad Adenauer's postwar Germany to commentaries on Marx. This wide range of topics continued throughout Habermas' career. As he developed more powerful ideas, and as these ideas appeared in books rather than scattered among many periodicals, his impact became widespread. As he once commented, "There has never been any need to complain about lack of attention among the scholarly and political public."

Habermas' overall goal was to construct a social theory that could affect the emancipation of people from arbitrary social constraint. Over the course of his writing (more than 200 articles and books) he pursued this goal in a variety of ways.

During his years as an assistant to Adorno, Habermas collaborated in a survey of the political disposition of Frankfurt University students which resulted in the book *Student and Politics*. He returned to this subject when he analyzed the student movement of the late 1960s.

He became an important spokesperson for academic reform on the one hand and against militant student behavior on the other. In a famous address at a student congress in 1968 he accused the students of mistaking their agitation for a revolution and, in the process, of threatening democratic processes in Germany. A lively debate ensued, which was published in *The Left Answers Jürgen Habermas*.

Habermas' early theoretical works examined broad changes in the way Western civilization treats political ideals; in *Theory and Practice* (1962) he traced the change from the study of Platonic ideas of goodness and decency to the study of effective means for manipulating citizens, as exemplified by modern social science. In *Strukturwandlung der öffentlichkeit* (1962) he examined changes in concepts of the public and the private spheres. During this period Habermas also engaged in a comprehensive examination of the methods of the social sciences (*Die Logik der Sozialwissenschaften,* 1967). He considered the differences between natural science research and social science research and reviewed the methods on which historical, sociological, and linguistic work was based. This work was the first which reflected his lifelong preoccupation with the ways in which social scientists study human behavior: the application of scientific measurement to human beings contains contradictions whose implications Habermas continued to explore.

This work was followed by *Knowledge and Human Interests* (1981), which contains his 1965 inaugural lecture at the University of Frankfurt, where he emphasized the importance of language. "What raises us out of nature," he stated, "is the only thing whose nature we can know: language. Through its structure autonomy and responsibility are posited for us."

The nature of contemporary society and the way it has been transformed by science and technology were of continuing concern to Habermas. In the early 1970s he examined the ideological roles science and technology play (*Toward a Rational Society,* 1971) and studied the social and cultural contradictions in modern societies in which the legitimacy of political systems has been increasingly challenged (*Legitimation Crisis,* 1973).

The Max Planck Institute

Habermas spent most of his work life as a professor in a university setting. However, between 1971 and 1983 he directed the Max Planck Institute for Social Research in Starnberg, near Munich. He assembled a group of young scholars from various disciplines—anthropology, economics, political science, developmental psychology, philosophy, sociology, and linguistics—and embarked upon an ambitious plan to comprehend the basic conditions for modern society. His theoretical perspective became even broader and began to include evolutionary anthropology and linguistic theory, as well as theories of moral development as espoused by Piaget and Kohlberg. From these diverse sources Habermas developed the broad interests that characterized his later studies, processes of what he called "communicative action" and "discourse ethics."

Habermas was often at the center of controversy. In the early 1980s, when he was still directing the Max Planck Institute, either his ideas or his politics were too controversial for the University of Munich to appoint him even as an adjunct professor. On the other hand, he received many prizes, awards, and honors, including the Hegel Prize, the

Sigmund Freud Prize, the Adorno Prize, and the Geschwister Scholl Prize. He served as Theodore Heuss Professor at the New School for Social Research in New York, which also awarded him an honorary degree, as did Cambridge University. He was invited to lecture at major universities in Europe, America, and Japan from the mid-1960s on.

Although Jürgen Habermas stated in an interview in the mid-1980s that he had been interested exclusively in problems of theory construction, he in fact continued to involve himself in political questions of the day. In the late 1970s, when the German government was suspending civil liberties in an effort to stop terrorism, he feared that there were threats to democratic institutions and a possible witch hunt of left-wing intellectuals. He sent a circular letter to 50 German critics, writers, and social scientists and asked them to contribute to a book that would express the diversity of concerns about the spiritual situation of the age (*Observations on "The Spiritual Situation of the Age,"* 1979).

In 1981 Habermas published what he called his "magnum opus," *The Theory of Communicative Action.* In this book he brought together much of his previous work and developed the concept of rationality; he constructed a concept of society that integrated what he called "the lifeworld paradigm" with a system paradigm; and he elaborated a critical theory of modernity. He carried out "historical reconstructions" of a number of classic and modern writers, such as Max Weber and Emile Durkheim, as well as such 20th-century figures as Adorno and Parsons. The aim was to "excavate and overcome their weaknesses."

When Habermas left the Max Planck Institute in 1983 he returned once again to the University of Frankfurt as professor of philosophy. He was married and had three children.

It was generally agreed that the scope of Habermas' work was encyclopedic. He was called the "leading social thinker in Germany today" and was compared to Hegel and Marx.

Certainly Habermas had close intellectual ties to Marx; however, he objected to the Marxian reduction of history and culture to mere economic processes, and humanized Marxian dialectic through his introduction of his theory of knowledge and ideas which forge historic changes.

With Hegel, Habermas shared the belief in the power of reason and discourse to establish social truths; but he placed greater emphasis on the individual's ability to reason and the social group's ability to reach a consensus of opinion on values and social norms of behavior.

Since his volume *Theory of Social Action*, (1981), Habermas has published a second volume, *The Critique of Functionalist Reason* (1984.) In both volumes he sought to integrate the individual's life experience with his total social context, the "system paradigm." He also took to task the views of several historic and contemporary social thinkers, such as Max Weber, Emile Durkheim, Theodor Adorno and Talcott Parsons, pointing out weaknesses in their reasoning and conclusions.

Habermas' 1996 volume in English, *Between Facts and Norms: Contributions to a Discourse Theory of Law and Democracy,* was reviewed by Cass R. Sunstein in the *New York Times Book Review* in August, 1996.

Further Reading

Many of Habermas' books are available in English, through the MIT Press and Beacon Press. A number of his articles have been translated; many appear in the journal *Telos.* The first volume of his "magnum opus," *The Theory of Communicative Action* (1981), is available in English, translated by Thomas McCarthy; the second volume was scheduled to be published in 1987. A convenient place to begin a study of Habermas is with Thomas McCarthy, *The Critical Theory of Jürgen Habermas* (1978, 1982). This book contains a clear exposition of his ideas, not including the ideas expressed in *The Theory of Communicative Action.* Also see Rick Roderick, *Habermas and the Foundations of Critical Theory* (1986). A lively interview with Habermas appears in the May/June 1985 issue of *New Left Review.* There is no biography of Habermas, but several works are devoted entirely to his ideas and give a good introduction to the wide range of his interests in philosophy and social science. See Richard J. Bernstein, editor, *Habermas and Modernity* (1985) and J. Thompson and David Held, *Habermas: Critical Debates* (1982).
More current secondary reading which explicates clearly Habermas' complex philosophy are Stephen K. White's *The Cambridge Companion to Habermas,* New York: Cambridge University Press, (1995); and Joanna Meehan's (editor) *Feminists Reading Habermas: Gendering the Subject of Discourse.* (New York: Routledge, 1995), the essays in which consider Habermas' social concepts from a feminist perspective. □

Hadrian

The Roman emperor Hadrian (76-138), or Publius Aelius Hadrianus, reversed the expansionist policies of Rome in a permanent shift to the defensive.

Hadrian was born in Rome on Jan. 24, 76. A ward of his uncle, Emperor Trajan, he spent the first 30 years of his life as a general and public official under Trajan's tutelage. There was a cloud over Hadrian's accession, for Trajan, though a relation, did not adopt him until on his deathbed, and there was some doubt even of that. The prompt execution of four possible rivals, though done without Hadrian's knowledge, also raised doubt.

Accession to the Throne

At Hadrian's accession the Jewish revolt over much of the East and Trajan's faltering Parthian War were his first concerns. He ended the war by abandoning Armenia and Trajan's Parthian conquests, quelled the Jewish revolt, and returned to Rome (118). His administration was marked throughout by great care for finances—Trajan's wars had proved too costly—and strict governmental supervision of an increasing number of sectors of public and private life. Of great importance was his policy of appointing equestrians (knights), the class below the senators, instead of freedmen to head the imperial bureaus. He thus recognized that these bureaus were organs of state, not household chores to be left to the Emperor's personal servants.

Hadrian's defensive policy posed problems of military discipline and morale, since it is always harder to maintain the efficiency of an army whose training may never be put to use. His answer was endless personal supervision, and he spent approximately half his reign touring the provinces on inspection. The system worked under Hadrian, but in time the efficiency of the armies declined.

Another result of Hadrian's defensive policy was the need for clearly marked frontiers and for border fortresses. He strengthened the defenses, notably in Germany and in Britain, where the most famous of all his frontier works, Hadrian's Wall, crosses Britain approximately along the border between England and Scotland.

Hadrian's last years were darkened by a new revolt of the Jews and the question of succession. He was responsible for the Jewish outbreak, since he decided to rebuild Jerusalem, in ruins since A.D. 70, as a Greek city with all Jews excluded save on one day a year. He also built a temple to Jupiter and the Emperor on the very site of the Jewish temple. This was too much to bear for the Jews of Judea, who had remained quiet during the previous revolt. They rose in 132, and the revolt lasted 3 1/2 years and cost the lives, it is said, of half a million people.

The Succession

Hadrian became ill about 135, and the quest for a successor was acute. For unknown reasons he executed his nearest relation (136) and adopted Aelius Verus. Hadrian continued to linger, however, and Verus died. He then adopted Aurelius Antoninus, making him in turn adopt Verus's son Lucius Verus and Antoninus's own nephew, the future emperor Marcus Aurelius. Hadrian died unlamented on July 10, 138.

The most many-sided of the emperors, Hadrian was interested in all the arts. In literature his taste ran toward the archaic; in sculpture he preferred the classic. But his favorite discipline was architecture; he built the Pantheon and Castel Sant' Angelo, his own tomb, in Rome; added a whole new quarter to Athens; and made of his palace at Tibur (modern Tivoli) a museum of replicas of buildings he had seen on his travels.

Further Reading

The only surviving ancient biography of Hadrian is in the collection known as the *Scriptores Historiae Augustae,* vol. 1, translated by David Magie (1921). The best modern treatment is Bernard W. Henderson, *The Life and Principate of the Emperor Hadrian* (1923). See also Sulamith Ish-Kishor, *Magnificent Hadrian* (1935). A brief but excellent discussion of Hadrian is in Edward T. Salmon, *A History of the Roman World from 30 B.C. to A.D. 138* (1944; 6th ed. 1968). Hadrian's buildings are considered in Paul MacKendrick, *The Mute Stones Speak* (1960).

Additional Sources

Lambert, Royston, *Beloved and God: the story of Hadrian and Antinous,* New York, NY: Viking, 1984.
Perowne, Stewart, *Hadrian,* London; Dover, N.H.: Croom Helm, 1986, 1960. □

Ernst Heinrich Philipp August Haeckel

The German biologist and natural philosopher Ernst Heinrich Philipp August Haeckel (1834-1919) was famous for his work in evolutionary theory, especially the construction of phylogenetic trees. In the late 19th and early 20th centuries he was as famous as Charles Darwin, whom he admired, though his views were closer to those of Jean Baptiste Lamarck.

Ernst Haeckel was born in Potsdam, Germany, on February 16, 1834, to Carl and Charlotte (Sethe) Haeckel. His father was the chief administrator for religious and educational affairs in Merseburg, while his mother was the daughter of a privy councillor in Berlin. Haeckel thus had the social advantage of growing up in an educated and cultured family. He was publicly educated at the *Domgymnasium* in Merseburg, graduating in 1852. He then, on the advice of his parents, studied medicine at Berlin, later at Würzburg and Vienna, before returning to Berlin to earn his medical degree in 1857.

In 1858 he passed the state medical examination, but he did not practice medicine. In fact, he had never been truly interested in being a physician, only pursuing that degree for his parents' sake. Yet he discovered, after initial reluctance, that medical school would provide him with the most solid foundation on which to build a scientific career. It was in this medical training that Haeckel met many of the most important biologists of his day. At Würzburg he studied under Albert von Kölliker and Franz Leydig, learning embryological and comparative anatomy as well as perfecting his skills in microscopical investigations—later to prove essential for his research in ontogeny and phylogeny.

It was also at Würzburg that Haeckel's philosophical views began to develop, confronted as he was by mechanistic and materialistic views of life developed by Rudolf Virchow and Carl Vogt and expressed by young scientists and physicians with whom he came into contact. In response to such strongly asserted materialism Haeckel's own Christian beliefs began to be transformed, and though he never relinquished the idea of god, his own god was eventually so radically changed that it seemed scarcely personal, perhaps nothing more than the principle of causality in the universe. Meanwhile, his medical education continued. At Berlin in 1854-1855 Haeckel studied under Johannes Müller, whom he greatly respected as the paradigm of the great scientist. Under Müller, he increased his understanding of comparative anatomy and he was introduced to marine zoology, one of Müller's specialties.

In 1858, after finishing his medical studies and final examination, Karl Gegenbaur offered him the chance of a future professorship in zoology at Jena if he would first undertake a zoological research expedition in the Mediterranean. This research occupied his time from 1859 to 1860 and resulted in the publication in 1862 of *The Radiolarians,* in which he announced his support of Darwinism. Haeckel determined to reinterpret all of morphology (study and comparison of animal forms) in terms of the theory of evolution, which meant the linking of animal species phylogenetically through "geneological" trees. He argued that all processes could be reduced to mechanical-materialistic causes, that evolution was driven by such causality, and that the true philosophy of nature should be Monism, a system stressing the unity of mind and matter, in contrast to all vitalistic or teleological dualism stressing the separation of mind and matter. He differed from Darwin in two fundamental ways—Haeckel's was the more speculative mind, and he relied much more upon the Lamarckian principle of the inheritance of acquired characteristics than Darwin ever did.

Also in 1862, Haeckel married his cousin, Anna Sethe, who died in 1864, at which time he married Agnes Huschke, daughter of anatomist Emil Huschke. They had three children. In 1861, upon his return from his research expedition, Haeckel had been given the post of *Privatdozent* at the University of Jena. In 1862 he was named professor extraordinary in comparative anatomy and was made director of the Zoological Institute. And in 1865 a chair in zoology was established for him, which he held until 1909. During that more than 40 year period Haeckel continued his herculean labors on behalf of his science, going on four major scientific expeditions (Canary Islands, 1866-1867; Red Sea, 1873; Ceylon, 1881-1882; Java, 1900-1901) and further elaborating on his evolutionary schemes.

In 1901 he was the recipient of the Turin Bressa Prize for his outstanding work in biology. Throughout his life he received many honors and was elected to many scientific societies, among them the Imperial Academy of Sciences at Vienna (1872), the American Philosophical Society (1885), and the Royal Society of Edinburgh (1888). His most characteristic ideas and tendencies are evident in his early work of 1886, *General Morphology*—all his subsequent efforts were reworkings of this book. He retired in 1909 and still lived in Jena when he died in 1919.

Further Reading

For a short but excellent intellectual and biographical sketch of Haeckel, see Georg Uschmann's article in the *Dictionary of Scientific Biography,* Volume 6. E. W. MacBride also wrote a short article in *Nature* 133 (1934) on the centenary of Haeckel's birth. Daniel Gasman in his *Scientific Origins of National Socialism* (1971) explored the way in which the Nazi's used Haeckel's ideas to support their own political ideology. For Haeckel's personal evolutionary views, see his *General Morphology* (1866). □

Shams al-Din Hafiz

Shams al-Din Hafiz (ca. 1320-1390) was a great Persian mystical poet who, as a professor of Koranic exegesis, composed some of the most sensitive and lyrical poetry ever produced in the Middle East.

Hafiz was born in Shiraz, the capital of the province of Fars. He grew up in an age when the finest Arabic literature had already been written and when Persian poetry had reached the zenith of its romantic era. What was left for Hafiz was the highest attainment yet of lyrical poetry, the ghazal.

As a student, Hafiz learned the Koran by heart (the name Hafiz means Koran memorizer), and his poetry proves also that he was very well versed in the sciences of his day. Like all Persian poets of the Middle Ages, Hafiz was a court poet and panegyrist dependent on the good will of his patrons. Since he was a Shiite Moslem rather than a Sunnite, as was the prescribed religion of the day, he had to be careful what he wrote.

His Cultural Heritage

However, there was another religious force underlying the poetry of Hafiz. This was Sufism, a mystical movement which grew in Islam as prosperity faded. By the 14th century it had acquired an elaborate and conventional system of symbolism, which formed the lingua franca for the poetic imagery of the day.

The tendency of Sufism is pantheistic. Each human soul is a particle of the Divine Absolute, and the mystic aims at a complete union with the Divine. This union is attained in the knowledge that a human being is himself that ultimate reality which he seeks. Only by abandoning the legalistic restraints of conventional religion can he attain this higher goal.

The sources of Sufism outside Islam included Zoroastrian or Magian worship, Nestorian Christianity, Greek Neoplatonism, and Indian Buddhism. When the Arabs conquered Persia in the 7th century, they took over a civilization much older and more complex than their own. Many of its elements undoubtedly persisted in the forms of Shiite Islam and other more esoteric movements such as Sufism, most of which exerted their influence on Hafiz.

By the age of 30 Hafiz recognized his poetic talents, and he was appointed to the court of the Indju vizier of Shiraz. Shiraz fell to a competing dynasty—the Muzaffarid—but their strict Sunni rule, technically hostile to the Shiism of Hafiz, did not prevent him from completing his most mature compositions. Although during these years his fame spread through the Islamic world, he declined all invitations to other courts. While Shah Shudja ruled Shiraz (1358-1384), Hafiz benefited from at least sporadic favor, and he left his home city only for 2 years, which were spent in nearby Isfahan and Yazd.

Hafiz's Poetry

In 1387, after Tamerlane had conquered all of Persia, he came to Shiraz to visit with Hafiz for 2 months. The most productive period of Hafiz's life was over, and he died 3 years later in Shiraz, but his fame was well deserved. No other poet up to his time in the Islamic world was such a superb linguist and literary craftsman. He took the poetic forms of the day so far beyond the work of his predecessors that he practically cut off all succession. Over 600 poems are attributed to Hafiz, most of them both mystical and lyrical. His work was meant to be understood on many levels, which was typical of the poetry of his day. Hafiz's major work, the *Divan,* was a collection of short odes known metrically as ghazals.

Further Reading

Gertrude L. Bell translated *Poems from the Divan of Hafiz* (1897; new ed. 1928), which includes an excellent introduction. A. J. Arberry, ed., *Fifty Poems of Hafiz* (1953), contains a good analysis. Other interpretive works on the poet include Thomas Wright, *Rose-in-Hood* (1925); Clarence K. Streit, *Hafiz: The Tongue of the Hidden* (1928); and Abbas Aryanpur, *Poetical Horoscope: or, Odes of Hafiz* (1965). For an intricate discussion of the rhythmics and meter of Hafiz's poetry see Walter Leaf, *Versions from Hafiz* (1898). □

Frank Hague

The American political leader Frank Hague (1876-1956), mayor of Jersey City, N.J., for three decades, was one of the major city bosses in the 20th century.

Frank Hague was born on Jan. 17, 1876, in Jersey City, N.J. At 16, after little schooling, he went to work. In 1896 he was picked by one of the Democratic district leaders to run for constable, given $80, and told to "use your head." Young Hague was elected and began his lengthy career in municipal politics.

Following his stint as constable, Hague held various other local offices. During those years he started to build his Democratic machine (an organization controlling politicians, patronage, and votes), which would later make him the most powerful man in the state. In 1917 he was elected mayor of Jersey City and went on to serve eight terms in office.

Hague's influence soon spread beyond the city. He controlled patronage in New Jersey and often had close ties with the state government. By 1922 he was elected a Democratic national committeeman and was a major figure in the party during the next 2 decades.

Hague's mayoralty brought much criticism, although by dispensing favors and courting the voters he remained enormously popular with his constituents. He kept a firm grip on his organization, and few doubted his words, uttered in a 1937 address, that "I am the law in Jersey City." David Dayton McKean alleged in *The Boss* (1940) that Hague

stayed in power by methods that included controlling newspapers, intimidating opponents, engaging in wiretapping, and making false arrests to silence his critics.

As mayor, Hague built a $1.8 million maternity hospital and the Jersey City Medical Center, which cost $16 million. The medical center was the largest hospital in any city of comparable size and provided treatment at nominal fees. At the same time, however, Jersey City was the highest-taxed American municipality and had the biggest bonded debt of any large city in the United States.

Deciding not to seek another term as mayor in 1947, Hague picked his nephew to succeed him. Although the nephew won, he was defeated 2 years later. Hague suffered another blow in 1952, when the New Jersey State Democratic Organization refused to retain him as a Democratic national committeeman.

After Hague left office, his nephew and a former deputy mayor were named defendants in a $15 million suit brought by the city administration on behalf of city employees who allegedly had been required to kick back 3 percent of their annual salaries to the Hague machine during the 1917-1949 period. Hague sought to block the action, and the suit ultimately was dismissed. He died in New York on Jan. 1, 1956.

Further Reading

The only work on Hague is David Dayton McKean, *The Boss: The Hague Machine in Action* (1940), a highly critical account of the mayor's political tactics. Ralph G. Martin, *The Bosses*

(1964), includes a popularly written account of Hague's whole career. Duane Lockard, *The New Jersey Governor: A Study in Political Power* (1964), deals with Hague's relationship with the governors of New Jersey. □

Otto Hahn

The German chemist Otto Hahn (1879-1968) was a joint discoverer of nuclear fission and a Nobel Prize winner in chemistry.

Otto Hahn was born in Frankfurt am Main on March 8, 1879. He was the youngest son of the owner of a prosperous glazing business. After leaving school in Frankfurt, he went to Marburg University with the intention of entering the chemical industry. Research on bromine derivatives of isoeugenol led to a doctorate in 1901, and after a year's military service he returned to Marburg to continue his research.

The turning point in Hahn's career came in 1904. He had in mind an industrial post for which knowledge of a foreign language was desirable, so he worked under Sir William Ramsay at University College, London. His task was to separate radium from a sample of impure barium chloride. Within a few months he showed that another radioactive substance was present and named it radiothorium. Urged by Ramsay to continue academic research in radioactivity, Hahn moved to Montreal, Canada, in 1905 to work with Ernest Rutherford. Here again success came quickly, and within a year he had recognized two other radioactive species, which he called thorium-C and radioactinium.

In 1906 Hahn returned to Germany, obtaining a place in Emil Fischer's Chemical Institute at Berlin University. Beginning work in a converted woodshop in the basement, he was soon joined by Lise Meitner, with whom he was to collaborate for 30 years. Here he discovered the radioelement mesothorium, studied beta emissions, and recognized the phenomenon known as radioactive recoil.

In 1913 Hahn was appointed head of radioactivity research in the new Kaiser Wilhelm Institute for Chemistry. Despite the interruptions of war service, Hahn made many major discoveries in the next 25 years. In an investigation of the radioactivity of rubidium he established a method for determining the geological ages of minerals that was in many cases more reliable than the traditional one using the radioactivity of uranium. A study of the radioactive precursors of actinium led to the discovery of the element protoactinium.

Following the discovery of artificial radioactivity by the Joliot-Curies in 1934, Meitner and Hahn repeated Enrico Fermi's experiment of bombarding uranium atoms with neutrons and agreed with his conclusion that new (transuranic) elements had been produced. Among the products isolated appeared to be new isotopes of radium; the suggestion that the "radium" was in fact barium by

Hahn and Fritz Strassmann in January 1939 was the first indication that the atomic nucleus had been split. This discovery of nuclear fission became, of course, the basis for the production of nuclear weapons, a development which Hahn always deplored.

Hahn was a prisoner of war in England for a few months in 1945, and the next year he received the Nobel Prize for chemistry, which he had been awarded for 1944. Twenty years later Germany's first nuclear vessel was appropriately named *Otto Hahn*.

Further Reading

A primary source is Hahn's *A Scientific Autobiography* (1962; trans. 1966). A detailed biographical profile of Hahn is in the Royal Society, *Biographical Memoirs of Fellows of the Royal Society* (vol. 16, 1970). See also Otto Robert Frisch, ed., *Trends in Atomic Physics: Essays Dedicated to Lise Meitner, Otto Hahn, Max von Laue on the Occasion of Their 80th Birthday* (1959), and Eduard Farber, *Nobel Prize Winners in Chemistry, 1901-1961* (1953; rev. ed. 1963). □

Haidar Ali

Haidar Ali (1721-1782) was the Indian ruler of Mysore. He was the most formidable enemy of the British in their struggle for supremacy in South India.

Born at Budikote in Mysore, Haidar Ali started his career as a soldier. In 1749 he was a petty officer in the Mysore army attending on the nizam, theoretically the Mogul deputy in South India. The nizam was assassinated in 1750, and in the ensuing confusion Haidar came by enough wealth to equip his own contingent and to distinguish himself in the service of Nanjraj, the new strong man of Mysore.

Nanjraj's involvement in the Anglo-French contest for supremacy in India gave Haidar the opportunity to master the art of warfare and learn the value of European as compared to Indian military training. Under Nanjraj, Mysore went bankrupt. Haidar, known for efficient leadership, first rose to be Nanjraj's most trusted lieutenant and later replaced him as usurper. Some nobles, in conspiracy with the Marathas, almost ousted him, but because of developments in North India the Marathas withdrew, and Haidar recovered full control in 1761. By 1764 he had extended his sway northward well beyond the Tungabhadra. For the rest of his life, with his superior diplomacy and strong army, Haidar Ali struggled to retain or add to his possessions against the Marathas in the northwest and the British on the east and west coasts.

The Marathas made four very damaging campaigns against Haidar. But after the death of their greatest leader, Madhava Rao I, in 1772, Haidar exploited their internal discords and their confrontation with the British to extend his control beyond the Tungabhadra to the Krishna, and then he enlisted their support against the British.

Haidar tried to gain the friendship of the British to be able to cope with the Marathas, but the British wanted to undermine his power. In the inevitable First Anglo-Mysore War (1767-1769), the British were forced to enter a treaty of mutual defense with him. But during the subsequent Maratha-Mysore wars, the British did not keep their promise. Knowing that his peace with the Marathas could not endure, in 1780 Haidar launched his second war against the British to eliminate their influence from South India. The French, hoping to regain a foothold in India, sent help but not enough for him to realize his goal. Still he was more than holding his own in 1782, when he died of cancer aggravated by overexertion.

Haidar owed his success to extraordinary determination, diligence, and a sense of realism which enabled him to always proceed from calm calculation. The last quality brought him many victories, but even in his repeated reverses it served to keep defeats from becoming utter routs. In diplomacy and civil administration, it enabled him to gear his policies to utility rather than passion and become the power that he was.

Further Reading

N. K. Sinha, *Haidar Ali* (1941), is a balanced biography. An old account is Lewin B. Bowring, *Haidar Ali and Tipu Sultan* (1893). Two works indispensable for an understanding of South Indian history during the 18th century are Robert Orme, *A History of the Military Transactions of the British Nation in Indostan* (2 vols., 1763-1778; vol. 1, rev. ed., 1799), a vivid picture of the period to 1761; and Mark Wilks, *Historical Sketches of the South of India, in an Attempt to Trace the*

History of Mysore (3 vols., 1810-1817; 2d ed., 2 vols., 1869), particularly valuable for evidence derived from "living characters." More recent surveys include K. M. Panikkar, *A Survey of Indian History* (1947; 4th rev. ed. 1964); J. C. Powell-Price, *A History of India* (1955); Percival Spear, *India: A Modern History* (1961); and Michael Edwardes, *A History of India* (1961).

Additional Sources

Fernandes, Praxy, *The Tigers of Mysore: a biography of Hyder Ali & Tipu Sultan,* New Delhi; New York, N.Y., U.S.A.: Viking, 1991. □

Alexander M. Haig Jr.

Alexander M. Haig, Jr. (born 1924), American military leader and diplomat, served as secretary of state and as adviser to two Republican presidents.

Accoording to a *TIME* special story on Alexander Haig in 1984, "Few American public figures have had such tempestuous careers. Alexander M. Haig, Jr. has spent much of his life in war zones—bureaucratic and geopolitical, as well as the kind for which he prepared in the U.S. Military Academy at West Point: Viet Nam, where he served as a battalion and brigade commander; as the indispensable aide-de-camp to National Security Adviser Henry Kissinger; as White House Chief of Staff during the climax of Watergate; and, after Richard Nixon's presidency fell, as Supreme Allied Commander in Europe. . . . But it was during his tenure as Ronald Reagan's Secretary of State that Haig found himself most embattled."

Haig was born in Bala-Cynwyd, Pennsylvania, a comfortable suburb of Philadelphia, on December 2, 1924, the elder of two sons of Alexander Meigs and Regina Anne Haig. He attended St. Matthias parochial school in Bala-Cynwyd and St. Joseph's preparatory school in Philadelphia, graduating from Lower Merion High School in 1942. Haig's father, an assistant city solicitor of Philadelphia, died when Haig was ten. Using savings from various afterschool jobs, Haig was able to enroll in Notre Dame in 1942.

After two years of reasonably serious study at Notre Dame, Haig obtained an appointment to West Point in 1944, thus realizing his childhood ambition of a military career. That career was to be far more spectacular than Haig's academic performance would suggest: he graduated in 1947 as the 217th ranked cadet in a class of 310. The 22-year old second lieutenant went first to the general combined arms course at Fort Riley, Kansas, and then to the Armored School at Fort Knox, Kentucky. Thereafter, he was assigned to the First Cavalry Division, then performed occupation duty and lackadaisical training in Japan. He married Patricia Antoinette Fox, the daughter of General Alonzo Fox, once his commanding officer, in May 1950. They had three children.

Haig early attracted the attention of highranking superiors, serving as administrative assistant to the chief of staff of the Far East Command and, during the early months of the Korean War, as aide to the X Corps commander. Promoted to captain in late 1950, he saw combat on several occasions and took part in the Inchon landings.

A bout with hepatitis resulted in Haig's reassignment to an armored unit at Fort Knox. After completing the advanced course there he served on the faculty of West Point and pursued graduate work in business administration at Columbia University. Thereafter, his career gained momentum. He served as S-3 (operations) of an armored battalion in West Germany, earned promotion to major in 1957, and spent 1958-1959 as a staff officer at USAEUR (United States Army in Europe). Haig then spent a year (1959-1960) at the Naval War College, took an M.A. in international relations from Georgetown University in 1961, and was promoted to lieutenant colonel in 1962.

Haig's staff service from 1962 to 1964 in the office of "DCSOPS," the deputy chief of staff for military operations, was a pivotal point in his career. When Cyrus R. Vance was named deputy secretary of defense in 1964, he took along this polished Pennsylvanian as his deputy special assistant. While dealing with a wide range of policy issues relating to such diverse areas as Berlin, the intervention in the Dominican Republic, and Cuba, Haig handled interagency politics and diplomatic crises with tact and impressive efficiency. This performance led to, first, a year at the Army War College, time as a battalion commander in Vietnam (and the Distinguished Service Cross during an engagement near An Loc), and brigade command.

Following promotion to colonel and another stint at West Point, Haig returned to Washington in 1969 as chief military assistant to National Security Adviser Henry Kissinger. His fortunes rose with the aggressive Kissinger, who swiftly became President Nixon's principal adviser on international security issues. Haig proved an invaluable "chief of staff" to Kissinger and soon began to deal directly with the White House. Preferring to work in anonymity, he served, as one journalist noted, "as gatekeeper to the summit." Promoted to brigadier general and then rapidly to major general, Haig was centrally involved with arrangements for Nixon's visit to China and the Vietnam peace initiative.

Haig moved into the spotlight and controversy when President Nixon promoted him over some 240 more senior officers to be a four-star general and the Army's vice-chief of staff. Nixon's action to push Haig into the military's front rank was consonant with the effort to get the "President's men" into positions of authority in various federal agencies. However, he was soon to return to the White House, serving as special assistant to the president in 1973-1974. In the months after the Watergate break-in, Haig, once termed "the ultimate professional," played a vital role for a beleaguered President Nixon. It is not coincidental that Haig was instrumental in the negotiations leading to Nixon's resignation in August 1974 and to Gerald Ford's accession to the presidency. Soon afterwards, Haig was named commander-in-chief, United States European Command, and supreme allied commander. He spent the next five years at the North Atlantic Treaty Organization (NATO), retiring in 1979 to become head of United Technologies Corporation. It appeared that a remarkable career in military administration had closed.

Alexander Haig's industrial sojourn ended with the election of his admirer Ronald Reagan as president in 1980. Against the advice of some intimates, Reagan chose Haig—whose impeccable military record, staunch anti-Communism, and links to the Republican establishment were great assets—to be his secretary of state. A sequence of stormy confirmation hearings occurred in January 1981, setting the tone for Haig's 18-month tenure as secretary of state. Critics charged that he was unqualified intellectually and emotionally for the position of chief proponent of United States foreign policy interests.

During his brief time at the helm, Haig battled with impressive vigor, if little apparent success, with his colleagues in the Reagan administration *and* for a tough stance toward the Soviet Union and its Third World clients. Obsessed with "turf" issues, Haig will be remembered for his controversial raising of the issue of executive authority in the aftermath of the attempted assassination of President Reagan. He devoted so much time to defending the prerogatives of the secretary of state against all comers (though, principally, the national security adviser) that the agenda of unfinished business at State began to alarm even the president. Haig's pugnacity and dogmatic views on policy toward the Soviet Union and public stumbles on such matters as Afghanistan, Poland, Lebanon, the Falklands crisis,

and Nicaragua eventually eroded Reagan's confidence in him.

On his side, Haig described Reagan's close advisers as "foreign policy amateurs" who cared only about the domestic political effects of global issues. His resignation as secretary of state, which finally came on June 25, 1982, ended what had become an impossible situation. Alexander Haig returned to private office bloodied but (as his memoirs, *Caveat: Realism, Reagan, and Foreign Policy,* published in 1984, make clear) unbowed by the experience. He returned to politics long enough to try to secure the Republican nomination for president in 1988 but dropped out early when it became apparent he did not have the support to win the nomination. He remained active as a speaker on foreign policy issues, but his focus shifted from politics to private business. He was hired by the international consulting firm of Worldwide Associates, Inc. and became chairman and president of that organization.

Haig is a key player in plans to build a controversial, multi-billion dollar natural gas pipeline from Central Asia across Iran into Turkey. He is co-chairman of US-CIS Ventures Inc., the Washington, D.C.-based company that is overseeing the pipeline project. Haig believes the area of Turkmenistan has tremendous, untapped oil reserves, and that by enabling the people of Turkmenistan to utilize them, he is helping them become more independent of Russia.

Haig is also a member of the Board of Directors of America Online, Inc., Interneuron Pharmaceuticals Inc., and MGM Grand Inc., and is on the American Board of Trustees of the A.F. Burns Fellowship. Haig's most current endeavor involves Sky Station International, a start-up company based in Chantilly, Virginia, that plans to offer inexpensive phone service and high-speed Internet access to consumers worldwide. Haig's son Alex acts as president of the company, which plans to float 250 inexpensive platforms suspended by Hindenburg-like airships, rather than launch satellites as its competitors have planned. This would result in a project costing only $800 millon dollars, compared to the billions of dollars a satellite project would require. Haig and his son hope to have the system deployed within the decade.

Further Reading

For additional information on Haig see his memoirs, *Caveat: Realism, Reagan, and Foreign Policy* (1984); and *Inner Circles: How America Changed the World: A Memoir* (1992); He is prominently mentioned in the two volumes of Henry Kissinger's memoirs: *The White House Years* (1979) and *Years of Upheaval* (1982). Haig is listed in *Who's Who in America* (1996); and *Who's Who in the World* (1996). Also see *Business Week* (June 3, 1996); *New York Times* (June 5, 1997); *Washington Post* (January 20, 1995). □

Douglas Haig

The British general Douglas Haig, 1st Earl Haig (1861-1928), commanded British forces on the Western front in Europe during World War I. He is

credited with the final British victories over the German armies in 1918.

Douglas Haig was born on June 19, 1861, in Edinburgh, Scotland. He was educated at Brasenose College, Oxford University, and the Royal Military College at Sandhurst. His first army duty was in India. He later attended the staff college and then went to join H.H. Kitchener for his campaign in the Sudan in 1898, where he was an outstanding officer. The following year, after having been assigned to duty in England, Haig was sent to South Africa to fight in the Boer War. He proved to be an excellent officer in action, and as a result Kitchener took him to India as inspector general of cavalry in 1903.

In 1906 R.B. Haldane, the war secretary, brought Haig back to England to serve on the general staff, which was implementing reforms in the War Office. In 1909 Haig was back in India as chief of staff to Kitchener, helping him in the completion of the reform of the Indian army. He was given a command in England in 1911 which included the leadership of the 1st Army Corps if and when it might be needed in a war on the Continent.

In August 1914, when England went to war, Haig took his 1st Army Corps to France. He was one of the few generals who saw the probability of a long war, and he urged that plans be made with that in mind. Haig won high praise for his leadership as a subordinate commander. When the government decided to replace Sir John French as commander in chief after the Battle of Loos in the fall of 1915, Haig was selected and took command on December 19. After 2 1/2 years of trench warfare and a crisis in cooperation among the Allies, the Germans were pushed toward defeat. Haig was among the first to sense the approaching victory. Just as he had foreseen a long war at the beginning, he saw the end before most of his colleagues, and he is given much of the credit for bringing the war to a conclusion before the end of 1918.

Haig was given the title of earl among other honors when he returned to England in 1919. He turned most of his attention to providing aid for the veterans of his armies. He was married and had one son. Haig died on Jan. 30, 1928.

Further Reading

The Private Papers of Douglas Haig, 1914-1919, edited by Robert Blake (1952), gives a firsthand view of Haig at the height of his career. The best full biography is Duff Cooper, *Haig* (2 vols., 1935-1936). Other studies are Sir George Arthur, *Lord Haig* (1928); John Charteris, *Field-Marshall Earl Haig* (1929); and Sir John Humphrey Davidson, *Haig: Master of the Field* (1953). More recent but less comprehensive are John Terraine, *Ordeal of Victory* (1963), and G.S. Duncan, *Douglas Haig as I Knew Him* (1966). Winston S. Churchill's sketch of Haig in *Great Contemporaries* (1937), reprinted in Barrett Parker, ed., *Famous British Generals* (1951), is the best brief study.

Additional Sources

Sixsmith, E. K. G. (Eric Keir Gilborne), *Douglas Haig,* London: Weidenfeld and Nicolson, 1976.
Smith, Gene, *The ends of greatness: Haig, Petain, Rathenau, and Eden: victims of history,* New York: Crown Publishers, 1990.
Terraine, John, *Douglas Haig: the educated soldier,* London: L. Cooper, 1990.
Warner, Philip, *Field Marshal Earl Haig,* London: Bodley Head, 1991.
Winter, Denis, *Haig's command: a reassessment,* London, England; New York, N.Y., USA: Viking, 1991. □

Haile Selassie

Haile Selassie (1892-1975) was an emperor of Ethiopia whose influence as an African leader far surpassed the confines of his country.

Haile Selassie was born on July 23, 1892, the son of Ras Makonnen, a cousin and confidant of Emperor Menilek II. Baptized Lij Tafari, Haile Selassie spent his youth at the imperial court of Addis Ababa, where, surrounded by constant intrigues, he learned much about the exercise of power. Menilek no doubt recognized Tafari's capacity for hard work, his excellent memory, and his mastery of detail when he rewarded the youth's intellectual and personal capabilities by appointing him, at the age of 20, *dejazmatch* (commander) of the extensive province of Sidamo.

Regent and Emperor

Upon the death of Menilek in 1913, his grandson, Lij Yasu, succeeded to the throne. Yasu's apparent conversion to Islam alienated the national, Christian church and gave impetus to the opposition movement led by Ras Tafari (as Haile Selassie was now designated), which joined noblemen and high church officials in deposing Yasu in 1916. Zawditu, the daughter of Menilek, then became empress, with Ras Tafari appointed regent and heir to the throne.

Throughout the regency the Empress, conservative by inclination and more concerned with religion than politics, served to counteract Ras Tafari's rising interest in national modernization; the result was an uneasy coalition of conservative and reforming forces which lasted for nearly a decade. In 1926 Tafari took control of the army, an action which, when coupled with his previous success in foreign affairs, including admission of Ethiopia to the League of Nations in 1923, made him strong enough to assume the title of *negus* (king). When Zawditu died in April 1930, he demanded the title *negasa negast* (king of kings) and took complete control of the government with the throne name of Haile Selassie I ("Power of the Trinity").

In 1931 the new emperor promulgated a written constitution to symbolize his interest in modernization and intention to increase the power of central authority, which had been waning since the death of Menilek. Haile Selassie's efforts were cut short, however, when Mussolini's Italy invaded the country in 1935. The Italian military deployed superior weaponry, airplanes, and poison gas to crush the

ill-fated resistance led by the Emperor; the ensuing Fascist occupation marked the first loss of national independence in recorded Ethiopian history. In 1936 Haile Selassie went into exile in England, where he appealed in vain to the League of Nations for help.

In early 1941 British expeditionary forces, aided by the heroic Ethiopian resistance, liberated the country, enabling Haile Selassie to triumphantly reenter his capital in May. The centralized Italian colonial administration, backed by force and with a vastly improved road network, meant that the Emperor returned to find that a great deal of provincial autonomy had been destroyed, leaving him in certain ways stronger than before he left. Throughout the next decade he rebuilt the administration, improved the army, passed legislation to regulate the government, church, and financial system, and further extended his control of the provinces by crushing revolts in Gojjam and Tigre. But in general the Emperor had gradually grown more cautious, and in his reluctance to antagonize conservative elements by any "hasty" modernization he allowed pitifully little infusion of new blood into the government.

In the 1950s Haile Selassie worked for the absorption of the important Red Sea province of Eritrea (accomplished in 1962), founded the University College of Addis Ababa, and welcomed home many Ethiopian college graduates from abroad. His Silver Jubilee of 1955 served as the occasion to present a revised constitution, followed in 1957 by the first general election. Haile Selassie's continued efforts to hold political balance between several major politicians and the recurrent frustration of many newly returned graduates, who still found few places in government, eventually led dissident elements to attempt a government coup in December 1960. The coup failed, but it gave a short and violent jolt to the heretofore uneventfulness of Ethiopian politics and hinted of future possibilities.

Pan-African Leader

In the 1960s the Emperor was clearly recognized as a major force in the pan-African movement, demonstrating his remarkable capacity for adapting to changing circumstances. It was a great personal triumph for him when, in 1963, the newly founded Organization of African Unity established its headquarters in Addis Ababa. Unlike other African leaders, Haile Selassie, of course, had not had to struggle once in office to prove his legitimate authority to his people; his control of government for over 40 years had given him enough time to identify with it.

By 1970 the Emperor had slowly withdrawn from many day-to-day administrative concerns and had become increasingly involved with foreign affairs. He probably made more state visits than any other head of state, enjoying such jaunts for their own sake even when they had little practical use. To him diplomacy seemed inseparable from prestige.

At home Haile Selassie more than ever evinced a trait of caution in his approach to modernization. Though receptive to Western innovations, he never throughout his long reign advanced faster than the consensus would allow, although by his fortieth year in power he appeared somewhat more concerned with adjustment to, and authorization of, change rather than with the active initiation of changes themselves.

A famine in Wello province in 1973 seriously undermined the credibility and legitimacy of Selassie's regime. With a strain on the nation, Selassie was forced to abdicate on September 13, 1974. The new octogenarian emperor Selassie spent his final year of life on house arrest. His death was announced by the Dergue on August 27, 1975. The man who led Ethiopia for 60 years, did not even have a funeral service. The exact location of his grave has never been revealed.

Further Reading

Christine Sandford, *The Lion of Judah Hath Prevailed* (1955); and Leonard Mosley, *Haile Selassie: The Conquering Lion* (1964); Edward Ullendorff, *The Ethiopians* (1960; 2d ed. 1965), analyzes Ethiopian culture; Christopher Clapham, *Haile-Selassie's Government* (1969), treats the political bureaucracy; Richard Greenfield, *Ethiopia: A New Political History* (1965), scans Ethiopian history with a perceptive interpretation of 20th-century developments. □

Richard Hakluyt

The English geographer and author Richard Hakluyt (c.1552-1616) was one of the first practical geographers in England and an important promoter of the English colonization of North America.

The second son of Richard Hakluyt, a London skinner, Richard Hakluyt attended Westminster School. A meeting with his cousin, the geographer Richard Hakluyt (ca. 1535-1591), aroused his interest in practical geography, cosmography, and trade. Young Richard performed well at Westminster and proceeded to Christ Church, Oxford, where he earned a bachelor of arts degree in 1575 and a master of arts degree in 1577. He was ordained priest a few years later. Meanwhile, he avidly pursued his geographical studies and lectured on geography at Oxford. He cultivated the acquaintance of men he called "the chiefest Captains at sea, the greatest Merchants, and the best Mariners of our nation." These men included Sir Francis Drake. In 1580 he sponsored the publication of two accounts of voyages by Jacques Cartier. John Florio, who was at Oxford, translated the originals.

Hakluyt became involved with the colonialist party in England. His first significant work, *Divers Voyages Touching the Discovery of America* (1582), served as an inspiration for English expansion. It was dedicated to Sir Philip Sidney. In addition to accounts of English voyages, it included a list of American products and a discussion of the Northwest Passage.

Within a few months after the publication of the *Voyages,* Hakluyt entered government service. He helped to promote Sir Humphrey Gilbert's voyage of 1583 and then went to France, where he served as chaplain to the ambassador, Sir Edward Stafford. During his years in France (1583-

1588) he collected geographical information from French, Portuguese, and Spanish sources. Meanwhile, he returned to England on various occasions. In behalf of Sir Walter Raleigh he presented the Queen with a plea for royal aid in Western planting (1584). The Queen rewarded him with a prebend at Bristol. He was in England when Raleigh's first colony sailed, when Drake brought it home again, and when Raleigh's second, or "lost," colony sailed. In France he sponsored the publication of books concerning geography and exploration.

In 1589 Hakluyt published the first edition of his major work, *The Principal Navigations, Voyages, and Discoveries of the English Nation,* a historical compilation of English enterprise abroad. Shortly thereafter he married. He continued to associate with those interested in the Virginia colony and in the East India Company. The second edition of the *Principal Navigations,* about twice as long as the first, appeared in three folio volumes between 1598 and 1600. It contained new material from all periods, including new information on the exploits of Sir Walter Raleigh. Hakluyt received a prebend at Westminster and was made chaplain of the Savoy.

Further Reading

Hakluyt's *Principal Navigations* was reprinted in 12 volumes by the Hakluyt Society (1903-1905). Several partial reprints have been published. There is a short biography by Foster Watson, *Richard Hakluyt* (1924). The standard work on Hakluyt's life and achievement is George B. Parks, *Richard Hakluyt and the English Voyages* (2d ed. 1961). The influence of the voyages on English literature was studied by Robert Ralston Cawley, *The Voyagers and Elizabethan Drama* (1938) and *Unpathed Waters: Studies in the Influence of the Voyagers on Elizabethan Literature* (1940). □

John Burdon Sanderson Haldane

John Burdon Sanderson Haldane (1892-1964) was an English biologist who utilized mathematical analysis to study genetic phenomena and their relation to evolution.

Born at Oxford on Nov. 5, 1892, J. B. S. Haldane was the son of John Scott Haldane, a distinguished physiologist. Educated at Eton and Oxford, Haldane taught at Oxford (1919-1922), Cambridge (1922-1933), and the University of London (1933-1957), where he was elected the first Weldon professor of genetics in 1957. A lifelong Marxist, he was a member of the British Communist party, and for a number of years he was also chairman of the editorial board of the *Daily Worker,* the party's newspaper. In 1950, following his differences with Soviet geneticists, he resigned from the party.

Refusing to live in what he called "a criminal and police state that had attacked Egypt," Haldane emigrated to

India in 1957 and became the director of the Orissa State Government Genetics and Biometry Laboratory. He was elected a fellow of the Royal Society in 1932, awarded the Darwin Medal in 1953, and given the Kimber Genetics Award in 1957. Author of at least 8 books, he wrote over 300 scientific papers, and over 500 articles for the *Daily Worker, Reynold News,* and many other publications.

Haldane's Work

A contemporary of Ronald Fisher and Sewall Wright, but working independently of them, Haldane mathematically investigated problems dealing with Darwinian "variation" and established the relationship of Mendelian genetics to evolution. He also explored the possibility of estimating spontaneous mutation rates through the observation of harmful or sex-linked genes in populations. For instance, he declared that the rate of mutation of the sex-linked gene among hemophiliacs was between 10 and 50 per million per generation. With Julia Bell he investigated how close the link was between the gene which caused color blindness and that which caused hemophilia.

Haldane was also known for his work in enzyme kinetics. He adduced proof that reactions produced by enzymes obey the known laws of thermodynamics, and he mathematically calculated the rates at which enzyme reactions occur. During World War II he conducted experiments to find out how men could escape from sunken submarines without great difficulty. He showed that, by controlling Eustachian tubes, pressure on eardrums could be lessened. He determined the safest mixture of gases for breathing,

depending upon depth and the duration of stay at that depth, to reduce the occurrence of bends. His outstanding contributions, however, were in mathematical genetics.

Haldane was married twice: his first marriage, in 1925, to Mrs. Charlotte Burghes almost led to his dismissal from Cambridge; in 1945 he married Dr. Helen Spurway, who survived him. Haldane died at Bhuvaneshwar, India, on Dec. 1, 1964.

Further Reading

Ronald William Clark, *JBS: The Life and Work of J. B. S. Haldane* (1968), is a readable study that includes a complete bibliography of Haldane's scientific papers. Haldane is memorialized in an anthology of essays and papers on his work and scientific contributions of his last 50 years, K. R. Dronamraju, ed., *Haldane and Modern Biology* (1968), which also includes some biographical information.

Additional Sources

Clark, Ronald William, *J.B.S., the life and work of J.B.S. Haldane,* Oxford Oxfordshire; New York: Oxford University Press, 1984, 1968.

Dronamraju, Krishna R., *Haldane: the life and work of J.B.S. Haldane with special reference to India,* Aberdeen: Aberdeen University Press, 1985. □

Edward Everett Hale

Edward Everett Hale (1822-1909) was an American Unitarian minister, a social reformer, and a prolific and versatile author.

E dward Everett Hale, born in Boston, was a descendant of eminent New England families on both sides. His father was a newspaper editor and his mother an author.

After preparation in private schools, Hale entered Harvard at the age of 13 and graduated at 17. While still in college he worked as a part-time reporter; soon after graduating he initiated his career by contributing to magazines. He studied theology independently and was licensed to preach in 1842. He became pastor of the Church of Unity, Worcester, Mass. (1846-1856), and of Boston's South Congregational Church (1856-1899). He married Emily Perkins, a member of the crusading Beecher family, in 1852.

Hale was a leader in the Social Gospel movement of the last half of the 19th century and a forceful advocate of emigrant aid, African American education, worker's housing, and world peace. In 1903 he became chaplain of the U.S. Senate and did not return to Boston until shortly before his death there, on June 10, 1909.

Two of Hale's stories became famous. "My Double and How He Undid Me" (1859) combines fantasy and realism in a humorous story about a harassed minister, Frederick Ingham, who has a double perform some of his many tasks. Ingham reappears as the narrator of "The Man without a Country" (1863). This story was inspired by a recent condemnation of America by a Southern sympathizer and was based, vaguely, upon an actual incident.

"The Man without a Country" concerns Philip Nolan, who, while on trial with Aaron Burr for conspiracy, shouts, "Damn the United States! I wish I may never hear of the United States again!" Taking him at his word, the court-martial condemns him "from that moment Sept. 23, 1807" never to hear his country's name again. A perennial prisoner aboard a U.S. naval vessel, Nolan "for that half-century and more" is "a man without a country." On his death bed, now a fervent patriot, he finally learns about his country's history since his punishment began. The story's verisimilitude and the public temper during 1863, the year of its anonymous appearance in the *Atlantic,* made it popular. It was reprinted as a pamphlet in 1865, collected in Hale's *If, Yes, and Perhaps* (1868), and republished scores of times. As late as 1937 it furnished the book for an opera.

Hale's other writings, though less popular, were much admired. The writings he esteemed most were collected in a 10-volume edition in 1898 and 1900.

Further Reading

Edward Everett Hale, Jr., *The Life and Letters of Edward Everett Hale* (2 vols., 1917), has the merits and defects of a biography written by a member of the subject's family. Jean Holloway, *Edward Everett Hale: A Biography* (1956), is the most useful study. □

George Ellery Hale

The American astronomer George Ellery Hale (1868-1938) designed and built three great observatories, invented the spectroheliograph, and discovered magnetic fields in sunspots.

George Ellery Hale was born on June 29, 1868, in Chicago, Illinois, the eldest surviving son of William Ellery Hale and Mary Scranton Browne. His father, a wealthy elevator manufacturer, instilled in Hale from an early age a love for tools and machinery and a deep interest in public affairs. Armed with a box of tools and small lathe for turning metal, Hale transformed his bedroom into a laboratory and later built with his own hands a workshop in the yard.

Hale's mother, a graduate of the Hartford Female Seminary in Hartford, Connecticut, cultivated his literary side, reading aloud the *Iliad* and the *Odyssey* and stocking the shelves of his personal library with books ranging from the unabridged *Robinson Crusoe* and *Don Quixote* in translation to *Grimm's Fairy Tales* and the poetry of Shelley and Keats. In biographical notes written in 1933 Hale spoke fondly of these and other classics that "helped greatly to arouse my imagination and prepare me for scientific research."

Early Interest in Astronomy

Hale attended the Oakland Public School and later the Allen Academy, taking also a shop course at the Chicago Manual Training School. But what mattered most to Hale were the studies he worked on at home. Astronomy headed the list. He first built a small telescope, then a spectroscope. Attached to the telescope, now a 4-inch Clark refractor purchased for him by his father, the homemade instrument allowed Hale to observe the solar spectrum. In 1884 he photographed a spectrum using a small commercial spectrometer. To measure more accurately the wavelengths of the dark Fraunhofer lines in the solar spectrum, Hale added a one-inch plane grating to the single prism spectrometer.

Reading everything he could find on spectra during these years, Hale bought Norman Lockyer's *Studies in Spectrum Analysis.* Inspired, he began laboratory observations of spectra and compared them with those of the sun's spectrum. Out of that work was born Hale's lifelong interest in the physical properties of the sun and stars. In explaining why classical astronomy with its emphasis on determining the positions, distances, and motions of celestial bodies did not appeal to him even then, Hale later wrote: "I was born an experimentalist, and I was bound to find the way of combining physics and chemistry with astronomy."

His First Observatory

Determined to leave his mark on the young science of astrophysics, Hale entered the Massachusetts Institute of Technology (MIT) in 1886, where he studied chemistry,

physics, and mathematics. For astronomy, he turned to Edward C. Pickering, director of the Harvard College Observatory, who took him on as a volunteer assistant. During summer vacations he continued his own solar and stellar research in a specially-equipped spectroscopic laboratory of his own design built for him by his father in 1888 on a lot adjacent to the family home in the Kenwood section of Chicago. This formed the nucleus of the Kenwood Physical Observatory.

At the time the standard method of recording solar prominences consisted of drawings based on visual observation. In his quest to find an adequate method of photographing prominences, Hale invented the spectroheliograph—an instrument for photographing phenomena in the solar atmosphere that would otherwise be invisible. The first tests of his new instrument, made in the winter of 1889-1890 at the Harvard Observatory, demonstrated that the basic principle was right. Then a senior at MIT, he wrote up the work for his thesis and received a B.S. in physics. Hale married Evelina Conklin in June 1890, two days after graduation. Upon their return to Chicago, Hale's father agreed to finance the construction of a 12-inch refractor telescope.

At the Kenwood Observatory, dedicated in 1891, Hale continued his experiments with the spectroheliograph. In examining the spectra of prominences, he observed two bright lines (H and K), which he had determined to be due to calcium, in the ultraviolet region. They proved ideal for photographing prominences, as photographic plates then in use were more sensitive to light in the ultraviolet. Moreover, his photographs of solar spectra showed H and K as bright lines all over the sun. Armed with this information and an improved instrument, Hale photographed these calcium clouds (flocculi) and prominences both at the solar limb and across the disc in 1892 for the first time. The success of this research tool sealed Hale's international reputation as a solar astronomer. Many of his findings appeared in *Astronomy and Astrophysics,* the forerunner of the *Astrophysical Journal,* a publication founded by Hale in 1895 and still the leading astronomical journal in the field.

Two More Observatories

In 1892 Hale joined the faculty of the new University of Chicago as associate professor of astrophysics and director of the observatory. An accomplished organizer and money-raiser, Hale persuaded streetcar millionaire C. T. Yerkes to provide the university with the largest refractor telescope in the world. Hailed in 1897 for its revolutionary design, the Yerkes Observatory at Williams Bay, Wisconsin, was, as Hale stated, "in reality a large physical laboratory as well as an astronomical establishment." There, with the aid of F. Ellerman and J. A. Parkhurst, Hale carried out a study on the spectra of low-temperature red stars (Secchi's fourth type). Besides continuing his own research on sunspot spectra, he also studied the distribution of calcium flocculi at different levels in the solar atmosphere and found the dark hydrogen flocculi using a large spectroheliograph of his own design built for the 40-inch telescope.

Hale lived by his own motto, "Make no small plans." He founded the Mount Wilson Observatory in Pasadena, California, in 1904 with funds provided by the Carnegie Institution and served as its director until 1923. In an effort to eliminate mirror distortion and air turbulence, Hale designed and built in 1908 a 60-foot tower telescope with a long vertical spectroheliograph in an underground well. By then he had discovered the low temperature of sunspots, the vortex structure of the dark hydrogen flocculi in the vicinity of sunspots, and the magnetic fields of sunspots. The discovery of hydrogen vortices around sunspots suggested to Hale that the double lines in sunspot spectra, photographed with the 60-foot tower telescope, were not due, as previously believed, to "reversals," but rather to intense magnetic fields (the Zeeman effect).

In 1908 Hale compared his astronomical work with the similar doubling of lines obtained with large electromagnets in the observatory's physical laboratory and demonstrated conclusively for the first time the existence of sunspot magnetic fields. Working later with the 150-foot tower telescope, Hale attempted to measure the general magnetic field of the sun; he also formulated the law of sunspot polarities and discovered the reversal of sunspot polarities in successive 11-year cycles.

A solar astronomer primarily, Hale also built stellar telescopes: a 60-inch reflector installed at Mount Wilson in 1908, and a 100-inch telescope inaugurated in 1917. In 1928 the International Educational Board of the Rockefeller Foundation agreed to finance Hale's $6 million proposal to build a 200-inch telescope on Mount Palomar (dedicated in 1948, it bears his name).

A Leader in the Science Community

A scientist bursting with educational, architectural, and civic ideas, Hale was elected to the National Academy of Sciences in 1902 and promptly set about to reform it. He created (and served as first chairman) the National Research Council, the operating arm of the academy, in 1916; aided in establishing a fellowship program in 1919; and raised the endowment for the council and the construction in 1924 of a permanent building for the academy in Washington, D.C. Back in Pasadena, he joined the board of trustees of Throop Polytechnic Institute in 1906 and played a major role in transforming it into the California Institute of Technology, a distinguished school of research and teaching in science and engineering. He influenced the creation of the Henry E. Huntington Library and Art Gallery and worked on the master plan for Pasadena's civic center.

Weakened by a series of nervous breakdowns, Hale resigned as director of the observatory in 1923 and built a small solar laboratory in Pasadena, where he continued to do research on the sun. Honors received during his life-time include the Royal Astronomical Society medal in 1904 and the Copley medal of the Royal Society in 1932 and election to the Accademia dei Lincei and the Royal Society of London, as well as membership in many scientific societies in the United States and abroad. He entered Las Encinas sanitarium in Pasadena following a stroke and died there of heart trouble on February 21, 1938.

Further Reading

Novelist Theodore Dreiser wrote Hale into his novel about Charles Yerkes, *The Titan* (1914). A first-hand account of Hale's work in California appears in *Ten Years' Work of a Mountain Observatory* (1915). The only full-length biography of Hale is Helen Wright, *Explorer of the Universe* (1966). Walter A. Adams, who succeeded Hale as director of the Mount Wilson Observatory, leaned heavily on Hale's unpublished autobiographical notes in the biographical introduction he prepared for the NAS *Biog. Mem.* (1940). Hale published six books and over 450 articles, all of which are chronologically listed in Adams' bibliography. Hale's work in astronomy and in developing scientific institutions is vividly revealed in pictures, documents, and essays in Helen Wright, Joan N. Warnow, and Charles Weiner (editors), *The Legacy of George Ellery Hale* (1972). Good background material is in Owen Gingerich (editor), *Astrophysics and Twentieth-Century Astronomy to 1950: Part A* (1984) and in Daniel Kevles, *The Physicists* (1978).

Additional Sources

Osterbrock, Donald E., *Pauper & prince: Ritchey, Hale & big American telescopes,* Tucson: University of Arizona Press, 1993.

Wright, Helen, *Explorer of the universe: a biography of George Ellery Hale,* Woodbury, N.Y.: American Institute of Physics, 1994. □

Sarah Josepha Hale

For nearly 50 years Sarah Josepha Hale (1788-1879) was the editor of America's most influential women's magazine.

Sarah Josepha Buell was born in Newport, N.H. She was educated at home and in October 1813 married David Hale, a lawyer. He encouraged her to write for local newspapers. When he died in 1822, leaving his widow with five children, Mrs. Hale attempted a full-scale literary career. Some early verse was well received, and in 1827 her first novel, *Northwood: A Tale of New England,* brought her serious critical attention. The Reverend John Laurie Blake was just about to found a monthly magazine for women in Boston, and he offered her the editorship. Accepting, she moved to Boston in 1828 and edited *Ladies' Magazine* there until 1837.

The magazine was a success, the first of its kind to take an important place in American periodical publication. It featured fiction, poetry, essays, and criticism and was characterized by its attempts both to define and to celebrate the wholesome and tasteful in American life. Hale wrote most of the material for each issue, and every month she pressed her arguments in favor of improved education for women and a role for women in the culture as teachers and moral guides. She rejected, with equal steadiness, the claims of the feminist movement for the right of women to occupy positions of executive authority in the political and business worlds.

In 1837 Louis A. Godey bought out the magazine, changed the name to *Godey's Lady's Book,* and promoted it to fame with impressive skill. Hale remained as editor, moved to Philadelphia, and for 40 years reigned as the taste maker of the American household. The magazine prided itself on being "a beacon light of refined taste, pure morals, and practical wisdom."

Though she always contributed freely to all departments of the magazine, as the years went by Hale concentrated most of her attention on the sections called "Literary Notices" and "Editor's Table." It was there that she tirelessly managed her campaign to establish standards of taste, delicacy, and decorum for American women.

Among her 36 volumes of essays, fiction, drama, poetry, cookbooks, and giftbooks, Hale published the huge *Women's Record: Sketches of Distinguished Women,* in at least three editions. Her poem "Mary Had a Little Lamb" first appeared in *Poems for Our Children* in 1830.

At the age of 90 Hale contributed her last article and retired, the acknowledged arbiter of 19th century American feminine manners and morals.

Further Reading

A scholarly, full-length study of Mrs. Hale is Ruth E. Finley, *The Lady of Godey's: Sarah Josepha Hale* (1931). Her career is also recounted in Helen Beal Woodward, *The Bold Women* (1953), and Walter Davenport and James C. Derieux, *Ladies, Gentlemen and Editors* (1960).

Additional Sources

Rogers, Sherbrooke, *Sarah Josepha Hale: a New England pioneer, 1788-1879,* Grantham, N.H.: Tompson & Rutter, 1985.
☐

Stephen Hales

The English scientist and clergyman Stephen Hales (1677-1761) pioneered the study of plant physiology, contributed the first major account of blood pressure, and invented a machine for ventilating buildings.

Stephen Hales was born in Bekesbourne, Kent, on Sept. 17, 1677. He entered Corpus Christi College, Cambridge, in 1697, where he studied theology and took a degree in arts in 1703. He received his doctorate from Cambridge in 1733. At Cambridge, Hales was caught up in the backwash of Isaac Newton's great work at the university, and he acquired an interest in astronomy, physics, and chemistry as well as in biology. In 1708 Hales became perpetual curate of Teddington in Middlesex, and here he remained until his death. In 1719 he married Mary Newce, who died 2 years later without issue.

In 1711 Hales began his studies on blood pressure. True to his mechanistic views, he carefully measured the blood pressure of three horses and produced the first recorded estimates of blood pressure. Furthermore, he studied the pulse rates of various-sized animals and measured the heart's capacity to pump blood through the pulmonary veins. Hales also studied the effects of heat, cold, and various drugs on the blood vessels and experimented with animal reflexes.

Even though some research had been carried out by Jan van Helmont and Marcello Malpighi, Hales rightfully merits the title of father of plant physiology. Certainly in a century given over almost exclusively to the taxonomy of Carl Linnaeus, Hales's work was unique. In 1718, the year he became a member of the Royal Society, he read a paper entitled "Upon the Effect of ye Sun's warmth in raising ye Sap in trees." He then carefully measured sap pressure, velocity, and circulation in plants. Until this time sap circulation in plants was believed to parallel blood circulation in animals. Hales, however, clearly demonstrated that the transpiration of leaves draws the sap toward them at the same rate that the roots push sap upward. Furthermore, he found that plants draw some of their food from the gases in the air. He invented the pneumatic trough for collecting gases and developed gages and techniques to measure sap pressure.

Hales published his findings in *Vegetable Staticks* (1727), reissued in 1733 as volume 1 of his *Statical Essays.* Volume 2 was *Haemastatics,* primarily a summary of his earlier work on blood circulation. For his work he received the Copley Prize in 1739.

Hales thought his invention of a ventilator was his greatest contribution to the well-being of mankind. As early as 1741 Hales presented to the Royal Society a description of a ventilator to rid mines, prisons, hospitals, and shops of noxious airs. He published *A Description of Ventilators* (1743) and *A Treatise of Ventilators* (1758). Hales also sought ways to distill pure water from seawater, preserve meat and water for long ocean voyages, preserve foods in tropical climates, measure earthquakes, and prevent forest fires.

In 1751 Hales became clerk of the closet of the princess dowager, and subsequently he was made chaplain to her and to her son, the future George III. Though offered the canonry of Windsor by the royal family, Hales maintained an active ministry at Teddington until his death on Jan. 4, 1761.

Further Reading

The best work on Hales is Archibald E. Clark-Kennedy, *Stephen Hales: An Eighteenth Century Biography* (1929). General background studies include Charles Singer and E. Ashworth Underwood, *A Short History of Medicine* (1928; 2d ed. 1962), and Abraham Wolf, *A History of Science, Technology, and Philosophy in the Eighteenth Century* (1938; 2d rev. ed. 1952). ☐

Élie Halévy

The French philosopher and historian Élie Halévy (1870-1937) wrote studies of the British utilitarians and a history of 19th-century England.

Élie Halévy was born on Sept. 6, 1870, at Étretat, where his mother had fled as the German army marched on Paris. His father was the playwright Ludovic Halévy, and Élie grew up surrounded by musicians, scholars, and politicians. After studying at the École Normale, he received his doctorate in philosophy in 1901 with the theses *The Platonic Theory of Knowledge* and *The Origins of Philosophical Radicalism*. The latter formed the base of his first major study, *The Formation of English Philosophical Radicalism* (3 vols., 1901-1904).

In an article of 1893 Halévy suggested that the great moral question of modern thought was how the abstract idea of duty could become a concrete aim of society. This question had first attracted him to the utilitarians, and he found at the core of their answer a fundamental contradiction. Utilitarianism, he said, was based on two principles: first, that the science of the legislator must bring together the naturally divergent interests of individuals in society; and, second, that social order comes about spontaneously through the harmony of individual interests. To Halévy this exemplified two fundamental human attitudes toward the universe: the contemplation of the astronomer and the intervention of the engineer.

In 1892 Émile Boutmy invited Halévy to lecture on English political ideas at the newly founded School of Political Science. After 1900 he alternated this course with another, on the history of socialism. At the same time he helped found the *Revue de métaphysique et de morale,* in which he retained an interest until his death.

Halévy's teaching led him to undertake annual trips to England, during which he became the intimate friend of many of the most important scholars and political figures of the age. He thoroughly explored the Jeremy Bentham manuscripts at Cambridge for his work on philosophical radicalism and over the years developed a deep and intensive knowledge of all the sources of 19th-century English history. In 1901 he began to work on the first volume of his masterpiece, the *History of the English People in the Nineteenth Century* (1912). In this book he described England in 1815 and sought to explain how England avoided violent social change. "If economic facts explain the course taken by the human race," he wrote, "the England of the nineteenth century was surely, above all other countries, destined to revolution, both politically and religiously." Neither the British constitution nor the Established Church was strong enough to hold the country together. He found the answer in religious nonconformity: "Methodism was the antidote to Jacobinism."

The second and third volumes of this history (1923) carried the story up to 1841. Then Halévy, profoundly moved by World War I, turned his attention to the period form 1895 to 1914. The tow volumes on this period (1926-1930) were written with considerable detachment, considering the immediacy of the problems he discussed.

In lectures of 1929, revised in 1936 (published in 1938; *The Era of Tyrannies*), Halévy argued that the world war had increased national control over individual activities and opened the way for de facto socialism. In opposition to those who saw socialism as the last step in the French Revolution, he saw it as a new organization of constraint replacing those that the Revolution had destroyed. A liberal individualist to the last, Halévy died at Sucy-en-Brie on Aug. 21, 1937.

Further Reading

Halévy's *The Era of Tyrannies: Essays on Socialism and War* (1938; trans. 1965) has a useful biographical and critical introduction, a preface, and a "Note" by different historians. There is a chapter on Halévy in Bernadotte E. Schmitt, ed., *Some Historians of Modern Europe: Essays in Historiography* (1942). An essay on Halévy appears in Herman Ausubel and others, eds., *Some Modern Historians of Britain: Essays in Honor of R. L. Schuyler* (1951).

Additional Sources

Chase, Myrna, *Élie Halévy, an intellectual biography,* New York: Columbia University Press, 1980. □

Alex Haley

Alex Haley (1921-1992) is the celebrated author of *Roots: The Saga of an American Family* (1976). By April 1977 almost two million hardcover copies of the book had been sold and 130 million people had seen all or part of the eight-episode television series. *Roots* is thus considered by many critics a classic in African-American literature and culture.

Haley, who was born in Ithaca, New York, and raised in the small town of Henning, Tennessee, became interested in his ancestry while listening to colorful stories told by his family. One story in particular, about an African ancestor who refused to be called by his slave name "Toby" and declared instead that his name was "Kintay," impressed Haley deeply. Young Haley was so fascinated by this account that he later spent twelve years researching and documenting the life of "Kunta Kinte," the character in his famous *Roots.* School records indicate that Haley was not an exceptional student. At the age of eighteen he joined the U.S. Coast Guard and began a twenty-year career in the service. He practiced his writing, at first only to alleviate boredom on the ship, and soon found himself composing love letters for his shipmates to send home to their wives and girlfriends. He wrote serious pieces as well and submitted them to various magazines.

Upon retiring from the Coast Guard, Haley decided to become a full-time writer and journalist. His first book, *The*

Autobiography of Malcolm X (1965), which he cowrote with Malcolm X, was widely acclaimed upon its publication. The work sold over five million copies and launched Haley's writing career. Malcolm X was at first reluctant to work with Haley. He later told the writer: "I don't completely trust anyone . . . you I trust about twenty-five percent." Critics praised Haley for sensitively handling Malcolm X's volatile life, and the book quickly became required reading in many schools. Two weeks after *The Autobiography of Malcolm X* was completed, Haley began work on his next project, *Roots.* The tale chronicles the life of Kunta Kinte, a proud African who is kidnapped from his village in West Africa, forced to endure the middle passage—the brutal shipment of Africans to be sold in the Americas—on the slave ship *Lord Ligonier,* and made a slave on the Waller plantation in the United States. To authenticate Kunta's life and that of Kunta's grandson, Chicken George, Haley visited archives, libraries, and research repositories on three continents. He even reenacted Kunta's experience on the *Lord Ligonier.* "[Haley] somehow scourged up some money and flew to Liberia where he booked passage on the first U. S. bound ship," an *Ebony* interviewer related. "Once at sea, he spent the night lying on a board in the hold of the ship, stripped to his underwear to get a rough idea of what his African ancestor might have experienced."

Although critics generally lauded *Roots,* they seemed unsure whether to treat the work as a novel or as a historical account. While the narrative is based on factual events, the dialogue, thoughts, and emotions of the characters are fic-

tionalized. Haley himself described the book as "faction," a mixture of fact and fiction. Most critics concurred and evaluated *Roots* as a blend of history and entertainment. Despite the fictional characterizations, Willie Lee Rose suggested in the *New York Review of Books* that Kunta Kinte's parents Omoro and Binte "could possibly become the African proto-parents of millions of Americans who are going to admire their dignity and grace." *Newsweek* applauded Haley's decision to fictionalize: "Instead of writing a scholarly monograph of little social impact, Haley has written a blockbuster in the best sense—a book that is bold in concept and ardent in execution, one that will reach millions of people and alter the way we see ourselves."

Some voiced concern, however—especially at the time of the television series—that racial tension in America would be aggravated by *Roots.* While *Time* did report several incidents of racial violence following the telecast, it commented that "most observers thought that in the long term, *Roots* would improve race relations, particularly because of the televised version's profound impact on whites. . . . A broad consensus seemed to be emerging that *Roots* would spur black identity, and hence black pride, and eventually pay important dividends." Some black leaders viewed *Roots* "as the most important civil rights event since the 1965 march on Selma," according to *Time.* Vernon Jordan, executive director of the National Urban League, called it "the single most spectacular educational experience in race relations in America." Speaking of the appeal of *Roots* among blacks, Haley added: "The blacks who are buying books are not buying them to go out and fight someone, but because they want to know who they are. . . . [The] book has touched a strong, subliminal chord."

For months after the publication of *Roots* in October 1976, Haley signed at least five hundred copies of the book daily, spoke to an average of six thousand people a day, and traveled round trip coast-to-coast at least once a week. Scarcely two years later, *Roots* had already won 271 awards, and its television adaptation had been nominated for a recordbreaking thirty-seven Emmys. Over eight million copies of the book were in print, and the text was translated into twenty-six languages. In addition to fame and fortune, *Roots* also brought Haley controversy. In 1977 two published authors, Margaret Walker and Harold Courlander, alleged separately that Haley plagiarized their work in *Roots.* Charges brought by Walker were later dropped, but Haley admitted that he unknowingly lifted three paragraphs from Courlander's *The African* (1968). A settlement was reached whereby Haley paid Courlander $500,000. The same year other accusations also arose. Mark Ottaway in *The Sunday Times* questioned Haley's research methods and the credibility of his informants, accusing Haley of "bending" data to fit his objectives. Gary B. and Elizabeth Shown Mills also challenged some of Haley's assertions. Writing in 1981 in *The Virginia Magazine of History and Biography,* they cited evidence that there was indeed a slave named Toby living on the Waller plantation. He was there, however, at least five years before the arrival of the *Lord Ligonier,* supposedly with Kunta on board.

Haley's supporters maintain that Haley never claimed *Roots* as fact or history. And even in the presence of controversy, the public image of *Roots* appears not to have suffered. It is still widely read in schools, and many college and university history and literature programs consider it an essential part of their curriculum. According to Haley himself, *Roots* is important not for its names and dates but as a reflection of human nature: "*Roots* is all of our stories. . . . It's just a matter of filling in the blanks . . . ; when you start talking about family, about lineage and ancestry, you are talking about every person on earth." Indeed, Haley's admirers contend, *Roots* remains a great book because it is the universal story of humankind's own search for its identity.

Further Reading

The Black Press U.S.A., Iowa State University Press, 1990.
Contemporary Literary Criticism, Gale, Volume 8, 1978, Volume 12, 1980.
Dictionary of Literary Biography, Volume 38: *Afro-American Writers After 1955: Dramatists and Prose Writers,* Gale, 1985.
Black Collegian, September/October, 1985.
Christianity Today, May 6, 1977.
Ebony, April, 1977.
Forbes, February 15, 1977. □

Margaret A. Haley

Margaret A. Haley (1861–1939) was a labor activist and leader of the Chicago Teachers' Federation who fought to improve public education and the working conditions of Chicago's elementary school teachers.

Margaret A. Haley headed the most militant teachers' organization in the United States, the Chicago Teachers' Federation (CTF), in the early decades of the twentieth century. Becoming leader of the group in January 1900, she continued in that position until her death thirty-nine years later. As labor advocate and social reformer, Haley fought for the cause of public education in Chicago and battled mightily to improve working conditions and pay for Chicago's elementary-school teachers. Haley's autobiography, *Battleground,* began with the words "I never wanted to fight;" but the slight but fiery "Maggie" never backed away from machine politicians, unscrupulous businessmen, inept school administrators, or anyone who sought to frustrate her efforts to improve schools for students and teachers.

Background

Haley was born in the town of Joliet, Illinois, on 15 November 1861 and spent her early childhood on a farm on the Illinois prairie. At sixteen, to help alleviate her family's financial troubles, Haley went to work as a teacher in a one-room country school. Finding she had a knack for teaching, she moved at age nineteen to Chicago and shortly thereafter began to teach in the urban Chicago public-school system.

Securing a job as a sixth-grade teacher, Haley remained in that position until 1900, when, at thirty-eight, she became the business representative for the Chicago Teachers' Federation.

The Tax Fight

Haley's first battle as head of the Chicago Teachers' Federation was waged because of her concern about insufficient revenues for Chicago's public-school system. An agreement between the Chicago Board of Education and the CTF in 1898 promised to grant teachers pay raises in three yearly installments. The board paid the first on time but failed to pay the second and third installments on the agreed dates. Even worse, in late 1899 the board threatened to cancel the earlier raise and close Chicago schools for two weeks because of a lack of funds. Wondering why the city was in such financial straits, Haley discovered that many of Chicago's major corporations were evading city taxes. With proof in hand, Haley and the CTF took five major utility and street-railway companies to court. The corporations lost, and new tax reassessments brought roughly $600,000 in back taxes to the city. Annual revenues available to Chicago increased by $250,000. Haley's fight with corporate scofflaws eventually made more money available for schools and ensured higher salaries for Chicago public-school teachers.

Affiliation with Labor Union

Following the tax fight, Haley urged the Chicago Teachers' Federation to join the most powerful labor union in the city, the Chicago Federation of Labor (CFL). Many people in Chicago—including many in the CTF—opposed such a step. The CTF was a voluntary organization of elementary-school teachers, 97 percent of whom were female; the labor union represented men who were teamsters, carpenters, horseshoers, and other blue-collar workers. Knowing that many teachers were uneasy about joining the union, Haley reminded the women in her organization that they could not legally vote in elections and that in any future political battles they would suffer a decided disadvantage. In Haley's words, "We realized that we had to fight the devil with fire, and, if we were to preserve not only our self-respect but the basic independence of public schools, we must make powerful political alliances." After weeks of deliberation the CTF finally agreed with Haley and joined forces with the labor union on 8 November 1902, thereby uniting the women of the CTF with the two hundred thousand working men of the CFL, all of whom could legally vote. The CTF became the first large body of teachers to affiliate with labor; and, in turn, organized labor became a strong supporter of public education in Chicago.

New Political Battles

After her success in 1902, Haley struggled for the rest of the decade to develop a partnership with working people whose interests included the factory, the home, and the school. During this period the CTF's influence on the civic life of Chicago grew. According to Haley, writing in 1903, "the Federation itself is as much an accepted fact and as essential a part of the business of Chicago now as the Board of Trade, the City Hall, or even the Board of Education itself." In 1905 the CTF energetically campaigned for reform candidate Edward F. Dunne in the city's mayoral election; following Dunne's victory, Chicago's public-school students and teachers continued to make new gains. Under Chicago's charter Mayor Dunne could appoint seven new members to the twenty-one-member school board each year. In his first year three of the seven appointees were women—one of whom was Jane Addams , head of the world-renowned Hull House settlement. In the second year Dunne's appointees were a majority of the board, and these appointees implemented needed reforms in school governance. Although Dunne failed to gain reelection for a second term, Margaret Haley and the CTF remained a vibrant organization fighting for school reform through the rest of the decade. Haley then continued to lead the Chicago Teachers' Federation for thirty more years. In the mid 1930s, she began devoting most of her energy to writing her autobiography, which she hoped would inspire continued faith in the teachers' union movement. Margaret Haley died on 5 January 1939 at the age of seventy-seven.

Further Reading

Margaret A. Haley, *Battleground: The Autobiography of Margaret A. Haley,* edited by Robert L. Reid (Urbana: University of Illinois Press, 1982). □

Christóbal Halffter

Christóbal Halffter (born 1930) was the most prominent of the group of composers who emerged in Spain in the 1950's, rejecting the folk-music orientation of earlier 20th-century Spanish composers and entering into the mainstream of European composition.

Christóbal Halffter, born in Madrid, was the nephew of Ernesto and Rodolfo Halffter, both prominent composers. Christóbal studied at the Madrid Conservatory; his gift for composing was discovered early, and he won numerous prizes while still a student. His earliest works, such as the *Antifonia Pascual* (1952) followed the spare Spanish style of Manuel de Falla and of some of his uncle's compositions. Others, such as the 1951 *Piano Sonata* and the 1956 *Mass* were in the tradition of Igor Stravinsky's neoclassicism. Halffter's *Dos Movimientos* (1956) for timpani and string orchestra, strongly influenced by Béla Bartók, won a prize in a contest for young composers sponsored by UNESCO.

After Halffter was introduced to the twelve-tone system in 1956, he began compositing in serial style. One of the most important is *Cinco Microformas* (1960) for orchestra, a set of five variations on a twelve-tone theme. His *Formantes* (1961) for two pianos was chosen to represent Spain at a UNESCO conference on contemporary music held in Tokyo. This piece employs aleatory (that is, chance) principles, in that the performers may choose the order in which they play various sections.

Halffter's first piece using electronic sounds was *Espejos* (1963) for four percussionists and magnetic tape. In this work, the first section is recorded and then played back while the instrumentalists continue playing new material. In 1964 Halffter became director of the Madrid Conservatory. He was instrumental in forming the Grupo Nueva Musica, which sponsored concerts of new music, until then virtually unknown in Spain. In *Simposium* (1967) for baritone, mixed chorus, and orchestra, Halffter showed his awareness of new trends in choral music by having his choir speak, whisper, and chant as well as sing.

In 1967 UNESCO commissioned Halffter to write a work commemorating the twentieth anniversary of the Universal Declaration of Human Rights. The cantata, *Yes, Speak Out, Yes,* was performed in New York City's United Nations Building in 1968. Norman Corwin wrote the texts for the early parts of the work to introduce settings of portions of the Declaration. The six-movement piece is written for two orchestras and two choruses and calls for two conductors. Halffter described his intent: "In each movement, I try to create a sonic environment which gives the words a new dimension, even at the cost of some loss of intelligibility. In the first movement, for instance, it is not possible to understand all the words. I have tried to create a brutal atmosphere of negation and violence." Halffter made effective use of many of the compositional techniques of his time. His works show fine craftsmanship, a sense of color, and expressive qualities.

By the mid-1960's, Halffter had established himself among the international avant-garde. Works for large orchestra like *Antillos* (1968) and *Lineas y Puntos* (1969), for 20 wind instruments and tape, established his ability to work freely with large sound masses as well as the more delicate combinations which at that time constituted the common language of young composers' orchestral writing. In a highly productive career, Halffter has written at least 37 pieces for orchestra, including concerti for cello, violin, and flute; 17 vocal compositions, many of which are choral works; an opera; music for a ballet; at least 10 works for chamber ensembles; and works for solo piano and for two pianos.

Among other posts, Halffter has been Director of the Royal Conservatory of Music, Madrid; Lecturer at the University of Navarra; guest conductor of major orchestras in Europe and the United States; and since 1989, Principal Guest Conductor of the National Orchestra in Madrid. King Juan Carlos of Spain awarded him the Gold Medal for fine Arts in 1983. He lives in Madrid.

Further Reading

Paul Henry Lang and Nathan Broder, eds., *Contemporary Music in Europe: A Comprehensive Survey* (1965).
H. H. Stuckenschmidt, *Twentieth Century Music* (trans. 1969). □

Thomas Chandler Haliburton

Thomas Chandler Haliburton (1796-1865) was a Canadian judge and author who is chiefly known for his humorous sketches and essays. He was also the first Canadian writer to achieve a significant international reputation.

Born in Windsor, Nova Scotia, of loyalist stock, Thomas Haliburton was educated at King's College, Windsor, and was called to the bar of his native province in 1820. He began his law practice at Annapolis Royal and represented that constituency in the legislative assembly from 1826 to 1829. In the latter year he succeeded his father as a judge of the Court of Common Pleas. He became a judge of the Supreme Court in 1841 but in 1856 moved from Nova Scotia to England, where he became a member of Parliament in 1859. He died in Isleworth-on-Thames.

Haliburton began his literary career in 1823 by publishing an anonymous pamphlet entitled *General Description of Nova Scotia*. In 1829 he published a history of his province, *A Historical and Statistical Account of Nova Scotia*. His literary fame was established, however, by the publication of *The Clockmaker; or, The Sayings and Doings of Sam Slick of Slickville*, first as a series of sketches in

Joseph Howe's magazine, the *Novascotian,* and then, in 1836, as a book.

This book is satire of a high order: it ridicules, chiefly in the person of Sam Slick, the itinerant Yankee clock salesman, the arrogance and sharp practices of Americans and at the same time pokes fun at the slothfulness, conservatism, and naiveté of his fellow Nova Scotians. The book was praised highly by reviewers in both the United States and the United Kingdom, and Sam Slick reappeared in later books by Haliburton—*The Attaché; or, Sam Slick in England* (1843-1844), *Sam Slick's Wise Saws and Modern Instances* (1853), and *Nature and Human Nature* (1853)—but lost some of his original luster.

Haliburton wrote a number of other books, including such serious political tracts as *The Bubbles of Canada* (1839), *A Reply to the Report of the Earl of Durham* (1839), and *Rule and Misrule of the English in America* (1851). The best of his later books, however, were three further collections of humorous sketches, *The Letter-Bag of the Great Western* (1840), *The Old Judge; or, Life in a Colony* (1849), and *The Season Ticket* (1860). Haliburton also edited two popular anthologies of American humor: *Traits of American Humour by Native Authors* (1852) and *The American at Home; or, Bye-ways, Back-woods and Prairies* (1855).

Haliburton's political position can best be described as that of a Tory radical: deeply conservative by nature, he was nevertheless quite ready to challenge the establishment. His most enduring achievements were, however, his comical portraits of persons, his shrewdly witty anecdotes, and his droll "tall tales."

Further Reading

The best book on Haliburton is still V. L. O. Chittick, *Thomas Chandler Haliburton* (1924). See also the sections on Haliburton in Ray Palmer Baker, *History of English-Canadian Literature to the Confederation* (1920); Desmond Pacey, *Creative Writing in Canada* (2d ed. 1961); and Carl F. Klinck, ed., *Literary History of Canada* (1965).

Additional Sources

Percy, H. R., *Thomas Chandler Haliburton,* Don Mills, Ont.: Fitzhenry & Whiteside, 1980. □

Halide Edip Adivar

Halide Edip Adivar (1884-1964) was a Turkish writer, scholar, and public figure dedicated to the rights of women and their emancipation. She attempted to analyze the rapid transition of Turkish society and to depict the deep-seated conflict the society faced through the clash between Eastern and Western culture.

Halide Edip was born in 1884 in Istanbul as the daughter of Mehmet Edip bey, private treasurer of Sultan Abdulhamit II, later director of the Régie Française de Tabac at Yanina and Bursa. Although she did not attend primary school, she received private lessons from well known personalities in the field of social sciences, philosophy, and mathematics. After graduating in 1901 from the American Girls College in Usküdar/Istanbul, she married her former tutor, the mathematician Salih Riza bey; two boys—Ayetullah and Hikmetullah—were born to the couple. After 1907 her articles were published in the newspaper *Tanin* and other reviews under the name of Halide Salih.

When her husband decided to take a second wife, she asked for a divorce in 1910. From that year on she taught history and concentrated her attention on issues of education. During World War I she was formally invited to Syria, where she organized the public instruction system and served as inspector of the girls' secondary schools in Beirut and Damascus. In 1918 she married Adnan Adivar, a well-known professor of medicine who later became minister of health under Mustafa Kemal's leadership. In 1918 Halide Edip was appointed professor of Western literature at the University of Istanbul. Following the armistice Halide Edip enthusiastically adopted the peace proposals of President Woodrow Wilson and became an activist in favor of an American mandate. After realizing that none of the defeated nations adhered to Wilson's principles, she changed her mind and espoused the nationalistic cause proclaimed by Mustafa Kemal, later Ataturk.

Halide Edip was the first woman speaker at a mass meeting in Istanbul in 1919, protesting the occupation of Izmir by the Greek armed forces. After the occupation of Istanbul in March 1919 by the British, she fled with her husband, Adnan bey, to Anatolia to join Mustafa Kemal's forces. The sultan's government condemned to death in absentia Mustafa Kemal and five of his closest collaborators; one among the condemned was Halide Edip. After joining the nationalist forces in Anatolia, the young woman writer began to work at the general staff headquarters; later she was moved to the Western front. In recognition of her military services she was promoted to the rank of sergeant.

After the establishment of the Turkish Republic, Halide Edip, her husband, and like-minded friends founded the Progressive Republican Party as the major opposition party. Following a ban on this party in 1925, the Adivars went abroad and lived from 1926 to 1939 in Europe and the United States. Halide Edip was invited by Columbia University as guest professor in 1928-1929. She taught courses on the intellectual history of the Near East and on contemporary Turkish literature. In 1935 Mahatma Gandhi invited her to India, where she taught in New Delhi. The couple returned to their home country in 1939. From 1940 on Halide Edip headed the chair of English literature at Istanbul University. After the transition to a multiparty system, Halide Edip served one term in parliament as an independent member from Izmir (1950-1954). She died on January 9, 1964, in Istanbul and was buried in the cemetery of Merkezefendi.

The most important characteristic of Halide Edip's novels is the broad social framework she built around her stories. Without neglecting the psychological dimensions, her main emphasis was on providing the reader with an insight into the major social issues of the time. Among her heroes women play an important role. In her writings one comes across nationalistic women, modernized women, women with strong personalities, women rising up against oppression, and idealistic women striving to educate the masses. Her male heroes are much more statue-like; they lack energy and drive. Her language was full of feelings, vivid and warm. Instead of detailed descriptions she preferred an impressionistic style. Her best known novel, *The Clown and His Daughter,* was first written in English, later rewritten in Turkish; the novel was given a literary prize in 1942. The book won international fame and went through 25 editions.

The first phase of her novel-writing reflected excitement and observation (1908-1928); the second phase attempted to achieve a cultural synthesis (1928-1952). In her two volumes on the history of English literature emphasis was placed upon the climatic, historical, social, and political factors which influenced the literary products. Halide Edip also wrote a successful detective story—the *Crime of Vol Palace*—and a number of short stories and essays. Her memoirs reflect the atmosphere of her early childhood in a typical Eastern setting as well as the problems she had to face upon confronting Western civilization. However, her inconsistent ideological tendency, vacillating between pan-Turkism and pro-Americanism or Turkish nationalism and the ideal of Westernization, prevented her from basing her analyses and her proposed solutions on solid ground.

Halide Edip during her 80 years achieved great distinction as a novelist, social philosopher, and academician. She was the first public speaker to mobilize Turkish public opinion. Halide Edip served in the army. She was a rebel against traditions and threw herself into the struggle of her nation for life and liberty, but never ceased to be aware of the moral and cultural conflicts of her time.

Further Reading

A considerable amount of Halide Edip's productions—including novels, plays, essays, and short stories—have been translated into a number of foreign languages, predominantly into English. Among her early novels dealing with pan-Turkism *Das neue Turan* was published in German (Weimar, 1916). Her novel *The Shirt of Flame,* dealing with issues pertaining to nationalist causes and the war of independence, was published in New York in 1924; this book appeared also over the years in German, Arabic, Russian, Swedish, and Urdu. A further volume dealing with nationalistic issues, *The Turkish Ordeal,* was published in English in London in 1928. Among her short stories, a collection entitled *The Wolf on the Mountain* was translated into English, German, and Norwegian. Another novel, *La fille de Smyrne,* appeared in French in Alger in 1948. Among Halide Edip's novels, the most famous one, translated into several languages and filmed twice, was *The Clown and His Daughter,* first written in English and published in London in 1935. The Turkish translation, entitled *Sinekli Bakkal* (*The Grocer of Sinekli*), won the literary prize given by the People's Republican Party in 1942.

Halide Edip wrote also a few theater plays, among them *Masks and Souls* (London, 1953). Most of her essays and some of her lectures were also published abroad, namely "Turkey Faces West" (London, 1930); "Conflict of East and West in Turkey" (Lahore, 1935); and "Inside India" (London, 1937). Her interesting, personal memories of her youth are also available in English under the title *Memoirs of Halide Edip* (London, 1928). For a discussion on Halide Edip's ideas on the status of Turkish women, see Emel Dogramaci, "The Novelist Halide Edip Adivar and Turkish Feminism" in *The World of Islam*, Vol. 14 (Leiden, 1971). For a broader outlook see Füsun (Altiok) Akatli, "The Image of Woman in Turkish Literature" in Nermin Abadan-Unat, editor, *Women in Turkish Society* (Leiden, 1981) and Kathleen Burrill, "Modern Turkish Literature," *Review of National Literatures,* special issue (Spring 1973).

Additional Sources

Advar, Halide Edib, *The Turkish ordeal: being the further memoirs of Halide Edib,* Westport, Conn.: Hyperion Press, 1981.
□

1st Earl of Halifax

The English statesman Edward Frederick Lindley Wood, 1st Earl of Halifax (1881-1959), was viceroy of India from 1926 to 1931. He later served as foreign secretary and as ambassador to the United States during World War II.

Edward Frederick Lindley Wood, the fourth son of the 2d Viscount Halifax, was born on April 16, 1881, in Powderham Castle near Exeter, Devonshire. He enjoyed an aristocratic childhood, although it was punctuated by tragedy. Like his father, who was president of the English Church Union for 51 years, he was a deeply religious person and developed a stoic ability to rise above personal tragedies. He was educated at Eton and Christ Church, Oxford; in 1906 he became a fellow of All Souls College, Oxford.

In 1909 Wood married Lady Dorothy Onslow, and the following year he entered Parliament as a Conservative member for Ripon, Yorkshire. His political advancement was steady but not spectacular. After serving (1915-1917) with the Yorkshire Dragoons in France, he became assistant secretary to the minister of national service and served in that capacity until the end of World War I. He was undersecretary of state for the colonies (1921-1922), president of the board of education (1922—1924), and minister of agriculture (1924-1925). In 1925 he was created Baron Irwin, and the following year he was appointed viceroy of India.

India in 1926 was a country in ferment. As viceroy, Lord Irwin labored to make India's constitutional development a reality and to reconcile British and Indian differences. He gained the respect of the Indians and enjoyed friendly relations with their leaders, including Gandhi. He returned to England in 1931 and again served as president of the board of education (1932-1935). After the death of his father in 1934, he became the 3d Viscount Halifax and left

the House of Commons to sit in the House of Lords. He continued to hold office—secretary for war (1935), lord privy seal (1935-1937), and lord president of the council (1937-1938). He was also leader of the House of Lords (1935-1938).

When Anthony Eden resigned in 1938 as foreign secretary in Neville Chamberlain's government, Halifax succeeded him. He supported the policy of appeasement, but after the signing of the Munich Pact he began to reconsider his views. After the outbreak of World War II he supported the war effort with determination. When Chamberlain resigned as prime minister in May 1940, Halifax was favored by many, including the King, to succeed him. However, as a member of the House of Lords, it was feared that he would be able to provide only token leadership in the Commons. Consequently, Winston Churchill was asked to form the new government. Halifax continued as foreign secretary until later in 1940, when Churchill appointed him ambassador to the United States.

The new ambassador was not well received in the United States. He was popularly denounced as a Tory reactionary and was the target of egg-throwing peace demonstrators. He ignored such remonstrances, however, and traveled widely throughout the United States to gain a firsthand impression of the American people. In time he became a respected and popular figure in the United States. He worked diligently to foster good Anglo-American relations throughout the war years, and in 1945 he attended the San Francisco Conference as a British delegate. When he concluded his ambassadorship in 1946, he stepped out of public life.

Halifax always conducted himself with quiet dignity. A serious and reserved person, he was considered an astute politician as well as an idealistic public servant. In appearance he was tall and angular and conveyed the impression of being an aristocratic country gentleman. He was also a person of high scholarly attainment. In 1909 he wrote a biography of the churchman John Keble, and in 1918 he coauthored *The Great Opportunity,* a volume that dealt with the future of the Conservative party. After his return from India, he published *Indian Problems* (1932). For his efforts in India he was awarded the Order of the Garter; in 1944 he was created an earl. He died on Dec. 23, 1959, after a short illness.

Further Reading

Lord Halifax's own recollections, *Fullness of Days* (1957), should be read in conjunction with his *Speeches on Foreign Policy* (1940) and *The American Speeches of the Earl of Halifax* (1947). The Earl of Birkenhead, *Halifax: The Life of Lord Halifax* (1965), is the best full-length biography. Alan Campbell Johnson, *Viscount Halifax* (1941), gives a satisfactory contemporary account of his life. For a perceptive appraisal of his work in India see Percival Spear, *India: A Modern History* (1961). These works refer to aspects of his later career: Sir Winston Churchill, *The Gathering Storm* (1948); Cordell Hull, *The Memoirs of Cordell Hull* (2 vols., 1948); John W. Wheeler-Bennett, *King George VI* (1958); Martin Gilbert and Richard Gott, *The Appeasers* (1963; 2d ed. 1967); and Sir Anthony Eden, *The Reckoning* (1965).

Additional Sources

Roberts, Andrew, *The Holy Fox: a biography of Lord Halifax,* London: Weidenfeld and Nicolson, 1991. □

Asaph Hall

The American astronomer Asaph Hall (1829-1907) discovered the two satellites of the planet Mars and was an important figure in government scientific circles during the period following the Civil War.

Asaph Hall was born in Goshen, Conn. He attended the district schools until he was 13. At 16 he was apprenticed to a carpenter, and he worked at that trade sporadically. His education in astronomy was spotty at best. He attended the Norfolk Academy to study mathematics one winter, spent a year and a half at Central College at McGrawville, N.Y., and received special instruction in astronomy from F. F. E. Brünnow during 3 months at the University of Michigan.

After a period as a schoolmaster in Ohio and some months working as a carpenter, in 1857 Hall finally secured a position at the Harvard Observatory. This gave him the opportunity to attend lectures and informally complete his education. He immediately proved to be a brilliant ob-

server, and in 1859 he began to send papers, chiefly on the orbits of comets and asteroids, to scientific journals. In 1862 he went to Washington as an aide in the Naval Observatory and the following year was appointed professor of mathematics there. In 1872 Hall was made chief of the Naval Observatory. Five years later Hall, using the observatory's new 26-inch telescope, discovered the satellites of Mars.

Hall achieved a reputation as an extremely careful observer and an accurate mathematician and computer. In his lifetime he was the recipient of numerous scientific awards in the United States and abroad. His nearly 500 published papers include investigations of the orbits of the various satellites, the mass of Mars, the perturbations of the planets, the advance of Mercury's perihelion, the parallax of the sun, stellar parallax, the distances of Alpha Lyrae and 61 Cygni, the mass of Saturn's rings, and the orbits of double stars, along with the solution of many mathematical problems suggested by these investigations. Disdainful of textbooks and popularizations, Hall refused to publish a book.

Following his retirement from the Naval Observatory in 1891, Hall taught at Harvard and continued to work in astronomy. His first wife died in 1892; in 1901 he married again. In 1902 he was elected president of the American Association for the Advancement of Science. He published his final paper in September 1906 and died on Nov. 22, 1907.

Further Reading

There is no book-length study of Hall. One source is David B. Hall's genealogical and biographical study, *The Halls of New England* (1883). □

Donald Hall

New England writer Donald Hall (born 1928) was a major poet in the lineage of Robert Frost. Memoirist, short story writer, essayist, dramatist, critic, and anthologist as well as poet, he was one of the most versatile and respected writers of his generation.

"I n the history of literature," wrote Donald Hall in a prose work, "Poetry Notebook," published in the *Seneca Review* (1982), "most poets have been so saturated in their own literature that they have used it without knowing what they were doing." This he considered "The Tradition," providing "models of greatness that we have the temerity to take as measures for our endeavors." Expressing a very different view, poet Alice Notley claimed that "There's only one poetic tradition," and "the moment I enter this tradition or this history...its entire nature changes."

Notley and Hall were both prominent contemporary poets, but they exemplified radically opposite poetic styles, one innovative and avant-garde, the other conservative and restrained. For Notley, the poetic tradition evolves in the act of writing; from Hall's somewhat more conservative position, it is an established authority against which one's own work is to be judged.

This distinction divided New England poets of Hall's generation into two very different groups. Poets such as Robert Creeley, Ted Berrigan, and Clark Coolidge accepted Ralph Waldo Emerson's vision of the universe in perpetual flux and evolution and consequently developed a poetry of process—a poetry that is realized in the act of composition. On the other hand, poets such as Hall, Richard Wilbur, and Robert Lowell followed the example of Robert Frost in shaping poems according to traditional forms and meters and in celebrating essentially fixed values and standards.

Early Years

Born in 1928, the son of a businessman, Hall spent his boyhood in Connecticut and New Hampshire. He attended local schools, graduated from Harvard in 1951, and received a B. Litt. from Oxford in 1953. After a year studying at Stanford University, he taught at Harvard until 1957 and then at the University of Michigan until 1975. A first marriage ended in divorce. In 1972 he married the poet Jane Kenyon. They lived and worked together until 1995 when Kenyon died of leukemia at the age of 47.

Conventional Poetry

Hall's conservative posture informed the influential anthology he edited with Robert Pack and Louis Simpson, *New Poets of England and America* (1957). This book, with an introduction by Robert Frost, exhibited the academic taste then in vogue and stood in rigid opposition to contemporary innovative work such as that gathered three years later in Donald Allen's anthology *The New American Poetry*. These two books were widely seen as defining an unbridgeable chasm in American poetry: in fact, no poet appeared in both.

Hall eventually modified his view, and his later anthology, *Contemporary American Poetry* (1962; revised 1972), included a number of poets, such as John Ashbery, who would have been uncomfortable in the earlier volume. Nonetheless, Hall continued to be seen as a spokesman for the more conventional side of American poetry.

New England Writer

Hall's admiration for tradition and custom underlies his highly regarded memoir, *String Too Short To Be Saved* (1961), in which he nostalgically recounts his boyhood summers on his family's New Hampshire farm. At the time the book was published he felt that the world he described had vanished forever, but in 1975 he left his job at the University of Michigan, moved back to the farm, and, as he wrote in an epilogue for the book's reissue in 1979, soon discovered that the essential character of rural New England life was unchanged: "The dead are dead enough, and their descendants occupy new bodies, but *everything is the same.*"

New England provided material for some of Hall's most admired prose works, including *Seasons at Eagle Pond* (1987), *Here at Eagle Pond* (1990), and *Life Work* (1993), a reflection on his life and heritage written when he was being treated for cancer. The book is by no means the bleak or self-indulgent meditation one might expect but finds strength rather in traditional New England values and "a community radiating the willingness or even the desire to be careful and loving."

Publications

Although written when he was still in his twenties, many of Hall's poems collected in *To the Loud Wind and Other Poems* (1955), *Exiles and Marriages* (1955), and *The Dark Houses* (1958) are marked by an elegiac, meditative sensibility as well as by an exceptional command of traditional poetics. An enthusiasm for Whitman led to experiments with free verse and the somewhat less formal poems in such books as *The Alligator Bride* (1969) and *The Yellow Room* (1971).

Most of Hall's major poetry was written after his return to New Hampshire. Many of these poems evoke the durable, seemingly immutable character of his region as seen through a deeply meditative or reflective sensibility. The books of this period include *Kicking the Leaves* (1978), *The Happy Man* (1986), *The Museum of Clear Ideas* (1993), *The Old Life* (1996), and *The One Day* (1988), a series of linked poems in blank verse that won the National Book Critics Circle Award. A selection from his poetry, *Old and New Poems,* was published in 1990.

Although primarily a poet and memoirist, Hall wrote books on baseball—*Dock Ellis in the Country of Baseball* (1976) and *Fathers Playing Catch with Sons: Essays on Sport (Mostly Baseball)* (1984)—and children's books, including *Ox-Cart Man* (1979), winner of the Caldecott Medal. More recent children's books include *When Willard Met Babe Ruth* (1996), *Old Home Day* (1996), and *I Am the Dog. I Am the Cat.* (1994). His short stories were collected in *The Ideal Bakery* (1987). Hall edited textbooks and anthologies such as *The Oxford Book of American Literary Anecdotes* (1981) and *The Oxford Book of Children's Verse in America* (1990). His plays include "An Evening's Frost," produced off-Broadway in 1965. He wrote about the sculptor Henry Moore in *Henry Moore: The Life and Work of a Great Sculptor* (1966) and in *As the Eye Moves* (1973). *Marianne Moore: The Cage and the Animal,* his study of that poet, appeared in 1970.

Remembering Poets, a series of sketches of modernist predecessors, including Ezra Pound and Robert Frost, was first published in 1978 and reissued in 1992 in a revised and considerably expanded version under the title *Their Ancient Glittering Eyes: Remembering Poets and More Poets.* His essays, reviews, and other short prose works have been collected in *Goatfoot Milktongue Twinbird* (1978), *To Keep Moving* (1980), *The Weather for Poetry* (1982), *Poetry and Ambition* (1988), and *Death to the Death of Poetry* (1994).

Further Reading

No major critical or biographical study of Hall has yet been published. The best sources for biographical information are his autobiographical works, particularly *String Too Short To Be Saved* (1961); and *Life Work* (1993); For information on his poetics, see the collected essays listed in the text: *Goatfoot Milktongue Twinbird, To Keep Moving, The Weather for Poetry,* and *Poetry and Ambition.*

Additional Sources

"Friends Pay Tribute to Late Poet, Janet Kenyon," *All Things Considered* (National Public Radio), 3 May 1996.

Hall, Donald, *Death to the Death of Poetry: Essays, Reviews, Notes, Interviews* Ann Arbor: University of Michigan Press, 1994.

McNair, Wesley, "Taking the World for Granite: Four Poets in New Hampshire," *The Sewanee Review* 104 (Winter 1996): 70-81.

"Noah Adams Talks with Poet Donald Hall" *All Things Considered* (National Public Radio), 26 November 1993. □

Granville Stanley Hall

The American psychologist and educator Granville Stanley Hall (1844-1924) pioneered in developing psychology in the United States. His wide-ranging and prolific writings reveal a central theme best characterized as genetic psychology or evolutionism.

On Feb. 1, 1844, G. Stanley Hall was born on his grandfather's farm in Ashfield, Mass. He graduated from Williams College in 1867 and then, apparently to please his mother, studied for a year at the Union Theological Seminary in New York. His lack of deep conviction must have been heard between the lines of his trial sermon, for at its close the members of the faculty knelt in prayer for the salvation of the young man's soul. With borrowed funds the heretic field to Germany, where for 2 years he wandered in poverty from one university to another in a constant state of intellectual ferment and euphoria.

On his return to America, Hall taught various subjects for 4 years at Antioch College, where, as he once said, he occupied not a chair but a whole bench. In 1878, under the guidance of his friend William James, he received from Harvard the first doctorate in psychology ever given in the United States. Hall then went back to Germany for 2 years, chiefly because he wanted to find out about the new psychology that was attracting so many scholars to Leipzig, and became Wilhelm Wundt's first American student.

In 1881 Hall was invited to lecture at Johns Hopkins University. As soon as he knew that his position there was reasonably secure, he set about building up the first American laboratory for psychology. In 1887 he founded and edited the *American Journal of Psychology,* the first journal of its kind in the United States.

When Jonas G. Clark, a wealthy merchant of Worcester, Mass., decided to found an institution of higher learning in his native city, he invited Hall to become its first president. Hall persuaded Clark that the institution should be exclusively for graduate students, and it opened in 1889. In a few years the distinguished faculty in mathematics, physics, chemistry, biology, and psychology made Clark University a unique and famous institution. In 1892 about 15 psychologists drew up plans for the American Psychological Association. Hall was its first president.

The twentieth anniversary of the founding of Clark had as one part of the celebration a conference attended by leading American and European psychologists, including Sigmund Freud. At that time Freud was almost unknown in academic circles.

Hall wrote scores of articles and dozens of books. Among his important works are *Adolescence* (1904), *Founders of Modern Psychology* (1912), and *Senescence* (1922). The theme of developmental psychology runs through almost everything Hall wrote in his application and extension of the doctrine of evolution to the growth of the individual, a view which Hall frequently referred to as recapitulation.

Further Reading

Hall's autobiography is *Life and Confessions of a Psychologist* (1923). A good biography is Dorothy Ross, *G. Stanley Hall: Psychologist as Prophet* (1972). The standard work for the lives and writings of psychologists is E. G. Boring, *A History of Experimental Psychology* (1929; 2d ed. 1950).

Additional Sources

Hall, Granville Stanley, *Life and confessions of a psychologist,* New York: Arno Press, 1977. □

Al-Husayn ibn Mansur al-Hallaj

Al-Husayn ibn Mansur al-Hallaj (857-922) was a Persian Moslem mystic and martyr. He reinforced ecstatic and pantheistic tendencies already present in the Islamic third century, and they became a continuing part of Islamic life after al-Hallaj's teaching and martyrdom.

Al-Hallaj was born in what is now southern Iran but was educated in Arabic-speaking Iraq, studying with one of the eminent Sufis, or mystics, of the time, Sahl al-Tustari. After his marriage in 877, al-Hallaj settled in the capital of the Abbasid Empire, Baghdad, and continued to study and experience mysticism. He made three pilgrimages to Mecca, each of which was a deep emotional experience for him, and he is also alleged to have traveled in India and central Asia.

A Teaching Sufi

Al-Hallaj early began to preach to crowds of listeners about his ecstatic mystical experiences. This brought him to the notice of the orthodox theologians. A political reform movement led by religious persons, in which al-Hallaj does not seem to have been personally involved, led to a reaction against the reformers. He was arrested and imprisoned in 911 with many others, but after being pilloried as a politicoreligious extremist (he seems to have been wholly inactive politically), he was kept under lenient arrest in the caliph's palace. There he influenced powerful personages such as the queen mother and the vizier Ibn Isa.

Financial corruption among candidates for the vizier's office led to the public trial in 921-922 of al-Hallaj, whose execution for heterodoxy was desired by one of the contenders to prove his own support of the orthodox position. The condemnation was pushed through, despite much popular sentiment in favor of al-Hallaj, on the grounds that he had said, "I am the Truth," that is, "I am God." He was tortured and executed in 922.

After al-Hallaj

The sordid political intrigues to which al-Hallaj fell victim are less important in historical perspective than the spiritual issues which he aroused during his lifetime and after. Orthodox Islam is a religion which stresses the remote transcendent quality of God, and the absolute monotheism which it preaches scarcely admits of even metaphorical and ecstatic expressions such as mystics in every religion are prone to utter. Later Sufis regarded al-Hallaj as a martyr and viewed his faults as primarily lack of discretion about the mystic experience; his example led to persecution for the Sufis for a time and to a certain care on their part that their sayings and poetry not be taken too literally.

Further Reading

There is no work on al-Hallaj in English. Useful introductions to the subject of Islamic mysticism, with references to al-Hallaj, are A. J. Arberry, *Sufism: An Account of the Mystics of Islam* (1950); R. C. Zaehner, *Hindu and Muslim Mysticism* (1960); and Majid Fakhry, *A History of Islamic Philosophy* (1970).

Additional Sources

Brewster, David Pearson, *Al Hallaj: Muslim mystic and martyr: translated extracts with a short biography and bibliography,* Christchurch: University of Canterbury, Dept. of Philosophy and Religious Studies, 1976.
Massignon, Louis, *The passion of Al-Hallaj: mystic and martyr of Islam,* Princeton, N.J.: Princeton University Press, 1994. □

Lewis Hallam Sr. and Jr.

Lewis Hallam, Sr. (ca. 1705-1755), and Lewis Hallam, Jr. (1740-1808), actors and theatrical managers, were members of America's first important theatrical family.

The elder Lewis Hallam was a moderately successful London actor when he decided to lead an acting company to the New World. Their production of *The Merchant of Venice* in Williamsburg, Va., in 1752 marks the beginning of truly professional theater in America. But strong opposition to stage plays existed, especially among the Puritans and Quakers, who considered drama irreligious. Hallam had difficulty getting licenses in New York and Philadelphia; he did not even try in Boston. He argued that his company could provide the drama of "the greatest geniuses of England" and could support "its dignity with proper decorum and regularity."

During 1753-1754 Hallam justified his assertion, for his actors were well trained, and he paid all his debts. In addition, his talented company provided a repertoire of almost all the important plays offered in London, including tragedies of Shakespeare and Joseph Addison and comedies of William Congreve and Richard Steele. Because of the elder Hallam's ability and integrity, Americans gained a trust in theater they had never known before. However, after the 1754 season the elder Hallam died and the group disbanded.

Though Lewis Hallam, Jr., was not so talented a manager as his father, he was a better actor. During his 50 years on the stage he was successful in most of the important roles of his time. He helped to reorganize the American Company in 1758, when at 18 he became its leading man. Up to the time of the American Revolution he was sovereign of the American stage as star and manager. When the theater was "outlawed" shortly before the Revolution, Hallam moved

to the West Indies. In 1784 he revived the old American Company. He sought, unsuccessfully, to prosper as a manager. Finally, in 1796, he resigned managership, though he continued as an actor until shortly before his death. In his time he had acted in the first American play (Thomas Godfrey's *The Prince of Parthia,* 1767) and the first successful American comedy (Royall Tyler's *The Contrast,* 1787), and his company had fostered a drama of high quality.

Further Reading

No book deals exclusively with the Hallams. However, every history of the American stage discusses their contribution. William Dunlap's *History of the American Theater* (1832) and his *Diary* (3 vols., 1930) detail the author's personal relationship with the younger Hallam. Arthur Hornblow, *A History of the Theater in America,* vol. 1 (1919), sufficiently details the Hallams' contributions. Among recent works see Glenn Hughes, *A History of the American Theater, 1700-1950* (1951); Barnard Hewitt, *Theater U.S.A., 1668 to 1957* (1959); Hugh F. Rankin, *The Theater in Colonial America* (1960); and Howard Taubman, *Making of the American Theater* (1965; rev. ed. 1967). □

Albrecht Von Haller

The Swiss physician Albrecht von Haller (1708-1777) conducted experiments in organic sensibility and irritability that are landmarks in the development of physiology.

Albrecht von Haller was born in Bern on Oct. 16, 1708. He lacked the strength to participate in the more ordinary pursuits of childhood and, under the guidance of a tutor, turned to scholarly activities. Among other things, he studied languages and wrote poetry. At 15 he entered the University of Tübingen to study medicine; he moved to the University of Leiden in 1725 and received a doctorate there in 1727.

For the next 2 years Haller studied in London and Paris and at the University of Basel. At Basel he became interested in botany, and studies started there culminated in the publication of a flora of Switzerland in 1742, *Enumeratio methodica stirpium Helveticarum.* More immediately, his botanical field studies in the Alps inspired him to write *Die Alpen,* his best-known poem, which was published in his *Versuch Schweizerischer Gedichte* in 1732. This poem introduced the concept of mountain beauty to the literary world. In 1729 he began medical practice in his native Bern. In 1736 he was appointed professor of anatomy, surgery, and botany at the newly founded University of Göttingen, where he stayed until 1753.

At Göttingen, Haller's interest turned to physiology, and in 1747 he authored the first textbook of physiology, *Primae lineae physiologiae.* His most important work was on the irritability and sensibility of organs. Although both concepts predated Haller, he was the first to demonstrate experimentally that sensibility (the ability to produce sensa-

tion) existed only in organs supplied with nerves, while irritability (a reaction to stimuli) was a property of the organ or tissue. His concept of irritability was particularly important in efforts to understand muscle physiology. His ideas were published in 1753 in *De partibus corporis humani sensibilibus et irritabilibus.*

In 1753 Haller returned to Bern. He took a position with the Swiss state service and then, from 1758 until 1764, was resident manager of the Bernese saltworks. His detailed, eight-volume compendium of information on physiology, *Elementa physiologiae corporis humani,* appeared between 1759 and 1766.

On Dec. 12, 1777, Haller died. His influence as a teacher and his publications, numbering in the thousands, guided development in physiology for a century. His research method laid the lasting foundations of experimental physiology.

Further Reading

There are several biographical sketches of Haller. These vary in their usefulness, but a good introduction is the chapter on Haller in Henry Sigerist, *The Great Doctors* (trans. 1933). Arturo Castiglioni, *A History of Medicine* (trans. 1941; rev. ed. 1947), and Ralph Hermon Major, *A History of Medicine* (vol. 2, 1954), discuss Haller and his work and are recommended for historical background.

Additional Sources

Haller, Albrecht von, *The natural philosophy of Albrecht von Haller,* New York: Arno Press, 1981. □

Edmund Halley

The English astronomer Edmund Halley (1656-1742) studied the orbital movements of the moon and of comets and discovered the proper motion of the fixed stars.

The son of a prosperous London soap-boiler, Edmund Halley was born on Nov. 8, 1656, in Haggerston near London. He attended St. Paul's School, where he excelled in classics and mathematics and early developed an interest in astronomy. At the age of 16, when he entered Queen's College, Oxford, he was already an accomplished astronomical observer. He continued his observations at Oxford and, before he was 20, had sent to the Royal Society an explanation of an improved means of calculating planetary orbits.

Recognizing the need for more accurate star charts, Halley, while still an undergraduate, proposed a plan for surveying the stars of the southern hemisphere as a supplement to the surveys then being made of the northern hemisphere by John Flamsteed and Johannes Hevelius. He left Oxford without a degree and in 1676 journeyed to the island of St. Helena in the South Atlantic. St. Helena's frequent cloud cover made it poorly suited for astronomical observations, although in 18 months on the island Halley managed to determine the position of approximately 350 stars. In addition, he made one of the first complete observations of a transit of Mercury; it occurred to him that similar transits might be used to accurately calculate the sun's distance from the earth. He returned to England in 1678, published his results, and was dubbed by Flamsteed "the Southern Tycho," a reference to the famous Danish astronomer Tycho Brahe.

Publication of Newton's "Principia"

Upon his return Halley received, by royal mandate, his Oxford degree and, at the age of 22, was elected a fellow of the Royal Society. After 2 years of traveling on the Continent, he returned to London, where he married and, in 1682, began a lengthy series of lunar observations. Designed to last for 18 years, these observations were to correct tables of the moon's position in an effort to solve the problem of accurately determining longitude. Such a lengthy project was not, however, well suited to Halley's temperament, and he was soon diverted to other concerns.

Intensely interested in the problem of gravitation, Halley had obtained by 1684 an inverse-square relationship, but since he was unable to deduce from it the planetary motions, in August that year he traveled to Cambridge to seek the assistance of Newton. What would be the orbit of a planetary body subjected to such a force? An ellipse, Newton replied. He had earlier proved that this was so and shortly thereafter sent Halley a copy of his demonstration. Realizing the significance of what Newton had done, Halley, utilizing great skill and tact, persuaded the reluctant Newton to develop and publish his ideas on celestial mechanics. Newton's *Principia* was published in 1687. Halley

1758 and suggested that other comets might also have elliptical orbits. Halley's comet, as it is known today, returned on schedule in 1835, 1910, and 1986.

Before Halley's discovery of the "proper motion" of fixed stars, it was believed that they (unlike the planets) never moved in relation to each other. In 1718, however, Halley pointed out that three of the brightest stars (Sirius, Procyon, and Arcturus) had apparently changed their relative positions markedly since having been observed by the Greeks. In fact, Sirius appeared to have moved perceptibly since observed by Tycho Brahe only a century and a half earlier. After carefully comparing the positions of other stars and establishing that this apparent movement could not be accounted for by any motion of the earth, Halley concluded that the three had actually shifted their relative positions and suggested that, if observed over sufficiently long periods, this proper motion might also be detected in other stars as well.

Halley's knowledge and interests were extensive. He pursued such varied topics as the magnetic origin of the aurora borealis, the design and construction of diving bells, and the establishment of quantitatively accurate mortality tables. He continued his astronomical observations until a few months before his death on Jan. 14, 1742.

Further Reading

Selections from Halley's correspondence and unpublished papers, together with two 18th-century biographical memoirs, are in Eugene Fairfield MacPike, ed., *Correspondence and Papers of Edmund Halley* (1932). The best biography of Halley is Angus Armitage, *Edmund Halley* (1966). Also useful is Colin A. Ronan, *Edmund Halley: Genius in Eclipse* (1969). For Halley's relations with contemporary astronomers see Eugene Fairfield MacPike, *Hevelius, Flamsteed and Halley* (1937).

Additional Sources

Standing on the shoulders of giants: a longer view of Newton and Halley, Berkeley: University of California Press, 1990. □

read the manuscript, corrected the proofs, and paid the publication costs out of his own pocket. A lasting friendship ensued, and in 1696, through Newton's influence, Halley was appointed deputy comptroller of the Mint at Chester.

Astronomical and Physical Observations

Halley maintained a lifelong interest in the declination of the magnetic compass, and he published two significant papers (1683 and 1692) discussing the causes of this variation and its change with time. Between 1698 and 1702 he undertook a series of government-sponsored expeditions to make extensive measurements of terrestrial magnetism in the South Atlantic and to study in detail the tides and coast of the English Channel. He correlated the data from his South Atlantic voyages with other measurements he had been collecting and in 1702 published for the first time a map showing lines of equal declination. Of great navigational value, these lines (known today as isogonics) were for years called "Halleyan lines."

Halley's calculation of the periodic nature of comets was perhaps his most significant contribution to astronomy. In his *Synopsis of the Astronomy of Comets* (1705) he collected and analyzed all known observations of comets and computed the parabolic orbits of 24 comets dating from 1337 to 1698. The orbital elements of three (1531, 1607, and 1682) were so similar as to suggest that they were in fact the successive returns of a single body whose orbit was an enormous elongated ellipse, rather than a parabola, and whose period of revolution was approximately 76 years. Halley successfully predicted the return of this comet in

Frans Hals

Frans Hals (c. 1581-1666) is one of the most admired masters of the great age of Dutch painting because of the spontaneity of his style and the vitality of his portrayals.

Frans Hals was probably born in Antwerp. It is likely that his parents were among the Protestants who fled from Catholic Flanders to the northern Netherlands after the Spanish took Antwerp in 1585. The earliest evidence of the presence of the Hals family in Haarlem is the record of the baptism in 1591 of Frans's brother, Dirck Hals, who also became a painter.

Between 1600 and 1603 Hals was a pupil of the Haarlem mannerist painter Karel van Mander. In 1610 Hals became a member of the Haarlem painters' guild. His earliest surviving dated portrait, of Jacobus Zaffius, is dated 1611. There must have been earlier works that either have not come down to us or have not yet been identified. Some scholars now accept the *Banquet in a Park,* destroyed in World War II, as a work by Hals painted about 1610, on the basis of the free brushstroke that characterizes his work.

Some 250 paintings by Hals still exist, of which almost 200 are portraits. Except for two pictures representing the Evangelists St. Luke and St. Matthew, the rest are genre subjects, mostly portraitlike single figures, almost all in half or three-quarter length.

Early Works

The *Merry Company* (ca. 1616) shows Hals's early genre style: hot colors, an overcrowded composition, the exuberance of holiday revelers. In 1616 he signed the first of his great group portraits; altogether he painted six civic guard groups and three groups of regents. From the first, he revolutionized the long Dutch tradition of portraying social groups. He devised a series of brilliant solutions to the problem of giving equal emphasis to each figure while relating them in an arrangement that is both natural and compositionally integrated. These works are masterpieces of the baroque style.

Hals was most productive in the 1630s, when he began to simplify and unify his pictures. They now tended toward the monochromatic, a trend that also prevailed in Dutch landscape and still-life painting at the time. The small por-

trait of Hendrick Swalmius, a Haarlem preacher (monogrammed and dated 1639), shows a striking variety of brushstrokes and a new richness of contrasts between warm and cool tones that Hals began to introduce about this time. He executed commissioned portraits with the same boldness that characterized his genre figures, of which he painted no more after 1640. He built the flesh tones and the blacks and whites of the sober costumes with an inimitable range of nuance.

While only two double portraits by Hals are known today, there are many pairs of portraits. Among the finest of his mature works of this kind are the portraits of De heer Bodolphe and Mevrouw Bodolphe (both monogrammed and dated 1643), which are notable for the liveliness of the characterizations and the related poses of the two sitters.

Late Works

After 1650 Hals's paintings became increasingly austere in color. The silvery grays and golden ochers that frequently dominated his early palette were replaced by darker tones. The alertness, vivacity, and elegance of the young couple known as the *Seated Man Holding a Hat* and *Seated Woman Holding a Fan* (ca. 1648-1650) were by the late 1650s replaced in most of his portraits by more serious expressions and somber colors.

Hals maintained his incisive observation and sure touch to the end. Over 80 years old when he painted the famous group portrait, *Lady Regents of the Old Men's Alms House* (traditionally dated 1664), he endowed it with a psychological intensity and technical brilliance that have made it one of the most admired works of Western art. His dynamic brushstroke was more fluid and free than ever before.

Though he received important commissions throughout his career, Hals was in financial difficulties most of his life. From 1662 until his death in 1666 he lived on a small subsidy granted him by the burgomasters of Haarlem. But the legend that he led a rowdy life is not well founded. He was a member of a respectable society of rhetoricians and of a militia company, as well as an officer of the painters' guild. His pupils, besides his sons Frans II, Reynier, and Claes, included his brother Dirck, Judith Leyster and her husband, Jan Meinse Molenaar, Adriaen van Ostade, Philips Wouwerman, and Adriaen Brouwer.

His Style

None of Hals's followers was able to reproduce the essence of his style. His apparently unrestrained brushstroke always succeeded in defining form. This was not a mere trick or a stylish device that could be imitated. It responded to a basic mode of observation. His fascinating variety of angular strokes and hatching, which give liveliness to the picture surface while they differentiate between the optical effects of different textures, foreshadowed the impressionist way of representing light falling on an object. His ability to communicate a moment of intense living has seldom been equaled.

Strangely, no drawing or print by Hals is known. There is reason to believe that some of his small-scale portraits were intended as models for engravers. There are only two self-portraits of Hals, the first as a member of the St. George militia company, in the group portrait *Officers of the Guild of Archers of St. George* (probably 1639), the second a small bust-length portrait (ca. 1650), of which a number of copies exist.

Further Reading

The best book on Hals in English is Seymour Slive, *Frans Hals* (2 vols., 1970). Biographical material is in Michael Kitson, *Frans Hals* (1965). See also Jakob Rosenberg, Seymour Slive, and E. H. ter Kuile, *Dutch Art and Architecture, 1600-1800* (1966).

☐

William Frederick Halsey

The popular and aggressive American naval officer Fleet Admiral William Frederick Halsey (1882-1959) commanded major Pacific Fleet units during World War II.

William F. Halsey was born in Elizabeth, N.J., on Oct. 30, 1882. The son of a Navy captain, he entered the Naval Academy in 1900. Most of Halsey's early sea duty was with destroyers. At the age of 51 he began flight training and after graduation took command of the aircraft carrier *Saratoga*. In 1938 he was given command of Carrier Division 2 and was promoted the following year to vice admiral and appointed commander of the Aircraft Battle Force.

Because the U.S. Navy's battleships had been crippled in the Japanese attack on the naval base at Pearl Harbor, Hawaii, on Dec. 7, 1941, Halsey's carrier force became the heart of the American fleet in World War II. Early in 1942 he led it on daring strikes against Japanese bases that culminated in a raid on Tokyo. While the damage inflicted by these raids was minor, they did much to bolster American morale and to make Halsey a popular hero.

On Oct. 18, 1942, Halsey was appointed commander of the South Pacific Area. He thus commanded America's initial Pacific offensive, the battle for Guadalcanal in the Solomon Islands. Operations there had reached a critical stage, and the appointment of Halsey, with his reputation for audacity and aggressiveness, was welcomed by the beleaguered Marine and Navy units. He lived up to his reputation, summarizing his strategy in a simple order to his carriers on October 26: "Attack—Repeat—Attack." In a series of fierce engagements Japanese naval forces in the area were defeated and American victory on Guadalcanal assured. President Franklin D. Roosevelt promptly promoted Halsey to admiral.

Throughout 1943 and early 1944 Halsey commanded naval operations around the Solomons, overrunning or isolating Japanese garrisons. On June 15, 1944, he was relieved as commander of the South Pacific Area and made

commander of the 3d Fleet. This force was the most powerful aggregation of naval striking power in American history.

Halsey and his staff began planning for reoccupation of the Philippines. Unfortunately, Halsey's operational performance failed to match his good planning. During the crucial battle for Leyte Gulf, he sent his main force after a Japanese decoy fleet; this allowed powerful enemy surface units to penetrate the Philippine Sea. Only frantic resistance by a small escort carrier group and a sudden Japanese retreat saved the American landing forces from major damage.

Two months later the admiral's reputation suffered another blow when he maneuvered directly into the path of a typhoon, losing three destroyers. In early summer 1945 Halsey again maneuvered the fleet into the path of a typhoon. Despite this error he retained command until the end of the war, directing the final, successful air and sea attacks upon the Japanese home islands.

Following Japan's surrender in 1945 Halsey was promoted to fleet admiral and assigned what were essentially public relations duties until his retirement in April 1947. In subsequent years he held several business positions and led an unsuccessful drive to raise funds for the preservation of the carrier *Enterprise*. He died on Aug. 16, 1959.

Further Reading

William F. Halsey and J. Bryan III, *Admiral Halsey's Story* (1947), contains material on the admiral's early career but is of limited value for the World War II period. Hans Christian

Adamson and George F. Kosco, *Halsey's Typhoons* (1967), summarizes the problems he encountered in the latter stages of the war. Perhaps the best concise history of naval operations in World War II is Samuel Eliot Morison, *The Two Ocean War* (1963). The role of American aircraft carriers in that conflict is admirably analyzed in Clark G. Reynolds, *The Fast Carriers: The Forging of an Air Navy* (1968).

Additional Sources

Halsey, William Frederick, *Admiral Halsey's story,* New York: Da Capo Press, 1976.

Merrill, James M., *A Sailor's admiral: a biography of William F. Halsey,* New York: Crowell, 1976.

Potter, E. B. (Elmer Belmont), *Bull Halsey,* Annapolis, Md.: Naval Institute Press, 1985. □

Johann Georg Hamann

The German philosopher Johann Georg Hamann (1730-1788) was known as the "Magus of the North." He held that truth is a matter of subjective belief, and he sought to reveal the divine in things and people.

Born on Aug. 27, 1730, in Königsberg, East Prussia, Johann Georg Hamann was the son of the local surgeon-barber and heir of generations of Protestant pastors, and this background helps explain his interests in science, medicine, and especially religion. The young Hamann was tutored at home, and the remarkable range of his intellectual pursuits was largely a product of self-education. He displayed an aptitude for languages and mastered Greek, Latin, French, Italian, English, and Hebrew in addition to his native German.

In 1746 Hamann enrolled at the University of Königsberg as a student of theology and later of law. There he was influenced by Martin Knutzen, the philosophy teacher of his fellow townsman Immanuel Kant. He withdrew in 1752 and spent the next 7 years working as a tutor and then for a business concern, the House of Barens. In the latter capacity he traveled as far as London, where he underwent a spiritual crisis. Returning to Königsberg, he spent the next few years in study, writing, and translating. Kant introduced Hamann to Johann Gottfried von Herder and also secured him a position with the local government, which he held for the next 24 years. About the same time, 1763, he entered into a lifelong domestic arrangement and fathered four children. Hamann died on June 21, 1788, while visiting a group of his admirers in Münster.

The main intention of Hamann's writings was to state the relationship between faith and philosophy. His early unpublished works—*Biblical Meditations* (1758) and *Thoughts on the Course of My Life* (1759)—culminated in his first major work, *Socratic Memorabilia* (1759). His reputation was increased by the publication of a collection of essays, *Crusades of the Philologian* (1762), which included "Aesthetics in a Nutshell;" political satires such as *Lost*

Letter of a Savage of the North to a Financier at Peking (1773) and *The Worm of the North* (1774); and his thoughts on sexuality, *Essay of a Sibyl on Marriage* (1775). *Konxompax* (1779), *Metacritique of the Purism of the Reason* (1784), and *Golgatha und Scheblimini* (1784) are various critiques of works by Gotthold Ephraim Lessing, Kant, and Moses Mendelssohn. He managed, however, to cultivate and maintain the friendship of the major figures of the German Enlightenment while criticizing their philosophies.

Hamann's writings focused on the study of the whole man of reason, emotion, language, and history. He believed that the rationalist gospel of the Enlightenment was inferior to facts and to true philosophy, which is "Socratic" or critical in the awareness of its own ignorance. Hamann's aim was to understand divine revelation and its workings in nature and history.

Further Reading

There are only two complete works of Hamann translated and one major study of him available in English. Ronald G. Smith, *J. G. Hamann, 1730-1788: A Study in Christian Existence—With Selections from His Writings* (1960), includes the *Metacritique,* and James C. O'Flaherty's edition of Hamann's *Socratic Memorabilia* (1967) is an excellent translation with commentary and biographical introduction. W. M. Alexander, *Johann Georg Hamann: Philosophy and Faith* (1966), is a thorough and full study. □

Fannie Lou Hamer

Fannie Lou Hamer (1917-1977), field secretary of the Student Nonviolent Coordinating Committee, was an outspoken advocate for civil rights for African Americans.

For more than half of Fannie Lou Hamer's life, she was a rural agricultural worker who saw no end to the cycle of poverty and humiliation that was the plight of most southern African Americans. Fannie Lou, born October 6, 1917, in Montgomery County, Mississippi, was the last of twenty children born to Jim and Ella Townsend. When she was two years old the family moved to Sunflower County, Mississippi, where Fannie resided for the rest of her life. At age six she joined the other family members working as a sharecropper picking cotton. By the time she was 13 she could pick between two and three hundred pounds of cotton a day.

In spite of intensive labor the Townsends were always in need because sharecroppers had to give a portion of their crop, as well as repayment for seeds and supplies they had purchased on credit, to the owner of the land on which they toiled. One year, when their crop was especially bountiful, Jim Townsend, hoping that his family's economic status would permanently improve, rented a parcel of land with a house and purchased some animals and farm implements to boost the farm's productivity. The family's hopes for prosperity were dashed, however, when a jealous white neighbor poisoned the Townsend's animals.

The condition of African Americans in the South caused young Fannie to wonder why they had to suffer such hardship while working so hard. In spite of her circumstances Fannie was able to attend school for a few months each year until she reached the sixth grade. After her formal schooling ended, she continued to study and read the Bible under the direction of teachers at the Stranger's Home Baptist Church. Fannie's religious beliefs and training were dominant influences during her entire life. She regularly prayed that someday she would have the opportunity to do something to improve the condition of African Americans in Mississippi.

During the 1940s Fannie Lou married Perry "Pap" Hamer, who worked on the W.D. Marlow plantation near Ruleville, Mississippi. Fannie also worked for the Marlows, first as a sharecropper and then—after the owner learned that she was literate—as the timekeeper. In the evenings she cleaned the Marlow's home. The Hamers supplemented their income by making liquor and operating a small saloon. Unable to have children of their own, the Hamers adopted two girls, Dorothy Jean and Vergie Ree.

In 1962, when she was in her mid-forties, Hamer's life changed drastically. She was invited to attend a Student Nonviolent Coordinating Committee (SNCC, pronounced "Snick") meeting at a church near her home. SNCC, an organization founded in 1960 by a group of young African Americans who used direct action such as sit-ins and other forms of civil disobedience as a means of ending segregation in the South, encouraged its workers to travel throughout the South to win grassroots support from African Americans. When Hamer heard the SNCC presentation she was convinced that the powerlessness of African Americans was based to a degree on their complacency and fear of white reprisals. She decided that no matter what the cost, she should try to register to vote. Though her first attempts to pass the voter registration test were unsuccessful they nevertheless resulted in the loss of her job and threats of violence against her and those who attempted to register with her for trying to alter the status quo.

In 1963 Hamer became a registered voter and a SNCC field secretary. She worked with voter registration drives in various locales and helped develop programs to assist economically deprived African American families. She was regularly threatened and faced beatings, a bombing, and ridicule. Nevertheless, she was a founding member of the Mississippi Freedom Democratic Party (MFDP), formed in April 1964 to challenge the all-white Mississippi delegation to the Democratic National Convention. The MFDP sent 68 representatives in August 1964 to the Democratic National Committee meeting in Atlantic City, New Jersey. Hamer was one of the representatives who testified before the party's Credentials Committee. In a televised presentation, Hamer talked about the formidable barriers that southern African Americans faced in their struggle for civil rights. She talked about the murders of civil rights activists such as Medgar Evers, James Chaney, Andrew Goodman, and Michael Schwerner.

"If the Freedom Democratic Party is not seated now, I question America," she said. "Is this America? The land of the free and the home of the brave? Where we have to sleep with our telephones off the hook, because our lives be threatened daily." Hamer discussed the abuse she had suffered in retaliation for attending a civil rights meeting. "They beat me and they beat me with the long, flat blackjack. I screamed to God in pain. . . ." As a compromise measure the Democratic Party leadership offered the MFDP delegation two seats, which they refused. Hamer said, "We didn't come for no two seats when all of us is tired." And no MFDP member was seated.

In 1965 Hamer, Victoria Gray, and Annie Devine ran for Congress and challenged the seating of the regular Mississippi representatives before the U.S. House of Representatives. Though they were unsuccessful in their challenge, the 1965 elections were later overturned. Hamer continued to be politically active and from 1968 to 1971 was a member of the Democratic National Committee from Mississippi.

Hamer was also a catalyst in the development of various programs to aid the poor in her community, including the Delta Ministry, an extensive community development program, and the Freedom Farms Corporation in 1969, a non-profit operation designed to help needy families raise food and livestock, provide social services, encourage minority business opportunities, and offer educational assistance. In 1970 Hamer became chair of the board of Fannie Lou Hamer Day Care Center, an organization established by the National Council of Negro Women. She also served as a member of the boards of the Sunflower County Day Care and Family Services Center and Garment Manufacturing Plant. She became a member of the policy council of the National Women's Political Caucus in 1971, and from 1974 to 1977 was a member of the board of trustees of the Martin Luther King Center for Nonviolent Social Change.

Hamer underwent a radical mastectomy in 1976 and died of cancer March 14, 1977, in the Mound Bayou, Mississippi, Hospital.

Further Reading

There are several biographies of Hamer, including Kay Mills, *This Little Light of Mine: the Life of Fannie Lou Hamer* (1993), and a children's book, *Fannie Lou Hamer: From Sharecropping to Politics,* by David Rubel with an introduction by Andrew Young (1990). Many histories of the civil rights movement in the South include information about Hamer. These include Vicki Crawford, Jacqueline Rouse, and Barbara Woods, *Women in the Civil Rights Movement: Trailblazers and Torchbearers, 1941-1965* (1990); Juan Williams, *Eyes on the Prize: America's Civil Rights Years, 1954-1965* (1987); and various histories of SNCC and its leaders. A collection of Fannie Lou Hamer papers is available on microfilm from the Amistad Research Center, Tulane University, New Orleans, Louisiana. □

Hamilcar Barca

Hamilcar Barca (ca. 285-c.229 B.C.) was a great Carthaginian general and statesman in the First Punic War who firmly established Carthaginian rule in Spain.

Hamilcar Barca was a daring, intelligent young man. He was appointed commander in chief in Sicily in 247 B.C., when, after 18 years of fighting, the Carthaginian forces were at their lowest. Entrusted with naval operations, he immediately set out to attack and ravage the coastline of Lucania and Bruttium. He then landed on the north coast of Sicily, seizing Mt. Hercte west of Panormus. From this vantage point he hoped to strike at the rear of the armies besieging Lily-baeum and Drepanum and possibly draw off their forces to the defense of Panormus. Meanwhile, he fortified the site, built a harbor for his fleet, and continued the raids on the Italian coast as far north as Cumae.

When, after 3 years of harassing the Romans and holding them at bay, Hamilcar was finally dislodged from Mt. Hercte, he captured the city of Eryx, thus driving a wedge between the Romans who occupied the Temple of Venus on top of Mt. Eryx and the army that besieged Drepanum. From this new strategic point Hamilcar sallied out with his fleet and continued to devastate the Sicilian and Italian shores.

Hamilcar's position became untenable, however, when the Roman victory over the Carthaginian fleet at the Aegates islands in 241 cut him off from the sea. His home government gave him full power to negotiate the best possible terms of peace with the Roman victor, Gaius Lutatius Catulus. Acting as a good and prudent leader, Hamilcar drew up a treaty with Lutatius, which, even though not fully accepted by the Roman people, put an end to the First Punic War. Hamilcar received free retreat for his troops, transferred them from Mt. Eryx to Lilybaeum, and laid down his command.

Revolt of the Mercenaries

Upon returning to Africa, Hamilcar's mercenary troops revolted because the Carthaginians were unable to pay them their arrears. When Hanno, the commander in chief in Africa, failed to suppress the revolt, Hamilcar replaced him. Hamilcar surrounded the mercenaries' position at the river Bagrades (Medjerda), defeated their leader Spendius, and relieved the siege of Utica. Trapped in turn by Spendius, Hamilcar extricated himself with the help of the young Numidian chief Naravas. In this battle 10,000 mercenaries were killed and 4,000 taken captive; Hamilcar either dismissed the captives or enrolled them in his own army. But he changed his policy of clemency when the rebel leaders inveigled the mercenaries to mutilate cruelly their Carthaginian prisoners.

An open quarrel between Hamilcar and Hanno resulted in the latter's recall and replacement. When the mercenaries laid siege to the city of Carthage, Hamilcar drove them into a defile and annihilated them. Having achieved a reconciliation with Hanno under pressure from the Carthaginian Senate, Hamilcar turned against the last contingent of rebellious mercenaries, who were laying siege to Tunis. He defeated their leader Matho in a decisive battle and finally reduced Utica in 238.

Conquest of Spain

Emerging as the most popular leader at the end of the war against the mercenaries, Hamilcar easily won the people's support for a new war intended to make up for the loss of Sicily and Sardinia. He was sent to Spain in the spring of 237, accompanied by his 9-year-old son Hannibal, whom he made swear eternal hatred against Rome. With the Phoenician colony of Gades as his base, Hamilcar fought successfully against Tartessians, Celts, and Iberians in southern and western Spain. Then he transferred his line of operations to the east, reduced the Iberians north of Cape Palos, pushed forward the Carthaginian frontier as far north as Cape Nao, and built a fortress at Akra Leuke on the rocky hill of Alicante to dominate the newly conquered territory. He thus overstepped the boundary line between Massilia and Carthage. Upon protestations from Rome, Massilia's ally, Hamilcar replied that his conquest was needed to pay his country's war indemnity to Rome.

Hamilcar died in the winter of 229/228, after 9 years of warfare in Spain, while besieging the town of Helice southwest of Alicante. As he was about to withdraw from the siege in order to meet an Iberian king in battle, he drowned in the river Alebos (Vinalapò).

It is difficult to give a fair estimate of Hamilcar's generalship in the First Punic War, since he arrived too late on the scene to change the tide. The historian Polybius—although conceding the Romans' superiority in individual courage—gave the palm of leadership to Hamilcar. The anti-Barcid tradition, found in Roman historians, blamed Hamilcar's personal ambition for his wars in Spain and denied that he was backed by his home government. Although this tradition is untrue, there can be no question that Hamilcar's conquests and the rising power of Carthage in Spain ultimately led to the great conflict with Rome in the Second Punic War.

Further Reading

The major ancient source for the life of Hamilcar is Polybius. For the historical background of Hamilcar's life and the Punic Wars see B. H. Warmington, *Carthage* (1960; rev. ed. 1969), and Gilbert Charles Picard and Colette Picard, *The Life and Death of Carthage,* translated by Dominique Collon (1969). Hamilcar received extensive treatment in Gavin de Beer, *Hannibal: Challenging Rome's Supremacy* (1969). □

Alexander Hamilton

The first U.S. secretary of the Treasury, Alexander Hamilton (1755-1804) was instrumental in developing the nation's first political party, the Federalists.

Alexander Hamilton's birth date is disputed, but he probably was born on Jan. 11, 1755, on the island of Nevis in the British West Indies. He was the illegitimate son of James Hamilton, a Scotsman, and Rachel Fawcett Lavien, daughter of a French Huguenot physician.

Hamilton's education was brief. He began working sometime between the ages of 11 and 13 as a clerk in a trading firm in St. Croix. In 1772 he left—perhaps encouraged and financed by his employers—to attend school in the American colonies. After a few months at an academy in New Jersey, he enrolled in King's College, New York City. Precocious enough to master most subjects without formal instruction and eager to win success and fame early in life, he left college in 1776 without graduating.

American Revolution

The outbreak of the American Revolution offered Hamilton the opportunity he craved. In March 1776 he became captain of a company of artillery and, a year later, a lieutenant colonel in the Continental Army and aide-de-camp to commanding general George Washington. Hamilton's ability was apparent, and he became one of Washington's most trusted advisers. Although he played no role in major military decisions, Hamilton's position was one of great responsibility. He drafted many of Washington's letters to high-ranking Army officers, the Continental Congress, and the states. He also was sent on important military missions and

drafted major reports on the reorganization and reform of the Army. Despite the demands of his position, he found time for reading and reflection and expressed his ideas on economic policy and governmental debility in newspaper articles and in letters to influential public figures.

In February 1781, in a display of pique at a minor reprimand by Gen. Washington, Hamilton resigned his position. Earlier, on Dec. 14, 1780, he had married the daughter of Philip Schuyler, a member of one of New York's most distinguished families. In July 1781 Hamilton's persistent search for active military service was rewarded when Washington gave him command of a battalion of light infantry in the Marquis de Lafayette's corps. After the Battle of Yorktown, Hamilton returned to New York. In 1782, following a hasty apprenticeship, he was admitted to the bar.

During the Revolution, Hamilton's ideas on government, society, and economic matured. These were conditioned by his foreign birth, which obviated a strong attachment to a particular state or locality, and by his presence at Washington's headquarters, where he could see the war as a whole. Like the general himself, Hamilton was deeply disturbed that the conduct of the war was impeded by the weakness of Congress and by state and local jealousies. It was this experience rather than any theoretical commitment to a particular form of government that structured Hamilton's later advocacy of a strong central government.

Confederation Era

From the end of the Revolution to the inauguration of the first government under the Constitution, Hamilton tirelessly opposed what he described as the "dangerous prejudices in the particular states opposed to those measures which alone can give stability and prosperity to the Union." Though his extensive law practice won him recognition as one of New York's most distinguished attorneys, public affairs were his major concern.

Attending the Continental Congress as a New York delegate from November 1782 through July 1783, he unsuccessfully labored, along with James Madison and other nationalists, to invest the Confederation with powers equal to the needs of postrevolutionary America. Convinced that the pervasive commitment to states' rights obviated reform of the Articles of Confederation, Hamilton began to advocate a stronger and more efficient central government. As one of the 12 delegates to the Annapolis Convention of 1786, he drafted its resolution calling for a Constitutional Convention "to devise such further provisions as shall appear . . . necessary to render the Constitution of the Federal Government adequate to the exigencies of the Union. . . ." Similarly, as a member of the New York Legislature in 1787, he was the eloquent spokesman for continental interests as opposed to state and local ones.

Ratification of the Constitution

Hamilton was one of the New York delegates to the Constitutional Convention, which sat in Philadelphia from May to September 1787. Although he served on several important committees, his performance was disappointing, particularly when measured against his previous (and subsequent) accomplishments. His most important speech called for a government close to the English model, one so high-toned that it was unacceptable to most of the delegates.

Hamilton's contribution to the ratification of the Constitution was far more important. In October 1787 he determined to write a series of essays on behalf of the proposed Constitution. First published in New York City newspapers under the pseudonym "Publius" and collectively designated *The Federalist,* these essays were designed to persuade the people of New York to ratify the Constitution. Though *The Federalist* was written in collaboration with John Jay and James Madison, Hamilton wrote 51 of the 85 essays. First published in book form in 1788, the *Federalist* essays have been republished in many editions and languages. They constitute one of America's most original and important contributions to political philosophy and remain today the authoritative contemporary exposition of the meaning of the cryptic clauses of the U.S. Constitution. At the New York ratifying convention in 1788, Hamilton led in defending the proposed Constitution, which, owing measurably to Hamilton's labors, New York ratified.

Secretary of the Treasury

On Sept. 11, 1789, some 6 months after the new government was inaugurated, Hamilton was commissioned the nation's first secretary of the Treasury. This was the most important of the executive departments because the new government's most pressing problem was to devise ways of paying the national debt—domestic and foreign—incurred during the Revolution.

Hamilton's program, his single most brilliant achievement, also created the most bitter controversy of the first decade of American national history. It was spelled out between January 1790 and December 1791 in three major reports on the American economy: "Report on the Public Credit"; "Report on a National Bank"; and "Report on Manufactures."

In the first report Hamilton recommended payment of both the principal and interest of the public debt at par and the assumption of state debts incurred during the American Revolution. The assumption bill was defeated initially, but Hamilton rescued it by an alleged bargain with Thomas Jefferson and Madison for the locale of the national capital. Both the funding and assumption measures became law in 1791 substantially as Hamilton had proposed them.

Hamilton's "Report on a National Bank" was designed to facilitate the establishment of public credit and to enhance the powers of the new national government. Although some members of Congress doubted this body's power to charter such a great quasi-public institution, the majority accepted Hamilton's argument and passed legislation establishing the First Bank of the United States. Before signing the measure, President Washington requested his principal Cabinet officers, Jefferson and Hamilton, to submit opinions on its constitutionality. Arguing that Congress had exceeded its powers, Jefferson submitted a classic defense of a strict construction of the Constitution; affirming the Bank's constitutionality, Hamilton submitted the best argument in American political literature for a broad interpretation of the Constitution.

The "Report on Manufactures," his only major report which Congress rejected, was perhaps Hamilton's most important state paper. The culmination of his economic program, it is the clearest statement of his economic philosophy. The protection and encouragement of infant industries, he argued, would produce a better balance between agriculture and manufacturing, promote national self-sufficiency, and enhance the nation's wealth and power.

Hamilton also submitted other significant reports which Congress accepted, including a plan for an excise on spirits and a report on the establishment of a Mint. Hamilton's economic program was not original (it drew heavily, for example, upon British practice), but it was an innovative and creative application of European precedent and American experience to the practical needs of the new country.

First Political Party

Hamilton's importance during this period was not confined to his work as finance minister. As the virtual "prime minister" of Washington's administration, he was consulted on a wide range of problems, foreign and domestic. He deserves to be ranked, moreover, as the leader of the country's first political party, the Federalist party. Hamilton himself, like most of his contemporaries, railed against parties

and "factions," but when the debate over his fiscal policies revealed a deep political division among the members of Congress, Hamilton boldly assumed leadership of the proadministration group, the Federalists, just as Jefferson provided leadership for the Democratic Republicans.

Prominent Lawyer and Army General

Because of the pressing financial demands of his growing family, Hamilton retired from office in January 1795. Resuming his law practice, he soon became the most distinguished member of the New York City bar. His major preoccupation remained public affairs, however, and he continued as President Washington's adviser. The latter's famous "Farewell Address" (1796), for example, was largely based on Hamilton's draft. Nor could Hamilton remain aloof from politics. In the election of 1796 he attempted to persuade the Federalist electors to cast a unanimous vote for John Adam's running mate, Thomas Pinckney.

The high regard in which most of the country's leading Federalists held Hamilton was matched by the dislike and distrust with which many others—notably the Republicans—viewed him. He was ambitious, arrogant, and opinionated. He was also indiscreet. For example, to refute a baseless charge by James Reynolds and others that as secretary of the Treasury he was guilty of corruption, he needlessly published a defense which included a confession of adultery with Mrs. Reynolds. Such an admission undoubtedly diminished the possibility of political preferment.

During the presidency of John Adams, however, Hamilton continued to wield considerable national influence, for members of Adams's Cabinet often sought and followed his advice. In 1798 they cooperated with George Washington to secure Hamilton's appointment—over Adams's strong opposition—as inspector general and second in command of the newly augmented U.S. Army, which was preparing for a possible war against France. Since Washington declined active command, organizing and recruiting the "Provisional Army" fell to Hamilton. His military career abruptly came to an end in 1800 after John Adams, in the face of the opposition of his Cabinet and other Federalist leaders (Hamilton among them), sent a peace mission to France that negotiated a settlement of the major issues.

Retirement and the Fatal Duel

Hamilton's role in the presidential campaign of 1800 not only was a disservice to his otherwise distinguished career but also seriously wounded the Federalist party. Convinced of John Adam's ineptitude, Hamilton rashly published a long Philippic which characterized the President as a man possessed by "vanity without bounds, and a jealousy capable of discoloring every object," with a "disgusting egotism" and an "ungovernable discretion of . . . temper." Instead of discrediting Adams, the pamphlet promoted election of the Republican candidates, Jefferson and Aaron Burr. When the Jefferson-Burr tie went for decision to the House of Representatives, however, Hamilton regained his balance. Convinced that Jefferson would not undermine executive authority, Hamilton also believed that Burr was "the most unfit and dangerous man of the community." He accordingly used his considerable influence to persuade congressional leaders to select Jefferson.

Although his interest in national policies and politics was unabated, Hamilton's role in national affairs after 1801 diminished. He remained a prominent figure in the Federalist party, however, and published his opinions on public affairs in the *New York Evening Post.* He was still an ardent nationalist and in 1804 severely condemned the rumored plot of New England and New York Federalists to dismember the Union by forming a Northern confederacy. Believing Aaron Burr to be a party to this scheme, Hamilton actively opposed the Vice President's bid for the New York governorship. He was successful, and Burr, now out of favor with the Jefferson administration and discredited in his own state, charged that Hamilton's remarks had impugned his honor. Burr challenged Hamilton to a duel. Although Hamilton was reluctant, he believed that his "ability to be in future useful" demanded his acceptance. After putting his personal affairs in order, he met Burr at dawn on July 11, 1804, on the New Jersey side of the Hudson River. The two exchanged shots, and Hamilton fell, mortally wounded. Tradition has it that he deliberately misdirected his fire, leaving himself an open target for Burr's bullet. Hamilton was carried back to New York City, where he died the next afternoon.

Further Reading

Henry Cabot Lodge, ed., *The Works of Alexander Hamilton* (2d ed., 12 vols., 1903), will be replaced by Harold C. Syrett and Jacob E. Cooke, eds., *Papers,* 15 volumes of which have been published (1961-1969). Hamilton's definitive biography is Broadus Mitchell's meticulous *Alexander Hamilton* (2 vols., 1957-1962). John C. Miller, *Alexander Hamilton* (1959), is an excellent one-volume life. Useful biographies are David Loth, *Alexander Hamilton: Portrait of a Prodigy* (1939), and Nathan Schachner, *Alexander Hamilton* (1946). Also recommended are Claude G. Bowers, *Jefferson and Hamilton: The Struggle for Democracy in America* (1925), and Richard B. Morris, *Alexander Hamilton and the Founding of the Nation* (1957). □

Alice Hamilton

The American physician Alice Hamilton (1869-1970) is recognized as the founder of industrial medicine in the United States. She was the first woman on the faculty of Harvard Medical School.

Alice Hamilton grew up in Fort Wayne, Ind., in an affluent home. Her parents entertained guests who discussed major topics of the day, and they stimulated the thinking of their children by raising doubts about society's religious and social assumptions. Hamilton attended Miss Porter's School in Farmington, Conn., and in 1893 graduated from the University of Michigan Medical School. She interned in the New England Hospital for Women in Boston. There she serviced working-class peo-

ple, the usual clientele of the first women doctors (who were seldom employed by the upper classes).

In 1894 Dr. Hamilton studied bacteriology in Germany and returned to accept her first teaching position at the Women's Medical College of Northwestern University in Chicago, Ill. Another important factor in her life seems to have been her decision to live at Chicago's settlement house, Hull House. Here she came into close contact with notable social reformers (including the founder of Hull House and one of America's first social workers, Jane Addams) and with the sick from the streets and the mills of the city. For several years she was torn between the medical-social work around Hull House and an equally strong desire to devote herself to research at the McCormick Institute for Infectious Diseases.

Eventually Dr. Hamilton's social passion and scientific skills combined as she plunged into the research and activity to control health hazards in the dangerous trades of mining and factory work. Her first real chance came in 1910, when the governor of Illinois appointed her to a commission to investigate occupational diseases. She inspected mines and factories to identify hazardous jobs. After the Federal government asked her to make her research nationwide, she spent 12 years identifying lead, arsenic, and mercury poisons, aniline dyes, picric acid, dust, bad ventilation, and other health hazards. On the basis of her research she was expected to present the needed antidotes and safeguards.

Always an outspoken feminist, Dr. Hamilton must have been excited to accept an invitation in 1919 to be the first woman to join the faculty of the Harvard Medical School. In 1935 she retired from Harvard but not from her national and international efforts to prevent industry from poisoning the earth. She was one of the first to warn of the lethal nature of atomic radiation.

Further Reading

The best book on Alice Hamilton is her autobiography, *Exploring the Dangerous Trades* (1943). For general background see George Rosen, *A History of Public Health* (1958). □

Sir William Rowan Hamilton

The Irish mathematical physicist Sir William Rowan Hamilton (1805-1865) reshaped theoretical optics by basing it on his law of varying action. His analysis of motion anticipated several basic notions of relativity and quantum mechanics.

William Rowan Hamilton was born on Aug. 4, 1805, in Dublin, the fourth child of Archibald Hamilton, a solicitor, and Sarah Hutton Hamilton. His father's family was known for a penchant for the gregarious and the romantic, while several members of his mother's family were distinguished scientists. It was the almost clashing union of the scientific and the romantic that became the most marked characteristic of William's personality. At the age of 2 he was entrusted to his uncle, a curate and an accomplished linguist. At the age of 3 William read English fluently; at 5 he was translating Greek and Hebrew; by the time he was 12, he not only had mastered German, French, Italian, and Spanish but also had a working knowledge of Syriac, Persian, Arabic, Sanskrit, and Hindustani. At his father's urging he wrote, at the age of 14, a letter in Persian to the Persian ambassador visiting in Dublin.

In 1820 Hamilton met the American mathematical prodigy Zerah Colburn, then studying in England, and thus became interested in mathematics. Later he began to read Euclid, from which came another powerful boost to Hamilton's single-minded, youthful pursuit of mathematical physics. He was hardly 17 when he mastered Isaac Newton's *Arithmetica universalis* and *Principia,* in addition to Pierre Laplace's *Mécanique céleste.* In the last, the self-taught young genius even discovered an error in connection with Laplace's demonstration of the parallelogram of forces.

Systems of Rays

In 1822 Hamilton submitted a paper on the osculation of certain curves of double curvature to John Brinkley, professor of astronomy at Trinity College and astronomer royal of Ireland. The following year Hamilton entered Trinity College, earning the highest honors in all examinations and winning practically all the prizes. In 1824 he presented to the Royal Irish Academy a paper, "On Caustics," the preface of which stated: "The Problems of Optics, considered mathematically, relate for the most part to the intersections of the rays of light proceeding from known surfaces, according to known laws. In the present paper, it is proposed to investigate some general properties common to all such Systems of Rays, and independent of the particular surface or particular law. It is intended in another paper to point out the application of these mathematical principles to the actual laws of Nature." These words prefaced in effect Hamilton's lifelong program in mathematical physics.

The committee appointed to report on the merits of Hamilton's paper requested him to elaborate further on the topic. In 1827 Hamilton, still an undergraduate, presented to the academy the enlarged form of the paper under the title "A Theory of Systems of Rays." His starting point was the well-established principle that light rays travel between two points (extremities, he called them) along the path of least time, or along the path of least action, depending on whether the wave theory or the corpuscular theory of light was considered.

This paper earned Hamilton not only fame but also meteoric rise in the academic world. Although still an undergraduate, he was appointed Andrews professor of astronomy (1827). Connected with the munificently endowed chair were the directorship of the Observatory of Dunsink, the title of astronomer royal of Ireland, and a spacious lodging on the observatory grounds. Furthermore, it was understood that he had no observational duties to perform lest his theoretical investigations be disturbed. The next 7 years in Hamilton's life were bathed in the sunshine of success and glory in every sense. His lectures on astronomy drew crowds that he kept spellbound with his soaring rhetoric. The prodigy was the toast of society, and he made lifelong friendships with Samuel Taylor Coleridge and William Wordsworth. At this time Hamilton's literary ambitions produced an outpouring of sonnets, many inspired by three romances, of which the last ended in his marriage to Helen Maria Bayley in 1833. The marriage was an unhappy one.

Conical Refraction and Quaternions

In early 1834 Hamilton made the most spectacular discovery of his career—the prediction that under certain circumstances an internal and an external conical refraction would occur. The prediction was soon verified by Humphrey Lloyd, a professor of physics at Trinity. In 1835 Hamilton was knighted. The next year he became president of the Royal Irish Academy.

In 1843 Hamilton announced to the Royal Irish Academy the definition of quaternions; in 1848 he began his "Lectures on Quaternions" (published 1853). The discovery of the quaternions represented for Hamilton the most important event in his life. In his letter of Oct. 15, 1858, to Tait, he described in detail what went on in his mind as he walked on Oct. 16, 1843, toward Broughman Bridge in Dublin: "I then and there felt the galvanic circuit of thought close; and the sparks which fell from it were the fundamental equations between i, j, k; exactly such as I have used them ever since." From another letter of his we know that on the spur of the moment Hamilton "cut with a knife on a stone of Brougham Bridge . . . the formula $i^2 - j^2 - k^2 - ijk = -1$." The theory included such points as the principles of noncommutative algebra, the generalized treatment of coordinates and momenta, and the correspondence of multiplication by imaginary numbers to rotation in space. All these topics now form indispensable parts of the mathematics of relativity and quantum mechanics. He also worked feverishly to achieve as much as possible of his great ambition, the detailed formulation of his quaternion theory, in which he saw the geometrical regularity embodied in the physical universe. His *Elements of Quaternions,* a huge volume comprising the efforts of his last 10 years, was published a year after his death.

Hamilton's last years were marked by alcoholism and by a routine of life that lacked any evidence of orderliness. His study resembled a pigsty; in his cabinets, rows of dry lamb chops alternated with heaps of precious manuscripts. For the most part he was living unmindful of fame, burning with zeal to produce the work that would honor Ireland in the same measure as Newton's *Principia* did glory to England. He felt immense satisfaction on learning shortly before his death, on Sept. 2, 1865, that the recently established National Academy of Sciences in the United States had elected him as its foreign associate. In fact, the academy put Hamilton's name on the top of the list by a majority vote of two-thirds.

Further Reading

Some of Hamilton's unpublished manuscripts are printed in the Royal Irish Academy's *The Mathematical Papers of Sir William Rowan Hamilton,* edited by A. W. Conway and others (4 vols., 1931-1941). The fullest biography of Hamilton is Robert Perceval Graves, *Life of Sir William Rowan Hamilton* (3 vols., 1882-1889). Shorter biographies of Hamilton are in Eric Temple Bell, *Men of Mathematics* (1937), and Scientific American, *Lives in Science* (1957). Dirk J. Struick, *A Concise History of Mathematics* (1948; 3d rev. ed. 1967), is recommended for general background.

Additional Sources

Hankins, Thomas L., *Sir William Rowan Hamilton,* Baltimore: Johns Hopkins University Press, 1980. □

Dag Hammarskjöld

The Swedish diplomat Dag Hammarskjöld (1905-1961) served as the secretary general of the United Nations from 1953 until his death.

Dag Hammarskjöld played a leading role in expanding the operations of the United Nations (UN), most notably through the establishment of peace-keeping forces and through technical and economic assistance to poor and newly independent nations. He practiced "quiet diplomacy" to reduce conflict and to build an international civil service that could carry out functions necessary to maintain peace and promote welfare. His extraordinary intellectual brilliance and courage were widely admired.

Dag Hammarskjöld was born on July 19, 1905, in Jönköping into one of Sweden's oldest aristocratic families, with a long history of government service. Hammarskjöld spent most of his childhood in Uppsala, where his father served as provincial governor. He attended a private school and then entered the university in 1923. He received his law degree at Uppsala in 1930, and in 1934 he earned a doctorate in political economics at the University of Stockholm.

Expert in Economics

In 1930 Hammarskjöld was appointed secretary of the Royal Commission on Unemployment. He served next as secretary of the Central Bank. His economic expertise brought him the high post of undersecretary in the Ministry of Finance at the age of 31. Five years later he was named chairman of the Central Bank and also assumed the duties of commissioner and assistant undersecretary in the State Financial Office. In 1946 he transferred to the Ministry of Foreign Affairs as an economic adviser. The next year he served as Swedish delegate to the Paris conference on economic recovery and later was responsible for Sweden's role in the Marshall Plan. He played a prominent role in establishing the Organization for European Economic Cooperation (OEEC), serving as vice-chairman of its executive committee. In 1949 he was appointed undersecretary in the

Ministry of Foreign Affairs. Two years later he was named a minister without portfolio in the Swedish Cabinet.

UN Secretary General

Hammarskjöld served as vice-chairman of the Swedish delegation to the General Assembly of the UN in 1952. The following year he became chairman of the delegation. In March 1953 Hammarskjöld received the recommendation of the Security Council to replace Trygve Lie as UN secretary general, and on April 7 the General Assembly adopted the recommendation. He took office 12 days later.

During his initial year at the UN, Hammarskjöld sought to streamline the operations of the Secretariat and to reduce the political interference of member states in Secretariat administration. He made it clear, however, that he felt the role of secretary general included serving as a trusted consultant to all sides in conflict and as a discreet channel of communications when normal diplomatic channels were inadequate. The practicality of this approach was proved in 1955, when Hammarskjöld successfully secured the release of 15 American fliers shot down over China and held by the Chinese.

Peace-keeping in the Middle East

Hammarskjöld's role as mediator became even more apparent in the 1956 Middle East crisis. In January he conferred with both President Gamal Abdel Nasser of Egypt and Premier David Ben Gurion of Israel, and his quiet diplomacy kept the explosive situation temporarily in check. After the nationalization of the Suez Canal in late 1956 and the subsequent military invasion of Egypt by Israel, France, and England, Hammarskjöld led in getting these forces removed and the canal reopened. A crucial factor was the establishment of a United Nations Emergency Force (UNEF), though previously the UN had only sent observers to areas of strife. Within a matter of weeks Hammarskjöld was able to establish the force and arrange for its operation along the lines between Israel and Egypt.

In 1958 Hammarskjöld was reelected as secretary general. He increasingly turned his attention to the emerging nations of Asia and Africa. Asian leaders sought his personal advice and diplomatic help. Hammarskjöld's trip to 24 African nations in 1960 deeply impressed him with the need for the UN to give assistance to newly independent countries, particularly with problems of public administration, economic development, and social reform.

Conflagration in the Congo

In July 1960 the Security Council authorized Hammarskjöld to give military assistance to the newly independent Republic of the Congo in order to restore and maintain law and order. Hammarskjöld organized a military force composed of contingents contributed by various countries, excluding the major military powers. He felt that maintaining order in the troubled country was the greatest single task the UN faced. His efforts were severely criticized by the U.S.S.R. and nations in its sphere of influence.

In September 1961 Hammarskjöld traveled to the Congo at the invitation of the Congolese government to mediate between the various factions within the country. During his stay fighting broke out between secessionist forces in Katanga and the UN peace-keeping troops stationed there. In Léopoldville, Hammarskjöld conferred with the government, then flew to meet Moise Tshombe, leader of the Katanga secessionists. En route, on September 17 Hammarskjöld and 15 others were killed when their plane crashed in Northern Rhodesia (Zambia). Hammarskjöld was awarded the Nobel Prize for peace posthumously in 1961.

The posthumous publication of Hammarskjöld's journal, *Markings,* revealed him as an intensely religious man, preoccupied with the spiritual problems of reconciling abstract ideals with human frailty.

Further Reading

Hammarskjöld revealed his literary and philosophical qualities in *Markings* (1964). *The Light and the Rock: The Vision of Dag Hammarskjöld,* (no date) edited by T. S. Settel, is a parallel volume of Hammarskjöld's statements that reflect his thoughts on many subjects. A helpful collection of Hammarskjöld's writings and speeches is Wilder Foote, *The Servant of Peace: A Selection of Speeches and Statements of Dag Hammarskjöld* (1962).

Among the many biographies and full-length portraits of Hammarskjöld are Joseph P. Lash, *Dag Hammarskjöld: Custodian of the Brushfire Peace* (1961); Sten Valdemar Söderberg, *Dag Hammarskjöld: A Pictorial Biography* (1962); Emery Kelen, *Hammarskjöld* (1966); Sven Stolpe, *Dag Hammarskjöld: A Spiritual Portrait* (trans. 1966); Charles May Simon, *Dag Hammarskjöld* (1967); Henry Pitney Van Dusen, *Dag Hammarskjöld: The Statesman and His Faith* (1967); Emery Kelen, ed., *Hammarskjöld: The Political Man* (1968); and Bo Beskow, *Dag Hammarskjöld: Strictly Personal; A Portrait* (1969). Gustaf Aulén, *Dag Hammarskjöld's White Book: The Meaning of "Markings"* (1969), is an investigation of the intellectual and theological background for Hammarskjöld's views recorded in his *Markings.* One of the most useful studies of Hammarskjöld's role in the UN is Marc W. Zacher, *Dag Hammarskjöld's United Nations* (1969).

Additional Sources

Hammarskjöld, Dag, *Markings,* Boston: G. K. Hall, 1976, 1964. Urquhart, Brian., *Hammarskjöld,* New York: Harper & Row, 1984, 1972. □

Hildegard Hamm-Brücher

Hildegard Hamm-Brücher (born 1921) was a prominent liberal politician in Germany. She held state secretary positions from 1969 to 1972 and from 1977 to 1982. In 1993 she became the Free Democratic Party's candidate for the federal presidency elections to be held the following year.

Born on May 11, 1921, in Essen in the heart of the Ruhr district, Hildegard Hamm-Brücher grew up with four siblings in a nonpolitical bourgeois family.

Her father was director of an electric firm; her mother maintained the household. Unexpectedly, her parents died within a year of each other when she was only ten and eleven years old. Her widowed grandmother, residing in Dresden, brought up young Hamm-Brücher and several of her siblings. The grandmother came from an industrial family whose ancestors had converted from Judaism to Protestantism. In the early 1930s young Hamm-Brücher made the acquaintance of Pastor Martin Niemöller, who later during the Hitler era was imprisoned in two concentration camps. She remained his close friend in the post-war period.

While Hitler governed, the nonconformist and antifascist Hamm-Brücher attended several secondary schools, was conscripted briefly into the Reich Labor Service, and during the war studied chemistry at the University of Munich. She was a sympathizer of the White Rose student resistance group at the university after her grandmother committed suicide rather than face imminent deportation to a concentration camp. These events later sparked Hamm-Brücher's interest in politics, even though with the Ph.D. that she received in 1945 she could have had a successful career in academia or industry.

Budding Politician

From 1945 to 1948 Hamm-Brücher worked as a journalist in Munich, becoming interested in educational policy questions. This led in 1949 to receipt of a U.S. Government-sponsored one-year grant to take courses at Harvard University. It gave her a chance to observe the American way of life, which she found most impressive. In the meantime, in 1946 she had interviewed Theodor Heuss, the future federal president of what was then West Germany and leader of the liberal Free Democratic Party (FDP), who urged her to go into politics. In 1948 she joined the newly founded party and gained a seat in the Munich city council.

From 1950 to 1966 she was a deputy in the Bavarian legislature and from 1954 on deputy chairwoman of the FDP parliamentary group. She fought hard for democratic educational reforms and supported the establishment of secular schools in rural areas having only denominational schools. As a result of her efforts, the voters had a chance to vote for a change in the educational provisions of the constitution through an initiative and referendum. In 1964 she was instrumental in forcing the resignation of the Bavarian minister of culture, who as a criminal lawyer in the Hitler era had written the legal commentaries justifying anti-Jewish laws.

In 1963 Hamm-Brücher became a member of the party's federal executive committee in Bonn and remained on it for 13 years. From 1972 on she served on the federal presidium, the top policy-making organ of the party. During this time she traveled abroad to study different educational systems.

State Secretary of Education

In 1966 when the FDP could not gain the minimum 5 percent of the vote necessary for its candidates to win election to the Bavarian legislature, Hamm-Brücher lost her seat. Having built up a reputation in the educational field,

the minister for education in the state of Hesse, who was a Social Democrat, asked her to become his state secretary. She hesitated, partly because of the heavy administrative duties of the job and partly because of her family obligations. Her husband, Erwin Hamm, a lawyer and city councilor in Munich, and her two children would not be able to join her in Wiesbaden, Hesse's state capital city, but they urged her to take the position. In 1967 she took up her new tasks, and she found great satisfaction in further developing a democratic educational system built on the principle of equal opportunity for all children.

When the Social Democratic Party formed a national coalition government with the FDP in Bonn in 1969, Chancellor Willy Brandt and the minister of education and science requested her to become state secretary in the federal ministry for education and science. She accepted, especially because she did not want to continue in her Hesse position under a new, more radical Social Democratic administration. In 1972 she returned to Munich to become chairwoman of the FDP parliamentary group in the Bavarian legislature.

In 1976 she won a seat in the Bonn federal Parliament, but soon accepted the post of state secretary (titled state minister) in the Foreign Office. In charge of cultural affairs, she urged the government to increase cultural contacts with other states. When Foreign Minister Hans-Dietrich Genscher (FDP) was abroad, Hamm-Brücher represented him in cabinet meetings, in Parliament, and at receptions for foreign dignitaries. Conversely, she represented Genscher on numerous official visits throughout the world. Thus she had to be familiar with all aspects of German foreign policy, rather than just the narrow segment of cultural policy.

Presidential Candidate

When the Social Democratic-FDP coalition broke apart in 1982 and the FDP allied itself with the conservative Christian Democratic Union/Christian Social Union, Hamm-Brücher and a minority of other liberal FDP leaders broke with their party and opposed the new coalition government headed by Chancellor Helmut Kohl. Hamm-Brücher resigned her post of state secretary but remained a deputy in the Bundestag (lower house of Parliament) until 1990. During this time she became active in the movement to reform and strengthen the Bundestag vis-à-vis the government. Although she announced her retirement from politics beginning in 1991, two years later she accepted her party's nomination to be its candidate for the federal presidency of a united Germany. She had no chance of being elected in 1994 because of the small number of FDP deputies in the federal assembly (the president is chosen by state and national legislators). However, her candidacy was a symbolic victory for women, demonstrating that they can succeed in German politics.

Further Reading

The best sources of information on Hamm-Brücher are in German. Two biographies shed some light on her: Paul Noack, *Hildegard Hamm-Brücher: Mut zur Politik—well ich die Menschen liebe* (1981); and Ursula Salentin, *Hildegard*

Hamm-Brücher: Der Lebensweg einer eigenwilligen Demokratin (1987); See also her own writings, such as *Der Politiker und sein Gewissen* (1987). ☐

Armand Hammer

Armand Hammer (1898-1992) was a physician turned entrepreneur and art collector whose natural talent for business made him a billionaire. His early, helpful relations with the Soviet Union made him an international figure.

Armand Hammer was born in New York City in 1898, one of three sons of Julius and Rose Robinson Hammer. Julius Hammer was the son of a Russian emigrant who worked his way through the Columbia University medical school, developed a successful medical practice, and then diversified into the wholesale drug business and retail drug stores. Armand Hammer also attended Columbia University, receiving his B.S. in 1919 and then entering the College of Physicians and Surgeons. While at the university Hammer worked with his two brothers to save and expand his father's pharmaceutical business. After World War I Hammer talked his family into buying up medical supplies after prices had plummeted. When the prices rose, the family earned a fortune; Hammer himself earned one million dollars. Hammer still found time to complete his medical degree in 1921, graduating among the top ten students in his class.

Impatient to begin medical practice and hearing of epidemics and famines in the Soviet Union, Hammer purchased a surplus army field hospital and set off to help. Upon arriving in Moscow in 1921 he concluded that the major problem was lack of food, and, using his natural business talent, he arranged a trade of Russian furs and caviar for a shipload of American wheat. He was invited to meet Lenin, who encouraged him to abandon medicine and, instead, to help the Soviet Union build up its economy. Lenin offered Hammer a concession to operate an asbestos mine in Siberia, which he was able to make profitable after several years. Hammer was also able to obtain sales concessions for several American firms, including Ford Motor Company, United States Rubber, Allis-Chalmers, and Underwood Typewriter. In 1925 the Soviet Union decided to handle its own foreign trade and offered Hammer a manufacturing concession in compensation for his agency, Allied American Corporation, which by then included 38 American businesses. Hammer asked for the right to manufacture pencils, at that time imported and expensive. He organized the A. Hammer Pencil Company, lured away the production manufacturer of a German company, started to operate in six months, and made a profit of $1 million at the end of the first year.

As the Soviet experiment with capitalism came to a close in 1926, the government asked Hammer to sell back his asbestos and later his pencil concessions. With the help and advice of his brother Victor, who had taken a degree in art history at Princeton University, Hammer used his profits to purchase Czarist works of art, which were disdained by the Soviets. Armand and his brother organized the Hammer Galleries in New York City and brought the works back with them in 1930 to sell here. As a result of that experience Hammer developed a passion for collecting and in 1936 wrote a book titled *The Quest for the Romanoff Treasure.* Hammer was forced by the Great Depression to adopt the radical technique of selling through department stores in order to move his merchandise. He used this same technique to dispose of a large portion of the William Randolph Hearst collection in 1940. He continued as president of the gallery into the 1980s.

Hammer also speculated successfully in Soviet promissory notes. Back in America, he cornered the market in Soviet oak barrel staves needed by the American liquor industry, reviving after the repeal of prohibition. He also saw opportunities in manufacturing the contents of the barrels. In 1940, noting a surplus of potatoes at the same time that there was a shortage of whiskey, he earned a multi-million dollar profit by turning the tubers into commercial alcohol and blended whiskey. He acquired 11 distillers and formed the J. W. Dant Distilling Company, making annual profits of $3 million before selling out to established distilleries in 1954.

Hammer married three times: Baroness Olga von Root in 1927 while he was in Europe; Angela Zevely in 1943, by whom he had a son, Julian; and Frances Barrett in 1956, with whom he retired to California. But retirement soon bored Hammer, and he began looking for new ventures. In 1957 he obtained control of the Mutual Broadcasting Company and turned it over for a profit. A year earlier he had agreed to finance two wildcat oil wells for tiny Occidental Petroleum Company, and when both were successful he increased his holdings and was soon named president and chairman of the board. The net worth of the company increased from $175,000 in 1957 to $300 million in 1967. Under Hammer's leadership Occidental diversified into chemicals, coal, and fertilizers, and in 1973 he returned to his Soviet connection, signing a multi-billion dollar, 25-year chemical fertilizer agreement under which a fertilizer plant would be built in the Soviet Union from which Occidental would receive supplies for sale abroad.

Art collecting was Hammer's principal hobby starting in the 1920s, but his approach was always to share his collection with as many people as possible, based on his conviction that art is an important force for understanding among people of all cultures. In 1965 he donated a multi-million dollar collection of works by Dutch, Flemish, German, and Italian masters of the 15th through 17th centuries to the University of California at Los Angeles and other works to the Los Angeles County Museum of Art. In 1971 he added more paintings to the County Museum and gave a large group of old masters to the National Gallery of Art in Washington, D.C. In 1972 he donated a painting by Goya worth $1 million to the Hermitage Museum in Leningrad, which had none. Hammer also owned three important collections, including more than 100 works by such masters as Rembrandt, Renoir, and Rubens, which traveled for exhibition throughout the world.

Hammer's concern for understanding among peoples led him in 1962 to donate the former Campobello Island estate of President Franklin Roosevelt, whom Hammer served as an adviser during World War II, as an international peace park. He also sponsored international conferences to bring experts together to discuss solutions to problems of human rights and world peace. In 1982 he founded the Armand Hammer United World College of the American West in Montezuma, New Mexico, the only U.S. campus of a movement dedicated to enhancing world peace and understanding through education.

Another of Hammer's concerns was the effort to find a cure for cancer. He was a board member of the Eleanor Roosevelt Cancer Foundation starting in 1960. He endowed the Armand Hammer Center for Cancer Biology at the Salk Institute in La Jolla, California, in 1969 and sponsored the annual Armand Hammer Cancer Conference there. In 1982 he established the Hammer Prize for cancer research, a 10-year, $1 million program to reward the scientists who do the most each year to advance cancer research. Hammer also pledged a $1 million prize for a cure for cancer, and he served three terms as the chairman of the panel which advises the U.S. president on the status of cancer research in the United States.

In his 80s Hammer still put in 16-hour days, seven days a week. (He once remarked that he would be willing to pay Occidental Petroleum for the privilege of letting him work.) In 1986 he sponsored medical aid for the Russians injured in the Chernobyl nuclear catastrophe. Along with his humanitarian work, Hammer also left himself open to severe criticism regarding his use of funds from Occidental stockholders. It is said he used company funds for many personal amenities and to buy works of art. He earned a reputation as a ''teflon tycoon,'' to whom charges of improprieties did not stick, though in 1976 he pleaded guilty to making illegal contributions to the Nixon 1976 presidential campaign and was fined. Hammer spent much of the 1980s trying to remove the blot on his good name, and in 1989 George Bush granted him a presidential pardon. However, some people continued to speculate about Hammer's ethics and he received his share of criticism.

Hammer made his last public appearance on November 25, 1992, at the grand opening of The Armand Hammer Museum of Art and Culture Center in Los Angeles, located just behind the Occidental Petroleum headquarters. (The museum has since come under the direction of the University of California-Los Angeles.) He died only two weeks later at the age of 92. He had suffered from chronic anemia, bronchitis, prostate enlargement, kidney ailments, an irregular heartbeat, and, most fatally, bone marrow cancer.

Further Reading

Additional information may be found in Bob Considine, *The Remarkable Life of Dr. Armand Hammer* (1975); the autobiography *Hammer* (1987); and Steve Weinberg, *Armand Hammer: The Untold Story* (1989).

Additional Sources

Art News (June 1997).

Christie Brown, ''The Master Cynic,'' *Forbes 400* (October 17, 1994; November 18, 1996).

Edward J. Epstein, ''The Last Days of Armand Hammer,'' *New Yorker* (September 23, 1996). □

Oscar Clendenning Hammerstein II

Oscar Clendenning Hammerstein II (1895-1960) was perhaps the most influential lyricist and librettist of the American theater. Major musicals for which he wrote the lyrics include *Showboat, South Pacific, The King and I,* and *The Sound of Music*.

Oscar Clendenning Hammerstein II was born into a great theatrical family on July 12, 1895, in New York City. His grandfather, Oscar I, was an opera impressario and showman. His father, William, was the manager of Hammerstein's Victoria, one of the most famous vaudeville theaters of its day. His uncle, Arthur, was a well known producer. All were famous in their own right, but all would be eclipsed by the success of Oscar II, the third generation theater Hammerstein. Oscar, or ''Ockie'' (his lifelong nickname), dabbled in theatrical activities as a youth, but when it came time for a career choice his father pushed him away from the theater. Oscar went to Columbia University in preparation for a career in law. It was at Columbia, however, that Oscar's career in theater actually began when, at age 19, he joined the Columbia University Players as a performer in the 1915 Varsity review *On Your Way.* He participated heavily in the Varsity shows for several years, first as a performer and later as a writer. It was at Columbia that Oscar first met the young man who would later collaborate with him and with Lorenz Hart, another Columbia alumnus: Richard Rodgers.

After Oscar's first year of law school, he convinced his uncle, Arthur, to hire him as an assistant stage manager on one of his upcoming shows. By 1919 he was promoted to production stage manager for all of Arthur's shows. In his position as production stage manager Oscar was able to do some writing and re-writing on scripts in development. Eventually he was writing musical comedies of his own. His first success as a librettist came in 1922 with *Wildflower,* written with Otto Harbach. A more major success in 1924, *Rose Marie,* written with Harbach, Rudolph Friml, and Herbert P. Stohart, led to his collaboration with composer Jerome Kern. Kern and Hammerstein had both been concerned with the "integrated musical," a musical in which the book, lyrics, and score all grow from a central idea and all contribute to the story line. They adapted Edna Ferber's sprawling novel about life on a Mississippi River boat into the landmark 1925 musical *Showboat,* with Kern composing the score and Hammerstein writing the book and lyrics. *Showboat* firmly established Oscar's success and reputation as a writer and lyricist.

In 1929 Oscar divorced his wife of 12 years, Myra Finn, and married Dorothy Blanchard Jacobson. The next decade turned out to be a happy one for Oscar personally, but unhappy professionally. He spent much of his time in Hollywood, working on contract to various studios. He discovered that he did not work well under the rigorous time demands of the movie industry, having achieved his greatest success with *Showboat's* one year writing period. In 1942 he returned to New York with Dorothy and began leisurely work on an adaptation of Bizet's *Carmen.* Oscar adapted the lyrics and story to create the Americanized, all-Black *Carmen Jones.* The opera received great acclaim.

When he had finished the libretto for *Carmen Jones,* Oscar was contacted by an old Columbia acquaintance, Richard Rodgers, whose partnership with Lorenz Hart had recently dissolved. Rodgers had read Lynn Riggs' *Green Grow the Lilacs* and wanted to collaborate with Hammerstein on a musical adaptation for the Theatre Guild. Hammerstein had also read the play, and the two began work on the musical, tentatively titled *Away We Go.* Rodgers and Hammerstein worked toward the concept of the integrated musical, with Hammerstein writing most of the lyrics before Rodgers wrote the score, the reverse of the normal process. Robert Mamoulian was signed on as director, Agnes deMille as choreographer, and Terry Helburn as producer for the Theatre Guild.

When the musical, retitled *Oklahoma,* opened on Broadway on March 31, 1943, it was an enormous success, both critically and popularly. *Oklahoma* ran for 2,243 performances in its initial Broadway engagement, and in 1944 it received a special Pulitzer Prize. The team of Rodgers and Hammerstein was a success. They produced their own work and promising works by other artists and at one time had five of the highest grossing shows running at the same time on Broadway. They followed up their success with collaborations on *Carousel* (1945), *Allegro* (1947), *South Pacific* (1949), *The King and I* (1951), *Me and Juliet* (1953), *Pipe Dream* (1955), *Flower Drum Song* (1958), and *The Sound of Music* (1960), for which Howard Lindsay and Russell Crouse wrote the book, Rodgers composed the score, and Hammerstein wrote the lyrics. *South Pacific* won the Pulitzer Prize in 1950. *South Pacific, The King and I,* and *The Sound of Music* all won Tony awards for best musical. Most of the Rodgers and Hammerstein musicals have been adapted for the screen, with the greatest success going to *Oklahoma* and *The Sound of Music.*

Hammerstein's talents as a lyricist and librettist are undeniable. Countless productions of Hammerstein musicals on Broadway, on tour, and in professional, amateur, and academic theaters around the world testify to the remarkable quality of his work. Hammerstein's influence on the next generation of lyricists and librettists was also direct and observable. Most notable was his influence on Stephen Sondheim, lyricist for such shows as *West Side Story, Sweeny Todd,* and *Sunday in the Park with George.* Sondheim was a close friend of the Hammerstein family from childhood and attributed his success in theater directly to Hammerstein's influence and guidance.

Oscar Clendenning Hammerstein II died in his home in Doylestown, Pennsylvania, on August 23, 1960, a victim of stomach cancer. He left behind three children, William and Alice by Myra Finn and James by Dorothy Blanchard Jacobson. On September 1, 1960, at 9 p.m., the lights were extinguished on Broadway in memory of Oscar Hammerstein II, the "man who owned Broadway."

Further Reading

Getting To Know Him (1977) by Hugh Fordin is the first authorized biography of Hammerstein. Fordin was given exclusive use of Hammerstein's archives and the right to tape the personal recollections of family and colleagues. Hammerstein's contribution to musical history is traced in David Ewen, *All the Years of American Popular Music* (1977) and Frederick Nolan, *The Sound of Their Music: The Story of Rodgers and Hammerstein* (1978). Stanley Green's *The Rodgers and Hammerstein Story* (1963) treats the careers of these two men separately and their actual 18 years collaboration.

Additional Sources

Citron, Stephen, *The wordsmiths: Oscar Hammerstein 2nd and Alan Jay Lerner,* New York: Oxford University Press, 1995.
Fordin, Hugh, *Getting to know him: a biography of Oscar Hammerstein II,* New York: Da Capo Press, 1995. □

Dashiell Hammett

Dashiell Hammett (1894-1961) was a seminal figure in the development of the peculiarly American contribution to crime fiction—the hard-boiled detective story.

Samuel Dashiell Hammett was born of English and French descendants on May 27, 1894, on the Eastern Shore of Maryland, the second of three children. His formal education was limited—he attended Baltimore Polytechnic Institute for just one year, leaving at the age of 13 to help his father run a small business. He worked in his teens as a newsboy, freight clerk, railroad laborer, messenger boy, and stevedore.

From 1915 to 1921 Hammett worked on and off as an operative for the Pinkerton detective agency, serving on the scandalous Fatty Arbuckle rape case and on the 1920-1921 Anaconda copper mine strike. Hammett's Pinkerton tenure, which was to provide the material for much of his fiction, was interrupted several times, first by his brief World War I service as a sergeant in the Motor Ambulance Corps, where he contracted tuberculosis, and then by the disease's recurrence a few years after the war. Throughout his life Hammett was to be plagued by poor health, aggravated no doubt by his heavy drinking and smoking.

In 1920, while a hospital patient, Hammett married his nurse, Josephine Dolan, by whom he had two daughters, but their cohabitation was only occasional. Much of the time, to avoid the danger of infecting her or the children with his highly contagious disease, Hammett occupied a separate room of their apartment and, at times, lived apart from the family in a hotel.

The Writing Years

Hammett's writing career began in earnest in 1922 with a story printed in *The Smart Set;* until then he had published only a handful of poems. In 1923, in the pioneering crime fiction magazine *Black Mask,* Hammett's story "Arson Plus" introduced a character later to become famous in two of his novels—a nameless San Francisco detective agency operative (based on an actual Baltimore Pinkerton agent) referred to only as "the Continental Op"; his persona ran counter to the familiar fictional detective types because he was neither a genius nor a dandy but a fat, fortyish, low-keyed professional matter-of-factly doing his unglamorous job.

Hammett's stories are less artistically successful than his novels. They display a sure hand at characterization, dialogue, and setting, but the plots tend toward an overcomplexity which then require too much authorial explanation in the wrap-up.

Hammett ground out a precarious living in the 1920s, supplementing his income from fiction by book-reviewing: in 1924 and 1925 he wrote three reviews for *Forum,* a prestigious literary journal; from 1927 to 1929, more than 50 mystery novel reviews for the *Saturday Review of Literature;* and in 1929 and 1930, 85 mystery novel reviews for the *New York Evening Post.*

The first Continental Op novel, *Red Harvest* (1928), was originally serialized in four parts in *Black Mask* . Anaconda, Montana, familiar to Hammett from his Pinkerton days, served as the model for its setting, Personville, which its cynical inhabitants pronounce "Poisonville." The novel is primarily a thriller but offers a big sociological bonus in its scathing dissection of small-town American corruption.

The Dain Curse (1929) was the second and last Op novel, although three more Op stories appeared later. It is a broken-backed novel, the plot of which seems exhausted a third of the way in but is then surprisingly reopened. It is less sociological than *Red Harvest* but even more sensational. It involves multiple murder (eight in all), madness, morphine addiction, sexual phobia, and religious cultism. Its theme is mythic: beauty and innocence traduced by evil but finally redeemed by a savior (the Op).

The Maltese Falcon (1930) was perhaps Hammett's masterpiece. A new hero-detective, Sam Spade, was introduced but, unlike the Op, he does not serve as the narrator of the novel, which was written in the third person. In his introduction to the 1934 Modern Library edition Hammett said of Spade: "He is a loner, operating outside of agencies and outside of the law, but has the same code as the Op—a *personal* sense of right which supersedes civil law." Also, like the Op, Spade is street-wise, and both "have the calloused emotions needed to do their jobs effectively." Sam Spade, more than the Op, served as the prototype for hundreds of tough, wise-cracking fictional detectives; the influence at its best resulted in Raymond Chandler's Philip Marlowe and Ross MacDonald's Lew Archer; at its worst it resulted in Mickey Spillane's sex-and-violence caricature, Mike Hammer.

The Maltese Falcon theme is the destructive power of greed and the illusory nature of wealth, which is expressed through a superb symbol: the much-sought-after jewel encrusted object never appears—all the scheming and killing, ironically, are done for a worthless imitation. The novel was a huge success, reprinted seven times in its first year, and the movie rights were sold to Warner Brothers. A later remake (1941) starring Humphrey Bogart, Mary Astor, Sidney Greenstreet, and Peter Lorre became a cult classic and is unquestionably the finest of the many film adaptations of Hammett's novels.

The Glass Key (1931) was Hammett's favorite among his novels. Written in one continuous writing session of 30 hours, it is a hard-boiled variation of the traditional love triangle, of two friends in love with the same woman, played out against a backdrop of political manipulation, upperclass decadence, and murder. Its theme is the dehumanizing effect of social and political power. The book is a model of novelistic objectivity: there is no sentimentalizing, no character evaluation, and no social editorializing. Hammett dedicated the book to Nell Martin, with whom he lived in New York from 1929 to 1931.

In the 1930s Hammett spent five years on Hollywood payrolls doing very little movie writing but living lavishly and flamboyantly, and occasionally involving himself in left-wing political causes. He also wrote stories for the better-paying slick magazines such as *Collier's, Liberty,*

Harper's Bazaar, Esquire, and *American Magazine.* Although he was one of the highest-paid writers of the 1930s, his expenses usually exceeded his income. It was in Hollywood that he struck up an enduring friendship with playwright Lillian Hellman, whose work he encouraged and even occasionally revised; although a romantic legend sprang up around their love affair, Hammett remained very much a loner all of his life and lived apart from Hellman much more than with her.

The Thin Man (1934), Hammett's last novel, was banned in Canada and was labelled "amoral" by a number of magazine editors who refused to serialize it. Nick Charles, an ex-private detective who retired after marrying into wealth, reluctantly investigates a man's disappearance and some related murders. Nick's investigative style is passive: he doesn't go out in search of anyone or anything—it all comes to him. What scandalized the bluenoses was the image of a married couple, Nick and Nora, who seemed less than monogamous (long before the voguish concept of the "open marriage"). The characters who populate the novel mark a reduction in Hammett's customary energy level, but it is still an engaging, well-plotted suspense tale. Ironically, though it was perhaps artistically the weakest of Hammett's novels, it was by far his greatest commercial success. Earnings from the novel, its characters, and spin-offs from 1933 to 1950 totaled about $1 million. An interesting sidelight was the public confusion as to the identity of "the thin man," which was compounded by the photograph of the tubercularly thin Hammett on the novel's dust jacket and by the film persona created by the elegantly slim William Powell. Actually, the sobriquet applied not at all to Nick Charles, but to the missing man that Charles was seeking.

The Later Years

Perhaps a bigger mystery than any Hammett created was the virtual end, at age 39, of his career. Undoubtedly poor health exacerbated by dissipation was part of the story, but another part was his temperament. Hammett never took fame seriously, nor did extremes of poverty and affluence ever seem to affect him deeply. Above all, he seems not to have been at all ambitious.

"Dash," as his friends called him, was a prematurely gray-haired, nattily-dressed, slender six-footer who was (despite his fondness for privacy) universally well-liked. He was a "night writer," one who preferred writing in the wee small hours. He was also an inveterate reader who especially admired the work of Scott Fitzgerald, Ernest Hemingway, Ben Hecht, Robinson Jeffers, and William Faulkner; the last, in fact, became a good friend and drinking companion.

During World War II, at the age of 48, Hammett enlisted as a private in the Army and edited an Alaskan army camp newspaper, *The Adakian,* from 1944 to 1945. He was honorably discharged as a sergeant in 1945 and began teaching writing courses at Jefferson School of Social Science, a Marxist institute in New York City. In the late 1940s Hammett was earning $1,300 a week for three weekly radio serials using his fictional characters Sam Spade, the Thin

Man, and the Fat Man (Caspar Gutman from *The Maltese Falcon*).

In 1951, however, Hammett's fortunes took a downward turn. He became one of many victims of the superpatriotic hysteria that characterized post-war American political life. Hammett had for some years been president of the New York Civil Rights Congress, and when it posted bail for a group of Communists on trial for conspiracy, four of whom jumped bail and disappeared, Hammett was subpoenaed. His subsequent refusal to reveal the sources of the bail fund resulted in a contempt citation, the cancellation of his Sam Spade radio series, and imprisonment. The irony of his political victimization was striking: Hammett's active connection with the Communist movement was, by all accounts, very slight. Lillian Hellman, in fact, later said that as far as she knew Hammett had never once been to the congress' offices and hadn't known the name of even one contributor. But he had told her, "If it were my life, I would give it for what I think democracy is . . . (but) I don't let cops or judges tell me what I think democracy is."

After serving five months in prison he was released but then immediately charged by the Internal Revenue Service with $100,000 in back taxes. In 1953 he appeared as a polite but unsympathetic witness before a Senate committee investigating pro-Communist books on overseas library shelves; the committee, headed by the infamous Joseph McCarthy, branded Hammett's books as "subversive" and recommended their removal!

Money and health gone forever, Hammett spent his last years in alcoholic seclusion, living in a small rural cottage in Katonah, New York, and spending his summers at Lillian Hellman's house on Martha's Vineyard, Massachusetts. Here he suffered a heart attack in 1955. He died on January 10, 1961, at Lenox Hill Hospital in New York City.

Further Reading

The two major biographical sources are Richard Layman's *Shadow Man: The Life of Dashiell Hammett* (1981) and Diane Johnson's *Dashiell Hammett* (1983). A more personal view may be found in Lillian Hellman's four memoirs, *Pentimento, Scoundrel Time, An Unfinished Woman,* and her introduction to a reprint of some of Hammett's work, *The Big Knockover* (1972). There is also a lovingly humorous fictional portrait in Joe Gores' parodistic thriller *Hammett* (1975).

Additional Sources

Johnson, Diane, *Dashiell Hammett, a life,* New York: Random House, 1983.
Layman, Richard, *Shadow man: the life of Dashiell Hammett,* New York: Harcourt Brace Jovanovich, 1984, 1981.
Nolan, William F., *Hammett: a life at the edge,* New York: Congdon & Weed: Distributed by St. Martin's Press, 1983.
Symons, Julian, *Dashiell Hammett,* San Diego: Harcourt Brace Jovanovich, 1985. □

James Henry Hammond

James Henry Hammond (1807-1864) was governor of South Carolina and a U.S. senator. He was a radical proponent of the doctrine of states' rights.

James Henry Hammond was born on Nov. 17, 1807, in the Newberry district of South Carolina. After graduating from South Carolina College (now the University of South Carolina), he established a successful law practice in Columbia. In 1831 he married Catherine E. Fitzsimmons, an heiress, and moved to a large cotton plantation on the Savannah River.

In 1832 Senator John C. Calhoun of South Carolina, outraged by new tariffs, engineered a state convention that passed an ordinance nullifying the federal policies and preparing the state for armed resistance to federal attempts to enforce them. During this crisis Hammond took an extreme position, advocating secession from the Union if the tariff was not repealed. As a member of the House of Representatives from 1834 to 1836, Hammond bitterly attacked the abolitionists, whom he felt should be subject to the death penalty.

During his term as governor from 1842 to 1844, Hammond converted the Citadel at Charleston, S.C., into a military academy, advocated public education, and conducted a state agricultural survey. He again urged the legislature to secede rather than accept tariff increases. This

proposal, originated by Robert Barnwell Rhett, was blocked by Calhoun, whose supporters persuaded the legislature to follow a more moderate course. In 1850 Hammond attended the Nashville Convention of Southern States as a secessionist.

Hammond's unwillingness to ally himself with either the Rhett or Calhoun factions prevented him from becoming a senator until 1857. During his term as senator, to the dismay of South Carolinians, he abandoned his secessionist views, for he had become convinced since 1850 that most Southerners had no desire to leave the Union as long as their rights were protected. He now urged Southerners to make concessions to Northern antislavery opinion, for he felt that Southern intransigence played into the hands of the abolitionists. His moderate views and his condemnation of proposals to reopen the slave trade lost him popularity at home. He did not favor secession after Abraham Lincoln's election for he saw no threat to Southern rights, but, yielding to pressure, he resigned from the Senate.

During the Civil War ill health kept Hammond from participating actively in Confederate politics, apart from one unsuccessful effort to persuade the Confederate government to make cotton the basis of credit. He died on Nov. 13, 1864, leaving an estate that included more than 300 slaves.

Further Reading

Elizabeth Merritt, *James Henry Hammond, 1807-1864* (1923), is a study of the man and his time. Charles Edward Cauthen, *South Carolina Goes to War, 1860-1865* (1950), describes Hammond's early views on secession. See also Chauncey Samuel Boucher, *The Nullification Controversy in South Carolina* (1916).

Additional Sources

Faust, Drew Gilpin., *James Henry Hammond and the Old South: a design for mastery*, Baton Rouge: Louisiana State University Press, 1982. □

Lawrence and Lucy Hammond

The English historians John Lawrence Le Breton Hammond (1872-1952) and Lucy Barbara Hammond (1873-1961) were joint authors of a number of histories of the English working class.

Lawrence Hammond was born at Drighlington, Yorkshire, on July 18, 1872. His future wife, Lucy Barbara Bradby, was born in London in July 1873. Both were children of Anglican clergymen with working-class parishes, Lawrence's in the industrial north, Barbara's among the London docks. Both Lawrence and Barbara attended Oxford University, he at St. John's College, where he studied classics, and she at Lady Margaret Hall, where she was known as one of the most brilliant students of her time. They were married in 1901.

In 1897 Lawrence Hammond entered a career in journalism as a writer for the *Leeds Mercury* and the *Liverpool Post*. Two years later he became editor of the new liberal weekly, the *Spectator*, which had been launched to oppose British imperialism in South Africa. In 1907 he left journalism to become secretary of the Civil Service Commission for six years. He returned to journalism after the war as correspondent for the *Manchester Guardian* and remained with this newspaper for the rest of his life.

After their marriage, the Hammonds began work on a series of social histories of the British labor class, extending from the later 18th to the mid-19th century. *The Village Labourer, 1760-1832* (1911) was the first to appear. In it they describe the changes that 18th-century parliamentary enclosures brought about in the villagers' way of life, the gradual isolation of the poor, and the laborers' revolts of the early 1830s. "The book," wrote Gilbert Murray, "had on its readers almost the effect of a revelation." Enclosures and the transformation of the laboring class had been looked upon as the necessary requisites for Britain's industrialization. Historians had emphasized the way these had contributed to Britain's progress in the 19th century. Here, however, the Hammonds assessed the cost of industrialization to its victims. They showed the suffering and degradation of the dispossessed amid the material success and the idealism of the early 19th century. Their next work, *The Town Labourer, 1760-1832,* appeared in 1917, and the last volume in the trilogy, *The Skilled Labourer, 1760-1832,* in 1919. They also wrote *Lord Shaftesbury* (1923), *The Rise of Modern Industry* (1925), *The Age of the Chartists* (1930), *The Bleak Age* (1934), and *C. P. Scott of the Manchester Guardian* (1934).

The Hammonds spent most of their later lives at Picott's End outside London. Here, wrote Arnold Toynbee, they lived in "Desert-Father austerity," surrounded by dogs, cats, and "a permanent congregation of birds, standing as expectantly as the birds in Giotto's picture of St. Francis."

Lawrence Hammond died on April 7, 1952. Barbara Hammond, grieving, went into a slow and irreversible decline. She died, after prolonged illness, on Nov. 14, 1961.

Further Reading

There is an excellent biographical study of Lawrence Hammond by R. H. Tawney in *Proceedings of the British Academy,* vol. 46 (1960). A charming personal memoir of the Hammonds is in Arnold J. Toynbee, *Acquaintances* (1967). See also Matthew A. Fitzsimons and others, eds., *The Development of Historiography* (1954), and Arthur Marwick, *The Nature of History* (1970). □

Hammurabi

Hammurabi (reigned 1792-1750 B.C.) was a Babylonian king. One of the outstanding rulers of early antiquity, he is especially known as a lawgiver, the author of the code which bears his name.

Nothing is known of the early life of Hammurabi. His name, sometimes written Khammurapikh, is West Semitic, and he was the sixth ruler of the Amorite dynasty founded by Shumu-Abum in 1894 B.C. On his accession Hammurabi inherited a kingdom of moderate size, one of a number of Mesopotamian city-states.

The first years of Hammurabi's reign were spent in consolidating his rule and in diplomatic maneuvers which strengthened his position; in alliance with Rim-Sin, king of neighboring Larsa, he repelled the Elamites from the eastern frontier, but in his thirtieth year he turned against his former ally; Rim-Sin capitulated, and Hammurabi became master of the south. He then conquered the kingdom of Mari, and in 1759 that city was razed by his orders. Eshnunna and Assyria soon fell to him as well.

These successes established Hammurabi as the leading power in western Asia. He controlled the trade routes to the west and may even have campaigned beyond the Euphrates, though the once popular identification of Hammurabi with "Amraphel, King of Shinar" (Genesis 14:9), does not nowadays find credence. His organization of the captured territories is known from letters he sent to his officials and the governors of provinces; these show him as an able administrator who supervised in person every aspect of his government.

Code of Hammurabi

The code of laws published by Hammurabi's order in every city of his realm has survived in several copies, the most complete being a stele of polished black diorite 8 feet high found at Susa, whither it had been carried by a later conqueror. The laws, originally 282 in number, do not form a complete code in the modern sense but are rather a series of enactments dealing with specific cases in which reform or clarification was needed.

They deal with a variety of subjects: marriage and inheritance, slavery, debt and usury, and the activities of trader, farmer, and tavern keeper. Compensation for specific injuries, the fees of surgeon and barber and veterinarian, a scale of punishments for assault and theft, the wages of laborers, and charges for the hire of boats and livestock are all laid down.

In the prologue to his code, the King declares his desire to "establish justice," and at the end he declares that through his enactments "the strong shall not injure the weak, and the orphan and the widow shall receive justice." Although this was not a new concept—earlier compilations of laws are known—Hammurabi yet stands out as one of the great humanitarian figures of history.

Further Reading

The Code of Hammurabi is translated and edited, with a good commentary, by Godfrey R. Driver and John C. Miles in *The Babylonian Laws* (2 vols., 1952-1955). For a brief summary of the contents see James G. Macqueen, *Babylon* (1964). Leonard W. King, *The Letters and Inscriptions of Hammurabi* (3 vols., 1898-1900), is a selection of the correspondence, but the letters are widely scattered in later publications too numerous to enumerate. *The Cambridge Ancient History,* 3d ed., vol. 2, pt. 1, has an excellent chapter by C. J. Gadd entitled "Hammurabi and the End of His Dynasty." F. M. T. Böhl, *King Hammurabi of Babylon in the Setting of His Time* (1946), should also be consulted. □

John Hampden

The English statesman John Hampden (1594-1643) was a leader of Parliament in its resistance to Charles I.

John Hampden was one of the largest landowners in Buckinghamshire. By his mother he was related to Oliver Cromwell. He received a Latin grammar school education and attended Magdalen College, Oxford. His principal interest was the reading of classical and modern history, from which he derived his political principles.

Hampden's estate would have fitted him to take up a peerage during the reign of James I, but he had already become opposed to the court. He sat in the Parliament of 1621 and in all succeeding parliaments until his death. In 1625 he opposed a loan to Charles I not sanctioned by Parliament. He was also the ally and literary executor of Sir John Eliot, the most ideologically extreme leader of the opposition in Charles I's early parliaments.

In 1632 the Earl of Warwick granted lands to Hampden and others in Connecticut, which showed Hampden's continued alliance with the leaders of the parliamentary opposition. When the refusal of Warwick and Lord Saye to pay ship money did not provoke the King to prosecute them, Hampden refused to pay his assessment in 1635. The King did prosecute Hampden. He was represented by Oliver St. John, and in the momentous decision of the case 5 of the 12 judges refused to uphold the government. This was a grave blow to the King's legal position; it became the most famous event in Hampden's career.

When Parliament met in 1640, Hampden was the spokesman of opposition to ship money. His chief importance in the Long Parliament, however, became that of a master political organizer and tactician. He never led in debate but always waited until the issues had been discussed at length before making a short and pithy speech to bring the issue to an apparently agreed conclusion, but one which actually conformed to his own policy. He worked closely with Lord Saye, the most effective opposition member of the House of Lords.

The attempt of Charles I to arrest Hampden, John Pym, and the other "Five Members" of the Commons determined Hampden on a militant course of resistance to the King. He raised troops in Buckinghamshire and was active in campaigning against the King. Although Parliament's lord general, the Earl of Essex, was more hesitant in his opposition to the King than Hampden, Essex relied heavily on Hampden's military and political advice. But Hampden's political leadership was cut short. In a typically vigorous attack on Prince Rupert's forces on June 18, 1643, Hampden received a wound in his shoulder at Chalgrove Field in his native Buckinghamshire. The wound became gangrenous, and he died a few days later.

Basically it was Hampden's principled support of Parliament which won the support of the political nation between 1635 and 1642. The same principles were adhered to by his son, Richard, and grandson, John Hampden, who were leading opponents of the later Stuarts and architects of the Glorious Revolution of 1688.

Further Reading

G. N. Grenville, Baron Nugent, *Some Memorials of John Hampden* (1832; 2d ed. 1854), remains the basic study. Hugh Ross Williamson, *John Hampden* (1933), is a popularized biography. John Drinkwater, *John Hampden's England* (1933), presents a highly favorable account of the man.

Additional Sources

Adair, John Eric, *A life of John Hampden, the patriot (1594-1643)*, London: Macdonald and Jane's, 1976. □

Wade Hampton

The American planter Wade Hampton (ca. 1751-1835) played a major role in the economic and political development of South Carolina and became one of the wealthiest planters in the South.

Born in Halifax County, Va., Wade Hampton was a descendant of a Jamestown settler of 1630. Prior to the American Revolution, his parents decided to seek their fortune on the frontier of South Carolina. There, except for Wade and three of his brothers, the family was massacred by Indians in 1776.

During the early years of the Revolution, Hampton was reluctant to declare his allegiance to either the Revolutionaries or the English crown. But after he began selling provisions to the American troops, he accepted a commission from the patriots and established a notable military reputation.

Shortly after the Revolution, Hampton purchased a sizable block of land near Columbia, the new capital of South Carolina. He cultivated tobacco and grains. By 1790 he owned 86 slaves and worked over 1,000 acres of land. After the invention of the cotton gin, he turned to cotton production. In 1799 he reportedly harvested nearly $90,000 worth of cotton. He is generally credited with being one of the first planters in South Carolina to demonstrate that large-scale production of cotton could be profitable. He also had extensive landholdings in Mississippi and Louisiana, where over 3,000 slaves produced cotton and sugarcane.

In the Southern tradition of public service, Hampton was active in South Carolina politics, serving as a delegate to the state assembly and as a member of the convention that ratified the U.S. Constitution. He represented South Carolina twice in the U.S. Congress. In addition, he was a justice of the peace and served briefly as sheriff.

At the threat of war with England, Hampton again became active in the Army. When the War of 1812 broke out, he was placed under the command of Gen. James Wilkinson as a brigadier general. But bad feelings erupted, and after the campaign against Montreal, Wilkinson held Hampton responsible for the defeat. Although Hampton was exonerated by the War Department, he resigned his commission and returned to South Carolina. At his death in 1835, he was reputed to be the wealthiest planter in the United States.

Further Reading

There is no full-length biography of Hampton. Extensive references to his careers in the Army and public service can be found in the work about his noted descendant written by Manly Wade Wellman, *Giant in Gray: A Biography of Wade Hampton of South Carolina* (1949). For references to Hampton's career as a planter see Ulrich B. Phillips, *Life and Labor in the Old South* (1929). A brief but accurate sketch of Hampton's life, written for public schools, is in Helen Kohn Hennig, *Great South Carolinians* (2 vols., 1940). □

Wade Hampton III

Wade Hampton III (1818-1902) was a Confederate general, South Carolina governor, and U.S. senator. In the 1880s he dominated politics in his native state.

Wade Hampton III was descended from a prominent South Carolina family. Born on March 28, 1818, in Charleston, he graduated from South Carolina College. He took up law studies briefly but abandoned them for the life of a planter and became a typical antebellum Southern aristocrat, with large land-holdings, many slaves, and several terms in his state's legislature.

With the coming of the Civil War in 1861, Hampton raised and commanded the elite "Hampton's Legion." Although he was wounded in action several times, his valor and determination brought him steady promotion. By 1865 he was a lieutenant general. By war's end he was commanding all cavalry in Robert E. Lee's Army of Northern Virginia. Hampton was an expert horseman and renowned for his physical strength. An associate described him as "six feet in height, broad-shouldered, deep chested, ... with legs which, if he chose to close them in a grip, could make a horse groan with pain."

After the war Hampton encouraged Southerners to accept their defeat graciously. He set an example for better race relations by constructing a school and a church for emancipated slaves. He also led in advocating civil and political rights for freed slaves.

Hampton spent the Reconstruction period on his Mississippi plantation, meanwhile serving as vice president of the Carolina Life Insurance Company. In 1876 he ran for governor of South Carolina against the incumbent, Daniel Chamberlain, a Maine carpetbagger (a Northerner seeking private gain under the Reconstruction). Whites banded together behind Hampton and simultaneously wooed and coerced African American votes. More ballots were cast than there were voters; each side claimed victory and installed rival legislatures. The intervention of President Rutherford B. Hayes in 1877 finally enabled Hampton to begin his 2-year term in office.

Hampton was elected to the U.S. Senate in 1878 and served for 13 uneventful years. From 1893 to 1897 he was U.S. commissioner of railroads. He died on April 11, 1902, in Columbia.

Historian Douglas Freeman wrote of Hampton: "To strangers he was reserved though always courteous, the gentleman as surely as the aristocrat; with his friends he was candid, cordial and free of any suggestion of the Grand Seigneur."

Further Reading

Manly Wade Wellman, *Giant in Gray: A Biography of Wade Hampton of South Carolina* (1949), the best study of Hampton, lacks balance. Hampton's wartime exploits are fully discussed in Edward L. Wells, *Hampton and His Cavalry in '64* (1899), and Douglas S. Freeman, *Lee's Lieutenants: A Study in Command* (1942-1944). For Hampton's postwar career see Francis B. Simkins, *The Tillman Movement in South Carolina* (1926), and William W. Ball, *The State That Forgot: South Carolina's Surrender to Democracy* (1932). □

Knut Hamsun

The novels of the Norwegian author Knut Hamsun (1859-1952) introduced a new style and concept of character into European literature. He received the 1920 Nobel Prize in literature.

Knut Hamsun was born on Aug. 4, 1859, in Lom (Gudbrandsdal). When he was 3, the family moved above the Arctic Circle, where the majestic Nordland nature left a lasting impression on his mind and art. After an impoverished and lonely childhood with little schooling, he worked for 14 years at a variety of jobs in Norway and America while struggling to become a writer.

Hamsun's breakthrough came when he was nearly 30, with the anonymously published first part of *Hunger* (1888), which made him immediately famous in Scandinavia. Based on his own experiences as a starving writer, the novel departed sharply from the prevailing literary realism. It does not give an objective picture of the world: everything is seen through the protagonist's eyes, and reality is shaped and colored by his physical and mental state. Hamsun is not concerned with social issues but with the mental activity and bizarre actions of his unique, tormented hero. Hamsun's style—lyric and brutal, serious and comic—was as individualistic as his hero.

In a famous essay, "On the Unconscious Life of the Mind" (1890), as well as in public attacks on Norway's reigning literary giants, Hamsun called for a radically new kind of literature, devoted to the individual, whom he saw as governed by psychic activity too delicate to be communicated through prevailing literary techniques. His views were based on personal experience and on his reading of Fyodor Dostoevsky and certain pre-Freudian philosophers of the unconscious.

Hamsun's authorship is usually divided into two periods. The greatest novels of the first period—*Hunger* (1890), *Mysteries* (1892), *Pan* (1894), and *Victoria* (1898)—deal with outsiders, socially and metaphysically alone. Beginning with *Pan,* one of Norwegian literature's most beautiful novels, a new lyric tone appears, as nature begins to play a more prominent role.

Hamsun's second period began in 1913, although not abruptly. From this time on, his novels are told in a fairly traditional third-person form and deal with the lives of many people. These novels also express a deep-rooted dislike for all aspects of modern culture and a love (which amounts to envy) for simple people who live out their lives close to the soil. Hamsun himself settled finally with his family on a large farm in southern Norway but spent much time away from it, writing novels which exhort others to return to the soil.

The most famous of Hamsun's later novels, *Growth of the Soil* (1917), is the monumental story of a man—the opposite in every respect of Hamsun's early heroes—who comes to the wilderness and carves out a farm with his bare hands, working in harmony, rather than in competition, with nature.

By far the richest of Hamsun's later books are the three novels about the fabulous liar, musician, and inventor August: *Vagabonds* (1927), *August* (1930), and *The Road Leads On* (1933). August is the restless, eternally dissatisfied wanderer from the first novels, now become a kind of cultural hero—or villain—who acts as a catalyst in the chemistry of man's discontent with the status quo.

During World War II Hamsun supported the Nazi government in occupied Norway. After the war he was heavily fined but escaped further punishment because he was judged mentally incompetent. His last book, *On Overgrown Paths* (1949), written when he was nearing 90, brilliantly contradicts this judgment. In its lyricism, its humor, its merciless study of the outsider—this time Hamsun himself—it compares favorably with his first novels. He died at his farm, Nørholm, on Feb. 19, 1952.

Further Reading

The finest study in English of Hamsun's early novels is James W. McFarlane, *Ibsen and the Temper of Norwegian Literature* (1960). Harold Beyer, *A History of Norwegian Literature* (1956), and Brian W. Downs, *Modern Norwegian Literature, 1860-1918* (1966), both contain balanced discussions of Hamsun's entire authorship. A useful examination of Hamsun's work is also in Alrik Gustafson, *Six Scandinavian Novelists* (1940).

Additional Sources

Ferguson, Robert, *Enigma: the life of Knut Hamsun,* New York: Farrar, Straus & Giroux, 1987. ☐

Hassan Hanafi

Egyptian philosopher Hassan Hanafi (born 1935) interpreted Islamic philosophy to the Western world and Western philosophy to the Arabic world.

B eginning in his student days and continuing throughout his career, Hanafi (also known as Hanfi in the Middle East) showed an interest in exploring both Islamic philosophic traditions and Western philosophy and in developing relationships between these cultural heritages that have sometimes clashed. Born in Cairo on February 13, 1935, Hanafi began teaching in the University of Cairo while he was still an undergraduate there. Gifted with an inquiring mind, he found himself wondering about the contradictions between what he learned from his instructors and what he read in books by such distinguished Islamic thinkers as Hassan al-Banna and Sayyid Qutb, the latter of whom influenced him deeply. Simultaneously he was attracted by writings of the French sociologist Guyau, the philosopher Bergson, and the German idealists Kant, Fichte, Schelling, and Hegel.

After earning his B.A. in 1956, Hanafi studied at the University of Paris (the Sorbonne) for ten years. Here he continued to explore the relations between Western and Arabic philosophy. He was greatly influenced by Jean Guitton, the foremost philosopher in Paris at that time. In 1959 and 1960 he read the complete works of Edmund Husserl in the German language. He came to admire the great philosophers of protest, Spinoza and Kierkegaard. From Paris he went to Rome for the 1964 sessions of Vatican Council II.

Already in the Paris years Hanafi did extensive writing. With colleagues he prepared for publication two volumes by Abu al Hussain al-Basri (*Al Mu'tamad Pi Usul al-Fiqh* 1964, 1965). At the same time he was completing and publishing his two doctoral dissertations and a third book in French. In these three volumes he investigated European Consciousness from the point of view of a non-European researcher, declaring the end of European Consciousness and a new beginning of Third World Consciousness. He also used phenomenological methods for the study of religion.

After completing his Ph.D. in 1966 Hanafi joined the faculty of Cairo University. In the following years he translated several European works into Arabic: an *Anthology of Christian Philosophy in the Middle Ages,* Spinoza's *Tractatus Theologico-Politicus* (to show the use of reason in religion and politics, to show the application of historical criticism to sacred scriptures, and to define the role of a free citizen in a free country), Gotthold Ephram Lessing's *Education of the Human Race,* and Jean-Paul Sartre's *The*

Transcendence of the Ego. Meanwhile, he was developing his own philosophy in a series of books. The titles of some of them (translated into English) gave significant clues to their purposes: *Contemporary Issues,* Volume I on Arabic thought (1976) and Volume II on Western thought (1977); *Tradition and Modernism* (1980); *Islamic Studies* (1981); and the five-volume *From Dogma to Revolution* (*Min al-Aqida ila al-thaura*; 1986).

Hanafi's reputation brought him many invitations for visiting professorships at the University of Toulouse (1969), the University of Louvain (1970), Temple University (1971-1975), the University of Khartoum (1976, 1977), the University of Kuwait (1979), the University of Fes, Morrocco (1982-1984), and the University of Tokyo (1984-1985). From 1985 to 1987 he was scientific consultant in the United Nations University in Tokyo. In 1988 he returned to his home base in Cairo University.

To those westerners who thought of Islam in terms of religious dogmatism and fanaticism, Hanafi's work came as a surprise. He saw it as a continuation of a classical Islamic tradition of rationality and universalism. Avicenna (ca. 980-1037), the Arabian physician and philosopher, was the author of treatises that influenced European medical thought from the late 12th to the 17th century; and Averroes (1126-1198), the Spanish-Arabian philosopher, made Aristotle familiar to Western Europe and thus influenced the Christian thought of Thomas Aquinas. In a comparable way Hanafi sought to develop out of the Islamic tradition a philosophy that welcomed the best in modern rationality. He stated his program in two "Platforms" issued in Egypt: "al-Turath wa al-Tajdid" and "Our Situation from Western Tradition: Introduction to Westernization."

In the structure of his philosophy, Hanafi developed a "triple feeling theory," appropriating historical feeling, speculative feeling, and practical feeling as resources for rebuilding Islamic culture. He found in Islamic monotheism the basis for a universalism of ethical principle, in which the norm and criterion is "the Good Deed." He sometimes referred to the "three horizons" of human experience: spiritual values, science, and technology. He advocated a synthesis of the three: "If Science affirms man as cognition, Technology links him to Nature and Spiritual Values incite him to face eternity."

Further Reading

The best source for Hanafi's thinking was his own publications. Additional information on Hassan Hanafi and on Islamic thought can be found in Kazuo Shimogaki, *Between Modernity and Post-Modernity: The Islamic Left* and *Dr. H. Hanafi's Thought: A Critical Reading* (Japan: 1988). Another Muslim philosopher, Shabbir Akhtar, in *A Faith for All Seasons* (1991) proposed that Islam should consider being more pluralistic and humanistic and less theistic. ☐

John Hancock

John Hancock (1737-1793) signed the Declaration of Independence and was a leader of the movement

toward revolution in the American colonies. Later prominent in the Continental Congress, he was elected Massachusetts governor for nine terms.

Born at Braintree, Mass., on Jan. 23, 1737, John Hancock was reared in the piety and penury of a Congregational minister's household. He was 7 when his father died and he became a ward of his uncle, a prominent Boston merchant. Hancock graduated from Harvard in 1754, served for a time in his uncle's office as a clerk, and went to London in 1760 as the firm's representative. In England he witnessed the pageantry unfurled for the new king, George III, but he was not enthralled by life in the imperial capital and returned to his Boston mansion. In 1763 Hancock became a partner in his uncle's prosperous importing and provisioning business.

When his uncle died in 1764, Hancock inherited property worth almost £70,000. As a merchant prince, he naturally resisted Britain's attempt to restrict colonial trading via the Stamp Act, which was later repealed. But Hancock's mercantile ventures soon led to evasive tactics that were, in fact, smuggling.

Pushed to prominence by more militant men, Hancock was elected to the Massachusetts General Court in 1766. The British seizure of one of his smuggling vessels, the *Liberty,* became a cause célèbre and made him a popular hero. He received more votes than Samuel Adams in the next General Court election. Meanwhile, he was threatened

by the Crown with fines of nearly £100,000 for the *Liberty* affair. Though the fines were never collected, neither was Hancock's ship returned.

Growing Anti-British Sentiment

British military and revenue policies after 1768 were exploited by Samuel Adams and other anti-British agitators. The Boston Massacre of 1770 increased colonial animosity and established a tension that was nurtured by the militant patriots. Hancock, for a time, wavered. However, when the tide of public opinion became clear, he announced that he was totally committed to the patriot cause, even if it cost him his life and his fortune. This took some courage.

In the rush of later events, as the Boston Tea Party of 1773 brought on more coercive laws and, finally, the Boston Port Bill of 1774, Hancock's reputation mounted. By 1775 his name was synonymous with American radicalism. How much of this was thoughtful leadership on his part and how far he had been pushed by Adams is uncertain. Hancock and Adams were, after all, the only two Americans denied amnesty when British general Thomas Gage belatedly decided to try for peaceful relations.

Continental Congress

Hancock was elected president of the Continental Congress in May 1775. He longed for command of the army around Boston and was undoubtedly disappointed when George Washington was selected. He voted for, and was the first delegate to sign, the Declaration of Independence. Then Hancock resigned as president in October 1777, pleading ill health.

Meanwhile, Hancock had married Dorothy Quincy in August 1775. Though he stayed on as part of the congressional delegation, he still longed for military glory. However, his one opportunity—in the Rhode Island campaign of 1778—was undistinguished.

Hancock was embarrassed in 1777, when Harvard College sought to regain its account books and funds. Hancock had been named treasurer of the college in 1773, and he now refused to give accounts or release funds in his care. He was forced to surrender £16,000 in 1777. In 1785 Hancock admitted that he still owed his alma mater £1,054—a sum eventually paid by his heirs.

Like most public men, Hancock had enemies. Though his detractors insisted that Hancock was a shallow man who lacked conviction and was merely an opportunist, they could not prevent his election as the first governor of Massachusetts, in 1780. He was reelected repeatedly, until an impending financial crisis coincided with his voluntary retirement in 1785. Though he claimed that his retirement was based on illness, Hancock's enemies asserted that he had seen the coming storm, which was caused in part by his ineptitude in fiscal matters. After Shays' Rebellion (1786), Hancock was reelected governor.

In 1788, elected president of the Massachusetts State Convention to ratify the new Federal Constitution, Hancock was approached by Federalists who recommended a set of amendments, hinting that—if he presented them, and if

Washington declined the presidency—Hancock himself might be in line for the nation's first office. Perhaps the story is unfair, but more than one witness attested to its truth. Hancock did offer the amendments, and Massachusetts ratified the Constitution. Perhaps Hancock waited for a call that never came.

Thereafter, Hancock remained as Massachusetts governor, his popularity unchallenged. He died in office on Oct. 8, 1793.

Further Reading

The best biography of Hancock is Herbert S. Allan, *John Hancock: Patriot in Purple* (1948). William T. Baxter, *The House of Hancock: Business in Boston, 1724-1775* (1945), is a specialized study. For general background John Richard Alden, *A History of the American Revolution* (1969), is recommended. Hancock's own preserved papers are few. □

Billings Learned Hand

Billings Learned Hand (1872-1961), American jurist, was a senior judge of the Federal Circuit Court of Appeals that had jurisdiction over Vermont, Connecticut, and districts of New York.

Learned Hand was born in Albany, N.Y., on Jan. 27, 1872. His father was a leading New York lawyer. At Harvard University, Hand majored in philosophy and graduated with highest honors and a Phi Beta Kappa key. As the editor of the *Harvard Advocate,* he had developed a strong leaning toward writing which showed later in his stylistically brilliant judicial decisions.

Hand remained in Cambridge to take his master's degree in philosophy in 1894. But pressure to become a lawyer was inevitable because there were so many lawyers in the family. In 2 years, during which he was editor of the *Harvard Law Review,* Hand earned his degree from the Harvard Law School.

By 1902 the young, vibrant lawyer had had his fill of closing mortgages and trying small negligence suits in Albany and moved to New York City. Within 2 years he became a partner in a first-class firm, where he remained until 1909. The American Bar Association *Journal* commented that during this period Hand was a "doughty opponent in civil cases as well as a trusted adviser of business concerns." The year he had arrived in New York, he had met and married Frances Amelia Fincke. The young couple bought a brownstone in midtown Manhattan and raised three daughters.

In 1909, as one of President William Howard Taft's first judicial appointments, Hand was made a Federal district judge for the Southern District of New York. During his tenure on the court he proved again and again his progressive leanings. During World War I, in a freedom-of-speech case concerning a possible violation of the Espionage Act of 1917 by a magazine, *The Masses,* Hand's ruling in favor of the publication and against the government was called "a notable example of fairness and self-restraint."

In 1924 Hand was named a judge of the U.S. Circuit Court of Appeals for the Second Judicial Circuit. He served there until his death in 1961, by which time he had filed over 2,400 opinions. In *Sheldon v. Metro-Goldwyn Pictures* (1936), one of the most famous opinions, the problem centered on violation of a copyright. A movie had been produced based on an actual situation; a novel covered the same incident. Hand decided that the film company had created its vehicle from the book rather than from the incident. This decision is considered one of the most critical studies of parallelism in creative expression.

His handling of lower-court decisions, in cases involving the charge of monopoly, many times set judicial precedence for decades. Hand took one year to render his decision in *United States v. Associated Press* (1943). He finally charged the Associated Press with violating the Sherman Antitrust Law when it refused to supply its news to competing papers. This decision has been called "one of the most important legal cases in the history of the American Press." Judge Hand's decisions have been used as models in many subsequent antitrust cases.

Justice Felix Frankfurter, in a *Harvard Law Review* tribute to Hand on his seventy-fifth birthday, declared, "Hand's many decisions will stand the test of time because of their insights, the morality of the mind which respects these insights, and the beauty with which they are expressed."

Further Reading

Many articles have been written on the work of Hand, but no full-length biography has appeared. The one book that summarizes his judicial and personal career is his *The Spirit of Liberty: Papers and Addresses,* edited by Irving Dilliard (1952; 3d ed. 1960). In his fine introduction to this volume Dilliard gives an incisive picture of Hand as a man of letters. *The Art and Craft of Judging: The Decisions of Judge Learned Hand,* edited by Hershel Shanks (1968), has a biographical introduction and annotation by the editor. □

George Frederick Handel

The dramatic English oratorios of the German-born English composer and organist George Frederick Handel (1685-1759) climaxed the entire baroque oratorio tradition. His Italian operas show a nobility of style and profundity of dramatic insight.

For half a century Handel was England's first composer. His lifelong ambition was to excel in creating Italian operas, and toward that end he developed a highly dramatic style of composition, which is to be found in all his works. Success eluded him during 30 years of Herculean labor to establish Italian opera in England until at last he turned to the creation of English oratorios, sacred and secular, which soon caught on in his adopted land and typify the English high baroque style.

George Frederick Handel (German, Georg Friedrich Händel) was born on Feb. 23, 1685, to Georg and Dorothea Händel in Halle. To study music he had to overcome his father's objections, at the same time yielding to insistence that he study law. But even before Handel had finished his course at the University of Halle in 1703, he had diligently pursued a musical career. About the age of 7 he performed at the keyboard before the duke and his court at Weissenfels and as a result became the pupil of Friedrich Wilhelm Zacchow, a composer and the organist at the Liebfrauenkirche in Halle. Zacchow taught him composition as well as organ, violin, and oboe, and by 1695 Handel was composing for these and other instruments. From 1696 until 1701, when he met the composer Georg Philipp Telemann, Handel composed voluminously. By his own testimony he "wrote like the very devil" in those days; the church cantatas and all but a few chamber works he composed at the time have disappeared.

Contact with Telemann and a meeting shortly afterward with the composer Agostino Steffani spurred Handel's operatic ambitions. In 1703 he resigned his post as organist at the Halle Domkirche and left the university, moving to Hamburg, where he joined the company of Rheinhard Keiser at the Goosemarket Theater as a violinist. Handel's exceptional skill at the keyboard soon brought him employment in that capacity in the performance of operas.

First Operas

Handel began his own operatic career with *Almira* (1704), which ran for some 20 performances at the Goosemarket Theater—a very successful run for those days. *Nero* followed in 1705, then *Florindo and Daphne,* which owing to its extraordinary length had to be produced as two separate works. (The scores for *Nero* and *Florindo and Daphne* are lost.)

Dismayed by Keiser's ineptitude and seeking richer operatic experience, Handel left for Italy in 1706. He visited Florence, Venice, Rome, and Naples during the next three seasons, meeting almost all the notable Italian musicians. His Italian journey resulted in two fine operas, *Rodrigo* (1707) and *Agrippina* (1709), produced in Florence and Venice, respectively; several dramatic chamber works, including two of the finest he ever wrote, *Apollo e Daphne* and *Aci, Galatea e Polifemo;* and equally dramatic sacred compositions, notably *La Resurezzione* and the grand motets *Dixit Dominus, Laudate Pueri,* and *Nisi Dominus.*

During a second visit to Venice in the season of 1709-1710 Handel met several persons interested in England who no doubt influenced his decision to try his luck as a freelance musician in London. However, he did not travel directly to England but stopped off at Hanover, where he accepted an offer made by the elector Georg Ludwig to be musical director of his court but requested leave almost immediately for his projected journey to England. A meeting with the manager of the King's Theatre furnished Handel with a chance to compose an opera; within 2 weeks he produced the opera *Rinaldo,* which marked the high point of the London season in 1710-1711. For better, as well as for worse, Handel's course was set for the rest of his life.

Settling in England

After a token visit to Hanover the following summer Handel returned to London, which became his permanent home. Between 1712 and 1715 he produced in rapid succession *Il pastor fido, Teseo, Silla,* and *Amadigi.* During this period he also composed a large amount of music for harpsichord, chamber ensembles, and orchestra, as well as various works for royal occasions, including the *Utrecht Te Deum and Jubilate* and the *Birthday Ode for Queen Anne,* both in 1713. These two so impressed the Queen that she awarded Handel an annual salary of £200.

Between 1715 and 1719 Handel produced several of his most famous works for orchestra and for smaller vocal ensembles. Queen Anne, who died in 1714, was succeeded by Georg Ludwig, Handel's former employer at Hanover, who now became George I, King of England. In 1715 Handel provided music for a royal pleasure cruise on the Thames for the King, his mistresses, and several barge-loads of courtiers—the famous *Water Music.*

In 1716 Handel accompanied his new monarch to Hamburg, while there composing the *St. John Passion* oratorio (based on a libretto by Berthold Heinrich Brockes), which, again, he finished within an incredibly short period. In 1717 he became musical director for the Earl of Carnarvon (later the Duke of Chandos) at his palatial home,

Cannons, where Handel composed the famous *Chandos Anthems,* wrote music for John Gay's *Acis and Galatea* and Alexander Pope's *Haman and Mordecai,* and composed a great quantity of instrumental music.

Operas for the Royal Academy

In 1719 Handel accepted an invitation to join forces with Giovanni Bononcini and Attilio Ariosti in the activities of the newly founded Royal Academy of Music. After traveling to Germany in search of singers, Handel wrote *Radamisto* for the academy's first season. In 1721 he collaborated in the composition of a composite opera, *Muzio Scaevola:* Bononcini composed the first act; Filippo Mattei, the second; and Handel, the third, which won the day.

Handel's operas *Floridante, Ottone,* and *Flavio* marked the third, fourth, and fifth seasons of the Royal Academy; despite their success the academy did not prosper. In 1724, to make up for the disastrous failure of Ariosti's opera *Vespasiano,* Handel very speedily brought *Giulio Cesare* to the boards, which had a resounding success. Bononcini was dismissed shortly before the production of Handel's *Tamerlano* in 1724, and Ariosti found himself without an engagement in 1725, the year for which Handel produced *Rodelinda,* another of his most successful operas.

In 1726 Handel became a naturalized Englishman and was appointed composer of music to the Chapel Royal. The season of 1727 saw the production of Handel's *Alessandro,* which marked the beginning of an intense rivalry between Faustina Bordoni and Francesca Cuzzoni, two prima donnas whose enmity greatly harmed the cause of Italian opera in London. Trouble between the two grew apace in the seventh season of the Royal Academy, during which Handel's *Admeto* and *Riccardo I* were performed, and at last erupted into violence during the production of Bononcini's *Astianatte,* when the ladies actually engaged in fisticuffs on stage, much to the delight of Joseph Addison, who described the event in the *Spectator,* and of John Gay, who inserted a parallel scene in his *Beggar's Opera.* Other factors no doubt lent weight to the growing public disenchantment, but this single event seemed to crystallize native opposition to Italian opera in London and introduced a succession of developments which led to its fall. The denouement came with the unprecedented success of the *Beggar's Opera* (1728). Despite Handel's best efforts with *Siroe* and *Tolomeo,* the first Royal Academy of Music failed.

Apparently undismayed, Handel immediately formed the New Royal Academy of Music in partnership with the Swiss entrepreneur Johann Jakob Heidegger. After a whirlwind trip to the Continent to audition new singers and to visit his mother, now blind and alone at Halle, Handel returned to London in time to open the new season with *Lotario,* following this in a few weeks with *Partenope.* Thereafter his operas flowed forth on the average of two per year. The quality of all these operas notwithstanding—the list includes such masterworks as *Sosarme* (1732), *Orlando* (1733), *Arianna* (1734), and *Alcina* (1735)—Italian opera grew ever less popular in London. In April 1737 Handel suffered a stroke; he took a quick cure during the summer at Aix-la-Chapelle and returned to London in time to start the next season. Finally, with the miserable failure of *Imeneo* (1740) and *Deidamia* (1741), he at last gave up and wrote no more new operas.

The Oratorios

Handel's ultimate failure with operas was offset, however, by ever-increasing success with his oratorios. These provided a new vehicle, the possibilities of which he had begun to explore and experiment with nearly a decade earlier. Indeed these, along with related forms such as masques, odes, and royal occasional music, soon established a new vogue, in which Handel fared better with London audiences than he had ever done with Italian opera. As if to test a possible market for dramatic compositions in English, Handel revived *Acis and Galatea* without choruses in a performance at Lincoln's-Inn-Fields Theatre in 1731. Prospects for such nonoperatic performances must have seemed favorable, for the very next season Thomas Arne pirated a production of *Acis and Galatea* for his own profit, with choruses. Thereupon Handel immediately mounted yet another production at the King's Theatre, going his competitors one better by adding various numbers from *Aci, Galatea e Polifemo,* a work written during his Italian travels, which otherwise had little or nothing in common with the English masque.

Esther, which derived from another composition finished during Handel's stay at Cannons, was produced three times in 1732; its success indicated that producing oratorios was a profitable business. As a direct consequence, the oratorio became a regular feature of each season, with Handel leading the field, as previously he had done with Italian opera.

Deborah graced the fourth season of the New Royal Academy of Music for London audiences in 1733, and in mid-1733 Handel produced *Athalia* for Oxford. Both oratorios were very successful, and it was obvious that the new form was on its way to becoming an established feature of English concert life. During the Lenten season in 1735 Handel gave no less than 14 concerts, consisting mainly of oratorios. His music set to John Dryden's *Alexander's Feast* (1736) was successful, which perhaps explains why he not only revived several oratorios, including *Esther* and *Deborah,* but mounted as well a new version of *Il trionfo del tempo,* composed in Italy 29 years earlier.

In 1737, after Handel returned from the cure at Aix-la-Chapelle miraculously restored, he set to work on the eloquent *Funeral Anthem for the Death of Queen Caroline;* again the performance was very successful. *Saul* and *Israel in Egypt* followed in quick succession, the latter being an impressive choral triptych for the first part of which Handel revised the text of the *Funeral Anthem.* In 1739 Handel prepared his *Ode to St. Cecilia.* For his next work in this genre, he turned to Milton's *L'Allegro ed il pensieroso,* undoubtedly the finest poem he ever set to music; the performance at Lincoln's-Inn-Fields in 1740 again was an outstanding success.

In the season of 1740-1741, in which his opera *Deidamia* failed, Handel produced the oratorios *L'Allegro* and *Messiah* in Dublin, along with a great many other works. On his return to London he supervised a production of *Saul,* as well as other music, including *Hymen,* a masque revised from his opera *Imeneo.* The following season (1743-1744) saw three new works: the *Dettingen Te Deum, Semele,* and *Joseph;* and each succeeding season, a new pair: *Hercules* and *Belshazzar* (1744-1745); the *Occasional Oratorio* and *Judas Maccabeus* (1745-1746); *Alexander Balus* and *Joshua* (1747-1748); *Susanna* and *Solomon* (1748-1749); *Theodora* and the grand anthem for the Peace of Aix-la-Chapelle, for which celebration Handel also wrote the *Royal Fireworks* music (1749-1750). After he composed *The Choice of Hercules* (1750-1751) and *Jeptha* (1751), total blindness set in. Thenceforward he was limited to revising earlier works with the aid of the two John Christopher Smiths, father and son, and to improvising on organ and harpsichord in public performances. Handel's accomplishment during the last creative decade of his life seems almost miraculous when to these 20 major works are added the Italian cantatas, several concertos and concerti grossi, and other miscellaneous works. He died in London on April 14, 1759.

Working Habits

Surveying Handel's entire creative life, one gains a sense of spontaneous and incredibly abundant creative flow. This sense is confirmed by the marvelous collections of autographs preserved at the Fitzwilliam and British museums in England, which reveal not only the enormous bulk of his creative achievement but also something of his uncompromising critical judgment. There is scarcely a page without deletions and emendations; frequently, he struck out whole passages. He obviously knew the art of heavy pruning, and his works profited greatly from it.

Handel's propensity to "write like the very devil" proved invaluable, in view of the demands imposed upon his time and energies in opera composition throughout most of his career. Time after time he found it necessary to meet crises without much time for creative gestation.

When Handel first arrived in London, for instance, it was urgent that he produce an opera quickly. By borrowing from *Rodrigo* and other works, he had the complete score ready within 2 weeks. Throughout his operatic career he achieved similar feats. When he turned to oratorio composition, the situation did not change greatly. To "save" the season of 1738-1739, Handel created both *Israel in Egypt* and *Saul* within an incredibly short period; no less than 17 of the 35 numbers of *Israel in Egypt* are derived from earlier pieces. The *Messiah* was written between Aug. 22 and Sept. 12, 1741. Again he depended heavily upon earlier works, mainly the *Italian Duets* composed earlier that summer. But in this instance, as in almost all others, the product bears the stamp of original, coherent unity so convincingly as to belie borrowing.

This paradoxical aspect of Handel's genius has received a great deal of scholarly attention. But all apologetics and moralizing indictments aside, it is clearly evident that Handel was at heart a dramatic composer for whom setting the scene and atmosphere and delineating character thrust all other considerations into the background.

Further Reading

The best-balanced study in the vast literature on Handel's life and works is Paul Henry Lang, *George Frideric Handel* (1966), which shows remarkable insight into the man, his works, and his times. Gerald Abraham, *Handel; A Symposium* (1954), is a very useful collection of essays on various aspects of Handel's creative life and an indispensable handbook for the Handel student. Three works established important milestones in Handel research and scholarship: Otto E. Deutsch, *Handel: A Documentary Biography* (1955); Jens Peter Larsen, *Handel's Messiah: Origins, Composition, Sources* (1957); and Winton Dean, *Handel's Dramatic Oratorio and Masques* (1959). □

Peter Handke

Peter Handke (born 1942) was an Austrian playwright, novelist, screenwriter, essayist, and poet.

There was little evidence very early in his life that Peter Handke would one day challenge the theatrical and literary conventions of his time. Born on December 6, 1942, in the small town of Griffen in Carinthia, Austria, Handke first dreamed of becoming a priest. He entered a Jesuit seminary while still in his teens and stayed there until 1961, when he decided to study law at the University of Graz.

Perhaps it was the haunting beauty and deep, mystical silences he experienced as a sensitive child growing up among the calm, majestical mountains and forests of the lake-studded Carinthian countryside that led to his early decision to enter the priesthood. Or perhaps it was just the nature of the young man himself, who seemed forever in search of something beyond himself and the conventional world. Years later he would describe his need to write in religious terms, stating that "it was a sort of fever, almost a religious necessity, coming out of a feeling of missing something, of wanting God."

Nevertheless, although Handke began writing highly structured, short prose pieces while still in law school for a little literary magazine called *Manuskripte,* it wasn't until he left the university in 1965 that he actively began writing. His first novel, *The Hornets,* was published in 1966, followed by *The Peddler* in 1967.

In the first work a blind man tried to reconstruct what he remembered himself and the world to be like, in his pre-blindness consciousness, while in the second work, described by critics as a Kafkaesque murder mystery, Handke explored the psychic states of dread and anxiety and their effects upon the physical world. The two were excellent early examples of the style of writing that Handke would later become famous for both in his plays and in his novels. This style, which scholar Nicholas Hern in his book *Peter Handke* described as "nonsequential, nondescriptive single-sentence statements," was, according to Handke, influenced by his law studies.

In his 1967 essay "I am an Ivory Tower Dweller," Handke described in considerable detail how terrifying it

was to discover the ways in which abstract, logically arranged language could be used for death and oppression. "They altered my previous ideas about the literary presentation of dying and death; they altered my ideas about dying and death itself. I then wrote a piece that transposed the lawbook's method into literature, and that in some sentences even consisted of the authentic legal code."

Most critics agreed that much of Handke's early prose reads like a long legal document, devoid as it is of emotion, decorative effect, and conventional narrative techniques, literary devices that Handke despised and condemned his fellow postwar German writers for using. This condemnation came in a virulent attack at the 28th meeting of German writers and critics, Gruppe 47, at Princeton in April 1966 when Handke lashed out at the group for writing nothing but idiotic and decorative prose which read like a "pictorial encyclopedia" and gave people a false view of reality. Only 24 years old, Handke was the youngest writer there, and although he had yet to write the works that would ensure his literary reputation, he was immediately hailed by Gruppe 47 for his brash courage in daring to speak out against the literary establishment.

This support, and all the hoopla and publicity which followed, helped to generate considerable excitement for the opening of Handke's first play, *Offending the Audience,* which premiered at the first "Experimenta" theater week in June in Frankfurt-on-the-Main. In October of the same year two more of his plays, *Prophecy* and *Self-Accusation,* opened together in Oberhausen.

The plays caused something of an uproar in the theater world, defying as they did the stage conventions of the times. Gone were illusion and any attempts at convincing the audience that what they were seeing on stage was real or smacked of real life. Actors were actors rather than characters, and they delivered speeches instead of dialogue. At times they even hurled insults at the audience, mocking them for their complacency and gullibility.

The following year in March Handke's "speaking piece" *Cries for Help* opened in Stockholm. Hern reported that it was described by critics as "a succession of unconnected slogans, mottoes, and catchwords, spoken by one set of actors and countered with repeated noes from the other set."

It wasn't until 1968, however, that Handke's literary reputation was thoroughly secured. In that year he won the prestigious Gerhart Hauptmann Prize in Berlin, and in May his first full-length play, *Kaspar,* opened to critical acclaim in Frankfurt and Oberhausen. Later it was nominated Play of the Year by the respected magazine *Theater Heute.*

A work with all the hallmarks of Handke's thematic and stylistic concerns over language and awareness and the ways in which an individual's consciousness and self-identity were shaped by society and its accepted conventions, *Kaspar* was seen by many as a brilliant and original *tour de force.* Some, however, found it boring and pretentious, criticisms that often accompanied his works when they first appeared.

In January 1969 Handke's play *My Foot My Tutor* opened at the Frankfurt Theater. The work astounded critics by daring to present characters who would say nothing for the entire length of the performance. Later *My Foot My Tutor* would be compared to Sam Beckett's *Play Without Words.*

In the spring of 1969 Handke's first collection of short prose poems, *The Inner World of the Outer World of the Inner World,* was published, followed several months later by the premiere of his play *The Ride over Lake Constance* in Berlin and the publication of his third novel, *The Goalkeeper's Anxiety at a Penalty Kick.* The story of a deeply confused, inarticulate young man who commits a senseless murder, *The Goalkeeper's Anxiety at a Penalty Kick* deals with the same themes of loneliness, alienation, violence, and social hypocrisy that haunt almost all of Handke's works, including his later novels, *Short Letter, Long Farewell* (1972) and *The Left-Handed Woman* (1978).

However, in 1974 Handke's style became much more personal and intimate when he wrote *A Sorrow Beyond Dreams: A Life Story,* a work that recorded with deep sensitivity and insight the events of his mother's life leading to her eventual suicide.

In the years to follow, Handke's work seemed to have mellowed somewhat. His later works included *Slow Homecoming* (1985), *Across* (1987), *Repetition* (1988), and *The Afternoon of a Writer* (1989). In 1996 *A Winter Journey to the Danube, Sava, Morava, and Drina Rivers: Or Justice for Serbia* was released. With this publication, Handke maintained that the international media had been unfair to Serbia in the Balkwan civil war. He charged a German newspaper with writing "the poison that never heals, the poison of words."(*World Press Review*, July 1996), while calling the war-torn Serbia "an orphaned, abandoned child."

Further Reading

Excellent sources of commentary for a more critical perspective on Handke's work were Guenter Heintz, *Peter Handke* (1971); Nicholas Hern, *Peter Handke* (1972); and Nicholas Hern, *Peter Handke: Theater and Anti-Theater* (1971). Further discussion can be found in Elizabeth Boa and J. H. Reid, *Critical Strategies: German Fiction in the Twentieth Century* (1972); Henning Rischbieter, *Peter Handke* (1972); Siegfried Mandel, *Group 47* (1973); Frederick Ungar, editor, *Handbook of Austrian Literature* (1973); Henning Falkenstein, *Peter Handke* (1974); and Richard Gilman, *The Making of Modern Drama* (1974). □

Oscar Handlin

Pulitzer Prize winner Oscar Handlin (born 1915) ranks as one of the most prolific and influential American historians of the twentieth century, with pioneering works in the fields of immigration history, ethnic history, and social history.

Oscar Handlin was born on Sept. 29, 1915, in Brooklyn, New York City, the son of Russian Jewish immigrants. His father was involved in running a grocery store, a steam laundry, and real estate. Handlin decided to become an historian at the age of eight and began reading avidly, even while delivering groceries for his father. He graduated from Brooklyn College in 1934 after only three years, winning the Union League History Prize; one year later, he earned his master's degree at Harvard University. He had intended to study medieval history, but specialized in American history because he thought the person one studied with was more important than the field itself; the medievalist had retired, so Handlin wrote his doctoral dissertation for Arthur M. Schlesinger, Sr. Handlin taught at Brooklyn College from 1936-1938, during which time he married Mary Flug, and began his long career on the Harvard University faculty in 1939.

Handlin's dissertation was published in 1941 as *Boston's Immigrants, 1790-1865: A Study in Acculturation*. The book was highly regarded for its innovative research involving sociological concepts, census data, and the previously untapped immigrant press; in 1941, the book won the prestigious Dunning Prize from the American Historical Association for being the outstanding historical work published by a young scholar that year. The book examined immigration from the Irish migrant's viewpoint and emphasized the high psychic cost of the transatlantic social dislocation.

Handlin was a prolific writer throughout his career. In 1947, in the first of several collaborations with Mary Flug, Handlin published a study of the role played by government in developing the economy in early Massachusetts. Two years later he published an anthology of writings by European visitors to the United States, and shortly after, *The Uprooted* (1951). This work was awarded a Pulitzer Prize and added considerably to Handlin's reputation. Opening with the now famous lines: "Once I thought to write a history of the immigrants in America. Then I discovered that the immigrants *were* American history". The work considered the nature and consequences of the alienation experienced by the more than 30 million immigrants who had come to America since 1820, considered from their point of view. In addition to traditional sources, Handlin based his work on folklore, novels, and newspapers, but the work was criticized by scholars who like footnotes. Handlin provided none, a practice he continued in other works written for the general public. Nevertheless, it became his most famous book.

In 1954, the year he became a full professor at Harvard, Handlin was chief editor of *The Harvard Guide to American History,* which was quickly recognized as "one of the most authoritative bibliographic tools in the field of American history"; the same year, he published a history of American ethnic groups (*The American People in the Twentieth Century,* tracing the history of racist thought in the early 1900s, and a history of Jews in America, (*Adventure in Freedom: Three Hundred Years of Jewish Life in America*), which among other things demonstrated elements of anti-Semitism in the early 1900's Populist movement.

In *Chance or Destiny* (1955), Handlin argues that history is "a line made up of a succession of points, with every point a turning point." In *Truth in History* and *The Distor-*

tion of American, responding to the political and intellectual turmoil of the '60's and '70's, Handlin expressed disapproval of New Left historians, whom he saw as partisans, and of academic faddishness, hiring quotas, overspecialization and fragmentation in all fields of history, and deficiencies in graduate training. Handlin was strongly anti-Communist and was critical of those who opposed the war in Vietnam.

By the late 1950's Handlin was publishing a book almost yearly, with works in the fields of civil rights, liberty, ethnicity, urban history, the history of education, foreign affairs, migration, biography, adolescence even a book of poetry. Sometimes, he wrote collaboratively with Mary Flug Handlin and, after her death in 1976 and his second marriage a year later, with Lilian Handlin. In the 1960's, Handlin produced 11 books, wrote a monthly book column for *The Atlantic Monthly,,* directed the Center for the Study of Liberty in America, helped manage a commercial television station in Boston, chaired a board that oversaw Fulbright Scholarship awards all this in addition to his regular teaching duties at Harvard. From 1979-1983, he was director of the university library.

In the 1960's, Handlin wrote eight books, including the controversial *Fire Bell in the Night: The Crisis in Civil Rights* in which he criticized separatists, segregationists, and suburban liberals but also disapproved of quotas, school busing, and affirmative action, saying, "Preferential treatment demands a departure from the ideal which judges individuals by their own merits rather than by their affiliations." He also edited a 42-volume collection of books on subjects relating to immigration and ethnicity, *The American Immigration Collection* (1969). During the next three decades, Handlin wrote 12 more books, many on the subject of liberty, and edited at least 20 biographies.

Handlin was honored in 1979 with a book by several former students, *Uprooted American: Essays to Honor Oscar Handlin,* which was praised for its craftsmanship and for the testimony it provided of his influence on the historical profession. Still, there is no "Handlin school of history," nor did he try to form one. He likely will be most remembered especially for his abundant demonstrations of the importance of immigration and its role in the history of the United States.

Further Reading

A mid-career evaluation of Handlin is Maldwyn Jones's essay in Marcus Cunliffe and Robin W. Winks, eds., *Pastmasters: Some Essays on American Historians* (1969). He is also mentioned in Arthur M. Schlesinger, Sr., *In Retrospect: The History of a Historian* (1963). Handlin's work is considered in Bruce Stave, "A Conversation with Oscar Handlin," in *The Making of Urban History* (1977); and Stephen J. Whitfield, "Handlin's History," *American Jewish History,* Vol. 70, (December 1980); For an autobiography of his teaching at Harvard University, see Oscar Handlin, "A Career at Harvard," *The American Scholar,* Vol 65 (Winter 1996). □

Handsome Lake (standing)

Handsome Lake

Seneca prophet Handsome Lake (ca. 1735-1815) played a major role in the revival of his own and other Iroquois League tribes.

Handsome Lake, a great leader and prophet, played a major role in the revival of the Senecas and other tribes of the Iroquois League. He preached a message that combined traditional Iroquois religious beliefs with specific white values. This message was eventually published as the Code of Handsome Lake.

Handsome Lake was born around 1735 in the Seneca village of Conewaugus, located on the Genesee River near Avon, New York. Very little is known of his parents. He was born into the Wolf clan and was named Hadawa'ko ["Shaking Snow"], but was eventually raised by the Turtle clan people. He was a half-brother to Cornplanter and an uncle of Red Jacket. Born during a time when the Seneca nation was at its peak of prosperity, Handsome Lake witnessed the gradual deterioration of his society.

Multiple factors led to the erosion of morale and the material welfare of the Iroquois. In the period after the American Revolution, the Iroquois lost most of their land and were forced to live on reservations. The reservations provided poor living conditions, and, within a relatively short period of time, many Iroquois began to suffer alcohol abuse, fighting, instability of the family unit, and accusations of witchcraft. This dismal situation was due, in part, to the basic incompatibility of the Iroquois social structure and reservation existence. The traditional religious rituals alone were inadequate to lessen the harshness of this situation. As a result, the Iroquois began searching for new solutions to their difficulties.

Brings a Message of Gaiwiio ("Good Word")

In 1799, after a period of illness due to many years of excessive alcoholic indulgence, Handsome Lake had the first of a series of visions. In his first vision, he was warned by three spiritual messengers about the dangers associated with alcohol; he was also told that witches were creating chaos within his tribe and that the persons guilty of witchcraft must repent and confess. Handsome Lake was directed to reveal these warnings to the people. His nephew Blacksnake and half-brother Cornplanter were with him during this time and believed in the power of his visions and their revelations. Shortly after Handsome Lake's first vision, he ceased drinking alcohol. When he regained his health, he began bringing a message of Gaiwiio (the "Good Word") to his people. He preached against drunkenness and other evil practices. His message outlined a moral code that was eventually referred to as the Code of Handsome Lake. The Code outlawed drunkenness, witchcraft, sexual promiscuity, wife beating, quarreling, and gambling. Handsome Lake presented his message along with a threat that fire would destroy the world if this Code was not obeyed.

Handsome Lake soon became obsessed with witch hunting and demanded confessions from those whom he suspected of witchcraft; some of those who refused to confess were killed. His witch hunting nearly became a catalyst for war with another tribe when he accused a prominent young man from that tribe of being a witch and demanded his punishment. Gradually, the sentiment of the people turned against Handsome Lake for what they considered an overzealous pursuit of witches. As a result of this change in attitude, he stopped his accusatory methods and briefly assumed a less prominent leadership role. Handsome Lake once again became popular during the War of 1812 and attracted many new followers.

The rise of Handsome Lake's religion was more successful than most religions during that time, apparently because his code combined traditional Iroquois religion with white Christian values. It stressed survival without the sacrifice of the Iroquois identity, and recognized the realistic need to make adjustments in order to survive in their changing world. *The Code of Handsome Lake,* published around 1850, played a significant role in the preservation of the Iroquois cultural heritage and was popular throughout the Iroquois nations in Canada and in the United States. Handsome Lake, referred to as Sedwa'gowa'ne, "Our Great Teacher," died on August 10, 1815, at the Onondaga Reservation. His religious beliefs were carried on by Blacksnake

and other disciples, and his teachings remain a compelling force among the Iroquois.

Further Reading

Dockstader, Frederick J., *Great North American Indians,* New York, VanNostrand Reinhold Co., 1977; 102-103.
Leitch, Barbara A., *Chronology of the American Indian,* St. Clair Shores, Michigan, Scholarly Press, 1975; 138.
Waldman, Carl, *Who Was Who in Native American History,* Facts On File, Maple-Vail Book Mfg. Group, 1990; 144.
Wallace, Anthony F. C., "Origins of the Longhouse Religion," in *Handbook of North American Indians,* edited by William C. Sturtevant, Smithsonian Institution, 1978; 445-448. □

William Christopher Handy

The African American songwriter William Christopher Handy (1873-1958), known as the father of the blues, was the first person to notate and publish blues songs. He wrote over 60 blues, spirituals, and popular tunes.

On Nov. 16, 1873, W. C. Handy was born in Florence, Ala., the son of two Methodist ministers. He studied at Kentucky Musical College, to the dismay of his father, who regarded secular music as a branch of the devil's activities. At an early age he left home to tour with a minstrel show. As a bandleader for Mahara's Minstrels for much of the period between 1896 and 1903, he first made contract with early blues and jazz. He moved to Memphis, Tenn., and led a band that featured his attempts to incorporate blues tunes and jazz motifs into written arrangements.

In 1909 Handy wrote his first song, "Mr. Crump," for a political campaign. He changed the title to "Memphis Blues" when he published it in 1912. His most famous number, "St. Louis Blues," appeared in 1914, followed by "Yellow Dog Blues" (1914), "Beale Street Blues" (1916), "Careless (or "Loveless") Love" (1921), and many others.

Handy is a somewhat enigmatic figure; in his lifetime he was bitterly accused by some musicians of plagiarism. It seems probable that he was less the original composer he claimed to be, more a sensitive collector of traditional material. Even if this is the case, his services as a folklorist should not be minimized; probably no one else has preserved such a wealth of blues material. As a performing musician, Handy was a competent instrumentalist in the European tradition, with no apparent ability as a jazz soloist.

Handy formed his own music publishing business in 1913. This, plus the royalties from his songs, brought him considerable wealth. But in the 1930s his sight began to fail, and by 1943 he was totally blind. In his later years he worked unceasingly for his W. C. Handy Foundation for the Blind and other charitable organizations.

His first wife, Elizabeth Price, with whom he had six children, died in 1937. In 1954, at the age of 80, he married

methodology of statecraft may have influenced the creation of authoritarianism by the Ch'in dynasty.

The main source of information on Han Fei's life is a short biography by the historian Ssu-ma Ch'ien (145-86 B.C.) in his *Records of the Historian*. Han Fei was a member of the royal family of Han, a small state located in north-central China. During the 5th century Han, along with two other states, had seceded from the large state of Chin, and for the following 2 centuries Han was an important power in the Chinese state system. In the 3d century, about the time of Han Fei's birth, Han found itself confronted with a newly emerging power to the west, the state of Ch'in. Toward the end of the 4th century Ch'in embarked on an extensive military campaign to expand its territory. Since Han was Ch'in's main neighbor to the east, it was inevitable that the two states would come into conflict. Han Fei's career revolved around this rivalry between his own state and Ch'in.

Han Fei studied under the great Confucian philosopher Hsün-tzu, who had established a school in Lan-ling, a small city-state in southern Shantung Province. According to Ssu-ma Ch'ien, Han Fei stuttered and had difficulty expressing himself orally. Eloquence was an absolute requirement for a statesman of this period, for almost all of the court business was conducted orally. To compensate for his handicap, he developed skill as a writer and sent all of his opinions to the court in writing. Han Fei was one of the best writers of rhetorical prose of his time, and his prose is still admired by the Chinese.

Career in Han

Because he was from the royal family, Han Fei was able to acquire an influential position in the government, probably as one of the principal advisers to the Han king. Han Fei was particularly alarmed by the increasingly aggressive posture of Ch'in, and he sent a series of memorials to the Han ruler, enjoining him to strengthen the army, reform the laws, and dismiss incompetent and corrupt officials to counteract the Ch'in threat. The King refused to comply with his requests, and Han Fei reportedly became extremely bitter and resentful. He wrote several essays at this time declaring in blunt terms the chief reasons for the current difficulty in his state.

One of the most outspoken of the essays Han Fei wrote at this time was the "Five Vermin" (*Wu tu*), in which he blamed what he called the "vermin" (scholars, sophists, knights-errant, sycophants, and merchants and artisans) for the disorder and bad government in the state. In a second essay, "Solitary Indignation" (*Ku fen*), he complained that it was virtually impossible for a man of character and integrity to make his views known to a ruler because it was first necessary to go through the ruler's corrupt and incompetent subordinates. A third essay, on rhetorical techniques, "Difficulties of Persuasion" (*Shui nan*), described the different strategies a person should use in trying to persuade his ruler.

Han Fei in Ch'in

In 234 Ch'in attacked Han, and Han Fei was summoned back to service. In the following year he traveled to

again. He was honored by having a theater and a park in Memphis, and a library in Philadelphia named after him during his lifetime. He died in 1958; in 1959 the W. C. Handy 6-cent postage stamp was issued.

Further Reading

Handy edited *Blues: An Anthology* (1926; reprinted in 1950 as *A Treasury of the Blues*), which contains a comprehensive selection of blues by him and others and includes biographical material on Handy. Handy's *Father of the Blues* (1941) is autobiographical, revealing Handy as likeable, generous, and at times naively conservative. See also Marshall Stern, *The Story of Jazz* (1958), and Gunther Schuller, *Early Jazz: Its Roots and Musical Development* (1968). □

Han Fei Tzu

Han Fei Tzu (ca. 280-233 B.C.) was a Chinese states-man and philosopher and one of the main formula-tors of Chinese Legalist philosophy.

Elements of Chinese Legalist philosophy can be traced to the 7th century B.C., but it was Han Fei Tzu who developed the precepts of this political philosophy into its definitive form. He emphasized the complete submission of the individual to the state and stressed the importance of law in maintaining state control. His elaborate

Ch'in to attempt to dissuade Ch'in from its aggressive policy. The King of Ch'in had received copies of his "Five Vermin" and "Solitary Indignation" and was favorably impressed with them. When Han Fei arrived in Ch'in, he submitted a memorial to the King proposing that it would be to Ch'in's advantage to attack the state of Chao instead of Han. The King was about to consent to Han Fei's plan, when Han Fei's former colleague, Li Ssu, prime minister of Ch'in, objected and wrote a long reply to Han Fei's memorial. Li Ssu then conspired with another court official to arouse the King's suspicion of Han Fei. They pointed out that he was a member of the Han royal house and that he was simply concerned about the welfare of his own state. They persuaded the King to imprison Han Fei until his loyalty could be investigated. As soon as Han Fei was placed in prison, Li Ssu sent poison to him, indicating that it would be best for him to commit suicide. Since he was held incommunicado and had no way of defending himself, he drank the poison.

His Legalism

Han Fei has traditionally been identified with the philosophical school known as the *Fa-chia,* or Legalist school. It is doubtful that Han Fei actually studied under a Legalist master, for the only teacher ever associated with his name is the Confucian Hsün-tzu. The primary emphasis of Han Fei's thought was not so much philosophical as political. Most of the writings attributed to him deal with the practical methods of statecraft, and particularly the maintenance and strengthening of the ruler's power. He encouraged the ruler to undertake a series of administrative reforms, such as appointing trained officials to replace the corrupt and incompetent bureaucrats who maintained their positions solely through special privilege. He sought to encourage more agricultural production, at the same time discouraging private commerce and craftsmanship. He advocated the drafting of an elaborate system of laws that would be strictly enforced and in which there was no room for mercy to the lawbreaker. This authoritarian system appealed to the Chinese despot, and many of the policies adopted under the Chinese Empire after 221 B.C. closely resemble ideas set forth by Han Fei.

Further Reading

A useful work is *Han Fei Tzu: Basic Writings,* translated by Burton Watson (1964). *The Complete Works of Han Fei Tzu,* translated by W. K. Liao (2 vols., 1959), also contains a biography by Ssu-ma Ch'ien in volume 1. H. G. Creel, *Chinese Thought: From Confucius to Mao Tse-tung* (1953), discusses Han Fei Tzu in historical context. See also Hou Wai-Lu, *A Short History of Chinese Philosophy* (1958). □

Han Kao-tsu

The Chinese emperor Han Kao-tsu (ca. 247-195 B.C.) was the founder of the Former Han dynasty, the first major Chinese dynasty for which there are reliable and fairly full historical records.

Kao-tsu is the posthumous title given to Liu Chi, the founder of the Former Han dynasty. Little is known of his early years (indeed, it is not certain whether his name was Liu Chi or Liu Pang). He was born a commoner and was one of only two commoners to become emperors of China. Part of his youth was spent as a peasant, but he managed to receive some education. He became a low-ranking local official under the Ch'in dynasty (221-207 B.C.).

The Ch'in rulers, who ruled under the influence of a Legalistic as opposed to a Confucian philosophy, were known for their excessively harsh application of laws and punishments and for their burdensome demands on the population for taxes and labor services. In 209 rebel bands began to arise in the eastern part of the empire in opposition to Ch'in policies.

Kao-tsu, in his official capacity, had been leading a group of convict laborers from his home in Kiangsu to the Ch'in capital, where they were supposed to work on the tomb of Ch'in Shih huang-ti, the dynasty's founder. When some of the convicts fled, Kao-tsu, knowing that he was responsible for them and would be punished because of their escape, also decided to turn bandit.

Kao-tsu developed a sizable following and then attached himself to Hsiang Yü, the descendant of a family which for generations had been well known as superb military commanders for the state of Ch'u. While he conquered areas in the eastern parts of the empire, Kao-tsu led his troops westward. In 207 Kao-tsu's army occupied the Ch'in capital, Hsien-yang, thus marking the end of the detested Ch'in dynasty. Kao-tsu, in later years, dated the founding of his own dynasty from the fall of the Ch'in capital.

Character of an Emperor

Actually, however, Kao-tsu did not become emperor until 202, when he defeated Hsiang Yü, who had become his major competitor for the throne of China. Kao-tsu's personality was an important factor in his ultimate victory. He tended to be magnanimous and forgiving where Hsiang Yü was cruel and vindictive. Kao-tsu also was well attuned to the suffering that people had endured under the Ch'in regime. Thus when he entered the Ch'in capital, one of his first acts was to announce that murderers were to be executed and thieves punished according to the gravity of the offense, but that all of the hated Ch'in laws were to be abolished.

Hsiang Yü was utterly lacking in this kind of appreciation for good propaganda. Kao-tsu was an excellent judge of men. While Hsiang Yü was a superior strategist, he was not able to surround himself with capable advisers and generals as Kao-tsu was able to do.

Organization and Consolidation

Since the Ch'in capital had been razed by Hsiang Yü, Kao-tsu built a new capital at Ch'ang-an. His state structure was very similar to that of Ch'in. There was, however, an important difference between the two. The Ch'in government had abolished the old feudal states and employed central government appointees in commanderies (*chün,* roughly equivalent to modern provinces but generally smaller) and prefectures (*hsien*).

During the wars that led to the rise of Han, generals had declared themselves kings of feudal states and Hsiang Yü had enfeoffed others. Kao-tsu had been forced to recognize some of these kings in order to gain their allegiance. The result of these earlier policies was that about half of the empire was not administered by the Emperor through his commanderies and prefectures but was ruled by seven highly autonomous kings. Throughout his reign Kao-tsu devoted most of his attention to eliminating these rulers over whom he had little or no control. By 196 all but one of the kings had been killed. The remaining kingdom was small and distant from the capital; hence it did not pose a threat to the imperial throne.

However, since one of the charges frequently made against the Ch'in dynasty had been its attempt to eradicate feudalism, Kao-tsu felt that some kind of a compromise was necessary. Accordingly, by the time of his death nine of his sons and brothers had been enfeoffed, and the principle had been established that only members of the imperial family, the house of Liu, could be made kings. But following the "Rebellion of the Seven Kingdoms" in 154, the kingdoms were reduced in size and ruled by officials sent out by the central government. In effect, although not entirely in name, the Han administrative system was the same as that of the Ch'in.

In the field of foreign policy Kao-tsu's major problem was the Hsiung-nu, nomadic tribes which raided the northern Chinese border settlements. In the course of one of Kao-tsu's campaigns against a rebel Chinese king in 201 the king joined forces with the Hsiung-nu. Kao-tsu was under siege for a week and barely managed to escape.

Following these battles, Kao-tsu pursued a policy of peace with the Hsiung-nu. In exchange for their pledge not to raid the border, Kao-tsu presented a Chinese princess to the Hsiung-nu ruler as his wife, and the Chinese made annual gifts to the nomadic warriors. With a few notable exceptions, including Hsiung-nu attacks that brought them within sight of the capital in 166, Kao-tsu's policy was effectively continued for about 60 years.

Further Reading

There is no scholarly work devoted exclusively to Han Kao-tsu. Excellent materials on him and his reign are available in Burton D. Watson, *Records of the Grand Historian of China, Translated from the Shih chi of Ssu-ma Ch'ien* (2 vols., 1961). A more critical translation (with annotations) of another Han history is Homer H. Dubs's translation of Pan Ku's *History of the Former Han Dynasty* (3 vols., 1938-1955). □

Nancy Hanks

Nancy Hanks (1927-1983) was called the "mother of a million artists" for her work in building federal financial support for the arts and artists. Her years as chairwoman of the National Endowment for the Arts and of the National Council on the Arts saw great expansion of their programs and budgets.

Nancy Hanks, named for her distant cousin, the mother of Abraham Lincoln, was born on December 31, 1927, in Miami Beach, Florida. Her parents Bryan Cayce Hanks, a corporation lawyer, and Virginia (Wooding) Hanks moved to Montclair, New Jersey, when Nancy was in high school. She attended Duke University in Durham, North Carolina, where she majored in political science and served as president of the student body. During the summer of 1948 she studied at Oxford University in England. Elected to Phi Beta Kappa, she received her B.A. *magna cum laude* from Duke in 1949.

In 1951 she went to Washington, D.C., where she began as a receptionist in the Office of Defense Mobilization set up during the Korean War. She moved from that position to secretary for the President's Advisory Committee on Government Operations, chaired by Nelson A. Rockefeller. Later she continued to serve as Rockefeller's assistant, first at the Department of Health, Education, and Welfare and later at the Special Projects Office of the White House.

In 1956 Hanks left Washington and moved to New York, where she worked for 13 years as executive secretary of the Special Studies Project set up by the Rockefeller Brothers Fund. There she directed a pioneering study project on the economic and social problems of the performing arts in America that laid much of the groundwork for federal funding of the arts. The study, *The Performing Arts: Problems and Prospects* (1965), recommended the development of state and community art councils throughout the country. Hanks became a member of the board of directors of the Associated Councils on the Arts (ACA), a private, nonprofit organization to promote the activities of the newly established arts councils. Elected president of the ACA in June 1968, Hanks coordinated conferences and supervised the publication of the journal *Cultural Affairs*.

In 1964, largely as a result of the work of the Rockefellers, the government created the National Endowment for the Arts as part of the National Foundation for the Arts and Humanities. For the first time since the Great Depression, the federal government committed funds to subsidize theater companies, symphony orchestras, museums, and other cultural institutions. The endowment agency worked closely with the National Council of the Arts, which set policy and determined projects worthy of aid.

When President Richard Nixon failed to reappoint Roger L. Stevens as head of the government art agencies in 1969, Hanks was selected to search for a successor. Several celebrated figures in the arts were approached and turned the position down. Six months after the search had begun, Hanks herself was nominated for the post. After her confirmation by the Senate in October, Hanks immediately confronted the task of creating a budget for 1970-1971. Within six weeks she submitted a detailed proposal not only to double the budgets for both the arts and the humanities endowments, but to plan for future increases and program strategies in anticipation of the nation's bicentennial celebration, at that time more than six years away. To lobby for her budget Hanks spoke personally to over 200 members of the Congress. What followed was a personal triumph of bureaucratic and political performance. Thanks to the administration's backing and Hanks' power of persuasion, the national endowment received $16 million of the $20 million she had requested.

Once in control, and with expanding budgets to work with, Hanks moved to make art accessible to all Americans. She allocated funds to send opera, theater, dance, and music groups on tour throughout the country. An Arttrain carried travelling exhibits to communities outside the big cities. Money was also made available to help small towns buy art works for local exhibition. Hanks made a special effort to reach the poor and the culturally disadvantaged. African American poets and authors went to teach in inner-city schools. The Artist-in-the-School program, begun under her auspices, gave students the opportunity to work with sculptors, painters, and writers.

Hanks began a systematic effort to increase the support for dance, for symphony, and for the development and improvement of museums. Believing that the United States had become the dance capital of the world, she liberally funded choreographers and dance companies. The American Ballet Theatre, the New York City Ballet, and the Jeffrey received funds, as did Merce Cunningham, Elliot Feld, Anna Sokolow, and many others. In 1970 the endowment began a sizable program of aid to orchestras, and in 1971 funds were set aside for museums.

As chairwoman of the National Endowment for the Arts and the National Council on the Arts from 1969 to 1977, Hanks proved an indefatigable champion of the visual and performing arts. Her goal was to transform and uplift society through art. Practical as well as visionary, she forged a coalition that included Democrats, Republicans, liberals, conservatives, business organizations, and artists of all types, from prima ballerinas to street artists. She was, according to one capital observer, "smart, tireless, funny, impassioned, shrewd, and tough." She could charm with a Southern magnolia manner one moment and be tough and businesslike the next.

Under Hanks' skillful leadership the agency saw its annual budget grow from $16 million to $100 million over her two terms as chairwoman. At the same time she remained committed to a policy of encouraging private contributions to the arts. Many of the endowment's grants were made on a matching funds basis, so Hanks estimated that in actual practice each dollar contributed by the agency generated about $3 of private money.

When she announced her resignation from the national endowment in 1977, she left as her legacy a much expanded network for the funding of the arts. Called "the mother of a million artists," Hanks died of cancer in 1983 at the age of 55. In 1986 the Old Post Office in Washington, D.C., renovated into a community center, was re-named the Nancy Hanks Center.

Further Reading

The Rockefeller Brothers Fund study Nancy Hanks helped to author provides a good starting place for understanding Hanks' later work: see *The Performing Arts: Problems and Prospects* (1965). Leonard Garment, special counsel to President Richard Nixon from 1969 to 1974, wrote an informative tribute to Hanks in *Art News,* April 1983. See also *The Annual Obituary 1983* (1984).

Additional Sources

Straight, Michael Whitney, *Nancy Hanks: an intimate portrait: the creation of a national commitment to the arts,* Durham N.C.: Duke University Press, 1988. ☐

Marcus Alonzo Hanna

Businessman, politician, and U.S. senator, Marcus Alonzo Hanna (1837-1904) managed the election of President William McKinley and was a leading spokesman for enlightened capitalism.

Mark Hanna was born on Sept. 24, 1837, in New Lisbon (now Lisbon), Ohio. His parents were well educated. Young Hanna enjoyed material comfort and relative social privilege. When the family moved to Cleveland in 1852, he completed public school and attended Western Reserve College briefly.

Business permeated Hanna's youthful environment and immediately absorbed his energies. He became a full partner in the family grocery firm after his father's death in 1862. Following his marriage in 1864, he launched ventures in lake transportation and oil refining, areas of enterprise that were also attracting his Cleveland schoolmate John D. Rockefeller. Hanna later joined his father-in-law in a large iron and coal firm.

Politics, a vigorous Ohio tradition, early engaged Hanna's attention, and he embraced the Republican party instinctively. To his father-in-law, a fervent Democrat, he seemed "a damned screecher for freedom." In reality, despite this appearance and later skirmishes with Cleveland's ward bosses in the 1870s, Hanna was no reformer, but he realized that business and politics were becoming increasingly related. He lent his organizational talents and money to the Ohio Republicans who sought the presidency between 1880 and 1900: James A. Garfield, John Sherman, and William McKinley. He helped elect McKinley governor of Ohio in 1891 and president in 1896 and 1900. His management of the McKinley campaigns marked the successful application of business skills to American politics. Between 1897 and his death Hanna served in the Senate. He was a trusted presidential adviser to McKinley and Theodore Roosevelt, despite his opposition to many of the latter's policies.

Although labeled "dollar Mark" by opponents, Hanna was no mere moneygrubber. The gold standard, high tariff, and large corporations—all of which he defended—

emy with the combined forces of infantry and cavalry.

As a boy of 9, Hannibal begged his father, Hamilcar Barca, to take him on the campaign in Spain, but Hamilcar, before fulfilling this childish wish, made him solemnly swear eternal hatred of Rome. As a young officer in Spain, Hannibal won his first laurels under the command of Hasdrubal, Hamilcar's successor and son-in-law.

Livy gives a remarkable portrait of Hannibal's physique and character at this time: to the old soldiers he seemed a Hamilcar reborn, as he possessed the lively expression and penetrating eyes of his father; the younger men were won over by his bravery, endurance, simplicity of life, and willingness to share all hardships with his troops. The accusations of cruelty, treachery, and lack of religion must be discounted as anti-Carthaginian war propaganda of Livy's Roman sources.

In Spain

Upon the assassination of Hasdrubal in 221 B.C., Hannibal, at the age of 26, was immediately proclaimed commander in chief by the entire army, an appointment soon afterward ratified by the Carthaginian Senate. Making New Carthage his headquarters, Hannibal consolidated Carthaginian power in Spain by attacking and defeating the Olcades on the upper Guadiana and the Vaccaei and

seemed means to ensure general prosperity by stabilizing capitalism. For similar reasons he defended labor's right to organize and strike. After 1900 he championed ship subsidies and an Isthmian canal to increase America's power through international trade.

Although Hanna introduced the phrase "stand pat" into the American vocabulary, his dream of domestic and international order through responsible capitalism was not a formula for do-nothingism. His instinctive idealism and his concern for the public weal represented the best of American Whig attitudes. Unfortunately for his reputation, he became, even before his death, a symbol of many reactionary business attitudes that he had personally condemned.

Further Reading

Herbert D. Croly, *Marcus Alonzo Hanna* (1912), the standard biography, is sometimes overly sympathetic. Thomas Beer, *Hanna* (1929), is a bright, cynical study by the son of one of Hanna's associates. H. Wayne Morgan, *William McKinley and His America* (1963), describes Hanna's role with balanced sympathy. □

Hannibal Barca

Hannibal Barca (247-183 B.C.) was a Carthaginian general and one of the greatest military leaders of the ancient world. A brilliant strategist, he developed tactics of outflanking and surrounding the en-

Carpetani beyond the Tagus. In the spring of 219 he besieged Saguntum, a city south of the Iberus River (Ebro) and an ally of Rome. Although he did not formally break the treaty of 226, which had defined the Iberus River as the line of demarcation between the Roman and Carthaginian spheres of influence, the blockade of Saguntum and its final destruction after an 8-month siege brought about the declaration of war.

Crossing the Alps

Aware of Roman supremacy on the sea, Hannibal conceived of an invasion of Italy from the north. He wanted to crush the Roman army with his superior land forces in their own territory, especially since he counted on the disaffection of Rome's Italian allies. Thus he crossed the Iberus in the spring of 218, and, after bloody battles with Spanish tribes, he marched with about 40,000 men across the Pyrenees. Once in Gaul, he hastened to the Rhone River without meeting resistance and, within a week, transported his army and war elephants across the river.

Meanwhile, the Roman consul Publius Cornelius Scipio, who had transported his troops by sea to Massilia (Marseilles), was moving north on the right bank of the Rhone, but when he heard that Hannibal had already crossed the river, he sent his brother Gnaeus with two legions to Spain, while he himself returned to northern Italy. Hannibal, on the other hand, wanted to cross the Alps and reach the Po Valley before the Romans were able to collect their forces against an unexpected invader. In 15 days he marched through rugged, unknown mountain passes, with his enormous army of diverse origin and language and his 38 war elephants, in the midst of enemy attacks, landslides, and early autumn snow—a heroic feat which has captured the imagination of historians and poets alike.

When Hannibal finally reached the Po Valley, his army was reduced to half its former size and most of his war elephants were lost. And yet, when he met the army of Publius Scipio at the Ticinus River, Hannibal's Numidian cavalry won a decisive victory over the Romans. Scipio, who was seriously wounded, withdrew to the Trebia River south of Placentia, where the consular army of Titus Sèmpronius Longus, recalled by the Senate from Sicily, joined him. Using the tactics of both ambush and outflanking the enemy, Hannibal defeated the combined armies, causing the loss of about 20,000 Roman soldiers.

In Italy

After spending the winter in the Po Valley, where he gained many recruits among the Gauls and Ligurians, Hannibal crossed the Apennines in the spring of 217. By ravaging Etruria he provoked the pursuit of the new consul Gaius Flaminius, whom Hannibal trapped with two legions in a defile on the northern shore of Lake Trasimenus. Rushing down from their ambush on the opposing hills, Hannibal's troops annihilated almost the entire army and, shortly afterward, intercepted and destroyed the cavalry that was sent to aid Flaminius.

Now Hannibal marched to Picenum, where he granted his troops a period of rest in the hope that Rome's Italian allies would defect. He continued to ravage Apulia and Campania without being able to involve the dictator Quintus Fabius, called Cunctator for his tactics of delay, in anything but minor skirmishes. But in the following year, when a new pair of consuls put into effect the aggressive war policy of the Senate, Hannibal beat the Romans in the worst defeat they had ever suffered. This happened at Cannae, where his strategy of outflanking the enemy again brought victory to the Carthaginians over superior numbers.

Now Capua and many other cities in southern Italy revolted against Rome, but Hannibal's weakened forces prevented him from taking full advantage of his victory. Making Capua his headquarters, he changed from an offensive to a defensive policy, mostly because his home government refused to send him adequate reinforcements. Although he was able to capture Tarentum, conquer Bruttium, and win a few minor victories, he gradually lost ground against the superior numbers of the Romans.

Negotiations with Philip V of Macedon and with Hieronymus of Syracuse proved ineffective, and the small band of Numidian cavalry sent to him from Carthage was insufficient for major warfare. In 211, when he was unable to relieve the Roman siege of Capua, Hannibal marched on Rome, pitched camp on the Anio River at a 3-mile distance from the city, but withdrew again to Apulia in the hope that his brother Hasdrubal would bring fresh troops across the Alps from Spain. This hope was shattered in 207, when his brother's bloody head was thrown at his feet as a testimony to the destruction of Hasdrubal's army in the battle of the Metaurus. Hannibal now concentrated his forces in Bruttium, where he held his ground for 4 more years, until he was recalled in 203 to defend Carthage against the victorious army of Publius Cornelius Scipio the Elder (Scipio Africanus Major).

In Africa

Back in his native land after 16 years of victorious warfare in enemy territory, Hannibal was finally defeated by Scipio Africanus in the battle of Zama. Ironically, Hannibal became the victim of his own strategy: Scipio outflanked and surrounded the Carthaginians with the aid of King Masinissa's Numidian cavalry. Hannibal escaped with only a few horsemen and rushed to Carthage, where he counseled peace. The treaty was concluded in 201.

Elected a suffete (civil magistrate) in 197, Hannibal broke the power of the Carthaginian oligarchy and worked for social and economic reforms. His political enemies accused him in Rome of intriguing with King Antiochus III of Syria. When the Romans sent a commission to investigate the matter, Hannibal fled, first to Antiochus's court at Ephesus, and, after the latter's defeat at Magnesia in 189, to King Prusias of Bithynia.

Hannibal helped his host successfully in a naval battle against King Eumenes of Pergamum, Rome's ally. When another senatorial commission was sent to demand from Prusias the surrender of the famous Carthaginian exile, Hannibal poisoned himself.

Further Reading

The major ancient sources for the life of Hannibal are Livy, Polybius, and Cornelius Nepos. Among the numerous modern biographies are T. A. Dodge, *Hannibal* (2 vols., 1891); W. O'C. Morris, *Hannibal* (1897); George P. Baker, *Hannibal* (1929); Harold Lamb, *Hannibal: One Man against Rome* (1958); Leonard Cottrell, *Hannibal: Enemy of Rome* (1960); Robert N. Webb. *Hannibal: Invader from Carthage* (1968), especially designed for young people; and Gavin de Beer, *Hannibal: Challenging Rome's Supremacy* (1969). On Hannibal's crossing the Alps see H. Spenser Wilkinson, *Hannibal's March through the Alps* (1911); Cecil Torr, *Hannibal Crosses the Alps* (1924); and Gavin de Beer, *Alps and Elephants: Hannibal's March* (1955). Recommended for general historical background are T. Frank, *Roman Imperialism* (1914); *The Cambridge Ancient History,* vol. 8 (1930); and A. J. Toynbee, *Hannibal's Legacy: The Hannibalic War's Effects on Roman Life* (2 vols., 1965). □

Lorraine Vivian Hansberry

Lorraine Vivian Hansberry (1930-1965) was an important American writer and a major figure on Broadway. Although her reputation grew with the posthumous publication of a range of works, she remained best known for the play and movie *A Raisin in the Sun*.

Lorraine Vivian Hansberry was born May 19, 1930, in Chicago, Illinois. Her father, Carl A. Hansberry, was prominent in Chicago's African American business and political community. He owned real estate, generously supported African American causes, and ran for Congress as a Republican; her mother, Nanny Perry Hansberry, taught school and also was active in politics. The Hansberry home, where Lorraine was the youngest of four children, was often visited by famous African Americans.

In 1938 the Hansberrys moved into a white neighborhood that excluded African Americans through the then widely used restrictive covenants. Carl Hansberry, while resisting attacks on his home and family from neighborhood hoodlums, took his case to court. Although armed guards protected the children, at one point a slab of concrete almost crushed Lorraine. In 1940 the U.S. Supreme Court ruled restrictive covenants unconstitutional in a case that came to be known as *Hansberry* v. *Lee,* although it did little to affect the actual practice of segregated housing in Chicago. Carl Hansberry died in 1946 before he could complete plans to move his family to Mexico City when Lorraine's two brothers had difficulties accommodating to segregation in the U.S. Army.

After graduating from high school in 1948 Lorraine is reported to have studied variously at the University of Chicago; at the Art Institute of Chicago; at the New School of Social Research in New York; in Guadalajara, Mexico; and at the University of Wisconsin, where she saw a production of Sean O'Casey's play *Juno and the Paycock* about the problems of a poor urban family in Dublin in 1922 during the early conflict between the Irish Republican Army and the British occupying forces. It is supposed to have inspired her to think of creating a comparable work about an African American family.

It was during her years in New York, living in Greenwich Village, that Hansberry became intimately involved with a number of the liberal causes of the period. In 1952 she attended the Intercontinental Peace Congress in Montevideo, Uruguay, as a substitute for Paul Robeson, who could not get a passport from the U.S. State Department. At the congress she met politically astute feminists from all over the world.

In 1953 she married Robert Nemiroff, who was a graduate student in history and English at New York University and participated, like his fellows, in the leftist political events of the time. The two met while picketing. The night before their wedding they joined a protest against the execution of Julius and Ethel Rosenberg for espionage. After a series of part-time jobs, including those of typist and assistant to a furrier, Hansberry settled down to the writing of a play, which eventually took its title from a poem by Langston Hughes, "Harlem," which declared that "a dream deferred" might "dry up/like a raisin in the sun." Nemiroff and his friends were to be instrumental in getting the play produced.

A Raisin in the Sun was finished in 1957 and opened on March 11, 1959, at the Ethel Barrymore Theater. It is unique in several respects. It was the first play to be produced on

Broadway written and directed by an African American and to have an all-black cast. The original production starred Sidney Poitier, Ruby Dee, and Claudia McNeil and was directed by Lloyd Richards. Ossie Davis eventually replaced Poitier. In May 1959 the New York Drama Critics Circle voted it Best Play of the Year for a season that included works by Eugene O'Neill, Tennessee Williams, and Archibald Macleish. Hansberry was the youngest American to win that award. The play had a long run and was made into a movie with a script by Hansberry and with Poitier repeating his stage role. Later it was turned into a Broadway musical, *Raisin.*

One of the more enthusiastic and perceptive assessments of *A Raisin in the Sun* came from the English critic Kenneth Tynan. "The supreme virtue of *A Raisin in the Sun,*" he wrote, "is its proud, joyous proximity to its source, which is life as the dramatist has lived it. The relaxed, freewheeling interplay of a magnificent team of African American actors drew me unresisting into a world of their making, their suffering, their thinking, and their rejoicing." Although Hansberry herself insisted that her play was essentially about an African American family in a particular time and place, some critics—of both races—suggested that it simply "happened" to be about African Americans.

Hansberry's next play, *The Sign in Sidney Brustein's Window,* opened and closed in 1965. Some critics felt that this play was an advance in subtlety and complexity over *A Raisin in the Sun.* It recorded some of the conflicts and paradoxes suffered by intellectuals in confronting the real world. One character, for example, an African American, while sensitive to white discrimination, is himself vicious about gay and white persons.

Hansberry's work continued to develop in ambition, breadth, sophistication, and depth. Although already ill, she wrote a parody of Samuel Beckett's *Waiting for Godot;* planned a musical adaptation of Oliver La Farge's novel about the Navajos, *Laughing Boy;* and worked on her major play, *Les Blancs,* the title of which ("The Whites") carried an obvious reference to Jean Genet's *The Blacks.* She also wrote a television drama on slavery, which, while it did not appear on television, was published in 1972 as *The Drinking Gourd.* Other works included *The Movement: Documentary of a Struggle for Equality,* which showed pictures of brutal attacks on African Americans in the South, and *What Use Are Flowers?*

In 1963 she left her hospital bed to give a talk to the winners of the United Negro College Fund writing contest, in which she used the phrase "To be young, gifted, and Black," which later became the title of her own autobiography, a collection of her assorted writings edited by Nemiroff. She died of cancer on January 16, 1965.

Further Reading

The best short summary of her career and writing appears in the *Dictionary of Literary Biography* (DLB), vol. 38. It was written by Steven R. Carter of the University of Puerto Rico, and much of the information in this article was taken from it. Carter also has an essay on her, "Commitment Amid Complexity: Lorraine Hansberry's Life-in-Action," *MELUS,* 7 (Fall 1980). A full biography is Catherine Scheader's *They Found a Way: Lorraine Hansberry* (1978). Doris E. Abramson's *Negro Playwrights in the American Theatre: 1925-1959* (1969) puts Hansberry's work in a larger context. A moving memoir by James Baldwin appears in *To Be Young, Gifted and Black* (1969). The standard bibliography is by Ernest Kaiser and Robert Nemiroff, "A Lorraine Hansberry Bibliography," *Freedomways,* 19 (Fourth Quarter 1979), although critical studies continued to appear more than 20 years after her death. ☐

Alvin Hansen

The influential economist Alvin Hansen (1887-1975) brought the 1930's Keynesian revolution in economics to the United States. He was a prolific writer who also played significant roles in the creation of the Social Security System and the Council of Economic Advisors.

Alvin Hansen was born at Viborg, South Dakota, on Aug. 23, 1887, to Danish parents. He graduated from Yankton College in South Dakota in 1910 and worked several years as a high school teacher, then principal, then county school superintendent, before returning to school for graduate studies, which he completed at the University of Wisconsin in 1918. He taught at Brown University until his appointment at the University of Minnesota in 1923. His major works in this period on business cycles and economic stabilization were in the neoclassical economics tradition.

In 1937 he accepted a prestigious appointment as Lucius N. Littauer Professor of Political Economy at Harvard University. Hansen's seminar on fiscal policy created a generation of graduate students, such as Paul Samuelson and James Tobin, who supported Keynesian economics. His 1938 book *Full Recovery or Stagnation?* was based on but a few paragraphs of Keynes's *The General Theory of Employment,* but it was an extended argument that employment stagnation would continue for decades to come. Ultimately, stagnation theories became more associated with Hansen, rather than Keynes. His 1941 book on fiscal policy and business cycles was the first major work in the United States to entirely support Keynes's analysis of the causes of the Great Depression, and he used that analysis to support Keynes's mainstay of deficit spending.

Hansen was much more than just a disciple of Keynes. He found serious mistakes in Keynes's presentation; he implemented Keynes, for example, by developing tax and spending models which clarified tax and spending policies as weapons in Keynes's arsenal, and he criticized Keynes for putting too much faith in interest rates and monetary policy. Still, one of his most influential teaching devices was his book, *A Guide to Keynes,* which took students through Keynes's *General Theory* chapter by chapter and, at times, paragraph by paragraph.

Hansen's teaching, in essence, was that government should not put the main burden of inflation control on

unemployment by its inaction. He thought inflation control should be exercised by timely changes in tax rates, by appropriate changes in the money supply, and by effective wage-price controls. He was said to be "a sparkling teacher." He wrote fifteen books, including an account of the Bretton Woods Conference that helped to establish the World Bank. His books were widely translated and read world-wide.

During the Roosevelt and Truman years, Hansen was of considerable influence in shaping fiscal policies as a member of numerous government commissions and as consultant to the Federal Reserve Board, the Treasury Department and the National Resources Planning Board. In 1935, he helped create the Social Security System and in 1946, he helped in the drafting of the Full Employment Act which among other things created the Council of Economic Advisors. Hansen also served as Vice President of the American Statistical Association and President of the American Economics Association.

After retiring from Harvard University in 1957, Hansen taught at the University of Bombay and at numerous American universities almost to his death in 1975.

Further Reading

Robert Lekachman, *The Age of Keynes* (1966), has a long and interesting analysis of the influence of Hansen on the development of Keynesian thought in America; Joseph Dorfman, *The Economic Mind in American Civilization,* vol. 5 (1959), focuses on Hansen's early career; Ben B. Seligman, *Main Currents in Modern Economics: Economic Thought since*

1870 (1962), discusses Hansen's entire career; For more recent works about Hansen, see the article by some of his former students in *Quarterly Journal of Economics,* Feburary, 1976; and W. Breit and R.L. Ransom, *The Academic Scribblers: American Economists in Collision* (1982). ☐

Julia Butler Hansen

Julia Butler Hansen (1907-1988) was a Washington state politician who served in the Washington State House of Representatives and in the U.S. House of Representatives. She was the first woman to serve on the House Appropriations Committee and the first woman to head a major appropriations subcommittee.

Julia Butler Hansen was born in Portland, Oregon, on June 14, 1907, the daughter of Donald C. and Maude (Kimball) Butler. She grew up and spent much of her life in Cathamet, Washington, a small town in the southeast of the state where her father had settled in 1891. She attended Oregon State College from 1924 to 1926 and received her B.A. in home economics from the University of Washington in 1930.

After graduation she returned to Cathamet, where she worked for a title company, wrote children's literature, and became involved in local politics. In 1935 she published *Singing Paddles* which won the Julia Ellsworth Ford Foundation Award for Juvenile Literature. In 1936 she entered politics on the grassroots level, serving as chairwoman of the county Democratic party and becoming the first woman to be elected to the Cathamet City Council. The popularity of *Singing Paddles* won her a statewide reputation, and in 1938 she was elected to a seat in the Washington House of Representatives, where she served until 1960. "My love is writing," she said, "politics is accidental."

In 1939, at the age of 32, she married Henry Hansen, a lumberman. Although her husband had little interest in politics, Hansen continued her political career. A veteran campaigner, she ran for reelection in one campaign from a hospital bed, where she had just given birth to a son (David) at the age of 38. In 1960 she left state politics, ostensibly to return to private life in Cathamet, but she was drafted to replace Russell Mack, the Republican representative to the U.S. Congress, upon his death.

Hansen moved to Washington, D.C. in 1960 and served under the administration of John F. Kennedy, first on the Interior and Insular Affairs Committee of the House of Representatives. By 1963 she had gained a seat on the influential House Appropriations Committee, becoming the first woman to serve on that committee. She later became chairwoman of the House Appropriations Sub-committee for the Interior, which controlled the purse strings for the Department of the Interior, including the National Parks Service, the Bureau of Indian Affairs, and the Bureau of Mines, as well as for all national arts and humanities projects. As

endless string of people who want everything from post offices to gasoline,'' she remarked with her usual candor.

A pioneer, Hansen had been the first woman in many different jobs: the first woman to chair the county Democratic Council, the first woman to serve on the Cathamet City Council, the first woman speaker pro tem of the Washington House, the first woman to chair its Roads and Bridges Committee, the first woman to serve on the U.S. House Appropriations Committee, and the first woman to head a major appropriations subcommittee.

As she was not a candidate for the ninety-fourth Congress, Hansen was appointed in 1975 to a six-year term on Washington State's Toll Bridge Authority and the state Highway Commission. She was also Chairman of Washinton State's Transportation Commission 1975-1981. She then retired completely to her home in Cathamet, Washington, where she died May 3, 1988.

Further Reading

For additional information on Julia Butler Hansen, see Esther Stineman, *American Political Women: Contemporary and Historical Profiles* (1980) and *Women in Congress, 1917-1976* (1977). There is also a lively article by Mike Heywood, ''Julia Butler Hansen: Alive, Well, Persnickety,'' in the Bellingham, Washington *Herald* (April 11, 1979).

For a chronological summary of Julia Butler Hansen's business and governmental positions, see the *Biographical Directory of the American Congress (1774- 1996),* however, this presented no biographical details. □

chairwoman Hansen managed budgets of over $2 billion. Because her home district contained almost all of the fish and timber resources in the state of Washington, it became Hansen's task to try to balance the interests of ecology against the business interests of manufacturers and developers. Her career in Congress was successful in part because of her skilled political maneuverings behind the scenes to obtain favorable legislation for her state, particularly on bills involving the fishing and lumber industries.

In her career in the House of Representatives Hansen managed to overcome obstacles that traditionally had kept women out of key positions in the Congress. Stressing competence and hard work, she became widely respected by her colleagues for her intelligence and knowledge of the House rules. She was selected to chair the Democratic Committee on Organization, Study and Review, known as the Hansen Committee, which was charged with the delicate task of reorganizing the committee system of the House of Representatives to give greater power to junior members.

In the early 1970s she shifted to a more conservative position, but she remained strongly pro-union, supported the Equal Rights Amendment, and voted to cut off funds for the Vietnam War after June 1972. Throughout her years in Congress she maintained a steady interest in the problems of Native Americans, working to improve education and living conditions on the Indian reservations.

When she announced her retirement in 1974 she had served longer than any other woman in elective office. ''Thirty-seven years is a long time to be pursued by an

Duane Hanson

The American sculptor Duane Hanson (1925-1996) was one of the leading sculptors working in a superrealist, or Verist, style. His work is highly illusionistic, but also has a social content. While his early works dealt with physical violence or social issues, his later work seems to portray passive, isolated figures as victims of society and negative values.

Duane Hanson was born January 17, 1925, in Alexandria, Minnesota. After attendance at Luther College and the University of Washington, he graduated from Macalaster College in 1946. Following a period teaching high school art, he received a Master of Fine Arts degree from the Cranbrook Academy in 1951.

Around 1966 Hanson began making figural casts using fiberglass and vinyl. Works that first brought him notice were of figures grouped in tableaux, usually of brutal and violent subjects, somewhat similar to the work of Edward Keinholz. Hanson's *Abortion* (1966) was inspired by the horrors of a backroom procedure; *Accident* (1967) showed a motorcycle crash; and *Race Riot* (1969-1971) included among its seven figures a white policeman terrorizing a African American man as well as a African American rioter attacking the policeman. Other works which dealt with physical violence or other explosive social issues of the 1960s were *Riot* (1967), *Football Players* (1969), and *Vietnam Scene* (1969). These works, cast from actual people, were made of fiberglass reinforced with fiber resin, then painted to make the revealed skin look realistic with veins and blemishes. Hanson then clothed the figures with garments from second-hand clothing stores and then theatrically arranged the action. Clearly these works contained strong social comment and can be seen as modern parallels to the concerns of 19th-century French Realists such as Honore Daumier and Jean Francois Millet, artists Hanson admired.

Around 1970 Hanson abandoned such gut-wrenching subjects for more subtle though no less vivid ones. In that year he made the *Supermarket Shopper, Hardhat,* and *Tourists; Woman Eating* was completed in 1971. These were also life-sized, clothed, fiberglass figures. Unlike the earlier works, however, these were single or paired figures, not overtly in a violent activity. Furthermore, whereas the earlier works tended to be more contained spatially, the later figures had no boundaries from the viewer. They quite literally *inhabited* the viewer's space—with amusing results at times, as in the cases of *Reading Man* (1977) or the *Photographer* (1978). Although detractors may liken his work to figures in a wax museum, the content of his sculptures is more complex and expressive than that normally found in waxworks.

The momentary confusion that Hanson's sculptures were real people sometimes shocked the viewer and put too

much attention on the technique, although Hanson argued that the technique was a means to an end. That end is an intense look at less exalted aspects of the world around the viewer. *Couple with Shopping Bags* (1976) shows two overweight people, wearing mismatched polyester clothes, carrying full bags. The woman's hairdo is complicated and her nails are painted. These certainly are not "beautiful" human figures in the traditional artistic sense, but they are without question typical of how many "average" middle-or lower-class Americans looked in the 1970s. Although for most sophisticated art viewers a work such as *Couple with Shopping Bags* has a pointed humor to it, poking fun at the poor taste so many Americans show in their dress and grooming, these works also have a more somber quality. The particularities make the figures vivid archetypes of American consumers and remind viewers that all people possess some unusual characteristics.

Individual works are made even more realistic because of the eccentricities Hanson chose to show, and his output may be seen as paying homage to common humanity. *Queenie* (1980) shows a dignified African American cleaning lady pushing a cart filled with mops, buckets, and cleaning compounds. Hanson, as is typical, searched for the right model, so that the figure is both distinctive but "average." This work, *Hardhat* (1971), and *Delivery Man* (1980) are especially good examples of Hanson's sympathy with workers, whose loss of independence to societal and governmental pressures is captured in their faces, postures, and clothing. Other examples of Hanson's work include *The Jogger* (1983-84), *Camper* (1987), and *Salesman* (1992).

Like his contemporary John de Andrea, Hanson's work is highly illusionistic, in the tradition of *trompe d'oeil* painting and sculpture. However, unlike Andrea, who stressed pose and attitude in his real-looking nude figures, or George Segal, who relied on surface expressiveness in his cast figures, Hanson placed much emphasis on paraphernalia and clothing and on body types. His work of the 1960s clearly had a social content, and, though it is more subtle, this interest in content continued in the work of the 1970s and 1980s. American greed, materialism, tastelessness, and narrow-mindedness seem to be a part of the later work. The characters within the art are passive, isolated beings, presented as victims of American society and negative values as much as the cause of them. In the 1990s Hanson created figures that challenged people's ideas about prejudice and social class.

Hanson experienced both criticism and praise during his lifetime. In addition to receiving numerous awards, Duane Hanson was honored with the proclamation of Duane Hanson day, by Broward County Florida in 1987, and in 1992 he was inducted into the Florida Hall of Fame.

Encountering a Hanson piece in a museum can be a shock because of the high degree of illusionism. That shock is in part due to the artist's impressive technique, but is also based on the recognition that the figure accurately mirrors us and the society of which we are a part. It reflects and informs. As Hanson once said, "Realism is best suited to convey the frightening idiosyncrasies of our time" (*Art News,* March 1996).

Hanson was 70 when he died in Boca Raton, Florida, on January 6, 1996, of non-Hodgkin's lymphoma.

Further Reading

Monographs on Duane Hanson include M. H. Bush, *Duane Hanson* (1976); and K. Varnadoe, *Duane Hanson* (1985); A brief 1972 interview for *Art in America* is reprinted in E. H. Johnson, editor, *American Artists on Art from 1940 to 1980* (1982); An excellent essay is J. Masheck, "Verist Sculpture: Hanson and de Andrea," reprinted in G. Battcock, editor, *Super Realism* (1975); Another study of super realism is F. H. Goodyear, *Contemporary American Realism Since 1960* (1981); For an excellent broader discussion of various art movements, including super realism, see C. Robins, *The Pluralist Era* (1984); Other more general studies of this period are S. Hunter and J. Jacobus, *Modern Art* (1985); E. Lucie-Smith, *Art in the Seventies* (1980); and E. Lucie-Smith, *Movements in Art Since 1945* (1985). See also *Art in America* (January 1993); *Art News* (March 1996); and *Who's Who in America* (1996); Two more books about Hanson are Robert Carleson Hobbs, *Duane Hanson: The New Objectivity* (1991); and Kirk Varnedoe, *Duane Hanson* (1985). ☐

Howard Hanson

Pulitzer Prize winner Howard Hanson (1896-1981), a major American composer and educator, founded the annual American Music Festival and directed the Eastman School of Music for 40 years.

Howard Hanson was born in October 1896 in Wahoo, Nebraska. He graduated from the Luther Academy and College in Nebraska in 1912, then studied under Percy Goetschius at the Institute of Musical Arts (later the Juilliard School) in New York City and under Arne Oldberg at Northwestern University in Evanston, Illinois. In 1916 Hanson became an instructor at the College of the Pacific in California. His teaching and administrative talents soon became evident, and in 1919 he was made dean of the College of Music at the age of 23.

Hanson received an American Prix de Rome in 1921 and spent the next two years in Rome. His most important compositions in this period were the *Nordic Symphony* and *The Song of Beowulf* for chorus and orchestra, works which show his sober and highly expressive musical personality. Throughout his career, Hanson's compositions reflected the strong influence of the Finnish composer Jean Sibelius.

Among Hanson's significant compositions are an opera, *Merry Mount,* commissioned in 1934 by the Metropolitan Opera in New York, and seven Symphonies, of which the Third, the *Romantic Symphony* is perhaps the best known. In 1943 he received a Pulitzer Prize for his Fourth Symphony, *Requiem.* His Seventh Symphony was first performed in 1977. Other works include a Piano Concerto, *Three Songs from Drum Taps* and *The Song of Democracy* for chorus and orchestra, *Concerto for Organ, Strings, and Harp,* and the *New Land, New Covenant,* an oratorio for chorus, two soloists, orchestra, and narrator, commissioned for the 1976 Bicentennial.

In 1924, the founder of Eastman Kodak Company, George Eastman, asked Hanson to became director of the new Eastman School of Music in Rochester, N.Y. Hanson accepted and held the post until his retirement in 1964. His energy and administrative skill made the Eastman School one of the most important conservatories in America.

Hanson became active in several national musical organizations. He was one of the founders, and later the president, of the National Association of Schools of Music, whose main purpose was to raise the standards of university and conservatory musical training. He also served as president of the Music Teachers' National Association, as a director of the Music Educators' National Conference, and as musical consultant to the U.S. State Department. One of Hanson's most significant achievements was the 1925 founding of the annual Festival of American Music, which featured the works of many American composers of all styles. In an era when European composers still dominated the music world, these festivals established the important fact that America had produced a large group of talented composers. In 1976, Hanson himself donated $100,000 to support the program.

Further Reading

Madeleine Goss, *Modern Music- Makers: Contemporary American Composers* (1952); Joseph Machlis, *American Composers of Our Time* (1963); For more recent works, see Donald J. Shetler *In Memoriam Howard Hanson* (1983); David Russell

Williams, *Conversations with Howard Hanson* (1988); and James E. Perone, *Howard Hanson: a Bio-Bibliography* (1993). ☐

Han Wu-ti

The Chinese emperor Han Wu-ti (157-87 B.C.) enlarged China's frontiers, instituted new means of income for the state, and made Confucianism the state orthodoxy.

Han Wu-ti was originally named Liu Ch'e. He came to the Han throne at the age of 16 but did not take the government into his own hands until 131 B.C. He was firmly determined to wield imperial power to a greater extent than any of his predecessors in the (Former) Han dynasty had done. In his administration of justice, for example, all but one of his seven prime ministers between 121 and 88 were convicted of crimes and met violent deaths. The numerous laws were harshly applied throughout the empire, thus creating a style of government unknown among his Han predecessors but strikingly similar to that of Ch'in Shih huang-ti.

Expansion of the Empire

Wu-ti (meaning "martial emperor") was a well-deserved title. His campaigns toward the south, into present-day North Vietnam, and toward the southeast, into the coastal regions, determined in large part the southern boundaries of China. His conquests along China's northern frontiers, if less permanent, were even more impressive. After a costly series of wars he drove the nomadic Hsiung-nu north as far as the Gobi Desert (119). In the northwest, China took control, for the first time, of Chinese Turkistan, and by 104 Emperor Wu's military might had reached beyond the Pamir Mountains to Russian Turkistan. Similarly, in the northeast, Chinese control stretched beyond the Liaotung Peninsula and into northern Korea. The empire that Wu-ti created, surpassing in size the contemporary Roman Empire, was the greatest in the world.

Economic Policies

When Emperor Wu came to the throne, the Han dynasty was financially very strong. But his wars were terribly costly. So too were construction projects that he initiated. Expenses were met by a variety of means. The tight net of the law meant that the government could remit punishments for cash or goods and thus add to the state's coffers. Those without money were condemned to penal servitude as soldiers or laborers.

Although new taxes were created and old ones increased, there was still not enough money. Hence, salt, iron, and liquor were made state monopolies. These measures produced widespread discontent and some uprisings. By the end of Wu-ti's reign the finances of the empire had been badly strained, and his successors had to institute ameliorative policies.

Emperor Wu is also famous for granting exclusive recognition to Confucianism as the official state philosophy. Soon after he ascended the throne, he ordered that students of the Legalist philosophy, which had been the dominant school of thought in the Ch'in period, be banished from the government. In 135 he established the Office of Erudites for the five Confucian classics. The Erudites served as advisers to the Emperor and as teachers of future officials.

The office was not new; there had earlier been Erudites for the Confucian classics, but Wu-ti's decree meant that from then on there would only be Confucian Erudites. Eleven years later he founded the Imperial University, where the Erudites taught the better students. It is difficult to overemphasize the importance of these decisions. From this time on, for over 2,000 years, men who wanted to become officials were expected to study the Confucian classics. Although the results of these policies were not immediate, they are of the most profound significance to all later Chinese history.

Further Reading

There is no scholarly monograph devoted to Han Wu-ti or his reign, but there are several works that deal with various aspects of the period. Homer H. Dubs's translation of the work by the 1st-century historian Pan Ku, *History of the Former Han Dynasty* (3 vols., 1938-1955), is a technical translation with interpretive essays of those parts that cover Wu-ti's reign in an annalistic manner. Parts of Ssu-ma Ch'ien's history dealing with the Han dynasty have been translated into English by Burton D. Watson in *Records of the Grand Historian of China, Translated from the Shih chi of Ssu-ma Ch'ien* (2 vols., 1961). Wu-ti's foreign policies are expertly treated in Ying-shih YU, *Trade and Expansion in Han China: A Study in the Structure of Sino-Barbarian Economic Relations* (1967). On Wu-ti's economic policies see Nancy Lee Swann, ed. and trans., *Food and Money in Ancient China* (1950). ☐

Han Yü

The Chinese writer Han Yü (768-824) is ranked high as a poet but, more importantly, is revered as a master of prose writing. His writing is characterized by a devotion to classicism both in form and in content.

With the early death of his parents, Han Yü grew up in difficult family circumstances, which, however, only spurred him to greater efforts in mastering the Confucian classics. Eventually he passed the civil service examination, but his advancement on the ladder of officialdom was interrupted by repeated banishment to posts of magistracy in one outlying region or another. His forthright opinions expressed in forceful language won him mostly fear and hatred. In 819 he presented a famed memorial against the royal reception of the relic of Buddha's finger bone, in which he condemned Buddhism in general and recommended the destruction of the "filthy object" by water and fire. The ensuing banishment was actually a merciful substitute for the capital punishment ordered by the infuriated emperor.

It was Han Yü's lifelong conviction that the restoration of the supremacy of Confucianism, with the corresponding suppression of Buddhism and Taoism, was the road to bringing forth order out of chaos in the land. His essays "On Man," "On the Tao," "On Human Nature," and on similar topics are considered harbingers of the Neo-Confucian movement in Chinese philosophy which flourished in the 11th century.

An administrator, military strategist, social reformer, and philanthropist, Han Yü is most of all remembered as a man of letters. More than anyone else, he was responsible for breaking the hold of the highly stilted and extravagant style of writing which was popular at the time. He attributed his own success as a classical literary stylist to his absorption in the Confucian classics, both in their teaching and in their expression.

Han Yü's collected works contain some 300 poems and an even larger number of letters and essays. Few are the Chinese who have completed their education without having learned a number of Han Yü's essays by heart, and many have been inspired by his example not only to say things clearly and elegantly but also to be fearless to say what is on one's mind. Han Yü was accorded the posthumous title of Master of Literature. In 1084 his tablet was placed in the Confucian Temple.

Further Reading

There is a dearth of English-language material on Han Yü. A treatment of the writer is found in any history of Chinese literature or of Chinese philosophy. Fung Yulan, *A History of Chinese Philosophy* (trans. 1937; 2 vols., 1952-1953), and Wu-chi Liu, *An Introduction to Chinese Literature* (1966), are among the best. □

Norman Hapgood

As an editor and author during the Progressive era in the United States, Norman Hapgood (1868-1937) was involved in vital issues affecting government policy and civil rights.

Norman Hapgood was born in Chicago, Ill., on March 28, 1868, of intellectual and affluent parents. The family prided itself on both Revolutionary and Tory ancestors. After graduating from Harvard College, he became a journalist.

In 1897 Hapgood joined the *New York Commercial Advertiser* as a literary and drama critic. He made a reputation for clear writing and independent opinion. *Literary Statesmen and Others* (1897) and *The Stage in America*

1897-1900 (1901) were informative and varied, though in their criticism of playwrights Henrik Ibsen and George Bernard Shaw and partiality for James M. Barrie they revealed Hapgood's bias for sweetness and light.

In 1902 Hapgood became editor of *Collier's Magazine* and a central figure in social and political muckraking (that is, exposé) writing and reform efforts. He entered cautiously into reform, repelled, for example, by the "sensationalism" of Upton Sinclair's *The Jungle*. Nevertheless, he found himself drawn into such major public events as the battle for pure food and drugs and the movement to curb the power of "Czar" Joseph G. Cannon, Speaker of the U.S. House of Representatives. *Collier's* quarrel with Secretary of the Interior Richard A. Ballinger concerning the disposal of government lands in Alaska was outstanding, and it cost William Howard Taft's administration its credibility with the general public.

Hapgood left *Collier's* in 1912 to edit *Harper's Weekly*. Now keenly aware of free-speech issues and eager to create a supranational body that could control militarism, he sought to aid President Woodrow Wilson in furthering both. In 1919 he was Wilson's controversial minister to Denmark and a founder of what became the Foreign Policy Association. As editor of *Hearst's International* (1923-1925), he opposed the Ku Klux Klan and also industrialist Henry Ford as a supporter of anti-Semitic propaganda. In 1927 Hapgood's *Professional Patriots* exposed organizations that suppressed civil liberties. His last political enthusiasm was Democratic presidential candidate Alfred E. Smith, whom he saw as a latter-day Lincoln, and whose campaign biogra-

phy, *Up from the City Streets* (1927), he wrote with Henry Moskowitz. Hapgood was editor of the *Christian Register* when he died on April 29, 1937.

Further Reading

Hapgood's autobiography, *The Changing Years* (1930), is given added dimensions in the richer book by his brother Hutchins Hapgood, *A Victorian in the Modern World* (1939). The Ballinger case is carefully retold in Alpheus Thomas Mason, *Bureaucracy Convicts Itself* (1941). Louis Filler, *Crusaders for American Liberalism* (1939; new. ed. 1961), places Hapgood in the era of reform.

Additional Sources

Marcaccio, Michael D., *The Hapgoods three earnest brothers,* Charlottesville: University Press of Virginia, 1977. □

Kei Hara

The Japanese politician and statesman Kei Hara (1856-1921) was the first commoner and the first professional politician to become prime minister of Japan, initiating the trend toward responsible party government that ended in 1932.

Born to a high-ranking samurai family in the Morioka fief in Iwate province, Hara was given the personal name of Kenjiro, later changed to Satoshi (written with a character read also as Takashi or Kei). The Tokugawa shogunate fell when Hara was 11, and since the Morioka had supported it, Hara's promised future in the feudal system seemed bleak.

Determined to succeed despite this bad luck, Hara made his way to Tokyo in 1872. He first entered a French Catholic seminary, where he was baptized, and later a law school, from which he was expelled for student activism. At 24 he joined the newspaper *Hochi* but left it when it was taken over by supporters of Toshimichi Okuma, who made it into an antigovernment paper.

Burning with political ambition, Hara decided not to join the opposition or fall in with the dominant Satsuma-Choshu factional leaders but to bore his way up into the oligarchy by making personal connections. Joining the progovernment paper *Daito,* he ingratiated himself with the oligarch Kaoru Inoue, who got him a post in the Japanese embassy in France and later in the Ministry of Agriculture. There Hara became the protégé of Munemitsu Mutsu, who had once opposed the oligarchy but now was making his way upward into it through his own abilities. Mutsu became foreign minister in 1893. He helped Hara into better positions but resigned for ill health. Hara then left the government, too, becoming president of the Osaka newspaper *Mainichi* for 3 years.

Learning of Hirobumi Ito's intention of launching a political party (the Seiyukai) in 1900, Hara rushed back to Tokyo and was made the party's chief secretary. Because of his ability to conduct delicate negotiations, manage the party, and collect political funds, Hara himself became Seiyukai president in 1914. Hara was elevated to the premiership in September 1918 with the reluctant approval of conservative oligarch Aritomo Yamagata, who disliked seeing a "party man," a member of the Lower House, and a commoner become premier, but he got Hara to promise to push through big defense appropriations.

While the Hara Cabinet was hailed as the first in Japanese parliamentary history to be made up entirely of party members and as initiating the trend toward responsible party government, it was full of ironies. Hara was a "commoner" only because he felt too aristocratic to accept a peerage from the Meiji oligarchs. His moves toward a party spoils system and his countenancing of political corruption not only caused his assassination by a disgruntled railway switchman on Nov. 4, 1921, but contributed to the eventual undermining of confidence in party government.

Further Reading

An interesting treatment of Hara's early political career is Tetsuo Najita's monograph *Hara Kei in the Politics of Compromise, 1904-1915* (1967). His later life and the significance of his premiership are discussed in Peter Duus, *Party Rivalry and Political Change in Taisho Japan* (1968). □

Irene Harand

Irene Harand (1900–1975) was an Austrian leader in Vienna who vigorously attacked the evils of Nazism, anti-Semitism, and religious intolerance and was honored by Israel for her efforts.

Only in the mid-1980s did it become apparent that not all of the horrors of Nazism originated in the nation that Adolf Hitler and his movement gained control over in 1933. A series of events made it clear that Hitler's Austrian homeland also played a significant role. For many decades Austria had enjoyed a reputation as a land of beautiful Alpine scenery, good food, and glorious musical traditions. Few Austrians and virtually no foreigners seemed interested in the darker sides of their country's recent past. Despite the fact that many Austrians had welcomed the German forces when Hitler annexed his homeland to Germany in March 1938, this was largely forgotten during World War II, when the Allied Powers issued their Moscow Declaration of November 1943, which solemnly proclaimed that Austria had been the "first victim" of Nazi aggression. This policy was as much based on a strong desire on the part of the anti-Nazi coalition to rapidly build up an independent Austrian nation, and thus ensure a permanently weakened Germany after the war, as it was grounded in an accurate understanding of contemporary history. Austrians took advantage of these attitudes after 1945 by creating a stable series of governments that played down internal political differences by ignoring ideology and emphasizing national solidarity. The bloody and deeply divisive Nazi past was simply swept under the rug, to most Austrians' immense relief.

In 1986 four decades of Austrian national amnesia about the Nazi past came to an abrupt end when it was revealed that one of the serious candidates for the office of president that year, former United Nations Secretary-General Kurt Waldheim, had not told the truth in his memoirs about his war service in the Nazi-occupied Balkans. The lively debate that grew out of this revelation opened a Pandora's box of details about that nation's recent past, particularly the difficult topic of its historic relationship with its Jewish citizens. This subject was discussed with even more passion starting in March 1988, when the 50th anniversary of the Nazi annexation (*Anschluss*) of Austria was commemorated by both government and private citizens. As a traumatic chapter of Austrian history finally began to be examined, nearly forgotten episodes surfaced from an often painfully repressed national memory.

The history of Christian hostility to Jews is a long and complex story with theological, economic, social, and psychological origins. In short, Europe's Jewish minority even in the Middle Ages was tolerated only when it served a purpose for the Christian majority in each nation. Christian moral teachings forbade the lending of money for interest (usury), but with the rise of a money economy such activity was necessary for any developing society; consequently, the presence of Jewish bankers, money lenders, and mer-

chants became essential for rulers if they wanted to rule strong and powerful states. However, when plagues, famines, or wars destabilized the social fabric it was common to single out the Jews as scapegoats and blame them for the calamities. Bloody persecutions followed. Being at the crossroads of central Europe, Austria had a thriving economic and intellectual life that attracted Jews at various times in its history, but while they enjoyed periods of prosperity and toleration, they also endured episodes of persecution.

Accompanying the religious fanaticism of the Crusades in the 11th and 12th centuries there came specific charges against Europe's Jews—including what was seen to be their collective murder of Jesus and continuing rejection of him as the Messiah. Jews were also accused of economic exploitation because of their involvement with money-lending. But most serious was the charge leveled by some of the clergy that held the Jews responsible for poisoning wells, murdering Christian children, and desecrating the consecrated wafers so as to mock the sacrifice of Jesus. As early as 1420-21, Archduke Albrecht V of Austria ordered that Jews be expelled from Vienna, blaming them for supplying arms to the forces of the Bohemian heretic Jan Hus. As would be the case in later centuries, these "reasons" were little more than pretexts for attacking the Jews. It was easy to find a scapegoat for one's woes in a group that had stubbornly remained religiously and ethnically distinct within the larger Christian society. Wiping clean the slate of indebtedness to Jewish money lenders was doubtless an attractive idea at a time when the costs of financing a war against Hussite rebels had become onerous. The combination of religious, cultural, and economic motives in Christian persecution of Jews would reappear in later centuries as the two communities continued to interact in an increasingly complex political and economic environment.

Austria's Jews began to emerge from their traditional ghetto world in the mid-18th century when the Empress Maria Theresa decreed in 1764 that they could engage in certain types of trade as well as continue their traditional activities as money lenders and changers, bankers, and jewel merchants. The Empress was by no means kindly disposed toward Jews, having once stated that she knew of "no worse plague" afflicting her empire, but she moved in the direction of a limited form of tolerance because her advisers made it clear that her realm stood to benefit economically. Far greater reforms affecting Jews in the Habsburg realm took place in the reign of Maria Theresa's son, Emperor Joseph II, which began in 1780. A thoroughgoing reformer, Joseph not only freed the Jews from such traditional burdens as having to wear a Jewish badge— a yellow Star of David —on their clothing but also encouraged their cultural as well as economic integration. The 1782 Patent of Toleration ended the requirement that Jews live in their own ghettos and opened up the trades and most professions to them.

By the mid-19th century, a significant number of Austrian and Hungarian Jews had broken away from traditional Jewish religious and cultural patterns and were now part of the modern economy, actively participating in the cultural and intellectual life of Budapest, Prague, and Vienna. Yet Jews remained second-class citizens, at least in part because the authoritarian nature of the regime denied all its subjects, not only Jews, basic constitutional rights that had been at least partially achieved in Great Britain and the United States. It was therefore not surprising that Jews participated when a massive 1848 uprising took place in Vienna against the reactionary regime of Prince Klemens von Metternich, who had headed the Austrian government for more than a generation. After the revolution was crushed, conservatives often blamed Jews for its excesses, suggesting that Jewish intellectuals were dangerous hotheads who could invariably be found in the vanguard of radical movements.

The Austrian Constitution of December 21, 1867, granted all of Emperor Francis Joseph II's subjects full civil liberties. Vienna's Jews took advantage of their new freedoms by engaging in commercial and financial enterprises as well as by preparing for the medical and legal professions by enrolling in universities. Many fortunes were made in the 1860s and early 1870s by Jewish financiers, and by the end of the 19th century a high percentage of Vienna's physicians and attorneys were of Jewish background; most of the city's newspapers were Jewish-owned. But these successes were threatened by a dark cloud. When the Vienna (as well as the Berlin) stock market experienced a severe crash in 1873, Jewish financiers and speculators involved in the collapse were blamed for the entire scandal despite the presence of non-Jews who were also implicated in the complex web of corruption. The financial catastrophe unleashed a general economic downturn. Workers and small shopkeepers lost their livelihood. While the causes of the depression were multi-factored, and few could prescribe a simple cure, many believed they knew the element responsible—the Jews.

By 1875, when the conservative publicist Baron Karl von Vogelsang founded his newspaper *Vaterland,* many Christian Viennese responded to his analysis of the modern causes of poverty and social instability. Vogelsang—whose Catholic conservatism was based on an idealized vision of the social harmony that characterized the Middle Ages—identified Jews with virtually all of the evils of his age, seeing them as the vanguard of such socially disruptive systems as capitalism, economic laissez-faire liberalism, materialism, and atheism. Although Vogelsang was harshly critical of what he defined as a corrosive "Jewish spirit," and advocated the creation of a new and "re-Christianized" social order, he did not attack the Jewish religion. Neither did he consider Jews to be biologically different or inferior to Christians. Rather, he hoped that the situation would be remedied when Jews converted to Roman Catholicism, abandoning their reputed love of secular wealth and power.

Others who criticized Austria's Jewish community looked at the problem from a different perspective. In France and Germany a number of writers claimed to have discovered objective, indeed "scientific," causes of the social ills of the time. First published in the 1850s, the racial theories of French author Count Arthur Joseph de Gobineau now appeared to some to hold the key to an understanding of the social chaos confronting the 19th century. Gobineau

argued that the only creative element in history was the white race, and that other human races, including the Jews and other Semitic peoples, had acted only as parasites. Gobineau himself was not hostile to Jews, and had hoped to make a strong case for the preservation of the privileges of the French aristocracy, arguing that they were racially the most creative and valuable segment of society. But others adapted Gobineau's pseudoscientific notions to their own ideological agendas, particularly in the troubled decade of the 1870s. In 1879 the German author Wilhelm Marr coined the term "anti-Semitic," contrasting the innocent and trusting German "race" to Jews who were forever rootless, cunning, and deceitful, while in the same year the German historian Heinrich von Treitschke defined the "Jewish problem" as a question of national survival.

By 1881 German and Austrian anti-Semitism was carried to new extremes when the University of Berlin professor Eugen Dühring published a violently anti-Semitic book entitled *The Jewish Question as a Race, Morals and Cultural Question.* Dühring asserted that the Jews were a distinct biological entity, a racial group that could never be assimilated or Christianized. These notions were highly attractive to ambitious politicians who could use them as a means of appealing to social groups in the population that had recently suffered from the ravages of unrestricted laissez-faire capitalism, or who felt themselves threatened by Jewish competitors in the job market. Fear of Jewish job competition was particularly strong at Austrian universities and technical institutes, where the number of Jewish students in many fields—particularly law and medicine—was much higher than that of the Jewish percentage of the overall population. By the late 1870s many student fraternities (*Burschenschaften*) had begun to exclude Jews from membership, arguing they did not possess German moral qualities, could never duel or drink beer as well as pure-blooded "Aryans," and were thus not fitted for membership in such exclusive circles.

By the mid-1880s the radicalized racist students of Vienna and Graz had found their champion in an up-and-coming politician named Georg von Schönerer (1842-1921). Schönerer's father had been an extremely successful railroad engineer who had at one time worked for the Jewish banking family the Rothschilds and who had become wealthy in his own right. Untroubled by money worries, the younger Schönerer entered political life in the 1870s as a left-wing liberal, championing some major social reforms. In June 1882 Schönerer turned decisively from liberalism, which was not a racist ideology, by founding the League of German Nationalists (*Deutschnationaler Verein*). This organization of several hundred journalists, teachers, and businessmen called for an all-out campaign against Jewish influences in the economy and political life, as well as in intellectual life and the arts. Using demagogic arguments, Schönerer and his followers agitated among students, middle-class Viennese shopkeepers, and artisans, trying to persuade them that all of their woes were due not to the economic slump of the period, or the capitalist system itself, but to the nefarious power of Jewish speculators and bankers. Although Schönerer's movement was able to score some successes, by the late 1890s it had been largely outdistanced by a new, much more effective vehicle for anti-Semitic demagoguery, the Christian Social party.

By the early 1890s anti-Semitic appeals had become commonplace in Austrian public life, and it was scarcely surprising that politicians more pragmatic and adaptive to changing moods should appear on the scene. The most successful of these figures was the Viennese-born popular leader Karl Lueger (1844-1910), whose personal charm and political astuteness was combined with a cynical use of anti-Semitic slogans that were immensely appealing to his lower middle-class constituency. In the 1890s, Lueger became undisputed leader of the Roman Catholic political party, the Christian Socials, by creating a mass political movement based largely on the fear artisans and shopkeepers had of "Jewish capitalism." In the closing decades of the 19th century tradesmen and artisans found their livelihoods increasingly threatened by competition from more efficient factories and retail distribution networks. Many of these were Jewish-owned enterprises, and anti-Semitic appeals fell on sympathetic ears—particularly if they were attractively presented in the folksy style perfected by such suave demagogues as Lueger.

Lueger's message was a peculiarly Viennese form of populist anti-capitalism that, while vague in its precise program of how to combat Jewish "threats to the Christian social order," nonetheless proved immensely appealing to the imperial city's populace. Even though Lueger refrained from proposing specific legislation to curb Jewish influences, his Christian Social party was able to win an absolute majority in the Vienna municipal elections of April 1895. Although Emperor Franz Joseph II refused on four occasions to appoint him to the office of Vienna's lord mayor, Lueger's continuing popularity finally forced the sovereign to relent in April 1897. Thus, Lueger became the first mayor of a major European city to rule on an anti-Semitic platform, and his Christian Social party was clearly the most successful political movement of the late 19th century to base its appeal on hostility toward the Jews.

In practice, Lueger's bark was much worse than his bite. Indeed, within a few years it became clear to the Jews of Vienna that Christian Social racism was almost entirely rhetorical in nature. No legislation was ever passed against Jews and, while they were greatly underrepresented in the bureaucracy, education and the professions were open to them. Ironically, the years 1897-1914 were a veritable Golden Age in Viennese Jewish history. In a society whose aristocracy continued to look contemptuously on money-making activities, Jews and other newly-arrived immigrants in Vienna found that with hard work they could often succeed in such areas as journalism, medicine, law, and the stock exchange. Although many Christian Austrians retained some anti-Semitic prejudices, in the prosperous years before 1914 even they reluctantly concluded that the many nationalities of the Habsburg empire would have to find ways to tolerate one another for the common good. Among the signs of growing toleration were the decline of Schönerer's influence among the fraternities and the rapid rise of the Social Democratic party, which included many

Jewish intellectuals and was based on an ideology of universal social transformation based on working-class fraternity.

This promise was shattered in August 1914 by the coming of World War I. At first, the war acted as a unifying force for the multinational state, and until 1916 there was a remarkable sense of common purpose among the different ethnic groups comprising the Habsburg realm. But by late 1916, war-weariness and extreme privations, particularly food shortages, had sapped the will of most Austrians to continue the war. The death of the aged Emperor Franz Joseph II in November 1916 symbolized the end of an era. By this time, anti-Semitism, particularly among a now impoverished middle class, was rampant. With Vienna overcrowded with tens of thousands of Jewish refugees from war-ravaged Galicia, rumors of black-market profiteering by Jews became a commonplace explanation for the sufferings of average Viennese. Politicians, particularly in the Christian Social party, seized upon the situation as one offering immense opportunities for increasing their own popularity at the expense of an increasingly unpopular minority.

The sudden collapse of the Habsburg military in October 1918, and the subsequent abolition of the monarchical regime in November, only accelerated a growing mass psychosis directed against a vaguely-defined "Jewish menace." Pacifist and Marxist Jews were now blamed for spreading defeatist propaganda among the frontline troops, thus hastening the military catastrophe. On the home front, too, Jews were seen as the major culprits of a spiraling inflation and black-market economy that made even the basic essentials of existence unaffordable to the middle class. For a resurgent anti-Semitic movement, Jews threatened the very existence of civilization in Austria, acting as either greedy capitalists or fomenting social unrest leading inevitably to a bloody civil war and Bolshevik dictatorship. At Austrian universities, and particularly at the world-famous University of Vienna, bloody student riots (Krawalle) regularly erupted in which Jewish students were beaten up and thrown down flights of stairs. In countless newspapers, magazines, and posters Jews were depicted as inhuman and depraved enemies of civilization whose cunning nature constituted an immediate threat to a supposedly pure Germanic spirit.

The end of inflation and the stabilization of the Austrian economy in the mid-1920s dampened but did not eliminate the deep-seated anti-Semitism. The fact that the leading religious and moral institution of Austria, the Roman Catholic Church, did little to combat such prejudices (and on many occasions actually endorsed and encouraged them), only emphasized the difficulties faced by those Christian groups and individuals who aspired to rid Austria of racial and ethnic hatreds.

In the troubled 1930s, before and during World War II, the individual who most effectively challenged Christians in Austria to live up to the teachings of their own religion in regard to the Jewish question was a woman, Irene Harand. Later, because the great majority of Austrians felt a need to suppress painful details of their recent history, and because her Nazi enemies almost succeeded in obliterating her memory from the consciousness of her fellow countrymen, the story of Irene Harand has only recently emerged from the shadows.

Irene Wedl was born into a prosperous Viennese family on September 6, 1900. Her father, a manufacturer, was Roman Catholic; her mother was Lutheran. To avoid any religious conflicts in the family, Irene and her three siblings were all raised as Catholics, but one of Irene's aunts was Jewish, making two of her cousins half-Jewish. Such religious and ethnic mixtures were quite common in pre-1914 Vienna, and among the educated elite toleration, rather than disapproval, was the general spirit in which such personal matches were viewed. But anti-Semitism was common among the poorer, less educated groups in society who had been propagandized by the demagogues.

During a summer holiday as a young girl, Irene had a firsthand experience with anti-Semitism when she, an older sister, and her two half-Jewish cousins were surrounded by a group of local peasant children who taunted them with pejorative anti-Semitic slogans. Decades later she recalled running, with her older sister in the lead, to the security of the family cabin. Vividly, she remembered what it had been like to be "on the receiving end" of racist hatred, noting that "one never forgets the first time one feels oneself frightened to death, and sees the world as being full of nothing but enemies."

In 1919 she married Frank Harand, who had served as a captain in the Austrian army during World War I. Like his bride, he was a devout Catholic who believed that if the world was to be spared another bloodletting such as the recently ended war, it would have to rebuild its moral values and social institutions on Christian principles of justice, love, and toleration. While both Harands were politically conservative and sympathetic to the principles of monarchism, during the first decade of their marriage they avoided political controversies, concentrating instead on creating a pleasant life for themselves. Although she had not attended a university during the 1920s, Harand read widely and familiarized herself with the major economic and political controversies of the time. During these years she increasingly came to read about, and sometimes discuss with friends, two closely intertwined problems that concerned politically active Austrians: the continuing hostility toward the nation's Jewish minority, and a small but growing ultraradical movement that pledged to solve once and for all Europe's "Jewish problem."

The Austrian Republic that came into existence in November 1918 with the demise of the Habsburg monarchy of Austria-Hungary was given little hope of survival. It was unable to feed itself and was burdened with the metropolis of Vienna that contained more than one-third of the new nation's impoverished population; indeed, most Austrians desired *Anschluss* (union) with the German Republic to the north. Furthermore, Austrian political life was a cauldron of deep-seated hatreds, with the ultraconservative Catholic party, the Christian Socials, facing an often implacably doctrinaire Marxist Social Democratic Workers' party. With small but militant Pan-German and Nazi parties appealing to returning veterans whose idea of politics was based on physical conflict and annihilation, Austrian political life in

the first half-decade of the Republic's existence was often violent and bloody. Ideologically, too, post-1918 Austrian politics exhibited extremely intolerant traits. Except for the Social Democrats, which most Austrian Jews supported, Austrian political parties during these years all campaigned on anti-Semitic platforms.

Although the Catholic Church did not condone the violent anti-Semitism of the Nazis, many Catholic clergymen including the nation's brilliant but often politically uncompromising federal chancellor, Ignaz Seipel, regarded the Jews as undesirable agents of social decomposition. The Church saw itself as a "nonpolitical" body that was leading the Austrian "spiritual" struggle against Jewry while the Christian Socials were to be found engaged in the often messy political arena. Yet, in practice, such lines were easily crossed.

This moral environment deeply distressed the Harands as well as others whose vision of a Christian society was built on justice and compassion, and who were convinced that for society to flourish Christians and Jews must be taught to tolerate and respect one another. But neither of the Harands had a pragmatic plan for infusing Christian ideals into a troubled land's public life. Indeed, Harand would continue to remain aloof from political controversies until a series of events inexorably led her into the arena of public debate. She had become interested in the plight of an aged nobleman whose poverty had recently been compounded by a deep personal disappointment. In the years of inflation, 1920-23, he had seen his fortune evaporate and now, in his extreme old age, he endured the pain of his son's refusal to assist him, though some years earlier he had given the son all of his lands and his castle. Believing she might be able to assist the old man, she set out to obtain justice through the law. She consulted a number of lawyers, and even though none accomplished anything of substance, all charged her substantially. After a number of such discouraging encounters, she met with well-known attorney Dr. Moritz Zalman.

Zalman differed from the other lawyers in that he showed great enthusiasm for the case, insisting that the old man could—indeed must—obtain justice. When the question of fees came up, Zalman told Harand that if she had managed to volunteer her time, energy, and funds on behalf of the poor nobleman, then he could certainly provide his legal skills gratis. This moment was the start of Harand's political career. Harand realized that even she—who had never knowingly harbored anti-Semitic feelings—had sought out only non-Jewish lawyers prior to consulting with Zalman, who was Jewish. The instant he volunteered assistance, the thought had crossed her mind that by refusing a fee for his work Zalman was not "behaving in a Jewish fashion." At this point, with a probing honesty characteristic of her personality, Harand concluded that she had initially interpreted the situation with an anti-Semitic mindset. Like most Viennese of her day, she had assumed that Zalman by definition would be an avaricious, unscrupulous individual. Immediately realizing that this was not the case, she decided to work closely with Zalman not only to help one old man, but to create the foundations of a movement that would bring new and better ideas into Austrian public life.

Besides being a respected attorney who often volunteered his time to help poor but deserving clients, Zalman had for years been deeply involved in political struggles on behalf of the poor and downtrodden. He was particularly involved in cases where impoverished old-age pensioners were denied their benefits. In one such instance, his efforts had resulted in the passing of a new law that guaranteed pensions to 40,000 men and women who had previously been denied any payments. Both Zalman's tough determination to find practical ways to accomplish a goal and his unquenchable moral concern for justice deeply impressed Harand. Together they created the Austrian People's party and, in what would turn out to be the last free parliamentary elections in Austria, campaigned in November 1930 on a platform calling for greater support for impoverished pensioners while condemning the increasingly virulent outbreaks of anti-Semitic propaganda and violence.

The election results were a disappointment, indeed a veritable disaster, for the fledgling party. Only 14,980 Austrians cast a ballot for the Austrian People's party (8,459 of these were in Vienna). As a consequence, no seats were won in the national legislature, and what few contributions had flowed into the party treasury before the election could now, in the middle of a worsening economic depression, no longer be counted on.

At this juncture, many might have withdrawn from political life, but a disturbing incident at the time of the election strengthened Harand's resolve to remain active. While walking on Vienna's busy Wiedner Hauptstrasse, she witnessed a parade of Nazi youths, characterizing them later as "a troop of half-grown youngsters." While marching by, they shouted a standard Nazi slogan: "*Juda verrecke*" (death to the Jews). Pedestrians at the scene seemed indifferent. Deeply shocked by this event, Harand noted that one boy of about 12 seemed transformed before her very eyes "from a human child to a little bloodthirsty beast." Alarmed by what she had seen, Harand decided that Nazism in Austria, while still not a mass movement in 1930, had clearly become a dangerous phenomenon because of its powerful appeals to young people seeking a cause. Nazism, she believed, was "guilty of robbing our children of their childhood, stealing our children from us and making criminals of them."

Soon after the incident, Harand appeared at a Catholic political meeting to warn of the growing menace of Nazism. Instead of a sympathetic reception, the audience dismissed her warnings, mocked her for a lack of political experience or judgment, and booed her off the stage as a "foolish, hysterical woman." But it would take more than public humiliation to discourage Harand, who was determined to awaken the people of her native Vienna to the evils growing in their midst. For over a year, she and Zalman continued to warn about the dangers of Nazism and racial hatred, spreading their message in small groups that met in apartments, cafes, and rented halls. But few seemed interested in their warnings. In both Germany and Austria, the Nazi movement grew alarmingly in size and aggressiveness. Most people were more concerned with the basics of economic survival during the depression and regarded Adolf Hitler as another Lueger, an unscrupulous demagogue whose anti-Semitism would quickly moderate once he was forced to deal with the responsibilities of actually wielding political power.

Harand's energies were galvanized when Hitler assumed control over Germany in early 1933. In a small pamphlet entitled "So? oder So?" which included on its cover sketches of a swastika and balanced scales of justice, she communicated with a mass audience on the burning issue of the day—whether Nazism, using anti-Semitism as one of its major arguments, would be able to seize power in Austria. Financed by herself and her husband, *So? oder So?* was printed in an edition of 30,000 copies, and sold for the low price of 20 Groschen. The main thesis of the work was that virtually all of the arguments used by anti-Semites were untruths, or gross distortions, and that Jews as individuals rarely behaved in the ways that racist stereotypes had depicted them. She gave as her motive for writing a basic belief that as an Austrian, a Christian, and an "Aryan" she had a responsibility to speak up for a historically maligned people, pointedly reminding her readers that Jesus Christ had also been a Jew.

Encouraged by a favorable response to her pamphlet, which soon went into a second printing of another 30,000 copies, Harand went about her work with a heightened sense of urgency in the summer of 1933. The Austrian Nazi party had been declared illegal in June of that year and was now engaged in numerous bomb attacks and other underground activities designed to destabilize and psychologically disarm the Austrian government. Attacks on Jewish shops and homes in Vienna became common, and it was clear that if Nazism triumphed in Austria the fate of its Jewish citizens would be grim at best. Seeking moral and financial support from both Catholics and Jews, Harand was able in early September 1933 to release the first issue of a newspaper dedicated to enlightening the public about the menace of Nazism. Called *Gerechtigkeit* (Justice), it declared as its guiding principles a strong desire to fight against racial hatred and to ameliorate human suffering. In a box featured on the first page of each issue, Harand proclaimed the reason for her defense of the honor of Austria's Jews: "I fight anti-Semitism because it defames our Christianity."

Gerechtigkeit quickly became a popular—and often controversial—publication. Many of Vienna's Jews felt their morale improve when they began reading this clearly written, courageous weekly newspaper. Some Catholics who had never given much thought to their anti-Semitic attitudes began to question some of their own assumptions (and prejudices) when confronted with powerful and passionately argued ideas. Within a short time of its founding, *Gerechtigkeit* reached a circulation of almost 30,000 copies. But Vienna's illegal Nazis regarded the paper as a dangerous weapon in the hands of their enemies and demonstrated their anger by disrupting Harand's rallies and meetings with stink bombs and firecrackers. Threatening letters were often addressed to Harand, warning that her defense of Jews made her a traitor to the "cause of pure Germandom."

Harand was not deterred. Encouraged by the initial successes of her publications, in 1933 she founded a "Movement against Anti-Semitism, Racial Hatred and Glorification of War." Anyone could join this organization, which was usually simply referred to as the Harand Movement. It appealed to Jews and Christians, young as well as old, and by May 1934 could claim 40,000 members. Although membership dropped slightly in 1936 to 36,000, in that year the Harand Movement could boast of 6,000 non-Austrian members. The religious affiliations of the Movement's Austrian members broke down into 25,000 Roman Catholics, 4,000 Jews, and 1,000 Protestants. Remembering that words alone would not suffice to combat ethnic and religious hatreds, the Harand Movement organized several shelters in Vienna that were able to provide hot drinks, food and warmth for 200 to 300 unemployed and homeless people daily in the city's bitterly cold winter months.

Aware that her message of religious toleration and resistance to Nazi racism could only be effective if disseminated to as many people as possible, Harand showed remarkable creativity in "packaging" the ideas of her movement in many different forms. The successful pamphlet *So? oder So?*, as well as the newspaper *Gerechtigkeit*, served to sound the alarm about Nazism, but other methods of recruitment and persuasion were constantly being tried. To win over alienated youth, an organization called the Austrian Youth League (*Österreichischer Jugendbund; ÖJB*) was created; many of its members came from the Social Democratic youth organizations banned in February 1934. Also popular was a youth chorus that served as an auxiliary of the ÖJB, which gave a number of successful concerts of Austrian folk songs. Another novel idea was the issuance of a phonograph record, one side of which contained a brief statement by Harand, with the other side reserved for a song, *"Gute Menschen"* (Good People), which summed up the humane optimism of the Harand Movement.

A final method of spreading the message was a series of perforated gummed labels which resembled postage stamps but had no postal validity. Printed in several languages, these labels depicted great Jewish thinkers, artists, and scientists and were meant to counter the Nazi slander that Jews had never been cultural benefactors. On at least one occasion, these labels were used in Nazi Germany by underground members of the Harand Movement who were in touch with their Vienna headquarters. In 1937 courageous members of the Movement entered the exhibition hall in Munich housing the Nazi regime's anti-Semitic propaganda exhibition *"Der ewige Jude"* ("The Eternal Jude"). Here they plastered the walls and exhibition frames with many of these labels, which depicted among other individuals the noted Jewish scientists Paul Ehrlich and Heinrich Hertz and politicians Benjamin Disraeli and Walter Rathenau.

In August 1935 Harand published a book that became her most compelling indictment of Nazism and anti-Semitism. Entitled *Sein Kampf*, this work was obviously meant to refute the arguments first raised a decade earlier by Hitler in *Mein Kampf*. By 1935 some conservative Austrians were clearly thinking of the day when an increasingly powerful Nazi Germany would be able to absorb the weak Alpine republic, and were thus less enthusiastic about supporting an outspoken anti-Nazi like Harand. It was probably for this reason that she was unable to find a publisher among the established publishing houses; undaunted, she had her manuscript privately printed and published. In the first chapter of in *Sein Kampf*, she defined as one essential feature of Nazism its reliance on lies, defining a lie as "a filthy weapon . . . a crime against God, against Nature and against Humanity."

While most of *Sein Kampf* was a vigorous defense of the Jews, Harand's book also analyzed and condemned other destructive forces in the modern world, particularly the long-existing spirit of rabid nationalism that made it possible for Hitler's movement to seduce and control otherwise decent human beings. Arguing that national feelings based on attitudes of superiority toward another people could only act as a poison and lead to war, she made it clear that, while she considered herself to be a good Austrian, such love of country was patriotism—not a narrow-minded and intolerant nationalism. Perhaps realizing that at least in the short run hers was to be a losing battle, Harand wrote in the Preface:

I hope that [this book] will bring consolation to the victims of National Socialism. It ought to assure them that there are still some people in this world who will not submit to the terror of the Third Reich but who will fight until the danger of Nazi expansion is banished from the earth and the victims of National Socialism are rescued from their torturers.

Sein Kampf ends with both a grim warning and words of shining hope: "National Socialism is the greatest menace of the century. In fighting it, we must use weapons which the Nazis scorn: Idealism and Courage, Common Sense and Love, Truth and Justice!"

The 1935 publication of *Sein Kampf* turned Harand into a declared enemy of the Third Reich. With its provocatively anti-Nazi title it quickly came to the attention of Nazi Germany's supreme censorship board, the *Reichsschrifttumskammer*, which kept tabs on any publication deemed dangerous to the regime. In the board's list of banned books issued in October 1935, *Sein Kampf* was described as being both "dangerous and undesired." With this listing, it became clear that Harand was now regarded as an active and dangerous foe of the Hitler regime. Not only Nazi literary agencies but Heinrich Himmler's feared SS and Gestapo placed her name on lists of those individuals in Austria who would be "dealt with accordingly" at such time that Nazi control extended to her country. Fortunately both Harands were in Great Britain at the time of the *Anschluss* which marked the annexation of Austria to Nazi Germany in March 1938. Had they been in Vienna, there is little doubt that they would have been sent to Dachau concentration camp, where the first anti-Nazis were transported when the Nazi rulers destroyed the vestiges of independent Austria.

After a brief period in Great Britain, the Harands emigrated to the United States, where Irene continued her defense of Jewish honor against Nazi propaganda. By the 1950s, her work was forgotten in both her native Austria and her new homeland America. Only in her final years did her life's work begin to receive the recognition it deserved. In 1969 she was honored by Israel's Yad Vashem Martyrs and Heroes Remembrance Authority as one of the non-Jewish individuals who helped Jews during the Holocaust period and thus deserved recognition as one of the "Righteous among the Nations." One of the members of the commission that recommended her for the award noted the courage necessary in her activities of the 1930s:

[T]o deliver public speeches at a time when Austria was swept by a wave of political assassinations meant exposing oneself to great risk. This woman waged a desperate and unceasing war which placed her in great peril. She sent her boys to hand out the newspaper at street corners. The children were beaten and she was beaten too. She stood her ground against vilification and threats. If this is not a struggle in which one risks one's life, then I don't know what risk means. She fought to save Austrian Jewry.

After decades of indifference, Harand's Austrian homeland began to take an interest in her achievements in the 1970s. She visited Vienna and was honored there in 1971. It was not, however, until 1990, some ten years after her death, when a public housing project in the heart of Vienna was named after her, that she became known again to the average Viennese. No doubt she would have appreciated the April 20th date chosen for the dedication ceremonies. Every April 20th had been celebrated in the Third Reich with elaborate ceremonies, for it was the birthday of Hitler. After many decades, at least symbolic justice had triumphed in a small corner of Hitler's homeland.

Further Reading

Bassett, Richard. *Waldheim and Austria*. Penguin Books, 1990.
"Champion of Justice: Irene Harand," in *Wiener Library Bulletin*, Vol. 9, nos. 3/4, May-August 1955, pg. 24.
Haag, John. "A Woman's Struggle Against Nazism: Irene Harand and Gerechtigkeit," *Wiener Library Bulletin*. Vol. 34, new series 53/54, 1981, pp. 64-72.
Harand, Irene. *His Struggle (An Answer to Hitler)*. Artcraft Press, 1937.
Paldiel, Mordecai. "'To the Righteous among the Nations Who Risked Their Lives to Rescue Jews,'" in *Yad Vashem Studies*. Vol. 19, 1988, pp. 403-425.
Pauley, Bruce F. *From Prejudice to Persecution: A History of Austrian Anti-Semitism*. University of North Carolina Press, 1992.
Weinzierl, Erika. "Christliche Solidarität mit Juden am Beispiel Irene Harands (1900-1975)," in Marcel Marcus et al., eds., *Israel und Kirche Heute: Beiträge zum christlich-jüdischen Dialog/Für Ernst Ludwig Ehrlich*. Herder, 1991, pp. 356-367.
Geehr, Richard S. *Karl Lueger: Mayor of Fin Vienna, de Siecle* Wayne State University Press, 1990.
Hallie, Philip. *Lest Innocent Blood be Shed: The Story of the Village of Le Chambon and How Goodness Happened There*. Harper & Row, 1979.
Parkinson, F., ed. *Conquering the Past: Austrian Nazism Yesterday & Today*. Wayne State University Press, 1989.
Pauley, Bruce F. *Hitler and the Forgotten Nazis: A History of Austrian National Socialism*, University of North Carolina Press, 1981.
Whiteside, Andrew G. *The Socialism of Fools: Georg Ritter von Schönerer and Austrian Pan-Germanism*. University of California Press, 1975. □

Ilyas al-Harawi

Ilyas al-Harawi (Elias Hrawi, born 1930) became president of Lebanon in 1989 at a time when his nation was torn by war, its economy crippled, and its defense and foreign policy dominated by neighboring Syria.

Ilyas al-Harawi was born in 1930 in Hawsh al-Umara', a suburb of the city of Zahle in the Bekáa valley in the eastern part of Lebanon. He obtained a degree in commerce from the Jesuit St. Joseph University in Beirut. He was a scion of a family of large landowners that was represented in the Chamber of Deputies beginning in 1943. He married Mouna Jammal and they had five children. He was elected a deputy of Zahle in the 1972 parliamentary elections. He served in the cabinet as the minister of public works during the period 1980-1982. In 1979 Harawi had joined the parliamentary bloc called the Independent Maronite Deputies Bloc, which included many presidential aspirants. He was elected president on November 24, 1989, two days after the assassination of President Rene Mu'awwad.

A Weak President

President Harawi and his predecessor were elected in accordance with the Ta'if Accord, a blueprint of reforms agreed upon by 62 Lebanese parliamentarians on October 22, 1989, in Ta'if, Saudi Arabia. Harawi was elected under unusual circumstances, which made him a weaker president than any of his predecessors since the independence of Lebanon in 1943. First, he succeeded an assassinated president. Secondly, he had to face an entrenched interim prime minister, General Michel Aoun, who refused to accept the Ta'if Accord and continued to operate from the presidential residence in Ba'abda. Thirdly, the Ta'if Accord itself changed the Lebanese political system from a quasi-presidential system to a cabinet-parliamentary system, and this was done at the expense of presidential powers. Fourthly, Harawi became president at a time when Syria under Hafiz Assad virtually dominated the Lebanese polity.

The first problem that Harawi had to deal with was General Aoun, who had emerged as the popular leader of those who opposed the Ta'if Accord. The conflict, which pitted Aoun's army against the Christian militia, the Lebanese Forces, during the period January-May 1990, weakened Aoun and prepared the ground for a Syrian air and land attack that dislodged Aoun from his headquarters in Ba'abda on October 13, 1990. Although Harawi gained in this action by forcing his rival to seek refuge in France, he lost in popular support, as he was perceived as an instrument of Syrian dominance in Lebanon.

The first two years of the Harawi presidency witnessed a greater Syrian hegemonic role in Lebanon. The Ta'if Accord, which had no provisions for eventual withdrawal of Syrian troops in Lebanon, was fully endorsed by the Chamber of Deputies on August 21, 1990. President Harawi and Syrian president Assad signed the Treaty of Brotherhood, Cooperation and Coordination between Syria and Lebanon in Damascus on May 22, 1991. The treaty called for joint Syrian-Lebanese institutions in the areas of defense, security, foreign policy, and the economy. Later, on September 1, 1991, Syria and Lebanon signed an agreement that established coordination in military strategy and internal security matters and in the exchange of intelligence information. This agreement was ratified by the Chamber of Deputies on September 17, 1991.

During Harawi's presidency all American hostages were released by December 4, 1991, when the radical party Hizballah (Hezbollah) freed Terry Anderson. By December 27, 1991, the remains of Lieutenant Colonel William Higgins and William Buckley, the former CIA bureau chief in Beirut, were returned. This, however, did not end the ban on travel to Lebanon for U.S. citizens, because Hizballah remained armed and operated freely in Lebanon. Although this was contrary to the stipulations of the Ta'if Accord, which called for the disarming of all militias, Syria prevented the disarming of Hizballah on the grounds that it was engaged in a war against the Israelis and their allies in southern Lebanon. This low-intensity conflict in southern Lebanon was a contrived conflict that Syria and Iran kept alive to serve their own national interests while the Lebanese president was not allowed to use the Lebanese Army to disarm Hizballah and put an end to the conflict.

Another drawback to the implementation of the Ta'if Accord was Syria's refusal to redeploy its troops to the eastern regions of Lebanon (as stipulated by the accord) two years after the passage of the reforms by the Chamber of Deputies, which became due in the autumn of 1992.

Successful Domestic Policies

The domestic achievements of Harawi's presidency were more successful. Internal conflict, except for that in southern Lebanon, came to an end. The free enterprise economic system, which has always been a hallmark of the Lebanese economy, survived the civil war and foreign military interventions and received a boost by the appointment of the billionaire Rafiq al-Hariri as prime minister in October 1992. The partnership of Christians and Muslims that characterized the consociational democratic system beginning in 1943 remained intact. The 1992 parliamentary elections for an expanded Chamber of Deputies (from 99 to 128 members) which equally divided between Christians and Muslims, should have been another step in the right direction. They were to be conducted under United Nations' supervision and after the redeployment of Syrian troops. But in fact, the elections were on the whole neither fair nor free and were boycotted by large segments of the electorate. Moreover, the curtailment of the press and the banning of news bulletins and political programs by private radio and television stations, which began on March 23, 1994, did not

augur well for the Lebanese polity, which had hitherto enjoyed this basic freedom. These developments marred the tangible positive advances achieved under President Harawi.

Continuing Rule

According to the Lebanese Constitution, each president was allowed only one six-year term and successive terms were prohibited. This meant that Harawi's term should have ended with elections in November of 1995. However, in October of 1995 the Lebanese government, with backing from Syria, amended the constitution so that Harawi could preside for three more years. This move was meant to encourage stability in the country, since Harawi was so successful at bringing peace to Lebanon, and because he had such good relations with Syria. Critics, though, saw this as a threat to democracy in Lebanon.

Further Reading

For additional information see the following works by Marius K. Deeb: *The Lebanese Civil War* (1980); "Lebanon in the Aftermath of the Abrogation of the Israeli-Lebanese Accord: The Dominant Role of Syria" in Robert O. Freedman (ed.), *The Middle East from the Iran-Contra Affair to the Intifada* (1991); and "Lebanon: Prospects for National Reconciliation in the Mid-1980s," *Middle East Journal* (Spring 1984); In Arabic, see Iliya Harik, *Man Yahkum Lubnan* (*Who Rules Lebanon*, Beirut, 1972).

Additional Sources

"Lebanon. Their Master's Voice." *Economist* 337 (October 21, 1995): 42+.

MacSwan, Angus. "Lebanon Cabinet Petitions President to Extend Term." *Reuters Ltd.,* 16 October 1995.

"President Elias Hraoui." *Biography from the Lebanese Embassy,* 1997.

Siblani, M. Kay. "Syrian Scales Seen Tipping in Favor of Keeping Lebanon's Hrawi In." *Arab American News,* 12 May 1995. □

Prince Karl August von Hardenberg

Prince Karl August von Hardenberg (1750-1822) served as chief minister of Prussia. He presided over the recovery of Prussia after the collapse of 1806 and guided the state's diplomacy.

Karl August von Hardenberg was born in Essenrode on May 31, 1750, and, as a young man, served in the bureaucracies of a number of small German states, including Hanover, Braunschweig, and Ansbach-Bayreuth. When the last was incorporated into Prussia in 1791, he was taken into the Prussian services, with the chief responsibility for governing that province. He also distinguished himself in various diplomatic assignments, so that by 1804 he was appointed Prussian foreign minister. The policy he recommended—strict neutrality in the Napoleonic Wars, combined with an attempt to acquire Hanover—would have been possible only with the help of Napoleon and was, to say the least, contradictory. Hardenberg was soon dropped by Frederick William III.

Hardenberg was recalled after the Prussian military collapse at Jena (1806) and at once attempted to salvage the situation by negotiating an alliance with Russia. At Napoleon's insistence he was dismissed a second time. He was, however, recalled in 1810 in the capacity of chief minister of Prussia, with the charge of administering the internal reforms proposed by Baron Stein. This he proceeded to do in a spirit rather more radical than Stein had proposed. All legislation favoring the restrictive craft guilds was abolished; the privileges of the nobility were severely curtailed; all taxation was consolidated into a general land tax; the remnants of serfdom, the forced labor still required of the peasantry on the large estates, were abolished. All of these radical steps were defended as the only means of raising the huge indemnity which Napoleon had imposed on Prussia.

At the same time Hardenberg presided most ably over the conduct of Prussian foreign policy. He saw to it that Prussia reentered the war at the right time and led the Prussian delegation to the Congress of Vienna (1815), where Prussia recovered all of the territory it had lost at Tilsit in 1807. Thereafter, Hardenberg, while remaining chief minister until his death, forfeited much of his influence by his vain attempts to persuade Frederick William III to honor his promise to give Prussia a constitution after the successful conclusion of the war. The King and the temper of the times were drifting toward reaction, and Hardenberg found himself representing, unwillingly, Prussia at a number of international congresses devoted to the suppression of liberalism in Europe. He died in Genoa on Nov. 26, 1822.

Further Reading

In the absence of English-language biographies of Hardenberg, the student should consult W. M. Simon, *The Failure of the Prussian Reform Movement* (1955); K. S. Pinson, *Modern Germany* (1963; 2d. ed. 1966); Hajo Holborn, *A History of Modern Germany,* vol. 2 (1964); and Klaus Epstein, *The Genesis of German Conservatism* (1966). ☐

James Keir Hardie

The British politician James Keir Hardie (1856-1915) helped to initiate the 20th-century labor movement in Britain.

Keir Hardie was born on Aug. 15, 1856, at Legbrannock, Lanarkshire, the illegitimate son of Mary Keir, domestic, and William Aitken, miner. He took the name of his stepfather, David Hardie, a ship's carpenter. He worked as a messenger boy when he was 8; from 1867 to 1879 he worked in or around the coal mines. Self-educated, he especially enjoyed what he read of Robert Burns, Thomas Carlyle, and Henry George. A convinced socialist at 21, he was converted to Christianity at 23, to the astonishment of his firmly atheistic mother.

Fired and blacklisted for union activity, Hardie was undismayed, and he married Lily Wilson, a publican's daughter, Aug. 3, 1879. After local union service he became secretary to the Scottish Miners' Federation in 1886. Hardie clashed with old-line "Lib-Lab" members of Parliament, whom he thought overly conservative about state intervention on the miners' behalf. Hardie's agitation for an 8-hour day brought cooperation from R. B. Cunninghame-Graham, a member of Parliament and a cofounder of the Scottish Labour party in 1888.

Hardie's election to Parliament for South West Ham in 1892 as an Independent Labour candidate won attention; publicity increased with his appearance at Westminster in a cloth cap, his maiden speech on the misery of the unemployed, and his dissent from congratulations on the birth (1894) of the future Edward VIII.

Hardie presided at the Bradford conference which inaugurated the Independent Labour party (ILP), pledged to socialism and intended as a weapon against unconverted Gladstonian Liberals. He lost his own seat in 1895 but pressed ILP candidates to challenge Liberals at by-elections. Returning to Parliament from Merthyr Tydfil in 1900, he denounced the Boer War constantly. Despite his feud with Liberals, Hardie approved the negotiation which reduced Liberal-Labour rivalry and produced 29 Labour members in 1906, who chose Hardie to lead them in Parliament.

In 1907 Hardie toured the world, expressing his sympathy with Egyptian independence, Indian home rule, and fairer treatment of native Africans in South Africa. He was often a difficult colleague within the Labour party before the war. He detested militarism and preached a general strike among workers internationally to prevent war. When war came, it crushed his spirit. He was howled down by his own constituents before he died of pneumonia on Sept. 26, 1915.

For years Hardie symbolized the working classes for cartoonists. He never forsook his soft hat for a bowler. Bearded, pipesmoking, with a mournful Celtic visage, his single-minded devotion to the workers' cause made him seem fanatical to some contemporaries but enhanced his reputation with later generations of the Labour party.

Further Reading

The earliest biography of Hardie is William Stewart, *J. Keir Hardie* (1921; new ed. 1925). It was followed by David Lowe, *From Pit to Parliament: The Story of the Early Life of James Keir Hardie* (1923); Hamilton Fyfe, *Keir Hardie* (1935); and Emrys Hughes, *Keir Hardie* (1956). Hardie's role in the Independent Labour party is treated by Henry Pelling in *The Origins of the Labour Party, 1880-1900* (1954; 2d ed. 1965), and by Philip P. Poirier in *The Advent of the British Labour Party* (1958).

Additional Sources

McLean, Iain., *Keir Hardie,* New York: St. Martin's Press, 1975.
Reid, Fred., *Keir Hardie: the making of a socialist,* London: Croom Helm, 1978. □

with all elements in the faction-ridden Ohio Republican party, he belonged to the Old Guard wing of the party. He ran unsuccessfully for governor in 1910. But in the Republican comeback in 1914 Harding was elected to the U.S. Senate. As a senator, Harding strongly supported business, pushing for high tariffs, favoring the return of the railroads to private hands, and denouncing radicals. He was a "strong reservationist" on the League of Nations, and he followed Ohio public opinion by voting for the prohibition amendment.

In 1919 Harding announced his candidacy for the Republican presidential nomination; he won the nomination on the tenth ballot. Legend has pictured Harding as a puppet in the hands of his wife or his campaign manager. But Harding was no one's puppet: he was an ambitious and calculating politician. Nor was he the handpicked nominee of a group of Old Guard senators. The convention was unbossed, and Harding, with his reputation as a loyal party man, his amiable personality, and his avoidance of controversial stands, was the second choice of the majority of the rank-and-file delegates. When the two front-runners deadlocked, the convention had swung to the handsome Ohioan.

In the election Harding successfully straddled the explosive League of Nations issue. By capitalizing on the public's yearning for a return to "normalcy" after World War I, Harding won by the largest popular majority yet recorded.

Warren Gamaliel Harding

The twenty-ninth president of the United States, Warren Gamaliel Harding (1865-1923), highly popular during his lifetime, was later regarded as one of the worst presidents in the country's history.

Warren G. Harding was born on Nov. 2, 1865, on a farm near Blooming Grove, Ohio. He attended local schools and graduated from Ohio Central College in 1882. His father moved the family to Marion that same year. After unsatisfactory attempts to teach, study law, and sell insurance, young Harding got a job on a local newspaper. In 1884 he purchased the struggling *Marion Star* with two partners (whom he later bought out). The growth of Marion and his own business skill and editorial abilities brought prosperity to the *Star* and to Harding. On July 8, 1891, he married Florence DeWolfe, a widow with one child; they had no children of their own.

Election to Office

Active in local Republican politics, Harding was elected in 1899 to the Ohio Senate, where he served two terms and became Republican floor leader. In 1903 he was elected lieutenant governor but retired in 1905. Although a born harmonizer who remained personally on good terms

The President

Despite the country's postwar position as a creditor nation, Harding gave his blessing to protective farm tariffs. Devoted to governmental economy, he supported establishment of the Bureau of the Budget, sharply cut government expenditures despite depressed economic conditions, and vetoed the World War I veterans' bonus passed by Congress. He backed Secretary of the Treasury Andrew Mellon's program for repealing the excess-profits tax and lowering the income tax on the wealthy; he gave Secretary of Commerce Herbert Hoover a free hand in his efforts to promote business cooperation and efficiency; he favored turning over government-owned plants to private enterprise; he packed regulatory commissions and the Supreme Court with conservative appointees; and he strongly favored immigration restriction.

Harding wished to remain neutral in labor disputes and worked behind the scenes for conciliation, but when his hand was forced, he took management's side. Thus, after his attempted mediation in the 1922 railroad shopmen's strike failed, he approved a sweeping injunction against the strikers—this won him the bitter enmity of organized labor.

But Harding was not the archreactionary of later myth. He supported the Sheppard-Towner Act (1921), extending federal aid to the states to reduce infant mortality. He unsuccessfully proposed establishing a department of public welfare to coordinate and expand Federal programs in education, public health, child welfare, and recreation. He was instrumental in ending the 12-hour day in the steel industry. He promoted increased federal spending on highways. He commuted the sentences of most of the wartime political prisoners, including Socialist leader Eugene V. Debs. While balking at government subsidies or price-fixing to assist farmers hard hit by postwar falling prices, he approved legislation for extending credit to farmers, for stricter federal supervision of the meat industry, for regulating speculation on the grain exchanges, and for exempting farm marketing cooperatives from the antitrust laws.

Foreign Policy

In foreign policy Harding was largely guided by his prointernationalist secretary of state, Charles Evans Hughes. Although Harding regarded the 1920 election as a popular mandate against American membership in the League of Nations, his administration cooperated with the nonpolitical activities of the League, and in 1923 he came out in favor of American membership on the World Court. Adamant in demanding full repayment of Allied war debts, he was flexible in arranging terms.

Efforts were made to restore good relations with Mexico and Cuba and to terminate military intervention in Haiti and the Dominican Republic. Colombia was indemnified for the loss of Panama. The Harding administration's most important diplomatic achievement was the Washington Conference. Meeting in November 1921, the conferees formulated a series of treaties, which secured Senate ratification, fixing ratios of warships for the United States, Britain, Japan, France, and Italy, guaranteeing the territorial status quo in the Pacific, and reaffirming the independence and territorial integrity of China and the open-door principle of commercial equality.

Scandals in the Administration

By 1923 Harding was increasingly disturbed by the rumors of corruption involving high administration officials and hangers-on. But he failed to act decisively, partly because he believed the attacks were politically motivated, partly because of a misplaced loyalty to old friends. Perhaps his worst mistake was in appointing his senatorial crony Albert B. Fall as secretary of the interior. Fall persuaded Harding to transfer naval oil reserves from the Navy Department to the Department of the Interior. Then, after Fall had corruptly leased the reserves at Elk Hills, Calif., and Teapot Dome, Wyo., to oilmen, he induced Harding to defend these transactions when questions were raised in the Senate.

Although the Republicans had suffered sharp losses in the 1922 congressional elections, Harding personally remained tremendously popular. However, his health was affected by overwork and anxiety over his wife's health and the multiplying evidences of corruption in his administration. He suffered a heart attack followed by bronchopneumonia while on his cross-country tour in the summer of 1923. He died on Aug. 2, 1923, probably from a cerebral hemorrhage. The posthumous exposure of the scandals in Harding's administration—including Fall's conviction for bribery, the attorney general's forced resignation and narrow escape from jail, and prison sentences for the head of two government bureaus—and the charges that Harding had fathered an illegitimate daughter and that he drank excessively all led to his decline in public esteem.

Yet Harding was not the affable, weak, and even stupid figure of popular legend. He was a hardworking, conscientious, well-intentioned, politically skillful chief executive who was not without courage or the capacity for growth. Most contemporaries praised his success in leading the country through the painful transition from the difficulties of the postwar years, and his administration did lay foundations for later prosperity. But he showed indecisiveness and lack of leadership when faced with conflict; his mind was untrained and undisciplined; and most important, the values of small-town America which he embodied were inadequate for dealing with the problems of the postwar world.

Further Reading

There is no satisfactory biography of Harding. Francis Russell, *The Shadow of Blooming Grove: Warren G. Harding in His Times* (1968), emphasizes the scandalous aspects of Harding's private and public life. Andrew Sinclair, *The Available Man: The Life behind the Masks of Warren Gamaliel Harding* (1965), contains shrewd insights but is superficial in its research. Robert K. Murray, *The Harding Era* (1969), is a well-researched but not wholly convincing attempt to rehabilitate Harding's presidential reputation. See also William Allen White, *Masks in a Pageant* (1928), and Samuel Hopkins Adams, *Incredible Era: The Life and Times of Warren G. Harding* (1939). On the election of 1920 see Arthur M. Schlesinger, Jr., ed., *History of American Presidential Elections,* vol. 3 (1971). □

Harriet Hardy

Harriet Hardy (1905-1993) identified the often-fatal respiratory disease berylliosis, making her one of the world's foremost authorities in the field of occupational medicine.

Harriet Hardy intended to be a simple general practitioner, but fortuitous events changed that plan. Through the investigation of a respiratory illness that was common among factory workers in two towns in Massachusetts, she discovered the often-fatal respiratory disease berylliosis—a discovery that led to her becoming one of the world's foremost authorities in the field of occupational medicine. In the course of her long career she battled against numerous diseases caused by dangerous substances to which workers are exposed, including silicosis and asbestosis.

Born on September 23, 1905 in Arlington, Massachusetts, Harriet Louise Hardy set her course early on for a career in medicine. In 1928 she graduated from Wellesley College, and four years later earned her M.D. from Cornell University. After interning and spending her residency at Philadelphia General Hospital, she started her practice at Northfield Seminary in Massachusetts as a school doctor. This simple practice, however, did not last long, and by 1939 she had accepted a post as college doctor and director of health education at Cambridge's Radcliffe College. It was here, while researching the fields of women's health and fitness, that Hardy's interests expanded to include industrial diseases.

In the early 1940s, Hardy began a collaboration with Joseph Aubt to study the effects of lead poisoning. Like Alice Hamilton and other pioneering pathologists of the time, Hardy began to recognize the dangers inherent in the modern factory, with workers coming into contact with all manner of toxic substances. There soon came word of a strange respiratory disease among the workers in the Sylvania and General Electric fluorescent lamp factories in nearby Lynn and Salem, Massachusetts. The sufferers all complained of shortness of breath, coughing, and loss of weight; in some cases, the disease was fatal. Hardy and her colleagues were initially baffled as to the cause of the disease, but it occurred to Hardy that the disease had to be occupationally related. Referring to research from Europe and Russia, Hardy finally found the connection to beryllium; a light metal used in the manufacture of fluorescent lamps, beryllium dust or vapor could be easily inhaled by factory workers. Hardy showed that this outbreak was indeed berylliosis, a condition whose symptoms sometimes are not manifested for up to 20 years after exposure to beryllium dust. Hardy subsequently became an expert in beryllium poisoning, writing papers which educated and alerted the medical community to its dangers. She also established a registry of berylliosis cases at the Massachusetts General Hospital (where she had been on staff since 1940); this registry later served as a model for the tracking of other occupation-related disorders.

Hardy went on to establish a clinic of occupational medicine at Massachusetts General Hospital in 1947, directing it for the next 24 years. She continued to explore the disease-producing properties of work-related substances, and in 1954 she was among the first scientists to identify a link between asbestos and cancer. Hardy was also concerned with the effects of radiation on the human body; she worked with the Atomic Energy Commission in Los Alamos, New Mexico, to study radiation poisoning, making a number of suggestions toward better working conditions in nuclear power plants. In 1949 she teamed up with Hamilton to write the second edition of *Industrial Toxicology,* which has become a standard text on the subject. Other areas of Hardy's research and investigation included mercury poisoning and treatments for lead poisoning. She also researched the harmful effects of benzene, and as a result of her findings the highest permissible concentration of the hydrocarbon used in industry was reduced by fifty percent.

In 1955 she was named Woman of the Year by the American Medical Women's Association. An outspoken and forceful critic for change, Hardy was appointed clinical professor at Harvard Medical School in 1971, and during the course of her long career authored over 100 scientific articles. She died of an immune system cancer, lymphoma, on October 13, 1993 at Massachusetts General Hospital.

Further Reading

Harvard Medical School Focus, October 21, 1993, p. 9.
Journal of the American Medical Women's Association, November, 1955, p. 402.
New York Times, October 15, 1993, p. B10. □

Thomas Hardy

The works of the English novelist, poet, and dramatist Thomas Hardy (1840-1928) unite the Victorian and modern eras. They reveal him to be a kind and gentle man, terribly aware of the pain human beings suffer in their struggle for life.

Thomas Hardy presented the spectacle of England from Napoleonic times to World War I and after. He revealed the changes that overwhelmed Victorian England and made it modern: the decline of Christianity, the shifts from reticence to openness in matters of sex and from an agricultural to a modern economy, and above all the growing sense of the disparity between the enormous universe and tiny man.

Hardy was born on June 2, 1840, in Higher Bockhampton in Dorset, which formed part of the "Wessex" of his novels and poems. A small baby, thought at birth to be dead, he became a small man only a little over 5 feet tall. He was taught by his father, a builder, to play the violin, and he often journeyed about the countryside playing for dances and storing up the impressions of rural life that make up so large a part of his work.

Early Writings

After attending local schools, Hardy was apprenticed in 1856 to John Hicks, an architect in Dorchester. At this time he thought seriously of attending university and entering the Church, but he did not do so. In 1862 he went to London to work. There he began to write poems and send them to publishers, who quickly returned them. He kept many of the poems and published them in 1898 and afterward. Back in Dorchester in 1867 working for Hicks, he wrote a novel, *The Poor Man and the Lady,* which he was advised not to publish on the ground that it was too satirical for genteel Victorian tastes. Told to write a novel with a plot, he turned out *Desperate Remedies* (1871), which was unsuccessful.

Meanwhile Hardy had begun to work for Gerald Crickmay, who had taken over Hicks's business. Crickmay sent him to Cornwall, where on March 7, 1870, he met Emma Lavinia Gifford, with whom he fell in love. Their courtship is recorded in *A Pair of Blue Eyes* and in some of Hardy's most beautiful poems, among them "When I Set Out for Lyonnesse" and "Beeny Cliff."

Hardy could have kept on with architecture, but he was a "born bookworm," as he said, and in spite of his lack of success with literature he decided to continue with it, hoping eventually to make enough money to enable him to marry. For *Under the Greenwood Tree* (1872) he earned £30. The book was well received, and he was asked to write a novel for serialization in a magazine. In September 1872 *A Pair of Blue Eyes* began to appear, even though only a few

chapters had been completed. *Far from the Madding Crowd* (1874), also serialized, was a success financially and critically. By then making a living from literature, Hardy married Gifford in September 1874.

Later Novels

Hardy preferred his poetry to his prose and thought his novels merely a way to earn a living. Certainly he was willing to write his novels to the requirements of magazines: a "thrill" in every installment and nothing to offend feminine readers. But his best novels—*The Return of the Native* (1878), *The Mayor of Casterbridge* (1886), and *Tess of the D'Urbervilles* (1891)—were, at least in book form, much more than magazine fiction. The main characters were individuals moving before a chorus of rural folk and a backdrop of unhuman and uncaring nature. The people were dominated by the countryside of "Wessex," Hardy's name for the area in south-west England where he set most of his novels, and the area is as vividly memorable as the people.

Even Hardy's best novels, however, were marred by a characteristically awkward prose and overuse of coincidence, as were the lesser novels: *The Hand of Ethelberta* (1876), a comedy of society; *The Trumpet-Major* (1880), about the Napoleonic Wars; *A Laodicean* (1881), written while sick in bed; *Two on a Tower* (1882), about an astronomer and a lady; and *The Woodlanders* (1887), about an unhappy marriage.

Good or bad, his novels brought Hardy money, fame, and acquaintance with the great. With his wife he traveled in Germany, France, and Italy; he built Max Gate near Dorchester, where he lived from 1886 until his death; he frequently dined out, meeting Matthew Arnold, Robert Browning, Alfred, Lord Tennyson, and others. Robert Louis Stevenson sought him out and visited him at Max Gate. It was a successful life and seemed happy enough, but he had a strained relationship with his wife.

Though Hardy's novels seldom end happily, he was not, he stated, a pessimist. He called himself a "meliorist," one who believed that man can live with some happiness if he understands his place in the universe and accepts it. He ceased to be a Christian; he read Charles Darwin and accepted the idea of evolution; later he took up Arthur Schopenhauer and developed the notion of the Immanent Will, the blind force which drives the universe and in the distant future may see and understand itself. This notion is not very optimistic for any one man's life, but it does leave room for hope.

Hardy was increasingly displeased by the restrictions imposed on his novels by the magazines. In the book version of *Tess* he restored several chapters cut out of the serial, and the book was attacked as immoral. In *Jude the Obscure* (1895) he did the same; there was an immense outcry. The story of a young man torn between the urgings of sex and the desire to go to the university, *Jude* presented the woes of marriage with a frankness not known till then in the Victorian novel. It is poorly constructed and too bitter to be one of Hardy's best novels, but it may be his most famous, because its reception was a main cause of his turning from novels to poetry.

Poetry and Drama

Collecting new and old poems, Hardy published *Wessex Poems* (1898) and *Poems of the Past and Present* (1902). Then he began to publish *The Dynasts,* an immense drama of the Napoleonic Wars which depicts all the characters, even Napoleon, as puppets whose actions are determined by the Immanent Will. The drama is commented on by "phantasmal Intelligences," who explain the workings of the Will. The "epic-drama" evolved into 19 acts and 130 scenes; it was published in three parts in 1903, 1905, and 1908. Meant to be read, not acted, it is frequently called Hardy's masterwork. Certainly it unites all his thoughts on the human condition in a vision remarkable for its scope.

Meanwhile Hardy continued to publish his shorter verse in *Time's Laughingstocks* (1909). His most famous single volume of poems, *Satires of Circumstance,* appeared in 1914. It revealed the extremes of Hardy's emotional range in the short, bitter poems referred to in the title and the longer poems about his first wife, who died in 1912. Any bitterness in their relationship had disappeared in the nostalgia with which he viewed their courtship and married life. *Selected Poems* (1916), *Moments of Vision* (1917), *Late Lyrics and Earlier* (1922), and *Human Shows* (1925) were published during the remainder of his life. *Winter Words* (1928) was published after his death.

Because in most cases Hardy published his poems years after he wrote them, the dates of composition can be determined only by his references to them in *The Early Life of Thomas Hardy* or *The Later Years.* Thus it is difficult to show Hardy's growth as a poet. In fact, he hardly grew at all. The last poems are remarkably similar in diction, meter, and feeling to the earliest. Because of this, his poems are customarily divided into three groups: naturalistic poems, or little slices of life; love poems, almost all about his first wife; and theological poems, about the workings of the Immanent Will. In the last kind, Hardy's macabre sense of humor is allowed full play.

In almost all his poems Hardy uses Victorian diction, regular meters, and neat stanzas. These cause him to be called a Victorian poet. But he also uses everyday words. These, with his bleak view of the human condition and his fusion of humor and pity, rank him with the moderns.

In 1914 Hardy married Florence Emily Dugdale, who had been his secretary for several years. He continued to receive famous visitors at Max Gate and to go to London for special occasions. He died on Jan. 11, 1928. His heart was buried in the churchyard at Stinsford, his ashes in Westminster Abbey.

Further Reading

The Early Life of Thomas Hardy, 1840-1891 (1928) and *The Later Years of Thomas Hardy, 1892-1928* (1930) were written mainly by Hardy rather than by the ostensible author, Mrs. Florence Emily Hardy. The life story is retold and Hardy's work interpreted by Carl J. Weber in *Hardy of Wessex: His Life and Literary Career* (1940; rev. ed. 1965). The true story of Hardy's relationship with his first wife appeared only in 1963 in *"Dearest Emmie": Thomas Hardy's Letters to His First Wife* (1963) and in *Hardy's Love Poems* (1963), both edited by Weber.

There is considerable critical material on Hardy. Albert J. Guérard, *Thomas Hardy* (1964), and Irving Howe, *Thomas Hardy* (1967), are astute studies of all of Hardy's work. Virginia Woolf's essay in *The Second Common Reader* (1932) bears the mark of greatness in its estimate of the novels.

John Crowe Ransom's comments on Hardy's short poems in *Poems and Essays* (1955) and *Selected Poems of Thomas Hardy* (1961) are indispensable. Harold Orel interprets *The Dynasts* in *Thomas Hardy's Epic-Drama* (1963). Excellent introductions to the historical background of Hardy's work are G. M. Young, *Victorian England: Portrait of an Age* (1936; 2d ed. 1953), and David Thomson, *England in the Nineteenth Century* (1950). □

Robert Hare

Robert Hare (1781-1858), considered the leading American chemist of his time, was a productive inventor and writer.

Robert Hare was born in Philadelphia on Jan. 17, 1781, the son of a prominent businessman and state senator. He was educated at home, then studied chemistry under James Woodhouse. While managing his father's brewery, he found time for chemical research and gained international fame in 1801 with his invention of the oxyhydrogen blowpipe, which provided the highest degree of heat then known. (Its application led to the founding of new industries such as production of platinum and limelight illuminants.)

After teaching briefly at the College of William and Mary in Virginia, Hare was appointed professor of chemistry at the University of Pennsylvania in 1818, where he remained until 1847. Hare's classes were noted for his spectacular experiments. His inventions included a calorimeter, a deflagrator for producing high electric currents, and an improved electric furnace for producing artificial graphite and other substances.

Although primarily noted as an experimental chemist and inventor of experimental apparatus, Hare was keenly interested in theoretical speculations about both chemistry and meteorology. He published articles in the *American Journal of Science,* edited by his close friend and collaborator Benjamin Silliman. His famous controversies were with Jöns J. Berzelius over chemical nomenclature, Michael Faraday over electricity, and William C. Redfield over the nature of storms. Hare was especially committed to the theory of the materiality of heat.

In 1850 Hare published a historical novel, *Standish the Puritan.* In 1854, near the end of his career, he became a convert to spiritualism, much to the dismay of his rationally minded colleagues. He produced a book on the subject and went so far as to claim that Benjamin Franklin's spirit had validated his electrical theories. But he was unsuccessful in getting the American Association for the Advancement of Science to listen to his views.

Hare was a member of the American Philosophical Society and the American Academy of Arts and Sciences. Though his only degrees were honorary, he represented the newly emerging professional university scientist in contrast to the traditional gentleman-amateur.

Hare had married Harriet Clark in September 1811; one son, John James Clark Hare, became a distinguished lawyer. Hare died on May 15, 1858.

Further Reading

The standard biography of Hare is Edgar F. Smith, *Life of Robert Hare* (1917). Additional material may be found in Henry Simpson, *The Lives of Eminent Philadelphians* (1859), and George P. Fisher, *Life of Benjamin Silliman* (1866). General background is available in Nathan Reingold, ed., *Science in Nineteenth Century America* (1964), and George H. Daniels, *American Science in the Age of Jackson* (1968).

Additional Sources

Smith, Edgar Fahs, *The life of Robert Hare: an American chemist, 1781-1858,* New York: Arno Press, 1980. □

Edward Hammond Hargraves

Edward Hammond Hargraves (1816-1891) was an Australian goldfields publicist whose astute assess-

ment of reports of gold discoveries in New South Wales played a part in the first Australian gold rush, in 1851.

Until recently Edward Hargraves had an undeserved reputation as the first discoverer of gold in Australia and consequently held an unduly high place in popular histories of the country, for the extensive gold rushes of the 1850s in both New South Wales and Victoria had important effects on economic and social changes in 19th-century Australia and some effect on international trade and monetary development.

Hargraves was born on Oct. 7, 1816, at Gosport, Hampshire, England, the son of an army officer. He joined the merchant marine and arrived in Sydney, New South Wales, in 1832. After working the land near Bathurst, in 1833 he sought bêche-de-mer in Torres Strait and returned to England.

The following year Hargraves returned to Bathurst as property overseer and familiarized himself with the country on which gold was later found. In 1836 in Sydney he married Eliza Mackie and settled in the Illawarra District. For the next 12 years he tried without success to make a living in the hotel trade and in cattle raising on the central coast of New South Wales.

Hearing of the California gold rush, Hargraves sailed for America in 1849. He found no gold and failed as a goldfields trader but did discuss with men who knew the western districts of New South Wales the strong likelihood of gold being discovered there because of similarities with the California fields. He returned to Sydney in January 1851 determined to test his opinions, chiefly in order to establish a claim for a government reward for the discovery of payable gold.

Appointed a commissioner of crown lands, Hargraves went to the Bathurst area in February 1851 during an unusually dry summer and found only minute quantities of gold in Lewis Ponds Creek, but he taught other prospectors to construct and use the wooden cradle and dish and encouraged them to persevere, especially John Lister and James and William Tom. Back in Sydney in March, Hargraves continued his pressure for a reward after he had heard of the discovery of 4 ounces of gold. By May he had returned to the Bathurst fields, which were now attracting numerous diggers. He named the richest area Ophir, where rain had revealed the presence of considerable alluvial gold, and presided over Australia's first gold rush.

Hargraves later received £10,000 for his trouble and in 1877 was granted a pension of £250. He also received £2,381 from the government of Victoria. In 1890 a New South Wales parliamentary committee decided that "Messrs. Tom and Lister were undoubtedly the first discovered of gold in Australia in payable quantities." Hargraves died in Sydney on Oct. 29, 1891.

Further Reading

There is no biography of Hargraves. His account of the Australian discoveries, *Australia and Its Gold Fields* (1855), was probably ghosted, possibly by Simpson Davison, whose own *The Discovery and Geognosy of Gold Deposits in Australia* (1860; 2d ed., entitled *The Gold Deposits in Australia,* 1861) gives valuable information on Hargraves. E. W. Rudder, *Incidents Connected with the Discovery of Gold in New South Wales* (1861), is also useful. The best modern account is in Geoffrey Blainey, *The Rush That Never Ended: A History of Australian Mining* (1963).

Additional Sources

King, John Anthony, *Edward Hammond Hargraves Esq.: an exuberant biography of the "discoverer" of payable gold in Australia,* Sydney; New York: Summit Books, 1977.
Silver, Lynette Ramsay, *A fool's gold?: William Tipple Smith's challenge to the Hargraves myth,* Milton, Qld.: Jacaranda Press, 1986. □

Keith Haring

Although invariably, and undeniably, tied to New York graffiti art of the 1980s, Keith Haring's (1958-1990) work represents a much more complex combination of primitive impulses, automatic writing, popular culture, and so-called "high" and "low" art.

Born on May 4, 1958, Keith Haring was raised in a traditional middle-class family in Kutztown, Pennsylvania. He would later remember fondly the creative drawing sessions he and his father, an amateur artist, would have together. Haring's early influences were not unlike those of many American children growing up in the 1960s—the cartoons of Walt Disney, Dr. Seuss, Charles Schulz, and the Looney Tunes characters he would watch on Saturday morning television's "The Bugs Bunny Show"; television sitcoms such as "I Dream of Jeannie" and "The Monkees"; and the powerful images in *Life* and *Look* magazines. These influences reflect the dominant role, emphasized by the Pop artists of the period, that mass media and popular culture had on American life.

After graduating high school in 1976, Haring attended the Ivy School of Professional Art in Pittsburgh, Pennsylvania. Feeling stifled by the constraints of a commercial art education, he left school after only two semesters. The catalyst for this decision was the chance reading of Robert Henri's *The Art Spirit* (1923), which inspired him to concentrate on his own art.

While working in a maintenance job for the Pittsburgh Center for the Arts (then the Pittsburgh Arts and Crafts Center), Haring explored on his own the art of Jean Dubuffet, Jackson Pollock, and Mark Tobey. His most critical influences at this time were a retrospective of the work of Pierre Alechinsky in 1977 and a lecture by the site sculptor, Christo, in 1978. Alechinsky's work, connected to the international Expressionist group CoBrA, gave Haring the confi-

dence to create larger paintings of calligraphic and automatic writing inspired images. Christo introduced him to the possibilities of involving the public with his art. Pittsburgh was also the host of Haring's first important one-man exhibition, at the Center for the Arts in 1978.

Haring's quest for a more vibrant artistic atmosphere, however, led him that same year to New York's School of Visual Arts where he studied semiotics with Bill Beckley and explored the possibilities of video and performance art. He was profoundly influenced at this time by the writings of William Burroughs, which inspired him to experiment with the cross-referencing and interconnection of images.

The social scene in New York's East Village was of immense importance to Keith Haring and his work. He became a prominent figure in the thriving underground art world, curating informal exhibitions at Club 57 and the Mudd Club. His active involvement with the gay lifestyle was reflected in his art, which often portrayed phallic images or explicit sexual encounters.

Inspired by his interest in language and by artist Jenny Holzer, Haring began to experiment with a more public art in the summer of 1980, pasting collages of fake *New York Post* headlines on lampposts or newsstands. His interest in automatic writing and semiotics, however, led him to explore the world of graffiti artists such as SAMO (Jean-Michel Basquiat) and Fab Five Fred (Fred Brathwaite). It was here, in the subways and on the streets of New York, that Haring created his own graffiti and developed his future vocabulary of primitive cartoon-like forms. Cryptic and yet accessible,

Haring's chalk-drawn "radiant babies" and "barking dogs" became familiar features on the matt black surfaces used to cover the old advertisements in the subways. Striving to make his art even more accessible, Haring passed out buttons illustrated with his drawings and collaborated on a book of his graffiti (*Art in Transit: Subway Drawings,* 1984) with photographer Tseng Kwong Chi.

Leaving school before the fall semester of 1980, Haring embarked upon a wide distribution of his semiotic forms. He began to disassociate himself from the graffiti scene, painting instead on tarpaulins and other objects, and had a one-man show at Shafrazi Gallery in 1982. His meteoric rise to world prominence after this show was truly remarkable. By the end of 1984 he had gained international recognition, exhibiting in Brazil, Spain, Japan, Italy, and England. Attempting to reach a larger public, he immersed himself in popular American culture, forming friendships with Andy Warhol and with such pop entertainers as Madonna and Grace Jones (whom he would body-paint). He became politically active, designing a Free South Africa poster (1985) and painting a section of the Berlin Wall in 1986. His interest in working with children inspired the enormous project *Citykids Speak on Liberty,* which involved 1,000 kids collaborating on a project for the Statue of Liberty centennial.

Ever increasing concern for making his art accessible led to commercial ventures such as the design for Swatch watches (1985); the Absolut Vodka advertisement (1986); and ultimately his Pop Shop (opened 1986) in which he sold T-shirts, posters, and other saleable items. It was these endeavors, as well as the graffiti images, that caused some critics and members of the art world to bemoan Haring's contribution, placing him instead among popular cultural figures. Haring maintained, however, that his intention was to make his art more accessible. Ideologically, he placed himself with Andy Warhol, the conceptual artists, and the earth artists—attempting to reach a broader public.

On February 16, 1990, at age 31, Keith Haring's life was cut short due to an AIDS-related illness. His work remains the most salient example of the diminishing line between consumerism, popular culture, and fine art in the 1980s. Despite their controversial nature, Haring's images reflect the 20th-century tradition of using primitive impulses to communicate the angst of modern times.

Further Reading

Keith Haring: The Authorized Biography by John Gruen (1991) includes interviews with the artist and those closest to him and is an invaluable source for understanding the art and life of Haring. The early work is illustrated in *Art in Transit: The Subway Drawings* (1984) and *Keith Haring* (Shafrazi Gallery, 1982). An enlightening interview by David Sheff appeared in *Rolling Stone* (August 10, 1989). Elizabeth Aubert directed an insightful video entitled *Drawing the Line: A Portrait of Keith Haring* (Biografilm, 1989). Later an attempt was made to place Haring within a broader art historical context in *Keith Haring,* edited by Germano Celant (1992). □

Georgia Harkness

A leading American Methodist and ecumenical theologian, Georgia Harkness (1891-1974) was named Churchwoman of the Year in 1958 by the Religious Heritage Society of America.

Georgia Harkness was born April 21, 1891, the youngest of four children of Joseph Warren and Lillie (Merrill) Harkness. She grew up in Harkness, New York, a small Adirondack town named for her grandfather, and graduated from Cornell University in 1912. She had long been interested in the Methodist Church, and after teaching high school for six years she went to Boston University for graduate studies in religion, earning the Ph.D. in 1923 with a dissertation titled "The Relations between the Philosophy of Religion and Ethics in the Thought of Thomas Hill Green."

Harkness then spent 15 years teaching religion and philosophy at Elmira College for Women in Elmira, New York. She studied for brief periods during this time at Harvard University, Yale Divinity School, and Union Theological Seminary in New York City. She also began to write regularly, eventually publishing more than 30 books. In 1937 she joined the faculty at Mount Holyoke College in Massachusetts, and in 1940 she became professor of applied theology at what was then called Garrett Biblical Institute, a Methodist graduate seminary in Evanston, Illinois. Harkness concluded her teaching career at the Pacific School of Religion in Berkeley, California, where in 1949 she became the first woman to hold the professorship in applied theology. For the year 1956-1957 she was a visiting professor at both the International Christian University of Japan and the Union Theological Seminary of Manila.

As these last positions suggest, Georgia Harkness long had an interest in global and ecumenical Christianity. She had planned to do missionary work after graduating from Cornell, but family problems prevented that. She contented herself with international work for the Methodist Church, and after World War II for the World Council of Churches. Through service on such Methodist organizations as the Board of World Peace and the Board of Social and Economic Relations and on different commissions of the World Council of Churches, she influenced many international meetings. In fact, her hymn "Hope of the World" was selected by the Hymn Society of America for use at the assembly of the World Council of Churches at Evanston, Illinois, in 1954. She served as a consultant for the 1937 Conference on Life and Work at Oxford, England, and worked on statements on social and economic matters for the World Council of Church's assembly in Amsterdam in 1948. She also served international Christian meetings in Madras, India, in 1938 and in Lund, Sweden, in 1952.

Harkness was ordained a minister of the Methodist Church in 1926 but, like all other women, she was not able to become a full member of a Methodist conference until 1956. Throughout her life she remained a loyal supporter of the church, and many of her books dealt with ecclesiastic themes. Her position on women's roles in the church was moderate. For example, it was typical of her to have advocated women's equality with men in aptitude for the Christian ministry prior to the 1956 Methodist meeting in Minneapolis that opened full pastoral status to women yet to not herself battle on the floor for this motion.

Harkness did, however, receive considerable notice as a leading female theologian and churchperson. In 1941 the General Federation of Women's Clubs awarded her a scroll for pioneer work in religion, and a poll taken by the magazine *Christian Advocate* in 1947 listed her as one of the ten most influential living Methodists. The magazine *The Christian Century* considered her one of six leading churchwomen in 1952, and in 1958 she was named Churchwoman of the Year by the Religious Heritage Society of America. She also received numerous honorary degrees from such schools as her alma mater Boston University in 1938 and MacMurray College in Texas in 1943.

Among Harkness' many books one might single out *Prayer and the Common Life* (1947), which was a cowinner of the $7,500 Abingdon-Cokesbury award for the book that would accomplish the most good for Christian faith and living, and her 1964 autobiography, *A Special Way to Victory*. Reviewers generally praised the lucidity and forcefulness of her style, although fellow scholars sometimes judged that she purchased availability to the laity at the price of originality or profundity. One regularly finds Harkness concerned for the significance that articles of faith ought to bear in practical life. This latter term she understood to include both the personal and the community life of prayer and the political realm of economic and social justice. From 1924 she followed a pacifist position, and in 1950 she went on record against the retaliatory use of atomic weapons.

Professionally Georgia Harkness was a model of clarity on the podium, and privately she enjoyed summers with her brothers and sisters in New York state and gardening and cooking at her own cottage there. From girlhood she found a home in the Christian church, and for all of her activity a certain peacefulness pervaded her books and the trail of her person, as though that home was quite pleasing.

Further Reading

Georgia Harkness' own books are quite readable. People interested in her life should begin with her autobiography, *A Special Way to Victory* (1964). Among the books probably considered both more important and more representative of the development of her thought the following stand out: *Prayer and the Common Life* (1948); *The Sources of Western Morality* (1954); *The Providence of God* (1960); *The Church and Its Laity* (1962); and *The Fellowship of the Holy Spirit* (1966).

Additional Sources

Keller, Rosemary Skinner, *Georgia Harkness: for such a time as this*, Nashville: Abingdon Press, 1992. □

John Marshall Harlan

John Marshall Harlan (1833-1911) was the lone voice on the U.S. Supreme Court supporting legal equality for African Americans during the late 19th and early 20th centuries.

John Marshall Harlan was born on June 1, 1833, in Boyle County, Ky. He graduated from Centre College in 1850, then studied law at the University of Transylvania and in the office of his father, a former congressman and Federal district attorney. In 1861 he moved to Louisville to begin his own lucrative law practice.

Originally a Whig, Harlan supported the Constitutional Union party in 1860 and remained a unionist when the Civil War broke out. He recruited a regiment which fought on the side of the North but resigned his colonelcy in 1863 in order to succeed his father as the state attorney general. After the war Harlan entered politics as a Republican, gaining the support of black and white Kentuckians.

Reconstruction in the South

The origins and social credentials of Harlan and many other Kentucky Republicans throw doubt on the often-used generalization that white Republicans in the Reconstruction South were all disreputable, out-of-state "carpetbaggers" who exploited unsophisticated former slaves. Indeed, Harlan regarded the electorate as discerning voters and anticipated close and even unfavorable attention from black voters when, during his race for governor, he agreed to represent an alleged member of the Ku Klux Klan accused of participating in a lynching. Harlan (who won the case) contended that every man, whatever his politics, deserved as good a lawyer as he could pay for.

In the Republican convention of 1876, Harlan nominated his law partner Benjamin H. Bristow but, seeing the contest deadlock between Bristow and James G. Blaine, released Bristow's delegates and secured the nomination of Rutherford B. Hayes. One personal result was a break between Harlan and Bristow, whose careers had been closely parallel. Meanwhile, Harlan, in strong presidential favor, was named associate justice of the U.S. Supreme Court, taking his seat in December 1877.

Supreme Court Justice

During the racially tense decades that followed, Justice Harlan was almost the only man in high Federal office who spoke for the equal rights of African Americans. This concern would have cost him any elective post, but life tenure on the Court allowed his voice to be heard. Harlan alone dissented in *U.S. v. Harris* (1882), in which the 14th Amendment was declared not to provide African Americans with Federal protection, even from lynching. He dissented again in the *Civil Rights Cases* (1883), in which the equal protection clause of the 14th Amendment was held *not* to guarantee equal access for African Americans to privately owned places of public entertainment or accommodation.

Harlan's most famous dissent was in *Plessy v. Ferguson* (1896). The 14th Amendment says, "No state shall make or enforce any law which shall abridge the privileges or immunities of citizens of the United States"; Harlan contended that a Louisiana law segregating African Americans into separate railroad cars was a violation thereof. Separate was not equal, he argued in a minority opinion, and he predicted, correctly, that "Jim Crow" segregation would soon extend far beyond railroad cars. He was also a dissenter in *Berea College v. Kentucky* (1908), which held that a Kentucky school segregation law could be made to apply to a long-integrated private college.

His Sense of Constitutionality

Harlan's contribution to racial justice was less an appeal to egalitarianism or to feelings of white guilt than to white feelings of self-confidence. In *Plessy,* he included an appeal to Anglo-Saxon pride which, he suggested, needed no assistance from segregation laws. Indeed, he saw no inconsistency in his championship both of the rights of oppressed African Americans and of burgeoning corporate enterprises. In his view each deserved protection from infringement on the basic right to develop to full capacity.

Harlan was also committed to the idea that the nation, as well as individuals, should maintain its strength. He dissented when the Supreme Court declared that the income tax was unconstitutional (*Pollock v. Farmer's Loan and Trust Company,* 1895). Similarly, in support of the premise that the states had "police power" to provide for the public

welfare, Harlan joined Oliver Wendell Holmes in dissenting in *Lochner v. New York* (1905).

A firm believer that the American Constitution and laws passed within its framework meant what they said, Harlan accepted neither Justice Stephen J. Field's appeal to "natural law" in the 19th century nor Chief Justice Edward Douglass White's doctrine of the "rule of reason" in the 20th, as he made clear in his dissent in *Standard Oil Company v. U.S.* (1911). The majority had held that certain monopolistic practices in restraint of trade were "reasonable" and, hence, allowable despite the Sherman Antitrust Act. Harlan died on Oct. 14, 1911, in Washington.

In 1857 Harlan had married Malvina F. Shanklin; they had six children. In 1955 his grandson and namesake was appointed to the court on which the first John Marshall Harlan had long been the most distinguished justice.

Further Reading

The only biography is Frank Latham, *Great Dissenter: John Marshall Harlan* (1970). The Bristow Papers at the Library of Congress are important. A study of Harlan is Floyd Barzilia Clark, *The Constitutional Doctrines of Justice Harlan* (1915; 2d ed. 1969). Allison Dunham and Philip B. Kurland, eds., *Mr. Justice* (1956; rev. ed. 1964), has a biographical sketch of Harlan. Leo Pfeffer, *This Honorable Court: A History of the United States Supreme Court* (1965), is a good background study.

Additional Sources

Beth, Loren P., *John Marshall Harlan: the last Whig justice,* Lexington, Ky.: University Press of Kentucky, 1992.
Yarbrough, Tinsley E., *Judicial enigma: the first justice Harlan,* New York: Oxford University Press, 1995. □

John Marshall Harlan

The second Justice John Marshall Harlan (1899-1971) preached the virtues of judicial restraint and federalism as a persistent dissenter from the reformist decisions of the Warren Court.

Dissenting was a Harlan family tradition. The grandfather whose name John Marshall Harlan bore had been a member of the turn-of-the-century Supreme Court whose lonely protests against racist rulings had made him a legend. The father and son of that first Justice Harlan were also lawyers. His namesake was born in Chicago on May 20, 1899. The second Justice Harlan attended elementary and secondary schools in the United States and Canada, then enrolled at Princeton in 1916. Following his graduation in 1920, he attended Balliol College, Oxford, as a Rhodes Scholar, staying on to study law there and ultimately receiving both B.A. and M.A. degrees. Upon his return to the United States he commenced an apprenticeship with the Wall Street law firm of Root, Clark, Buckner &

Howland, meanwhile completing his formal education as a part-time student at the New York Law School, which awarded him an LL.B. in 1924.

Law Practice

Harlan's association with Root, Clark continued for three decades. The firm made him a partner in 1931, and he became its leading trial lawyer in 1941. Harlan handled a number of spectacular and highly publicized cases for his law firm. He represented boxer Gene Tunney in a contract dispute and the New York City Board of Education in litigation arising out of its attempt to employ Bertrand Russell. Especially impressive was his defense of the Ella Wendell will against imposters claiming to be heirs of the multimillionaire spinster. Harlan also argued several appeals before the Supreme Court, in one case winning a ruling that became a landmark in the fields of corporate law and civil procedure.

Although lengthy, his service with Root, Clark was not continuous. He interrupted it several times for public service. When one of the firm's senior partners, Emory R. Buckner, was appointed U.S. attorney for the southern district of New York in 1925, Harlan became his assistant. In that capacity he participated in the prosecution of former Attorney General Harry Daugherty for official misconduct and in efforts to enforce prohibition. After returning to Root, Clark in 1927, Buckner and Harlan took leave again the following year to serve as special prosecutors for the state in an investigation of municipal graft in Queens.

During World War II Harlan joined the armed forces, rising to the rank of colonel and winning several decorations for his work as head of the Operational Analysis Section of the Eighth Air Force in England. He also served with the Air Force's Post-War Planning Section. After a few years back in private practice, in 1951 Harlan became the general counsel of the New York State Crime Commission, a body created to study the relationship between organized crime and state government.

Supreme Court Justice

Soon after he completed that assignment, President Eisenhower appointed Harlan to the U.S. Court of Appeals for the Second Circuit. Harlan spent less than a year there before being elevated to the Supreme Court on November 8, 1954. His nomination encountered resistance from southerners, who feared this Harlan might share his grandfather's well known hostility to legalized segregation and hoped that delaying his confirmation might keep the Court from implementing its recently announced ruling in *Brown v. Board of Education* (1954). Not until March 28, 1955, was Harlan able to take his seat.

He quickly established a reputation as a "lawyer's judge" who wrote carefully crafted and scholarly opinions which explicated in great detail the reasons for his decisions. Harlan also worked hard. During the ten year period beginning with the Court's 1958 term, he authored more opinions per term than any other Justice. The reason was that he so seldom agreed with his colleagues. During his 17 years on the Court, Harlan wrote 613 opinions. Of these,

296 were dissents and another 149 were concurrances. Only 168 times did he speak for the majority.

Judicial Philosophy

Harlan served on a Court, headed throughout most of his tenure by Chief Justice Earl Warren, which was revolutionizing American constitutional law, making it an instrument for the promotion of egalitarianism, the protection of the disadvantaged, and the accomplishment of a wide variety of reforms. In the process, the Warren Court greatly expanded the role and power of the federal judiciary and considerably reduced the autonomy of the states. Harlan marched to a different drummer. Although conservative in the sense that he believed the Court should consider historical tradition and not lightly overrule its earlier decisions, he did not oppose the substance of the Warren Court's liberal reforms. Harlan was personally committed to racial justice, adopted forward positions on the enforcement of the Bill of Rights in a federal context, and sometimes took quite libertarian stands in speech and privacy cases. But he thought reform should come about through legislative action which reflected popular consent rather than through imposition by judicial fiat. Harlan preached endlessly about the need for judicial self-restraint.

An even more persistent theme in his dissents was federalism. Harlan idealized diversity and pluralism and loathed what he viewed as the compelled uniformity the Court was forcing on the country. He protested his colleagues' insistence that virtually all elected members of state and local government represent districts of equal population. He also fought a long losing battle against imposing most federal criminal procedures on the states by incorporating them into the Due Process Clause of the Fourteenth Amendment. Harlan thought the Constitution required of state criminal procedure only fundamental fairness, not compliance with every rule the federal courts had to follow. By binding the states to national standards of its own making, he argued, the Supreme Court was precluding them from engaging in potentially productive experimentation.

His futile fight for federalism and restraint continued until cancer forced him to resign in September 1971. Although often defeated, Harlan was never vanquished, and after his death on December 29, 1971, his reputation, like that of his famous grandfather, continued to grow.

Further Reading

There is no book-length biography of Harlan, and his personal papers at Princeton remain a largely untapped resource. There is a good "Biographical Note" in David L. Shapiro, editor, *The Evolution of a Judicial Philosophy: Selected Opinions and Papers of Justice John M. Harlan* (1969). Norman Dorsen's "John Marshall Harlan," in *The Justices of the United States Supreme Court 1789-1969: Their Lives and Major Opinions,* edited by Leon Friedman and Fred L. Israel (1969), Volume 4, and the same author's nearly identical "The Second Mr. Justice Harlan: A Constitutional Conservative," in *New York University Law Review* (April 1969) are also informative. Dorsen's "John Marshall Harlan," in *The Burger Court 1969-1978,* edited by Leon Friedman (1978) analyzes the last years of Harlan's tenure on the Court. Henry J. Bourguignon, "The Second Mr. Justice Harlan: His Principles of Judicial Decision Making,'' in *Supreme Court Review 1979* (1980) and J. Harvie Wilkerson III, ''Justice John M. Harlan and the Values of Federalism,'' in *Virginia Law Review* 57 (October 1971) are perceptive studies of Harlan's jurisprudence. Stephen M. Dane, '''Ordered Liberty' and Self-Restraint: The Judicial Philosophy of the Second Justice Harlan,'' *University of Cincinnati Law Review* 51 (1982) is not as good.

□

Robert Harley

The English statesman Robert Harley, 1st Earl of Oxford and Earl Mortimer (1661-1724), revived and unified the Tory party at the end of the 17th century and was its leader until the death of Queen Anne in 1714.

Robert Harley was born in London on Dec. 5, 1661, eldest son of a well-known Presbyterian squire of Herefordshire and member of Parliament. He was educated at a Nonconformist academy and read law for a while. When England expelled its Catholic king James II in 1688, Harley supported the Dutch Prince of Orange, who supplanted James, taking the throne as William III. Harley began his political career as a Whig-Presbyterian member of Parliament but soon moved into leadership of the coalition that opposed William III and his Whig government.

Leader of the Tories

This coalition was made up of Church Tories, former Tory courtiers, independent gentry, and dissatisfied Whigs. It combined reverence for the monarchy with dislike of the Dutch king, loyalty to the Church of England with attacks on Nonconformists, and respect for the landed interest with scorn for city financiers and war contractors. These were to be lasting elements of Toryism. A skilled parliamentarian and born intriguer, by 1701 Harley had become a leader of this new Tory party and was chosen Speaker of the House of Commons.

When William III died in 1702 and was succeeded by Queen Anne, Harley continued as Speaker. He was now on close terms with Sidney Godolphin, whom Anne had named lord treasurer and head of the government. While the Duke of Marlborough managed the great war with France (War of the Spanish Succession, 1702-1713) and Godolphin the government finances, Harley managed the government's business in the Commons—first as Speaker, then (1704-1708) as secretary of state. In 1708 this three-man team broke up. Marlborough and Godolphin found it impossible to continue the war without the support of the Whigs, who were strong among the Non-conformists and commercial class.

This approach to the Whigs alienated the pious Anglican queen, as it did Harley. Harley persuaded the Queen to let him form a new administration, purged of Whig elements; but the scheme was discovered before it could be put into effect. The leading political figures refused to accept

Harley in place of Godolphin and Marlborough, and Harley was forced out of office in late 1708. Two years later, taking advantage of general weariness with the long war, Harley successfully brought down the Marlborough-Godolphin administration. His influence with the Queen and the political mistakes of the government in rejecting a peace overture from France and apparently attacking the Church of England by the impeachment of an antiadministration High Church parson contributed to Harley's success.

Lord High Treasurer

Harley became the new lord treasurer and was made Earl of Oxford and Earl Mortimer. His administration made peace with France on favorable terms at Utrecht (1713). He himself improvised financial backing for his regime in the face of Whig hostility in London business circles through the foundation of the South Sea Company—a legitimate corporation in its early years though later tainted by the scandals of the ''South Sea Bubble'' of 1720. Harley had a brilliant public relations man in Jonathan Swift, whose *Four Last Years of Queen Anne* is a classic. He also used Daniel Defoe as a government journalist.

Harley's leadership did not go unchallenged. The chief architect of the peace with France was Henry St. John, Viscount Bolingbroke. While Harley tried to preserve his communications with Low Church and Whig groups, Bolingbroke rallied the young High Church squires around him. As Harley slipped into indolence and overindulgence, he let the initiative fall into the hands of Bolingbroke and the young Tory extremists. Schemes for a Stuart restoration were afoot, but the sudden death of the Queen on Aug. 1, 1714, came before they could be carried out. When George of Hanover was proclaimed king of England, Bolingbroke fled to France, and Harley remained to face the music.

Impeached for high treason by the unanimous vote of the Commons, Harley spent nearly 3 years in the Tower until acquitted by the House of Lords. Thereafter he attended the upper house regularly until his death in London on May 24, 1724.

During his lifetime Harley acquired a notable collection of printed books plus some 25,000 manuscripts later bequeathed to the British Museum. Much of his correspondence has survived; it adds to the enigma of his devious and secretive personality.

Further Reading

A short but excellent biography is Oswald B. Miller, *Robert Harley, Earl of Oxford* (1925). Also recommended is Elizabeth Hamilton, *The Backstairs Dragon: A Life of Robert Harley, Earl of Oxford* (1970). Geoffrey Holmes deals with Harley in *British Politics in the Age of Anne* (1967), an introductory work to a projected biography of Harley. See also Robert Walcott, *English Politics in the Early Eighteenth Century* (1956), to which Holmes's work is a rejoinder.

Additional Sources

Biddle, Sheila, *Bolingbroke and Harle,* New York, Knopf; distributed by Random House 1974.
Hill, Brian W., *Robert Harley, speaker, secretary of state, and premier minister,* New Haven: Yale University Press, 1988. □

Adolf von Harnack

The German theologian and scholar Adolf von Harnack (1851-1930) fashioned the historicopositivist approach to the theology and origin of Christianity, which characterized the study of religion in the first half of the 20th century.

Adolf von Harnack was born on May 7, 1851, in Dorpat, Estonia. His father, Theodosius Harnack, was professor of practical theology at Dorpat University. When Harnack had finished his university studies in 1874, he became an instructor in Church history and, 2 years later, professor extraordinarius at Leipzig. He was appointed full professor at Giessen in 1879.

Harnack's intellectual approach to Christianity started off within the orthodoxy of the Erlangen and Dorpat schools. He was soon drawn to the historicocritical approach of the Tübingen school, which emphasized the need of historical structures in order to understand the Christian message. From this, it was but one step to the view of Albrecht Ritschl, who held that an understanding of Christianity could be had only by relating it to the culture in which it originated and developed.

Harnack progressed beyond the Ritschlian position and proposed to separate dogma (ecclesiastical formulation of the Christian faith) from what he called the essence of Christianity. To do this, he proposed to avoid all abstract speculation and metaphysical deduction. Instead he set out to study the sources of knowledge about Christianity with a strictly scientific method of factual verification, historical cross-reference, and verification of documentary authenticity.

In 1882 he initiated with O. von Gebhardt the publication of a text series: *Texte und Untersuchungen zur Geschichte der Altchristlichen Literatur* (Texts and Examinations on the History of Old Christian Literature). Harnack contributed 49 monographs to this series. In 1886 he became a professor at Marburg and in 1889 professor at the University of Berlin. Between 1886 and 1889 he produced his greatest work, *Lehrbuch der Dogmen Geschichte* (The History of Dogma), with his theory of Christian development.

Harnack's thesis was simple: Christianity of the first 1,500 years resulted from the Greek spirit which the early Greek theologians of the Church infused into the originally Judaic message of Jesus. Furthermore, he maintained, in the 16th-century Reformation a first attempt was made to recover the essence from its 1,500-year-old overlay of dogma. Harnack proposed that this work of the Reformation be completed by a strict historicocritical approach to Christianity. Harnack's view laid the foundation for the later Form School criticism and the demythologizing theology of the 20th century.

Harnack also composed a three-volume history of the Prussian Academy of Sciences, of which he was a member. In 1902 he founded and became first president of the Evangelical-Social Congress. He was director of the royal library (1905-1921), and in 1914 he received a noble title. He continued writing and teaching and lecturing almost to his death on June 10, 1930, in Heidelberg.

In addition to the works mentioned above, some of Harnack's more important ones have been translated into English: *What Is Christianity?* (1901) and *The Mission and Spread of Christianity in the First Three Hundred Years* (1904-1905).

Further Reading

Some English-language sources on Harnack are in volume 2 of Kenneth S. Latourette, *Christianity in a Revolutionary Age* (5 vols., 1958-1962); John Macquarrie, *Twentieth-Century Religious Thought* (1963); and Fritz K. Ringer, *The Decline of the German Mandarins: The German Academic Community, 1890-1933* (1968). Also useful is James H. Nichols, *History of Christianity, 1650-1950* (1956). □

William Michael Harnett

The American painter William Michael Harnett (1848-1892) was his era's leading trompe l'oeil still-life painter.

William Harnett was born on Aug. 10, 1848, in County Cork, Ireland, and taken to Philadelphia by his parents when he was a child. Harnett learned the engraver's trade and found employment as a silver engraver. When he was 19, he attended night classes at the Pennsylvania Academy of Fine Arts. Two years later he moved to New York, where he worked for jewelry firms during the day and studied painting at the National Academy of Design and the Cooper Union at night.

A still-life painter from the start, Harnett was not tormented by dreams of artistic grandeur. In an age when many portrait painters wished to paint historical subjects, he was happy to paint his cabbage and, according to legend, eat it too. His first picture of a pipe and a beer mug not only was accepted at the National Academy's annual exhibition but was sold for a welcome $50. His future course was clear: he had hit upon a popular vein, and with rate single-mindedness he stayed with it all his life.

Harnett returned to Philadelphia and, between 1873 and 1879, sold enough pictures to go to Europe. His work was appreciated by the Europeans. While abroad he painted *After the Hunt*. His greatest success, it is a startling, realistic rendering of an old barn door, dead game birds, a hunting horn, a shotgun, a powder horn, and a Tyrolean hat.

In 1886 Harnett returned to New York and exhibited *The Old Violin* at the National Academy that year. From then on he lived a moderately successful, if uneventful, life; his pictures sold steadily, though at modest prices.

Harnett's art was undoubtedly influenced by his Philadelphia predecessor Raphael Peale, but he carried American trompe l'oeil (as this style, which seeks to "fool the eye," is known) to new heights. He probably found inspiration for some of his effects in the 17th-century Dutch still lifes he had seen abroad.

Harnett's work, and that of other painters in the trompe l'oeil school, has an appeal beyond art: people who do not respond to other kinds of painting like it. Trompe l'oeil is intriguing because it is fascinatingly close to visual reality. Harnett gave the nonart public pegs on a wall so real that people tried to hang their hats on them, and dollar bills that they tried to pick up. The seemingly naive Americanism of his work is one of his greatest illusions, but he played all his tricks with the consummate skill of a magician. On his death on Oct. 29, 1892, he left few pictures and very little money.

Further Reading

A good sampling of reproductions is in Harnett's *Nature-vivre* (1939), compiled from an exhibition in New York. The basic book on Harnett is Alfred Frankenstein, *After the Hunt* (1953; rev. ed. 1969), which gives a fascinating account of the whole school of American trompe l'oeil painters. See also Barbara Novak, *American Painting of the Nineteenth Century* (1969). □

Harold I

Harold I (ca. 840-933), the first king of Norway, reigned from 860 to 930. He became the ideal for unification at the time of his great-grandson Olaf I Tryggvason.

Harold Haarfarer ("Fairhair") was a catalyst in his day and place. On the death of his father, Halfdan the Black in 860, Harold succeeded to the sovereignty of several small and somewhat scattered kingdoms which had come into his father's hands through conquest and inheritance. After his father's accidental death by drowning, his mother's brother, Guthorm, held his father's enemies at bay.

Harold was a man of legends. His mother, Ragnhild, perceived his rise to power from a thorn. The daughter of a neighboring king induced Harold to take a vow not to cut or comb his hair until he was the sole ruler of Norway. Two years later he was justified in trimming it, and henceforth he was known as "Fairhair" rather than "Shockhead."

From his ancestral lands in southeast Norway, Harold began in 866 a series of conquests over the many petty kingdoms which Norway then comprised. A smashing victory in 872 at Hafrisfjord near Stavanger made him king of the entire country. That battle was one of the most decisive battles in medieval Scandinavian history. There Harold met enemies from Iceland, the Orkneys, Shetlands, Hebrides, and Faeroes and from Scotland who were aided by malcontents who opposed Harold's land taxes.

As Snorri Sturluson pointed out, Hafrisfjord did not make it possible for Harold to trim his hair with royal ease. Norway was not accustomed to one-man rule. When Harold gained power, he appropriated hereditary estates, and all farmers were taxed. He appointed a jarl in each shire (*fylki*) to administer law and justice and to collect fines, one-third reserved for the Crown.

Actually Harold's policies in some ways added to the power of the jarls. Landlords who supported him held their hereditary rights, and he used assemblies of the strong to confirm his position and his authority. Thus the power of the assembled congregations was enhanced. Wealthy in his own right, Harold adopted measures to strengthen coastal defenses by increasing ship service. During his reign the Scottish islands came under Norwegian rule.

The latter part of Harold's reign was troubled by strife among his sons, who numbered between 16 and 20. One, Haakon the Good, was fostered in England under Athelstan. To all Harold assigned titles, lands, and rights of governing in designated areas. Toward the end of his life, he bestowed supreme authority upon a child of his old age, Erik "Bloody Axe."

Harold was the greatest Viking warrior chief of the 9th century. He controlled trade and collected gifts from traders. He confiscated estates but recognized the rights of legislative assemblies. He withdrew support from the Vikings in Northumbria, England, and was the only heathen able to claim kingship of all Norway. Under him the old Viking civilization of the 9th century reached a climax. His ideal for a united Norway became imperishable.

Further Reading

Accounts of Harold I are in Knut Gjerset, *History of the Norwegian People* (2 vols., 1915); Karen Larsen, *A History of Norway* (1948); and Gwyn Jones, *A History of the Vikings* (1968). A detailed but not always accurate treatment of him is in Snorri Sturluson, *Heimskringla* and *Egils Saga.* □

Harold II

Harold II (died 1066) was the last Anglo-Saxon king of England. During his 9-month reign in 1066 he turned back the invasion of the king of Norway, only to succumb to that of William of Normandy.

Harold II was the second son of Godwin, Earl of Wessex, one of the most powerful men in 11th-century England. When Edward the Confessor returned from exile in Normandy to become king in 1042, reinstating the ancient house of Wessex in England after 25 years of rule by Danish kings, Godwin attempted to retain the power he had accumulated as royal adviser to the Danes. Not until 1051 did Edward feel strong enough to banish Godwin and his sons. Less than a year later, however, Godwin was reconciled with Edward under threat of civil war, and when Godwin died in April 1053, Harold became Earl of Wessex.

After his father's death Harold gradually became Edward's most powerful adviser and general. Between 1055 and 1063 he commanded the English forces in a series of campaigns against the aggressive Welsh king, Gruffydd ap Llewelyn. When Harold finally crushed Gruffydd and stabilized the English-Welsh border, the triumph greatly enhanced his authority and his reputation throughout England. It also established his claim to succeed King Edward, whose only remaining relative was a very young cousin living at the court of Hungary.

Then, in 1064, in a mysterious incident recorded in the famous Bayeux Tapestry, Harold was sent by King Edward on a mission of unknown nature to the Continent but was blown off course and landed in Normandy. There he was imprisoned and taken to Duke William, to whom he swore an oath which probably committed him to helping William secure the English kingship after Edward's death. There is no way of determining whether Harold gave his word freely or under duress; in any case, when Edward died in January 1066, Harold was clearly in the best position to preserve the continuity of rule in England and was at once chosen by the English nobility as Edward's successor.

Harold's brief reign was one of frantic activity in defense of England against invasion both by William and by Harald Hardrada, King of Norway. Harald struck first, in September 1066, landing with a large army in Yorkshire.

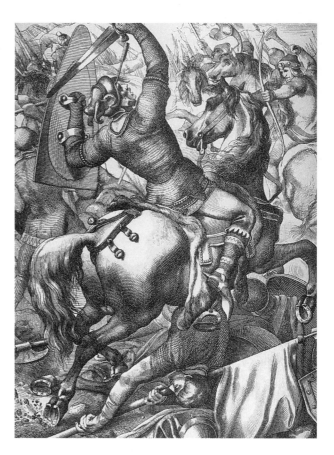

Harold II (on horse)

Harold, who had been in the south awaiting William's attack, raced northward and crushed the invaders at Stamford Bridge on September 25. Two days later William, whose plans had been delayed by unfavorable winds, sailed from Normandy with an army of Normans and mercenaries. Harold had to rush south to face William with an exhausted and undermanned army. The two sides met near Hastings on October 14, and after a day of furious fighting Harold was killed and his army defeated. With Harold's gallant death Anglo-Saxon history comes to an end, and the Anglo-Norman age begins.

Further Reading

The main source of information on Harold II is *The Anglo-Saxon Chronicle,* edited and translated by G. N. Garmonsway (1953; rev. ed. 1954). The "D" version of the *Chronicle* in particular supplies the fullest detail on the events of 1066. For Harold's encounter with, and oath to, William of Normandy see Sir Frank Stenton and others, eds., *The Bayeux Tapestry* (1957; 3d ed. 1965). An analysis of the events of Harold's life and reign is in F. M. Stenton, *Anglo-Saxon England* (1943; 2d ed. 1947), and in D. C. Douglas, *William the Conqueror: The Norman Impact upon England* (1964).

Additional Sources

Three lives of the last Englishmen, New York: Garland Pub., 1984. □

Harold III

Harold III (1015-1066), who is surnamed Haardraade, or "Ruthless," was king of Norway from 1047 to 1066. He was the last of the great Viking aristocratic rulers whose fame extended throughout Europe.

Son of King Sigurd and half brother to King Olaf II (the Saint), Harold was severely wounded at Stiklarsladir fighting at the age of 15 against the largest army ever assembled in Norway. Leaving his dead half brother, he took refuge in a lonely farmhouse. His health recovered, he crossed into Sweden. From there he went to Novgorod, where he was well received by Prince Yaroslav and in 1032 assisted him in a Polish campaign.

Accompanied by a personal following of 500 warriors, Harold followed the traditional Varangian route to Constantinople. He arrived there in 1035 and until 1042 seems to have been the leader of the Varangian guard of the Empress Zoë. During that period he campaigned in the Greek islands, Asia Minor, the Caucasus, Palestine, Sicily, and Bulgaria. He was resourceful, cunning, resilient, and persevering, and if it suited his purpose, could be treacherous, vengeful, and cruel. As Gwyn Jones (1968) pointed out, he was "the epitome of the Viking who lived by rapine and war, believed in fame, riches and power, and employed fair means and foul." Through his sword and courage, he amassed a fortune; his standard, the famed "Land-waster," became an object of dread to his foes and of pride and reverence to his followers.

Harold left Constantinople because of a dispute with Zoë over a woman and returned home by way of Novgorod, where he married Elizabeth, the daughter of Yaroslav. Almost immediately he allied himself with Sven of Denmark against his nephew Magnus, now king of Norway, and deserted Sven when Magnus for a considerable sum of money offered him part of Norway. In 1047, upon the death of Magnus, he absorbed the rest of Norway and until 1064 carried on a senseless and devastating was against Sven. During this same period he brought to terms the warrior chieftains of Norway and, on the site of an old marketplace, established the city of Oslo.

In 1066, drawn by the never-failing Viking compulsion for wealth and fame overseas, Harold III embarked on the last effective Viking intervention in the affairs of western Europe. Probably urged on by the invitation of Earl Tostig of England but probably more by greed and by the tales and deeds of earlier Vikings, the 50-year-old warrior claimed the throne of England. Defeated at Stamford Bridge by the forces of Harold II, he won only the 7 feet of land that the victor had promised him, but his doom in a Viking holocaust that rivaled the battles told by the skalds of old made possible the conquest of England by a remoter brand of Norseman, William the Conqueror. His was indeed a Viking exit and the exit of the Viking age.

Further Reading

King Harold's Saga: Harald Hardrodi of Norway, translated with an introduction by Magnus Magnusson and Hermann Pálsson (1966) from Snorri Sturluson's *Heimskringla,* contains most known information on Harold III. Other translations of Snorri Sturluson's *Heimskringla* are also useful, such as *Heimskringla: History of the Kings of Norway,* translated with introduction and notes by Lee M. Hollander (1964). Karen Larsen, *A History of Norway* (1948), has an excellent summary, as does Gwyn Jones, *A History of the Vikings* (1968). □

William Rainey Harper

The American educator and biblical scholar William Rainey Harper (1856-1906) was the first president of the University of Chicago.

Born in New Concord, Ohio, on July 24, 1856, William Rainey Harper attended Muskingum College in New Concord, where his interest in Hebraic studies began. He graduated in 1870 and went on to receive a doctorate from Yale in 1874 for studies in the Indo-Iranian and Semitic languages. After teaching at Masonic College in Macon, Tenn., and then at Denison University, he moved on to a professorship in Hebrew at the Baptist Union Theological Seminary in Chicago. He held the chair of Semitic languages at Yale from 1886 to 1891, earning a national reputation as a teacher, lecturer, and writer. In 1889 he was also appointed Woolsey professor of biblical literature at Yale. He was active in the Chautauqua movement, serving as principal of the Chautauqua College of Liberal Arts from 1885 to 1891 and lecturing on biblical topics there and at William Dwight Moody's summer conferences at Northfield, Mass.

Harper's reputation was that of a sound, though not especially creative, scholar and an outstanding teacher whose lectures and books helped to spread the more scholarly criticism of the Bible in America. He was always a devout Christian, and his obvious piety and mild-tempered approach to controversy made him widely welcome among American religious groups. The best received of his books on the Bible were *The Priestly Element in the Old Testament* (1902), *The Prophetic Element in the Old Testament* (1905), and *Critical and Exegetical Commentary on Amos and Hosea* (1905).

In 1892 Harper became the first president of the University of Chicago, founded by John D. Rockefeller. From the start Harper insisted that academic excellence and academic freedom should characterize the school. He used the generous financial support of Rockefeller and others to offer substantial salaries to outstanding scholars, winning the enmity of other college presidents who resented his raiding, but rapidly assembling an outstanding faculty that soon made Chicago a leading center of research and graduate study. Harper built up the library, started a university press, and vigorously defended his faculty against sectarian attacks. Other characteristics of his institution included university extension, division of the year into quarters, separation of the two upper years of the college into a senior college, and faculty control of athletics.

Although busy with administrative problems raised by the rapid growth of the university, and continually striving to increase his endowment, Harper insisted on teaching full time and serving as chairman of his department. Even with his strong constitution, the heavy work schedule proved a drain on his vitality. He died in Chicago on Jan. 10, 1906.

Further Reading

The only full biography of Harper is Thomas Wakefield Good-speed, *William Rainey Harper* (1928), written at the request of Harper's family. An excellent account of his work at Chicago is in Richard J. Storr, *Harper's University, the Beginnings: A History of the University of Chicago* (1966).

Additional Sources

Wind, James P., *The Bible and the university: the messianic vision of William Rainey Harper,* Atlanta, Ga.: Scholars Press, 1987. □

Edward Henry Harriman

Edward Henry Harriman (1848-1909), executive of the Union Pacific Railroad, was one of the dominant American figures in that industry in the late 19th century.

B orn on Feb. 20, 1848, in Hempstead, N.Y., E. H. Harriman was raised in a relatively affluent environment. Although his father was a clergyman, the rest of the family engaged successfully in business. At the age of 14 Harriman became an office boy in a Wall Street firm. When he turned 21 he borrowed $3,000 from an uncle and purchased a seat on the stock exchange.

Harriman's first venture in transportation was the modest purchase of a Hudson River boat running between New York City and Newburgh. Mary Williamson, whom he married in 1879, was the daughter of the president of an upstate New York railroad. From this time Harriman began rebuilding bankrupt railroads in that region.

In 1883 Stuyvesant Fish, vice president of the Illinois Central Railroad, secured a seat for Harriman on the board of directors, and when Fish moved to the presidency in 1887, Harriman became vice president. Through Harriman's brilliant financial acumen the Illinois Central survived the devastating depression of the 1890s.

During this period Harriman was also eyeing the Union Pacific Railroad. When the line went into receivership in 1893, Harriman joined the reorganization syndicate. Four years later he gained a seat on the board of directors. He soon was made chairman of the executive committee, becoming, in effect, the voice of the Union Pacific. Harriman moved first to restore the physical condition of the road. He also gained control of two Oregon railroads and thus en-

sured the Union Pacific an entrance to Portland. He then turned his attention to California. A golden opportunity arose in 1900, when the Southern Pacific Railroad holdings were put up for sale. Harriman purchased enough securities to control the vast transportation network operating along the entire Pacific Coast and east to New Orleans.

Meanwhile, Harriman wanted to extend the eastern terminus of the Union Pacific, then at Omaha, to Chicago. He attempted to gain control of the Chicago, Burlington and Quincy Railroad but ran headlong into James J. Hill of the Great Northern Railway. Harriman, backed by the Kuhn-Loeb financial group, and Hill, supported by financier J. P. Morgan, battled for stock control. The antagonists eventually agreed to create a holding company, the Northern Securities Company, which was to control a vast majority of the railroads west of the Mississippi River.

To their surprise, U.S. president Theodore Roosevelt instigated an antitrust suit against Northern Securities. In 1904 the Supreme Court ordered the company dissolved. Harriman suffered another setback when, in 1906-1907, the Interstate Commerce Commission's investigation revealed his part in a group of ''robber barons'' who had set about to financially destroy the Chicago and Alton Railroad.

Harriman also dabbled in steamships, banks, and insurance companies. In 1899 he organized and accompanied a research expedition to Alaska. He was also active in New York boys' club work. In 1885 he began buying acreage in Orange County, N.Y., for the purpose of preserving forest lands; some 20,000 acres plus funds to purchase additional tracts were given to the state to create Harriman Park, now over 45,000 acres in extent.

Harriman was the father of six children, the most famous of whom was W. Averell Harriman.

Further Reading

The most extensive treatment of Harriman is George Kennan, *E. H. Harriman: A Biography* (2 vols., 1922). The only other study is the journalistic account by Hamilton J. Eckenrode and Pocahontas Wight Edmunds, *E. H. Harriman: The Little Giant of Wall Street* (1933).

Additional Sources

Eckenrode, H. J. (Hamilton James), *E.H. Harriman: the little giant of Wall Street,* New York: Arno Press, 1981.
Kennan, George, *E. H. Harriman, a biography,* New York: Arno Press, 1981, 1922.
Memoirs of three railroad pioneers, New York: Arno Press, 1981.
□

W. Averell Harriman

W. Averell Harriman (1891-1986), American industrialist and financier, had a distinguished second career as a top-level diplomatic negotiator for five Democratic presidents. He was Governor of New York for one term.

Harriman was born in 1891 during the administration of President Benjamin Harrison and died in 1986 during Ronald Reagan's first term; he first visited Siberia under the reign of Czar Nicholas II at age 7, and at age 91 made his last visit to Moscow to meet the new Soviet leader, Yuri Andropov. As a 35 year-old investment banker and industrialist, Harriman conducted mining negotiations with Leon Trotsky, and subsequently dealt directly as a diplomat with every Soviet leader from Stalin to Andropov. He worked on New Deal projects for President Franklin Roosevelt, and in 1943 was appointed Ambassador to the Soviet Union by FDR. After the war, he was President Harry Truman's ambassador to Great Britain and later, secretary of commerce, chief negotiator in Europe for the Marshall Plan, and special assistant to the president. In the Kennedy administration, Harriman served as ambassador at large, reporting directly to the president; as assistant secretary for Far Eastern affairs, he negotiated the Laos neutrality accords; and, at 71 years of age, as undersecretary of state for political affairs, he conducted successful negotiations with Soviet leader Nikita Khrushchev for the historic limited Nuclear Test Ban Treaty. Under Lyndon Johnson, Harriman was again named Ambassador at Large, and then, more vaguely, "Ambassador for Peace;" in both capacities, he met with heads of state around the globe, and in 1968 spent the last seven months of his negotiating career as Johnson's emissary to the Paris Peace talks on Viet Nam. Finally, at age 84 and in Moscow once again, Harriman gave Leonid

Brezhnev assurances that candidate Jimmy Carter was seriously interested in nuclear arms reduction. At a celebration of Harriman's 90th birthday, Senator Edward Kennedy saluted the honoree by saying, "We couldn't have held the twentieth century without him."

Son of E.H. Harriman, the last and perhaps greatest of the 19th century "railroad barons," William Averell Harriman was born in 1891 to a world of riches and power. His father taught his that "great wealth is an obligation", and he always followed his father's admonition to "be something and somebody." Traveling with his parents, Harriman had toured Europe in some depth before he went to prep school, and he was in Tokyo in 1905 when riots broke out over Japanese opposition to the terms of the treaty ending the Russo-Japanese war. His worldly experience led him to see the United States as part of a global community. He thought of the oceans as avenues of commerce instead of shields isolating America from foreign enemies.

Harriman graduated from Yale University in 1913, having already been elected to the board of the Union Pacific Railroad. Although vice president of the Union Pacific Railroad from 1915-1917, the young Harriman was wealthy enough to afford other business interests. During the next decade, with the perception that the United States had no significant merchant marine fleet, he bought a shipyard and began producing "prefabricated" freighters. He ventured into mining operations in Soviet Georgia, copper in Silesia (eastern Europe), oil in Iran, a power plant in Poland, gold in South America. In 1927, Harriman and his younger brother Roland went into banking; at the end of two years, they were handling accounts for hundreds of importers and exporters; at the end of another year, and not too long after the great Wall Street crash, they merged with their biggest competitor to become Brown Brothers Harriman and Company. Harriman became involved in aviation, as an original investor in a forerunner of Pan American Airways, and in publishing, with a national magazine called *Today*, "an independent journal of public affairs" whose first subscriber was FDR; *Today* eventually merged with *News Week*

In his earlier years, Harriman was something of a sportsman, vigorously involved with polo, racehorses, and bird dogs. After the 1932 Winter Olympics in Lake Placid, NY, Harriman began to think about developing a destination ski resort somewhere in the western United States, accessible of course by Union Pacific passenger trains. He hired a young Austrian count and skier to scout the entire American west for the spot that met all of Harriman's requirements. The count was about to give up when he heard about Ketchum, "a backwater sheep town" in south central Idaho. It met all the requirements, and with the help of a (non-skiing) publicist who came up with a name and sold Harriman on the idea of making it a destination resort for the famous and glamorous, Sun Valley was born. In a short time, it was a big success, and while not a big profit-maker for the railroad, for Harriman Sun Valley "was the most satisfying venture of his business career."

The elder Harriman had been a Republican, but the son had never taken an active interest in politics, becoming a Democrat partly because of his sister Mary Harriman's friendships in the White House (the president was "Franklin") and her enthusiasm for the New Deal. He spent a good deal of time in Washington in the administration's first two years, looking after his own business interests rather than for a job; nevertheless, Harriman understood that real power in America has shifted from New York's financial district to Washington, and he "found joy in the exercise of power." Harriman's public career began in January, 1934, administering the National Recovery Administration's codes for heavy industry.

As Ambassador to the Soviet Union, Harriman performed services of the first importance. He attended the international conferences at Teheran and Yalta and provided excellent information regarding Soviet affairs. Optimistic at first about the possibility of good relations with Moscow, by 1945 Harriman changed his mind and began advocating a firm attitude toward the Soviets. Still, he never became an ideologue about the Soviets and always believed in treating them with firmness and patience.

Interspersed with Harriman's life as a globe-trotting diplomatic, there was Harriman the politician. He sought the Democratic party nomination for president in 1952 and 1956 and had considered running for the U.S. senate. In 1954, he won the New York Democratic nomination for governor, beating FDR, Jr., and managed to turn what had looked like a landslide victory in the general election into a "squeaker" victory of 11,000 votes. Harriman's oratorical skills have been described as "wooden" and "paralytically boring." He was said to be "incapable of humor or repartee," and people thought him aloof and reserved. Harri-

man tried for a second term but lost to Nelson Rockefeller; nevertheless, for years after, he was called "Governor."

Harriman's 14-year marriage to his first wife, Kitty, ended in divorce; his second wife, Marie, died after 41 years of marriage; his third wife, Pamela Churchill Harriman, was with him for the last 15 years of his life (she later served as ambassador to France in the Clinton administration until her death in 1997).

The last half or more of Harriman's life was spent as a public figure in the company of almost all the world leaders who defined and drove the twentieth century. The British political scientist Isaiah Berlin said Harriman "was an irreplaceable asset to the U.S. government and to the entire West because of an uncanny sense of what, as negotiator, could work, and what could not. In the most essential aspects of international relations, he seemed to be virtually infallible." Harriman's longevity at the top levels of government was said to be "because power and access to power, influence, and knowledge were his mother's milk." Of Averell Harriman's passing Pamela Churchill Harriman said, "He just decided that enough was enough."

Further Reading

Various aspects of Harriman's work are discussed in Robert E. Sherwood, *Roosevelt and Hopkins: An Intimate History* (1948; rev. ed. 1950); Harry S. Truman, *Memoirs* (2 vols., 1955-1956); Arthur Schlesinger, Jr., *The Age of Roosevelt*, vol. 2 (1959); Clarence B. Randall, *Adventures in Friendships* (1965); Roger Hilsman, *To Move a Nation: The Politics of Foreign Policy in the Administration of John F. Kennedy* (1967); George F. Kennan, *Memoirs, 1925-1950* (1967); and Robert H. Jones, *The Roads to Russia: United States Lend-Lease to the Soviet Union* (1969); for an excellent and complete biography, see Rudy Abramson, *Spanning the Century: The Life of W. Averell Harriman, 1891-1986* (1992) □

James Harrington

The English political theorist James Harrington (1611-1677) is best known for "The Commonwealth of Oceana," a utopian treatise which advocates the establishment of an aristocratic republic.

The eldest son of Sir Sapcotes Harrington, James Harrington was born into an old and extremely well-connected family. After showing much academic promise as a child, he entered Trinity College, Oxford. Upon the death of his father, he left Oxford without taking a degree and began a tour of the Continent.

Harrington became a frequent visitor at The Hague and, after meeting the Prince of Orange, was introduced to the Elector and Electress Palatine. He accompanied the elector on at least one state visit to Denmark. His discretion so impressed the elector that Harrington was later commissioned to look after his affairs at the court of his brother-in-law, Charles I. Before returning to England, Harrington passed from Holland, through France, into Italy. Venice greatly interested him, and he proved a keen observer of the Venetian republican government, as his later works demonstrated.

Upon returning to England, Harrington sought to retire from court life and devote his time to study, but in 1638-1639 was co-opted by Charles as a member of his privy chamber. He then accompanied the King in the First Bishops' War against the Scots, but this appears to have been the extent of his active involvement in the events precipitated by that unsuccessful campaign. He does not seem to have taken part in the Short or Long Parliament, nor does he seem to have played a role in the Second Bishops' War or in the civil wars which ensued.

After Charles's defeat Harrington was named as one of the King's attendants. Although he was not in sympathy with the excesses of monarchy, he apparently got along very well with the King and is reported to have been with Charles at the time of his execution in 1649.

Harrington then turned his attention to the problem of choosing the best of all possible governments for England and began work on *The Commonwealth of Oceana.* He proposed a society in which all men of property would have a share; property was to be balanced by laws which limited the extent of individual wealth. A senate (drawn from historical examples) was to be elected by all men of property and was to propose laws. Once the laws had been ratified by the people, they were to be executed by an elected magistracy. All officials were to serve for limited terms to ensure the maximum participation on the part of the citizens of the

Commonwealth. A community of interest served to hold the society together. Harrington's work reflected conditions in England, but in a sense the reflection was all too clear. "Olphaus Megaletor" was so obviously Oliver Cromwell that the government seized his manuscript. Only with the greatest difficulty did Harrington succeed in convincing Cromwell of his good intentions, but his work was restored to him and finally published in 1656.

Once in print, the work was violently attacked by monarchists and extreme republicans alike. These attacks led Harrington to pen a defense called *The Prerogative of Popular Government,* to abridge his work for a wider audience under the title *The Art of Law Giving,* and to further develop his views in a series of essays which were printed in 1659, the last year of the Commonwealth.

With the Restoration, Harrington retired from public life but at the end of 1661 was arrested as a traitor and thrown into the Tower. There appears to have been no basis for the accusations made against him, but Charles II's ministers evidently felt that his writings made him a dangerous foe of monarchical government. Transferred to a jail in Plymouth, he suffered from disease and from mistreatment at the hands of a prison physician, and he ultimately became insane. His release soon followed, but Harrington never recovered the full use of his faculties, nor did his health improve significantly. A late (and unhappy) marriage was followed by the onset of the gout and palsy; he died of a stroke on Sept. 11, 1677.

Further Reading

The Commonwealth of Oceana is the only work of Harrington's readily available. Henry Morley includes it in his *Ideal Commonwealths* (1893; 6th ed. 1968) and appends a short sketch of Harrington's life. See also Charles Blitzer, *An Immortal Commonwealth: The Political Thought of James Harrington* (1960). □

Michael Harrington

The American political activist and educator Michael Harrington (1928-1989) was a tireless advocate of democratic socialism. He helped develop the War on Poverty conducted by Presidents Kennedy and Johnson.

ichael Harrington was born into a middle class family and educated at Holy Cross College (A.B., 1947), Yale Law School, and the University of Chicago (M.A., 1949). He was drawn to the political left early in his career, becoming a conscientious objector to the Korean War and serving as associate editor of a Christian anarchist publication, *The Catholic Worker,* in 1951-1952. Harrington soon converted to socialism and was one of its most eloquent voices for over 30 years. During that time he supported himself by writing, lecturing, and, after 1972, teaching at Queens College of the City University of New York, where he was a professor of political science.

He always managed to give prodigious amounts of time and energy to socialist activities. Among other things Harrington served as a delegate to international socialist bodies, conventions, and congresses; as chairman of the board of the League for Industrial Democracy; as chairman and co-chairman of the executive board of the Socialist Party; as chairman of the Democratic Socialist organizing committee, and as chairman of the resulting Democratic Socialists of America. He was active also in the American Civil Liberties Union and other organizations concerned with labor, poverty, civil rights, and civil liberties.

In these ways Harrington showed himself to be a worthy heir of Norman Thomas, his predecessor as chief spokesman for American social democracy. Like Thomas he tirelessly advocated fair and humane socio-economic policies. But, again like Thomas, he was constrained by his role in the political system. Outside the United States, even in democracies, socialists can rise to the top. But in America, owing to the movement's narrow base, they can only be marginal politically no matter how great their talents. Harrington, like his forebears, chose this road all the same out of a deep faith in socialist ideas and as a matter of principle. By keeping the democratic socialist tradition alive they insured that the American left would not consist solely of totalitarians. The cost of doing this is that socialists generally, and Harrington in particular, had to give up even the hope of exercising power. For men and women of their persuasion,

only the Democratic Party holds out this possibility, and Harrington, though often a supporter of Democrats, never joined them.

Yet lacking power does not necessarily deprive one of influence, and Harrington acquired a good deal through his writings. Few authors can claim to have affected history. Harrington did this with his first book, *The Other America: Poverty in the United States* (1962). Written at a time when his fellow citizens were busy celebrating their country's affluence, *The Other America* had tremendous impact. In it he spoke up for what he called the "invisible poor": industrial rejects, migrant workers, minorities, and the aged. Harrington's book came to the attention of President John F. Kennedy. As Kennedy biographer Arthur M. Schlesinger, Jr. explained it, the book "helped crystallize his determination in 1963 to accompany the tax cut (with) a poverty program." Kennedy died before his plan could be realized, but it was put into effect with impressive results by President Lyndon Johnson. If Harrington had done nothing else his place in history would be assured.

In fact, Harrington wrote a great deal more. His first book was followed in 1965 by *The Accidental Century.* Here he argued that the "accidental revolution" of the 20th century was the gap between technological progress and economic, social, and religious consciousness. A more ambitious book than *The Other America,* it sought to draw a complete picture of the defects in Western society that made socialism imperative. As with his previous book, Harrington was more interested in establishing the problem than arriving at solutions to it.

In his next book, *Toward a Democratic Left* (1968), Harrington addressed the question of how to bring about the good society. He called for a new political movement based on Black power, white youth, white collar labor unions, the new left, and religious groups. It seemed to Harrington, as to others at the time, that the elements for such a party already existed and needed only organization and leadership to become operational. Events, as usual, were against Harrington. The year 1968 witnessed not a new socialist or pre-socialist democracy, but the election of a conservative, Richard Nixon, and a setback to hopes of turning America leftward.

Of his later works, *The Twilight of Capitalism* (1976) is a critique based on his own revised version of Marxism. Some reviewers thought Harrington was a surefooted guide through treacherous political swamps. Sidney Hook, the foremost philosophical critic of Marxism, disagreed, maintaining that Harrington was out of his intellectual depth. In *The Next America: The Decline and Rise of the United States* (1981) Harrington attacked the new conservative mood, taking his customary view that America must go further left than was possible under New Deal liberalism. *The Politics at God's Funeral* (1983) argues that as God is dead man must henceforth rely upon democratic socialism. In making his familiar case Harrington continued to display the attributes that set him apart from most social critics. Though an apostate, he treated religion with great respect. Also, though a socialist he recognized that capitalism had shown a remarkable ability to reform itself, admitting that it had made great contributions to democracy.

Though some regarded his many books, articles, and speeches on behalf of his movement as fatiguing and irrelevant, no one doubts that Harrington is unmatched as a socialist champion. Even to his critics he never appeared to be anything less than decent and humane. His anti-Communism, which runs through all of Harrington's work, is in contrast to much of the writing by leftist intellectuals. Despite his professorship, Harrington was not a conventional scholar. He practiced what might be called the "higher journalism": a mixture of fact, analysis, and polemic. Few Americans have so successfully called attention to national shortcomings or raised more important questions. His books were coherent and well thought out. He took the reader seriously. His arguments were honestly made and did not distort or ignore inconvenient facts. Though his style wavered between the eloquent and the slipshod, as one reviewer put it, Harrington at his best was, in the words of another, "lucid, brilliant, and epigrammatic." As a political program socialism made little progress in America. But with spokesmen like Harrington it will remain a moral and intellectual force.

Harrington argued that his brand of socialism was essentially a highly modified Marxism which had been refined through the twentieth-century disasters of communism and various forms of state-sponsored socialism. His utopian socialist state would be similar to Sweden's recent experiments with worker-ownership and to some similar plans which have been undertaken in the United States as a consequence of bankruptcies and/or under-capitalization.

Michael Harrington was working on his final book and carrying a full load of academic and public lectures when he died of cancer in 1989.

Further Reading

Other books by Harrington include *American Power in the Twentieth Century* (1967), *The Seventies: Problems and Proposals* (1972), *Fragments of the Century* (1974), *The Conservative Party* (1974), *The Vast Majority: A Journey to the World's Poor* (1977), and *The New American Poverty* (1986). The best history is Daniel Bell, *Marxian Socialism in the United States* (1967).

Other books by Michael Harrington include *Decade of Decision: The Crisis of the American System*, New York: Simon & Schuster (1980); *The Next Left: The History of a Future*. New York: Henry Holt (1986); *The Politics at God's Funeral: The Spiritual Crisis of Western Civilization:* New York: Penguin Books (1983); *Taking Sides: The Education of a Militant Mind*. New York: Holt, Rinehart and Winston (1985); and *Socialism: Past and Present*. New York: Little, Brown (1989).

Other excellent secondary readings are Dorrien, Gary. *The Vision of Michael Harrington. The Democratic Socialist Vision.* Totowa, NJ: Rowman and Littlefield (1986), pp. 5, 98-135; and Dorrien, Gary, Editor. *Leaders from the 1960s: A Biographical Sourcebook of American Activism*, Westport, Connecticut: Greenwood Press (1994), pp. 517- 522. □

Abram Lincoln Harris Jr.

Abram Lincoln Harris, Jr. (1899-1963), was the first African American to achieve prominence in the economics profession in the United States as an academic. Harris' influence touched fields as disparate as economic anthropology, African American studies, institutional economics, and the history of economic doctrines.

Abram Lincoln Harris, Jr., was born into a comparatively middle-class African American family in Richmond, Virginia, on January 17, 1899. His father, a butcher, and his mother, a schoolteacher, together made it possible for their son's upbringing to occur in the midst of relative economic security with a high degree of intellectual stimulation. The elder Harris worked at a meat shop owned by a German-American in Richmond, and the younger Harris, as a consequence of his interaction with the owner's family, developed fluency in German at an early age. This would serve him well in his mature years when he devoted much of his attention to the writings of German or German-trained economists' proposals for social reform.

Harris' earliest writings displayed a deep commitment to the analysis of conditions of and solutions to the problems of African Americans. His perspective took the tone of the left; he was for many years a consistent and radical advocate of the development in the United States of a multiracial labor movement aimed at redressing the class-based grievances of the majority of Americans. It was Harris' presumption that only such a working-class movement could lead to sharp change and improvement in the status of most African Americans.

He was fully attuned to the profound racial division that existed among American laborers, particularly through the long-standing practice of unions to exclude African American workers from their membership rolls. Having finished his undergraduate degree in 1922 at the local black institution in Petersburg, Virginia State University, Harris went on to earn an M.A. in economics from the University of Pittsburgh in 1924. His masters' thesis, "The Negro Laborer in Pittsburgh," inaugurated his examination of African American workers in the steelmaking and coal-mining industries and led to two articles published in the mid-1920s in the National Urban League's journal, *Opportunity,* on the difficulties confronting African American miners. One of the central issues he explored was the antagonism African American miners faced from their white peers in the coal sector. He even addressed the phenomenon of "race prejudice" among white workers, native born versus new immigrants, as an additional factor inhibiting labor organization among all the miners.

After teaching for a year (1924-1925) at West Virginia State University (then called West Virginia Collegiate Institute), Harris took a position as director of the Minneapolis Urban League. During his year in Minnesota he prepared a detailed report on the condition of African Americans in

Minneapolis. Relying heavily on statistics from surveys and from census reports, Harris documented in dramatic fashion the extent of social and economic inequality faced by African Americans in the northern city. He also devoted a substantial portion of the report to the extensive pattern of wage and employment discrimination faced by African Americans seeking work in Minneapolis, providing additional evidence of a racially split workforce.

In 1925 Harris published a semi-apocryphal essay entitled "Black Communists in Dixie" in *Opportunity*. The essay was accompanied by an editor's note reading, "This interesting narrative by Mr. Harris is an actual experience. The name of the city and the three leading figures have been changed." Presumably the city was either Harris' native Richmond or Institute, West Virginia, during the period when he taught at West Virginia State. Harris exposed with sardonic humor the prevalence of racism among Southern white leftists, who would seek African American political support but exclude them from the central committees of the Communist Party. Harris also displayed decided cynicism about Bolshevist rhetoric.

A Doctorate in Economics

The best evidence suggests that Harris was the second African American to receive a Doctorate in Economics in the United States, following Sadie Mosell Alexander. But Alexander had not pursued an academic career. Harris' dissertation research at Columbia involved further work that examined the gulf between African American and white labor in the United States. He merged his Ph.D. thesis, completed and defended in 1930, with that of the political scientist Sterling Spero to produce a now-classic study of African American labor history, *The Black Worker*, published in 1931. Racial antagonism between workers, founded on economic conflict, was a central theme of the volume. White union exclusion of African Americans and the role of African Americans as strikebreakers played a prominent role in the analysis in *The Black Worker*.

Nevertheless, Harris tended to believe that the only viable course of action for African Americans was to contribute to the development of a working-class political party in the United States. He dismissed such alternative strategies as rebellion, secession, "Back to Africa" (described derisively by Harris as "Negro Zionism"), and an independent African American economy as the stuff of fantasy. Strategies such as interracial conciliation, civil libertarianism, passive resistance, or reliance on the judiciary for relief were either superficial or ephemeral.

Spero and Harris contended in the pages of *The Black Worker* that the basis for racial antagonism in the working class had roots that could be dug out. First, they argued that distrust of African Americans by whites dated from slavery times; second, many African Americans were recent urban immigrants with a peasant background that led them to be ignorant of the advantages of trade unionism; and third, the anti-union ideology of the African American middle-class leadership of such organizations as the National Urban League fostered racial division among the working class. The first two factors would vanish with the passage of time

and with active promotion of working-class enlightenment by progressive labor organizations. The third factor could be reversed by new patterns of education of younger university-trained African Americans who would be at the center of the next generation's middle class.

Harris was consistent in endorsing construction of a racially united militant labor movement. Having joined the Howard University faculty in 1927, before completing his Ph.D., Harris and his colleagues Ralph Bunche and E. Franklin Frazier formed a radical triumvirate of social scientists at the institution. They were principal figures in the attack on the older generation of "race men" at the NAACP's 1933 Amenia Conference. Harris was the main author of the so-called Harris Report, which urged the NAACP to embrace a more militant protest and class-based course of action, rather than a race-based approach. Harris also was the author of a Progressive Labor Party pamphlet in 1930 that called for the formation of a working-class political party in the United States.

But like Bunche, Harris' radicalism became more muted as the Great Depression era came to a close. He was to claim in his introduction to a 1957 collection of his essays that he was "emerging from a state of social rebellion [while] still adher[ing] somewhat to socialistic ideas by the late 1920s." However, the evidence suggests that Harris was solidly a socialist throughout the entire decade before World War II; indeed, he even advanced a critique of the New Deal based on its failure to address the fundamental problem of class inequality in the United States.

Still, it seems that Harris underwent an ideological conversion after the Great Depression. His writings took on more of the tone and flavor of orthodox economics. Whereas he had defended Karl Marx from the conventional charges of the economists in a contribution to the Wesley Clair Mitchell *festschrift* in 1935, by the mid-1940s he was publishing essays explicitly critical of Marx. While he may have flirted intellectually with some of the most extreme libertarian perspectives in economics in the 1940s and 1950s—Harris even was associated with the Mount Pelerin Society—he eventually came to describe himself as a proponent of an individualistic brand of socialism patterned after the thinking of John Stuart Mill.

What was the cause of the conversion? Perhaps it was a sincere repudiation of views held in his younger years. Perhaps it was a reaction to the negatives of the Soviet experiment, although Harris seemed to harbor no illusions about the Soviet Union under Stalin in the 1930s, based upon his published work. Perhaps it was, and this is most likely, an accommodation made to facilitate his 1945 move from Howard to the University of Chicago.

Work at the University of Chicago

With the move Harris became one of the first African American academics with an appointment at an historically white institution of the first rank. This was apparently an appointment he valued deeply, despite the fact that he never held a regular position with the faculty of the economics department, presumably due to his race. His position was exclusively in the undergraduate college.

The move was facilitated by the efforts of the renowned Chicago economist Frank Knight, who began publishing several of Harris' papers on themes in economic doctrinal history in the prestigious *Journal of Political Economy* as early as the late 1920s. The move also was aided in a negative sense by Harris' deteriorating relationship with Howard's tyrannical president, Mordecai Johnson.

It was the papers in the *Journal of Political Economy* that made Harris' reputation in the economics profession at large. Painstaking, careful, sometimes turgid, the papers were brilliant examinations of the perspectives of a variety of economists who had staked positions on how best to bring about social reform. These papers included critiques, comparisons, and reassessments of the perspectives of Thorstein Veblen, Werner Sombart, Karl Marx, Heinrich Pesch, and John Stuart Mill, among others. Harris' critical acumen was at its best here.

With the move to Chicago, where Harris was to continue teaching until his death in 1963, not only did Harris' work lose its prior radicalism but he wrote very little on questions of race relations and the economic status of African Americans. In fact, there was no further published work on race and economics until an essay of his appeared posthumously in a 1964 Rand McNally volume celebrating a century of Black emancipation. Here Harris can be found expressing views that would be echoed two decades later by the neoconservative African American economist Thomas Sowell. Harris minimized the role of discrimination in explaining African American economic disadvantage and emphasized the role of racial differences in human capital endowments, attributable to differences in familiar socialization processes in African American and white homes.

Harris' earlier work, including the fiery attack on African American entrepreneurs in his *Negro as Capitalist,* can lay a foundation for contemporary African American radical thought. His later work anticipated the posture of African American neoconservatives. All of his writings on race relations squarely address themes of interest in African American studies courses. His *Journal of Political Economy* essays continue to play an important role for economists who form an institutionalist school and for economists who are students of the history of economic doctrines.

But Harris also had an important, albeit indirect, influence on economic anthropology. While at Columbia he was a research assistant for Melville Herskovits and, in effect, designed Herskovits' reading course in economics. What Herskovits gleaned from Harris became the basis for the economic component of the theory that informs Herskovits' classic work *The Economic Life of Primitive People.*

As for Harris' personal life, for an individual with a somewhat austere demeanor and a taste for understated sartorial splendor, it was somewhat colorful. Twice married—first to California (Callie) McGuinn and later to Phedorah Wynn—his intensely personal correspondence with the journalist Benjamin Stolberg reveals that Harris had several extramarital affairs, at least during his first marriage. But what seems to have defined Abram Harris more than all else was his intellectual career and accomplishments.

While Frank Knight may have been exaggerating a bit when he described Harris as the greatest intellect at the University of Chicago to a younger African American economist named Marcus Alexis, who was later to join the faculty at Northwestern and to serve as a commissioner with the Interstate Commerce Commission, the observation was surely not far from the mark.

Further Reading

The thinking of Abram Harris, Jr., is available in three major sources: the aforementioned work with Spero, *The Black Worker* (1931); his study of African American entrepreneurial history in the United States, *The Negro as Capitalist* (1936), which included a savage attack on the impact of African American businessmen on the African American masses; and his essays and book reviews, virtually all of which are available in a volume entitled *Economics and Social Reform* (1957) and a volume entitled *Race, Radicalism, and Reform: Selected Papers* (edited by William Darity, Jr., 1989). The last includes an introductory essay with an appraisal of Harris' life and accomplishments as well as a series of appraisals of each bloc of essays in the volume, both prepared by the editor. For additional biographical information on Harris' career see William Darity, Jr., and Julian Ellison, "Abram Harris, Jr.: The Economics of Race and Social Reform" in *History of Political Economy* (Winter 1990). □

Barbara Clementine Harris

In 1989, Barbara Clementine Harris (born 1930) became the first woman bishop in the Worldwide Anglican Communion. Prior to this appointment, Harris was a noted social activist, and her views on social issues continue to inform her actions as a religious leader.

Destined never to take the well-traveled or easy path to success, Barbara Clementine Harris made history in 1989 when she became the first woman bishop in the Worldwide Anglican Communion. Harris, an African American Episcopal pastor, had always chosen to be a leader and not a follower, both within and outside her church. Her elevation to bishop amazed many, as it provided a towering example of how far women had come in their struggle for equality in mainline Protestant churches. Harris's goal was to extend the boundaries of her church, continually pushing for a more progressive message from Episcopalians on issues of civil rights, sexism, and fairness. Harris's history as a social activist before joining the priesthood remained ingrained and served as a guide in all her religious actions.

Background

Harris was born on 12 June 1930 in Philadelphia, Pennsylvania. As a youth Harris attended Saint Barnabas Episcopal Church in Philadelphia and developed a strong relationship with her church and its vision. Harris completed high school and enrolled in college, but did not

complete her course work. In 1958 a public relations firm, Joseph Baker Associates, hired Harris, believing that she had great potential to enter this field and succeed. Two years later, Harris married. The relationship was short-lived and she was divorced by 1963. Politically, Harris was greatly affected by her surroundings. As a young African American woman, she felt it her duty to be a part of the civil rights struggle. Her participation in freedom rides, voter registration, and marches with Dr. Martin Luther King in Selma, Alabama, focused Harris's attention on the importance of fighting injustice and inequality. She went on to work as a chief public relations executive at the Sun Oil Company but always held her interests in the Episcopal Church, religion, and in the struggle for justice. Harris's voice increased in the church in 1974 when she lent her support to a group of Episcopal bishops who defied a ban on ordaining women as priests. Harris became so engulfed in the issue of women's rights in the church that she contemplated becoming a priest herself. By October 1980 her dream became a reality as she was ordained. Harris's early assignments varied from serving as chaplain in a Philadelphia County prison and working in small parishes to becoming executive director of the Episcopal Church Publishing Company. While at the publishing company Harris wrote for the liberal Episcopal magazine *Witness* and began to receive worldwide coverage in the Anglican community.

Election

Harris's ascension as bishop was a major event in the religious world. The Lambeth Conference, the once-a-dec-

ade meeting of the international Anglican hierarchy, decided in early August 1988 to allow for the ordination of women as bishops in the church, and this decision set the stage for Harris to be elected. Her election in September 1988 to be the Episcopal bishop for the state of Massachusetts occasioned great celebration as well as turmoil. She defeated many prominent candidates, including other female priests, in order to achieve her status. In response to her victory counterprotests were launched. Several conservative priests revolted, some breaking ties with the church completely, while top Anglican leaders, such as Robert Runcie, the archbishop of Canterbury, refused to acknowledge female bishops in England. Ecumenical ties between the Roman Catholic Church and the Anglican Church were also strained as the Catholic Church wholeheartedly opposed women entering the priesthood. Harris, for her part, took the controversy in stride and did not let the spotlight detract her from her mission. She had always been outspoken, and she was willing to battle potential challenges to her election as bishop, a stand that won her the admiration of many of her critics.

Aftermath

Once elected and consecrated bishop, Harris continued to advocate for diversity in the Episcopal Church and the entire Anglican community. Her command of a 96,000–member Boston-based diocese made her a powerful force to be reckoned with in deciding church policy and programs. Realizing that with great power came greater responsibility, Harris toned down her rhetoric but did not alter her message. She remains what she always was—an activist critic of the status quo who constantly strives to break new ground.

Further Reading

Larry G. Murphy, J. Gordon Melton, and Gary L. Ward, eds., *Encyclopedia of African American Religions* (New York: Garland, 1993).
Richard N. Ostling, ''The Bishop is a Lady,'' *Time*, 132 (26 December 1988): 80. □

Frank Harris

The writings of the Irish-American author and editor Frank Harris (1856-1931) ranged from the scandalous to the distinguished.

F rank Harris was born on Feb. 14, 1856, in Galway, Ireland. A small, ugly, passionate boy with a quick mind, he won a scholarship to Cambridge University but took the prize of £10, and ran off to the United States. His odd jobs in New York, Chicago, and Texas are recounted with dubious accuracy in *On the Trail: Being My Reminiscences as a Cowboy* (1930).

At the University of Kansas, Harris mixed law studies with precocious sensuality, became an American citizen, and attained admission to the bar. His decision to leave for

England and then to write as a correspondent in the Russo-Turkish War reflected his stormy, ambitious disposition. He subsequently studied at German universities and sought out distinguished contemporaries, whom he tried to impress with his reading, rich voice, and eloquent pronouncements.

In the early 1880s Harris became editor of the *London Evening News.* Absorbed in "kissing and fighting," he also sought fame. He became editor of the *Fortnightly* and married for money but soon abandoned the review. He then purchased his most notable publication, the London-based *Saturday Review,* drawing such new talents as Bernard Shaw and H. G. Wells to it.

Harris stirred interest. Thomas Carlyle saw him as earnest and idealistic. George Meredith admired his writing. But A. E. Housman resented his "truculent praise," and Joseph Conrad found him unimpressive. A raconteur, Harris fascinated some; others, aware of his shady business intrigues and undiscriminating amorous adventures, resented or even despised him. However, his friendship with Oscar Wilde and his generosity toward needy writers appear to have been genuine.

In 1898 Harris sold the *Saturday Review.* Subsequent editorships included *Vanity Fair* (1907-1910), *Hearth and Home* (1911-1912), and *Modern Society* (1912-1913). All were downhill operations, the last occasioning a prison term for libel.

Harris's own writing included *Elder Conklin* (1894), a group of naturalistic tales that impressed critics. *Montes, the Matador* (1900) increased his prestige. *The Man Shakespeare* (1909) and *The Women of Shakespeare* (1911) were praised as fresh and penetrating. *Contemporary Portraits* (1915), the first of five volumes, attempted to make art out of Harris's friendships and contacts. *Oscar Wilde* (1916) was hailed by some critics as a masterpiece in both its human perceptions and its literary style.

Back in the United States Harris bought and edited *Pearson's Magazine,* which was harassed by the U.S. Post Office for its pro-Germanism and eventually suspended. Having remarried, he and his second wife returned to France. Here he wrote his most sensational book, *My Life and Loves,* which was circulated from under booksellers' counters. *Bernard Shaw* (1931), published posthumously, was largely prepared by others.

Further Reading

A favorable view of Harris is in A. I. Tobin and Elmer Gertz, *Frank Harris: A Study in Black and White* (1931), and in Edward Merrill Root, *Frank Harris* (1947). See also *Lies and Libels of Frank Harris,* edited by Gerrit Smith and Mary Caldwell Smith (1929); Robert Harborough Shepard, *Bernard Shaw, Frank Harris, and Oscar Wilde* (1937); and Vincent Brome, *Frank Harris* (2d ed. 1959).

Additional Sources

Bain, Linda Morgan, *Evergreen adventurer: the real Frank Harris,* London: Research Pub. Co., 1975.
Harris, Frank, *My life and loves,* New York: Grove Weidenfeld, 1991.

Lunn, Hugh Kingsmill, *Frank Harris,* New York, Haskell House, 1974.
Pullar, Philippa, *Frank Harris,* London: Hamilton, 1975, New York: Simon and Schuster, 1976. ☐

Joel Chandler Harris

American writer Joel Chandler Harris (1848-1908) used folklore, fiction, dialect, and other devices of local color to picture both black and white Georgians under slavery and Reconstruction.

Joel Chandler Harris was born in Eatonton, Ga., the illegitimate son of Mary Harris. Scantily educated, at 13 Harris became an apprentice printer on a little newspaper edited and published by Joseph Addison Turner, a highly literate planter, lawyer, and writer, and learned about writing under Turner's tutelage. Harris then worked on newspapers in several Southern cities. While in Savannah he met and married Esther LaRose; they had nine children. In 1876 Harris began a 24-year association with the *Atlanta Constitution.*

Harris's work as a columnist led to his creation of Uncle Remus, the black singer of songs and teller of stories. The tales, collected in *Uncle Remus: His Songs and Sayings* (1880), are based upon folklore and are told by the venerable family servant to a little boy on a Georgia plantation. The book's favorable reviews and large sales led to magazine publication of stories later collected in *Nights with Uncle Remus* (1883), *Uncle Remus and His Friends* (1892), *Told by Uncle Remus* (1905), and others.

Remus, the old storyteller, is wise, perceptive, imaginative, poetic, and gifted with a sly sense of humor. The stories can be read for the larger picture they give of the exploited blacks who invented them. Their hero, Brer Rabbit, as Harris observed, is "the weakest and most harmless of all animals," but he is "victorious in contests with the bear, the wolf, and the fox." Thus "it is not virtue that triumphs, but helplessness; it is not malice, but mischievousness." However, since Uncle Remus's casual revelations often picture idyllically the lives of slaves and kindly whites on an antebellum plantation, these tales cultivated sympathy for Harris's people and his South. Critics believe that Harris's conscious aim was to end sectional antagonism.

In other fictional works Harris enlarged his portrayal of Southerners to include aristocrats, members of the middle class, mountaineers, and poor white farmers. Genre stories appeared in *Mingo and Other Sketches* (1884), *Free Joe* (1887), and other collections. There were two novels: *Sister Jane, Her Friends and Acquaintances* (1896) and *Gabriel Tolliver: A Story of Reconstruction* (1902). Harris died on July 3, 1908, in Atlanta.

Further Reading

Harris's *On the Plantation: A Story of a Georgia Boy's Adventures during the War* (1892), gives an autobiographical account of

the National Association for the Advancement of Colored People and led a demonstration which helped integrate a white restaurant located in a black section of Washington.

After graduation Harris returned to Chicago and pursued graduate studies in industrial relations at the University of Chicago. During this time she also worked as program director of the local Young Women's Christian Association. In 1949 she journeyed back to Washington and enrolled in American University for further graduate study. Along with her education, Harris kept busy as assistant director of the American Council of Human Rights and, after 1953, as executive director of Delta Sigma Theta, an African American sorority. She kept that position until 1959, when she entered the George Washington University Law School, partially because of the urging of William Beasley Harris, a Washington attorney whom she married in 1955. Patricia Harris graduated first in her class in 1960 and took a position as attorney with the appeals and research section of the criminal division of the Department of Justice. After serving there for two years she joined Howard University as assistant professor and associate dean of the law school. While at Howard, President John Kennedy appointed her chairperson of the National Women's Committee for Civil Rights, an unpaid position to create and coordinate support from women's groups for a new civil rights bill.

The hard work and loyalty of this life-long Democrat paid off when she was asked to second the presidential nomination of Lyndon Johnson at the 1964 Democratic National Convention. Later that year the president named Harris to the 13-member Commission on the Status of Puerto

an important period in his life. Julia C. Harris contributed valuable intimate details in *Life and Letters of Joel Chandler Harris* (1918) and *Joel Chandler Harris as Editor and Essayist* (1931). Probably the best biographical and critical account is Paul M. Cousins, *Joel Chandler Harris* (1968). A useful specialized study is Stella B. Brookes, *Joel Chandler Harris, Folklorist* (1950).

Additional Sources

Bickley, R. Bruce, *Joel Chandler Harris,* Athens: University of Georgia Press, 1987. □

Patricia Roberts Harris

Patricia Roberts Harris (1924-1985) became the first African American woman in the Cabinet when President Jimmy Carter appointed her secretary of housing and urban development in 1977.

B orn on May 31, 1924, in Mattoon, Illinois, to working class parents, Patricia Roberts Harris exemplified a true American success story. Educated in the Chicago public schools, Harris attended Howard University in Washington, D.C., where she was elected to Phi Beta Kappa and graduated *summa cum laude* in 1945. While at Howard, she served as vice-president of a student chapter of

Rico. Impressed with her diplomatic skills, Johnson appointed Harris the first female African American ambassador in U.S. history when he made her ambassador to Luxembourg in 1965.

After serving there two years Harris returned to Howard and eventually became the first female African American chosen dean of a law school. At the same time she served as the first U.S. African American delegate to the United Nations. She left Howard in 1969 in protest against what she felt was a lack of support from the university's president for her strong stand against protesting students. Following her departure she joined the law firm of Freed, Frank, Harris, Shriver, and Kampelman. Besides practicing corporate law, she served on the board of directors of Chase Manhattan Bank, I.B.M., and Scott Paper. Throughout this period she remained active in Democratic politics. Her star rose rapidly, and her fellow Democrats selected her permanent chairperson of the powerful Credentials Committee for the 1972 Democratic National Convention.

When the Democrats won the presidency in 1976, President Jimmy Carter named Harris secretary of housing and urban development. Although the appointment of this African American woman to a cabinet post proved controversial, much of the concern came from liberals who feared her lack of experience in housing and her close connection with the "establishment." During her confirmation hearing came the famous exchange between Sen. William Proxmire and Harris. Proxmire questioned whether Harris had empathy for the poor and disadvantaged. "Senator," she replied, "I am one of them. You do not seem to understand who I am. I'm a black woman, the daughter of a dining car waiter. . . . I am a black woman who could not buy a house eight years ago in parts of the District of Columbia. . . . If my life has any meaning at all, it is that those who start out as outcasts may end up being part of the system."

Once installed in office, Harris quickly dispelled doubts about her commitment. A fighter characterized by some as self-righteous, brittle, and excessively partisan, Harris breathed new life into a disorganized and demoralized agency of 16,000 workers. Not only did she demand excellence from those under her, but she lobbied hard and successfully for additional funding from Congress. As a result, the number of subsidized housing starts quadrupled under her tenure. Even more important, she helped reshape the focus of the department. A staunch supporter of housing rehabilitation, Harris funneled millions of dollars into upgrading deteriorating neighborhoods rather than wiping them out through slum clearance. For example, she pushed a Neighborhood Strategy Program that subsidized the renovation of apartments in deteriorated areas. In addition, she expanded the Urban Homesteading Plan and initiated Urban Development Action Grants to lure businesses into blighted areas. Although she ultimately wanted to replace public housing by some type of voucher system so as to provide the poor with more choice for housing, she poured millions of dollars into renovating deteriorating projects throughout the nation.

For her successful efforts, President Carter appointed Harris to the largest cabinet post, Health, Education, and Welfare (HEW), in 1979. Her most important work there was the protection of social programs during a period of budget cutting. When Congress created a separate education department in 1980, Harris became the first secretary of health and human services.

Although swept out of office by the Reagan landslide in 1980, Harris remained active in politics. In 1982, she ran for mayor of Washington, but lost to incumbent Mayor Marion Barry in the primary. After her unsuccessful bid, she returned to her position as professor of law at George Washington University Law Center. Harris died of cancer on March 23, 1985, five months after the death of her husband of 29 years.

Further Reading

Little has been written about Harris. One of the better analyses of her early tenure in office is found in Herman Nickel, "Carter's Cactus Flower at HUD," *Fortune* (November 1978). For an example of Patricia Harris' fighting spirit while at HUD, see Laurence E. Lynn, Jr., and David deF. Whitman, *The President as Policymaker: Jimmy Carter and Welfare Reform* (1981). □

Roy Harris

American composer Roy Harris (1898-1979) was a leading figure of the "American" movement in music in the 1930s and 1940s; he composed over 200 works.

Roy Harris was born on Feb. 12, 1898, in Lincoln County, Oklahoma. He migrated to California with his parents while still a boy. After military service in World War I, he began serious musical study at the University of California at Berkeley. His mentor was composer Arthur Farwell, who introduced him to the poetry of Walt Whitman and encouraged him to develop a distinctive style. He also studied with Charles Demarest, Fannie Dillon, Henry Schoenfeld, and Modest Altschuler.

Harris's first orchestral composition, *Andante,* was performed by the New York Philharmonic in 1926. With the encouragement of Aaron Copland, Harris then spent three years working with composer/pianist Nadia Boulanger in Paris. Under her tutelage, he wrote a Concerto for piano, clarinet, and string quartet which established him in Paris as one of the premier young American composers. His return to the United States was followed during the 1930s by a rapid rise to prominence, with numerous performances, recordings of most of his major works, and many commissions. One of his best known works, *The Third Symphony* dates from this period.

Harris's name and music has been associated with a visionary view of the United States and is linked with poets Walt Whitman and Carl Sandburg. He composed music for ballet, orchestra (including 16 symphonies), chamber ensembles, and one film. Some of his explicitly American themes are suggested by such titles as *What So Proudly We*

Hail, Gettysburg Address, The Abraham Lincoln Symphony, Kentucky Spring, Epilogue to Profiles in Courage: JFK, and the well-known overture, *When Johnny Comes Marching Home.*

Harris's highly original style reveals constant development and cultivation, most characteristically expressed in his Symphony No. 3 (1938). His most frequently performed work, this symphony is classical in attitude, tonally organic, and intensely dramatic. Melodies spin out in long, free lines, evolving gradually into direct and affirmative motifs. The symphony has a sense of open spaces and harmonies, rugged rhythmic inventiveness, modal character, and hymnlike sections. It displays qualities considered American that are characteristic of many of his compositions.

Harris was associated with a number of academic institutions as a teacher of composition, as composer-in-residence, and as recipient of creative grants. During World War II he was chief of the Music Division of the Office of War Information. In 1958 he visited the Soviet Union as a cultural representative, becoming the first American to conduct his own symphony with a Soviet orchestra. His academic posts were at Westminster Choir School, Cornell University, Colorado College, Utah State Agricultural College, Peabody College for Teachers, Pennsylvania College for Women, University of Southern Illinois, Indiana University, the Inter-American University in Puerto Rico, the University of California at Los Angeles, and, as composer-in-residence, California State University, Los Angeles. Among his many honors was the title, Composer Laureate of the State of California.

Roy Harris died in 1979, in Santa Monica, California. The Roy Harris Archive is housed at the Kennedy Memorial Library, California State University, Los Angeles.

Further Reading

Biographical details, Harris's own remarks, and stylistic observations are in David Ewen, *The New Book of Modern Composers* (1942; 3rd ed. 1961); Major works are discussed in Ewen's *The World of Twentieth-Century Music* (1968); for an evaluation see Wilfrid Mellers, *Music in a New Found Land: Themes and Developments in the History of American Music* (1965); For recent works, see Dan Stehman's *Roy Harris: An American Musical Pioneer* (1984); and *Roy Harris: A Bio-Bibliography* (1991). □

Townsend Harris

American merchant and diplomat Townsend Harris (1804-1878), the first U.S. envoy to reside in Japan, opened commercial relations between Japan and the United States.

Townsend Harris was born on Oct. 3, 1804, in Sandy Hill, N.Y., and educated at the local primary school. In 1817 he began work at a dry goods store and later joined his father and brother in importing china and earthenware. Harris read and studied widely and became proficient in French, Spanish, and Italian. Elected to the New York Board of Education in the 1840s, he served as its president. Harris was almost solely responsible for legislation creating the New York Free Academy, a public institution that provided free higher education for the poor and eventually became the College of the City of New York. After his mother died in 1847, Harris left for California. He purchased a ship and started trading with ports in China and the British and Dutch East Indies.

In 1853 Harris applied for a consular position in Hong Kong or Canton but was appointed instead to Ningpo (modern Ningbo) in eastern China. Rejecting this, he went to Washington to apply to Secretary of State William Marcy, an old friend, for a position as consul to Japan, which had just established treaty relations with the United States. Named consul general in 1855, Harris traveled by way of Siam (Thailand), where he negotiated a new commercial treaty, and arrived at his post, a small seaport near Yokohama, in August 1856.

After many difficulties, in 1857 and 1858 Harris finally persuaded Japanese officials to agree to commercial treaties which secured rights of American residence and trade at certain ports, regulated duties, provided for extraterritoriality and religious freedom for Americans, and established diplomatic representation at Edo (modern Tokyo). Named minister resident, Harris advised the Japanese in their conflicts with other countries. Opening a door to the West caused internal troubles in Japan resulting in violence that included assassination of the U.S. legation secretary and translator. Harris rejected military retaliation; his

William T. Harris was born in North Killingly, Conn., on Sept. 10, 1835, into a Congregationalist farming family. He entered Yale College in 1854 and completed 2 years before traveling west. In St. Louis, Mo., he tried editing, tutoring, selling, and teaching shorthand. His permanent career in education started in 1858, when he was appointed to teach in a St. Louis grammar school. He married a childhood friend, Sarah Tully Bugbee, on Dec. 27, 1858.

In 1859 Harris became principal of one of St. Louis's expanding public schools. In 1867 he was appointed assistant superintendent of the entire school system, and the following year he became superintendent.

Harris's ascendancy in education was paralleled by his study of philosophy, particularly of G. W. F. Hegel and German idealism. His superintendency drew notice for its philosophical base and its well-organized management. His *Annual Reports* stressed the idea of education as a means of achieving the social and moral progress of civilization. He promoted new ideas, notably the kindergarten, making the St. Louis public school system the first in the nation to experiment with this European concept. He traveled, lectured, and published extensively.

Harris's service to St. Louis lasted until 1880, when he resigned to travel and analyze European education. On the advice of other American educators, President Benjamin Harrison appointed Harris commissioner of education in 1889. He held this influential office until 1906, gathering

friendly but firm diplomacy won the admiration of the Japanese people.

Harris submitted his resignation to President Abraham Lincoln in 1861. He retired to New York City and continued his involvement in the temperance movement and church, civic, and foreign affairs. He died on Feb. 25, 1878.

Further Reading

The best source on Harris is his own work, *The Complete Journal of Townsend Harris, First American Consul General and Minister to Japan,* edited by Mario Emilio Cosenza (1930; rev. ed. 1959). The only good biography is Carl Crow, *He Opened the Door of Japan: Townsend Harris and the Story of His Amazing Adventures in Establishing American Relations with the Far East* (1939). Oliver Statler, *The Shimoda Story* (1969), is a nearly day-to-day coverage of Harris's stay in Shimoda. Harris is featured in Payson Jackson Treat, *The Early Diplomatic Relations between the United States and Japan, 1853-1865* (1917), and Tyler Dennett, *Americans in Eastern Asia* (1922). □

William Torrey Harris

William Torrey Harris (1835-1909) was a dominant influence in American education through his writings and by his own example as a school administrator.

and disseminating national and international information concerning educational developments.

During the 1890s Harris served on significant investigatory committees of the National Education Association. In 1895, on a committee seeking to remodel elementary education, he articulated his theory of coordinated subjects as "windows of the soul" through which children might gain an understanding of people and nature.

Harris published more than 475 educational and philosophical works. He died on Nov. 5, 1909, in Providence, R.I.

Further Reading

The best account of Harris's life is Kurt F. Leidecker, *Yankee Teacher: The Life of William Torrey Harris* (1946). A comprehensive study of Harris's educational and philosophical viewpoints is John S. Roberts, *William T. Harris* (1924). A good short summary of his life and work appears in Merle Curti, *The Social Ideas of American Educators* (1935; new ed. 1963). □

Benjamin Harrison

U.S. president Benjamin Harrison (1833-1901), though possibly the dullest personality ever to inhabit the White House, was nevertheless a competent enough president during one of the most eventful administrations of the late 19th century.

Benjamin Harrison was born in North Bend, Ohio, on Aug. 20, 1833. The Harrison had been among the most illustrious families of colonial Virginia, and Benjamin was the namesake of a Revolutionary soldier and signer of the Declaration of Independence. His grandfather, William Henry Harrison, who had transported the family to Ohio, was elected president as "Old Tippecanoe" in 1840.

Harrison graduated from Miami University in Oxford, Ohio, in 1852. He Married Caroline Scott of Oxford the following year. He read law for 2 years in Cincinnati, then moved to Indianapolis, Ind., where he established a prosperous practice.

Republican Politics

Harrison became a Republican immediately. He was known as a good political orator, although today his speeches seem to combine only triteness and pedantry with 19th-century bombast. His political career advanced slowly but steadily until the Civil War: he was city attorney of Indianapolis in 1857, secretary of the Republican State Central Committee in 1858, and reporter of the Indiana supreme Court in 1860. The last position proved profitable, as Harrison drew large royalties for many years from his compilation of Indiana laws.

Unlike many political contemporaries, Harrison sat out the first campaign of the Civil War. In 1862, however, he organized the Union's 70th Indiana Infantry and was commissioned as its colonel. A typical volunteer officer, he knew nothing of war making and was fortunate in being assigned to guard the newly captured Louisville and Nashville Railroad.

Harrison was not popular with his troops; apparently he was something of a martinet, and the personal coldness of which many contemporaries would later complain was already manifest. The dullness of guard duty also may have affected the unhappy command, but that was relieved in 1864, when Harrison and his men joined Gen. William T. Sherman. Harrison stayed at the front only briefly, as he was quickly requested to return to Indiana in order to head off a Democratic political threat in the fall elections. He rejoined Sherman, but only after Sherman's famous, devastating march through Georgia was complete; Harrison was brevetted as brigadier general, more for political than military services.

Postwar Career and Character

After the war Harrison built his legal practice into one of the most successful in Indiana. Still, he never neglected Republican politics. He supported the victorious radical faction of the party and during the 1870s became a spokesman for the equally dominant fiscal conservatives. He was unsuccessful as candidate for governor of Indiana in 1876 but continued to serve the party. In 1877 he again donned military uniform briefly to command troops during the national railroad strike. He was a solidly conservative Republican.

Harrison's career improved sharply in 1880. He was elected to the U.S. Senate and played an important role in winning the Republican presidential nomination for James A. Garfield. Harrison was himself a "dark horse" candidate for the nomination in 1884, but, realizing that it was the charismatic James G. Blaine's year, he refused to allow his name before the convention. It was this combination of stern party regularity and fortuitous personal decisions—rather than any particular brilliance—that accounted for Harrison's rise.

Harrison's years in the Senate were undistinguished. He played on Civil War emotionalism and appealed to anti-British sentiment but made no significant contributions to the great issues of the day. Rather, he turned his considerable legal talents to constructing interminable constitutional briefs for petty and partisan purposes. But his services paid off when he was nominated to run for president in 1888.

Harrison as President

In the presidential campaign Harrison lost the popular vote but won in the Electoral College. More than any previous Republican president, he committed his party to certain high financial and "big business" interests when, through his postmaster general, he systematized the solicitation of party funds. His administration sat during the "Billion Dollar Congress" elected in 1890, the first Congress ever to expend more than $1 billion. That famous Congress also passed a high tariff law containing reciprocity provisions (which Harrison largely wrote) that facilitated American economic expansion abroad, the landmark Sherman Antitrust Act, and the ill-fated Sherman Silver Purchase Act. Harrison's term also saw the Republican party finally abandon its commitment to defend the civil rights of Southern African Americans when Congress failed to pass a law designed to protect them.

Harrison kept in touch with his Congress on the various questions although, in the fashion of the time, he took a minimal part in the public debates. The accomplishments of the "Billion Dollar Congress," however, bear his mark: the carelessly drawn acts, intended as much to obfuscate as clarify, showed the lack of interest or inability to comprehend long-term effects which characterized Harrison's career.

Harrison was ultimately no more popular with his own party than with the Democrats. Short and portly with a stony, uncomely countenance, he seemed incapable of a warm personal relationship, let alone of the glad-handing conviviality which late-19th-century American politics frequently required. Still, he was the incumbent in 1892 and secured his party's renomination—only to lose the election to Grover Cleveland.

Actually, Harrison was to be just as happy about his defeat. Cleveland's second term was a disaster, marked by agricultural and industrial unrest with which Harrison could hardly have better coped. And Harrison was personally more suited for private life. His first wife had died in the White House, leaving him with two children. He married Mary Dimmick, by whom he had another child. He returned to his legal practice in Indiana, represented Venezu-

ela in a celebrated boundary dispute with Great Britain, and wrote several books, including *Views of an Ex-President* (1901) and *This Country of Ours* (1897), a popular textbook for several years. He died of pneumonia on March 13, 1901.

Further Reading

Harry J. Sievers, *Benjamin Harrison* (3 vols., 1952-1968; vol. 1, 2d ed. 1960), is scarcely inspiring but includes an exhaustively detailed source book. John A. Garraty, *The New Commonwealth: 1877-1890* (1968), provides an antidote to Sievers's uncritical admiration. The presidential election of 1888 is covered in Arthur M. Schlesinger, Jr., ed., *History of American Presidential Elections* (4 vols., 1971). H. Wayne Morgan, *From Hayes to McKinley: National Party Politics, 1877-1896* (1969), is the best recent survey of late-19th-century politics. □

Peter Harrison

Peter Harrison (1716-1775), American colonial architect and merchant, provided a number of distinguished edifices for British and American patrons.

Peter Harrison was born of a Quaker family in Yorkshire, England. He became a seaman and on a voyage to America visited Newport, R.I., about 1738. In 1745 his vessel was captured by a French warship, and he was imprisoned in the fortress of Louisbourg, Nova Scotia. After his release he drew a map of Louisbourg and otherwise assisted a later colonial expedition against the fort.

Harrison settled in Newport in 1746, married Elizabeth Pelham that year and established himself as a dealer in rum, mahogany, molasses, and wines. Shirley Place, the house he built in Roxbury, Mass., in 1746 for Governor Shirley of Massachusetts, was apparently his first architectural design.

One of Harrison's best-known buildings is the Redwood Library in Newport (1748). He designed it by combining plates from various English architectural design books he owned. Later Harrison provided plans for Touro Synagogue (1759-1763) and the Brick Market (ca. 1760) in Newport, King's Chapel in Boston (1749-1754), and Christ Church in Cambridge, Mass. (1759-1761). Sometimes attributed to Harrison are St. Michael's Church in Charleston, S.C. (1759-1761), and a number of houses with facades distinguished by two-story central sections framed by pilasters, such as the Vassall-Longfellow House in Cambridge (1760), the Apthorpe Houses in Cambridge and New York (1760 and 1767), and the Lady Pepperell House in Kittery Point, Maine (1760).

What essentially distinguishes Harrison's work is not so much an artistic personality as a generally recognizable preference for certain architectural plans and forms. As a gentleman architect, Harrison, like other refined men of his day, chose the form a building would take and left the construction details to artisans.

Politically, Harrison was a Tory. Toward the end of his life he became customs collector for the port of New Haven,

Conn. However, it was an inauspicious moment, for Revolutionary tempers were running high, and as an officer of the Crown Harrison was suspect. Fortunately for him, perhaps, he died in 1775; unfortunately for history, a mob of "patriots" broke into his office and burned his books and papers, including his architectural designs.

Further Reading

The standard biography is Carl Bridenbaugh, *Peter Harrison* (1949). Hugh S. Morrison, *Early American Architecture* (1952), gives a short summary of Harrison's sources. For an analysis of Harrison's style and place in American architecture see Alan Gowans, *Images of American Living* (1964). John F. Millar, *The Architects of the Colonies* (1968), provides a useful series of line drawings of all works attributed to Harrison, including some attributed to him only by Millar. □

William Henry Harrison

William Henry Harrison (1773-1841), the ninth president of the United States, was an early administrator of the American territorial system. He gained fame as an Indian fighter and military hero before becoming president.

William Henry Harrison was born in Charles City County, Va., on Feb. 9, 1773, into one of the state's leading families. His father, Benjamin Harrison, was a signer of the Declaration of Independence and governor of Virginia during the Revolution. William Henry studied at Hampden-Sidney College and at the University of Pennsylvania before receiving a commission in the U.S. Army in 1792.

Harrison served in the Ohio Territory and was aide-de-camp to Gen. Anthony Wayne at the Battle of Fallen Timbers (1794), which temporarily destroyed Indian power in the Northwest Territory. He married an Ohio girl, Anna Tuthill Symmes, in 1795. Three years later he left the Army, having attained the rank of captain. He soon was appointed secretary of the Northwest Territory and elected representative to the U.S. Congress. In Congress, Harrison's Land Act of 1800 was a major contribution to the development of America's territorial policy. Under its terms the Federal government provided cheap land and extended each settler 5 years' credit to pay for his property.

President John Adams appointed the experienced Harrison as governor of the Indiana Territory in 1801, when it was carved out of the Northwest Territory. During his 12 years in that post, Harrison's main accomplishments were the establishment of a legal system, the settlement of land disputes, and the management of Indian affairs. Harrison gained a national reputation through his victory over an Indian confederation organized by Tecumseh and his brother, the "Prophet," at the Battle of Tippecanoe. This was one of the last efforts at resistance by Indians east of the Mississippi River.

When the War of 1812 started, Harrison received a major general's commission in the U.S. Army and, after Gen. William Hull surrendered at Detroit, took command of the Northwest forces. Although failing to achieve his primary military objectives—the recapture of Detroit and the conquest of Canada—Harrison was victorious at the battle on Canada's Thames River. After the war Harrison was one of the commissioners who negotiated the Spring Wells Treaty in 1815, which completed the Federal takeover of Indian lands in the Northwest.

Political Career

Upon his return to Ohio, Harrison was elected to the U.S. House of Representatives (1816-1819). In 1825 he was elected to the U.S. Senate, where he served until 1828.

In 1828 Whig president John Quincy Adams appointed Harrison ambassador to Colombia. Having little knowledge of diplomacy, Harrison promptly tangled with Colombia's ruler, Simón Bolívar, who accused Harrison of complicity in an uprising. Incoming president Andrew Jackson, a Democrat, recalled him.

With the Whig party in temporary eclipse, Harrison returned to Ohio and went into political retirement until 1834. But the celebration that year of the twentieth anniversary of the Battle of the Thames returned him to prominence. A movement to make Harrison president gained strength in the Middle Atlantic states, where he had the backing of the leaders of the Antimasonic party, which by 1836 had largely combined with the Whigs. Since the Whig party was without a candidate for the 1836 contest and was composed of a number of discordant elements, several sectional candidates emerged to challenge the Democratic nominee, Martin Van Buren. They hoped collectively to throw the election into the House of Representatives, where one of the Whigs would emerge victorious. This strategy failed, but Harrison had proved the strongest contender.

The President

Soon after Van Buren's inauguration the movement for Harrison picked up new steam. Aided by a decline in Van Buren's popularity as a consequence of the Panic of 1837, Harrison received the Whig party's nomination at its 1839 convention with John Tyler, of Harrison's native county in Virginia, as his running mate.

The Whigs used a purposely vague program to carry Harrison to victory. Harrison refused to take a stand during the course of the campaign. He was portrayed as a simple, hardworking western farmer who lived in a log cabin and loved farm work, as contrasted to Van Buren, who was described as an eastern aristocrat living in luxury. Although the campaign rhetoric may have influenced the election, the dire economic condition of the country led to a general desire for changes, which worked in Harrison's favor.

Between his election and inauguration, Harrison was beset by numerous party quarrels over patronage. On April 4, 1841, one month after he took office, amid signs that his party was breaking up, Harrison died of pneumonia. The nation was stunned, having witnessed the first death of a president in office.

Further Reading

Dorothy Burne Goebel, *William Henry Harrison: A Political Biography* (1926), is a warm and interesting account of the life of the frontier hero, but quite outdated. Beverley W. Bond, Jr., *The Civilization of the Old Northwest, 1788-1812* (1934), is a good account of Harrison's early career and the difficulties encountered by territorial officials. Other studies include Freeman Cleaves, *Old Tippecanoe: William Henry Harrison and His Time* (1939), and James A. Green, *William Henry Harrison: His Life and Times* (1941). For the election of 1840 see Robert G. Gunderson, *The Log-Cabin Campaign* (1957), and Arthur M. Schlesinger, Jr., ed., *History of American Presidential Elections* (4 vols., 1971). □

Harsha

One of North India's most celebrated heroes, Harsha (ca. 590-647) was a gifted warrior-administrator, a sensitive poet and playwright, and a generous patron of religions and the arts.

From the middle of the 5th century North India was subjected to the incursions of marauding Huns. Their activity hastened the decline of the Gupta Empire, which dissolved by the mid-6th century, leaving North India again fractured politically into several independent sover-

eignties. Two dominant among these were the Maukhari, who ruled the region around the city of Kanyakubja (Kanauj), and the Pushyabhuti, who controlled lands north of Kanauj from their capital at Sthanvisvara (Thaneswar).

Harsha was the younger of two sons of the Pushyabhuti ruler Prabhakaravardhana. In 604 Prabhakara ordered his older son, Rajyavardhana, to march against the still-active Huns. During that campaign Prabhakara died. Shortly thereafter the young princes learned that their sister's husband, Grahavarman—the Maukhari ruler of Kanauj—had been killed and that she had been imprisoned by forces from the east under the joint leadership of the Malava Gupta king and the Bengali prince Sasanka. Rajyavardhana marched south and defeated the Malava but was slain—treacherously, according to Bana—by the Bengali. Harsha dispatched an army to meet the Bengali's forces while he went himself in search of his widowed sister. Bana's story concludes with Harsha's rescuing his sister from a funeral pyre and rejoining his army. There is no record of a military encounter between his troops and Sasanka's.

In addition to ruling traditional Pushyabhuti lands, Harsha accepted regency of the Maukhari territory and soon made Kanauj his major city. As regent, he took the title Kumara (Prince) Siladitya (Sun in Virtues).

Warrior and Administrator

The first 6 years of the young king's reign were years of almost ceaseless military campaigning. It is held that during this period Harsha brought much of North India under his control—from Gujarat and the Punjab in the west to Assam (but presumably not Bengal) in the east.

Tradition has it that Harsha suffered his only military defeat in a battle against the Chalukya king Pulakesin II, but since some historians date the battle in 612 and others in 620, it is possible that the testimony refers not to a single great military setback but rather to Harsha's inability to extend his political authority into the Deccan.

With the exception of the Thaneswar and Kanauj territories which were under Harsha's immediate control, the lands in his empire were administered by feudatories, who were often the traditional rulers recommissioned as viceroys. Harsha does not seem to have devised any new administrative policies or techniques, nor does it appear that the network of political and economic control was as secure as that of the Mauryas or the imperial Guptas before him. What could not be provided through a system Harsha attempted to give personally. It is said that he spent far the greater part of his time traveling from one district to another, holding court and giving audience.

Patron and Artist

Harsha was a distinguished and creative patron of religions and the arts. He lavished gifts on Buddhist institutions, and it is clear that he was profoundly influenced by Buddhist thought and practices. Still, there is no evidence that he became a Buddhist; rather it would seem that he remained a devotee of Shiva. Late in his life he may have become more concerned with the prosperity of Buddhist institutions as he emulated the manner of Asoka Maurya.

Kings and princes of India prided themselves on the accomplishments of artists, scholars, and poets whom they attracted to their courts. Harsha was no exception. And he had reason to be proud, for in his court were such great literary personalities as Banabhatta and Mayura.

Harsha's participation in the cultured life of his court was more direct than that of most kings, and it is in his personal contribution to Sanskrit literature that he clearly overshadows them. To him are assigned three plays: *Priyadarsika, Ratnavali,* and the *Nagananda.* In addition, he is credited with two significant poems on Buddhist themes—the *Ashtamahasricaityastotra* (Praise to Eight Grand Caityas [Buddhist assembly halls]) and *Suprabhatastotra* (Laud to Morning)—and a tract on grammatical gender, the *Linganusasanam.* Harsha's authorship has been disputed on several occasions, but no decisive contrary arguments have been proposed.

The *Priyadarsika* appears to be the earliest of Harsha's plays. It and the *Ratnavali* deal with the amorous adventures of the king Vatsa, his queen Vasavadatta, and newcomers to the royal harem. Both plays borrow from the earlier works of Bhasa and Kalidasa (especially the latter's *Malavikagnimitra*) and are based ultimately on material in the collection *Brhatkatha.* These plays lack thematic novelty but sustain interest through brisk dialogue. Both are frequently cited by later writers on dramatic theory and technique.

Harsha's *Nagananda* is his most important play. It is, in fact, a singular creation in Sanskrit drama. This five-act drama draws again on the *Brhatkatha* for the substance of its first three acts. In them, the hero, Jimutavahana, Prince of the Vidyadharas, meets and marries the Siddha princess Malayavati. To that point, the romance of the fairy prince and princess is quite conventional.

The mood of the play changes sharply in the fourth act. Jimutavahana discovers mounds of skeletons which evidence the daily sacrifice of serpents to the celestial bird Garuda. The hero resolves to offer his own body so that the serpents may be spared (a type of resolution very familiar in Buddhist literature). At the drama's conclusion it is the non-Buddhist goddess Gauri, however, who restores the bodhisattva, Jimutavahana, to life. In this attractive and moving drama, Harsha combined Buddhist and "Hindu" themes adroitly and uniquely, and through it one sees clearly his artistic and political genius.

With Harsha's death passed an age unduplicated in Indian history. There would be other Hindu political structures more extensive and longer-lived than Harsha's; and there would appear Sanskrit authors more facile and ingenious than he. But India has not produced again an individual of such wide-ranging talents who could wield the sword, the scepter, and the pen with equal authority.

Further Reading

Harsha's most important literary works—his three plays—are available in a single, convenient volume with Sanskrit text and English translation: *Sri Harsa's Plays,* translated by Bak Kun Bae (1964). The major biographical study of Harsha is still Radha Kumud Mookerji, *Harsha* (1926). Additional im-

portant material is in Rama Shankar Tripathi, *History of Kanauj to the Moslem Conquest* (1937). A recent popular biography is V. D. Gangal, *Harsha* (1968). D. Devahuti, *Harsha: A Political Study* (1971), concentrates on the imperial system Harsha developed. □

Gary W. Hart

Gary W. Hart (born 1936) came to national attention as a political campaign organizer, a two-term U.S. senator, and a presidential candidate.

Gary Warren Hart was born on November 28, 1936, in Ottawa, Kansas, an agricultural community where his father farmed and sold farm equipment. The family moved to Colorado several years later. At college, he shortened his family name from Hartpence to Hart. He married the former Oletha (Lee) Ludwig in 1958. They had two children, Andrea (born in 1964) and John (born in 1966).

Throughout his youth, Hart had considered the ministry as his life's vocation. He entered Bethany Nazarene College in Oklahoma and earned his B.A. degree in 1958. After graduation, he entered Yale Divinity School, where he planned an academic program in philosophy and religion. At Yale he discovered there were alternatives of service, and his career goals changed with his entry into the world of politics. Though his interest in a religious career changed, he stayed at Yale to receive a B.D. degree in 1961. Hart's new objective was to study law. He entered Yale's School of Law and earned his LL.B. degree in 1964.

Hart began his career in Washington, D.C., working as an attorney in the Department of Justice. Two years later he became a special assistant to Secretary of the Interior Stewart Udall and specialized in oil shale issues in the Western states. He left government service and moved to Denver, Colorado, in 1967. There he practiced law and taught natural resources law at the University of Colorado School of Law in Boulder.

Hart got his first experience in politics when he was a student volunteer in the 1960 presidential campaign of Senator John F. Kennedy. He volunteered again in the 1968 presidential primaries to work for Senator Robert F. Kennedy.

Senator George S. McGovern persuaded Hart to coordinate his 1972 presidential bid. Hart agreed to help McGovern by organizing a campaign structure in the Western states. He soon undertook the task of national campaign director. He helped create a coalition of liberals and anti-Vietnam War believers to support McGovern. Hart's major achievement in that campaign was to create a grassroots organization—an army of volunteers—which relied heavily on door-to-door visits, neighborhood canvassing, and raising small, individual campaign donations. McGovern lost the election in a Richard Nixon landslide, winning only about 38 percent of the popular vote nationwide and ob-

taining electoral votes only in Massachusetts and the District of Columbia.

The time had arrived, Hart felt, to run for office himself. He entered the 1974 Senate race in Colorado. He began his campaign as an underdog against the incumbent two-term Republican senator Peter H. Dominick. Hart ran as a new voice in politics and relied on his grassroots network of supporters. He won with over 57 percent of the vote statewide. In 1980 Hart ran for a second term. He barely won the office with a majority of less than 20,000 votes out of nearly 1.2 million cast.

In the Senate Hart liked to think, ask questions, shape ideas about long range strategies, and do his homework. He was considered an intellectual force and a loner rather than a persuader or wheeler-dealer. He served on the Environment and Public Works Committee, the Armed Services Committee, and the Budget Committee.

On environmental policy, Hart considered himself a conservationist rather than an environmentalist. He wanted natural resources to be guarded by the government, but believed that they should be developed. He supported the need for nuclear energy, but pushed for safety precautions and solutions to the problem of nuclear waste disposal. Hart also promoted the development of solar energy.

America's military policy became a special interest of Hart's. The senator wanted to redirect the country's defense strategy. Hart's emphasis was to shift conventional warfare to maneuver warfare. In naval operations, for example, Hart wanted a shift from huge aircraft carriers to a more mobile

fleet of smaller, less costly ships. He supported a nuclear weapons freeze, nuclear test bans, and arms limitation.

Senator Hart founded the bipartisan Congressional Military Reform Caucus to develop reforms in military strategy. His interest in America's military defense can best be illustrated by a dramatic personal move. At the age of 44, never having served in the armed forces, he joined the Naval Reserve.

Hart sought the presidential nomination in the 1984 primaries. Again, he seemed the underdog, for 1983 polls showed him to be near the rear of a group of prospective candidates. Underfinanced, he relied on his traditional grassroot volunteers strategy.

The 1984 campaign slogan was "New Ideas, New Generation." Hart's new ideas were to avoid traditional means of treating problems. Instead of a choice between conservatism and liberalism, he wanted to create a third option and focused on trying to convince the public that the real choice is between the past and the future. He attempted to reinforce the Democratic Party's image of social concerns, while repudiating its emphasis on big government and governmental regulation of business. Hart spoke for individual rights and a respect for free enterprise and economic productivity. He claimed independence from party leaders and special interests. His appeals were directed to the emerging group of young, upwardly mobile professionals ("yumpies" or "yuppies," as the terms were popularized at the time)—a new generation of educated men and women born after World War II.

Almost overnight his long-shot candidacy vaulted from the back of an eight-candidate race to the forefront after unexpected victories in the New Hampshire primary and the Iowa party caucuses. Riding a wave of momentum, he captured party delegates in New England and other states during February and March 1984. The fast pace of success could not keep up with the need for organization in many states. His momentum was lost to a well-organized campaign and support from labor and other interest groups for former Vice-President Walter F. Mondale. Hart floundered in the South and found little electoral support in the urban, industrialized areas. At the Democratic nominating convention, Hart lost to Mondale by 1,200.5 delegate votes to 2,191 votes.

In 1986 Hart did not seek a third term in the Senate. He continued to advance his issues and causes, and in 1987 he began another campaign for the presidency. Hart's campaign was hampered by rumors of his womanizing, so Hart openly challenged the press to follow him. Shortly thereafter, reporters from the *Miami Herald* "caught" Hart with 29-year-old model/actress Donna Rice. It was revealed that the pair had vactioned together, and Hart withdrew from the race.

The former senator resumed his law practice and hosted a radio talk show in his home state of Colorado. Many of his political supporters urged him to "get back into politics," by running for his former senatorial seat.

Further Reading

Hart has written several books which explain his activities and issue focus. *Right From the Start: A Chronicle of the McGovern Campaign* (1973) is a personalized account of the operations, decisions, and strategies of the 1972 presidential race. *The Good Fight: The Education of an American Reformer* (1993), detailed his political education and provided insight into his reform philosophy. For additional biographical detail on ex-Senator Gary Hart, consult *Biographical Directory of the American Congress 1774-1996;* and *U.S. News and World Report,* April 10, 1995, which carried a brief summary of Hart's political involvement.

For an overall report of the 1972 election struggles, read Theodore White, *The Making of the President 1972* (1973). Hart detailed his "new ideas" proposals that were to be the basis for his 1984 campaign themes in *A New Democracy: A Democratic Vision for the 1980s and Beyond* (1983). Hart's 1984 presidential campaign is discussed in Elizabeth Drew, *Campaign Journal: The Political Events of 1983-1984* (1985) and in Peter Goldman and Tony Fuller, *The Quest for the Presidency 1984* (1985). The senator's ideas on military policy were presented in Gary Hart and William S. Lind, *America Can Win: The Case for Military Reform* (1986). Lastly, Hart co-authored a spythriller with Senator William Cohen entitled *The Double Man* (1985). Information about Hart's ill-fated preseidential campaign can be accessed at http://www.80s.com/Timeline/1987/ (August 7, 1997). □

Francis Brett Harte

Francis Brett Harte (1837-1902), known as Bret Harte, an American poet and fiction writer who specialized in local color and regional stories, set the fashion in fiction for a number of writers in the era following the Civil War.

Bret Harte, born in Albany, N.Y., had a somewhat sketchy education in the East before he followed his widowed and recently remarried mother and her family to the Pacific Coast in 1854. There he taught school for a year, visited the Mother Lode mining country, and worked briefly for an express company.

Early Career

Harte got his professional start between 1857 and 1860, when he was a journalist in Union, Calif. He moved to San Francisco, worked in government offices, and contributed writings to the *Golden Era* and the *Californian* which brought him prominence in literary circles. A collection of poems, *The Lost Galleon,* and a volume of parodies, *Condensed Novels,* appeared in 1867. The next year Harte became editor of a new West Coast magazine, *Overland Monthly,* and began to write a series of local sketches.

When stories set in the mining country, such as "The Luck of Roaring Camp" and "The Outcasts of Poker Flat," were read and reprinted in the East and elsewhere, Harte skyrocketed to fame. His renown increased when his comic ballad "Plain Language from Truthful James"—relating how Ah Sin, a Chinese gambler, outwitted two confidence men—became nationally famous.

By the time Harte's first collection of western local-color stories appeared in book form in 1870, eastern publishers were competing for Harte's services. In 1871 he signed a contract with the *Atlantic Monthly* at a record figure for an American writer—$10,000 for 12 monthly contributions. He left California, never to return, and journeyed eastward, receiving a triumphant welcome everywhere.

Harte as Stylist

It seemed to his contemporaries that Harte had written the first authentic fiction about gold rush California on the basis of intimate knowledge. Actually he had arrived in the West several years too late, and was in the mining camps too briefly, to know them intimately. He did what most authors who achieve immediate success do—combined old elements with new ones in a way that initially seemed to be quite novel.

For one thing, Harte used the techniques of the fiction writer most popular in America during the 1860s, Charles Dickens—despite the deft parody of Dickens included in *Condensed Novels.* Harte repeatedly borrowed some of the very elements he had burlesqued—the linking of settings with moods and actions, and the creation of memorable characters by assigning them unusual names and grotesquely incongruous characteristics.

Harte also owed a debt to the most popular American writers of the day: the native humorists. He himself claimed that the unique qualities of the American short story derived from the native comic story, and in describing this genre he might well have been analyzing his own narratives: "condensed, yet suggestive . . . delightfully extravagant—or a miracle of understatement. It voiced not only the dialect, but the habits of thought of a people or locality . . . often irreverent; it was devoid of all moral responsibility."

Like antebellum humorists, Harte stressed regional characters and mores. Like postbellum humorists, he used a style marked by fanciful figures of speech, unusual word combinations, and eccentrically shaped sentences. Not surprisingly, despite his frequent pathos, Harte was classified often as a humorist.

New Ingredient

When Harte appeared on the scene, American popular fiction was largely preachy and sentimental, showing noble characters doing noble deeds. The new ingredient in Harte's typical tale was another kind of character: his rough miners, prostitutes, dance hall girls, gamblers, and badmen proved that beneath their rugged exteriors beat hearts of gold. Many of these characters became stereo-types in western fiction, particularly in cowboy stories; so did others, such as the schoolmarm imported from the East and the aristocratic colonel from the South.

These qualities appeared in early tales and in later collections: *Mrs. Skagg's Husbands* (1873), *Tales of the Argonauts* (1875), *An Heiress of Red Dog and Other Sketches* (1878), and *Colonel Starbottle's Client, and Some Other People* (1892); and in novels: *M'Liss* (1873), *Gabriel Conroy* (1876), and *Jeff Briggs's Love Story* (1880).

As time passed, it became clear that Harte was repeating himself and that his powers—except in an occasional story—were waning. Two plays, one written in collaboration with Mark Twain, were failures. Domestic difficulties and personal problems were factors that prompted Harte to accept United States consulships in Germany and in Scotland. He went to London in 1885 and stayed there for the last 17 years of his life. His considerable reputation deteriorated steadily, and scholars eventually agreed that his chief importance derived from the fact that he set a fashion in fiction writing that would be adopted by many American writers, some of them great.

Further Reading

Geoffry B. Harte edited *The Writings of Bret Harte* (19 vols., 1896-1907) and *Letters of Bret Harte* (1926). Two good biographies are George Rippey Stewart, *Bret Harte: Argonaut and Exile* (1931), and Richard O'Connor, *Bret Harte* (1966). Margaret Duckett, *Mark Twain and Bret Harte* (1964), treats their relationship and its deterioration and reflects favorably on Harte.

Additional Sources

Stewart, George Rippey, *Bret Harte, Argonaut and exile: being an account of the life of the celebrated American humorist . . . ,* New York: AMS Press, 1979, 1931. □

David Hartley

The British physician and philosopher David Hartley (1705-1757) is often referred to as one of the fathers of physiological psychology.

D avid Hartley, the son of a British clergyman, was born on Aug. 30, 1705. He received a private education before attending Cambridge, where he earned a bachelor's degree in 1726 and a master's degree in 1729. Although he intended to follow his father into the clergy, Hartley's disagreement with certain speculative doctrines adhered to by the Church of England prevented him from doing so. It did not, however, prevent him from remaining a lifelong member and defender of the Church or from writing on the subjects of theology and morals, as well as medicine and psychology. Forced to seek a new profession, Hartley turned to medicine and enjoyed considerable success.

Often the major contributions of self-effacing men are known best to those who come after them. Hartley's reputation as one of the founding fathers of the science of psychology rests on his two-volume work, *Observations on Man*, published, almost unnoticed, in 1749. Volume 2 deals with theology, and though of great importance to its author, it is of historical significance only as an example of the conviction held by many 18th-century scientists that there was no necessary conflict between science and revealed religion. Volume 1 is a systematic description of the emergence of highly complex emotional and mental states out of simple physical sensation.

Hartley's psychology can best be summarized under the twin headings of physiological determinism and associationism. All ideas and emotions are merely the coming together, or association, of various separate ideas which in turn can be traced to individual sensations that have been transmitted along the various nerves by a process of physical vibrations.

Hartley's private life was relatively uneventful: twice married, he fathered a number of children. Though he made little impression on the contemporary world at large, he communicated with many first-rate English minds of his day. In every way a gentleman, he was a kindly and expert doctor, well versed in subjects as diverse as shorthand and poetry and mathematics, devoutly religious, well organized and methodical though neither pedantic nor coldly efficient, and loved and admired by all who knew him. Hartley died at Newark, London, where he had practiced medicine, on Aug. 28, 1757.

Further Reading

The Transactions of the Halifax Antiquarian Society (1938-1939) contains a series of letters from Hartley to John Lister. These letters include personal information and show his interest in theological matters as well as algebra and shorthand. A facsimile of the first edition of Hartley's *Observations on Man*, edited by Theodore L. Huguelet (1966), contains a 12-page introduction which discusses Hartley's influence and life. □

Marsden Hartley

Marsden Hartley (1877-1943) was an American painter whose finest, most original works depict Maine's rocky shoreline and the fishermen who depend upon the sea for their livelihood.

Marsden Hartley's family left England to settle in Maine, where he was born. His first drawings were inspired by his interest in natural history. He studied on a scholarship at the Cleveland School of Art (1892-1898). Then he went to New York City to study painting under William Merritt Chase and Frank Dumond.

Hartley's earliest paintings after leaving school are impressionist and suggest the influence of the Italian painter Giovanni Segantini, whose work Hartley knew only through reproductions. Alfred Stieglitz gave Hartley his first exhibition at his "291" gallery. The show consisted mostly of "black landscapes," done in the manner of Albert P. Ryder.

In 1912 Hartley traveled to Paris, Munich, and Berlin. Although he experimented with cubism, in Germany he discovered the style which provided the expressive pictorial elements he would develop during the rest of his career. He exhibited with the Blaue Reiter group in Munich and made friends with Wassily Kandinsky, Franz Marc, and Paul Klee. A characteristic painting of this expressionist phase is *Portrait of a German Officer* (1914). Here Hartley expresses military pomp by showing only the officer's epaulets, abstracted with heightened color in contrast with coarse, black contours. This emblematic approach was modified some 3 years later when he turned to Paul Cézanne's work for direction. The influence of Cézanne is evident in Hartley's work as late as 1928.

In 1930 Hartley returned to America, where, except for brief visits to Mexico and Germany, he remained, doing his finest work. In Nova Scotia and in Bangor, Maine, he painted the craggy shoreline, dramatizing the dolmenlike rocks that were tilted as if to pit their bulk against a surging sea and a threatening sky. The sailboats that venture out in this inhospitable setting epitomize human indomitability and man's skill at harnessing natural powers. Hartley's most impressive paintings are his "archaic memory portraits" of Nova Scotia seamen, first exhibited in 1938. Hieratic and frontal, these figures are as austere and spiritualized as the saints depicted in Russian icons. It is as if these fishermen and their wives are immobilized and transfixed by the constant fear inherent in their perilous profession. Hartley painted a series of pictures of Mt. Katahdin, emulating, as he noted, the Japanese painter Ando Hiroshige, and, one might add, Cézanne.

Hartley also wrote verse. His first book, *Twenty-five Poems,* was published in Paris in 1922. He died at Ellsworth, Maine, on Sept. 2, 1943.

Further Reading

Elizabeth McCausland, *Marsden Hartley* (1952), is an extensive work on the artist. The Museum of Modern Art's catalog *Lyonel Feininger—Marsden Hartley* (1944) includes a brief text with some statements by the artist and a chronology of significant biographical events.

Additional Sources

Hartley, Marsden, *Somehow a past: the autobiography of Marsden Hartley,* Cambridge, Mass.: MIT Press, 1996.

Ludington, Townsend, *Marsden Hartley: the biography of an American artist,* Boston: Little, Brown, 1992.

Robertson, Bruce, *Marsden Hartley,* New York: Abrams in association with the National Museum of American Art, Smithsonian Institution, 1995. □

Charles Hartshorne

Charles Hartshorne (born 1897) was one of the leading American developers and exponents of process philosophy. He also made significant contributions to the contemporary theological understandings of God, creation, suffering, and evil.

Charles Hartshorne was born in Kittanning, Pennsylvania, on June 5, 1897. His father, Francis C. Hartshorne, was an Episcopal clergyman and his mother, Marguerite Haughton, was the daughter of an Episcopal clergyman. Although in his own life not identified with a particular denomination, Hartshorne's religious background provided a definitive direction for his philosophical thinking. A serious youth given to much reading and reflection, he entered Haverford College in 1915. With the advent of World War I he became a hospital orderly in Normandy, France, and, as with many other participants in the war, the enormous toll in human lives and injury deeply upset him. Hartshorne returned from the war and entered Harvard, majoring in philosophy. He completed his undergraduate work in 1921 and in quick succession received the doctor's degree in philosophy in 1923.

There is a direct line between the philosophical system Hartshorne developed in his formative years and his mature thinking. William Ernest Hocking's metaphysics, Clarence I. Lewis's idealism, Ralph Barton Perry's ethics: the teachers and the courses at Harvard all influenced him. Fellowships allowed him to spend two years in Europe where he studied under Edmund Husserl and Martin Heidegger, leading exponents of phenomenology and existentialism, respectively. Returning to Harvard in 1925 he began the monumental task, along with Paul Weiss, of editing the papers of Charles Sanders Peirce, the founder of pragmatism. This difficult task resulted in the publication of six volumes of Peirce's writings. At the same time Hartshorne worked as assistant to Alfred North Whitehead, who along with Peirce and Henri Bergson strongly influenced Hartshorne's thinking. It was Whitehead who was considered his intellectual mentor.

Hartshorne combined a capacity for brilliant philosophical analysis with an outgoing social nature. In 1928, after accepting a teaching position at the University of Chicago, he married Dorothy Eleanore Cooper. They had a daughter, Emily Lawrence. His prolific and distinguished publishing career began in 1929, and his first book, *The Philosophy and Psychology of Sensation,* was published in 1934. He early on developed a pattern of lecturing and writing, both of which continued within the framework of a teaching career at Chicago (1928-1955), Emory (1955-1962), and the University of Texas (1962 to 1980s), along with visiting professorships at, among other universities, Stanford, the Sorbonne (France), Kyoto (Japan), and Goethe (Germany).

In *The Brothers Karamazov,* Fyodor Dostoyevsky described two paths taken by young men in the pursuit of truth. The easier path involved immediate action, even to the point of sacrificing one's life. The more difficult path demanded years of tedious study which multiplied tenfold the ability to serve the truth. In Charles Hartshorne, one finds a person who chose the second path. He was the contemporary scholar who provided direction for the human community's search for self-understanding. What is it in the teaching and writing of Hartshorne that commands our attention?

Hartshorne was a pre-eminent philosopher and had a decided influence on 20th-century American thinking for several reasons. He was a shaper of the idealist tradition through his seminal works in process philosophy and theology, wherein all reality, God included, was seen in a state of eternal change and becoming. This process philosophy sharply challenged many of the fundamental ideas about the universe and God that had been the cornerstone of Western philosophy and theology.

Hartshorne developed a metaphysics—that is, a theory of meaning whereby we understand being, the universe, humans, and God. He thus provided an anchor for philosophy as it sought to gain stability in a period reacting to linguistic analysis and logical positivism. He also offered a challenge to the rapidly developing disciplines in applied ethics (e.g., business, engineering, and medical ethics) to press their arguments to more fundamental levels of philosophical and theological discourse.

He made a significant contribution to theology's never-ending quest to understand the nature of God. According to Hartshorne's "neo-classical theism," God changes along with temporal creation and is enriched by it. All reality moves toward the future, but this future has no ending, just as the past had no beginning. The God of process thought shares creation in a most intimate way with creatures, for divinity moves from present to future in the closest of relationships with the cosmos in joy and sorrow, not in distant all-knowing omnipotence or static perfection. Hartshorne's theological reflections picture a God not caught up in solitary splendor, a notion prevalent in Christian thinking. This God is incapable of being truly loving. In one of his important works, *Reality as Social Process,* Hartshorne stated: "For to love a being yet be absolutely independent of and unaffected by its welfare or suffering seems nonsense." In Hartshorne's view, God-with-us, in the tragedies made possible or inevitable by freedom, should receive more attention from theologians.

Hartshorne summarized his own religious credo, a belief worked out in countless books, essays, and lectures: "I definitely believe in God, in divine love as the key to existence, in love for God as (ideally) the all-in-all of our motivation, and in love for fellow creatures as valuable and important, judged by the same principle of value-to-God as we should judge ourselves by" (*Omnipotence and Other Theological Mistakes*). This affirmation by a maker of modern philosophy gives contemporary society pause to think of how it understands itself religiously as well as secularly since we are all believers, a people which must come to terms with meaning and ultimacy even if that belief does not assent to divinity as traditionally understood.

Charles Hartshorne was a most prolific writer on theological and philosophical subjects throughout his career. He had the ability to translate complex abstractions into language which made his ideas available to the non-academic reader.

Hartshore retired from teaching at 80 years of age, and became Professor Emeritus at the University of Texas at Austin. He also continued his active interest in bird song and published a book on the subject in 1973. He lived in Austin, Texas, and maintained an office on the university campus there. The University celebrated his one-hundredth birthday with him in 1997.

Further Reading

Eugene H. Peters, *Thinkers of the Twentieth Century,* (Pages 328-329) contains a detailed bibliography of Charles Hartshorne's publications, and of several secondary studies which explicate his academic theology and philosophy, to 1985. □

Harun al-Rashid

Harun al-Rashid (766-809) was the fifth caliph of the Abbasid dynasty. During his reign the power and prosperity of the dynasty was at its height, though its decline is sometimes held to have begun at that time.

I n 750 the Abbasid dynasty replaced the Umayyad as rulers of the Islamic Empire, and for a generation they were busy consolidating their rule and overcoming internal disorders. They moved the capital eastward from Damascus to their new city of Baghdad. By 786 the reorganization of the empire was bearing fruit in greater trade and greater wealth, which made possible the luxury now associated with the caliphal court.

Harun al-Rashid was born at Rey near Teheran in 766 (or perhaps 763), the third son of the third Abbasid caliph, Mohammed al-Mahdi. His mother was Khayzuran, a Yemeni slave girl, later freed, who through her husband and son came to have great political influence. As a boy, Harun was nominal leader of military expeditions against the Byzantines in 780 and 782. Because of his victories he received the honorific name al-Rashid (the Upright). He also gained experience as governor of various provinces under the supervision of a high official, Yahya ibn Khalid the Barmakid. In 782 Harun had been named as second in succession to the throne, but on his father's death in 785, the new caliph, his brother al-Hadi, treated him very badly. Al-Hadi, however, died mysteriously in September 786, and Harun was proclaimed caliph. He at once appointed Yahya the Barmakid as his vizier.

His Reign

For the first 17 years of his reign Harun relied to a great extent on his vizier and two of the vizier's sons, al-Fadl and Jafar. Yahya appears to have been an exceptionally competent administrator and to have shown great wisdom in the selection and training of subordinates; his two sons had similar qualities. The Barmakid family fell from power suddenly with the execution of Jafar on the night of Jan. 28/29, 803, and with the arrest of his father and al-Fadl. The fundamental reason was that they were too powerful and left too little scope to the caliph.

Although the caliphate was now mostly pacified and there were no major revolts, there was an almost constant series of local insurrections. In the earlier part of the reign there were troubles in Egypt, Syria, Mesopotamia, Yemen, and Daylam (south of the Caspian Sea), and in 806 a more serious revolt in Khurasan under Rafi ibn Layth. The difficulty of holding together an empire as vast as Harun's led to the establishment of an independent principality in Morocco by the Idrisid dynasty in 789 and of a semi-independent one in Tunisia by the Aghlabid dynasty in 800. These marked a loss of power by the central government. The danger of disintegration was increased by Harun's unwise arrangement for succession. It provided for one son, al-Amin, to become caliph and for another son, al-Mamun, to have control of certain provinces and of a section of the army.

Harun took a personal interest in the campaigns against the Byzantines, leading expeditions in 797, 803, and 806. In 797 the empress Irene made peace and agreed to pay a large sum of money. The emperor Nicephorus denounced this treaty but was forced to make an even more humiliating one in 806. Cyprus was occupied in 805. Though not mentioned in Arabic sources, there seem to have been diplomatic contacts between Harun and Charlemagne, in which the latter was recognized as protector of Christian pilgrims to Jerusalem. Harun died at Tus in eastern Persia on March 24, 809, during an expedition to restore order there.

His Personality

Although the poet, thinking of some of the stories of the *Arabian Nights*, could speak of ''the good Haroun Alraschid,'' the scholar R. A. Nicholson thought he was rather ''a perfidious and irascible tyrant, whose fitful amiability and real taste for music and letters hardly entitle him to be described either as a great monarch or a good man.''

Yet with all its violence and cruelty and its readiness to have human beings executed and tortured, the court of Harun al-Rashid undoubtedly had something which later ages admire. It was far from being without a conscience, and in the quality of its living there were elements of grandeur and nobility of style; and the tone of this life was set by Harun and the Barmakids.

Further Reading

There is no recent scholarly work on Harun. E. H. Palmer, *Harun Alraschid: Caliph of Bagdad* (1881), is out of date. H. St. J. B. Philby, *Harun al Rashid* (1933), is popular but based on secondary sources. F. W. Buckler, *Harunu'l-Rashid and Charles the Great* (1931), deals in detail with the diplomatic exchanges between the monarchs. Nabia Abbott, *Two Queens of Baghdad* (1946), describes court life and shows the influence of Khayzuran, Harun's mother, and of Zubayda, his wife. There are also brief accounts in general histories. The stories about Harun may be found in translations of the *Arabian Nights* (or *Thousand and One Nights*), with great differences between different versions.

Additional Sources

Glubb, John Bagot, Sir, *Haroon al Rasheed and the great Abbasids,* London: Hodder and Stoughton, 1976. □

Suzuki Harunobu

Suzuki Harunobu (ca. 1725-1770) was one of the six great masters of the Japanese wood-block print and was responsible for inventing the fully developed color print called nishiki-e, or brocade painting.

orn in Edo (modern Tokyo), Harunobu was one of the large group of artists whose work was devoted to the portrayal of scenes from contemporary life, especially the Kabuki theater and the courtesans of Yoshiwara, the amusement district of Edo. Tradition has it that Harunobu was a pupil of the famous Kyoto printmaker Sukenobu, but it is clear that he must also have studied the printmakers of the Torii school as well as Toyonobu and Chinese figure painters of the Ming period.

Harunobu's early works are of little distinction, generally following the conventional style of the day. At the age of 40 Harunobu emerged as the master of the color print. The event which established his reputation took place in 1765, when a group of amateur poets decided to print a deluxe edition of an illustrated calendar which they wished to distribute among their friends. Due to the genius of Harunobu and the excellence of the engraving and printing, which for the first time used multiple colors, this work at once became the rage of Edo. Encouraged by the enthusiastic reception of the color prints, the artist embarked upon a period of great activity during which he produced no less than 600 prints in 6 years, but his brilliant career was cut short when he died at the age of 45.

The prints of Harunobu, which many Ukiyo-e collectors regard as the best ever made, are outstanding both for the beauty of their design and the superb quality of their execution, in which the finest natural colors and the best-quality cherry wood were used. Harunobu's subjects were graceful and slender young girls, some of whom were courtesans, though he was more apt to portray beauties from the streets and shops of Edo. Another group of his prints dealt with erotic subjects, which were treated with the refinement and sophistication for which he was famous. His vision of life is a very poetic one in which 18th-century Edo is transformed into a world of charm and elegance, with willowy beauties in colorful kimonos meeting their lovers, viewing nature, or simply pursuing the daily activities of their domestic life.

Although Harunobu was merely one of hundreds of Ukiyo-e artists who made prints dealing with these subjects, he is outstanding for the lyrical quality of his images and the delicate beauty of his colors and designs. Reducing the forms to flat, clearly defined, decorative patterns of color and showing a technical mastery rarely achieved in the history of Ukiyo-e, Harunobu produced some of the masterpieces of this art, works which were much admired in his own life and aroused the enthusiasm of artists like Édouard Manet and Edgar Degas when the prints were introduced to Paris in the late 19th century.

Further Reading

Studies of Harunobu include Yoné Noguchi, *Harunobu* (1940); Ichitaro Kondo, *Suzuki Harunobu,* English adaptation by Kaoru Ogimi (1956); and Lubor Hajek, *Harunobu* (trans. 1958). □

William Harvey

The English physician William Harvey (1578-1657) was the founder of modern experimental physiology and the first to use quantitative methods to establish verifiability in the natural sciences.

orn in Folkestone, Kent, on April 1, 1578, William Harvey came from a prosperous family. After 6 years at King's School, Canterbury, he entered Caius College, Cambridge, in 1593, indicating a preference for a medical career. When he was 20, he went to the University of Padua, the center for western European medical instruction, where he studied under the famed anatomist Fabricius of Aquapendente. In 1602 Harvey was awarded degrees at Padua and at Cambridge.

Harvey was admitted as a candidate of the Royal College of Physicians of London in 1604, and that year married Elizabeth Browne, daughter of Lancelot Browne, physician to King James I. In 1609 Harvey became physician to St. Bartholomew's Hospital, London, and in 1616 he gave the first of his Lumleian Lectures before the Royal College of Physicians, the manuscript notes of which contain the first account of blood circulation. In 1618 Harvey was appointed physician extraordinary to King James I.

Although Harvey's practice suffered because of his radical views, he was appointed physician in ordinary to King Charles I in 1630, and in 1633 he was with Charles's court in Scotland. Professionally, Harvey made news by examining and exonerating several suspected witches and by performing a postmortem examination on Thomas Parr, reputed to have lived 152 years. In 1642, the year he fled from London with the court, he was made doctor of physic at Oxford. When his brothers died in 1643, Harvey retired from St. Bartholomew's Hospital. In 1646 he fled with the court from Oxford back to London and retired to live with his remaining brothers.

Harvey's great contribution, *Exercitatio anatomica de motu cordis et sanguinis in animalibus,* appeared in 1628. It was a poorly printed 72-page book, done by an obscure printer in Frankfurt. Harvey probably arranged it this way in order to avoid trouble in England, for he realized that his ideas flaunted the conventional teaching about the heart, which had been derived from the writings of Galen. *De motu cordis* was a landmark in the history of science. In it Harvey demonstrated the circulation of blood in animals, thus giving a firm foundation for the scientific development of the health professions. It must have been composed at different times, for the introduction is more vigorous, and in its critical attitude more youthful, than any of the rest of the 17 chapters.

Harvey's *De generatione* (1651; *On the Generation of Animals*) pioneered modern embryology and comparative sex psychology. This work was important in holding that the embryo builds gradually from its parts, rather than existing preformed in the ovum. His studies here were balked by the same difficulty which beset him in his studies on the circulation: he had no microscope. He could neither demonstrate directly how blood would move from arteries to veins, although he postulated the capillary anastomoses, nor could he see directly how the embryo gradually aggregated. In most cases the demonstration was completed by Marcello Malpighi, the great Italian biologist, who was one of the first to have and use a microscope.

In 1653 appeared the first English edition of *De motu cordis,* and Harvey's genius was fully recognized. He gave buildings and a library to the Royal College of Physicians, although he refused its presidency. He died of a stroke on June 3, 1657, and, "lapt in lead," was buried in Hempstead church.

Further Reading

The Works of William Harvey, a translation with a notice of his life by R. Willis, first appeared in Everyman's Library in 1907. Biographies of Harvey are Archibald Malloch, *William Harvey* (1929); Louis Chauvois, *William Harvey: His Life and Times* (trans. 1957); K. D. Keele, *William Harvey the Man, the physician, and the Scientist* (1965); and Sir Geoffrey Keynes, *The Life of William Harvey* (1966). □

al-Hasan ibn al-Haytham

The Arabian physicist, astronomer, and mathematician al-Hasan ibn al-Haytham (ca. 966-1039), or Alhazen, established the theory of vision that pre- **vailed till the 17th century. He also defended a theory of the physical reality of Ptolemy's planetary models.**

Al-Hasan was born at Basra in southern Iraq, where he must have received all his education. He gained sufficient fame for his knowledge of physics in his youth that he was called to Egypt by the Fatimid ruler al-Hakim to attempt to regulate the flow of the Nile. Failing in this effort, he was disgraced and established himself as a copyist of mathematical manuscripts; there still exists in Istanbul a manuscript of the Banu Musa's version of Apollonius's *Conics* copied by him in 1024. He continued to practice the scribal art in Cairo for the remainder of his life.

He did not cease to pursue his scientific studies, however, and published a large number of highly original works. He produced two catalogs of his own work, which are preserved by Ibn abi Usaybia. The first of these, compiled in 1027, comprises 25 books on mathematics and 44 on physics and metaphysics, including *On the Structure of the World.* The second, supplementary catalog was complied in 1028.

Work in Astronomy

The primary interest of al-Hasan was the explanation of phenomena by both mathematical and physical hypotheses. His interest in astronomy was motivated by the discrepancy between the Aristotelian physical and mechanistic model of the celestial spheres and the Ptolemaic mathematical model. *On the Structure of the World,* of which only the Latin translation has been published, describes the Aristotelian sublunar world of four elements and the Ptolemaic celestial spheres in all their complexity (his only change is to accept the theory that the solar apogee is fixed with respect to the fixed stars) as if they were material. He inserts a discussion of the perception of lunar and solar eclipses based on the assumption that the moon and sun are solid physical bodies.

This problem al-Hasan takes up again in *On the Light of the Moon,* in which he refutes the ancient theory that the moon reflects the sun's light like a mirror. Rather he believes that the moon is a self-illuminating body because each point on its surface broadcasts light rays in all directions, whereas each point on the surface of a mirror reflects a light ray from a single source (here the sun) in only one direction. However, he further believes that the eye receives two primary impressions in the act of vision: light and color. Therefore he concludes that only some physical effect of the sun's light rays on the moon renders the latter's color (and thereby its light) visible. This explanation opens the possibility of reconciling Aristotle and Ptolemy, for the element of which the heavenly bodies are constituted is now seen to be, though qualitatively unchangeable as Aristotle insisted, yet subject to some quantitative change which renders their light visible when they are struck by the sun's light.

Work in Optics

Al-Hasan's greatest scientific achievements were in the field of optics. In the discussion of the nature of vision at the beginning of *Optics,* he argues that light physically affects the eye, citing the pain experienced by looking directly at the Sun and the afterimage experienced by staring at fire and then looking into a weakly illuminated place. From this he argues that the assumption of emission of visual rays from the eye utilized by mathematical opticians, though convenient for their geometric analysis, must be physically wrong. Light rays rather proceed from the visible object to the eye and are always accompanied by color.

These mixed rays of light and color issue in all directions from a visible object, whether it is self-illuminating or an illuminated nontransparent body. They are perceived when the object lies in the visual field of the eye, each point on the surface of the visible object emitting a ray perpendicular to the front surface of the "glacial humor" (or "crystalline lens"); nonperpendicular rays are not perceived by the eye. The eye physically receives only the rays of light and color, but the mind interprets the patterns produced on the glacial humor as certain forms at certain distances. This theory of vision, after al-Hasan's book was translated into Latin in the late 12th or early 13th century, became the basis of all discussions of optics in the West until the 17th century.

In the latter part of *Optics* and in several other works, al-Hasan investigates problems of reflections from various sorts of mirrors. His famous solution is of "al-Hasan's problem," which he encountered in examining spherically concave mirrors: given two points A and B on the plane of a circle with center O and radius $R,$ find the point M on the circumference of the circle where a ray of light emitted from A must be reflected in order that it pass through $B.$ This leads to a biquadratic equation which al-Hasan solves geometrically by the intersection of an equilateral hyperbole with a circle.

His Influence

Al-Hasan, who has been called, with some exaggeration, the founder of modern physics, seems certainly to have been the greatest Moslem student of physical theory, with the possible exception of the less well-known Qutb al-Din al-Shirazi. It is unjustified to be too emphatic about his originality until more is known about his predecessors. His contributions to science were, however, uniformly of the highest order.

Further Reading

The best book on al-Hasan is in German: Matthias Schramm, *Ibn al-Haythams Weg zur Physik* (1963). Scholarly background works in English are Charles Singer, ed., *Studies in the History and Method of Science,* vol. 2 (1921); A. C. Crombie, *Medieval and Early Modern Science,* vol. 1: *Science in the Middle Ages: V-XIII Centuries* (1959; originally published as *Augustine to Galileo: The History of Science, A.D. 400-1650,* 1952); and Seyyed Hossein Nasr, *Science and Civilization, in Islam* (1968). George Sarton, *Introduction to the History of Science,* vol. 1: *From Homer to Omar Khayyam* (1927), includes a survey of the state of science in the 11th century. □

Charles Homer Haskins

American historian Charles Homer Haskins (1870-1937) was a leading authority on Norman culture and an important academic administrator.

Charles Homer Haskins was born in Meadville, Pa., on Dec. 21, 1870. He learned Latin at the age of 5 and Greek a little later and entered Allegheny College at 12. Transferring to Johns Hopkins, he graduated at 16 and began advanced work in history, receiving his doctorate in 1890.

Appointed an instructor at the University of Wisconsin, Haskins became a full professor in 2 years. In 1902 he moved to Harvard, where he held a number of chairs in history and in 1908 became dean of the Graduate School of Arts and Sciences. In 1911 he served on the American Historical Association committee which reported on *The Study of History in Secondary Schools*. The next year he married Clare Allen.

Meanwhile, Haskins became Harvard's first Henry Charles Lea professor in medieval history. His initial book in this area, *The Normans in European History* (1915), was a collection of lectures. Most of his books were based on his lectures or on papers. Haskins's next book, often considered his best, *Norman Institutions* (1918), followed this pattern.

Following World War I, President Woodrow Wilson appointed Haskins chief of the Division of Western Europe on the American Commission to Negotiate Peace. Haskins and Robert H. Lord, the chief of the Division of Eastern Europe, gave their impressions of this task in a series of lectures that became *Some Problems of the Peace Conference* (1920). This volume remains valuable for historians of the Versailles Treaty.

During the 1920s Haskins lectured, wrote, and worked in scholarly organizations. He helped form the American Council of Learned Societies and served as chairman from 1920 to 1926. He was president of the American Historical Association in 1922 and of the Medieval Academy, which he helped found, in 1926-1927.

The breadth of Haskins's interest in medieval history is reflected in the titles of his books: *The Rise of Universities* (1923), *Studies in the History of Medieval Science* (1924), *The Renaissance of the 12th Century* (1927), and *Studies in Medieval Culture* (1929). His work, a pioneer effort, has become dated in parts but still remains impressive. He retired in poor health from Harvard in 1931 and died in Cambridge, Mass., on May 14, 1937.

Further Reading

Evaluations of Haskins as a historian are in John Higham and others, *History* (1965); as a peacemaker, in Edward Mandell House and Charles Seymour, *What Really Happened at Paris: The Story of the Peace Conference, 1918-19* (1921); and as a graduate dean, in Samuel Eliot Morison, ed., *The Development of Harvard University since the Inauguration of President Eliot, 1869-1929* (1930). The *Anniversary Essays in Mediaeval History, by Students of Charles Homer Haskins,* edited by Charles H. Taylor and John L. LaMonte (1929), includes a bibliography of Haskins's writings but no biography. □

Frederick Childe Hassam

Frederick Childe Hassam (1859-1935) was a pioneer American impressionist painter whose work always retained a definitely native flavor.

Childe Hassam was born in Dorchester, Mass., on Oct. 17, 1859. He was early interested in art, and instead of going to college he went to work in a wood engraver's shop in Boston. Those were the great days of American illustration, and soon his work appeared in all kinds of magazines. During the evenings he drew nudes at the Boston Arts Club, and on weekends he worked outdoors with landscape painters. He soon had his own studio and his own students.

In 1883 Hassam went to Europe for a year. On his return he married a childhood friend, Kathleen Maude Doane. The couple moved to Paris for 3 years, where Hassam earned a good living doing magazine illustrations and painting pictures which he sent home to dealers. His early Paris street scenes are among his finest works. He continued studying, at the Académie Julian, but his painting, propelled by the rising wind of impressionism, soon veered away from the academic.

Hassam easily absorbed the bright colors, the white light, and the pale palette of impressionism. His main concern from this time on was light; his figures, not his best work, are flat patterns, and even his excellent etchings are studies in light. The striking results of his interest in light are best seen in his paintings of landscapes, rocky coasts, and the white churches of Gloucester and East Hampton.

As soon as he could, Hassam devoted himself entirely to painting. He early received honors—a bronze medal at the Paris Exposition (1889) and a silver medal at Munich (1892). A born painter, he certainly enjoyed painting more than anything else. However, he was somewhat touchy about his debt to the French impressionists, insisting that the modern movement in painting was founded on John Constable, William Turner, and Richard Bonington. But the fact is that he painted more like Claude Monet than did Theodore Robinson, who was Monet's avowed disciple; and Hassam's work was far more derivative than Alden Weir's or John Twachtman's, and hence, possibly, all the easier to understand and accept.

Hassam never gave up painting the figure, particularly after he settled in New York in 1889. His colorful New York is not unrelated to Camille Pissarro's Paris, and his famous flag series is heavily dependent on Édouard Manet's influence. Hassam was a member of "The Ten" and a regular exhibitor at the Carnegie International and at the annual exhibition of the Pennsylvania Academy.

Hassam was a large, red-faced gentleman, proud of his New England ancestry. His life was without trials. He was lively and cheerful, rather aggressive and outgoing. He died in East Hampton, Long Island, on Aug. 27, 1935, leaving all his work to the American Academy of Arts and Letters.

Further Reading

Adeline Adams, *Childe Hassam* (1938), is an indispensable study of Hassam. Hassam is discussed in James Thomas Flexner, *Nineteenth Century American Painting* (1970).

Additional Sources

Hoopes, Donelson F., *Childe Hassam,* New York: Watson-Guptill Publications, 1988. □

King Hassan II

After inheriting the throne of Morocco in 1961, King Hassan II (born 1929) became a stabilizing force in northwest Africa.

Mouley Hassan, son of King Mohammed V, was born on July 9, 1929, taking the name of his great grandfather who was Sultan of Morocco from 1874 to 1897. He received a classical education in both French and Arabic at the palace and at the imperial college, completing his higher education in the field of law at the University of Bordeaux in France.

By training and outlook, the future king was a "modernist." He soon became weary of the decorative character of the Moroccan leadership under the French protectorate and aware of the need to build a modern and independent state. He persuaded his father to embrace the nationalist cause and, when the French arrested Moroccan activists, followed him in exile to Corsica and Madagascar (1953-1955). Yet he was also a man who upheld the importance of the monarchial tradition of power: the king is both caliph (religious leader) and zaim (national leader), directly linked to his people.

At independence from France in 1956, Mouley Hassan was named chief of staff of the royal armed forces, which he successfully reorganized. In 1957, and again in 1959, he took charge of suppressing uprisings in the south and in the Riff in the north.

After the split of the Istiqlal, the nationalist party, the election of 1960 was won by the leftist wing, the National Union of popular forces (led by Ben Barka and Ben Seddick, the leader of the Moroccan workers union). King Mohammed V then took over the government and named his son his vice-premier. At the unexpected death of Mohammed V in 1961, Mouley Hassan, now King Hassan II, assumed the post of premier and head of the Ministries of Defense, Interior, and Agriculture. The following year he proposed a constitution patterned on the 1958 French model and providing for two elected chambers.

But the increasing tensions with emerging social/political forces—notably those of the National Union—led the young king to end the constitutional experiment. The next two years saw the dismantling of the opposition, marked by the elimination or arrest of its key leaders, including Ben Barka. The king chose to rule alone with the support of liegemen and technocrats, in many ways like the traditional and patrimonial mode of the Moroccan sultans. The constitutions of 1970 and 1972, which established a strong executive in the hands of the monarch, gave a legal-rational authority to this system of power. From time to time referenda permitted the expression of the people's loyalty to the regime while allowing a political intercourse evoking a parliamentary monarchy.

The sovereign relied in turn upon three forces: the people, the bourgeoisie, and the military. The popular attachment to the regime was stronger in the countryside than in cities. Such measures as periodic land redistribution and the suppression of an agricultural tax revitalized the perennial devotion of the fellahs to the commander of the faithful. Hassan II kept the support of the bourgeoisie by encouraging the formation of political parties, but at the same time he limited their power and fostered internal divisions within the organizations.

The military establishment, which had been the favored instrument of power at the beginning of Hassan II's rule, lost prestige after the failed coups of Skhirat (1971) and Kenitra (1972). The king himself took over its control, acting not only as the armed forces supreme commander but also as general chief of staff. However, involvement in combat

operations (in Syria and Egypt in 1973, in Mauritania from 1977 to 1979, or in Zaire in 1977 and 1978, and especially in the war of the Sahara) offered the armed forces opportunities to recover a sense of professional purpose.

A key characteristic of Hassan II's reign rested on his desire to assert himself as a leading international actor in Africa and in the Middle East. He aided negotiations between France and Libya in Chad in 1984. In the continuing Middle East unrest Hassan II played an arbiter's role. He met regularly with the chiefs of state of the region and organized international meetings, such as the Islamic Congress of Casablanca in 1984 and the Arab summits in Rabat in 1974 and in 1985. Choosing moderation and appeasement, he sought the recognition of Israel and invited the Jewish Communities Council to Rabat in 1984. He also presided over the Al Qods committee for the settlement of the status of Jerusalem, a theme discussed during his visit to the Vatican in 1980 and during that of Pope John Paul II in Morocco in 1985.

But the most troublesome issue remained that of the former Spanish Sahara, which Morocco claimed against the Sahrawi resistance upheld by Algeria and Libya. This conflict in which Hassan II involved his people tightened the links between the masses and the throne. Morocco left the OAU (Organization of African Unity) in November 1984 after the admission of the Arab Sahrawi Democratic Republic. On the other hand, Hassan II created the Arabic-African Union with Libya in August 1984. At home, the royal armed forces fought off the claims of the Polisario guerrillas to the key area of Western Sahara (the Saguia el Hamra with its rich phosphate deposits) through a strategy of "mobile walls" (the fourth and most advanced one was completed in 1985). However, Hassan II agreed in 1984 to accept the result of a referendum to determine the status of the troubled province.

In July 1986 King Hassan broke ranks with other Arabic states by holding two days of talk with Israeli prime minister Shimon Peres. Syria, Algeria, Iraq, and Libya criticized the attempt to find a basis for Middle East peace. Only Hosni Mubarak of Egypt applauded the effort. The brief union with Libya was dissolved.

Political Moderation and Democratization

Always a political moderate and an able negotiator, Hassan's talks with Shimon Peres led to the establishment of closer relations between Moroccan Jews and Israel, and permission for Israelis to visit Morocco.

During the 1990-1991 Gulf War between Iraq and the United States-backed international coalition, Hassan sent a contingent of the Moroccan Army to defend Saudi Arabia and oppose Iraq, despite mass demonstrations in Rabat and pro Saddam Husseim public opinion.

In September, 1996, King Hassan II initiated a referendum on the Moroccan constitution, which provided for a second chamber for the country's parliament. He removed one-third of the indirectly-elected membership of the single chamber representative body enabling Hassan and his ministers to veto the opposition parties. Elections to the newly designed bicameral parliamentary system were scheduled for spring of 1997; however, the major opposition parties and the government had to prepare new electoral laws, and the election was postponed until late 1997.

King Hassan was a skillful ruler of a turbulent country in a troubled region for nearly four decades, and modernized and democratized Morocco as rapidly as was feasible; considering the political and social unrest fostered by extreme Islamic fundamentalist propaganda and the armed terrorism of Hamas inspired groups.

Further Reading

Douglas E. Ashford's *Political Change in Morocco* (1961) ends with the reign of Mohammed V. Two interesting sources are in French: King Hassan's own book, *Le defi* (The Challenge) (Paris, 1976), and John Waterbury's *Le commandeur des croyants* (The Commander of the Faithful) (Paris, 1975).

The magazine *Presidents and Prime Ministers* (May/June 1996), featured a section on Diplomacy and World Peace which covered the summit talks in Egypt and Hassan's role as mediator. *The Economist* (September 28, 1996) discussed Morocco's election and Hassan's constitutional changes; and a later edition (January 2, 1997) of the same magazine discussed Hassan's relations with the Islamic fundamentalist and Moroccan militants. Yaacov Shimoni's *Biographical Dictionary of the Middle East* (1991), although an Israeli publication, outlined a sympathetic sketch of Hassan II as a just and fair-minded ruler beset by a myriad of political problems. □

Muhammad Abdille Hassan

Muhammad Abdille Hassan (1864-1920) was a politico-religious leader and poet who is considered the father of Somali nationalism for his inspiration and leadership in a 20-year war against European and Ethiopian imperialism in Somaliland.

Muhammad Abdille Hassan was born on April 7, 1864, in northern Somaliland, and by age 12 he had decided to dedicate his life to the religion of Islam. His subsequent travels throughout Arabia and East Africa in search of knowledge, his reputation for learning, and his abilities as a teacher soon earned him the honorary title of sheikh. While in Mecca he met leaders of certain Moslem revivalist movements, and when he returned to Somalia in 1897, he began to condemn all excessive indulgences and luxuries and exhorted his people to return to a strict path of Moslem devotion.

During that era of the European partition of Africa, Sheikh Muhammad's contact with Catholic missionaries and British colonial officials convinced him that Christian colonization sought to destroy the Islamic faith of the Somalis. He believed that his passion to deepen Somali faith would never be realized until they were free, so he intensified his efforts by urging his countrymen to remove the European "infidels."

Sheikh Muhammad was clearly a man of great energy and broad imagination. In his attempt to create a national movement, he used kinship ties as bases for political alliances and deftly utilized marriage ties to cement alliances with clans with whom his relations were poor. To ensure a continued broad-based appeal, he was assisted in decision making by a small group of lieutenants who belonged to no single clan.

Mediator and Guerrilla Leader

Sheikh Muhammad's success as a mediator in disputes between clans and tribes over water and grazing rights—main concerns for the pastoral Somalis—and his remarkable abilities as a poet further enhanced his fame, so that by 1899 he had attracted 3,000 followers, whom he called "dervishes." His subsequent raids on British outposts and threats to Italian and Ethiopian holdings in the area led to the dispatch of four expeditions between 1901 and 1904, all of which failed to kill the sheikh or inflict serious damage on his followers. The disgruntled British officials denounced him as a madman and an outlaw and dubbed him the "Mad Mullah."

Unable to defeat Sheikh Muhammad's nomadic guerrillas, the Europeans accused him of alleged violations of Islamic law in an attempt to undercut his power, a maneuver that failed owing to a lack of evidence and the sheikh's obvious magnetism. Financial stringency finally led the British to evacuate the interior of their protectorate from 1910 to 1912. Many Somalis unsympathetic to the sheikh's movement were then subjected to reprisals, and Somaliland lapsed into a state of unparalleled confusion and chaos.

The British returned to the Somaliland interior in 1912, but the military commitments of World War I allowed for little more than defensive operations in their small Somali colony. In January 1920, however, the British government organized a carefully combined air, sea, and land attack on the dervishes. Planes bombed Taleh, a semipermanent, fortified center the sheikh had built for his dervish theocracy, and he was forced to abandon it to reorganize. With haughty disdain he rejected a British offer of free pardon upon surrender. Further attacks forced his dwindling forces into eastern Ethiopia, where he eventually succumbed to an attack of influenza and died on Dec. 21, 1920.

The Poet

A national figure who appealed to the Somalis as Moslems regardless of their clan and lineage allegiance, Sheik Muhammad had as a formidable weapon of propaganda his scathing poems. As a poet, he relied on the traditional Somali art of alliterative poetry, which is used as a means to preserve the past and as an effective vehicle for communicating political ideas. He contributed to his charisma by assigning to certain dervishes the sole task of memorizing his poetry. In the innumerable poetic polemics his style alternated from violent denunciation and vituperation to soft words of conciliation, but the content always revealed a shrewd appreciation of the colonial situation in Somaliland. His poetry is still sung in Somali oral form, to the enrichment of the Somali poetic heritage.

Further Reading

The best statement on Sheikh Muhammad is the chapter by R. L. Hess in Norman R. Bennett, ed., *Leadership in Eastern Africa* (1968), and the best scholarly treatment of Somali history is I. M. Lewis, *The Modern History of Somaliland* (1965). Lewis' *A Pastoral Democracy* (1961) is an outstanding anthropological analysis of Somali society. ☐

Warren Hastings

The English statesman Warren Hastings (1732-1818) was the first governor general of British India. He established the system of civil administration that was the basis of Anglo-Indian security and prosperity.

Warren Hastings was born on Dec. 6, 1732, in Churchill, near Daylesford, of an old but poor family. His mother died immediately after his birth, and his father, a clergyman, disappeared in the West Indies. Raised by an uncle, Hastings had a good education and attended Westminster. He became a clerk in the East India Company and reached Calcutta in October 1750. As was the custom, he augmented his salary by private trading. He was placed in charge of a factory weaving silk and cotton goods in Kasimbazar (Cossimbazar) and by 1756 was a member of the council, the local governing body of the company.

When Suraja Dowla (Siraj-ud-Daula), the nawab of Bengal, attacked and took Calcutta, Hastings was taken prisoner but was soon released to act as intermediary for the prisoners in the Black Hole. He joined Robert Clive's relief force, which recaptured the city.

In August 1758 Clive appointed Hastings resident at Murshidabad to deal with the new nawab, Mir Jafar. Three years later Hastings was named to the Calcutta council under Henry Vansittart, Clive's successor. Disgusted by the widespread corruption, Hastings retired to England in 1764 with a modest fortune. His funds gone after 4 years, he applied for reemployment and was appointed to the Madras council, arriving there in 1769. In 1772, after Vansittart and two other members were lost at sea, Hastings became governor of Bengal. Two years later he was governor general of India, a post he held until 1785.

Hastings's tenure of office was marked by constant strife in his council and in England. He faced and dealt with continual opposition to his policies. Yet by strength of character, firmness of resolve, and sense of duty he overcame all obstacles, many of which arose from the difficulty of defining his new position and its responsibilities.

Hastings carried out an aggressive policy of administrative, judicial, and fiscal reform to improve government and eliminate abuse. He suppressed banditry in the country. He put down a serious Maratha conspiracy supported by the French. He reestablished British prestige, which had declined after Clive's departure. He used military forces throughout India to prevent the fragmentation and dissolution of British power. He perhaps occasionally overstepped his prerogatives by making British forces available to the nawab of Oudh, by using questionable methods to recover from the dowager of Oudh money illegally withheld. But he vigorously maintained his authority over subordinate provincial governors despite objections to what at times seemed like his autocratic or dictatorial control.

Hastings also fostered education, encouraged the codification of Hindu law, stimulated the study of Sanskrit by European scholars, founded a Mohammedan college in Calcutta and an Indian institute in London, opened a trade route to Tibet, sponsored a survey of Bengal, and organized expeditions to explore the seas.

The passage in 1784 of Pitt's India Act, which provided a new constitution, persuaded Hastings there was little point for him to remain. Resigning, he returned to England in 1785. He was immediately charged with "high crimes and misdemeanors," which he denied vigorously. He was impeached by Parliament in 1786, but the trial opened 2 years later and lasted 7 years. The House of Lords found him not guilty, but his personal fortune was exhausted by his defense. The East India Company came to his aid and granted him funds and an annuity.

In 1813 Hastings was asked to discuss Indian matters in Parliament and was received with extraordinary respect. In 1814 he was made a privy councilor. He died at Daylesford on Aug. 22, 1818.

Hastings was said to have "looked like a great man, and not like a bad man." He was physically slight, temperate in his habits, and reserved in his behavior. Personally neither corrupt nor cruel, he has been characterized as "the scapegoat upon whose head parliament laid the accumulated sins, real and imaginary, of the East Indian company."

Further Reading

There are three standard biographies of Hastings: Cuthbert C. Davies, *Warren Hastings and Oudh* (1939); Penderel Moon, *Warren Hastings and British India* (1947); and Keith Grahame Feiling, *Warren Hastings* (1954). Hastings the man is revealed in *Letters of Warren Hastings to His Wife,* edited by Sidney C. Grier (1905), and in H. H. Dodwell, ed., *Warren Hastings' Letters to Sir John Macpherson* (1927). □

William Henry Hatch

William Henry Hatch (1833-1896), American reformer, sponsored the Hatch Act of 1887, which gave Federal aid to agricultural research.

William Hatch was born in Scott County, Ky., on Sept. 11, 1833, the son of a pioneering Protestant (Campbellite) minister. Called to the bar at the age of 21, Hatch moved to Hannibal, Mo. There he became a noted lawyer, joined the Democrats, and was elected a circuit attorney (1858-1862).

With the outbreak of the Civil War, Hatch joined the Confederate forces. He returned to Hannibal to practice law after the war. Following the defeat of the Radical Republicans in 1871, he began seeking elective office in Kentucky. He became the Democratic congressman for the solidly agricultural First District in 1878, thereafter winning eight successive 2-year terms.

Hatch's influence in Congress was exerted mainly through his chairmanship of the Committee on Agriculture. He was defeated for the Speakership in 1892 and never achieved his ambition of becoming secretary of agriculture, though he successfully led the movement to raise that post to Cabinet rank (1889).

Hatch's pure-food reforms included the Bureau of Animal Husbandry Act of 1884; the first Oleomargarine Act of 1886 (which brought Federal inspection of margarine production and earned him the nickname "Bull Butter Hatch"); the Meat Inspection Act of 1890; and various measures to check grain speculation, to control the "tobacco trust," and to establish national standards of hygiene in the control of communicable animal diseases.

"Farmer Bill" Hatch made his greatest contribution to American agriculture with the Hatch Act of 1887. This gave direct Federal support to each state and territory for agricultural experimental stations closely associated with the Morrill land-grant colleges. The agricultural colleges were suffering from low enrollments, poorly trained faculty, and bad morale owing to the relatively undeveloped state of the agricultural sciences in the United States. The Hatch Act brought immediate improvement: 50 or 60 research stations were eventually created, and their discoveries helped revolutionize American agriculture and the life of the farmer. The colleges grew rapidly after 1887, and it was soon taken for granted that Federal and state governments should work together in a national system of agricultural teaching, research, and (later) extension education work. The Office of Experimental Stations was created in the U.S. Department of Agriculture in 1888.

Defeated for reelection in 1894, Hatch retired to his farm in Hannibal, where he died on Dec. 23, 1896.

Further Reading

General background information and a discussion of the Hatch Act are in Whitney H. Shepardson, *Agricultural Education in the United States* (1929). □

Hatshepsut

Hatshepsut (reigned 1503-1482 B.C.) was an Egyptian queen of the Eighteenth Dynasty. Usurping the throne after her husband's death, she held effective power for over 20 years.

he daughter of Thutmose I by his queen Ahmose, Hatshepsut was married to her half brother Thutmose II, a son of Thutmose I by a lesser queen named Mutnofre. During Thutmose II's lifetime Hatshepsut was merely a principal queen bearing the titles King's Daughter, King's Sister, God's Wife, and King's Great Wife.

On the death of Thutmose II the youthful Thutmose III, a son of Thutmose II by a concubine named Ese (Isis), came to the throne but under the tutelage of Hatshepsut, who for a number of years thereafter succeeded in keeping him in the background. At the beginning she had only queenly status but soon assumed the double crown of Egypt and, after some initial hesitation, had herself depicted in male dress.

Although both she, and later Thutmose III, counted their reigns from the beginning of their partnership, Hatshepsut was the dominant ruler until Year Twenty. Thutmose III was also shown as a king but only as a junior coregent. In an inscription of Year Twenty in Sinai, however, Thutmose III is shown on an equal footing with his aunt.

For obvious reasons warlike activities were barred even to so virile a woman as Hatshepsut, and with the exception of a minor expedition into Nubia, her reign was devoid of military undertakings. But an inscription on the facade of a small rock temple in Middle Egypt, known to the Greeks as Speos Artemidos, records her pride in having restored the sanctuaries in that part of Egypt, which she claimed had been neglected since the time of the alien Hyksos rulers.

Among the many officials on whose support Hatshepsut must have depended at least initially was one Senmut, whom she entrusted with the guardianship of the heir to the throne, the princess Ranefru, her daughter by her marriage to Thutmose II. According to Senmut himself, he was responsible for the many buildings erected by the Queen at Thebes. Among these was her splendid terraced temple at Deir el-Bahri, which was inspired by the earlier structure there of the Eleventh Dynasty king Mentuhotpe I.

Apart from the customary ritual ceremonies, the colored reliefs on the walls of this temple depicted the two main events of Hatshepsut's reign, the transport of two great red granite obelisks from Elephantine to Karnak and the famous expedition of Year Nine to the land of Punt, an unidentified locality which probably lay somewhere on the African Red Sea littoral.

Once having proclaimed herself king, Hatshepsut had a tomb excavated for herself in the Valley of the Kings. How she died is unknown, but after her death her memory was execrated by Thutmose III, who caused her name to be erased from the monuments wherever it could be found.

Further Reading

The reign of Hatshepsut is discussed in some detail in James H. Breasted, *A History of Egypt from the Earliest Times to the Persian Conquest* (1905; 2d ed. 1909), and by William C. Hayes in *The Cambridge Ancient History* (12 vols., 1923-1939). Leonard Cottrell, *Queens of the Pharaohs* (1966), discusses Hatshepsut. On the Queen's temple see E. Naville, *The Temple of Deir el Bahari* (7 vols., 1894-1906). □

Mohammad Hatta

Mohammad Hatta (1902-1980), one of the foremost intellectuals in the Afro-Asian anticolonial movement, was a leader of the Indonesian nationalist movement leading to its independence in 1945. He was a champion of non-alignment and of socialism grounded in Islam.

Mohammad Hatta was born in Bukittinggi, West Sumatra, Indonesia, on August 12, 1902. Although his father died while he was an infant, he was raised in a secure, well-to-do family environment which encouraged scholarly achievement and faithfulness to Islam. These characteristics became his signature during his career as one of the foremost intellectuals in the Afro-Asian anti-colonial movement.

Education and Political Activism

As a child Hatta received the best education available in the Netherlands Indies, including Dutch-language secondary schooling in Jakarta. By the time he left for the Netherlands to continue his studies at the Rotterdam School of Commerce he had already developed a keen interest in political affairs, having served while still in his teens as an officer of youth organizations in West Sumatra and Jakarta. Shortly after arriving in Rotterdam he became treasurer of the Indonesian Union (Perhimpoenan Indonesia) at a time when it was adopting explicitly political programs.

Hatta did not return to Indonesia, as he and his nationalist compatriots called the colony, until 1932. During these ten years he emerged as the overseas leader of the Indonesian nationalist movement and became acquainted with counterparts representing other independence movements, including the Indian leader Jawaharlal Nehru. In 1927 Hatta was accused by Dutch authorities of writing treasonous articles. After being imprisoned for a year and a half, Hatta successfully defended himself and his associates in a rousing, uncompromising courtroom speech which, upon publication in Indonesia, set a militant tone for the independence movement.

After his return to Indonesia Hatta and his compatriot Sutan Sjahrir sought to join forces with other nationalist leaders, including Sukarno. The organizational efforts of these men were thwarted by the repressive policies of the colonial state. First Sukarno was arrested and exiled to Flores; in 1934 Hatta and Sjahrir were arrested and eventually imprisoned in the much harsher prison camp at Digul, Western New Guinea. They later were relocated to the island of Banda, where they continued to formulate their ideas and express them in articles which were circulated in many Indonesian cities. When the Dutch in the Far East surrendered to Japan in early 1942, Hatta, back in Jakarta, assumed a new leadership role.

Occupation and Independence

Together with Sukarno and Sjahrir, Hatta participated in the Japanese occupation government. He remained in communication with underground elements of the nationalist movement, and he used his position as vice-chairman of Putera—a mass organization created in 1943—to continue political preparations for independence. With the collapse of Japan's imperial ambitions, Indonesia became independent on August 17, 1945. The days leading up to this event were tumultuous and included a brief "kidnapping" of Sukarno and Hatta by youths who were pressing for dramatic action on the part of their leaders. Sukarno and Hatta signed the proclamation of independence and quickly were designated president and vice-president, respectively, by the provisional parliament.

The next four years were a period of armed struggle against the Dutch, who were intent upon regaining control of the East Indies. For Hatta it was a time of intense political activity which included another detention by the Dutch and a deepening rift with Sukarno. As negotiations leading to the December 1949 Dutch cession of sovereignty proceeded, Hatta's international stature and his ease and competency in dealing with Europeans were instrumental in determining the outcome. Among other things he successfully opposed imposition of a federal system designed by the Dutch.

Political Ideas and Influence

Although Hatta subsequently was overshadowed by the more flamboyant and aggressive Sukarno, many of his positions became important not only in Indonesia but internationally. He was an articulate champion of non-alignment and of socialism based mainly on cooperatives and decentralization. He also believed that Indonesian socialism should be firmly grounded in Islam.

Because he was from Sumatra and was so different in personal style from Sukarno, a Javanese, the two came to be regarded as thoroughly complementary. But these same differences caused their partnership to break down, and when Sukarno abandoned parliamentary processes in favor of "guided democracy" in the later 1950s the gulf between them became unbridgeable. The collapse of Sukarno's regime in confusion and disrepute in 1966 did not lead to Hatta's return to a formal political position, however; the successor government under Suharto was dominated by the army, an organization which Hatta regarded as corrupt, inefficient, and unsuited for governance under any circumstances.

Mohammad Hatta remained in the background of Indonesian politics throughout the 1970s except for a brief period in 1978 when he agreed to serve as general chairman of the Foundation for the Institute of Constitutional Awareness. The foundation provided a forum for bold expressions of criticism from a wide range of opponents to the Suharto government. It was unable to weaken significantly the army's control of public institutions, however, and it lost much of the momentum which it may have been gaining when Hatta died on March 14, 1980.

Further Reading

In view of the long and complex relationship between the two men, it should be no surprise that biographies of Sukarno are a good source of information on Hatta. See, for example, J. D. Legge, *Sukarno: A Political Biography* (1972). George Kahin's study of *Nationalism and Revolution in Indonesia* (1952) is a thorough account of the movement in which Hatta was absorbed. The best source for the post-independence period (not covered by Kahin) is Herbert Feith, *The Decline of Constitutional Democracy in Indonesia* (1962). A brief but insightful tribute to Hatta by Kahin appears under the title, ''In Memorium: Mohammad Hatta (1902-1980),'' in *Indonesia* (1980). A selection of Hatta's writings may be found in Herbert Feith and Lance Castles, editors, *Indonesian Political Thinking, 1945-1965* (1970).

Additional Sources

Hatta, Mohammad, *Mohammad Hatta: memoirs,* Jakarta: Tintamas Indonesia, 1979.

Hatta, Mohammad, *Mohammad Hatta, Indonesian patriot: memoirs,* Singapore: Gunung Agung, 1981.

Rose, Mavis, *Indonesia free: a political biography of Mohammad Hatta,* Ithaca, N.Y.: Cornell Modern Indonesia Project, Southeast Asia Program, Cornell University, 1987. ☐

Gerhart Johann Robert Hauptmann

The German dramatist and novelist Gerhart Johann Robert Hauptmann (1862-1946) is best known for his pioneering naturalistic dramas. His subsequent work treats in various forms and styles the role of the individual in an apparently deterministic universe.

Gerhart Hauptmann as naturalist, was the leader of the literary school which flourished especially from 1880 to 1900, a period coinciding with German imperialist expansion and industrialization. The naturalists reflected with photographic and frequently harrowing realism the resultant dislocations in a society that confused material progress with its destiny. Scientific and political theorists drew attention to the formative effects of heredity and environment, the exploitation of workers, the subservient role of women, and the general decay of moral fiber. In treating such themes, the naturalists hoped to alert their contemporaries to the need for reform.

Hauptmann was born in Obersalzbrunn, Silesia, on Nov. 15, 1862, the son of a hotel owner. As a dreamy and restless young art student in Breslau, he experienced lean and frustrating years after a decline in the family fortunes. His marriage to Marie Thienemann brought financial independence and made possible his studies at the University of Jena and journeys to Italy (1883).

Upon his return Hauptmann produced an autobiographical epic poem, *Promethidenlos* (1885), anticipating the materialistic-idealistic conflict prominent in his subsequent work. Settling in Berlin, he studied Charles Darwin, Karl Marx, and contemporary schemes of social reform and developed an interest in Henrik Ibsen. The result was the pioneering naturalistic drama *Vor Sonnenaufgang* (1889; *Before Dawn*), which caused a sensation and inaugurated a series of related dramas.

Naturalistic Dramas

Vor Sonnenaufgang, first performed in Berlin on Oct. 20, 1889, supported by the society Freie Bühne, typifies Hauptmann's naturalism with its ''analytic'' technique, the ''completed'' characters, the stifling force of milieu and heredity, and the incompetence of the ''savior'' from the outside world. For a time it appears that the arrival of the socialist reformer Alfred Loth means for the virtuous Helene salvation from the degradation of a family utterly corrupted by sudden wealth and now burdened by alcoholism, infidelity, and other vices. But when Loth becomes aware of this domestic situation, he abruptly breaks with Helene and departs, unwilling to risk deeper involvement with one who, he fears, may later fall victim to a hereditary taint. In despair Helene commits suicide.

The ''analytic'' technique thus reveals not a development in response to conflict, but rather the static situation created by forces and events preceding the opening of the play. Similarly, the characters respond to situations in a manner preordained by immutable forces.

A comparably burdened and flawed family group is displayed in *Das Friedensfest* (1890), while Hauptmann's third drama, *Einsame Menschen* (1891), presents another incompetent and "misunderstood" central character. Johannes Vockerat harbors scientific and scholarly ambitions, but his loving wife, Käthe, who supports his life of scholarship, is intellectually incapable of understanding him. His own capacities appear paralyzed in consequence. The arrival of Miss Anna Mahr, a student who shares Johannes's interests, creates a triangular impasse. Johannes and Anna fall in love, but he cannot bring himself to choose between the two women and the sharply differing life-styles that they represent. Anna departs, and Johannes commits suicide. (Similarly flawed and "misunderstood" husbands appear in the "artist dramas"—*Kollege Crampton,* 1892; *Michael Kramer,* 1900; and *Gabriel Schillings Flucht,* 1912.)

Die Weber (1892; *The Weavers*), based on a historical incident of 1844, established Hauptmann's international reputation. Here the sociological problem overshadows the personal—machines are replacing the handwork of the weavers—and the mass of exploited Silesian workers emerges as "hero," taking on a character and identity of its own: a novelty in German drama. The workers' revolt is put down, but it is clear that their cause is just.

A similar attention to the psychological implications of the mass characterizes the broadly conceived drama *Florian Geyer* (1896), based on the ill-fated 16th-century Peasant Revolt. The peasant troops represent the tragic hero, whose fate is paralleled in Geyer, the well-intentioned leader who lacks the ruthless will to act.

Three further naturalistically oriented plays represent a climactic achievement, although they transcend strict naturalistic technique. In *Fuhrmann Henschel* (1898) a lowly trucker takes his own life, consumed by remorse at breaking a solemn oath to his wife on her deathbed that he would not marry Hanne, their unpleasant maid. (The situation is similar in an early novella—*Bahnwärter Thiel,* 1887.) In *Rose Bernd* (1903), however, the shame and remorse of an unmarried mother guilty of infanticide are assuaged by the forgiveness of her fiancé. In *Die Ratten* (1911) a comic element is overshadowed by the tragedy arising from Frau John's pathologically intense and frustrated maternal instinct. The work reveals expressionistic elements and symbolizes the ethical brittleness of imperial Germany's social fabric. (In one of German literature's outstanding comedies—*Der Biberpelz,* 1893; *The Beaver Coat*—Hauptmann had already satirized a prominent flaw of the Prussian establishment: its stiff-necked and ethically myopic officialdom.)

The drama *Vor Sonnenuntergang* (1932) closes the naturalistic cycle. Here the hope of the aging Clausen for happiness in marriage to his young secretary is thwarted by the ungenerous conniving of his children by a previous marriage. The grasping materialism of the new generation drives the humanistic Clausen to suicide.

Neoromanticism and Legend

With his most successful fairy-tale drama, *Hanneles Himmelfahrt* (1893), Hauptmann transcends the naturalistic limits. In this work a young girl who despairs because of mistreatment by her stepfather attempts to drown herself and is rescued, but her ensuing fever is fatal, and her

fantasies as death approaches are realized onstage—the language reflects the transition in passing from lowly prose to exalted verse—projecting her attainment of the fulfillment impossible on the plane of reality.

Hannele provides a bridge between naturalism and the neoromantic myth drama in verse, *Die versunkene Glocke* (1896; *The Sunken Bell*), in which the bell caster (artist) Heinrich, though incapable of living on the normal plane of reality, is made tragically aware that the artist cannot attain the life of pure spirit. The conflict mirrors a similar struggle in Hauptmann's own career, climaxed in 1904 by his decision to divorce his first wife and marry a gifted musical artist. The prose drama *Und Pippa tanzt!* (1906) projects the fragile quality of beauty, or of longing, pursued and victimized by crass reality.

The epic element characterizes three dramas: *Der arme Heinrich* (1902) reworks the themes of blood sacrifice and compassion in the old legend; *Kaiser Karls Geisel* (1908) treats the love of the 80-year-old emperor Charlemagne for the 16-year-old Saxon hostage Gersuind, while *Griselda* (1909) examines the patience of this legendary figure in terms of abnormal psychology.

Comparable treatments of legendary and historical themes are found in the drama *Der weisse Heiland* and the dramatic poem *Indipohdi* (both 1920), which protest the inhumanities of the Spanish in their New World conquests. The dramas *Winterballade* (1917) and *Veland* (1925) offer analyses of abnormal or morbid psychological states.

Narrative Work

Hauptmann's 20 novels and narratives develop similar psychological themes, frequently combined with an autobiographical element. *Der Narr in Christo Emanuel Quint* (1910) treats the messianic complex and the conflict of spirit and flesh in modern terms. *Atlantis* (1912) reflects Hauptmann's own struggle to choose between two women of sharply differing qualities.

Der Ketzer von Soana (1918) and *Die Insel der grossen Mutter* (1924) celebrate the overpowering force of the erotic impulse. *Das Buch der Leidenschaft* (2 vols., 1929-1930) analyzes the psychological complexities for the man torn between two women, while *Mignon* (published posthumously in 1947) recreates, with demonic overtones, this remarkable figure from Goethe's *Wilhelm Meister.* In *Im Wirbel der Berufung* (1936) the basic pattern is again the triangle, and opportunity is created, again as in *Wilhelm Meister,* for a long analysis of Shakespeare's *Hamlet.*

Classical Epilogue

Classical settings and themes predominate in the four verse dramas of the late *Atriden tetralogy,* in which Hauptmann seeks to interpret the events of the Greek past in terms of a catastrophic present (Nazi domination and World War II). The results are at best ambiguous and the prospect for man's further development clouded.

In Hauptmann's literary output one finds a compendium of the contending forces, from materialism to mysticism, active in German literature during his long career. In his lifelong efforts to encompass them in art, the view of man as a powerless victim of higher forces is balanced in some measure by a recurrent faith in the redemptive power of human compassion.

Hauptmann died on June 6, 1946, and was buried on the Baltic Island of Hiddensee, his favorite summer retreat. His extensive travels included two trips to America (1894 and 1932). He received the Nobel Prize in 1912.

Further Reading

Informative older studies of Hauptmann are Otto Heller, *Studies in Modern German Literature* (1905; repr. 1967), and Camillo von Klenze, *From Goethe to Hauptmann: Studies in a Changing Culture* (1926). The sociological implications of Hauptmann's work are stressed in Margaret Sinden, *Gerhart Hauptmann: The Prose Plays* (1957), and Leroy R. Shaw, *Witness of Deceit: Gerhart Hauptmann as Critic of Society* (1958). A good general analysis is by Hugh F. Garten, *Gerhart Hauptmann* (1954). Hauptmann and his times are well treated in Jethro Bithell, *Modern German Literature 1880-1950* (1939; 3d ed. 1959).

Additional Sources

Holl, Karl, *Gerhart Hauptmann, his life and his work, 1862-1912,* Norwood, Pa.: Norwood Editions, 1977.
Maurer, Warren R., *Understanding Gerhart Hauptmann,* Columbia, S.C.: University of South Carolina Press, 1992. ☐

Karl Haushofer

Karl Haushofer (1869-1946) was a German professional soldier who, on his retirement at the age of 50, became a geopolitician whose views were influential in Germany especially under the Hitler regime, from 1933 to 1945.

Born in Munich on Aug. 27, 1869, Karl Haushofer belonged to a family of artists and scholars and on his graduation from the Munich Gymnasium (high school) contemplated an academic career. However, service with the Bavarian army proved so interesting that he stayed to work, most successfully, as an instructor in military academies and on the general staff. He fought in World War I and in 1919 retired with the rank of major general.

The cultivated atmosphere of his childhood gave Haushofer an outlet for retirement. He had visited Japan on a military mission in 1908 and traveled extensively in Asia; in 1911 he had received a doctorate of philosophy from Munich University for a thesis on Japan. Joining the staff of Munich University in 1921, he quickly became, as the major general-professor-doctor, a respected figure.

A New View of Geopolitics

In 1924 Haushofer published a book on the geopolitics of the Pacific Ocean and, with a group of young geographers and social scientists, founded the *Zeitschrift für Geopolitik,* conceived as political geography with a dy-

namic purpose. This gave many Germans what they wanted, a *Weltanschauung,* meaning a view of the world, a philosophy, a sense of purpose, a living faith. Haushofer appealed to the heroic virtues of discipline and obedience. Aristocratic in origin and temperament, he believed that the army could be the abiding power in Germany.

For a long time his attitude to the Nazi domination from 1933 was cautious. Prophesying that the Soviet Union was potentially a greater power than the United States, he wished to see a German-Soviet alliance, with Japan in friendly association. In Haushofer's view, the days of France and England were finished, and the future lay with the resurgent nations, Germany, Italy, and Japan. His views were expressed in books and numerous articles.

Though Haushofer was an adviser to Hitler, his last years were bitter, for his son Albrecht, professor of political geography and geopolitics at Berlin University, was murdered by National Socialist agents. Haushofer's hopes for Germany perished, and with his wife he died by suicide on March 13, 1946, at Paehl bei Weilheim.

Further Reading

Detailed studies of Haushofer are in Andreas Dorpalen, *The World of General Haushofer: Geopolitics in Action* (1942), and Edmund Aloysius Walsh, *Total Power: A Footnote to History* (1948). See also Franz Leopold Neumann, *Behemoth: The Structure and Practice of National Socialism 1933-1944* (1942; rev. ed. 1944), and Russell Humke Fitzgibbon, ed., *Global Politics* (1944). ☐

Baron Georges Eugène Haussmann

Baron Georges Eugène Haussmann (1809-1891), as French prefect of the Seine, carried out under Napoleon III a huge urban renewal program for the city of Paris.

During the administration of Baron Haussmann, 71 miles of new roads, 400 miles of pavement, and 320 miles of sewers were added to Paris; 100,000 trees were planted, and housing, bridges, and public buildings were constructed. Elected a member of the Académie des Beaux-Arts in 1867, the year of the International Exhibition in Paris, Haussmann stated, "My qualification? I was chosen as demolition artist" (*Memoires,* 3 vols., 1890-1893).

Admittedly Haussmann destroyed a considerable portion of the historic city, but the purpose was to tear down the worst slums and discourage riots, make the city more accessible, accommodate the new railroads, and beautify Paris. Long, straight boulevards for parades and for the circulation of traffic could also foil would-be rioters, since the mob could not defend boulevards as readily as barricaded slum alleyways.

Georges Eugène Haussmann was born in Paris. Exceedingly ambitious, he studied law solely with the aim of becoming an administrator within the prefectorial corps. He was appointed prefect of the Seine in 1853.

The instigator of the beautification of Paris was Napoleon III, who admired London, especially its squares. Such a program of beautification would in addition stimulate the banks and solve the problems of unemployment. Haussmann spent a total of 2,115,000,000 francs, the equivalent of $1.5 billion in today's currency.

Haussmann began by continuing the Rue de Rivoli as a great east-west link across Paris and by developing the areas of the Louvre and the Halles. He brought a competent engineer named Alphand from Bordeaux to continue the development of the Bois de Boulogne. Other acquaintances were introduced into the administration, notably in the construction of the famous sewers. The sewers, although underground, did not go unnoticed; Haussmann ensured that they became showplaces and even provided transportation for their viewing. One critic cynically considered the sewers "so fine that something really great should happen in them" (*Memoires*).

Three-quarters of the Île de la Cité was destroyed to create a central area for the Palais de Justice and police headquarters and barracks. The Boulevard de Sebastopol, beginning at the Gare de l'Est, was extended across the Île to provide a north-south route across Paris. The Gare du Nord was linked to the business district by the Rue La Fayette. Radial roads linked the core of the city to the suburbs. A green belt around the fortifications linking the Bois de Boulogne in the west to the Bois de Vincennes in the east did not materialize.

Haussmann was forced to retire in 1869, having succumbed to his critics, who accused him of "Haussmannomania," heavy spending, and disrespect for the laws governing finance. One of his last acts for Napoleon III was the drafting of a proclamation for the siege of Paris in 1870.

Further Reading

J.M. and Brain Chapman, *The Life and Times of Baron Haussmann: Paris in the Second Empire* (1957), is good background, although opinionated, particularly on Garnier's Opéra, and not well illustrated. Sigfried Giedion, *Space, Time and Architecture: The Growth of a New Tradition* (1941; 5th ed. 1967), contains superior illustrations. See also David H. Pinkney, *Napoleon III and the Rebuilding of Paris* (1958). □

Vaclav Havel

A world-renowned playwright and human rights activist, Vaclav Havel (born 1936) became the president of Czechoslovakia in December 1989, a unique position in European history. His literary brilliance, moral ascendancy, and political victories served to make him one of the most respected figures of the late 20th century and led his country to be one of the first Eastern European nations to be invited into NATO.

Vaclav Havel was born in Prague, Czechoslovakia, on October 5, 1936, to a wealthy and cultivated family. His father was a restaurateur, real estate developer, and friend of many writers and artists, and his uncle owned Czechoslovakia's major motion picture studio. The coming of World War II did not much disturb the Havels' lifestyle, and young Vaclav grew up amid the trappings of luxury, with servants, fancy cars, and elegant homes.

Deprived of High School Education

The 1948 Communist takeover of Czechoslovakia radically changed the Havels' lives. Their money and properties were confiscated, and Vaclav's parents had to take menial jobs. The worst deprivation for the family was that Vaclav and his brother were not allowed to attend high school. Fortunately he discovered a loophole in the system by which he could attend night school, and so for five years he combined a full-time job as a laboratory assistant with school. The busy teenager also enjoyed an active social life, which revolved around a group of friends who, like Vaclav, wrote poetry and essays, endlessly discussed philosophical matters, and sought out the company of writers and intellectuals. In the fall of 1956 he first attracted widespread attention when, at a government-sponsored conference for

young writers, he appealed for official recognition of several banned poets, an act which earned him much criticism.

Became a Playwright

From 1957 to 1959 Havel served in the Czech army, where he helped found a regimental theater company. His experience in the army stimulated his interest in theater, and following his discharge he took a stagehand position at the avant-garde Theater on the Balustrade. The eager would-be playwright attracted the admiration of the theater's director and he progressed swiftly from manuscript reader to literary manager to, by 1968, resident playwright. It was while at the Theater on the Balustrade that Havel met and in 1964 married Olga Splichalova. Of working-class origin, his wife was, as Havel later said, "exactly what I needed. . . . All my life I've consulted her in everything I do . . . She's usually first to read whatever I write. . . ."

His wife did a great deal of reading as Havel's career took off. Heavily influenced by Theater of the Absurd playwrights, Havel's early plays were clever, rather depressing exposés of the relationship between language and thought. These plays, which included *The Garden Party* (1963), *The Memorandum* (1965), and *The Increased Difficulty of Concentration* (1968), were instant successes in Czechoslovakia and abroad, where they were translated and performed to critical and popular acclaim.

Human Rights Activities

The Russian invasion of Czechoslovakia in August 1968 brought an abrupt end to the cultural flowering of the "Prague Spring" and marked a watershed in Havel's life. He felt he could not remain silent, and so began his long career as a human rights activist with an underground radio broadcast asking Western intellectuals to condemn the invasion and to protest the human rights abuses of the new and repressive regime of Gustav Husak. The government responded by banning the publication and performance of Havel's works and by revoking his passport. Although he was forced to take a job in a brewery, he continued to write, and his works were distributed by clandestine, "samizdat" means—typewritten copies and illegal tapes, many of which were sent abroad for publication.

Like many of his countrymen, and in particular many intellectuals and artists, Havel could have fled Czechoslovakia to the freedom of the West. He was offered several opportunities to leave, and the government encouraged him to do so. He declined, however, saying, "The solution of this human situation does not lie in leaving it. . . ." His courageous decision to remain and face what he termed the "interesting" future in his own country made him a hero to many Czechs.

Havel's human rights activities continued with April 1975's "Open Letter to Doctor Gustav Husak," which decried the state of the country as a place which had lost all sense of values and in which people lived in fear and apathy. The "Letter," disseminated through samizdat channels, attracted much notice and clearly put Havel at risk.

Jailed For Protest

In January 1977 hundreds of Czech intellectuals and artists, Marxists and anti-Communists alike, signed Charter 77, which protested Czechoslovakia's failure to comply with the Helsinki Agreement on human rights. Havel took an active part in the Charter movement and was elected one of its chief spokesmen. As such, he was arrested and jailed early in 1977, tried on charges of subversion, and given a 14-month suspended sentence. Havel was unrepentant: "The truth has to be spoken loudly and collectively, regardless of the results. . . ."

Havel and some other Charter 77 activists founded the Committee for the Defense of the Unjustly Persecuted, or VONS, in 1978. The members of VONS were arrested, and in October 1978 Havel was tried, convicted, and sentenced to four and one-half years at hard labor. He served his sentence at a variety of prisons under arduous conditions, some of which are chronicled in his book *Letters to Olga* (1988), based on his prison letters to his wife. A severe illness resulted in his early release in March 1983.

Henceforth Havel was viewed both at home and abroad as a symbol of the Czech government's repression and the Czech people's irrepressible desire for freedom. He continued his dissident activities by writing a number of significant and powerful essays, many of which are collected in 1987's *Vaclav Havel or Living in Truth*. Highly critical of the totalitarian mind and regime while exalting the human conscience and humanistic values, the essays contain some splendid and moving passages. The government responded by tapping his telephone, refusing to let him accept literary prizes abroad, watching his movements, and even shooting his dog.

In January 1989 Havel was arrested again following a week of protests and was sentenced to jail for nine months. On November 19, 1989, amid growing dissatisfaction with the regime in Czechoslovakia and similar discontent throughout Eastern Europe, Havel announced the creation of the Civic Forum. Like Charter 77, a coalition of groups with various political affiliations and a common goal of nonviolent and nonpartisan solution, the forum was quickly molded by Havel and his colleagues into a responsive and effective organization.

The Collapse Of the Communist Regime

The week following the creation of the forum marked the beginning of the so-called "Velvet Revolution," by which Czechoslovakia's Communist regime collapsed like a house of cards. With almost dizzying speed, a new, democratic republic was smoothly and bloodlessly established. Havel and the Civic Forum played a decisive role in this revolution, meeting with the government and applying pressure by mass demonstrations. On December 10, 1989, Husak resigned as president. On December 19, Parliament unanimously elected Havel to replace him. To the cheering throngs which greeted him after his election Havel said, "I promise you I will not betray your confidence. I will lead this country to free elections. . . ."

The new president was a new type of leader for Czechoslovakia. The long-persecuted but never silenced dissident was a modest, diffident intellectual, who, lacking a professional politician's self-conscious self-confidence, readily admitted his fears for the future and amazement at his success. In his first months in office he accomplished much. His very presence as president manifested Czech unity and freedom, and he retained his great personal popularity both at home and abroad. He was enthusiastically received in Germany and accorded respect in Moscow, where Premier Gorbachev agreed to withdraw Soviet troops from Czechoslovakia. He was deliriously applauded in the United States, where he addressed Congress, met with the president, and was lionized by celebrities. His government began the long, and, as he warned his people, often painful process of social and economic change to democracy and a free market economy. Most importantly, in June 1990 the promised free elections—the first since 1946—were held, with Havel's Civic Forum's candidates winning large majorities in both houses of Parliament. On July 5, 1990, Parliament reelected an unopposed Havel as president for a two-year term.

Vaclav Havel as President

Havel's government had considerable success in its first year and managed to avoid some of the awkward adjustments faced by other Eastern European countries. Nonetheless, Havel and his country faced some weighty problems. The first of these was the resurgence of Slovakian nationalism, which was stayed by Havel's popularity and a constitution which ensures a Slovakian prime minister. Then there was Havel himself, who as a dissident criticized the government but did not have—and could not have had—a realistic program as an alternative. He therefore had to do a great deal of learning on the job, a process not without its hazards. When he released prisoners, for example, he crippled Czechoslovakia's main automobile factory, which depended on convict labor, causing severe though temporary economic dislocations.

More serious was the split of the Civic Forum between those wanting a complete and rapid transformation of the Czech economy to a free market system, led by Vaclav Klaus, and Havel's more cautious followers, who believed in a gradual approach. To the surprise of most observers, and of Havel himself, Klaus was elected chairman of the Civic Forum in October 1990, defeating Havel's candidate. Many viewed this as Havel's first serious political setback, and the split of the forum into two distinct factions did not bode well for its long-term survival as a political entity.

In August 1992, the Slovak parliament passed its own constitution, and Havel resigned as president. In December, parliament passed a law dividing Czechoslovakia into the Czech Republic and Slovakia, a separation Havel had tried to prevent. However, Havel's political career was not yet over. In 1993 parliament elected him first president of the Czech Republic.

Tumor Removed

In January 1995 a crisis occurred. Havel's wife of 32 years died of cancer. One year later, Havel married Czech actress Dagmar Veskrnova. In just a few months, Havel entered a clinic with what was thought to be pneumonia. While performing exploratory surgery, doctors found a tumor on his right lung. The tumor was removed on December 2, along with half the lung. During this time, his nation waited anxiously. Supporters called Havel the "chief stabilizing force in this country." Fortunately, Havel was released in good condition on December 27, and three days later was addressing the nation on Czech television.

Invitation to NATO

The positive changes in the former Soviet block country under Havel's leadership led to a landmark event. On July 8, 1997, NATO invited the Czech Republic, along with Poland and Hungary, to be the first Eastern European nation to become a part of the Western Alliance. According to the Associated Press, United States President Bill Clinton told his fellow leaders, some of whom were opposed to the expansion of NATO, that "they have met the highest standards of democratic and market reform. They have pursued those reforms long enough to give us confidence they are irreversible." NATO planned to admit the new members in April of 1999, the 50th anniversary of NATO. Havel called the invitation from NATO "the crowning achievement of enormous efforts by those countries to shed their communist pasts."

Of Havel's survival as a national figure there can be no doubt. It is impossible to predict if he will remain president after his term expires or if, as he often indicated, he will return to his writing career. Whatever his plans, he will leave a formidable legacy. His career demonstrated what he called "the power of the powerless"—of one courageous writer, unable to "live within a lie," who inspired his countrymen to overturn the oppression of 40 years despite the obvious dangers and despite a natural fear of change. Havel also inspired others, and will continue to serve as a symbol for those whose revolutions are still in progress or have not yet begun.

Further Reading

Of his own works, *Disturbing the Peace* (1990), set in the form of answers to an interviewer's questions, presents a great deal of otherwise unavailable autobiographical information as well as an explanation of his philosophies. For the general reader, this is the most accessible of his works. Several of his plays, notably *The Memorandum* (1965) and *Largo Desolato* (1984), provide insight into Havel's beliefs. George Galt's "Gentle Revolutionary," *Saturday Night* (September 1990), is a temperate but admiring review of *Living in Truth, Letters to Olga,* and *Disturbing the Peace*

The usually silent Olga Havel eloquently describes her situation in John Tagliabue's "Prague Playwright Is Jailed Again," *New York Times* (February 5, 1989). For two fascinating accounts of reporters' visits with a harassed, pre-revolutionary Havel, see *TIME* (May 29, 1989), and John Keane's "Rebel With A Cause," *New Statesman and Society* (December 8, 1989). "The Conscience of Prague," *TIME* (December 11, 1989), and Mervyn Rothstein's "A Master of Irony and Humor," *New York Times* (December 30, 1989), are excellent introductions to Havel's life and careers. A good overview of the revolution and Havel's part in it is in *Newsweek* (December 18, 1989).

For a look at Havel as the new president, see Craig R. Whitney's interview in the *New York Times* (January 12, 1990), which reveals the chaotic good humor with which the new regime was initiated. More sober are Michael Meyer's "End of the Affair," *Newsweek* (April 30, 1990) and Richard Z. Chesnoff's "The Prisoner Who Took the Castle," *U.S. News and World Report* (February 26, 1990) which provide cogent analyses of the problems facing the new government. Finally, an important and balanced profile of Havel is given in William A. Henry III's "Dissident to President," *TIME* (January 8, 1990). See also *Vaclav Havel: The Authorized Biography* (St. Martin's Press, 1993); Alfred Horn, ed., *Czech and Slovik Republics* (Houghton Mifflin, 1993); Vaclav Havel, "The Need for Transcendence in the Postmodern World," *The Futurist* (July-August, 1995); Vaclav Havel, "The Hope for Europe," *The New York Review of Books* (June 20, 1996); and "The Responsibility of Intellectuals" (June 22, 1995). □

Robert James Lee Hawke

The Honorable Robert James Lee Hawke (born 1929) was first elected as a Labor member of the Australian House of Representatives in 1980. After becoming prime minister in 1983, he led the Labor Party government to reelection four times through 1990, a new record for Australia.

obert Hawke was born on December 9, 1929. He earned his bachelor of law degree and bachelor of arts in economics from the University of Western Australia and was an honorary fellow at University College, having won a Rhodes scholarship to Oxford in 1953. He married Hazel Masterson in 1956 and had one son and two daughters.

He made labor his career. Between 1958 and 1969 he was research officer and advocate for the Australian Council of Trade Unions (A.C.T.U.), the peak and powerful organization of the trade union movement. He was its president between 1970 and 1980. As a union leader Hawke was committed to the trade union movement as an instrument for social reform. He began discount trading in Victoria with the acquisition of Bourke's Melbourne Pty. Ltd. in 1971 and the New World Travel Agency in Sydney in 1973. Between 1971 and 1973 he was a member of the National Executive of the Australian Labor Party, after which he was president until 1978. He was also a member of the governing body of the International Labor Organization (I.L.O.).

Ascending to the Labor Helm

After a false start in 1963 when Hawke unsuccessfully contested the Federal seat of Corio, he was elected as a Labor member of the House of Representatives for the Melbourne constituency of Wills in 1980. In that year he was awarded the United Nations Association Media Peace Prize for his series of Boyer Lectures: "The Resolution of Conflict." Hawke became leader of the Australian Labor Party (A.L.P.) in February 1983 and prime minister on electoral

victory in March 1983. His rapid parliamentary ascent from first election to prime minister in three years was unique, reflecting both his own popularity and the pragmatism of the post-Whitlam Labor Party, which was willing to "parachute" him into the leadership in the belief that Hawke would lead the Labor Party to victory.

Hawke's political style made him an extraordinary politician. He remained popular between 1983 and 1990, despite the variable fortunes of the Labor Party and the unpopularity of most of its policies. He was a deeply committed Labor politician, yet counted among his closest friends some of the richest capitalists in Australia, to whom he was publicly devoted. He was also extremely friendly with U.S. President Ronald Reagan, with whom he shared almost no ideological belief.

Prototype Australian

In many ways Hawke was seen as a prototype Australian male: before entering politics he was an extremely heavy drinker; indeed, he set a Guinness record for beer drinking while at the university in England. His accent remained broad Australian despite his Oxford degrees, and he specialized in portraying himself as "Australia's mate," frequently appearing at the victory celebrations of sporting events. He liked to be "one of the boys." On the other hand, in defiance of the traditions of Australian mateship, Hawke was highly emotional in public, breaking down and crying on a number of occasions on television, once when discussing the drug addiction of one of his children and on another occasion when admitting to his marital infidelities. Despite such admissions, Hawke remained popular with the Australian electorate. He was frequently described as having two unintegrated sides: passionate and puritanical, Christian and atheist, scholar and sportsman, vulnerable and insensitive, sentimental and calculating.

Certain aspects of his policy commitments also reflected his passionate nature. He became committed to the cause of Israel and in particular to the plight of Russian Jews after a visit to Israel and a meeting with Golda Meir, whose humanity touched him. His handling of a pilots' dispute during 1989 and the compensation granted to the airlines by the government were also seen as a commitment on a personal level to his friends who owned one of the airlines.

Political Strengths

Hawke's great strength was generally seen as a mediator and a conciliator. On the A.C.T.U. his greatest victories were ones in which he could play the role of peacemaker, and as prime minister he acted, by and large, as first minister, but did not necessarily insist on center stage or his own way. He allowed ministers to run their own policy areas and to take the credit and the blame as appropriate. He attempted to run Australian politics by consensus, a dramatic change following the autocratic seven years of Malcolm Fraser and the chaotic crash through three years of Whitlam.

Despite a consensus style, dramatic reforms were enacted by the Labor government: the financial markets and banking were deregulated; the dollar floated; the public service was totally restructured; and the domestic budget

was turned around to run in surplus rather than deficit. Definitions of policy areas were changed so that, for example, foreign affairs and trade were run as one "megadepartment" in an attempt to integrate their policies. Education policies, especially at the tertiary level, were also dramatically redefined and the Department of Education joined to Employment and Training, signaling a redefinition of the role of the universities.

Hawke's period as prime minister also saw a turnaround in the relationships between the parliamentary wing of the Labor Party and its organizational wing. Traditionally the extra-parliamentary party was able, when it so determined, to dictate policies to the parliamentarians. Partly due to the domination of the extra-parliamentary party by its conservative right faction, which supported Hawke, the parliamentary party in general and Hawke in particular were able to dominate the policy direction of the party. At times they successfully ignored the explicit decisions of the Labor Party Conference, which theoretically was the supreme policy-making body. More usually Hawke was able to gain conference endorsement of his policy directions. Altogether, Labor under Hawke—in contrast to the vacillating inconsistencies of conservative parties—showed a remarkable solidarity, which was reflected in electoral success.

The greatest achievement of the Hawke prime ministership was the successful establishment and continuation since 1983 of a wages accord among unions, government, and employers that reduced real wages and improved the potential for Australia's industries to become competitive with the rest of the world. While many other policy successes can be attributed to the skill of his treasurer, Paul Keating, the successful negotiation and implementation of the wages accord through the device of a summit at which the three relevant parties met was generally seen as a direct result of Hawke's particular style and ability to straddle the camps of both labor and capital.

Just one and a half years into a fourth term, however, Hawke's Labor party ousted him in December 1991 and replaced him with his former treasury minister and bitter rival, 47-year-old Paul Keating. In a nation beset by rising unemployment and a severe recession, Hawke's popularity rating had fallen to just 25 percent, down from a high of 75 percent in his first term.

Further Reading

Additional information on Bob Hawke can be found in Allen Patience and Brian Head, editors, *From Fraser to Hawke* (Melbourne: 1989); Blanche d'Alpuget, *Robert J. Hawke, A Biography* (East Melbourne: 1982); Paul Kelly, *The Hawke Ascendancy 1975-1983* (Sydney: 1984); and John Hurst, *Hawke, The Definitive Biography* (Sydney: 1979). □

Stephen William Hawking

The theories of British physicist and mathematician Stephen William Hawking (born 1942) placed him in the great tradition of Newton and Einstein. Hawking

made fundamental contributions to the science of cosmology—the study of the origins, structure, and space-time relationships of the universe.

Stephen W. Hawking was born on January 8, 1942, in Oxford, England. His father, a well-known researcher in tropical medicine, urged his son to seek a career in the sciences. Stephen found biology and medicine too descriptive and lacking in exactness. Therefore, he turned to the study of mathematics and physics.

Hawking was not an outstanding student at St. Alban's School, Hertfordshire, nor later at Oxford University, which he entered in 1959. He was a sociable young man who did little schoolwork because he was able to grasp the essentials of a mathematics or physics problem quickly and intuitively. While at Oxford he became increasingly interested in relativity theory and quantum mechanics, eventually graduating with a first class honors in physics (1962). He immediately began post-graduate studies at Cambridge University.

The onset of Hawking's graduate education at Cambridge marked a turning point in his life. It was then that he embarked upon the formal study of cosmology that focused his intellectual energies in a way that they had never been previously. And it was then that he was first stricken with amyotrophic lateral sclerosis (Lou Gehrig's disease), a debilitating neuromotor disease that eventually led to his total confinement to a wheelchair and to a virtual loss of his speech functions. At Cambridge his talents were recognized

by his major professor, the cosmologist Dennis W. Sciama, and he was encouraged to carry on his studies despite his growing physical disabilities. His marriage in 1965 to Jane Wilde was an important step in his emotional life. Marriage gave him, he recalled, the determination to live and make professional progress in the world of science. Hawking received his doctorate degree in 1966 and began his life-long research and teaching association with Cambridge University.

Hawking made his first major contribution to science with his theorem of singularity, a work which grew out of his collaboration with theoretician Roger Penrose. A singularity is a place in either space or time at which some quantity becomes infinite. Such a place is found in a black hole, the final stage of a collapsed star, where the gravitational field has infinite strength. Penrose proved that a singularity was not a hypothetical construct; it could exist in the space-time of a real universe.

Drawing upon Penrose's work and on Einstein's General Theory of Relativity, Hawking demonstrated that our universe had its origins in a singularity. In the beginning all of the matter in the universe was concentrated in a single point, making a very small but tremendously dense body. Ten to twenty billion years ago that body exploded in a big bang which initiated time and the universe. Hawking was able to bring current astrophysical research to support the big bang theory of the origin of the universe and refute the rival steady-state theory.

Hawking's research into the cosmological implications of singularities led him to study the properties of the best-known singularity: the black hole. Although a black hole is a discontinuity in space-time, its boundary, called the event horizon, can be detected. Hawking proved that the surface area of the event horizon of a black hole could only increase, not decrease, and that when two black holes merged the surface area of the new hole was larger than the sum of the two original surface areas. Working in concert with B. Carter, W. Israel, and D. Robinson, Hawking was also able to prove the "No Hair Theorem" first proposed by physicist John Wheeler. According to this theorem, mass, angular momentum, and electric charge were the sole properties conserved when matter entered a black hole.

Hawking's continuing examination of the nature of black holes led to two important discoveries. The first of them, that black holes can emit thermal radiation, was contrary to the claim that nothing could escape from a black hole. The second concerned the size of black holes. As originally conceived, black holes were immense in size because they were the end result of the collapse of gigantic stars. Using quantum mechanics to study particle interaction at the subatomic level, Hawking postulated the existence of millions of mini-black holes. These were formed by the force of the original big bang explosion.

Hawking summarized his scientific interests as "gravity—on all scales," from the realm of galaxies at one extreme to the subatomic at the other extreme. In the 1980s Hawking worked on a theory that Einstein unsuccessfully searched for in his later years. This is the famous unified field theory that aims to bring together quantum mechanics and relativity in a quantum theory of gravity. A complete unified theory encompasses the four main interactions known to modern physics: the strong nuclear force, which operates at the subatomic level; electromagnetism; the weak nuclear force of radioactivity; and gravity. The unified theory would account for the conditions which prevailed at the origin of the universe as well as for the existing physical laws of nature. When humans develop the unified field theory, said Hawking, they will "know the mind of God."

As his physical condition grew worse Hawking's intellectual achievements increased. Not content with causing a revolution in cosmology, he presented a popular exposition of his ideas in *A Brief History of Time: From the Big Bang to Black Holes*. First published in 1988, this book acquired great popularity in the United States. It sold over a million copies and was listed as the best-selling nonfiction book for over a year.

In 1993 Hawking wrote *Black Holes and Baby Universes and Other Essays,* which, in addition to a discussion of whether elementary particles that fall into black holes can form new, "baby" universes separate from our own, contains chapters about Hawking's personal life. He co-authored a book in 1996 with Sir Roger Penrose titled *The Nature of Space and Time,* which is based on a series of lectures and a final debate by the two authors. Issues discussed in this book include whether the universe has boundaries and if it will continue to expand forever. Hawking says yes to the first question and no to the second, while Penrose argues the opposite. Hawking joined Penrose again the following year, as well as Abner Shimony and Nancy Cartwright, in the creation of another book, *The Large, the Small, and the Human Mind* (1997). In this collection of talks given as Cambridge's 1995 Tanner Lectures on Human Values, Hawking and the others respond to Penrose's thesis on general relativity, quantam physics, and artificial intelligence.

Hawking's work in modern cosmology and in theoretical astronomy and physics was widely recognized. He became a fellow of the Royal Society of London in 1974 and five years later was named to a professorial chair once held by Sir Isaac Newton: Lucasian professor of mathematics, Cambridge University. Beyond these honors he earned a host of honorary degrees, awards, prizes, and lectureships from the major universities and scientific societies of Europe and America. These included the Eddington Medal of the Royal Astronomical Society, in 1975; the Pius XI Gold Medal, in 1975; the Maxwell Medal of the Institute of Physics, in 1976; the Albert Einstein Award of the Lewis and Rose Strauss Memorial Fund (the most prestigious award in theoretical physics), in 1978; the Franklin Medal of the Franklin Institute, in 1981; the Gold Medal of the Royal Society, in 1985; the Paul Dirac Medal and Prize, in 1987; and the Britannica Award, in 1989. By the last decade of the 20th century Stephen Hawking had become one of the best-known scientists in the world.

Hawking's endeavors include endorsing a wireless connection to the internet produced by U.S. Robotics Inc., beginning in March 1997, and speaking to wheelchair-bound youth. In addition, Hawking made an appearance on the television series *Star Trek* that his fans will not soon forget.

Hawking does not readily discuss his personal life, but it is generally know that he was divorced from his first wife in 1991 and they have two sons and a daughter.

When asked about his objectives, Hawking told Robert Deltete of *Zygon* in a 1995 interview, "My goal is a complete understanding of the universe, why it is as it is and why it exists at all."

Further Reading

Stephen W. Hawking's work can best be approached by reading his books, which include *Is the End in Sight for Theoretical Physics* (1980); *A Brief History of Time* (1988); and *Black Holes and Baby Universes and Other Essays;* Sources on Hawking and his work include John Boslough, *Stephen Hawking's Universe* (1985); Alan Lightman and Roberta Brower, editors, *Origins: The Lives and Worlds of Modern Cosmologists* (1990); Michael Harwood, "The Universe and Dr. Hawking," *New York Times Magazine* (January 1983); Elizabeth Devine, et al., editors, *Thinkers of the Twentieth Century* (1983); David Blum, "The Time Machine," *New York* (October 1988); Kitty Ferguson, *Stephen Hawking: A Quest for a Theory of the Universe* (1992); Melissa McDaniel, *Stephen Hawking: Physicist* (1994); Harry Henderson, *Stephen Hawking* (1995). See also Russ Sampson, "Two Hours with Stephen Hawking," *Astronomy* (March 1993); *Publishers Weekly* (February 12, 1996; March 10, 1997); Michael Lemonick, "Hawking Gets Personal," *Time* (September 27, 1993); and Robert J. Deltete, "Hawking on God and Physical Theory," *Zygon* (December 1995); Stephen Hawking also has his own web page at http://www.darntp.carn.ac.uk/user/hawking/home.html. □

Coleman Hawkins

The American jazz musician Coleman Hawkins (1904-1969) transformed the tenor saxophone from a comic novelty into jazz's glamour instrument. He was one of the music's all-time preeminent instrumental voices.

Coleman Hawkins was born on November 21, 1904, in St. Joseph, Missouri. His mother, an organist, taught him piano when he was 5; at 7, he studied cello; and for his 9th birthday he received a tenor saxophone. By the age of 12 he was performing professionally at school dances; he attended high school in Chicago, then studied harmony and composition for two years at Washburn College in Topeka, Kansas.

His first regular job, in 1921, was with singer Mamie Smith's Jazz Hounds, and he made his first recording with them in 1922. Based in Kansas City, the band played the major midwestern and eastern cities, including New York, where in 1923 he guest recorded with the famous Fletcher Henderson Band. A year later he officially joined Henderson's band and remained with it until 1934.

The first half of his tenure with Henderson served as a valuable apprenticeship, and by 1929, inspired by Louis Armstrong's improvisational concepts, Hawkins had developed the hallmarks of his mature style—a very large tone, a heavy vibrato, and a swaggering attack. Hitherto the tenor saxophone had been regarded as a novelty instrument serving chiefly for rhythmic emphasis (achieved by a slap-tonguing technique) or for bottoming out a chord in the ensemble, but not as a serious instrument and certainly not as a serious *solo* instrument. Hawkins' artistry singlehandedly altered its status.

Fame on Two Continents

The Henderson band played primarily in New York's Roseland Ballroom, but also in Harlem's famous Savoy Ballroom, and made frequent junkets to New England and the Midwest. As a result, Hawkins' fame grew as much from public appearances as from his showcase features on Henderson's recordings. When he finally left the band, he was a star.

From 1934 to 1939 Hawkins lived in Europe. He was guest soloist with the celebrated Jack Hylton Band in England, free-lanced on the Continent, and participated in a number of all-star recording sessions, the most famous of which was a 1937 get-together with the legendary Belgian gypsy guitarist Django Reinhardt and the great American trumpeter-alto saxophonist Benny Carter.

In a move very likely prompted by the imminence of war, Hawkins in 1939 returned to the United States, where

he formed a nonet and played a long engagement at Kelly's Stables on New York's jazz-famed 52nd Street. The highlight of that year, however, was his recording of "Body and Soul," illustrating in three masterful choruses his consummate melodic and harmonic command—a stunning performance that had the jazz world buzzing. That year *Down Beat* voted him #1 on tenor saxophone, the first of many such honors. Late in 1939 Hawkins formed his own big band, which debuted at New York's Arcadia Ballroom and played at such other locales as the Golden Gate Ballroom, the Apollo Theatre, and the Savoy Ballroom. In 1941 Hawkins disbanded and reverted to small groups, including in 1943 a racially mixed sextet (a rarity in that era), which toured primarily in the Midwest.

Most of Hawkins' contemporaries bitterly resisted the mid-1940s bebop revolution, with its harmonic and rhythmic innovations, but Hawkins not only encouraged the upstart music but also performed frequently with its chief practitioners. As early as 1944 with modernists Dizzy Gillespie, Max Roach, and Oscar Pettiford he recorded "Woody'n You," probably the first bop recording ever. In 1945, a watershed year for the new music, he performed and recorded in California with modern trumpeter Howard McGhee.

His long tenure, begun in 1946, with the Jazz at the Philharmonic (JATP) tour brought him inevitably into musical contact with virtually all the top-flight younger players. Also, as a leader on his own American and European engagements in the late 1940s and early 1950s he enlisted the talents of such outstanding young musicians as trumpeters Fats Navarro and Miles Davis, trombonist J.J. Johnson, and vibraphonist Milt Jackson. Hawkins' democratic acceptance of the newer jazz idiom is admirable and somewhat surprising considering the difficulties he had in adapting his own sharply-defined style to it. There is frequently a rhythmic stiffness in his attempts to integrate his sound with theirs, and he thrived best in that period when he collaborated with his fellow swing era stalwarts, playing more traditional material.

In the 1950s Hawkins teamed often, both in and out of JATP, with swing era trumpet giant Roy Eldridge. He made television appearances on "The Tonight Show" (1955) and on the most celebrated of all television jazz shows, "The Sound of Jazz" (1957). His working quartet in the 1960s consisted of the great pianist Tommy Flanagan, bassist Major Holley, and drummer Eddie Locke, but his finest recording of the decade was a collaboration with a small Duke Ellington unit in 1962.

By the late 1960s Hawkins' chronic alcoholism had resulted in a deterioration of his health. He collapsed in 1967 while playing in Toronto and again a few months later at a JATP concert. In 1968, on a European tour with the Oscar Peterson Quartet, ill health forced the cancellation of the Denmark leg of the tour. Despite failing health, he continued to work regularly until a few weeks before his death. He appeared on a Chicago television show with Roy Eldridge early in 1969, and his last concert appearance was on April 20, 1969, at Chicago's North Park Hotel. He died of bronchial pneumonia, complicated by a diseased liver, at New York's Wickersham Hospital on May 19, 1969.

The Man and His Music

Hawkins, despite the snappy nicknames "Hawk" and "Bean," was a private, taciturn man, and an attentive listener to all kinds of music: among his favorite recordings were those of opera singers, whose rhapsodic quality he captured in his own fiercely passionate playing. A married man with three children, Hawkins' consumption of alcohol seemed to be his only vice.

Hawkins is perhaps overly identified with "Body and Soul." Masterwork though it certainly is, it is only one of a great number of sublime performances. A partial listing of his best work would include: "Out of Nowhere" (1937, *Hawk in Holland*); "When Day Is Done" (c. 1940, *Coleman Hawkins Orchestra*); "I Surrender, Dear" and "I Can't Believe That You're in Love with Me" (1940, *The Tenor Sax: Coleman Hawkins and Frank Wess*); "I Only Have Eyes for You," "'S Wonderful," "Under a Blanket of Blue," "I'm Yours," and "I'm in the Mood for Love" with Roy Eldridge equally featured (1944, *Coleman Hawkins and the Trumpet Kings*); "April in Paris," "What Is There to Say?" and "I'm Through with Love" (1945, *Hollywood Stampede*); "Say It Isn't So" (1946), "Angel Face" (1947), and "The Day You Came Along" (1956, *Body and Soul*); "La Rosita" and "Tangerine" in tandem with tenor great Ben Webster (1957, *Tenor Giants*); "Mood Indigo" and "Self Portrait of the Bean" (1962, *Duke Ellington Meets Coleman Hawkins*); and "Slowly" and "Me and Some Drums" (1962, *Shelly Manne: 2,3,4*).

Further Reading

There are many treatments of Coleman Hawkins' art, but not many on the life of this private man. The most valuable articles are Humphrey Lyttleton's in *The Best of Jazz* and Stanley Dance's in *The World of Swing*. The first full-length study is British critic Albert J. McCarthy's *Coleman Hawkins* (London: 1963). British trumpeter and critic John Chilton has written a landmark biography, *The Song of the Hawk: The life and Recordings of Coleman Hawkins* (1990).

Additional Sources

Chilton, John, *The song of the Hawk: the life and recordings of Coleman Hawkins,* Ann Arbor: University of Michigan Press, 1990.
James, Burnett, *Coleman Hawkins,* Tunbridge Wells Kent: Spellmount; New York: Hippocrene Books, 1984. □

Sir John Hawkins

The career of the English naval commander Sir John Hawkins (1532-1595) touched all aspects of the Elizabethan maritime world from the illegal and inglorious to the patriotic and profitable. His skills helped to ensure the defeat of the Spanish Armada in 1588.

The second son of William Hawkins, a wealthy West Country merchant trader, John Hawkins was born at Plymouth. As a youth, he made a number of voyages to the Spanish-held Canary Islands, where he first learned of the profits to be made from selling African slaves in Spain's American colonies. In 1559 he married Katharine Gonson, the daughter of the treasurer of Queen Elizabeth I's navy. Gonson and his friends helped supply Hawkins with three ships for his first slaving voyage, in 1562.

Ignoring Portugal's nominal control over Africa, Hawkins captured several hundred people into slavery. Sailing to Cuba, he exchanged his live cargo for enough "hides, ginger, sugar, and pearls" to fill his original fleet and two more ships. By September 1563 he and three of his vessels were safely back in England; the others had been sent to Spain.

English trading rights with Spain and its possessions had been secured by treaties in the reign of Henry VII. The Spanish maintained that their American colonies were not included in these agreements and virtually prohibited foreign trade with the New World. Since Hawkins had failed to obtain a proper license, his ships which reached Spain were seized, and their rich cargoes confiscated.

Although Hawkins's efforts to regain his goods proved futile, his profits were enormous. Courtiers and nobles joined merchants and naval officials in backing a new expedition in 1564, and Elizabeth loaned Hawkins a ship, the *Jesus of Lubeck*. After some fighting against Africans, the slave-laden fleet made a slow passage to the Venezuelan coast. There the English found that the Spanish government, alarmed by Hawkins's earlier activities, had forbidden the colonists to trade with foreigners. To persuade them to break the law, Hawkins landed armed parties which (without actually fighting anyone) "captured" towns long enough to set up a brisk trade and to provide alibis for nervous local authorities. The profits of this voyage far exceeded those of the first, and a third expedition seemed inevitable.

Moderates on the Privy Council blocked the intended voyage for a year, during which time Hawkins's fleet, anchored in Plymouth harbor, fired on several Spanish ships which had attempted to approach too closely. By October 1567, while the Spaniards were still protesting this incident, Hawkins sailed for the west coast of Africa. With him again was the Queen's *Jesus* and, among some smaller ships, the *Judith,* commanded by his relative Francis Drake.

At first all went as before. Portuguese and Africans alike were unable to resist the English, and the Spaniards in the New World were readily coerced into illicit trade. Then, in September 1568, pleading the effects of a storm on his flotilla, Hawkins put into the Mexican port of San Juan de Ulla (Veracruz), where he hoped to sell his remaining cargo while refitting. A day later a well-armed Spanish fleet anchored in the harbor. Despite pledges of good faith, fighting broke out, and the English had the worst of it. Hawkins was forced to abandon most of his companions, goods, and ships and, after an agonizing passage, reached England in January 1569.

Forbidden to attempt the forcible release of his friends, Hawkins pretended to join the service of the King of Spain.

With the approval of the Privy Council he so deceived Philip II that the King released the captives, made Hawkins a grandee, and sent him £40,000; the voyage had finally shown a profit.

During the 1570s and 1580s Hawkins left the sea. He became member of Parliament for Plymouth, survived an attempted assassination, and succeeded his late father-in-law as treasurer and then as comptroller of the navy. Hawkins prospered in his new posts; while his ethics were certainly questionable, he made many improvements in naval construction.

When war came with Spain in 1587-1588, the English ships designed and fitted by Hawkins proved far superior to those of the enemy. As commander of the *Victory* (built to his specifications) and rear admiral of the fleet, Hawkins was knighted for his part in the English victory. Paradoxically, Spain's navy improved after its defeat, and Hawkins's first post-Armada venture in company with Martin Frobisher was a dismal failure.

By August 1595 Hawkins was at sea once more; as second-in-command to Drake, he went again to the West Indies on what was to prove an English disaster. Hawkins, however, died before the voyage was well under way and was buried at sea off Puerto Rico on Nov. 12, 1595. Hawkins willed a large sum of money to Elizabeth, but his most valuable legacy was to the nation as a whole: the eminently seaworthy ships he had designed and built.

Further Reading

Hawkins's *A True Declaration of the Troublesome Voyage of M. John Haukins* (1569) provides autobiographical information. James A. Williamson wrote two excellent biographies of Hawkins, *Sir John Hawkins: The Time and the Man* (1927) and *Hawkins of Plymouth* (1949). The achievements of the Hawkins family are dealt with in Sir Clements R. Markham, ed., *The Hawkins' Voyages during the Reigns of Henry VIII, Queen Elizabeth, and James I* (1878). Hawkins's role in the building of the British navy is discussed in James A. Williamson, *Age of Drake* (1938; 4th ed. 1960).

Additional Sources

Andrews, Kenneth R., *The last voyage of Drake & Hawkins,* Cambridge Eng. Published for the Hakluyt Society, at the University Press, 1972.

Williamson, James Alexander, *Hawkins of Plymouth: a new history of Sir John Hawkins and of the other members of his family prominent in Tudor England,* London: Black, 1969.

Williamson, James Alexander, *Sir John Hawkins; the time and the man,* Westport, Conn.: Greenwood Press, 1970. □

Nicholas Hawksmoor

Nicholas Hawksmoor (1661-1736) was a leading English architect. His very original church designs are baroque in their monumentality and sense of mass.

Nicholas Hawksmoor was born in Nottinghamshire, probably at Ragnall. He entered the service of Sir Christopher Wren at the age of 18 and was closely concerned with most of Wren's commissions from 1684 on, especially at Winchester Palace (begun 1683) and Chelsea Hospital (1687-1692). Hawksmoor also played an important part in the building of Wren's City of London churches during the 1680s and St. Paul's Cathedral between 1691 and 1712.

In 1689 Hawksmoor obtained through Wren the post of clerk of works at Kensington Palace and Greenwich Hospital, retaining the latter post until his death. From 1715 he was clerk of works at Whitehall Palace, Westminster Abbey, and St. James's Palace and secretary to the Board of Works. Dismissed from these posts in 1718, in 1726 he was restored as secretary, a post he held for the rest of his life.

As Wren's "supervisor," "gentleman," and "scholar," Hawksmoor made a far greater contribution to his master's achievement than that of mere assistant or draftsman. In particular, he remedied Wren's deficiencies in the handling of the fundamental masses and proportions of a building. This feeling for mass and movement, which Hawksmoor derived from his studies of Roman and medieval architecture, was the basis of the baroque spirit in English architecture.

Hawksmoor was employed by Sir John Vanbrugh at Castle Howard, Yorkshire, from 1699 on and at Blenheim Palace from 1705, taking entire charge of the work there after Vanbrugh's final rupture with Sarah, Duchess of Marlborough, until its completion in 1725. Their partnership was extremely close and successful: both understood the importance of mass, stability, and the element of movement in the relative advance and recession of the various planes of a building. Of Castle Howard and Blenheim it might truly be said that, while the total dramatic conception in each case was Vanbrugh's, many of the decorative features and details were due to Hawksmoor. The Long Library and Triumphal Arch Gateway at Blenheim were built entirely to his designs; so also was his masterpiece, the great Mausoleum at Castle Howard.

At Easton Neston, Northamptonshire (1702), entirely designed by Hawksmoor, he introduced elements that were of critical importance in the development of the English country house. He is famous chiefly for his London churches, especially St. George's, Bloomsbury (1720-1730); Christchurch, Spitalfields (1723-1729); and St. Alphege, Greenwich (1712-1714).

Hawksmoor was of lowly station in life, dourly reserved and self-effacing, and somewhat embittered by his failure to achieve worldly success. He died in his house at Millbank, Westminster, on March 25, 1736.

Further Reading

The only full-length comprehensive monograph on Hawksmoor is Kerry Downes, *Hawksmoor* (1959), a well-documented and well-illustrated study of his life and career, incorporating the results of recent researches. A valuable short essay on Hawksmoor's achievement is H. S. Goodhart-Rendel, *Nicholas Hawksmoor* (1924), which contains excellent photographs, especially of his churches. His relations with Wren and Vanbrugh and his significance in the development of the English baroque movement are considered in Sir John Summerson, *Architecture in Britain, 1530-1830* (1954; rev. ed. 1963). See also Laurence Whistler, *Sir John Vanbrugh* (1938), and *The Imagination of Vanbrugh and His Fellow Artists* (1954).

Additional Sources

Colvin, Howard Montagu, *Unbuilt Oxford,* New Haven: Yale University Press, 1983.

Downes, Kerry, *Hawksmoor,* New York: Praeger, 1970, 1969; Cambridge, Mass.: MIT Press, 1980, 1979; London: Thames & Hudson, 1969; London: A. Zwemmer, 1979.

Downes, Kerry, *Hawksmoor: an exhibition selected by Kerry Downes, held at Whitechapel Art Gallery, 23 March-1 May 1977,* London: The Gallery, 1977.

Kaiser, Wolfgang, *Castle Howard: ein englischer Landsitz des fruhen 18. Jahrhunderts: Studien zu Architektur und Landschaftspark,* Freiburg im Breisgau: Gaggstatter, 1984.

Saumarez Smith, Charles, *The building of Castle Howard,* Chicago: University of Chicago Press, 1990. □

Nathaniel Hawthorne

The work of American fiction writer Nathaniel Hawthorne (1804-1864) was based on the history of his Puritan ancestors and the New England of his own day but, in its "power of blackness," has universal significance.

Nathaniel Hawthorne was born in Salem, Mass., on July 4, 1804, into the sixth generation of his Salem family. His ancestors included Puritan magnates, judges, and seamen. Two aspects of his heritage were especially to affect his imagination. The Hathornes (Nathaniel added the "w" to the name) had been involved in religious persecution with their first American forebear, William, and John Hathorne was one of the three judges at the 17th-century Salem witchcraft trials. Further, the family had over the generations gradually declined from its early prominence and prosperity into relative obscurity and indigence. Thus the Pyncheons and the Maules of Hawthorne's Salem novel *The House of the Seven Gables* represent the two different faces of his ancestors, and his feelings about his birthplace were mixed. With deep and unbreakable ties to Salem, he nevertheless found its physical and cultural environment as chilly as its prevalent east wind.

Early Life and Education

Nathaniel's father, a sea captain, died in 1808, leaving his wife and three children dependent on relatives. Nathaniel, the only son, spent his early years in Salem and in Maine. A leg injury immobilized the boy for a considerable period, during which he developed an exceptional taste for reading and contemplation. His childhood was calm, a little isolated but far from unhappy, especially since as a handsome and attractive only son he was idolized by his mother and his two sisters.

With the aid of his prosperous maternal uncles, the Mannings, Hawthorne attended Bowdoin College from 1821 to 1825, when he graduated. Among his classmates were poet Henry Wadsworth Longfellow; Franklin Pierce, the future president of the United States, who was to be at his friend's deathbed; and Horatio Bridge, who was to subsidize the publication of Hawthorne's *Twice-Told Tales* in 1837. At Bowdoin, Hawthorne read widely and received solid instruction in English composition and the classics, particularly in Latin. His persistent refusal to engage in public speaking prevented his achieving any marked academic distinction, but he made a creditable record. On one occasion he was fined 50 cents for gambling at cards, but his conduct was not otherwise singled out for official disapproval. Though small and isolated, the Bowdoin of the 1820s was an unusually good college, and Hawthorne undoubtedly profited by his formal education, as well as making steadfast friends. Such men as Longfellow, Pierce, and Bridge remained devoted to him throughout life, and each would render him timely assistance.

Years as a Recluse

Hawthorne's life was not externally exciting or remarkable, but it presents an interesting symbolic pattern. As John Keats said of Shakespeare, he led a life of allegory and his works are the comments on it. Returning from Bowdoin, Hawthorne spent from 1825 to 1837 in his mother's Salem household. Later he looked back upon these years as a period of dreamlike isolation and solitude, spent in a haunted chamber, where he sat enchanted while other men moved on. The "solitary years" were, however, his literary apprenticeship, during which he learned to write tales and sketches that are still unrivaled and unique.

Recent biographers have shown that this period of Hawthorne's life was less lonely than he remembered it to be. In literal truth, he did have social engagements, played cards, and went to the theater and the Lyceum; his sister Elizabeth remarked that "if there was any gathering of people in the town he always went out; he liked a crowd." Nevertheless, he consistently remembered these 12 years as a strange, dark dream, though his view of their consequences varied.

"In this dismal chamber Fame was won," Hawthorne wrote, perhaps a little ironically, in 1836. To his fiancée, Sophia Peabody, he later confided, "If ever I should have a biographer, he ought to make great mention of this chamber in my memoirs, because so much of my lonely youth was wasted here, and here my mind and character were formed." On the whole, he felt that his isolation had been beneficial: " . . . if I had sooner made my escape into the world, I should have grown hard and rough, and been covered with earthly dust, and my heart would have become callous by rude encounters with the multitude"—an observation that he made more than once.

Writing the Short Stories

Most of Hawthorne's early stories were published anonymously in magazines and giftbooks. In his own words, he was "for a good many years, the obscurest man of letters in America." In 1837 the publication of *Twice-Told Tales* somewhat lifted this spell of darkness. In the preface to the 1851 edition he spoke of "the apparently opposite peculiarities" of these stories. Despite the circumstances under which they were written, "they are not the talk of a secluded man with his own mind and heart . . . but his attempts, and very imperfectly successful ones, to open an intercourse with the world." The *Twice-Told Tales* he supplemented with two later collections, *Mosses from an Old Manse* (1846) and *The Snow-Image* (1851), along with *Grandfather's Chair* (1841), a history for children of New England through the Revolution; the *Journal of an African Cruiser* (1845), edited from the observations of his friend Horatio Bridge while he was purser on an American frigate; and the second edition of the *Tales* (1842).

Hawthorne's short stories came slowly but steadily into critical favor, and the best of them have become American classics. It may well be claimed for them as a whole that they are the outstanding achievement in their genre to be found in the English language during the 19th century. Lucid, graceful, and well composed, they combine an old-fashioned neoclassic purity of diction with a latent and hard complexity of meaning. They are broadly allegorical but infused with imaginative passion. The combination has produced very different opinions of their value, which Hawthorne himself acutely foresaw, remarking that his touches "have often an effect of tameness," and that his work, "if you would see anything in it, requires to be read in the clear,

brown, twilight atmosphere in which it was written; if opened in the sunshine, it is apt to look exceedingly like a volume of blank pages" (1851 Preface, *Twice-Told Tales*).

Hawthorne is a master of balance and suggestion who inveterately understates: the texture of his tales, as of his novels, is so delicate that some readers cannot see it at all. But many, too, will testify as Herman Melville did to his "power of blackness." Of Hawthorne's story "Young Goodman Brown," Melville wrote, "You would of course suppose that it was a simple little tale. . . . Whereas it is as deep as Dante: nor can you finish it, without addressing the author in his own words: 'It is yours to penetrate, in every bosom, the deep mystery of sin.'"

Out in the World

By his own account it was Hawthorne's love of his Salem neighbor Sophia Peabody that brought him from his "haunted chamber" out into the world. His books were far from profitable enough to support a prospective wife and family, so in 1838 he went to work in the Boston Custom House and then spent part of 1841 in the famous Brook Farm community in hopes of finding a pleasant and economical haven for Sophia and himself. It is curious that the seclusive Hawthorne was always interested in experiments in community living: in Brook Farm, in the New England Shaker settlements, and later in Greenwich Hospital in London. He was to record his mingled feelings of sympathy and skepticism about Brook Farm in *The Blithedale Romance* (1852).

At any rate, Hawthorne and Sophia, whom he married in 1842, resorted not to Brook Farm but to the Old Manse in Concord, where they spent several years of idyllic happiness in as much solitude as they could achieve. Concord, however, contained Ralph Waldo Emerson, Henry David Thoreau, and Ellery Channing, and Hawthorne was in frequent contact with these important thinkers, though his was not a nature for transcendental affirmations.

Writing the Novels

Facing the world once more, Hawthorne obtained in 1846 the position of surveyor in the Salem Custom House, from which as a Democrat he was expelled after the Whig victory in the 1848 presidential election. He did not leave without a fight and considerable bitterness, and he took revenge in the "Custom-House" introduction to *The Scarlet Letter* (1850) and in *The House of the Seven Gables* (1851), in which he portrayed his chief Whig enemy as the harsh and hypocritical Judge Pyncheon. His dismissal, however, turned out to be a blessing, since it gave him leisure in which to write his greatest and crucial success, *The Scarlet Letter*. Except for his early *Fanshawe* (1828), which he suppressed shortly after publication, *The Scarlet Letter* was his first novel, or, as he preferred to say, "romance"; thus his literary career divided into two distinct parts, since he now almost wholly abandoned the shorter tale.

The period 1850-1853 was Hawthorne's most prolific. Doubtless stimulated by the enthusiastic reception accorded *The Scarlet Letter*, he went on with *The House of the Seven Gables* and *The Blithedale Romance*, along with *A*

Wonder Book (1852) and *Tanglewood Tales* (1853), exquisitely fanciful stories for children from Greek mythology. During 1850 the Hawthornes lived at the Red House in Lenox in the Berkshire Hills, and Hawthorne formed a memorable friendship with novelist Herman Melville, whose Arrowhead Farm was some miles away on the outskirts of Pittsfield. The association was more important to Melville than to Hawthorne, since Melville was 15 years younger and much the more impressionable of the two men. It left its mark in Melville's celebrated review of *Mosses from an Old Manse,* in the dedication of his *Moby-Dick,* and in some wonderful letters. Hawthorne's share in their correspondence has not survived, but he clearly aided Melville with insight and sympathy.

Years Abroad

In 1852 Franklin Pierce was elected to the presidency of the United States, and Hawthorne, who was induced to write his campaign biography, was appointed to the important overseas post of American consul at Liverpool, in which he served form 1853 to 1857 with considerable efficiency. These English years resulted in *Our Old Home* (1863), a volume drawn from the since-published "English Note-Books." It was to give considerable offense to the English public. Hawthorne felt a very deep affinity for "our old home," but as with his other "old home," Salem, his feelings were mingled, and he did not hesitate to express them.

In 1857 the Hawthornes left England for Italy, where they spent their time primarily in Rome and Florence. They returned to England, where Hawthorne finished his last and longest complete novel, the "Roman romance" *The Marble Faun* (1860). They finally returned to the United States, after an absence of seven years, and took up residence in their first permanent home, The Wayside, at Concord, which Hawthorne had bought from Bronson Alcott.

Last Years

Hawthorne was to live only four more years. Although he had always been an exceptionally vigorous man, his health inexplicably declined; and since he refused to submit to any thorough medical examination, his malady remains mysterious. During these last years in Concord he struggled with no less than four romances, *The Ancestral Footstep, Dr. Grimshawe's Secret, Septimius Felton,* and *The Dolliver Romance,* but completed none of them. Ironically, they are obsessively concerned with the theme of "earthly immortality" and the "elixir of life," which he had earlier touched upon in stories like "Dr. Heidegger's Experiment" (*Twice-Told Tales*).

Hawthorne died on May 19, 1864. He had set off for the New Hampshire hills with Franklin Pierce. He had always been fond of such expeditions and hoped to benefit from this one. But he died the second night out in Plymouth, N.H., presumably in his sleep. The circumstances of his end were somehow representative of the man, at once settled and at the same time restless when too long in one place. He once said that New England was enough to fill his heart, yet he sought the broader experience of Europe. Modest in expectations, he had yet desired to live fully.

Hawthorne's Literary Background

The case of Hawthorne is complex, in his life and in his writings. A born writer, like Edgar Allan Poe he suffered the difficulties of the writer in early-19th-century America: an unsympathetic environment, the materialism of a physically expanding nation, the lack of an artistic tradition. His Puritan heritage was both a support and a drawback. Its tradition of soul-searching encouraged profundity, and its penchant for seeking God's Providence in natural events provided Hawthorne with a way of seeing and interpreting. It was a highly literate tradition as well. It was, however, notoriously unfriendly to art—fiction as make-believe was mere vanity, and as imitation of God's creatures and creations it was idolatry. A natural artist, Hawthorne was always to worry about the morality of imitating and analyzing human nature in his art of fiction.

With his Puritanism, Hawthorne also inherited the Augustan culture of the early 18th century—a common case in New England, but especially powerful in his. Thus came the purity of his prose style, and its coolness and balance, in a sense retrogressive in his own time. Yet he was also responsive to the influence of his near contemporaries, the English romantics. He read widely and was vitally influenced by all the chief romantic poets, William Wordsworth, Samuel Taylor Coleridge, Lord Byron, Percy Bysshe Shelley, and John Keats. Hawthorne drew especially upon Coleridge's critical principles for his own theory of the prose romance. Like the romantics, he too desired to live fully and make the best use of his sensibilities, but his impulses were tempered by Augustan moderation and Puritan self-distrust.

A serious and conscientious craftsman, Hawthorne yet was not committed (as was Henry James) to the craft of fiction, not being minded to sacrifice either himself or those who depended upon him to its demands. He held a rather too pessimistic view of his own talent, and his deep Puritan skepticism of the value of merely human effort was also a deterrent to complete dedication to fiction; the volume of his writing is substantial but not great.

Power of Darkness

Hawthorne's belief in Providence could be discouraging, but it was also a source of strength. Along with Melville, he was one of the great "no-sayers" of 19th-century America. He accepted, imaginatively if not literally, the doctrine of the Fall of Man, and thus the radical imperfection of man. In his work there is as much light as darkness, but the dark is perhaps the more dramatic hue. In imaginative literature evil can be an esthetic element with the dark as a contrast to light; and Hawthorne used contrast so effectively that Henry James believed his "darkness" to be mere fanciful playing, with evil and pain used simply as counters in his fictional game. Melville, however, perceived more deeply that Hawthorne might be fascinated with the problem of evil as an element of his design, yet at the same time treat it with the utmost seriousness ("Hawthorne and his Mosses").

Tragedy is traditionally the most complex literary form, while it is also an imaginative testing ground, in which the human spirit is broadened and deepened by its struggle with the utmost imaginable adversity. In *The Scarlet Letter,* for example, the protagonists Hester and Dimmesdale are opposed not only by Puritan society but by something in themselves, and by a mysterious and invisible principle of reality still more powerful.

Allegorical Structures and Themes

Hawthorne's fictional structures are basically allegorical confrontations of good and evil, and his characters can usually be classified as types. He writes, however, not to prove points or teach moral lessons, which are themselves his fictional materials rather than his conclusions. *The House of the Seven Gables,* for instance, has a message, "the truth, namely, that the wrongdoing of one generation lives into the successive ones, and, divesting itself of every temporary advantage, becomes a pure and uncontrollable mischief." But Hawthorne reflects that when romances do teach anything, "it is usually through a far more subtle process than the ostensible one. . . . A high truth, indeed, fairly, finely, and skillfully wrought out, brightening at every step, and crowning the final development of a work of fiction, may add an artistic glory, but is never any truer, and seldom any more evident, at the last page than at the first" (Preface, *The House of the Seven Gables*).

Isolation or "alienation" is Hawthorne's principal theme and problem, and loss of contact with reality is the ultimate penalty he envisions. Characteristically, this results from a separation of the "head," or intellect, and the "heart," a term that includes the emotions, the passions, and the unconscious. The heart is the custodian of man's deepest potentialities for good and evil, and it is man's vital connection with reality. Too much "head" leads always to a fatal intellectual pride, which distorts and finally destroys the wholeness of the real world. This, for Hawthorne, is the worst sin or calamity that man is heir to.

Further Reading

Randall Stewart, *Nathaniel Hawthorne* (1948), is the standard biography. Newton Arvin, *Hawthorne* (1929), contains criticism and psychological analysis. Mark Van Doren, *Nathaniel Hawthorne* (1949), presents a balanced interpretation of Hawthorne's life and principal works. Older works include Henry James, Jr., *Hawthorne* (1879).

Notable treatments of Hawthorne's art in its historical and national contexts appear in Yvor Winters, *Maule's Curse: Seven Studies in the History of American Obscurantism* (1938); F. O. Matthiessen, *American Renaissance: Art and Expression in the Age of Emerson and Whitman* (1941); Charles Feidelson, Jr., *Symbolism and American Literature* (1953); and Richard Chase, *The American Novel and Its Tradition* (1957), which is illuminating on the tradition of "romance" in America.

More specialized interpretations of Hawthorne's fiction are Richard Harter Fogle, *Hawthorne's Fiction: The Light and the Dark* (1952, rev. ed. 1964) and *Hawthorne's Imagery* (1969); Hyatt H. Waggoner, *Hawthorne: A Critical Study* (1955, rev. ed. 1963); and Roy R. Male, *Hawthorne's Tragic Vision* (1957). □

John Hay

John Hay (1838-1905) was important for shaping America's open-door policy toward the Far East. He set guidelines for much of America's diplomacy in the 20th century, involving the United States in maintaining China's territorial integrity.

Rapid change characterized the United States during the years of John Hay's public service. Retarded briefly by the Civil War, dynamic forces of urbanization and industrialization began to transform both the landscape and the mood of America. Though the railroad tie and the sweatshop were as foreign to the aristocratic world of John Hay as the reaper and the grain elevator, they combined to support a new economic system that knew few boundaries, wrenching America out of its quiet isolation and into the highly competitive arena of international politics, where Hay's contribution would be made.

Hay was born on Oct. 8, 1838, in Salem, Ind. He attended Brown University (1855-1858), where he reluctantly prepared for a career in law. In 1859 he entered a Springfield, Ill., law firm, next door to the office of Abraham Lincoln. When Lincoln was elected U.S. president, Hay became his assistant private secretary. After Lincoln's death, Hay took minor diplomatic posts in Paris, Vienna, and Madrid. Socially successful, he had no serious influence on foreign policy. In 1870 he returned to the United States.

Between 1870 and 1896 he moved in and out of Republican politics, journalism, and business, surrounding himself with a patrician set of friends, including Boston aristocrats, intellectuals, and prominent politicians. His widely acclaimed poems and novels were overshadowed in 1890 by his *Abraham Lincoln: A History,* a ten volume work completed with John Nicolay.

Hay became close to presidential candidate William McKinley during his 1896 campaign. As president, McKinley appointed Hay ambassador to Great Britain, where Hay smoothed out issues concerning the Spanish-American War and subsequent annexations. He returned to become McKinley's secretary of state in 1898.

Secretary of State

As secretary of state, Hay was concerned with policy in four major areas: conducting peace negotiations after the Spanish-American War, setting policy toward the Far East, improving the United States position in Latin America, and settling the dispute with Great Britain over the Alaskan boundary.

Whereas McKinley had shaped the Spanish-American War settlement (and, later, President Theodore Roosevelt was the force behind policies in Latin America), Hay exerted considerable influence in making American policy toward the Far East and in the Canadian boundary dispute. Regarding England, Hay was considered a good friend to Britain by both the English and the Americans. Though committed to United States interests, he sought solutions in the Canadian dispute that would not endanger Anglo-American understanding.

Regarding the Far East, America watched the establishment of spheres of influence in China by European powers, Russia, and Japan with apprehension, fearing that United States trade rights might be limited by new political arrangements. In 1899 Hay asked the six governments directly involved to approve a formula guaranteeing that in their spheres of influence the rights and privileges of other nations would be respected and discriminatory port dues and railroad rates would not be levied and that Chinese officials would continue to collect tariffs. Although the six nations responded coolly, Hay announced that the open-door principle had been accepted, and the American press described the policy as a tremendous success. When an antiforeign uprising broke out in China in 1900, Hay sent a second set of notes, urging the open-door policy for all of the Chinese Empire and maintenance of the territorial integrity of China. Traditional protection of American economic interests thus was tied to the overly ambitious task of preserving the territory of China; under the guise of America's historic mission to support the cause of freedom, this would lead the United States to ever stronger commitments in the Far East.

When the assassination of McKinley made Roosevelt president, Hay increasingly gave way to presidential leadership in foreign policy. Following Roosevelt's lead concerning the building of an Isthmian canal, Hay obtained British consent to a United States canal under the Hay-Pauncefote treaties of 1900 and 1901. Though he supported Roosevelt's

policy toward the new Panamanian Republic and the acquisition of the Canal Zone in 1903, Hay did little to actually shape Latin American policy.

The 1903 Alaskan-Canadian boundary dispute with Great Britain was settled amiably by commissioners, as Hay had suggested. Soon after, serious illness forced Hay to assume a virtually inactive role as secretary of state. He retained the office until his death on July 1, 1905, in Newbury, N. H.

Further Reading

Hay's correspondence is gathered in William R. Thayer, *The Life and Letters of John Hay* (2 vols., 1915). Tyler Dennett's biography, *John Hay: From Poetry to Politics* (1933), treats Hay's career colorfully and sympathetically. Scholars have generally focused their attention on Hay's role as secretary of state. An able assessment by Foster R. Dulles is in Norman A. Graebner, ed., *An Uncertain Tradition: American Secretaries of State in the Twentieth Century* (1961), and a general description of the diplomacy of the period is in Thomas McCormick, *A Fair Field and No Favor* (1967). For contrasting interpretations of the origins of the open-door policy see George F. Kennan, *American Diplomacy, 1900-1950* (1951), and William A. Williams, *The Tragedy of American Diplomacy* (1959; rev. ed. 1962). □

Victor Raul Haya de la Torre

Victor Raúl Haya de la Torre (1895-1979) was the founder and leader of the American Popular Revolutionary Alliance (APRA), principal theorist of Aprismo, and three-time presidential candidate (in the 1930s and 1960s) of the Peruvian Aprista Party. He spent most of his adult life in jail, in exile, or in hiding from the police.

V ictor Raúl Haya was born in Trujillo, Peru, on Feb. 22, 1895; his father was a newspaper publisher and his mother a descendant of a president of Peru. He studied at Trujillo National University and San Marcos University, but did not graduate. From the beginning, he took up popular causes and involved himself in radical movements. He said, "I have always preferred doing to discussing," and he believed *doing* and *organizing* were inseparable. He became involved in agitation on student reform issues, but was jailed in 1923 and then deported over an incident involving freedom of religious conscience. While in Mexico in 1924, he founded APRA, which he first saw as a continent-wide anti-imperialist movement.

Operationally, *Aprismo's* three main themes are to champion the three underprivileged classes—workers, farmers and middle class; to re-focus government activities in the interests of the national economy, as opposed to foreign interests; and to develop the necessary moral force to support practical action. Specific programmatic ideas

included reorganizing the state; extending voting rights; decentralizing police power; controlling foreign investment in the Peruvian economy; nationalizing certain industries; expropriating certain estates (with compensation) and converting them to production for domestic markets; creating collective farms; incorporating Indians into national life and preserving their culture; establishing the eight-hour day and paid annual vacations, equal pay for women, and maternity leave; and freedom for the armed forces and the police from political interference.

From 1923 to 1931, Haya de la Torre traveled widely in Mexico, France, England, the Soviet Union, and the United States, studying, writing, and spreading his ideas. While a student at San Marcos, Haya de la Torre had been inspired by the Mexican Revolution (1911) and the Russian Revolution (1917), but in 1924 he broke with orthodox Marxism and came up with his own theory for developing "Indo-America" (by which he meant all of Central and Latin America).

When the Peruvian dictatorship was overthrown in 1931, Haya de la Torre returned as the Aprista party's candidate for president. He was officially given 35 percent of the vote, but the party thought it a fraud and staged an unsuccessful uprising. The military awarded the presidency to Col. Sánchez Cerro, who quickly established a dictatorship and tried to destroy the Aprista movement. Haya de la Torre was jailed in May 1932 and kept in solitary confinement until August 1933, after Sánchez Cerro's was assassinated. In 1934 Haya de la Torre went underground for eleven years.

During this time, the Aprista party extended its power by organizing sugar estate unions, school teachers, and miners. In 1939 the party provided the votes that elected a liberal as president, but nine years later it was unable to bring Haya de la Torre to power through a strike and the Apristas were outlawed once again by a military-led government. In 1949, Haya de la Torre took asylum in the Colombian embassy in Lima. The Peruvian dictatorship refused to allow him to leave Peru. Twice the International Court of Justice at the Hague took up his case and, under heavy international pressure, the regime finally allowed him to leave the country in 1954.

Haya then lived in Latin America and Europe until 1956, when he was allowed to return to Peru. After that, he alternated living in Peru with traveling in all parts of the world. Haya led all other candidates for the presidency in the election of 1962, but the armed forces canceled the election. In 1963 Haya, again a candidate, was defeated, but the Apristas won a dominant position in the legislature. In 1968 it appeared as if Haya would be elected president for the 1969-1975 term, but the military reinstituted dictatorship. He spent most of his remaining years in Paris. A month before Haya de la Torre's death in 1979, APRA announced that once again, he was to be their presidential candidate.

Haya was a great orator who addressed meetings of up to 250,000 Peruvians. His significant contributions to political theory were to emphasize that Latin America's political parties must seek indigenous roots and to oppose violence as a means of achieving political power. His ideas have been adopted by political parties in all parts of Latin America.

Further Reading

No good biography of Haya has been published in English. Robert J. Alexander, *Prophets of the Revolution: Profiles of Latin American Leaders* (1962), has a chapter on Haya. Recommended for an understanding of the man and the Aprista movement are Harry Kantor, *The Ideology and Program of the Peruvian Aprista Movement* (1953); and Grant Hilliker, *The Politics of Reform in Peru: The Aprista and Other Mass Parties of Latin America* (1971). □

Thomas Emmet Hayden

The American writer and political activist Thomas Emmet Hayden (born 1939) was one of the few radical leaders of the 1960s to outlast the movement. He was admired for remaining alive politically without sacrifice of his principles.

Tom Hayden was born Dec. 11, 1939, in Royal Oak, Michigan, into a middle class family and attended the University of Michigan, graduating with an A.B. in 1960. During his college years he joined the Student Nonviolent Coordinating Committee, participating in its dangerous work for civil rights in the South. During a voter registration campaign he was beaten and jailed in McComb, Mississippi. Hayden was a co-founder of the Economic Research and Action Project (ERAP), which attempted to mobilize poor people in their own behalf. Hayden led the ERAP program in Newark, New Jersey, until the riots of 1967 put an end to it. He also co-founded the Students for a Democratic Society (SDS) and was an author of its manifesto, "The Port Huron Statement." Genuinely democratic and nonviolent at first, the SDS fell victim to the revolutionary posturing of the times. As it drifted toward terrorism and extinction, Hayden became caught up in the anti-Vietnam War movement.

He twice visited North Vietnam in the 1960s, returning from his second trip with three American prisoners of war placed in his custody by the North Vietnamese government. Unlike some Americans who opposed the war chiefly because of its cost in blood and treasure, Hayden favored a Communist victory. He argued the point in a book co-authored with Staughton Lynd, *The Other Side* (1967). As a project director of the National Mobilization Committee to End the War in Vietnam, he helped organize antiwar demonstrations during the Democratic National Convention in 1968. As a result he became one of the "Chicago Seven" defendants in what was probably the most celebrated political trial of the era. He and three others were convicted of crossing state lines to incite riot, and all seven were indicted for contempt of court. But on appeal their convictions and indictments were dismissed. In 1971 Hayden participated

in a demonstration on behalf of People's Park in Berkeley, California, during which state troopers killed a student.

As the radical era drew to a close Hayden, like his peers, was in danger of becoming politically obsolete. Most New Leftists failed to make the transition. A few became urban terrorists. Others clung to the old faith and sank out of sight. Still others made their peace with a system that had proved to be both more resistant and more resilient than expected. Hayden almost alone found another way. After several years of travel and speeches, including campaign work for George McGovern in his run for the presidency in 1972, Hayden took up electoral politics. With the valuable aid of his second wife, actress Jane Fonda, he ran for a California seat in the U.S. Senate in 1976. Though defeated in the Democratic primary, Hayden captured 40 percent of the vote, a remarkable feat for someone so notorious. He then organized the Campaign for Economic Democracy (CED), which advocated liberal reforms. With its help he was elected to the California State Assembly in 1982.

Hayden wanted to democratize the economy by means of tax reform, public ownership of utilities, greater equality of income among the races and between the sexes, and curtailment of corporate abuses. Hayden opposed nuclear energy, promoting solar power as the desirable alternative. Even at his most radical Hayden never entirely lost sight of the real world. He was the New Left's best organizer and one of its most prolific writers. As a working politician he made ample use of these talents and would probably have been heard from even had he married less spectacularly. There is no doubt, however, that Fonda's wealth and glamour and the publicity the couple commanded benefitted his career in no small measure.

In the mid-1980s, Hayden's CED was reorganizied as Campaign California and began to "support entrepreneurial activity" in the legislative fight against environmental damage. Despite his emotional involvement with Hanoi during the Vietnam War, Hayden's belief in participatory democracy enabled him to engage his ideas and energies within the system and make valuable contributions toward environmental and educational initiatives as a member of the California State Assembly (1982-1991).

In 1992, Hayden ran successfully for the California State Senate, in which body he espoused environmental and educational issues. However, his radical past disturbed the more conservative elements among politicians and the electorate, and impeded his political goals. His opponents on the right recalled to public attention his radical past and anti-war involvement in order to defeat his legislative initiatives. In 1994, he was defeated in his bid for the state governorship largely due to his past extremist activities. This opposition tended to make Hayden more conservative, and he has even spoken in favor of the death penalty.

In the California State Senate, Tom Hayden chaired or was a member of committees on Energy, Natural Resources and Wildlife, Housing and Urban Affairs, Transportation and Public Safety.

Further Reading

Several recent volumes are dedicated to studying the student upheavals and political upheavals and turmoil of the Vietnam Era, e.g., David DeLeon's *Leaders from the 1960s: A Biographical Sourcebook of American Activism*, Westport, Connecticut: Greenwood Press (1994). *The Los Angeles Times* (August 13, 1995) ran an article by Elizabeth Mehren which traced the subsequent careers of the figures involved in the Activist Movement of the 1960s.

Tom Hayden's many books include *Rebellion in Newark* (1967), *Trial* (1970), *The Love of Possession Is a Disease with Them* (1972), and *The American Future* (1980). The standard history, in which Hayden figures prominently, is Kirkpatrick Sale, *SDS* (1973). ☐

Franz Joseph Haydn

The Austrian composer Franz Joseph Haydn (1732-1809) in his instrumental music, especially the symphonies and string quartets, essentially founded and brought to first mature realization the formal and structural principles of the classical style.

Joseph Haydn virtually created the classical formal structures of the string quartet and symphony, which were developed later by Wolfgang Amadeus Mozart and Ludwig van Beethoven. He participated in the development of other forms of 18th-century instrumental music, in addition to composing prolifically in the fields of sacred music, opera, and song. Throughout a lifetime of experimentation he developed in the quartet and symphony a fully mature classical tonal idiom, characterized externally by the four-movement structure (allegro, slow movement, minuet and trio, and finale) of the majority of these works and internally by emphasis on thematic and motivic development within a balanced tonal framework. Haydn evolved a tonal language that exhibited a gradual growth toward contrapuntal complexity and a vast range of expression in comparison to the technical simplicity and expressive triviality of much mid-18th-century instrumental music of the *style galant.*

Haydn was born in Rohrau, Lower Austria, on March 31, 1732. At the age of 8 he became a choirboy at the Cathedral of St. Stephen's in Vienna, remaining there until his dismissal in 1749. By his own account his early years were largely given to self-instruction in music: he developed some facility as a violinist and keyboard player (but he was never a virtuoso performer); he studied briefly with the Italian opera composer and singing master Niccolò Porpora; and he became thoroughly acquainted with Viennese musical life of the period 1740-1760 and knew its leading figures.

Haydn made his first attempts at composition; as he later described them, "I wrote industriously but not quite correctly." His early works included a *Singspiel* entitled *Der krumme Teufel* (1752), a few keyboard sonatas and trios, and his first string quartet, written during the 1750s. This first period of his development concluded with 2 years (1758-1760) in private service in Bohemia, during which he evidently composed his first symphony (generally dated 1759).

In Service of Esterházy Family

In 1761 Haydn entered the private service of the noble Hungarian Esterházy family, serving under Prince Paul Esterházy and then, on his death in 1762, under Prince Nicholas. Haydn embarked on the longest and most productive period of private service at a single court enjoyed by any major composer of the 18th century and perhaps of the entire epoch of court patronage of musicians. He remained in the Esterházy service until 1790. At first he held the post of *vice kapellmeister,* or conductor. In 1766 Prince Nicholas opened a new estate at Esterházy (the previous one had been at Eisenstadt), and that year, on the death of Gregor Werner, Haydn was promoted to kapellmeister.

Haydn was in charge of the musical forces of the court, which included an orchestra of 12 musicians and a group of singers. His duties were to provide two operas and two concerts a week plus a Sunday Mass and whatever additional music might be wanted. Under these conditions his productivity and originality were equally remarkable. As he described it in a famous statement: "As head of an orchestra I could experiment, observe what heightened the effect and what weakened it, and so could improve, expand, cut, take risks; I was cut off from the world, there was no one near me to torment me or make me doubt myself, and so I had to become original."

During the 3 decades of his Esterházy service Haydn's output was prodigious. By 1770 he had produced some 40 symphonies, the quartets up to the six of Opus 9 (1769), much chamber music for baryton (an instrument of the viol family, played by Prince Nicholas), several concertos, operas, keyboard music, and his first Masses. During the period 1771-1780 (called by some biographers his "romantic" period) his music deepened in seriousness and elaborative richness, and he struck out in new paths; as one biographer, E.L. Gerber, put it in 1812: "Haydn's finest symphonic period begins with the year 1770 and from then on gains each year in magnificence." From 1771 and 1772 come the 12 quartets of Opus 17 and Opus 20, with special importance attaching to the latter group, several of which have fugal finales; about 30 more symphonies, including the *Mourning* Symphony, No. 44, and the *Farewell,* No. 45 (1772); and about 18 keyboard sonatas, 6 operas and other dramatic music, and two Masses.

Friendship with Mozart

During his last decade in private service, a most important influence on Haydn's music arose from his contact with Mozart. This relationship dates from the time Mozart took up residence in Vienna in 1781; in the next years Haydn came to know him during his trips to Vienna, and they admired each other's music beyond that of any other contemporary. Haydn commented often on Mozart's remarkable gifts and complained bitterly over the lack of recognition and the absence of any permanent post for Mozart comparable to the one Haydn enjoyed. When an official of Prague asked him for an opera in 1787, 2 months after the premiere of Mozart's *Don Giovanni* there, Haydn declined, saying in part: "It is hardly possible for anyone to stand beside the great Mozart. For if I could impress Mozart's inimitable works as deeply, and with that musical understanding and keen feeling with which I myself grasp and feel them, upon the soul of every music lover . . . the nations would compete for the possession of such a jewel within their borders."

Haydn's major works of this period seemed to his younger contemporaries to show a considerable influence of Mozart's mature style, and the relationship was openly reciprocal. In this decade Haydn produced about 20 symphonies, including the 6 *Paris* Symphonies, Nos. 82-87 (1786), and the *Oxford Symphony,* No. 92 (1788). He also produced the 25 quartets constituting Opus 33 (1781), "written in a new and special manner"; Opus 42 (1785); Opus 50 (1787); Opus 54 and Opus 55 (1789); and Opus 64 (1790). His reputation had by now spread throughout Europe, despite his isolation, owing in part to his being regularly published by a leading Viennese music publisher, Artaria.

Last Years

In 1791 the death of Prince Nicholas freed Haydn from private service, and he embarked on the last and most international phase of his career. He made his first visit to England, at the invitation of the impresario J. P. Salomon, to give concerts of his own works. This visit was a triumph in every respect: Haydn was awarded a degree by Oxford University, met and was honored by members of English society, and gave a highly successful series of concerts. In 1792 he returned to the Continent, passing through Bonn, where he met the young Beethoven, who became his pupil in Vienna. In 1794 he returned to London for another successful tour, then in 1795 settled in Vienna for good. In these years of his travels to England, Haydn, already in his sixties, produced many of his finest late works: his 12 last and greatest symphonies, Nos. 93-104, called the *London Symphonies,* and the last of his piano trios and piano sonatas.

In 1795-1800, on his return to the Continent, Haydn not only continued his extraordinary productivity but turned once again in a new and progressive direction as a composer. The quartets of Opus 71 belong to 1793; the six of Opus 76 (including the *Emperor* and *Sunrise* Quartets) were composed as late as 1797-1798; and the final quartets of Opus 77, Nos. 1 and 2, and the unfinished Opus 103 come from 1799 and 1803. In 1797 Haydn wrote the "Kaiser-Hymn" as a deliberately patriotic gesture in time of war, and it became, as he intended that it should, the Austrian national anthem. In 1796-1798 he set to work on the first of his two final major works—the oratorios *The Creation* and *The Seasons.*

The Oratorios

The Creation was based on a German translation by Baron Gottfried van Swieten of an anonymous English oratorio libretto that had been prepared for George Frederick Handel and was based on John Milton's *Paradise Lost.* With this work Haydn produced a work deliberately planned on the grand scale, based on a religious subject but freely developed in content, for solo voices, chorus, and orchestra. The work as a whole set him at once in the great tradition of oratorio that he had come to know in Handel's works during his visits to England. Although the strain of writing *The Creation* virtually exhausted him, Haydn in 1800 set to work on another oratorio of similar magnitude: *The Seasons,* again with libretto by Van Swieten based on James Thomson's poem.

In these oratorios Haydn came as close as he was ever to come to matching Mozart's sense of dramatic action articulated through music. Neither oratorio is truly a stage work, but both have strong elements of the dramatic and the pictorial, and at times have musicodramatic moments of the highest order. Among these is the entire first part of *The Creation,* beginning with a representation of "Chaos" as orchestral introduction, and then narrating the creation of the world. After the first recitative the chorus enters sotto voce with the words "And the spirit of God moved upon the waters; and God said, 'Let there be light.'" The arrival of the chorus at a fortissimo climax on the word "light" electrified the audiences of Haydn's time, and at his last appearance in public before his death in Vienna on May 31, 1809, at a performance of *The Creation* in 1808 given as a tribute to him, he rose at this point and attributed, in effect, all his creative ability to divine power.

Enormous Output

Haydn's output was so large that at the end of his life he himself could not be absolutely sure how many works he had written. The problems of compiling an accurate catalog of his works, sorting out spurious compositions, and producing an accurate and complete edition have still not been solved. For example, the six string quartets of Opus 3 have been attributed on good grounds to a minor contemporary named Hoffstetter, whose name appeared on the title page of the original edition but was effaced and replaced with that of Haydn.

But the essential mass of Haydn's output remains unshakable in its attribution to him, and it is of formidable proportions: 104 symphonies; 78 string quartets (omitting Opus 3 and counting as separate items the seven movements of *The Seven Last Words of Christ* as arranged for quartet); numerous concertos for keyboard, violin, and violoncello; over 125 baryton trios; numerous divertimenti for winds and for mixed ensembles; 52 keyboard sonatas; over 30 piano trios; 12 Masses and a number of other sacred works; approximately 13 operas; and arias and songs.

Further Reading

A valuable primary source is *The Collected Correspondence and London Notebooks of Joseph Haydn,* edited by H. C. Robbins London (1959). The most important early biographies of Haydn are those by G.A. Griesinger (1809) and A.C. Dies (1810), both based on interviews with Haydn in his last years and available in English translation by Vernon Gotwals, *Joseph Haydn: Eighteenth-Century Gentleman and Genius* (1963). Modern biographies include K. Geiringer, *Haydn: A Creative Life in Music* (1946; 2d rev. ed. 1963), and Rosemary Hughes, *Haydn* (1950). Major studies in English on sectors of Haydn's work are few. Excellent contributions are H.C. Robbins Landon, *The Symphonies of Joseph Haydn* (1955), and D. F. Tovey, "Haydn's Chamber Music," in his *The Main Stream of Music and Other Essays* (1949). Perceptive analytic studies of a number of works are in Felix Salzer, *Structural Hearing: Tonal Coherence in Music* (2 vols., 1952).

Additional Sources

Bobillier, Marie, *Haydn,* Freeport, N.Y.: Books for Libraries Press 1972; New York: B. Blom, 1972.

Butterworth, Neil, *Haydn: his life and times,* Tunbridge Wells, Eng.: Midas Books, 1977.

Geiringer, Karl, *Haydn: a creative life in music,* Berkeley: University of California Press, 1982.

Greene, Carol, *Franz Joseph Haydn: great man of music,* Chicago: Children's Press, 1994.

Landon, H. C. Robbins (Howard Chandler Robbins), *Haydn: chronicle and works,* Bloomington: Indiana University Press, 1976-1980.

Landon, H. C. Robbins (Howard Chandler Robbins), *Haydn: chronicle and works,* London: Thames and Hudson, 1976-c1980.

Landon, H. C. Robbins (Howard Chandler Robbins), *Haydn: his life and music,* Bloomington: Indiana University Press, 1988.

Landon, H. C. Robbins (Howard Chandler Robbins), *Haydn, a documentary study,* New York: Rizzoli, 1981.

Lasker, David., *The boy who loved music,* New York: Viking Press, 1979.

Thompson, Wendy, *Joseph Haydn,* New York: Viking, 1991.

Vignal, Marc, *Joseph Haydn,* Paris: Fayard, 1988. □

Friedrich A. von Hayek

The Austrian-born British free market economist and social philosopher, Nobel Laureate Friedrich Auguste von Hayek (1899-1992) was one of the most distinguished social thinkers of the 20th century.

Friedrich A. von Hayek was born on May 8, 1899, in Vienna into a modest family that could lay claim to a great academic tradition. He left school to enlist in World War I in March 1917. Shortly after returning from the Italian front in November 1918 he began to study law at the University of Vienna. Hayek obtained his Juris Doctor degree only three years later, but continued to study political science, receiving his second doctorate from the same university in 1923.

Hayek in 1921 helped found the "*Geistkreis,*" a small circle of young social scientists in Vienna. More than half of its participants later became world-famous. In 1923 Hayek visited New York and worked part-time as a research assistant at New York University. Greatly stimulated by the newly developed advanced techniques for analyzing time series and forecasting industrial fluctuations, he returned to Vienna in 1924 and published several articles in this field and in monetary theory that paved the way for his later work. Together with his teacher Ludwig von Mises (1881-1973), the eminent scholar of Liberalism, he founded the Austrian Institute for Business Cycle Research in 1927 and directed it until 1931. In 1929 he became a lecturer at Vienna University. That same year his first book on *Geldtheorie und Konjunkturtheorie* (1929) appeared and set a standard in modern business cycle theory.

Becoming an International Scholar

Hayek's series of guest lectures at the London School of Economics in 1931, published as his important *Prices and Production* (1931), led to his appointment as Tooke Professor of Economic Science that same year. There, Hayek immediately became the only intellectual opponent of the new theories of under–consumption and under-investment of Lord John Maynard Keynes. All eminent economists of the time were involved in this major intellectual controversy.

To the big debate (which continues to this day) over the impossibility of socialist calculation and 'market socialism' in the 1930s, with Mises and Hayek on one side and Lange and H. D. Dickinson on the other, Hayek contributed a number of essays which refuted the socialist approach to economic planning. They are collected in his *Individualism and Economic Order* (1948). His seminal essay on "Economics and Knowledge" (1937), in which he first formulated the 'division of knowledge' in society, led him increasingly to socio-philosophical problems, although his interest in technical economics culminated in his *The Pure Theory of Capital* (1942). He was elected Fellow of the British Academy in 1944.

Hayek's *The Road to Serfdom* (1944) made him world-famous overnight and aroused heated discussions. In this best-seller of the immediate post-war years, since translated into sixteen languages, he showed that socialism carries with it no adequate provision for the preservation of freedom and that the convergence of economic systems is rooted in an economic error.

Hayek's important contributions to the methodological problems of the social sciences and scientism were later collected in his *The Counter-Revolution of Science* (1952). In his crucial essay on "The Use of Knowledge in Society" (1945), Hayek refined his idea of the price system as a mechanism for communicating information.

In 1947 Hayek founded the exclusive Mont Pelerin Society, an international association of like-minded scholars. By the end of 1949 he left London and accepted a professorship at the University of Chicago. *The Sensory Order* (1952), a discourse in pure psychology containing some of his most original and important ideas, was published in 1952, though the preliminary thoughts dated back to the early 1920s when he had been uncertain whether to become a psychologist or an economist. Hayek's socio-philosophic approach, however, led to his *The Constitution of Liberty* (1960), regarded as one of the great books of the mid-20th century. Here he further developed his idea of spontaneous order and laid down the ethical, legal, and economic principles of freedom.

Hayek's next move, in 1962, was to the University of Freiburg (Germany). Among many pathbreaking works, he published there his famous *Studies in Philosophy, Politics, and Economics* (1967). After becoming professor emeritus at Freiburg in 1968, he returned to his native Austria and joined the University of Salzburg. In this period, besides some important essays, the first and second volumes of his fundamental trilogy *Law, Legislation, and Liberty* (1973-1976) were published.

In 1974 he was awarded the Nobel Prize in Economics. Hayek's courageous Nobel Prize lecture on "The Pretence of Knowledge" (1974) to some extent again initiated the intellectual revival of liberalism. After Hayek's return to Freiburg in 1977 he published his widely discussed *Denationalization of Money* (1978), his *New Studies in Philosophy, Politics, Economics and the History of Ideas* (1978), and the third volume of his trilogy.

When not lecturing throughout the world, Hayek devoted himself entirely to the completion of his next work, significantly entitled *The Fatal Conceit*. This book presents a most important fundamental critique of rationalism, socialism, and constructivism. Hayek's career as scholar and teacher was international, and he held honorary degrees from universities all over the world. Among his honors, awards, and orders, he received the Order Pour le Merite from Germany and in 1984 the Companion of Honour from Britain.

Hayek's Leading Ideas

Hayek represented the subjective approach of the free-market oriented Austrian School of Economics, distinguished by its methodological individualism. His economic analysis, therefore, rested upon the insight that every individual chooses and acts in pursuit of his purposes and in accordance with his perception of his options for achieving them. His early writings, as shown above, were in pure economic theory.

Hayek's trade cycle theory explained that overinvestment leads to scarcity of capital compelling a cutback in investment and even the abandonment of a part of the real capital produced because of the excessive investment rate.

His most important discovery was the "division of knowledge" and the spontaneous order. The spontaneous interaction of millions of individuals, each possessing unique information of which beneficial use might be made, created circumstances that cannot be conveyed to any central authority. A system of signals—the price system—was therefore the only mechanism that communicates information and enables people to adapt to circumstances of which they know nothing. The whole modern order and well-being rested on the possibility of adapting to processes that were unknown. It was not scientific knowledge which matters, but the unorganized particular knowledge of time and place.

While for most social philosophers the chief aim of politics consisted in setting up an ideal social order through utopian reforms, Hayek's main task was the finding of rules that enable men with different values and convictions to live together. These rules were established so as to permit each individual to fulfill his aims and to limit government action.

In his "Denationalization of Money" (1976) he convincingly argued that inflation could be avoided only if the monopolistic power of issuing money was taken away from government and state authorities and the task given to private industry to promote competition in currencies.

According to Hayek, cultural evolution was not a result of human reason consciously building institutions, but a process in which culture and reason developed concurrently. The spontaneous social order generated by individuals interacting according to these general rules was distinguished from the constructivist approach exemplified by socialist ideas, which interpreted all order as the product of conscious design.

Hayek's seminal work arose and developed from a comprehensive approach to various intellectual disciplines that condition and influence one another. Although there were only a few direct disciples in academia, Hayek's influence on pure economics, public policy, and social, political, and legal philosophy were tremendous.

Classical Liberalism

During the 1980s, Hayek's interdisciplinary theories gained wider dissemination, especially his opposition to the concept that publc institutions could be designed to meet human requirements and intentions. He preferred an almost laissez-faire approach in which public order evolved from specific ideas and actions. Thus, he was opposed to the highly-centralized economics of the various forms of socialism, which denied the economics of the marketplace.

British Prime Minister Margaret Thatcher, was greatly influenced by Hayek's ideas of personal liberty and market economics and based many of her government's conservative policies upon her interpretation of his concepts.

In 1991, Hayek published his final volume, *Economic Freedom*, in which he argued that political/economic coercion is the greatest threat to individual freedom and best achieved through the natural evolution of market forces.

Since Hayek's death in March 1992, there has been continuing debate concerning his interdisciplinary system. It was thought that he diminished the role of reason, and failed to reconcile the value of such liberal institutions as have evolved with their role as preservers and nurturers of reason and freedom.

Further Reading

Probably the best collection of Hayek's most important and influential essays and chapters available is Kurt R. Leube and Chiaki Nishiyama, *The Essence of Hayek* (1984), which includes a biography and an introduction. A good popular presentation of Hayek's ideas can be found in Eamonn Butler, *Hayek: His Contribution to the Political and Economic Thought of Our Time* (1983). His political philosophy is penetratingly treated in John N. Gray, *Hayek on Liberty* (1984), which includes a comprehensive bibliography compiled by John Cody. Two Festschrifts are dedicated to Hayek: Erich Streissler et al. (editors), *Roads to Freedom: Essays in Honour of Friedrich A. von Hayek* (1969), and Kurt R. Leube and Albert H. Zlabinger (editors), *The Political Economy of Freedom: Essays in Honor of F. A. Hayek* (1985). Hayek's publication list covered 19 books and some 240 essays and articles.
There were several in-depth studies of Hayek's interdisciplinary theories which seek to make his concepts accessible to the uninformed but interested reader. Margaret Thatcher's *The Path to Power* (1995) acknowledged her debt to Hayek's *The Road to Serfdom* for his insights into the economic and social slavery of the authoritarian forms of socialism which were coming into vogue in the late thirties and early forties. Keith Graham in *The London Times* obituary of Hayek (March, 1992) presented a concise but lucid analysis of his major concepts, and contained an extensive bibliography of Hayek's main publications and secondary reading. □

Helen Hayes

Helen Hayes (1900-1993) was an American actress whose long career made a lasting impression in the American theater world.

Helen Hayes was born on October 10, 1900, in Washington, D.C., daughter of Francis Brown Hayes and Catharine Estelle Hayes. The young Helen appeared on stage even before she went to school: at five years old she played the part of Prince Charles in *The Royal Family*. Other roles quickly followed this one, and she made her first appearance on Broadway as Psyche Finnegan in *The Summer Widowers* when she was ten years old. Much later, in 1958, Hayes wrote of this period: "when I was five, everything was certain and known, and I was positive that life was long and art short . . . even in 1905, Broadway was merely 230 miles away."

Though she appeared on the New York stage numerous times before she was even of age, the young Helen was educated at the Academy of the Sacred Heart Convent in her native Washington. She graduated in 1917, having already spent three years with the Columbia Players in Washington. Upon graduation she moved to New York City, where she was to spend a large portion of her life. Acting came naturally to her, and it was not until her role as Cora Wheeler in *Clarence* (Booth Tarkington's 1919 play) that she ever felt that acting was a challenging profession. This was the first part where she felt her natural talents insufficient. After this performance, she began to take lessons in dance, mime, and even fencing—all as means through which to learn how to control even the most minute muscle of her body, which she thought of as her "actor's instrument."

In 1921 Booth Tarkington wrote a play especially for Hayes entitled *The Wren*. She had starred in *Penrod* as well as *Clarence*, and they had struck up a friendship that inspired Tarkington to make his next protagonist, Seeby Olds, perfect for Hayes. He did not realize, however, something that she had not told anyone: Helen Hayes always reached outward for inspiration for her parts and did not know how to play a part so close to herself. In 1958 she commented, "the twenty-fourth performance brought down the final, merciful curtain."

Hayes had many other successes, however, not the least of which was her marriage to Charles MacArthur, a playwright, in 1928. She had a daughter, Mary, and a son, James. Though they got along very well, the couple seldom worked together. The most notable exception was a highly successful one, however: in 1931 Hayes won an Academy Award for her film debut in *The Sin of Madelon Claudet,* which her husband had written for her. In it Hayes portrayed an old woman; in her autobiography, she explained that it was the memory of Mme. Curie, whom she had seen once on a boat crossing the Atlantic, that enabled her to play the part.

One of her most celebrated performances in the theater came four years later, when she played the part of Queen Victoria in *Victoria Regina.* Immediately previous to this performance she had played the role of Mary Stuart in *Mary of Scotland,* thus starting what she dubbed her "queen kick" that was to last over four years. *Victoria Regina* itself ran for four years, including a coast-to-coast tour. Hayes received the Drama League of New York medal of 1936 for "the most distinguished performance of the year" for her portrayal of Victoria. She later said that this performance had been inspired by the memory of her grandmother, who had been in London during Queen Victoria's wedding procession and who subsequently at least physically imitated the queen.

Helen Hayes continued to tour the United States with various successful plays both before and after World War II. She appeared in London for the first time in 1948 at the Haymarket. There she played the role of Amanda Wingfield in *The Glass Menagerie,* a role that she was to play in several different locations quite a few more times in her career. The Sarah Bernhardt Theater in Paris saw the debut in 1955 of another role that she would play often—that of Mrs. Antrobus in *The Skin of Our Teeth.* Hayes toured Europe and Israel for the U.S. State Department playing both of these roles in 1961, following that tour with one of South America.

She made her first appearance at the Helen Hayes Theater in New York in October 1958 as Nora Melody in *A Touch of the Poet.* This role became special to her in many ways—not the least of which was that the play was Eugene O'Neill's last. Although Nora was not the protagonist of the play, Hayes felt that it was around her spirit that the entire play revolved, and this spirit reminded her very much of her husband's, who had died in 1956.

In the summer of 1962 Hayes appeared with Maurice Evans at the recital entitled "Shakespeare Revisited: A Program for Two Players" in Stratford, Connecticut. This recital inspired her to form the Helen Hayes Repertory Company in 1964, which sponsored tours of Shakespeare readings in universities around the country.

Hayes published her autobiography, *A Gift of Joy,* in 1965. Rather than a chronological account of her life, the book is a delightful collection of impressions and anecdotes about her career, her family, and herself, interspersed with passages from her favorite poems and plays. She also co-authored *Twice Over Lightly* with Anita Loos in 1972.

Hayes received an honorary Doctor of Fine Arts from Princeton University in 1956. She received many other honorary degrees—from Columbia, Brown, New York University, and others. She was awarded the Medal of the City of New York as well as the Finnish Medal of the Arts. The United Service Organization nominated her Woman of the Year in 1974, and she was president of the American National Theater Academy from 1951 to 1953. She received a Tony Award in 1947 for her performance as Addie in *Happy Birthday* and a second Oscar (as supporting actress) for her performance in *Airport* in 1970.

The First Lady of the American Theater retired from live performance in 1970, following her appearance in a revival of *Harvey.* She was honored with a professorship at the University of Illinois and taught speech and drama for several semesters.

She returned to acting before the camera in a television series *The Snoop Sisters* (1973-1974) with Mildred Natwick. She also made many cameo appearances in feature and television films, from the delightful characterization of a professional stowaway little old lady in *Airport* (1970) to her portrayal of Agatha Christie's Miss Marple in *A Caribbean Mystery* (1983), directed by Robert Lewis.

Although she appeared in several short silent films and won an Oscar for *The Sin of Madelon Claudet* (1931), Helen Hayes's film career was somewhat abortive. She followed her early success with a series of failures, from *Arrowsmith* (1931) by John Ford, to *Vanessa, Her Love Story* (1935) by William K. Howard and her public lost interest in her as film star material. She often referred to her career as "the triumph of plain Jane."

Helen Hayes lived in her home in Nyack, New York, until her death from congestive heart failure, March 17, 1993. As a tribute to her position as of America's greatest actresses, the lights of Broadway went dim for one minute at 8:00 P.M. the day she died.

Further Reading

Articles on Helen Hayes can be found in *Who's Who in American Theater* (1977) and the *Oxford Companion to the Theatre* (1966). Her autobiography, *A Gift of Joy,* was published in 1965. She also wrote an article for the *New York Times* in 1958 entitled "Helen Hayes Relives Her Roles."

Helen Hayes published her memoir *On Reflection* (1968) and her biography *My Life in Three Acts* (1990), written with Katherine Hatch.

Variety Magazine Obituaries, New York and London: Garland Publishing Inc., (1993-94) paid tribute to Helen Hayes, March 22, 1993, with a lengthy and detailed account of her achievements on stage and in films. She also appears in *Notable Women in the American Theater: A Biographical Dictionary* and in *A Biographical Dictionary of Film,* New York: Alfred A. Knopf, (1995). □

Cardinal Patrick Joseph Hayes

Cardinal Patrick Joseph Hayes (1867-1938) was a leader of the Catholic hierarchy, best known for his

work in expanding and organizing the outstanding program of Catholic charities in his diocese.

Patrick Joseph Hayes was born in New York City on Nov. 20, 1867, the son of Irish immigrants. Five years later his mother died, and he went to live with relatives. He attended parochial schools conducted by the Christian Brothers and graduated in 1888 from Manhattan College. To study for the priesthood he attended the diocesan seminary at Troy, N.Y., and was ordained in 1892. Two years later he earned a licentiate of sacred theology at the Catholic University of America.

Father Hayes's first assignment was in New York's St. Gabriel's parish, serving under John M. Farley. When his pastor became auxiliary bishop of New York in 1895, Hayes became his secretary. After Archbishop Michael A. Corrigan died, Farley succeeded to his post with Hayes continuing as his secretary. Later Hayes served also as diocesan chancellor and president of the new preparatory seminary.

In 1914 Hayes was consecrated auxiliary bishop of New York, and in 1919 he succeeded Farley as head of the diocese. During World War I Hayes was named bishop of the American Armed Forces and mobilized a group of 900 Catholic chaplains. He also served on the administrative board of the National Catholic War Council, which coordinated Catholic war work at home and abroad. Hayes was a signatory of the Bishops' Program of Social Reconstruction, a series of proposals for postwar social reforms issued in the name of the Catholic hierarchy in 1919.

In his 20 years as New York's archbishop, Hayes devoted himself to local matters, avoiding the spotlight and shunning national controversies. With the assistance of the Reverend Robert J. Keegan, he completed the centralization and incorporation of diocesan charities, including over 200 agencies, providing a model for other prelates and dioceses. Named to the College of Cardinals in 1924, he was frequently referred to as the "Cardinal of Charities."

Occasionally Cardinal Hayes did speak out on public issues which he felt involved moral principles or the welfare of the Church. He opposed prohibition, backed legislation to limit indecency on the stage, and, in a rare step, denounced the work of the American Birth Control League in 1935. Widely respected by prominent citizens, he joined in efforts to combat bigotry and endorsed unemployment relief during the Depression. He died on Sept. 4, 1938.

Further Reading

A full-length study of Hayes is John Bernard Kelly, *Cardinal Hayes: One of Ourselves* (1941). There is an account of Hayes's life in Brendan A. Finn, *Twenty-Four American Cardinals* (1947). For general background see Thomas T. McAvoy, *A History of the Catholic Church in the United States* (1969). □

Roland Hayes

One of the highest paid musicians of his time, tenor Roland Hayes (1887-1977) was a masterful interpreter of both classical songs and black spirituals.

Tenor Roland Hayes is acknowledged as a masterful interpreter of both classical songs and black spirituals. In a career that spanned more than thirty years, he performed throughout the United States and Europe. Hayes shattered the color barrier in the world of classical music, becoming one of the highest paid musicians of his time and paving the way for later African American singers. Summing up Hayes's career, Marva Griffen Carter wrote in the *Black Perspective in Music:* "Hayes's life of almost ninety years reveals a remarkable story of a man who went from the plantation to the palace, performing before kings and queens, with the finest international and American orchestras, in segregated communities before blacks and whites alike.... When he sang, art became more than polished excellence. It appealed to something beyond the intellect, something one could call the soul."

One of six children, Roland Hayes was born on June 3, 1887, in Curryville, Georgia. Although neither of his parents were afforded any formal educational opportunities, they recognized the value of good schooling. Hayes's father, William, a former slave turned farmer and carpenter, had an intense appreciation of music; his mother, Fannie, also a former slave, was determined to see that all of her children were educated—and that Roland would pursue a religious vocation.

Music was a natural part of Hayes's life. A timid child, he nevertheless liked to sing while at work on the farm and at the Baptist church the family attended. Hayes learned to read music from a man who conducted a seasonal singing school, and he also played the quills—joints of bamboo tied together like panpipes—to music of African origin.

When Hayes was eleven years old, his father died from injuries suffered several years earlier in a work-related accident. Young Roland and his brother Robert were forced to quit school and work to support the family. In 1900 the Hayes family—then consisting of Fannie, Roland, and his two brothers, Robert and Jesse—moved to Chattanooga, Tennessee. There, Hayes worked at an iron foundry, awaiting his turn to attend school. At age sixteen, after he had been made a foreman at the foundry, he returned to his studies part-time. Determined to succeed despite the embarrassment of reciting lessons with students much younger than himself, Hayes even hired a tutor. He also started singing lessons with W. Arthur Calhoun, an Oberlin University music student who opened Hayes's ears to classical music. After three months, Hayes knew that regardless of his mother's objections, he must aspire to a career in music.

In 1905 Hayes entered the preparatory division at Fisk University in Nashville, Tennessee. After three years, during which he received a scholarship and helped support himself through housework and vocal performances with various groups, Hayes reportedly left the university because of a

misunderstanding. He worked at a men's club in Louisville for a short time and began to gain notoriety for his singing. After performing a few years at small social functions, he gave a concert in Boston with the Fisk Jubilee Singers in 1911. After that, he stayed in Boston, where he found work as a hotel bellboy, a waiter, and a messenger for an insurance company. He continued his studies with operatic bass Arthur Hubbard and sent for his mother—who finally accepted her son's career choice—to come and live with him in the Northeast.

Early Performances

Hayes performed with American educator Booker T. Washington and singer-composer Harry Burleigh, whose reputations and experience enhanced that of the budding singer. However, early in the twentieth century, no professional manager was willing to sponsor a black performer; thus, in 1915 Hayes gave his first concert—self-managed—with little success. Two years later the undeterred singer rented Symphony Hall in Boston, then an unprecedented step for an African American. His performance of *lieder*, or classical songs, by Franz Schubert and arias by Mozart and Tchaikovsky created a sensation.

In early 1918 Hayes began a U.S. tour, which he managed himself, and in 1920 he set sail for London, England. After a year of scraping by with whatever small performances came their way, Hayes and his accompanist, Lawrence Brown, were booked to perform at the prestigious Wigmore Hall. Although he was suffering from pneumonia, Hayes sang masterfully. Two days later he gave a command performance for King George V and Queen Mary. While in London, Hayes also studied lieder singing with Sir George Henschel.

Toured the United States

Upon his return to the United States in 1922, the world famous Hayes performed at Symphony Hall in Boston to rave reviews. Shortly afterward he became the first black singer to appear at Carnegie Hall in New York City. Hayes then began a series of concert tours that took him to nearly every corner of the country. By 1924 he was performing more than eighty concerts per year, many with major orchestras, such as those in Boston, Philadelphia, New York, and Detroit. He was widely praised for his interpretations of German and French songs, as well as his renditions of black folk songs and spirituals, which he later compiled in a single volume titled *My Songs*.

In 1925 Hayes gave a command performance for Queen Mother Maria Christian of Spain. That same year, he was awarded the Spingarn Medal, given annually by the National Association for the Advancement of Colored People for the "most outstanding achievement among colored people." Hayes toured Italy in 1927 and the Soviet Union the following year. He was hailed wherever he went as one of the greatest lieder singers of his era for his silken smooth tone and sensitive lyrical interpretations. Although Hayes often performed concert renditions of arias, he never appeared in an opera because interracial casting was frowned upon during his era.

Expressed Musical Philosophy

In a 1947 *Christian Science Monitor* interview, Hayes spoke about the universality of his work, "When I began my career I realized that if I would speak to all men, I must learn the language and the ways of thought of all men. What good could I do if I knew only my own ways and the thoughts of my own people? So I learned to sing the songs of all people. . . . The song I sing is nothing. But what I give through the song is everything. I cannot put into words what I try to do with this instrument that is nearest to me—my voice. If I were to frame it in words, I would lose some of the ability to make it effective."

Remembered as a Master of Song

In addition to his exceptionally long singing career, Hayes taught voice at Boston University beginning in 1950. In 1954 he toured Europe, where he was greatly admired in England, Holland, and Denmark. At age seventy he still garnered rave reviews: "What Mr. Hayes does is live each song he sings," wrote *Boston Herald* music critic Rudolph Elie. "To be sure, there are many others who so the same thing. . . . The essential difference here, however, is that Mr. Hayes knows what he is living: there is a classic balance between his intellectual comprehension and his emotional concept. The consequence is an atmosphere so intense as to be gripping. . . . [The listener] is in the presence of a master." In 1962, on his seventy-fifth birthday, Hayes gave his farewell concert at Carnegie Hall.

Although Hayes recorded for a number of labels, including Vocalion, American Columbia, Vanguard, and Veritas, few recordings are available. In 1990, however, the Smithsonian Institution issued *The Art of Roland Hayes,* an audio recording of various performances by Hayes from 1939 to 1965.

Hayes was a groundbreaking figure in the field of music who helped pave the way for classical African American artists such as Marian Anderson, Paul Robeson, Leontyne Price, Simon Estes, William Warfield, and George Shirley to name but a few. In a television documentary titled *The Musical Legacy of Roland Hayes,* William Warfield recalled a conversation with Hayes, who advised African American singers: "I started all this. . . . Now, you can't stop where I stopped; you've got to go on."

Further Reading

Hayes, Roland, *My Songs: Aframerican Religious Folk Songs Arranged and Interpreted by Roland Hayes,* Little, Brown, 1948.
Helm, MacKinley, *Angel Mo' and Her Son, Roland Hayes,* Little, Brown, 1942.
Atlanta Journal, November 25, 1990.
Black Perspective in Music, Fall 1974; Fall 1977.
Boston Globe, June 17, 1990.
Boston Herald, October 21, 1957.
Christian Science Monitor, November 22, 1947.
Record Collector, Volume 10, 1955.
Washington Post, February 19, 1990.
Hayes was also the subject of the television documentary *The Musical Legacy of Roland Hayes.* □

Rutherford Birchard Hayes

Rutherford Birchard Hayes (1822-1893), nineteenth president of the United States, supervised the Republican party's unsuccessful attempt to build a Southern wing based on old white "Whig" elements.

Rutherford B. Hayes was born Oct. 4, 1822, in Delaware, Ohio. His family, recently moved from New England, was well-to-do. Born 2 months after his father's death, Hayes was dominated by his neurotic mother and sister and patronized by his wealthy uncle Sardis Birchard.

Birchard was a critical influence in Hayes's life and helped pay for his education. Graduating from Kenyon College with highest honors in 1842, Hayes went to Harvard Law School in 1843. In 1845 he moved to Lower Sandusky (now Fremont), Ohio, to practice law under his uncle's sponsorship. Easygoing and pliable, Hayes was inclined to accept the conservative ideals surrounding him, and he adopted his uncle's Whig politics and distaste for abolitionists. The tall, handsome Hayes was a congenial and ready conversationalist, and he enjoyed considerable popularity in the town. Nevertheless, in 1849 he moved to Cincinnati, then the most important city in the West.

The young lawyer's personability and good showing in a celebrated homicide case soon won Hayes some reputation and political notice. Like most Northern Whigs during the late 1850s, Hayes had turned to the Republican party. However, he was not excessively interested in political questions; during the momentous election of 1860 he wrote, "I cannot get up much interest in the contest." He preferred the casual society of the "best people," travel, and occasional lectures on temperance.

War Years

Hayes's life of genteel idleness ended with the Civil War. He accepted a commission as major of the 23d Ohio Infantry. Now, for the first time in his life, he truly reveled in an all-masculine world, and he later looked back on the war as "the best years of our lives." He was brave to the point of recklessness and was wounded four times, once seriously. He rose to the rank of major general. What was more significant, his war record catapulted him into prominence in Ohio politics. While he was still in the military, he was nominated by the Republicans to serve in Congress and was elected without campaigning. He went to Washington for two terms, beginning in 1864.

In 1867 Hayes was elected governor of Ohio. He compiled a "moderate" record on all issues and retired to what he regarded as a permanent private life in 1871. However, in 1875, Republican leaders prevailed on him to stand again for governor, with the possibility of the presidential nomination the next year clearly understood. Successful, he entered his third term.

Disputed Election

Hayes entered the Republican nominating convention of 1876 as a minor candidate. The favorite, James G. Blaine, faced a number of opponents. In addition, the Republicans were sensitive to charges of political corruption, as the administration of Ulysses S. Grant had been blackened by scandal and Blaine had been implicated in a stock manipulation deal. Blaine's rivals withdrew one by one in favor of the deliberately "passive" Hayes.

The election, which pitted Republican Hayes against Democrat Samuel J. Tilden, proved more difficult. Owing to questions of the legitimacy of vote casting and counting in several states, the whole election was questioned and the country plunged into debate. Finally, a congressional commission was established to decide the election. By a curious twist the commission was composed of eight Republicans and only seven Democrats. However, the dispute was settled, and Hayes took office in March 1877 without further serious incident because the Republicans had made informal agreements with Southern Democrats to work toward establishment of a new political alliance between men of means in both the North and the South. Hayes's party thus hoped to drive a wedge between the two wings of its opposition.

Hayes was more than happy with the plan. He was naturally a "Whig" and had been uncomfortable with Grant's "bloody shirt" politics. He did not personally regard deals with the Southern Democrats as abandoning the Republican commitment to Southern blacks; rather, he hoped

to win paternalistic protection for them by encouraging the growth of the Republican party among whites.

As president, Hayes withdrew the last Federal troops from the South and, as a symbol of the end of this phase of the Reconstruction, decorated Confederate graves on Memorial Day, 1877. "My task was to wipe out the color line, to abolish sectionalism; to end the war and bring peace," Hayes remembered, but by 1878 he had to state, "I am reluctantly forced to admit that the experiment was a failure."

Though Hayes was as meticulous with detail as ever and dispensed his presidential duties ably, he abhorred active leadership. He pledged to serve only one term, and the Republicans were happy to retire him. Hayes spent his final years in prosperous retirement in Lower Sandusky, distracting himself with active participation in the Grand Army of the Republic and other veterans' organizations. He died on Jan. 17, 1893.

Further Reading

Hamilton J. Eckenrode, *Rutherford B. Hayes: Statesman of Reunion* (1930), is highly favorable to Hayes but suffers from a blatantly racist approach to the questions of Reconstruction that loomed so large in Hayes's career. Harry Barnard, *Rutherford B. Hayes and His America* (1954), is a model of thorough historical research and possesses shrewd insights. T. Harry Williams, *Hayes of the Twenty-third* (1965), is a fascinating account of Hayes's war years. C. Vann Woodward, *Reunion and Reaction* (1951; rev. ed. 1956), is the indispensable insight into the ending of Reconstruction, and H. Wayne Morgan, *From Hayes to McKinley* (1969), is the best recent overall account of the period. For the election of 1876 see Arthur M. Schlesinger, Jr., ed., *History of American Presidential Elections,* vol. 2 (1971). □

J. E. Casely Hayford

J. E. Casely Hayford (1866-1903) was a Gold Coast lawyer, politician, journalist, and educator. He was a leading pan-African nationalist.

On Sept. 29, 1866, J. E. Casely Hayford was born of a prominent family in the coastal town of Cape Coast. He attended the Wesleyan Boys' High School there and Fourah Bay College in Freetown, Sierra Leone (1872-1874). In Freetown, at this time the leading educational and pan-African center in western Africa, Hayford became a staunch admirer and disciple of Edward Wilmot Blyden, the foremost pan-African figure of his time, who edited the *Negro,* the first explicitly pan-African journal in West Africa.

Although a militant advocate of African and pan-African causes, Hayford never became bitter and always acted "constitutionally." He was a dapper man of medium height, charming, and with a keen sense of humor. To point up the hypocrisy of "Christians," he often referred to himself as a "pagan." He was no prig: he enjoyed a social drink and the company of women. He was twice married. He had a son, Archie Hayford, the well-known Ghanaian lawyer, by his first wife, and a daughter, Gladys, by his second.

Journalist and Educator

Hayford began his career as a journalist, serving as an assistant editor on the *Western Echo* (1885-1887) and as editor of the *Gold Coast Echo* (1888-1890). He edited the *Gold Coast Chronicle* and contributed articles to the *Gold Coast Independent* (1891-1893). Later he helped edit the *Gold Coast Methodist Times* and was closely associated with the *Gold Coast Aborigines*. In 1902 Hayford and three other colleagues founded the *Gold Coast Leader,* which became the main organ of his propaganda until his death.

Hayford's formal career as a teacher was short-lived. He was headmaster of the Wesleyan Boys' High School at Accra (1891-1893). But throughout his entire adult life he was a staunch advocate of education at all levels along "racial and national lines." In 1902 he became one of the founders of the Mfantsi National Education Fund to provide for the "proper education" of the children of the Gold Coast. Children were to be taught to read and write in Fante, and the study of Gold Coast history, geography, institutions, and customs was to be emphasized. But the scheme aborted.

In 1911, in his book *Ethiopia Unbound,* Hayford publicly advocated the establishment of a national university with a curriculum relevant to African needs and conditions. In 1919 he and other colleagues sought unsuccessfully to

establish secular independent high schools through the newly formed Gold Coast National Education Scheme. Hayford's educational dream was partly realized when the Gold Coast government opened Achimota College in 1927. Its curriculum was Africanized, and throughout the remainder of the colonial period it was the premier primary and secondary educational institution in the Gold Coast. Hayford was a member of the Achimota Council and also served on the Gold Coast Board of Education.

Lawyer and Politician

Hayford saw the knowledge of law as an important asset in promoting his political ambitions. In the late 1880s he worked as a law clerk in Cape Coast. During the academic year 1893/1894 he studied jurisprudence at St. Peter's College, Cambridge, and during the next 2 years continued his study of law at Inner Temple, London. He was called to the bar on Nov. 17, 1896, and shortly thereafter returned to the Gold Coast.

As a lawyer-politician, Hayford successfully argued and agitated against two measures which would have resulted in the alienation of African lands to the British crown: the Lands Bill of 1897 and the proposed Forest Bill of 1911. The research for his briefs against these two bills formed the basis of three of his books: *Gold Coast Native Institutions* (1903), *Gold Coast Land Tenure and the Forest Bill* (1911), and *The Truth about the West African Land Question* (1913). In the Legislative Council he fearlessly criticized the shortcomings of colonial rule and constantly demanded a larger African say in running their affairs. He himself served on several government commissions.

Pan-African Leader

Early in his career Hayford came to see the essential problem of Africans—both in the ancestral home and abroad—as regaining self-confidence and self-respect, which had been crushed by European exploitation and degradation. He therefore inveighed strongly against the uncritical acceptance of European ideas, customs, and institutions. In 1888 he publicly stressed the need to retain African languages and African dress. In his newspapers he regularly recalled the achievement of outstanding Africans so as to foster racial pride. In 1916 he published *William Waddy Harris: The Man and His Message,* a biography of an outstanding African religious prophet.

Hayford took an especially keen interest in Afro-Americans and encouraged the pan-African aspirations of Dr. W. E. B. Du Bois and Marcus Garvey and their followers. Hayford's last pamphlet, *The Disabilities of Black Folk and Their Treatment, with an Appeal to the Labour Party,* was in the tradition of pan-African protest.

In West Africa, Hayford's pan-African dream took the form of an independent federation of the British colonies— Gambia, Sierra Leone, Gold Coast, and Nigeria—within the British Commonwealth. In 1914 he began seriously to discuss the idea of a conference of representatives from the four British colonies. In 1919 he made the case for west African unity in a pamphlet, *United West Africa.*

In March 1920 he succeeded in convening a conference in Accra of some 50 British West African delegates which resulted in the National Congress of British West Africa. The Congress met on three subsequent occasions: Freetown in 1923, Bathurst at the turn of the year 1925/1926, and Lagos in 1929. The Congress lacked mass support and did not realize any of its goals. However, it did act as an important stimulus to African nationalism. With Hayford's death on Aug. 11, 1930, the guiding spirit of the Congress was removed, and it became defunct.

Further Reading

There is no biography of Hayford. His *Ethiopa Unbound: Studies in Race Emancipation* (1911; 2d ed. 1969) includes an analysis of his work and a biographical sketch by F. Nnabuenyi Ugonna. There is a short biographical sketch of Hayford in Magnus J. Sampson, *Gold Coast Men of Affairs* (1937), but the chronology is often weak or confused. His political activities are briefly analyzed in David Kimble, *A Political History of Ghana* (1963). □

Muhammad Husain Haykal

Muhammad Husain Haykal (or Heikal) (born 1923) was a powerful journalist and editor of *Al Ahram* (1957-1974), widely read in the Arab world and internationally. He also served as an adviser to Egyptian Presidents Nasser and Sadat.

Muhammad Husain Haykal (or Heikal) was born in Cairo in 1923 into a family of middle class origin. He finished his studies at Cairo University with a degree in economics and journalism. At the age of 19 he began his lifelong career in journalism, which not only took him nearly everywhere in the world, but brought him in close contact with many of the world's statesmen and politicians, most notably Egypt's president, Gamal Abdel Nasser. His writings gave him world renown; during the peak of his career in the 1960s and 1970s he may have been the most powerful journalist in the world.

Early Career

Fame and power came rather quickly to Haykal. He began his career as a simple editor of a Cairo English language daily, *The Egyptian Gazette,* and it was for this paper that he covered the famous World War II Battle of El Alamein. Between 1942 and 1957 he worked for almost all of Egypt's leading newspapers and weekly magazines, including *Rus al-Yusuf; Akhar Sa'a; Akhbar al-Yawm,* and *al-Akhbar.* He not only covered domestic events but travelled extensively as a foreign correspondent reporting on world events and international crises. He covered the Arab-Israeli war in 1948 (when he met King Abdullah ibn Husein of Jordan and Prime Minister David Ben Gurion of Israel), the Greek civil war (in 1947 and 1949), and the Korean War (in 1949). By the age of 25, when he won the King Farouk Prize in journalism for the first—but not the last—time, he was

already a celebrity in Egypt. Between 1953 and 1956 he was the editor of the weekly *Akhir Sa'a;* then he became editor of *Akhbar al-Yaum,* a daily. Finally in 1957 he became the editor of the powerful, semi-official Egyptian newspaper *al-Ahram,* a post he retained until he was removed by President Anwar al-Sadat in 1974.

Haykal and Nasser

Haykal first met Gamal Abdel Nasser in 1948 during the Arab-Israeli war, when Nasser was a major commanding a batallion in the Negev desert. In July 1952 the Egyptian monarchy was ended by a military coup planned and executed by a group of officers led by Nasser. After holding several high offices, Nasser became president of the new Egyptian Republic in 1956.

The real beginning of the relationship between Nasser and Haykal took place in 1952 when Nasser asked Haykal to edit and publish his memoirs. Haykal persuaded Nasser to turn his memoirs into a book which would explain Nasser's thinking to the Egyptian public. Thus was born Nasser's famous work, *The Philosophy of the Revolution* (1959).

Thereafter, Nasser and Haykal became friends. Nasser was charmed by Haykal's lively mind and attentive ear and eagerly sought the insights Haykal brought him on social and political life in Egypt. Soon Haykal was as powerful as most Egyptian cabinet ministers; indeed, many ministers sought Haykal in an effort to gain Nasser's ear.

For ten years in the 1960s Haykal was Nasser's unofficial political and press adviser, working closely with Nasser in formulating the ideology and policies of the Egyptian government. His Friday editorial in *al-Ahram,* "Bi-Saraha" ("Frankly Speaking"), was the barometer of Egyptian policy. In it he explained and justified the actions of the Egyptian state. These articles were closely read not only in Egypt, but throughout the Arab world for what they told of Arab and Egyptian politics, and they were regularly quoted and analyzed in the international press.

Haykal was an advocate of Arab nationalism and patriotism, of the need for a united Arab front against Israel, and of democracy in Egypt. He felt that Egypt could never stand against the Israeli challenge unless it fought backwardness at home and created a more open society based on the rule of law.

Haykal was generally considered a moderate in Nasser's entourage and a man of pro-Western sentiments. This reputation created some enmity toward him among Egyptian Leftists, chief among them Ali Sabri, prime minister from 1954 to 1957 and later secretary general of the Arab Socialist Union, Egypt's sole political party under Nasser. The rivalry between Sabri and Haykal only ended in 1973 when Sabri and his men were arrested for plotting a coup against Sadat.

For a brief time in 1970 Haykal was minister of national guidance, and in this position he played an important role in the formation of a joint Egyptian-Libyan-Sudanese information service and in creating the Egyptian Radio and Television Federation. He resigned from this post after Nasser's sudden death in October of the same year.

At the height of Haykal's political influence in 1970 he was the editor of *al-Ahram,* minister of information, acting minister of foreign affairs, a member of the National Security Council, and a member of the Central Committee of the Arab Socialist Union.

The history of *al-Ahram* will always be inextricably associated with Haykal's name. It was Haykal who gave the paper the organization and direction which made it the best newspaper in Egypt and in the Arab world. He built an impressive news building as *al-Ahram's* headquarters and equipped it with the latest and most sophisticated technology. Under his guidance, *al-Ahram's* daily circulation reached nearly one million, making it the most widely read newspaper in the Arab world. In association with the newspaper he developed a publishing house, a large advertising agency, and a computer service used by many Egyptian companies.

Haykal and Sadat

After Nasser's death and the subsequent election of Anwar Sadat as president, Haykal resigned as minister of information, but he kept his post as head of *al-Ahram.* At first, his relationship with Sadat was close; he became Sadat's adviser and helped Sadat foil the plot against him led by Sabri. Haykal is credited with having persuaded Sadat to follow moderate policies and to establish close ties with the United States. However, the relationship soured after 1973, when Haykal managed to convey the impression that Sadat was not a competent successor to Nasser. In 1974, after *al-Ahram* printed a series of articles critical of Sadat's policies, Haykal was removed as editor. From then on he worked as a free-lance journalist and writer. When domestic opposition to the Sadat regime grew more vocal in 1978, Sadat accused Haykal, among other things, of atheism and plotting to establish a rival "center of power" and had him arrested. Haykal denied the allegations. His arrest was followed by such strong international protest and indignation that Sadat was compelled to release him, although he was prohibited from writing in the Egyptian press and from travelling abroad. These restrictions were removed in 1981 after Sadat's assassination and the election of Hosni Mubarak as president. Haykal returned to his role as a free-lance journalist.

Haykal maintained his prestigious position as Egypt's leading journalist, writer and intellectual; and was considered as a negotiator between Egypt and other Arab states which were hostile to Egypt, notably Libya.

Haykal was the author of several books in Arabic and English, all known for their lively style and clarity. Among the most famous are those dealing with Nasser and his foreign policy: *The Cairo Documents* (1973), *The Road to Ramadan* (1975), and *The Sphinx and the Commissar* (1979). *Autumn of Fury: The Assassination of Sadat,* New York: Random House, (1983) provided insight into the political history of Egypt, especially the post-Nasser period, and clarified the confusion of extremist groups which operated in the Middle East.

Further Reading

The best works on Haykal are those written by Haykal himself, especially the three mentioned above: *The Cairo Documents, The Road to Ramadan,* and *The Sphinx and the Commissar.* A good biography of Haykal by Edward R. Sheehan is found in the introduction of the edition of *The Cairo Documents* published by Doubleday (1973).

Yaacov Shimoni's *Biographical Dictionary of the Middle East,* Jerusalem: The Jerusalem Publishing House Ltd., (1991) provides an encapsulated biography of Muhamed Heykal (sic) which is clear and detailed. □

Robert Young Hayne

United States senator Robert Young Hayne (1791-1839), a notable defender of the Southern states'-rights position, distinguished himself in the 1830 Senate debates on the nature of the Union.

Robert Hayne was born on a rice plantation in South Carolina on Nov. 10, 1791. He studied law and was admitted to the bar just before he was 21. In 1814 he was elected as a Jeffersonian Republican to the lower house of the South Carolina Legislature and 4 years later became its speaker. After serving as state attorney general for 2 years, he was elected to the U.S. Senate in 1822, with the backing of John C. Calhoun.

As senator, Hayne took a lead in opposing Federal efforts to increase the tariff. He attracted national attention and became the idol of the South when he joined Senator Thomas Hart Benton of Missouri in opposing a resolution to curtail the sale of western land. Hayne based his case on the argument that the Federal government lacked such power, for the territories were joint possessions of all the states. Any restriction on the sale of lands would be an infringement of the rights of citizens of the states.

Hayne's brilliant exposition of the states'-rights interpretation of the Union was forcefully challenged by Daniel Webster in 1830. In the course of their debates (waged for 2 weeks before crowded Senate galleries) the two men ranged over a vast number of topics: slavery, nullification, the basic character of the Constitution, and the objectives of the Hartford Convention of 1814. These speeches defined the arguments that would be repeated endlessly by Northern and Southern leaders until the Civil War.

Hayne withdrew from the Senate in 1832 to make way for John C. Calhoun, who had resigned from the U.S. vice presidency. Hayne next participated in South Carolina's nullification convention and then, as governor, prepared to resist if President Andrew Jackson used force to execute Federal laws. However, when a compromise tariff was proposed, Hayne promptly suspended action.

After one term as governor and one year as mayor of Charleston, Hayne concentrated on his business interests. He was an active promoter of the Louisville, Cincinnati, and Charleston Railroad Company, which sought to link

William Haywood was born in Salt Lake City, Utah, into a working-class family. His father died when Haywood was 3 years old. After a few years of school he took his first job as a miner in Nevada about 1884. He married, then floated from job to job, working as cowboy and construction worker but mostly as a miner.

In 1896, working in Silver City, Idaho, Haywood became a charter member of the local Western Federation of Miners (WFM). Demonically energetic, he held every office in the local union and was largely responsible for its success, helping administer its hospital and maintaining virtually unanimous organization of the miners. Also active in the WFM's central office, in 1899 Haywood was elected to its executive board. In 1900, elected secretary-treasurer, he left the mines for good.

"Big Bill" Haywood spoke for the militant, radical wing of the WFM and led the union's strikes between 1903 and 1905. In 1906 he was indicted for the murder of a former Idaho governor and, after being legally kidnaped from Denver, was acquitted in an internationally noted trial. Although eased out of the WFM after the trial, he had gathered a large personal following because of the publicity.

Haywood had joined the Socialist party in 1901 and was its candidate for governor of Colorado in 1906. Between 1908 and 1912 he spent most of his time on speaking tours in the United States and abroad. In 1910 he attended the International Socialist Congress and in 1911 was elected to the Socialist party's executive committee.

By 1912 Haywood was devoting himself largely to the Industrial Workers of the World (IWW), the "Wobblies," which he had helped found in 1905 as a revolutionary alternative to the American Federation of Labor. In 1914, after moderate Socialists removed him from his party post, Haywood became secretary-treasurer of the IWW.

Haywood traveled constantly, organizing for the IWW and leading the union's famous strikes at Lawrence, Mass. (1912), and Paterson, N.J. (1913). He impressed an administrative stability upon the erratic union so that by 1916 it seemed a permanent fixture on the American industrial scene. With World War I, however, the IWW was attacked by groups ranging from patriotic lynch mobs to the Federal government. Haywood and a hundred other "Wobbly" leaders were indicted under the Espionage Acts, and after a long (and subsequently discredited) trial Haywood was sentenced to 20 years in prison and a large fine.

In 1921, out on bail pending appeal, Haywood fled the country for the Soviet Union, where he was lionized for a short time. But he lapsed quickly into obscurity and lived forgotten on a small pension in Moscow until his death on May 17, 1928.

Further Reading

Haywood's autobiography, *Bill Haywood's Book* (1929), is reliable, if incomplete. The only full-length biography is Joseph R. Conlin, *Big Bill Haywood and the Radical Union Movement* (1969). Two good essays on Haywood are by Carl Hein in Harvey Goldberg, ed., *American Radicals* (1957), and by

Charleston to the major cities of the South and West. The Panic of 1837 curtailed development of the company, but the planned route was later used by the Southern Railway. Hayne died suddenly of a fever on Sept. 24, 1839.

Further Reading

Theodore Dehon Jervey, *Robert Y. Hayne and His Times* (1909), is the standard biography. There is good material on Hayne in Charles Maurice Wiltse, *John C. Calhoun* (3 vols., 1944-1951).

Additional Sources

Jervey, Theodore D. (Theodore Dehon), b. 1859, *Robert Y. Hayne and his time,* New York: Da Capo Press, 1970, c1909.
Winthrop, Robert C. (Robert Charles), 1809-1894, *Webster's reply to Hayne, and his general methods of preparation:* R.C. Winthrop, 1893 or 1894. □

William Dudley Haywood

American labor leader and one of his era's most notorious radicals, William Dudley Haywood (1869-1928) led the Industrial Workers of the World during that union's heyday.

Melvyn Dubofsky in Alfred F. Young, ed., *Dissent: Explorations in the History of American Radicalism* (1968). On the IWW, Melvyn Dubofsky, *We Shall Be All* (1969), provides a good narrative history, while Joseph R. Conlin, *Bread and Roses Too* (1970), focuses on specific problems of IWW history.

Additional Sources

Bird, Stewart., *The Wobblies: the U.S. vs. Wm. D. Haywood, et al.: a play,* New York: Smyrna Press, 1980. □

Rita Hayworth

In the 1930s, Rita Hayworth (1918-1987) was confined to leads in "B" pictures, but through much of the 1940s she became the undisputed sex goddess of Hollywood films and the hottest star at Columbia Studios.

Whether illuminating the screen with a song and dance or beaming from a magazine photo, Rita Hayworth was an unforgettable sight. Capitalizing on her inherited beauty and talent to become a legendary motion picture star, Hayworth captured the hearts of countless American servicemen during the 1940s. At her peak, she epitomized American beauty, and her career produced several memorable moments: dance routines with Fred Astaire in *You'll Never Get Rich* (1941); a glamorous photo in *Life* magazine; a scandalous striptease in *Gilda* (1946); and mature sophistication in *The Lady From Shanghai* (1949). While Hayworth's death in 1987 saddened America, it alerted the nation to the plight of those threatened by Alzheimer's disease, the illness that slowly killed her.

Born Margarita Carmen Cansino to Eduardo and Volga Haworth Cansino on October 17, 1918, in New York City, Rita Hayworth was no stranger to show business. Her father, a headliner on vaudeville, was descended from a line of famous Spanish dancers, and her mother, a Ziegfeld showgirl, came from a family of English actors. When the girl was nine years old, the family moved to Los Angeles, California, where the motion picture industry was rapidly growing. There, Eduardo taught dancing and directed dance scenes for various studios. She began her education at the Carthay School and later spent her first and only year of high school at Hamilton High. Throughout her school years, she continued family tradition by taking acting and dancing lessons.

At eleven, the girl found her first acting role in a school play, and by 1932, she had made her professional debut. She appeared in a stage prologue for the movie *Back Street* at Carthay Circle Theater. At this point, Eduardo Cansino decided that his attractive twelve-year-old daughter was ready for work. The perfect dance partner, she was introduced as Eduardo's wife when they danced at the Foreign Club in Tijuana, Mexico, for a year and a half, and then later on a gambling boat off California's coast. The "Dancing Cansinos" performed twenty times per week.

Makes Film Debut in Dante's Inferno

Rita Cansino, as she was called during this time, received her first big break when she was noticed dancing with her father in Agua Caliente, Mexico. Winfield R. Sheehan of the Fox Film Corporation hired the young woman, then sixteen, for a role in a movie starring Spencer Tracy entitled *Dante's Inferno* (1935). Though the film was not successful, Rita Cansino was given a year-long contract with Fox. During this year she held minor, ethnic roles in the motion pictures *Charlie Chan in Egypt* (1935), *Under the Pampas Moon* (1935), *Paddy O'Day* (1935), and *Human Cargo* (1936), in which she played Egyptian, Argentinean, Irish, and Russian dancers respectively. When her contract expired and was not renewed, the actress spent a year playing Mexican and Indian girls; she earned $100 for each role.

When Rita Cansino was 18, she married Edward C. Judson, a car salesman, oil man, and businessman who became her manager. According to the *New York Times,* Judson "transformed" the actress "from a raven-haired Latin to an auburn-haired cosmopolitan" by altering Rita's hairline and eyebrows with electrolysis and changing her professional name. Rita Cansino took her mother's maiden name, added a "y" to ensure its proper pronunciation, and became Rita Hayworth. Magazines and newspapers captured the image of the new Rita, who won the favor of Harry Cohn and a seven-year contract with his Columbia Pictures.

After fourteen low-budget movies, Hayworth was finally given a leading role. She was hired by Howard W. Hawks to portray an unfaithful wife in *Only Angels Have Wings* (1939), which starred Cary Grant. Good reviews of her performance attracted attention: she was borrowed from Columbia by Warner Brothers Pictures for the film *Strawberry Blonde* (1941) with James Cagney, and in that same year, she made *Blood and Sand* (1941) with Fox. Hayworth began to shine. According to *Time*, "something magical happened when the cameras began to roll"; the woman who was "shy" and "unassuming" offstage "warmed the set." The *New York Times* wrote that Hayworth "rapidly developed into one of Hollywood's most glamorous stars."

Hayworth achieved celebrity status when she starred as Fred Astaire's dance partner in *You'll Never Get Rich* (1941) for Columbia. She appeared on the cover of *Time* and was dubbed "The Great American Love Goddess" by Winthrop Sargent in *Life*. In 1942, she made three hit movies: *My Gal Sal, Tales of Manhattan* and *You Were Never Lovelier,* with Fred Astaire. As her career skyrocketed, however, Hayworth's marriage failed; she divorced Edward Judson that same year.

Marries Orson Welles

During the early forties, Hayworth's personal life improved and she established her professional allure. She married Orson Welles, the famous actor, director, and screenwriter, in 1943; they had a daughter, Rebecca, two years later. Hayworth was earning more than $6,000 a week as Columbia's leading actress. After she starred in *Cover Girl* (1944) with Gene Kelly, *Life* presented a seductive photograph of the actress wearing black lace which, according to the *New York Times,* "became famous around the world as an American serviceman's pinup." The *Times* also noted that, in what was "intended . . . as the ultimate compliment, the picture was even pasted to a test atomic bomb that was dropped on Bikini atoll in 1946."

Hayworth's fame continued to grow after she made *Tonight and Every Night* (1945) and *Gilda* (1946). Of these films, critics contend that *Gilda* is the most memorable. A scene in which Hayworth sang "Put the Blame on Mame" and stripped off her long, black gloves scandalized conservative viewers. It was testimony to her popularity that her 1947 film, *Down to Earth,* was included in a twentieth-century time capsule despite the fact that the film itself received some bad reviews.

Hayworth did not mind the attention she garnered. "I like having my picture taken and being a glamorous person," she was quoted as saying in the *New York Times.* "Sometimes when I find myself getting impatient, I just remember the times I cried my eyes out because nobody wanted to take my picture at the Trocadero." Hayworth's daughter Yasmin Aga Khan confirmed this in *People:* "Mother was very good with her fans, very giving and patient."

While Hayworth starred as a sophisticated short-haired blonde in *The Lady From Shanghai* (1948) with her husband Orson Welles—who also directed the movie—she was in the process of divorcing him. She was later quoted in *People*

as saying, "I just can't take his genius anymore," and in *Time,* she noted, "I'm tired of being a 25-percent wife." After making *The Loves of Carmen* (1948), she married Prince Aly Kahn, with whom she had been having an affair, in 1949. This was an off-screen scandal, for Hayworth was already pregnant with their daughter, the Princess Yasmin Aga Kahn. Although she was quoted in *Time* as saying, "The world was magical when you were with him," this marriage did not last as long as her second; the couple divorced in 1953.

Hayworth's career began to wane. After making the movies *Affair in Trinidad* (1952), *Salome* (1953), and *Miss Sadie Thompson* (1953), she once again entered a marriage (1953-1955) that would prove to be unsuccessful as well as destructive. This fourth husband, the singer Dick Haymes, "beat her and tried to capitalize on her fame in an attempt to revive his own failing career," said Barbara Leaming, a Hayworth biographer, in *People*. While Hayworth came out of her temporary retirement after her divorce to make *Fire Down Below* (1957), which met with some positive reviews, she had only a supporting role in the film *Pal Joey* (1957). Failing to maintain her glamour, this movie was Hayworth's final appearance as a contracted actress.

At this point in the actress's life, Hayworth's personal life seemed to parallel her professional career. She married producer James Hill in 1958 and divorced him in 1961. *People* reported that Hill had wanted Rita to continue to make movies instead of "play golf, paint, tell jokes and have a home." After the failure of this fifth and final marriage, it was apparent that Hayworth did not have good luck with the men in her life. While Hayworth was quoted in *People* as saying, "Most men fell in love with *Gilda* but they woke up with me," biographer Barbara Leaming asserted that these "doomed" relationships were due to Hayworth's abusive father, Eduardo Cansino. Leaming told *People,* "Eduardo raped her [Hayworth] in the afternoons and danced with her at night." In her biography of Hayworth, *If This Was Happiness,* Leaming elaborates on this revelation, which she says was given to her by Orson Welles.

Develops Alzheimer's Disease

While critics agreed that Hayworth gave one of her best performances as a traitorous American in *They Came to Cordura* (1959), they also noted that her trademark beauty was fading. As a free-lance actress, Hayworth found fewer roles. *The Story on Page One* (1960), *The Poppy Is Also a Flower* (1967), and *The Wrath of God* (1972) were some of her last films. Hayworth's 1971 attempt to perform on stage was aborted; the actress could not remember her lines.

Biographers, relatives, and friends now believe that the first stages of Alzheimer's disease were responsible for Hayworth's memory lapses, alcoholism, lack of coordination, and poor eyesight during the last three decades of her life. Although Alzheimer's, a disease which was relatively unknown at the time, was not diagnosed as the source of Hayworth's problems, it was obvious that Hayworth was ill. In 1981 she was legally declared unable to care for herself. Her daughter, Princess Yasmin Aga Khan provided shelter, care, and love for her mother, and sought to enlighten the public to the symptoms of the obscure neurological disease by helping to organize Alzheimer's Disease International and serving as its president.

Hayworth's mind slowly began to deteriorate. When she died in her New York apartment on May 14, 1987, she did not even know her own family. Nevertheless, the "All-American Love Goddess," as *Time* called her, was not forgotten by her fans. The *New York Times* reported at the time of her death that President Ronald Reagan, a former actor, stated: "Rita Hayworth was one of our country's most beloved stars. Glamorous and talented, she gave us many wonderful moments . . . and delighted audiences from the time she was a young girl. [First Lady] Nancy and I are saddened by Rita's death. She was a friend whom we will miss."

Further Reading

Leaming, Barbara, *If This Was Happiness,* Viking, 1989.
American Film, July, 1986, pp. 69-72.
Good Housekeeping, August, 1983, pp. 118-27; September, 1983, pp. 74-82.
Harper's Bazaar, November, 1989, pp. 156-59.
Ladies' Home Journal, January, 1983, pp. 84-89.
Ms., January, 1991, pp. 35-38.
New York Times, May 16, 1987.
People, November 7, 1983, pp. 112-17; June 1, 1987, pp. 72-79; November 13, 1989, pp. 129-32.
Time, May 25, 1987, p. 76.
Variety, May 20, 1987, pp. 4-6. □

William Hazlitt

The English literary and social critic William Hazlitt (1778-1830) is best known for his informal essays, which are elegantly written and cover a wide range of subjects.

Born at Maidstone, Kent, on April 10, 1778, William Hazlitt was the son of the Reverend William Hazlitt, a Unitarian minister. In 1783 the family sailed for America. Three years later, after preaching Unitarianism from Maryland to Maine, the Reverend Hazlitt returned to seek a home for his family in England. Eight-year-old William wrote his father that it would have been "a great deal better for America if the white people had not found it out." The family was reunited at Wem in Shropshire, where William grew happily until 1793, when he went to New College, Hackney, to study divinity. In 1795 he withdrew from New College, feeling unfitted for the ministry.

In January 1798 Hazlitt heard Samuel Taylor Coleridge preach in Shrewsbury and wrote that "until then . . . I could neither write nor speak . . . the light of his genius shone into my soul." Coleridge, however, later described him as "brow-hanging, shoe-contemplative, strange." That May, Hazlitt spent 3 weeks with Coleridge in Somerset, meeting William Wordsworth. That fall he began painting in London and in 1802 had a portrait hung in the academy. In 1802 he

lived in Paris for 4 months, studying painting in the Louvre and making his living expenses by copying his favorite masterpieces. He returned to England in 1803 and painted Coleridge and Wordsworth, from whom he now differed politically, since he nearly worshiped and they detested Napoleon Bonaparte. In May war with France was renewed, and Hazlitt was driven out of the Lake District, both for his pro-French views and because of a sexual involvement. In 1804 he made friends with Robert Southey and with Charles and Mary Lamb.

Hazlitt published *An Essay of the Principles of Human Action* in 1805, *Free Thoughts on Public Affairs* in 1806, and *Reply to the Essay on Population* and an anthology of parliamentary speeches in 1807. He married Sarah Stoddart on May 1, 1808, and lived for 4 years on her small property at Winterslow. In 1811 he gave up painting and in 1812 returned to London and gave lectures at the Russell Institute. In the same year, on Lamb's recommendation, he became parliamentary correspondent for the *Morning Chronicle,* then the leading Whig (Liberal) daily.

In 1813 Hazlitt began writing drama criticism for the *Morning Chronicle* but left it in 1814 for the *Examiner.* He also became art critic of the *Champion.* From 1814 to 1830 he was a regular contributor to the *Edinburgh Review.* From 1816 on he wrote political articles for the *Examiner.* There he expounded his idea that all nations are part of "the great society of mankind" and each must defend all against the aggressions of any single one upon the whole society. In 1818-1820 he lectured on English poets and in 1820 wrote drama criticism for the *London Magazine.*

Hazlitt left his wife in 1819, going to board at a Holborn tailor's, with whose 20-year-old daughter, Sarah Walker, he fell passionately in love. He analyzed his "insane passion" in the *Liber Amoris,* published in 1823. He got a divorce, but Sarah would not marry him. In 1824 he married a rich widow, Mrs. Bridgwater, and went with her on a tour of European art galleries, making friends with Walter Savage Landor in Florence. On his return to London his wife left him. In 1826 he was in Paris writing his life of Bonaparte, which was completed in four volumes in 1830. It disappointed his friends. He declared, "I have loitered my life away, reading books, looking at pictures, hearing, thinking, writing what pleased me best." Hazlitt died on Sept. 18, 1830, his last words being, "I have had a happy life."

Further Reading

Among the full-length biographies of Hazlitt are Percival P. Howe, *The Life of William Hazlitt* (1922; rev. ed. 1928; new ed. 1947), and Herschel C. Baker, *William Hazlitt* (1962). John Boynton Priestly, *William Hazlitt* (1960), is a short study. See also Marie H. Law, *The English Familiar Essay in the Early Nineteenth Century* (1934), and William Price Albrecht, *Hazlitt and the Creative Imagination* (1965).

Additional Sources

Albrecht, William Price, *William Hazlitt and the Malthusian controver,* Port Washington, N.Y.: Kennikat Press 1969.
Birrell, Augustine, *William Hazlit,* Westport, Conn.: Greenwood Press 1970.

Brett, R. L., *Hazlitt,* Harlow, Eng.: Published for the British Council by Longman Group, 1977.

Bromwich, David, *Hazlitt, the mind of a critic,* New York; Oxford: Oxford University Press, 1983.

Cafarelli, Annette Wheeler, *Prose in the age of poets: romanticism and biographical narrative from Johnson to De Quincey,* Philadelphia: University of Pennsylvania Press, 1990.

Chandler, Zilpha Emma, *An analysis of the stylistic technique of Addison, Johnson, Hazlitt, and Pater,* Norwood, Pa.: Norwood Editions, 1978.

Hazlitt, William, *The letters of William Hazlitt,* New York: New York University Press, 1978.

Hazlitt, William, *Liber amoris, or, The new Pygmalion,* Oxford; New York: Woodstock Books, 1992.

Hazlitt, William, *My first acquaintance with poets,* Oxford; New York: Woodstock Books, 1993.

Hazlitt, William Carew, *Lamb and Hazlitt; further letters and records hitherto unpublished,* Folcroft, Pa.: Folcroft Library Editions, 1973.

Heller, Janet Ruth, *Coleridge, Lamb, Hazlitt, and the reader of drama,* Columbia: University of Missouri Press, 1990.

Houck, James A., *William Hazlitt: a reference guide,* Boston: G. K. Hall, 1977.

Howe, Percival Presland, *The life of William Hazlitt,* Westport, Conn.: Greenwood Press 1972.

Jones, Stanley, *Hazlitt: a life, from Winterslow to Frith Street,* Oxford England; New York: Oxford University Press, 1991.

Keynes, Geoffrey, Sir, *Bibliography of William Hazlitt,* Godalming, Surrey: St. Paul's Bibliographies, 1981.

Kinnaird, John, *William Hazlitt, critic of power,* New York: Columbia University Press, 1978.

Lamb, Charles, *Lamb and Hazlitt: further letters and records hitherto unpublished,* New York: AMS Press, 1973.

Mahoney, John L., *The logic of passion: the literary criticism of William Hazlitt,* New York: Fordham University Press, 1981.

McFarland, Thomas, *Romantic cruxes: the English essayists and the spirit of the age,* Oxford: Clarendon Press; New York: Oxford University Press, 1987.

Park, Roy, *Hazlitt and the spirit of the age: abstraction and critical theory,* Oxford: Clarendon Press, 1971.

Priestley, J. B. (John Boynton), *William Hazlit,* London: Published for the British Council and the National Book League by Longmans, Green 1969.

Ready, Robert, *Hazlitt at table,* Rutherford N.J.: Fairleigh Dickinson University Press; London: Associated University Presses, 1981.

Stoddard, Richard Henry, *Personal recollections of Lamb, Hazlitt, and others,* Folcroft, Pa.: Folcroft Library Editions, 1976 c1875.

Uphaus, Robert W., *William Hazlitt,* Boston, Mass.: Twayne, 1985.

William Hazlitt, New York: Chelsea House, 1986. □

Martin Johnson Heade

Martin Johnson Heade (1819-1904), American painter, was a central figure in American luminism, a movement primarily concerned with the painting of light.

Martin Johnson Heade was born on Aug. 11, 1819, in Lumberville, Pa. He received his early training in painting from the primitive artist Edward Hicks. About 1838 Heade went to Rome to study; during the 2 years there he painted several portraits, which were exhibited later in New York City and Philadelphia. Again in Rome in 1848, he painted his only extant genre piece, the *Roman Newsboys.* A year later Heade traveled to St. Louis and Chicago; by 1854 he had moved east to Trenton, N.J. Later he was at work in Providence and along the Rhode Island coast, where he painted his first landscapes in a somewhat hard and flat style.

A new phase of development came in 1859, when Heade took a studio in New York City. There he formed a close friendship with the artist Frederic E. Church. Probably under his influence, Heade's work during the next decade became more dramatic, his subjects more exotic, and his colors more intense.

In the early 1860s Heade traveled often along the New England coast in search of subjects to paint, and he found them most frequently among the salt marshes. During a journey inland he painted one of his finest pictures of this period, *Lake George* (1862). Heade's luminist style was now characterized by firm draftsmanship, cool and clear lighting, and a sense of timeless suspension. While painting along the Massachusetts coast, he met the Reverend James C. Fletcher, who persuaded him to go to Brazil. There in 1863 Heade began a new type of painting—the scientific depiction of hummingbirds in their natural habitat. For his accomplishments he was knighted by Dom Pedro II, Emperor of Brazil, although a subsequent effort to publish chromolithographs after these paintings in London brought little success. By 1865 Heade was back in New York. Two years later he was painting in Central America.

During this period Heade began to paint still lifes, especially flowers—roses, orchids, and magnolias—an interest he maintained throughout the rest of his career. In the late 1870s he settled down in New York City for a longer period. His style became looser and more painterly, although he retained his sure sense for color, atmosphere, and texture. By 1883 he had bought a house in St. Augustine, Fla., and had married. For the most part he spent the last 20 years of his life in Florida. He still traveled, continuing to paint his familiar subjects up to his death on Sept. 4, 1904.

Further Reading

The most comprehensive work on Heade is Theodore E. Stebbins's exhibition catalog, *Martin Johnson Heade* (1969). It is carefully researched, thoughtful, and extensively illustrated. Prior to its publication, the standard but incomplete monograph was Robert G. McIntyre, *Martin Johnson Heade* (1948).

Additional Sources

Cash, Sarah, *"Ominous hush": the thunderstorm paintings of Martin Johnson Heade,* Fort Worth, Tex.: Amon Carter Museum, 1994.

Stebbins, Theodore E., *The life and works of Martin Johnson Heade,* New Haven: Yale University Press, 1975. □

Bernadine Patricia Healy

Bernadine Patricia Healy (born 1944) was the first woman to head the National Institutes of Health.

Bernadine Patricia Healy is a cardiologist and health administrator who was the first woman to head the National Institutes of Health (NIH) from 1991 to 1993. Known for her outspokenness, innovative policymaking, and sometimes controversial leadership in medical and research institutions, Healy has been particularly effective in addressing medical policy and research pertaining to women. She spent the early part of her career at Johns Hopkins University where she rose to full professor on the medical school faculty while also undertaking significant administrative responsibilities. She served as deputy science advisor to President Ronald Reagan from 1984-1985. In 1985 she was appointed Head of the Research Institute of the Cleveland Clinic Foundation where she remained until her appointment as director of the NIH in 1991. Healy was also president of the American Heart Association from 1988-1989 and has served on numerous national advisory committees. Her awards include two American Heart Association special awards for service and the 1992 Dana Foundation's Distinguished Achievement Award for her work on promoting research on the health problems of women.

The second of Michael J. and Violet (McGrath) Healy's four daughters, Bernadine Patricia Healy was born August 2, 1944, in New York City and grew up in Long Island City, Queens, New York. Her parents, second generation Irish-Americans, operated a small perfume business from the basement of their home. Healy attended Hunter College High School, a prestigious public school in Manhattan and graduated first in her class. At Vassar College she majored in chemistry and minored in philosophy, graduating summa cum laude in 1965. One of ten women in a class of 120 at Harvard Medical School, she received her M.D. cum laude in 1970.

Healy completed her internship and residency at Johns Hopkins Hospital in Baltimore and spent two years at the National Heart, Lung, and Blood Institute at NIH before returning to Johns Hopkins and working her way up the academic ranks to professor of medicine. During these years, she also served as director of the coronary care unit (1977-1984) and assistant dean for post-doctoral programs and faculty development (1979-1984). From there, Healy served the Reagan Administration as deputy director of the White House Office of Science and Technology Policy. President George Bush nominated her for director of NIH in September 1990 and she was later confirmed by the U.S. Senate. Her tenure with NIH ended when incoming President Clinton appointed a new director in 1993. Healy has been married to cardiologist Floyd D. Loop since 1985. With Loop she has a daughter, Marie McGrath Loop; her other daughter, Bartlett Ann Bulkley, is from her previous marriage to surgeon George Bulkley, whom she divorced in 1981.

Despite her various administrative posts, Healy has treated patients during much of her career. Her research has led to a deeper understanding of the pathology and treatment of heart attacks, especially in women. Her colleagues at Johns Hopkins described her as someone who often challenged conventional wisdom and created new directions in research. In addition, unlike many scientists and physicians, Healy viewed management positions as important and challenging. As she told Erik Eckholm of the *New York Times,* "I guess I tended to see those administrative issues, often seen as dreary work burdens, in terms of their broader policy implications." Healy demonstrated her administrative talents during her five-year directorship at the research institute of the Cleveland Clinic Foundation where research funding rose from eight million to thirty-six million dollars. Her responsibilities at the clinic, in addition to being a staff member of the cardiology department, involved directing the research of nine departments, including cancer, immunology, molecular biology, and cardiology.

Healy has manifested her talent and interest in shaping research policy through her many appointments to federal advisory panels, editorial boards of scientific journals, and other decision-making bodies. As the president of the American Heart Association she initiated pioneering research into women's heart disease and demonstrated that medical progress depends on the public and medical community's perception that there is a problem to be solved. Previously, heart disease was perceived as a male affliction despite the fact that it kills more women than men. Medical practitioners for years treated women's heart disease far less aggressively than men's, and most research on coronary heart disease (like most other medical research) used male subjects either predominantly or exclusively. Healy has set out to "convince both the lay and medical sectors that coronary heart disease is also a woman's disease, not a man's disease in disguise," she wrote in *New England Journal of Medicine.*

At the time that Healy was appointed director of the National Institutes of Health in 1991, the agency included thirteen research institutes, sixteen thousand employees, a research budget of over nine billion dollars, and was a world leader in bio-medical research. Yet when Healy assumed control, the agency was beset with problems, its effectiveness was in decline, and it had been without a permanent director for twenty months. Scientists were leaving in record numbers because of non-competitive salaries, politicization of scientific agendas (a prime example was the ban on fetal-tissue research because the Republican administration believed it encouraged abortion), and congressional investigations into alleged cases of scientific misconduct. The agency had been accused of sexism and racism in hiring and promotion. Low morale and bureaucratization added to the institute's problematic image. Healy brought an aggressive and visible management style to the NIH. Her appointment was viewed positively by many because of her outstanding experience in dealing with science policy issues. In addition, because she had been a member of a panel that advised continuation of fetal-tissue research, her appointment was also seen as a move away from politicized science. She also held a series of "town meetings" with NIH scientists to pinpoint problems and form committees to make recommendations concerning NIH research priorities. Furthermore, she initiated a large scale study of the effects of vitamin supplementation, hormone replacement therapy, and dietary modification on women between the ages of forty-five and seventy-nine. She established a policy whereby the NIH would fund only those clinical trials that included both men and women when the condition being studied affected both genders. She has written a book on the subject of women's health care, *A New Prescription For Women's Health: Getting the Best Medical Care in a Man's World* (1995).

Healy's policy decisions at times proved controversial. For example, Healy charged the NIH Office of Scientific Integrity (OSI), whose job it was to investigate ethical matters, with improper conduct, including leaking confidential information and failing to protect the rights of scientists being investigated. In response, the head of OSI accused Healy of mishandling a scientific misconduct case at the Cleveland Clinic Foundation. The allegations led to a hearing in 1991 in which Healy vigorously defended herself, as well as the changes that she had implemented at OSI.

Another controversy involved gene patenting. Despite the objections of Nobel Laureate James Watson, head of NIH's human genome project, Healy approved patent applications for 347 genes. She believed that patenting genes would promote, not hinder, the ability to access information about them and also spark much-needed international debate on the subject. A third controversy strained her relationship with the Congressional Caucus for Women's Issues. Healy lobbied against provisions in a congressional bill concerning the NIH that would make the inclusion of women and minorities in clinical studies a legal requirement, arguing that it represented "micro-management" of NIH. Attempting to negotiate a political compromise on another issue, she lobbied against overturning the Bush Administration's ban on fetal tissue research, despite her previous support for such research.

Healy has described herself as a life-long Republican and a feminist. She credits her father's belief in the importance of education for girls as the reason for her enrollment in an academically competitive high school—an unorthodox move for a Catholic girl during that era. In both medical school at Harvard and during her career at Johns Hopkins she was forced to deal with incidents of sexism. Among her achievements at mid-career point is her success in pointing out and undermining the subtle but pervasive bias against women in medical research. Healy continues to provoke both criticism and praise for the vocal stances and decisive actions that have defined her career.

Further Reading

Newsmakers: The People Behind Today's Headlines, Gale, 1993, pp. 35–36.
Chronicle of Higher Education, April 8, 1992, pp. A28–29.
New York Times, November 3, 1992, p. B2.
New York Times Biographical Service, December 1991, pp. 1285–1287.
Science, February 1, 1991, pp. 508–511; August 30, 1991, p. 963; September 6, 1991, pp. 1087–1089.
Washington Post, July 14, 1993, pp. A1 ff.
Working Woman, September 1992, pp. 61–63 ff. □

Seamus Justin Heaney

The poetry of Seamus Justin Heaney (born 1939) reveals his skill with language and his command of form and technique. In his poems, Heaney balances personal, topical, and universal themes. He approaches his themes from a modest perspective, creating depth of meaning and insight while remaining accessible to a wide audience.

Seamus Justin Heaney's attempts to develop poetic language in which meaning and sound are intimately related result in concentrated, sensually evocative poems characterized by assonant phrasing, richly descriptive adjectives, and witty metaphors. Critics note that Heaney is concerned with many of contemporary Northern Ireland's social and cultural divisions. For example, Irish and Gaelic colloquialisms are often intermingled with more direct and straightforward English words for a language that is both resonant and controlled. Viewing the art of poetry as a craft, Heaney stresses the importance of technique as a means to channel creative energies toward sophisticated metaphysical probings. He explores a wide range of subjects in his poems, including such topics as nature, love, the relationship between contemporary issues and historical patterns, and legend and myth. Although some critics debate Robert Lowell's assessment of him as "the greatest Irish poet since Yeats," they agree that Heaney is a poet of consistent achievement. Heaney was awarded the Nobel Prize for literature in 1995.

Born April 13, 1939, Heaney's childhood in a rural area near Ulster, Northern Ireland, informs much of his poetry, including his first volume, *Death of a Naturalist* (1966), for which he won immediate popular and critical success. In most of these poems, Heaney describes a young man's responses to beautiful and threatening aspects of nature. In "Digging," the poem which opens this volume, he evokes the rural landscape where he was raised and comments on the care and skill with which his father and ancestors farmed the land. Heaney announces that as a poet he will metaphorically "dig" with his pen. In many of the poems in his next volume, *Door into the Dark* (1969), he probes beneath the surface of things to search for hidden meaning. Along with pastoral poems, Heaney focuses on rural laborers and the craftsmanship they display in their work.

Heaney left Northern Ireland when the "troubles" resumed in 1969. After teaching in the United States, he settled with his family in the Republic of Ireland. The poems in *Wintering Out* (1972) reveal a gradual shift from personal to public themes. Heaney begins to address the social unrest in Northern Ireland by taking the stance of commentator rather than participant. After having read P. V. Glob's *The Bog People,* an account of the discovery of well-preserved, centuries-old bodies found in Danish bogs, Heaney wrote a series of poems about Irish bogs. Some of the bodies found in Danish bogs are believed to have been victims of primitive sacrificial rituals, and in *Wintering Out* Heaney projects a historical pattern of violence that unites the ancient victims with those who have died in contemporary troubles. In *North* (1975), which some consider his finest collection, Heaney continues to use history and myth to pattern the universality of violence. The poems in this volume reflect his attempt to tighten his lyrics with more concrete language and images.

The poems in *Field Work* (1979) concern a wide range of subjects. Critics praised several love poems dealing with marriage, particularly "The Harvest Bow," which Harold Bloom called "a perfect lyric." In the ten-poem sequence "The Glanmore Sonnets," Heaney describes a lush landscape and muses on such universal themes as love and mortality, ultimately finding order, meaning, and renewal in art. Other books of significance by Heaney include *Preoccupations: Selected Prose 1968-1978* (1980) and *Sweeney Astray* (1984). The former, which includes prose pieces on the origins and development of his poetry as well as essays on other poets, lends insight into Heaney's poetics. *Sweeney Astray,* a story-poem based on the ancient Irish tale *Buile Suibhne,* relates the adventures of Suibhne, or Sweeney, as he is transformed from a warrior-king into a bird because of a curse. The narrative follows Sweeney's exile from humanity and his wanderings and hardships as a bird, mixing prose descriptions of events with lyrical renderings of Sweeney's ravings as he responds to the harshness and beauty of nature.

Heaney's next volume of poetry, *Station Island* (1984), is made up of three sections. The opening part consists of lyrical poems about events in everyday life. The title sequence, which comprises the second section, is based on a three-day pilgrimage undertaken by Irish Catholics to Station Island, where they seek spiritual renewal. While on Station Island, Heaney ruminates on personal and historical events and encounters the souls of dead acquaintances and Irish literary figures who inspire him to reflect upon his life and art. In the third section, "Sweeney Redivivus," Heaney takes on the persona of Sweeney, attempting to recreate Sweeney's highly sensitized vision of life. Although critics debated the success of the three individual sections, most agreed that *Station Island* is an accomplished work that displays the range of Heaney's talents.

Further Reading

Abse, Dannie, editor, *Best of the Poetry Year 6,* Robson, 1979.

Begley, Monie, *Rambles in Ireland,* Devin-Adair, 1977.

Broadbridge, Edward, editor, *Seamus Heaney,* Danmarks Radio (Copenhagen), 1977.

Brown, Terence, *Northern Voices: Poets from Ulster,* Rowman & Littlefield, 1975.

Buttel, Robert, *Seamus Heaney,* Bucknell University Press, 1975.

Concise Dictionary of British Literary Biography: Contemporary Writers, 1960 to the Present, Gale, 1992.

Contemporary Literary Criticism, Gale, Volume 5, 1976, Volume 7, 1977, Volume 14, 1980, Volume 25, 1983, Volume 37, 1986. □

Lafcadio Hearn

Lafcadio Hearn (1850-1904), European-born American author, wrote novels and articles with exotic themes in highly precise and polished prose.

L afcadio Hearn was born June 27, 1850, on the Greek island of Santa Maura. His mother was Maltese and his father a British army surgeon of Anglo-Irish extraction. When Hearn was 2, his mother abandoned him to an aunt in Dublin, who later sent him to St. Cuthbert's College to prepare for the priesthood. There he lost his left eye in an accident; he lost much of his religious faith as well. His other eye, strained by incessant reading, bulged badly.

At 19, extremely short, disfigured, and psychologically maimed, Hearn arrived in Cincinnati, Ohio, where he eventually became a reporter for the *Inquirer.* In 1874 he married a local African American girl, breaking the Ohio laws against miscegenation. The marriage lasted 3 years and cost Hearn his job. Sent by another periodical to New Orleans, he found there the colorful, exotic ambience that would energize his pen.

By 1881 Hearn had become the successful literary editor of the *New Orleans Times Democrat,* to which he contributed local-color sketches, obscure folktales and legends, and translations of French writers. His first book, *One of Cleopatra's Nights* (1882), was a perceptive translation of six Théophile Gautier stories. He also contributed to *Harper's Weekly* and the *Century.* His literary propensities were becoming more obvious; he was attracted by the romantic, strange, and grotesque, but he presented these against real backgrounds or with real people. He published a book of obscure legends and stories, *Stray Leaves from Strange Literature* (1884) and *Some Chinese Ghosts* (1887). He lived for 2 years in the West Indies, where he wrote his first novels, *Chita* (1889), a Rousseauesque romance, and *Youma* (1890), concerning a slave rebellion. Both narratives illustrate his deft, polished, precise prose and emphasis on description which often overshadow the brittle and abstract plot and characterization.

In 1890 Hearn was commissioned to go to Japan, but shortly after arriving there he quarreled with his publisher and found himself unemployed. For a while he taught English at a government school in Matsue and freelanced newspaper articles. His life in Japan was greatly enhanced by his marriage to Setsuko Koizumi, whose family adopted him. As Yakumo Koizumi, Hearn found his final nationality and an estimable academic position as professor of literature at the Imperial University of Tokyo. During this happy period Hearn composed his best prose—minute examinations of Japan, its people, and its folkways: *Glimpses of Unfamiliar Japan* (1894); *Kokoro* (1896); *Gleanings in Buddha-fields* (1897); *Exotics and Retrospectives* (1898); *In*

Ghostly Japan (1899); *Shadowings* (1900); and *Kwaidan and Japan: An Attempt at Interpretation* (1904). He died in Okubo, Japan, on Sept 26, 1904.

Further Reading

Vera S. McWilliams, *Lafcadio Hearn* (1946), is the important biography. Also useful are Elizabeth Stevenson, *Lafcadio Hearn* (1961), and Arthur E. Kunst, *Lafcadio Hearn* (1970). The authorized study by Elizabeth Bisland, *The Life and Letters of Lafcadio Hearn* (2 vols., 1906), contains indispensable material but appears more apologetic than definitive. For perceptive criticism see Nina H. Kennard, *Lafcadio Hearn* (1911), and Edward Larocque Tinker, *Lafcadio Hearn's American Days* (1924; 2d ed. 1925). P. D. and Ione Perkins, *Lafcadio Hearn: A Bibliography of His Writings* (1934), is reliable but incomplete.

Additional Sources

Ball, Charles Edward, *Lafcadio Hearn: an appreciation,* Norwood, Pa.: Norwood Editions, 1976.

Bellair, John, *In Hearn's footsteps: journeys around the life of Lafcadio Hearn,* Huntington, W. Va.: University Editions, 1994.

Cott, Jonathan, *Wandering ghost: the odyssey of Lafcadio Hearn,* New York: Knopf, 1991; New York: Kodansha International, 1992.

Dawson, Carl, *Lafcadio Hearn and the vision of Japan,* Baltimore: Johns Hopkins University Press, 1992.

Hearn, Lafcadio, *The Japanese letters of Lafcadio Hearn,* Wilmington, Del., Scholarly Resources 1973.

Hearn, Lafcadio, *Lafcadio Hearn: Japan's great interpreter: a new anthology of his writings, 1894-1904,* Sandgate, Folkestone, Kent: Japan Library; New York: Distributed in the U.S. by Talman Co., 1992.

Hearn, Lafcadio, *Letters,* New York: AMS Press, 1975.

Hearn, Lafcadio, *Manuscripts,* New York: AMS Press, 1975.

Hearn, Lafcadio, *Some new letters and writings of Lafcadio Hearn,* Folcroft, Pa. Folcroft Library Editions, 1973.

Hearn, Lafcadio, *Writings from Japan: an anthology,* New York, N.Y., U.S.A.: Penguin Books, 1984.

Hughes, Jon Christopher, *The tanyard murder: on the case with Lafcadio Hearn,* Washington: University Press of America, 1982.

Kennard, Nina H., *Lafcadio Hearn; containing some letters from Lafcadio Hearn to his half-sister, Mrs. Atkinso,* Port Washington, N.Y., Kennikat Press 1967.

Koizumi, Setsu, *Reminiscences of Lafcadio Hearn,* Folcroft, Pa.: Folcroft Library Editions, c1978.

Kunst, Arthur E., *Lafcadio Hearn,* New York, Twayne Publishers c1969.

Noguchi, Yonâe, *Lafcadio Hearn in Japan,* Folcroft, Pa.,: Folcroft Library Editions, 1978.

Perkins, Percival Densmore, *Lafcadio Hearn; a bibliography of his writing,* New York: B. Franklin 1968.

Stevenson, Elizabeth, *Lafcadio Hearn,* New York: Octagon Books, 1979, 1961.

Thomas, Edward, *Lafcadio Hearn,* Folcroft, Pa.: Folcroft Library Editions, 1977.

Thomas, Edward, *Lafcadio Hearn,* London: Constable; Boston: Houghton Mifflin, 1912.

Webb, Kathleen M., *Lafcadio Hearn and his German critics: an examination of his appeal,* New York: P. Lang, 1984. □

Samuel Hearne

Samuel Hearne (1745-1792) was an English explorer who surveyed the Coppermine River, discovered the "Northern Ocean," and searched for the Northwest Passage.

Samuel Hearne was born in London, the son of Samuel and Diana Hearne. Upon his father's death in 1750 the family moved to Beaminster in Dorsetshire. The attempts of Samuel's mother to educate him seem to have failed: his spelling and grammar left much to be desired, although his mathematics was surprisingly reliable.

Soon after the commencement of the Seven Years War, Hearne joined the Royal Navy at age 11 or 12. He went to sea as servant to Capt. Samuel Hood, who had lived in Beaminster. Hearne's years at sea gave him useful experience for his future travels in Canada: he fought the French in 1759 and took part in bombarding the French coast. Thus, he grew hardened by the life and weather at sea. Perhaps, also, he gained some insight into the importance of navigation and the attendant sciences of geography and astronomy.

In 1766 Hearne joined the Hudson's Bay Company as a seaman, sailed from Churchill on summer whaling expeditions, gained a knowledge of Eskimo life, and sought a future as a master in one of the company's ships. But after 1769 the incompetent Moses Norton, the governor of Prince of Wales Fort at Churchill, sent him on three fruitless voyages in search of copper over what became known, after Hearne's discoveries, as the "Barren Lands."

Hearne's Three Arctic Expeditions

Hearne's first Arctic journey originated from Prince of Wales Fort and lasted from Nov. 6 to Dec. 11, 1769. It was poorly organized by Norton. Without knowledgeable guides, Hearne could not go into the vast spaces—Hudson Bay and Great Slave Lake. From this expedition Hearne learned that Indians could not be pushed and that he would not travel with other Europeans, for he had found them unable to take the hardships of travel in the Canadian subarctic.

Norton sent Hearne on his second expedition in February 1770. Again Hearne had a poor Indian guide, both in the sense of geographical knowledge and influence among his fellow natives. In August the party was plundered, and in latitude 70°N they became totally lost. The accidental breaking of Hearne's quadrant forced their return on November 25, for without this instrument he would have been unable to fix the exact positions of the Coppermine River according to instructions.

In December 1770 Hearne began his third and most important journey. In this he had a good guide, Matonabbee, and did his own planning. On July 15, 1771, Hearne reached the Arctic Ocean at the mouth of the Coppermine River, traveling en route via Artillery, Aylmer, and Contwoyto lakes. He was thus the first European to reach the Arctic Ocean overland from Hudson Bay. On this expedition he exhibited no great abilities as an astronomer, and the accuracy of his readings was justifiably questioned by contemporaries such as Alexander Dalrymple. Yet his principal objective—the examination of the practicability of exploiting the copper ore deposits near the river—was completed, even if the findings were negative. He returned to Hudson Bay on June 30, 1772, via Great Slave Lake and thereby proved the nonexistence of a Northwest Passage in the territory that he had traversed.

Hearne's later service in the company included founding Cumberland House in 1774, being in charge of Prince of Wales Fort after 1776, and defending it unsuccessfully against the French under La Pérouse in 1782. He died in England in November 1792 of dropsy.

Further Reading

The best work on Hearne's life and travels is his *A Journey from Prince of Wales's Fort in Hudson's Bay, to the Northern Ocean,* which appeared in 1795 and was subsequently edited by J. B. Tyrrell (1911) and Richard Glover (1958). His experiences at Cumberland House are recorded in *Journals of Samuel Hearne and Philip Turnor,* edited by J. B. Tyrrell (1934). See also A. C. Laut, *Pathfinders of the West* (1904), and Gordon Speck, *Samuel Hearne and the Northwest Passage* (1963).

Additional Sources

Lambert, Richard Stanton, *North for adventure:* Toronto, McClelland and Stewart, 1952.

Laut, Agnes C. (Agnes Christina), *Pathfinders of the West; being the thrilling story of the adventures of the men who discovered the great Northwest, Radisson, La Verendrye, Lewis, and Clar,* Freeport, N.Y.: Books for Libraries Press, 1969.

Speck, Gordon, *Samuel Hearne and the Northwest Passage:* Caldwell, Idaho: Caxton Printers, 1963.

Syme, Ronald, *On foot to the Arctic; the story of Samuel Hearn,* New York; W. Morrow, 1959. □

George Hearst

George Hearst (1820-1891), American publisher and U.S. senator, began as a prospector and acquired vast claims in gold and copper mines.

George Hearst was born on Sept. 3, 1820, in Franklin County, Mo. His boyhood work in the Missouri lead mines induced him to enroll in the Franklin County Mining School. He graduated in 1838. In 1850 he went to the California goldfields but found little gold.

For a time Hearst operated a general store at Nevada City, Calif., but an attempt to establish a branch in Sacramento proved financially disastrous. Returning to mining, he at last struck a paying prospect—the Lecompton mine—at Nevada City. In 1859 he joined the rush to the Washoe Valley of Nevada. In partnership with James Haggin and Lloyd Tevis, Hearst became owner of several of the most promising mines on the Comstock Lode. Hearst continually expanded his holdings and also acquired mining properties in Utah, Nevada, and California, and also in Peru, Chile, and Mexico.

By the early 1870s the firm of Hearst, Haggin, Tevis and Company was becoming the single largest firm of private mine owners in the nation. However, Hearst suffered severe reversals in the depression of 1873. Yet, at the very moment when his fortune seemed on the wane, he invested in what became the two most profitable mining ventures of his career: the Homestake gold mine in the Black Hills of South Dakota and the Anaconda copper prospect in Montana.

Like other business titans, Hearst made large contributions to political parties and ultimately sought public office. In 1865 California's pro-South element elected him to the state legislature. He served one term and cast the only vote against ratification of the 13th Amendment. He then devoted himself to business activities until 1882, when he sought the Democratic gubernatorial nomination and was narrowly defeated.

Needing a public forum to further his political ambition, Hearst entered the newspaper business in 1880, acquiring the *San Francisco Daily Examiner.* When he achieved his political goal 7 years later, he turned the *Examiner* over to his son, William Randolph Hearst.

In 1885 the Democrats supported Hearst for the Senate, but he was defeated by railroad magnate Leland Stanford. The following year, however, on the death of California's senior senator, Hearst was appointed to fill the vacancy. In

1889 he was elected to a full term. He died on Feb. 28, 1891, while serving in Washington.

Further Reading

Mr. and Mrs. Fremont Older, *The Life of George Hearst* (1933), is an official biography. Other works containing relevant material include Edith Dobie, *The Political Career of Stephen Mallory White* (1927), and Oliver Carlson and Ernest Sutherland Bates, *Hearst: Lord of San Simeon* (1936).

Additional Sources

Older, Fremont, *The life of George Hearst, California pioneer,* Beverly Hills, Calif.: William Randolph Hearst, 1933 (San Francisco: John Henry Nash). □

Patricia Hearst

Patricia Hearst (born 1954) was heiress to a wealthy newspaper publisher when she was kidnapped and held for ransom by a small leftist terrorist group in California. She was later tried and sent to prison, along with her kidnappers, on charges of bank robbery.

Patricia Hearst became an American celebrity, victim, and criminal in February 1974 when she was kidnapped by a leftist terrorist group, the Symbionese Liberation Army (SLA). This obscure Oakland, California, revolutionary group held her for a $2 million ransom. Patricia was the granddaughter of William Randolph Hearst , the wealthy California newspaper publisher, but during months of harsh captivity she was allegedly brainwashed and renamed "Tania." To obtain her release, her parents donated millions of dollars worth of food to the poor, but the giveaway became a fiasco and did not result in her release.

Urban Guerrilla

When Hearst was filmed in April 1974 assisting the SLA in a San Francisco bank robbery, the kidnapping victim was transformed in the public mind into another spoiled, rich college student whose unconventional lifestyle led to crime as a self-confessed "urban guerrilla" and "radical feminist." Patty was captured a year later during a police shoot-out. She was convicted of bank robbery in a sensational California trial in January 1976. On 24 September she was sent to prison for seven years, but President Carter commuted her sentence on 29 January 1979.

Public Skepticism

This was a major news story, but with a bizarre twist. The victim received little sympathy because the public was disgusted with assassins, radicals, and revolutionaries. The naive college student who became a gun-toting bank robber found little understanding or forgiveness. The story did not end when she was released from prison. Public fascination with the abduction of the newspaper heiress was stimulated by a 1975 biography, her own memoirs published in 1982, and a movie, *Patty Hearst,* in 1988.

Further Reading

Patricia Campbell Hearst and Alvin Moscow, *Every Secret Thing* (Garden City, N.Y.: Doubleday, 1982).
Patricia Campbell Hearst and Cordelia Frances Biddle, *Murder at San Simeon,* Scribner, 1996.
Don West, *Patty/Tania* (New York: Pyramid, 1975). □

William Randolph Hearst

William Randolph Hearst (1863-1951) was the American publisher, editor, and proprietor—for almost half a century—of the most extensive journalistic empire ever assembled by one man.

On April 29, 1863, William Randolph Hearst was born in San Francisco. He received the best education that his coarse-grained, multimillionaire father and his refined, schoolteacher mother (more than 20 years her husband's junior) could buy: private tutors, private schools, grand tours of Europe, and Harvard College. Hearst inherited his father's ambition and energy, but neither his father's fortune nor need to make his own way in the world. George Hearst had amassed millions in mining properties, which he left, not to his son but to his wife—who compensated for his crass unfaithfulness by wantonly spoiling their only offspring.

Young Hearst's journalistic career began in 1887, 2 years after he was expelled from Harvard. "I want the San Francisco Examiner," he wrote his father, who owned the newspaper and granted the request. The *Daily Examiner* became young Hearst's laboratory, where he indulged a talent for making fake news and faking real news in such a way as to create maximum public shock. From the outset he obtained top talent by paying top prices. Ambrose Bierce, at the peak of his fame, became Hearst's first star performer.

Building a Journalistic Empire

But to get an all-star cast and an audience of millions, Hearst had to move his headquarters to New York City in 1895, 4 years after his father's death. By this time his mother had liquidated $7,500,000 of her husband's mining properties and turned over the proceeds to her son, who immediately purchased the decrepit *New York Morning Journal.* Within a year Hearst ran up the circulation from 77,000 to over a million by spending enough money to beat the aging Joseph Pulitzer's *World* at its own sensationalist game. Sometimes Hearst hired away the *World*'s more aggressive executives and reporters; sometimes he outbid all competitors in the open market, as when he got Richard Harding Davis to report and Frederick Remington to illustrate the ongoing Spanish-American War.

The *Journal* had got its start by raiding the *World* of its talents and its readers. Next, to Arthur Brisbane's portentous

front-page column entitled "Today," and to black-and-white daily comic strips and colored Sunday supplements, Hearst added frenetic reporting of sports, crime, sex, scandal, and human-interest stories. "A Hearst newspaper is like a screaming woman running down the street with her throat cut," said Hearst writer Arthur James Pegler. Hearst's slam-bang showmanship attracted new readers and nonreaders, but on no one did the *Journal* cast so potent a spell as on its master of ceremonies.

During the last 5 years of the 19th century Hearst set his pattern for the first half of the 20th. The *Journal* supported the Democratic party, yet Hearst opposed the free-silver campaign of Democratic presidential candidate William Jennings Bryan in 1896. In 1898 Hearst backed the Spanish-American War, which Bryan and the Democrats opposed. Further, Hearst's wealth cut him off from the troubled masses to whom his newspapers appealed. He could not grasp the rudimentary problems raised by the issues of free silver and the war with Spain. Thus, for 5 years Hearst stood in the mainstream of the history of his time and did not even get his feet wet.

Entering Politics

Having shaken up San Francisco with the *Examiner* and New York with the *Journal,* Hearst established the *Chicago American* in 1900, the *Chicago Examiner* in 1902, and the *Boston American* and the *Los Angeles Examiner* in 1904. These acquisitions marked more than an extension of Hearst's journalistic empire, they reflected his sweeping decision to seek the U.S. presidency. However, he had chosen the wrong path to the wrong goal at the wrong time. To begin with, journalism and politics rarely mix; each is a full-time occupation. Furthermore, Hearst never even qualified as a great journalist. At most he was a showman whose very flair for a certain type of metropolitan journalism did him more harm than good in national politics. Finally, he had little preparation and less aptitude to win success in either field in the rough-and-tumble atmosphere of 20th-century America. The contrasts between his towering presence and his close-set eyes, his courtly manner, and his high-pitched voice did not present the typical image of a successful politician.

In 1902 and 1904 Hearst won election to the House of Representatives as a New York Tammany Democrat. But his journalistic activities and his $2 million presidential campaign left him little time to speak, vote, or answer roll calls in Congress. His absenteeism disgusted his colleagues and dismayed his constituents. Nevertheless, he found time to run as an independent candidate for mayor of New York in 1905 and, in 1906, as Democratic candidate for governor. His loss in both elections ended Hearst's political career.

The 45 years of anticlimax that followed gave ample scope to those defects of character, inheritance, and environment which a perverse fate had bequeathed Hearst. In 1903, the day before his fortieth birthday, he married 21-year-old Millicent Willson, a show girl with whom he had been smitten for several years, giving up Tessie Powers, a waitress he had supported since his Harvard days. The Hearsts had five boys, but in 1917 Hearst fell in love with another show girl, 20-year-old Marion Davies of the Ziegfeld Follies. He maintained a liaison with her that ended only at his death. He spent millions on her career as a movie actress, backing such sentimental slush as *When Knighthood Was in Flower* and *Little Old New York,* while ignoring her real talents as a comedienne.

When Hearst's mother died in 1919, he came into his patrimony and took up permanent residence on his father's 168,000-acre San Simeon Ranch in southern California. There he spent $37 million on a private castle. He put $50 million into New York City real estate and another $50 million into his art collection—the largest ever assembled by a single individual.

Hearst Publications

During the 1920s one American in every four read a Hearst newspaper. Hearst owned 20 daily and 11 Sunday papers in 13 cities, the King Features syndication service, the International News Service, the *American Weekly* (a syndicated Sunday supplement), International News Reel, and six magazines, including *Cosmopolitan, Good Housekeeping,* and *Harper's Bazaar.*

Yet, for all his getting and spending, Hearst had few powers to lay waste and none to hoard. Originally a progressive Democrat, he had no truck with the Republican expressionists—Theodore Roosevelt, Henry Cabot Lodge, Elihu Root—who supported the Spanish-American War, which Hearst claimed he had made but which actually had made his *Journal.* Hearst then fought every reform Demo-

cratic leader from Bryan to Franklin Roosevelt; he opposed American participation in both world wars.

In 1927 the Hearst newspapers printed unchecked, forged documents charging that the Mexican government had paid several U.S. senators more than $1 million to support a Central American plot to wage war against the United States. (Ironically, this fiasco led President Calvin Coolidge to appoint Dwight Morrow as ambassador to Mexico, thereby launching a new era in U.S.-Latin American relations.) From this scandal the Hearst press suffered not at all. Nothing was lost save honor, and that had gone long since.

In the next 10 years, however, Hearst's funds and the empire suddenly ran out. In 1937 the two corporations that controlled the empire found themselves $126 million in debt. Hearst had to turn them over to a seven-member conservation committee, which managed to stave off bankruptcy only at the expense of much of Hearst's private fortune and all of his public powers as a newspaper lord. He died on Aug. 14, 1951.

Some of Hearst's biographers have stressed his split personality—as if that differentiated him from the rest of mankind. The word "nihilist" provides a more precise clue. Not that Hearst's nihilism incorporated any of the revolutionary passion that impelled the Bolshevik Lenin or the destructive passion that impelled the Nazi Hitler. Hearst's nihilism had no more substance than Hearst himself possessed. In fact, no notable of his time left so faint an imprint on its sands.

Further Reading

Edmund D. Coblentz, ed., *William Randolph Hearst: A Portrait in His Own Words* (1952), is a compilation of Hearst's public and private documents. Judicious interpretations of Hearst's life are Oliver Carlson and Ernest Sutherland Bates, *Hearst: Lord of San Simeon* (1936); John William Tebbel's sympathetic *The Life and Good Times of William Randolph Hearst* (1952); and William A. Swanberg, *Citizen Hearst* (1961). Ferdinand Lundberg, *Imperial Hearst: A Social Biography* (1936), is a scathing attack. See also John K. Winkler, *William Randolph Hearst: A New Appraisal* (1955). □

Edward Richard George Heath

Edward Heath (born 1916) was Prime Minister of Great Britain from 1970 to 1974. His major achievement was to gain membership for Britain in the European Common Market.

The Rt. Hon. Sir Edward Richard George Heath K.G., M.B.E., was born in Broadstairs, Kent, on July 9, 1916, the son of a builder. He won a music scholarship to Chatham House (a grammar school in Ramsgate) and attended Balliol College, Oxford, where in 1939 he received a degree in politics, philosophy, and economics. Heath's political interests developed at Oxford. He was president of the Oxford Union and of the University Conservative Association. As a student he strongly opposed the aggressive foreign policies of Hitler and Mussolini.

Heath joined the army shortly after World War II began. In 1940 he was assigned to the Royal Artillery, where he advanced to the rank of lieutenant-colonel. His distinguished war record included time spent on the Normandy front and in the crossing of the Rhine River. In the immediate postwar years he began to prepare for a career in politics. He worked successively as a civil servant in the Ministry of Civil Aviation, as news editor of the *Church Times,* and for a merchant bank in the City of London.

In 1950 Heath was elected Conservative Member of Parliament (MP) for Bexley, Kent, a constituency that (taking into account changes in boundary and title) he continued to represent into the 1980s. When the Conservatives were returned to power (over the Labour Party) under Winston Churchill in 1951, Heath was appointed to a junior position in the government. Two years later he was made government chief whip, a position he held until 1959. The chief whip is in charge of party discipline, and Heath's skills at conciliation served him well. He helped to preserve the unity of the Conservative Party during the controversial Suez invasion of 1956.

In 1959, with Harold Macmillan as Prime Minister, Heath was appointed Minister of Labor with a seat in the Cabinet. A year later he became Lord Privy Seal. Then from

1963 to 1964 he was secretary of state for industry, trade, and regional development as well as president of the board of trade. These were years of transition within the Conservative Party. An older generation of leaders, including Anthony Eden, Macmillan, and Sir Alec Douglas-Home, was passing from the scene. Heath was among the younger politicians who were competing for the future leadership of the party. Though not an ideologue, he was identified with the moderate wing of the party on social and economic questions. Above all, he was a "European" who wanted Britain to join the Common Market. As lord privy seal, he conducted lengthy negotiations to that end, only to have President Charles de Gaulle of France exercise a veto in January 1963.

Heath was elected leader of the Conservative Party in 1965 in succession to Douglas-Home. At 49, he was the youngest Conservative leader in a century; he was also the first to be chosen by members of Parliament rather than private consultation. Although he was defeated by Harold Wilson in the election of 1966, Heath worked hard to prepare his party for power, emphasizing personal initiative and a reduction of the role of the central government as elements of modern conservatism. In 1968 he dismissed Enoch Powell from his shadow cabinet as a "racist" after the latter made an extreme anti-immigrant speech.

In the election of 1970 Heath won the prime ministership with a narrow victory over Wilson. From the outset he turned his attention to the unresolved question of the Common Market. He and President Georges Pompidou of France reached an historic agreement in 1972, and the following year Britain entered the Common Market. This attempt at unity with the continent of Europe was almost certainly Heath's major achievement in politics.

On domestic matters, Heath pursued a "quiet revolution" involving fewer governmental controls, reduced taxation, and the reform of trade union law. However, by 1972 he had reversed some of his policies. The Industrial Relations Act, passed in 1971, was not enforced effectively, and his Chancellor of the Exchequer, Anthony Barber, carried out a policy of increased expenditure to deal with rising unemployment. In February 1974, in the midst of a miners' strike that led to severe power cuts, the Conservatives were defeated in a general election and Wilson returned to power with the Labour government.

Heath fought and lost another election to Wilson in October, 1974. The following February he was replaced as leader of the opposition by Margaret Thatcher. After that he was on poor terms with Thatcher and lost much of his influence within the Conservative Party. He continued to be a vigorous spokesman for the Conservative "wets," who favor a consentual approach to social and economic problems and have generally been critical of Thatcher's policies.

Internationalist

Losing the General Election of October 1974 to Margaret Thatcher and the Party Election to Harold Wilson in 1975 did not remove Sir Edward Heath from political life, as he retained his seat in Parliament as the Member for Old Bexley and Sidcup. Thus, he was still a Member of the

House and of the ruling Conservative Party. As such, he chaired important governmental committees which determined national policy. During the 1990-1991 war in the Persian Gulf, Heath was the British government's negotiator with Saddam Hussein of Iraq, and succeeded in gaining the release of many British hostages.

Renaissance Man

Like the aristocrats of the past, Edward Heath cultivated his multiple talents to a high degree of skill. Not only was he an able negotiator and international statesman, but also a first-class recital and concert organist who conducted classical orchestras in Britain and on the Continent. He took up yachting when he was fifty years old and won the Sydney, Australia to Hobart, Tasmania Race, with his personal yacht. He was also chosen to captain the British Admiral's Cup Team in 1971 and 1979. He was a consummate politician, sportsman, organ virtuoso, journalist, writer and investment counsellor. He was truly a man of universal talents.

In April 1972, Edward Heath was appointed Knight of the Garter by Queen Elizabeth II, i.e., an ancient British title which elevated Heath to the peerage (British aristocracy). He had already been decorated with the Order of the British Empire in November 1965, for meritious service to the nation. He was now addressed formally as The Rt. Hon. Sir Edward (Richard George) Heath, KG, MBE. In Parliament he was termed the Father of the House of Parliament and, as such, he presided over the internal elections.

Sir Edward Heath figures in history as the man who brought Great Britain back into the European community of nations as Britain had been so many centuries ago.

Further Reading

Margaret Thatcher's two volumes of political memoirs presented portraits of Edward Heath as her political opponent, *The Downing Street Years* (1993) and *The Path to Power* (1995). For an encapsulated but detailed biographical listing of Edward Heath's achievements and positions held, *Who's Who 1997: An Annual Biographical Dictionary,* has all the facts chronologically arranged.

Although not an adequate biography of Edward Heath, George Hutchinson's, *Edward Heath: A Personal and Political Biography* (1970) provides an interesting portrait. The published accounts of Heath's tenure as Prime Minister have been generally critical. The best of these are Martin Holmes, *Political Pressure and Economic Policy: British Government, 1970-4* (1982) and Robert Blake, *The Conservative Party from Peel to Thatcher* (1985). Edward Heath has written three non-political books, all of which are entertaining to read: *Sailing: A Course of My Life* (1975); *Music: A Joy for Life* (1976); and *Travels: People and Places in My Life* (1977). □

Charles Heavysege

Charles Heavysege (1816-1876) was a Canadian poet and dramatist. He was one of the first serious poets to emerge in Canada, and his play "Saul" was hailed on its appearance as the greatest verse drama in English since the time of Shakespeare.

Charles Heavysege was born at Huddersfield, Yorkshire, left school at the age of 9, and was apprenticed to a carpenter and cabinetmaker. As a youth, he saw a production of *Macbeth* and bought a cheap edition of Shakespeare: Shakespeare and the Bible were the chief influences on all his own writings. Heavysege's first book of verse, *The Revolt of Tartarus,* appeared in England in 1852.

In 1853 Heavysege emigrated to Canada, settled in Montreal, and supported his large family by working as a cabinetmaker. A second volume of verse, *Sonnets,* appeared in 1855. His chief work, the long verse drama *Saul,* was published in Montreal in 1857. Coventry Patmore, reviewing *Saul* in the *North British Review,* ranked it as the greatest English poem published outside Great Britain. Hawthorne, Emerson, and Longfellow were all enthusiastic in their praise, and the play went into three editions.

In the 1860s Heavysege published six more books. In 1860 there appeared *Count Filippo; or, The Unequal Marriage,* a five-act tragedy in blank verse; in 1864, *The Owl,* a narrative poem in direct imitation of Poe's "The Raven," and *The Dark Huntsman;* in 1865, *Jepthah's Daughter,* a long biblical narrative in blank verse, and *The Advocate,* a historical romance in prose; and in 1867, *Jezebel,* another biblical narrative poem. In his later years Heavysege gave up his trade as a cabinetmaker and became a journalist, writing first for the *Montreal Transcript* and later for the *Montreal Witness.*

At its best, Heavysege's work is marked by its massive dignity, its acute analysis of morbid mental states, its descriptive accuracy, and its melancholy atmospheric effects. Perhaps because of his defective education, however, his taste was uncertain, and his dignity often lapsed into grandiloquence, his delight in subtlety into a kind of fantastic eccentricity. His language is often inflated in the manner of the pseudo-Miltonists of the 18th century, and he never overcame a tendency toward garrulousness and verbosity. Although his work is now seen to be somewhat pompous and derivative, he is of interest because, at a stage in Canadian literary history when there was little to encourage literary excellence, he persevered in his attempts to express his vision in memorable form.

Further Reading

There is no book-length study of Heavysege. Information on him is in Ray Palmer Baker, *A History of English-Canadian Literature to the Confederation* (1920); Desmond Pacey, *Creative Writing in Canada* (2d ed. 1961); and Carl F. Klinck, ed., *Literary History of Canada* (1965). □

Friedrich Hebbel

The plays of the German author Christian Friedrich Hebbel (1813-1863) combine realistic presentation with highly theoretical and philosophical principles.

Friedrich Hebbel was born on March 18, 1813, in Wesselburen, Holstein, the son of a poverty-stricken mason. Harboring youthful literary ambitions, he journeyed to Hamburg as the protégé of Amalie Schoppe, a popular writer. He failed to qualify for the university but met and established a relation with Elise Lensing, who later bore him two illegitimate sons. With her financial support he sought in vain to enter Heidelberg University in 1836 and then moved on to Munich.

After nearly 3 years of private study and privation Hebbel returned to Hamburg and completed a successful first drama, *Judith* (1840), a study of motivation in which altruism gives way to a self-centered desire for revenge leading to tragedy. A second drama, *Genoveva* (1840), treats the vicissitudes of a virtuous 8th-century Countess of Brabant. In 1843 Hebbel described his dramatic theory in the essay *Mein Wort über das Drama:* the individual ego, whether willing good or ill, must in its unavoidable drive toward expression conflict with the totality of mankind existing in the flow of time; that is, the developing individual inevitably clashes with historical development.

In the bourgeois tragedy *Maria Magdalena* (1844) the conflict originates for the first time, as Hebbel said, "within the bourgeois milieu itself," where custom and tradition exert a paralyzing effect upon the principals. After an Italian sojourn Hebbel settled in 1845 in Vienna and in 1846 married Christine Enghaus, a prominent actress. His subsequent career was successful and prosperous. Hebbel himself considered *Herodes und Mariamne* (1848) a "masterpiece." Here theory and dramatic effectiveness combine to expose the motives of two equally guilty and innocent principals, while the remarkable drama *Agnes Bernauer* (1852) depicts the innocently destructive power of great beauty in conflict with interests of state.

Hebbel's later dramas display a classicizing shift to verse. In *Gyges und sein Ring* (1854) he examines psychological motivation in ethical and religious terms, indicating how a Hegelian synthesis may emerge from antithetical views. His most ambitious undertaking is the trilogy *Die Niebelungen* (1855-1860), where, as he said, he sought to motivate in "purely human" terms the vital historical "turning point" when the Germanic peoples accepted Christianity.

Hebbel's verse tends toward the analytical and reflective, while his extensive diaries trace the development of his thought. He died in Vienna on Dec. 13, 1863.

Further Reading

The most recent full-length treatment of Hebbel in English is Sten G. Flygt, *Friedrich Hebbel* (1968). An excellent analysis of Hebbel's work is T. M. Campbell, *The Life and Works of Friedrich Hebbel* (1919). Useful background information on the development of 19th-century German drama is the "introduction" to T. M. Campbell, ed., *German Plays of the Nineteenth Century* (1930).

Additional Sources

Flygt, Sten Gunnar, *Friedrich Hebbe,* New York, Twayne Publishers, c1968.

Flygt, Sten Gunnar, *Friedrich Hebbel's conception of movement in the absolute and in history,* New York, AMS Press, 1966, c1952.

Friedrich Hebbel, Agnes Bernauer, Stuttgart: P. Reclam, 1974.

Garland, Mary, *Hebbel's prose tragedies: an investigation of the aesthetic aspect of Hebbel's dramatic language,* Cambridge Eng. University Press, 1973.

Gerlach, U. Henry (Ulrich Henry), *Hebbel as a critic of his own works: "Judith", "Herodes und Mariamne," and "Gyges und sein Ring,"* Gèoppingen, A. Kèummerle, 1972.

Hebbel, Friedrich, *Three plays,* Lewisburg Pa. Bucknell University Press 1974.

Kofman, Sarah, *Freud and fiction,* Cambridge, UK: Polity Press, 1991; Boston: Northeastern University Press, 1991.

Niven, William John, *The reception of Friedrich Hebbel in Germany in the era of national socialism,* Stuttgart: H.-D. Heinz, 1984. □

Jacques René Hébert

The French journalist and revolutionist Jacques René Hébert (1757-1794) published the journal "Le Père Duchesne" and was a spokesman for the sansculottes, the extreme republicans of revolutionary France.

Like other popular leaders of the French Revolution, Jacques René Hébert was a member of the bourgeoisie. He was born in Alençon, the son of a successful master jeweler who was a member of the municipal nobility. At the beginning of the French Revolution he was a destitute in Paris, but by 1790 he had established himself as a successful pamphleteer of political satires, appealing to popular antagonisms toward the nobility and the clergy. After the flight of the King, he attacked the Crown as the enemy of the Revolution.

In June 1792 Hébert founded the Revolutionary journal *Le Père Duchesne*, which became his vehicle for expounding his conception of proletarian interests and for venting his own frustrations. Its symbol was the caricature of a well-known braggart—a sinister-looking man, a revolver in one hand and a hatchet in the other, standing over a kneeling priest, continually calling for the death of the enemies of the people. On Dec. 22, 1792, Hébert was elected assistant prosecutor of the Paris Commune.

During 1793 Hébert became the advocate of sansculottism, which demanded all-out war against the enemies of the people. These enemies included the Church, counterrevolutionaries, profiteers, and political moderates. Although he has been associated with the dechristianization movement, Hébert claimed he was not an atheist. He maintained that all good Jacobins ought to see Christ as the first Jacobin.

Hébertists were closely linked to the program of the Terror. Their fierce hatred of those classified as "enemies of the people" was influential in the Law of the Suspects, which made official their demands for justice. Their demands for price-fixing and enforced consumer protection led to the Laws of the Maximum of September and December 1793. Hébertists were also fanatical terrorists, and their influence was great in the police apparatus of the Committee of General Security. As such, they were deeply implicated not only in the Reign of Terror in Paris but also in the massacres of Lyons, Nantes, and the Vendée.

Hébert's base of power was the Commune and the influence it wielded on the Committee of Public Safety. The Committee's actions in December 1793 in suppressing the Commune did much to arouse the ire of Hébert and the sansculottes. They began to attack the Committee, blaming it for the failure of price controls and for complicity with war profiteers. Finally, on March 4, 1794, Hébert—egged on by his supporters—called for an insurrection of the Commune. His call met with little success, but it served as a reason for his proscription as a counterrevolutionary. He was arrested on March 14, 1794, and was executed on March 24.

All historians have agreed that Hébert was an opportunist, but recently social historians have suggested that his opinions were widely held by the people. In particular, he seems to have been representative in his belief that by 1794 a conspiracy of sellers against consumers did exist.

Further Reading

Hébert's role in the French Revolution is discussed in Georges Lefebvre, *The French Revolution* (1930; 3d ed. rev. 1963; trans., 2 vols., 1962-1964); Ralph Korngold, *Robespierre and the Fourth Estate* (1941); Robert Roswell Palmer, *Twelve Who Ruled: The Committee of Public Safety during the Terror* (1941); and Albert Soboul, *The Parisian Sans-Culottes and the French Revolution, 1793-4* (1964).

Additional Sources

Slavin, Morris, *The Hébertistes to the guillotine: anatomy of a "conspiracy" in revolutionary France*, Baton Rouge: Louisiana State University Press, 1994. □

Ben Hecht

A leading American journalist and playwright, Ben Hecht (1894-1964) became Hollywood's most prolific and sought-after scriptwriter of his time.

Ben Hecht was born on February 28, 1894, in New York City, although he grew up and attended school in Racine, Wisconsin, where his mother owned a store. On graduation from high school, he worked as an acrobat and then owned and managed a theater.

In 1910 he went to Chicago, where he got a job as a reporter for the *Chicago Journal*. At the time there were seven news-gathering organizations in the city, so the competition was cutthroat. Hecht proved himself one of the best at getting exclusives, although his methods were at least unorthodox. On one occasion he was sent by his city editor to get a photograph of a girl who had joined in a suicide pact with a married clergyman; of course, reporters from other newspapers had been given the same order. But the dead girl's mother and brothers barricaded themselves in their home and refused to have anything to do with the press. The newsmen waited all day with no developments, and the others left. Noticing that the family had lit a fire in their fireplace, Hecht secured a ladder and some boards, climbed up onto the roof, put the boards over the top of the chimney, waited until the resultant smoke had driven the residents from the house, dashed inside, and grabbed a photo.

But at the same time as he was establishing himself as one of the wilder members of a wild journalistic fraternity, Hecht had hopes of making a reputation as a serious writer. Among the literary figures he met and befriended were the leaders of the "Chicago Renaissance," Sherwood Anderson, Carl Sandburg, Maxwell Bodenheim, and Vincent Starrett. He began to publish short stories in Margaret Anderson's *The Little Review*, the voice of the movement.

In 1914 he moved from the *Chicago Journal* to the *Chicago Daily News*, where he stayed for nine years, with a brief interval (1918-1919) spent as a correspondent in Berlin. It was during these years that he began to publish vignettes about Chicagoans, mostly the dispossessed and the

downtrodden. These pieces purported to be about real people, but in his autobiography Hecht later confessed: "It was not my talents as a news gatherer that I offered my paper but a sudden fearless flowering as a fictioneer. . . . I made them all up."

Many of these pieces were anthologized in his first collection, *One Thousand and One Afternoons in Chicago* (1922), but by that time his reputation had been solidly established by his novel *Erik Dorn,* the first of 11. Published to wide acclaim in 1921 and soon snapped up for inclusion in the prestigious Modern Library, *Erik Dorn,* the story of a newspaper editor and his loves, now seems sentimental romanticism more like 1891 than 1921. Hecht published many more volumes of short stories and sketches (a total of 17), and his early reputation as a *litterateur* rested principally on them.

He also had aspirations as a playwright, completing *The Egotist* in 1922, and began to write screenplays, winning an Academy Award in 1927 for *Underworld.*

In 1928 he joined with fellow Chicago newsman Charles MacArthur (later the husband of Helen Hayes) to compose one of the major American plays of the 20th century, *The Front Page.* The plot concerns an addled leftist condemned to death for murder who escapes on the eve of his execution and hides in the pressroom of the Chicago jail. While an emissary from the governor seeks to deliver a commutation, the venal mayor and the sheriff hope to deliver the escapee dead to ensure their re-election. The subplot involves a reporter who is about to marry and leave for a lucrative public relations job in New York and his city editor, who wants to keep him in Chicago.

Yet the whole play is really about the Chicago newspaper business and, in an epilogue often appended to published versions, Hecht and MacArthur wrote that their intention had been to expose "inequities, double dealings, chicaneries and immoralities which . . . we knew so well," but that they had ended up with "a Valentine thrown to the past, a Ballad . . . full of *Heimweh* and Love."

It was very much a *drame à clef,* with the mayor based on a combination of Fred Busse and William Hale (Big Bill) Thompson, Jr.; the hapless leftist, Earl Williams, based on Terrible Tommy O'Connor who, sentenced to hang in 1921, escaped and was never recaptured; Hildy, the reporter, on Hilding Johnson, a Swedish immigrant who rose from copyboy to top reporter; and Walter Burns, the city editor, on Walter C. Howey, for whom MacArthur had worked on the *Chicago Tribune* and the *Chicago Herald and Examiner.* Other acquaintances of the two show up in minor roles: Roy Benzinger of the *Chicago Evening American* appears as Bensinger, the hygiene-conscious reporter for the *Chicago Tribune.*

The great success of this play led its authors to Hollywood, where Hecht became the top script writer of the 1930s and 1940s. He won a second Oscar for *The Scoundrel* in 1935 and was nominated for four others: *Viva Villa* in 1934, *Wuthering Heights* in 1939, *Angels over Broadway* in 1940, and *Notorious* in 1946.

It is actually impossible to assess the totality of Hecht's work in the movies because so many of the films turned out in Hollywood's Golden Age were the result of collaboration, with one writer providing the script idea, another preparing the treatment, and two or three or four others writing the screenplay. Hecht showed his versatility by working on everything from gangster stories like *Scarface* (1932) and *Kiss of Death* (1947) to sophisticated comedy like *Design for Living* (1933) to arrant sentimentalism like *The Miracle of the Bells* (1948). He himself said that he was involved in more than 70 films, but he kept no close count and the total may well have been more than that. He never felt, however, that cinema was a significant art. In his autobiography he wrote: "I can understand the literary critic's shyness toward me. It is difficult to praise a novelist or a thinker who keeps popping up as the author of innumerable movie melodramas."

It was in 1939, at the height of his fame and influence, that Hecht became conscious of his Jewishness and began a fight which lasted for nine years to help found the state of Israel. As he put it: "I had before then been only related to Jews. In that year I became a Jew and looked on the world with Jewish eyes."

At that time he joined "Fight for Freedom," a group dedicated to taking the United States into the war against the Germans, and later began a column for the now-defunct New York newspaper *P.M.,* urging a moral outcry against the fate of European Jewry.

In 1941 he became a supporter of and fund-raiser for Irgun Tzevai Leumi, the most militant of the groups in Palestine trying to force Great Britain to turn that nation into a Jewish homeland. So successful was he in his efforts that the British declared a boycott against him and his work.

In 1943 in the *Reader's Digest* he published the article "Remember Us," the first generally circulated exposé of what was happening to the Jews under the Nazis, and in that same year, working with Kurt Weill and Billy Rose, he staged the pageant "We Will Never Die" on Jewish indomitability at Madison Square Garden in New York.

After the state of Israel was established, he became one of its foremost supporters in America and raised funds for the young nation until his death. He continued to write films and, in print, turned more to non-fiction. Ben Hecht died on April 18, 1964.

Further Reading

Hecht's autobiography, *A Child of the Century* (1954) is the best source, although it is rambling and unfocussed. Other autobiographical works include *Gaily, Gaily* (1963) and *Letters from Bohemia* (1964). The best biography is *The Five Lives of Ben Hecht* by Doug Fetherling (1977), which includes as complete a filmography as readers are ever likely to get. Also worth mentioning is *The Novels of Ben Hecht* by Ronald M. Roberts (1970), although now few would agree that the subject merits a book.

Additional Sources

Fetherling, Doug, *The five lives of Ben Hecht,* Toronto: Lester and Orpen, 1977.

Hecht, Ben, *The Ben Hecht show: impolitic observations from the freest thinker of 1950s television,* Jefferson, N.C.: McFarland, 1993.

Hecht, Ben, *A child of the century,* New York: Primus, 1985, 1982.

Hecht, Ben, *A thousand and one afternoons in Chicago,* Chicago: University of Chicago Press, 1992.

MacAdams, William, *Ben Hecht: a biography,* New York: Barricade Books, 1995.

MacAdams, William, *Ben Hecht: the man behind the legend,* New York: Scribner, 1990.

Martin, Jeffrey Brown, *Ben Hecht, Hollywood screenwriter,* Ann Arbor, Mich.: UMI Research Press, 1985. □

Isaac Thomas Hecker

Isaac Thomas Hecker (1819-1888), American Catholic churchman, was the founder of the Congregation of Missionary Priests of St. Paul the Apostle, known as the Paulist Fathers.

Isaac Thomas Hecker was born on Dec. 18, 1819, in New York to German Protestant immigrants. After 6 years of schooling he went to work. The family was close, and Isaac's mother was an admirable woman who greatly influenced him. Hecker's thoughts increasingly turned to religion and theology, and in his quest he sojourned at two utopian colonies, Brook Farm and Fruitlands. His mentor was Orestes A. Brownson, a Catholic convert and social reformer.

In 1844 Hecker converted to Roman Catholicism. He soon became a priest in the Redemptorist order, which worked with German immigrants. Frustrated by the crippling regulations of this order and finally expelled from it, he founded a new order in 1858 with St. Paul as patron. Hecker served as superior general of the Paulists until his death in 1888. Although plagued by ill health, he displayed prodigious energy—planning, directing, writing, speaking, traveling—all in the hope that the Roman Catholic Church might find itself at home in America and that increasing numbers of Americans might find their spiritual home in Catholicism.

Though the Paulists remained small in number, their influence was great. Hecker was not a rebel, but he held that a rigid authoritarianism would blight the development of Christian perfection. The Paulists demanded no vows of its members, shifting emphasis from rules to conscience and the guidance of the Holy Spirit. Hecker was convinced that the Church would prosper in the free environment of the United States and that the way to make Catholicism attractive to Protestants was by infusing it with the "American" spirit. He won converts by emphasizing partial agreement and inviting Protestants to inspect the virtues of the True Church, and by not denouncing all Protestants as heretics. A confirmed humanitarian, Hecker understood that the Church must serve man's needs and that Catholicism would spread to the degree that the Church's deeds matched its creeds.

Hecker was angrily denounced by conservative churchmen both in America and abroad. After his death the controversy over what some termed the heresy of "Americanism" (sparked in part by the French translation of an 1891 biography of Hecker) resulted in the condemnatory papal letter *Testem benevolentiae* (1899).

Further Reading

Biographical accounts of Hecker are Vincent F. Holden, *The Early Years of Isaac Thomas Hecker (1819-1844)* (1939), and Joseph McSorley, *Father Hecker and His Friends* (1952). For information on Hecker's order see James M. Gillis, *The Paulists* (1932). Robert D. Cross, *The Emergence of Liberal Catholicism in America* (1958), is an excellent examination of the "Americanism" question.

Additional Sources

The Brownson-Hecker correspondence, Notre Dame: University of Notre Dame Press, 1979.

Elliott, Walter, *The life of Father Hecker,* New York, Arno Press, 1972.

Farina, John, *An American experience of God: the spirituality of Isaac Hecker,* New York: Paulist Press, 1981.

Hecker, Isaac Thomas, *Isaac T. Hecker, the diary: romantic religion in ante-bellum America,* New York: Paulist Press, 1988.

Hecker, Isaac Thomas, *Questions of the soul,* New York: Arno Press, 1978.

Hecker studies: essays on the thought of Isaac Hecker, New York: Paulist Press, 1983.

Holden, Vincent F., *The early years of Isaac Thomas Hecker (1819-1844),* New York, AMS Press, 1974.

Kirk, Martin J., *The spirituality of Isaac Thomas Hecker: reconciling the American character and the Catholic faith,* New York: Garland, 1988.

O'Brien, David J., *Isaac Hecker: an American Catholic,* New York: Paulist Press, 1992.

Portier, William L., *Isaac Hecker and the First Vatican Council,* Lewiston, N.Y.: E. Mellen Press, 1985. □

Margaret Mary O'Shaughnessy Heckler

Margaret Mary O'Shaughnessy Heckler (born 1931) was an attorney, congressional representative, Secretary of Health and Human Services, and Ambassador to the Republic of Ireland.

Margaret Heckler was born in Flushing, New York, in 1931, the daughter of John and Alice O'Shaughnessy. She graduated from Albertus Magnus College, where she had been a political science major and active in student politics, in 1953. She met her husband, John, a stockbroker, while in college, and, although they were divorced in 1984, he was a strong supporter of her political ambitions during most of their 30-year marriage. The Hecklers had three children: Belinda, Alison, and John.

In 1956 Heckler was the only woman in her graduating class at Boston College Law School, where she had been elected editor of the Law Review. She entered Massachusetts politics in 1962 as the first woman elected to the Governor's Council. In 1966 she was elected as a Republican to the U.S. House of Representatives and represented Massachusetts' 10th District for 16 years.

Despite negligible support from the Republican Party, she had won her first term in the House and attributed her victory to the support of women constituents. Her campaign slogan, "Massachusetts needs a Heckler in the House," symbolized the frequently independent stance she took during her subsequent eight terms in Congress. During the Nixon administration (1969-1974) she criticized the president on such issues as the conduct of the war in Vietnam and cuts in federal support for child-care for children of working mothers.

During her years in public service Heckler demonstrated a firm commitment to supporting such women's issues as equal credit laws and the passage of the Equal Rights Amendment. In 1977 she helped found the Congresswomen's Caucus, "a bipartisan group of women in the House and Senate working on legislative issues 'to improve the rights, representation, and status of women in America.'" Concerns of the caucus included: revision of the Social Security system's treatment of women, improvements in monitoring programs and procedures specifically directed to women's health, displaced homemakers, sexism in public education, women in small business, domestic violence, legal rights for women, and older women. Heckler

was criticized by feminist groups, however, for her "right-to-life" position on abortion.

While in Congress Heckler also served on the House Committee on Agriculture, the Committee on Veteran Affairs, and the Committee on Science and Technology. There are those who saw her support for such programs as home health care as an alternative to institutionalization and co-sponsorship of Arthritis Institute legislation as preparation for her cabinet position.

In 1982 Heckler lost her congressional seat due in large part to re-districting in Massachusetts. In 1983 President Reagan nominated Heckler to be Secretary of Health and Human Services. The department had the third largest budget in the world ($274 billion in 1984) and 142,000 employees. The vast array of problems and issues facing the prospective secretary included discouragement of smoking, ethical problems in medicine and biomedical research, protection of the rights of handicapped persons, the cost of health care, studies about Agent Orange, the resettlement of Indochinese refugees, and the funding and administration of ongoing social programs such as medicare and social security.

In a statement made during Senate confirmation hearings, Heckler posed two goals for her administration: "First, I want the Health and Human Services Department to focus more on long-range problems and long-range solutions. Second, I want to be a catalyst for caring in America: for the young, the elderly, the sick, the handicapped and the needy."

During her two years as Secretary, however, Heckler was criticized for her inability to delegate authority, her combative personal style, and—by conservatives—for her liberalism. Supporters pointed out that her efforts toward reform were consistently hampered by budget cuts and by repeated attempts by the Office of Management and Budget to dictate Health and Human Services policy. Secretary Heckler targeted significant health problems such as AIDS, Alzheimer's disease, and breast cancer for research and commitment of departmental resources.

In 1984, Heckler divorced her husband in a highly publicized divorce trial which brought to light the strains put upon marriage by public life. John Heckler initially sued for divorce, claiming that his wife "deserted and abandoned" him twenty years previously; and Margaret Heckler, in a counter-suit, claimed a share of her husband's business since it had benefitted by her political connections in Washington.

In October, 1985, President Reagan asked Heckler to resign her Cabinet position and appointed her Ambassador to Ireland. Many felt Reagan was influenced in his decision by White House Chief of Staff Donald Regan, a critic of Heckler's performance at Health and Human Services. Heckler, who frequently spoke of her Irish descent, was seen as a suitable candidate for the ambassadorship.

Margaret Heckler's post as Ambassador to the Republic of Ireland lasted from December, 1985, until August, 1989. She retired from political office but maintained her affiliations with the Catholic Women's College Alumnae Association and the American Bar Association from her home in Wellesley, Massachusetts.

Further Reading

Biographical profiles of Margaret Heckler can be found in Hope Chamberlin, *A Minority of Members* (1973); Peggy Lamson, *Few Are Chosen* (1968); Esther Stineman, *American Political Women: Contemporary and Historical Profiles* (1980); and Judith Paterson and Lavinia Edmunds, "Cabinet Member Margaret Heckler: Reagan's Answer to the Gender Gap," *Ms.* (July 1983). □

Sven Anders Hedin

Sven Anders Hedin (1865-1952) was a Swedish explorer and geographer whose investigations in Tibet and western China make him one of the most eminent explorers of Asia.

Sven Hedin was born on Feb. 19, 1865, in Stockholm to professional, middle-class parents. He received his undergraduate education at Uppsala and in 1881-1883 studied at Berlin and Halle. In Germany he became a staunch admirer of Prussian ways and culture and continued so throughout his life. Also, he came under the influ-

ence of the distinguished explorer of China, F. P. W. von Richthofen, and decided to devote his career to opening up unexplored areas of the map of Asia.

Hedin's first chance came in 1885, when he became a private tutor in Baku, a post that allowed him to travel in Mesopotamia and Persia. In 1890 he was appointed Sweden's ambassador to Persia and received support from King Oscar II for a trip to the Chinese border. Starting in 1891 from Teheran, he crossed the Khurasan region and Bukhara to Samarkand, reaching Kashgar in Sinkiang.

Early Explorations

Between 1893 and 1932 Hedin led five major expeditions and several lesser ones. The first (1893-1897) started from Orenburg, crossed the Ural and Pamir mountains, went over the Takla Maklan Desert twice, the second trip nearly proving fatal, and reached Lop Nor, the great salt lake of the ancient Chinese geographers. From kashgar he visited the Pamirs again and then made his first entry into Tibet. After returning to Khotan, he followed the Tarim River to Lop Nor, crossed Inner Mongolia, and arrived at Peking. He had covered 6,300 miles in 1,300 days.

On the second journey (1899-1902) Hedin followed the Tarim River, crossed the desert, visited Lop Nor, and discovered the ruins of the archeologically important ancient city Loulan. The Lama turned the expedition back before they reach Lhasa, and they had to cross the Karakoram Range to kashgar in order to return to Europe. The main achievement was to study the mystery of the

"wandering" lake, Lop Nor. It had been visited first by Nikolai Przhevalsky and later by four other expeditions before Hedin offered his solution, now accepted, that the ancient lake had not changed its location but had dried up and been replaced by new, small lakes.

On Hedin's greatest journey (1906-1908) he crossed Persia and Afghanistan, entered Tibet, and identified the true sources of the Indus, Sutlej, and Brahmaputra rivers. He discovered and mapped the Transhimalayan Mountains, crossing the range eight times and overcoming formidable obstacles of winter weather, mountain passes never crossed before, and hostile local tribesmen, who kept Hedin prisoner for a time.

Travel was not easy during World War I, but Hedin did make short trips in the Middle East. His vigorous support of the German cause lost him the confidence of the governments of India, Russia, and China and hampered his exploration for some years.

Last Travels

Hedin's fourth journey (1923-1924) was a trip around the world, through the United States, Mongolia, and the Soviet Union.

Hedin's last big expedition (1928-1932) was a joint Swedish-Chinese-German effort. It made surveys in Mongolia, western kansu, Sinkiang, and the Gobi Desert, making extensive use of motor vehicles. His last trip (1934, aged 69) was to retrace some of the old silk-caravan routes in China.

After 1934 Hedin ceased traveling in order to write. He also became involved politically in support of Germany and in 1944 traveled to Munich to receive an honorary doctorate. During his lifetime Hedin was recognized as a great explorer. He was given their highest awards by leading geographical societies; made a Swedish noble (1902); elected one of the 18 members of the Swedish Academy; and knighted by India (1909).

Hedin's style of travel was to rely on small parties assisted by well-chosen natives. He had great physical strength and moral courage, with the originality to recognize great problems and the ingenuity to solve them. He never married, and he died in Stockholm on Nov. 26, 1952.

Further Reading

Hedin's autobiography is *My Life as an Explorer* (1925). A biographical study of Hedin appears in John L. Cook, *Six Great Travellers: Smith, Anson, Stanhope, Stanley, Fawcett, Hedin* (1960). Charles E. Key, *The Story of Twentieth-Century Exploration* (1938), has a section of Hedin's Tibetan adventures.

Additional Sources

Hedin, Sven Anders, *My life as an explorer,* Hong Kong; New York: Oxford University Press, 1991.
Hedin, Sven Anders, *Sven Hedin as artist: for the centenary of Sven Hedin's birth,* Stockholm: Sven Hedins Stiftelse: Statens Etnografiska Museum, 1964.
Hedin, Sven Anders, *Trans-Himalaya; discoveries and adventures in Tibet,* New York, Greenwood Press 1968.
Kish, George, *To the heart of Asia: the life of Sven Hedin,* Ann Arbor: University of Michigan Press, 1984. □

Hugh Hefner

Hugh Hefner (born 1926), founder and publisher of *Playboy* magazine, helped usher in a new era of openness in American Culture.

When *Playboy* first hit the newsstands in 1953, it represented a new openness about sexuality that was beginning to influence American life. The magazine, which was the brainchild of a would-be cartoonist from Chicago named Hugh Hefner, was originally to be called "Stag Party," but Hefner, who wanted to suggest sophistication as well as high living and wild parties, eventually settled on *Playboy*. Hefner hoped to make his magazine the equal of others that featured female nudity as well as articles, such as *Esquire,* for which Hefner had also worked and which had recently stopped featuring suggestive photography.

Marilyn Monroe

Playboy was an instant sensation, mainly because Hefner had shrewdly purchased a nude photograph of actress Marilyn Monroe; it had been taken before her success in Hollywood, and Hefner used it as the centerfold of his first issue. Monroe was a star by the time the magazine was published, and the first issue sold out quickly. That issue included an editorial by Hefner that espoused the *Playboy* philosophy that was to become familiar over the years:

> We like our apartment. We enjoy mixing up cocktails and an *hors d'oeuvre* or two, putting a little mood music on the phonograph and inviting in a female acquaintance for a quiet discussion on Picasso, Nietzsche, jazz, sex. . . . . If we are able to give the American male a few extra laughs and a little diversion from the anxieties of the Atomic Age, we'll feel we've justified our existence.

Trappings of Success

The immediate success of the magazine prompted Hefner to establish a proper office and staff for the magazine, and as of the fourth issue the *Playboy* empire was officially under way. Hefner's devotion to the magazine in its early years precipitated the breakup of his marriage: Hefner and his wife Millie were separated in 1957 and divorced in 1959. As he and his wife became increasingly estranged, Hefner and his associates began to embody the life-style about which they wrote, having almost weekly parties at the *Playboy* editorial offices. When the success of the magazine came to the attention of the mainstream public, Hefner was happy to portray himself as the playboy his magazine described. In 1959 he even hosted the television series "Playboy's Penthouse," a weekly talk show set in a bachelor pad, featuring plenty of the magazine's "playmates" and celebrities such as comedian Lenny Bruce and singers Ella Fitzgerald and Nat King Cole.

"We're extremely popular on the Internet and are going to be launching a pay site. You can actually get an electronic version of the magazine and go through archival things. We are also launching a Playmate fan club in which you can get information, download images and communicate with Playmates from all through the decades." But as a parent himself, Hefner believes that parents should be empowered with a device to block their children from viewing certain Internet features. □

Georg Wilhelm Friedrich Hegel

The German philosopher and educator Georg Wilhelm Friedrich Hegel (1770-1831) took all of knowledge as his domain and made original contributions to the understanding of history, law, logic, art, religion, and philosophy.

L iving in a time of geniuses and revolutions, G. W. F. Hegel claimed his own work to be not so much a revolution as the consummation of human development, and not so much the product of genius as the final expression of all philosophy up to that time. Among the great figures living then were the writers Johann Wolfgang von Goethe, Gotthold Ephraim Lessing, and Novalis; the philosophers Immanuel Kant, Jean Jacques Rousseau, Johann Gottlieb Fichte, and F. W. J. von Schelling; and the composers Wolfgang Amadeus Mozart and Ludwig van Beethoven. When Hegel was 19 the French Revolution began, and for most of his lifetime all Europe was in foment.

Hegel was born in Stuttgart on Aug. 27, 1770, the son of an official serving the Duke of Württemberg. He received a classical education and was a precocious pupil. Urged by his Pietist father to enter the clergy, he registered in the Tübingen Lutheran seminary in 1788. A fair student, Hegel generally preferred the conviviality of cafés and country walks to scholarly asceticism. His love of wine and company, his passion for the secular writings of Jean Jacques Rousseau, and his interest in practical political matters prevailed over the stern demands of a religious calling. Nevertheless, he studied philosophy for 2 years and theology for 3, completing his theological examination in 1793.

At the seminary Hegel read deeply in German poetry and Greek literature, in the company of Friedrich Hölderlin, the poet, and Schelling, who was to reach early eminence as a philosopher of romanticism. The three friends professed ardent sympathy with the French Revolution and took for their motto "Freedom and Reason."

Employment as Tutor

For the next 3 1/2 years Hegel was engaged as a private tutor in Berne. Though his duties left him little time for study and writing, he acquainted himself with the Bernese political situation. His first published work, in 1798, consisted of

Pursuit of Pleasure

For Hefner, his magazine and image were responses to the new mood of the country. He felt that the puritan ethic was eroding and that the pursuit of pleasure and material gain was the way of life for many Americans. As Hefner has been quoted, "If you had to sum up the idea of *Playboy,* it is antipuritanism. Not just in regard to sex, but the whole range of play and pleasure." For many the *Playboy* philosophy proved to be a welcome antidote from the repressive atmosphere of the 1950s. Over the years it has continued to have its followers, and Hefner's small magazine for men has become an empire extending well beyond magazine publishing.

New Directions

In the 1990s, the glamorous life-style at the Playboy Mansion began to change. After suffering a minor stroke in 1985, Hefner reevaluated his life and made several dramatic modifications to his life-style. Gone were the all-night pool-side parties, replaced with more restrained celebrations, and in 1988, Hefner turned over the business operations of Playboy Enterprises to his daughter Christie, one of two children he had with his first wife. After a second marriage to a former Playmate of the Year produced two sons, Hefner continued to enjoy his new role as a husband and father.

He also decided to focus on electronic communication, particularly the Internet, to promote his magazine. In 1996 Hefner told Associated Press writer Jeff Wilson,

notes accompanying his translation of letters by an exiled Bernese lawyer criticizing the city's oligarchy.

Thanks to Hölderlin's initiative, in 1797 Hegel was rescued from his cheerless situation through an appointment as a private tutor in Frankfurt. His employer owned a fine library and allowed him time to be with friends, especially Hölderlin. Most importantly, he had time to write. Among his many concerns were the "conditions of profit and property" in England, the history of Christianity, love, the Prussian penal code, and theology. Some of his Frankfurt writings were published posthumously by Hermann Nohl (1907) and were translated by T. M. Knox and R. Kroner in *Early Theological Writings* (1948).

Hegel's father died in January 1799, leaving a legacy that enabled him to leave tutoring and prepare seriously for an academic career. In 1801 he lived with Schelling, already a professor, at the great University of Jena. There he worked fervently; he wrote a detailed, critical study of the Constitution of the German Empire and completed his first published book, *The Difference between Fichte's and Schelling's Systems of Philosophy* (1801). Challenging the popular view that Fichte and Schelling were master and disciple, Hegel brought out their obscured but basic differences. Each, to be sure, had made significant discoveries; but both were ingenious at the expense of systematic thoroughness. Recognizing that their philosophies were irreconcilable on their own terms, Hegel resolved to work out a complete system that would account for the common aim and many differences of previous philosophies. Hegel's would have to be the system of all philosophy.

In 1801 Hegel also submitted a Latin dissertation on the orbits of the planets and consequently was granted the right to teach in any German university (the *venia legendi*). He began to give lectures at Jena and eventually became one of the better-known lecturers. A student wrote about him later: "Hegel succeeded in captivating his students with the intensity of his speculation. . . . [His eyes] were large but introverted, the refracted gaze filled with deep ideality, which at certain moments would exert a visible and poignant power. . . . The earnestness in his noble features at first had something that, although not intimidating, kept others at a distance; but the gentleness and amiability of his expression were winning and inviting." In addition to teaching and writing, Hegel worked with Schelling to found and edit the *Kritisches Journal der Philosophie* (1802-1803), to which he contributed several articles and reviews.

Phenomenology of Spirit

While at Jena the idea of a wholly reconciling philosophy was gestating in Hegel's mind. It came to fruition in 1806 as the dense but exciting tome called *Phänomenologie des Geistes* (*Phenomenology of Spirit*). It is the reflective study (*logos*) of the historical self-manifestation (*phenomenon*) of the Spirit, which all men have in common.

The stages in the development of the general Spirit, as shown in the conflicts and reconciliations of history, are also the stages of the individual's growth. Thus, the *Phenomenology of Spirit* can be read as a discipline of self-education, through which the individual absorbs and prepares to go beyond the present development of Spirit. The *Phenomenology* develops from the simplest level of experience, sense perception, to the richest, here called "absolute knowledge."

This movement of Spirit is "dialectical"; that is, Spirit develops in stages, undergoing successions of internal opposition and reconciliation. The stages must necessarily evolve in a continuous pattern, omitting none. There can be no short cuts to truth—a point Hegel stressed in criticizing romantic philosophers. The dialectical process of Spirit is always going on; it is what is "most real," though men are rarely conscious of it. Hegel's achievement was to cast the universal experience in the language appropriate to it, enabling consciousness to grasp it.

The entire book was written in haste and was completed on October 13, the very day Napoleon and his troops occupied Jena. Later, Hegel said of Napoleon, "It is truly a wonderful sensation to see such an individual, concentrated here on a single point, astride a single horse, yet reaching across the world and ruling it."

Since the university was in disarray and his own financial situation desperate, Hegel arranged through his friend F. I. Niethammer to become editor of a newspaper, the *Bamberger Zeitung*. He held this position for a year, and on Nov. 15, 1808, thanks once again to Niethammer, he was appointed headmaster of the gymnasium, or secondary school, at Nuremberg.

For 8 years Hegel taught philosophy and occasionally Greek literature and calculus. His administration was conservative and effective, but the position was ill-suited to his genius. In 1811 Hegel married Marie von Tucher, only 20 years old, after a tender courtship. Soon a daughter was born to them, but she died only a few months later. Then, in 1813, a son, Karl, was born, and a year later a second son, Immanuel. Hegel had had another son, Ludwig, born in 1807 to his landlord's wife; in 1816 Hegel invited him to join his household.

Science of Logic

While at Nuremberg, Hegel completed his second major work, *Wissenschaft der Logik* (*Science of Logic*), publishing part I of the first volume in 1811. Part II appeared in 1813, and the second volume in 1816. This difficult book presents the science of thought, purified of all reference to experience, to acts, or to facts of nature. In fact, the *Logic* consists of a closed series of "thought determinations"—for example, quantity and quality, form and matter—and displays both the differences between them and the way each meshes with every other. This pure science "contains thought insofar as it is just as much the thing in itself, or the thing in itself insofar as it is just as much pure thought." In other words, the *Logic* deals with reality, not solely with man's instruments for knowing or discussing it. "Logic [is] . . . the system of pure reason . . . the kingdom of pure thought. This kingdom is the truth as it is, without covering, in and for itself." But this kingdom of pure thought, for Hegel, presupposes man's rootedness in the complex, developing world of experience. The *Phenomenology* and the *Logic,* then, are interdependent portions of a single system. The study of logic, Hegel says, "is the absolute education and discipline of consciousness."

Heidelberg and the Encyclopedia

In 1816 Hegel was called to the University of Heidelberg. In his opening lecture he remarked that the peace following on Napoleon's exile might revive "the courage of truth, a faith in the power of the spirit," which is the "prime requirement of philosophy." "Man, being spirit, may and should consider himself worthy of the highest . . . if he retains this faith, nothing will be so hard and unyielding that it will not open up to him." Feeling the need for a restatement and improvement of his earlier work, he published *The Encyclopedia of the Philosophical Sciences in Outline* (1817). This summary of his system was later revised considerably, in 1827 and again in 1830. The book began with a section on logic, followed by "the philosophy of nature" and "the philosophy of spirit," and concluded with the self-knowledge vouchsafed only to philosophy. Another name for this self-knowledge is freedom. Since philosophy includes every kind of knowledge, true freedom is not separation but the most complete relatedness. The free man is actively at home in and with both nature and history.

Berlin and Fame

In 1817 Hegel was granted a professorship at Berlin. There he quickly found himself the center of a following, though he was hardly a seeker of followers. On the contrary, he took pains to discourage what he called "tutelage." It is

reported, moreover, that he preferred the company of affable and urbane folk to that of earnest intellectuals.

By this time Hegel's enthusiasm for the French Revolution had waned, and to some it appeared that he was an apologist for Prussian reaction. However, his major political work—the only book he published while at Berlin—confounds such a simple interpretation. Here he insists, "Whatever happens, every individual is a child of his time; so philosophy too is its own time apprehended in thought." It is for statesmen, not philosophers, to prescribe for tomorrow. Published in 1821, the book has a double title: *Naturrecht und Staatswissenschaft im Grundrisse* and *Grundlinien der Philosophie des Rechts* (translated by T. M. Knox as *Hegel's Philosophy of Right,* 1952).

The sphere of reality examined in political philosophy is "objective Spirit." But the highest sphere, in which the accidents of nationality, economics, geography, and climate are transcended, is "absolute Spirit," which develops through three kinds of activity: art, religion, and philosophy. Although Hegel lectured on these subjects regularly, he did not write a book on them. However, some former students, after his death, compiled and published their notes from the lectures. A portion of these notes has been published as *On Art, Religion, and Philosophy,* edited by J. Glenn Gray (1970). Hegel's attempt to ferret out the truth of Spirit is a study of history, but a special kind of study since history is comprehended as the development of human freedom, rather than as a series of events and stories.

Hegel became rector of the university in 1830. The next year he wrote a critical study of the situation in England, *On the English Reform Bill,* parts of which were published in a Prussian journal. The remainder was censored by state authorities to avoid antagonizing the English. For the fall semester of 1831, he announced two lecture courses: philosophy of law and the history of philosophy. He gave his first lectures on November 10; on November 14 Hegel succumbed to cholera, then epidemic in Europe.

Hegel's influence on subsequent generations is incalculable. It has been said that the history of European thought since Hegel has been a series of revolts against his ideas. No thinker since has combined such ambition with such rigor and insight, and many who are sympathetic to his achievement regard his legacy as the "crisis of philosophy" which so preoccupies philosophers a century later.

Further Reading

An easily accessible biography of Hegel in English is Franz Wiedmann's admiring *Hegel: An Illustrated Biography* (trans. 1968). Hegel's political thought is discussed in Herbert Marcuse, *Reason and Revolution: Hegel and the Rise of Social Theory* (1941; 2d ed. 1954), and in an introductory essay by Z. A. Pelczynski in *Hegel's Political Writings,* translated by T. M. Knox (1964). A wealth of material is presented in Walter Kaufmann, *Hegel: Reinterpretation, Texts, and Commentary* (1965). Two good introductions to Hegel's work are J. Glenn Gray, *Hegel's Hellenic Ideal* (1941), and John N. Findlay, *Hegel: A Re-examination* (1958). The place of Hegel's work in 19th-century German thought is lucidly examined by Karl Löwith in *From Hegel to Nietzsche: The Revolution in Nineteenth-Century Thought* (trans. 1964). □

Martin Heidegger

German philosopher Martin Heidegger (1889-1976) has become widely regarded as the most original 20th century philosopher. Recent interpretations of his philosophy closely associate him with existentialism (despite his repudiation of such interpretations) and, controversially, with National Socialist (Nazi) politics.

Martin Heidegger was born in Messkirch, a small town in Baden in southwest Germany, on Sept. 26, 1889. His father was a verger in the local Catholic church, and the boy received a pious upbringing. After graduation from the local gymnasium, he entered the Jesuit novitiate; later, he studied Catholic theology at the University of Freiburg. The markedly philosophical cast of medieval theology helped attract Heidegger to philosophy, and he finished his education in that subject. In 1914 he presented a doctoral thesis entitled "The Theory of Judgment in Psychologism," which showed the strong influence of Edmund Husserl's writings. A year later he was admitted to the faculty of Freiburg as a lecturer. His habilitation thesis was on a work of medieval logic, then thought to be by John Duns Scotus.

In 1916 Husserl was called to Freiburg as professor of philosophy, and when Heidegger returned from brief military service in World War I (spent in part at a meteorological station), he sought out the teacher whose works he had admired. In the following years Heidegger became an academic assistant for Husserl and edited the latter's manuscripts for *The Phenomenology of Internal Time-consciousness*.

Heidegger was called to a professorship in Marburg in 1923. Among his colleagues there were Rudolf Bultmann and Paul Tillich, theologians whose own work was profoundly shaped by discussions with Heidegger and by the publication in 1927 of his major work, *Being and Time*. In the autumn of 1928 Heidegger was recalled to Freiburg to take Husserl's chair, singled out by Husserl as his only qualified successor. Though Heidegger had been, in effect, designated as the leader of the developing phenomenological movement, it soon became clear that his own philosophical aims differed radically from those of Husserl.

In *Being and Time* Heidegger had made it plain that he was fundamentally interested in one great question, about the meaning of Being. Later, in the *Introduction to Metaphysics* (1935) he accepted G.W. von Leibniz's formulation: "Why should there be any being at all and not rather nothing?" But the bulk of *Being and Time* has to do with a fundamental analysis of human existence. Heidegger regarded this as only a preparation for ontology, arguing that it is characteristic of the human being (*Dasein*) to raise the question of Being (*Sein*). The promised second half of *Being and Time,* which was to provide the new ontology, did not appear.

His analysis introduced a number of concepts that later received wide currency in existential philosophy: for example, "human finitude," "nothingness" "being-in-the-world," "being-unto-death," and "authenticity." When these ideas were picked up and developed by French philosophers during and after World War II, Heidegger explicitly repudiated the designation of his views as existentialist in a *Letter on Humanism* (1949). Nevertheless, his reputation and considerable influence stem from *Being and Time* "a work that, though almost unreadable, was immediately felt to be of prime importance."

After 1930, Heidegger turned to a more historical approach, presenting man's understanding of the "nature of being" in different epochs (especially in Ancient Greece) leading up to the 20th century, which he found to be deeply flawed in large part because it was technologically overboard. But his works did not become easier to understand because of the historical turn. His articles and short books were Delphic in their obscurity and mystical in tone. (Contemporary mainstream British and American academic philosophers who read Heidegger "tend to divide into two camps: those who believe his writings are largely gibberish and those who believe they are entirely gibberish.") Heidegger laments man's forgetfulness of Being. But it seems that Being now hides itself from man. "We come too late for the gods and too early for Being." The true calling of the philosopher, shared only with the poet, is to "watch for Being" and, in rare moments, "to name the Holy" or "speak Being."

Beginning in the 1920's Heidegger lived in a primitive ski hut high on an isolated mountain in the Black Forest. He did not know how to drive a car. Dressing in the Swabian peasant costume of his family, he and his wife lived a simple, ascetic life close to nature, from which, with the help of his favorite poet, Friedrich Hölderlin, Heidegger attempted to learn the secret of Being.

Shortly after the electoral triumph of the National Socialist party in 1933, Heidegger began an association with the Nazis which is the subject of much contemporary controversy. The leaders of the Third Reich were determined to enforce conformity on all the institutions of Germany and immediately began to pressure the universities. The rector at Freiburg resigned, and in April 1933, shortly after Hitler was elected Chancellor, Heidegger was unanimously elected rector by the teaching faculty. Heidegger later claimed that the faculty "hoped that my reputation as a professor would help to preserve the faculty from political enslavement." But in his inaugural address and particularly in addresses to students in July and November of that year, Heidegger went far beyond what would have been required of any rector under the regime. In these speeches he rejected the concept of academic freedom as "implying uncommittedness in thought and act," and he urged students to make an "identification with the New Order." In his declaration to students on Nov. 3, 1933, Heidegger said, "Doctrine and 'ideas' shall no longer govern your existence. The Führer himself, and only he, is the current and future reality of Germany, and his word is your law." Despite the strength of these statements, Heidegger left his position as rector within a year, but he continued to see a unique destiny for German culture. Philosophy, he said, can be written only in Greek or German, and Germany to him was still entrusted with the fate of European culture, a nation caught in great pincers between two powers, Russia and America, which share "the same dreary technological frenzy, the same unrestricted organization of the average man."

Until the late 1980's most Heideggerians viewed his encounters with Nazism as an error of enthusiasm or philosophical misunderstanding or both, and it was not much of an issue. But in 1987 Victor Farías published *Heidegger and Nazism* (in French); the book "dropped like a bomb on the quiet chapel where Heidegger's disciples were gathered, and blew the place to bits." The story Heidegger had offered after the war that he supported the Nazis briefly and only to protect the university was overwhelmed by evidence of Heidegger's deep and long-lasting commitment to National Socialism, his blatant anti-Semitism, and his blackballing of colleagues for holding pacifist convictions, associating with Jews, or being "unfavorably disposed" toward the Nazi regime.

Heidegger was by no means the only German philosopher who signed up, but he was the most important, by far, and the only one who "saw himself as one of the greatest thinkers in the history of the West." After the war, a "de-Nazification" committee of Heidegger's peers at the university, many of them favorably disposed to him, were unconvinced by his claims of "intellectual resistance" to Nazism and removed him from his job, denying him emeritus status, and pensioning him off. Heidegger himself finally admitted that his lectures after he left the rectorship were anything but tough attacks on Nazism. Otherwise, after the war, he maintained "an almost hermetic silence" about the Holocaust. For some, this was "Heidegger's crime:" he was a thinker and writer who believed such people should be "the guardian of the memory of forgetting," but who "lent to extermination not his hand and not even his thought but his silence and nonthought. . .he 'forgot' the extermination."

Heidegger spent his last 20 years writing, publishing, and guest-lecturing at various places. He died in Freiburg in 1976.

Further Reading

Heidegger is the subject of much scholarship. Collections of essays on his work include Charles Guignon (ed.) *The Cambridge Companion to Heidegger* (1993); Hubert L. Dreyfus and Harrison Hall (eds.), *Heidegger: A Critical Reader* (1992); and Michael Murray (ed.), *Heidegger and Modern Philosophy* (1978); On Heidegger's politics, see Julian Young, *Heidegger, Philosophy, Nazism* (1997); James F. Ward, *Heidegger's Political Thinking* (1995); Hugo Ott, *Martin Heidegger A Political Life* (1993); Hans Sluga, *Heidegger's Crisis, Philosophy and Politics in Nazi Germany* (1993), Richard Wolin, *The Heidegger Controversy* (1993); Victor Farías, *Heidegger and Nazism* (1987); For more listings, articles, and book reviews, see the Heidegger page at *www.webcom.com/~paf/ereignis.html*. □

Carl Gustaf Verner Von Heidenstam

The Swedish author Carl Gustaf Verner von Heidenstam (1859-1940) is known for his lyric poetry and historical novels. He received the 1916 Nobel Prize in literature.

Verner von Heidenstam was born on July 6, 1859, the son of aristocratic parents. Because of illness he was sent to the milder climate of the Middle East when he was 15. He returned to Sweden in 1887 and debuted the following year with a book of poetry, *Pilgrimage and Wander-years,* which made him famous. These poems stood in the sharpest contrast to the sober, pessimistic Swedish literature of the time. Heidenstam's poetry celebrated the joy of life and individualism. The exotic subject matter, taken from his years in the Orient and southern Europe, as well as the style, was virtually without precedent in Swedish literature.

In articles Heidenstam advocated a literature that combined fantasy, imagination, and a sense of the beautiful with a "bold, drastic realism." His call was quickly answered by young writers, some of whom, with Heidenstam, created a new golden age in Swedish poetry. In 1892 he published an autobiographical novel, *Hans Alienus,* in which the hero searches for an alternative to the hedonistic way of life Heidenstam had earlier celebrated. In his second volume of poetry, *Dikter* (1895), he moved toward nationalism.

Heidenstam's historical fiction begins with *The Charles Men* (1897-1898), stories concerning Charles XII's last years, one of the darkest periods in Swedish history. Heidenstam attempted to justify the self-sacrifice of the Swedes in following their King by showing that man achieves his greatest stature in moments of trial and suffering for his country. *The Tree of the Folkungs* (1905-1907), perhaps his greatest novel, is a study of an aristocratic Swedish state emerging from barbarism. Like all his historical novels, it is distinguished by powerful character portrayal and a sensuous evocation of the past.

Heidenstam dreamed of arousing in his countrymen some of the greatness of the past, which, he felt, was absent in a Sweden moving swiftly into the industrial age. But he failed in his role as "poet chieftain" and found himself more and more isolated from his times. His greatest collection of poems, *Nya Dikter* (1915), demonstrates a clear, classical form far different from his earlier poetry.

Except for a book of childhood memories published posthumously, Heidenstam wrote nothing in the last 25 years of his life. He died on May 20, 1940.

Further Reading

An anthology of Heidenstam's poetry is *Sweden's Laureate: Selected Poems of Verner von Heidenstam,* translated, with an introduction, by Charles W. Stork (1919). For further information in English see Alrik Gustafson, *Six Scandinavian Novel-*

ists (1940; 2d ed. 1966) and *A History of Swedish Literature* (1961). ☐

Heinrich Heine

The German author Heinrich Heine (1797-1856) is best known for his lyric poems, a number of which are considered among the best in German literature. His essays on German literary, political, and philosophical thought contain remarkable and frequently prophetic insights.

The career of Heinrich Heine spans the later years of the German romantic movement and the era of the socially and politically conscious literary movement called Young Germany. His work reflects the influence of both schools, but an ingrained satirical sense and a sharp wit prevent his complete subscription to the tenets of either. He hoped to secularize romanticism in a "new (pagan) Hellenism," but his liberal political philosophy rejected contemporary reactionary German regimes as well as revolutionary "mob rule." His self-imposed exile from Germany after 1831 demonstrates his independence and isolation in a lifelong search for personal and national identity.

Heine was born on Dec. 13, 1797, in Düsseldorf. The son of middle-class Jewish parents, he was named Harry after an English friend of the family. His early education included training in both Hebrew and Jesuit schools, and at the insistence of his ambitious mother he was sent to Frankfurt and then to Hamburg to learn banking and business. But the dreamy youth proved unsuited to a life in trade, even with the support of his wealthy uncle Solomon in Hamburg. The principal legacy of Heine's Hamburg years was his unrequited love for his cousin Amalie (and later for her younger sister Therese); his double disappointment was the theme of many of his early lyrics.

University Years

With the financial support of his uncle, Heine entered the University of Bonn in 1819, planning to study law. Here A. W. von Schlegel, professor of literature and a cofounder of German romanticism, encouraged his literary bent. Heine was delighted by such attention but was alienated by the political conservatism of the university administration and by the anti-Semitism he encountered. In 1820 he removed to the University of Göttingen. Conditions there were even less appealing; his inevitable opposition to them soon led to his suspension, and he moved on to the University of Berlin. He attended the lectures of G. W. F. Hegel, and literary sponsors helped him to publish *Gedichte* (Poems) in 1822. These poems followed romantic conventions but were also marked by a novel use of language and imagery. *Lyrisches Intermezzo* (1823) and the lyric cycle *Heimkehr* (1826; Homecoming) show improved command of lyric form and frequently project the simplicity and directness of the folk song and the folk ballad. The dominant theme remains his unhappy love for Amalie and then, in the latter work, for Therese.

After an interlude at home, Heine, at the insistence of his uncle, returned to Göttingen. Upon Christian baptism (a necessary step for Jews who would handle Christian legal clients) he took the name Heinrich and received his law degree in July 1825.

His Travels

A journey on foot through the Harz Mountains and a vacation on the North Sea coast inspired the first volume of Heine's *Reisebilder* (1826; Travel Pictures), containing the *Heimkehr* cycle, *Die Nordsee* (lyrics which introduced sea themes into German literature and which are frequently considered Heine's finest achievement in the form), and *Die Harzreise,* an account of the Harz journey after the manner of the 18th-century English novelist Laurence Sterne. The freedom of form, which combined prose and poetry and was marked by many fanciful and philosophical digressions, proved congenial to the poet and popular with the public. Heine produced three further volumes in this vein, mirroring his reactions to subsequent travels and experiences in Germany, England (1827), and Italy (1828).

In 1827 Heine gathered together his best lyrics, publishing them as *Buch der Lieder* (Book of Songs), a collection that enjoyed immense popularity. No previous work had revealed so clearly his lyric range and versatility, wit, and unique mixture of sentiment and satire. The singing quality of his verse appealed to a number of 19th-century composers, including Johannes Brahms, Franz Schubert, and Robert Schumann; many poems were given musical settings and remain staples of the concert stage.

Between 1828 and 1831 Heine sought in vain for a secure position. His attempt at political journalism in Munich failed in a few months; by attempting to avoid censurable writing, he succeeded only in stifling his unique gifts. Thereafter the prospects for a university professorship dissolved in the face of conservative opposition and intrigue, and by 1831 he was delighted to be able to emigrate to Paris, hoping for a more congenial atmosphere in the wake of the July Revolution of 1830.

Parisian Exile

Heine's "romantic" period was now virtually at an end, and he determined to devote his energies henceforth to the "realistic" demands of the times. His announced purpose as self-appointed German cultural ambassador was to interpret German thought to the French. The essays in *De l'Allemagne* (1835) exhibit his own free-wheeling analysis of current German religious, philosophical, and literary theory. The three principal essays are entitled *Zur Geschichte der Religion und Philosophie in Deutschland, Die Romantische Schule,* and *Elementargeister* . A second edition included Heine's *Geständnisse* (Confessions).

In these essays Heine advocated a species of pantheism influenced by Saint-Simonianism. He urged the reestablishment of the fundamental German values that he professed to find in German folklore and the political realization of the revolutionary potential of contemporary German philosophy. In discussing German romanticism, Heine found its otherworldly "spiritualism" exaggerated and outmoded, and he advocated a renewed recognition of sensualistic claims and the joys of the here and now. (His last major blow against an outmoded romanticism, including its tendentious and patriotic wing, was delivered in 1843 in the delightful mock epic poem *Atta Troll.*) The great variety of pieces published in several volumes under the title *Der Salon* (1834 and later) brought to the German public much of Heine's thought, including his reactions to his French experiences.

Later Years

Heine's middle and later poetry—*Zeitgedichte* (1832-1844; Poems of the Times), *Romanzen* (1839), *Romanzero* (1851), and *Letzte Gedichte* (1853; Last Poems)—reinforce the theme of secularization sounded so strongly in the essays. These works often reflect his pessimism and disillusionment at witnessing the rising tide of 19th-century materialism. In this period there is also a withdrawal from the paganism advocated in his earlier work, induced in some part by the sufferings of Heine's last 8 years, when a spinal affliction and progressive paralysis confined him to his bed. Near the end, it was necessary for him to prop an eyelid open with one hand while writing with the other and, eventually, to dictate his work. To the last he was faithfully cared for by his "Mathilde" (Crescencia Eugenie Mirat), a simple French girl whom he had married in 1841.

In this reduced state Heine acknowledged, but without a trace of self-pity, that he had become convinced of the existence of "one religion for the healthy, and an entirely different one for the sick" and that he no longer regarded himself "the freest German since Goethe."

Heine died on Feb. 17, 1856, and was buried, in accord with his wishes, in the cemetery of Montmartre in Paris.

Further Reading

An extensive selection of Heine's work and a biographical essay are in Frederic Ewen, ed., *The Poetry and Prose of Heinrich Heine* (1948). Although no single work is generally accepted as definitive, a selection of studies can provide a cross section of the varying treatments of Heine. Eliza M. Butler, *Heinrich Heine: A Biography* (1956), is a sensitive and enthusiastic appreciation of the manifold and frequently incompatible facets of Heine's personality and work. Max Brod, *Heinrich Heine: The Artist in Revolt* (1934; trans. 1956), stresses Heine's antiestablishment orientation and re-creates the 19th-century milieu through extensive quotations from Heine and his contemporaries. Heine's political attitudes and his relation to his Jewish heritage are examined in William Rose, *Heinrich Heine: Two Studies of His Thought and Feeling* (1956). Still useful is Ludwig Marcuse, *Heinrich Heine: A Life between Past and Future* (1932; trans. 1934).

The critical study by Barker Fairley, *Heinrich Heine: An Interpretation* (1954), deals with recurrent images and motifs in Heine's poetry and prose and postulates a theory of the unity in Heine's work. A recent study is Jeffrey L. Sammons, *Heinrich Heine: The Elusive Poet* (1969). Solomon Liptzin, *The English Legend of Heinrich Heine* (1954), attempts to elucidate the mystery of Heine's international appeal through the context of English criticism from pre-Victorian times to the present. Surveys which discuss Heine are August Closs, *The Genius of the German Lyric* (1938), and Hermann Boeschenstein, *German Literature of the Nineteenth Century* (1969). For historical background see Hajo Holborn, *A History of Modern Germany* (2 vols., 1959-1964).

Additional Sources

Arnold, Matthew, *Essays in criticis,* London, Cambridge, Macmillan and co., 1865.

Brod, Max, *Heinrich Heine: the artist in revolt,* Westport, Conn.: Greenwood Press, 1976, 1957.

Butler, E. M. (Eliza Marian), *Heinrich Heine, a biography,* Westport, Conn., Greenwood Press 1970, 1956.

Fairley, Barker, *Heinrich Heine: an interpretation,* Westport, Conn.: Greenwood Press, 1977.

Heine, Heinrich, *Confessions,* Malibu, Calif.: J. Simon, 1981.

Heine, Heinrich, *Memoirs, from his works, letters, and conversations,* New York, Arno Press, 1973.

Hofrichter, Laura, *Heinrich Heine,* Westport, Conn.: Greenwood Press, 1987, 1963.

Kossoff, Philip, *Valiant heart: a biography of Heinrich Heine,* New York: Cornwall Books, 1983.

Pawel, Ernst, *The poet dying: Heinrich Heine's last years in Paris,* New York: Farrar, Straus and Giroux, 1995.

Robertson, Ritchie, *Heine,* New York: Grove Press, 1988.

Sammons, Jeffrey L., *Heinrich Heine,* Stuttgart: J.B. Metzler, 1991.

Sammons, Jeffrey L., *Heinrich Heine: a modern biography,* Princeton, N.J.: Princeton University Press, 1979.

Spencer, Hanna, *Heinrich Heine,* Boston: Twayne Publishers, 1982. □

Anthony Philip Heinrich

The giant orchestral works of Anthony Philip Heinrich (1781-1861), an American of Bohemian extraction, won him the sobriquet "Beethoven of America." He was the first American composer to use Indian themes in his work.

Anthony Philip (originally Anton Philipp) Heinrich was born in Bohemia (now part of the Czech Republic) on March 11, 1781. As a boy, he learned to play the violin. In 1816, following the failure of a business he had inherited, he emigrated to the United States and decided to make music his career.

After a few years in Philadelphia directing music in the Southwark Theater, Heinrich moved to Pittsburgh, where he conducted the earliest known American performance of a Beethoven symphony. Later he moved to Kentucky. While convalescing from a serious illness, he taught himself how to compose, and in 1820 his Opus 1 was published. This was "a collection of original, moral, patriotic and sentimental songs for the voice and pianoforte interspersed with airs, waltzes, etc." entitled *The Dawning of Music in Kentucky, or the Pleasures of Harmony in the Solitudes of Nature.*

The cordial reception of this work induced Heinrich to move to Boston in 1823. Although held in high esteem by his colleagues and the public, he had difficulty earning a living. By 1826 he had resettled in London, where he played the fiddle in the orchestra at the Drury Lane Theatre and tried, with minimal success, to advance his reputation as a composer. He returned to Boston in 1831, but by 1833 he was back at Drury Lane. The Continent beckoned, and in 1835 he went to Germany and Austria, enjoying a small degree of public favor. Performances of his orchestral music are recorded in Dresden, Prague, Budapest, Graz, and elsewhere.

In 1837 Heinrich settled in New York City. He threw himself into composing and teaching with unflagging energy, and within a short time he had gained considerable renown and notoriety as "Father Heinrich," eccentric genius. Enthusiasm for him culminated in monster "Heinrich Musical Festivals" in New York in 1842, 1846, and 1853, and in Boston in 1846.

Heinrich returned to Europe in 1857, receiving an especially warm welcome, climaxed by an all-Heinrich concert in Prague. His reception in Germany was less enthusiastic, and in late 1859 he was in New York again, where he died in abject poverty on May 3, 1861.

None of Heinrich's music outlived him. Some characteristic titles of large works are *The Columbiad, or Migration of American Wild Passenger Pigeons; Pocahontas, the Royal Indian Maid and the Heroine of Virginia, the Pride of the Wilderness; The Wildwood Troubadour;* and *The Wild Wood Spirit's Chant.*

Further Reading

William T. Upton, *Anthony Philip Heinrich: A Nineteenth-Century Composer in America* (1939), is a definitive biography. The Boston musical festival of 1846 is examined at some length in Irving Lowens, *Music and Musicians in Early America* (1964). □

Werner Karl Heisenberg

German physicist Werner Karl Heisenberg (1901-1976) was a pioneer in the formalization of atomic theory. He won the 1932 Nobel Prize in physics for his discovery of the uncertainty principle, which states that it is impossible to specify the precise position and momentum of a particle at the same time. Heisenberg also developed the theory of matrix mechanics. During World War II he was director of the German atomic bomb project, which led to his brief imprisonment following the war and some controversy during the remainder of his career.

Werner Karl Heisenberg was born on December 5, 1901, in Würzburg, Germany, the son of August and Annie Wecklein Heisenberg. He received his education at the Maximilian Gymnasium in Munich and at the University of Munich, where his father was professor of Greek language and literature. Shortly before he began his university studies, he worked on a farm for several months and took active part in youth movements, searching for a way out of the social collapse that hit Germany at the end of World War I.

Heisenberg was also a talented pianist, an avid hiker, and an eager student of classical literature and philosophy. At the university, where he enrolled in 1920, Heisenberg soon established close contact with Arthur Sommerfeld, a chief figure in early modern physics, and with Sommerfeld's most outstanding student, Wolfgang Pauli, later a Nobel laureate. Heisenberg spent the winter of 1922-1923 at the University of Gettingen, where the physics department was rapidly establishing itself, with the help of Max Born, James Franck, and David Hilbert, as a center of theoretical physics. After taking his doctorate in Munich in 1923, Heisenberg went on a Rockefeller grant to Niels Bohr's institute in Copenhagen, where he eagerly studied the most creative and up-to-date speculations on atomic theory.

His Landmark Papers

The fusion of the influence of these mentors with the receptiveness of a most talented mind worked unusually well. No sooner had Heisenberg completed his stay in Copenhagen than he worked out, while recuperating on the shores of Helgoland from a heavy attack of hay fever, a comprehensive method of calculating the energy levels of "atomic oscillators." The method yielded very good results but appeared so strange that Heisenberg was undecided

whether to submit his report for publication or "to throw it into the flames." Happily for science, he sent a copy of it to Pauli and, after receiving a favorable reply, he showed it to Born on his return to Gettingen in June 1925. Born realized its importance and had it sent to the Physikalische Zeitschrift, where it was immediately printed under the title, "On Quantum Mechanical Interpretation of Kinematic and Mechanical Relations." The person most preoccupied with the "strange" mathematical formalism in Heisenberg's paper was Born himself, who after eight days of constant reflection discovered that it corresponded to the rules of matrix calculus.

Heisenberg's paper earned its author immediate fame and recognition. At Bohr's recommendation, in 1926 he was appointed lecturer in theoretical physics at the University of Copenhagen. It was there that Heisenberg gave much thought to the apparent discrepancy between two formulations of quantum theory, one based on matrix calculus, the other on wave equations elaborated by Erwin Schroedinger. In the course of his work on this question, Heisenberg realized that only those physical situations are "meaningful" in quantum mechanics in which the differences of the noncommutative products of conjugate variables occur. He immediately saw that, because of these differences, one cannot determine simultaneously the position and velocity of an atomic particle or the energy level and its timing of an atomic oscillator.

The recognition of this fact led Heisenberg to the formulation of the famous uncertainty principle, which appeared in 1927 on the pages of the *Physikalische Zeitschrift*

in an article entitled, "On the Visualizable Content of Quantum Theoretical Kinematics and Mechanics." Heisenberg's *The Physical Principles of the Quantum Theory* (1930) also is considered a classic in this field. Heisenberg's rise was now as rapid in the academic as in the scientific world. In 1927, at the age of 26, he became professor of theoretical physics at the University of Leipzig. He was the recipient, along with Schroedinger and Paul Dirac, of the Nobel Prize for physics for 1932. In 1941 he took the chair of theoretical physics at the University of Berlin and the directorship of the Kaiser Wilhelm Institute for Physics. During this flurry of academic activity, in 1937 he married Elisabeth Schumacher, and they had seven children.

Questionable Role in War

As a theoretical scientist, Heisenberg was initially held in low regard and even considered suspect by the Nazi government. However, when World War II began, the government appointed him as director of the German uranium project, and he worked on developing an atomic bomb for Germany throughout the war. Heisenberg was arrested and placed in Allied captivity in England from April 1945 until the summer of 1946. His role during the war continues to be a source of controversy.

Later Career

After World War II Heisenberg did much to reorganize scientific research as head of the Max Planck Institute of Physics and of the Alexander von Humboldt Foundation. In the early 1950s Heisenberg turned with great vigor toward the formulation of a "unified theory of fundamental particles," stressing the role of symmetry principles. This theory was intensively discussed at an international conference in 1958, the year he moved to the University of Munich as professor of physics. He presented his thought on this subject in *Introduction to the Unified Field Theory of Elementary Particles* (1966).

In 1955-1956 Heisenberg gave the Gifford Lectures at the University of St. Andrews, Scotland, which were printed under the title *Physics and Philosophy: The Revolution in Modern Science*. He also published the autobiographical *Physics and Beyond* (1971) and several books dealing with the philosophical and cultural implications of atomic and nuclear physics, all of which are available in English translation.

Heisenberg retired in 1970, although he continued to write on a variety of topics. His health began to fail in 1973, and shortly thereafter he became seriously ill. He died on February 1, 1976 in Munich.

Further Reading

The best treatment of the conceptual foundations of Heisenberg's achievements in physics is the study by Patrick A. Heelan, *Quantum Mechanics and Objectivity: A Study of the Physical Philosophy of Werner Heisenberg* (1965); The place of Heisenberg's discoveries in the development of modern physics is given with all the technical details in the work by Max Jammer, *The Conceptual Development of Quantum Mechanics* (1966); For a popular but still informative presentation of the origins and techniques of quantum mechanics see Banesh

Hoffmann, *The Strange Story of the Quantum* (1959); For an account sprinkled with anecdotal details see the works of George Gamow, *Biography of Physics* (1961) and *Thirty Years That Shook Physics: The Story of Quantum Theory* (1966).

Additional Sources

Finkelstein, David, *Quantum Relativity: A Synthesis of the Ideas of Einstein and Heisenberg,* Springer-Verlag, 1996.
Peierls, Rudolf Ernst, *Atomic Histories,* American Institute of Physics, 1996.
See Walker, Mark, *Nazi Science: Myth, Truth, and the German Atomic Bomb,* Plenum Press, 1995, for a critical examination of Heisenberg's role in developing an atomic bomb for Germany during World War II. □

Joseph Heller

Joseph Heller (born 1923) is a popular and respected writer whose first and best-known novel, *Catch-22* (1961), is considered a classic of the post-World War II era. Presenting human existence as absurd and fragmented, this irreverent, witty novel satirizes capitalism and the military bureaucracy.

Heller's tragicomic vision of modern life, found in all of his novels, focuses on the erosion of humanistic values and highlights the ways in which language obscures and confuses reality. In addition, Heller's use of anachronism reflects the disordered nature of contemporary existence. His protagonists are antiheroes who search for meaning in their lives and struggle to avoid being overwhelmed by such institutions as the military, big business, government, and religion. *Catch-22* is most often interpreted as an antiwar protest novel that foreshadowed the widespread resistance to the Vietnam War that erupted in the late 1960s. While Heller's later novels have received mixed reviews, *Catch-22* continues to be highly regarded as a trenchant satire of the big business of modern warfare.

Heller was born in Brooklyn, New York, to first generation Russian-Jewish immigrants. His father, a bakery-truck driver, died after a bungled operation when Heller was only five years old. Many critics believe that Heller developed the sardonic, wisecracking humor that has marked his writing style while growing up in the Coney Island section of Brooklyn. After graduating from high school in 1941, he worked briefly in an insurance office, an experience he later drew upon for the novel *Something Happened* (1974). In 1942, Heller enlisted in the Army Air Corps. Two years later he was sent to Corsica, where he flew sixty combat missions as a wing bombardier, earning an Air Medal and a Presidential Unit Citation. It is generally agreed that Heller's war years in the Mediterranean theater had only a minimal impact on his conception of *Catch-22*. Discharged from the military in 1945, Heller married Shirley Held and began his college education. He obtained a B.A. in English from New York University, an M.A. from Columbia University, and

attended Oxford University as a Fulbright Scholar for a year before becoming an English instructor at Pennsylvania State University. Two years later Heller began working as an advertising copywriter, securing positions at such magazines as *Time, Look,* and *McCall's* from 1952 to 1961. The office settings of these companies also yielded material for *Something Happened.* During this time Heller was also writing short stories and scripts for film and television as well as working on *Catch-22.* Although his stories easily found publication, Heller considered them insubstantial and derivative of Ernest Hemingway's works. After the phenomenal success of *Catch-22,* Heller quit his job at *McCall's* and concentrated exclusively on writing fiction and plays. In December of 1981, he contracted Guillain-Barre syndrome, a rare type of polyneuritis that afflicts the peripheral nervous system. Heller chronicled his medical problems and difficult recovery in *No Laughing Matter* (1986) with Speed Vogel, a friend who helped him during his illness.

Catch-22 concerns a World War II bombardier named Yossarian who believes his foolish, ambitious, mean-spirited commanding officers are more dangerous than the enemy. In order to avoid flying more missions, Yossarian retreats to a hospital with a mysterious liver complaint, sabotages his plane, and tries to get himself declared insane. Variously defined throughout the novel, "Catch-22" refers to the ways in which bureaucracies control the people who work for them. The term first appears when Yossarian asks to be declared insane. In this instance, Catch-22 demands that anyone who is insane must be excused from flying missions.

The "catch" is that one must ask to be excused; anyone who does so is showing "rational fear in the face of clear and present danger," is therefore sane, and must continue to fly. In its final, most ominous form, Catch-22 declares "they have the right to do anything we can't stop them from doing." Although most critics identify Yossarian as a coward and an antihero, they also sympathize with his urgent need to protect himself from this brutal universal law. Some critics have questioned the moral status of Yossarian's actions, noting in particular that he seems to be motivated merely by self-preservation, and that the enemy he refuses to fight is led by Adolf Hitler. Others, however, contend that while Catch-22 is ostensibly a war novel, World War II and the Air Force base where most of the novel's action takes place function primarily as a microcosm that demonstrates the disintegration of language and human value in a bureaucratic state.

Heller embodies his satire of capitalism in the character of Milo Minderbinder, whose obsessive pursuit of profits causes many deaths and much suffering among his fellow soldiers. Originally a mess hall officer, Milo organizes a powerful black market syndicate capable of cornering the Egyptian cotton market and bombing the American base on Pianosa for the Germans. On the surface Milo's adventures form a straightforward, optimistic success story that some commentators have likened to the Horatio Alger tales popular at the turn of the twentieth century. The narrative line that follows Yossarian, on the other hand, is characterized by his confused, frustrated, and frightened psychological state. The juxtaposition of these two narrative threads provides a disjointed, almost schizophrenic structure that reasserts the absurd logic depicted in Catch-22.

Structurally, Catch-22 is episodic and repetitive. The majority of the narrative is composed of a series of cyclical flashbacks of increasing detail and ominousness. The most important recurring incident is the death of a serviceman named Snowden that occurs before the opening of the story but is referred to and recounted periodically throughout the novel. In the penultimate chapter, Yossarian relives the full horror and comprehends the significance of this senseless death as it reflects the human condition and his own situation. This narrative method led many critics, particularly early reviewers, to condemn Heller's novel as formless. Norman Mailer's oft-repeated jibe: "One could take out a hundred pages anywhere from the middle of Catch-22, and not even the author could be certain they were gone" has been refuted by Heller himself, and has inspired other critics to carefully trace the chronology of ever-darkening events that provide the loose structure of this novel.

Heller poignantly and consistently satirizes language, particularly the system of euphemisms and oxymorons that passes for official speech in the United States Armed Forces. In the world of Catch-22 metaphorical language has a dangerously literal power. The death of Doc Daneeka is an example: when the plane that Doc is falsely reported to be on crashes and no one sees him parachute to safety, he is presumed dead and his living presence is insufficient to convince anyone that he is really alive. Similarly, when Yossarian rips up his girlfriend's address in rage, she disap-

pears, never to be seen again. Marcus K. Billson III summarized this technique: "The world of [Catch-22] projects the horrific, yet all too real, power of language to divest itself from any necessity of reference, to function as an independent, totally autonomous medium with its own perfect system and logic. That such a language pretends to mirror anything but itself is a commonplace delusion Heller satirizes throughout the novel. Yet, civilization is informed by this very pretense, and Heller shows how man is tragically and comically tricked and manipulated by such an absurdity."

Heller's second novel, Something Happened, centers on Bob Slocum, a middle-aged businessman who has a large, successful company but who feels emotionally empty. Narrating in a monotone, Slocum attempts to find the source of his malaise and his belief that modern American bourgeois life has lost meaning, by probing into his past and exploring his relationships with his wife, children, and co-workers. Although critics consider Slocum a generally dislikable character, he ultimately achieves sympathy because he has so thoroughly assimilated the values of his business that he has lost his own identity. Many commentators have viewed Slocum as an Everyman, a moral cipher who exemplifies the age's declining spirit. While initial reviews of Something Happened were mixed, more recent criticism has often deemed this novel superior to and more sophisticated than Catch-22, particularly citing Heller's shift from exaggeration to suggestion. In his critical biography Joseph Heller, Robert Merrill described Something Happened as "the most convincing study we have of what it is like to participate in the struggle that is postwar America."

Good as Gold (1979) marks Heller's first fictional use of his Jewish heritage and childhood experiences in Coney Island. The protagonist of this novel, Bruce Gold, is an unfulfilled college professor who is writing a book about "the Jewish experience," but he also harbors political ambitions. Offered a high government position after giving a positive review of a book written by the president, Gold accepts, leaves his wife and children, and finds himself immersed in a farcical bureaucracy in which officials speak in a confusing, contradictory language. In this novel, Heller harshly satirizes former Secretary of State Henry Kissinger, a Jew who has essentially forsaken his Jewishness. As a result, the author draws an analogy between the themes of political powerlust and corruption with Jewish identity. Similarly, Gold's motives for entering politics are strictly self-aggrandizing, as he seeks financial, sexual, and social rewards. When his older brother dies, however, Gold realizes the importance of his Jewish heritage and family, and decides to leave Washington. Throughout the novel, Heller alternates the narrative between scenes of Gold's large, garrulous Jewish family and the mostly gentile milieu of Washington, employing realism to depict the former and parody to portray the latter.

Heller's next novel, God Knows (1984), is a retelling of the biblical story of King David, the psalmist of the Old Testament. A memoir in the form of a monologue by David, the text abounds with anachronistic speech, combining the Bible's lyricism with a Jewish-American dialect reminiscent of the comic routines of such humorists as Lenny Bruce, Mel Brooks, and Woody Allen. In an attempt to determine the origin of his despondency near the end of his life, David ruminates on the widespread loss of faith and sense of community, the uses of art, and the seeming absence of God. In *Picture This* (1988), Heller utilizes Rembrandt's painting '' Aristotle Contemplating the Bust of Homer'' to draw parallels between ancient Greece, seventeenth-century Holland, and contemporary America. Moving backward and forward among these eras, this novel meditates on art, money, injustice, the folly of war, and the failures of democracy. Critics questioned whether *Picture This* should be considered a novel, a work of history, or a political tract.

Heller's first play, *We Bombed in New Haven* (1967), concerns a group of actors who believe they are portraying an Air Force squadron in an unspecified modern war. The action alternates between scenes where the players act out their parts in the ''script'' and scenes where they converse among themselves out of ''character,'' expressing dissatisfaction with their roles. This distancing technique, which recalls the work of Bertolt Brecht and Luigi Pirandello, alerts the audience to the play's artificiality. As in *Catch-22,* this drama exposes what Heller perceives as the illogic and moral bankruptcy of the United States military. Many critics have also interpreted *We Bombed in New Haven* as a protest against America's participation in the Vietnam War. Heller has also adapted *Catch-22* for the stage, but critics generally consider this work inferior to the novel.

While Heller's place in twentieth-century letters is assured with *Catch-22,* he is also highly regarded for his other works, which present a comic vision of modern society with serious moral implications. A major theme throughout his writing is the conflict that occurs when individuals interact with such powerful institutions as corporations, the military, and the federal government. Heller's novels have displayed increasing pessimism over the inability of individuals to reverse society's slide toward corruption and degeneration. He renders the chaos and absurdity of contemporary existence through disjointed chronology, anachronistic and oxymoronic language, and repetition of events. In all his work, Heller emphasizes that it is necessary to identify and take responsibility for our social and personal evils and to make beneficial changes in our behavior.

Further Reading

A Dangerous Crossing, Southern Illinois University Press, 1973.
Aichinger, Peter, *The American Soldier in Fiction, 1880-1963,* Iowa State University Press, 1975.
American Novels of the Second World War, Mouton, 1969.
Authors in the News, Volume 1, Gale, 1976.
Bergonzi, Bernard, *The Situation of the Novel,* University of Pittsburgh Press, 1970.
Bier, Jesse, *The Rise and Fall of American Humor,* Holt, 1968.
Bruccoli, Matthew J. and C. E. Frazer Clark, Jr., editors, *Pages: The World of Books, Writers, and Writing,* Gale, 1976. □

Walter Heller

Catapulted into the spotlight as chairman of the Council of Economic Advisors during the Kennedy-Johnson years, Walter Heller (1915-1987) became the chief spokesman and exemplar of the "New Economics" which attempted to maximize economic growth through "fine tuning."

Walter Heller's life and career was fairly conventional until he reached the age of 45. Born in Buffalo, New York, the son of German immigrants, he travelled with his family to Washington state and then to Wisconsin, where he attended public schools and entered Oberlin College in 1931.

After graduating in 1935 Heller went on to the University of Wisconsin for advanced work in economics, being awarded the Ph.D. in 1941. From there Heller took a post at the Department of the Treasury, where he served as senior analyst for tax research, an area in which he was to specialize. By 1945 Heller was assistant to the head of the division, and in that year he left government service for an associate professorship at the University of Minnesota.

Throughout this period Heller published a number of papers on taxation, winning a growing reputation in the field. Because of this he was asked to serve as chief of finance for the American military government in Germany, and in this capacity he helped devise the tax and banking programs which became the basis for the German economic recovery in the 1950s. Heller went to Washington during the Korean War to develop taxation programs, and later in the 1950s he helped reform Minnesota's tax system. The early 1960s found him in the Hashemite Kingdom of Jordan fashioning a graduated tax system for that country.

By then Heller's philosophy regarding the role of taxes in the economy was well established, and it turned out to be a blend of old conservative notions and newer liberal ones. Conservatives supported lower taxes in the belief that government should be limited, and so less by way of revenues would be required. They also thought it a matter of simple justice to take as little as possible from those who earned the money. In addition, they would cut taxes during economic turndowns to stimulate the economy. Heller, who considered himself a liberal, wanted to employ tax reductions when a gap developed between actual and potential performance of the economy and would do so even if this meant an increase in the deficit, which might stimulate inflation.

Inflation wasn't much of a concern at the time; from 1951 to 1960 the rate was generally below 3 percent, and in one year, 1954, prices actually declined. Moreover, Heller felt that a decline in the unemployment rate and an increase in gross national product was well worth a little inflation. Then too, over time increased tax revenues coming from an expanded economy would more than make up for any immediate shortfall. In addition, Heller believed in what later was known as "fine tuning," meaning that economists had progressed to the point where they could apply short term stimuli or dampen growth so as to assure smooth progress, unmarked by severe recession or inflation.

It was ideas like this which attracted the attention of Democratic presidential candidate John F. Kennedy, who after his election selected Heller to head the Council of Economic Advisors. Little happened during Kennedy's first year in office, as the economy turned upward after the 1960 recession. But as growth slowed down Kennedy sought ideas regarding stimulative measures.

In the summer of 1962 Heller created and Kennedy accepted a draft bill to reduce taxes. Heller's hand could be seen in the budget message sent to Congress early in 1963. In it Kennedy predicted a slight surplus for the coming year, but "to plan a deficit under such circumstances (through a tax cut) would be to increase the risk of inflationary pressures." He went on to say that "on the other hand, we are still short of full capacity use of plant and manpower. To plan a large surplus would risk choking off economic recovery."

This was followed by a statement that was straight out of Heller: "Faster economic growth in the United States requires, above all, an expansion of demand, to take up existing slack and to match future increases in capacity." Although he was somewhat vague, clearly the president was coming out in favor of a tax cut.

Kennedy continued to discuss tax cuts throughout the spring and summer of 1963, and increasingly became convinced it was the best way to stimulate the economy. Yet he was unable to push a bill embodying these ideas through Congress.

Kennedy's successor, Lyndon Johnson, had better fortune. Upon taking office he said: "No act of ours could more fittingly continue the work of President Kennedy than the early passage of the tax bill for which he fought all this long year." The measure was signed into law on February 26, 1964, and it provided for a cut of $14 billion in 1964 and $11 billion in 1965. Heller considered this his most important accomplishment. Later on he wrote that the willingness of Kennedy and Johnson "to use, for the first time, the full range of modern economic tools, underlies the unbroken U.S. expansion since early 1961."

In 1964 Heller spoke of the "fiscal dividend" which would result from the tax cut. "Our federal tax system is so powerful that—even after reducing our income taxes by about 12 percent—on the average, each year, it generated about $5 billion more revenues than it did the year before." Some claim that Johnson took this to mean that he could conduct a war in Vietnam and one against poverty at the same time, without raising taxes. Indeed, Heller indicated that Johnson would have to accelerate his domestic spending programs if peace came to Vietnam.

Heller resigned his post in November 1964 to return to his academic duties in Minnesota. Inflationary pressures developed the following year, by which time Heller was considering a shift in position. By 1966 he was calling for either an end to the Vietnam War or an increase in taxes to combat growing inflationary pressures.

Heller continued to speak out on economic issues through a regular column in *The Wall Street Journal* and as a member of *TIME*'s editorial board. But his ideas seemed discredited by the combination of inflation and stagnation ("stagflation") which developed in the early 1970s.

In the 1980s Heller was deemed a respected member of the old liberalism, while his new economics was rarely discussed by his compatriots. Ironically, the use of tax cuts to stimulate economic growth was taken up by the "supply side economists" who supported President Ronald Reagan, while Heller and other liberal economists of the Kennedy-Johnson era talked of the need for balanced budgets. In the 1984 presidential campaign the Republicans praised Heller's 1960s approach, even while he supported Democratic nominee Walter Mondale, who sounded much like a fiscal conservative of the 1960s. Heller died of a heart attack in 1987.

Further Reading

Although there is no full-scale biography of Walter Heller, a discussion and analysis of his life and works may be found in Robert Sobel, *The Worldly Economists* (1980); Edward Flash, Jr., *Economic Advice and Presidential Leadership* (1965); William Breit and Roger Ransom, *The Academic Scribblers* (1971); and Herbert Stein, *The Fiscal Revolution in America* (1969). For his career in the Kennedy-Johnson years see J. Ronnie Davis, *The New Economics and the Old Economists* (1971). Among Heller's books, the most useful are *New Dimensions of Political Economy* (1966), *The Economy: Old Myths and New Realities* (1976), and *Perspectives on Economic Growth* (1968). □

Lillian Florence Hellman

Lillian Florence Hellman (1906-1984), American playwright, wrote a series of powerful, realistic plays that made her one of America's major dramatists. She explored highly controversial themes, with many of her plays reflecting her outspoken political and social views.

Lillian Florence Hellman was born in New Orleans on June 20, 1906, of Jewish parentage. In 1910 her family moved to New York City, where she attended public schools. She studied at New York University (1923-1924) and Columbia University (1924). Her marriage to Arthur Kober in 1925 was dissolved in 1932.

She worked as a manuscript reader for Liveright Publishers before becoming main play reader for producer Herman Shumlin. In 1930, ready to drop her idea of being a writer, she was dissuaded by Dashiell Hammett, who became her lifelong mentor and partner.

Major Works Invited Controversy

After a "year and a half of stumbling stubbornness," Hellman finished *The Children's Hour* (1934), based on an actual incident in Scotland. The action of the play is triggered by a child's accusation of lesbianism against two teachers, which leads to one woman's suicide. The play reveals Hellman's sharp characterizations and explicit, moral comment on a theme considered dramatically untouchable at the time.

In Days to Come (1936), a play of family dissolution as well as of the struggle between union and management, Hellman's dramatic touch faltered. However, her next play, *The Little Foxes* (1939), ranks as one of the most powerful in American drama. Set in the South, it depicts a family almost completely engulfed by greed, avarice, and malice.

During World War II Hellman wrote two plays. *Watch on the Rhine* (1941), an anti-Nazi drama about an underground hero, received the New York Critics Circle Award. *The Searching Wind* (1944) championed anti-fascist activity and criticized the failure of influential Americans to halt the rise of Hitler and Mussolini. In *Another Part of the Forest* (1946), Hellman again portrayed the Hubbard family of *The Little Foxes;* she also directed the play. *Autumn Garden* (1951) lacked the usual ferocity of her dramas but was a touching and revealing insight into a Southern boardinghouse. The style of the play is sometimes compared to Anton Chekhov's work. *Toys in the Attic* (1960), a devastating portrait of possessive love set in New Orleans, won her another New York Critics Circle Award.

Work Outside of the Theater

Hellman demonstrated her versatility as an author with a witty book for the musical *Candide* (1956); adaptations of two plays, *Montserrat* (1949) and Jean Anouilh's *The Lark* (1956); and her departure from realism in the humorous play of Jewish family life, *My Mother, My Father and Me*

(1963). She also edited *The Letters of Anton Chekhov* in 1955.

Hellman published three memoirs dealing with her career, personal relationships, and political activities (including her scathing criticism of the House Unamerican Activities Committee headed by Joseph McCarthy): *An Unfinished Woman* (1969), *Pentimento: A Book of Portraits* (1973), and *Scoundrel Time* (1976). There was much discussion at the time about whether the content of these memoirs was greatly enhanced by Hellman.

Hellman received honorary doctorates from several colleges and universities. Her theatrical awards included the New York Drama Critics Circle Award (1941 and 1960); a Gold Medal from the Academy of Arts and Letters for Distinguished Achievement in the Theatre (1964); and election to the Theatre Hall of Fame (1973). She also received the National Book Award in 1969 for *An Unfinished Woman* and a nomination in 1974 for *Pentimento: A Book of Portraits*.

Further Reading

For insights into Hellman's personal world, see Lillian Hellman, *An Unfinished Woman: A Memoir* (1969), *Pentimento: A Book of Portraits* (1973), and *Scoundrel Time* (1976). Critical assessments of her writings can be found in Barnard Hewitt, *Theatre U.S.A., 1668 to 1957* (1959); Allan Lewis, *American Plays and Playwrights of the Contemporary Theatre* (1965); Walter J. Meserve, ed., *Discussions of Modern American Drama* (1965); Jean Gould, *Modern American Playwrights*

(1966); and John Gassner, *Dramatic Soundings: Evaluations and Retractions* (1968).

See also Mellen, Joan, *Hellman and Hammett,* HarperCollins, 1996, for a highly criticized account of the stormy relationship between these two talented writers. □

Hermann Ludwig Ferdinand von Helmholtz

The German physicist and physiologist Hermann Ludwig Ferdinand von Helmholtz (1821-1894) made the first mathematical analysis of the principle of the conservation of energy and invented the ophthalmoscope. He also investigated the physics of tone and color perception.

B orn on Aug. 31, 1821, in Potsdam, Hermann von Helmholtz was the eldest of six children of August Helmholtz, a teacher of philosophy and classics in the local gymnasium, and Caroline Penne Helmholtz, a descendant of the family which took prominent part in the founding of Pennsylvania. At the age of 17 he entered the Friedrich Wilhelm Institute as a scholarship student of medicine. Happily for science, Helmholtz had the genius to absorb medical and physiological training with the mind of a physicist. A great help in this respect was a teacher of his at the institute, Johannes Müller, the foremost German physiologist at that time, who insisted on carrying as far as possible the physical and chemical explanation in all problems of physiology. For Helmholtz this also meant the utmost use of mathematics, which he learned on his own to a very advanced degree by studying in his free time such mathematical classics as the works of Euler, Bernoulli, D'Alembert, and Lagrange. His doctoral dissertation (1842) described and analyzed the connections between nerve fibers and nerve cells, a discovery which he made by skillful use of the microscope and which forms the histological basis of the physiology and pathology of the nervous system.

Helmholtz's scholarship status implied the obligation to serve for 8 years as army doctor. His first post (1842-1843) was that of a house surgeon at the Charité Hospital in Berlin, followed by a stint of 5 years as assistant surgeon to the Royal Hussars at Potsdam. Despite time-consuming duties, Helmholtz found ways of developing his scientific interests. While at the Charité, he published a demonstration of the strictly chemical nature of fermentation and noted that a vitalistic account would be equivalent to assuming a perpetual-motion process. His papers on metabolism during muscular activity (1845) and on physiological and animal heat (1846, 1847) clearly indicated the great goal toward which his creative mind inevitably tended. In February 1847 he sent the first draft of the introduction of "The Conservation of Force" to Emil Du Bois-Reymond, who immediately declared that it was "an historical document of great scientific import for all time." The 26-year-old

Helmholtz read the paper on July 23 before the Physical Society of Berlin. He was not the first to enunciate the idea that physical force (energy) was conserved in its various transformations, but his originality consisted in giving the principle a generalized mathematical form, which readily yielded expressions for kinetic and potential energy in mechanics, thermodynamics, electricity, and magnetism.

Academic World

The impact of the lecture and the availability of a teaching post in anatomy at the Academy of Arts in Berlin made it possible for Helmholtz to transfer to the academic world. In 1849 he accepted the invitation to serve as professor of physiology at the University of Königsberg, where he married Olga von Velten the same year. Among his first papers at Königsberg was "On the Method of Measuring Very Small Intervals of Time and Their Application to Physiological Purposes" (1851). The purpose was the determination of the rate of transmission of sense impressions along the nerves. The value he found shortly afterward was approximately 30 meters per second, in good agreement with subsequent determinations. The next year Helmholtz wrote of a marvelous new device to investigate the eye, the ophthalmoscope, which made its inventor world famous almost overnight.

In 1855 Helmholtz went to Bonn as professor of physiology and anatomy. During the following 3 years he started his incisive analysis of the mathematical relationships underlying tone perception and the esthetical judgment about various tonalities. At the same time he began publishing in a mature form his previous studies of the physiology of vision. The first volume of his famous *Handbook of Physiological Optics* appeared in 1856. The massive volume was a systematic application of physics to the phenomenon of vision. "On the Integrals of the Hydrodynamic Equations Which Express Vortex Motions" (1858) represented not only a brilliant solution of seemingly insoluble equations, but it also became the foundation for late-19th-century physicists who tried to devise a so-called vortex model of the ether.

Helmholtz spent the next 13 years at the University of Heidelberg. During his first year there his wife died. In 1861 Helmholtz married Anna von Mohl, who became mother of three children. He spent 13 years at Heidelberg, officially a physiologist but in reality a physicist.

The second part of Helmholtz's *Handbook of Physiological Optics* was published in 1862. The next year saw the publication of another systematic application of physics in physiology, *Theory of the Sensations of Tone as Physiological Basis of the Theory of Music*. In 1867 followed the third, and final, volume of the *Handbook*. Helmholtz's last 3 years at Heidelberg were marked by portentous investigations in theoretical physics. His interest was now in fluid mechanics, the foundations of geometry and electricity. Characteristically enough, when the chair of physics became vacant in Bonn, the university tried to get Helmholtz back as professor of physics. Helmholtz declined the opportunity, but in his reply he made no secret of his lifelong ambition: "Physics was really from the outset the science which principally attracted my interests. I was mainly led to medicine and thereby to physiology by the force of external circumstances. What I have accomplished in physiology rests mainly upon a physical foundation."

Life in Berlin

The same letter also gives a clue to the inspiration that animated Helmholtz during the last two major assignments of his life. The first of these was the professorship of physics at the University of Berlin (1871-1888). Following the Franco-Prussian war of 1870-1871, Berlin emerged as the capital of the First Reich, and as a professor of physics at the University of Berlin Helmholtz could be most influential in promoting the cause of scientific instruction in German schools and universities. There was much to be done if, in a predominantly humanistic and classical educational system, science courses were to gain a rightful place. It was the professorship of physics at the University of Berlin which he finally found most promising to reward him "for taking the new work of a new post" upon himself. His request was immediately granted that a chair in physics be complemented by an Institute of Physics reserved exclusively for advanced research. Shortly after his arrival in Berlin, Helmholtz gave evidence of the high level in physical research which he had in mind. His memoir read in 1872 before the Berlin Academy of Sciences, "On the Theory of Electrodynamics," represented a remarkable effort to provide a generalized form of electrodynamics, of which even James Clerk Maxwell's theory was but a particular case. In 1873 he was invited to lecture in the United States, but he felt that acceptance would hinder his researches at his

institute, which had begun to attract the most promising young physicists in Germany. The foremost among them was Heinrich Hertz, who developed under Helmholtz's guidance the interest to test experimentally a chief consequence of Maxwell's theory, the propagation of electromagnetic oscillations in space. A high point in Helmholtz's own reflections on the problems of electricity was his Faraday lecture in 1881, in which he emphasized the essentially atomic structure of electricity, a contention fully confirmed a few years later by J. J. Thomson's work with cathode rays.

During this period Helmholtz began to achieve the status of a chief adviser to the state in scientific matters. He played a prominent part in the establishment of the Imperial Physico-Technical Institute (Physikalisch-Technische Reichsanstalt), of which he became the first director in 1888. Although a chief aim of the new institute was to carry out high-precision measurements, Helmholtz wanted the new institute to serve pure science as well as technology. During his last years acclaim and honors poured in from every side. His seventieth birthday became an occasion for nationwide celebrations. He died on Sept. 8, 1894, after months of struggle with paralysis. In no small measure, through his inspiration physics in Germany rose to unparalleled heights by the end of the 19th century, a position which remained unchallenged for another generation.

Further Reading

Leo Koenigsberger's classic three-volume biography is available in English in a one-volume abridgment by Frances A. Welby as *Hermann von Helmholtz* (1906). It covers equally well the personal and scientific aspects of Helmholtz's career and discusses his influence on science in the second half of the 19th century. A specialized study of Helmholtz is Richard M. Warren and Roslyn P. Warren, *Helmholtz on Perception, Its Physiology and Development* (1968). A detailed biographical account of Helmholtz's life is in Bessie Zaban Jones, ed., *The Golden Age of Science: Thirty Portraits of the Giants of 19th-Century Science by Their Scientific Contemporaries* (1966). Good discussions of Helmholtz are also in Henry Ernst Sigerist, *The Great Doctors: A Biographical History of Medicine* (1933), and Ralph Hermon Major, *A History of Medicine* (vol. 2, 1954). □

Jan Baptista van Helmont

The Flemish chemist and physician Jan Baptista van Helmont (1579-1644) attempted to construct a natural philosophical system based on chemical concepts. He also developed the concept of gas.

Jan Baptista van Helmont was born of a noble family in Brussels in January 1579. He studied the classics at the University of Louvain until 1594, but he did not accept a degree because he considered academic honors a mere vanity. He also studied aspects of magic and mystical philosophy in courses given by Jesuit teachers at their recently founded Louvain school, and then he turned to the study of such mystical spiritual writers as Thomas à Kempis. Dissatisfied with all these studies, he turned to medicine. In his new undertaking he was inspired by religious zeal and by the desire to be of service to society.

After obtaining his license to practice, Van Helmont was invited to lecture on surgery at the University of Louvain. However, he contracted a case of scabies and found the orthodox treatment by harsh purgatives to be debilitating and ineffective. He was eventually cured by Paracelsian mineral remedies, but meanwhile, disillusioned with the medical science of the time, Van Helmont abandoned his medical career and for 10 years traveled through Europe. He married a wealthy noblewoman, Margaret van Ranst, in 1609 and settled on an estate in Vilvorde near Brussels to devote himself to chemical philosophy.

Following the publication of his treatise on the magnetic cure of wounds, which was directed against a Jesuit, Van Helmont came to the attention of the Inquisition. A charge was brought against him, and this affair cast a shadow over the remainder of his life, which ended on Dec. 30, 1644; he was not acquitted until 2 years after his death. This circumstance possibly made him reluctant to publish much during his lifetime. His son Franciscus Mercurius published his papers posthumously in 1648 under the title *Ortus medicinae* (*Origins of Medicine*).

Van Helmont lived precisely in that era of the 17th century when modern scientific method based upon observation and experiment was being forged, but as yet science was not identified either uniquely or exclusively with this approach. For Van Helmont knowledge was a divine gift of God: there was no one way to understand the creation; man had to utilize all the means God had given him, including study of the Scriptures, prayer, meditation, mystical illumination, and direct observation of nature. Like most Paracelsians, Van Helmont distrusted the dialectical mode of reasoning that the scholastic philosophers of the Middle Ages used and the natural philosophy of the Greeks. Experience, both mystical and empirical, was the route to knowledge, not verbal reasoning.

Theory of the Elements

These varied aspects of Van Helmont's thought are nowhere better illustrated than in his theory of the elements. Rejecting the four elements, earth, air, fire, and water, of Aristotle and the three principles, salt, sulfur, and mercury, of Paracelsus, Van Helmont settles on two elements as the basic constituents of the material universe: air and water. Only one of the elements, water, undergoes chemical change: air is simply a physical matrix which contains various vapors and exhalations but does not enter into chemical combination. All material substances, with the exception of air, are thus modified forms of water.

Van Helmont found support for his elemental water theory in the account of creation given in Genesis. To account for the diversity of material forms derived from the primal water, Van Helmont postulated a series of directing and generating principles which he called ferments or seminal principles. They were links between the material world and the spiritual world and as such had a key place in Van Helmont's natural philosophy.

Van Helmont tried to demonstrate his water theory by means of quantitative experiment. He planted a tree in a pot containing a weighed amount of earth. For 5 years he nourished the tree only with water. He found that the weight of the tree had gained 164 pounds while the weight of the earth in the pot was approximately the same as at the beginning of the experiment. He thus attributed the increase in weight of the tree to the assimilation and transformation of water into the substance of the tree.

Concept of Gas

Van Helmont's concept of gas, a word he coined from the Greek *chaos,* was an integral part of his water-ferment theory of matter. He recognized gases as specific individual chemical entities distinguished from air, but here the comparison with the modern chemical idea of gas ends. A gas to Van Helmont was primal water modified by a specific ferment: each body in nature contains such a gas and under specific conditions, for example, by heating, this gas can be liberated. Van Helmont described the production of such a gas. After burning 62 pounds of charcoal, only 1 pound of ashes remained. He assumed the other 61 pounds had changed into a wild spirit or gas (he called it gas sylvestre) that could not be contained in a vessel. He obtained the same gas by burning organic matter and alcohol and by fermenting wine and beer.

Ferments also play a major role in Van Helmont's biological and medical theories. He hypothesized that each of the principal organs of the body contained an individual

ferment which controlled and directed the function of that organ, particularly the assimilation of foodstuff into the tissue of the body. This view led him to study the particular action of the various organs and to the recognition of the role of acid in the digestive process of the stomach.

To Van Helmont, diseases were caused by the invasion of the body by foreign ferments which interfered with the controlling action of the ferments of particular organs. Thus diseases had to be studied and treated as individual specific complaints with their own individual and specific cures. Although the Helmontian view of nature did not claim many adherents in the second half of the 17th century, his works were widely read and appreciated as a source of novel ideas and experiments.

Further Reading

Van Helmont's chemical work is treated in some detail in J. R. Partington, *A History of Chemistry,* vol. 2 (1961). Walter Pagel, *The Religious and Philosophical Aspects of Van Helmont's Science and Medicine* (1944), offers a more penetrating but difficult analysis.

Additional Sources

Pagel, Walter, *From Paracelsus to Van Helmont: studies in Renaissance medicine and science,* London: Variorum Reprints, 1986.
Pagel, Walter, *Joan Baptista van Helmont: reformer of science and medicine,* Cambridge Cambridgeshire; New York: Cambridge University Press, 1982. □

Jesse Helms

Jesse Helms (born 1921), conservative Senator from North Carolina, is well liked by the religious right for his position on abortion rights, school prayer, and school busing.

Born in Monroe, North Carolina, Jesse Helms studied at Wingate Junior College and Wake Forest University before serving in the navy during World War II. He became active in politics while working as a journalist in Raleigh, North Carolina, and served as an adviser to Willis Smith during his campaign for the U.S. Senate in 1950. After Smith's victory in what is regarded as the most virulently racist election in North Carolina history, Helms worked in Washington as an administrative assistant for Smith (1951-1953) and then briefly for Sen. Alton Lennon (1953). Returning to North Carolina in 1953, he worked as a television commentator and as a lobbyist for the banking industry before his election to the Senate as a Republican in 1972. He has been reelected by close margins in 1978, 1984, and 1990. In 1972 and 1984, presidential election years, he ran behind the Republican presidential nominee.

Ideological Purity

Helms has developed a reputation as an ideological purist. His record in the Senate has been consistently anti-

United Nations, anti-Communist, anti-government spending, anti-welfare, anti-arms control, anti-foreign aid, and pro-military. His only major political about-face was his 1985 switch from an anti-Israeli position to one that is pro-Israel—one said to have been prompted in part by the narrowness of his 1984 victory over an opponent who received substantial contributions from pro-Israel individuals and groups outside North Carolina.

Support from the Religious Right

Helms is known for his derisive treatment of those he opposes—from Martin Luther King to the Soviet Union to homosexuals—and he has an old-time southern politician's visceral appeal for conservative, mostly rural, white North Carolinians. Said to have an Old Testament sense of good and evil, he has had close ties to the religious right throughout his career, and during his campaigns he has made frequent appearances on the shows of the televangelists Jim Bakker and Pat Robertson. Leaders of Jerry Falwell's Moral Majority have spoken on his behalf at political rallies.

Pushing Conservative Causes

Helms has not often been successful in getting his own legislation passed. In 1982 he failed to implement measures that would have stripped the Supreme Court of jurisdiction over cases involving abortion, school prayer, and school busing. He has cast dozens of votes to outlaw or restrict abortion, to eliminate busing for school integration, and to do away with food stamps. In 1989—after he became enraged over the inclusion of homoerotic photographs by

Robert Mapplethorpe and Andres Serrano's photograph of a crucifix in a glass of urine in exhibits funded by the National Endowment for the Arts (NEA)—he tried unsuccessfully to convince the Senate to pass a bill that banned the funding of "obscene" art by the NEA or any other federal agency.

Blocking Nominations

Helms has also used his position on the committee to block or hold up nominations regardless of which party controlled the White House. He opposed Republican Gerald Ford's nominations of Nelson Rockefeller for vice president and Donald Rumsfeld for secretary of defense. Many of Democrat Jimmy Carter's nominees faced the same treatment, as did Caspar Weinberger , whom Republican Ronald Reagan nominated for secretary of defense. In 1981 Helms stalled Senate approval of several Reagan appointees as undersecretaries of state, including Lawrence Eagleburger, Chester Crocker, Robert Hormats, and Thomas Enders. In 1985 Helms held up the confirmation of Thomas Pickering as ambassador to Israel at a time of crucial discussions over possible exchanges of western hostages in Beirut for Arabs in Israeli prisons.

Right-Wing Ties

The animosity between Helms and Pickering stemmed from Pickering's service as ambassador to El Salvador, where he was actively trying to work with the Duarte government while Helms had close ties to Duarte's ultraright-wing opponent, Roberto D'Aubuisson. Helms has been closely tied to various right-wing governments, including the regime of Augusto Pinochet in Chile. Beginning in 1986 Helms served as chairman of the editorial advisory board of the International Freedom Foundation, a front organization for the South African Defense Fund, which set up and funded the foundation to conduct political warfare against opponents of apartheid in the United States. Other prominent conservative Republicans connected to the foundation included representatives Dan Burton and Robert Dornan of California and African American political activist Alan Keyes. In 1988 Helms led the fight to pass legislation that required the United States to maintain two embassies in Israel, one in Tel Aviv, the secular capital, and one in Jerusalem, in the contested West Bank region.

The Foreign Relations Committee

Throughout the 1980s Helms was consistently a thorn in the sides of Democratic and Republican administrations as he tried to promote his own ultraconservative foreign-policy agenda. But as chairman of the Senate Foreign Relations Committee he had the power to do so. His staff included former intelligence personnel who have retained ties within their agencies, and he promoted the hiring of his staffers and aides for key positions in the various national security agencies. After the GOP took control of both houses of Congress, Helms attempted to dismantle U.S. foreign policy. In March of 1995 he introduced a bill to get rid of USAID, the United States Information Agency, and the Arms Control and Disarmament Agency. The Democrats filibustered the bill, but to get even Helms shut down the

Foreign Relations Committee for four months. Even though foreign aid makes up only one percent of the federal budget, Helms thinks that foreign aid is "the greatest racket of all time" and "the ripoff of the American taxpayers." Informational holds can be placed on projects to temporarily delay funding. The last time the GOP controlled the Senate, there were five holds placed in four years; Helms placed eighty-four holds in 1995. He maintained his presence in the Senate after the 1996 election, defeating former Charlotte mayor Harvey Gantt with a 52.6% share of the vote.

In March 1996 the Helms-Burton Act was signed into law, sponsored by Helms and Republican Representative Dan Burton of Indiana. The law was designed to pressure Cuba to adopt democratic reforms and was approved a month after Cuban warplanes shot down two civilian aircraft, killing four Cuban-Americans on board. It was bitterly criticized by Canada and the European Union.

On April 18, 1997, Clinton approved a plan to reorganize the State Department, a decision that responded to a long-standing demand by Helms. The plan aimed to consolidate the Arms Control and Disarmament Agency and the U.S. Information Agency into the State Department by 1999. Helms remained feisty, as in the fall of 1997, he refused to hold a hearing on President Clinton's nomination of moderate Republican William Weld to be ambassador to Mexico, noting that the former Massachusetts governor was soft on drugs. Although he began to face mounting criticism, "Senator No" wasn't budging. Helms won the battle, as Weld asked the White House to withdraw his nomination in mid-September.

His next battle appears to be federal arts funding, as Helms is among politicians who want to eliminate the National Endowment for the Arts. He stated in a speech to his colleagues, "It is self-evident that many of the beneficiaries of NEA grants are contemptuous of traditional moral standards."

Further Reading

Furgurson, Ernest B., *Hard Right: The Rise of Jesse Helms*, Norton, 1986.
Mother Jones, May 1995.
New Republic, November 12, 1990.
New York Times, April 18, 1997.
New York Times Magazine, October 28, 1990. □

Hinton Rowan Helper

Hinton Rowan Helper (1829-1909), American author and railroad promoter, wrote a brilliant antislavery tract based on economic analysis, as well as producing several denunciatory books on the African Americans.

Hinton Rowan Helper was born on a small farm near Mocksville, N. C., the youngest of six children. Upon the father's death, the family was forced to turn to a maternal uncle who ran the farm and paid for Hinton's education at the Mocksville Academy. Helper worked as an apprentice to a storekeeper in Salisbury until 1850, when he left for California with $300 in embezzled funds, which he agreed to pay back.

Helper's California adventure failed, and he returned home to write his first book, *The Land of Gold,* perhaps the most derogatory account of California ever written. Complaining that the proslavery publisher of the book had deleted his comments on slavery, he decided to write a criticism of the slave system. *The Impending Crisis: How To Meet It* was an instant success despite the 1857 depression. Using the census statistics of 1850, Helper developed a superb economic critique of slavery, a version of which the young Republican party distributed for campaign purposes in the 1860 election.

Helper was destitute in late 1861, when President Abraham Lincoln made him consul to Buenos Aires. He served competently until 1866, married a well-born Argentinian, but plunged deeply in debt.

Distraught at the failure of middling Southern whites to assume control of the South during the early Reconstruction period, he produced *Nojoque* (1867), a vitriolic attack on African Americans. He followed it the next year with *Negroes in Negroland,* another catalog of disaffection.

After limited success as a real estate promoter and agent for Americans with claims against South American republics, Helper turned to railroads, which occupied his attention for nearly 40 years. He inspired essay contests, compiled statistics, wrote tracts and letters, lobbied incessantly, and produced a visionary feasibility study of intercontinental railroads. During this period he authored three books: the semiautobiographical *Noonday Exigencies in America,* an acerbic treatise on South American nations; *Oddments of Andean Diplomacy;* and *The Three Americas Railway.* He also tried to organize a third political party, encouraged the growth of the American Anthropological Society, and traveled extensively abroad. His wife, childless and blind, returned to Argentina. Helper committed suicide at the age of 79 and was buried in a pauper's grave.

Further Reading

The most detailed and exhaustive treatment of Helper is an unpublished 1967 doctoral dissertation at the University of Wisconsin by Joaquin Jose Cardoso, *Hinton Rowan Helper: A Nineteenth Century Pilgrimage.* Hugh C. Bailey, *Hinton Rowan Helper: Abolitionist-Racist* (1965), is sketchy on Helper's early life and relies on secondary materials. See also Hugh Talmadge Lefler, *Hinton Rowan Helper: Advocate of a "White America"* (1935).

Additional Sources

Peissner, Elias, *The American question in its national aspect. Being also an incidental reply to Mr. H. R. Helper's "Compendium of the impending crisis of the South,* Freeport, N.Y., Books for Libraries Press, 1971.

Wolfe, Samuel M., *Helper's impending crisis dissected,* New York, Negro Universities Press, 1969. □

Claude Adrien Helvétius

The French philosopher Claude Adrien Helvétius (1715-1771) advocated political and social equality for all men and held that education and legislation were the means to attain this goal.

Claude Adrien Helvétius was born on Jan. 25, 1715, in Paris into a family of noted physicians. Taught by private tutor until 11, Claude attended France's leading school, the Jesuits' Louis-le-grand. To prepare Helvétius for the remunerative post of tax collector, his father apprenticed him to his uncle, already in such a position. At Caen, Helvétius studied more than finance: he wrote poetry; he read John Locke, Baron de Montesquieu, Thomas Hobbes, Voltaire, and Sir Isaac Newton; and he indulged himself in the pleasures of the town.

Through influence of the Queen, his father procured for Helvétius a post as tax collector. This position required him to travel much in the provinces, and he became painfully aware of the state of the rural economy. From 1738 to 1751 his home was Paris. Handsome, a good dancer, with a great passion for women, he circulated vigorously in Parisian society. But by 1749 he longed for a life of repose so as to write. In 1751 he married and retired to a country estate at Voré.

By 1755 Helvétius had produced *De l'esprit.* On July 15, 1758, the book was offered for sale in Paris. By early August difficulties began for Helvétius and lasted until his death in 1771. He was exiled for 2 years from Paris, and the sale of his book was forbidden. Publicly burned, placed on the Index, condemned by Jansenist and Jesuit alike, the work was attacked even by other *philosophes.* Some of them found it narrow and empty; others thought its boldness frightening.

In 1764 Helvétius visited England and in 1765, Prussia. He was struck by the great disparity of wealth found among the "free" English. England's commercialism, he said, had "made corruption legal." Except for these tours and occasional trips to Paris, Helvétius' remaining years were spent at Voré and were for him rather melancholy ones. Harvests were poor, and attacks of gout prevented his participation in sports, which, in addition to women, were said to be his real passion.

By 1769 Helvétius had finished *De l'homme* and turned to reworking his early poem *Du bonheur.* On Dec. 4, 1771, he and his family left Voré for the winter's stay in Paris. On December 26, following severe gout attacks, Helvétius died surrounded by his family.

Helvétius taught that man depended for all his knowledge on sensation and that his motives were those of self-love. For Helvétius the truly virtuous man is he who finds his pleasure—not just his obligation—in working for the com-

mon good. Most religions, he held, were ineffectual and offered hypocritical bases for morality. Differences in men's behavior stem from differences in station and education rather than from inherent differences. So, legislation that pertains to the structure of society and education accorded to all by the state are the fit means to procure an increase in man's happiness. In economics too Helvétius' views were radical, and he traced the unhappiness of men and nations to unequal distribution of wealth.

Further Reading

A good recent work on Helvétius is David Warner Smith, *Helvétius: A Study in Persecution* (1965). Mordecai Grossman, *The Philosophy of Helvétius, with a Special Emphasis on the Educational Implications of Sensationalism* (1926), is a still useful introduction. For Helvétius as an educational theorist see Ian Cumming, *Helvétius: His Life and Place in the History of Educational Thought* (1955). Irving Louis Horowitz, *Claude Hevétius: Philosopher of Democracy and Enlightenment* (1954), is a forthright appreciation of Helvétius' political and economic thought and influence.

Additional Sources

Grossman, Mordecai, *The philosophy of Helvetius, with special emphasis on the educational implications of sensationalism,* New York, AMS Press, 1972.

Hazlitt, William, *An essay on the principles of human action, and some remarks on the systems of Hartley and Helvetius,* Gainesville, Fla., Scholars' Facsimiles & Reprints, 1969.

Smith, David Warner., *Helvétius: a study in persecution,* Westport, Conn.: Greenwood Press, 1982, 1965. □

Ernest Miller Hemingway

Ernest Miller Hemingway (1898-1961), American Nobel Prize-winning author, was one of the most celebrated and influential literary stylists of the 20th century.

Ernest Hemingway was a legend in his own life-time—in a sense, a legend of his own making. He worked hard at being a composite of all the manly attributes he gave to his fictional heroes—a hard drinker, big-game hunter, fearless soldier, amateur boxer, and bullfight *aficionado*. Because the man and his fiction often seemed indistinguishable, critics have had difficulty judging his work objectively. His protagonists—virile and laconic—have been extravagantly praised and vehemently denounced. In his obsession with violence and death, the Hemingway creation has been rivaled only by the Byronic myth of the 19th century. Despite sensational publicity and personal invective, Hemingway now ranks among America's great writers. His critical stature rests solidly upon a small body of exceptional writing, distinguished for its stylistic purity, emotional veracity, moral integrity, and dramatic intensity of vision.

Ernest Hemingway was born in Oak Park, Ill., on July 21, 1898. His father was a country physician, who taught his son hunting and fishing; his mother was a religiously puritanical woman, active in church affairs, who led her boy to play the cello and sing in the choir. Hemingway's early years were spent largely in combating the repressive feminine influence of his mother and nurturing the masculine influence of his father. He spent the summers with his family in the woods of northern Michigan, where he often accompanied his father on professional calls. The discovery of his father's apparent cowardice, later depicted in the short story "The Doctor and the Doctor's Wife," and his suicide several years later left the boy with an emotional scar.

Despite the intense pleasure Hemingway derived from outdoor life, and his popularity in high school—where he distinguished himself as a scholar and athlete—he ran away from home twice. However, his first real chance for escape came in 1917, when the United States entered World War I. He volunteered for active service in the infantry but was rejected because of eye trouble.

After spending several months as a reporter for the *Kansas City Star,* Hemingway enlisted in the Red Cross medical service, driving an ambulance on the Italian front. He was badly wounded in the knee at Fossalta di Piave; yet, still under heavy mortar fire, he carried a wounded man on his back a considerable distance to the aid station. After having over 200 shell fragments removed from his legs and body, Hemingway next enlisted in the Italian infantry, served on the Austrian front until the armistice, and was decorated for bravery by the Italian government.

Learning His Trade

Shortly after the war Hemingway worked as a foreign correspondent in the Near East for the *Toronto Star*. When he returned to Michigan, he had already decided to commit himself to fiction writing. His excellent journalism and the publication in magazines of several experimental short stories had impressed the well-known author Sherwood Anderson, who, when Hemingway decided to return to Europe, gave him letters of introduction to expatriates Gertrude Stein and Ezra Pound. Hemingway and his bride, Hadley Richardson, journeyed to Paris, where he served his literary apprenticeship under these two prominent authors. Despite the abject poverty in which he and his wife lived, these were the happiest years of Hemingway's life, as well as the most artistically fruitful.

In 1923 Hemingway published his first book, *Three Stories and Ten Poems*. The poems are insignificant, but the stories give strong indication of his emerging genius. "Out of Season" already contains the psychological tension and moral ambivalence characteristic of his mature work. With *In Our Time* (1925) Hemingway's years of apprenticeship ended. In this collection of stories, he drew on his experiences while summering in Michigan to depict the initiation into the world of pain and violence of young Nick Adams, a prototype for later Hemingway heroes. The atrocities he had witnessed as a journalist in the Near East became the brief vignettes about intense suffering that formed interchapters for the collection. One story, "Indian Camp," which sets the tone for the entire volume, has Nick accompanying his

father, Dr. Adams, on a call during which the physician performs a caesarean operation with no anesthetic. They discover afterward that the squaw's husband, unable to bear his wife's screams, has killed himself by nearly severing his head with a razor. The story is written in Hemingway's characteristically terse, economic prose. "The End of Something" and "The Three Day Blow" deal with Nick's disturbed reaction to the end of a love affair. "The Big Two-hearted River" describes a young man just returned from war and his desperate attempt to prevent mental breakdown.

Major Novels

Hemingway returned to the United States in 1926 with the manuscripts of two novels and several short stories. *The Torrents of Spring* (1926), a parody of Sherwood Anderson, was written very quickly, largely for the purpose of breaking his contract with Boni and Liveright, who was also Anderson's publisher. That May, Scribner's issued Hemingway's second novel, *The Sun Also Rises*. This novel, the major statement of the "lost generation," describes a group of expatriate Americans and Englishmen, all of whom have suffered physically and emotionally during the war; their aimless existence vividly expresses the spiritual bankruptcy and moral atrophy of an entire generation. Hemingway's second volume of short stories, *Men without Women* (1927), contains "The Killers," about a man who refuses to run from gangsters determined to kill him; "The Light of the World," dealing with Nick Adams's premature introduction to the sickening world of prostitution and homosexuality; and "The Undefeated," concerning an aging bullfighter whose courage and dedication constitute a moral victory in the face of physical defeat and death.

In December 1929 *A Farewell to Arms* was published. This novel tells the story of a tragically terminated love affair between an American soldier and an English nurse, starkly silhouetted against the bleakness of war and a collapsing world order. It contains a philosophical expression of the Hemingway code of stoical endurance in a violent age: "The world breaks everyone," reflects the protagonist, "and afterward many are strong in the broken places. But those that it will not break it kills. It kills the very good and the very gentle and the very brave impartially. If you are none of those you can be sure that it will kill you too, but there will be no special hurry."

Hemingway revealed his passionate interest in bullfighting in *Death in the Afternoon* (1932), a humorous and inventive nonfiction study. In 1933 Scribner's published his final collection of short stories, *Winner Take Nothing*. This volume, containing his most bitter and disillusioned writing, deals almost exclusively with emotional breakdown, impotence, and homosexuality.

Hemingway's African safari in 1934 provided the material for another nonfiction work, *The Green Hills of Africa* (1935), as well as two of his finest short stories, "The Short Happy Life of Francis Macomber" and "The Snows of Kilimanjaro." Both stories concern attainment of self-realization and moral integrity through contact with fear and death.

Hemingway wrote *To Have and Have Not* (1937) in response to the 1930s depression. The novel, inadequately conceived and poorly executed, deals with a Florida smuggler whose illegal activities and frequent brutalities mask his sense of ethics and strength of character. Mortally wounded by the gangsters with whom he has been dealing, the individualistic hero comes to the startling realization that "One man alone ain't got no—chance."

The chief political catalyst in Hemingway's life was the Spanish Civil War. In 1936 he had returned to Spain as a newspaper reporter and participated in raising funds for the Spanish Republic until the war's end in 1939. In 1937 he collaborated on the documentary film *The Spanish Earth.* Hemingway's only writing during this period was a play, *The Fifth Column* (1936; produced in New York in 1940), a sincere but dramatically ineffective attempt to portray the conditions prevailing during the siege of Madrid.

Seventeen months after that war ended, Hemingway completed *For Whom the Bell Tolls* (1940). His most ambitious novel, it describes an American professor's involvement with a loyalist guerrilla band and his brief, idyllic love affair with a Spanish girl. A vivid, intelligently conceived narrative, it is written in less lyrical and more dramatic prose than his earlier work. Hemingway deliberately avoided having the book used as propaganda, despite its strained attempt at an affirmative resolution, by carefully balancing fascist atrocities with a heartless massacre by a peasant mob.

World War II

Following the critical and popular success of *For Whom the Bell Tolls,* Hemingway lapsed into a literary silence that lasted a full decade and was largely the result of his strenuous, frequently reckless, activities during World War II. In 1942 as a *Collier's* correspondent with the 3d Army, he witnessed some of the bloodiest battles in Europe. Although he served in no official capacity, he commanded a personal battalion of over 200 troops and was granted the respect and privileges normally accorded a general. At this time he received the affectionate appellation of "Papa" from his admirers, both military and literary.

In 1944 while in London, Hemingway met and soon married Mary Welsh, a *Time* reporter. His three previous marriages—to Hadley Richardson, mother of one son; to Pauline Pfeiffer, mother of his second and third sons; and to Martha Gelhorn—had all ended in divorce. Following the war, Hemingway and his wife purchased a home, Finca Vigia, near Havana, Cuba. Hemingway's only literary work was some anecdotal articles for *Esquire;* the remainder of his time was spent fishing, hunting, battling critics, and providing copy for gossip columnists. In 1950 he ended his literary silence with *Across the River and into the Trees,* a narrative, flawed by maudlin self-pity, about a retired Army colonel dying of a heart condition in Venice and his dreamy love affair with a pubescent girl.

Last Works

Hemingway's remarkable gift for recovery once again asserted itself in 1952 with the appearance of a novella about an extraordinary battle between a tired old Cuban fisherman and a giant marlin. *The Old Man and the Sea,* immediately hailed a masterpiece, was awarded the Pulitzer Prize in 1953. Although lacking the emotional tensions of his longer works, this novella possesses a generosity of spirit and reverence for life which make it an appropriate conclusion for Hemingway's career. In 1954 Hemingway won the Nobel Prize for literature.

Hemingway's rapidly deteriorating physical condition and an increasingly severe psychological disturbance drastically curtailed his literary capabilities in the last years of his life. A nostalgic journey to Africa planned by the author and his wife in 1954 ended in their plane crash over the Belgian Congo. Hemingway suffered severe burns and internal injuries from which he never fully recovered. Additional strain occurred when the revolutionary Cuban government of Fidel Castro forced the Hemingways to leave Finca Vigía. After only a few months in their new home in Ketchum, Idaho, Hemingway was admitted to the Mayo Clinic to be treated for hypertension and emotional depression and was later treated by electroshock therapy. Scornful of an illness which humiliated him physically and impaired his writing, he killed himself with a shotgun on July 2, 1961.

Shortly after Hemingway's death, literary critic Malcolm Cowley and scholar Carlos Baker were entrusted with the task of going through the writer's remaining manuscripts to decide what material might be publishable. The first posthumous work, *A Moveable Feast* (1964), is an elegiac reminiscence of Hemingway's early years in Paris, containing some fine writing as well as brilliant vignettes of his famous contemporaries. A year later the *Atlantic Monthly* published a few insignificant short stories and two long, rambling poems. In 1967 William White edited a collection of Hemingway's best journalism under the title *By-Line Ernest Hemingway.*

Further Reading

The authorized biography of Hemingway is Carlos Baker, *Ernest Hemingway: A Life Story* (1969). A controversial portrait is A. E. Hotchner, *Papa Hemingway: A Personal Memoir* (1966). Among the major full-length critical studies are Carlos Baker, *Ernest Hemingway: The Writer as Artist* (1952; 3d rev. ed. 1963), a textual study with emphasis on structure and symbolism; Philip Young, *Ernest Hemingway* (1952; rev. ed. 1966); Earl Rovit, *Ernest Hemingway* (1963); Richard B. Hovey, *Hemingway: The Inward Terrain* (1968); and Leo Gurko's more general *Ernest Hemingway and the Pursuit of Heroism* (1968).

The most valuable early critical essays on Hemingway are Edmund Wilson, "Hemingway: Gauge of Morale," in *Wound and the Bow* (1941); Robert Penn Warren, "Ernest Hemingway," in *Selected Essays* (1958); and Malcolm Cowley, "Nightmare and Ritual in Hemingway," reprinted in Robert Percy Weeks, ed., *Hemingway: A Collection of Critical Essays* (1962). The two major critical collections are John K. McCaffery, ed., *Ernest Hemingway: The Man and His Work* (1950), and Carlos Baker, ed., *Hemingway and His Critics: An International Anthology* (1961). See also the relevant sections in Joseph Warren Beach, *American Fiction, 1920-1940* (1941); Edwin Berry Burgum, *The Novel and the World's Dilemma* (1947); Wilbur M. Frohock, *The Novel of Violence in America, 1920-1950* (1950; 2d rev. ed. 1958); Frederick J. Hoffman, *The Modern Novel in America, 1900-1950* (1951); and

Ray B. West, *The Short Story in America, 1900-1950* (1952). □

Louis Hémon

Louis Hémon (1880-1913) was a French novelist best known for his "Maria Chapdelaine," in which the pioneering regions of Quebec are so vividly presented that the work long overshadowed novels by native Canadians.

Born in Brest, Louis Hémon was educated in Paris, where his father was an inspector general in the education ministry. Hémon qualified for the colonial service but decided not to become a civil servant. Instead, he traveled in England, working occasionally as a commercial traveler. He developed an interest in various sports and wrote for sporting journals. In these he also published his first stories, mostly based on his observations in England. Little is known about his personal life except that he had a daughter in 1909.

In 1911 Hémon arrived in Canada, spending his first winter in Montreal. Then he set out for Lake St. John, where he was engaged as a farmhand in Peribonka. Hémon's taciturn nature and laconic correspondence have left the way open for legends, such as that of the overcivilized Parisian seeking a simple natural life or the atavistic Breton in need of adventurous travel. What is certain is that he was a keen observer, detached enough to record the externals of pioneer life, yet involved enough to comprehend the myths of the French Canadians.

It is the combination of detachment and involvement that makes *Maria Chapdelaine: Récit du Canada français* into a major Canadian novel, despite the objections of many Canadians who feel it gives a distorted picture of their life. The premature death of the hero results from a heroic gesture but also from an impossibly hard environment. The death of the heroine's mother is precipitated by ignorance and isolation but at the same time reveals the courage and endurance which give the people its pride. The final choice of the heroine, to marry a poor pioneer like her father instead of a neighbor who has "deserted" to become an American factory worker, has excited both disgust and admiration.

The style of the novel ranges from cold, naturalistic description to lyrical effusion. Its general import goes beyond a mere local problem to evoke a feeling for human dignity in a bleak world. Hémon apparently wrote the novel in his sparse leisure time at Peribonka and left during the following spring. He dispatched the manuscript to *Le Temps,* a onetime sporting journal, where it was published in serial form (1914). The author meanwhile had set out for the West but was killed in a train accident at Chapleau, Ontario, in July 1913.

Maria Chapdelaine was published in book form in 1916 but not rescued from oblivion until 1921. Four other books were subsequently published from Hémon's manuscripts.

Further Reading

There is scant information on Hémon in English, but he is mentioned in several works that also serve as useful background: Lorne Pierce, *An Outline of Canadian Literature* (1927); Ian Forbes Fraser, *The Spirit of French Canada: A Study of the Literature* (1939); and Jack Warwick, *The Long Journey: Literary Themes of French Canada* (1968).

Additional Sources

Deschamps, Nicole, *Le mythe de Maria Chapdelaine,* Montreal: Presses de l'Universite de Montreal, 1980.

Dube, Marcel, *Jean-Paul Lemieux et le livre,* Montreal: Art Global, 1988.

Hémon, Louis, *Itineraire de Liverpool a Quebec,* Quimper France: Calligrammes, 1985.

Hémon, Louis, *Lettres a sa famille,* Montreal: Boreal Express, 1980.

Lemieux, Jean Paul, *Jean Paul Lemieux retrouve Maria Chapdelaine,* Montreal; Paris: Stanke, 1981.

Levesque, Gilbert., *Louis Hémon, aventurier ou philosophe?,* Montreal: Fides, 1980.

Thom, Ian M., *Maria Chapdelaine: illustrations,* Kleinburg, Ont.: McMichael Canadian Art Collection, 1987. □

Arthur Henderson

The British statesman Arthur Henderson (1863-1935) was an architect of the Labour party and served as foreign secretary from 1929 to 1931.

Arthur Henderson, the second son of a Scottish cotton spinner, David Henderson, was born in Glasgow on Sept. 13, 1863. He grew up in a poor but hardworking family and attended school in Glasgow and in Newcastle upon Tyne in Northumbria. At age 12 he terminated his schooling and began working in a local foundry.

In his late teens several things happened that profoundly influenced Henderson for the remainder of his life. He happened to hear the famed evangelist Gipsy Smith, who was a captain in the Salvation Army. Henderson was captured by the evangelist's eloquence and joined a local Wesleyan Methodist church. He also became interested in the trade union movement and joined the Friendly Society of Ironfounders (later renamed the National Union of Foundry Workers).

Henderson entered politics as an admirer of William Gladstone, who was then in the twilight of his long career. He engaged in local politics as a member of the radical wing of the Liberal party, and in 1892 he was elected a member of the Newcastle City Council. It was the first of several local positions that he held. Throughout this period of his life he remained active in trade union activities and rightfully deserves to be considered one of the founders of the emerging Labour party. In 1911 he became secretary of the Labour party and retained this position until 1934. He entered

ward ways and throughout his life revealed a great strength of character based upon his strong religious convictions. In 1888 he married Eleanor Watson; they had three sons and one daughter. His family was extremely close and a source of great satisfaction to him. Henderson suffered a heart attack and died on Oct. 20, 1935.

Further Reading

The best biography of Henderson is Mary Agnes Hamilton, *Arthur Henderson* (1938). Edwin Alfred Jenkins, *From Foundry to Foreign Office* (1933), is a less complete, journalistic account of his life. Both authors knew Henderson and are sympathetic toward him. For his role in the Labour party, G. D. H. Cole, *A History of the Labour Party from 1914* (1948), should be consulted. A perceptive chapter on Henderson's years at the Foreign Office can be found in Gordon A. Craig and Felix Gilbert, eds., *The Diplomats, 1919-1939* (1953).

Additional Sources

Carlton, David, *MacDonald versus Henderson: the foreign policy of the second Labour Government,* New York, Humanities Press, 1970.

Carlton, David, *MacDonald versus Henderson: the foreign policy of the second Labour Government,* London, Macmillan, 1970.

Leventhal, F. M., *Arthur Henderson,* Manchester, UK; New York: Manchester University Press; New York: Distributed exclusively in the USA by St. Martin's Press, 1989.

Wrigley, Chris, *Arthur Henderson,* Cardiff: GPC Books, 1990. ☐

Parliament in 1903 as a member of the Independent Labour party.

In the House of Commons, Henderson quickly won the respect of his colleagues for his keen knowledge of social and labor problems. When World War I broke out in 1914, he replaced Ramsay MacDonald as Labour leader in the House, and in 1915 he was brought into H. H. Asquith's Cabinet as president of the board of education. Later he resigned this post and accepted the less demanding one of paymaster general. In 1916 the new prime minister, David Lloyd George, made him a member of his War Cabinet. After the first Russian revolution of 1917, Lloyd George sent him on an important mission to Russia. After his return from Russia, however, he broke with Lloyd George over the question of British representation at the proposed conference of international socialists to be held at Stockholm. Consequently, he resigned his Cabinet position and redirected his energies to Labour party affairs.

After the war Henderson remained an instrumental figure in party activities, and he continued to serve, with some interruptions, in the House of Commons. He is best remembered for the 2 years (1929-1931) he spent at the Foreign Office, where he championed policies such as support for the League of Nations and disarmament. He later presided over the World Disarmament Conference which met in Geneva in 1932. He received the Nobel Peace Prize for 1934.

Henderson was known in Labour party ranks as "Uncle Arthur" and was recognized internationally as an "Apostle of Peace." He was respected for his sincere and straightfor-

Richard Henderson

Richard Henderson (1735-1785), American jurist and land speculator, was important in the early expansion of the frontier. He established the short-lived Transylvania Colony in Kentucky.

Richard Henderson was born on April 20, 1735, in Hanover County, Va. During the early 1740s his family moved to Granville County, N.C., where his father became sheriff. Richard served as constable and, later, as deputy to his father. After studying law for a year, he passed the bar examination in 1763 and, about the same time, married Elizabeth Keeling. The couple had two sons.

In 1764 Henderson organized Richard Henderson and Company to take advantage of opportunities for land and profit in the West. He hired Daniel Boone to explore the region beyond the mountains, sending Boone into Kentucky in 1769.

Because of his family position and his legal training, Henderson was appointed an associate justice of the Superior Court of North Carolina in 1768. But his judgeship brought considerable difficulties; thus, when his term expired in 1773, he returned to western land speculation.

During the winter of 1774-1775 Henderson organized the Transylvania Land Company and soon opened negotiations with Cherokee Indian leaders for several million acres between the Kentucky and Cumberland rivers on which to found a new colony. In March 1775 the Transylvania leaders concluded the Treaty of Sycamore Shoals, thereby, theoretically, clearing the area of Indian claims.

During the summer, settlement began, and Henderson himself led settlers through the Cumberland Gap into Kentucky. There he tried to establish the new colony of Transylvania. However, conflicting land claims of North Carolina and Virginia, continuing warfare with marauding Indian bands, and the unwillingness of the frontiersmen to accept Henderson's autocratic views, prevented this. When, in December 1776, Virginia created Kentucky County, Henderson's colonizing was effectively ended.

Henderson eventually received some 400,000 acres of western lands to compensate for his expense and effort. He later helped survey the Virginia—North Carolina boundary, was instrumental in establishing a settlement at Nashville, and served several terms in the North Carolina Legislature.

Further Reading

There is no biography of Henderson, although his activities are discussed in many works about the early trans-Appalachian settlement. Archibald Henderson in *The Conquest of the Old Southwest* (1920) gives a laudatory account of Richard Henderson, his ancestor. The best discussion is William Stewart Lester, *The Transylvania Colony* (1935). For Henderson's relationship with Boone see John Bakeless, *Daniel Boone* (1939). James Alton James, *The Life of George Rogers Clark* (1928), relates Clark's role in the fight against Henderson in Kentucky.

Additional Sources

Brashers, Howard Charles, *A snug little purchase: how Richard Henderson bought Kaintuckee from the Cherokees in 1775,* La Mesa, Calif.: Associated Creative Writers, 1979. ☐

Jimi Hendrix

Jimi Hendrix (1942-1970) is perhaps the most innovative electric guitarist of all time, combining blues, hard rock, modern jazz, and soul into his own unmistakable sound.

In the few years between his emergence as a solo artist and his death from a barbiturate overdose at the height of his fame, Jimi Hendrix wrought a slew of radical changes on pop music. Arguably the most innovative electric guitarist of all time, he combined the raw passion of the blues, the sonic aggression of hard rock, the aural adventure of psychedelia and modern jazz, and the symphonic lyricism of progressive soul, melding these disparate inclinations into a style that, even when heard in fragments, remains unmistakably his own.

Had his instrumental prowess been his only contribution, Hendrix would remain a towering figure in modern music. But he was also a supremely gifted songwriter, as the myriad cover versions of his songs by such diverse artists as Eric Clapton, the Pretenders, Frank Zappa, Rickie Lee Jones, Living Colour, The Cure, jazz composer Gil Evans, and many others attest. When funk pioneer George Clinton was asked by a *Rolling Stone* interviewer how Hendrix had influenced Clinton's band Funkadelic, he responded, ''He was it. He took noise to church.''

At the time of his death, Hendrix was working desperately on an ambitious project that seemed designed to bridge a dazzling array of musical territories. Though he never completed that record, he did lay the groundwork for a range of bold stylistic hybrids, and he continues to influence those who hear his work. ''Hendrix left an indelible, fiercely individual mark on popular music,'' wrote David Fricke in *Rolling Stone,* ''accelerating rock's already dynamic rate of change in the late 1960s with his revolutionary synthesis of guitar violence, improvisational nerve, spacey melodic reveries and a confessional intensity born of the blues.'' Indeed, as one of the late musician's friends told the authors of the biography *Electric Gypsy,* Hendrix revealed, ''I sacrifice part of my soul every time I play.''

Raised by His Father

The man who would achieve fame as Jimi Hendrix was born Johnny Allen Hendrix in Seattle, Washington, in 1942. His father, Al—a gifted jazz dancer who worked at a number of jobs including landscape gardening—bore much of the responsibility of raising the boy and his brother, Leon, as did their grandmother and various family friends. This was due to the unreliability of Al's wife, Lucille, who drank excessively and would disappear for extended periods. Al

Hendrix won custody of his sons and exercised as much discipline as he could, but the boys—young Johnny especially—worshipped their absentee mother; numerous biographers have hypothesized that in later years the guitarist looked to her as his muse. Al later changed his older son's name to James Marshall Hendrix.

Jimmy Hendrix wanted a guitar early on; before acquiring his first real instrument, he plucked a number of surrogates, including a broom and a one-stringed ukelele. Al at last procured a guitar for him, and the precocious 12-year-old restrung it upside down—as a left-hander, he was forced to turn the instrument in the opposite direction from how it is usually played, which left the low strings on the bottom unless he rearranged them—proceeding to teach himself blues songs from records by greats like B. B. King and Muddy Waters. The guitar rarely left his side and even lay beside him as he slept. By his mid-teens, Hendrix was playing blues and R&B with his band the Rocking Kings. He played behind his back, between his legs, and over his head—as had many blues guitarists before him. Thus he endeared himself to audiences, if not to all musicians.

It was therefore a shock to his father and friends when Hendrix joined the armed forces at age 17 and left his guitar behind. He volunteered for the 101st Airborne Division as a paratrooper and was soon jumping out of airplanes (he would later use his instrument to evoke the otherworldly sounds and sensations of freefall). Eventually he sent for his guitar and became the object of much derision and abuse from his peers, who considered Hendrix's extravagant devotion to the instrument freakish.

Performed on the "Chitlin Circuit"

An exception was a young private named Billy Cox. Himself an aspiring bassist with a taste for jazz as well as R&B, Cox overheard guitar music coming from inside a club on the camp that sounded, as he told *Electric Gypsy* authors Harry Shapiro and Caesar Glebbeek, "somewhere between [German classical composer Ludwig von] Beethoven and [blues icon] John Lee Hooker." He immediately suggested that he and Hendrix form a band; soon their quintet was entertaining troops all over the region. Eventually, though, Hendrix tired of army discipline and managed—with the help of a well-timed and overdramatized injury—to obtain a discharge. Cox got out two months later.

After a few unproductive months, the two musicians headed for Nashville, Tennessee, which was just gaining a national reputation for its recording scene. Their new band, the King Kasuals—a revamped version of their service combo—landed a regular gig at the El Morocco club. Hendrix rapidly established himself as one of the hottest guitarists in town. At the time, however, he had no confidence in his singing and was content to back R&B artists, among them Curtis Mayfield, whose soulful guitar playing combined rhythm and lead and strongly influenced Hendrix's later balladry.

Over the next few years, Hendrix logged time in several R&B road shows—on what came to be known, somewhat disparagingly, as the "Chitlin Circuit"—though he didn't last long with any one act; his wild hair and compelling stage presence often stole the thunder from bandleaders who expected their musicians to play their assigned parts and stay in the background. From the seminal rocker Little Richard, Hendrix lifted much of what would become his signature look as an artist. Richard admired the guitarist's playing but viewed his taste for the limelight as a threat. The Isley Brothers gave Hendrix a bit more freedom; he was allowed to stretch out onstage and contributed a fiery solo to their 1964 single "Testify." The Isley Brothers hit showcases the passion and budding virtuosity that would soon make Hendrix a sensation.

Hendrix then played with saxophonist King Curtis and later with friend Curtis Knight (cowriting and recording some sides with the latter that would be exploited after he achieved fame). In 1965 he signed—for a one-dollar advance—a record contract with Knight's manager and PPX Productions head Ed Chalpin, the first of many costly and ill-advised legal entanglements that characterized Hendrix's career. It was around this time that he formed his own group, Jimmy James & the Blue Flames (which included a future member of the psychedelic rock group Spirit), moved to New York, and played endless low-paying gigs at the Cafe Wha? in Greenwich Village. His increasingly daring guitar work would make itself known, however.

Gave "Experience" New Meaning

Linda Keith, then girlfriend of Rolling Stones guitarist Keith Richards, was sufficiently impressed by Hendrix to recommend him to Chas Chandler, bassist for British rock sensations the Animals and an aspiring manager. Chandler was stunned by Hendrix and urged him to come to London.

The road-weary Hendrix was justifiably skeptical, but Chandler turned out to be the real thing. Soon the guitarist was en route to the United Kingdom.

Chandler suggested changing the spelling of Hendrix's first name to Jimi, though the oft-cited assertion that he made this suggestion on the flight to London may be untrue. In any event, they touched down in September of 1966 and immediately put a band together with two British musicians, guitarist Noel Redding—who came to Chandler's office hoping to audition for the Animals but would, instead, be handed a bass for the first time—and jazz-influenced drummer John "Mitch" Mitchell, who won a coin toss to beat out his only competitor.

Mitchell's exuberant, round-the-kit playing combined the frenetic psychedelic blues attack of his most famous British peers with a post-bop virtuosity that recalled Elvin Jones, one-time skinsman for visionary jazz saxophonist John Coltrane. Many critics would later suggest that the Hendrix-Mitchell chemistry paralleled that between the two jazz players. Thus was born the Jimi Hendrix Experience. "Together, they complemented the rhythmic idiosyncrasies of Hendrix's songs and playing style with their own turbulent blend of hardy soul dynamics and breathtaking acid-jazz breakaways," wrote Rolling Stone's Fricke. "The sound was fluid enough for open-ended jamming yet free of excess instrumental baggage, tight and heavy in the hard-rock clutches."

Meanwhile, Hendrix had found his voice not only as a songwriter but as a singer. Both his vocalizing and lyrics were profoundly influenced by folk-rock trailblazer Bob Dylan, whose unpretty plainsong voice and personal, surrealistic writing inspired Hendrix to cover his work—witness the rocking hit version of "All Along the Watchtower"—and to emulate it.

The Experience coalesced in a whirlwind couple of weeks, playing its debut gig in Paris opening for French pop star Johnny Hallyday at the Paris Olympia. Having signed with Track Records, they commenced recording their debut album the following month and by December had released their first single, a cover version of the folk-rock standard "Hey Joe." Hendrix's relaxed take on this often frantically rendered song added menace to the violent imagery of the lyrics and lent the title character's flight from justice considerable heft with concise, emotional bursts of lead guitar.

"Hey Joe" became a hit, and Hendrix proceeded to terrify London's biggest rock stars with his electrifying stage show. "It's the most psychedelic experience I ever had, going to see Hendrix play," guitarist Pete Townshend of The Who told Charles Shaar Murray, author of Crosstown Traffic. "When he started to play, something changed: colours changed, everything changed." Townshend—who claims never to have been a heavy user of psychedelic substances—recalled "flames and water dripping out of the ends of his hands." Eric Clapton, guitar "God" of rock until Hendrix's arrival, invited the young American onstage to play with his group Cream; soon "God" slunk offstage and was found in his dressing room with his head in his hands. Cream later wrote their psychedelic riff-rock smash "Sunshine of Your Love" in tribute to the American

firebrand; he eventually adopted it into his live set without knowing he'd inspired it.

Unlike Townshend, Hendrix had a special fondness for hallucinogens like LSD and was also an enthusiastic marijuana smoker. In addition, scores of women flocked to him, and his "Wild Man of Borneo" reputation made him seem—to those who didn't know him—like some kind of omnivorous Yank tornado. Yet he is almost universally remembered as a shy, diffident person, occasionally explosive but largely gentle and naive; he was in no way prepared for the stormy sea of fame or the cynical manipulations of the music business. As Shapiro and Glebbeek pointed out in Electric Gypsy, he was dashed between the extremes of sporadic hero worship and institutional racism. "Feted as the greatest rock guitarist in the world, acclaimed as a Dionysian superstud and refused service at the tattiest redneck lunch counters—Jimi Hendrix was treated as superhuman and subhuman, but rarely just human," the authors attest. Even so, he seemed to care little about issues of color and was especially frustrated by the suggestion that he played "white music" or "black music."

Stirred Up a "Purple Haze"

The Experience's debut album, Are You Experienced?—released in the United States on the Reprise label—was a watershed in popular music, only kept from the top chart position by one of the few albums that arguably exceeds it in importance: the Beatles' Sgt. Pepper's Lonely Hearts Club Band. Hendrix produced a psychedelic rock anthem in the disoriented "Purple Haze," elegiac soul with the ballad "The Wind Cries Mary," R&B brimstone with "Fire," and proto-jazz rock with "Third Stone from the Sun." The U.K. version of the record included the signature Hendrix blues "Red House," released the following year in the United States on a singles collection. Are You Experienced? was an epochal debut, full of innovative studio effects and Hendrix's advanced use of feedback and tremolo. Then, in 1967, the band took the landmark Monterey Pop Festival by storm; Hendrix's ceremonial burning of his guitar—a highly theatrical routine that he somehow invested with the solemnity of a ritual sacrifice—left audiences stunned and appropriately worshipful.

Hendrix returned to the United States a hero. Crowds swarmed to watch this "wild man" play with his teeth, play behind his head, make relatively explicit love to—and, with any luck, torch—his Fender Stratocaster, and otherwise update the blues showman tradition with revolutionary fervor. What sometimes got lost in this impressive performance, to Hendrix's eternal dismay, was the music.

In the meantime, Chas Chandler made the best of the Experience's disastrous, abortive tour with wholesome TV popsters the Monkees by starting a rumor that the ultraconservative Daughters of the American Revolution had forced out the group. When Hendrix wasn't playing concerts or engaging in marathon studio sessions, he could invariably be found jamming at local clubs with anyone and everyone.

The Jimi Hendrix Experience's follow-up album, Axis: Bold as Love, demonstrated Hendrix's balladry and general songcraft to even greater effect, particularly on "Little Wing," which has been covered numerous times. Yet Hendrix was deeply dissatisfied by the way his albums had been cut and mixed and by a number of other factors. The trio format limited him—Redding played the bass parts Hendrix wrote but added little spice to the band dynamic—and he quickly tired of the theatrics audiences had come to expect. When he neglected to play the flashy guitar hero, crowds often grew restless, filling him with frustration and even contempt.

Hendrix longed to expand his musical range and to this end began work on the one album over which he exercised complete control, the sprawling double-length *Electric Ladyland.* Featuring a vast crew of guest players, the epic blues "Voodoo Child," and the plaintive mini-symphony "Burning of the Midnight Lamp"—as well as the hit single "Crosstown Traffic"—it was the most far-reaching achievement of his brief recording career. "You don't care what people say so much," he told *Down Beat,* "you just go on and do what you want to do." Increasingly, this would not be as easy as Hendrix made it sound.

It was at this point that the unscrupulous Ed Chalpin sued Hendrix's management over his 1966 contract with the guitarist, disrupting his affairs for several years. Meanwhile, the enormous recording costs Hendrix had amassed making *Electric Ladyland* induced Chandler and comanager Mike Jeffreys to build a custom studio—Electric Ladyland Studios—that would be rented out when the guitarist wasn't using it. But this, too, cost a fortune, necessitating endless touring that resulted in extreme road fatigue. The Experience broke up, and Hendrix began working with bassist Cox again, also recruiting drummer Buddy Miles for a soul-rock trio he called Band of Gypsys.

Revamped the National Anthem

In 1969 Hendrix appeared at the famed Woodstock festival in New York state, where his performance of the "Star-Spangled Banner"—complete with apocalyptic guitar noise—captured the anguish of the Vietnam War era and became a legend and a vital component of every time-capsule summary of the period. As Living Colour guitarist and Black Rock Coalition founder Vernon Reid told *Crosstown Traffic* author Murray, "At that moment, he became one of the greats, like Coltrane or [bop saxophone luminary Charlie] Parker or [woodwind innovator Eric] Dolphy. He plugged into something deep, something beyond good or bad playing. It was just 'there it is.'"

Various interested parties hoped to team Hendrix with trumpeter-bandleader-composer Miles Davis, one of the preeminent creative forces in post-bop jazz; though this never materialized, Hendrix did play with a number of musicians in Davis's circle and showed a marked interest in elements of what would come to be called "fusion," an amalgam of jazz and rock. He also declared, in a late interview quoted by Murray, that he wanted a "big band" and expressed the desire for "other musicians to play my stuff," saying, "I want to be a good writer."

The Band of Gypsys recorded a live album and, of legal necessity, handed it over to Chalpin; it is the only document

of their short-lived band dynamic, one that tantalizingly demonstrates how a different rhythm section affected Hendrix's guitar work. Cox and Miles—who, as black sidemen, symbolized to Hendrix's more literal-minded political advisors a welcome concession to the black militancy of the day—did something Redding and Mitchell hadn't: they grooved. Much of the funk-rock and funk-metal that followed owes a huge debt to this corner of Hendrix's creativity. The scorching "Machine Gun" has been hailed by critics as a masterpiece.

But the trio was short-lived; soon Miles was out, Mitchell returned, and Hendrix recorded a number of tracks for what was to be perhaps the fullest realization of the sound he heard in his head: another double album, this one titled *First Rays of the New Rising Sun.* All available evidence suggests it would have melded soul, jazz, psychedelia, hard rock, and a few styles as yet unimagined. Tragically, after a slew of dispirited performances and perpetual self-medication, Jimi Hendrix died of a sleeping-pill overdose on September 18, 1970, before he could complete the ambitious work. He was buried in Seattle.

The Hendrix estate was mired in litigation for many years; Al Hendrix at last found an aggressive lawyer and in 1994—after a protracted struggle—looked to regain control of much of his son's music. In the years after the guitarist's death, hundreds of "new Hendrix albums" appeared, featuring everything from studio outtakes to pre-Experience club performances to rambling interviews. Consumers have gotten the shortest end of the stick, with a sizeable group of what rock industry consensus regards as the ultimate bottom-feeders profiting from these paltry and often grotesquely misrepresented scraps. Such exploitation, however, has scarcely tarnished Jimi Hendrix's shining legacy.

Bits and pieces of what would have been First Rays appeared on three of many posthumous releases—*The Cry of Love,* the soundtrack to the meandering hippie film *Rainbow Bridge,* and 1995's *Voodoo Soup,* of which *Vibe's* Joseph V. Tirella commented, "The title is silly but apt, since this album is a delicious soup of sorts, a bouillabaisse of musical flavors." Of all his posthumous recordings, *Voodoo Soup* garnered the best general reviews. *Entertainment Weekly* queried, "Another Hendrix hodgepodge? Yes . . . The catch is that this one . . . is as fluid and cohesive as a preconceived record, without a bad song in the bunch."

In less than four years, Hendrix had established himself as one of the most important figures in pop music history. His influence extends to virtually every corner of contemporary music, from funk to heavy metal to fusion to the "harmolodic" school of New York free jazz to alternative rock. Well into the 1990s, Hendrix's presence on the rock scene practically makes a myth of his physical absence: MCA Records released remastered versions of his classic albums on CD as well as a compilation of his blues pieces and his complete Woodstock set.

In 1992 Hendrix was inducted into the Rock and Roll Hall of Fame. The following year he received the Grammy Awards Lifetime Achievement Award. And notable rock, rap, and blues artists contributed cover versions of his songs to the high-profile 1993 tribute album *Stone Free.* That same year Hendrix archivist Bill Nitopi published *Cherokee Mist: The Lost Writings,* an ensemble of various forms of personal memorabilia including Hendrix's unpublished writings such as letters to family and friends, "never-before-seen" photographs, and notes on unrecorded music. The book title was meant to pay homage to Hendrix's Native American heritage.

Hendrix mania even extended into mid-1990s cyberculture when the Jimi Hendrix Foundation created an Internet web site (http://www.wavenet.com/~jhendrix) for aficionados. Named after the classic Hendrix tune "Room Full of Mirrors," the web site was characterized in *Newsweek* as "part shrine, part fanzine . . . [with] high-culture and low-culture perspectives on Hendrix." Considering the amount of unreleased Hendrix music—of varied quality and in the hands of those with varied integrity—he will likely remain as prolific posthumously as any new artist. Meanwhile, his groundbreaking, heartfelt body of work will certainly continue to inspire musicians and listeners with every new rising sun.

Further Reading

Murray, Charles Shaar, *Crosstown Traffic: Jimi Hendrix and the Rock 'N' Roll Revolution,* St. Martin's, 1989.
Rees, Dafydd, and Luke Crampton, *Rock Movers & Shakers,* Billboard, 1991.
Shapiro, Harry, and Caesar Glebbeek, *Jimi Hendrix: Electric Gypsy,* St. Martin's, 1991.
Billboard, December 14, 1968, p. 10; September 26, 1970, p. 3.
Down Beat, February 1994, pp. 38-39.
Entertainment Weekly, April 21, 1995, p. 54.
Jet, January 31, 1994, p. 61.
Musician, February 1993, p. 44.
Newsweek, January 16, 1995, p. 64; August 7, 1995, p. 10.
Q, July 1994, pp. 46-49.
Rolling Stone, September 20, 1990, pp. 75-78; February 6, 1992, pp. 40-48, 94.
Vibe, May 1994; August 1995. □

Heng Samrin

Heng Samrin (born 1934) was a relatively minor Cambodian Communist leader who suddenly, in January 1979, rose to international prominence as president of the People's Republic of Kampuchea (PRK) after the Vietnamese invasion and occupation of his country. His earlier obscurity had left him untainted by the odious reputation of the bloody Pol Pot regime which had preceded him.

Heng Samrin was born on May 25, 1934, the son of a well to do peasant-trader in the Ponhea district of Kompong Cham province. Some accounts also list a hamlet in Prey Veng province as the abode of his youth. He attended local schools, and it is not certain that he completed any secondary level of education. In the early 1950s he joined a group of Cambodians who were fighting together with the Viet Minh against the French colonial government. Official statements claim membership for him both in the Khmer People's Revolutionary Party (KPRP) and in the United Khmer Issarak (Freedom) Front. The former was Cambodia's first Communist party, organized in 1951 as an offshoot of the Indochinese Communist Party, and it, like its parent organization, remained under Hanoi's influence. Though hazily structured, it provided Heng Samrin with his first ideological and organizational training. The Issarak, led by nationalist and Marxist radicals of various hues, shaped his initial combat experience.

The deft political maneuvering in 1953-1954 by Cambodian ruler Prince Norodom Sihanouk in order to achieve his country's complete independence from French colonial rule left Cambodian Communists and leftist nationalists increasingly divided. After the 1954 Geneva Conference Heng Samrin, along with other Viet Minh oriented KPRP members, left for Hanoi and further organizational and ideological training. He returned in 1956 to join the Krom Pracheachon (Citizens Association). The latter had been established in 1954 by KPRP and other underground anti-Sihanouk radicals as a legal Communist organization to participate in national elections.

The Growing Influence of Viet Nam

How deep Heng Samrin's loyalties went to any one of the various developing factions within Cambodian Communism at this time is not clear. The founding in 1960 of the Workers Party of Kampuchea, later the Communist Party of Kampuchea (CPK), by Pol Pot gradually quickened the anti-Sihanouk Marxist insurrectionary resistance in Cambodia. Vietnamese party cadres and followers of the National Liberation Front of South Vietnam increasingly infiltrated the Krom Pracheachon. It was in considerable measure under their tutelage that Heng Samrin acquired further guerrilla combat experience. During the 1960s and early 1970s his military service reportedly was interrupted by new sojourns to Hanoi. The Vietnamese in this period were intensifying their recruitment of younger middle level Cambodian Communist leaders in an attempt to affirm their hegemony over the Cambodian party.

Upon their return most of the approximately 1,500 members of this so-called Khmer Hanoi group to which Heng Samrin belonged eventually developed party and military bases close to the Vietnamese-Cambodian border, including the Cambodian part of the Ho Chi Minh Trail. Collectively they came to be identified as the Eastern Zone group within the CPK. It was in this area that Heng Samrin eventually rose to intermediate command position in the CPK's Revolutionary Army of Kampuchea, which had been formally established on January 12, 1968.

The name of Heng Samrin did not win any attention, however, amidst increasing popular unrest. There were strikes and demonstrations against Sihanouk's rule and clashes of Sihanouk's forces with the Khmer Rouge (the Sihanouk regime's catchall term for the Communist or Communist-influenced political and military resistance). After the overthrow of Sihanouk on March 18, 1970, Communist resistance against the new Lon Nol regime intensified.

In the common struggle against Lon Nol, ideological and tactical differences between pro-and anti-Hanoi factions tended to be submerged. This circumstance, along with his party and military service, allowed Heng Samrin to establish himself in the Eastern Zone after Lon Nol was driven out in April 1975.

The Rise and Fall of Pol Pot

In early 1976, shortly before Pol Pot rose to the premiership of Kampuchea, Heng Samrin was named political commissar and commander of the Fourth Infantry Division of the government's Revolutionary Army. This unit was stationed in the Eastern Zone, and the new position gave Heng Samrin considerable authority over local party policy and military preparedness. His appointment, however, appears to have been part of a general trade-off of party and military command posts among the CPK factions at the time. Heng Samrin's new position should be seen primarily as reflecting the appointment of Heng Samrin's superior, So Phim, to head the Eastern Zone and So Phim's membership in the new CPK Politburo, rather than as any sign of favor by Pol Pot himself.

In the next two years, Pol Pot's extensive purges decimated the ranks of senior CPK leaders. Heng Samrin, though known to be a part of the Hanoi-oriented party faction, managed to escape liquidation. This probably was due less to his political astuteness and more to his second rung party status and his relative harmlessness as perceived by the Pol Pot leadership. In May 1978, however, Heng Samrin and other Eastern Zone party dissidents led by So Phim rose up in revolt against Pol Pot. The details of the plot and Heng Samrin's exact role in it are still unclear, but it would appear that Heng Samrin, So Phim, and their associates sought to mobilize military and party units in other zones and called for the aid of Vietnam against Pol Pot. The revolt failed, however, in part because of the rumored betrayal of some key plotters. Amidst bloody new purges (So Phim committed suicide), Heng Samrin managed to escape to Vietnam as clashes between Vietnamese and Kampuchean troops continued to intensify.

With the Vietnamese already controlling much of the Eastern Zone in Cambodia and poised for a final invasion to oust Pol Pot, Heng Samrin and other fellow pro-Hanoi party associates who had escaped met in Snuol in Kompong Chom province in Cambodia on December 2, 1978. Here they drafted a political alternative to the Pol Pot regime. This was the United Front for the National Salvation of Kampuchea, and Heng Samrin was proclaimed president of the front and of its central committee. To these posts he subsequently added that of the presidency of the Revolutionary People's Council, the formal executive arm of the new People's Republic of Kampuchea (PRK). The PRK had been proclaimed jointly by the Vietnamese and Heng Samrin on January 7, 1979, as Vietnamese forces, having driven out the Pol Pot regime, installed themselves in Phnom Penh.

Heng Samrin in Control

Already in his capacity as leader of the National Salvation Front, Heng Samrin in December 1978 had announced a commitment to the abolition of the excesses of the Pol Pot regime and to the establishment of an independent democracy "moving towards socialism." Restoration of family life and freedom of expression and association also were assured in this declaration. After coming to power, Heng Samrin's PRK government, though heavily dependent on the continuing presence of 180,000 Vietnamese military and political cadres in Cambodia, restored a measure of the rule of law and attempted to begin the recovery of the country's shattered economy. The brutalities of the Pol Pot era did not disappear, however. The Heng Samrin regime was criticized by such human rights groups as Amnesty International (London) and The Lawyers Committee for International Human Rights (New York) for arbitrary arrest, extensive confinement of suspected dissenters or old regime officials in "re-education camps," torture of prisoners, and severe restrictions on all movement of people, on those engaging in trade or other occupations, and even on those wishing to get married.

Heng Samrin apparently was seen even by supporters of his regime as a puppet of Hanoi, but he was also viewed by many as preferable to a possible return of Pol Pot and his bloody policies. Cambodian enthusiasm for Heng Samrin's regime remained lukewarm at best. The KPRP (the name assumed again by the pro-Hanoi Communist followers of Heng Samrin) probably numbered no more than 1,000 and Heng Samrin himself complained that the level of political and ideological training of his cadre followers was low. Foreign recognition of the Heng Samrin regime was confined to Soviet bloc nations, with the notable exception of India. Already, on December 5, 1981, Heng Samrin forced the resignation of party secretary Pen Sovan, his closest rival. Hanoi appeared uninterested in replacing Heng Samrin so long as the Cambodian conflict persisted. The forces of the Coalition Government of Democratic Kampuchea continued to battle the Vietnamese and Heng Samrin's regime.

Nothing is known for certain about Heng Samrin's private life. Reportedly, he was married to a former Eastern Zone cadre and had four children.

The War Continues

The Cambodia conflict, with its multiple political factions, splinter groups and guerilla armies, was reported daily in news dispatches, factional press releases and questionable government statements. The Supreme National Council, established as a result of the 1991 peace treaty, and representing the four major factions, began to govern the country under United Nations supervision. Vietnam continued to support Heng Samrin, but he no longer held the post of Chairman of the Council of State. He continued to disavow his former Khmer Rouge alliance and military position, and apparently retained his position as Chairman of the People's Revolutionary Council. Norodom Ranaridh and Hun Sen shared the Royal Government's Deputy Prime

Minister position; both also being co-Chairmen of the Provisional National Government.

The Cambodian army, together with Heng Samrin's well-trained and well-equipped Vietnamese forces, temporarily ousted the Khmer Rouge from the capital, Phnom Penh, and other sensitive areas. However, the Khmer Rouge were still a major factor, both politically and militarily, and could counter-attack anytime.

Peace

The Paris Peace Accord was attended by most of the major factions, with Heng Samrin representing the Council of State. This led to the general elections of 1993. Funcinpec, The United National Front for and independent, neutral, peaceful and Co-operative Cambodia, won the election by a narrow margin. This was the monarchist Party and Prince (now King) Sihanouk was now head of state. He persuaded both the Cambodian People's Party (CPP) and the Funcinpec faction to resolve their differences to create a stable government. Heng Samrin was apparently a member of the CPP, though he seemed to be non-participatory.

Chaos Again

The re-establishment of King Sihanouk as head of state, a new constitution (1993), and the elections, seemed to be what Cambodia required for stability and the re-establishment of social order. However, the Khmer Rouge controled the northern and western portions of the country and increased their guerilla attacks every dry season. The Vietnamese-backed forces impinged on the border and occasionally made forays against key areas, increasing their control. This was Heng Samrin's allegiance, and Vietnam continued to back and support him. Both established political parties (Funcinpec and CPP) fragmented into several interest groups, and no one faction seemed able to rule the country—least of all Sihanouk, the titular head of state.

The economic situation worsened daily; battles and skirmishes were won and lost by the Cambodian army, the Khmer Rouge guerilla forces, and the Vietnamese force along the border. King Sihanouk's shaky government became increasingly repressive, violating human rights and suppressing all political opposition. The bloody Pol Pot was captured, tried, and sentenced to several years' house arrest. Apparently, the political situation collapsed and the fight for control of the country was between Heng Samrin's Vietnamese forces and the Khmer Rouge rebels who controled most of the northern and western provinces already.

In July 1997, Mary Kay Magstad, an NBC correspondent, reported from Phnom Penh that the Cambodian populace had lost faith in the Hun Sen government, which had resorted to mass political arrests and inhuman torture of prisoners in a desperate attempt to control the country.

Further Reading

There was no published biography, not even one issued by official PRK quarters, of Heng Samrin. Various glimpses of his career were offered in Michael Vickery, *Cambodia, 1975-1982* (1984) and in Serge Thion, "Chronology of Khmer Communism, 1940-1982," in David Chandler and Ben Kiernan, editors, *Revolution and Its Aftermath in Kampuchea* (Yale University Southeast Asia Studies, Monograph Series, no. 25, 1983). See also the interview of Heng Samrin by the Swedish journalist Sven Oste in the Stockholm daily *Dagens Nyheter,* February 5, 1984 (reprinted in *Foreign Broadcast Information Service reports,* Washington, D.C., February 15, 1984).
For a graphic account of the horrors of daily life under Heng Samrin's army and government, Dr. Haing Ngor's book, *A Cambodian Odyssey* (1987), was an excellent source. Haing Ngor was the Cambodian refugee medical doctor who finally escaped to Thailand and came to Los Angeles. His case and his country's plight came to world attention when he won an Academy Award as best supporting actor in *The Killing Fields* (1984).
For general background information regarding the ongoing turmoil in Southeast Asia, Heng Samrin and other factional leaders, consult: William Colby's *Lost Victory,* Chicago: Contemporary Books, (1989); *Asian Affairs: An American Review* (Winter 94, Vol. 20, Issue 4, pp. 187, 218); *The Economist Newspaper NA Inc.,* (January 12, 1991, Vol. 318, Issue 7689, p. 28 and October 26, 1994, Vol. 321, Issue 7730, p.39); or *The UN Chronicle* (September, 1990, Vol. 27, Issue 3, p. 24; December 1990, Vol. 27, Issue 4, p. 25; and March 1991, Vol. 28 Issue I, p. 65.) □

Henry I

Henry I (876-936), or Henry the Fowler, was king of Germany from 919 to 936. The first monarch of the Saxon dynasty, he allowed autonomy to the various German duchies and concentrated his resources on defense against the Danes and the Magyars.

The son of Otto of Erlauchten, Duke of Saxony, Henry I was a great grandson of Louis the Pious. What education he had was from tutors, and he was trained to succeed his father as Duke of Saxony. In 909 Henry married Mathilda, daughter of Count Dietrich, whose possessions in Westphalia helped to increase the power of the Saxon duke in that area.

In 912, upon the death of his father, Henry became Duke of Saxony. His relations with King Conrad I were not always peaceful, but the struggle for control of Thuringia, a territory that lay adjacent to Saxony and Franconia (Conrad's duchy), was settled by the Treaty of Grona in 915.

Shortly before his death in 918, Conrad designated Henry as his successor, and Henry was acclaimed king at Fritzlar in May 919. As king, he ruled a federation of duchies which were recognized as autonomous units. Henry concentrated on building up his own power in Saxony and expanding his control into lower Lorraine. After an unsuccessful attempt to unseat Duke Gilbert (Giselbert) of Lorraine, who was aided by the king of the West Franks, Charles the Simple, Henry was recognized as king of the East Franks at the Treaty of Bonn in 921. In 923 Henry again tried to enter Lorraine, only to be driven back by Rudolf, Duke of Burgundy. In 925 he attempted a third campaign and, besieging Gilbert at Zülpich, forced his submission.

tion is G. Barraclough, *The Origins of Modern Germany* (1946; 2d ed. 1947). ☐

Henry then turned eastward to protect Saxony and Thuringia against the incursions of the Danes, the Wends, and the Magyars. Henry was able to halt the Danes and Wends and, through the capture of a Magyar chieftain, forced peace on the Magyars for 9 years, during which time they paid tribute to the Saxon king.

Henry used this period of peace to consolidate his power in Saxony. He fortified his major cities, Merseburg, Hersfeld, Goslar, Gandersheim, Quedlinburg, and Pöhlde, which were to become centers of trade, justice, and social and military activity. The lands that had been taken from the Wends were distributed in the form of fiefs among his followers and servants.

During the years 928-932 Henry pushed eastward into Slavic lands and set up administrative centers at Brandenburg and Meissen. In 929 he entered Bohemia, where he forced King Wenceslas to recognize German sovereignty and to pay a yearly tribute. In 933 and 934 Henry concentrated on attacking and defeating in turn the Magyars and the Danes.

Sick with paralysis, Henry designated his eldest son, Otto, as king and called the nobles to Erfurt in early 936 to elect him. On July 2, 936, at Memleben, Henry died and was buried in the church of St. Peter, which he had founded at Quedlinburg.

Further Reading

An account of the reign of Henry I is in *The Cambridge Medieval History,* vol. 3 (8 vols., 1911-1936). A more recent interpreta-

Henry I

Henry I (1068-1135) was king of England from 1100 to 1135. His reign was dominated by his struggle to conquer and defend Normandy and to make his government in England more efficient and more profitable.

The third surviving son of William I and Matilda of Flanders, Henry I received a good education and could read and write Latin, an accomplishment rare among laymen at that time. On his father's death in 1089, Henry's brothers, Robert and William II, inherited Normandy and England respectively; Henry was left £5,000, with which he bought land in western Normandy. Robert could not govern efficiently, and Henry therefore allied with William, who in 1096 took over Normandy as security for a loan to enable Robert to go on a crusade.

On Aug. 2, 1100, when Robert was on his way home, William was shot, possibly with Henry's connivance, when hunting in the New Forest. Henry seized the royal treasure in nearby Winchester and was hastily crowned on August 5 at Westminster. Here he issued a charter promising reforms, most of which were designed to win support from the great landowners and the Church. He imprisoned William's unpopular minister Ranulf Flambard and recalled the exiled Anselm, Archbishop of Canterbury. In November 1100 he married Edith, later called Matilda, daughter of Malcolm III, King of Scots and descendant of the Saxon kings; this marriage secured peace with Scotland and the goodwill of the English. These measures helped him to survive an attack by Duke Robert in 1101. In 1104 and 1105 Henry attacked Normandy and in 1106 finally defeated his brother at Tinchebrai and took over the duchy, keeping Robert a prisoner till his death in 1134.

In 1107 Henry reached a statesmanlike compromise with the Pope and the archbishop of Canterbury in the long-standing dispute about elections of bishops and abbots, which had caused Anselm to retire to a second period of exile. Henry gave up the ancient custom of lay investiture (giving prelates the ring and staff which were the symbols of their spiritual office), while the Pope agreed that prelates should be elected in the King's presence and do homage for their estates before consecration. In this way Henry and his successors retained control of Church appointments, giving up only a formal ceremony.

As well as watching constantly to suppress rebellion in Normandy, Henry made diplomatic moves to protect it from attack. In 1109 his daughter Matilda was promised to the emperor Henry V; in 1113 he agreed that his son and heir William should marry the daughter of Fulk, Count of Anjou. He paid a large pension to the Count of Flanders and gave substantial estates in England and Normandy to his nephew

Stephen, brother of another potential ally, the Count of Blois. Thus fortified, he was able to repel several attacks led by Louis VI, King of France, in support of the claim to Normandy of Duke Robert's son, William Clito. Though defeated at Brémule in 1119, Louis continued to support William and made him Count of Flanders in 1127. Fortunately for Henry, William Clito died in 1128.

Though he gave much of his time to Normandy, Henry's reign produced notable developments in the government of England. He increased the number of professional administrators, employing men of comparatively humble origins. Many of these were laymen, but their chief was Roger, Bishop of Salisbury. Roger was the King's right-hand man and was probably responsible for the organization of the Exchequer, the royal accounting office, which had its own staff and its own records, the Domesday Book and the Pipe Rolls, of which the first surviving specimen belongs to the year ending Michaelmas (sept. 29), 1130. In judicial matters more cases were claimed for the King's court, and the King's controlling position was emphasized by sending justices to visit the county courts and by the brutal, but methodical, punishment of criminals.

The great problem of Henry's later years was the succession. He had at least 20 illegitimate children but only one legitimate son, William, and one daughter, Matilda. William's death by drowning in 1120 was a political disaster. Henry, in hope of an heir, married Adeliza, daughter of Godfrey, Duke of Lower Lorraine (another potential ally of France's flank), but the union was childless. Matilda, however, became a widow in 1125; Henry summoned her

home and in December 1126 made the nobles swear to accept her as domina (lady) of England and Normandy. He then arranged her marriage to Geoffrey, son of the Count of Anjou. But when Henry died on Dec. 1, 1135, his nephew Stephen ascended the English throne.

Further Reading

A basic study of Henry is in Richard William Southern, *Medieval Humanism and Other Studies* (1970). A contemporary account of Henry I is *Eadmer's History of Recent Events in England* (trans. 1964). Good accounts of Normandy and England in this period are in Charles Homer Haskins, *Norman Institutions* (1918), and Frank Barlow, *The Feudal Kingdom of England, 1042-1216* (1955; 2d ed. 1961). Edward J. Kealey, *Roger of Salisbury* (1972), is an important study of the man who was Henry's viceroy for over 30 years.

Additional Sources

Brett, M., *The English Church under Henry I,* London: Oxford University Press, 1975.
Dymoke, Juliet, *Henry of the high roc,* London, Dobson, 1971.
Dymoke, Juliet, *The lion's legacy,* London: Dobson, 1974.
Plaidy, Jean, *The lion of justice,* London: Hale, 1975.
Plaidy, Jean, *The lion of justice,* New York: Putnam, 1979, 1975.

□

Henry II

Henry II (1133-1189) was king of England from 1154 to 1189. He restored and extended royal authority, supervised great legal reforms, and clashed with Thomas Becket.

B orn on March 5, 1133, Henry II was the eldest son of Geoffrey, Count of Anjou, and Matilda, daughter of King Henry I. On her father's death Matilda failed to secure England and Normandy, but Geoffrey of Anjou conquered Normandy and in 1150 invested Henry with the duchy. On Geoffrey's death a year later Henry became Count of Anjou. To these lands he added the duchy of Aquitaine by his marriage (May 18, 1152) to Eleanor, daughter of the late duke. These lands were not independent states; they were separate fiefs of the kingdom of France, and for each of them Henry did homage to King Louis VII as his overlord. Louis, like other kings in this period, was trying to convert feudal overlordship into real authority to govern and deeply resented Henry's strength. The duchy of Aquitaine, often regarded as a great loss to Louis, was in many ways a liability to Henry; it had no internal unity, and it had never been effectively governed.

Recovery of England

In 1153 Henry led an expedition to claim the throne of England from his mother's rival, King Stephen. Many of the nobles had objected to a woman ruler; now they were ready to accept Henry, influenced no doubt by his power as Duke of Normandy to seize their Norman lands. The death of Stephen's son Eustace in August made a settlement possible,

and at Winchester in November Stephen recognized Henry as his heir, while Henry left the throne to Stephen for the rest of his life. When Stephen died (Oct. 25, 1154), Henry succeeded peacefully and was crowned on December 19 at Westminster.

The new king was a tough, intelligent young man of 21, well educated, ambitious, and ruthless. His violent temper and his enormous energy soon became proverbial; he was constantly on the move, surprising friend and foe and exhausting his followers by his long journeys.

Henry's first objective was to regain all the rights and powers of his grandfather King Henry I. He reclaimed royal lands and castles, destroyed castles built without royal permission, and reorganized the machinery of finance, justice, and administration. He had a wise adviser in Theobald, Archbishop of Canterbury, and the service of able and experienced administrators such as Nigel, Bishop of Ely, and Richard de Lucy, justiciar till 1179. In the next 4 years he reasserted his overlordship of Scotland, the Welsh princes, and Brittany and married his eldest son to the daughter of the King of France; she brought as her dowry the Norman Vexin. He had already forced his brother Geoffrey to take money instead of the county of Anjou, promised to Geoffrey by their father.

Quarrel with the Church

Triumphant elsewhere, Henry met some opposition in his attempts to assert his authority over the clergy. On the death of Archbishop Theobald in 1161, he arranged the election as archbishop of Canterbury of his chancellor and friend Thomas Becket, hoping for his cooperation. But Thomas opposed him, and Henry's reaction was bitter and violent. The first serious quarrel was about the punishment of clergy accused of crimes; Henry wanted at least the right to punish them when convicted, but Thomas claimed them for the Church courts.

In October 1163 Henry demanded general acceptance of the customs of his grandfather's time. The following January at Clarendon the customs setting out the king's rights over the Church were defined in writing in 16 clauses, now known as the Constitutions of Clarendon. Thomas withdrew his acceptance, and Henry now determined to humiliate him. At Northampton in October 1164 Thomas was accused on trumped-up charges, and ruinous fines were imposed on him; it was clear that his resignation was required. Finally he fled secretly from England after appealing to the Pope. Henry had the support of some of the bishops and a reasonable case, for most of the disputed customs had indeed been exercised in Henry I's time. Pope Alexander III, hard pressed in his own quarrel with Emperor Frederick I, did not dare to offend Henry. Negotiations dragged on, but Thomas remained in exile till 1170.

In that year the dispute took a new turn. Henry put himself in the wrong by having his son crowned by the archbishop of York, in defiance of the known right of the archbishop of Canterbury to perform the ceremony. He now allowed a patched-up peace to be arranged, not mentioning the customs, and carefully avoided giving Thomas the formal kiss of peace, which would have been regarded as binding him not to harm the archbishop. Reports of Thomas's actions soon drove the king into one of his violent rages, and four of his knights, hoping to please him, hurried to Canterbury and murdered Thomas in his Cathedral on Dec. 29, 1170.

Henry made a great show of distress and prudently removed himself to Ireland while tempers cooled. The Pope still had to take care not to drive him into the party of the Emperor, and as all parties now desired a settlement, peace was made and Henry was reconciled to the Church on May 21, 1172, at Avranches. He promised to give up any customs which had been introduced in his time against the Church and to permit appeals from the Church courts in England to the Pope's court. The appeals were allowed from that date to the Reformation. The problem of "criminous clerks" was settled by a compromise in 1176. Broadly speaking, Henry conceded the point disputed with Thomas in return for the right to judge clergy accused of forest crimes.

Rebellion of 1173

By 1173 Henry seemed to have overcome all opposition. But in that year he had to meet rebellion and attack from all sides, partly as the result of his high-handed treatment of his own family. He had been constantly unfaithful to his proud wife, and he gave his sons, now growing up, titles but no power and no independent income. Eleanor and his three eldest sons now allied against him with King Louis VII of France, the Count of Flanders, King William of

Scotland, and disaffected nobles in many places. But Henry had some warning (he had spies in his eldest son's household); he also had effective, paid soldiers and loyal, capable officials. His wife was captured and the rebels defeated. The Scottish king, defeated and imprisoned, had to make humiliating concessions to gain his freedom (Treaty of Falaise, December 1174).

Later Years

In the British Isles, Henry's triumph was decisive and final. In France too his prestige had never been greater. He made generous terms with his sons; the king of France was cowed. The king of Sicily sought his daughter Joanna in marriage; the kings of Castile and Navarre chose him to arbitrate between them in 1177. But his sons were dissatisfied and jealous, always ready to fly to arms and to ally with the most dangerous enemy of their house, the young king of France, Philip II. Philip had many grievances against the king of England, and he exploited the situation for his own advantage. The heir to the throne, Henry "the young king," died while in rebellion against his father (June 11, 1183); the new heir, Richard, opposed by force Henry's plan to endow his youngest son, John, with Aquitaine. Finally both allied with Philip against their father, who was forced to make a humiliating peace and died 2 days later (July 6, 1189). He was buried in the abbey church of Fontevrault, where his effigy remains.

Administration and Justice

The most constructive and enduring part of Henry's work lay in England. Here his reign saw continuing advances in the techniques of government, based on those made under his grandfather. The administration became more elaborate, more professional, and better documented, but always under the King's control, as Henry demonstrated in 1170, when he suspended all the sheriffs, sent commissioners to inquire into their behavior, and subsequently dismissed all but seven of them. The King's court was still a general center of government, but finance and justice were becoming provinces for experts, such as the treasurers Nigel, Bishop of Ely, and his son Richard, Bishop of London, who wrote the first account of the working of a government office, the *Dialogue of the Exchequer*.

In law and the administration of justice, progress was dramatic. Only a few points can be noted out of many. Judges were sent out on circuit from the royal court with increasing regularity, ensuring uniformity and central control. The Assizes of Clarendon (1166) and Northampton (1176) laid down new rules for the presentment of criminals by sworn freemen, who had to cooperate with sheriffs and the itinerant justices. Henry and his lawyers also made use of the Roman legal concept of a distinction between the possession of property and the absolute right to property. By the Assizes of Novel Disseisin and of Mort d'Ancestor those who had been violently dispossessed of their land could get trial in the king's court, not by the old crude method of duel but by the evidence of sworn neighbors. The treatise *On the Laws of England* describes the new system. King Henry wanted order, power, and the profits of justice; his lawyers,

Richard de Lucy and Ranulf de Glanville chief among them, could draw on great experience and the revived knowledge of Roman law to carry out his wishes.

Further Reading

The best biography remains L. F. Salzman, *Henry II* (1914). Also useful is John T. Appleby, *Henry II: The Vanquished King* (1962). General accounts with emphasis on England are given in J.E.A. Jolliffe, *Angevin Kingship* (1955; 2d ed. 1963), and Frank Barlow, *The Feudal Kingdom of England, 1042-1216* (1955; 2d ed. 1961). Important legal developments of the reign are lucidly treated in Sir Frederick Pollock and Frederic William Maitland, *The History of English Law before the Time of Edward I* (2 vols., 1895; 2d ed. 1899). Amy Kelly, *Eleanor of Aquitaine and the Four Kings* (1950), is a fascinating story told from the point of view of Henry's queen.

Additional Sources

Amt, Emilie, *The accession of Henry II in England: royal government restored, 1149-1159,* Woodbridge, Suffolk, UK; Rochester, NY, USA: Boydell Press, 1993.

Barber, Richard W., *The devil's crown: Henry II, Richard I, John,* Conshohocken, PA: Combined Books, 1996.

Barber, Richard W., *The devil's crown; Henry II, Richard I, John,* London: British Broadcasting Corporation, 1978.

Bingham, Caroline, *The crowned lions: the early Plantagenet kings,* Newton Abbot Eng.; North Pomfret, Vt.: David & Charles, 1978.

Butler, Margaret, *The lion of Christ,* New York: Coward, McCann & Geoghegan, 1977.

Butler, Margaret, *The lion of England,* New York, Coward, McCann & Geoghegan 1973.

Butler, Margaret, *The lion of England: a novel of Henry I,* London, Macmillan, 1973.

Butler, Margaret, *The lion of justice,* New York: Coward, McCann & Geoghegan, 1975.

Butler, Margaret, *The Lion of Justice,* London; New York: MacMillan London, 1975.

Butler, Margaret, *This turbulent priest,* London: Macmillan, 1977.

Cooke, Carol Phillips, *Through a glass darkly: the story of Eleanor of Aquitaine,* S.l.: M.H.I., 1990 (Concord, N.C.: Concord Print. Co..

Corfe, Tom, *Archbishop Thomas and King Henry II,* Cambridge; New York: Cambridge University Press, 1975.

Corfe, Tom, *The murder of Archbishop Thomas,* Minneapolis: Lerner Publications Co., 1977, 1975.

Duggan, Alfred Leo, *Devil's brood: the Angevin family,* Bath: Chivers, 1976.

Fry, Christopher, *Play,* London, New York, Oxford University Press, 1971.

Gillingham, John, *The Angevin empire,* New York: Holmes & Meier, 1984.

Gittings, Robert, *Conflict at Canterbury: an entertainment in sound and light,* London, Heinemann Educational, 1970.

Goldman, James, *The lion in winter,* Harmondsworth, Middlesex; New York: Penguin Books, 1983, 1964.

Warren, Wilfrid Lewis, *Henry,* London, Eyre Methuen 1973.

York, Robert, *The swords of December,* New York: Scribner, 1978. □

Henry III

Henry III (1017-1056) was Holy Roman emperor and king of Germany from 1039 to 1056. The medieval empire is generally considered to have attained its greatest power and solidity during his reign.

The only son of Conrad II, the first Salian emperor, Henry was designated by his father to be co-king of Germany in 1028. He was made Duke of Swabia in 1038, and on the death of his father the following year he succeeded as emperor. Within Germany itself Henry III weakened the power of the great nobles by ruling most of the great tribal duchies directly—with Lorraine as the only major exception. He also won effective overlordship of Poland, Bohemia, and Hungary, and in Hungary he actually had his own candidate, Peter, placed on the throne. He intervened in Italy as well, where he not only controlled the north and the region around Rome but in 1046 recognized the Norman Guiscards as dukes of Apulia. Concerned with keeping the peace within his empire, he personally proclaimed the Peace of God from the pulpit of the Cathedral of Constance in 1043.

Henry's most controversial actions involved his dealings with the Church and especially the papacy. He was well educated and pious like his namesake, the emperor Henry II, and a patron of the arts as well. Unlike his father, Conrad II, however, he was actively involved in Church

reform, especially in reorganizing monasteries and removing unworthy clerics. It was this interest which led to his intervention in papal affairs.

The papacy had fallen upon evil days, with three popes, each claiming the office and all tainted with scandal. Angered at this, Henry in 1046 entered Italy and at a synod held in Sutri deposed all three popes—Sylvester III, Gregory VI, and Benedict IX—and selected a pope of his own, Clement II. After the death of Clement, Henry appointed still another pope, Leo IX, who was his friend and cousin Bishop Bruno of Toul, a Lorrainer. It was this pope who surrounded himself with northern and Tuscan reformers and started freeing the papacy from secular control and thus began to establish the popes as leaders of the entire Western Church. It was Henry III, therefore, who unwittingly laid the foundations of a papal reform with which his successors had to cope. He also failed to build up in Germany itself any institutions of government or an imperial domain upon which later German emperors could rely for strength.

During his reign Henry III dominated much of eastern Europe, kept Germany peaceful, controlled much of Italy, and intervened almost as head of the Church in papal affairs. Yet his power was more superficial than it appeared, and his policies within both the empire and the Church were to lead to a crisis for his son and successor, Henry IV.

Further Reading

For the era of Henry III see Gerd Tellenbach, *Church, State and Christian Society at the Time of the Investiture Contest* (trans. 1940); Geoffrey Barraclough, *Origins of Modern Germany* (1946; 2d rev. ed. 1966); Walter Ullmann, *The Growth of Papal Government in the Middle Ages* (1955; 2d ed. 1962); and Jeffrey Russell, *Dissent and Reform in the Early Middle Ages* (1965). □

Henry III

Henry III (1207-1272) was king of England from 1216 to 1272. His reign saw the rise of English nationalism and the development of a strong baronial claim to participate in government.

The eldest son of King John and Isabella of Angoulême, Henry III was born on Oct. 1, 1207. At the death of his father, he ascended the throne on Oct. 19, 1216, and was crowned at Gloucester. Ten days later William Marshall, Earl of Pembroke, was appointed regent. On Pembroke's death in 1219, Hubert de Burgh, who served as justiciar, became the most powerful man in government. In the first years of the regency, England was under papal influence due to Henry's father, John. Efforts were made to maintain peace through negotiating with Louis of France in 1217, reconfirming the Great Charter in 1223 and making peace with Wales.

In 1223 Pope Honorius III allowed Henry to be declared of age for certain limited purposes. In January 1227

Henry declared himself of full age and commenced to attempt to regain the overseas French possessions that had been lost. In the preceding years he had lost most of his French possessions but by 1225 had recovered Gascony, and in 1228, for baronial support, he agreed to restore the forest liberties. By 1230 he was invading Poitou and Gascony, and the following year to obtain scutage (a form of revenue) he reaffirmed the liberties of the Church.

Henry, by 1232, hoped to act as his own minister and caused the dismissal of Hubert de Burgh. He then alienated the English barons by replacing English officers with Poitevin friends and was forced to back down in 1234 due to pressure from Hubert de Burgh and the barons. In 1235 to gain foreign support he married his sister Isabella to the emperor Frederick II, and on January 20 the following year he married Eleanor of Provence. This marriage, which resulted in two sons and three daughters who survived infancy, caused England to be flooded with his wife's worthless relations, and the period is marked by the rise of English nationalism as the barons saw the government passing into the control of foreigners.

By 1239 Henry's behavior was such that even his brother-in-law Simon de Montfort and his brother Richard, Earl of Cornwall, joined the opposition. Henry, while making minor concessions, continued to fill state and Church offices with foreigners. Baronial opposition to the misgovernment of the King continued to grow. In 1242 they refused a grant for the French war, and 2 years later both barons and the Church protested, but these efforts failed due to lack of leadership as Henry detached his brother Richard

from the opposition through the marriage arranged with Sanchia, daughter of Raymond Berenger IV, Count of Provence.

In 1252 Henry alienated Simon de Montfort, who had been governor of Gascony, and a crisis developed when Henry agreed to finance Pope Alexander II's struggle with Manfred in return for the grant of the crown of Sicily to Prince Edmund, Henry's son. This "Sicilian Venture" would be of no value to England, and so the barons came to Parliament at Westminster, clad in armor and ready for a confrontation. With Montfort as their leader, in 1258 the barons met at the "Mad" Parliament and drew up the "Provisions," which gave the barons control of the executive and the right to nominate half of the Council as well as establishing a committee of 24 to institute reforms.

The barons soon quarreled as Montfort aimed at a more popular government, and the Earl of Gloucester became the leader of the more autocratic-minded barons. As a result, in 1261 Henry was able to regain power and obtained a papal bull absolving him from the terms of the "Provisions." In 1264 the conflict with the barons was referred to Louis IX of France for arbitration, and by the Mise of Amiens a favorable decision was given for the King. Although the decision was upheld by Pope Urban IV, the barons refused to accept the award, and civil conflict developed. After capturing Leicester and other areas, the baronial forces marched into the south for provisions. At the Battle of Lewes on May 14, 1264, Montfort defeated the King and forced a calling of Parliament.

Montfort's position now being too powerful, some of the barons deserted to the side of the King, whose forces led by Prince Edward defeated and killed Montfort at the Battle of Evesham in 1265. With the death of the opposition leader, Henry revoked all his recent acts, confiscated the lands of the rebels, and in the Battle of Kenilworth ensured peace for the rest of his reign. By now power had slipped from the hands of the King to his son Edward, and the last years of the reign saw the passage of some reforms at the 1267 Parliament of Marlborough.

Perhaps one of Henry's greatest achievements was the completion of Westminster Abbey in 1269. On Nov. 16, 1272, Henry died at Westminster, and his body was buried in the abbey 4 days later before the high altar, his heart being buried at Fontevrault.

Further Reading

There is much literature on Henry III's long and important reign. F. M. Powicke, *King Henry III and the Lord Edward* (2 vols., 1947), is the best biography. Kate Norgate, *The Minority of Henry the Third* (1912), surveys the early years. The baronial system and Henry's relationship to it are examined in E. F. Jacobs, *Studies in the Period of Baronial Reform and Rebellion, 1258-1267* (1925), and R. F. Treharne, *The Baronial Plan of Reform* (1932). An excellent narrative is Tufton Beamish, *Battle Royal: A New Account of Simon de Montfort's Struggle against King Henry III* (1966). For general background on the period see F. M. Powicke, *The Thirteenth Century, 1216-1307* (1953; 2d ed. 1962).

Additional Sources

Bennetts, Pamela., *The de Montfort legac,* New York, St. Martin's Press 1973.

Carpenter, David., *The minority of Henry III,* Berkeley: University of California Press, 1990.

Carpenter, David., *The minority of Henry III,* London: Methuen London, 1990.

Carpenter, David., *The reign of Henry III,* London; Rio Grande, Ohio: The Hambledon Press, 1996.

Colvin, Howard Montagu., *Building accounts of King Henry II,* Oxford, Clarendon Press, 1971.

Turner, Ralph V., *The king and his courts; the role of John and Henry III in the administration of justice, 1199-12,* Ithaca, N.Y., Cornell University Press 1968. □

Henry IV

Henry IV (1050-1106) was Holy Roman emperor and king of Germany from 1056 to 1106. An able, ruthless, and secretive monarch, he led the empire into a disastrous confrontation with Pope Gregory VII in the Investiture Controversy.

Born in Goslar, Saxony, Henry IV was the only son of Emperor Henry III and Agnes of Poitou. His father died when he was only 6, and he had a long and difficult minority as king, since early in 1062 he was taken from his mother and raised by a bevy of quarreling, scheming bishops. In 1066 he came of age and began governing on his own. He was married twice, first to Bertha of Savoy and late in his reign, after her death, to Praxedis of Russia.

Henry attempted, initially, to reassert his father's old imperial rights throughout the empire and also to build up a new, strong imperial domain in Saxony. This led to serious uprisings in 1073 in which Saxons and southern German nobles combined against him. By 1075 he had suppressed these revolts, only to begin a quarrel with Pope Gregory VII over the imperial right to appoint or invest churchmen with their offices. Gregory and Church reformers claimed that neither rulers nor any other laymen could exercise this right—despite long precedent. Angry at Gregory's opposition to his appointing an archbishop of Milan, in 1076 Henry hastily summoned a council of German bishops who declared Pope Gregory deposed. Gregory answered by declaring Emperor Henry excommunicated and suspended from office.

This encouraged German nobles again to rebel and to summon the Pope to come to Augsburg and sit in judgment on their ruler. Fearing the results of such collaboration between the Pope and German magnates, Henry slipped through the Alpine passes and met Pope Gregory at Canossa in northern Italy in 1077, where, as a penitent, he prevailed upon the Pope to forgive him. This prevented Gregory, much against his will, from continuing to work with the German nobles against Henry, which, of course, was Henry's objective.

Despite lack of papal support, Henry's German opponents chose an antiking, Rudolf of Swabia. But Henry returned across the Alps and defeated him. Rudolf died soon thereafter, in 1080, and Henry reopened hostilities with Pope Gregory. Despite a renewal of his excommunication, he led another army into Italy and by 1084 had marched on Rome and set up an antipope there who crowned him emperor. Gregory was saved from capture only by a large Norman force, which rescued him at the cost of a severe plundering of the city of Rome itself. The Pope had to retire with the Normans south toward Naples and died in exile the following year.

After Gregory's death, Henry IV continued to resist the popes who were chosen as his successors and to set up antipopes of his own against them. In this he was relatively unsuccessful, since his papal opponents were men like Urban II, capable of rallying all Europe behind them in the First Crusade and similar enterprises. Henry also had much trouble due to opposition to his rule in both Germany and Italy, especially from his eldest son, Conrad, and from Duke Welf of Bavaria and Countess Matilda of Tuscany. Not until 1098 did the revolts they encouraged collapse, and soon afterward Conrad died. But Emperor Henry had to pay a heavy price to Saxon rebels and others to secure peace. Finally, in 1105, his second son and heir, later Henry V, joined his father's enemies, imprisoned him, and forced him to abdicate. Escaping in 1106, he had just defeated this ungrateful son when he died, leaving a weakened imperial power in Germany and the struggle with the papacy over investitures still unresolved.

Further Reading

There is an immense literature dealing with Henry IV. Among the more important accounts are those found in Gerd Tellenbach, *Church, State and Christian Society at the Time of the Investiture Contest* (trans. 1940); Geoffrey Barraclough, *Origins of Modern Germany* (1946; 2d rev. ed. 1966); and Walter Ullmann, *The Growth of Papal Government in the Middle Ages* (1955; 2d ed. 1962). See also shorter accounts in Ralph H. C. Davis, *A History of Medieval Europe* (1957), and Christopher Brooke, *Europe in the Central Middle Ages, 962-1154* (1964). □

Henry IV

Henry IV (1367-1413), the king of England from 1399 to 1413, was the first monarch of the Lancastrian dynasty. His reign was marked by the development of parliamentary government in England.

Henry IV was the only son of John of Gaunt, the son of Edward III, and Blanche, the daughter of Henry Grismond, Duke of Lancaster. Known as Henry Bolingbroke after his birthplace in Lincolnshire, he was made a knight of the Garter in 1377. In 1380, at the age of 13, he married Mary de Bohun, the youngest daughter and coheiress of Humphrey, the last Earl of Hereford. They had four sons and two daughters before her death at the age of 24, in 1394. As the Earl of Darby, Henry entered the House of Lords in 1385. In 1387 he supported his uncle Thomas, Duke of Gloucester, in his opposition to Richard II. (Gloucester was also Richard's uncle, and Henry was the King's first cousin.)

While taking part in the "Merciless" Parliament of 1388, Henry regained the favor of the King and in 1390 departed on the Crusade to Lithuania and then to Jerusalem. Visiting the kings of Bohemia and Hungary and the Archduke of Austria and then Venice in 1392-1393, he went only as far as Rhodes and then returned to England as a popular hero. He soon entered the government; he served on the Council while Richard was absent in Ireland in 1395 and for his efforts was made Duke of Hereford in 1397.

Henry soon quarreled with the Duke of Norfolk, each accusing the other of arranging the murder of the Duke of Gloucester and calling for a trial by battle. Both men were banished from the realm, Norfolk for life and Henry for 10 years with a proviso that he would be allowed to inherit from his father. But on the death of John of Gaunt in 1399, the Lancastrian estates were confiscated by the King, and Henry decided to return, ostensibly to claim his promised inheritance.

Taking advantage of the King's absence in Ireland, Henry landed on July 4, 1399, at Ravenspur, near Bridlington, where he was soon joined by the northern nobles who were unhappy with the policies of the monarchy. By the end of the month Henry and his followers had raised an

army and marched to Bristol. When Richard returned in August, the royal army started to desert; Henry claimed the throne for himself, and on August 19 he captured Richard near Conway. He then went with his prisoner to London and there, on September 29, Richard abdicated. On October 13 Parliament formally deposed Richard and transferred the crown to Henry. This parliamentary action had constitutional importance, since it revived the claim that Parliament had the power to create monarchs. Prior to his coronation, Henry condemned Richard to imprisonment, where the deposed monarch soon died, possibly due to starvation.

Once on the throne, Henry spent his reign solidifying his position and removing the threat posed by the nobles who supported Richard. Starting in 1400, Henry made expeditions in Scotland against the Duke of Albany and the 4th Earl of Douglas and in Wales against Owen Glendower. He was an active supporter of the Orthodox Church against the Lollards, and in 1401 *De heretico comburendo,* one of the most important medieval statutes, was passed. In 1402 he married Joan of Navarre, the widow of John V, Duke of Brittany, who survived him without issue. In the north the Percy family rose against the King, but Henry checked them in July 1403 at Shrewsbury and the following year at Dartmouth. A revolt by the 1st Earl of Northumberland, Archbishop Scrope, and the Earl Marshal was checked in 1405, and 2 years later the Beauforts' claims to the throne were ended.

By the Battle of Brabham Moor in 1408, the domestic threats to the throne were ended, and Henry could turn his attention to the civil wars in France as well as reforming his household administration. He was able to check an attempt to force him to resign in favor of his more popular son (later Henry V), but his health declined, perhaps because of epilepsy. On March 20, 1413, he was seized with a fatal attack while praying at Westminster Abbey and died in the Jerusalem Chamber. He was buried at Canterbury.

Further Reading

An excellent modern biography of Henry IV is J. L. Kirby, *Henry IV of England* (1971). The standard biography remains James Hamilton Wylie, *History of England under Henry the Fourth* (4 vols., 1884-1898). For the background of the period see May McKisack, *The Fourteenth Century, 1307-1399* (1959), and Ernest Fraser Jacob, *The Fifteenth Century, 1399-1485* (1961). See also V. H. H. Green, *The Later Plantagenets: A Survey of English History between 1307 and 1485* (1955; rev. ed. 1966). □

Henry IV

Henry IV (1553-1610) was king of France from 1589 to 1610. The first Bourbon monarch, he faced internal discord caused by the Wars of Religion and the economic disasters of the late 16th century and external danger posed by the powerful Hapsburg monarchy of Spain.

Born at Pau in Béarn on Dec. 14, 1553, Henry IV was the son of Antoine, Duc de Bourbon, and Jeanne d'Albret, daughter of the king of Navarre. Henry's parents were sympathetic to the Huguenot (Calvinist) faith, and Henry was raised a Huguenot. Through his father, Henry was a descendant of King Louis IX of France and hence a prince of the blood royal, next in succession to the French throne should the children of Henry II and Catherine de Médicis have no issue.

Henry's early childhood was supervised by his grandfather, Henri d'Albret, the king of Navarre, and, after his grandfather's death in 1555, by his mother, now queen of Navarre. He was trained in physical as well as intellectual disciplines, and his later career showed the results of both aspects of his early life. His physical endurance and vigor were matched by a quick and tolerant mind, his skill as a soldier matched by his diplomatic and political astuteness in the course of his reign.

Historical Background

From 1559 to 1590 France was the scene of internal political and religious conflicts exacerbated by the constant threat of military intervention by Spain, the greatest military power in Europe. During this period France was ruled by the three children of Henry II and Catherine de Médicis in succession: Francis II (1559-1560), Charles IX (1560-1574), and Henry III (1574-1589). All three were weak-willed, and the first two had political minorities, thus making political power a prize to be controlled either by the queen mother, Catherine, or by one of the rival aristocratic factions, whose

dynastic rivalry was further embittered by their religious differences.

The greatest of these rival clans were the ducal house of Lorraine, the family of Guise, and the house of Bourbon, led by Antoine of Navarre, Henry's father, and Antoine's brother, Louis, Prince of Condé. The Guise faction was the champion of orthodox Roman Catholicism, while the Bourbon faction spoke for French Protestantism. During the reign of Francis II the Guise faction acquired greater influence. Catherine's regency during the minority of Charles IX, however, favored playing off one faction against the other, and the French Wars of Religion began in 1562 and continued until 1598. The rival aristocratic houses used warfare or the threat of warfare to increase their own political power, calling for aid from their coreligionists outside France— Spain, the papacy, England, or the Protestant princes of Germany. Warfare, religious hatred, economic disorder, and the continual threat of outside intervention dominated the late 16th century in France.

The Reformation and its ensuing political complications thus struck France in a different way from that in which it had affected Germany and England. Exacerbating political rivalries, playing upon the instability and minority of French kings, and affording all dissident social elements the opportunity of evening old scores, the Reformation in France was not so much the arguing of theological points (as in Germany) or the vehicle of increasing royal authority (as in England), but the unleashing of political forces which the French monarchy was unable to contain. It was to be the task of Henry IV to create a monarchical state out of political and religious anarchy.

King of Navarre

Henry was brought into the center of political infighting before he was 20. Catherine de Médicis arranged for a marriage between Henry and her daughter, Margaret of France. Henry's mother, Jeanne, was in Paris to be persuaded that her son should marry the Catholic princess but died in 1572. Henry then became King Henry III of Navarre. He and Margaret were married in August 1572, a week before Catherine, fearful of Huguenot influence over Charles IX, ordered the execution of Huguenots in Paris and other French cities. Henry himself was spared, but he was kept a prisoner in various degrees of security from 1572 to 1576, when he escaped to his own kingdom.

Henry's appearance and personality in these years made him a favorite not only of his own subjects but even of many people at court who had every reason to wish him dead. A description of him in 1567 reads: "He demeans himself towards all the world with so easy a carriage that people crowd around wherever he is. He enters into conversation as a highly polished man. He is well informed and never says anything which ought not to be said. . . . He loves play and good living." Henry's physical skill and military prowess brought him the friendship of many men, and his passionate nature brought him the love of many women (too many, his wife and subjects often thought).

Between his amorous adventures (which continued all his life) and his new role as king of Navarre and leader of

French Huguenots, Henry's life moved out of Navarre exclusively and out of the choking world of the court into France itself. From 1576 to his conversion to Catholicism in 1594, Henry was the center of opposition both to Catholic persecution of Huguenots and to the powerful political League, which the Duke of Guise had created to control the crown of France under the semblance of defending it from Protestants.

King of France

In 1584 the Duke of Anjou, the youngest son of Catherine de Médicis, died, thus making Henry of Navarre the heir apparent to the reigning king, Henry III. The League immediately became more powerful, fearing a Protestant king. The League, allied with Philip II of Spain, exceeded in power even Henry III, who in despair arranged the assassination of the Duke of Guise and allied himself with Henry of Navarre.

When Henry III was assassinated in 1589, France faced the prospect of a Protestant king, kept from most of his kingdoms by a League of Catholics backed by the power of Spain. Henry had to fight his way to his own throne. But Henry IV refused to fight in the way his predecessors had done. Although he agreed to be instructed in the Catholic faith, he promised his coreligionists that he would end persecution on both sides, and from the death of Henry III to his own death, Henry IV had to create a political state over the skepticism of both Catholics and Protestants and in the presence of bitter memories of a kind that few states have been able to survive.

Between 1589 and 1594 Henry fought his way to the throne. He slowly wore down the Catholic front, declared war on Philip II of Spain in 1595, and guaranteed his earlier promises of religious toleration with the Edict of Nantes in 1598, the first successful attempt in modern European history to reconcile the presence of two religions within a single kingdom. Henry's actions were dictated by political necessity as well as personal conviction. France was in dire economic straits and in the midst of a social crisis. He was aided by a strong civil service and by a minister of exceptional talents, Maximilien de Bethune, Duc de Sully, his director of finance. In 1599 Henry IV divorced his wife and in 1600 married Marie de Médicis, who in 1601 bore him a son, his successor Louis XIII.

In the course of his reign Henry turned his attention vigorously to those aspects of the kingdom which had virtually been ignored during the period of the civil wars: justice, finance, agriculture, the exploitation of foreign acquisitions in Canada, the calming of old religious and social hatreds, and the perennial task of the 16th-century French monarchy, the control of Spain and Hapsburg Austria through alliances with England and the United Provinces. In the case of Hapsburg power, Henry devised a general program for checking the ambitions of this great imperial house. Whether or not Henry was responsible for the famous "Grand Design" which Sully later attributed to him is doubtful, but his last act in the area of foreign affairs was to launch an invasion of the Spanish Netherlands.

As he left Paris for the new war, Henry IV was stabbed by the assassin Ravaillac on May 14, 1610. He died before he could be brought back to the Louvre. Henry's reign had witnessed the worst of the civil wars which had been fought in many parts of Europe in the name of religion. It had witnessed the immense threat of Spanish power as well as the fire of internal rebellion. It had begun the slow political, social, and economic reconstruction of France. Much of the success of the reign was directly the result of Henry's personality and political and military ability. In an age when monarchy is no longer considered a viable form of government, it is well to be aware of a point in European history when a victory for absolute monarchy meant social and political reform on a scale that no other form of government could provide—and meant, too, a victory for a monarch who was as personally appealing as any other figure in those 2 centuries his life touched.

Further Reading

The most recent, and the best, biography in English of Henry IV is Desmond Seward, *The First Bourbon* (1971). A well-balanced study is Henry D. Sedgwick, *Henry of Navarre* (1930). Other biographies are Paul F. Willert, *Henry of Navarre and the Huguenots in France* (1893), and Quentin Hurst, *Henry of Navarre* (1938). The best account of the period in recent literature is *The New Cambridge Modern History*, vol. 4: R.B. Wernham, ed., *The Counter-Reformation and Price Revolution, 1559-1610* (1968). The complex political and diplomatic affairs of the period are brilliantly described in Garrett Mattingly, *The Armada* (1959).

Additional Sources

Provinces et pays du Midi au temps d'Henri de Navarre, 1555-1589: colloque de Bayonne, Pau: Henri IV 1989, 1989. □

Henry V

Henry V (1081-1125) was Holy Roman emperor and king of Germany from 1106 to 1125. The last of the Salian line of emperors, he continued the struggle with the papacy over lay investiture that had been carried on by Henry IV.

In 1106 Henry V succeeded his father, Emperor Henry IV, against whom he had rebelled the previous year. He was, like his father, a man of great ability who had to spend most of his reign in a struggle against the papacy over investitures and in attempts to keep his unruly German nobles under some form of control.

Henry began his reign by restoring a measure of order in Germany. Then, in 1110, he crossed the Alps into Italy; he marched on Rome with a large army and forced Pope Paschal II, whom he held prisoner for a time, to crown him emperor and to accept his terms for settling the Investiture Controversy. Circumstances soon forced him, however, to release the Pope and leave Italy. As soon as he had done so, Paschal proceeded to repudiate his agreement with his imperial opponent. From this time on, though Henry did invade Italy again, he was never able to exert much authority in the Italian portion of his empire, which became increasingly independent.

As for the Investiture Controversy itself, it dragged on until 1122, when a new pope, Calixtus I, negotiated a compromise settlement of the dispute with Henry called the Concordat of Worms. By this compromise the Emperor lost effective control over the appointment of churchmen in Italy and Burgundy, while still maintaining a good deal of power over their choice in Germany itself. In all cases churchmen were now to receive the spiritual symbols of their authority, the ring and the staff, directly from the pope. So ended this controversy, which had caused trouble between pope and emperor for almost 5 decades, with a settlement which represented in essence a victory for the papacy.

Though Henry was concerned during most of his reign with the struggle over investitures, he seems to have been particularly busy attempting to reassert his imperial authority in Germany itself. Here the problem he faced was that of a new nobility which was arising and which competed with him for authority. Perhaps the best examples of this new nobility are to be found in examining the rise of two powerful families, the Hofenstaufens in Swabia and the neighboring Rhinelands regions and the Welfs in Bavaria. Both made use of new feudal concepts and loyalties, previously largely unknown in Germany, as a basis for consolidating their authority over wide areas. To them, and others like them, the future of Germany was to belong.

Finally, once the Investiture Controversy had ended, Henry in his last days became interested in increasing his authority in the Low Countries along the borders of France. In 1114 he had married Matilda, the daughter of King Henry I of England and the future mother of the English king Henry II by another husband. In alliance with his English father-in-law, he attempted to increase his power in Flanders, but their actions led to friction with the French king Louis VI, who had an interest in the region as well. Finally, in 1124, he attempted an invasion of northern France itself. This provoked strong opposition and so rallied the northern French to their Capetian king that the imperial troops were forced to retreat without gaining any success. A year later, still childless, Henry V died. He left an Italy where imperial power had all but ceased to exist and a Germany ready for that long struggle between Welf and Hofenstaufen which was to disturb it for many decades.

Further Reading

Geoffrey Barraclough's *Medieval Germany* (2 vols., 1938) and his *Origins of Modern Germany* (1946; 2d rev. ed. 1966) cover this period well. See also James W. Thompson, *Feudal Germany* (1928), and Gerd Tellenbach, *Church, State and Christian Society at the Time of the Investiture Contest* (trans. 1940). ☐

Henry V

Henry V (1387-1422) was king of England from 1413 to 1422. His reign marked the high point in English attempts to conquer France. While the long-term effects of his reign were minimal, Henry V became a folk hero in English literature.

The eldest son of Henry of Lancaster and Mary de Bohun, Henry V was born at Monmouth on Aug. 9, 1387. His early military training was under Thomas Percy, Earl of Worcester, and he is believed to have been educated at Queen's College, Oxford, under his uncle Henry Beaufort (later bishop of Winchester). Henry's early years were spent in various military campaigns, and in Ireland in 1398-1399 he was a hostage of Richard II. (Richard was deposed in 1399 by Henry's father, who then became King Henry IV.)

At the age of 15 Henry was leading royal forces against Conway, Merioneth, and Carnarvon, fighting Owen Glendower. By 1403 he was fighting with his father at Shrewsbury; 2 years later he was fighting in Wales, capturing Aberystwith, and by 1407 was invading Scotland. All this military activity negates the idea that he spent his youth in dissipation with no regard for his reputation, an idea that Shakespeare took from the work of Edward Hall. He also fought in France against the Armagnacs but withdrew from the Council in 1412, when his French policy was rejected. Coming to the throne on March 21, 1413, Henry was so secure that he pardoned the Percy family, who had con-

uniting the thrones of England and France. The terms of the treaty included Henry's marriage to Catherine of France.

The French Dauphin and his followers, who did not accept the treaty, continued to oppose Henry, who returned to campaigning, capturing Melun in November and making a triumphal entrance into Paris the following month for the treaty's ratification by the Parliament of Paris. After making plans for the governing of Normandy, Henry took his bride to England to be crowned queen and devoted time to internal affairs, reforming the Benedictine monasteries and dealing with James I of Scotland.

After the defeat of the English forces under the Duke of Clarence at Beauge, Henry was forced to return to France to reestablish his control in March 1421; there he relieved Chartres and drove the forces of the Dauphin across the Loire. After capturing Meaux the following year while on the way to help his ally, the Duke of Burgundy, Henry came down with a fatal fever and died on Aug. 31, 1422, at Bois de Vincennes at the age of 35. After a funeral procession back to England, he was buried in Westminster Abbey.

Further Reading

There are many good biographies of Henry V, beginning with the 16th-century study *The First English Life of King Henry the Fifth*, edited by Charles Lethbridge Kingsford (1911). Other biographies include James Hamilton Wylie, *The Reign of Henry the Fifth* (3 vols., 1914-1929); Ernest Fraser Jacob's short and interesting *Henry V and the Invasion of France* (1947); Harold F. Hutchinson, *King Henry V: A Biography* (1967); and C. T. Allmand, *Henry V* (1968). The military campaigns are discussed in such works as Edouard Perroy, *The Hundred-Years War* (trans. 1951), and Christopher Hibbert's shorter *Agincourt* (1964). Background information is in Ernest Fraser Jacob, *The Fifteenth Century, 1399-1485* (1961).

Additional Sources

Allmand, C. T., *Henry V,* Berkeley: University of California Press, 1992.

Barbie, Richard A., *Good King Hal,* Chicago, Ill.: Dramatic Pub. Co., 1981.

Brennan, Anthony., *Henry V,* New York: Twayne Publishers, 1992.

Candido, Joseph, *Henry V: an annotated bibliography,* New York: Garland Pub., 1983.

Earle, Peter, *The life and times of Henry,* London, Weidenfeld and Nicolson, 1972.

Gesta Henrici Quinti = The deeds of Henry the Fifth, Oxford Eng.: Clarendon Press, 1975.

Labarge, Margaret Wade., *Henry V: the cautious conquerer,* New York: Stein and Day, 1976, 1975.

Labarge, Margaret Wade., *Henry V: the cautious conqueror,* London: Secker and Warburg, 1975.

Lindsay, Philip, *King Henry V: a chronicle,* London, Howard Baker Publishers Ltd., 1969.

Seward, Desmond, *Henry V: the scourge of God,* New York, N.Y., U.S.A.: Viking, 1988, 1987. □

spired against his father, and gave the remains of Richard II an honorable burial.

In internal matters Henry seems to have followed his father's religious policies: the abolition of alien priories, the repression of the Lollards in 1414, and the arrest of Sir John Oldcastle 3 years later. However, he appears to have been favorable to the plan of the lay peers to confiscate some of the Church's wealth.

In external matters Henry revived the English claims to the French crown and is best remembered for his military activities to achieve this end. In August 1415, after dealing with a conspiracy to remove him from the throne, he led an army of 20,000 foot soldiers and 9,000 horsemen to attack Harfleur and, after sending a large part of his army home due to illness, marched to Calais to secure a base for further operations. On the way, unable to avoid a vastly superior French army, he gave battle at Agincourt on Oct. 25, 1415, gaining a great victory and capturing the constable of France and the Duke of Orléans.

Henry soon returned to England to gain new supplies and men, to solidify English support for his further campaigns, and to build a navy. By 1417 he was back in France, attacking Cherbourg, Coutances, Avranches, and Évreux as well as capturing most of Normandy and the key city of Rouen. By making an alliance with Philip the Good, Duke of Burgundy, Henry was able to make the Treaty of Troyes (May 21, 1420), by which he was declared the heir to Charles VI, regent of France and lord of Normandy, thus

Henry VI

Henry VI (1421-1471) was king of England from 1422 to 1461 and in 1470-1471. He was known for his piety and charity, but his reign was marred by the rivalries of his uncles and ministers and by the loss of the achievements of his Lancastrian predecessors.

The only son of Henry V and Catherine of France, Henry was born on Dec. 6, 1421, at Windsor. At less than 9 months of age he succeeded to the throne on Sept. 1, 1422, and he was proclaimed king of both England and France. During his minority he ruled through a council consisting of his uncle, Humphrey, Duke of Gloucester, as protector; Richard Beauchamp, Earl of Warwick, as master; and another uncle, John, Duke of Bedford, as governor of his French possessions. Things went well at first, and at the Battle of Verneuil (August 1424) Bedford was able to check the Dauphin (later Charles VII), who had hoped to take advantage of the minority. But soon the advantage was lost as Gloucester drove the dukes of Burgundy and of Brittany to the French side.

After his coronations in London in 1429 and in Paris the following year, Henry tried to take an active part in government. He mediated in the feud between his uncles in 1434 and sided with the peace policy of Cardinal Beaufort. When Joan of Arc rallied the French, English interest in continuing the war declined for the next decade. Henry reached legal majority in 1442 and concluded a 2-year truce with France the next year.

In 1445 Henry married Margaret of Anjou, the daughter of René, Duke of Anjou and Lorraine and titular king of Sicily, Naples, and Jerusalem. She persuaded him to cede to Charles VII many of the possessions that England held in France. This resulted in her unpopularity with the English and was eventually to lead to her downfall, for she was to be imprisoned for 4 years after Henry's death. From this point on, interest in foreign matters depended mainly on their effect upon public feeling in England and the rivalries that later led to civil war. In 1448 Henry surrendered Maine in order to prolong the truce with France. To please public opinion, in 1450 Henry was forced to exile one of his ministers, John, Duke of Suffolk, who had been instrumental in the downfall of the popular Duke of Gloucester, and in the same year he faced his first major internal crisis in the rebellion of Jack Cade.

Wars of the Roses

This period saw the loss of more English holdings in France (Normandy in 1450 and Guienne by 1453) and the rise of a popular leader, Richard, Duke of York (Suffolk's father-in-law), as the head of the prowar party that had been led by Gloucester. Henry, deeply in debt, tried to calm the parties and granted a general pardon in 1452. In August 1453 he suffered temporary mental illness, and in April 1454 the Duke of York was appointed protector. Henry's only son, Edward, was born in October 1453. While the King was insane, the two rival parties for power, one side led by the Queen and the Duke of Somerset and the other by the Duke of York, started to prepare for civil war. When Henry recovered in January 1455, Edmund Beaufort, Duke of Somerset, was restored to favor, and the Duke of York was excluded from the Council. After Henry went to the north to gain support, the two sides met at the first Battle of St. Albans in May, where the King was slightly wounded, Somerset was killed, and the fighting of the Wars of the Roses commenced. (The house of York was associated with the white rose, the house of Lancaster with the red rose.)

The next year Henry again became ill, and York was made protector until the King's recovery. York was removed from office when the king's health returned but was allowed to remain on the Council. The war broke out again 4 years later, and in the Battle of Blore Heath on Sept. 23, 1459, the royal forces were defeated. On the approach of the King, however, the Yorkists fled, and 2 months later at the Parliament at Coventry the Duke of York and his followers were dishonored. But by July 1460 the Yorkists had been able to recover and gain London, and in the Battle of Northampton (July 10) Henry was taken prisoner. While the Queen fled to the north to gather allies, the Duke of York claimed the throne, and the two forces met at the Battle of Wakefield (December 30), where the Duke of York was killed. The Queen was unable to follow up the victory, even after a second battle at St. Albans (Feb. 17, 1461), where the King was rescued.

Early in March, Edward, Duke of York, declared himself King Edward IV with the support of London as Henry

fled. Henry's followers continued to battle on his behalf unsuccessfully, at the Battle of Towton (March 29, 1461) and at Hexham (May 15, 1464). After hiding first with the Scots and then on the Lancashire-Yorkshire border, Henry was finally captured in 1465 and put in the Tower of London for 5 years. He was briefly restored to the throne after his release (Oct. 3, 1470) due to the support of Richard Neville, Earl of Warwick ("Kingmaker"). Warwick, however, was slain at the Battle of Barnet (April 14, 1471), and Henry's son, Edward, was killed a month later at the Battle of Tewkesbury. Henry was recommitted to the Tower, where he was murdered, possibly by Edward IV's brother, Richard, Duke of Gloucester (later Richard III). On May 22 Henry's body was placed on display at St. Paul's Cathedral and then buried with little ceremony at Chertsey Abbey.

Henry was worshiped as a martyr by people in the north of England, and Henry VII had his remains reburied at St. George's Chapel, Windsor, giving up an attempt to have Henry VI canonized as being too costly. Henry VI was the first monarch to establish the royal motto *Dieu et Mon Droit*, and as a patron of learning he founded Eton (1440) and King's College, Cambridge (1441), as well as suggesting to his queen the foundation of Queen's College, Cambridge (1448).

Further Reading

There is no standard biography of Henry VI, although much of the source material is in print. Detailed studies of the period include Sir Charles W. C. Oman, *Warwick the Kingmaker* (1891); Cora L. Scofield, *The Life and Reign of Edward the Fourth* (1923); and Jack R. Lander, *The Wars of the Roses* (1966). General histories of the period are Alec Reginald Myers, *England in the Later Middle Ages* (1952), and Ernest Fraser Jacob, *The Fifteenth Century, 1399-1485* (1961).

Additional Sources

Alexander, Peter, *Shakespeare's Henry VI and Richard III,* Norwood, Pa.: Norwood Editions, 1975; Philadelphia: R. West, 1977.

Alexander, Peter, *Shakespeare's Henry VI and Richard II,* New York, Octagon Books, 1973; Folcroft, Pa. Folcroft Library Editions, 1973.

Barton, John, *The Wars of the Roses: adapted for the Royal Shakespeare Company from William Shakespeare's Henry VI, Parts 1, 2, 3 and Richard II,* London, British Broadcasting Corporation, 1970.

Crown, Mr. (John), *Henry the Sixth, the first part, 168,* London, Cornmarket P., 1969.

Crown, Mr. (John), *The misery of civil war, 168,* London, Cornmarket P., 1969.

Dicks, Samuel E., *Medieval and Renaissance studies: Henry VI and the daughters of Armagnac; a problem in medieval diploma,* Emporia, Kansas State Teachers College, Graduate Division, 1967.

Dombrowa, Regina., *Strukturen in Shakespeares King Henry the Sixth,* Amsterdam: B.R. Grèuner, 1985.

Doran, Madeleine, *Henry VI, parts II and III: their relation to the Contention and the True tragedy,* Folcroft, Pa.: Folcroft Library Editions, 1977; Norwood, Pa.: Norwood Editions, 1978.

Gaw, Allison, *The origin and development of 1 Henry VI: in relation to Shakespeare, Marlowe, Peele, and Greene,* Philadelphia: R. West, 1978 c1926; Folcroft, Pa. Folcroft Library Editions, 1974 c1926.

Goy-Blanquet, Dominique., *Le roi mis áa nu: l'histoire d'Henri VI, de Hall áa Shakespeare,* Paris: Didier âerudition, 1986.

Griffiths, Ralph Alan., *The reign of King Henry VI: the exercise of royal authority, 1422-1461,* Berkeley: University of California Press, 1981.

Henke, James T., *The Ego-King: an archetype approach to Elizabethan political thought and Shakespeare's Henry VI plays,* Salzburg: Inst. f. Engl. Sprache u. Literatur, Univ. Salzburg, 1977.

Hinchcliffe, Judith, *King Henry VI, parts 1, 2, and 3: an annotated bibliography,* New York: Garland Pub., 1984.

Kleine, Peter., *Zur Figurencharakteristik in Shakespeares "Henry VI": e. Vergleich mit d. Quellen unter Berèucksichtigung d. Textèuberlieferung u. d. Konzeption moderner Historik,* Mèunchen: Minerva-Publikation, 1980.

Long, Freda Margaret., *The coveted cro,* London, Hale, 1966.

Mescal, John, *Henry VI,* London: Catholic Truth Society, 1980.

Plaidy, Jean, *Red rose of Anjou,* New York: Putnam, 1983, 1982; London: Hale, 1982.

Ricks, Don M., *Shakespeare's emergent form; a study of the structures of the Henry VI play,* Logan, Utah State University Press, 1968.

Riggs, David, *Shakespeare's heroical histories; Henry VI and its literary traditio,* Cambridge, Mass., Harvard University Press, 1971.

Ruvigny et Raineval, Melville Henry Massue, marquis de, *The blood royal of Britain: being a roll of the living descendants of Edward IV and Henry VII, Kings of England, and James III, King of Scotland,* Baltimore: Genealogical Pub. Co., 1994.

Saltmarsh, John, *King Henry VI and the royal foundations: a commemorative oration delivered at Eton Colleg,* Cambridge, Printed for the Provost and Fellows of Eton College and King's College Cambridge, 1972.

Tull, George Francis., *Henry of Windsor, the scholarly King: a public lecture given in Caxton Hall, Westminster on 27th January 196,* Tonbridge (Kent), Henry VI Society 1969.

Watts, John Lovett., *Henry VI and the politics of kingship,* New York: Cambridge University Press, 1996.

Wolffe, B. P. (Bertram Percy), *Henry VI,* London: Eyre Methuen, 1981, 1980. ☐

Henry VII

Henry VII (c. 1274-1313) was Holy Roman emperor and king of Germany from 1308 to 1313. He is often called the last medieval emperor, since his vision of the grandeur of the imperial office resembled that of his much more powerful predecessors.

When he was elected Holy Roman emperor in November 1308, Henry, Count of Luxemburg, was the ruler of a modest territory between Germany, France, and Flanders. The German ecclesiastical and lay princes to whom fell the lot of electing the emperor had established the policy since 1273 of electing a comparatively obscure candidate to the imperial throne in order to avoid the creation of too powerful an imperial monarchy. In that year they had elected Rudolf I of Hapsburg, and in 1291 Adolf of Nassau. Henry was elected precisely because of his meager personal resources, and, like his predecessors, he used some of the imperial resources to increase the wealth and power of his dynasty.

Not only Henry's relative obscurity, however, but his personal character and ability also appealed to the electors. Educated in France, he was a fair, slim man with intelligent features, courtly behavior, and considerable kindness. He was pious and temperate in his life-style, but he was also an excellent administrator who had succeeded in increasing his power and intelligently using his modest wealth even before his election. His reign as emperor was occupied with two major concerns: the extension of the Luxemburg family influence and the pacification of Italy.

In 1310 Henry took an oath to the Pope, promising to fulfill his imperial duties properly but also demanding a quick coronation in Rome. In the same year Henry raised Luxemburg to the status of a duchy and named his son John its duke. He then married John to Elizabeth of Bohemia. He backed a military expedition that placed Elizabeth and John on the Bohemian throne and began the aggrandizement of the Luxemburg house, whose Bohemian kingdom would provide three more emperors in the next century: Henry's grandson Charles IV and Charles's sons Wenceslaus and Sigismund.

In 1310 Henry also began his journey to Italy to pacify the faction-ridden cities and receive the Lombard crown at Milan and the imperial crown at Rome. Henry's arrival was hailed by many Italians, including the great poet Dante, as the coming of the "King of Peace." Indeed, something of Henry's character may be inferred from the tributes which Dante paid him, ranging from the poet's letters, to his political tract *On Monarchy,* to the moving lines in the *Paradiso* which depict the glorious throne and crown which await the Emperor in Heaven.

Henry was not, however, to bring the peace he wanted to Italy. As soon as he arrived in Milan, the political rivalries which tore the city involved the Emperor, and Henry found himself forced to take sides in political quarrels and successfully led his army against the cities of Cremona and Brescia. By 1312 he arrived in Rome, by then opposed by many cities, the King of Naples, and even the Pope himself. On June 29, 1312, Henry was crowned emperor by the cardinal bishop of Ostia, the papal legate, in the church of St. John Lateran, his enemies having occupied St. Peter's.

Faced with papal opposition to his continued presence in Italy and furious with the King of Naples for opposing his imperial mission to Rome, Henry called an imperial Diet at Pisa in 1313, assembled another army, and marched again toward Rome, determined to free the city from Neapolitan occupation. On his way, Henry, who was recovering from malaria, unwisely exerted himself, caught fever, and died on Aug. 24, 1313. His body was returned to Pisa, where it was buried in a magnificent tomb in the Cathedral.

Henry's sincere idealism, his respect for the imperial office and its duties, and his promise of justice attracted many men to him, including some of the most astute minds of Italy. Dante was not alone in his praises of the Emperor. But Italian political rivalries, traditional suspicion of a German emperor in the Italian cities, and the concerted opposi-

tion of Pope Clement V and King Robert of Naples destroyed any hope that Henry had of being able to accomplish his mission as imperial peacemaker. His frustrated Italian campaign weakened his diplomatic arrangements in Germany. His glorious concept of the imperial ideal was not sufficiently realistic to deal with the complex diplomatic forces which opposed the notion of a universal political authority—the power of France, the Avignon papacy, and the rising signorial power of city rulers and city alliances. For Italy as well as for Germany, Henry was indeed the last medieval emperor.

Further Reading

The most important work in English on Henry VII is William M. Bowsky, *Henry VII in Italy: The Conflict of Empire and City-state, 1310-1313* (1960). Useful information is in J. R. Tanner and others, eds., *The Cambridge Medieval History* (8 vols., 1913-1936), and in a number of studies of Dante's work and thought, such as Charles T. Davis, *Dante and the Idea of Rome* (1957). □

Henry VII

Henry VII (1457-1509) was king of England from 1485 to 1509. He was a successful usurper, the founder of the Tudor dynasty, and an accomplished practitioner of Renaissance diplomacy.

Born on Jan. 28, 1457, at Pembroke, Wales, Henry VII was the only son of Edmund Tudor and Margaret Beaufort. Through the Beaufort family, Henry was descended from Edward III, and in 1470 he was given the title of Earl of Richmond by Henry VI, last of the Lancastrian Kings.

The Yorkist victories of 1471 brought death to Henry VI and his son, and Henry Tudor became a refugee in Brittany as well as heir to the claims of Lancaster. The death of Edward IV in April 1483 left the Yorkist monarchy to his 12-year-old son Edward V, soon deposed and imprisoned by his uncle, regent, and successor, Richard III. Henry attempted a Lancastrian uprising in October 1483 but was balked by bad weather and Richard's soldiers.

Aided by Charles VIII of France, Henry landed at Milford Haven in August 1485 with 2,000 men. A large Welsh troop under the banner of Cadwalader were among the following of 5,000 with whom Henry won the Battle of Bosworth Field (Aug. 22, 1485), where Richard was killed at the head of his forces. The victor was proclaimed King Henry VII by his own soldiers and some of Richard's. There were only three post combat "reprisal slayings" at Bosworth, and Henry made broad use of "temporary forfeiture" to encourage former opponents to earn back their estates by service to the king.

Henry's coronation on Oct. 30, 1485, was marked by expensive pageantry, as he considered an appearance of splendor appropriate to a monarch. On November 7 Henry

Attempted collection led to tax riots, and only after a further grant of £60,000 was Henry able to stage a brief campaign in Picardy in 1492. By the Treaty of Étaples, Henry agreed to give up the invasion, and Charles agreed to pay Henry an indemnity and a pension of £5,000 per year.

This settlement was viewed in England as a betrayal of the national investment to the profit of the King's treasury, and Henry's 1492 unpopularity encouraged one Perkin Warbeck to an impersonation of Richard of York (younger brother of Edward V). For 5 years the elusive Warbeck cultivated anti-Tudor interests in Ireland, Scotland, and on the Continent, with occasional forays into England to encourage a Yorkist faction. The attainder of Sir William Stanley was one result of these disorders. Another was the appointment of Edward Poynings to govern Ireland, resulting in "Poynings' Laws" on the relation of the English and Irish governments.

While Charles VIII's 1494 invasion of Italy preoccupied Europe, Henry remained neutral and solvent in anticipation of troubles at home. The prudence of this policy was shown when Charles's campaign collapsed in 1495 and when the Scots invaded England in 1496. Taxes for an army in 1497 provoked riots and a full-scale rebellion in Cornwall. Henry left the Scots to Thomas Howard, Earl of Surrey, who ended a successful campaign with the Truce of Ayton in September. The Cornish rebels advanced on London with a force of 15,000 but were driven back by Henry and an army of 25,000. Perkin Warbeck linked his fortune to the Cornish rebellion only to share its failure in the summer of 1497. Warbeck was captured, confessed his imposture, and was removed to the Tower.

These events were the last serious challenges to Henry's throne. Ralph Wilford's 1499 "Warwick" gained him only a speedy hanging. At the same time, Henry used a futile Warbeck and Warwick plot to escape as an excuse to make an end of both. Warbeck was hanged on Nov. 23, 1499, at Tyburn. Warwick, imprisoned since childhood, was beheaded at Tower Hill on Nov. 29, 1499, and the male line of York was no more.

Diplomatic and Domestic Policies

Henry negotiated marriage alliances for his children as part of his diplomacy. The 1503 marriage of his daughter Margaret to James IV of Scotland aimed at detaching James from the "Auld Alliance" with France and ultimately led to a union of English and Scottish governments.

Prince Arthur's Nov. 14, 1501, marriage to Catherine of Aragon was ended by Arthur's death on April 2, 1502, from a respiratory infection. Ferdinand and Isabella suggested Henry's younger son and namesake as a husband for their daughter, but the June 25, 1503, marriage contract made this dependent on Prince Henry's consent when he came of age on June 28, 1509. Consummation of the marriage to Arthur was a point in dispute, and Henry VII thoughtfully collected testimony that Henry VIII later used in his divorce of Catherine of Aragon.

Henry VII's 1508 proxy marriage of his daughter Mary to Prince Charles of Castile did not become a real union, and as a widower Henry was unsuccessful in his attempts to

opened Parliament, which accepted him as king, and attainted Richard for usurpation and "shedding of infants' blood," presumably explaining the fate of Edward V and Richard of York. Customs for life and an act of resumption were voted. On Jan. 18, 1486, Henry fulfilled a parliamentary petition, and his own promise to unite the families of York and Lancaster, by marrying Elizabeth of York, daughter of Edward IV.

Threats to His Crown

But the Yorkist faction was not to be romanced out of existence. Lambert Simnel, son of an Oxford tradesman, was coached to an impersonation of Edward of Warwick, son of Edward IV's brother, George of Clarence. Henry demonstrated Simnel's imposture by having Warwick taken from the Tower of London long enough to attend High Mass at St. Paul's. Nevertheless, a serious Yorkist movement developed, supported by several councilors and the King's mother-in-law, among others. This uprising was checked only by Henry's victory in the Battle of Stoke (June 16, 1487). The captured Simnel was made a palace servant.

By 1489 Henry had settled on a foreign policy of limited rivalry with Charles VIII. This suited England's anti-French prejudices and gave Henry a diplomatic rationale for alliances with the emperor Maximilian I, the Duchess of Brittany, and Ferdinand and Isabella of Spain. The 1489 Treaty of Medina del Campo linked England and Spain in policy and a promise of marriage alliance. Henry asked the 1489 Parliament for a subsidy of £100,000 to finance war against France. The policy was popular, but not the price.

marry his own way into the control of another kingdom. He could not prevent Spain and France from growing into kingdoms of increasing solidity and strength, but Henry at least helped to save England from becoming the victim of France or Spain.

Henry VII continued the restoration of governmental effectiveness begun by Edward IV, following the bankruptcy and collapse of government under Henry VI. A more general enforcement of law and order earned Henry much of his support, despite particular abuses in Star Chamber cases or in the field of jury tampering. Government income more than doubled in Henry's reign, and he showed great sense in the use of money. The structure of Henry's government remained medieval in organization, but the King's investments in commerce, attention to technological changes in shipbuilding and mining, and sponsorship of John Cabot's voyage to America all gave to the general impression of Henry's government an effect which was both modern and national.

Henry's selfishness and capacity for foresighted calculation won him many advantages but few admirers, and in later life Henry at times appeared dissatisfied with the ungenerous methods by which he had prospered. By any account, however, he was one of England's more successful diplomatists.

Further Reading

A study of Henry and his era is A.F. Pollard, ed., *The Reign of Henry VII from Contemporary Sources* (3 vols., 1913-1914). Biographies of Henry include James Gairdner, *Henry the Seventh* (1889), a standard work; Eric N. Simons, *Henry VII: The First Tudor King* (1968), a popular biography; and R. L. Storey, *The Reign of Henry VII* (1968), a fresh assessment. Henry is discussed in Kenneth Pickthorn, *Early Tudor Government: Henry VII* (1934), which is a brief commentary; J. D. Mackie, *The Earlier Tudors, 1485-1558* (1952), a concise survey; and G. R. Elton's excellent *England under the Tudors* (1955).

Additional Sources

Alexander, Michael Van Cleave, *The first of the Tudors: a study of Henry VII and his reign,* Totowa, N.J.: Rowman and Littlefield, 1980.

Chrimes, S. B. (Stanley Bertram), *Henry V,* Berkeley, University of California Press, 1972; London, Eyre Methuen 1972.

Farrington, Robert, *Tudor agent,* New York: St. Martin's Press, 1974.

Fox, Alistair, *Politics and literature in the reigns of Henry VII and Henry VIII,* Oxford, UK; New York, NY, USA: Blackwell, 1989.

Gairdner, James, *Henry the Seventh,* St. Clair Shores, Mich., Scholarly Press 1969?; New York, AMS Press 1970.

Gellis, Roberta, *The Dragon and the Rose,* Chicago: Playboy Press, 1977.

Ide, Arthur Frederick, *The mercantile policies of Henry VII,* Irving, Tex.: Scholars Books, 1987.

Jones, Michael K., *The King's mother: Lady Margaret Beaufort, Countess of Richmond and Derby,* Cambridge England; New York: Cambridge University Press, 1992.

Macalpine, Joan, *The shadow of the tower: Henry VII and his England, background to the BBC tv serie,* London, British Broadcasting Corporation, 1971.

Pitt, Derek William, *Henry VI,* London, Oxford U.P., 1966.

Plaidy, Jean, *Uneasy lies the head,* New York: Putnam, 1982, 1984; London: R. Hale, 1982.

Randall, Dale B. J, *"Theatres of greatness": a revisionary view of Ford's Perkin Warbeck,* Victoria, B.C., Canada: University of Victoria, 1986.

Rees, David, *The son of prophecy: Henry Tudor's road to Bosworth,* London: Black Raven Press, 1985.

Simon, Linda, *Of virtue rare: Margaret Beaufort, matriarch of the House of Tudor,* Boston: Houghton Mifflin, 1982.

Simons, Eric N., *Henry VII, the first Tudor king,* New York: Barnes & Noble, 1968; London: Muller, 1968.

Sisson, Rosemary Anne, *The dark horse: a play,* London; New York: French, 1979.

Stephens, Peter John, *Battle for destiny,* New York: Atheneum, 1967.

Stubbs, Jean, *An unknown Welshman; a novel based on the early life of Henry Tudor, Earl of Richmond, later King Henry VII of England, from 1457 to 1485,* London: Macmillan, 1972.

Temperley, Gladys, *Henry VI,* Westport, Conn.: Greenwood Press, 1971.

Williams, Glanmor, *Harri Tudur a Chymru = Henry Tudor and Wales,* Cardiff: Gwasg Prifysgol Cymru, 1985.

Williams, Neville, *The life and times of Henry VI,* London: Weidenfeld and Nicolson, 1973. □

Henry VIII

Henry VIII (1491-1547) was king of England from 1509 to 1547. As a consequence of the Pope's refusal to nullify his first marriage, Henry withdrew from the Roman Church and created the Church of England.

The second son of Henry VII, Henry VIII was born on June 28, 1491, at Greenwich Palace. He was a precocious student; he learned Latin, Spanish, French, and Italian and studied mathematics, music, and theology. He became an accomplished musician and played the lute, organ, and harpsichord. He composed hymns, ballads, and two Masses. He also liked to hunt, wrestle, and joust and drew "the bow with greater strength than any man in England."

On his father's death on April 21, 1509, Henry succeeded to a peaceful kingdom. He married Catherine of Aragon, widow of his brother Arthur, on June 11, and 13 days later they were crowned at Westminster Abbey. He enthused to his father-in-law, Ferdinand, that "the love he bears to Catherine is such, that if he were still free he would choose her in preference to all others."

Foreign Policy

In short order Henry set course on a pro-Spanish and anti-French policy. In 1511 he joined Spain, the papacy, and Venice in the Holy League, directed against France. He claimed the French crown and sent troops to aid the Spanish in 1512 and determined to invade France. The bulk of the preparatory work fell to Thomas Wolsey, the royal almoner, who became Henry's war minister. Despite the objections of councilors like Thomas Howard, the Earl of Surrey, Henry

went ahead. He was rewarded by a smashing victory at Guinegate (Battle of the Spurs, Aug. 13, 1513) and the capture of Tournai and Théorouanne.

Peace was made in 1514 with the Scots, who had invaded England and been defeated at Flodden (Sept. 9, 1513), as well as with France. The marriage of Henry's sister Mary to Louis XII sealed the French treaty. This diplomatic revolution resulted from Henry's anger at the Hapsburg rejection of Mary, who was to have married Charles, the heir to both Ferdinand and Maximilian I, the Holy Roman emperor. Soon the new French king, Francis I, decisively defeated the Swiss at Marignano (Sept. 13-14, 1515). When Henry heard about Francis's victory, he burst into tears of rage. Increasingly, Wolsey handled state affairs; he became archbishop of York in 1514, chancellor and papal legate in 1515. Not even his genius, however, could win Henry the coveted crown of the Holy Roman Empire. With deep disappointment he saw it bestowed in 1519 on Charles, the Spanish king. During 1520 Henry met Emperor Charles V at Dover and Calais, and Francis at the Field of Cloth of Gold, near Calais, where Francis mortified Henry by throwing him in an impromptu wrestling match. In 1521 Henry joyfully received the papally bestowed title "Defender of the Faith" as a reward for writing the *Assertion of the Seven Sacraments,* a criticism of Lutheran doctrine. He tried to secure Wolsey's election as pope in 1523 but failed.

English Reformation

Catherine was 40 in 1525. Her seven pregnancies produced but one healthy child, Mary, born May 18, 1516.

Despairing of having a legitimate male heir, Henry created Henry Fitzroy, his natural son by Elizabeth Blount, Duke of Richmond and Somerset. More and more, he conceived Catherine's misfortunes as a judgment from God. Did not Leviticus say that if a brother marry his brother's widow, it is an unclean thing and they shall be childless? Since Catherine was Arthur's widow, the matter was apparent.

The Reformation proceeded haphazardly from Henry's negotiations to nullify his marriage. Catherine would not retire to a nunnery, nor would Anne Boleyn consent to be Henry's mistress as had her sister Mary; she grimly demanded marriage. A court sitting in June 1529 under Wolsey and Cardinal Campeggio heard the case. Pope Clement VII instructed Campeggio to delay. When the Peace of Cambrai was declared between Spain and France in August 1529, leaving Charles V, Catherine's nephew, still powerful in Italy, clement revoked the case to Rome. He dared not antagonize Charles, whose troops had sacked Rome in 1527 and briefly held him prisoner.

Henry removed Wolsey from office. Actually, Wolsey's diplomacy had been undermined by Henry's sending emissaries with different proposals to Clement. Catherine had a valid dispensation for her marriage to Henry from Pope Julius II; furthermore, she claimed that she came a virgin to Henry. She was a popular queen, deeply hurt by Henry's forsaking her bed in 1526. Henry's strategy matured when Thomas Cromwell became a privy councilor and his chief minister. Cromwell forced the clergy in convocation in 1531 to accept Henry's headship of the Church "as far as the law of Christ allows."

Anne's pregnancy in January 1533 brought matters to a head. In a fever of activity Henry married her on Jan. 25, 1533, secured papal approval to Thomas Cranmer's election as archbishop of Canterbury in March, had a court convened under Cranmer declare his marriage to Catherine invalid in May, and waited triumphantly for the birth of a son. His waiting was for naught. On Sept. 7, 1533, Elizabeth was born. Henry was so disappointed that he did not attend her christening. By the Act of Succession (1534) his issue by Anne was declared legitimate and his daughter Mary illegitimate. The Act of Supremacy (1534) required an oath affirming Henry's headship of the Church and, with other acts preventing appeals to Rome and cutting off the flow of annates and Peter's Pence, completed the break. Individual unwilling to subscribe to the Acts of Succession and Supremacy suffered, the two most notable victims being John Fisher, Bishop of Rochester, and Thomas More (1535). Their executions led to the publication of the papal bull excommunicating Henry.

Although Henry allowed the publication of an English Bible (1538), the Henrician Reformation was basically conservative. Major liturgical and theological revisions came under his son, Edward VI. Henry's financial need, however, made him receptive to Cromwell's plan for monastic dissolutions via parliamentary acts in 1536 and 1539, in which the Crown became proprietor of the dissolved monasteries. The scale of monastic properties led to important social and economic consequences.

Later Marriages

Anne's haughty demeanor and moody temperament suited Henry ill, and her failure to produce a male heir rankled. She miscarried of a baby boy on Jan. 27, 1536, 6 days after fainting at the news that Henry had been knocked unconscious in a jousting accident in which the king fell under his mailed horse. It was a costly miscarriage, for Henry was already interested in Jane Seymour. He determined on a second divorce. He brought charges of treason against Anne for alleged adultery and incest; she was executed on May 19. The following day Henry betrothed himself to Jane and married her 10 days later. Jane brought a measure of comfort to Henry's personal life; she also produced a son and heir, Edward, on Oct. 12, 1537, but survived his birth a scant 12 days.

Henry was deeply grieved, and he did not remarry for 3 years. He was not in good health. Headaches plagued him intermittently; they may have originated from a jousting accident of 1524, in which Charles Brandon's lance splintered on striking Henry's open helmet. Moreover his ulcerated leg, which first afflicted him in 1528, occasionally troubled. Both legs were infected in 1537. In May 1538 he had a clot blockage in his lungs which made him speechless, but he recovered.

The course of diplomatic events, particularly the fear that Charles V might attempt an invasion of England, led Henry to seek an alliance with Continental Protestant powers; hence, his marriage to the Protestant princess Anne of Cleves on Jan. 12, 1540. His realization that Charles did not intend to attack, coupled with his distaste for Anne, led to Cromwell's dismissal and execution in June 1540 and to the annulment of his marriage to Anne on July 9, 1540.

Cromwell's fall was engineered by the conservative leaders of his Council, Thomas Howard, Duke of Norfolk, and Bishop Gardiner. They thrust forward the 19-year-old niece of Norfolk, Catherine Howard, and Henry found her pleasing. He married Catherine within 3 weeks of his annulment and entered into the Indian summer of his life. He bore his by now tremendous girth lightly and was completely captivated, but his happiness was short-lived. Catherine's indiscretions as queen consort combined with her sexual misdemeanors as a protégé of the old dowager Duchess of Norfolk ensured her ruin. Inquiry into her behavior in October 1541 led to house arrest and her execution on Feb. 13, 1542, by means of a bill of attainder.

Henry's disillusionment with Catherine plus preoccupation with the Scottish war, begun in 1542, and plans for renewal of hostilities with France delayed remarriage. The French war commenced in 1543 and dragged on for 3 years, achieving a solitary triumph before Boulogne (1545). Henry married the twice-widowed Catherine Parr on July 12, 1543. Though she bore him no children, she made him happy. Her religious views were somewhat more radical than those of Henry, who had revised the conservative Six Articles (1539) with his own hand. During his last years he attempted to stem the radical religious impulses unleashed by the formal break with Rome.

No minister during Henry's last 7 years approached the power of Wolsey or Cromwell. Henry bitterly reflected that Cromwell was the most faithful servant that he had ever had. He ruled by dividing his Council into conservative and radical factions. When Norfolk's faction became too powerful, he imprisoned him and executed his son the poet Henry Howard, Earl of Surrey. The King was unwell in late 1546 and early 1547, suffering from a fever brought on by his ulcerated leg. Before he died on Jan. 28, 1547, Henry reflected that "the mercy of Christ [is] able to pardon me all my sins, though they were greater than they be."

Appearance and Assessment

A contemporary described Henry in his prime as "the handsomest potentate I have ever set eyes on; above the usual height, with an extremely fine calf to his leg; his complexion fair and bright, with auburn hair . . . and a round face so very beautiful that it would become a pretty woman. . . . He is much handsomer than any other sovereign in Christendom; a great deal handsomer than the King of France." Henry was "a capital horseman, a fine jouster," and "very fond of hunting," tiring 8 or 10 horses in the course of a day's hunting. "He is extremely fond of tennis, at which game it is the prettiest thing in the world to see him play, his fair skin glowing through a shirt of the finest texture."

Henry came to the throne with great gifts and high hopes. Ministers like Wolsey and Cromwell freed him from the burdensome chores of government and made policy, but only with Henry's approval. His relentless search for an heir led him into an accidental reformation of the Church not entirely to his liking. Ironically, had he waited until Catherine of Aragon died in 1536, he would have been free to pursue a solution to the succession problem without recourse to a reformation. His desire to cut a figure on the European battlefields led him into costly wars. To pay the piper, it was necessary to debase the coinage, thus increasing inflationary pressures already stimulated by the influx of Spanish silver, and to use the tremendous revenues from the sale of monastic properties. Had the properties been kept in the royal hand, the revenue could have made the Crown self-sufficient—perhaps so self-sufficient that it could have achieved an absolutism comparable to that of Louis XIV.

Though personally interested in education, Henry sponsored no far-reaching educational statutes. However, his avid interest in naval matters resulted in a larger navy and a modernization of naval administration. He brought Wales more fully into union with the English by the Statute of Wales (1536) and made Ireland a kingdom (1542). Through the Statute of Uses (1536) he attempted to close off his subjects' attempts to deny him his feudal dues, but this was resisted and modified in 1540. The great innovations came out of the Reformation Statutes, not the least of which was the Act in Restraint of Appeals, in which England was declared an empire, and the Act of Supremacy, in which Henry became supreme head of the Anglican Church. The politically inspired Henrician Reformation became a religiously inspired one under his son, Edward VI, and thus

Henry's reign became the first step in the forging of the Anglican Church.

Henry ruled ruthlessly in a ruthless age; he cut down the enemies of the Crown, like the Duke of Buckingham in 1521 and the Earl of Surrey. He stamped out the Pilgrimage of Grace (1536-1537), which issued from economic discontent, and set up a council in the north to ensure that there would be no more disorder. Though he had political gifts of a high order, he was neither Machiavelli's prince in action nor Bismarck's man of blood and iron. He was a king who wished to be succeeded by a son, and for this cause he bravely and rashly risked the anger of his fellow sovereigns. That he did what he did is a testament to his will, personal gifts, and good fortune.

Further Reading

A. F. Pollard, *Henry VIII* (1902; new ed. 1913), the traditional interpretation of Henry VIII, has been challenged in recent years by G. R. Elton, *Henry VIII: An Essay in Revision* (1962), and J. J. Scarisbrick, *Henry VIII* (1968). Scarisbrick, unlike Pollard, does not view Henry as England's savior. He believes that Henry created England's difficulties and censures him for his lack of social responsibility. He also provides a detailed analysis of the technical aspects of the divorce. Lacey Baldwin Smith, *Henry VIII: The Mask of Royalty* (1971), concentrates on Henry's last years and brilliantly portrays his personal despotism and naked pride and power. Melvin J. Tucker, *The Life of Thomas Howard, Earl of Surrey, Second Duke of Norfolk, 1443-1524* (1964), gives a good case study of Henry's relationship to his aristocracy. Joycelyne G. Russell, *The Field of Cloth of Gold* (1969), supplies an interesting analysis of the pageantry that accompanied state affairs. Lacey Baldwin Smith, *Tudor Prelates and Politics, 1536-1558* (1953), effectively deals with conciliar factions.

A variety of studies deal with the historical background: J. W. Allen, *A History of Political Thought in the Sixteenth Century* (1928; 3d ed. 1951), ably handles political theory; S. T. Bindoff, *Tudor England* (1951), is a brilliantly written general survey and is good on economics; G. R. Elton, ed., *The Tudor Constitution: Documents and Commentary* (1960), unravels complicated constitutional matters; A. G. Dickens, *The English Reformation* (1964; rev. ed. 1967), deals incisively with the Henrician Reformation; and R. B. Wernham, *Before the Armada: The Emergence of the English Nation, 1485-1588* (1966), is essential on Tudor foreign policy. □

Henry the Navigator

The Portuguese prince Henry the Navigator (1394-1460) launched the first great European voyages of exploration. He sought new lands and sources of revenue for his kingdom and dynasty and searched for eastern Christian allies against Islam.

Born at Oporto on March 4, 1394, Henry was the third son of John I of Portugal and Philippa of Lancaster. He grew to maturity at a time when John I was bringing to a close a confused period of civil strife and war with Castile and securing Portugal's independence. The conflicts of this period had left the nobility decimated and impoverished and the monarchy's revenues greatly depreciated. Thus the ruling families began to look abroad for new worlds of wealth, land, and honors to conquer.

John and his sons became involved in a threefold movement of Portuguese expansion, comprising the campaign to conquer Moorish North Africa; the movement to explore and conquer the Atlantic island groups to the west and south; and the exploring, trading, and slaving expeditions down the West African coast. These ventures were united not by geographical curiosity but by Henry's overreaching desire to continue abroad the traditional Portuguese crusade against Moors and Berbers in the peninsula itself. He hoped also to catch Islam in a gigantic pincers movement by joining forces with the mythical "Indies" Christian kingdom of Prester John, the wealthy and powerful priest-king of medieval legend. The Prester's domains had been variously located in present-day India and in East Africa (Ethiopia).

North Africa and the Atlantic Islands

King John wished to satisfy the avarice and lust for battle of his warriors; Prince Henry and his brothers wanted to prove their manhood and strike a blow for the faith on the battlefield. A campaign launched in July 1415 during a civil war in North Africa left the port of Ceuta stripped of its navy. Henry was knighted and made Duke of Viseu. With the fall of Ceuta the Portuguese learned of the long-established gold trade with black Africa conducted by caravan across the Sahara. Gold hunger had been growing in late medieval Europe in response to the growth of commerce, but Portugal had lacked gold coinage since 1383. Prince Henry may thus have sought to tap the supply at its source by venturing down the West African coast.

Henry's first sponsored voyages of exploration were to the Atlantic islands of Madeira and Porto Santo (1418-1419); colonization followed. These islands, as well as the Azores and Canaries, had been known to the earlier Middle Ages; they were now rediscovered and exploited by the Portuguese (the Azores ca. 1439), except the Canaries, which fell under the control of Castile. The Cape Verde Islands, much farther to the south, were discovered and settled in 1455-1460. Colonization of these islands was important for the entire subsequent history of Iberian expansion: they provided bases for voyages to the New World and for the development of practices used later in American colonization. More immediately, they brought in returns on capital loans extended by Prince Henry to island settlers.

Meanwhile, the Portuguese involvement in North Africa was proving to be a costly and dangerous undertaking. During Henry's disastrous attempt in 1437 to conquer Tangier, the Moslems roundly defeated the Portuguese and took Prince Henry's younger brother, Fernando, as a hostage against the return of Ceuta. Over the objections of Henry and his eldest brother, Duarte (then king), the royal council refused to make the trade, and Fernando lived out the rest of his days in a dungeon at Fez.

African Voyages

The repeated probes made down the West African coast at Henry's behest constitute the most significant achievement of his career. Only the most important of these expeditions will be mentioned here.

After many unsuccessful attempts Gil Eannes in 1434 rounded Cape Bojador on the North African coast. This point was the southernmost limit of previous European exploration, and Eannes's feat in sailing beyond it—and returning—constitutes the most important navigational achievement of the early Portuguese maritime enterprise. Further voyages under Nuno Tristão led to the rounding of Cape Blanco (1442), the occupation of Arguin Island (1443), and the discovery of the mouths of the Senegal (1444) and Gambia (1446) rivers. Cape Verde was attained by Dinas Dias in 1444, and the islands of that name were first visited by Alvise da Cadamosto in 1555. The mouths of the Geba and Casamance rivers were discovered by Diogo Gomes in 1456, and in 1460 Pedro da Sintra reached Sierra Leone. A total of about 1,500 miles of African coast had been explored by these expeditions.

The economic and political consequences of African "discovery" were momentous. The Portuguese obtained an ever-increasing flow of gold through trade with inhabitants of the coastal regions and in 1457 resumed minting gold coins. With a coarse African red pepper (*malagueta*) the Portuguese made their first incursion into the Italian monopoly of the spice trade. However, the most important long-range economic development was the beginnings of the African slave trade, which became significant after 1442. The Portuguese obtained slaves through raids on coastal villages and trade with the inhabitants of Gambia and Upper Guinea. In this way the Portuguese, at the very beginning of Europe's overseas expansion, provided the "woeful solution" for the problem of colonial labor power.

Equally important for future patterns of colonization were developments in economic, religious, and political policy. At this time the papacy commenced to issue its long series of bulls defining the rights of the colonizing powers. The Portuguese crown was awarded an exclusive monopoly over both present and future exploration, commerce, and conquest all the way to South Africa and the "Indies," as well as a spiritual monopoly over these same regions.

Henry supported and defined the missions of his captains and patronized map makers and others who could make practical contributions to the progress of discovery. But he sponsored no "school" of pure science and mathematics, and his reputation as a patron of learning has been grossly inflated. Henry died at Vila do Infante near Sagres on Nov. 13, 1460.

Further Reading

There are several biographies of Prince Henry, of which one of the best is C. Raymond Beazley, *Prince Henry the Navigator: The Hero of Portugal and of Modern Discovery, 1394-1460 A.D.* (1895; new ed. 1923). The standard work on Portuguese expansion in the 15th century is Edgar Prestage, *The Portuguese Pioneers* (1933), but this should now be supplemented with C.R. Boxer, *The Portuguese Seaborne Empire, 1415-1825* (1969). The history of Portugal in this period is best conveyed by H. V. Livermore, *A New History of Portugal* (1947). The history of European expansion overseas from the 15th through the 17th century is considered in Boies Penrose, *Travel and Discovery in the Renaissance, 1420-1620* (1952), and J. H. Parry, *The Age of Reconnaissance* (1963).

Additional Sources

Age of exploration and discovery: Prince Henry and the Portuguese navigators (1394-1498), Philadelphia, Westminster Press 1969.

Chubb, Thomas Caldecot, *Prince Henry the Navigator and the highways of the sea,* New York, Viking Press 1970.

Fisher, Leonard Everett, *Prince Henry the Navigator,* New York: Macmillan; London: Collier Macmillan, 1990.

Jacobs, William Jay, *Prince Henry, the Navigator,* New York, F. Watts, 1973. □

Aaron Henry

Aaron Henry (born 1922) a champion of civil rights, leader the Mississippi chapter of the NAACP and a member of the Mississippi House of Representatives, he is one of the most revered civil rights leaders in Mississippi.

Described by one biographer as "the oldest, best known, and most respected civil rights activist in Mississippi," Aaron Henry has served as president of the Mississippi chapter of the NAACP since 1960. Henry grew up near Clarksdale, Mississippi, and later earned a degree in political science at Xavier University in New Orleans. During World War II, he served as a staff sergeant with the U.S. Army in the Pacific. After the war, the African American veteran attended pharmacy school, and eventually returned to Clarksdale to open a drug store.

As a leader of the NAACP, Henry participated in virtually every aspect of the struggle for equality in Mississippi, while serving as a voice of moderation and an advocate of racial conciliation. In 1961, he joined the Freedom Rides to protest segregation in interstate bus facilities and was arrested when the group reached Jackson, Mississippi. Two years later, Henry ran for governor—and won handily—in the Freedom Vote, a mock election held to demonstrate African American interest in politics and to mobilize the African American community for further political action. During the Freedom Summer of 1964, Henry served as chairperson of the Council of Federated Organizations, an umbrella agency which attempted to coordinate the activities of the NAACP, the Student Nonviolent Coordinating Committee, the Southern Christian Leadership Conference, and the Congress of Racial Equality. Under his leadership, the various civil rights organizations launched a large-scale voter registration drive and conducted "Freedom Schools," which combined adult education with training in community activism.

When African American activists and white liberals organized the Mississippi Freedom Democratic Party, they elected Henry chairperson of the biracial coalition, and he led the MFDP's challenge to the seating of the regular Mississippi delegation at the 1964 Democratic National Convention in Atlantic City, New Jersey. The leadership of the national party proposed a compromise under which the regulars would be seated along with Henry and Ed King, the white chaplain at Tougaloo College and a member of the MFDP. In addition, the compromise would have prohibited the exclusion of blacks or other minorities from future delegations. Henry and other moderate NAACP members within his delegation supported the compromise, but they were outvoted by more militant activists whose primary loyalty was to the MFDP itself. Nevertheless, Henry believed that the highly publicized attack on the exclusion of blacks from the Mississippi Democratic Party represented a significant moral victory for the forces of change. The MFDP challenge, Henry said later, "Wrote the beginning of the restructuring of politics in the nation." Indeed, in 1965, the NAACP withdrew support for COFO, and formed a new coalition with white liberals and organized labor. Known as the Loyalist Democrats, to distinguish themselves from Mississippi's conservative white Democrats who often bolted the national party to support Republican and third-party candidates, the new coalition won the right to represent Mississippi at the Democratic convention in 1968. By the 1970s, the Loyalists had gained a dominant role within the state party organization.

Henry Elected to NAACP National Board

In 1964, Henry attempted to run for Congress as an independent, but white election officials ruled that the NAACP leader, along with other African American candidates, failed to obtain the required number of signatures on the petitions to put their names on the ballot. In another "Freedom Vote" in 1965, however, Henry overwhelmingly defeated incumbent John C. Stennis in a mock election for the U.S. Senate. In the same year, Henry was also elected to the national board of directors of the NAACP.

A subject of frequent abuse for his civil rights views, Henry was convicted in March 1962 for sexually harassing a young white hitchhiker. An appellate court reversed the conviction. When Henry claimed he had been the victim of a racial vendetta by the local prosecutor and police chief, the white officials sued him and won an $80,000 award. The jury verdict, however, was also reversed on appeal. Henry fended off the legal threats, but white supremacists bombed his home and his drugstore, and his wife was fired from her job as a public school teacher. Through three tumultuous decades, the steady, modest Henry endured. "I think," he said, "that every time a man stands for an ideal or speaks out against injustice, he sends out a tiny ripple of hope." In 1982, Henry was elected to the Mississippi House of Representatives.

One of the founding members of Rural America, Henry served on its board from 1967–1989. He served as Rural America's Board Chairman from 1983–1989. □

Joseph Henry

Joseph Henry (1797-1878), American physicist and electrical experimenter, was primarily important for his role in the institutional development of science in America.

Joseph Henry was born Dec. 17, 1797, in Albany, N. Y. He attended the common school until the age of 14, when he was apprenticed to a jeweler. He later studied at the Albany Academy and in 1826 became professor of mathematics there. He immediately began researching a comparatively new field—the relation of electric currents to magnetism. The important result of this work was Henry's discovery of induced currents. In 1832 he was appointed professor of natural philosophy (chemistry and physics) in the College of New Jersey at Princeton.

In 1846 Henry became the first secretary and director of the Smithsonian Institution in Washington, D.C., a position he held for the rest of his life. Under his direction the institution encouraged and supported original research. Although a large portion of the income settled on the institution by Congress was for the support of the museum, art gallery, laboratory, and library, Henry took every opportunity to divest the institution of such burdens.

As the Smithsonian's director, Henry acted as one of the major coordinators of government science. Among the projects he originated was the system of receiving simultaneous weather reports by telegraph and basing weather predictions on them. From these beginnings came the U.S. Weather Bureau. During the Civil War he served on the Navy's permanent commission to evaluate inventions and on the Lighthouse Board.

Henry was elected to the American Philosophical Society in 1835. He helped organize the American Association for the Advancement of Science in 1847 and was an original member of the National Academy of Sciences, chartered by Congress in 1863. He became vice president of the National Academy in 1866 and was president from 1868 until his death. He was responsible for reorganizing the academy and transforming it from a society that emphasized governmental service to an honorary organization which recognized "original research."

Henry died on May 13, 1878. By concurrent resolution a memorial service was held in his honor on the evening of Jan. 16, 1879, in the hall of the House of Representatives, and by act of Congress a bronze statue was erected at Washington in his memory.

Further Reading

The only modern biography of Henry is Thomas Coulson, *Joseph Henry: His Life and Work* (1950), a largely uncritical account that does not adequately stress Henry's institutional contributions. Detailed accounts of Henry's life and work are in James Gerald Crowther, *Famous American Men of Science* (1937); Bernard Jaffe, *Men of Science in America* (1944; rev. ed. 1958); and Bessie Zaban Jones, ed., *The Golden Age of Science,* containing a memoir by Asa Gray (1966). Henry's

Indicted in 1896 for embezzling bank funds (actually a result of technical mismanagement), Porter fled to a reporting job in New Orleans, then to Honduras. When news of his wife's serious illness reached him, he returned to Texas. After her death he was imprisoned in Columbus, Ohio. During his 3-year incarceration, he wrote adventure stories set in Texas and Central America that quickly became popular and were collected in *Cabbages and Kings* (1904).

Released from prison in 1902, Porter went to New York City, his home and the setting of most of his fiction for the remainder of his life. He wrote, under the pen name O. Henry, at a prodigious rate—a story a week for a newspaper, plus still other stories for magazines. Books made up of his stories followed rapidly: *The Four Million* (1906); *Heart of the West* and *The Trimmed Lamp* (both 1907); *The Gentle Grafter* and *The Voice of the City* (both 1908); *Options* (1909); and *Whirligigs* and *Strictly Business* (both 1910).

O. Henry's most representative collection was probably *The Four Million*. The title and the stories answered the snobbish claim of socialite Ward McAllister that only 400 people in New York "were really worth noticing" by detailing events in the lives of everyday Manhattanites. In his most famous story, "The Gift of the Magi," a poverty-stricken New York couple secretly sell valued possessions to buy one another Christmas gifts. Ironically, the wife sells her hair so that she can buy her husband a watch chain, while he sells his watch so that he can buy her a pair of combs.

Incapable of integrating a book-length narrative, O. Henry was skilled in plotting short ones. He wrote in a dry,

career and influence are discussed at length in Paul Henry Oehser, *Sons of Science: The Story of the Smithsonian Institution and Its Leaders* (1949), and Bessie Zaban Jones, *Lighthouse of the Skies: The Smithsonian Astrophysical Observatory: Background and History, 1846-1955* (1965). *A Memorial of Joseph Henry*, containing several biographical sketches and a complete bibliography, was published by order of Congress in 1880 (published also as *Smithsonian Miscellaneous Collections*, vol. 21, 1887). □

O. Henry

The American short-story writer William Sydney Porter (1862-1910), who wrote under the pseudonym O. Henry, pioneered in picturing the lives of lower-class and middle-class New Yorkers.

William Sydney Porter was born in Greensboro, N.C., on Sept. 11, 1862. He attended school for a short time, then clerked in an uncle's drugstore. At the age of 20 he went to Texas, working first on a ranch and later as a bank teller. In 1887 he married and began to write free-lance sketches. A few years later he founded a humorous weekly, the *Rolling Stone*. When this failed, he became a reporter and columnist on the *Houston Post.*

humorous style and, as in "The Gift of the Magi," frequently used coincidences and surprise endings to underline ironies. Even after O. Henry's death on June 5, 1910, stories continued to be collected: *Sixes and Sevens* (1911); *Rolling Stones* (1912); *Waifs and Strays* (1917); *O. Henryana* (1920); *Letters to Lithopolis* (1922); *Postscripts* (1923); and *O. Henry Encore* (1939).

Further Reading

The best biographical and critical studies are Eugene H. Long, *O. Henry: The Man and His Work* (1949), and Dale Kramer, *The Heart of O. Henry* (1954). See also Gerald Langford, *Alias O. Henry: A Biography of William Sydney Porter* (1957), and a good recent study, Richard O'Connor, *O. Henry: The Legendary Life of William Sydney Porter* (1970).

Additional Sources

Blansfield, Karen Charmaine, *Cheap rooms and restless hearts: a study of formula in the urban tales of William Sydney Porter,* Bowling Green, Ohio: Bowling Green State University Popular Press, 1988.

Current-Garcia, Eugene, *O. Henry: a study of the short fiction,* New York: Twayne Publishers; Toronto: Maxwell Macmillan Canada; New York: Maxwell Macmillan International, 1993.

Current-Garcia, Eugene, *O. Henry (William Sydney Porter),* New York, Twayne Publishers 1965.

Eikhenbaum, Boris Mikhailovich, *O. Henry and the theory of the short story,* Ann Arbor Dept. of Slavic Languages and Literatures, University of Michigan 1968.

Engel, Elliot, *A Dickens of a Christmas,* Raleigh, NC: Dickens Fellowship, 1994.

Gallegly, Joseph, *From Alamo Plaza to Jack Harris's Saloon. O. Henry and the Southwest he knew,* The Hague, Mouton, 1970.

Harris, Richard C., *William Sydney Porter (O. Henry), a reference guide,* Boston: G. K. Hall, 1980.

Henry, O., *Four short stories: English, Francais, Deutsch,* Hanover, USA: Hanover Print., 1987.

Knight, Jesse F., *The world of O. Henry: five one-act plays,* Indianapolis: Lion Enterprises, 1977.

Langford, Gerald, *Alias O. Henry: a biography of William Sidney Porter,* Westport, Conn.: Greenwood Press, 1983, 1957.

Long, E. Hudson (Eugene Hudson), *O. Henry, the man and his world,* New York, Russell & Russell 1969, 1949.

Longo, Lucas, *O. Henry, short story writer,* Charlotteville, N.Y.: SamHar Press, 1976.

O'Connor, Richard, *O. Henry papers; containing some sketches of his life together with an alphabetical index to his complete work,* Folcroft, Pa.: Folcroft Library Editions, 1973.

O'Quinn, Trueman E., *Time to write: how William Sidney Porter became O. Henry,* Austin, Tex.: Eakin Press, 1986.

Pike, Cathleen., *O. Henry in North Carolina,* Folcroft, Pa.: Folcroft Library Editions, 1978.

Smith, C. Alphonso (Charles Alphonso), 1864-1924, *O. Henry,* New York: Chelsea House: distributed by Scribner Book Companies, 1980.

Stuart, David, *O. Henry: a biography of William Sydney Porter,* Chelsea, MI: Scarborough House, 1990.

Toepperwein, Fritz Arnold, *O. Henry almanac through the years 1862 to 1910, containing an account of some of the highlights in the life of William Sydney Porter, pseudonym O. Henry,* Boerne, Tex., Highland Press, 1966?. □

Patrick Henry

Patrick Henry (1736-1799), American orator and revolutionary, was a leader in Virginia politics for 30 years and a supremely eloquent voice during the American Revolution.

Patrick Henry was born into a family of lesser gentry in Hanover County, Va. He received a good education from his father and his uncle, an Anglican clergyman. He largely failed at attempts to become a storekeeper and a farmer, and his early marriage to Sarah Shelton made him at 35 the father of six children, whom he was always hard-pressed to support. A cursory training in law at Williamsburg about 1760, admission to the bar, and a modest beginning in a crowded profession did not at first improve his standing.

Eloquent Patriot

In 1763, defending a Louisa County parish against claims by its Anglican rector, Henry discovered the twin foundations of his public career—a deep empathy for injustice to the plain people and an eloquent voice that could overwhelm a jury. After he had scorned ecclesiastical arrogance and the British power supporting it, Henry's listeners carried him triumphantly from the courtroom. Two years later, as a member of the House of Burgesses, he made his stirring speech denouncing the Stamp Act. Henry also sponsored resolves against the Stamp Act, denying the power of Parliament to tax Virginians, which, published throughout the Colonies, marked him as an early radical leader. For 10 years Henry used his powerful voice and popular support to lead the anti-British movement in the Virginia Legislature.

During the crisis precipitated by the Boston Tea Party and the Coercive Acts, Henry was at the pinnacle of his career. He spurred the House of Burgesses to repeated defiances of the stubborn royal governor, Lord Dunmore. In August 1774 Henry, George Washington, Richard Henry Lee, and others traveled to Philadelphia as the Virginia delegation to the First Continental Congress. Henry stood with the Adamses of Massachusetts and other radicals, urging firm resistance to Britain, and union among the Colonies. "The distinctions between Virginians, Pennsylvanians, New Yorkers, and New Englanders are no more," Henry said. "I am not a Virginian, but an American." John Adams referred to Henry as the "Demosthenes of America." Back home in Virginia, Henry resumed his leadership of the radical party, "encouraging disobedience and exciting a spirit of revolt among the people," reported Lord Dunmore, who, as a result of Henry's exertions, was soon driven from the colony.

Elected to the first Virginia Revolutionary Convention, of March 1775, Henry made one of the most famous orations in American history. Attempting to gain support for measures to arm the colony of Virginia, Henry declared that Britain, by dozens of rash and oppressive measures, had proved its hostility. "We must fight!" Henry proclaimed. "An appeal to arms and to the God of Hosts is all that is left

us! . . . Is life so dear, or peace so sweet, as to be purchased at the price of chains and slavery? Forbid it almighty God! I know not what course others may take; but as for me, give me liberty or give me death!'' The delegates were entranced by Henry's eloquence and swept away by his fervor. Virginia rushed down the road to independence.

Henry capped his seditious activities during the spring of 1775 by leading a contingent of militia that forced reparations for gunpowder stolen by British marines from the Williamsburg arsenal. In the Second Continental Congress, of May-September 1775, Henry again spoke boldly for the radicals. In Virginia for 6 months he commanded the state's regular forces, but exhibiting no particular military talent, he resigned to resume civilian leadership. At the Virginia Convention of May-July 1776, Henry sponsored resolves calling for independence that eventuated in the Declaration of Independence by Congress on July 4, 1776. ''His eloquence,'' wrote a young listener, ''unlocked the secret springs of the human heart, robbed danger of all its terror, and broke the key-stone in the arch of royal power.'' Henry was elected first governor of Virginia under its constitution as an independent commonwealth.

Revolutionary Governor

In three terms as wartime governor (1776-1779), Henry worked effectively to marshal Virginia's resources to support Congress and George Washington's army. He also promoted George Rogers Clark's expedition, which drove the British from the Northwest Territory. During the years of Henry's governorship, the legislature, led by Thomas Jeffer-

son, passed reforms transforming Virginia from a royal colony into a self-governing republic.

Henry's retirement from the governorship gave him time to attend to pressing family concerns. His first wife had died in 1775, leaving him six children, aged 4 to 20. Two years later he married Dorothea Dandridge, who was half his age and came from a prominent Tidewater family. Beginning in 1778, Henry had 11 children by his second wife, thus giving him family responsibilities that taxed his resources and provided abundant distraction from public life.

Meanwhile, Henry continued to serve in the Virginia Assembly, engaging in oratorical battles with Richard Henry Lee and sharing leadership during the breakdown in government after the British invasion of Virginia in 1780-1781. Though Henry backed some measures for strengthening the Continental Congress, his concern increasingly centered on Virginia and on efforts to expand its trade, boundaries, and power.

After the Revolution, Henry served two further terms as governor of Virginia (1784-1786). Increasingly opposed to a stronger federation, he refused to be a delegate to the Constitutional Convention of 1787. As an old revolutionary, he distrusted the ambitions of men like Virginia's James Madison and New York's Alexander Hamilton, fearing that they would sacrifice simple, republican virtues to the alleged needs of a grandiose nation.

''Peaceable Citizen'' Henry

At the Virginia Convention of 1788, Henry engaged Madison and his colleagues in a dramatic debate. He called upon all his oratorical powers to parade before the delegates the tyrannies that would result under the new Constitution: Federal tax gatherers would harass men working peacefully in their own vineyards, citizens would be hauled off for trial in distant courts before unknown judges, and the president would prove to be a worse tyrant than even George III. Furthermore, in his most telling practical arguments, Henry insisted the new Federal government would favor British and Tory creditors and negotiate away American rights to use the Mississippi River. The Federalists nevertheless managed to win a narrow victory, which Henry accepted by announcing that he would be ''a peaceable citizen.'' He had enough power in the legislature, however, to see that Virginia sent Antifederalist senators to the first Congress, and he almost succeeded in excluding Madison from a seat in the House of Representatives.

Finally, shorn of his domination of Virginia politics, Henry largely retired from public life. He resumed his lucrative law practice, earning huge fees from winning case after case before juries overwhelmed by his powerful pleas. He also extended his real estate interests, which, through skillful speculations, made him at his death one of the largest landowners in Virginia, with huge tracts in Kentucky, Georgia, and the Carolinas as well. His continuing national fame, and his switch by 1793 to support of President Washington and the Federalists, led to a series of proffered appointments: as senator, as minister to Spain and to France, as chief justice of the Supreme Court, and as secretary of state. In poor health and content to stay amid his huge progeny,

Henry refused them all. Only one final cause—repeal of the Virginia Resolutions of 1798—prompted his return to politics. In 1799 Henry won election to the Assembly, causing the Jeffersonians to fear that he would carry the state back under the Federalist banner. Henry was mortally ill, however. On June 6, 1799, he died of cancer at his Red Hill plantation and was laid to rest under a plain slab containing the words "His fame his best epitaph."

Further Reading

Two early accounts of Henry, often inaccurate but filled with the drama of his life and containing extracts from the small surviving body of his earlier papers, reminiscences of his associates, and "reconstructions" of his speeches, are William Wirt, *Sketches of the Life and Character of Patrick Henry* (1817; 15th ed. 1852), and William Wirt Henry, *Patrick Henry: Life, Correspondence and Speeches* (3 vols., 1891). The standard biography of Henry is Robert D. Meade, *Patrick Henry* (2 vols., 1957-1969). A hostile view of Henry's career is given in Irving Brant, *James Madison* (6 vols., 1941-1961). □

Josiah Henson

The autobiography of Josiah Henson (1789-1883), an African American slave who escaped to freedom in Canada, was widely read by abolitionists, and he became mistakenly known as the model for Uncle Tom in the novel "Uncle Tom's Cabin."

Josiah Henson was born June 15, 1789, in Charles County, Md. As a child, he saw his father beaten and his family sold away. After almost dying of neglect, he was sold to rejoin his mother, a slave of Isaac Riley. Henson grew to be an intelligent, strong worker and was made superintendent of his owner's farm. After conversion at the age of 18, he became a respected preacher. In a quarrel with a white man, he suffered an arm injury that crippled him for life. At the age of 22 he married a slave girl and fathered 12 children.

Henson was so trustworthy that Riley entrusted him with supervising the move of 18 slaves to his brother's farm in Kentucky. Though the group had opportunities to escape, Henson honored his promise and delivered them to Kentucky. After 3 years there he returned to Maryland, having earned enough as a preacher in the Methodist Episcopal Church to purchase his freedom. However, Riley raised the price beyond Henson's reach, then sent him to New Orleans to be sold away from his family. The owner's son decided not to sell Henson, however, and returned him to Kentucky.

In 1830 Henson fled with his wife and four children to Canada. Working as a farmer, first for hire and then on land owned jointly by a group of escaped slaves, he adjusted quickly to freedom. He became a preacher in Ontario. Other blacks acknowledged his leadership, and whites also regarded him highly. In 1842 he moved to the all-black community of Dawn, Ontario, founded with the support of American and English abolitionists. Henson was the community's natural leader and, although funds were short, the settlement prospered. He was also an agent for the Underground Railroad, by which American slaves escaped to freedom in Canada.

To raise more funds, Henson told his life story to Samuel A. Eliot, who published it as *The Life of Josiah Henson, Formerly a Slave, Now an Inhabitant of Canada* (1849). This would probably have remained just another slave narrative among the many then circulating were it not for the widespread success of *Uncle Tom's Cabin,* by Harriet Beecher Stowe. Though Stowe probably had neither met Henson nor read his story until after her novel was published (1852), Henson became popularly identified with Uncle Tom, and he did not discourage this mistake. Fame followed, and he met celebrities in America and Britain, including Queen Victoria. His autobiography was revised under various editors and titles, with introductions and forewords by various notables, including Stowe. During his later years Henson continued working for Dawn's development. However, he did not wear his fame lightly and offended many associates. Nevertheless, he successfully raised money for Dawn. He died in Dresden, Ontario, on May 5, 1883.

Further Reading

The numerous accounts of Henson's life are all essentially based on his autobiography. The most complete edition, *An Autobiography of the Rev. Josiah Henson* (1881), was republished in 1969 with a thorough introduction by Robin W. Winks. Other relevant works are Brion Gysin, *To Masta—A Long*

Goodnight: The Story of Uncle Tom, A Historical Narrative (1946), and Jesse L. Beattie, *Black Moses: The Real Uncle Tom* (1957). A biographical sketch is in Wilhelmena S. Robinson, *Historical Negro Biographies* (1968), in the *International Library of Negro Life and History*.

Additional Sources

Bleby, Henry, *Josiah, the maimed fugitive; a true tale,* Miami, Fla., Mnemosyne Pub. Co. 1969.

Cavanah, Frances, *The truth about the man behind the book that sparked the War Between the States,* Philadelphia: Westminster Press, 1975.

Henson, Josiah, *Uncle Tom's story of his life: an autobiography of the Rev. Josiah Henson, 1789-1876; introduction by C. Duncan Ric,* London, Cass, 1971. □

Matthew A. Henson

Matthew A. Henson (1866-1955) always accompanied Robert Peary on his Arctic explorations. As a result, he was part of the first expedition to reach the North Pole.

Matthew A. Henson was born in Charles County, Maryland, south of Washington, D.C. on August 8, 1866. Henson was an African-American, whose parents had been born free. When he was young, he moved with his parents to Washington. Both of his parents had died by the time he was seven. He was raised by an uncle and attended a segregated school in Washington for six years. At the age of 13, he went to Baltimore and found a job as a cabin boy on a ship bound for China. He was befriended by the ship's captain, Captain Childs, and worked his way up to being an able-bodied seaman. During that period he sailed to China, Japan, the Philippines, North Africa, Spain, France, and Russia. Childs died when Henson was 17, and he left the sea to look for work on land.

In 1888 Henson was working in a clothing store in Washington when he met a young U.S. Navy lieutenant, Robert Peary, who had come in to buy a tropical helmet. Peary offered to hire him as a valet. Henson did not like the idea of becoming a personal servant, but he thought it would be worthwhile to accompany Peary to Nicaragua where he was headed to survey for a possible canal across Central America. They spent a year together in Nicaragua and then Henson worked as a messenger when Peary was stationed at League Island Navy Yard. Peary was interested in the possibilities of Arctic exploration and had made a first trip to Greenland in 1886 with the intention of being the first to cross the Greenland ice cap. He was beaten by Roald Amundsen and he then set himself the goal of being the first person to reach the North Pole.

Peary returned to northern Greenland in June 1891, and Henson accompanied him along with Peary's wife, Josephine, and other assistants, including Frederick Albert Cook. During this first trip Henson started to learn about the way of life of the Inuit who lived at the northern end of

Greenland, to learn to speak their language and to learn how to use their knowledge of survival in the Arctic. Henson became very popular among the Inuit where he was credited with learning their language and adapting their customs better than any other outsider. He was nicknamed Maripaluk—"kind Matthew."

Henson returned with Peary to Greenland in June 1893, at which time he adopted a young Inuit orphan named Kudlooktoo and taught him to speak English. On this expedition Peary and Henson crossed the northern end of Greenland from their base at Etah to the northeastern corner of the island at Independence Bay in "Peary Land." Henson later wrote, "The memory of the winter and summer of 1894 and 1895 will never leave me . . . the recollections of the long race with death across the 450 miles of the ice-cap of North Greenland in 1895 . . . are still the most vivid." They returned to the United States in September 1895, and Henson vowed never to return.

But he did return—in the summers of 1896, 1897, 1898, 1900, and 1902. In July 1905 Peary and Henson went back north to Greenland again, this time with the intention of traveling over the polar ice cap to the North Pole. Starting in early 1906 they traveled by dog sled over the frozen sea, but it turned out to be an unusually warm winter and early spring, and they encountered too many stretches of open water to be able to continue. They got to within 160 miles of the Pole, the farthest north any one had reached to that time.

Peary and Henson set out again on July 6, 1908 on a ship named after the U.S. president, the *Roosevelt*, with an expedition that included 21 members. They sailed to Etah in Greenland and took on board 50 Inuit who were to help set up the supply bases on the route to the Pole. They then went to Cape Columbia at the northern end of Ellesmere Island. Peary and Henson set out from there on the morning of March 1, 1909. They were accompanied by or met up with various advance teams along the way. One of these support teams was headed by Professor Ross Marvin of Cornell University. It set up its last supply depot 230 miles from the Pole and then headed back for Cape Columbia. Marvin never made it. One of the Inuit in the party, Kudlukto, said that he had fallen into a stretch of open water and drowned. Years later Kudlukto confessed that he had shot Marvin and dumped his body in the water when he refused to let one of Kudlukto's young cousins ride on a dog sled.

On March 31 Peary and other members of the expedition were at 87°47', the farthest north any man had reached—about 150 miles from the Pole. At that point Peary told Captain Bob Bartlett, commander of the *Roosevelt,* to return to Cape Columbia. He would make the last dash to the Pole accompanied by Henson. Bartlett was bitterly disappointed, and the next morning walked alone to the north for a few miles as though he would try to make it on his own. He then turned around and headed south. It made sense for Peary to take Henson: he had much more Arctic experience and was an acknowledged master with the dog teams. But there have always been suggestions that Peary sent Bartlett back because he did not want to share the honor of reaching the Pole with anyone else. Given the racial prejudice at the time, Henson and the four Inuit—Ootah, Seegloo, Ooqueah, and Egingwah—did not "count."

A couple of days later, on April 3, Henson was crossing a lane of moving ice, and one of the blocks of ice that he was using for support slipped and he fell into the water. Fortunately one of the Inuit was next to him and was able to pull him out immediately or he would have frozen and drowned. The normal day's procedure was for Peary to leave the night's camp early in the morning and push ahead for two hours breaking the trail ahead. The others would pack up the camp and then catch up with Peary. Then Peary (who at the age of 52 was already suffering from the leukemia that would later kill him) would ride in one of the dogsleds while Henson went ahead and broke trail. They would not see each other until the end of the day.

On April 6, 1909 Henson arrived at a spot that he, just by calculating the distance traveled, thought must be the North Pole. When Peary arrived 45 minutes later, Henson greeted him by saying, "I think I'm the first man to sit on the top of the world." Peary was furious. Peary then attached an American flag to a staff, and the whole expedition went to sleep. At 12:50 p.m. there was a break in the clouds, and Peary was able to take a reading of their location. It showed that they were 3 miles short of the Pole. After another nap, Peary took another reading and then set out with Egingwah and Seegloo to where he thought the Pole must be—without telling Henson. They then spent 30 hours in the vicinity of the Pole, and Henson officially raised the flag over what Peary's calculations told him was the North Pole.

(Whether it really was the Pole or not has been a source of controversy ever since.)

Peary and Henson and the four Inuit arrived back at the spot where they had left Bartlett at midnight on April 9, an incredible speed—and reached Cape Columbia on April 23. They stayed there until July 17 when the ice had melted enough for the *Roosevelt* to steam into open water. They telegraphed news of their triumph from Labrador on September 6, 1909. But by that time, the world already thought that Frederick Cook had been the first one to reach the Pole. Peary spent the next few years defending his claims and was eventually vindicated.

By the time Henson got back to the United States he weighed 112 pounds (his normal weight was 155 pounds), and he was forced to spend several months recovering. For a while, he accompanied Peary on his lecture tours, where he would be exhibited in his Inuit clothes. In 1912 he wrote a book about his experiences (*A Negro at the North Pole*). However, the book died quickly, and Henson was forced to take a job as a porter working for $16 a week. Thanks to some politically influential friends he was later given a job as a messenger at the United States Customs house in New York at a salary of $20 a week, which was later raised to $40 a week. He retired in 1936, at which time there was an effort to have him awarded the Congressional Medal of Honor, but nothing came of it.

As racial attitudes in the United States changed, Henson began to receive more recognition. He was elected a full member of the Explorers Club in New York in 1937, the first Black member. In 1945 all of the survivors of the North Pole expedition received the Navy Medal, but Henson's was awarded in private. When he went to attend a banquet in his honor in Chicago in 1948, none of the downtown hotels would allow him to register because of his race. In 1950, however, he was introduced to President Truman and in 1954 was received by President Eisenhower in the White House. He died in New York in 1955 at the age of 88 and was buried in a private cemetery there. Years later, in 1988, when news of his achievements received more publicity, he was reburied at Arlington National Cemetery with full military honors in a plot next to Peary's.

Since Peary and Henson were both married at the time of their Arctic expeditions, it is not surprising that there was no public knowledge that both of them had liaisons with Inuit women. Dating from the 1905 expedition, they both fathered children—Peary had two sons and Henson had a boy named Anaukaq. This information came to light in 1986 when it was revealed that the small Greenland village of Moriussaq was largely made up of Henson's descendants, who had prospered as traders and hunters.

Further Reading

Henson's autobiography, *A Negro Explorer at the North Pole* was first published in 1912 (New York: 1912). It was reprinted in 1969 with a slightly different title: *A Black Explorer at the North Pole* (New York: Walker and Company). This edition was reprinted as a paperback by the University of Nebraska Press in Lincoln in 1989.
There are two biographies of Henson: Bradley Robinson, *Dark Companion* (New York: Robert M. McBride & Co., 1947) and

Floyd Miller, *Ahdoolo!: The Biography of Matthew A. Henson* (New York: E.P. Dutton & Co., 1963).
The story of Henson's descendants is told in "The Henson Family" by S. Allen Counter in the 100th anniversary edition of the *National Geographic* magazine (September 1988, pp. 422-429). □

Hans Werner Henze

Hans Werner Henze (born 1926) is a German composer of unusual productivity and diversity of style. He is best known for unorthodox operas such as *Boulevard Solitude* (1952), with its unique treatment of the "Manon" story used by Puccini, and the comic opera *Der junge Lord* (1965). His later works show his political affiliation with socialism, as in a requiem for Che Guevara, the Cuban revolutionary.

Born in Gütersloh, Germany, on July 1, 1926, Hans Werner Henze majored in piano and percussion at the Staatsmusikschule in Braunschweig. He was drafted into the Germany army in 1943 and served in the tank corps before being taken prisoner by the British.

Early Training and Work

After World War II, Henze became a student of composer Wolfgang Fortner at Heidelberg. The style of Henze's first mature compositions—a violin sonata, a chamber concerto, and the *First Symphony* (1947)—was neoclassic in the manner of Igor Stravinsky and Béla Bartók. After his introduction to the 12-tone technique, Henze's next scores showed his mastery of this technique: the piano variations and a violin concerto (1948); Symphonies no. 2 (1949) and no. 3 (1951); a piano concerto (1950); *The Idiot* (1952), a ballet; the First String Quartet (1952); and a Wind Quintet (1953). He also exploited jazz idioms in *Jack Pudding* (1951) and *Maratona di danza* (1956).

Henze was musical director of the German Theater in Konstanz (1948-1950) and composer and adviser on ballet for the Wiesbaden State Theater (1950-1952).

Later Work and Awards

Henze considers his opera *König Hirsch* (1952-1956) and the *Fourth Symphony* (1955-1963) as the end of his "exploratory" period. In his later compositions many styles and techniques are assimilated, including polytonality, neoclassicism, romanticism with elements of jazz, and an Italianate lyricism. Out of these, says Joseph Machlis (1961), Henze "forged an original language marked by brilliance of instrumentation, rhythmic urgency, and lyric intensity." His theatrical works, especially, aroused heated controversy because of the bold librettos and astringent musical idiom.

In 1959 Henze won the Berlin Kunstpreis and in 1962 the Grand Prize for Artists at Hanover. In 1961 he became professor of composition at the Mozarteum in Salzburg.

Henze's important compositions include *Undine* (1958), a ballet; *The Prince of Homburg* (1960), a semihistorical opera; *Elegy for Young Lovers* (1961), with a libretto by W.H. Auden and Chester Kallman; and *The Bassarids* (1966), an opera with a libretto by Auden and Kallman, which many consider Henze's most felicitous score. He also wrote the *Second Piano Concerto* (1968); an oratorio, *Das Floss der Medusa* (1969); *Concerto for Double Bass* (1969); and the opera *El Cimarron* (1970).

In 1963 Henze remarked: "The twelve-tone problem does not now play a great part in my music. . .I have always been concerned with musical substance, particularly with melody, and have tended to express the most difficult musical processes in the simplest forms I could devise. My music has as much to offer the naive listener as it has for the expert who can base his judgment on extensive technical knowledge."

Henze visited the United States in 1963 for the world premiere of his Fifth Symphony, performed by the New York Philharmonic for the inaugural of Lincoln Center for the Performing Arts in New York City.

Hans Werner Henze continues to capture the attention of music critics. The English National Opera celebrated his 70th birthday in 1996 by performing some of his works. His Symphony no. 7, which was called "bone-rattling and exciting," was reviewed in *Stereo Review* (April 1994), by David Patrick Stearns, who claims that Henze has "been through more stylistic changes than Madonna."

Further Reading

David Ewen, *The World of Twentieth-Century Music* (1968), treats Henze briefly but thoughtfully and analyzes six major works; Joseph Machlis, *Introduction to Contemporary Music* (1961), and Otto Deri, *Exploring Twentieth-Century Music* (1968), are good background studies.

Additional Sources

Stereo Review, April 1994. □

Audrey Hepburn

Audrey Hepburn (1929-1993) was an engaging screen actress who won an Academy Award in 1954 for her work in *Roman Holiday*. She also worked with the United Nations to alleviate the misery of the poor.

Peerless in her screen presence, actress Audrey Hepburn had huge brown eyes, a husky voice, and a dancer's gracefulness—qualities that seduced the entire moviegoing world. While Hepburn was never an actress with a wide range and had very little acting training, she was never boring. According to *People,* Humphrey Bogart once said of her style, "With Audrey it's kind of unpredictable. She's like a good tennis player—she varies her shots." Certainly every fan has chosen his or her favorite

Hepburn moment; for some its Hepburn's regal entrance in the denouement of *My Fair Lady,* with her towering hairdo and sweetly serious expression, while others may prefer her playful dance sequence in a book store in *Funny Face.* In any case, Hepburn's most successful movies capitalized on her childlike qualities, pairing her with an older actor whose character was eventually disarmed by her inestimable charm. Several years after she was chosen by Colette to star in the Broadway version of the French author's *Gigi,* Hepburn burst onto the Hollywood scene with 1953's *Roman Holiday.* Costarring Gregory Peck, the film tells the tale of a runaway princess who is shown around Rome by a reporter smitten with love for her. He nonetheless convinces her to resume her royal duties. The role landed Hepburn an Oscar at the tender young age of 24 for best actress. Full of adoration, Jay Cocks described the last scene of the film in *Time,* remarking that Peck's close up expressions of loss "would have been nonsense if Peck did not have something wonderful and irreplaceable to miss. He had Audrey Hepburn."

Her Humanitarian Work

In turn, Hepburn yielded to a calling other than acting, preferring to spend her time with her two sons and working for UNICEF. "If there was a cross between the salt of the earth and a regal queen," Shirley MacLaine told *People,* "then she was it." An articulate and impassioned spokeswoman, Hepburn was named the goodwill ambassador for the international children's relief organization UNICEF in 1988. Instead of using the title for travel privi-

leges and charity balls, Hepburn worked in the field, nursing sick children and reporting on the suffering she witnessed. Her last plea proved most moving; Hepburn had traveled to Somalia in the fall of 1992, and her sad but hopeful account galvanized the world's response to the dreadful famine and warfare that would eventually kill thousands in that West African country. For all her otherworldly good looks, Hepburn was a down-to-earth, sensible actress in a Hollywood of excess.

Her Background

Perhaps Hepburn's humility sprung from her childhood. Her father, an English-Irish banker, deserted her family when she was only 8 years old. Another traumatic mark was left by the Nazi occupation of Holland during World War II. Her mother, a Dutch baroness, had sent the youngster to the Germanic nation at the beginning of the war to live with relatives. *People* noted that "along with her grandparents, she received food from a relief agency—UNICEF's precursor. 'Your soul is nourished by all your experiences,' she once said.'It gives you baggage for the future—and ammunition, if you like.'" The once chubby Hepburn was whittled down by a diet that sometimes consisted only of flour made from tulip bulbs; nonetheless, as a fledgling ballet dancer, she sometimes carried messages for the Resistance in her toe shoes. Many years later she politely refused to make a movie of *The Diary of Anne Frank* as she felt the young Jewish girl's experience of World War II too closely mirrored her own. While memories of fear, deprivation, and cattlecars full of deportees populated her dreams for the rest of her life, Hepburn utilized her experiences in ministering to the world's starving children, many of whom did not know that the beautiful woman was a movie star.

Hepburn and her mother moved to England to pursue her dance career after the war. She was cast in bits parts on stage and screen in both Holland and England before she had the good fortune to be discovered by Colette in Monte Carlo, Monaco. Because Colette insisted Hepburn play Gigi, the young woman was thrust into an entertainment world that would compete fiercely for her. In 1952 she won a Theatre World Award for *Gigi,* followed a year later by the Academy Award she won for *Roman Holiday.* A hot commodity, director Billy Wilder snapped her up in 1954 for his new film. *Sabrina,* about a chauffeur's daughter whose education in Paris makes her the toast of Long Island society, costarred William Holden and Humphrey Bogart as her love interests. Eventually Hepburn shared the screen with all the best leading men of her time: Cary Grant, Fred Astaire, Rex Harrison, Mel Ferrer (whom she wed in 1954 and divorced in 1968), and Sean Connery. Of Hepburn's 27 films, quite a few have become classics and only a few films are generally acknowledged to be bad. Although Hepburn had knocked everyone out with her 1956 portrayal of Natasha in *War and Peace,* another big movie did not fare so well. *Green Mansions* was a fantasy in which Hepburn gamboled as a birdgirl. Directed by Ferrer, the adaptation from W. H. Hudson's novel of the same name was thought laughable by some. The same year, 1959, she made her first serious film, *The Nun's Story.* Seeking meatier roles, Hepburn disintegrating during a motorcycle trip across France. Hepburn and Albert Finney were applauded for their realistic portrayals. After l967's spooky *Wait Until Dark,* in which she plays a blind woman who ultimately bests a psychotic, Hepburn took on an extended sabbatical. Acting became secondary in her life, as she bore a child at age 40 during her 13-year marriage to Italian physician Andrea Dotti. Hepburn made only four more movies between 1976 and 1989. The last, *Always,* featured her in a cameo as an angel. Money was not a consideration; besides her own income, Hepburn lived in Switzerland with Robert Wolders, the wealthy widower of actress Merle Oberon, for the last 12 years of her life (she died in 1993). Though Hepburn was nominated for three Oscars after *Roman Holiday,* she never won again. Shortly before her death, she was given the Screen Actors Guild award for lifetime achievement. Unable to accept in person she sent actress Julia Roberts to accept the honor in her place. While Hepburn's acting was highly appreciated in her lifetime, she would doubtless prefer to be remembered as UNICEF's hardworking fairy godmother.

Further Reading

Chicago Tribune, January 21, 1993
Detroit Free Press, January 21, 1993
Entertainment Weekly, February 5, 1993
New York Times, January 25, 1993
People, February 1, 1993
Time, February 1, 1993
Times (London), January 22, 1993 □

Katharine Hepburn

Katharine Hepburn (born 1907) was a critically successful actress on the stage and on the screen for over 50 years, delighting audiences with her energy, her grace, and her determination.

K atharine Hepburn was born in Hartford, Connecticut. Her birthdate is variously given; the years most frequently cited are 1907 and 1909. In her autobiography (1991), Hepburn stated her birthdate as 1907. She was one of six children (three of each gender) born to a socially prominent, well-to-do, activist family. Her mother was a well-known and passionate suffragette; her physician father was an innovative pioneer in the field of sexual hygiene. Educated by private tutors and at exclusive schools, she entered Bryn Mawr College in 1924. Upon graduating four years later she immediately embarked on a successful career in the theater. Her critical success as an Amazon queen in the satire *The Warrior's Husband* led to a contract with the film studio RKO. In 1932 she made her film debut in that company's *A Bill of Divorcement,* playing opposite John Barrymore. She received rave reviews for her performance and achieved overnight stardom.

Her screen career lasted for over 50 years and was based on a persona whose essentials included energy, grace, determination, trim athletic good looks, and obvious

upper class breeding (as indicated, among other things, by a clipped manner of speaking). This persona, when intelligently utilized by producers and directors, led her to four Academy Awards as "Best Actress:" *Morning Glory,* 1933; *Guess Who's Coming to Dinner,* 1967; *The Lion in Winter,* 1968; and *On Golden Pond,* 1981. Hepburn also garnered an additional eight Oscar nominations over the years: *Alice Adams,* 1935; *The Philadelphia Story,* 1940; *Woman of the Year,* 1942; *The African Queen,* 1951; *Summertime,* 1955; *The Rainmaker,* 1956; *Suddenly Last Summer,* 1959; and *Long Day's Journey Into Night,* 1962. Her role in the 1975 made-for-television film *Love Among the Ruins* won her an Emmy award.

Hepburn's career, however, was not without its setbacks, most notably in the 1930s. A return to the Broadway stage in 1934 in a flop play—*The Lake*—led to the well-known quip by the acerbic wit Dorothy Parker that the actress "runs the gamut of emotion, all the way from A to B." In 1937 Hepburn, along with various other female stars, was described as "box office poison" in a trade paper advertisement placed by an important exhibitor. RKO's indifferent response led Hepburn—at a cost to her of over $200,000—to buy out her contract from the company. Shortly thereafter she was rejected for the role of Scarlett O'Hara in the film version of *Gone with the Wind.*

Determined to re-establish herself, she returned to the Broadway stage, playing the lead in a successful production of Philip Barry's comedy of manners, *The Philadelphia Story.* Having invested in the production she controlled the screen rights, which she ultimately sold to MGM in return

for a tidy profit and a guarantee by the studio that she would play the lead in the film version. She did, and the film was a critical and a commercial success. Her Oscar nomination was but one manifestation of the dramatic way she had re-established herself in Hollywood.

Hepburn's next MGM film brought into her life Spencer Tracy, with whom she began a liaison that lasted for over two decades until his death in 1967. Although separated from his wife, Tracy never divorced her, and his romance with Hepburn was a quiet, tender, and private affair. In the 1960s Hepburn interrupted her career to care for the ailing Tracy. They were a team professionally as well as personally and made nine films together over a period of 25 years: *Woman of the Year,* 1942; *Keeper of the Flame,* 1942; *Without Love,* 1945; *Sea of Grass,* 1947; *State of the Union,* 1948; *Adam's Rib,* 1949; *Pat and Mike,* 1952; *The Desk Set,* 1957; and *Guess Who's Coming to Dinner,* 1967. These films were not all either commercially or critically success-ful, but whether comedies or dramas they were provocative and interesting, especially for their emphasis on the per-sonal interplay between the sexes. Both Tracy and Hepburn played strong characters in these films, but neither was forced to give in to the other.

Hepburn had been married in 1928 to the social and well-to-do Ludlow Ogden Smith, who had changed his name to Ogden Ludlow because she did not want to be Kate Smith. The marriage actually lasted about three weeks be-fore they separated, but they were not divorced until 1934 and they remained friendly. Among her other romantic at-tachments in the 1930s was the eccentric tycoon Howard Hughes.

The actress was not particularly fortunate in her choice of vehicles in any medium after the beginning of the 1970s. But for a few notable exceptions, such as *On Golden Pond* (1981), the roles, whatever their promise, did not make really good use of her considerable talents. Her television debut in 1972 as the mother in a version of Tennessee Wil-liams' moving *The Glass Menagerie* was not auspicious. A pairing with the rugged action star John Wayne *Rooster Cogburn,* (1975), while apparently a great deal of fun for the stars on location proved to be lackluster. She had some success playing the noted French designer Coco Chanel in a Broadway musical which opened in 1969; *Coco* had a long run but did not make impressive use of her capabilities. Several later Broadway ventures proved abortive.

Katharine Hepburn never conformed to the conven-tional star image, but there is no doubt that she was a super star in more than one medium. A strong-minded indepen-dent woman, she governed her life and her career to suit herself. In the process she entertained and delighted and aroused millions and did so without compromising her cherished beliefs. Hepburn, without any doubt, was, as one of her biographers claimed, "a remarkable woman."

Although she suffered some significant injuries in a 1985 automobile accident, and illnesses usual to one of her years, Hepburn golfed, cycled, and swam in the sea into her nineties.

Katharine Hepburn provided some new perspectives on her personality and the roles she played on stage and screen in her autobiography, published after she retired from performance. In it she stressed the important influence of her liberal intellectual family, and her continued close-ness with her siblings and their offspring. Through this charming, witty and frank summing up of herself may be discerned the natural aristocracy of the person and the solidity and permanence of her character.

Further Reading

Biographies of Hepburn were by Charles Higham (1975), Mi-chael Freedland (1984), and Anne Edwards (1985). A moving and witty book is *Tracy and Hepburn: An Intimate Memoir* (1971) by Garson Kanin.
See also Katharine Hepburn's autobiography, *Me: Stories of My Life* New York: Alfred A. Knopf, 1991.
For a detailed listing to 1983 of Katharine Hepburn's stage ap-pearances, tours, awards and films, refer to *Contemporary Theater, Film and Television Biographies,* Volume I, pps. 240-241. Hepburn has also written *The Making of the African Queen* for those who are film fans and want to see behind the scenes. □

George Hepplewhite

George Hepplewhite (died 1786) was an English fur-niture designer whose name has become synony-mous with grace and elegance. His work was instrumental in disseminating the neoclassic style of Robert Adam.

Little is known of George Hepplewhite's life. He was an apprentice with the firm of Gillow in Lancaster and then moved to London, where by 1760 he was estab-lished in Redcross Street, St. Giles', Cripplegate. He died in 1786, and his widow, Alice, carried on the business as A. Hepplewhite and Company. It seems likely that the firm existed by supplying designs for cabinetmakers rather than by manufacturing furniture, for not a single piece of furni-ture is authenticated by a bill or other document as having come from his workshop.

Two years after Hepplewhite's death his widow pub-lished *The Cabinet-Maker and Upholsterer's Guide,* a folio volume of 300 designs that was the largest book of its sort to appear since Thomas Chippendale's *Director* (1754). The immediate success of Hepplewhite's work resulted in a sec-ond edition in 1789, and a third edition in 1794.

The Adam spirit in furniture may be said to have found its chief fulfillment in Hepplewhite designs. His oval-, wheel-, and shield-back chairs, bookcases with vase-shaped door glazing and urn-capped pediments, beds with delicately carved or painted posts and cornices, and bowfront commodes are among the most beautiful in the history of furniture. Hepplewhite was much influenced by Chippendale, especially in his designs for sideboard-tables with accompanying urns and pedestals and in the simpler types of domestic furniture such as chests of drawers, book-cases, and wardrobes. Hepplewhite never used human or animal figures in his designs, or sphinxes or military trophies, as did Adam and Thomas Sheraton; Hepplewhite's decorative motifs consisted chiefly of stylized foliage, urns, and vases and occasionally of ornaments in the Louis XVI manner, such as ribbon entwining a fluted chair leg. Several designs for chairs and stools with curved legs in the Louis XV manner reflect the revival of interest in the rococo from about 1770 to 1790.

Sheraton, whose *Drawing Book* (1791) seems to have been produced in emulation of Hepplewhite's work, refers in his preface to the "outmoded character" of some of his rival's designs, particularly for chairs. The third edition of Hepplewhite's book included some 20 designs for chairs in the new square-back manner introduced by Sheraton, but they lack the exquisite grace of Hepplewhite's earlier oval- and shield-back designs.

Further Reading

There is a selection in facsimile, *Hepplewhite Furniture Designs* (1947), from the third edition (1794) of *The Cabinet-Maker and Upholsterer's Guide,* with an introduction by Ralph Edwards. The only comprehensive account of Hepplewhite and a description of his designs, including a comparison with those of Sheraton, are in Clifford Musgrave, *Adam and Hepplewhite and Other Neo-Classical Furniture* (1966). See also Ralph Edwards and Margaret Jourdain, *Georgian Cabinet-Makers* (1944; new rev. ed. 1955); Peter Ward-Jackson, *English Furniture Designs of the Eighteenth Century* (1958); Ralph Fastnedge, *English Furniture Styles: 1500-1830* (1962); and Ralph Edwards and L. G. G. Ramsey, eds., *The Connoisseur Period Guides, Late Georgian 1760-1810* (1968).

Additional Sources

Hinckley, F. Lewis., *Hepplewhite, Sheraton & Regency furniture,* New York: Washington Mews Book, 1987. □

Barbara Hepworth

British-born (1903-1975) sculptor Barbara Hepworth has been called one of the outstanding women artists of the twentieth century. Throughout her working life and until her death, she never received the recognition of male contemporaries such as another—and more famous—British sculptor, Henry Moore. Comparing the two, art critic Leslie Judd Portner, in *Washington Post and Times Herald,* noted that "Where Moore concerns himself with natural forms, Hepworth's work is almost entirely abstract."

Born in Wakefield, Yorkshire, England, on Jan. 10, 1903, Jocelyn Barbara Hepworth was the eldest of four children. As a young girl, she often traveled about the Yorkshire countryside with her father for his work as county surveyor. She spoke of Yorkshire as a "curiously rhythmic patterning of cobbled streets. . .most ungracious

houses dominated by. . .slagheaps, noise, dirt, and smell." These early impressions of the contradiction between industrial town and quiet countryside later became an integral part of her work.

The Years Abroad

By the age of 16, Hepworth was modeling life portraits in clay, which helped to win her a scholarship to the Leeds School of Art, where she studied for a year. At Leeds, she met another young artist who would become a lifelong friend, the renowned sculptor, Henry Moore. Although Hepworth would never receive the recognition of her colleague, he was an important influence on her work.

Another scholarship gave Hepworth three years in London as a student at the Royal College of Art. In 1924, at the age of 21, her work earned her a year's study in Italy. From the art-filled city of Florence, Hepworth toured the countryside, and the sights and sounds of the Tuscany landscape became an integral part of her work, just as Yorkshire had years before.

Hepworth stayed in Italy for 18 months after her scholarship ended. She studied in Rome with master carver Ardini, who taught her that "marble changes color under different people's hands." She later said she understood him to mean that the artist must learn to understand, not dominate the material. Besides her studies, Hepworth found time for marriage to John Rattenbury Skeaping, also a sculptor from Britain. Their only child, Paul, was born in 1929. A year earlier, the work of both Hepworth and Skeaping was

exhibited at the Beaux Arts Gallery in London. Hepworth's doves in Parian marble from this exhibition are now in the Art Gallery of Manchester. She and Skeaping were divorced in 1933. That same year she married another British artist, Ben Nicholson. Under his influence, her sculpture became more severe and geometrical.

Hepworth and Nicholson traveled through France for most of the year, visiting the studios of such famous artists as Pablo Picasso and avant-garde sculptors Constantin Brancusi and Jean Arp. They joined the Abstraction-Création group in Paris. Hepworth's work from this period includes a kneeling figure in rosewood, now in the Wakefield Art Gallery.

Work in a New Direction

The birth of triplets, Simon, Rachel, and Sarah, in 1934 marked a profound change both in Hepworth's life and her life's work. Always short of money in recognition of her art, she said that after the birth of the triplets, she knew fear for the first time. She and Nicholson had about $100 in the bank at the time and were living in a basement flat. Her work changed, too. Relationships in space began to absorb her creativity, and her sculpture became more formal. For some time she had been drifting away from recognizable human forms, but now her pieces became far more abstract. An example is *Three Forms* (1935), consisting of a sphere and two nearly oval shapes. Critics have suggested this may symbolize the birth of her triplets.

By 1935, Hepworth and Nicholson had become involved with an international artistic group that included such names as Dutch abstract artist Mondrian and German-born Walter Gropius, an influential leader in the development of modern architecture. But World War II was now approaching and Hepworth, worried about the safety of her children, moved with them to Cornwall in southwestern England. The influence of what she called the "pagan landscape" and the sea is evident in her work from this period, such as *Tides* (1946), with a hollowed interior that contrasts in color with the polished grain on each side. By the mid-1940s, Hepworth's sculpture had become increasingly open and hollowed out so that the interior space became as important as what surrounded it.

Recognition and Honors

Hepworth and Nicholson were divorced in 1951. For the next two decades, her work received broader recognition and honors. It was part of an exhibition in Venice, the Twenty-fifth Biennale, which she attended, sitting every day in the Piazza San Marco and watching the way people reacted to her use of space. She produced *Contrapuntal Forms* in blue limestone (1950) for the Festival of Britain, which stresses the opposition of vertical forms to the horizontal. For a change of pace in 1954 she designed sets for Michael Tippett's opera, *Midsummer Marriage*. By this time, Hepworth had started to work with metals. One of her best-known works, which now guards the United Nations Plaza in New York City, is *Single Form* (1963), a towering shield-like mass of bronze. She received a number of commissions in the 1960s for truly huge sculptures, most of them

about 20 feet high. An example is *Four-Square Walk Through* (1966), a gigantic geometrical piece.

Barbara Hepworth's life and work were honored by her country in 1965 when she was made a Dame Commander of the Order of the British Empire. She died on May 20, 1975, in a tragic fire in her home at St. Ives, Cornwall. The house is now a museum and features many of her works.

An artist who never received the level of attention given to her male contemporaries, Hepworth strongly felt that women artists could contribute greatly to an understanding of the visual arts. "Perhaps especially," she said, "in sculpture, for there is a whole range of formal perception belonging to feminine experience."

Further Reading

For Barbara Hepworth's work, see her own publications: *Carvings and Drawings* (1952), *Drawings from a Sculptor's Landscape* (1966), and *A Pictorial Autobiography* (1970); A good introduction to her work is A. M. Hammacher, *Barbara Hepworth* (1968); J. P. Hodin, *Barbara Hepworth* (1961), contains a biography and an analysis of the development and style of the artist; See also: *Who's Who in Art* (1956); *Encyclopedia Americana* (Vols. 10,14, 1996 □

Heraclides of Pontus

The Greek philosopher Heraclides of Pontus (ca. 388 B.C.-310 B.C.) proposed the theory that the apparent daily revolution of the fixed stars is in fact due to the actual daily rotation of the earth about its own axis.

Born at Heracleia in Pontus, the son of the wealthy Euthyphron, Heraclides was a descendant of one of the founders of Heracleia. He was probably forced to leave in 364/363 B.C. because of the tyranny of Clearchus and went to Athens to study under Plato at the Academy. He was left in charge of the Academy when Plato went to Sicily in 360 B.C. He later studied under Aristotle, but, when a successor to Speusippus was elected in 339 B.C., his candidacy was defeated by Xenocrates and he returned to Pontus.

Heraclides was a most prolific writer, composing dialogues on ethics, natural science, literary criticism, music, rhetoric, and the history of philosophy. However, his works are now known only through some quotations by later writers. His most interesting theories are those in astronomy. Contradicting the Platonic and Aristotelian doctrine that the earth must stand still, he hypothesized that it rotates once daily on its own axis. On this assumption he was free to assert as a corollary that the universe is infinite, then to speculate on the existence of other earths in the stellar systems that appear to be fixed stars. This daring theory could not explain as much about motion as did Aristotle's and therefore was regarded merely as an oddity.

Heraclides also possibly indicated, in one fragment which can be otherwise interpreted, that he believed that Venus and Mercury revolve around the sun, a theory also contrary to Aristotelian physics. This deduction, if his, was probably due only to the identity of the sidereal periods of the sun and the two inferior planets, as these sidereal periods were the common criteria for determining the order of the planetary spheres. It is not an adumbration of the planetary system advocated by Tycho Brahe in the 16th century. Another theory doubtfully attributed to Heraclides is that the apparent anomalous motion of the sun can be explained as well by the earth's revolving about the sun as by the sun's about the earth. The mathematical identity of the geocentric and heliocentric systems, however, is irrelevant to the problem of anomalous motion, and the meaning of the fragment is thereby rendered very dubious indeed.

Further Reading

Heraclides' astronomy is discussed in Sir Thomas Heath, *Aristarchus of Samos: The Ancient Copernicus* (1913). Background studies that discuss Heraclides are George Sarton, *A History of Science: Ancient Science through the Golden Age of Greece* (1952); Marshall Clagett, *Greek Science in Antiquity* (1955); Benjamin Farrington, *Greek Science: Its Meaning for Us* (2 vols., 1949; repr. with revisions, 1 vol., 1961); and W. K. C. Guthrie, *A History of Greek Philosophy* (2 vols., 1962).

Additional Sources

Gottschalk, H. B., *Heraclides of Pontus,* Oxford: Clarendon Press; New York: Oxford University Press, 1980. □

Heraclitus

The Greek philosopher Heraclitus (active 500 B.C.) attempted to explain the nature of the universe by assuming the existence of the *logos,* that is, order or reason, as the unifying principle which guides all things and by specifying fire as the basic substance which underlies physical reality.

Heraclitus was born in the Ionian city of Ephesus and is said to have renounced the privileges to which his social rank entitled him (perhaps the kingship) in favor of his brother. The available evidence for his life is too scanty for a clear picture to emerge. He is a solitary figure who claims to have sought the truth within himself, and although his work shows familiarity with the writings of other philosophers, particularly those of Anaximander, both his unique ideas and his peculiar literary style set him apart.

Many fragments of Heraclitus's work, commonly known as *On the Nature of the Universe,* have survived, although their interpretation is made difficult by their lack of context and by the abbreviated, oracular style in which they were written. Because of the difficulty of his thought, Heraclitus was known throughout the ancient world as "the

Obscure" (*skoteinos*). The basis of his philosophy is the world of appearance, the sensible world. All things are constantly changing, and thus it is impossible to step into the same stream twice. Change is due to the mutual resolution of opposites such as hot and cold, day and night, hunger and satiety, although underlying all change and guiding it is a basic unity expressed by the idea of the *logos.* He also believes that that which seems to be at variance with itself through conflict or tension is in reality expressive of a kind of harmony. He asserts that the truth of the *logos* is partially expressed by the concept of Zeus.

Although the cosmos, in Heraclitus's view, has always existed and therefore did not come into being at some arbitrary point in time, fire, under the influence and guidance of the *logos,* is the basic substance in it, and all elements are some transformation of it. It is not completely independent but is infused with the *logos,* as is the human soul, and it is for this reason that the soul may come to grasp the truth of the cosmos, although human understanding may reach only childish limits.

Heraclitus enjoins men to learn the nature of the universe through an understanding of their own souls and has been considered as the first mental philosopher. Exact language and thought are of paramount importance to him, since he conceives of the *logos* as both the underlying order in the cosmos and the soul's discourse upon it. Since the truth is complex and difficult to grasp, he uses the oracular style of Delphi and merely hopes to "indicate" the truth.

He is important as one of the first Greek philosophers to take up the problem of knowledge, and he is undoubtedly the first to stress the importance of an understanding of the soul as a step toward understanding the external world order. His writing provided much of the theoretical basis for Stoicism.

Further Reading

Selected passages of Heraclitus's work with English translation and commentary are in G. S. Kirk and J. E. Raven, *The Presocratic Philosophers* (1965). Excellent discussions of Heraclitus's importance are in John Burnet, *Early Greek Philosophy* (1920), and Kathleen Freeman, *The Presocratic Philosophers* (1948). See also Philip E. Wheelwright, *Heraclitus* (1959). General discussions of Pre-Socratic philosophy in its intellectual tradition are in the standard histories of Greek literature, such as that by Albin Lesky, *A History of Greek Literature* (1966). □

Heraclius

Heraclius (ca. 575-641) was Byzantine emperor from 610 to 641. Ascending the throne when the empire seemed on the point of dissolution, he saved it from its immediate foes and gave it new institutional and cultural direction.

orn in Cappadocia, Heraclius was apparently of Armenian origins. His father, Heraclius, was a leading general under Emperor Maurice and became exarch (viceroy) of North Africa. When the regime of the usurper Phocas (602-610) degenerated into chaos, dissident elements in Constantinople urged the elder Heraclius to seize the throne; but the old exarch sent his son instead. The rebellion succeeded in overthrowing Phocas and enthroning Heraclius in October 610.

Because of Phocas's mismanagement, Heraclius faced a seemingly impossible situation. The Slavs and the Avars had overrun the Balkans and threatened anew the empire's remaining European territories. Meanwhile, the Sassanid king of Persia, Chosroes (or Khusru) II, began a war of conquest against the empire's eastern territories and soon detached Syria-Palestine (613-614) and Egypt (616). The Persians also menaced Asia Minor and the paths to the capital.

The empire's military and financial resources were inadequate to cope with these threats, and the ensuing years were spent in laborious preparations for defense. Precarious peace was purchased from the Avars, and in 622 Heraclius was ready to begin his counteroffensive. The Emperor assumed personal command of his troops and during the next 6 years campaigned vigorously. The Avars and the Slavs mounted a fierce siege on Constantinople in 626; but the city resisted successfully, and Heraclius remained free to fight. His efforts gradually cleared Asia Minor, won the support of allies in the Caucasus, and even carried the war into Persian territory in Mesopotamia (627). Peace was settled with the weakened Persian government in 629. Having secured the eastern frontier, Heraclius made a triumphant return to Constantinople. Probably in 630, he solemnly restored to Jerusalem the True Cross and other Christian relics the Persians had carried off.

Heraclius attempted to restore the battered empire internally. With the promulgation of the Ékthesis (683) Heraclius unsuccessfully sought to end the religious strife among Christian factions. More far-reaching were the institutional changes of the period. Heraclius has been associated with the initiation of the Byzantine system of "themes," the military provinces organized around local native forces. This system would become the basis of the empire's strength for the next 4 centuries. Heraclius also defined the "Byzantine" character more clearly in terms of Greek language and culture.

Before Heraclius could complete his work of reconstruction, the Arabs, under the new banner of Islam, began assaults on the restored provinces. Possibly because of poor health, the Emperor failed to respond effectively. Worn out and disillusioned as much of his life's work crumbled, Heraclius died on Feb. 11, 641. He had, however, founded the dynasty that would direct the Byzantine Empire boldly and successfully through its most perilous period of transformation and survival.

Further Reading

The most recent and detailed account of Heraclius is in the opening volumes of Andreas N. Stratos, *Byzantium in the Seventh Century,* vol. 1 (1968). General accounts are in J. B. Bury, *A History of the Later Roman Empire from Arcadius to Irene, 395 A.D. to 800 A.D.,* vol. 2 (1889); J. B. Bury, ed., *The Cambridge Medieval History,* vol. 2 (1913); George Ostrogorsky, *History of the Byzantine State* (1940; trans. 1957; rev. ed. 1969); and Romilly J. H. Jenkins, *Byzantium: The Imperial Centuries, A.D. 610-1071* (1966).

Additional Sources

Feistner, Edith, *Ottes "Eraclius" vor dem Hintergrund der französischen Quelle,* Göppingen: Kümmerle, 1987.

Gallo, Nicola Ugo, *Eraclio: il colosso di Barletta nella storia e nella leggenda,* Barletta: La gazzetta della provincia, 1976.

Kyriazåes, Kåostas D., *Håerakleios,* Athåenai: Vivliopåoleion tåes "Hestias", I.D. Kollarou, 1968.

Pratt, Karen, *Meister Otte's Eraclius as an adaptation of Eracle by Gautier d'Arras,* Göppingen: Kümmerle Verlag, 1987. □

Johann Friedrich Herbart

Johann Friedrich Herbart (1776-1841) was a German philosopher-psychologist and educator, noted for his contributions in laying the foundations of scientific study of education.

ohann Friedrich Herbart was born on May 4, 1776, in Oldenburg, the son of the state councilor for Oldenburg. He attended the University of Jena (1794-1799). While there he studied under Johann Gottlieb Fichte and met Friedrich von Schiller. Upon graduation Herbart went to Interlaken, Switzerland, where he served as tutor to the governor's three sons. In Switzerland he met Johann Pestalozzi and visited his school at Burgdorf.

Herbart taught philosophy and pedagogy at Göttingen (1802-1809). He began to seek a sound philosophical base upon which to rest his educational theories. His major works during this time include *ABC's of Observation* (1804), *The Moral or Ethical Revelation of the World: The Chief Aim of Education* (1804), *General Pedagogics* (his chief educational work, 1806), *Chief Points of Logic* (1806), *Chief Points of Metaphysics* (1806), and *General Practical Philosophy* (1808).

In 1809 Herbart accepted the chair of philosophy at Königsberg University. He met Wilhelm von Humboldt, the Prussian commissioner of education, and at his request served on the commission for higher education. Herbart, a believer in normal schools and teacher education, sponsored the establishment of a pedagogical school and practice (laboratory) school at Königsberg in 1810. He then married Mary Drake, an English girl.

Herbart wrote *System of Psychology* (1814), *Text-book of Psychology* (1816), *Psychology as a Science* (1825), and a two-volume work, *General Metaphysics* (1829). His work cast him as a liberal thinker in many minds, and this did not fit well into the reactionary tone then gaining headway in Prussia. It cost him an appointment to Hegel's vacated chair of philosophy at Berlin University in 1831. Dissatisfied with

the way things were progressing in Prussia, Herbart returned to Göttingen in 1833. He lectured at the university and published *Outline of Pedagogical Lectures* (1835). He died on Aug. 11, 1841.

Philosophy of Education

Herbart's influence on educational theory is very important, even at the present time. He not only developed a philosophical-psychological rationale for teaching but a teaching method as well. Herbart believed that the mind was the sum total of all ideas which entered into one's conscious life. He emphasized the importance of both the physical and the human environment in the development of the mind. To Herbart, ideas were central to the process. He felt they grouped themselves into what he called "apperceptive masses." By assimilation (or apperception) new ideas could enter the mind through association with similar ideas already present. This was the learning process.

Herbart's method of instruction has been identified by his students as involving the "Five Formal Steps of the Recitation." These are preparation, presentation, association, generalization, and application. Herbart went further to emphasize that through the proper correlation of subjects (curriculum materials) the student would come to understand the total unity of what is the world.

In Germany, Leipzig and Jena became centers for Herbartianism. It was through the influence of Americans who studied at Jena that the ideas of Herbart reached the United States (ca. 1890). The advocates formed the National Herbartian Society in 1892 (now the National Society for the Study of Education). Its purpose was to promote Herbart's ideas as they might relate to America's needs. The principal criticism which has been leveled at the Herbartians is the extreme formality into which they let Herbart's instructional method fall.

Further Reading

Charles De Garmo, *Herbart and the Herbartians* (1895), is an old but worthwhile study. The application of Herbartian psychology to the instructional process is covered in John Adams, *The Herbartian Psychology* (1899), and in Gabriel Compayre, *Herbart and Education by Instruction,* translated by M. E. Findlay (1906; trans. 1907). For modern accounts of Herbart's influence consult such sources as James Mulhern, *History of Education* (1946; 2d ed. 1959); John S. Brubacher, *A History of the Problems of Education* (1947; 2d ed. 1966); and Harold B. Dunkel, *Herbart and Herbartianism: An Educational Ghost Story* (1970).

Cole, Percival Richard, *Herbart and Froebel: an attempt at synthesis,* New York, AMS Press, 1972.

De Garmo, Charles, *Herbart and the Herbartians,* Folcroft, Pa.: Folcroft Library Editions, 1979.

Dunkel, Harold Baker, *Herbart & education,* New York, Random House 1969.

Dunkel, Harold Baker, *Herbart and Herbartianism; an educational ghost story,* Chicago, University of Chicago Press 1970.

MacVannel, John Angus, *The educational theories of Herbart and Froebe,* New York, AMS Press, 1972.

McMurry, Dorothy, *Herbartian contributions to history instruction in American elementary school,* New York, AMS Press, 1972.

Mossman, Lois (Coffey), *Changing conceptions relative to the planning of lesson,* New York, AMS Press, 1972. □

Will Herberg

Will Herberg (1906-1977), Jewish theologian, social thinker, and biblical exegete, represented an independent strand in American Jewish leadership. While working from the standpoint of a Conservative Jew, he interacted with other Americans of many faiths, reflecting on the cultural and social conditions which challenged all those who took religion seriously.

Herberg was born August 4, 1906 (some sources say 1909), to Russian immigrant parents in New York City where he grew up and was educated. His father died when he was ten years old, leaving him to be educated by a mother who believed strongly in self-taught learning. He excelled in high school, graduating at 16, and from there entered Columbia University where in 1928 he earned both an A.B. and an M.A. degree, receiving the Ph.D. in 1932.

From the age of 17 he had been a leading organizer of the Young Workers League, being attracted to Marxism by its utopian ideals. When, however, the controversial Jay

Lovestone was ousted from the Communist Party in 1929, Herberg followed him and then grew more and more distant from Marxism. His essays revealed his concerns with racism and his praise of the politics of the New Deal. By the early 1940s he had made a complete break with Marxism, declaring it a false faith, an idolatrous parody of Jewish and Christian values. His growing conservatism could be seen in his later ambivalence towards McCarthyism and his selection as contributing editor of the National Review, a post he held from 1961 onwards. He felt he had advanced from following the false God of Marxism to worship of the true God, a God that could not be confused with any secular or political reality.

He described this transformation well in an autobiographical essay first published in 1947 and reprinted in 1970, "From Marxism to Judaism: Jewish Belief as a Dynamic of Social Action." That rejection of Marxism became the touchstone of Herberg's later writing and thinking. An early essay, "The Christian Mythology of Socialism" (1943), claimed that socialism is a secular distortion of the Jewish and Christian messianic vision. In his study of *Judaism and Modern Man* (1951) he rejected the false idols of political or social utopias, recognizing that ideology can become a substitute for true religion. In a later article, "The Great Society and the American Constitutional Tradition" (1967), he warned that even the most humanistic projects can lead to a destructive idolatry. His contention that politics can be dissolved into ideology led to disagreement with other thinkers, as was evident in a 1952 public conference on "The Ethics of Controversy" held at New York's Tamiment Institute.

Jewish Theology and Sociology

After leaving Marxism Herberg devoted himself to education. From 1935 to 1948 he worked as a research analyst and education director of the International Ladies' Garment Workers Association. During 1948 to 1955 he developed a distinctive theological and social perspective expressed in his writings and lecturing. These works showed the influence of the Protestant theologian Reinhold Niebuhr, who convinced him not to convert to Christianity but rather to develop a modern Jewish theology. Herberg united this theology with sociological insight in his classic work *Protestant-Catholic-Jew* (1955). The book combined careful review of research on the ways Americans of the 1950s were religious with reflection on the perils of the diluted religiousness prevalent during the "religious revival" of the Eisenhower years.

In this book Herberg claimed that the traditional religious communities in America were tending to blur their distinctive views and affirm instead "the American Way of Life." He suggested that the sociological data pointed to a growing belief that the various traditions could be reduced to a common system of ideas which were identical with Americanism. His theological argument demonstrated the danger such dilution of biblical religion had for the prophetic task of opposing any actual human system with the divine ideal. He later claimed that the "American Way of Life" need not be a competitor to traditional religions but

could exist beside them ("Society, Democracy and the State: A Biblical Realist View," 1959, and "America's Civil Religion: What It Is and Whence It Comes," 1974). Herberg believed that American democracy when correctly understood could be held up as an example of biblical pessimism, a self-critical system that recognized its own limitations. The influence of Reinhold Niebuhr became refined in a conservatism that was still prophetic in its view of American religious life.

Education and Ecumenical Thinking

Herberg's leadership became evident through his influence on students and in ecumenical dialogue while he was on the faculty of Drew University (1955-1976). Through his teaching and lecturing Herberg communicated the biblical heritage that Jews and Christians shared as well as the conceptual differences that separated them. He saw both traditions as affirming "salvation history" in the sense of a lived re-experiencing again and again of the events of salvation. Thus his exposition of the redemptive holidays of Easter and Passover emphasized a common view of ritual combined with a divergence of symbols.

Herberg's freedom from institutional ties enabled him to build bridges with other religious groups. He taught Jewish students to appreciate Christian thinkers like Kierkegaard and Maritain. His helpful anthology *Four Existentialist Theologians* (1957) is an ecumenical collection including Catholic, Protestant, and Jewish thinkers. He affirmed the distinctiveness of the Jewish way of life to Christian audiences. He was frequently a participant in ecumenical events, even preaching in the context of Christian worship. This interaction made him a significant figure not only in Jewish life but among Christians as well. Bernhard W. Anderson, a well known Christian biblical scholar, commented on Herberg's influence on the Christian community: "As a philosopher and theologian he has helped Christians to reach a deeper understanding of their own faith." When he died on March 27, 1977, both Jews and Christians mourned his passing.

Further Reading

There is no full scale study of Will Herberg currently available. John P. Diggins in *Up From Communism: Conservative Odysseys in American Literary History* (1975) devotes two chapters to Herberg—one to his Marxist quest and one to his Jewish response. An interesting article is that by S. Daniel Breslauer, "Will Herberg: Intuitive Spokesman for American Judaism," in *Judaism* (1978). His autobiographical essay "From Marxism to Judaism: Jewish Belief as a Dynamic of Social Action," now found in *Arguments and Doctrines: A Reader of Jewish Thinking in the Aftermath of the Holocaust*, edited by Arthur A. Cohen (1970), can also be consulted with profit.

Additional Sources

Ausmus, Harry J., *Will Herberg, a bio-bibliography*, Westport, Conn.: Greenwood Press, 1986.
Ausmus, Harry J., *Will Herberg, from right to right*, Chapel Hill: University of North Carolina Press, 1987. □

Edward Herbert

The English philosopher, poet, diplomat, and historian Edward Herbert, 1st Baron Herbert of Cherbury (1583-1648), is considered the father of English deism. His major work, "On Truth," is one of the few metaphysical treatises in English philosophy.

Edward Herbert was born on March 3, 1583, the first son of Richard and Magdalen Herbert, at Eyton, Shropshire. Edward was precocious in his early studies, and the poet John Donne was employed as a tutor for the Herbert children. On the death of Richard Herbert in 1596 the family moved to Oxford, where the young philosopher studied at University College. When he was barely 15, Edward married. The poetry of his younger brother, George Herbert, has been widely recognized, but Edward's Latin and English verse has also earned him recognition as an important disciple of Donne.

For the next 20 years Herbert divided his time between attendance at the courts of Elizabeth and James I and travels on the Continent. He served as a soldier, wrote verses, and dabbled in philosophy. All of this is recounted with enormous self-esteem in *The Life of Edward Lord Herbert of Cherbury, Written by Himself.* Horace Walpole's publication of Herbert's autobiography in 1764 created a literary sensation.

In 1618 James I appointed the 35-year-old Herbert as English ambassador to France, and he served with distinction for 6 years until he was recalled by the King. As a reward he was given an Irish peerage as Baron of Castle Island in 1624, and 5 years later he received an English title as the 1st Baron of Cherbury. But, in effect, his public career was ended, and he suffered the vicissitudes of English aristocracy during a period of great political turmoil. He unsuccessfully applied to court and to Parliament for redress and compensation. He died on Aug. 20, 1648, in London.

Deism holds that all elements of religion should be amenable to reason and therefore criticizes private revelation, priesthood, and dogma. In *De veritate* (1624; *On Truth*) Herbert begins with the attempt to find a medium between faith and skepticism. Truth is that which is universal and eternal and known by the interaction of the faculties—instinct, will, sensation, and reason—with the apprehension of objects, appearances, concepts, and truths of intellect. This view is supported with the thesis that man is born with implicit "common notions" which provide the foundations for all truth, law, and religion. John Locke later attacked this naive form of innatism. In *De causis errorum* (1645; *The Causes of Error*) Herbert expanded his notion of the uniformity, harmony, and universality of truth by defining falsity as that which is neither true, probable, nor possible.

In *De religione laici* (1645; *The Religion of the Laity*) Herbert anticipated the theory of the natural history of religion adopted by David Hume a century later. Religious documents should be treated historically, and true religion is that which expresses the greatest conformity to the universal common notions. Herbert further developed the application of common notions to religion in *De religione gentilium* (1663; *Ancient Religion of the Gentiles*). The universal characteristics of true religion are identified as the notions that there is one God, that He is worthy of worship, and that He rewards and punishes man, judging him according to his practice of virtue and his sorrow for sin.

Further Reading

Useful studies of Herbert's life and work are in the introductions to the English translations of his works: *De veritate,* with an introduction by Meyrick H. Carre (1937), and *Lord Herbert of Cherbury's De religione laici,* introduced by the editor and translator, Harold R. Hutcheson (1944). *The Autobiography of Edward, Lord Herbert of Cherbury* contains a useful introduction to his life and work together with letters and a continuation of his life by Sidney Lee (1886; 2d rev. ed. 1906). For deism, in general, Clement C. J. Webb, *Studies in the History of Natural Theology* (1915), and Peter Gay, *Deism: An Anthology* (1968), are recommended. □

George Herbert

The English metaphysical poet and Anglican priest George Herbert (1593-1633) is best known for "The Temple," a monument of brilliant rhetoric which

expertly combines private experience with a demonstration of the way to salvation.

Descended from soldiers and administrators, George Herbert was born on April 3, 1593, in or near Montgomery Castle on the Welsh border. In 1596 his mother, Magdalen, daughter of a landowner, Sir Richard Newport, was left a widow with 10 children—like Job, as she remarked. She was much admired by John Donne, who later influenced Herbert's poetry. She brought up George in Oxford and then London, where he attended Westminster School. In 1609 she married Sir John Danvers.

In that year Herbert became a scholar of Trinity College, Cambridge, where he earned a bachelor of arts degree in 1613 and a master of arts degree in 1617. Appointed a fellow of Trinity, he taught Latin and Greek grammar until he was made university praelector in rhetoric in 1617. Instead of giving conventional lectures on the classics, he used an oration by James I as his text, thus flattering his way to prospects of a career at court. By lecturing on a modern author, he also identified himself with a progressive academic effort to break the educational stranglehold of Ciceronianism. In addition, he lauded the "New Science" of Francis Bacon. Such bold modernity was typical of this enlightened young aristocrat, who dressed expensively, disdaining the sober university regulations about clothing.

Though committed by his fellowship to enter the priesthood, Herbert wanted to emulate his brothers: the eldest,

Edward, Lord Herbert of Cherbury, was an ambassador who became a minor poet and the founder of English deism; another, Henry, was a courtier and parliamentarian who became the master of revels. In 1620 George was elected to "the finest place in the University," that of public orator. As such, he wrote official letters to dignitaries and delivered Latin orations to them when they visited Cambridge.

Doubly moved by conviction and an ambition to become a secretary of state, Herbert supported the peace policy of King James I and denounced the horrors of war in an oration before one of those visitors, Prince Charles, who was eager for war with Spain. The same motives induced Herbert to become a member of Parliament in 1624. But the King's death in the next year put the militarists in power and ended his secular prospects. About 1626 he entered deacon's orders. In 1627 his mother died, and the funeral sermon preached by Donne was published with Latin and Greek poems written by Herbert in her memory. Two years later he resigned his university post and married Anne Danvers. Ordained a priest on Sept. 19, 1630, he officiated for less than 2 1/2 years as rector of Bemerton in Wiltshire, occupying the parsonage with his wife, six servants, and three orphaned nieces. His charity extended to generous donations to repair churches.

At Bemerton, Herbert completed *A Priest to the Temple* (published in 1652), a prose work on how to be an ideal parson. He also revised and greatly added to some 72 religious poems which he had previously composed. These poems were published posthumously as *The Temple: Sacred Poems and Private Ejaculations* (1633). This work won high praise in the 17th century, but after the 13th edition (1709) it was not published again for 90 years. Since 1799, however, it has been printed with growing frequency. The Victorians found it uplifting and quaint but were biased by Izaak Walton's charming, inaccurate life of George Herbert (1670), which overconcentrates on his brief priesthood and transforms him into a saintly paragon.

The poems in *The Temple* are sequentially related. Though superficially simple, they are profoundly complex in art, meaning, and allusiveness, reflecting Herbert's expert knowledge and love of music. They conduct the reader from the Church Porch into the Church, tracing man's spiritual and physical growth as a resistant soul struggling against a God who seeks to establish His temple in the human heart. The volume concludes with a versified history of the Church Militant and an envoi.

Further Reading

The standard edition of Herbert's works is F. E. Hutchinson, ed., *The Works of George Herbert* (1941). The chief, though misleading, biographical source, Izaak Walton, *The Lives of John Donne, Sir Henry Wotton, Richard Hooker, George Herbert and Robert Sanderson* (1670; often reprinted), should be read as charming Anglican propaganda. Its fallacies are noted in David Novarr, *The Making of Walton's Lives* (1958). There is no definitive biography, but Marchette Chute, *Two Gentle Men: The Lives of George Herbert and Robert Herrick* (1959), is reliable and interesting. The best general study is Joseph H. Summers, *George Herbert: His Religion and His Art* (1954). See also Margaret Bottrall, *George Herbert* (1954). More specialized studies are Rosemond Tuve, *A Reading of George Herbert* (1952), and Mary E. Rickey, *Utmost Art: Complexity in the Verse of George Herbert* (1966).

Additional Sources

Asals, Heather A. R. (Heather Anne Ross), *Equivocal predication: George Herbert's way to God,* Toronto; Buffalo: University of Toronto Press, 1981.

Benet, Diana, *Secretary of praise: the poetic vocation of George Herbert,* Columbia: University of Missouri Press, 1984.

Beresford, John, *Gossip of the seventeenth and eighteenth centurie,* Freeport, N.Y., Books for Libraries Press, 1968.

Bloch, Chana, *Spelling the word: George Herbert and the Bible,* Berkeley: University of California Press, 1985.

Bottrall, Margaret (Smith), *George Herbert,* Folcroft, Pa.: Folcroft Library Editions, 1971; Norwood, Pa.: Norwood Editions, 1975; Philadelphia: R. West, 1977.

Caulkins, Richard Leonard, *George Herbert's art of love: his use of the tropes of eros in the poetry of agape,* New York: P. Lang, 1996.

Charles, Amy Marie, *A life of George Herbert,* Ithaca, N.Y.: Cornell University Press, 1977.

Clements, Arthur L., *Poetry of contemplation: John Donne, George Herbert, Henry Vaughan, and the modern period,* Albany, NY: State University of New York Press, 1990.

Di Cesare, Mario A., *A concordance to the complete writings of George Herbert,* Ithaca, N.Y.: Cornell University Press, 1977.

Dickson, Donald R., *The Fountain of living waters: the typology of the waters of life in Herbert, Vaughan, and Traherne,* Columbia: University of Missouri Press, 1987.

Eliot, T. S. (Thomas Stearns), *George Herbert,* Plymouth: Northcote House in association with The British Council, 1994, 1962.

Essential articles for the study of George Herbert's poetry, Hamden, Conn.: Archon Books, 1979.

Fish, Stanley Eugene, *The living temple: George Herbert and catechizing,* Berkeley: University of California Press, 1978.

Flesch, William, *Generosity and the limits of authority: Shakespeare, Herbert, Milton,* Ithaca: Cornell University Press, 1992.

Freer, Coburn, *Music for a king; George Herbert's style and the metrical psalm,* Baltimore: Johns Hopkins University Press, 1972.

George Herbert journal, Bridgeport, Conn., s. n. Semiannual.

Harman, Barbara Leah., *Costly monuments: representations of the self in George Herbert's poetry,* Cambridge, Mass.: Harvard University Press, 1982.

Higgins, Dick, *George Herbert's pattern poems: in their tradition,* West Glover, Vt.: Unpublished Editions, 1977.

Hodgkins, Christopher, *Authority, church, and society in George Herbert: return to the middle way,* Columbia: University of Missouri Press, 1993.

Kumar, Kailash, *George Herbert, heart in pilgrimage,* Liverpool: Lucas Publications, 1988.

Kyne, Mary Theresa, *Country parsons, country poets: George Herbert and Gerard Manley Hopkins as spiritual autobiographers,* Greensburg, PA: Eadmer Press, 1992.

Like season'd timber: new essays on George Herbert, New York: P. Lang, 1987.

Lull, Janis., *The poem in time: reading George Herbert's revisions of the church,* Newark: University of Delaware Press; London: Associated University Presses, 1990.

Mann, Cameron, bp., *A concordance to the English poems of George Herbert,* Folcroft, Pa.: Folcroft Press, 1970; St. Clair Shores, Mich., Scholarly Press, 1972; Folcroft, Pa.: Folcroft Library Editions, 1977; Norwood, Pa.: Norwood Editions, 1978.

Miller, Edmund, *Drudgerie divine: the rhetoric of God and man in George Herbert,* Salzburg: Institut für Anglistik und Amerikanistik, Universität Salzburg, 1979.

Miller, Edmund, *George Herbert's kinships: an ahnentafel with annotations,* Bowie, Md.: Heritage Books, 1993.

Nuttall, A. D. (Anthony David), *Overheard by God: fiction and prayer in Herbert, Milton, Dante, and St. John,* London; New York: Methuen, 1980.

Nuttall, A. D. (Anthony David), *Overheard by God: fiction and prayer in Herbert, Milton, Dante, and St. John,* London; New York: Methuen, 1983, 1980.

Page, Nick., *George Herbert: a portrait,* Tunbridge Wells England: Monarch, 1993.

Pahlka, William H., *Saint Augustine's meter and George Herbert's will,* Kent, Ohio: Kent State University Press, 1987.

Ray, Robert H., *A George Herbert companion,* New York: Garland Pub., 1995.

Roberts, John Richard., *George Herbert: an annotated bibliography of modern criticism, 1905-1984,* Columbia: University of Missouri Press, 1988.

Schoenfeldt, Michael Carl, *Prayer and power: George Herbert and Renaissance courtship,* Chicago: University of Chicago Press, 1991.

Seelig, Sharon Cadman., *The shadow of eternity: belief and structure in Herbert, Vaughan, and Traherne,* Lexington, Ky.: University Press of Kentucky, 1981.

Shaw, Robert Burns, *The call of God: the theme of vocation in the poetry of Donne and Herbert,* Cambridge, MA: Cowley Publications, 1981.

Sherwood, Terry G. (Terry Grey), *Herbert's prayerful art,* Toronto; Buffalo: University of Toronto Press, 1989.

Singleton, Marion White, *God's courtier: configuring a different grace in George Herbert's Temple,* Cambridge Cambridgeshire; New York: Cambridge University Press, 1987.

Stein, Arnold Sidney, *George Herbert's lyrics,* Baltimore: Johns Hopkins Press, 1968.

Stewart, Stanley, *George Herbert,* Boston: Twayne Publishers, 1986.

Strier, Richard, *Love known: theology and experience in George Herbert's poetry,* Chicago: University of Chicago Press, 1983.

Taylor, Mark, *The soul in paraphrase; George Herbert's poetic,* The Hague, Mouton, 1974.

Thorpe, Douglas, *A new earth: the labor of language in Pearl, Herbert's Temple, and Blake's Jerusalem,* Washington, D.C.: Catholic University of America Press, 1991.

Todd, Richard, *The opacity of signs: acts of interpretation in George Herbert's "The Temple",* Columbia: University of Missouri Press, 1986.

Toliver, Harold E., *George Herbert's Christian narrative,* University Park, Pa.: Pennsylvania State University, 1993.

"Too rich to clothe the Sunne": essays on George Herbert, Pittsburgh, Pa.: University of Pittsburgh Press, 1980.

Tuve, Rosemond, *A reading of George Herbert,* Chicago: University of Chicago Press, 1982.

Veith, Gene Edward, *Reformation spirituality: the religion of George Herbert,* Lewisburg: Bucknell University Press; London: Associated University Presses, 1985.

Vendler, Helen Hennessy., *The poetry of George Herbert,* Cambridge: Harvard University Press, 1975.

Wall, John N., *Transformations of the word: Spenser, Herbert, Vaughan,* Athens: University of Georgia Press, 1988.

Westerweel, Bart, *Patterns and patterning: a study of four poems by George Herbert,* Amsterdam: Rodopi, 1984.

White, James Boyd, *This book of starres: learning to read George Herbert,* Ann Arbor: University of Michigan Press, 1994. □

Johann Gottfried von Herder

The German philosopher, theologian, and critic Johann Gottfried von Herder (1744-1803) is best known for his contribution to the philosophy of history.

Johann Gottfried von Herder was born into a religious middle-class family in East Prussia on Aug. 25, 1744, and was raised in the town of Mohrongen, where his father was the schoolmaster. A surgeon in the occupying Russian army offered to be young Herder's patron and finance his university education in the capital city of Königsberg. In 1762 Herder enrolled as a medical student only to discover that he was unable to attend dissections or operations without fainting. He transferred to theology, and during this period he met Immanuel Kant and Johann George Hamann. Despite their later disagreements, Herder wrote a moving description of Kant, then a young teacher, and Kant, equally impressed, remitted his usual lecture fees. In Hamann, Herder discovered a kindred spirit who wished to preserve the integrity of faith by exposing the limitations of "enlightened" rationalism. Their lifelong friendship and correspondence reinforced the interests of both philosophers in literature, language, translation, and esthetics.

Between 1764 and 1769 Herder lived in Riga, where he worked as a teacher and minister and wrote a number of reviews and essays. His first important works—*Fragments concerning Recent German Literature* (1767) and *Critical Forests* (1769)—display an early tendency to treat problems of esthetics and language historically.

In the following years Herder traveled throughout Europe and held a minor pastorate. In Paris he met the *encyclopédistes* Denis Diderot and Jean d'Alembert, and in Strasbourg he began his lifelong association with the poet J. W. von Goethe. Through Goethe's intervention, Herder eventually secured a permanent appointment as superintendent of the Lutheran clergy at Weimar in 1776. Herder worked conscientiously at his considerable administrative and clerical career in order to provide for his family of four children. Nonetheless, his prolific writings run to 33 volumes and include *Letters for the Advancement of Humanity, Christian Writings,* two works criticizing Kant (*Metakritik* and *Kalligone*), as well as collections of folk literature, translations, and poetry. He died in Weimar on Dec. 18, 1803.

His Thought

The speculative dimension of history is concerned with the search for philosophic intelligibility or meaning in the study of human events. Ancient historians saw the repetitive pattern of history, and in this *cyclical* perspective the justification for studying the past was to anticipate the future. Christianity introduced a linear conception of time and the notion of *Providence* by dating history from a specific event and envisioning a definite end. Beginning with the late 17th century, philosophers secularized Providence: God's story

was replaced by a belief in human *progress* and man's future perfectibility. By and large, professional historians and philosophers have discarded such theories in favor of a position known as *historicism*. In this view there are no general patterns, and each historical epoch is unique in its individual character and culture.

Herder's work is the first to incorporate elements of historicism. In an early work, ironically entitled *Another Philosophy of History for the Education of Mankind* (1774), and his later four-volume *Idea for a Philosophy of History for Mankind* (1784-1791), he displays an ambivalence toward the goals of rationalism and the Enlightenment. In the *Idea* Herder's Protestant pessimism about the perfectibility of human nature is reinforced by physical-cultural relativism: on a star among stars, man, as a creature among creatures, plays out his unique destiny in proportion to the "force" or "power" resulting from the interaction between individual, institution, and environment. Like Kant, Herder was among the first to strike upon the ingenious solution, later favored by G. W. F. Hegel and Karl Marx, of locating progress in the species rather than in the individual. Thus humanity progresses, through God's mysterious ways, in spite of the individuals who compose it. History offers a synthesis of Providence, progress, and individuality since "whatever could be has been, according to the situation and wants of the place, the circumstances and occasions of the times, and the native or generated character of the people."

Further Reading

Robert T. Clark's biography *Herder: His Life and Thought* (1955) is excellent and contains the fullest analysis in English of Herder's work. G. A. Wells, *Herder and After* (1959), discusses Herder's conception of both man and history and its critical reception from the 19th century to current times. Other brief studies include Alexander Gillies, *Herder* (1945), and portions of Arthur O. Lovejoy, *Essays on the History of Ideas* (1948).

Additional Sources

Barnard, F. M. (Frederick M.), *Self-direction and political legitimacy: Rousseau and Herder,* Oxford, England: Clarendon Press; New York: Oxford University, 1988.

Berlin, Isaiah, Sir., *Vico and Herder: two studies in the history of ideas,* New York: Viking Press, 1976.

Berlin, Isaiah, Sir., *Vico and Herder: two studies in the history of ideas,* New York: Vintage Books, 1977, 1976.

Berlin, Isaiah, Sir., *Vico and Herder: two studies in the history of ideas,* London: Hogarth, 1976.

Bluestein, Gene, *Poplore: folk and pop in American culture,* Amherst: University of Massachusetts Press, 1994.

Ergang, Robert Reinhold, *Herder and the foundations of German nationalis,* New York, Octagon Books, 1966 c1931.

Fugate, Joe K., *The psychological basis of Herder's aesthetic,* The Hague, Mouton, 1966.

Johann Gottfried Herder: language, history, and the enlightenment, Columbia, SC: Camden House, 1990.

Johann Gottfried Herder, innovator through the ages, Bonn: Bouvier, 1982. □

José Hernández

The Argentine poet José Hernández (1834-1886) was an active social force during the period of consolidation of the Argentine nation. He is best known for his classic gaucho epic, "Martín Fierro."

José Hernández was born on Nov. 10, 1834, on a ranch not far from Buenos Aires. His family was engaged in cattle raising, and various difficulties prevented him from obtaining any sort of formal education. Political events of the mid-19th century in Argentina—most directly the civil wars then being fought—dictated his being sent to live with relatives in Brazil. He eventually returned to Argentina and came to know and sympathize with the life and tribulations of the gauchos of the plains, who were frequently little more than pawns in the raging struggles for political dominance in the young nation.

By 1863 Hernández had settled in Buenos Aires and, after experimenting with several professions, had secured a job as a journalist with the paper *El Argentino.* Six years later he founded the newspaper *Río de la Plata,* but it was soon shut down by order of his political adversary, the celebrated Argentine author Domingo Faustino Sarmiento, who was then serving as the nation's president.

During these difficult years Hernández not only had formed strong sympathies for the gauchos' cause but had also developed profound scorn for those Europeanized fellow countrymen who viewed the gaucho as a subject unworthy of serious literary treatment and believed he could serve only as the model for quaint and picturesque caricatures.

"Martín Fierro"

Encouraged by a friend to write a "fundamental" gaucho poem, Hernández began composing in his Buenos Aires hotel room the verses of the first part of the long epic poem he would entitle *Martín Fierro* . In the 2,325 lines of the poem, which first saw print in 1872, he succeeded in capturing the authentic speech of the gaucho and in fashioning with his dominant sestinas and quatrains an eloquent attack on the social and political attitudes he opposed.

At the outset of the epic, the gaucho Martín Fierro announces that he will sing the song of his sorrows and with that song and the accompaniment of his guitar will seek consolation. There is an acute tone of social protest in Fierro's account of how the good old days had changed and how the government had come to abuse and cheat the gauchos it recruited for the Indian wars. Fierro becomes an outlaw, unites with a fellow gaucho, Cruz, and eventually goes off to live with the Indians, thus rejecting the society of civilized man.

The success of the first part of *Martín Fierro* was resounding. It was read in the cities and recited and enjoyed by the gauchos themselves on their ranches and around the country store-taverns, where they gathered for diversion. The second part, *La vuelta de Martin Fierro* (1879), is twice the length of the original poem and recounts Fierro's return to civilization, his search for his lost wife and sons, and further injustices perpetrated by the government. In the end, Fierro rides off aimlessly, with no future, but once more embracing society.

Under a new administration Hernández became a senator, serving in the Congress in Buenos Aires. He held this office until his death, which occurred on Oct. 21, 1886, as the result of a heart attack.

Further Reading

Two studies of Hernández in English are of special note: Henry Alfred Holmes, *Martin Fierro: An Epic of the Argentine* (1923), and Walter Owen's introduction to his translation of Hernández's *The Gaucho Martin Fierro* (1936). See also Enrique Anderson-Imbert, *Spanish-American Literature: A History* (1954; trans. 1963; 2d ed., 2 vols., 1969).

Additional Sources

Albarracín-Sarmiento, Carlos, *Estructura del Martín Fierro,* Amsterdam: Benjamins, 1981.

Amaral, Anselmo F., *As origens do gaúcho na temática de Martin Fierro: ensaio crítico,* Porto Alegre: Martins Livreiro Editor, 1988.

Azeves, Angel Héctor, *José Hernández, el civilizador,* La Plata, Argentina: Departamento de Historia, Facultad de Humanidades y Ciencias de la Educación, Universidad Nacional de La Plata, 1986.

Barski, León., *Vigencia del "Martín Fierro",* Buenos Aires: Editorial Boedo, 1977 or 1978.

Borges, Jorge Luis, *El "Martín Fierro,"* Madrid: Alianza; Buenos Aires: Emecé, 1983.

Cárdenas de Monner Sans, María Inés, *Martín Fierro y la conciencia nacional,* Buenos Aires: Editorial La Pléyade, 1977.

Chávez, Fermín, *La vuelta de José Hernández del federalismo a la república libera,* Buenos Aires, Ediciones Theoria, 1973.

Chiappini, Julio O., *Borges y José Hernández,* Rosario, Prov. Santa Fe, República Argentina: Zeus Editora, 1994.

Corro, Gaspar Pío del, *Facundo y Fierro; la proscripción de los héroes,* Buenos Aires: Ediciones Castaäneda, 1977.

Corte, José C., *De Hernández y de Lugones: breviario conmemorativo,* Santa Fe, Argentina: Librería y Editorial Castellví, 1975.

Dellepiane, Angela B., *Concordancias del poema Martín Fierro,* Buenos Aires: Academia Argentina de Letras, 1995.

Di Candia, Alcides J., *Ayudando a leer el Martín Fierro,* Montevideo: Comisión Nacional de Homenaje del Sesquicentenario de los Hechos Históricos de 1825, 1975.

Díaz Araujo, Enrique, *La política de Fierro; José Hernández ida y vuelt,* Buenos Aires, Ediciones La Bastilla, 1972.

Fernández Latour de Botas, Olga, *Prehistoria de Martín Fierro,* Buenos Aires: Librería Editorial Platero, 1977.

Galarza, Pedro Ignacio, *Presencia de la mujer en el Martín Fierr,* Catamarca Argentina, Dirección General de Cultura, 1970.

Gálvez, Manuel, *José Hernánde,* Buenos Aires, Editorial Huemul, 1964.

Gandía, Enrique de, *José Hernández: sus ideas políticas,* Buenos Aires: Ediciones Depalma, 1985.

Giménez Vega, Elías S., *Hernandismo y martinfierrismo (geopolítica del Martín Fierro),* Buenos Aires: Plus Ultra, 1975.

González Lanuza, Eduardo, *Temas del "Martín Fierro,"* Buenos Aires: Academia Argentina de Letras, 1981.

Haboba Tobal, Víctor J., *Martín Fierro (José Hernández): crítica literaria,* Montevideo: Librería Editorial Ciencias, 1978 or 1979.

Halperín Donghi, Tulio, *José Hernández y la formulación de una ideología rural en la Argentina,* Montevideo: Departamento de Historia Americana, Facultad de Humanidades y Ciencias, 1985?

Halperín Donghi, Tulio, *José Hernández y sus mundos,* Buenos Aires: Editorial Sudamericana: Instituto Torcuato di Tella, 1985.

Isaacson, José, *Encuentro político con José Hernández: notas y digresiones,* Buenos Aires: Ediciones Marymar, 1986.

José Hernández (estudios reunidos en conmemoración del centenario de El gaucho Martín Fierro) 1872-197, La Plata, Universidad Nacional de La Plata, Facultad de Humanidades y Ciencias de la Educación, 1973.

Leumann, Borges, *Martínez Estrada: Martín Fierro y su crítica, antología,* Buenos Aires: Centro Editor de América Latina, 1980.

Lugones, Leopoldo, *El payado,* Buenos Aires, Otero Impresores, 1916.

Lugones, Leopoldo, *El payador y antología de poesía y prosa,* Caracas, Venezuela: Biblioteca Ayacucho, 1979.

Martín Fierro: cien aänos de crítica, Buenos Aires: Editorial Plus Ultra, 1986.

Martín Fierro en su centenari, Washington, D.C.: Embajada de la República Argentina en los Estados Unidos de América, 1973.

Martínez Estrada, Ezequiel, *Muerte y transfiguración de Martín Fierro: ensayo de interpretación de la vida argentina,* Buenos Aires: Centro Editor de América Latina, 1983.

Neyra, Juan Carlos., *Introducción criolla al Martín Fierro,* Buenos Aires: Librería Huemul, 1979.

Paso, Leonardo, *La idea del cambio social,* Buenos Aires: Centro Editor de América Latina, 1993.

Paz, Carlos, b. 1886., *Hernández y Fierro contra la oligarquía,* Buenos Aires?: Ediciones del Mirador, 1974?

Rela, Walter, *De Martín Fierro a D. José Hernández,* Montevideo: Editorial Ciencias, 1979.

Sansone de Martínez, Eneida, *La poesía gauchesca en Martín Fierro,* Montevideo, Uruaguay: Ediciones de la Casa del Estudiante, 1981.

Scroggins, Daniel C., *A concordance of Josée Hernández' Martín Fierro,* Columbia University of Missouri Press, 1971.

Catalogue of Martín Fierro materials in the University of Texas Library, Austin: Institute of Latin American Studies, University of Texas at Austin, 1972, c1973.

Verdugo, Iber, *Teoría aplicada del estudio literario: análisis del Martín Fierro,* México: Universidad Nacional Autónoma de México, 1980. □

Rafael Hernández Colón

Rafael Hernández Colón (born 1936), Puerto Rican political leader and twice-elected governor, was one of the foremost defenders of commonwealth status for his country.

R afael Hernández Colón was born on October 24, 1936, in Ponce, Puerto Rico, the son of Rafael Hernández Matos, a lawyer who served as an associate justice of the Supreme Court of Puerto Rico, and Dorinda Colón Clavell. After receiving his elementary education at private schools in Ponce he attended high school at Valley Forge Military Academy in Wayne, Pennsylvania, graduating in 1953. He then entered Johns Hopkins University, from which he graduated with honors in 1956 with a B.A. degree in political science.

Upon returning to Puerto Rico he studied law at the University of Puerto Rico; where he received his law degree in 1959, graduating *magna cum laude* and as valedictorian of his class. That same year he married Lila Mayoral, the daughter of a prominent Ponce industrialist. The couple had four children.

From 1959 to 1965 he practiced law, appearing before the Puerto Rican and U.S. federal courts, including the U.S. Supreme Court. Between 1961 and 1965 he was lecturer on civil procedure at the Catholic University in Ponce. During this time he wrote various articles on legal matters, including several explaining and defending the commonwealth status of Puerto Rico, of which he was to become an authoritative proponent. He wrote a textbook on civil law which was published in 1968.

He showed an early interest in public affairs and in a career in politics. During the early 1960s he became one of the most prominent of the younger leaders of the Popular Democratic Party, and his talents were soon recognized by the party's founder and leader, Luis Muñoz Marín, and his associates. He was appointed to be a member of the Public Service Commission and served from 1960 to 1962. Muñoz's successor as governor, Roberto Sánchez Vilella, who was elected in 1964, named Hernández to his cabinet as attorney general (secretary of justice). Sánchez later broke with Muñoz Marín and the Popular Party; Hernández stayed in the party and resigned as attorney general in 1967.

He ran for the Senate as an at-large candidate in 1968, and although the opposition New Progressive Party won the governorship that year, the Popular Democrats won control of the Senate, and Hernández was elected its president. From this position he became principal spokesman and the highest ranking elected official of his party. In 1969 he became president of the Popular Democratic Party, and in 1972 he was its undisputed candidate for governor. In the elections of that year he won the governor's office from incumbent Luis Ferré. His administration coincided with the "petroleum crisis" of 1974 and a period of economic recession which adversely affected the Puerto Rican economy. Hernández ran for re-election in 1976 but was defeated by Carlos Romero Barceló of the New Progressive Party.

After temporarily relinquishing the formal presidency of the party he continued to work diligently in its re-organization and re-established himself as chairman and gubernatorial candidate. He was again defeated in 1980 by the incumbent Romero, but by a razor-thin plurality. In 1984 he succeeded, by a small but comfortable margin, in defeating his by now arch-rival Romero and on January 2, 1985, was sworn in as governor for the second time.

Throughout his political career Hernández was diligent in the defense of the commonwealth status and in attempts to modify and expand it in the direction of more autonomy for Puerto Rico. His role as the political inheritor of the legacy of Muñoz Marín seemed secure in the mid-1980s.

Governor Hernández Colón Popular Democratic Party ran the island colony from 1985 to 1993, having been re-elected in 1989. His inaugural address that year put forth a plan to petition Congress and President Bush for a island-wide plebiscite to determine the future political status of Puerto Rico. Of the three options: continued commonwealth status, statehood or full independence; President Bush favored statehood, but supported the plebiscite proposal. Congress struck seventeen of Hernández Colón's twenty proposals from the petition, and found his plan for greater island autonomy within the existing commonwealth framework totally unacceptable on constitutional grounds, arguing that Congress must maintain ultimate authority over all U.S. territories. Nevertheless, Congress gave approval of the plebiscite, which was promised for 1998.

The rejection by Congress of Hernández Colón's plan for greater Puerto Rican autonomy within the colonial framework led to the defeat of the P.D.P. in 1993. Governor Pedro Rosello stated that he favors statehood and the continuation of tax credits and loans to bolster the chaotic island economy. The president of the statehood party, Baltosar Corrado del Rio, criticized the past governorship of Hernández Colón and employed scare tactics in an attempt to sway Congress and the island's electorate toward statehood.

Further Reading

There are some good volumes on Puerto Rican politics and Hernández Colón's contributions toward the resolution of the island's multiple problems. Examples are: Kal Wagenheim, *Puerto Rico: a Profile* (1970); Jorge Heine and J. M. Garcia-Passalacqua, *The Puerto Rican Question* (1983); Jorge Heine, editor, *Time for Decision* (1983); Raymond J. Carr, *Puerto Rico: a Colonial Experiment*, New York and London: New York University Press, (1984); Richard J. Bloomfield, editor, *Puerto Rico and the Search for National Policy*, Boulder, Colorado, and London: Westview Press, Inc., (1985); and Ronald Fernandez' *The Disenchanted Island: Puerto Rico and the United States in the Twentieth Century, 2nd edition,* Westport, Connecticut: Praeger Publishers, (1996.) All are clear, thorough and precise discussions of the island's political and economic problems and Hernández Colón's attempts to resolve these problems in a manner which is beneficial and amicable to both sides. □

Herodotus

Herodotus (ca. 484 B.C.-ca. 425 B.C.) was the first Greek writer who succeeded in writing a large-scale historical narrative that has survived the passage of time.

In the lifetime of Herodotus the writing of history, and indeed of prose of any sort, was still something of a novelty. The earliest writings in prose had been the work of a group of Greek intellectuals from the Ionian cities of Asia Minor who, from about 550 B.C. onward, wrote works on science and philosophy or on historical subjects. However, at this early date there were as yet few clear-cut distinctions between the various disciplines, and historical writing included much that today would be regarded rather as the concern of the geographer, the anthropologist, or the economist. Herodotus was heir to this tradition, and he was greatly influenced by his few predecessors, and especially by the ablest of them, Hecataeus of Miletus.

Herodotus's Life

Little is known of Herodotus's life beyond what can be deduced from his writings. He was born in 484 B.C., or perhaps a few years earlier, in Halicarnassus, a small Greek city on the coast of Asia Minor. His family was wealthy and perhaps aristocratic, but while he was still quite young they were driven from the city by a tyrant named Lygdamis. Herodotus lived for several years on the island of Samos and at a later date, is said to have returned to Halicarnassus to take part in the overthrow of the tyrant, but he did not remain there.

Herodotus spent several years of his early manhood in unusually extensive traveling. One early trip was to the Black Sea, where he appears to have sailed along both the south and west coasts. Later he went by sea to the coast of Syria, then overland to the ancient city of Babylon, and on his way back he may have traveled through Palestine to Egypt. He certainly visited Egypt at least once, probably

It is possible that he originally conceived his subject as being limited to the Persian attack on Greece made in 480, an event of his own boyhood, but in the end it expanded to embrace the whole history of the relations between the Greek world and Persia and the other kingdoms of Asia. The narrative of the *Histories* starts with the accession of Croesus, the last king of Lydia, and gives an account of his reign, including his conquest of the Asiatic Greeks and his overthrow by the Persian King Cyrus. These events take up the first half of Book I. (The division of the work into nine books is not Herodotus's own but was carried out later by Alexandrian scholars.) In the rest of Book I and the three following books the basic theme is the expansion of the Persian kingdom from the accession of Cyrus to about 500 B.C., but there are also several long digressions on the habits of the Persians and their subjects—the whole of Book II is one enormous digression on the customs and early history of Egypt. There are also several sections devoted to the history of some of the Greek states, and in particular, in a series of digressions, Herodotus gives us what is virtually a continuous history of Athens from 560 B.C. onward.

Books V and VI cover primarily the Ionian Revolt (499-494 B.C.) and the subsequent Persian expedition that was defeated by the Athenians at Marathon (490 B.C.), but again there are many digressions on contemporary events in the Greek states. In the last three books the story is rounded off by a detailed account, comparatively free from digressions, of the expedition of Xerxes (480-479 B.C.) and of its wholly unexpected defeat by the Greeks.

Herodotus's Sources

In compiling the materials for his *Histories* Herodotus depended mainly on his own observations, the accounts of eyewitnesses on both sides, and, for earlier events, oral tradition. There was very little in the way of official records available to him, and few written accounts. The results of modern archeological investigations show that he was a remarkably accurate reporter of what he saw himself. But when he depended on others for information, he was not always critical enough in deciding what was reliable and what was not and in making due allowances for the bias of his informants.

Herodotus was particularly uncritical in dealing with military operations, since he had no personal experience of warfare and therefore could not always assess accurately the military plausibility of the stories he heard. At the same time it is clear that he did not always believe what he was told and sometimes related stories of doubtful reliability because it was all he had, or because they were such good stories that he could not resist them. It is also sometimes said that he did not take enough care over matters of chronology, but it was very difficult indeed for anyone to work out and present a detailed and accurate chronological scheme in an age when every little Greek city-state had its own way of counting years and, often, its own calendar of months and days.

Herodotus's chief weakness, however, lies in his often naive analysis of causes, which frequently ascribes events to the personal ambitions or weaknesses of leading men when,

after 455 B.C. It is possible that he went on his travels primarily as a trader, for in his writings he shows great interest in the products and methods of transport of the countries he describes, and few Greeks of his generation could have afforded to make such lengthy journeys purely for pleasure. He made excellent use of his opportunities, inquiring everywhere about the customs and traditions of the lands through which he passed and amassing a great store of information of all kinds.

About 450 B.C. Herodotus went to live for a time in Athens. During his stay there he is said to have become a close friend of the poet Sophocles. Another tradition, that he also became intimate with the great Athenian statesman Pericles, is much less reliable. After a time, however, Herodotus migrated to the Athenian colony of Thurii in southern Italy, which remained his home for the rest of his life. The date of his death is uncertain; the latest events he mentions in his writings took place in 430 B.C., and it is usually supposed that he died not long afterward.

Herodotus's Work

The writing of Herodotus's great work, the *Histories* (the name is simply a transliteration of a Greek word that means primarily "inquiries" or "research"), must have occupied a considerable portion of his later life, but we do not know when, where, or in what order it was written. In its final form it could not have been completed until the last years of his life, but parts were undoubtedly written much earlier, as we are told that he gave public readings from it while he was living in Athens.

as his own narrative makes clear, there were wider political or economic factors at work.

Herodotus wrote, in the Ionic dialect, a fascinating narrative in an attractively simple and easy-flowing style, and he had a remarkable gift for telling a story clearly and dramatically, often with a dry ironic sense of humor; the best of his stories have delighted, and will continue to delight, generations of readers.

An Evaluation

But Herodotus was much more than a mere storyteller. He was the first writer successfully to put together a long and involved historical narrative in which the main thread is never completely lost, however far and often he may wander from it. Moreover, he did this with a remarkable degree of detachment, showing hardly any of the Greeks' usual bias against the hereditary enemy, Persia, or of their contempt for barbarian peoples. And if he does not often achieve the depth of understanding of his great successor, Thucydides, his range of interests is much wider, embracing not only politics and warfare but also economics, geography, and the many strange and wonderful ways of mankind. He was the first great European historian, and the skill and honesty with which he built up his complex and generally reliable account and the great literary merit of his writing fully justify the title that has been bestowed on him: "Father of History."

Further Reading

The best short account of Herodotus's life is the one in the "Introduction" to vol. 1 of W. W. How and J. Wells, *A Commentary on Herodotus* (2 vols., 1912; rev. ed. 1928). Recommended longer accounts are Terrot R. Glover, *Herodotus* (1924), and the first half of John Linton Myres, *Herodotus: Father of History* (1953). More specialized is Henry R. Immerwahr, *Form and Thought in Herodotus* (1967). There is an excellent analysis of some of Herodotus's material in James A. K. Thomson, *The Art of the Logos* (1935).

There are a number of works that deal with the developing art of historiography. Good but rather technical accounts of Herodotus's predecessors are in Lionel Pearson, *Early Ionian Historians* (1939). Chester G. Starr, *The Awakening of the Greek Historical Spirit* (1968), gives an interesting account of the early development of Greek historiography. There are useful comments in Arnold W. Gomme, *The Greek Attitude to Poetry and History* (1954). Herodotus is discussed in studies of classical historiography such as Stephen Usher, *The Historians of Greece and Rome* (1969), and Michael Grant, *The Ancient Historians* (1970). For background Aubrey de Selincourt, *The World of Herodotus* (1962), is lively but lacks depth. Good modern accounts of the period of history that Herodotus covered are in A. T. Olmstead, *History of the Persian Empire: Achaemenid Period* (1948), and A. R. Burn, *Persia and the Greeks: The Defence of the West* (1962).

Additional Sources

Arieti, James A., *Discourses on the first book of Herodotus,* Lanham, Md.: Littlefield Adams Books, 1995.

Armayor, O. Kimball, *Herodotus' autopsy of the Fayoum: Lake Moeris and the Labyrinth of Egypt,* Amsterdam: J.C. Gieben, 1985.

Benardete, Seth, *Herodotean inquirie,* The Hague, Martinus Nijhoff, 1969, 1970.

Drews, Robert, *The Greek accounts of Eastern history,* Washington, Center for Hellenic Studies; distributed by Harvard University Press, Cambridge, Mass., 1973.

Evans, J. A. S. (James Allan Stewart), *Herodotus,* Boston: Twayne, 1982.

Evans, J. A. S. (James Allan Stewart), *Herodotus, explorer of the past: three essays,* Princeton, N.J.: Princeton University Press, 1991.

Fehling, Detlev., *Herodotus and his "sources": citation, invention, and narrative art,* Leeds, Great Britain: Francis Cairns, 1990.

Flory, Stewart, *The archaic smile of Herodotus,* Detroit: Wayne State University Press, 1987.

Fornara, Charles W., *Herodotus: an interpretative essay,* Oxford, Clarendon Press, 1971.

Gaines, Ann, *Herodotus and the explorers of the Classical age,* New York: Chelsea House Publishers, 1994.

Glover, T. R. (Terrot Reaveley), *Herodotus,* Freeport, N.Y., Books for Libraries Press, 1969; New York, AMS Press 1969.

Gould, John, *Herodotus,* New York: St. Martin's Press, 1989.

Hart, John, *Herodotus and Greek history,* New York: St. Martin's Press, 1982.

Hartog, François., *The mirror of Herodotus: the representation of the other in the writing of history,* Berkeley: University of California Press, 1988.

Heidel, William Arthur, *Hecataeus and the Egyptian priests in Herodotus, Book II,* New York: Garland Pub., 1987.

Hohti, Paavo, *The interrelation of speech and action in the histories of Herodotus,* Helsinki: Societas Scientiarum Fennica, 1976.

A commentary on Herodotus with introduction and appendixes, Oxford Oxfordshire; New York: Oxford University Press, 1991.

Hunter, Virginia J., *Past and process in Herodotus and Thucydides,* Princeton, N.J.: Princeton University Press, 1982.

Huxley, George Leonard, *Herodotos and the epic: a lecture,* Athens: G. Huxley, 1989.

Immerwahr, Henry R., *Form and thought in Herodotus,* Cleveland, Published for the American Philological Association Chapel Hill, N.C. by the Press of Western Reserve University, 1966.

Lang, Mabel L., *Herodotean narrative and discourse,* Cambridge, Mass.: Published for Oberlin College by Harvard University Press, 1984.

Lateiner, Donald, *The historical method of Herodotus,* Toronto; Buffalo: University of Toronto Press, 1991.

Linforth, Ivan M. (Ivan Mortimer), *Studies in Herodotus and Plato,* New York: Garland Pub., 1987.

Lister, R. P. (Richard Percival), *The travels of Herodotus,* London: Gordon & Cremonesi, 1979.

Lloyd, Alan B., *Herodotus, book II,* Leiden: E. J. Brill, 1975-1988.

Long, Timothy, *Repetition and variation in the short stories of Herodotus,* Frankfurt am Main: Athenèaum, 1987.

Mandell, Sara, *The relationship between Herodotus' history and primary history,* Atlanta, Ga.: Scholars Press, 1993.

Myres, John Linton, Sir, *Herodotus, father of history,* Chicago, H. Regnery Co. 1971.

Plutarch, *The malice of Herodotus = De malignitate Herodoti,* Warminster, England: Aris & Phillips, 1992.

Powell, J. Enoch (John Enoch), *A lexicon to Herodotus,* Hildesheim, Georg Olms, 1966.

Pritchett, W. Kendrick (William Kendrick), 1909-, *The liar school of Herodotos,* Amsterdam: J.C. Gieben, 1993.

Shimron, Binyamin, *Politics and belief in Herodotus,* Stuttgart: F. Steiner Verlag Wiesbaden, 1989.

Solmsen, Friedrich, *Two crucial decisions in Herodotus,* Amsterdam: North-Holland Pub. Co., 1974.

Stork, Peter, *Index of verb-forms in Herodotus on the basis of Powell's Lexicon,* Groningen: E. Forsten, 1987.

Thompson, Norma, *Herodotus and the origins of the political community: Arion's leap,* New Haven: Yale University Press, 1996.

Vandiver, Elizabeth, *Heroes in Herodotus: the interaction of myth and history,* Frankfurt am Main; New York: P. Lang, 1991.

Waters, Kenneth H., *Herodotos on tyrants and despots; a study in objectivity,* Wiesbaden, F. Steiner, 1971.

Waters, Kenneth H., *Herodotos, the historian: his problems, methods, and originality,* Norman: University of Oklahoma Press, 1985.

Wells, J. (Joseph), *Studies in Herodotus,* Freeport, N.Y., Books for Libraries Press, 1970.

Wilson, John Albert, *Herodotus in Egypt,* Leiden, Nederlands: Instituut voor het Nabije Oosten, 1970.

Wood, Henry, *The histories of Herodotus. An analysis of the formal structure,* The Hague, Mouton, 1972. □

Herod the Great

Herod the Great (ca. 73 B.C.-4 B.C.), King of Judea, was an example of a class of client princes who kept their thrones by balancing between being overthrown by their own peoples for too much subservience to Rome and being dismissed by the Romans for too much independence.

Judea was one among the many petty states into which the Hellenistic East had fragmented, ruled by high priests of the Hasmonean dynasty, descendants of the leaders who had freed the country from Seleucid rule. These Hasmoneans, however, were eager to raise revolts and engage in civil wars against each other, and Palestine was a cockpit of contending factions and forces. Against this background Herod's family rose to prominence; a Hasmonean, King Alexander Jannaeus, had appointed Herod's grandfather, who was probably an Idumean, to some sort of governorship in Idumea. Herod's father, Antipater, took a prominent part in a civil war between two further Hasmoneans, Hyrcanus II and Aristobulus II and his descendants, and became one of Hyrcanus's chief ministers; he also established close relations with the Romans.

Herod's mother's family were perhaps Nabatean Arabs—Herod himself never lived down the charge that he was only a half Jew—and he seems to have spent part of his childhood among the Nabateans.

Political Career

In 47 B.C., when Caesar momentarily settled Palestinian affairs, he seems to have entrusted Antipater with the effective civil government. Antipater named his eldest son, Phasael, governor of Jerusalem and his second son, Herod, governor of Galilee. Herod won favor with the Romans by his success in dealing with local guerrilla bands, but he executed a guerrilla leader out of hand, and opponents of the upstart Idumean family got the matter brought before the

Sanhedrin. Herod was accused of murder. He did not quite dare ignore the summons of the Sanhedrin, but he did appear in Jerusalem with a large armed bodyguard, and the matter was dropped. He seems, however, to have lost his position in Galilee.

In 46 B.C. Herod was appointed governor of Coele-Syria and Samaria by Caesar's representative, but with the death of Caesar and the arrival of Cassius in Syria, Herod was quick to line up with the republicans. He won Cassius's favor by raising the 700 talents' tribute which Cassius exacted. He also married Mariamne, a Hasmonean princess and granddaughter of the high priest Hyrcanus II.

A Parthian invasion in 40 B.C. brought another change: Antigonus, a rival Hasmonean, became king of Judea, and Herod had to flee. He left his family in the fortress of Masada and went via Egypt to Rome. There both Antony and Octavian, the future Augustus, accepted him as a useful counter against the Parthians, and the Senate named him king of Judea.

Herod as King

The Jews of course did not recognize Rome's right to choose their king for them, and Herod, with Roman help, had to conquer his kingdom. Not until July 37 B.C. did he get Jerusalem. Antigonus and his chief followers were put to death, but on the whole Jerusalem was spared. Herod turned to the problem of the high priesthood; he himself had not the blood to claim the office, and he needed a priest who could not rival him in dignity. But the Hasmoneans, even those connected with Herod by marriage, would not forego their claims. By the end of this struggle, which raged for most of the reign, the priesthood had become only a temporary office held at the King's pleasure.

Herod's other chief difficulty during the first part of his reign stemmed from Cleopatra's desire to restore the lost empire of the Ptolemies. She did gain some territories, including the Jericho district, from Herod, but the coolness between them ultimately helped Herod as it kept him from being too close to Antony's party. When Antony fell, Herod found it relatively easy to shift his loyalty to Octavian. He, on his part, saw no reason to prefer some different puppet to Herod, who was eager to please, not fanatically Jewish, and already in possession. Octavian not merely confirmed Herod but restored Jericho and gave him other, particularly non-Jewish, territories.

The reason first Antony and then Augustus supported Herod for so long was that he pursued a policy they thoroughly favored, that of bringing Judea out of its isolation and religious exclusiveness and of putting it into the mainstream of Greco-Roman civilization. Herod consciously undertook to Hellenize every aspect of life in his kingdom. Officials were given the titles and functions of royal ministers elsewhere, and non-Jews were given many of the highest posts; the army was reconstructed and made into a mainly mercenary and non-Jewish force; theaters and circuses were built; and several of Herod's sons were sent to Rome for their training.

Herod also brought his kingdom considerable prosperity. He stabilized the coinage and maintained taxation at a bearable level. He encouraged trade and built the splendid port city of Caesarea. Indeed, he was a tremendous builder generally, and this too provided jobs. Much of his building naturally had a military purpose—fortresses like Masada were built or enlarged, military colonies were planted on the frontiers, and even many of Herod's numerous palaces were partly fortresses. His building in the cities had the further purpose of increasing Hellenization, for many of his cities, like Caesarea and Samaria (rebuilt and renamed Sebaste), were intentionally Hellenistic rather than Jewish, even to having a predominantly non-Jewish population.

During nearly his whole reign Herod faced trouble within his own family, stemming partly from the Hasmoneans' regal scorn for the Idumaean upstart, partly from Herod's Hellenizing policies, and partly from his paranoid tendency, when his suspicions were aroused, to turn and rend those he loved best. As early as 29 B.C. he had killed his wife, Mariamne, from jealousy. As the years went by, the whole matter was further complicated by the question of the succession, for like many people with a strong will to power, Herod showed little ability at facing the idea of losing it, even to death.

In the years of intricate scheming and counterscheming between Herod and his heirs, three of Herod's sons were put to death, and his brother "escaped death only by dying." And when Herod finally did die in 4 B.C., he left a disputed succession with two further sons both having some claim to the throne. Augustus finally resolved the matter by splitting the inheritance between these two sons and still a third one, and not allowing the title of king to any of them.

Herod's Accomplishment

In an age when even the existence of the smaller states depended not on their own strength but on the will of Rome, Herod kept Judea safe, secure, and prosperous. And yet, throughout his career Herod suffered from being caught somewhere between Jew and Gentile. He loved Greek culture and showered money on the cities of the Greek East, but he began the rebuilding of the Temple and acted as protector and spokesman for various Jewish communities scattered about the world. He sought the favor of Rome and was ostentatious in his loyalty to it, yet he wished to strengthen the position of the Jewish state. In the final analysis, he failed to judge the temper of his people, and, though the great crisis did not come until the reign of Nero, his attempt to make the Jewish kingdom another civil state of the customary Mediterranean type was already a failure at his death.

Further Reading

The chief source of information on Herod is the two works by the ancient Jewish historian Josephus, *The Jewish War* and *The Antiquities of the Jews*. Among the modern works see W. O. E. Oesterley, *A History of Israel*, vol. 2 (1932); Stewart Perowne, *The Life and Times of Herod the Great* (1959); and Samuel Sandmel, *Herod: Profile of a Tyrant* (1967), which is interesting but perhaps too psychological in its interpretation. □

Heron of Alexandria

The engineer, mathematician, and inventor Heron of Alexandria (active ca. 60) ranks among the most important scientists of the ancient Roman world in the tradition of Aristotelian experimentation.

Heron, about whose personal life virtually nothing is known, resided in Alexandria, Egypt, among the scientists and men of letters of the late Ptolemaic and Roman eras who dwelled around the famed library and museum. A brilliant theoretical scientist and a prolific writer, Heron wrote with clarity and insight. The knowledge of his writings and scientific investigations was preserved in the writings of the late Roman, Byzantine, and Arabic scientists and encyclopedists.

One of Heron's outstanding treatises was the *Metrica*, a geometrical study, in three volumes, on the measurement of simple plane and solid figures from polygons to hendecagons. It approximates the areas of triangles, polygons, quadrilaterals, ellipses, spheres, circles, and cones, and the volumes of various solids, including the cone, cylinder, and pyramid. In developing the mathematical studies, Heron solved complex quadratic equations arithmetically, approximated the square roots of nonsquare numbers, and calculated cube roots. Heron's other mathematical works include the *Definitions, Geometrica, Geodaesia* (Land Measurements), *Stereometrica* (Solid Measurement), *Mensurae* (Measures), and *Liber geëponicus* (Book on Agriculture).

In the *Mechanica,* preserved only in Arabic, Heron explored the parallelograms of velocities, determined certain simple centers of gravity, analyzed the intricate mechanical powers by which small forces are used to move large weights, discussed the problems of the two mean proportions, and estimated the forces of motion on an inclined plane. The *Pneumatica,* possibly derived from the works of Philo of Byzantium and Ctesibus, describes mechanical devices operated by compressed air, water, or steam. Included are the steam engine, siphon, fire engine, water organ, slot machines, and water fountains. Other works by Heron dealing with the problems of mechanics and engineering are the *Barulcus* (On Raising Heavy Weights), *Belopoeica* (Making Darts), *On Automaton-making, Catoptrica* (On Mirrors), and *On the Dioptia.* In the last treatise Heron describes a machine called the "Cheirobalistra," which depended on a refined screw-cutting technique and could be used to bore a tunnel through a mountain. He also described an instrument called the hodometer for measuring distances traveled by wheeled vehicles.

Beyond gadgetry, the practical application of Heron's ideas in antiquity was minimal, although they did influence Arabic and Renaissance construction of fountains, clocks, and automated objects. In Heron's time the widespread use of slave labor throughout the Roman world negated most interests in labor-saving devices.

Further Reading

Some fragments of Heron's writings appear in English in Morris R. Cohen and Israel E. Drabkin, *A Source Book in Greek Science* (1958). Heron's scientific ideas are best presented in A. G. Drachman, *The Mechanical Technology of Greek and Roman Antiquity* (1963), and Robert S. Brumbaugh, *Ancient Greek Gadgets and Mechanics* (1966). General books which discuss Heron and ancient science are Marshall Clagett, *Greek Science in Antiquity* (1955), and L. Sprague de Camp, *The Ancient Engineers* (1963). □

Juan de Herrera

The Spanish architect Juan de Herrera (ca. 1530-1597) helped to plan the Escorial and introduced there a style that influenced Spanish architecture for over a century.

Juan de Herrera was born in Mobellán, Santander Province. He completed his studies at the University of Valladolid in the spring of 1548. The following October he joined Prince Philip (later Philip II) for a 3-year tour of Italy, Germany, and the Netherlands. He returned to Italy in 1553 in the service of Emperor Charles V and subsequently fought in the campaign of Flanders.

Herrera called his service to the monarch his "highest ideal." Not surprisingly, then, he followed Charles V into retirement in a monastery in Yuste, Estremadura region, and remained until the Emperor's death in 1558. Thereafter Herrera entered the service of Philip II. Herrera declared that, from 1565 onward, he made it a point "to follow His Majesty constantly wherever he might go." He also considered it to be his obligation to dress elegantly and to spend "excessively" in the best places as a living proof of "so great a prince."

One evidence of Herrera's ambition to be the very model of a multitalented Renaissance man is his geometrical illustrations for an abridgment (1562) of Alphonse the Wise's book on astronomy. Herrera also applied his knowledge of mathematics to the invention of navigational instruments that have been said to have increased the accuracy of nautical calculations.

In 1563 Philip II appointed Herrera to assist Juan Bautista de Toledo, the court architect, in the plans and construction of the Escorial (1561-1584), which the monarch described as "a palace for God and a little house for me." Some authorities insist that Herrera's real contribution to the Escorial design and construction did not begin until 1572, 5 years after Toledo's death. Letters between Philip II and Pedro de Hoyo in 1564, however, indicate that Herrera was playing an important role even then.

The Escorial is a complex of monastery, church, royal mausoleum, and palace. The site chosen was near the Guadarrama Mountains in the little town of El Escorial. All controversy over the extent of Herrera's contribution aside, the completed monument was the introduction of a style known traditionally as Herreran. The style is austere, symmetrical, and majestic, influenced by an Italianate, classicistic mannerism. Yet it is unique: its majesty is unforced; its formality is polyphonically muted; and its severity is a sovereign simplicity. Like the Gregorian chant, it is a paradox, simultaneously solemn and profoundly intimate.

Later works by Herrera, such as the Alcázar of Toledo (1571-1585) and the Palace of Aranjuez (ca. 1564-1586; finished in the 18th century), justify his fame. Among his disciples were Jorge Manuel Theotocopuli, the son of El Greco; and Francisco de Mora and his nephew Juan Gómez de Mora. Owing to what has been called the metaphysics of Herrera's principles, his style has been largely inimitable.

Herrera fell seriously ill in 1584 and was obliged to rely heavily upon the assistance of his pupils, particularly Francisco de Mora. He died on Jan. 15, 1597, in Madrid. He had married twice and was survived by his only child, Lorenzo.

Further Reading

The most informative source on Herrera in English is Fernando Chueca y Goitia's article in the *Encyclopedia of World Art,* vol. 7 (1963). George Kubler and Martin Soria, *Art and Architecture in Spain and Portugal and Their American Dominions: 1500-1800* (1959), provides sufficient information on the number of architects involved with the Escorial to give the reader an excellent idea of the controversy, which may continue until further documentation is discovered.

Wilkinson-Zerner, Catherine., *Juan de Herrera: architect to Philip II of Spain,* New Haven: Yale University Press, 1993. □

Felipe Herrera Lane

Felipe Herrera Lane (born 1922), a Chilean banker and economist, became one of the major architects of economic development because of his key position as president of the Inter-American Development Bank.

Felipe Herrera was born in Valparaiso, Chile, on June 17, 1922. Although he was originally intended for a military career, he did not complete his studies at the Escuela Militar but transferred to the law school of the University of Chile in Santiago. He received his degree in 1946 and became an attorney for the Central Bank of Chile, continuing a relationship begun in 1943, when he had been employed by the bank's legal department. He married Rosa Alamos in June 1947. In 1961 he was remarried, to Ines Olmo.

Successful Economist

Although Herrera for a time maintained a private law practice, his major energies soon became focused on banking and economic affairs. He had become interested in the study of economics while at the university, and through his studies there, and at the London School of Economics, prepared himself for a second, and concurrent, career as a professor of economics. Between 1947 and 1958 he regularly taught fiscal and monetary policy. He also had a brief career in politics, as undersecretary of economics and commerce (1952) and minister of finance (1953) in the administration of Carlos Ibañez.

In 1953 Herrera returned to the Central Bank as its general manager. He continued to occupy that position for the next 5 years, though he became increasingly involved in international economic affairs. At first he was his nation's representative to the World Bank (International Bank for Reconstruction and Development) and to the International Monetary Fund (IMF). In 1958 he became the executive director of the IMF for Argentina, Bolivia, Chile, Ecuador, Paraguay, and Uruguay.

Inter-American Development Bank

With the creation, in 1960, of the Western Hemisphere's own bank, the Inter-American Development Bank, Herrera reached a climactic point in his career. He was elected its president and then reelected, for 5-year terms, in 1964 and 1969. Accepted, to a considerable degree, by both the "monetarists" and "structuralists," he attempted to create a "bank of ideas," as well as a lending agency. As the head of an institution which was second only to the World Bank itself as an international lender, he influenced a whole generation of Latin American economists and played a key part in determining the course of Latin American economic development.

In October 1970 Herrera suddenly resigned to resume his teaching post at the university so that he could be in a position, if that proved to be desirable, to participate in the "general aspirations" of his country under the government of Salvador Allende Gossens. He died in 1996 of natural causes.

Further Reading

Herrera's views on some of the economic problems of Latin America can be found in his *The Inter-American Bank: Instrument for Latin American Development* (1962); His career as Chilean finance minister is briefly recounted in Albert O. Hirschman, *Journey toward Progress: Studies of Economic Policy-Making in Latin America* (1963); For a brief description of his work for the bank and background on the Alliance for Progress see Jerome Levinson and Juan de Onis, *The Alliance That Lost Its Way: A Critical Report on the Alliance for Progress* (1970).
Green, Robert. "Chilean Economist Felipe Herrera Dies at 74." *Reuters Ltd.,* 18 September 1996. □

Robert Herrick

The English poet and Anglican parson Robert Herrick (1591-1674) invented a fanciful world compounded of pagan Rome and Christian England, of reality and fantasy, which he ruled as his poetic domain.

Robert Herrick's 83 years stretched from Elizabethan times, when Shakespeare was writing history plays and Edmund Spenser was publishing *The Faerie Queene,* to the Restoration period, when John Dryden was composing heroic drama and John Milton was publishing *Paradise Lost.* He was contemporary with the metaphysical poets John Donne and George Herbert and is classified with the neoclassic or Cavalier poets Edmund Waller, Thomas Carew, Sir John Suckling, and Richard Lovelace.

Little is known about Herrick other than what may be gathered from a few extant letters and the 1,403 poems in his only book, *Hesperides; or, The Works both Humane and Divine of Robert Herrick, Esq.* (1648). Unknown are what school he attended, what he was doing in 1620-1622, 1624-1626, and 1648-1660, and even the days of his birth and death. Although he probably preached at least 1,500 times, no sermon has survived.

In 1556 Nicholas Herrick, son of an ironmonger in Leicester, went to London. After 10 years as a goldsmith's apprentice, he set up a prosperous business in that craft. In 1582 he married Julian Stone, daughter of a prominent London mercer. Their fifth son, Robert, was born in their Cheapside mansion on Goldsmith's Row, and he was baptized on Aug. 24, 1591. From his father's craft Robert derived the delight in metals, jewels, and amber which shines in his poetry; and his maternal grandfather's trade inspired the fascination which silks, sheer linens, and other fine textiles had for him.

Early Years

His eldest brother died when Robert was 14 months old, and a few days later his father fell from the fourth floor of their home to his death. Legally a suicide's property could be confiscated, but since the cause of death was uncertain, his widow managed to retain the estate, worth £5,000 at a time when a laborer's hire was a few pennies a day.

Robert had an excellent schooling in Latin, but when he was 16 his practical, bourgeois relatives apprenticed him to his uncle, Sir William Herrick, a leading goldsmith. But Robert proved more proficient with words than metal. About 1610, when his brother took up farming, Robert memorialized the occasion in "A Country Life," a poem imitative of Horace and Ben Jonson but distinctively his own. He had already begun to invent his poetic world and populated it with friends and relatives, imaginary mistresses and faithful servants, rascals and fairies, and peasants who made sacrifices to Jove and danced around Maypoles.

With Herrick's twenty-first birthday, in 1612, he inherited £800 from his father's estate, left its management to his uncle, and arranged to leave his apprenticeship in 1613. Shortsightedness may have handicapped Herrick for goldsmithing; he later mentioned his waning eyesight, and throughout his poetry he tends to concentrate on things seen close up—flowers, miniatures, a pipkin of jelly, and those "little spinners," the spiders.

At 22 Herrick was about 6 years older than most undergraduates when he entered St. John's College, Cambridge, as a fellow commoner, paying double fees. Ever eager to enjoy what was available, he participated in student pleasures, made lifelong friends of John Weekes and Clipseby Crew, and laid a foundation in experience for his poems about sack. In them he hailed that potent sherry as "the drink of Gods and Angels," urging the wine to come to him "as Cleopatra came to Anthonie."

Despite the gusto with which Herrick celebrated inebriation and imaginary mistresses in poetry, he had his family's common sense, and from Horace he had learned the value of moderation. So he suggested to his uncle that it might be wise for him to transfer to a less expensive college and study law. This he did, entering sober, intellectual Trinity Hall and assuring his uncle that he would live economically as a recluse, with no company but upright thoughts. He earned his bachelor of arts and master of arts degrees in 1617-1620.

Clerical Career

In the next 3 years Herrick may have tried to practice law. Perhaps he studied divinity. At any rate, on April 24, 1623, he and his friend Weekes were ordained deacons and, on the next day, priests in the Church of England. This uncanonical haste suggests that he became some nobleman's chaplain. So does his presence as a chaplain to the Duke of Buckingham in 1627, when that royal favorite led a naval attack against the French at the Île de Ré. Two-thirds of the English forces were killed, but Herrick survived to be rewarded by Charles I with the vicarage of Dean Prior in Devonshire.

While waiting for this benefice, Herrick wrote songs and carols which were set to music by the leading court musicians, Henry Lawes and Nicholas Lanier, and were sung before the King. He also celebrated the birth of Prince Charles in a pretty pastoral.

In September 1630 Herrick began his clerical duties at Dean Prior. Typically, he made the best of his environment, thanking God for his "little house" and writing poems about his spaniel Tracie, his pet sparrow, and his maid Prue, "by good luck sent." For 17 years he conducted services, baptisms, marriages, and funerals; interested himself in local folklore; flattered female parishioners in verse; exposed the vices of men named Scobble and Mudge, Groynes and Huncks, in biting epigrams; and "became much beloved by the gentry."

The peace of Devonshire was blasted by the civil war which broke out in 1642. The fact that the conquering Puritans were slow to oust Herrick from his vicarage suggests that he was popular with his parishioners and faithful in his duties. In religion he was moderate and reasonable; his sacred poems express a broad Protestantism based on Scripture and common sense. It was his outspoken royalism which caused his expulsion in 1647.

Presumably Herrick returned to London to see his book into print in 1648. Then he drops out of sight until 1660, when he was restored to his vicarage. If he wrote more poems, they have not survived. He was buried at Dean Prior on Oct. 15, 1674. His successor 30 years later reported that he had been a "sober and learned man"; and after more than a century locals recalled "that he kept a pet pig, which he taught to drink out of a tankard."

His Poetry

The many roles which he played in his poetry only partially correspond to the real Herrick. Indeed, it is misleading to identify the "I" in his verse with all the personae he assumed—inebriate, lover, and sensualist; scholar, moralist, and royalist; innocent child, advocate of moderation, and obscene epigrammatist. The fact is that he ranges over the whole human comedy, singing of nature, seasons, youth and love, physical dews and rains, and balms which symbolize the spiritual heaven. He extends to the causes of things and the twilight realm of fairies; and he meditates upon hell, death, and heaven, urging readers to gather the roses of joy while they may. And he concludes his volume with *His Noble Numbers; or, His Pious Pieces, Wherein* (*amongst other things*) *he sings the Birth of his Christ: and sighes for his Saviour's suffering on the Crosse.*

The first edition of Herrick's *Hesperides* seems to have been large and popular with royalists but unsuited to Restoration and 18th-century taste. Not until 1810 did a second edition appear. Despite some attacks on his "naughty" material, the fame which he was certain he deserved came to him, and today his position as one of the great lyrical artists is secure. Moreover, scholars are beginning to recognize that his technical brilliance is complemented by complex profundities.

Further Reading

The standard editions are *The Poetical Works of Robert Herrick,* edited by L. C. Martin (1956), and *The Complete Poetry of Robert Herrick,* edited by J. Max Patrick (1963). The sparse biographical data and the background are attractively set forth in Marchette Chute, *Two Gentle Men: The Lives of George Herbert and Robert Herrick* (1959). There is perceptive criticism of the poetry in Roger B. Rollin, *Robert Herrick* (1966). The cultural background and debt to Jonson are considered in Kathryn Anderson McEuen, *Classical Influence upon the Tribe of Ben* (1939). For the general literary milieu see Douglas Bush, *English Literature in the Earlier Seventeenth Century* (1946; 2d ed. 1962). Rose Macaulay's novel *The Shadow Flies* (1932) gives an imaginary but delightful treatment of Herrick. He is also treated fictionally in Emily Easton, *Youth Immortal: A Life of Robert Herrick* (1934).

Additional Sources

Aiken, Pauline, *The influence of the Latin elegists on English lyric poetry, 1600-1650, with particular reference to the works of Robert Herrick,* New York, Phaeton Press, 1970.

Braden, Gordon, *The classics and English Renaissance poetry: three case studies,* New Haven: Yale University Press, 1978.

Budd, Louis J., *Robert Herrick,* New York, Twayne 1971.

Coiro, Ann Baynes, *Robert Herrick's Hesperides and the epigram book tradition,* Baltimore: Johns Hopkins University Press, 1988.

Deming, Robert H., *Ceremony and art. Robert Herrick's poetry,* The Hague, Paris, Mouton, 1974.

Deneef, A. Leigh, *"This poetick liturgie": Robert Herrick's ceremonial mode,* Durham, N.C.: Duke University Press, 1974.

Ferrari, Ferruccio, *L'influenza classica nell'Inghilterra del Seicento e la poesia di Robert Herrick,* Messina; Firenze: G. D'Anna, 1979.

Ferrari, Ferruccio, *La poesia religiosa inglese del Seicento,* Messina; Firenze: G. D'Anna, 1975.

Gertzman, Jay A., *Fantasy, fashion, and affection: editions of Robert Herrick's poetry for the common reader, 1810-1968,* Bowling Green, Ohio: Bowling Green State University Popular Press, 1986.

Hageman, Elizabeth, *Robert Herrick: a reference guide,* Boston, Mass.: G.K. Hall, 1983.

Holloway, Robin, *The consolation of music: for unaccompanied mixed voices, op. 38, no. 1, on poems by Herrick and Strode,* London; New York: Boosey & Hawkes, 1979.

Horlacher, Friedrich W., *Die Romane Robert Herricks: Empirie u. Fiktion,* Frankfurt am Main; Las Vegas: Lang, 1978.

Ishii, Shôonosuke, *The poetry of Robert Herrick,* Tokyo: Renaissance Institute, Sophia University, 1974.

Johnston, Jack, *Diverse voices of Herrick: songs for medium voice and piano,* Geneseo, N.Y.: Leyerle Publications, 1986.

Macaulay, Rose, Dame, *The shadow flies,* St. Clair Shores, Mich., Scholarly Press, 1971.

Macaulay, Rose, Dame, *They were defeated,* Oxford: Oxford University Press, 1981.

MacLeod, Malcolm Lorimer, *A concordance to the poems of Robert Herrick,* New York, Haskell House Publishers, 1971; Folcroft, Pa.: Folcroft Library Editions, 1977; Norwood, Pa.: Norwood Editions, 1978 c1936.

Musgrove, S. (Sydney), *The universe of Robert Herrick,* Folcroft, Pa.: Folcroft Library Editions, 1975; Norwood Editions, 1978 c1869.

Robert Herrick Memorial Conference, University of Michigan, Dearborn, *"Trust to good verses": Herrick tercentenary essays,* Pittsburgh: University of Pittsburgh Press, 1978.

Rollin, Roger B., *Robert Herrick,* New York, Twayne Publishers 1966; Toronto: Maxwell Macmillan Canada; New York: Maxwell Macmillan International, 1992.

Scott, George Walton, *Robert Herrick, 1591-1674,* London, Sidgwick & Jackson 1974; New York, St. Martin's Press 1974.

□

Édouard Herriot

The French statesman and author Édouard Herriot (1872-1957) was prominent in interwar politics and personified the radical-liberal tradition in French political and cultural life. He was also a biographer and historian of note.

The son of an army officer, Édouard Herriot was born at Troyes on July 5, 1872. After graduating with highest honors from the École Normale Supérieure in 1894, he rapidly acquired a reputation for outstanding scholarship and teaching. His doctoral thesis, *Madame Récamier et ses amis* (1904), followed by his brilliant *Précis de l'histoire des lettres françaises* (1905), secured that reputation.

Like many young turn-of-the-century French intellectuals, Herriot was politicized by the Dreyfus Affair. As an ardent Dreyfusard, he joined the Radical party, and for more than half a century he had few peers in his passionate dedication to justice and eloquent defense of liberalism and republican democracy.

Herriot began his active political career as municipal councilor of Lyons in 1904. Elected mayor the following year, Herriot held that post until his death except for a brief period under the Vichy regime during World War II. This energetic and innovative mayor imaginatively guided the city's development as a modern industrial city. In 1910 he was elected to the departmental general council and 2 years later as senator from the Rhône Department.

In November 1919 Herriot resigned as senator and was elected a member of the Chamber of Deputies, where he became leader of the Radical party. After directing the opposition to the right-wing Bloc National, which had won a parliamentary majority in 1919, he organized a left-wing coalition of Radicals and Socialists called the Cartel des Gauches, which won the elections of May 1924. Herriot was then asked to form the next government.

Herriot's first ministry lasted 10 months. Acting as his own foreign minister, he supervised the evacuation of the Ruhr in 1924 and recognized the Soviet Union the following year. He also unsuccessfully sponsored at the League of Nations proposals for arbitration, security, and disarmament. At home, his program of financial reforms was killed in the Senate, and he resigned in April 1925. As Raymond Poincaré's minister of public instruction from 1926 to 1928, he devoted his energies to the struggle for free secondary education.

Herriot served again as prime minister from June to December 1932 after his left-leaning coalition won the parliamentary elections of that year. Infuriated at his decision to pay the December installment of the French war debt to the United States, the Chamber overturned his government. Herriot served as vice-premier under Gaston Doumergue in 1934 and P. E. Flandin in 1934-1935 and was elected president of the Chamber of Deputies in 1936. He remained in that office until the fall of France in June 1940; he abstained the following month when the French Parliament voted full powers to Marshal Pétain. Though he took no active role in the Resistance, his hostility to the Vichy regime was widely known. In 1944 he lived under house arrest in Lyons until he was deported to Germany.

Liberated in April 1945 by Soviet armies, Herriot returned to Lyons, where he had already been elected mayor. Resuming his leadership of the depleted Radical party, he was elected to the first and second constituent assemblies. In 1947 he was returned to his old post as president of the new National Assembly of the Fourth Republic and retained it until his retirement in January 1954.

In his later years Herriot was the recipient of numerous honors. In 1946 he was elected to the prestigious French Academy, and following his retirement from active politics he was made honorary life president of his beloved French Chamber of Deputies. In June 1955 the Soviet government awarded him its annual Peace Prize in recognition of his long advocacy of international cooperation. Grossly overweight and in declining health for several years, Herriot died at Lyons on March 26, 1957, a patriarch venerated by virtually all Frenchmen.

Further Reading

The first volume of Herriot's two-volume memoirs was translated as In *Those Days* (1948; trans. 1952). There is extensive biographical coverage of Herriot in Francis De Tarr, *The French Radical Party: From Herriot to Mendès-France* (1961). Herriot's career is also well covered in the more specialized Peter J. Larmour, *The French Radical Party in the 1930's* (1964). For general background see Denis W. Brogan, *The Development of Modern France, 1870-1939* (1 vol., 1947; rev. ed., 2 vols., 1966).

Additional Sources

Jessner, Sabine, *Edouard Herriot, patriarch of the Republic,* New York, Haskell House Publishers, 1974. □

Sir John Frederick William Herschel

The English astronomer Sir John Frederick William Herschel (1792-1871) is noted for his observations of the stars in the southern hemisphere.

John Herschel was born at Slough on March 7, 1792, son of William Herschel, the most eminent astronomer of the period. His early training was in mathematics at Cambridge, where he graduated first in his class in 1813. He quickly established himself with the production of mathematical papers, which earned him the Copley Medal of the Royal Society.

Soon after graduation Herschel and two classmates composed a textbook on the calculus, which was aimed at, and succeeded in, introducing into England the more powerful mathematical methods that had been developed on the Continent during the preceding century. This work, however, signaled both the beginning and the end of Herschel's career as a mathematician. Interested primarily in chemistry, he spent the next few years pursuing it and dabbling variously in law, optics, and astronomy. Not until 1820 did he yield to what he seems always to have regarded as a "birth debt" and turn seriously to astronomy. After serving an apprenticeship to his father for the grinding of an 18-inch telescope mirror, he won his spurs as an astronomer with a 2-year program of double-star observations.

Having fulfilled his obligation for a time, Herschel retired into less intensive observation after 1823, while serving vigorously as secretary of the Royal Society and president of the Royal Astronomical Society. By 1830 his restless but superb intellect had carried him through pioneering efforts in what is now called philosophy of science, to a treatise, *On the Study of Natural Philosophy*. He was knighted in 1831.

Rather early in his astronomical career Herschel had determined to do a systematic follow-up and extension of his father's imaginative surveys of double stars and nebulas. By 1833 he was through with the northern hemisphere. In the fall of that year, therefore, he moved his family to South Africa for 4 years of observation of the southern skies. This was the first real step toward putting knowledge of the two hemispheres on a comparable basis, and a chief feature in this endeavor was Herschel's inauguration of photometry, the precise measurement of stellar brightness.

Returning to England in 1838, Herschel received honors at Queen Victoria's coronation. He relaxed in chemical researches. Already, in 1819, he had discovered the crucial property of the chemical that has since been used as the photographer's "hypo." Only during Herschel's African sojourn, however, was photography itself actually accomplished, and the art was still in a very primitive state. By 1839 Herschel was right in the thick of things, with the invention of methods of producing images on paper and glass rather than metal, and he introduced "positive" and "negative" in the photographic context.

Herschel devoted most of the rest of his life to the reduction, evaluation, and publication of astronomical data. He died on May 11, 1871, and was buried in Westminster Abbey.

Further Reading

An interesting biography of Herschel by a noted German scholar is Günther Buttmann, *The Shadow of the Telescope: A Biography of John Herschel* (trans. 1970). Also valuable is Agnes M. Clerke, *The Herschels and Modern Astronomy* (1895).

Additional Sources

Buttmann, Günther, *John Herschel. Lebensbild eines Na-turforschers. Mit 13 Ab,* Stuttgart, Wissenschaftliche Ver-lagsgesellschaft, 1965.

Buttmann, Günther, *The shadow of the telescope; a biography of John Herschel,* New York, Scribner 1970; Guildford: Lutterworth Press, 1974.

Clerke, Agnes M. (Agnes Mary), *The Herschels and modern astronomy,* London, New York etc.: Cassell and company, limited, 1901.

Herschel, John F. W. (John Frederick William), Sir, *Herschel at the Cape; diaries and correspondence of Sir John Herschel,* Cape Town, Balkema (A.A.), 1969; Austin: University of Texas Press, 1969.

Herschel, John F. W. (John Frederick William), Sir, *Letters and papers of Sir John Herschel from the archives of the Royal Society,* Frederick, MD: University Publications of America, 1990.

Schaaf, Larry J. (Larry John), *Out of the shadows: Herschel, Talbot & the invention of photography,* New Haven: Yale University Press, 1992.

Schaaf, Larry J. (Larry John), *Tracings of light: Sir John Herschel & the camera lucida: drawings from the Graham Nash collec-tion,* San Francisco: The Friends of Photography, 1989.

Warner, Brian, *Maclear & Herschel: letters & diaries at the Cape of Good Hope, 1834-1938,* Cape Town: A.A. Balkema, 1984.

□

Sir William Herschel

The German-born English astronomer Sir William Herschel (1738-1822) discovered the planet Uranus, the intrinsic motion of the sun in space, and the form of the Milky Way.

William (originally Friedrich Wilhelm) Herschel was born in Hanover on Nov. 15, 1738. His father was a musician in the Hanoverian guard, which William joined at the age of 14.

In 1757 Herschel went to England. In Yorkshire he conducted a small military band, and from 1762 to 1766 he was a concert manager in Leeds. His notebook of 1766 has these laconic entries: "Feb. 19. Wheatly. Observation of Venus" and "Feb. 24. Eclipse of the moon at 7 o'clock A.M. Kirby." These are the first signs of Herschel's future inter-ests. By the end of the year he became organist at the fashionable spa town of Bath. In 1772 his sister, Caroline Lucretia Herschel, came to live with him at Bath. She col-laborated with her brother on astronomical researches.

Not until 1773 is there another scientific entry in Her-schel's notebooks: "April 19. Bought a quadrant and Emerson's Trigonometry." That this entry heralded a new phase in his life is shown by the fact that it is followed by others of a similar nature: "Bought a book of astronomy . . . bought an object glass . . . bought many eye glasses . . . hire of a 2 feet reflecting telescope." These entries show that he was proposing to make his first (metal) telescope mirror.

Herschel's First Telescope

Obsessed with astronomy, Herschel progressed through pasteboard and tin-tubed telescopes to a hired Gregorian reflector. When he tried to buy a much larger reflecting telescope in London, he could find nothing suit-able which he could afford. For this reason he began to build his own. By September 1774 he was observing the heavens with a (Newtonian) reflecting telescope of 6-foot focal length of his own construction.

Herschel now entered into a long and tedious period of his life, when he and his brother and sister worked away at grinding and polishing telescope mirrors. He had to keep the mirror moving unceasingly on the grinding tool for long periods of time. His sister fed him as he worked. Some idea of his astonishing industry may be had from his statement, made in 1795, that he had made "not less than 200 7 feet, 150 10 feet and about 80 20 feet mirrors." Of the various mountings he devised for these, he was very pleased with a 7-foot Newtonian telescope stand, completed in 1778.

Early Observations

Herschel began to keep a record of what he saw in the heavens from March 1, 1774. He observed the rings of Saturn, the moons of Jupiter, and the markings of the moon. It is interesting to see how in his eagerness to make novel discoveries he was deluded into thinking that he had found signs of a forest on the moon, even supposing that he could make out the shadows cast by the trees at the edge of the wood. His next lunar observations were 3 years later, when he began to calculate the height of the lunar mountains.

This self-taught astronomer of Bath was by his own efforts soon to be transmuted into the world's leading observational astronomer. He possessed instruments as powerful as any to be found and all the perseverance needed to use them effectively. In 1777 he began observations of a well-known but neglected star, Mira Ceti, which varies in brightness periodically. Soon he had the idea of determining the annual parallax of stars (the shift in the apparent relative positions of the stars as the earth goes around the sun). Whether the stars were so far away as to make this apparent movement unobservable was not then known. In fact, no annual parallax was measured until 1838, when Friedrich Wilhelm Bessel measured that of star 61 Cygni. Herschel, nevertheless, observed the relative positions of pairs of stars close together (called double stars). He measured hundreds of double stars, but in March 1778 he recorded his disappointment at finding "the stars in the tail of Ursa Major just as I saw them three months ago, at least not visibly different."

Discovery of Uranus

In recording double stars systematically, on March 13, 1781, Herschel entered a pair of which "the lowest of the two is a curious either nebulous star or perhaps a comet." Four days later he looked for the object and found that it had moved. He recorded the new position of the "comet" and proceeded to follow it regularly. What he had discovered was the planet Uranus, as it is now known—the first planet to be discovered in historical times.

Herschel was given the Copley Medal of the Royal Society and elected a fellow. Col. John Walsh wrote to him that he had spoken with the king, George III, and had taken "occasion to mention that you had a twofold claim as a Native of Hanover and a Resident of Great Britain, where the Discovery was made, to be permitted to name the Planet from his Majesty." The planet was thus at first called "Georgium sidus" ("star George"), and it appears in this form on early maps and models.

King's Patronage

George III asked Herschel to move his telescope to an observatory the King had built in the Deer Park at Richmond. Herschel moved to Windsor, near the King's residence, and in due course was given the patronage for which he had long hoped—a salary for himself and his sister, upkeep for the telescope, and later a very large sum for a 40-foot telescope, the largest ever made before the mid-19th century.

Herschel eventually settled at Slough, where he wrote the paper announcing his second great discovery, "Motion of the Solar System in Space" (1783). He carefully noted the proper motions of seven bright stars and showed that the movement in the intervening time seemed to converge on a fixed point, which he interpreted correctly as the point from which the sun is receding. Other discoveries followed. He found that "Georgium sidus" had satellites. Some of those he discovered are now known to be spurious, but the diffi-

culties of observing, especially with the crude mounting available to him, were very great.

Structure of the Universe

Many double stars are seen as such merely because they happen to be in a straight line as seen from the earth. Herschel reasoned that if one member of a double-star system was much brighter than the other this must be the result of such a coincidence, the brighter star of the pair being much the closer of the two. He continued to record the relative positions of all such systems, and in 1782 and 1785 he presented long lists of his observations. He was, of course, assuming that the stars were all more or less uniformly bright, intrinsically speaking, and that they were uniformly distributed throughout space. This being so, he believed that by taking counts of stars over a given small area of sky the number of stars visible would give him the extent of the Milky Way in that direction. He thus formulated a picture or map of the Milky Way, which was quite remarkable in his time, and which even now is not wildly wrong.

Later Years

In 1788 Herschel married Mary Pitt, a wealthy widow, by whom he had his only son. Herschel was able to make a useful additional income by selling telescopes, and he invested money in building machines to help grind mirrors. He corresponded with the leading astronomers of England and Europe and received many distinguished visitors at Slough who were anxious to see the telescope he had completed on Aug. 28, 1789; it had a 40-foot focal length and 4-foot aperture.

Herschel was knighted in 1816 and received honors from states and academies the world over. He died at Slough on Aug. 25, 1822.

Further Reading

The most important volumes for an appreciation of Herschel are *The Scientific Papers of Sir William Herschel* (2 vols., 1912), the first volume of which has an invaluable short account of Herschel's life by J. L. E. Dreyer. Biographies include Edward S. Holden, *Sir W. Herschel: His Life and Works* (1881); James Sime, *William Herschel and His Works* (1900); and J.B. Sidgwick, *William Herschel: Explorer of the Heavens* (1953). Michael A. Hoskin, *William Herschel and the Construction of the Heavens* (1963), is composed largely of extracts from Herschel's writings, intended to show his views on the structure of the universe. For a short account of Herschel's views and the way in which they were developed by others see J. D. North, *The Measure of the Universe: A History of Modern Cosmology* (1965).

Additional Sources

Armitage, A. (Angus), *William Herschel,* London, New York, Nelson 1962.

Clerke, Agnes M. (Agnes Mary), *The Herschels and modern astronomy,* London, New York etc. Cassell and company, limited, 1901.

Crawford, Deborah, *The king's astronomer, William Herschel,* New York, J. Messner 1968.

Hoskin, Michael A., *William Herschel and the construction of the heaven,* New York, Norton 1964, 1963.

Lubbock, Constance A. (Constance Ann), 1855?-1939, ed., *The Herschel chronicle; the life-story of William Herschel and his sister, Caroline Herschel,* New York, The Macmillan company; Cambridge, Eng., The University press, 1933.

Moore, Patrick, *William Herschel, astronomer and musician of 19 New King Street, Bath,* Sidcup, Kent, England: P.M.E. Erwood in association with The William Herschel Society, Bath, England, 1981. □

Alfred Day Hershey

Alfred Day Hershey (1908-1997) shared the Nobel Prize in medicine for his research on viruses.

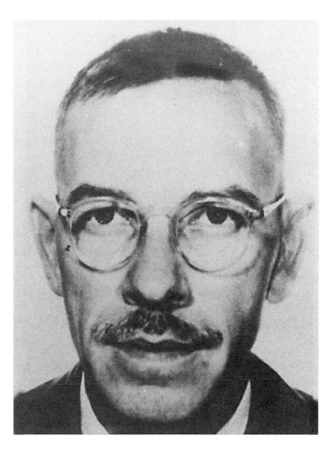

By seeking to understand the reproduction of viruses, the simplest form of life, Alfred Day Hershey made important discoveries about the nature of deoxyribonucleic acid (DNA) and laid the groundwork for modern molecular genetics. Highly regarded as an experimental scientist, Hershey is perhaps best known for the 1952 "blender experiment" that he and Martha Chase conducted to demonstrate that DNA, not protein, was the genetic material of life. This discovery stimulated further research into DNA, including the discovery by James Watson and Francis Crick of the double-helix structure of DNA the following year. Hershey's work with bacteriophages, the viruses that prey on bacteria, was often carried out in loose collaboration with other scientists working with bacteriophages. Hershey shared the Nobel Prize in Physiology or Medicine in 1969 with Max Delbrück and Salvador Edward Luria. The Nobel Committee praised the three scientists for their contributions to molecular biology. Their basic research into viruses also helped others develop vaccines against viral diseases such as polio.

Hershey was born on December 4, 1908, in Owosso, Michigan, to Robert Day Hershey and Alma Wilbur Hershey. His father worked for an auto manufacturer. Alfred attended public schools in Owosso and nearby Lansing. He received his B.S. in bacteriology from Michigan State College (now Michigan State University) in 1930 and his Ph.D. in chemistry from the same school in 1934. As a graduate student, Hershey's interest in bacteriology and the biochemistry of life was already evident. His doctoral dissertation was on the chemistry of *Brucella,* the bacteria responsible for brucellosis, also known as undulant fever. Undulant fever is transmitted to humans from cattle and causes recurrent fevers and joint pain. After receiving his Ph.D., Hershey took a position as a research assistant in the Department of Bacteriology at the Washington University School of Medicine in St. Louis. There he worked with Jacques Jacob Bronfenbrenner, one of the pioneers in bacteriophage research in the United States. During the sixteen years he spent teaching and conducting research at Washington University, from 1934 to 1950, Hershey was promoted to instructor (1936), assistant professor (1938), and associate professor (1942).

Bacteriophages—known simply as phages—had been discovered in 1915, only nineteen years before Hershey began his career. Phages are viruses that reproduce by preying on bacteria, first attacking and then dissolving them. For scientists who study bacteria, phages are a source of irritation because they can destroy bacterial cultures. But other scientists are fascinated by this tiny organism. Perhaps the smallest living thing, phages consist of little more than the protein and DNA (the molecule of heredity) found in a cellular nucleus. Remarkably efficient, however, phages reproduce by conquering bacteria and subverting them to the phage particles' own needs. This type of reproduction is known as replication. Little was known about the particulars of this process when Hershey was a young scientist.

By studying viral replication, scientists hoped to learn more about the viral diseases that attack humans, like mumps, the common cold, German measles, and polio. But the study of bacteriophages also promised findings with implications that reached far beyond disease cures into the realm of understanding life itself. If Hershey and other researchers could determine how phages replicated, they stood to learn how higher organisms—including humans—passed genetic information from generation to generation.

Hershey's study of phages soon yielded several discoveries that furthered an understanding of genetic inheritance and change. In 1945 he showed that phages were capable of spontaneous mutation. Faced with a bacterial culture known to be resistant to phage attack, most, but not all, phages would die. By mutating, some phages survived to attack the bacteria and replicate. This finding was significant because it showed that mutations did not occur gradually, as one school of scientific thought believed, but rather occurred immediately and spontaneously in viruses. It also helped explain why viral attack is so difficult to prevent. In 1946 Hershey made another discovery that changed what scientists thought about viruses. He showed that if different strains of phages infected the same bacterial cell, they could combine or exchange genetic material. This is similar to what occurs when higher forms of life sexually reproduce, of course. But it was the first time viruses were shown to combine genetic material. Hershey called this phenomenon genetic recombination.

Hershey was not the only scientist who saw the potential in working with bacteriophages. Two other influential scientists were also pursuing the same line of investigation. Max Delbrück, a physicist, had been studying phages in the United States since he fled Nazi Germany in 1937. Studying genetic recombination independently of Hershey, he reached the same results that Hershey did in the same year. Similarly, Salvador Edward Luria, a biologist and physician who immigrated to the United States from Italy in 1940, had independently confirmed Hershey's work on spontaneous mutation in 1945. Although the three men never worked side by side in the same laboratory, they were collaborators nonetheless. Through conversation and correspondence, they shared results and encouraged each other in their phage research. Indeed, these three scientists formed the core of the self-declared "phage group," a loose-knit clique of scientists who encouraged research on particular strains of bacteriophage. By avoiding competition and duplication, the group hoped to advance phage research that much faster.

In 1950 Hershey accepted a position as a staff scientist in the department of genetics (now the Genetics Research Unit) of the Carnegie Institute at Cold Spring Harbor, New York. It was at Cold Spring Harbor that Hershey conducted his most influential experiment. Hershey wished to prove conclusively that the genetic material in phages was DNA . Analysis with an electron microscope had showed that phages consist only of DNA surrounded by a protein shell. Other scientists' experiments had revealed that during replication some part of the parental phages was being transferred to their offspring. The task before Hershey was to show that it was the phage DNA that was passed on to succeeding generations and that gave the signal for replication and growth.

Although Hershey was not alone in having reached the belief that DNA was the stuff of life, many scientists were unconvinced. They doubted that DNA had the complexity needed to carry the blueprint for life and believed instead that the genetic code resided in protein, a far more elaborate molecule. Furthermore, no one had yet demonstrated the technical skill needed to design an experiment that would answer the question once and for all.

With Martha Chase, Hershey found a way to determine what role each of the phage components played in replication. In experiments done in 1951 and 1952, Hershey used radioactive phosphorus to tag the DNA and radioactive sulfur to tag the protein. (The DNA contains no sulfur and the protein contains no phosphorus.) Hershey and Chase then allowed the marked phage particles to infect a bacterial culture and to begin the process of replication. This process was interrupted when the scientists spun the culture at a high speed in a Waring blender.

In this manner, Hershey and Chase learned that the shearing action of the blender separated the phage protein from the bacterial cells. Apparently while the phage DNA entered the bacterium and forced it to start replicating phage particles, the phage protein remained outside, attached to the cell wall. The researchers surmised that the phage particle attached itself to the outside of a bacterium by its protein "tail" and literally injected its nucleic acid into the cell. DNA, and not protein, was responsible for communicating the genetic information needed to produce the next generation of phage.

Clearly DNA seemed to hold the key to heredity for all forms of life, not just viruses. Yet while the blender experiment answered one question about DNA, it also raised a host of other questions. Now scientists wanted to know more about the action of DNA. How did DNA operate? How did it replicate itself? How did it direct the production of proteins? What was its chemical structure? Until that last question was answered, scientists could only speculate about answers to the others. Hershey's achievement spurred other scientists into DNA research.

In 1953, a year after Hershey's blender experiment, the structure of DNA was determined in Cambridge, England, by James Dewey Watson and Francis Harry Compton Crick. Watson, who was only twenty-five years old when the structure was announced, had worked with Luria at the University of Indiana. For their discovery of DNA's double-helix structure, Watson and Crick received the Nobel Prize in 1962.

Hershey, Delbrück, and Luria also received a Nobel Prize for their contributions to molecular biology, but not until 1969. This seeming delay in recognition for their accomplishments prompted the *New York Times* to ask in an October 20, 1969, editorial: "Delbrück, Hershey and Luria richly deserve their awards, but why did they have to wait so long for this recognition? Every person associated with molecular biology knows that these are the grand pioneers of the field, the giants on whom others—some of whom received the Nobel Prize years ago—depended for their own great achievements." Yet other scientists observed that the blender experiment merely offered experimental proof of a theoretical belief that was already widely held. After the blender experiment, Hershey continued investigating the structure of phage DNA. Although human DNA winds double-stranded like a spiral staircase, Hershey found that some phage DNA is single-stranded and some is circular. In 1962 Hershey was named director of the Genetics Research Unit at Cold Spring Harbor. He retired in 1974 and died of cardiopulmonary failure at the age of 88 on May 22, 1997.

Hershey was "known to his colleagues as a very quiet, withdrawn sort of man who avoids crowds and noise and most hectic social activities," according to the report of the 1969 Nobel Prize in the October 17, 1969, *New York Times*. His hobbies were woodworking, reading, gardening, and sailing. He married Harriet Davidson, a former research assistant, on November 15, 1945. She later became an editor of the *Cold Spring Harbor Symposia on Quantitative Biology.* She and Hershey had one child, a son named Peter Manning. Born on August 7, 1956, Peter was twelve years old when Hershey won the Nobel Prize.

In addition to the Nobel Prize, Hershey received the Albert Lasker Award of the American Public Health Association (1958) and the Kimber Genetics Award of the National Academy of Sciences (1965) for his discoveries concerning the genetic structure and replication processes of viruses. He was elected to the National Academy of Sciences in 1958.

Further Reading

Fox, Daniel M., editor, *Nobel Laureates in Medicine or Physiology: A Biographical Dictionary,* Garland, 1990.

Magner, Lois N., *History of the Life Sciences,* Dekker, 1979.

McGraw-Hill Modern Scientists and Engineers, McGraw-Hill, 1980.

Wasson, Tyler, editor, *Nobel Prize Winners,* H. W. Wilson, 1987.

New York Times, October 17, 1969, p. 24; October 20, 1969, p. 46.

Science, October 24, 1969, p. 479–481.

"Three Americans Share Nobel Prize for Medicine for Work on Bacteriophage," in *Chemical and Engineering News,* October 27, 1969, p. 16.

Time, October 24, 1969, p. 84. □

Melville Jean Herskovits

The American anthropologist Melville Jean Herskovits (1895-1963) is famous for his research on Africa and his pioneer studies in African American ethnology.

Melville Herskovits was born in Belefontaine, Ohio, on Sept. 10, 1895. He received his education at Columbia University. Later he founded the program of African studies at Northwestern University, where many of the first American African specialists were trained. When the African Studies Association was formed, he became its first president.

Herskovits is chiefly famous for his much-debated thesis that African American culture owes much to the African way of life, expressed in his *Myth of the Negro Past* (1941). The "myth" that he tried to destroy was that the ancestral cultures of blacks were primitive, with Africans making no contribution to the history of the world, and that under the slave regime of the antebellum South virtually all traces of African culture—except, perhaps, certain survivals in music and the dance—had been destroyed. Not only did Herskovits maintain that Africanism existed in a black American subculture, but he argued that certain of these cultural traits had been transmitted to the whites.

Herskovits held that African survivals were less common in the United States than in Brazil or the Caribbean because of the higher proportion of whites to blacks in the American South and the absence of mountain or jungle retreats where escaped slaves could have developed stable communities without white interference. African survivals were thus strongest among the inhabitants of the coastal islands off South Carolina and Georgia because of their relative isolation. He tried to show that their speech and syntax, once thought to be derivative from archaic dialects of 16th-century England, were derived from Africa. Although the African influence upon black music and dance, both of which in turn influenced white culture, was recognized and accepted, Herskovits contended that much of black folklore, magic, and folk medicine could also be traced to African origins, as could their mutual aid societies and funeral practices.

African American scholars and liberal whites involved in bettering race relations at first opposed Herskovits's thesis on the existence of a black subculture in North America. The inescapable implication of his thesis was that African Americans were an unassimilable group, unable to adjust to white middle-class society, a group immalleable to the "melting pot." In opposition to Herskovits's thesis, his antagonists attempted to explain the existence of the black pattern of culture not on the basis of African derivations but on the basis of social oppression and economic degradation. With the rise of the black power ideology and such movements as the Black Panthers, the difference or uniqueness of African Americans was gloried in, and the notion of a black subculture was exalted. Herskovits's theories thus enjoyed a tremendous revival as African Americans sought the origins of their identity. Thus it appears that the validity of his theories remains to be determined at a time when they are not so emotionally involved in contemporary political movements.

Herskovits is also known as one of the leading exponents of ethical relativism in politics, the position that maintains that there is no objective order of justice, but that what is just in one culture may be unjust in another. Thus he wrote that "the relativist point of view brings into relief the *validity* of every set of norms *for* the people whose lives are guided by them." One of the objections made to this position is that it would make the set of norms which guided the lives of most Germans under Hitler *valid.* Thus, it would be "immoral" to judge another culture (such as Nazi Germany) by one's own moral norms since morality is determined by the culture, and a member of that culture could not do other than what he did do.

Further Reading

Information on Herskovits is in Hoffman R. Hays, *From Ape to Angel: An Informal History of Social Anthropology* (1958), and Marvin Harris, *The Rise of Anthropological Theory* (1968).

Additional Sources

Simpson, George Eaton, *Melville J. Herskovits,* New York, Columbia University Press, 1973. □

Heinrich Rudolf Hertz

The German physicist Heinrich Rudolf Hertz (1857-1894) demonstrated experimentally the propagation of electrical oscillations in space.

orn on Feb. 22, 1857, in Hamburg, Heinrich Hertz was the oldest of the five children of Gustav Hertz, a lawyer and later a senator and the head of the judiciary of the city of Hamburg, and Elizabeth Pfefferkorn Hertz. Heins, as the boy was called in the family, soon gave evidence of his extraordinary aptitudes in mathematics, science, languages, and manual skills. The galvanometer and the spectroscope which he constructed as a teen-ager served him well during his university studies.

In addition to a thorough acquaintance with Homer and the Greek dramatists, Hertz acquired through his own efforts a knowledge of Sanskrit and Arabic. Following his graduation with highest honors from the gymnasium in Hamburg in 1875, he thought that his future lay with engineering. He spent a year in Frankfurt with an engineering firm, and in the summer of 1876 he attended courses at the Polytechnic in Dresden. After a year of volunteer military service in Berlin he began his regular engineering studies at the University of Munich in 1877.

No sooner had the classes gotten under way than it dawned on Hertz that he would prefer physics to engineering. He spent the winter of 1877/1878 studying the treatises of Pierre Simon de Laplace and Joseph Louis Lagrange and the spring in the laboratory working under G. von Jolly. To achieve the best training, he sought out the best teachers, and these were at the University of Berlin. Soon after his arrival there he became Hermann von Helmholtz's student. By spring 1879 Hertz completed the experimental verification of a question about electrical inertia, and his work won a gold medal at the university on August 4.

Demonstration of Electromagnetic Oscillations

Hertz's combination of theoretical and experimental work was so remarkable that during the next spring he was allowed to present his research as his doctoral dissertation, "On Induction in Rotating Spheres," and received the degree *magna cum laude*. He became Helmholtz's assistant at the Physikalisches Institut at the University of Berlin, and during his 3 years there Hertz's most remarkable achievement was his work on the pressure arising between two plates in contact. The influence of his conclusions on the construction of precision instruments was so great that his paper "On the Contact of Elastic Solids" was simultaneously published in a scientific and a technical magazine. But the promise of the future lay with his work on electric and cathode-tube discharge, published in 1883 in two papers.

Hertz next went to the University of Kiel, where he did some work on meteorological and thermoelectric problems, but his real interest was in James Clerk Maxwell's theory as

shown by his paper from 1884, "On the Relations between Maxwell's Fundamental Electromagnetic Equations and the Fundamental Equations of the Opposing 'Electromagnetics.'" Hertz was at Karlsruhe as the head of the Physics Institute at the Polytechnic when he began his experimental research on the effect of electric and cathode-tube discharges. In Karlsruhe he met Elizabeth Doll, the daughter of a well-known geodesist, and married her on July 31, 1886.

On surveying the equipment in his laboratory, Hertz came across two Riess spirals and found "that it was not necessary to discharge large batteries through one of these spirals to obtain sparks in the other; ... that even the discharge of a small induction coil would do, provided it had to spring across a spark gap." He soon noticed that the oscillations thus produced were rather regular. By spring 1887 Hertz knew that sparks were more readily formed when the metal spheres forming the gap were exposed to ultraviolet radiation.

This discovery put Hertz within reach of producing with relative ease oscillations of sufficiently high frequency with corresponding wavelengths that could be detected with apparatus tailored to the dimensions of ordinary laboratories. By summer he succeeded in showing the effect of a rectilinear electric oscillation upon a neighboring circuit. On Nov. 10, 1887, he sent to the Berlin Academy the now historic report "On Electromagnetic Effects Produced by Electrical Disturbances in Insulators," disclosing that he had obtained oscillatory inductive action at distances up to 12 meters. While the result was a triumph for Maxwell's theory,

Hertz knew that one also had to settle the question of the finite velocity of the propagation of the inductive effect across space. This he did in 1888, and the same year he also proved that electromagnetic waves could be reflected as predicted by Maxwell's theory. Later that year he accepted the chair of physics at the University of Bonn, which had been vacant since the death of R. J. E. Clausius.

Hertz's work at Bonn aimed at a generalization of a cherished idea of his revered teacher, Helmholtz, that electromagnetic effects were products of the motion of the ether atoms, obeying the law of least action. Hertz now wanted a formulation of the whole science of physics along these lines. His *Principles of Mechanics* took him 3 years to write; it was published posthumously.

In 1889 Hertz was the principal speaker at the Congress of German Scientists at Heidelberg, where he described the impact of the verification of Maxwell's theory on the physics of the future. Needless to say, he believed with the rest of the late-19th-century physicists that it was to become a physics of the ether. Hertz succumbed to an infection of the inner ear on Jan. 1, 1894. Most likely Hertz would have been among the first to perceive the fallacies inherent in the concept of the ether and to usher in a new age of physics.

Further Reading

The chapter on Hertz in Rollo Appleyard, *Pioneers of Electrical Communication* (1930), gives a short but informative account of his life and scientific work. The best account of the status of electromagnetic theory during Hertz's time is in E. T. Whittaker, *A History of the Theories of Aether and Electricity* (2 vols., 1951-1953).

Additional Sources

Bryant, John H., *Heinrich Hertz, the beginning of microwaves: discovery of electromagnetic waves and opening of the electromagnetic spectrum by Heinrich Hertz in the years 1886-1892,* New York: Institute of Electrical and Electronics Engineers; Piscataway, NJ: IEEE Service Center, Single Publication Sales Dept. distributor, 1988.

Buchwald, Jed Z., *The creation of scientific effects: Heinrich Hertz and electric waves,* Chicago: University of Chicago Press, 1994.

Hertz, Heinrich, *Heinrich Rudolf Hertz (1857-1894): a collection of articles and addresses,* New York: Garland Pub., 1994.

Hertz, Heinrich, *Memoirs, letters, diaries / Charles Susskin,* San Francisco, Calif.: San Francisco Press, 1977.

O'Hara, J. G. (James G.), *Hertz and the Maxwellians: a study and documentation of the discovery of electromagnetic wave radiation, 1873-1894,* London: P. Peregrinus Ltd. in association with the Science Museum, 1987. □

James Barry Munnik Hertzog

James Barry Munnik Hertzog (1866-1942) was a South African soldier and political leader. His government isolated Africans from the political process and laid the groundwork for the separatist apartheid system, which allowed the white minority to oppress blacks.

James Hertzog was born in the Wellington district of the Cape Province on April 3, 1866, a descendant of German immigrants. Educated at Stellenbosch University near Cape Town, Hertzog studied law in Holland, France, and Germany. Returning to South Africa in 1893, he served as reporter to the Transvaal High Court and subsequently became a judge of the High Court of the Orange Free State. Hertzog resigned this post when the Anglo-Boer war broke out in 1899, enlisted for service, and assumed command of the burgher forces in June 1900. The Treaty of Vereeniging, which ended the war, set him on a public career that was to make Afrikaner nationalism the most important influence in South African politics.

Advocate of Afrikaner Nationalism

At the time, an Afrikaner leader was judged mainly by his attitudes to the British connection, the relations between the Afrikaners and the English minority, and inevitably the race problem. Hertzog's thinking on these had developed during his student days. "A distinctive nation," Oswald Pirow, his confidant and lifelong friend, quotes him as having written from Europe, "has thus come into being, with a distinctive language of a separate and independent character." Hertzog, who had been pleased to speak Dutch in Stellenbosch, then rejected "the folly of trying to introduce

into South Africa a highly synthetic language like Neder-lands.''

For Hertzog, the destiny of the Afrikaner was defined in terms of ''a severe and sustained struggle for dominance in South Africa.'' What Hertzog really had in mind emerged during a heated session of the Vereeniging peace conference. Angered by Boer demands for the equal treatment of the English and Dutch languages, Lord Milner, the British administrator, shouted: ''I want only one official language in South Africa!'' Hertzog's retort was ''So do I!''

Louis Botha invited Hertzog to join his Cabinet when the Union (now Republic) of South Africa was formed in 1910. The partnership was doomed almost from the beginning. Where Botha cooperated with Britain, conciliated the English minority, and treated the Africans with paternalistic benevolence, Hertzog preferred a different political style. He was in a hurry to free South Africa from domination by ''foreign fortune seekers,'' wanted the Afrikaners and the English to develop along separate though equal cultural lines, and insisted on segregating the Africans.

A keen admirer of John Milton's puritanical sternness and an untiring reader of Carlyle's *Frederic the Great,* Hertzog moved to his goals with a rigidity and single-mindedness which thrilled his followers, exasperated his enemies, and finally brought about his downfall. His version of language equality created crises in the Free State's educational system, which forced Botha to resign (1912) and reconstitute his Cabinet—without Hertzog.

The Nationalist party, led by Hertzog, came into being in 1914. It formed an alliance with the mainly English-speaking Labour party after the Rand disturbances in 1922. The alliance emerged victorious from the 1924 elections. Hertzog became Afrikaner nationalism's first prime minister. Two years later he was in London, pressing the Imperial Conference for clarification of the status of members of the British Commonwealth. The Statute of Westminster (1931), which recognized South Africa's independence, and the legislation giving the country a separate flag constitute the crowning achievements in Hertzog's struggle to remove the humiliations of Vereeniging.

Apostle of Apartheid

Hertzog's attitude to the African was rooted in the long history of conflict between black and white and in the Afrikaner's fear of miscegenation. Urgency was given to it by his fear of an African-English alliance against the Afrikaner. In the Cape, where the Africans had the vote, they used it against Afrikaner nationalism. One of the three British columns which had harassed Hertzog's armies in the Free State had been African. The first Nationalist-Labour Cabinet had fallen (1928) because the English-speaking labor minister had met a black delegation from Clements Kadalie's Industrial and Commercial Workers Union.

Hertzog's government introduced the bans to isolate and silence political dissent, removed the Africans from the common voters' roll in the Cape, and passed legislation upholding the industrial color bar. His successors were to build on these foundations to cast apartheid in its present form.

The depression forced Hertzog to form a coalition government with Gen. Jan C. Smuts, who led the South African party. The coalition developed into the United party (1934). The clouds of war were rising in Europe. Hertzog advocated a policy of neutrality. He adopted this attitude, he told the Imperial Conference in 1937, ''because England continues to associate itself with France in a policy with reference to East and Central Europe which is calculated to endanger Germany's existence or which refuses to eliminate any injustice flowing from the Treaty of Versailles.'' With this in mind he tabled a neutrality motion in Parliament on Sept. 4, 1939, which was rejected by 80 votes to 67. His government fell.

He later joined D. F. Malan to form the Reunited party, which split in 1940 when the militants rejected Hertzog's moderate policies toward the English in favor of what he had earlier termed Afrikaner ''dominance in South Africa.'' The remnants of his followers formed the Afrikaner party and persuaded Hertzog to lead it. Speaking out for national socialism for the Afrikaners, Hertzog alienated both the Afrikaner militants and those fighting Hitler. Embittered and lonely, Hertzog died on Nov. 21, 1942.

Further Reading

The most authoritative work on Hertzog is Christian Maurits van den Heever, *General Hertzog* (1946). Oswald Pirow, *James Barry Munnik Hertzog* (1958), discusses the intrigues that brought about Hertzog's downfall. Lawrence E. Neame, *General Hertzog: Prime Minister of the Union of South Africa since 1924* (1930), is an English view of the Boer statesman.

Additional Sources

Coetzer, Alta, *Generaal Hertzog in beeld,* Johannesburg: Perskor; 1991.

Esterhuysen, Matthys van As., *The era of the generals = Die era van die generaals: a portrayal of the medals and commemorative awards in honour of General Louis Botha, Jan Christiaan Smuts and James Barry Munnik Hertzog . . . ,* Pretoria: National Cultural History and Open Air Museum, 1974.

Nienaber, Petrus Johannes, 1910- ed. *Gedenkboek Generaal J. B. M. Hertzog,* Johannesburg, Afrikaanse Pers-Boekhandel, 1965.

Generaal J.B.M. Hertzog: sy strewe en stryd, Johannesburg: Perskor, 1987.

Meiring, Piet, *Generaal Hertzog, 50 jaar daarna,* Johannesburg: Perskor, 1986.

Scholtz, Gert Daniel, *Generaals Hertzog en Smuts en die Britse Ryk,* Johannesburg: Randse Afrikaanse Universiteit, c1974. □

Heruy Wäldä-Sellasé

Heruy Wäldä-Sellasé (1878-1938) was an Ethiopian writer and director of the government press who encouraged and significantly advanced the writing and publication of books in Amharic, Ethiopia's national language.

Heruy Wäldä-Sellasé was born on May 7, 1878, in Shoa. His early years are shrouded in mystery, but he probably was one of the gifted young men of humble origin whom Emperor Menilek selected for high civil service posts. Heruy's interest in learning and literature first showed in his catalog of the Geez and Amharic manuscripts in Ethiopia. The third book to be printed in Addis Ababa, it appeared in 1911-1912.

When Ras Tafari (later Haile Selassie) was chosen as regent in 1917, Heruy was appointed mayor of Addis Ababa and director of the government press. In this latter capacity he considerably increased the printing of books, which were mostly of a devotional or educational kind, but which also included praise poems in honor of the Empress Zawditu and Ras Tafari and anonymous pamphlets in verse advocating modernization of the country. Heruy himself contributed several volumes: a biography of Emperor Yohannes, a collection of funeral songs, and a volume of moral meditations.

During the early 1920s Heruy traveled widely in Europe and the Middle East, accompanying the regent on his journeys, of which he wrote the official accounts: this was an excellent way of bringing knowledge of the outside world to the semiliterate Ethiopian audience. Besides producing further volumes devoted to religion, practical ethics, and the history of Ethiopia, he published an important collection of qenè, the traditional hymns of the Coptic Church. In 1927-1928 Heruy set up his own press in the hope of stimulating the production of creative literature more efficiently than could be done by the government press.

After Ras Tafari's accession to the imperial throne as Haile Selassie in 1930, Heruy was appointed foreign minister. In spite of the duties of his office and of his travels to Japan and Europe, his literary activity continued unabated. In addition to his educational writings, he promoted the growth of Amharic prose fiction. The first novel in Amharic, by Afäwärq Gäbrä Lyasus, had been printed in Rome in 1909. The second was Heruy's *Thoughts of the Heart: The Marriage of Berhané and Seyon Mogasa* (1930/1931), a slight story designed to discourage the Ethiopian custom of child marriage. More ambitious was *The New World* (1932/1933), which deals with a young Ethiopian who has an opportunity to study in Europe; on returning to his native country, he meets almost insuperable difficulties in his attempts to eradicate obsolete customs, to purify the corrupt clergy, and to introduce such emblems of Westernization as the telephone and the phonograph. This story, somewhat crude and unappetizingly edifying, is probably the first treatment of an African's direct contact with Europe in African prose fiction.

One of Heruy's most significant works of the early 1930s was the chronicle of his journey to Japan, a country which held peculiar fascination for Ethiopia because of its success in resisting European imperialism and in assimilating nonetheless the technological civilization of the West.

After the Italian invasion and the defeat of Ethiopia in 1936, Heruy followed the Emperor to his British exile. He

died in the monarch's residence in Bath on Sept. 29, 1938, after several months' illness.

Further Reading

A section on Heruy is in Edward Ullendorff, *The Ethiopians: An Introduction to Country and People* (1960; 2d ed. 1965). A detailed discussion of Heruy's writings is in Albert S. Gérard, *Four African Literatures* (1971). □

Gerhard Herzberg

The German-born Canadian chemist/physicist Gerhard Herzberg (born 1904) was famous for his spectral analysis of molecules and atoms. He was one of only three Canadians to win a Nobel Prize.

Born in Hamburg, Germany, on Christmas day, 1904, he was the younger son of Albin and Ella Herzberg. Gerhard early showed an interest in science. However, his life was disrupted at the age of 10 when his father died, and his mother was later forced to emigrate alone to the United States to work as a housekeeper.

He originally had hoped to become an astronomer but was told by the director of a German observatory that there was no point in going into the field unless he had a private income. So he went on to take a course in engineering physics, supported in part by a scholarship offered by a wealthy industrialist.

His genius showed early, and by the age of 24 he had already published 12 papers on atomic and molecular physics.

In 1924, while at the Darmstadt Technical University, he embarked on work in the area that eventually brought him his Nobel award. After reading Sommerfeld's classic book on atomic structure and spectral lines he fixed on spectroscopy—the study of light waves and other radiation which molecules and atoms can be made to emit or absorb—as his central scientific interest. Having obtained his doctorate in 1928, he spent the following year at the University of Gottingen. There he and a group of other young physicists eagerly applied the principles of quantum mechanics to obtain a fuller understanding of the electronic structures of atoms and molecules.

In 1929 he spent a second post-doctoral year at the University of Bristol in England where he photographed and analyzed the spectra of phosphorus carbide molecules, among others. During this year he returned briefly to Gottingen and married Luise Dettinger, a Jewish physics student. This marriage was to have significant ramifications in Herzberg's life after the Nazis came to power.

From 1930 to 1935 he worked as a *privatodozent* at Darmstadt Technical University. A *privatodozent* in the German academic system is able to give private lectures at the university for which he receives a fee. In addition, Herzberg supervised undergraduate laboratories.

At Darmstadt he collaborated in research with the Hungarian-born inventor of the hydrogen bomb, Edward Teller. He also began the first of his attempts to apply his spectroscopic efforts to astrophysics—in this case, the oxygen molecule observed in the atmosphere of the sun.

In 1933 he began to look for work outside of Germany because the Nazis introduced laws banning professors with Jewish wives from teaching at universities. His wife had already begun collaborating with him on a number of papers. In 1935 a former student of his named John Spinks obtained for him a post at the unlikely site of the University of Saskatchewan, located in the middle of the Canadian prairies. He arrived there with the equivalent of $2.50 in his pocket.

Even though the university was nearly bankrupt, Herzberg was able to turn it into a world center for spectrographic research in the ten years he stayed there. He and his wife also began a family, starting with his son Paul, born in 1936, and followed by his daughter Agnes, born in 1938.

While in Saskatchewan he started his work on "free radicals." These are molecular fragments which appear for millionths of a second when molecules are breaking apart and combining in new structures. These chemical reactions are of increasing interest to atmospheric scientists who are studying their relation to pollution in the Earth's upper atmosphere.

"Knowledge of their (free radicals) importance is of fundamental importance to our understanding of how chemical reactions proceed," said the Nobel committee in giving Herzberg his prize. It took Herzberg 14 years of research before he could identify one of these free radicals.

Herzberg also was one of the first to suggest the existence of molecules in space. His claim was initially disputed by other scientists who thought that the ultraviolet rays which are partially blocked out by the Earth's atmosphere would break down all space-born molecules into simple elements. Herzberg also was able to identify some of the elements that make up comets from spectrographic readings.

Before he left Germany, Herzberg completed the first of his classic books of spectroscopy, entitled *Atomic Spectra and Atomic Structure* (1937, 1944). Barred from working on major wartime research during much of World War II because he was legally an alien, Herzberg produced the first two volumes of his three-volume work on the structure and spectra of molecules (*Molecular Spectra and Molecular Structure,* 1939, 1945, 1966). Toward the end of the war the Canadian government put his talents to work analyzing the detonation characteristics of explosives.

In 1945 Herzberg went to Yerkes Observatory, which belongs to the University of Chicago, and stayed there for three years. It was in Chicago that his youthful interest in astronomy and his chemical training were reunited in an extensive analysis of various stellar substances. Unhappy with living in Chicago, he returned to Canada in 1948 to become director of physics at the Canadian government's National Research Council (NRC) in Ottawa, Ontario.

In the region around Ottawa he was able to continue his life-long love of hiking and regularly entertained colleagues and friends alike with his other passion—Germanlieder singing. At the NRC he became a mentor for several generations of Canadian and foreign researchers, impressing them with the unfailing good humor with which he approached life and an almost superhuman capacity for work. When he reached retirement age in 1969, the NRC created its highest grade, distinguished research officer, to allow him to continue his personal research. This he continued to do into his 80s.

It was during this time that he became a leading spokesman against Canadian government efforts to gain more political control over science. He remained a strong advocate of pure research in a Canadian political milieu that increasingly emphasized industry-directed research.

His wife died in 1971, the same year he received the Nobel Prize in chemistry. In 1972 he married Monika Tenthoff, the niece of a close friend he had known during high school.

The Nobel Prize was only one of a number of awards Herzberg received during a scientific career which produced 246 publications. He lectured extensively around the world and received honorary degrees from 35 universities.

About his method of approaching science, Herzberg said in 1984, "In a good sense, I am like a beaver . . . I don't have all that many problems which are brilliant but if it is a problem I think is important I persist in it."

His contributions to Canadian science were further recognized in 1975 when the NRC's astrophysics and spectroscopy units were reorganized as the Herzberg Institute of Astrophysics, where he continued his research and teaching into his 90s.

Herzberg has added to the lengthy list of accolades and prizes he has already won with awards for scientific achievement from Europe, North America and Japan. In 1987, minor planet 3316 = 1984 CN1 was officially named Herzberg in his honor.

In 1992, Herzberg was appointed a Member of the Queen's Privy Council for Canada, which is that democratic country's equivalent of a British title. Thus, he became formally addressed as the Honourable Gerhard Herzberg, PC.

Further Reading

There are no book-length accounts of Herzberg's life. A shorter account appears in the *The Canadian Who's Who,* Toronto: University of Toronto Press, Lumley, Elizabeth, (editor) (1996).

The Internet web facilities provided by the Centre for Systems Science at Simon Fraser University should be browsed for a detailed listing of Herzberg's international scientific awards and an encapsulated biography of his life and achievements. Good information can be found by doing a general search on the internet for "Gerhard Herzberg." □

Aleksandr Ivanovich Herzen

The Russian author and political agitator Aleksandr Ivanovich Herzen (1812-1870) developed a socialist philosophy that was the ideological basis for much of the revolutionary activity in Russia.

Aleksandr Herzen, whose real surname was Yakovlev, was born on March 25, 1812, in Moscow. He was the illegitimate son of a wealthy Moscow aristocrat, Ivan Alexeevich Yakovlev, and a German woman of humble birth. Herzen was 13 when the Decembrist rising took place, and he was present at the thanksgiving service in the Kremlin after the hangings. The scene made a lasting impression on him. His foreign tutors exposed him to radical ideas, and in his early teens he dedicated himself to the fight for freedom. In 1829 Herzen entered the University of Moscow to study natural sciences and became the leader of a small group of like-minded students. The news of the fighting on the barricades in Paris in July 1830 and the November rebellion in Warsaw profoundly moved them.

Influence of Saint-Simon

During his university years Herzen and his friends discovered the writings of the Comte de Saint-Simon and Charles Fourier. Socialist teachings were just beginning to take root in Russia. What impressed Herzen most was Saint-Simon's vision of mankind totally regenerated by a new Christianity, a faith that exalted both the individual and the community. He was fascinated by Saint-Simon's doctrines that denounced the failings of the existing order and promised to stop the exploitation of man by man. He was somewhat repelled by Saint-Simon's emphasis on the role of government and was inclined to accept Fourier's plan for phalansteries that relied on private initiative and the free cooperation of the workers. The French Revolution, the Polish uprising, and the teachings of Saint-Simon made him feel that the time was ripe for change.

Arrest and Deportation

Herzen completed his studies in 1833, and his circle broke up the following year, when he and his lifelong friend Nikolai Ogarev were arrested. The charge against them was that they sang songs containing "vile and ill-intentioned expressions against the oath of allegiance to the monarch." The official investigators considered Herzen to be "a bold free thinker, very dangerous to society." Herzen and Ogarev were suspected of having founded a secret organization aiming to overthrow the existing order through the propagation of revolutionary ideas permeated with Saint-Simon's pernicious doctrine. The two friends were deported to the provinces, where Herzen remained until 1842.

Toward the end of his confinement and afterward Herzen studied the works of G. W. F. Hegel. He perceived in the Hegelian dialectical conception of history a sanction for political and social change. If, as Hegal maintained, everything real is rational, Herzen then thought that rebellion against the order of things grown oppressive is also justified by reason. Herzen concluded that the "philosophy of Hegel is the algebra of revolution."

Protagonist of Westernism

Moscow was the Slavophile center, and Herzen participated in the endless disputations that raged in the literary salons there. He found Slavophile theories extremely dangerous, seeing in them "fresh oil for anointing the Czar, new claims laid upon thought." By 1845 the relations between the Slavophiles and the Westerners were severed. Nevertheless, Herzen retained a certain predilection for some ideas of the Slavophiles. He shared the Slavophiles' partiality for everything Russian and their faith in the common people, and he was impressed by the Slavophile emphasis on the collectivist spirit of the Russian folk, as it was embodied in the *obshchina* (village commune).

Travel Abroad

Herzen went abroad with his family in 1847 to escape the suffocating atmosphere of despotism of Nicholas I. He never returned to Russia. His first experience with life in western Europe was disheartening. Herzen discovered that France was dominated by the bourgeoisie, the segment of the population that had appropriated all the gains of the Revolution. He thought the bourgeoisie had all the vices of the nobleman and the plebeian and none of the virtues, and he rarely wavered in his dislike of the European middle class.

As Herzen's disillusionment with the West deepened, his country appeared to him in a different light. He came to believe that the Slavophiles were right: unlike effete Europe, Russia was full of vigor, self-confidence, and courage. Like most Slavs, Russians "belonged to geography, rather than to history." Above all, Russia possessed the village commune, "the life-giving principle of the Russian people." Herzen argued that the commune was in effect the seed of a socialist society because of its tradition of equality, collective owner-ship of land, and communal self-government. The Russian *muzhik* (peasant) was the man of destiny. Since the Russian *muzhik*'s whole existence was keyed to a collective way of life, Russia, or rather Slavdom, was in a position to assure the triumph of socialism. Taking advantage of Russian back-wardness and European experience, Russia might indeed bypass capitalism and middle-class culture on its way to socialism.

In 1852 Herzen arrived in London. He was a bereaved and heartbroken man; one of his small sons and his mother had been drowned, and his wife had died in childbirth afterward. He desperately needed work in which he could submerge himself, and he used a portion of his considerable inheritance to set up the Free Russian Press in 1853.

The first pages produced were an appeal to the gentry to take the initiative in liberating the serfs. Otherwise, Herzen held that the serfs would be emancipated by the Czar, strengthening his despotism, or else abolition would come as the result of the popular uprising. He went on to tell the landlords that Russia was on the eve of an overturn, which would be close to the heart of the people living out their lives within the commune. Herzen concluded, "Russia will have its rendezvous with revolution in socialism."

The "Bell"

On July 1, 1857, Herzen with Ogarev's help launched *Kolokol* (the *Bell*), first as a monthly, then as a biweekly. The *Bell* summoned the living to bury the past and work for the glorious future. It spoke for freedom and against oppression, for reason and against prejudice, for science and against fanaticism, for progressive peoples and against backward governments. Specifically, the *Bell* was dedicated to the "liberation of Russia."

Since Herzen had the privilege of freedom from censor-ship, his office at the *Bell* was flooded with communications from Russia, and there was a constant stream of Russian visitors. With their help and that of scores of correspondents scattered through Russia, the *Bell* conducted a most suc-cessful muckraking campaign. It cited particulars and named names. Minutes of secret sessions of the highest bodies appeared in its columns. The journal was read by all literate Russia. Fear of exposure in the *Bell* became a deter-rent to administrative corruption, and there was talk in high government places of buying Herzen off, perhaps with an important post.

After the failure of the Polish rebellion of 1863 Herzen continued to berate the administration and to preach "Russian socialism," stemming from the *muzhik*'s way of life and reaching out for that "economic justice" which is a universal goal sanctioned by science. But the *Bell* was now

reduced in readership and influence. Herzen antagonized the many who had drifted to the right, as well as the few who had moved to the left. In 1868 the *Bell* was silenced for good, and on Jan. 9, 1870, Aleksandr Herzen, a crusading journalist possessed of a powerful pen, died in Paris.

Further Reading

Herzen's *My Past and Thoughts* (trans., 6 vols., 1924-1927), is a classic autobiography and an unsurpassed source of informa-tion and insight into the life of the Russian intelligentsia in the reign of Nicholas I. Martin E. Malia, *Alexander Herzen and the Birth of Russian Socialism, 1812-1855* (1961), is a bio-graphical study and an examination of the western European intellectual sources of Herzen's thought. Recommended for general historical background is Thomas G. Masaryk, *The Spirit of Russia: Studies in History, Literature, and Philosophy*, translated from the German by Eden and Cedar Paul (2 vols., 1919; 2d ed. 1955), a comprehensive survey of Russian spiritual culture that is significant for exploration of values of Russian culture. Franco Venturi, *Roots of Revolution: A His-tory of the Populist and Socialist Movements in Nineteenth Century Russia*, introduction by Isaiah Berlin (trans. 1960), is focused upon a single aspect of the development of 19th-century Russian thought. The treatment begins with Herzen and ends with the assassination of Alexander II.

Additional Sources

Acton, Edward, *Alexander Herzen and the role of the intellectual revolutionary*, Cambridge Eng.; New York: Cambridge Uni-versity Press, 1979.

Carr, Edward Hallett, *The romantic exiles: a nineteenth-century portrait gallery*, New York: Octagon Books, 1975; Cam-bridge, Mass.: MIT Press, 1981.

Herzen, Alexander, *Childhood, youth, and exile: parts I and II of My past and thoughts*, Oxford; New York: Oxford University Press, 1980.

Herzen, Alexander, *Letters from France and Italy, 1847-1851*, Pittsburgh, Pa.: University of Pittsburgh Press, 1995.

Herzen, Alexander, *The memoirs of Alexander Herzen, parts I and I*, New York: Russell & Russell, 1967; Westport, Conn.: Greenwood Press, 1976.

Herzen, Alexander, *My past and thoughts: the memoirs of Alex-ander Herzen*, New York: Knopf; distributed by Random House, 1973; New York, Vintage Books 1974, 1973.

Partridge, Monica, *Alexander Herzen, 1812-1870*, Paris: Unesco, 1984.

Zimmerman, Judith E., *Midpassage: Alexander Herzen and Euro-pean revolution, 1847-1852*, Pittsburgh, Pa.: University of Pittsburgh Press, 1989. ☐

Theodor Herzl

The Hungarian-born Austrian Jewish author Theodor Herzl (1860-1904) founded the World Zionist Orga-nization and served as its first president.

Theodor Herzl, son of Jacob and Jeanette Herzl, was born on May 2, 1860, in Budapest, Hungary, where he attended elementary and secondary schools. In 1878 he was admitted as a law student to the University of Vienna, but after a year of legal studies he switched to journalism. He worked for the *Allgemeine Zeitung* of Vienna until 1892, when he took an assignment in Paris as correspondent for the Vienna *Neue Freie Presse*. In this capacity he reported on the Dreyfus Affair in 1894, and he was greatly troubled by the anti-Semitism he saw in France at the time. In 1896 Herzl started his political career with the publication of his pamphlet *The Jewish State: An Attempt at a Modern Solution of the Jewish Question.*

According to *The Jewish State,* persecution could not destroy the Jewish people but would accomplish the opposite: it would strengthen Jewish identification. In Herzl's view, effective assimilation of the Jews would be impossible because of the long history of prejudice and the competition between the non-Jewish and Jewish middle classes. Because of conditions in the Jewish Diaspora, some communities might disintegrate, but the people as a whole would always survive. Herzl believed that the Jews had little choice but to begin the concentration of the Jewish people in one land under its own sovereign authority. To achieve this purpose, he organized the First Zionist Congress, which met in Basel, Switzerland, in August 1897. This meeting marked the establishment of the World Zionist Organization, whose executives were to be the diplomatic and administrative representatives of the Zionist movement. Herzl became president of the organization, a post he held until his death.

The official goal of the World Zionist Organization was the establishment of ''a secured homeland in Palestine for the Jewish people.'' Because Palestine was part of Turkey and because Germany enjoyed a special relationship with

Turkey, in 1898 Herzl met with Kaiser William II in an unsuccessful effort to win his support. In May 1901 Herzl was received by the sultan of Turkey, Abdul-Hamid II. But this meeting too had no positive results, since Turkey was not willing to allow mass immigration without restrictions to Palestine.

In view of the deteriorating situation of eastern European Jewry, Herzl considered other territorial solutions for the Jewish problem. The British government suggested Uganda for the Jewish mass immigration, but this plan was rejected by the Fourth Zionist Congress in 1903, which again stated the ultimate goal of Zionism as the establishment of a Jewish national home in Palestine.

During the Uganda polemics Theodor Herzl showed signs of grave illness. On July 3, 1904, he died and was buried in Vienna. According to his wishes, his remains were transferred by the government of the independent state of Israel to Jerusalem in 1949 and buried on Mt. Herzl, the national cemetery of Israel.

Further Reading

The Complete Diaries of Theodor Herzl was edited by Raphael Patai (5 vols., 1960) and is also available in several abridged editions. Two biographies are Alex Bein, *Theodor Herzl: A Biography* (trans. 1940), and Israel Cohen, *Theodor Herzl* (1959).

Additional Sources

Beller, Steven, *Herzl,* New York: Grove Weidenfeld, 1991.

Blau, Eric, *The beggar's cup,* New York: Knopf, 1993.

Braham, Mark, *Jews don't hate: how a Jewish newspaper died,* London, Nelson, 1970.

Elon, Amos, *Herz,* New York: Holt, Rinehart and Winston 1975; Schocken Books, 1986, 1975.

Falk, Avner, *Herzl, king of the Jews: a psychoanalytic biography of Theodor Herzl,* Lanham: University Press of America, 1993.

Finkelstein, Norman H., *Theodor Herzl,* New York: F. Watts, 1987; Minneapolis, MN: Lerner Publications Co., 1991.

Gurko, Miriam, *Theodor Herzl, the road to Israel,* Philadelphia: Jewish Publication Society, 1988.

Handler, Andrew, *Dori, the life and times of Theodor Herzl in Budapest (1860-1878),* University, Ala.: University of Alabama Press, 1983.

Hein, Virginia Herzog., *The British followers of Theodor Herzl: English Zionist leaders, 1896-1904,* New York: Garland Pub., 1987.

Herzl, Theodor, *The Jewish state,* New York: Dover Publications, 1988.

Jewish Community House of Bensonhurst. *Herzl comes home: 22nd anniversary Jewish Community House, Nov. 20, 1949,* Brooklyn: Jewish Community House, 1949.

Kornberg, Jacques, *Herzl year book,* New York: Herzl Press, 1958-.

Kotker, Norman, *Herzl, the kin,* New York, Scribner, 1972.

Mystics, philosophers, and politicians: essays in Jewish intellectual history in honor of Alexander Altmann, Durham, N.C.: Duke University Press, 1982.

Pawel, Ernst, *The labyrinth of exile: a life of Theodor Herzl,* New York: Farrar, Straus & Giroux, 1989.

The Psychoanalytic interpretation of history, New York, Basic Books, 1971.

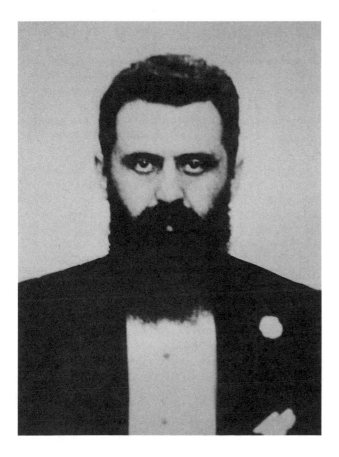

The Rise of Israel: From precursors of Zionism to Herzl, New York: Garland Pub., 1987.

The Rise of Israel: Herzl's political activity, 1897-1904, New York: Garland Pub., 1987.

Sela, Jaim, *Teodoro Herzl,* Jerusalem, Israel: La Semana Publicaciones, 1983.

Sternberger, Ilse, *Princes without a home: modern Zionism and the strange fate of Theodore Herzl's children, 1900-1945,* San Francisco: International Scholars Publications, 1994.

Stewart, Desmond, *Theodor Herzl,* Garden City, N.Y., Doubleday, 1974.

Theodor Herzl: a memorial, Westport, Conn.: Hyperion Press, 1976, 1929.

Vital, David, *The origins of Zionism,* Oxford Eng.: Clarendon Press, 1975. □

Chaim Herzog

Sixth president of the state of Israel, Chaim Herzog (1918-1997) was appointed by the Knesset in 1983 and reelected to a second five-year term in 1988.

At a troubled time for Israel, President Chaim Herzog came to represent one of the country's few effective unifying forces in the early 1990s, earning respect in most quarters of a divisive society through his high visibility, personal dignity, and political tact. Exercising limited, largely ceremonial powers of office, he missed no occasion to remind countrymen of those historical, religious, and cultural roots that, reinforced by present common security concerns, ultimately bind together the Jewish state and the peoples of Israel.

Reviewing Chaim Herzog's biography suggests how his background, education, and entire professional experience—lawyer, career military officer, author, ambassador to the United Nations, member of the Israeli parliament—may have prepared him for the sensitive role he was to play in Israeli nation-building during his presidency.

From Ireland to Israel

Chaim Herzog was born in Belfast on September 17, 1918, but immigrated to Palestine at the age of 17 when his father, then chief rabbi of Ireland, was appointed in 1935 spiritual leader of the Jewish homeland. As a result, Chaim received a diversified education: three years of talmudic training at the Hebron Yeshiva, then on to Wesley College (Dublin), the Government of Palestine Law School (Jerusalem), London University, and Cambridge University, eventually earning a law degree from London University (LL.B, 1941).

The advent of World War II fundamentally altered his career plans. Enlisting in the British Army (1939-1945), Herzog attended officer candidate school at the Royal Military College (Sandhurst), was wounded in tank combat, and eventually directed British intelligence operations in northern Germany. Following discharge in 1945 with the rank of lieutenant colonel, he proceeded to join *Haganah,* the Jewish underground movement in Palestine, taking part in

the fighting in the Jerusalem sector during Israel's 1948 war of independence. Prime Minister David Ben-Gurion then appointed him director of military intelligence for the Israel Defense Forces (IDF) from 1948 to 1950.

Herzog's next posting was military attaché in North America: first in Washington, D.C. (1950-1953), and then in Ottawa, Canada (1953-1954). Returning to Israel, he was given field command in the years 1954-1959 and then completed a second stint as chief of IDF intelligence before retiring from active military service as a major general in 1962.

While building up his private legal practice Herzog also concentrated on various business enterprises, serving as managing director of G.U.S. Industries in Tel-Aviv from 1962 to 1972. Once again, however, war intervened; this time the 1967 Middle East crisis. During the stressful period preceding Israel's stunning victory in the June Six Day War, Reserve General Chaim Herzog gained wide public recognition and acclaim for his insightful radio commentary on the daily geopolitical currents and later battlefield developments in and around Israel which helped to boost the nation's morale. Immediately following the conflict he briefly accepted appointment as first military governor of the administered West Bank territory.

Public and Private Life

This pattern of transition from public to private life and back again repeated itself in 1973 when the sudden and traumatic Yom Kippur War launched against Israel by Syria and Egypt once more called Chaim Herzog to the role of military analyst. Once the crisis was weathered he spent the next three years writing an acclaimed book on the 1973 war, lecturing abroad, and heading his successful Tel-Aviv law firm. But then followed three challenging years in New York as head of the Israeli mission to the United Nations at a time when his country was threatened with international isolation and the increased popularity of the rival Palestinian Liberation Organization (PLO). Nevertheless, Herzog rose to the occasion, defending Israel with both eloquence and conviction. His finest moment came on November 10, 1975, when Ambassador Herzog, in a defiant gesture of contempt from the rostrum of the UN General Assembly, tore in two the recently-adopted resolution defining Zionism as "a form of racism," denouncing it as an infamous act against the Jewish people.

Returning to Israel in 1978, Herzog combined legal practice with domestic political and party activity on behalf of the Ma'arach Labour alignment and was rewarded by a seat in the Knesset following the 1981 elections. When the presidency became vacant in March 1983, he was chosen in a Knesset secret ballot to the position, in spite of the fact that the rival Likud coalition enjoyed a majority in the house. Many observers attributed the surprise outcome to interparty political maneuvering, but others saw the explanation in Herzog's national stature and obvious qualifications.

President Herzog

Once inaugurated, President Herzog worked hard at reaffirming his commitment to preserve the symbolic, apolitical, nonpartisan nature of the position. As the only president to serve two terms, he boldly spoke out on issues of burning and national concern, denouncing excessive violence in the territories; opposing ethnic, religious, or ideological extremism; campaigning for road safety and environmental protectionism; calling for greater governmental and bureaucratic efficiency; and promoting the absorption of Ethiopian and Russian Jewry. While calling for greater national unity, he also undertook the assignment of goodwill ambassador, unflinchingly objecting to unfair criticism of Israel abroad while paying state visits to the United States, the Far East, and a number of European countries. After the establishment of diplomatic relations between Israel and China on January 24, 1992, he was invited to Beijing in December, becoming the first Israeli president to visit China. President Herzog came to represent the conscience and voice of Israel both at home and within the international community.

Since leaving Beit Hanassi in 1993, Herzog has been invited to sit on national and international boards of both commercial and noncommerical organizations and institutions. He took an active part in the activities of the Council for Promoting Israel-China relations after it was established in Tel Aviv in 1996.

Chaim Herzog died of pnuemonia in April 1997.

Further Reading

Although no biography has been written on Chaim Herzog, he is himself the author of several books about Israel which intersperse autobiographical material and personal viewpoints with the larger struggle by Israel for security in both peace and war. These books include *Israel's Finest Hour* (1967); *Days of Awe* (1973); *The War of Atonement* (1975); a compilation of his UN speeches, *Who Stands Accused?* (1978); *Battles of the Bible* (1978); and *The Arab- Israeli Wars* (1982). □

Roman Herzog

Roman Herzog (born 1934) was a politician and, beginning in 1987, president of the German Federal Constitutional Court. He was elected president of Germany in 1994 as the candidate of the Christian Democratic Union and Christian Social Union.

Roman Herzog was born on April 5, 1934, in Landshut, a small city in Bavaria. His father was an employee in a tobacco plant and later became an archivist and director of a museum. The young Herzog, who had taken Latin at the secondary school, taught it to his father, who needed it in his new career.

Recipient of a Bavarian state scholarship, Roman Herzog studied law in Munich. In 1958, one year after passing the first bar examination, he received the degree of doctor of jurisprudence. For the next six years he was assistant to an ultraconservative law professor. From 1964 to 1966 Herzog taught law at the University of Munich. In 1966 he became professor of law and politics at the Free University of Berlin. Three years later he accepted a similar position at the University of Administrative Sciences in Speyer, where he also served as president from 1971 to 1972.

Early Political Career

In 1970 Herzog joined the Christian Democratic Union (CDU), the conservative party, which at the time was the chief national opposition party to the government in Bonn, the capital of what was then West Germany. Helmut Kohl, then the CDU minister-president of Rhineland-Palatinate and future German chancellor, was impressed by Herzog's successful academic and administrative career. In 1973 Kohl, as minister-president, appointed Herzog to the position of state secretary. For the next five years Herzog was the chief representative of the state of Rhineland-Palatinate in Bonn and became one of Kohl's close unofficial advisers.

After moving to Stuttgart in 1978, Herzog became minister of culture and then minister of the interior in the Baden-Wuerttemberg CDU-led cabinets. In the latter position he pursued a tough law and order policy. For instance, he required participants in illegal sit-down demonstrations to pay fines that were used to offset the cost of the extra police units marshaled to break up the demonstrations. In 1982 Herzog recommended that the police be better armed to

fight the state's radical opponents. Civil libertarians, including the state commissioner for data protection, took issue with his policies limiting the civil rights of individuals.

In 1983 Herzog gave up his post as deputy in the state parliament, to which he had been elected three years earlier, and his post in the cabinet in order to serve as a judge on the Federal Constitutional Court. He was appointed vice-president of the court to the consternation of the Social Democratic Party, then in opposition in Bonn. Despite his earlier conservative political positions, Herzog, who became president of the court in 1987, voted with the majority of judges in an important case declaring a state prohibition against demonstrations near a nuclear power plant unconstitutional. The judges said that the law had violated the citizens' right to assemble freely.

Presidential Candidate

In 1993 the major political parties selected candidates for the federal presidency in an election scheduled for mid-1994. The Christian Democratic Union (CDU) and its Bavarian ally, the Christian Social Union (CSU), chose Steffen Heitmann, Saxony's minister of justice; the Social Democratic Party chose Johannes Rau; the liberal Free Democratic Party chose Hildegard Hamm-Brücher; and independents chose Walter Jens. Soon after Chancellor Kohl nominated Heitmann for the candidacy in October 1993 a bitter controversy erupted over the nominee. Heitmann not only alienated his party's foes but also many of his party's members with his ultraconservative statements on social and political issues. When the controversy could

not be contained, Heitmann withdrew his candidacy, which was a bitter defeat for Kohl.

The CDU/CSU had to choose a new nominee for the five-year post. In January 1994 the executive committees of the CDU and the CSU nearly unanimously endorsed the candidacy of Herzog for the presidency. Only weeks earlier he had said in jest that the party should choose any candidate as long as the name was not Herzog. Once nominated, he said on a more somber note that the president should, through nonpartisan speeches, set a moral tone for the country and thereby play more than the role of ceremonial chief of state that the constitution specifies. Some presidents, such as Richard von Weizsäcker, in office from 1984 to 1994, fit such a model. The president is to be selected by a special assembly made up of all members of Parliament and an equal number of electors from the state parliaments. They choose among the candidates nominated by the parties. A majority of votes is necessary in the first two rounds, but in the third round a plurality of votes suffices for election, and on this ballot Herzog triumphed with 696 votes to 605 for Social Democrat candidate Johannes Rau.

More than a Symbolic Head of State

In his effort to set a moral tone for the country, Herzog tried to reconcile Germany's past with the present. He reminded Germans not to forget about their history, particularly the tragedies of World War II, but he also encouraged them not to be overwhelmed by their past. Racial prejudice and old wounds from history were seen by Herzog as issues dividing Germany. While the presidency of Germany is a ceremonial position and the president is not allowed to engage formally in political issues, Herzog nonetheless made his opinions known. He was a strong supporter of European integration and won the Charlemagne Prize in 1997 for promoting European unity. He also sought to mitigate tensions among opposing political parties through informal means, so that they could better deal with the country's problems, such as high unemployment rates.

Private Life

Herzog's political and judicial activities did not hinder him from devoting time to his high positions in the Protestant Church, including his six-year chairmanship of the CDU/CSU Protestant Working Group. In addition, he was a prolific writer, co-editing a leading law commentary on the constitution and a Protestant encyclopedia. He continued to teach part-time at the universities in Speyer and Tübingen.

Further Reading

There is no biography of Herzog in English. He wrote or coedited many volumes on constitutional law, including *Verfassungsrecht* (1978) and *Unser Recht: die wichtigsten Gesetze für den Staatsbürger* (1991); For an analysis of the Constitutional Court on which Herzog served see Donald P. Kommers, *Judicial Politics in West Germany: A Study of the Federal Constitutional Court* (1976).

"Germany's Herzog Urges Europe to Back Integration." *Reuters Ltd.*, 8 May 1997.

"Germany's Herzog Warns Against Danger of Prejudice." *Reuters Ltd.*, 2 March 1997.

Heneghan, Tom. "Herzog Honours Nazi Victims, Urges New Ways to Remember." *Reuters Ltd.,* 19 January 1996.

Herbst-Bayliss. "Kohl's Policies Attacked After Record Jobless Rate." *Reuters Business Report,* 9 February 1997.

Konstantinova, Elisaveta. "Hecklers Call Herzog "Traitor" Over German Border." *Reuters Ltd.,* 8 September 1996.

"Roman's Law." *The Economist* 342 (March 22, 1997): 66. □

Theodore Martin Hesburgh

Theodore Martin Hesburgh (born 1917) was an activist American Catholic priest who was president of Notre Dame, 1952-1987. He served on the Civil Rights Commission from 1957 to 1972, becoming both its most outspoken member and its chairman. He was also active in the anti-Vietnam War movement and in efforts to improve the treatment of illegal aliens.

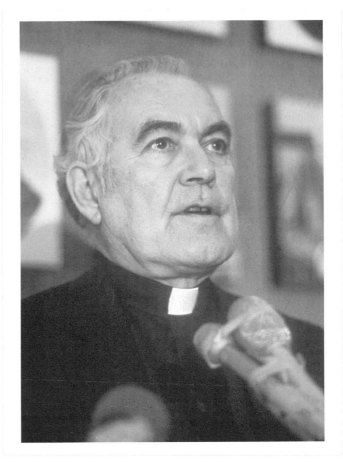

Theodore Martin Hesburgh was born May 25, 1917, in Syracuse, New York, to Theodore Barnard Hesburgh and Ann Marie Murphy Hesburgh. A product of the "Catholic ghetto," he attended only Roman Catholic schools and felt called to be a priest while only in grade school. Following graduation from high school in 1934 he entered the Order of the Congregation of the Holy Cross and began his undergraduate studies at the University of Notre Dame that fall. He was graduated from Gregorian University in 1939 with a Ph.D. degree and entered the seminary at Holy Cross College, Washington, D.C., in 1940. Hesburgh was ordained a Roman Catholic priest in 1943 and was awarded an S.T.D. degree by Catholic University in 1945.

With the massive return of war veterans to college, Notre Dame called him to be chaplain to the student veterans, which he did until becoming assistant professor and head of the Department of Religion in 1948. One year later he was named executive vice president of Notre Dame and in 1952 succeeded Reverend John J. Cavanaugh as president. The institution's reputation at that time centered on its football prowess, academic mediocrity, and production of loyal Catholics. Notre Dame's faculty were often chosen more for their orthodoxy than intellect.

Cavanaugh had succeeded in persuading alumni that academic quality was as important as athletic success, and the 32-year-old Hesburgh inherited an institution ready for excellence. He quickly let it be known that he was no great lover of football nor did he reverently value all the school's tradition. His consummate skill in public relations enabled him to convince alumni that football was not enough and that he had a dream of taking Cardinal Newman's 19th century "idea of a university" and forming Notre Dame into "America's first truly great Catholic university."

He began reforming by undertaking an eight-year building program which dramatically altered the campus skyline. He also restructured the control of the university away from the church and into the hands of a lay-dominated board of trustees. This act in itself set a precedent for other Catholic colleges and universities to follow. Over the first 20 years of Hesburgh's presidency the academic standards were raised, a high-quality faculty became relevant to both the hiring of staff and recruitment of students, salaries were brought up to a competitive level, the budget and endowment were increased tremendously, the curriculum was modernized, and in 1972 Notre Dame became coeducational. All of this was accomplished while continuing to retain the moral quality of the school. The basic thrust of a Notre Dame education continued to be the molding of character.

By 1955 Theodore Hesburgh began to catch the eye of the establishment. The National Science Foundation was the first to ask him to serve, and then the invitations for him to be a member here or an adviser there began to snowball. In 1957 President Eisenhower tapped him to be one of the first members of the newly formed Civil Rights Commission, and it was through membership on this body that Hesburgh derived his public fame. The commission recommended far-ranging legislative solutions to racial problems, most of which were not acceptable to Congress or the president. Hesburgh quickly became the commission's most outspoken member, advocating fair housing legislation and especially busing "as a solution to the 'hopeless' cycle of poor education in poor neighborhoods." He served 15 years on the commission, the final three (1969-1972) as chairman.

The same deep commitment to civil rights which brought him to Eisenhower's attention in 1957 cost him his participation on the Civil Rights Commission. President

Nixon's Southern strategy—opposition to fair housing laws and the use of busing to achieve desegregation—was seriously challenged by the commission under Hesburgh's leadership. Shortly after the 1972 election he, along with 2,000 other appointed officials, was replaced in what the White House labeled a massive "housecleaning." Nixon showed his disdain for the Civil Rights Commission by neglecting to appoint a new chairman.

Hesburgh received a plethora of invitations to join private foundations, public commissions, and other service bodies. Capable as he was, it seemed at times as if he was simply "the necessary Catholic." He served on the National Science Board, as a trustee of the Rockefeller Foundation, and on the Carnegie Commission on Higher Education. The Vatican appointed him representative to the International Atomic Agency, and when President Johnson asked him in 1964 to take control of the space program he declined: "I couldn't see a Catholic priest handing out six billion dollars in contracts." He also refused President Nixon's 1969 offer to head the poverty program.

Despite the responsibilities of the Notre Dame presidency, Theodore Hesburgh remained very much involved in political and social affairs. He became extremely vocal in opposition to the Vietnam War and the draft, particularly following the Cambodian invasion. To many, this stance contradicted the tight control and suspension policy he exercised over student disruption at Notre Dame. He continued to be outspoken in many areas of concern, even publicly disagreeing with his church. His opposition to abortion was unwavering, but he believed the Vatican position on birth control to be a mistake. He supported celibacy for himself and those who choose it, but reminded his audience that the apostles were married and clergy in the Middle Ages "kept women." He disapproved of sex outside of marriage and was exceedingly proud of the fact that 93 percent of the marriages of Notre Dame alumni held together. He was an ardent supporter of the Equal Rights Amendment and answered his critics who said passage would have pushed women to become like men by saying, "I think women will have to work overtime to catch up with men at evildoing." He also advocated creation of a Palestinian homeland as part of an overall Middle East peace settlement.

Hesburgh's concern for the plight of illegal aliens (especially Hispanic) surfaced during the Johnson administration when he criticized the plight of the farmworkers in the president's own state of Texas. In 1979 he became chairman of the Select Commission on Immigration and Refugee Policy, a body created by Congress and the president. He continued to be vocal about widespread abuses of aliens and the seeming public indifference toward these people. This activism extended to root causes of political immigration, repression, and the sanctuary movement. In 1979 he also became chairperson of the Overseas Development Council. His ministry was focussed on Notre Dame, but obviously he saw the world as his parish. His success in reforming that institution extended to the necessity he saw for reforming society's ills. In 1986 he announced that he would retire after delivering the commencement address to the Notre Dame class of 1987. His successor was associate provost Reverend Edward A. (Monk) Malloy.

After his retirement from academic life, Father Hesburgh was elevated to Professor Emeritus status (from 1987), and maintained an active involvement on the several boards and committees to which he was elected. He has written *God, Country and Notre Dame,* (1990), and *Travels with Ted and Ned* (1992.) He has also written and edited, with George Marsden, *What Can Catholic Universities Learn from Protestant Examples?* in *The Challenge Promise of a Catholic University,* University of Notre Dame Press, (1995); and the foreword to *The Encyclopedia of Catholicism,* San Francisco: Harper/Collins, (1995).

Father Ted, as he preferred to be known, received many awards, including the Presidential Medal of Freedom, the U.S. Navy Distinguished Service Award, the Freedom Foundation Award, and the Hughes Award of the National Conference of Christians and Jews. He was also decorated as a Commander in *l'Ordre des Arts et des Lettres* by the French government. He was a member of the Catholic Theological Society, American Philosophical Society, Council on Foreign Relations, and National Academy of Education.

Further Reading

The only biography of Hesburgh in general circulation is Joel R. Connelly and Howard J. Dooley, *Hesburgh's Notre Dame* (1972), which is a non-scholarly slick view of limited value. The popular periodical press of the 1960s and 1970s (*TIME, Newsweek, LIFE,* etc.) contain many articles on the man and by him as issues at Notre Dame and causes he was involved in became newsworthy. He also wrote numerous essays for a myriad of periodicals. The following books by Hesburgh should provide additional insight: *Foreign Policy and Morality: Framework for a Moral Audit* (with Louis J. Halle, 1979); *God and the World of Man* (1950); *Patterns for Educational Growth* (1958); *The Hesburgh Papers: Higher Values in Higher Education* (1979); *The Humane Imperative: A Challenge for the Year 2000* (1974); *Theology of Catholic Action* (1945); and *Thoughts for Our Times* (a series beginning in 1962). □

Abraham Joshua Heschel

Abraham Joshua Heschel (1907-1972) was a Polish-born theologian, educator, and philosopher who sought to build a modern philosophy of religion on the basis of ancient Jewish tradition. Among other posts, he held the chair of professor of Jewish ethics and mysticism at the Jewish Theological Seminary of America, New York City.

With his birth in Warsaw, Poland, in 1907, Abraham Joshua Heschel entered a family that counted back seven generations of Hasidic rabbis. His father was Rabbi Moshe Mordecai, and his ancestors helped to found the Polish Hasidic movement, a Jewish sect of mystics, in the eighteenth century. Both his father and his mother, Reisel Perlow Heschel, instilled in him a love of learning as he grew up in the orthodox ghetto of Warsaw. As a young man, he wrote poetry, and his collection of Yiddish verse was published years later (1933) in his home city.

Student and Teacher Years

Following a traditional Jewish education in Warsaw, Heschel went to Berlin, where he studied at the university and also taught the Talmud, during 1932-33, at the Hochschule fur die Wissenschaft des Judentums. He earned his PhD degree from Berlin University in 1933 and accepted a fellowship at the Hochschule, graduating the following year. Over the next three years, three published works established him as a scholar and author of note: *Maimonides: Eine Biographie,* concerning the medieval Jewish philosopher (1935); *Die Prophetie,* on Hebrew prophesy (1936); and *Don Jizchak Abravalel,* about the fifteenth-century Jewish statesman of Spain (1937).

In 1937, Heschel went to Frankfurt am Main to teach at the noted Judisches Lehrhaus. But war clouds were gathering in Europe, and he was deported from Nazi Germany in 1938. He returned to Warsaw for a few months of teaching at the Institute of Judaistic Studies, but the Nazi invasion of his homeland forced him to London where he founded the Institute for Jewish Learning.

The United States had not yet entered World War II when Heschel arrived in Cincinnati, Ohio, where he joined the faculty of Hebrew Union College in 1940. Five years later he took the chair of professor of Jewish ethics and mysticism at Jewish Theological Seminary of America in New York City. Heschel, who became an American citizen in 1945, married concert pianist Sylvia Straus in 1946, and they had one daughter, Hannah. He remained at the Jewish Theological Seminary until his death in New York City on December 23, 1972.

Teachings and Published Works

Abraham Heschel wished to construct a modern philosophy of religion on the basis of ancient Jewish tradition and teachings. In traditional Jewish piety, he observed an inner depth of devotion that he sought to convey to twentieth-century humans. "The Jew is never alone in the face of God," he said, "for the Torah is always with him."

Heschel's concern for the piety of the individual involved him in the civil rights demonstrations of the 1960s and early 1970s to end discrimination against blacks in America. He was one of the first religious leaders in the United States to speak out against the escalating war in Vietnam. And he risked the wrath of fellow Jews by meeting with Pope Paul VI at the Vatican in Rome to discuss Jewish feelings concerning Vatican Council II. Some Jewish leaders objected to the trip, but Heschel felt it important that Jewish approval be added, if possible, to some of the Council's decrees, such as the denial of any Jewish guilt in the crucifixion of Jesus.

In addition to his teachings, Heschel is well known for his writings. They include: his magnum opus, *Man Is Not*

Alone: A Philosophy of Religion (1951), *The Sabbath: Its Meaning for Modern Man* (1951), *Man's Quest for God: Studies in Prayer and Symbolism* (1954), *God in Search of Man* (1955), *The Prophets* (1962), *Who Is Man?* (1965), and *The Insecurity of Freedom: Essays on Human Existence* (1966). These books provide insights into his existentialist philosophy of Judaism with its central concept based on a "theology of pathos," in which God is a god of pathos, "revealed in a personal and intimate relation to the world. . . . He is also moved and affected by what happens in the world and reacts accordingly." This divine pathos, in turn, evokes a human response of sympathy for God, by which "man experiences God as his own being"—Heschel's "religion of sympathy."

The element of time occupies an important place in Heschel's theology, since "Time is perpetual innovation, a synonym for continuous creation," and human existence in time is communion with God and a reaction to the continuous action of God. From this concept of time, Heschel derived his theory of human freedom as "a spiritual event." According to Heschel, the individual learns about God not by reason and intellect, but through experience, divine revelation, and sacred deeds, all of which enable the individual to form a relationship—a "leap of action" rather than of faith—with God.

In addition to his scholarly and philosophical writings, Heschel authored several works on Jewish life in eastern Europe. Chief among them is *The Earth Is the Lord's: The Inner World of the Jew in East Europe* (1950), in which he theorizes that the "golden age" of European Jewish life was in the Jewish culture of eastern Europe. In the 1960s Heschel was active in the movement to aid the Jews of the Soviet Union.

Further Reading

An excellent introduction to Heschel's thought is in *Between God and Man: An Interpretation of Judaism, from the Writings of Abraham J. Heschel,* selected, edited, and introduced by Fritz A. Rothschild (1959); See also: *Who's Who in America, New York Times,* Dec. 24, 1972. □

Michael Heseltine

One time defense secretary and environment secretary, Michael Heseltine (born 1933) was a key figure in British politics from the 1980s into the mid-1990s, first as a member of the Thatcher governments, then as an alternative Conservative voice to that of then Prime Minister Thatcher, and later as a member of the John Major government.

Michael (Ray Dibdin) Heseltine, having served as a junior and middle rank minister through the government of Edward Heath (1970-1974), became secretary of state for the environment when the Conservative Party returned to power in 1979 under Margaret Thatcher. Later he was secretary of state for defense, but he left the government dramatically, walking out of a Cabinet meeting in January 1986 in protest at her style of running the government. He then became on the backbenches a focus of an alternative Conservatism, preaching what he characterized as a "caring capitalism," taking a more enthusiastically pro-European Community line than Thatcher, and opposing some of the government's more controversial policies, such as the (community charge) poll tax. He succeeded in defying the laws of gravity which normally ensure that ministers who resign office steadily disappear from public view. Instead, Heseltine toured the country speaking at countless Tory meetings, remaining through this period a likely successor to Thatcher as party leader.

Born in Swansea, South Wales, on March 21, 1933, the grandson of a coal merchant and son of a structural engineer who was a colonel in the Territorial Army, Michael Heseltine went to a private boarding school, Shrewsbury School. This was followed by three years at Pembroke College, Oxford, where he took a degree in philosophy, politics, and economics and where his debating skills and already perceived business sense led to his becoming president of the Union in 1954. He also founded there a non-establishment Tory society called the Blue Ribbon Club.

Entering Politics

After university he studied accountancy from 1955 to 1957 and set out early on a career that made him a millionaire property developer when he used a legacy to buy a

house in an unfashionable part of London and rented rooms. He then worked as a magazine publisher with Haymarket Publishing. He had joined the Conservative Party in Swansea at age 17, and after only nine months of his two years of National Service Michael Heseltine took terminal leave in October 1959, as the rules allowed, to contest the parliamentary seat of Gower, a forlorn hope for the Tories. He tried again in marginal Coventry North in October 1964 but by the next general election had been picked for the safe Tory seat of Tavistock, which he won in 1966. Tavistock, which he represented until 1974, then disappeared as a result of boundary changes, and he was selected as Member of Parliament (MP) for Henley, which he represented into the 1990s.

A close ally of the left-wing Heathite Conservative Peter Walker, Heseltine first made his name in Parliament attacking the Labour government's transport legislation. During the Heath government he was a junior minister first in the Transport Department and then on Local Government before becoming minister for aerospace from 1972 to 1974. In opposition from 1974 to 1979, he was successively spokesman for industry and for the environment, and when the Conservatives returned to power under Margaret Thatcher in 1979 he became secretary of state for the environment.

A Career Haunting Episode

In an episode in May 1976 that has haunted his career since, he became infuriated when Labour leftwingers began singing the "Red Flag" in the Commons chamber after a key vote. Heseltine seized the ceremonial mace and swung it around his head, offering the symbol of parliamentary authority in mockery to the Labour benches. Fellow Tories were shocked and he had to apologize the next day. But from then on the nickname "Tarzan," occasioned also by his abundant blonde mane, stuck with him.

About this time, too, Heseltine became a favorite of the Conservative Party conference, delighting party activists with an annual series of tub-thumping theatrical speeches attacking the Labour Party and extending well beyond his front-bench brief. As secretary of state for the environment he was responsible for reducing the departmental workforce and introducing the MINIS (Management Information for Ministers) system, which set specific tasks and responsibilities for civil servants.

Always a socially conscious politician, he was given specific charge of the Merseyside area after Liverpool riots in 1980. He and the city made a considerable impression on each other as he sought to counter the deprivation, which had appalled him, with inner-city development plans and new initiatives for dockland areas involving private industry.

He was forced to back away from a plan he produced as environment minister for local referenda to be held before councils could impose extra rate (local tax) increases on residents. He set his face against the "poll tax" idea which, when introduced after he had left the Cabinet, caused major political problems for the Thatcher government.

In January 1983 Michael Heseltine was made defense secretary in the hope that he would succeed in reducing manpower and budgets at that department, too. He became an enthusiastic crusader against the Campaign for Nuclear Disarmament and a strong supporter of the stationing in Britain of cruise missiles, part of the effort later held to have pushed the Soviet Union toward arms reduction talks.

Conflict with Thatcher

A keen supporter of the developing European Community, (European Union) Heseltine argued through the autumn of 1985 that the crisis in a small British helicopter-making company, Westland, should be solved by European co-operation. Thatcher, with the support of other ministers, chose a rescue deal with the U.S. Sikorsky firm. Heseltine quit the government in consequence, storming out in the middle of a Cabinet meeting in Downing Street in protest against the prime minister's style. Another minister, Leon Brittan, later to become one of Britain's EC commissioners, was forced to resign over the leaking of a critical letter about Heseltine from the solicitor general. The affair produced a major crisis for Thatcher's government, and relations between her and Heseltine were bitter from then on.

Instead of accepting obscurity on the backbenches, Heseltine became the highest-profile politician in his party, traveling ceaselessly around the country as a popular speaker at an endless round of Conservative functions in MPs' constituencies. Offering general loyalty to the government's line but differing on certain specific issues, as in his enthusiasm for British participation in the European monetary system and for closer relations between business and government, Heseltine was able to take his Thatcherism ''a la carte.'' He remained an ever-present threat to Thatcher as the government ran into deep political difficulties in 1989 and 1990. As alternative leader in waiting, Heseltine finally challenged Thatcher for leadership of the party (and thus prime minister). In an election limited to Conservative MPs on November 20, 1990, Heseltine received 152 votes. Thatcher received 204, but that was still four votes short of preventing a second round of balloting. Thatcher then resigned, forcing a wide-open election between Heseltine, Foreign Secretary Douglas Hurd, and Chancellor of the Exchequer John Major. Major won and promptly named Heseltine as secretary of state for environment and local government.

Major later bestowed other titles on Heseltine: Deputy Prime Minister and First Secretary of State, titles not held by one person since 1962. He and Major discussed his role in the government before the election, and it appears that he was rewarded for encouraging his followers to vote for Major instead of abstaining. In exchange for his loyalty, Heseltine was rewarded a new suite of offices over twice the size of Major's. Heseltine also snagged a new press nickname to go with the job—''Lion King'' instead of ''Tarzan.

While in office, Heseltine met with Chinese Premier Li Peng in Beijing and Chinese President Jiang Zemin. While on the trip to China, wife Anne donated medical equipment and medicine to the Beijing Children's Hospital on behalf of the British Chamber of Commerce.

In May of 1997, Heseltine announced that he would not seek the post of prime minister because of poor health, although he was widely considered a front-runner to replace John Major. His decision not to run probably spelled the end of his career at the top of politics, political analysts said.

Further Reading

More can be found about Heseltine in *Heseltine, the Unauthorised Biography* by Julian Critchley (London: 1987). His own works include *The Challenge of Europe: Can Britain Win* (London: 1989). ☐

Hesiod

The Greek poet Hesiod (active ca. 700 B.C.) was the first didactic poet in Europe and the first author of mainland Greece whose works are extant. His influence on later literature was basic and far-reaching.

T he facts about Hesiod are shrouded in myth and the obscurity of time; what we can say with certainty about him comes from his own writing. His father, a merchant ''fleeing wretched poverty,'' migrated from Cyme in Asia Minor and became a farmer near the town of Ascra in Boeotia, where Hesiod lived most or all of his life. Hesiod undoubtedly spent his early years working his father's land. He says that the Muses appeared to him as he was tending sheep on the slopes of Mt. Helicon and commanded him to compose poetry, and it is likely that he combined the vocations of farmer and poet.

After his father's death Hesiod was involved in a bitter dispute with his brother, Perses, about the division of the property. Later legend relates that Hesiod moved from Ascra and that he was murdered in Oenoe in Locris for having seduced a maiden; their child is said to have been the lyric poet Stesichorus. The poet relates that the only time he traveled across the sea was to compete in a poetry contest at the funeral games of Amphidamas at Chalcis (in Euboea).

The dates of Hesiod's life are much disputed; some of the ancient chroniclers make him a contemporary of Homer; most modern critics date his activity not long after the Homeric epics but presumably before 700 B.C. The titles of a number of poems have come down to us under the name of Hesiod; two complete works survive, which are generally believed to be genuine.

Major Works

The *Theogony* (*Theogonia,* or *Genealogy of the Gods*) is a long (over 1,000 lines) narrative description of the origin of the universe and the gods. Beginning with the aboriginal Chaos (Emptiness) and Gaia (Earth), Hesiod describes the creation of the natural world and the generations of the gods. His account concentrates on the struggles between the generations of divine powers for dominion of the world. Uranus (Sky), the original force, is succeeded by his son,

Kronos, who, at the instigation of his mother, Gaia, castrates Uranus. Kronos, in turn, is deposed after a fierce battle waged between the Olympian gods (the sons and daughters of Kronos and Rhea), led by Zeus, and the Titans (children of Uranus and Gaia), led by Kronos. In the course of the narrative the births of the gods, major and minor, the evolution of the natural world, and the emergence of personified abstractions like Death, Toil, and Strife are detailed.

Although many of the myths which Hesiod incorporates are extremely primitive and probably Eastern in origin, the *Theogony* is a successful attempt to give a rational and coherent explanation of the formation and government of the universe from its primal origins through the ultimate mastery of the cosmos by Zeus, "the father of men and gods." Of special interest in the *Theogony* are the vivid description of battle between the gods and the Titans and the story of Prometheus, the Titan, who defied Zeus by stealing fire for man and was doomed to be chained forever to a rock with a stake through his middle as punishment.

The Works and Days (*Erga Kai Hemerai*), another long poem (over 800 lines), is much more personal in tone. It is addressed to Hesiod's brother, Perses, who had taken the bigger portion of their inheritance by means of bribes to the local "kings" and then had squandered it. Around this theme of admonition to his brother, Hesiod composed a didactic poem consisting of practical advice to farmers and seafarers, maxims (again, mostly practical) on how to conduct oneself in everyday affairs with fellowmen, moral and ethical precepts, and warnings to the local "kings" to observe righteousness in their disposition of justice. A long section at the end is a list of primitive taboos followed by a catalog of lucky and unlucky days. The authenticity of these lines is doubted, but they are characteristic of the unsophisticated peasant outlook.

The two major themes that Hesiod sounds again and again are the necessity for all men to be just and fair, since justice comes from Zeus, who will punish the wrongdoer, and the formula that success depends on unceasing hard work. If you desire wealth, he says, then "work with work upon work." The world which Hesiod describes in the *Works and Days* is not the heroic arena of the Trojan War but the difficult life of the small peasant farmer. Hesiod's view is essentially pessimistic; Ascra, his home, is "bad in winter, harsh in summer, good at no time"; and, in one famous passage, he details the five "Ages of Man." From the Golden Age of the reign of Kronos through the Silver, Bronze, and Brass ages of heroes, mankind has degenerated; Hesiod finds himself in the Age of Iron, where there is nothing but trouble and sorrow, labor and strife. Also included in the *Works and Days* is the story of Pandora, the first woman. The myth states that she was created at Zeus's command as a punishment for men.

Other Works

A number of other poems, attributed to Hesiod in antiquity and now generally ascribed to the "Boeotian," or "Hesiodic," school, are known by title or from fragmentary remains. The most important of these "minor works," possibly by Hesiod himself, was the *Catalog of Women,* which seems to have described the loves of the gods and their offspring. A number of fragmentary excerpts survive. A longer fragment, called the *Shield of Herakles,* most likely not by Hesiod, narrates the battle between Herakles and the robber Kyknos. A large portion of this substantial (480 lines) fragment is devoted to a description of Herakles's shield—an inferior imitation of the famous description in the *Iliad* of the shield of Achilles.

Like Homer, Hesiod wrote in the Ionian dialect and employed the dactylic hexameter, the meter of the epic poets; but the soaring elegance of the Homeric poems is replaced by a simpler, more earthy style. Portions of the Hesiodic poems are mere "catalogs" of names and events, but often his words ring with an eloquence and conviction that reveal true literary genius. Hesiod was the first European poet to speak in a personal vein and to stress social and moral ethics. The *Theogony* won immediate acceptance as the authentic account of Greek cosmogony, and it stands today as one of the important basic documents for the study of Greek mythology. Hesiod's professed intent was to instruct and inform, not to amuse; thus he stands at the head of a long line of teacher-poets in the Western world.

Further Reading

Excellent critical analyses of Hesiod's writings are in Werner Wilhelm Jaeger, *Paideia: The Ideals of Greek Culture,* vol. 1 (trans. 1939; 2d ed. 1945), and Friedrich Solmsen, *Hesiod and Aeschylus* (1949). Useful for general historical background and cultural interpretation of the poems is Andrew Robert Burn, *The World of Hesiod* (1936; 2d ed. 1967). See also Alfred Eckhard Zimmern, *The Greek Commonwealth: Politics and Economics in Fifth-century Athens* (1911; 5th rev. ed. 1931), and Chester G. Starr, *The Origins of Greek Civilization* (1961). □

Victor Francis Hess

The Austrian-American physicist Victor Francis Hess (1883-1964) shared the Nobel Prize in Physics for his discovery of cosmic rays.

Victor Francis (originally Franz) Hess was born on June 24, 1883, at Schloss Waldstein, Styria. He studied physics at the universities of Graz (1901-1905) and Vienna (1905-1908) and graduated as a doctor of philosophy at Graz in 1906. From 1910 to 1920 Hess was a lecturer at the Institute for Radium Research in the University of Vienna.

In 1900 C. T. R. Wilson proved that air is a slight conductor of electricity. Thereafter it was held that this property of the air was due to ionization by gamma rays emitted by radioactive substances in the air or in the earth. It was known that gamma rays are almost completely absorbed by 300 meters of air. To test the theory, balloon ascents were made between 1909 and 1911. Each showed that the ionization was too great to have been due to gamma rays emitted from the earth. But in each case the instruments were defective. In 1910 Theodore Wulf obtained similar results from readings at the foot and at the top of the Eiffel Tower, which is 300 meters high.

Hess became interested in Wulf's account of his experiment. Hess designed new instruments, and he made two balloon ascents in 1911, seven in 1912, and one in 1913. He showed that, as the height increased, the degree of ionization decreased at first and then rapidly increased. At a height of 5 kilometers it was many times greater than at the earth's surface. He concluded that the phenomenon was due to hitherto unknown rays of high penetration which entered the earth's atmosphere from space. On one ascent, during an almost total eclipse of the sun, the radiation was not diminished. Hess therefore concluded that the rays could not be emitted by the sun. At a later date R. A. Millikan named the radiation discovered by Hess "cosmic rays."

In 1920 Hess was appointed associate professor at Graz. From 1921 to 1923, while on leave of absence, he was director of research at the United States Radium Corporation, New York. In 1925 he became professor of experimental physics at the University of Graz and in 1931 professor of physics at Innsbruck. In 1931 he established an observatory for the study of the diurnal and nocturnal fluctuations of the cosmic rays, at which he had hinted in 1912. In 1938 Hess accepted the chair of physics at Fordham University, New York, and he became a naturalized American citizen in 1944. He died in New York on Dec. 18, 1964.

Hess's discovery encouraged the study of subatomic particles and led to the discovery of the positron by C. D. Anderson. In 1936 Hess shared the Nobel Prize for Physics with Anderson, and he received many other honors.

Further Reading

There is a biography of Hess in *Nobel Lectures, Physics, 1922-1941* (1965), which also includes his Nobel Lecture. For a discussion of his work see N. H. deV. Heathcote, *Nobel Prize Winners, Physics, 1901-1950* (1953). For the effects of cosmic rays see F. K. Richtmyer and E. H. Kennard, *Introduction to Modern Physics* (1950), and S. Glasstone, *Sourcebook of Atomic Energy* (1958). □

Walter Richard Rudolf Hess

Walter Richard Rudolf Hess (1894-1987) was Deputy Reichsführer for Adolf Hitler from 1933 to 1941. He lived longer than any other major war criminal.

Rudolf Hess was born April 26, 1894, in Cairo, Egypt, eldest son of Fritz H. Hess and Klara Münch. He was educated in a German school at Alexandria and also in Germany at Godesberg am Rhein. In World War I Hess served in the Bavarian infantry and trained as a pilot. In 1919, he attended Munich University briefly and was a student of geopolitical professor Karl Haushofer. In 1920 Hess joined the Nazi Party and soon after became a private secretary to Adolf Hitler. Following the 1923 Munich putsch and 1924 trial, Hess was imprisoned at Landsberg, where he helped Hitler in preparing the book *Mein Kampf*. In 1927 Hess married Ilse Pröhl, and one son, Wolf Rüdiger, was born in 1937. In 1933 Hess was chosen by Hitler as a cabinet member and deputy reichsführer.

Hess oversaw the employment, promotion, and training of Nazis in government, party, and business positions; had significant responsibility for administering the Nuremberg Laws on citizenship; and adjudicated claims and appeals on a broad range of subjects. Hess's administration was honest in that he did not profit financially or build a following. Presumably it suited Hitler to have a deputy who was politically neutral and ethically "decent," but adamant in upholding authoritarian and anti-Semitic principles. Hess "saved" a few victims of persecution, but his administration established categories of people later sent to labor camps and extermination camps. In September of 1939 Hermann Göring was named war-time "successor" to Hitler, with Hess as a successor to Göring.

During the French campaign of 1940 Hitler discussed with Hess and others his wish for an Anglo-German "good will" peace settlement giving the Germans a free hand in Eastern Europe. Hitler's speech of July 19, 1940, and his "peace feelers" via Switzerland, the Vatican, the United States, and several private channels put his broad ideas in clear enough terms. In September 1940 Hess began air pilot practice and related preparations of his own for a flight to Britain as an emissary of Hitler's peace policy, but without

Rudolf Hess (center, holding pencil)

Hitler's consent or knowledge. On May 10, 1941, Hess flew an ME110 fitted with auxiliary gas tanks from Augsburg to Scotland, landing by parachute south of Glasgow. Hitler expressed surprise and displeasure and was concerned as to what and how much Hess might tell the British about "Barbarossa," the projected invasion of Russia. Hitler ordered death for Hess should he return to Germany, but made no effort to have Hess rescued or killed and later spoke of him as a loyal but misguided "Old Comrade." Martin Bormann succeeded Hess as deputy with malign efficiency.

The surprised British confined Hess to varying forms of comfortable imprisonment and much highly-publicized censorship. According to Hess's own later account he early on asked to see the Duke of Hamilton and then explained to the duke that he came to offer peace and asked for the king's "parole" to protect and assist his efforts. Hess's subsequent interviews with Ivone Kirkpatrick of the Foreign Office and Sir John Simon, then lord chancellor, were entirely fruitless. Hess later wrote "things as I apparently imagined them are not possible in England." However, the central defect of Hess's "mission" was its lack of practical meaning. He brought no new proposals and had no authority to negotiate or even to be in Britain. In Churchill's later words, "this escapade . . . had no relation to the march of events."

In 1946 Hess was tried at Nuremberg as one of the major war criminals. The record of his suicide attempts and

amnesia while in custody led to examinations and reports by psychiatrists who agreed that Hess was sane in terms of criminal law—that is, he could distinguish right from wrong and understood the consequences of his actions. Apart from this legal issue, Hess's amnesia was never complete, with no fixed temporal "bloc" associated with any sudden trauma. His active delusion that his failures were caused by the secret powers of his "Jewish enemies" was not unique among Nazis. The Nuremberg Tribunal confined itself to the counts of the indictment, convicted Hess of committing aggression and conspiracy to commit aggression, and imposed a sentence of life imprisonment. It seems possible that a better memory and mental condition would have increased Hess's chance of being hanged.

After 1946 Hess was kept at Spandau Prison in West Berlin. The Western powers and many Western leaders made efforts for his release, chiefly on grounds of age and time served. The Russians, however, appeared to believe Hess morally responsible for "Barbarossa" and its 20 million Russian victims. Rudolf Hess died in 1987.

The uncertain possibilities of the Hess case compelled the attention of national leaders at the time, and the combination of sensational elements continued to attract speculative pens. As Hitler's deputy Hess could wield great power over others, but without Hitler's authority Hess's own role was humiliatingly inconsequential.

Further Reading

No extended biography of Hess has so far been published. *Hess* (1973) by Roger Manwell and Heinrich Fraenkel is the most judicious work available. Brigadier J. R. Rees's *The Case of Rudolf Hess* (1948) includes medical reports and Hess's own short account of his mission. J. Douglas-Hamilton's *Motive for a Mission* (1971) covers Haushofer's role. Other memoirs, medical reports, or studies of the period relate in part to the Hess case, and Wolf Rüdiger Hess has published his own account. However, Peter Allen's *The Windsor Secret* (1984) is not convincingly documented, and W. Hugh Thomas's *The Murder of Rudolf Hess* (1979) presents an impersonation theory of massive improbability. Alfred Seidl's *Der Fall Hess* (1984) summarizes arguments in international law at Nuremberg and since.

Additional Sources

Allen, Peter, *The crown and the swastika: Hitler, Hess, and the Duke of Windsor,* London: R. Hale, 1983.

Bird, Eugene K., *The loneliest man in the world: the inside story of the 30-year imprisonment of Rudolf Hess,* London: Secker & Warburg, 1974.

Bird, Eugene K., *Prisoner #7, Rudolf Hess: the thirty years in jail of Hitler's deputy Führer,* New York: Viking Press, 1974.

Brenton, Howard, *H.I.D.: (Hess is dead),* London: N. Hern Books, 1989.

Costello, John, *Ten days that saved the West,* London; New York: Bantam Press, 1991.

Costello, John, *Ten days to destiny: the secret story of the Hess peace initiative and British efforts to strike a deal with Hitler,* New York: W. Morrow, 1991; 1993.

Douglas-Hamilton, James, *Motive for a mission: the story behind Rudolf Hess's flight to Britain,* New York: Paragon House, 1986, 1979.

Douglas-Hamilton, James, *The truth about Rudolf Hess,* Edinburgh: Mainstream, 1993.

Gabel, Charles A., *Conversations interdites avec Rudolf Hess: 1977-1986,* Paris: Plon, 1988.

Hutton, Joseph Bernard, *Hess: the man and his mission,* New York, Macmillan 1971, 1970.

Kilzer, Louis C., *Churchill's deception: the dark secret that destroyed Nazi Germany,* New York: Simon & Schuster, 1994.

Manvell, Roger, *Hess: a biography,* New York, Drake Publishers 1973.

Padfield, Peter, *Hess: flight for the Fuhrer,* London: Weidenfeld & Nicolson, 1991.

Schwarzwaller, Wulf, *Rudolph Hess, the last Nazi,* Bethesda, Md.: National Press, c1988. ☐

Walter Rudolf Hess

A Swiss neurophysiologist, Walter Rudolf Hess (1881-1973) won the 1949 Nobel Prize for Physiology or Medicine (with Antonio Egas Moniz) for discovering the role played by certain parts of the brain in coordinating the functions of internal organs.

The son of Professor Clemenz Hess, Walter Rudolf Hess was born at Frauenfeld, Switzerland, on March 17, 1881. In 1900 he became a medical student at the University of Lausanne, and after more study in Switzerland and Germany, he graduated from the University of Zurich in 1906. He became a practicing ophthalmologist, but in 1912 he turned to physiology. In 1917 Hess was appointed professor of physiology and director of the Institute of Physiology at the University of Zurich.

The Experiments

Hess soon became interested in the study of the autonomic nervous system, the nerves that originate at the base of the brain and extend throughout the spinal cord. These nerves control such functions as digestion and also trigger the response of organs to such stimuli as stress. In 1925 Hess began work on the influence of the diencephalon (interbrain)—especially the hypothalamus—in relation to the regulation of involuntary activities that enable the individual to function as an integrated organism.

At the time, it was known that the autonomic nervous system was divided into the sympathetic and the parasympathetic and that these two divisions were in general mutually antagonistic. Involuntary muscles and glands were supplied by two types of fibers, one excitatory and the other inhibitory. But much less was known about the action of the central origins of the autonomic nervous system in the brain, mainly in the hypothalamus. A few scientists had observed the reactions in animals following stimulation of poorly localized areas of the hypothalamus. It thus came to be realized that the hypothalamus, through the autonomic nervous system, controlled the automatic functions of the body, such as the blood supply to muscles and organs, mechanism of heat regulation, activity of the gastrointestinal tract, and the regulation of basal metabolism, of the sugar content of the blood, and of blood pressure. But to a large extent, the exact areas responsible for such functions had never been precisely localized.

Hess developed his own brilliant technique for the investigation of such problems. Others had used needle electrodes implanted in the hypothalamus to pass an electric current to a desired area, but locations were generally not precise. Hess implanted his electrodes accurately under general anesthesia. The needle electrode, insulated except at the very tip, was connected to a frame fixed to the skull. When the animal had recovered from the operation, a very weak current was passed through the electrode, and the animal's reaction, giving the result of stimulation at the site of the tip of the electrode, was very carefully recorded. After repeated observations of this type, the minute area around the tip of the electrode was coagulated by a current, and the animal's reaction was again recorded. At autopsy, serial sections were made of the animal's brain in order to identify the exact situation at the tip of the electrode. The correlation of these clinical and anatomical findings involved a very careful recording technique. Hess's experiments were carried out on a scale never previously attempted.

Hess proved conclusively that bodily functions, triggered by the sympathetic division of the autonomic nervous system, are related to the posterior and middle parts of the hypothalamus. Stimulation of a certain area of the hypothalamus of a cat produces all the symptoms of rage. Stimulation of another defined area produces parasympathetic, not sympathetic, effects; the cat relaxes and falls asleep. By these methods Hess mapped out the influence of the hypothalamus, and for his work he was awarded a Nobel Prize, with Antonio Egas Moniz, in 1949.

After his official retirement in 1951, Hess continued to work in the Institute of Physiology. He was already the author of several books, and in 1956 he published an atlas of sections of the hypothalamus and the thalamus. In 1962 he published a work that related his research to psychosomatic phenomena and the behavior pattern of the individual (2d ed., 1968). Hess received many honors, including honorary degrees from four universities and in 1971, the Johannes Müller Medal. He died in Locarno, Switzerland, on Aug. 12, 1973.

Further Reading

There is a biography of Hess in *Nobel Lectures, Physiology or Medicine, 1942—1962* (1964), which also includes his Nobel Lecture. For the physiology of the autonomic system and hypothalamus see J. F. Fulton, *Physiology of the Nervous System* (3d ed. 1949). For the historical aspects see J. Beattie in W. E. LeGros Clark and others, *The Hypothalamus* (1938). ☐

Eva Hesse

The sculptor Eva Hesse (1936-1970) pioneered the use of plastic and other nontraditional materials in order to visualize her essential concern, the

absurdity of relationships within contradictory systems.

Although Eva Hesse worked as a sculptor for only five years before her untimely death at 34 in 1970, she made a significant contribution to contemporary art and aesthetics. Born in Hamburg, Germany, on January 11, 1936, she and her sister Helen escaped the Nazi program via a children's train to Amsterdam in 1938. There Eva was rejoined with her parents and together they travelled to England and then to the United States, arriving in New York City on June 23, 1939. Hesse's father kept a record of these events and continued to document Eva's activities as she grew up in New York. Eva kept diaries as well, and her obsession with autobiography can be found in the strongly personal nature of her work.

The trauma of Hesse's early childhood strongly affected her emotional development, as did her parents' separation and divorce and her mother's subsequent suicide in 1945. These events left Hesse insecure and anxious, and in 1954 she began psychiatric therapy which she maintained throughout her life. This therapy encouraged her to examine herself more closely, and with the help of this intense self-analysis, Hesse created original and innovative sculpture: "I think art is a total thing. A total person giving a contribution. It is an essence, a soul. . . . In my inner soul, art and life are inseparable."

Interest in Many Styles

Hesse's creative talent had been evident since childhood. At 16 she graduated from the New York School of Industrial Arts. In the fall of 1952 she began studies at the Pratt Institute of Design, but she dropped out in December 1953. She then studied figure drawing at the Art Student's League while she worked as a layout artist for *Seventeen* magazine. In 1957 she graduated from Cooper Union in New York and then studied at Yale University with the assistance of a Norfolk Fellowship, receiving her B.A. in 1959.

While at Yale Hesse studied color theory with Joseph Albers. During this period she worked as a painter, and her work was heavily influenced by the Abstract Expressionist movement. Most of her work from 1960 to 1965 was abstract, small in size, and intensely personal. Her drawings were strongest. Filled with circular and box-like shapes and reflecting a concern for chaos and order, they anticipated her later sculptural configurations. Hesse's emerging spatial interest was especially evident in the broad overlapping planes of collages she created in 1962 and 1963 with ink, pencil, watercolor, and gouache.

In 1962 Hesse married the sculptor Tom Doyle (they would separate in 1966), and two years later they moved to Ketturg-Am-Ruhr, Germany. There they were guests for a year of the textile manufacturer and collector F. Amhard Scherdt. This visit proved crucial to Hesse's development, as it was during this time that she executed a large body of drawings and created her first sculpture. Her drawings emerged from the gestural and pictographic symbols of the early 1960s to sharply defined flowing contours positioned in a non-atmospheric space. Much of the imagery was inspired by machine parts Hesse had found in an abandoned factory and the large crescent and plough shapes of Doyle's sculpture. These drawings of machine-line forms were often humorous, reminiscent of the "erotic machines" of Francis Picabia or Marcel Duchamp. Hesse was intrigued by the Dada notion of the absurd and later incorporated this attitude into her sculpture: "If I can name the content, then . . . it's the total absurdity of life. . . . Absurdity is the key word. It is to do with contradictions and oppositions. . . . I was always aware that I should take order versus chaos, stringy versus mass, huge versus small and I would try to find the most absurd opposites or extreme opposites."

While Hesse enjoyed drawing, she found it difficult to translate her ideas into paintings. Slowly, she began to explore three-dimensional form, first in relief and then in sculpture. *Ring Around Arosie* (1965), a bright pink breastlike projection made of paper mache, cloth, and wire on a masonite panel, alludes to the sexual nature of much of her early relief works and points to Hesse's concern for exploring the self in terms of the female experience. At the same time, the artist intentionally broke down conventions, using non-traditional materials such as plastic and industrial wire, in her quest to explore a personal vision: "My idea now is to counteract everything I've ever learnt or been taught about those things—to find something inevitable that is my life, my thought, my feelings." Hesse exhibited many of these reliefs, along with her "machine" drawings, at the Kunsthalle in Dusseldorf, Germany, in August 1965.

When Hesse returned to New York the next month, she was filled with a new sense of confidence gained from 15 months abroad. Soon she began exploring, through sculpture, the emotional terrain of her experience. *Hang-Up* (1966) alludes to her desire to move off the canvas into space: here, a curved metal rod springs from a latex and cheesecloth bound rectangular frame. With one image, Hesse dissolved the boundaries between drawing, painting, and sculpture. Many of the works of this 1966-1968 period contain rectangular box and grid forms or circular spherical shapes, reductive structures and systems also found in the work of her friends, the sculptors Sol LeWitt, Mel Boucher, and Carl Andre.

Metronomic Irregularity I (1966) and *Addendum* (1967) employ logical arrangement to create random results. In these works Hesse stated directly her essential concern for inter-relating contradictory systems: order and chaos, logic and absurdity, the geometric and organic. Her grid drawings of this time also interface a regular repeated module with the individual variation of her markings in each unit.

A Restless Search for Expression

Constantly experimenting with new processes and materials, Hesse began in 1967 to use latex and fiberglass to build up forms layer by layer or to cover found objects. These transparent, translucent plastic mediums captured light and color and enabled the artist to broaden the vocabulary of her forms. *Expanded Expansion* (1969) is typical of this period.

From 1968 to 1970 Hesse exhibited many of these sculptures at the Fishbach Gallery, directed by her dealer and friend Donald Droll. During this time she also taught at the School of Visual Arts. Her work was included in group exhibits at the Art Institute in Milwaukee, Kunsthalle, Berne, and the Whitney and Museum of Modern Art in New York.

Hesse's "window" gouaches of 1968-1969 point to the constant interaction between her drawings and her sculpture. In this series, like the fiberglass layers of her sculpture, saturated colors are built up by thin washes of color. Hesse was always aware of the ironic interplay between two-dimensional and three-dimensional form. *Contingent,* executed the summer of 1969, addresses this concern. Eight parallel banner-like elements hang from the ceiling to the floor. Suspended within each panel is a large rectangular stretch of latex and fiberglass covered cheesecloth. From the front, *Contingent* looks like a layered abstract painting or one of her "window" gouaches, while from the side it expands into space. The thin sheets of organic material move with the wind and deny any sense of the solidity usually associated with sculpture. Color and light dance among the panels, creating a poetic and meditative feeling from raw matter.

Although Hesse died before the feminist movement of the 1970s, she imbued her sculpture with values associated with the female experience. Her work emphasized the intuitive and self-reflective; it sought to temper the intellectual with feeling and to undermine monumentality with intimate and personal forms.

Untitled, completed shortly before her death of brain cancer in May 1970, suggested a new direction for Hesse's work. Here a system of knotted ropes is suspended from the ceiling, the connection of elements determining its final shape. This sculpture has no plan or actual form—only relationships suspended in space waiting for the observer to give them definition and meaning. Rejecting the idea of a singular style, Hesse made her own definition: " . . . how to achieve by not achieving? How to make by not making? it's all in that./it's not new. it's what is not yet known, thought seen touched—but really what is not, and that is."

Further Reading

The most complete and informative text on Hesse remains Lucy R. Lippard, *Eva Hesse* (1976). On Hesse's drawings, see Ellen H. Johnson, *Eva Hesse: A Retrospective of the Drawings* (1980). Her last interview was published the month of her death: Cindy Nemser, "An Interview with Eva Hesse," *ArtForum,* VII (May 1970).

Additional Sources

Eva Hesse: a retrospective, New Haven: Yale University Art Gallery: Yale University Press, 1992.

Hesse, Eva, *Eva Hesse: drawing in space: Bilder und Reliefs,* Ostfildern: Cantz, 1994.

Johnson, Ellen H., *Eva Hesse, a retrospective of the drawings,* Oberlin, Ohio: Allen Memorial Art Museum, Oberlin College, 1982.

Lippard, Lucy R., *Eva Hesse,* New York: Da Capo Press, 1992.

Wagner, Anne Middleton, *Three artists (three women): modernism and the art of Hesse, Krasner, and O'Keeffe,* Berkeley: University of California Press, 1996. □

Hermann Hesse

The novels of the German author Hermann Hesse (1877-1962) are lyrical and confessional and are primarily concerned with the relationship between the contemplative, God-seeking individual, often an artist, and his fellow humans.

Hermann Hesse was born on June 2, 1877, in Calw, Württemberg. His father worked for the publishing house directed by his maternal grandfather, Hermann Gundert, a scholarly Orientalist. Both his parents, as well as his grandfather, had seen service as missionaries with the Basel Mission in the East Indies. The atmosphere in which Hesse grew up was therefore pious, but the household was nonetheless an educated one and relatively urbane.

In 1893 Hesse won a scholarship to the Protestant Theological Seminary at Maulbronn; but he soon rebelled against the intellectual and clerical discipline there and ran away. This experience of flight was evidently of decisive significance in his imaginative development, and it recurs in one form or another in almost all his major works. After some time at another high school and a short period as a machine-shop apprentice, Hesse found employment in the book trade. He read widely in German and foreign literature and began to write lyric poetry, sketches, and stories. His first published works, *Romantische Lieder* (1899) and *Eine Stunde hinter Mitternacht* (1899), are mannered tributes to the neoromantic conventions of the day, pseudoexotic, melancholic, and tinged with irony.

Early Works

The novel *Peter Camenzind* (1904) made Hesse's name. An attempt to overcome decadence by portraying the cure of a melancholic outsider by means of altruistic activity and a return to nature, *Peter Camenzind* presents an early, half-formed version of that life pattern found in almost all Hesse's novels. It was followed in 1905 by *Unterm Rad* (*Beneath the Wheel*), a contribution to the then fashionable subgenre of "school novels." The book portrays the miseries and sad decline of a sensitive youth crushed by the intellectual demands and unfeeling attitudes encountered in school. In this novel Hesse divides his interest, as so often in his later work, between two characters, Hans Giebenrath who regresses and dies, and Hermann Heilner who breaks out and lives, albeit by eventually finding a compromise with the bourgeois world.

Hesse himself had compromised by marrying and settling down in Gaienhofen on Lake Constance. He lived there until 1912, when he moved to Berne. He published a number of short stories and novellas: *Diesseits* (1907),

Nachbarn (1908), and *Umwege* (1912) are collections of tales of small-town and country life, after the manner of Gottfried Keller. *Knulp,* three whimsical sketches of the vagabond existence, dates from this period, as do the full-length novels *Gertrude* (1910) and *Rosshalde* (1913). All these works show Hesse as a careful and talented writer, with a keen psychologist's eye and a supple style, but they rather mute the serious conflicts incipiently suggested by his first two novels. Hesse's journey to the Malayan archipelago in 1911 is, however, some indication of his inner restlessness. The interest in Oriental cultures which originated in his childhood now takes deeper root.

During World War I there occurred an extremely sharp break in Hesse's life and work. His third son, Martin, fell seriously ill, his wife began to show the first signs of mental disease, and his family life disintegrated. The war, in which he was directly involved only through his relief work for German prisoners of war, shocked him terribly; he denounced it at its outset and was in his turn denounced by the German press as a pacifist traitor. He never returned to live in Germany and became a Swiss citizen in 1922. In 1916 he underwent a course of Jungian analysis in Lucerne.

"Demian" and "Siddhartha"

The product of all these diverse traumatic experiences was the novel *Demian,* published pseudonymously in 1919, which won the Fontane Prize for first novels (Hesse returned the prize and later admitted his authorship). *Demian* reestablished Hesse in the forefront of German letters and perhaps rescued him from a creeping mediocrity

in his creative work. It deals with the "awakening" of a youth, Emil Sinclair, under the influence of an older boy of mysterious presence and powers, Demian. Critics have shown that the primary key to the book is the structure of a typical Jungian analysis. But the novel contains gnostic as well as overtly psychoanalytic material and works out mythical and biblical motifs, such as that of the Prodigal Son.

From this point onward in Hesse's work discrimination between the psychoanalytic and the religious elements in his symbolic motifs and patterns is extremely difficult. *Siddhartha* (1922) is a hagiographic legend, but it is also a very personal confession which reworks the psychological material of earlier novels in a fresh garb; and the mystical conclusion of *Siddhartha* proves on examination to be as much Christian as Buddhist or Hindu.

Between 1916 and 1925 Hesse composed several of his most distinguished novellas, notably *Iris* (1918), *Klein and Wagner* (1920), *Klingsors letzter Sommer* (1920; *Klingsor's Last Summer*), and *Piktors Verwandlungen* (1925; *Pictor's Transformations*). In 1919 he had taken up residence in Montagnola near Lugano, entirely alone and impoverished, resolved to live now only for his literary work. *Iris* is a beautifully wrought allegory on the search for selfhood, *Klein und Wagner* a study of sexual conflict, loss of identity, and rediscovery of self, *Klingsor's Last Summer* a series of passionately colored sketches of the life of a declining artist, and *Pictor's Transformations* an exotic fairy tale designed to impart a vision of the ultimate androgynous unity and of eternal change and flow.

Meaning of "Steppenwolf"

This insight into a divine reality and unity which may be glimpsed for a moment when the usual order of the mind is momentarily shaken or dissolved, in some trauma (such as Klein's suicide) or in sexual or artistic experience, is the positive vision which Hesse seeks increasingly to convey. Thus *Der Steppenwolf* (1927) should not be mistaken, as it often is, for a pessimistic and desperate work; on the contrary, this account of a psychopathic outcast, close to suicide, who finds remission and self-insight through friendship with a prostitute, dancing, and drugs is a reassertion of the omnipresence of the higher reality for those sensitive to it. The "golden thread" of this reality is often discernible, especially in the music of Mozart or, indeed, the life and art of any of the "Immortals"—Goethe, Leonardo, Rembrandt, among others. *Steppenwolf* is formally the most consummate of all Hesse's books, an extremely intricate experimental novel. It reflects something of its author's experiences in the 1920s, after the failure of his second marriage.

In 1930 Hesse published *Narziss und Goldmund,* a long picaresque work in a medieval setting, which is his most overt treatment of the relentless struggle between the mind and the senses. By no means his best novel, *Narziss und Goldmund* has been one of his most popular; sometimes trite, it has, however, an undercurrent of pain, failure, and bitterness which is often overlooked.

In 1932 appeared *Die Morgenlandfahrt* (*The Journey to the East*), an ironic allegory on the subject of the inner pilgrimage, full of secret allusion and whimsical onomastic games; extremely elusive, *The Journey to the East* subsumes with anecdotal brevity the spiritual experience of several decades.

"The Glass Bead Game"

Das Glasperlenspiel (1943; *The Glass Bead Game*), Hesse's longest and perhaps his most famous novel, took 11 years to write. It is concerned with a futuristic society in which a scholars' utopia, Castalia, exists as a separate province with the task of preserving the austere ideals of the Spirit and the unsullied service of Truth, as well as training teachers to work in the schools of the outside world. The protagonist, Joseph Knecht, is followed through his years of training until he is eventually elected Master of the Glass Bead Game, a game "with all the contents and all the values of our culture," which is Castalia's supreme cult. Through the game an element of art, and of numinous experience, infiltrates a sphere which has become too much the province of the intellect.

The Glass Bead Game depicts Knecht's gradual insight into the decadence which has overtaken Castalia and his apostasy as he resolves to leave for the outside world and to become a simple teacher. The ambivalence of this delicately written and elaborate novel lies in the question whether Knecht's act is a true breakthrough to ethical action or the expression of an unrepentant individualism, or both. Ethical and esthetical, saintly and artistic elements blend and separate deceptively again and again in this novel as throughout Hesse's work.

Hermann Hesse's poetry has been published in several collections, for example, *Gesammelte Gedichte* (1942), and has been widely anthologized. There is also the remarkable collection of "Steppenwolf" poems, *Krisis* (1928). In his verse he is generally more derivative and less searching than in his prose works. Having married for the third time in 1931, he continued to live in Montagnola, devoting a good deal of his time to a voluminous correspondence, particularly with young people interested in his work and philosophy of life. Hesse was awarded the 1946 Nobel Prize in literature. He died in August 1962.

Further Reading

There are three studies of Hesse in English: Ernst Rose, *Faith from the Abyss* (1965); Theodore J. Ziolkowski, *The Novels of Hermann Hesse* (1965); and Mark Boulby, *Hermann Hesse: His Mind and Art* (1967). Rose gives a short introduction to the author, Boulby a detailed analysis of eight novels and several novellas, and Ziolkowski a study of *Demian* and later novels, also placing Hesse in the contemporary literary scene. For bibliographical material see Joseph Mileck, *Hermann Hesse and His Critics* (1958). Ralph Freedman, *The Lyrical Novel* (1963), illuminates the analogies between Hesse, André Gide, and Virginia Woolf. □

Mary B. Hesse

Mary B. Hesse (born 1924) was a British philosopher who specialized in the philosophical interpretation of the logic, methods, and foundational assumptions of natural and social science. She was a member of the British Academy and was elected president of the Philosophy of Science Association in 1979.

Mary Hesse was born on October 15, 1924, in Reigate, England. Her father was Ethelbert Hesse and her mother was Brenda (Pelling) Hesse. She was educated at the Imperial College of Science and Technology, London, and received her Ph.D. from this institution in 1948. She also earned a M.SC. from University College, London, in 1949.

Her university career began when she accepted a position as lecturer in mathematics in 1951 at the University of Leeds in England. From 1955 until 1959 she taught at the University of London as a lecturer in the history and philosophy of science. In 1960 she began her long and distinguished association with Cambridge University, England. She was first appointed lecturer in history and philosophy of science. In 1968 she was appointed university reader. In 1975 she was appointed to the position of professor of philosophy of science at Cambridge, which she continued to hold into the 1990s.

Hesse became familiar to American scholars by accepting invitations to serve as visiting professor at numerous universities in the United States. She came to Yale University in 1962, the University of Minnesota in 1966, the University of Chicago in 1968, and the University of Notre Dame in 1972. She was the Stanton lecturer at Cambridge from 1977 through 1980 and was the Gifford lecturer at the University of Edinburgh in 1983. She was a long-standing member in the following societies: Philosophy of Science Association, the British Society for the Philosophy of Science, and the British Society for the History of Science. Finally, she was made a fellow of the British Academy.

Her writings included numerous articles in professional journals on topics in philosophy of science. Her books included *Science and the Human Imagination* (1953), *Forces and Fields* (1961), *Models and Analogies in Science* (1963), *The Structure of Scientific Inference* (1974), *Applications of Inductive Logic* (editor; 1979), *Revolutions and Reconstructions in the Philosophy of Science* (1980), and *The Construction of Reality*, with Michael Arbib (1987).

As a philosopher of science, Hesse was concerned with the nature, methods, foundations, and human implications of natural and social sciences. Furthermore, if philosophy of science could be somewhat artificially divided into its "critical" and "speculative" aspects, then a good portion of Hesse's critical philosophy of science could be defined in terms of her famous attack on the hypothetical deductive theory of scientific justification. (Henceforth we will refer to this as the H-D theory.) H-D theorists such as Karl Popper argued that deductive logic alone was sufficient for the purposes of scientific inference. According to the H-D model, scientific research began with hypotheses and then one used deductive logic to derive observable implications from the hypotheses.

But when should we consider the hypotheses justified? According to H-D theorists, one ought to accept a scientific hypothesis only after rigorous attempts at "falsifying" the hypothesis have failed. One accomplishes this goal by first deductively deriving "empirical result" statements from the hypothesis under consideration and then returning to the laboratory to determine whether these empirical result statements were experimentally true or false. If the expected results obtain, then the failure to falsify has been accomplished and confirmation has been accomplished. However, if the expected results do not obtain, then the hypothesis has been falsified. H-D theorists held that if the expected results obtained, one was not thereby justified in holding the hypothesis as true or even probably true. Such a strategy could establish the truth or probable truth of the hypothesis only by committing the logical fallacy of affirming the consequent. For example, merely because the theory that the earth was at the center of the universe implied that we would observe the sun rising over the horizon in the morning did not imply that the geocentric theory was true. Other theories might explain this observable fact. However, data which were inconsistent with the theory could falsify the hypothesis, and thus H-D theorists held that falsification was the only legitimate goal of the scientist.

Hesse consistently argued that while this H-D picture of science had the virtue of being easy to understand, it did not correspond with how actual scientists justified their hypotheses. For one thing, it asserted that evidence in favor of a hypothesis was always irrelevant to the justification of the hypothesis since only failure to falsify hypotheses counted within confirmation. This did not square well with how actual scientists operated. It was, she argued, inaccurate with respect to both contemporary science and the history of science. Numerous case studies as well as logical shortcomings were presented throughout her work to demonstrate the inadequacy of this viewpoint.

Her speculative or creative philosophy of science focused on the development and articulation of the inductivist view of science, which had fallen out of favor with many scientists and philosophers of science during the middle part of the 20th century. The reason for this disfavor was that inductive inference rules were very complex and they frequently yielded paradoxes of absurdities if not carefully formulated. Scientists and logicians were thus suspicious of these inductive rules. Moreover, because deductive inference rules were less complex and not nearly as paradoxical as inductive rules, scientists were eager to support the deductivist picture of science.

Inductive inferences were inferences whose conclusions follow with only a degree of probability. According to Hesse, these inferences were obviously more complex than deductive inferences. However, they were, she argued, essential for scientific argumentation. Furthermore, while inductive inferences have many forms, Hesse emphasized

three particular types of inductive inference that have played a vital role in both contemporary science and the history of science. These three forms may be referred to as inferences based on analogies, inferences based on models, and inferences based on metaphors. Analogical arguments involve comparisons between individuals A and B with the aim of attributing a known property of A to B. Thus an object or set of objects A may be known to have a property of having a frequency, but B was not known to have this property. But in virtue of the other similarities between A and B, we attributed frequency to B. She claimed that the wave theory of sound developed in much this way. For Hesse, the history of scientific breakthroughs was full of such analogies, and failing to appreciate their significance would lead to a misunderstanding of the logic of science. Analogies were as necessary for science as hypotheses.

The second type of inference that concerned her were inferences involving models. Models were sets of theoretical or observable objects that are used as theoretical pictures of complex substances. For example, Newtonian laws of motion are true of Newtonian point masses. To use these point masses as a picture of what the makeup of a gas was involved using these point masses as a model of the gas. This was an example of a theoretical model, but models could also be observable physical objects that were used to partially represent objects that were difficult to see. For example, wind tunnels were frequently used as models of atmospheric conditions. Hesse argued that such models are essential within our justification of the gas laws as well as our hypotheses about the atmosphere. Once again, models were as necessary for science as hypotheses.

Finally there was the role of metaphor in science. Obvious metaphors such as "humans are computers" said something true of humans, but they also said something false. However, what they supplied for the scientist was a global perspective of "a point of view"; perhaps a very limited one from which to think about the objects under consideration. According to Hesse, metaphors with all their virtues and vices were present throughout contemporary and historical science, and failing to appreciate their role in scientific argument would prevent an accurate understanding of science. For example, the above metaphor played a crucial role in the development of contemporary cognitive science. Once again, metaphors are as necessary for science as hypotheses.

In the 1980s Hesse turned away from purely logical questions about science and focused on social analyses of science. Here she was concerned with the ways in which science is similar and dissimilar to political, philosophical, and religious systems of thought. Within this context she argued for the claim that science is not essentially distinct from these enterprises and that the virtues and vices that are to be found within these admittedly impure domains of human activity were also to be found in science. In effect, she argued for the view that there is no rigid criterion, like falsifiability, that distinguished science from other forms of human belief. Consequently, she was quite happy with the notion that science was best viewed as "one among many" forms of human knowledge. Hesse believed that science was as subject to the same biases as these other ideologies.

Further Reading

Among the many commentators on Mary Hesse's philosophical perspective, the following were some of the most helpful: Frederick Suppe, *The Structure of Scientific Theories,* 2nd edition (1977). Suppe's critical introduction to this anthology was useful in contrasting Hesse's views on scientific models with the views of traditional positivists. Robert Ackermann's review of Hesse's *Models and Analogies in Science* in the *"British Journal for the Philosophy of Science"* (1965) offered a sustained criticism of her attack on formalism within the philosophy of science. Also, her views on the question of whether science can be interpreted realistically was discussed at length within Brendan Minogue's "Realism and Intentional Reference," *Philosophy of Science* (Winter 1979). Hesse's rejoinder to Minogue was entitled "Minogue on Intensional Reference," *Philosophy of Science* (December 1980). □

George Charles de Hevesy

The Hungarian chemist George Charles de Hevesy (1885-1966) was a pioneer of isotope labeling and codiscoverer of the element hafnium.

George de Hevesy was born in Budapest on Aug. 1, 1885. He studied at Freiburg, Zurich, and Karlsruhe and in 1911 joined Ernest Rutherford at Manchester. His assignment there, to separate radium-D from lead, proved impossible, because radium-D, as was later demonstrated, actually comprises isotopes. Yet the 2 years were not wasted, for Hevesy gained valuable technical experience in the new field of radiochemistry. In 1913 he left for Vienna to join F. A. Paneth, whose experience with radium-D had been similar. They studied the exchange between radioactive and nonradioactive lead atoms, showing that, for all ordinary processes, the chemical and physical behavior of these atoms was identical. Also, by using radioactive (labeled) samples to determine the solubilities of various lead salts, they introduced the technique of radioactive tracers.

In 1920 Hevesy moved to Niels Bohr's institute at Copenhagen, where his attention was directed to the possibility of separating isotopes. In 1922 Hevesy, working with J. N. Brønsted, effected a partial separation of the isotopes of mercury by repeated fractional distillation; he had similar success with chlorine and potassium. Hevesy then joined D. Coster in a search for missing element number 72. In examining zirconium minerals they found six unaccountable lines in x-ray spectra and attributed them to the new element, which they named hafnium. Hevesy began using radioactive isotopes as tracers: he studied the absorption of lead by the bean plant (1923) and the distribution and elimination of bismuth injected into rabbits (1924). These were the earliest applications of tracer techniques to biological problems.

In 1926 Hevesy moved to the University of Freiburg, where he developed the use of x-ray fluorescence for mineral analyses and began tracer experiments with stable isotopes. With some deuterium-enriched ("heavy") water, received as a gift from its discoverer, H. Urey, Hevesy studied water exchange between a goldfish and its surroundings, and within the human body. He showed that the human body retains water molecules much longer.

Political pressure compelled Hevesy to move again in 1934, and he returned to Copenhagen. There biology dominated his research, as the recently produced radiophosphorus had become available for studies on metabolism. He examined the rates of exchange of phosphorus in plants, yeast cells, and animal organs, as well as the excretion of phosphate and its exchange between plasma and corpuscles, and the effects of x-rays on the metabolism of malignant tumors.

Aware of the growing hostility of the Nazis, Hevesy escaped to Stockholm in 1944. There he continued his biological tracer work with much success, including studies on the formation and fate of red corpuscles in the blood. He was awarded the Nobel Prize in chemistry in 1944 and for another 20 years made further explorations in the field that he had pioneered. In 1959 he received the Atoms for Peace Prize. Hevesy died in Freiburg on July 5, 1966.

Further Reading

An extensive sketch of Hevesy's life is in The Royal Society, London, *Biographical Memoirs of Fellows of the Royal Society,* vol. 13 (1967). Biographical information is also in Eduard Farber, *Nobel Prize Winners in Chemistry, 1901-1961* (1953; rev. ed. 1963), and Nobel Foundation, *Chemistry: Including Presentation Speeches and Laureates' Biographies,* vol. 3 (1964). For background see Aaron J. Ihde, *The Development of Modern Chemistry* (1964).

Additional Sources

Frontiers in nuclear medicine, Berlin; New York: Springer, 1980. Levi, Hilde, *George de Hevesy: life and work: a biography,* Bristol; Boston: A. Hilger, 1985. □

Abram Stevens Hewitt

Abram Stevens Hewitt (1822-1903) was a major figure in the American iron and steel industry. His public career included service as mayor of New York City.

Abram S. Hewitt was born at Haverstraw, N.Y., on July 31, 1822, the son of a British-born mechanic. Educated in New York City public schools, Hewitt was a brilliant student, won a scholarship to Columbia College, and distinguished himself before graduating in 1842. For several years he read law, although he was never formally admitted to the bar.

In 1843 Hewitt and a college associate, Edward Cooper, traveled in Europe. On the voyage home their ship foundered in a storm; they were cast adrift, rescued, and became friends and business associates for the rest of their lives. They became the operators and proprietors of an ironworks which had been founded by Edward's father, Peter Cooper, in Trenton, N.J. The Cooper and Hewitt enterprise quickly became one of the country's leading iron manufacturing companies, making not only the raw product but producing it in semifinished and finished form.

During the Civil War, Hewitt established the first open-hearth furnace in America. It produced great quantities of the gun-barrel steel needed for war material and made Cooper, Hewitt and Company one of America's outstanding steel companies. As his business reputation grew, Hewitt became a director or corporate officer of a number of allied concerns.

In 1845 Hewitt had married Sarah Amelia Cooper, the only daughter of Peter Cooper. When the elder Cooper laid plans to establish a coeducational school, he called upon the talents of his son-in-law. Hewitt drew up the first charter of Cooper Union and became involved in the administration of the institution for almost 40 years. He also made it a gift of nearly $1 million.

Hewitt was also a public man, a longtime friend of Samuel J. Tilden, and a major figure in the Democratic party of New York. In 1874 he was elected to the U.S. Congress. He was reelected four times. He became chairman of the Democratic National Committee in 1876 and played a major role in the Tilden-Hayes campaign.

In 1886 Hewitt defeated Henry George and Theodore Roosevelt in an exciting three-way race for the mayoralty of New York City. His reform administration made improvements in a number of city departments, initiated construction of the rapid transit railroad, and fought the city's corrupt political machine. Upon his retirement from politics, Hewitt focused on public service. He was a trustee of Columbia University, chairman of the Board of Trustees of Barnard College, and chairman of the Board of Trustees of the Carnegie Institution. He died at 81, survived by his wife and six children.

Further Reading

The definitive biography of Hewitt is Allan Nevins, *Abram S. Hewitt: With Some Account of Peter Cooper* (1935). Nevins also edited *Selected Writings of Abram S. Hewitt* (1937).

Additional Sources

Post, Louis Freeland, *Henry George's 1886 campaign: an account of the George-Hewitt campaign in the New York municipal election of 1886,* Westport, Conn.: Hyperion Press, 1976. □

Paul Johann Ludwig Heyse

The German author Paul Johann Ludwig Heyse (1830-1914) is best known for his novellas. Marked by careful construction, nobility and dignity of content, and economy of form, these works reveal his relation to the classical tradition.

P aul Heyse was born in Berlin on March 15, 1830. The son of a professor, he pursued studies leading to a doctorate in philology. During an extended visit to Italy in 1852, he determined to abandon formal scholarship for a career in literature. In 1854 he was summoned to Munich by Maximilian II, king of Bavaria, who granted him a lifetime stipend. His subsequent career as a leader of the Munich Poets' Circle was marked by professional and popular success.

Heyse's half dozen novels avoid the political and sociological and tend to emphasize ethical views and goals. *Kinder der Welt* (1873) attests to his advocacy of "nature" and individual "freedom" as criteria in opposition to religious dogmatism. *Im Paradiese* (1875) is anti-Philistine in its ethical orientation. The element of classical balance and restraint and his opposition to the tenets and tactics of naturalism emerge in the novel *Merlin* (1892).

In his 120 novellas Heyse's imaginative and formalistic gifts are most fully realized. Here, too, his emphasis upon freedom, individuality, and instinct comes to the fore, although instinct is not presented as incompatible with spirituality or a sense of duty. Even the humblest or most unfortunate characters are endowed with dignity and nobil-

ity, which can provide a redemptive force if the individual remains "true to himself." *L'Arrabbiata* (1852) is perhaps his most famous novella.

As coeditor, Heyse published two extensive collections of 19th-century novellas: *Deutscher Novellenschatz* (24 vols., from 1871) and *Neuer deutscher Novellenschatz* (24 vols., 1884-1888). In his introduction to the former work he describes his "falcon theory" of the novella, advocating the utmost simplicity and clarity of content and form and urging the necessity for an inward conflict culminating in an abrupt turning point or change, which should be represented by a concrete symbol (as the falcon in a Boccaccio story).

Heyse's 60 carefully constructed dramas and many lyrics lack force, but his translations from the Italian poets are admired. In 1910 Paul Heyse received the Nobel Prize for literature. He died in Munich on April 2, 1914.

Further Reading

Georg Brandes's essay "Paul Heyse," reprinted in his *Creative Spirits of the Nineteenth Century,* translated by Rasmus B. Anderson (1923), is an enthusiastic appreciation. A balanced view of Heyse as author and theoretician is in E. K. Bennett, *A History of the German Novelle* (1934; 2d ed. rev. 1961). □

Thomas Heywood

The English playwright Thomas Heywood (c.1573-1641) worked successfully in a wide range of dramatic forms. A competent craftsman, he lacked the brilliance of the greater Elizabethan and Jacobean dramatists.

Thomas Heywood, in all probability the son of the clergyman Robert Heywood, was born in Lincolnshire. He attended Cambridge but left without a degree when his father died in 1593. He seems to have moved directly from Cambridge to London, where he soon became an actor and playwright. By 1598 he had done enough dramatic writing to impress a contemporary as one of the best comic writers of the time. Unfortunately, none of Heywood's plays from this early period of his career has survived.

Most of Heywood's significant literary activity was done between 1600 and 1620. In 1633, in the preface to his play *The English Traveller* (probably written about 1623), he claims to have had "either an entire hand, or at the least a main finger" in 220 plays. Because Heywood, like most of his fellow playwrights, had little interest in printing works written for stage production, it is impossible to identify more than a small fraction of this amazing output. *The Four Prentices of London* (ca. 1600), *A Woman Killed with Kindness* (1603), and *The Rape of Lucrece* (1608) are the most important surviving plays which can be assigned with confidence to his pen.

A Woman Killed with Kindness, one of the finest tragedies of the "bourgeois," or "domestic," type, is universally regarded as Heywood's masterpiece. Mistress Anne Frankford, a virtuous and happy middle-class wife, unaccountably surrenders her honor to Wendoll, a man whom Master Frankford had befriended and received as a guest in his house. Mistress Frankford's punishment, repentance, and deathbed reconciliation with her husband are skillfully presented. Heywood throughout preserves sympathy for his heroine without relaxing his high moral tone.

Heywood also produced a number of nondramatic works, including translations, poems, and pamphlets on various topics. The most notable of these nondramatic works is the *Apology for Actors* (ca. 1608; printed 1612), a well-informed response to the criticism frequently leveled against the drama. Like most apologists of the time, Heywood rests his defense on the neoclassic idea that art serves a moral function.

From the mid-1620s on, Heywood devoted himself more and more to nondramatic writing, although in his later years he did produce several lord mayor's pageants. His long and fruitful but unspectacular career came to an end sometime before Aug. 16, 1641, when he was buried in St. James's Church in the Clerkenwell section of London.

Further Reading

The standard biographical study of Heywood is Arthur Melville Clark, *Thomas Heywood, Playwright and Miscellanist* (1931), a detailed and judicious examination of the relatively meager documentary evidence about Heywood's life. Frederick S. Boas, *Thomas Heywood* (1950), is valuable but less comprehensive.

Additional Sources

Baines, Barbara J. (Barbara Joan), *Thomas Heywood,* Boston: Twayne, 1984.

Boas, Frederick S. (Frederick Samuel), 1862-1957., *Thomas Heywood,* St. Clair Shores, Mich., Scholarly Press 1974; Folcroft, Pa. Folcroft Library Editions, 1974; New York: Phaeton Press, 1975; Norwood, Pa.: Norwood Editions, 1977.

McLuskie, Kathleen, *Dekker and Heywood: professional dramatists,* New York: St. Martin's Press, 1993.

Wentworth, Michael D., *Thomas Heywood, a reference guide,* Boston, Mass.: G.K. Hall, 1986. □

James Butler Hickok

James Butler Hickok (1837-1876), American gunfighter, scout, and spy, brought law to the untamed West. In his lifetime he became the symbolic western hero.

James Hickok was born on May 27, 1837, in Troy Grove, Ill. The Hickok family was abolitionist and evidently schooled him in the "genteel tradition." In 1855 he left home for Kansas. He filed land claims in Johnson County and apparently wanted to become a farmer.

By 1858, after serving briefly as constable, Hickok was working for the famous express company Russell, Majors and Waddell. Early in 1861 the firm stationed him at their Rock Creek, Nebr., station as assistant stock tender. There Hickok and fellow employees killed David McCanles and his two companions, who had come—unarmed—to collect the delinquent payments on the Rock Creek station land. Tried for murder, Hickok and the express company workers pleaded self-defense and were acquitted.

During the Civil War, Hickok served the Union forces creditably as wagon master, scout, and spy. Just after the war, while gambling, Hickok killed David Tutt, a former Confederate, in the prototype setting for later stories and movies—an iron-nerved shoot-out in the public square of Springfield, Mo. Tried for murder, he was again acquitted. Shortly afterward an inflated story about Hickok was published in *Harper's Magazine,* and from this grew the legend of "Wild Bill," the western hero.

Early in 1866, as deputy U.S. marshal at Fort Riley, Kans., Wild Bill was told to establish order. Conditions were close to chaos, with growing enmity between emigrant train scouts and discontented soldiers. Hickok quieted the fort. When the ordinarily reticent and soft-spoken marshal shouted, "This has gone far enough," it usually intimidated even the most unruly. If not, his fist or pistol barrel reinforced his voice. Later he rounded up deserters, horse thieves, and illegal timber cutters. He also gambled and drank.

In late 1869 Hickok became sheriff of Hays City, Kans., where drinking, gambling, and prostitution often led to violence. In 4 months as sheriff there Hickok helped establish law and order, although in doing so he killed two men. The lawless element understandably resented Hickok, and several attempts were made on his life. Thus he developed a habit of standing or sitting with his back to a wall.

Hickok appeared briefly in a Wild West show before becoming city marshal of Abilene, Kans., in 1871. Abilene was a railhead, and many cowboys ended their trail drives with pistol shots and uninhibited drinking. Once again Hickok used weapons and threats to keep order. In October one man was killed by Hickok's bullet during a group "spree." A policeman was also killed by running into the cross fire. Citizens supported Hickok's actions, but he was discharged in December.

Hickok was about 6 feet tall, with a good physique and pale blue eyes. He often wore fancy shirts, a red vest, the latest design in trousers, and a flat, wide-brimmed hat. Many thought him handsome, and women found him attractive. In manner he reflected the genteel tradition of quiet courtesy.

During 1872 and 1873 Wild Bill drifted around Kansas and Missouri gambling. Once he wrote to a St. Louis newspaper denying he had been killed by some Texans. He next appeared in Cheyenne and stayed nearby during 1874 and

1875. Here Wild Bill probably met "Calamity Jane" Cannary. He married a widowed circus owner in Cheyenne in 1876. He also gambled considerably and was several times dubbed a vagrant and ordered out of town.

Hickok left Cheyenne for the Black Hills soon after his marriage, arriving at Deadwood, Dakota Territory, in July with "Colorado Charlie" Utter and Calamity Jane. He looked briefly for a mining claim and gambled in various saloons. On Aug. 2, 1876, while playing cards, he was shot in the back of the head; Hickok had forgotten to keep his back to the wall. His hand—two aces, two eights, and a jack—became known as the "dead man's hand."

Further Reading

Frank J. Wilstach, *Wild Bill Hickok: The Prince of Pistoleers* (1926), is interesting and fairly accurate. Well researched and factually correct is Joseph G. Rosa, *They Called Him Wild Bill: The Life and Adventures of James Butler Hickok* (1964). Another reliable work is William Elsey Connelley, *Wild Bill and His Era* (1933). A useful biography is Richard O'Connor, *Wild Bill Hickok* (1959). Kent Ladd Steckmesser, *The Western Hero in History and Legend* (1965), is a study of the folklore that created myths about the West and its rugged heroes. □

Edward Hicks

Edward Hicks (1780-1849) was an American folk painter whose chief subject was the "Peaceable Kingdom," based on the biblical prophecy from Isaiah.

Edward Hicks was born on April 4, 1780, in a small Pennsylvania town (now Langhorne). He was orphaned early and boarded out at the age of 3 to David Twining, a Quaker, civic leader, and prosperous farmer near Newtown, Pa.

At 13 Hicks was apprenticed to a coach maker. In 1800 he began working as a journeyman coach painter and 6 months later struck out on his own. When he came of age in 1801, Hicks began to attend Quaker meetings at nearby Middletown. Two years later he applied for Quaker membership there and married Sarah Worstall, whom he had known since childhood. The couple began married life in Milford, Pa., where the first of their four children was born.

Hicks painted an elaborate tavern sign, probably in 1813, the same year that he turned from coach painting to farming. Failing as a farmer, he returned in 1815 to Newtown and to painting. That year a Friends' meeting was established there, and the painter met his cousin, Elias Hicks of Long Island, who had founded the Hicksite movement, which urged a return to the principles of the early Quakers. A fireboard painted in 1817 may have been Hicks's first easel painting.

Hicks's 1819 visit to Niagara Falls was used later as the subject of at least two paintings. In 1820, with few painting commissions to occupy him, Hicks visited Elias's Long Island meetings to work for peace among disparate Quaker factions. That year he also painted the first version of the "Peaceable Kingdom," a favorite subject of which almost 60 versions are extant. In 1827, when a schism developed among the Quakers, Hicks joined his cousin as a member of the dissenting Hicksites.

Hicks continued to paint "Peaceable Kingdom" pictures, both as gifts and as commissions from relatives and friends. In the 1840s he painted the first of several landscapes that range from beautiful and romantic versions of Bucks County, Pa., farms to renditions of the *Grave of William Penn,* based on a print or book illustration. He painted several versions of other subjects, including *Penn's Treaty with the Indians* and *Washington Crossing the Delaware.*

On Aug. 23, 1849, Hicks died in Newtown. According to a contemporary account, his funeral was the largest ever held in Bucks County. More than 100 paintings by this supremely talented, intensely personal, and unique folk artist still exist.

Further Reading

The painter's own *Memoirs of the Life and Religious Labors of Edward Hicks* was published in 1851. The definitive biography is Alice Ford, *Edward Hicks: Painter of the Peaceable Kingdom* (1952). The most comprehensive exhibition of Hicks's paintings took place in 1960 at the Abby Aldrich Rockefeller Folk Art Collection in Williamsburg, Va.; the exhibition's catalog, with an introduction and chronology by Alice Ford, deals directly with his work.

Additional Sources

Andrew Crispo Gallery., *Edward Hicks, a gentle spirit: catalog of an exhibition, May 16 thru June 28, 1975,* New York: A. Crispo Gallery, 1975.

Ford, Alice, *Edward Hicks, his life and art,* New York: Abbeville Press, 1985.

Ford, Alice, *Edward Hicks, painter of the Peaceable Kingdom,* Millwood, N.Y., Kraus Reprint Co., 1973.

Goldstein, Ernest, *Edward Hicks' The Peaceable Kingdom,* Champaign, Ill.: Garrard Pub. Co., 1982.

Haynes, George Emerson, *Edward Hicks, Friends' minister,* Doylestown, Pa.: C. Ingerman at the Quixott Press, 1974.

Hicks, Edward, *A peaceable season,* Princeton, Pyne Press; distributed by Scribner, New York, 1973.

Mather, Eleanore Price, *Edward Hicks, his peaceable kingdoms and other paintings,* Newark: University of Delaware Press; New York: Cornwall Books, 1983.

Pullinger, Edna S., *A dream of peace; Edward Hicks of Newtown,* Philadelphia, Dorrance 1973. □

Miguel Hidalgo y Costilla

Miguel Hidalgo y Costilla (1753-1811), a Mexican revolutionary priest, is considered the foremost patriot of Mexican independence. He led a revolt against Spanish rule that inaugurated a series of military and political episodes culminating in the achievement of Mexican independence in 1821.

Miguel Hidalgo was born a Creole on May 8, 1753. His father was the administrator of a *hacienda* in the Bajío (in the present state of Guanajuato). Miguel was trained briefly in a Jesuit school before the order was expelled from the empire in 1767. Later that year he matriculated in the diocesan College of San Nicolás in Valladolid (now Morelia). Hidalgo was intellectually oriented and chose to remain part of the academic community long after he had earned degrees in theology and had been ordained. By 1776 he was a member of the San Nicolás faculty and remained in Valladolid until 1792 as an academician, an exponent of the Enlightenment, and a Don Juan. In 1790 he became rector of the college, but his advanced ideas and mismanagement of funds soon led to his ouster.

From 1792 until 1810 Hidalgo served as parish priest in a succession of curacies. While in San Felipe (1793-1803), he made his house a salon and promoted French theatrical works (which he translated), orchestral music, dances, and literary discussions. The Inquisition investigated his activities (1800-1801) but did not press charges. On his arrival in Dolores near Guanajuato in 1803, Hidalgo turned to more socioeconomic interests. These he expressed through his development of local craft industries (ceramics, tanning, sericulture) for the benefit of the Indian and caste population.

Start of a Rebellion

With the Napoleonic invasion of Spain in 1808, Mexico's own crisis began. Hidalgo's search for intellectual

companionship had brought him into contact with prominent Creoles throughout the Bajío, Michoacán, and adjacent areas. When the Creoles in Querétaro organized a plot to expel the dominant peninsular Spaniards and to substitute themselves in power, Hidalgo joined. Articulate, well informed, and charismatic, he soon emerged as the uprising's leader, with Ignacio Allende, a militia captain, as second in command.

Exposed in early September 1810, the conspirators were forced to revolt prematurely. In a dramatic episode, Hidalgo put the plan into effect on September 16 by delivering an impassioned speech, the *Grito de Dolores,* to his parishioners. Avoiding abstractions like "independence," which were meaningless to the untutored villagers, he couched his revolutionary appeals in traditional protest language: the Catholic religion and the exiled king, Ferdinand VII, were extolled, and "death to bad government," represented by the peninsular Spaniards, was urged. The native patroness, the Virgin of Guadalupe, was added to the slogans, and her image became the banner of the revolt.

Hidalgo permitted Indians and castes to join his holy war of redemption in such numbers that the original white Creole motives of the insurrection were obscured. The jacquerie swept through the Bajío, burning and looting, until it engulfed the mining center of Guanajuato on September 28. The massacre of the Spanish defenders of the fortress granary and the subsequent sack of the city set the tone for the Hidalgo revolt. Hidalgo took Valladolid in mid-October and then marched on Mexico City. His horde numbered some 80,000 as it approached the viceregal capital.

Turn of the Tide

Meanwhile, the royalist government in Mexico City, under the leadership of Viceroy Francisco Venegas, had prepared defenses as much psychological as military. An intensive propaganda campaign had advertised the destructive horrors of the social revolution and revealed its threat to vested Creole interests. Hidalgo won a Pyrrhic victory on October 30 at Monte de las Cruces on the divide between Toluca and the capital but found the sedentary Indians and castes of the Valley of Mexico as much opposed to the Bajío intruders as were the Creoles and Spaniards. Threatened from the north by an army under the royalist general Félix Calleja, Hidalgo withdrew to Guadalajara to recoup without attacking Mexico City.

From his new base, Hidalgo made rudimentary efforts to establish a separatist government and to ameliorate the economic plight of the lower sectors of society (abolition of slavery and tribute were confirmed, and lands were ordered restored to Indian communities). Hidalgo, a strong egoist, however, assumed grandiose airs and exacerbated a growing schism with Allende's Creole faction. In January 1811 Calleja threatened Guadalajara, and Hidalgo advanced east to meet him at the bridge of Calderón with nearly 100,000 men. Calleja's disciplined army of 7,000 men defeated Hidalgo's horde on January 17, and Hidalgo fled north.

Suspended from command by the Allende party, Hidalgo was only a figurehead during the retreat. Allende's attempt in March to reach the United States was thwarted at Baján north of Saltillo, and the major leaders of the rebellion were captured. Hidalgo and his companions were removed to Chihuahua for trial and the inevitable executions. Aware that his enterprise had been a catastrophe, Hidalgo repented and apparently signed a public retraction. He was shot on July 30, 1811, and his body decapitated.

After Hidalgo's death his cause languished in spite of the efforts of José María Morelos, for the Creole majority remained opposed. In 1821 Agustín de Iturbide engineered a conservative independence and established a short-lived empire. After the republican overthrown of Iturbide, Hidalgo emerged as a patriotic hero. Modern Mexico venerates him as the *Padre de la Patria,* and the anniversary of his *Grito* is celebrated on September 16 as Mexico's independence day.

Further Reading

Hugh M. Hamill, Jr., *The Hidalgo Revolt: Prelude to Mexican Independence* (1966), is more concerned with the nature of the rebellion than with the man. For the general background see Lesley Byrd Simpson, *Many Mexicos* (1941; 4th ed. 1966), and Charles C. Cumberland, *Mexico: The Struggle for Modernity* (1968). A wealth of detail about the independence movement is in Hubert H. Bancroft, *History of Mexico,* vol. 4 (6 vols., 1883-1888).

Additional Sources

De Varona, Frank, *Miguel Hidalgo y Costilla: father of Mexican independence,* Brookfield, Conn.: Millbrook Press, 1993.
Hamill, Hugh M., *The Hidalgo revolt: prelude to Mexican independence,* Westport, Conn.: Greenwood Press, 1981.
Noll, Arthur Howard, *The life and times of Miguel Hidalgo y Costilla,* New York, Russell & Russell, 1973.
Perlin, D. E., *Father Miguel Hidalgo: a cry for freedom,* Dallas, Tex.: Hendrick-Long Pub. Co., 1991.
Scott, Bernice, *The grito of September sixteenth: biography of Padre Miguel Hidalgo, father of Mexican independence,* Ingleside, Tex.: Hemisphere House Books, 1981. □

Sadiq Hidayat

Sadiq Hidayat (1903-1951) is considered the father of modern Persian fiction. Although his works show a variety of literary forms, he was essentially a short-story writer.

Only since the beginning of the 20th century, because of the development of journalism and the influence of the West, has Persian prose been given the same status as poetry. Sadiq Hidayat contributed greatly to this literary revolution.

Hidayat was born on Feb. 17, 1903, in Teheran, Persia, to an aristocratic family of great landowners from the northern province of Mazandaran. His ancestors gave Persia (especially in the 19th century) many prominent statesmen and men of letters, and his family played an important role during the constitutional revolution of 1906, in this period of confrontation of the past with the new.

Very little is known about Hidayat as an individual, as he preferred to live modestly and in solitude. However, it is known that he cared for the underprivileged and the humble people of his country and that he was a patriot, but at the same time he was obsessed with an idea of self-destruction, of suicide.

In his 20s Hidayat went to France to study dentistry but soon changed to engineering. His engineering studies did not last long as he got interested in the study of pre-Islamic Persia. He turned to writing and in 1927 published *The Advantages of Vegetarianism,* a second attempt (the first was a short book, *Man and Animals,* an unsuccessful literary debut) to show man's cruelty to animals. The first sign of his new, simple style is seen in his short play, *The Legend of Creation.*

Hidayat returned to Persia in 1930, and his first collection of short stories, *Buried Alive,* was published that year. *The Blind Owl* (1937), his masterpiece, is his self-analysis. Through Kafka-like dream technique, Hidayat brings about unreality. The hero of the book seeks an escape from his misery and poverty in alcohol and opium, which cause his dream life. The atmosphere of *The Blind Owl* reminds one of the grimmest passages of E. A. Poe, F. Kafka, F. Dostoevsky, C. Dickens, and E. Zola. The recurring motif in Hidayat's stories is the vanity of human existence and its uselessness and absurdity.

During the 1930s Hidayat not only published eight other important works but was engaged with other progressive artists and writers in the movement against the old-fashioned bombastic style. His interest in Persian studies can be seen in the writing of this period as he tried to show the continuity of long Persian civilization and its glorious past. At the same time Hidayat was one of the pioneers in bringing folklore into his literary works. He was still under the influence of the famous Persian writer Omar Khayyam. Hidayat devoted three books to Khayyam and his philosophy, which touches on the everlasting puzzles of humanity.

The characters in Hidayat's short stories are mostly small people with their problems, sorrows, hates, and weaknesses—sympathetic yet repulsive. But as Henry D. G. Law writes: "Hidayat does not write objectively; with his reckless soaring genius he infuses into each of his tales his own personality, his own mood of pity, indignation, or tenderness, so that you may enter fully into the mind and thoughts of his characters, whoever they may be—seeing them as he sees them. They live and they haunt you long after you have closed the book."

In his stories Hidayat paints the abnormalities of human characters, who in most cases suffer from suicidal temptations. The satirical tone in some of his short stories in indirect criticism of the society which obstructs the education and advancement of the masses. Hidayat is particularly sympathetic toward the position of women, and the women in his stories are symbols of revolt against backwardness.

Hidayat's search for the glorious past of Persia led him to India, where he studied with Parsee scholars. But India did not cure him of his melancholy and gloomy pessimism. After returning to Persia, he published new collections of his grimmest short stories, *The Stray Dog* and *The Dead End,* which show his belief that man cannot liberate himself from his fate. Hidayat committed suicide in Paris on April 9, 1951.

Further Reading

Hidayat is considered in two studies that also provide useful background: Hassan Kamshad, *Modern Persian Prose Literature* (1966), and Jan Rypka, written in collaboration with Otaker Klima and others, *History of Iranian Literature* (1968).

Additional Sources

Bashiri, Iraj., *The fiction of Sadeq Hedayat,* Lexington, Ky., USA: Mazdea Publishers, 1984. □

Marguerite Higgins

American journalist Marguerite Higgins (1920-1966) gained respect among fellow reporters, the U.S. military, and the American public for her courage and determination as a war correspondent. She was most recognized for her front-line reports of the Korean War in the 1950s, which earned her the Pulitzer Prize for international reporting.

American newspaper journalist Marguerite Higgins gained a reputation for her courage and talent in reporting stories from the front lines of battle. She began her war writing by providing eyewitness accounts of the liberation of German concentration camps at the end of World War II. In the 1950s, she worked alongside soldiers in the field to produce vivid reports of the Korean War. For her Korean War stories, Higgins became the first woman to receive the Pulitzer Prize for international reporting. In addition to her newspaper work, she was also the author of several books that recount her journalistic adventures in Korea, Vietnam, and the Soviet Union.

Higgins was born in British-controlled Hong Kong, on September 3, 1920. She was the only child of Lawrence Daniel Higgins, an American who had served as a pilot in World War I, and Marguerite Goddard, a French woman he had met while in Europe. Early in her life, Higgins contracted malaria and was taken to Vietnam to recover in a treatment center there. When she was three, her father left his job with a Hong Kong shipping company and took his family to Oakland, California. Her family did not fare well in their attempts to adjust to life in suburban, middle-class America. After losing his job as a stockbroker, due to the stock market crash of 1929, Lawrence Higgins secured a position as a bank manager. Dissatisfied with his life, Lawrence Higgins began to drink heavily. His wife went to work as a French teacher to help boost the family income, but she too experienced distress that manifested itself in fainting spells. Their daughter, meanwhile, distinguished herself as

an excellent student. Already fluent in a number of languages due to her international background, she received a scholarship to attend the Anna Head school in Berkeley where her mother taught.

Began Career at the *Tribune*

At the age of 17, Higgins enrolled in the Berkeley campus of the University of California. In her first year at the college she began to work on the campus newspaper, the *Daily Californian,* which was known as one of the top university papers in the country. Higgins was enthralled by the world of journalism and set her sights on becoming a professional foreign correspondent. She graduated with honors and a degree in journalism in 1941. Unable to land a job at that time, she entered a master's program in journalism at Columbia University in New York City. During her graduate studies, she also held a part-time position for the *New York Tribune* as a college correspondent.

When Higgins graduated with her master of science degree in journalism in the summer of 1942, she found a much more receptive job market. Many men in the newspaper business had joined the armed forces to serve in World War II, providing new opportunities for women in positions previously unavailable to them. Higgins was hired full-time by the *Tribune* and set her sights on top assignments. Her ambition was aided not only by wartime shortages of reporters, but probably also by her numerous affairs with men on the staff. Her reputation as a temptress willing to use her sexual allure to gain professional favors did not do much for the success of her first marriage. She wedded Stanley

Moore, a Harvard philosophy professor, in 1942, but shortly afterward, her husband was drafted. The separation caused by war and the public reports of Higgins's romantic escapades brought a quick end to the relationship.

Covered Fall of Nazi Germany

Higgins's work earned her the use of a byline in the *Tribune* by 1943—she was one of the few staff writers to be so recognized. But, despite her success in New York, she was unable to convince her editors to give her the foreign correspondent assignment for which she longed. More interested in seeing the war than abiding by professional policy, she finally went over the heads of her editors to Helen Rogers Reid, the wife of the paper's owner. Reid had a hand in the operation of the *Tribune* and she also was known for her support of feminist issues. She sympathized with Higgins and arranged a post for her in London, England, in 1944. But covering events in London still did not satisfy the reporter's desire to be on the battlefront. With much persistence, she finally received permission to travel to Paris, and in the beginning of 1945, she landed an assignment at the Berlin bureau.

Although she did not get to the front lines until the very end of the war, Higgins's reporting still had an impact. She was one of a group of reporters that were allowed to tour parts of Germany decimated by bombing raids, she was on hand to cover the arrival of Allied forces at the Nazi concentration camps of Dachau and Buchenwald, and she witnessed the fall of Munich. Her work earned her a number of awards following the war, including an Army campaign ribbon for distinguished service, and the New York Newspaper Women's Award for best foreign correspondent of 1945.

Higgins remained in Europe in the late 1940s, covering such events as the Nuremburg war trials and the Berlin blockade. She was promoted to bureau chief in Berlin in 1947 at the age of 26, but it was evident that supervising a news office was not one of her strengths. Higgins became obsessed with staying ahead of competitors on every story, placing a great deal of stress on herself and her staff. Her personal life of this period was somewhat happier, but no less controversial; she began a relationship with Major General William Hall, the director of Army intelligence, who at that time was married with a family of four children back in America. Their attachment proved to be a strong one, however, and the two were married in 1953; they would later have two children of their own.

Gained Fame for Korean Exploits

Higgins was assigned to Tokyo, Japan, as Far East bureau chief in May of 1950. She took the transfer as a professional affront because stories on events in the Far East rarely appeared in the *Tribune*. But international events soon made it clear that she couldn't have been in a better place as a reporter. That June, communist North Korea invaded the U.S. supported country of South Korea, launching the Korean War. Higgins traveled to the South Korean capital of Seoul, recounting the events in the final days before the fall of that city to North Korean forces—barely escaping before the arrival of the communists. When the *Tribune* sent the more experienced war reporter Homer Bigart to cover Korea, Higgins was instructed by the paper to return to her Tokyo post. She refused to leave the action in Korea, however, and continued her coverage of the growing hostilities, beginning a rivalry with Bigart to get the best stories. Her ability to cover combat was threatened when American Lieutenant General Walton W. Walker banned all women from the front, stating that females could not be accommodated by facilities at the battlefield. Higgins, who was quite willing to don combat fatigues and join in the hardships of a soldier's life, again turned to Helen Rogers Reid for assistance. Reid contacted Walker's superior, General Douglas MacArthur, and permission was granted for Higgins to resume her front-line reporting.

Her reporting during the Korean War firmly established Higgins's image as a glamorously daring war correspondent. She won the respect of soldiers and male reporters alike for her pursuit of information under the most difficult and dangerous conditions. She gave readers a personal view of the war by working alongside military men, going so far as to join the Marines in landing in enemy territory at Inchon. The *Tribune* ran her stories on a regular basis, sometime placing them side-by-side with reports by her competitor, Bigart. Her popularity reached even greater heights when she was the subject of an article in the October 2, 1950, edition of *Life* magazine featuring photographs of Higgins outfitted in battle fatigues. She capitalized on interest in her wartime exploits by publishing *War in Korea* in 1951. Documenting her experiences as a reporter in Korea, the book became a best-selling hit in the United States.

Received Pulitzer Prize

Higgins's war correspondence was honored with a number of awards in the early 1950s. In 1951, she became the first woman to win a Pulitzer Prize for international reporting when she shared the prize with five other journalists. The same year she was named Woman of the Year by the Associated Press news organization. Her other honors included the George Polk Award of the Overseas Press Club and the Marine Corps Reserve Officers Award.

In 1953, Higgins covered the defeat of the French in their colony of Vietnam at Dien Bein Phu, resulting in the formation of North and South Vietnam. During the fighting there she narrowly escaped injury when the photographer Robert Capra was killed by a land mine just a few feet from her. Despite the harrowing experience, Higgins did not relent in her work. About this time, she received a visa to travel behind the Iron Curtain in the Soviet Union. Cold War tensions were at a high point, and she was the first reporter allowed on such a visit in many years. She traveled the nation extensively, covering 13,500 miles and getting a picture of life under Communism that had been previously unavailable to the West. The journey became the basis for another book, *Red Plush and Black Bread*, published in 1955. The same year she released another volume, *News is a Singular Thing*.

Over the next decade, Higgins continued to cross the globe, following her instinct for newsworthy international developments. In 1961 she reported on the civil war in the Congo, becoming the first member of the *Tribune* to cover the central African region since the search for David Livingstone by Henry Morton Stanley in the 1870s. She returned to Vietnam in 1963 and documented her concerns about American military involvement there in the 1965 book, *Our Vietnam Nightmare.*

Higgins ended her association with the *Tribune* in 1963 and began contributing weekly columns to *Newsday.* She established a home in Long Island, New York, at this time, but continued to travel, returning to Vietnam in 1965. There she was stricken with leishmaniasis, a tropical disease, and returned to the United States to be treated at Walter Reed Hospital in Washington, D.C. She fell into a coma and died on January 3, 1966, at the age of 45. Higgins's outstanding career as a journalist and her service to her country as a war correspondent were honored with her burial at Arlington National Cemetery.

Further Reading

Edwards, Julia, *Women of the World: The Great Foreign Correspondents,* Houghton Mifflin, 1988.
Kluger, Richard, *The Paper: The Life and Death of the New York Tribune,* Knopf, 1986.
May, Antoinette, *Witness to War: A Biography of Marguerite Higgins,* Beaufort Books, 1983.
Mydans, Carl, "Girl War Correspondent," *Life,* October 2, 1950, pp. 51-52. □

Thomas Wentworth Higginson

American reformer and editor Thomas Wentworth Higginson (1823-1911) led the first black regiment to serve in the Civil War. He also supported women's suffrage and encouraged many female writers.

Thomas W. Higginson was born on Dec. 23, 1823, in Cambridge, Mass. He graduated from Harvard in 1841. In 1847 he graduated from the Harvard Divinity School and married a distant cousin, Mary Channing. The couple moved to Newburyport, R.I., where Higginson served the Unitarian congregation, preaching social reform in general and abolition in particular. He was asked to resign after 2 years.

Free of the pulpit, Higginson worked for women's rights, the Free Soil party, and abolitionist causes, which brought him into contact with such men as Henry David Thoreau and Orestes Brownson. In the 1850s, while pastor of the Free Church of Worcester, Mass., Higginson lectured and wrote poetry and essays for the *Atlantic Monthly.* As an abolitionist, he was one of the "secret six" who sponsored John Brown's raid. In *Ought Women to Learn the Alphabet?*

(1859) he argued for education and professional opportunities for women.

While trying to recruit a regiment to fight in the Civil War, Higginson continued publishing essays in the *Atlantic.* One, "A Letter to a Young Contributor," elicited a response from an unknown poet in Amherst, Mass., who enclosed four poems. The inquirer was Emily Dickinson. Thus Higginson became the first person outside Emily Dickinson's small circle of friends to read her verse and offer criticism.

Higginson entered the Army as a captain of volunteers in August 1862, but he soon was offered the unique challenge of commanding the Army's first black regiment. These volunteers, recruited from freed slaves, became the model for later black units. Higginson's recollections appeared in *Army Life in a Black Regiment* (1870).

After the war Higginson settled in Newport, R.I. At first he devoted his energies to writing and lecturing in favor of radical reconstruction, but by 1867 he had turned to fiction. His novel, *Malbone,* was badly received.

Higginson's wife died in 1877. His second wife, Mary Thatcher, was one of the many authors he had encouraged. Two daughters were born to the couple. Profits from his *Young Folks' History of the United States* (1875) enabled the family to move to Cambridge. Here Higginson wrote his *Larger History of the United States* (1885).

Two years after Emily Dickinson's death, Higginson and Mabel Loomis Todd began preparing her poems and letters for publication. Higginson's reputation won Emily Dickinson a large and appreciative readership. But for his efforts, one of America's greatest poets might have gone unrecognized. Higginson continued as an active writer and leader until his death on May 9, 1911.

Further Reading

Three fine biographies of Higginson appeared in the 1960s: Anna Mary Wells, *Dear Preceptor* (1963); Howard N. Meyer, *Colonel of the Black Regiment* (1967); and Tilden G. Edelstein, *Strange Enthusiasm* (1968). A collection of Higginson's autobiographical essays, *Cheerful Yesterdays,* originally published in 1898, was reissued in 1968.

Additional Sources

Higginson, Thomas Wentworth, *Army life in a Black regiment,* Alexandria, Va.: Time-Life Books, 1982; New York: W.W. Norton, 1984.
Tuttleton, James W., *Thomas Wentworth Higginson,* Boston: Twayne Publishers, 1978. □

Johann Lucas von Hildebrandt

The Austrian architect Johann Lucas von Hildebrandt (1663-1745) introduced a lighter, more decorative quality into Austrian baroque architecture. In his works he emphasized structural clarity enlivened by ornamental touches.

Johann Lucas von Hildebrandt was born in Genoa, Italy, on Nov. 14, 1663, the son of a German officer in the imperial army stationed there. He was trained in Rome under Carlo Fontana in civil architecture, but he also studied town planning, military architecture, and fortification. In 1695-1696 Hildebrandt served as a military engineer under Prince Eugene of Savoy during his campaigns in the Piedmont. Late in 1696 Hildebrandt arrived in Vienna, where he remained for the rest of his life. By 1698 he was an imperial councilor and by 1699 court architect (surveyor general of imperial buildings). In spite of his official position, Hildebrandt found most of his clients among the aristocracy of the empire, for Johann Bernhard Fischer von Erlach, as chief court architect, dominated official building in Vienna. Although Hildebrandt received some commissions for religious buildings, he was largely a secular architect, constructing palaces and summer residences for the nobility.

Hildebrandt's greatest and most understanding patron was Count Friedrich Carl Schönborn, vice-chancellor of the empire and a passionate builder, who showed the greatest sympathy for his temperamental and erratic architect. For the Schönborn family Hildebrandt constructed their summer palace in Vienna (1706-1717) and their summer palace (1710-1717) and Loreto Church at Göllersdorf not far from the city; he also built churches on several of their properties, the family chapel in the Cathedral of Würzburg, and other chapels on their estates in Lower Austria, Bohemia, and Moravia.

Hildebrandt built the palace on the Freyung in Vienna for Count Wierich Daun (1713-1716), which is considered one of his best works and the most successful city palace of the period. Constructed on a small, narrow plot of land, the palace (now called the Daun-Kinsky Palace) is noteworthy for the ornamentation that enlivens the flat facade and for the ingenious interior features, particularly the grand stairway, where Hildebrandt achieved the monumentality the period required of a main stairway through brilliant exploitation of the extremely limited space at his disposal.

The Belvedere

At the same time, Hildebrandt was working for Prince Eugene of Savoy in the construction of his summer palace outside the city walls on the Rennweg. Situated on the street, with a long formal garden running up the slope behind it, the Belvedere Palace (1714-1716) was based on the plan of French city palaces with their walled courtyards in front of the building. This palace, planned to house the prince himself as well as his staff and some of his collections, proved to be too small, and the prince decided to have another palace built, at the other end of the garden on top of the hill, to be used primarily for entertaining and formal receptions. This palace (1721-1722), now called the Upper Belvedere to distinguish it from the first building, the Lower Belvedere, is Hildebrandt's masterpiece. With its intricate silhouette, clearly showing that it was meant to be seen from a distance, the Upper Belvedere, part suburban villa, part fantastic reception room, part garden pavilion, is joined to the relatively simpler Lower Belvedere by formal gardens with terraces, pools, fountains, mazes, and trimmed avenues of greenery, all as much part of the ensemble as the two buildings.

Fischer von Erlach's Karlskirche and Hildebrandt's Belvedere are the two major baroque monuments of Vienna. The Belvedere now houses the Österreichische Galerie (Austrian State Galleries of Art).

Other Works

Hildebrandt also collaborated with Balthasar Neumann in the planning and construction of the Residenz palace at Würzburg from 1720 to 1723 and again from 1729 to 1744. During this period Hildebrandt was busy on a score of projects, and his fame and esteem increased. In 1723 he was ennobled by the Emperor, and upon Fischer von Erlach's death that year Hildebrandt achieved the position of first court architect, for which he had worked and intrigued for years, only to lose it to Fischer's son shortly afterward. For Prince Eugene the architect planned the terraces at Schlosshof (1725-1732) and his palace of Rackeve on an island in the Danube near Budapest.

Of Hildebrandt's religious buildings the most noteworthy are the church of Maria-Treu (1698) and the Peterskirche (1702-1707), both in Vienna and both among the outstanding baroque monuments of the city. His grandiose plans for rebuilding and enlarging the monastery of Göttweig (1719), although left incomplete, reveal his abilities as an engineer in the fortifications and as an architect in the main building of the monastery, where the great staircase is one of his most successful creations.

For the prince-bishop of Salzburg, Count Franz Anton Harrach, Hildebrandt designed rooms in the Salzburg Residenz (1710-1711) and largely rebuilt Schloss Mirabell (1722-1725) in Salzburg, which contains one of his finest staircases. For the Harrach family he designed a garden pavilion for their city palace in Vienna and a summer palace outside the city.

Hildebrandt also designed monuments, temporary festival decorations, and even sarcophagi, such as the splendid lead tombs for several of the Hapsburgs in their burial crypt in the Capuchin Church in Vienna, the most notable being those for Emperor Leopold I (1705) and Joseph I (1712). During his last years Hildebrandt was working on Schloss Werneck, on illuminations celebrating the birth of the archdukes Joseph and Charles, and on the monastery of Klosterbruck (Louka) near Znaim in Moravia. He died on Nov. 16, 1745, in Vienna.

Further Reading

Hildebrandt's work is discussed in John Bourke, *Baroque Churches of Central Europe* (1958; 2d ed. rev. 1962); Nicholas Powell, *From Baroque to Rococo* (1959); and Eberhard Hempel, *Baroque Art and Architecture in Central Europe* (1965). See also Henry-Russell Hitchcock, *Rococo Architecture in Southern Germany* (1968). □

Richard Hildreth

Richard Hildreth (1807-1865), American historian and political theorist, wrote one of the first multivolume histories of the United States.

R ichard Hildreth was born in Deerfield, Mass., on June 22, 1807. He went to Phillips Exeter Academy, where his father was teaching, and then enrolled at Harvard, graduating in 1826. After an apprenticeship in a law office at Newburyport, he was admitted to the Massachusetts bar in 1832. During his legal studies Hildreth was a correspondent for several newspapers and afterward turned to newspaper work permanently, becoming editor of the *Boston Atlas.*

Hildreth was an antislavery, free-bank Whig whose first published work was a popular antislavery novel, *The Slave; or, Memoirs of Archy Moore* (1836). In 1840 he published *Despotism in America,* an attack on slavery; *The Contrast; or, William Henry Harrison versus Martin Van Buren,* a campaign tract for Harrison; and *Banks, Banking, and Paper Currencies,* a book favoring free banking.

In 1840 Hildreth traveled to British Guiena to recover his failing health. There he worked on newspapers and wrote two books: *Theory of Morals* (published 1844) and *Theory of Politics* (published 1853). In the latter he claimed that wealth controls political power and unequal distribution of wealth results in the destruction of democracy.

Hildreth returned to the United States in 1843. He began the *History of the United States* in 1847. Six volumes, published between 1849 and 1852, covered the periods from the Age of Discovery to the Missouri Compromise. Failing to obtain an appointment in history at Harvard, he became a political reporter for the *New York Tribune.* For his support of the Republican party, President Abraham Lincoln named Hildreth consul at Trieste during the Civil War. While in Europe, Hildreth became ill, and he resigned. He died on July 11, 1865, in Florence.

Hildreth's multivolume history did not gain acceptance in his lifetime. His astringent criticism of Puritan rule alienated New Englanders, while his adamant opposition to slavery put off Southern readers. He lacked the rampant nationalism of the historian George Bancroft and thus failed to tap the romantic patriotism of the day. However, critics today suggest that Hildreth was some 40 years ahead of his time, and his reputation has improved with the years.

Further Reading

Donald E. Emerson's book, *Richard Hildreth* (1946), and his chapter "Hildreth, Draper, and 'Scientific History'" in Eric F. Goldman, ed., *Historiography and Urbanization: Essays in American History in Honor of W. Stull Holt* (1941), claim that Hildreth was the first American historian to conceive of the use of scientific methods in history. A detailed examination of Hildreth's philosophy is in Martha Mary Pingel, ed., *An American Utilitarian: Richard Hildreth as a Philosopher* (1948). Two other appraisals of Hildreth are Alfred H. Kelly's chapter on Hildreth in William T. Hutchinson, ed., *The Marcus W.* *Jernegan Essays in American Historiography* (1937), and Harvey Wish's chapter "Richard Hildreth, Utilitarian Philosopher" in his *The American Historian: A Social-Intellectual History of the Writing of the American Past* (1960). □

Anita Hill

It was during the Senate confirmation hearings in October 1991, for United States Supreme Court Justice Clarence Thomas that Anita Hill became famous. She came forward with sexual harassment charges against Judge Thomas that shocked the nation, and many watched as she poured out painful details of Thomas's alleged sexual harassment, purportedly committed when both had worked for the Equal Employment Opportunities Commission.

O n October 6, 1991, Anita Hill's life was dramatically and irrevocably changed when her charges of sexual harassment against a former employer, Clarence Thomas, were made public on the eve of his confirmation as a Supreme Court justice. In the ensuing days, Hill was grilled by the Senate Judiciary Committee about the graphic details of the alleged harassment and about her personal life. Her compelling testimony before the committee was broadcast live around the globe, sweeping her from the quiet obscurity of her life as a professor of law at the University of Oklahoma. Her charges produced a stunning collision of race and gender issues, and reactions to her and her story were highly polarized; some viewed her as a hero and a martyr, while others vilified her as mentally unstable, a liar, and even a racist.

In the end, the U.S. House and Senate chose to dismiss her allegations, and as a result, Thomas was given a seat on the highest court in the nation. Yet, Hill's appearance in Washington, D.C., was by no means without far-reaching effects. Her testimony, and the committee's reaction to it, have since been credited with revitalizing feminism, greatly increasing the public's awareness of sexual harassment, inspiring women to run for office in record numbers, and significantly increasing the numbers of women willing to speak out publicly about their own experiences of sexual harassment when they might otherwise have suffered in silence.

Nothing in Anita Hill's upbringing could have prepared her for the glare of international publicity she would eventually face. The youngest in a family of 13 children, she was raised in a deeply religious atmosphere on her parents' farm in rural Morris, Oklahoma, located some 45 miles south of Tulsa. Sundays were spent at the Lone Pine Baptist Church, while the rest of her week was filled with farm chores and schoolwork. She attended Okmulgee County's integrated schools, where she earned straight As and graduated as class secretary, valedictorian, and a National Honor Society student. After graduation, she attended Oklahoma State University, where she continued her outstanding academic

performance and graduated with a degree in psychology and numerous academic honors.

An internship with a local judge had turned her ambitions to the field of law, and she sought and won admission into Yale University's demanding School of Law, where she was one of 11 black students in a class of 160. After graduation, she took a full-time job as a professional lawyer with the Washington law firm of Ward, Harkrader, and Ross.

Association with Clarence Thomas

In 1981, after working with the firm for about a year, Hill accepted a job as the personal assistant to Clarence Thomas, who was then head of the Office of Civil Rights at the Education Department in Washington. It was at this time, according to her sworn testimony, that he made repeated advances toward her and, when she rebuffed him, began to make vulgar remarks to her and to describe in vivid detail various hard-core pornographic films he had seen. When he began dating someone else, Hill stated, the harassment stopped, and she accepted an offer to follow him to a better job when he was made chairman of the Equal Employment Opportunity Commission. The alleged harassment began again, however, according to Hill's version of the events. In 1983, after being hospitalized with stress-related stomach problems, she left Washington to accept a position as a professor in the area of civil rights at Oral Roberts University in Tulsa. As a faculty member of this conservative religious school, Hill took an oath that said in part: "I will not lie, I will not steal, I will not curse, I will not be a talebearer."

In 1986, the university was reorganized, and the law school moved to the state of Virginia. Because she preferred to be near her family in Oklahoma, Hill declined to move with the school and instead sought employment at the University of Oklahoma, where she became a specialist in contract law. Six years of teaching are usually required before tenured status is granted to a professor there, but Hill was tenured after only four years. In addition to her teaching duties, she served on the faculty senate and was also named the faculty administrative fellow in the Office of the Provost, which made her a key voice in all major academic policy decisions.

Call from the Senate

Such was the state of Hill's life on September 3, 1991, when she was approached by the Senate Judiciary Committee and asked to supply background information on Clarence Thomas, who was then being considered as a replacement for Supreme Court Justice Thurgood Marshall. In a news conference given at the University of Oklahoma by Hill, which was excerpted at length in the *New York Times,* Hill elaborated: "They asked me questions about work that I had done there, and they asked me specifically about harassment and issues involving women in the workplace. Those questions, I have heard, were prompted by rumors that individuals who had worked at the agency had understood that I had been subject to some improper conduct . . . while at the agency." Hill, who had never filed a complaint against Thomas, found herself reluctant to go public with her story some ten years after the fact.

Initially, she decided to protect herself and her privacy by remaining silent. On further reflection, however, she apparently felt an obligation to tell the truth as she knew it, no matter how difficult that might be. "Here is a person [Thomas] who is in charge of protecting rights of women and other groups in the workplace and he is using his position of power for personal gain for one thing," she said in an interview with National Public Radio, also quoted by the *New York Times.* "And he did it in an very ugly and intimidating way."

By September 9, Hill had decided to cooperate in the investigation of Thomas on the condition that her identity be kept confidential. But she was informed on September 20 that the Judiciary Committee could not be told her story unless Thomas was notified of her identity and given a chance to respond to her allegations. Furthermore, if she agreed to cooperate, she and Thomas would both be questioned by the FBI. Hill pondered these new facts as the confirmation hearings for Thomas, already underway, drew near their close. On September 23, she agreed to allow her name to be used in an FBI investigation. She also requested permission to submit a personal statement to the committee.

Hill has since criticized the handling of her complaint, in part because copies of the FBI report were given to just two committee members, and her personal statement also failed to reach all those who should have seen it. Thomas, meanwhile, had issued a sworn statement forcefully denying all of Hill's allegations against him. In his version of the events, he had simply asked Hill out for dates a few times. He and his supporters characterized her eleventh-hour appearance as a ploy designed to keep him off the bench, engineered by liberals opposed to his appointment to the court. Hill answered such suggestions in her press conference at the University of Oklahoma: "There is absolutely no basis for that allegation, that I am somehow involved in some political plan to undermine the nominee. And I cannot even understand how someone could attempt to support such a claim. . . . This has taken a great toll on me personally and professionally, and there is no way that I would do something like this for political purposes."

Televised Hearings

After considerable debate, the U.S. Senate decided that new hearings on Thomas's confirmation would be held and that Hill would be called to Washington to testify before the Senate Judiciary Committee—which was made up of 14 white, male legislators. The televised hearings, which included Hill's and Thomas's appearances, drew an audience of millions, who were riveted by the drama of race and sex unfolding on the screen. Hill remained dignified and composed throughout the proceedings—in the face of repetitive questioning by the senators. Her credibility and character were vehemently attacked by some observers, who questioned why she maintained a speaking relationship with Thomas after the alleged incidents occurred and why she never filed a formal complaint. Republican legislator Arlen Specter went so far as to imply that Hill had fantasized the whole scenario; others suggested that she was acting out of jealousy because Thomas had failed to provide her the attentions she secretly desired from him.

Racial issues were in evidence during the hearings and influenced reaction among both the general public and the Judiciary Committee. Thomas himself fueled that fire when he denounced the proceedings as a "high-tech lynching," effectively accusing Hill of participating in a racist plot to keep him out of the Supreme Court because he is black. In the book *Race-ing Justice, En-gendering Power,* essayist Carol M. Swain discussed another race-related phenomenon that turned the tide of black opinion against Hill: "For African Americans generally, the issue was not so much whether Hill was credible or not; she was dismissed because many saw her as a person who had violated the code . . . which mandates that blacks should not criticize, let alone accuse, each other in front of whites."

In the Aftermath

The nomination of Clarence Thomas was confirmed on October 16, 1991. Hill, who had by then returned to Oklahoma, accepted the news with the composure that had marked her appearance before the committee. Disregarding all the racial, political, and feminist implications of the decision, she told Roberto Suro of the *New York Times:* "For me it is enough justice getting it heard. I just wanted people to know and understand that this had happened. . . . You just have to tell the truth and that's the most anyone can expect from you and if you get that opportunity, you will have accomplished something."

Many of Hill's detractors had predicted that she would capitalize on her experience by making high-paid speaking appearances, writing a book, or even selling her story as a television movie-of-the-week, but in the months following her testimony, she proved them wrong. She resumed her usual teaching duties and returned to her regular routine as nearly as was possible, given the reporters and others who constantly sought her out. In time she took a sabbatical from teaching, using the interlude to study the sociology and psychology of sexual harassment. Aside from an appearance on the CBS News program *60 Minutes,* and, much later, one on the *Today* show, she turned down all interview requests. She made carefully selected appearances on the speaking circuit, often for no fee, and at such appearances, she declined to talk in detail about the hearings or her own personal experience, focusing instead on the larger issues of sexual harassment and discrimination in general.

Following the hearings, former Minnesota House representative Gloria M. Segal approached Hill with a plan to establish an endowed fund for a special professorship in her name—devoted to the study of sexual harassment and workplace equity—at the University of Oklahoma. In spite of the fact that half of the $250,000 needed for the project was easily raised, by mid-1993 work on establishing the professorship had stalled, due mainly to the adverse publicity and political fallout felt at the University of Oklahoma. The future of the fund remains in doubt, although several other colleges and universities across the country have reportedly expressed an interest in assuming control of the money and following through on the institution of the professorship.

The Thomas-Hill hearings continued to resonate long after the headlines had faded. Public opinion polls taken at the time of the Senate hearings showed that a majority of those polled discredited Hill's story. Yet a poll taken one year later showed that twice as many people had come to believe her version of the events. Then, in the spring of 1993, investigative journalist David Brock published his controversial book *The Real Anita Hill,* in which he claims to offer hard evidence that Hill lied about her relationship with Thomas. Political commentator George F. Will commented in *Newsweek:* "To believe that Hill told the truth you must believe that dozens of people, with no common or even apparent motive to lie, did so. Brock's book will be persuasive to minds not sealed by the caulking of ideology. If Hill is a 'victim,' it is not of sexual harassment. . . . Rather, she may be a victim of the system . . . that taught her to think of herself as a victim and made her fluent in the rhetoric of victimization."

Still, Anita Hill has, for many, become a symbol of a new and powerful wave of feminism. Women's groups continue to credit Hill's appearance before the Senate Judiciary Committee with vastly increasing the public's awareness of sexual harassment and making it much less tolerated in the workplace. In an Associated Press news story dated October 11, 1992, Helen Neuborne, executive director of the NOW Legal Defense and Education Fund, stated: "A lot of women had felt so isolated and perhaps couldn't even define sexual harassment. . . . The hearings made an enormous difference even though they were horrible."

The Equal Employment Opportunity Commission, where Hill and Thomas once worked, reported a 50 percent increase in complaints filed for harassment in the year following Hill's testimony. Additionally, in the aftermath of the hearings, numerous women ran for and won election to government office for the first time, citing their dissatisfaction with the all-male Senate Committee's response to Hill's allegations as their primary reason for doing so. And debate about the truth or falsity of Hill's allegations went on. Tonya Bolden, a *Black Enterprise* contributor commenting on the various analyses of the Hill-Thomas affair, suggested that the entire incident may have sparked a vital understanding of broader issues. As she put it in the April 1993 issue: "At the end you care less about who was lying and more about what you can do to counter racism and sexism."

In the fall of 1995, Hill retuned to her teaching position at the University of Oklahoma. During her leave, she authored two books. In 1995, she co-edited the book *Race, Gender, and Power in America: the legacy of the Hill-Thomas hearing* with Emma Coleman Jordan. Hill left the University of Oklahoma at the end of the fall 1996 semester.

Further Reading

The Black Scholar staff, editors, *Court of Appeal: The Black Community Speaks Out on the Racial and Sexual Politics of Thomas vs. Hill,* One World/Ballantine, 1992.

Brock, David, *The Real Anita Hill,* Free Press, 1993.

Morrison, Toni, editor, *Race-ing Justice, En-gendering Power: Essays on Anita Hill, Clarence Thomas, and the Construction of Social Reality,* Pantheon, 1992.

American Spectator, March 1992.

Associated Press wire report, October 11, 1992.

Black Enterprise, April 1993, p. 12.

Essence, March 1992, pp. 55-56, 116-17.

Ms., January-February 1992.

Nation, November 4, 1991.

National Law Journal, January 20, 1992.

Newsweek, December 28, 1992, pp. 20-22; April 19, 1993, p. 74.

New York Times, October 7, 1991; October 8, 1991; October 9, 1991; October 10, 1991; October 11, 1991; October 14, 1991; October 16, 1991; October 17, 1991; November 2, 1991; December 18, 1991; February 3, 1992; April 26, 1992; October 7, 1992; October 17, 1992; October 19, 1992.

New York Times Book Review, October 25, 1992.

Oakland Press (Oakland County, MI), October 11, 1992; April 24, 1993, p. A4.

Time, October 21, 1991; October 19, 1992.

U.S. News and World Report, November 2, 1992.

Working Woman, September 1992, p. 21. □

Archibald Vivian Hill

English physiologist Archibald Vivian Hill (1886-1977) shared the Nobel Prize in Physiology or Medicine (1922) for his discoveries relating to the production of heat in muscles.

The son of a timber merchant, A(rchibald) V(ivian) Hill was born in Bristol, England, on Sept. 26, 1886. In 1904 he entered Trinity College, Cambridge, to begin a brilliant career, first in mathematics, then in physiology, in which he obtained a first-class honors degree in 1909.

From 1909 until World War I broke out in 1914, Hill did research work in the Physiological Laboratory at Cambridge. Advised to investigate "the efficiency of cut-out frog's muscle as a thermodynamic machine," this would become Hill's life work. During the war he was director of an official group of scientists who produced revolutionary recommendations on antiaircraft gunsights. In 1920 Hill became Brackenbury professor of physiology in the University of Manchester and in 1923 Jodrell professor of physiology at University College, London. Two years later he was appointed as the Royal Society's Foulerton Research Professor in biophysics at University College. He retired from this chair in 1956 but continued to work in the physiology department.

Early Investigations in Muscle Physiology

Following the suggestion of English physiologist J.N. Langley, Hill began research into the production of heat by a contracting muscle. Practically all that was known at the time was that the total energy involved in contraction of a muscle, that is, the sum of the work done and the heat evolved, was related to the length of the muscle and to the load. But in a single muscle twitch, the heat evolved does not exceed 0.003°C, and the available instruments could

not measure such small amounts. The successive events in a muscle contraction are all chemical reactions, but these cannot be analyzed immediately after they occur, and chemistry can give only the end result. The physical changes can be measured as soon as they occur—hence the emphasis on heat production.

Using a strap-like thigh muscle in the frog, Hill demonstrated that oxygen is needed not for the contractile phase of muscular activity but only for the recovery phase. This led to the discovery of the numerous biochemical reactions that occur in muscle cells and result in contraction.

Hill's studies of the heat in muscle contraction continued through the years. There was no early chemical proof of his deductions, but they were confirmed chemically by Otto Meyerhof in 1920.

Hill wrote many of his papers in collaboration with William Hartree, who worked in Hill's laboratory. Shortly after the war, Hill found a sudden, large production of heat at the onset of contraction and another during relaxation. In 1920, with Hartree, he discovered that, with muscles in nitrogen, there was indeed a smaller heat production during the three minutes following the stimulus. In 1922 they wrote a standard paper on recovery heat, in which they gave the first clear description of the characteristics of this "anaerobic delayed heat" (a.d.h.) found in muscles in nitrogen. In 1923 they gave its value as about 0.25 of the initial heat. The explanation of the a.d.h. had to await the further chemical work of Meyerhof and others. In 1922 Hill shared the Nobel Prize in Physiology or Medicine with Meyerhof.

More Theories and Publications

During World War II, Hill's laboratory was closed, and he held important public and advisory offices, such as chairman of the Executive Committee of the National Physical Laboratory, Member of Parliament for the University of Cambridge, and member of the War Cabinet Scientific Advisory Committee. He also visited India as a consultant to the Indian government on scientific matters.

Hill returned to experimental work after the war and published numerous important papers. He also derived his "Hill equation," a mathematical expression for the uptake of oxygen by hemoglobin.

In 1967 Hill stopped all experimental work and moved to Cambridge. His last book *First and Last Experiments in Muscle Mechanics* (1970) contains the results of his difficult experimental and mathematical investigations.

For many years Hill carried out experiments on muscular activity in trained athletes. In 1922 he introduced the fruitful conception of the "oxygen debt," which explains how a person can for a short period produce without exhaustion far larger quantities of lactic acid than the maximum oxygen intake can oxidize at the time. In many experiments Hill found that the maximum speed in running was usually reached in 30 to 50 yards; it then began to decline. In 1925 Hill was the first to plot speed against distance for world running records. In 1928 he studied the effects of different winds on running, and he later investigated the force-velocity relationship in human muscle.

Hill's important books include: *Muscular Activity* (1926), *Muscular Movement in Man* (1927), *Chemical Wave Transmission in Nerve* (1932), and *Trails and Trials in Physiology* (1965). *Trails and Trials*, although nominally an annotated and classified bibliography of his own scientific papers and those of his coworkers, contains critical discussions of his work and that of others.

Honors

Hill received many honors in addition to his Nobel Prize. He became an Officer of the Order of the British Empire in 1918 and a Companion of Honour in 1946. In 1918 he was elected a Fellow of the Royal Society, of which he was Biological Secretary (1935-1945) and Foreign Secretary (1945-1946). He was awarded its Royal Medal in 1926 and its highest honor, the Copley Medal, in 1948. He received honorary degrees from 17 universities and was elected to many foreign scientific societies. He was an Honorary Fellow of both King's College (1927) and Trinity College (1941), Cambridge, and an Honorary Fellow of University College, London (1948). In the early 1930s he was a founding member of the Society for the Protection of Science and Learning, established to assist foreign scholars suffering under Nazi oppression, and later its president. A.V. Hill died in Cambridge on June 3, 1977.

Further Reading

There is a biography of Hill in *Nobel Lectures, Physiology or Medicine, 1922-1941* (1965), which also contains his Nobel Lecture. For Hill's later work see his *Trails and Trials in Physiology* (1965). For the general background of muscle physiology see G. H. Bourne, ed., *The Structure and Function of Muscle,* vol. 2 (1960). □

Benjamin Harvey Hill

The American Benjamin Harvey Hill (1823-1882) was a prominent Georgia politician during the Civil War and Reconstruction eras.

Benjamin H. Hill was born on Sept. 14, 1823, into a Georgia frontier family. He graduated with first honors from the University of Georgia in 1843. Admitted to the bar, he established a highly profitable practice in LaGrange, Ga., which he maintained throughout his public career.

Hill began his political life as a Whig, devoted to the union of the states and the Constitution. In 1851, as a member of the lower house of the Georgia Assembly, he encouraged acceptance of the Compromise of 1850 to quiet the slavery issue. After a 4-year retirement from public life, Hill was defeated in a bid for the U.S. Congress. He then cast his lot with the American, or "Know-Nothing," party. In 1857 Hill ran unsuccessfully for the governorship of Georgia. In the presidential race of 1860, he attempted vainly to effect a fusion in Georgia of the three tickets opposing Abraham Lincoln.

In January 1861, in the state convention, Hill opposed the motion to secede from the Union but finally signed the Ordinance of Secession. As a member of the Provisional Congress, he actively participated in organizing the Confederate government. In November 1861 Hill was elected to the Confederate Senate, where he remained throughout the war. Recognized as a spokesman for President Jefferson Davis, he was called upon to defend such controversial policies as conscription and suspension of the writ of habeas corpus; he justified them as war measures. After the war he was arrested and imprisoned for 3 months.

From 1867 until 1870 Hill conducted a strenuous campaign against the reconstruction program. But by late 1870 he advised Georgians to accept the Reconstruction Acts as accomplished facts and to involve themselves in new issues. His address before the Georgia Alumni Society in 1871 stated the case for a "New South." At about the same time, Hill provoked the anger of conservatives by participating in the sale of the state railroad with a group of Republicans.

In 1875, despite violent opposition, Hill was elected to the U.S. Congress. In Washington he was characterized as a Southern champion, defending Jefferson Davis and the Confederate government against charges of inhumanity. He was elected to the U.S. Senate in January 1877 but did not live out his term. He died of cancer in Atlanta on Aug. 16, 1882.

Further Reading

There are no recent studies of Hill. The most definitive work is Haywood Jefferson Pearce, *Benjamin H. Hill: Secession and*

Reconstruction (1928), a general but competent and scholarly study based largely on printed sources. Background studies of the period include Paul Herman Buck, *The Road to Reunion, 1865-1900* (1937), and C. Vann Woodward, *Reunion and Reaction: The Compromise of 1877 and the End of Reconstruction* (1951).

Additional Sources

Pearce, Haywood Jefferson, *Benjamin H. Hill, secession and reconstruction,* New York, Negro Universities Press, 1969. ☐

Herbert Hill

An American scholar and civil rights activist, Herbert Hill (born 1924), national labor director for the National Association for the Advancement of Colored People from 1948 to 1977, was widely recognized as a leading authority on race, labor, and employment discrimination in the United States.

Herbert Hill was born January 24, 1924, in Brooklyn, New York. He was educated in the public school system of the city and attended the New School for Social Research and New York University, receiving his bachelor's degree from the latter in 1945. In 1947 he became an organizer for the United Steel Workers of America, and in 1948 he joined the staff of the National Association for the Advancement of Colored People (NAACP), where he served as national labor director until 1977.

As NAACP labor director, Hill, a white man, became a leading figure in the struggle to achieve job equality for African American workers in the United States. His work involved both scholarship and political activism. He conducted extensive research on employment discrimination in American industry and labor unions resulting in the publication of numerous papers and monographs. This body of research became the basis for the NAACP's litigation in the federal courts on issues involving discrimination by labor unions and industrial firms.

Hill frequently testified in federal courts as an expert witness in employment discrimination cases and was invited to appear before numerous state legislative bodies, the U.S. Department of Labor, the U.S. Commission on Civil Rights, and the Equal Employment Opportunity Commission. As an outspoken critic of racism and discrimination in American industry and organized labor, Hill through his research and advocacy made a major contribution to the development of jurisprudence, legislation, and administrative procedures prohibiting employment discrimination and assuring fair and equitable employment practices in the United States.

In his career Hill published more than 50 monographs, essays, and articles dealing with the problems of race and labor. Studies by Hill appeared in many of the nation's leading journals of law, industrial relations, social policy,

and liberal opinion. In 1979 he published volume one of *Black Labor and the American Legal System,* hailed as the definitive study of the development of American law and legislation regarding employment discrimination.

In addition to his work on race and labor, Hill also contributed to the literature on African American arts and letters, including two edited collections *Soon One Morning: New Writings by Black American Writers* and *Anger and Beyond: The Negro Writer in the United States.* In 1964 Hill was director of the University of California, Berkeley's seminar on "The Negro Writer in the United States," and in 1966 he was program consultant for the University of California, Los Angeles' year long series "American Art and Culture: The Negro's Contribution."

Hill served as special consultant to the United Nations Conference on the Prevention of Discrimination and the Protection of Minorities and as a consultant on manpower policy to Israel's Ministry of Labor and to the U.S. Equal Employment Opportunity Commission and was chairperson of the Wisconsin State Advisory Commission to the U.S. Commission on Civil Rights. Appointed visiting professor at several American universities, after his retirement in 1977 as NAACP labor director Hill held a joint appointment as professor in the Department of Afro-American Studies and the Industrial Relations Research Institute at the University of Wisconsin, Madison. Hill also continued to write, lecture, and consult on issues of employment discrimination and worked on volume two of *Black Labor and the American Legal System,* which deals with developments since passage of Title VII of the Civil Rights Act of 1964.

A member of the Progressive Editorial Advisory Board, Hill, along with James E. Jones, Jr., edited *Race in America: The Struggle for Equality* in 1994. It includes essays by writers such as Julius Chambers, Kenneth Clark, Derrick Bell and Eddie Williams. The collection focuses on the persistence of racial discrimination. Hill also published *Black Labor and the American Legal System: Race, Work and the Law* in 1985.

Further Reading

Hill's work as NAACP labor director is discussed in Phillip S. Foner, *Organized Labor and the Black Worker, 1619-1981,* and in Ray Marshall, "The Negro and the AFLCIO", in John H. Bracey, Jr., August Meier, and Elliot Rudwick (editors), *Black Workers and Organized Labor.* Hill himself wrote two articles on the Black worker for the *Journal of Negro Education,* vol. 30 (Spring 1961) and vol. 38 (Spring 1969). See also "Race and Ethnicity in Organized Labor: The Historical Sources of Resistance to Affirmative Action" in *The Progressive* (July 1985). □

James Jerome Hill

James Jerome Hill (1838-1916), American railroad builder, was the major force in the construction and management of the Great Northern Railway and is often referred to as the "Empire Builder of the Northwest."

James J. Hill was born on Sept. 16, 1838, near Rockwood, Ontario, Canada, of parents of Irish background. His formal education ended with his father's death in 1852, and he began clerking in the local general store. At the age of 18 he left Canada for St. Paul, Minn., at that time a small frontier trading post at the head of the navigable portion of the Mississippi River. During his first years there Hill worked as agent and clerk for various packet companies, meanwhile making valuable contacts and establishing a reputation for integrity. When the Civil War started in 1861, Hill's attempt to enlist was rejected because of the sightless eye that was the result of a childhood accident.

Hill ventured into an independent forwarding business in 1865 and a year later agreed to provide fuel for the St. Paul and Pacific Railroad. This experience, together with his involvement in companies transporting goods and passengers between St. Paul and Winnipeg, provided Hill with a thorough grasp of the area's transportation opportunities. He also entered into a partnership in the Red River Transportation Company. However, his major interest remained the fuel business, which provided him with an increased standing in the community and some much-needed capital.

In 1878 Hill and his associates purchased enough securities in the St. Paul and Pacific Railroad (which extended into the region northwest of St. Paul) to control it. Hill's brilliant management not only resurrected the road but extended it to the Canadian border and westward through the

Dakotas to Great Falls, Mont. (1887), and on, finally, to Seattle, Wash. During construction the company was reorganized as the St. Paul, Minneapolis and Manitoba Railway. It now occupied all of Hill's time.

Hill's expansion policy required using steel rails instead of iron ones and called for connecting all the region's important towns. The expanded railroad encouraged settlement in the region and corresponding improvements in agricultural methods, as well as improvement of terminal facilities. Unlike many railroad men, Hill preferred financing through stocks rather than bonds; this led him to reorganize the railroad in 1890 as the Great Northern Railway Company. (No basic changes in corporate organization occurred after 1890 until the 1970 merger of the Great Northern with the Northern Pacific and the Burlington lines.)

Competition from the rival Northern Pacific Railroad led Hill to attempt to get control of that line during the 1890s, after the Northern Pacific had fallen into receivership. However, his effort to merge the two lines failed when the U.S. Supreme Court upheld an injunction stating that the action would create a monopoly. Hill personally still owned a large block of Northern Pacific stock, and in 1901 the two companies purchased 97 percent of the Burlington Railroad's outstanding stock. This gave Hill's roads entrance into Chicago and access to new markets in the Midwest and South and checked E. H. Harriman of the Union Pacific Railroad, who also had wanted the Burlington.

Harriman's group then bought control of the Northern Pacific, an action which precipitated a stock war. The issue was resolved in 1901 with the creation of the Northern Securities Company, a holding company which included the Great Northern, Northern Pacific, and Burlington lines. This new organization was immediately attacked as monopolistic, a view which the Supreme Court sustained in 1904. Three years later Hill resigned as president of the Great Northern and turned his attention to public interests.

Hill also had been a member of the original syndicate that financed the Canadian Pacific Railway and formed the Great Northern Steamship Company. He collected art and endowed the Hill Reference Library in St. Paul. In 1867 he had married Mary Theresa Mehegan, who bore him 10 children.

Further Reading

Hill's *Highways of Progress* (1910) presents his ideas on railroad building and management. The most complete work on Hill is Joseph Gilpin Pyle's authorized study, *The Life of James J. Hill* (2 vols., 1917). Stewart Holbrook, *James J. Hill: A Great Life in Brief* (1955), is a sympathetic account. See also Frank L. Eversull, *Empire Builder: And a Part of His Empire* (1945).

Additional Sources

Comfort, Mildred Houghton, *James Jerome Hill, railroad pioneer,* Minneapolis, Denison 1973.
Malone, Michael P., *James J. Hill: empire builder of the Northwest,* Norman: University of Oklahoma Press, 1996.
Martin, Albro, *James J. Hill and the opening of the Northwest,* New York: Oxford University Press, 1976; St. Paul: Minnesota Historical Society Press, 1991.

Memoirs of three railroad pioneers, New York: Arno Press, 1981. □

Edmund Hillary

Edmund Hillary (born 1919) was one of the greatest explorers and mountaineers of the 20th century.

Edmund Hillary was born in Auckland, New Zealand, on July 20, 1919. He spent his childhood in Tuakau, a rural area just south of Auckland where he went to the local primary school. Later he traveled daily to the city for secondary schooling. He discovered his joy in the mountains on a school trip to Mount Ruapehu, and it never left him.

During the 1940s he made many climbs in New Zealand, particularly in the Southern Alps. He quickly became recognized for his daring, strength, and reliability. Then came climbs in Europe which brought the invitation to join Sir John Hunt's expedition to Everest in 1953. It is history that Hillary and his Nepalese Sherpa guide Tenzing Norgay (who died in 1986 at the age of 71) were the first to climb Everest, reaching the summit on May 29. On returning to base camp in a state of exhaustion Hillary's laconic comment was, "We knocked the bastard off."

Vivian Fuchs (later to be knighted) asked Hillary to become part of the Trans-Antarctic expedition in 1957 and 1958. Hillary's job was to set up supply dumps from Scott Base towards the South Pole so that Fuchs' party could complete the crossing of Antarctica.

Hillary would have liked to use the sophisticated Snow-Cats available to Fuchs, but he had to settle for Ferguson farm tractors for transport and hauling. When the last dump was established Hillary—on his own decision—headed for the Pole, which he reached with his three tractors on January 4, 1958. He was the first person to come there by land in 46 years.

Through the 1960s and 1970s Hillary continued to explore the Himalayas. He also led a renowned expedition by jet boat and on foot from the mouth of the Ganges to its source. Like his other adventures it was animated by his zest, good humor, and joy.

Out of love, respect, and concern for the Sherpa people, Hillary built hospitals and schools in the mountains of Nepal. He raised the money, bought the materials, and worked on many of the buildings.

His social concerns were also expressed in New Zealand with comments on public issues that were noted for their bluntness and good sense. He was president of Volunteer Service Abroad and patron of an Outdoor Pursuit Centre and of the Race Relations Council. He was also active in the Family Planning Association, in abortion law reform, and in conservation campaigns. He was strongly opposed to nuclear tests and to ocean dumping in the South Pacific or elsewhere.

His achievements were recognized internationally with the award of numerous decorations and honorary degrees, beginning with his knighthood in 1953. They reflect the rare warmth and respect in which he was held. In 1985 he was appointed New Zealand high commissioner to India. He was also honorary president for New York's Explorers Club.

In 1975, Hillary's wife and teenage daughter were killed in an airplane crash. He later remarried, and, after leading one last expedition in 1977, he retired to his bee farm outside of Auckland.

Even in retirement, Hillary remained an important voice in the sport of mountain climbing. He wrote the forward for a book by Helen Thayer titled *Polar Dream* (1993). In 1996 he reacted to the death of eight mountain climbers in a storm on Mount Everest with the comment to *Time*'s David Van Biema, "I have a feeling that people have been getting just a little too casual about Mount Everest. This incident will bring them to regard it rather more seriously."

Hillary has also kept active in the region where he made his famous climb. The Sir Edmund Hillary Himalayan Trust provides funds and expertise to support reforestation, build schools and hospitals, and use technology such as solar power. He personally raised funds for the Nepal people throughout the 1990s through public speaking engagements and lectures in the United States. In a 1995 interview with James Clash, Hillary said, "I think the most worthwhile things I've done have not been on the mountains or in the Antarctic, but doing projects with my friends, the Sherpa

people. The 27 schools we've now established, the hospitals-those are the things I would like to be remembered for."

Further Reading

Hillary's own books can be read by all ages with ease and pleasure. They are all autobiographical, but only in *Nothing Venture, Nothing Win* (1975) is there a lot about Hillary as a person. *High Adventure* (1955), *No Latitude for Error* (1961), *Schoolhouse in the Clouds* (1964), *Two Generations* (1984), and *From the Ocean to the Sky* (1979) are splendid adventures. He also wrote *East of Everest* (1956) with George Lowe, *Crossing the Antarctica* (1958) with Sir Vivian Fuchs, *High in the Thin Cold Air* (1962) with Desmond Doig, and *Two Generations* (1983) with Peter Hillary.

There are some useful biographies of Hillary. In historical order they are: Kenneth Moon, *Man of Everest: The Story of Sir Edmund Hillary* (1962); Mark Sufrin, *To the Top of the World: Sir Edmund Hillary and the Conquest of Everest* (1966); Showell Styles, *First Up Everest* (1966); Faith Knoop, *A World Explorer: Sir Edmund Hillary* (1970); Julian May, *Hillary & Tenzing: Conquerors of Everest* (1973); and Terence Bell, *Hillary of Everest* (1973). Some of the most perceptive comments on Hillary appear in *Because It Is There* (1959) by his great friend George Lowe. Hillary relates his experiences as a child, a climber, and a diplomat in *Architectural Digest* (January 1988). Also see *Who's Who in the World* (1996); *Denver Post* (June 4, 1991; June 9, 1991); *Time* (May 27, 1996); and the web site for the Academy of Achievement at http://www.achievement.org. □

Hillel

Hillel (ca. 60 B.C.-A.D. ca. 10) was a Jewish scholar and founder of a dynasty of patriarchs who were the spiritual heads of Jewry until the 5th century.

Sources of information about Hillel are meager and must be sifted from many legends which subsequent generations have spun about him. Hillel, known as Hillel Hazaken, or Hillel the Elder, was born in Babylonia and was said to have descended from the house of David. Impelled by a thirst for learning, he migrated to Palestine at a mature age (ca. 40 B.C.) and arrived in Jerusalem only a few years before Herod the Great ascended to the Judean throne. In Jerusalem, Hillel studied at the academy of two highly reputed scholars, Shmaiah and Abtalion, while earning a meager livelihood as a manual laborer. Half of Hillel's wages went for the support of his family, while the remainder was used for tuition at the academy.

Hillel devoted himself to his studies with great zeal and skill and succeeded in attaining the rank of *nasi,* prince or president of the Bet Din Hagadol, the High Court of ordained scholars known as the Great Sanhedrin. This was the supreme legal and judicial body in Judea.

Hillel's Teachings

Hillel appears to have laid great stress on the practice of Babylonian schools to derive doctrine and law directly from the scriptural text rather than merely relying on established tradition, memorized and transmitted orally from one generation to another. This method of textual deduction, called *midrash,* or exposition, involved the use of Hillel's Seven Rules of Logic. These rules enabled the rabbis in Hillel's and subsequent generations to apply the law to new conditions on the theory that the new laws were implicit in the Mosaic law.

Hillel was a man of saintly and noble character and disposition. A popular anecdote tells of the heathen who asked Hillel to teach him the entire Torah in the time he could stand on one foot. Unperturbed, Hillel answered, "What is hateful to thee, do not do unto your neighbor. This is the whole Torah and the rest is commentary; go and study it further!" This version of the golden rule is believed by many to be a less utopian and more practical precept than the affirmative one to love one's neighbor as oneself (Leviticus 19:18).

The sayings attributed to Hillel in the tractate Abot (Fathers) reveal his humanity and virtue. Hillel was a great lover of peace who urged his followers to "be of the disciples of Aaron [who was famed as a peacemaker in rabbinic lore]; loving thy fellow creatures and drawing them nigh to Torah." "Judge not thy neighbor till thou art in his place," he urged. "If I am not for myself, who will be for me, yet if I am only for myself, then what am I?" he taught. He also preached the social tenet, "Do not separate thyself from the community."

For 2 1/2 years the Hillelites and Shammaites are said to have debated the question of the worthwhileness of existence, the Hillelites characteristically taking a positive viewpoint and the Shammaites the negative. On this basic issue the two opposing schools agreed that theoretically the Shammaites may be correct, but practically, since existence is a fact, man should live constructively and effectively. Life-affirming Judaism permits of no other attitude.

Further Reading

Solomon Zeitlin, *The Rise and Fall of the Judaean State,* vol. 2 (1967), offers a good sketch of the life and work of Hillel. Nahum N. Glatzer, *Hillel the Elder: The Emergence of Classical Judaism* (1956), presents a well-written, popular account of Hillel's life, works, and ideas. Recommended for a brief historical survey of Hillel's times is Judah Goldin, "The Period of the Talmud," in Louis Finkelstein, ed., *The Jews: Their History, Culture, and Religion,* vol. 1 (1946; 3d ed. 1960). Louis Ginzberg, *On Jewish Law and Lore* (1955), contains an essay "The Significance of the Halacha." Hillel's doctrines are expounded in George Foote Moore, *Judaism in the First Centuries of the Christian Era,* vol. 1 (1927).

Additional Sources

Blumenthal, Aaron H., *If I am only for myself; the story of Hillel,* New York United Synagogue Commission on Jewish Education 1973.
Buxbaum, Yitzhak., *The life and teachings of Hillel,* Northvale, N.J.: Jason Aronson, 1994.
Neusner, Jacob, *Judaism in the beginning of Christianity,* Philadelphia: Fortress Press, 1984. □

Nicholas Hilliard

The English painter Nicholas Hilliard (ca. 1547-1619) executed miniature portraits of Queen Elizabeth I and her courtiers, set in jeweled lockets, that are the most original and characteristic pictures painted in England in the late 16th century.

Nicholas Hilliard was born in Exeter. His father was a goldsmith, and Nicholas was apprenticed to a goldsmith by 1562. About 1570 he entered the royal service as limner (miniature painter) and goldsmith, in which capacity he designed the Second Great Seal of the Kingdom.

Hilliard's earliest surviving miniatures, painted when he was 13, are reminiscent of the little round portraits decorating the illuminated manuscript *Commentairs de la Guerre Gallique* (ca. 1519). They also resemble the work of Hans Holbein the Younger, who had produced superb miniatures in London before 1543. "Holbein's manner of limning I have ever imitated," wrote Hilliard. But he defined eyes, lips, curls, and lace with needlesharp precision, creating a brittle arabesque that distinguishes his style from the broader approach of Holbein.

In 1572 Hilliard painted his first dated portrait of Queen Elizabeth. One of his finest miniatures, it marks the arrival of the Elizabethan costume piece, that curiously insular product of a court by now culturally as well as politically isolated from Catholic Europe. The Queen is shown half-length, wearing a typically elaborate black dress with white embroidered sleeves and a small frill ruff, with a white rose pinned to her shoulder. Brightly colored and evenly lit, with gold lettering surrounding the head over a blue background, the miniature is painted in watercolor on the back of a playing card, the queen of hearts.

In 1576 Hilliard went to France, where, in the service of the Duc d'Alençon, he was in close touch with the French court. One of Hilliard's best-known works, the *Youth among Roses* (ca. 1588), seems to echo in microcosm the courtly and artificial world of Shakespeare's early comedies.

About 1600 Hilliard wrote the *Treatise concerning the Art of Limning* (published 1911-1912), partly consisting of technical hints and partly a theoretical treatise deriving from Italian mannerist art theory. At that time painters in England were still looked upon as craftsmen, and Hilliard insists on their status as practitioners of a liberal art. "None should meddle with limning," he writes, "but gentlemen alone." He goes on to record conversations with the Queen on portrait painting, which, they agree, is "best in plain lines without shadowing."

After Elizabeth's death in 1603 Hilliard worked for James I. But by this time his style was going out of fashion, to be superseded by the shadowed and more realistic approach of his pupil Isaac Oliver.

Further Reading

Erna Auerbach, *Nicholas Hilliard* (1961), is the standard monograph and has a full bibliography. Other relevant documents are in Auerbach's *Tudor Artists* (1954). □

Sidney Hillman

Sidney Hillman (1887-1946), Lithuanian-born American labor leader, was a founder of the Congress of Industrial Organizations and an important figure in reshaping national labor and welfare legislation during the New Deal.

S idney Hillman was born on March 23, 1887, in Žagare, into a middle-class Jewish family. In 1901 he was sent to a Jewish seminary to study for the rabbinate. However, a year of religious study convinced Hillman that his interests were primarily secular, and he became involved in the Jewish Bund, a radical workers' organization dedicated to trade unionism and socialism. The small part he played in the Russian Revolution of 1905 resulted in a 4-month prison term. Fearful of the postrevolutionary wave of repression, he left Russia for England, where he stayed briefly.

Early Union Career

Arriving in the United States in 1907, Hillman went to Chicago and became an apprentice fabric cutter for a men's clothing manufacturer. In 1910 he went out on strike with his fellow employees, and despite obstacles thrown up by the leaders of the United Garment Workers of America (UGWA), the workers won a notable victory.

Hillman's active participation in union affairs as business agent for the UGWA coat-makers' local in Chicago taught him that "Power is always seized, never bestowed." His success in building the Chicago local brought him to the attention of the International Ladies' Garment Workers' Union (ILGWU), which called Hillman to New York in 1914 to serve as chief clerk of its arbitration machinery.

However, a revolt was brewing within the UGWA; the workers had grown dissatisfied with the conservative policies of the union's leaders. The revolt erupted in 1914, when the immigrant tailors seceded from the UGWA to form their own national organization. The rebels invited Hillman to become president; he readily accepted. The new union, known as the Amalgamated Clothing Workers of America (ACWA), was opposed by the American Federation of Labor (AFL) because it drew membership away from the UGWA, an AFL affiliate.

The ACWA

Despite its existence outside the mainstream of the labor movement, the ACWA flourished under Hillman's astute leadership. During the 1920s, when most American

trade unions were foundering, the ACWA not only survived but also pioneered in a whole range of activities, from labor banks and unemployment insurance to cooperative housing projects and a Russian-American Industrial Corporation. The union also maintained an extensive education program for its members. These activities won Hillman a reputation as the "labor statesman." But even the labor statesman was unable to save his union from the ravages of the Great Depression, when membership and funds declined precipitously.

New Deal

Hillman was prepared to grasp the opportunities opened to unions by Franklin Roosevelt's New Deal labor legislation. Hillman rebuilt the membership and finances of the ACWA and then united with other labor leaders in an aggressive campaign to bring industrial unionism to the mass-production industries.

After finally winning membership in the AFL, the ACWA, led by Hillman, bolted in 1936, when the AFL refused to support the Committee on Industrial Organization's program for industrial unionism. When the committee became permanent as the Congress of Industrial Organizations (CIO) in 1938, Hillman was elected vice president. From 1937 to 1939 he was also chairman of the CIO's Textile Workers Organizing Committee. The massive industrial unions, under the guidance of such men as Hillman, David Dubinsky, and John L. Lewis, drastically altered the nature of labor-management relations and made organized labor a significant force in national politics.

Political Activities

In the 1930s Hillman shed the last remnants of his socialist background and became an ardent New Deal Democrat. But because he retained a broader social vision than most labor leaders and felt comfortable among intellectuals, he became a confidant of President Franklin Roosevelt. He served on Roosevelt's first labor advisory board (1933-1936). To guide socialist voters in New York into the Roosevelt camp in the 1936 presidential election, Hillman helped establish the American Labor party, a sort of halfway house between the Socialist and Democratic parties.

In gratitude, Roosevelt in 1940 made Hillman labor's representative on the Advisory Commission to the Council of National Defense and, during World War II, associate director of the Office of Production Management. Hillman was Roosevelt's major adviser on labor affairs.

Hillman was an accommodator and an opportunist who sought to offer workers a better living and society a reasonable degree of social stability. On July 10, 1946, at the height of his national reputation and influence, he died of a heart attack.

Further Reading

Two laudatory biographies provide the best introduction to Hillman: George H. Soule, *Sidney Hillman: Labor Statesman* (1939), is excellent up to the time Hillman became important in Washington politics, and Matthew Josephson, *Sidney Hillman: Statesman of American Labor* (1952), discusses his whole career. Two books which offer the fullest introduction to the development of unionism in the garment industry are Joel Seidman, *The Needle Trades* (1942), a brief but thorough survey, and Benjamin Stolberg, *Tailor's Progress: The Story of a Famous Union and the Men Who Made It* (1944), which treats Hillman unfairly. Irving Bernstein's *The Lean Years: A History of the American Worker, 1920-1933* (1960) and *Turbulent Years: A History of the American Worker, 1933-1941* (1970) provide important information on the milieu in which Hillman worked.

Additional Sources

Records of the Amalgamated Clothing Workers of America, Bethesda, MD: University Publications of America, 1989.
Fraser, Steve, *Labor will rule: Sidney Hillman and the rise of American labor,* New York: Free Press; Toronto: Maxwell Macmillan Canada; New York: Maxwell Macmillan International, 1991; Ithaca: Cornell University Press, 1993. □

Morris Hillquit

Morris Hillquit (1869-1933), Russian-born American lawyer and author, figured prominently in the organization of the Socialist Party of America.

Morris Hillquit, born Moses Hilkowitz in Riga on Aug. 1, 1869, received his early education abroad. Soon after emigrating to New York City in 1886, he began a lifelong involvement in left-wing political activities, participating in the establishment of the United Hebrew Trades, a union for impoverished Jewish garment workers formed in 1888. About the same time, he worked as a clerk for the Socialist Labor party and soon began writing for the *Arbeiter Zeitung,* a Yiddish-language newspaper. In 1891 he entered New York University Law School, receiving a degree in 1893. From 1893 to 1899 he mainly devoted himself to building a successful legal practice.

In 1899 Hillquit emerged as an important Socialist leader. He and others had become restive under Daniel De Leon's heavy-handed leadership of the Socialist Labor party, and the dissidents—known as the "Kangaroo" faction—bolted the party. In 1900 Hillquit and his allies supported the presidential candidate of the Social Democratic party, Eugene V. Debs. The next year, with Hillquit as a central figure in the unity move, the Kangaroo faction and the Debs party joined to form the Socialist Party of America.

Hillquit served the party as promoter, platform writer, legal adviser, author, and candidate. He wrote numerous articles and books on the party's behalf. On five occasions—in 1906, 1908, 1916, 1918, and 1920—he ran for Congress in East Side New York districts. Twice he ran for mayor of New York City. An evolutionary socialist, he argued that the party would discredit itself if it promised an instant socialist utopia. He nevertheless repeatedly supported the leadership of Debs, though he was closer to the party's radical wing.

Hillquit was conspicuously hostile to American involvement in World War I. In 1915 the Socialist party adopted a platform (largely written by Hillquit) urging Americans to withhold economic and diplomatic support from all the belligerents. When the United States entered the war in 1917, another Hillquit platform condemning the war was approved by the party. When, in 1917, Hillquit ran for mayor, it was in the face of great hostility to the Socialists' peace platform; still, he received more than 20 percent of the vote.

After World War I Hillquit's poor health and the demoralized condition of the Socialist party limited his political effectiveness, although in 1932 he again entered the New York City mayoralty race and won nearly a quarter-million votes. He died on Dec. 31, 1933.

Further Reading

Hillquit's many writings include an autobiography, *Loose Leaves from a Busy Life* (1934). Three excellent studies of socialism in America provide background for Hillquit's career: Ira Kipnis, *The American Socialist Movement, 1897-1912* (1952); Howard H. Quint, *The Forging of American Socialism* (1953); and David A. Shannon, *The Socialist Party of America* (1955).

Additional Sources

Pratt, Norma Fain., *Morris Hillquit: a political history of an American Jewish socialist,* Westport, Conn.: Greenwood Press, 1979. □

Carla Anderson Hills

A moderate Republican official, Carla Anderson Hills (born 1934) served three presidents as lawyer, cabinet member, and US trade representative.

Carla Anderson Hills was born in Los Angeles on January 3, 1934, the daughter of Carl H. and Edith (Hume) Anderson. A tomboy nicknamed Butch, she grew up in affluence, living in Beverly Hills and attending private schools. Her father, a self-made millionaire, ran a lucrative building supply business. Under his tutelage Carla became a fierce competitor who excelled in sports. She captained the tennis team at Stanford, where she graduated *magna cum laude* in 1955, after spending a year abroad at St. Hilda's College, Oxford University.

Her desire to become a lawyer, which she claimed dated from grade school, clashed with her father's plans to bring her into the business. In 1955 she entered Yale Law School, working as a bank teller and bookkeeper to pay her tuition until her father relented and financed her schooling. She graduated in the top 20 of her class at Yale in 1958, but she could not land a job at a major firm. One San Francisco law office told her, "Sorry, there are no 'separate facilities' for women lawyers." Hills would later downplay the sexual discrimination she encountered. "I never really think about it," she stated, offering her own formula for success. "Somewhere in your presentation, the audience stops thinking of you as a 5-foot, 6-inch woman with freckles on your nose. If people think you are immersed, are serious, have done your homework, then they take you seriously."

In 1958 she married Stanford law school graduate Roderick M. Hills and went to work for the US Attorney in Los Angeles arguing civil cases. She and her husband joined with others to form the law firm of Munger, Tolles, Hills, and Rickershauser in 1962. Hills and her husband worked together a great deal during their marriage, practicing in their Los Angeles firm from 1962 to 1974. Hills specialized in antitrust and securities cases and published three books on the subjects. She served as president of the Los Angeles chapter of the American Bar Association in 1963 and of the National Association of Women Lawyers in 1965. That same year she was admitted to the bar of the US Supreme Court. In 1971 she taught as adjunct professor of antitrust law at the University of California, Los Angeles (UCLA). During these years in Los Angeles, Hills had four children: a son Roderick and three daughters, Laura, Megan, and Lisa. Hills liked to boast that in spite of her active career she never missed a school play or birthday party.

Carla Hills became involved in government work almost by accident. In 1973 Elliot Richardson, then serving as President Richard Nixon's secretary of defense, flew to Los Angeles to recruit Hill's husband to become assistant secretary. He refused, but Richardson was impressed with Carla and later, after becoming attorney general, he offered her the job of assistant. Almost immediately after he made the offer, Richardson resigned to protest Nixon's firing of Watergate special prosecutor Archibald Cox in an incident

known as the "Saturday Night Massacre." Hills went to work for the new attorney general, William Saxbe, working with the White House as Nixon became increasingly ensnared in legal battles. At the Justice Department she earned a reputation as a tough and able administrator.

In February of 1975 President Gerald Ford nominated her as secretary of Housing and Urban Development (HUD). Hills became the third woman to hold a cabinet position, joining Frances Perkins, Franklin Delano Roosevelt's secretary of labor, and Oveta Culp Hobby, Dwight Eisenhower's secretary of health, education, and welfare. Critics in the Senate complained that Hills had no background in urban affairs and had been named only to give Ford a woman appointee, but she was confirmed and later gained a reputation for her grasp of details and consummate skill at bureaucratic infighting.

As HUD secretary, Hills came into conflict with many city mayors and planning commissions who criticized her tight-fisted policies. Although she favored the restoration of urban centers, arguing that "it is far less costly to recycle a city than to build a suburb," she opposed government funding, fearing it would add to the national deficit. Carla Hills served as secretary of Housing and Urban Development from March 1975 to January 1977.

During the Democratic administration of President Jimmy Carter, Hills returned to private practice as partner in the Washington firm of Latham, Watkins, and Hills. She served on the boards of directors of a number of prominent corporations, including Chevron, IBM, and American Air-

lines. She sat on several national commissions, including the Trilateral Commission and the Sloan Commission on Government and Higher Education. She also held advisory positions at a number of top educational institutions, including the University of Southern California, Stanford's and Yale's law schools, and Princeton's Woodrow Wilson School of Public and International Affairs.

A moderate Republican, Hills did not accept a position in the Reagan administration. Instead, she practiced law and served as chair of the Urban Institute, a Washington think tank that produced some sharp critiques of President Ronald Reagan's domestic policies. She also served on the Lawyers Committee for Civil Rights Under the Law, co-chaired the Alliance To Save Energy, and acted as vice chair of the advisory council on legal policy of the American Enterprise Institute. In 1986 she became a managing partner in the Washington law offices of Weil, Gotshal & Manges.

In December of 1988 President George Bush named Hills US trade representative, a cabinet level position that carries with it the title of ambassador. Although Hills had no background in trade, at her confirmation hearing before the Senate she won unanimous approval by declaring, "We will open foreign markets with a crowbar where necessary, but with a handshake whenever possible." Delighted Washingtonians, including President Bush, sent Hills hundreds of crowbars. Her tough negotiating style, coupled with her feminine demeanor, won her the nickname the "velvet crowbar."

Hills faced an extremely demanding first six months as US trade negotiator. With no background in trade policy and no staff to speak of, she put herself through a crash course to get up to speed on trade disputes. Senator Lloyd Bentsen, chair of the Senate Finance Committee, who initially termed Hills "a disappointing choice," praised her for her hard work and acknowledged she "had proved herself to be a quick study."

Hills, known as a "very lawyerly lawyer," pored over details of agreements and then stuck to the text when she negotiated. "I think it is very important to know all the facts you possibly can about your position," Hills insisted. "If you have all the facts, it will nudge [your trade strategy] along." Admirers praised her keen sense of US interests and her relentless bargaining style. Critics contended that she was cold, abrupt, and often impolitic. They complained that she was too much the lawyer, that she lacked vision and took "too legalistic an approach to trade."

According to *Fortune* magazine, in the years ahead the US trade representative faces formidable problems. As Europe moved toward economic unification in 1992, American business was increasingly worried about higher tariff walls. Japan continued its commercial dominance, and other Asian countries, particularly South Korea, were generating big trading surpluses with the United States. The trade negotiator's task will be to use the 1988 Trade Act to take action against the worst international offenders without destroying the fragile philosophy of free trade.

In 1991, Hills made a veiled threat of trade sanctions against Japan until further efforts were made to increase the US semiconductor industry's market share in the Japanese market. The US expected to have a 20% share by the end of 1992. Hills has had her share of successes. By 1993 she had opened Japanese markets to American goods and fought European Community Trade Barriers. In 1993, the former US trade representative joined the law firm of Shea and Gould. Although she was nominated for corporate directorship, she ended her work there by resigning. Her chief concerns continued to lie with US trade agreements and President Clinton's foreign and domestic trade policies.

Further Reading

Further information on Carla Hills can be found in the cover story on Carla Hills in *Business Week* (January 22, 1990); "Two for the Trade," in *National Journal* (August 12, 1989); Ann Reilly Dowd, "What To Do about Trade Policy," in *Fortune* (May 8, 1989); I. Ross, "Carla Hills Gives the Woman's Touch a Brand New Meaning," in *Fortune* (December 1975); and in "Call Her Madam," in the *Washington Post* (February 26, 1975). □

Gertrude Himmelfarb

The American professor, writer, and scholar Gertrude Himmelfarb (born 1922) was noted for her work on Victorian intellectual history and for her conservative point of view.

Gertrude Himmelfarb was born in Brooklyn, New York, on August 8, 1922, the daughter of Bertha and Max Himmelfarb, a manufacturer. She graduated from New Utrecht High School in Brooklyn in 1939 and attended Brooklyn College, studying history and philosophy. She graduated from Brooklyn College in 1942 and in the same year married Irving Kristol but retained her maiden name for professional purposes. In the late 1990s, one writer wrote: "No family has had a greater impact on today's conservatism than the Kristols," writes Jacob Weisberg in the New Yorker of [then] editor Bill; his mother, historian Gertrude Himmelfarb; and his father, public philosopher Irving.

The young couple moved to Chicago, where Himmelfarb began graduate work in history at the University of Chicago. Himmelfarb wrote her Master's thesis on Robespierre under the direction of well-known historian Louis Gottschalk and received her MA in 1944. She continued her graduate studies while Kristol served with the U.S. Army. After Kristol's discharge in 1946, they went to England, where Himmelfarb had been awarded a fellowship to Girton College, Cambridge University. At Cambridge she continued her doctoral research on Lord Acton, a fascinating and paradoxical Victorian figure, both European and English, a political thinker and historian.

First Book

Back in the United States, Himmelfarb published her first book, an edition of Lord Acton's *Essays on Freedom and Power,* in 1948. In 1950 she received her Ph.D. from the University of Chicago. During the late 1940s and early 1950s Himmelfarb wrote several articles and began to establish her area of expertise in Victorian intellectual history. In 1952 her book *Lord Acton: A Study in Conscience and Politics* was published and received high praise from reviewers.

Between 1950 and 1965 Himmelfarb was an "independent scholar" with no official academic affiliation. Her work attracted sufficient interest, however, for her to be awarded several prestigious grants, including two Guggenheim fellowships. This independence further allowed her to spend several years in London, where Kristol was serving as the co-editor of the intellectual journal *Encounter.*

In 1959 Himmelfarb's second monograph, *Darwin and the Darwinian Revolution,* was published. The book was a study of the influence of Darwin's theory of natural selection on his contemporaries, particularly those concerned with politics and religion, and like its predecessor was widely praised. Himmelfarb published an edition of Thomas Malthus' *On Population* in 1960 and an edition of John Stuart Mill's *Essays on Politics and Culture* in 1962.

Her long academic "holiday" ended in 1965, when she was appointed professor of history at Brooklyn College. In 1978 Himmelfarb was named distinguished professor of history at the graduate school of the City University of New York.

Politics, Religion and Moral Values

Himmelfarb was an individual with strong ideas on a variety of topics. She believed that among mankind's most important ideas are those relating to politics, religion, and moral values. In her youth a classic liberal, she became increasingly appreciative of the conservative point of view. In this process she was joined by her brother, Milton Himmelfarb, and her husband, both eminent "neo-conservative" thinkers and writers about American political and intellectual life. Her opinions had an obvious impact on her work as an historian, and among other things helped determine who would be her heroes (i.e., Edmund Burke and Adam Smith) and her villains (i.e., Jeremy Bentham and Karl Marx). Her political views were well-known and gave rise, in particular in the 1960s and 1970s, to criticism, much of it unwarranted, of her work as an historian.

In 1968 one of Himmelfarb's most important works, *Victorian Minds,* was published. The book is a series of essays on Victorian men of ideas ranging from Edmund Burke (to whom two very different essays, indicative of Himmelfarb's changing views of the great conservative theorist, are devoted) to J.S. Mill to Leslie Stephen to John Buchan. One essay is devoted to the "Victorian ethos," the changing and inclusive community of ideas and values shared by the majority of Victorians. *Victorian Minds* attracted much critical attention, both negative and positive, but all critics were aware of Himmelfarb's massive research and the book had a large impact on Victorian studies.

Two books on John Stuart Mill appeared in 1974. The first was an edition of Mill's *On Liberty.* The second book, *On Liberty and Liberalism: The Case of John Stuart Mill,* was an exploration of the "two" Mills—the one who wrote *On*

Liberty and the one who wrote Mill's other works. There is, Himmelfarb stipulated, a qualitative difference between the writings of the two, the former being strongly influenced by his long-time companion and later wife, Harriet Taylor, and the latter, whom Himmelfarb clearly preferred, belonging "to an older liberal tradition."

The Idea of Poverty: England in the Early Industrial Age (1984) was the first of two projected volumes. Comprehensively researched using economic, political, sociological, and literary sources and brilliantly written, the book describes changes in what late 18th-and early 19th-century people actually meant by the terms "poverty" and "the poor" and what these contemporaries thought should be done about both. According to Himmelfarb, the Industrial Revolution saw a change in the idea that poverty was a "natural, unfortunate, often tragic fact of life, but not necessarily a demeaning or degrading fact" to its portrayal as "an urgent social problem" that threatened the fabric of society and must, at all costs, be abolished. *The Idea of Poverty* received widespread applause from the historical profession and from the more general reading public.

In 1986 Himmelfarb's *Marriage and Morals Among the Victorians* was published. A series of essays which, she said, "reflect a sense of the intellectual and moral nature of the Victorians," the book is largely concerned with the Victorian "moral imagination," an offshoot of the Victorian ethos. Himmelfarb wrote in tribute to Victorian morality and to Disraeli's "Tory Imagination" while harshly criticizing the methodology of a contemporary study on Victorian marriage as well as the morals of the literary and artistic Bloomsbury Group.

Another volume of essays, *The New History and the Old* (1987), is a scathing critique of the "new" or social history and its methods. As a political conservative and a traditional historian (one does not necessarily imply the other), Himmelfarb was alarmed at the "hegemony" of the new history within the profession. Each essay deals with a specific type of new history—psycho-history, quanto-history, sociological history, Marxist history—or problem raised by the new history's methods. She was deeply concerned with the new history's belittlement of the importance of ideas, of politics, and of traditional narrative. This book received much attention from reviewers, who admired Himmelfarb's wit and writing skill. Reviews of the contents of the book, understandably, seem to be divided along party lines, with traditional historians applauding and new historians highly critical.

In 1987 Himmelfarb was honored when she emerged as a strong though unsuccessful candidate for the position of Librarian of Congress. In 1988 she retired from her job with the City University of New York and became a professor emerita at that institution.

After her retirement Himmelfarb continued to write a large number of articles on a variety of topics in both popular and professional periodicals, and her work continued to be informed by her conservative views. For example, she wrote opinion articles in the *New York Times* against changes in academic curricula, academic affirmative action quotas, and radical feminism. She pursued her interest in

the Victorian moral imagination in articles in the *Wilson Quarterly* and in *Commentary*. And she furthered her examination of the new history in an important article in the *American Historical Review* (June 1989) that deplores historical deconstructionism. Deconstructionism, a theory which has come and gone, she said, in other disciplines, has been adopted by some historians "to liberate the study [of history] from the tyranny of facts."

Himmelfarb's critically well received 1991 volume *Poverty and Compassion: The Moral Imagination of the Late Victorians* argues that the lives of the era's poor, while wretched by many modern standards, were not all that bad relative to the average Englishman's. They were also better than the lives of the poor in most of the European countries from which the critics came. She writes of the Victorians' realistic approach to helping the poor and the destitute, and for their determination to frame the issue of relief in moral terms. The evil of poverty, they held, resided less in material deprivation than in character deformation.

Her *On Looking Into the Abyss: Untimely Thoughts on Culture and Society* (1994) took its title from a remark Lionel Trilling made to his students to "look into the Abyss." Their pervasive nihilism, that threatens to engulf everyone, prevented them from grasping just how subversive, how hostile to civilization the assigned readings were. Though she does not say so, her subtitle comes from Nietzsche's Unzeitgemasse Betrachtungen (Untimely resections). In this way, she wished to signal her intention of pitting the moral imagination against the spiritual descendants of Bloomsbury, the active proponents of immorality and nihilism. Since the years when Trilling lectured to uncomprehending students, she writes, the abyss has opened wider. "The beasts of modernism have mutated into the beasts of postmodernism—relativism into nihilism, amorality into immorality, irrationality into insanity, sexual deviancy into polymorphous perversity."

The Demoralization of Society: From Victorian Virtues to Modern Values (1995) follows *On Looking Into the Abyss: Untimely Thoughts on Culture and Society,* with further speculations on the effects on present-day society of the abandonment of Victorian standards of moral behavior. She devotes a chapter to crime statistics in England and in America and to levels of illegitimacy and single parenthood. She deduces from these that moral standards have changed for the worse, and questions what new standards, if any, have replaced the old. "The Victorian virtues were neither the classical nor the Christian virtues; they were more domesticated than the former and more secular than the latter," but were believed to be perennial. "For Victorians, virtues were fixed and certain, not in the sense of governing the actual behavior of all people all the time . . . [rather], they were the standards against which behavior could and should be measured. When conduct fell short of those standards, it was judged in moral terms as bad, wrong or evil—not, as is more often the case today, as misguided, undesirable or (the most recent corruption of the moral vocabulary) 'inappropriate'." This is the major distinction between the Victorian age and our own, argues Himmelfarb.

In other words, Victorian virtues—which included work, discipline, thrift, self-help, self-discipline, cleanliness, chastity, fidelity, valor and charity—provided a continuity that unified society. Certainly there were "class distinctions, social prejudices, abuses of authority, [and] constraints on personal liberty" in England during the 19th century. But Victorians from royal dukes to stevedores and scullery maids were confident that being English and Christian was superior to being anything else.

Her call for a return to Victorian values coincided with a national debate about "family values" and a general national discussion regarding a rising crime rate, lower education test scores, single parenthood and so her work enjoyed more popular attention than her previous writings.

Gertrude Himmelfarb occupied a unique place in the historical profession and among American scholars. She was one of the few women of her generation to pursue graduate education and successfully complete a Ph.D. In addition, her political views and her work were often controversial and subjected to harsh criticism. She led a highly unconventional career, with 15 years as an "independent scholar" and marriage (and enduring "intellectual companionship," according to Kristol) to a prominent political thinker and writer. Universally recognized and respected for the depth of her scholarship, her gift of analysis, and the incisiveness of her arguments, she was justly described by another eminent American historian of Victorian Britain as "the most eminent American scholar to have written acutely on the history of Victorian ideas."

Further Reading

There are no full-length books about Gertrude Himmelfarb or articles devoted exclusively to a retrospective of her career. Nonetheless, as an important and controversial historian she has attracted much attention. A highly favorable but sensible review of *Victorian Minds* by John Gross in the *Observer* (October 6, 1968) provides an excellent introduction to Himmelfarb and her work. An interesting counter to this is Robert E. Bonner's review of *Victorian Minds* in the *Carleton Miscellany* (Fall 1968), which castigates Himmelfarb for her conservative views and finds much fault with her husband, Irving Kristol. A review of books by Himmelfarb and another historian by Bernard Semmel in *Partisan Review* (1985) enthusiastically discusses *The Idea of Poverty* and Himmelfarb's place among contemporary historians. Favorable but balanced views of *Marriage and Morals* are provided by Neil McKendrick in the *New York Times Book Review* (March 23, 1986) and John Gross in the *New York Times* (February 28, 1986). □

Heinrich Himmler

The German National Socialist politician Heinrich Himmler (1900-1945) commanded the SS, Hitler's elite troops, and was head of the Gestapo. He was perhaps the most powerful and ruthless man in Nazi Germany next to Hitler himself.

B orn in Munich, Bavaria, on Oct. 7, 1900, Heinrich Himmler was the son of the former tutor of one of the Bavarian princes. In World War I he took his first opportunity to join the army (1917), but owing to his frail health he never reached the front. Yet he continued soldiering in veterans' bands after the war while a student at the university in Munich, and in November 1923 he marched in Hitler's ill-fated Beer Hall Putsch. After a brief flirt with the leftist Strasser faction of the Nazis, the young anti-Semitic fanatic joined Hitler in 1926 as deputy propaganda chief.

In January 1929 Himmler found his "calling" with his appointment as commander of the blackshirt SS (*Schutzstaffel*)—then still a small, untrained bodyguard. With characteristic drive and pedantic precision he rapidly turned this organization into an elite army of 50,000—including its own espionage system (SD). After the Nazis came to power in 1933, Himmler took over and expanded the Gestapo (*Geheime Staatspolizei,* secret police). In 1934 he liquidated Ernst Roehm, chief of the SA (storm troopers), and thus gained autonomy for the SS, which took charge of all concentration camps.

From this power base, to which he added the position of chief of all German police forces in June 1936 and that of minister of the interior in August 1943, Himmler coordinated the entire Nazi machinery of political suppression and racial "purification." From 1937 on, the entire German population was screened for "Aryan" racial purity by Himmler's mammoth bureaucratic apparatus. After the invasion of eastern Europe it became Himmler's task to "Germanize"

the occupied areas and to deport the native populations to concentration camps.

After the plot of July 1944 against Hitler, Himmler also became supreme commander of all home armies. In 1943 he made contacts with the Western Allies in an attempt to preserve his own position and to barter Jewish prisoners for his own safety—an action which caused his expulsion from the party shortly before Hitler's death. On May 21, 1945, Heinrich Himmler was captured while fleeing from the British at Bremervoerde. Two days later he took poison and died.

Further Reading

Roger Manvell and Heinrich Fraenkel, *Himmler* (1965), a carefully researched and fair-minded biography, is the best personal portrayal in English. Willi Frischauer, *Himmler: The Evil Genius of the Third Reich* (1953), is more concerned with the SS itself, as is Heinz Höhne, *The Order of the Death's Head,* translated by Richard Barry (1969). Felix Kersten, *The Kersten Memoirs,* translated by Constantine Fitzgibbon and James Oliver (1956), is a fascinating and invaluable close-up look at Himmler by his personal physician.

Additional Sources

Breitman, Richard, *The architect of genocide: Himmler and the final solution,* New York: Knopf: Distributed by Random House, 1991; Hanover, NH: University Press of New England, 1992.

Kersten, Felix, *The Kersten memoirs: 1940-1945,* New York: H. Fertig, 1994; Alexandria, VA: Time-Life Books, 1992.

Lee, Robert J., *Fascinating relics of the Third Reich,* Franklin, Tenn. (P.O. Box 465, Franklin 37065): R.J. Lee, 1985.

Padfield, Peter, *Himmler: Reichsfuhrer-SS,* New York: Holt, 1991. □

Paul Hindemith

Paul Hindemith (1895-1963) was a prolific and versatile German composer and also an important teacher of musical composition.

Paul Hindemith was born on Nov. 16, 1895, in Hanau am Main. At the age of 9, he began violin lessons; advancing rapidly, he was soon able to enter a conservatory in nearby Frankfurt, where he studied composition. In 1923 he became concertmaster of the Frankfurt Opera orchestra. More important, however, was his career as violist, first in the Rebner Quartet and later (1922-1929) in the Amar Quartet, which toured Europe playing many major contemporary works.

In 1919 Hindemith signed his first contract with a music publisher (Schott), a connection he maintained throughout his life. That same year he wrote his first important compositions: the First String Quartet in F Minor, Op. 10, and the one-act opera *Mörder, Hoffnung der Frauen.* These were rapidly followed by two more stage works: *Das Nusch-Nuschi,* a one-act play for Burmese marionettes, and the one-act opera *Sancta Susanna.* All these works were controversial, and Hindemith was considered a radical. Yet, later, his music remained firmly rooted in tonality; he rejected the twelve-tone method and was not interested in electronic composition.

From 1926 to 1929 Hindemith was active in the direction of the contemporary chamber-music festivals at Donaueschingen and Baden-Baden. During these years he wrote chamber music, including chamber concertos for piano, cello, violin, viola, and organ. *Cardillac* (1926) was an opera of major importance in his career. In 1927 he produced typical examples of his *Gebrauchsmusik,* that is, music intended for specific purposes or particular occasions: the *Spiel-und Jugendmusiken* Music for Youth), Op. 43 and 44.

In 1927 Hindemith accepted a professorship of composition at the Staatliche Hochschule für Musik in Berlin. He remained there until 1934, when he was suspended as part of the Nazi campaign against "degenerate" (modern) music. It was under the impact of such turbulent political events that he composed his finest stage work, *Mathis der Maler.* Dealing with the problems and the duties of the artist in troubled times, this work draws deeply on Hindemith's own spiritual experiences while telling the story of the 16th-century German painter Matthias Grünewald. It was completed in July 1935 and premiered 3 years later in Zurich, Switzerland.

Also in 1935 Hindemith made his first journey to Turkey, where, at the request of the Turkish government, he drew up plans for the organization of Turkish musical life. While these plans were carried out over the next 2 years, he visited Turkey three more times. In 1937 he finally resigned from the Staatliche Hochschule; the following year he moved to Switzerland. In 1940 he emigrated to the United States and settled at Yale University, where he taught for the next 13 years.

During his American period Hindemith produced some of his most popular works, such as *Symphonic Metamorphosis of Themes by Carl Maria von Weber* (1943) and *When Lilacs Last in the Door-yard Bloom'd* (*A Requiem for Those We Love;* 1946). However, he became nostalgic for Europe and in 1953 returned to Switzerland, where he lived for the last 10 years of his life. Among the major works of these years were two operas: *The Harmony of the World* (1957) and *The Long Christmas Dinner* (1960). On his last journey to America, in 1963, he heard the first American performance of the latter work, as well as the premiere of the Concerto for Organ and Orchestra, which he had written to celebrate the opening of Philharmonic Hall in New York City. His last work, a Mass for mixed choir a cappella, was premiered in November 1963 in Vienna under his direction. On December 28 he died in Frankfurt.

Hindemith's philosophy of music is summed up in the speech he gave upon receipt of the Balzan Prize in 1963. "In which direction," he asked," can music still develop? Certainly not . . . in the ever greater extension and expansion of the limits of sound. . . . To express what has never been said before, the musician must enter another dimension. He must explore the heights and the depths, the heights of the spiritual and the depths of the human soul."

Such rejection of new sound possibilities weakened Hindemith's influence on musical developments of the 1950s and 1960s. More influential are his theoretical textbooks, *The Craft of Musical Composition* (1941), *Traditional Harmony* (1943), and *Elementary Training for Musicians* (1946), which are widely used in American universities.

Further Reading

Hindemith's Charles Eliot Norton Lectures of 1949-1950 were published as *A Composer's World: Horizons and Limitations* (1952). They offer interesting insights into the composer's views and experiences. A pictorial biography is *Testimony in Pictures,* with an introduction by Heinrich Strobel (trans. 1968). An excellent general study which discusses Hindemith is Joseph Machlis, *Introduction to Contemporary Music* (1961).

Additional Sources

Hindemith, Paul, *Selected letters of Paul Hindemith,* New Haven: Yale University Press, 1995.

Noss, Luther, *Paul Hindemith in the United States,* Urbana: University of Illinois Press, 1989.

Skelton, Geoffrey, *Paul Hindemith: the man behind the music: a biography,* New York: Crescendo Pub., 1975.

Yale University Music Library, *The Paul Hindemith collection: Yale University Music Library archival collection mss 47,* New Haven, Conn.: The Library, 1994. □

Paul Ludwig Hans von Beneckendorff und von Hindenburg

The German field marshal and statesman Paul Ludwig Hans von Beneckendorff und von Hindenburg (1847-1934) commanded the German forces during the last 2 years of World War I. He was president of Germany from 1925 to 1934.

Paul von Hindenburg was one of the last prominent representatives of the old Prussian Junkerdom— once the mainstay of Prussia's military power and its honest and efficient civil service—and he profoundly shared its values of honor, duty, and total dedication to the state. As president during the critical years of the Depression, he also symbolized the curious inability of the old Prussian aristocrats to deal with the barbaric nationalism and reckless militarism of Hitler's national socialism.

Hindenburg was born in Posen (now Poznań, Poland) on Oct. 2, 1847, to a family of old Junker stock. Trained in the Prussian Cadet Corps, he fought bravely in the wars against Austria (1866) and France (1870), earning a citation for bravery and the Iron Cross.

Never a man of outstanding strategic or tactical talents, Hindenburg made his mark as a hardworking, loyal, and dedicated soldier. His sincerity and noble bearing earned him the respect of both superiors and subordinates and assured him of a steady rise through the ranks in the long years of peace after 1871. By 1904 he had become commanding general of the IV Army Corps, a post he held until his retirement in 1911.

World War I

As an experienced officer, Hindenburg was recalled to active duty shortly after the outbreak of World War I and sent to command the 8th Army on the Eastern front with the extremely talented but highly temperamental Erich Ludendorff as his chief of staff. On the morning after its arrival on the front, the new command team commenced the Battle of Tannenburg (August 26-29), which resulted in the most decisive German victory on the Eastern front and made its official victors, Hindenburg and Ludendorff, into almost legendary German heroes. In this battle the German forces virtually annihilated a Russian army twice the size of the German detachment and cleared East Prussian territory for the balance of the war. By November 1914 Hindenburg had advanced to supreme commander in the east with the rank of field marshal.

When the German armies were increasingly driven into the defensive on the decisive Western front in the summer of 1916, Hindenburg was made chief of general staff, with Ludendorff at his side as chief of operations. Thus Hindenburg and Ludendorff—with the latter always in the driver's position—increasingly determined the direction of German politics. Their policy consisted primarily of a stub-

born, increasingly suicidal insistence on an all-out military effort and sizable annexations and a wooden resistance to all reforms at home. For the German military fortunes, however, even the unification of the supreme command of the Central Powers under Hindenburg and desperate all-out offensives in the west were not enough. By the summer of 1918 German offensive strength had run out, and an Allied counteroffensive, reinforced by fresh American troops, threatened to carry the war into Germany.

The subsequent surrender did not diminish Hindenburg's prestige, however. He prepared what he believed to be the temporary resignation of the emperor, William II, to make an armistice possible. He gained the lasting gratitude of his nation by bringing every German soldier across the armistice line along the Rhine before the deadline set by the Allies. Only after the signing of the Peace Treaty of Versailles did he finally lay down his command—still the most popular public figure in Germany.

Years as President

After the first president of the postwar republic died in 1925, Marshal Hindenburg was nominated by the parties of the right and was elected with a slight plurality over the candidate of the center and moderate left. Although he continued to hope for a return of his beloved monarchy, he loyally supported the various governments of the republic in the 1920s.

An abrupt shift in Hindenburg's position took place with the outbreak of the Depression and the subsequent breakdown of majority coalition governments in the German Parliament. Under an emergency paragraph in the constitution, he now supported Chancellor Heinrich Brüning's government of the center against the combined antirepublican majority of Nazis and Communists. Widely regarded as the last bulwark against Hitler, the 82-year-old war hero was reelected with the support of the center-left parties in the spring of 1932.

Hindenburg soon turned against Brüning, however, because of a moderate land reform thought disadvantageous to Hindenburg's fellow landed aristocrats. He replaced this last genuinely republican chancellor with Franz von Papen and then Kurt von Schleicher, both personal friends. Finally, on Jan. 30, 1933, he overcame his initial dislike and distrust of Nazi leader Adolf Hitler and appointed him to the chancellorship, thereby inaugurating 12 years of Nazi dictatorship.

Failing in health, Hindenburg increasingly lost control over the radicalization and terrorization of German politics. In March 1933 he symbolically presided over the opening of Hitler's newly purged Reichstag and in the following year had to tolerate the army purges accompanying the infamous Roehm Purge. On Aug. 2, 1934, Paul von Hindenburg died at Neudeck, a broken man. His death removed the last restraints on Hitler.

Further Reading

Hindenburg's early autobiography, *Out of My Life* (1920), was translated by F. A. Holt (1933). Of the many biographies of Hindenburg, mostly by admirers, the best in English are John W. Wheeler-Bennett, *Wooden Titan: Hindenburg in Twenty Years of German History, 1914-1934* (1936; republished as *Hindenburg: The Wooden Titan*, 1967), a full biography, and Andreas Dorpalen, *Hindenburg and the Weimar Republic* (1964), which is limited to the time of the republic. Margaret Goldsmith and Frederick Voigt, *Hindenburg: The Man and the Legend* (1930), is a generally favorable, scholarly account. Emil Ludwig, *Hindenburg* (trans. 1935), is popularized but is an accurate appraisal. Recommended for general historical background are Walter Görlitz, *The German General Staff: Its Historical Structure, 1657-1945* (1950; trans. 1953); Gordon A. Craig, *The Politics of the Prussian Army, 1640-1945* (1955); and Erich Eyck, *A History of the Weimar Republic* (trans., 2 vols., 1962-1963). □

Gregory Oliver Hines

Dancer and actor Gregory Oliver Hines (born 1946) began his career when he was still a toddler. He tapped his way to fame in nightclubs with his brother, Maurice Hines, on Broadway and in Hollywood.

Valentine's Day, 1946, marks the birth of Gregory Hines in New York City. His father was Maurice Sr., who worked as a soda salesman, a nightclub bouncer, and a semi-pro baseball player. His paternal grandmother, Ora Hines, was a showgirl at the Cotton Club, the famous Prohibition-era nightclub in Harlem where African American entertainers performed for a wealthy white clientele.

His brother, Maurice Jr., was two years old when Gregory was born, and already in tap shoes. The boys grew up in Harlem and Brooklyn, and it was their mother who steered them toward tap-dancing careers as a way "out of the ghetto." Envisioning them as the new Nicholas Brothers, she enrolled them in dancing school as soon as they could walk. The boys made regular visits to Harlem's vaudeville mecca, the Apollo Theatre, and Gregory's idols were the improvisational tap masters "Sandman" Sims and Teddy Hale.

The brothers first performed locally together when Gregory was five and Maurice seven. Their education took place at professional children's schools; summer vacations were booked with tours of their dance act, called the Hines Kids. Their Broadway debut was in 1954 as the newspaper boy (Maurice) and the shoeshine boy (Gregory) in the musical comedy "The Girl in Pink Tights," starring French ballerina Jeanmarie.

Under the tutelage of tap coach Henry LeTang, the Hines Kids became an international attraction. When Maurice reached his teens, they became the Hines Brothers, and briefly they were Hines, Hines and Brown when singer and pantomimist Johnny Brown joined the act. The next member of the act joined in 1962, when Maurice Sr., having learned to play the drums, made possible Hines, Hines and Dad. Maurice Jr. was the straight man for Gregory's com-

edy, and the three of them played such venues as "The Ed Sullivan Show," "The Tonight Show," the Palladium in London, and the Olympia Theatre in Paris.

By the late 1960s, the interests of the two brothers took divergent paths. Maurice wanted to concentrate on "legitimate theatre," and Gregory, more influenced by the times, wanted to write songs and perform rock-style music.

In 1973 the brothers' act broke up, and Gregory moved to Venice, California, where he became, in his words, "a long-haired hippie." He organized a jazz-rock group, Severence, for which he wrote songs, sang, and played guitar. He worked as a waiter, busboy, and karate instructor (he is a Black Belt), and joined a men's consciousness-raising group. He met his second wife, Pamela Koslow, during this period. Hines had been married once before to dance therapist Patricia Panella, and his daughter from that marriage, Daria, lived with her mother in Manhattan.

Hines missed his daughter and moved back to New York in 1978. He landed a tap-dancing spot in "The Last Minstrel Show," a Broadway hopeful that opened and closed in Philadelphia.

His next effort was his first joint appearance in five years with his brother, in the African American musical revue "Eubie!" (1978-1979). Choreographed by their mentor Henry LeTang, the show was an homage to then 95-year-old composer Eubie Blake. Gregory sang a soulful rendition of "Low Down Blues," and he "machine-gun" tapped out "Hot Feet," a number that was repeatedly interrupted by audience applause. Gregory and Maurice sang

and danced "Dixie Moon" as a duet and joined others in the tango "There's a Million Little Cupids in the Sky." Hines won several awards for his performance in "Eubie!", including one from the Outer Critics' Circle, and was nominated for a Tony as Outstanding Featured Actor in a Musical.

A musical-comedy version of "A Christmas Carol" called "Comin' Uptown" (1979-1980) was Hines' first vehicle for genuine acting. Although it flopped at the box office, Hines, who played the lead, was nominated for a Tony as Outstanding Actor in a Musical.

His next effort was to choreograph "Blues in the Night," a revue based on classic blues songs. This show ran for six weeks off-Broadway in early 1980.

In May 1980, Hines participated with Charles "Honi" Coles, John Bubbles, Nell Carter, and others in "Black Broadway," George Wein's salute to African American Broadway musicals of the past. The same year, a pair of Hines' tap shoes was placed on the "Wall of Fame" at Roseland, the venerable Manhattan dance hall, alongside the shoes of Fred Astaire and Ruby Keeler.

"Sophisticated Ladies" was a showcase of Duke Ellington's music conceived by director-choreographer Donald McKayle, with its tap segments choreographed by LeTang. After its Philadelphia tryout, reviewers complained it was too long and encumbered with wooden narration, which minimized the song-and-dance talents of Hines and co-star Judith Jamison. The show moved to Washington, D.C. in early 1981, where Hines criticized the show publicly and was dismissed. The cast rallied on his behalf, threatening to walk out; Hines was rehired, and McKayle was replaced by Michael Smuin.

The revamped show reached Broadway in March 1981. It was no longer a drawn-out tour of Ellington's musical life and times, but a slick, elegant bundle of nostalgia for a Saturday night party at the old Cotton Club. With Mercer Ellington, Duke's son, conducting the on-stage orchestra, Hines sang the title song as well as "Don't Get Around Much Anymore" and "Something to Live For"; a duet with Jamison, "I Let a Song Go Out of My Heart," and others including "Take the A Train" and "It Don't Mean a Thing (If I Ain't Got That Swing)." For "Sophisticated Ladies," Hines received his third straight Tony nomination, this one for Best Actor in a Musical. The show didn't close until January 1983. In January 1982 Hines turned over the role to his brother in order to help produce the West Coast production of the show.

During this period he made his first film appearance, opening up yet another venue for his talents. In Mel Brooks' farce "The History of the World—Part I" (1981), Hines brief comic scene featured him as Cleopatra's long-tongued slave. That same year, he appeared in the horror film "Wolfen" (1981), and in 1983 he co-starred with Chevy Chase and Sigourney Weaver in "Deal of a Century."

While in Los Angeles for "Sophisticated Ladies," he heard about a jazz-era film titled "The Cotton Club." For two weeks, he begged the film's producer, Robert Evans, for the part of Sandman Williams, a promising, young Cotton

Club tap dancer. Evans had his mind set on Richard Pryor for the part, and when Pryor turned it down, Hines got his wish.

Francis Ford Coppola relied on his cast's real-life experiences in rewriting the screenplay for "The Cotton Club" 40 or 50 times, with the help of William Kennedy, before it was satisfactory. After hearing Hines describe the breakup of the Hines, Hines and Dad act, Coppola decided to make Gregory's character half of a feuding brother act, with Maurice Hines playing the other half. The film was released in 1984, to lukewarm reception by critics and audiences.

Hines appeared on the star-studded two-hour NBC network show "Motown Returns to the Apollo" (May 19, 1985), a condensed version of a six-hour taping that took place at the official re-opening of the historic Harlem theater two weeks earlier. The same year, he co-starred with Mikhail Baryshnikov in "White Nights" (1985), which impressively juxtaposed the tap and ballet talents of the two stars, but critics agreed that not much else about it was impressive. Other films for Hines include "Running Scared" (1986) with Billy Crystal and "Off Limits" (1988) with Willem DeFoe. "Tap" (1989), a tribute to his old idols, included appearances by Sammy Davis, Jr., and Sandman Sims and was choreographed by Henry LeTang.

Nineteen-ninety-two marked a turning point in Hines' career. He received his fourth Tony Award nomination for his role as Jelly Roll Morton in "Jelly's Last Jam," and this time he won. Dinitia Smith reviewed the performance in *New York* and called Hines "perhaps, the greatest tap dancer in the world." In the 1990s, Hines became well known in the film industry, earning important roles in many films, including "White Lie," "A Rage in Harlem," "Eve of Destruction" (1991); "T Bone N Weasel," "Dead Air" (1992); "Renaissance Man," "Dying for a Smoke" (1994); "Waiting to Exhale" (1995); and "The Preacher's Wife" (1996). He has directed an independent film, "White Man's Burden," released in 1994. Hines' next move appears to be into television, with the advent of the prime-time sitcom "The Gregory Hines Show," in which Hines plays a widower trying to get back into the dating scene while also raising his 12-year-old son.

Despite his many successful endeavors in other areas, Hines continued to think of himself as a tap dancer. He told Leslie Bennetts of *Vanity Fair,* "Whenever I go to Europe and have to fill out that landing card that asks what your occupation is, I always put down 'tap dancer.'"

Further Reading

Although no biographies of Hines have been published, numerous newspaper and magazine articles give in-depth profiles of him, including the *Christian Science Monitor* (March 1981); *New York* (March 1981); *New York Daily News* (December 1984); *People* (August 1981); *Time* (April 1981); *Jet* (March 1988); and the *Washington Post* (January 1981, February 1985, September 1988, and February 1989). See also *Essence* (November 1993); *Who's Who in America* (1996); and *Who's Who Among African Americans* (1996). ☐

Rolando Hinojosa

Rolando Hinojosa is one of the most prolific and well-respected Hispanic novelists in the United States. Not only has he created memorable Mexican American and white characters, but he has completely populated a fictional county in the lower Rio Grande Valley of Texas through his continuing generational narrative that he calls the Klail City Death Trip Series.

The first Chicano author to receive a major international literary award, Rolando Hinojosa won the prestigious Premio Casa de las Américas for *Klail City y sus alrededores* (*Klail City*), part of a series of novels known to English-speaking readers as "The Klail City Death Trip." Hinojosa's fiction, often infused with satire or subtle humor, is widely praised for its multiple narratives that unite many characters' individual perspectives into the unique combined voice of the Chicano people. Hinojosa has also produced essays, poetry, and a detective novel titled *Partners in Crime.*

Hinojosa was born in Texas's Lower Rio Grande Valley to a family with strong Mexican and American roots: his father fought in the Mexican Revolution while his mother maintained the family north of the border. An avid reader during childhood, Hinojosa was raised speaking Spanish until he attended junior high, where English was the primary spoken language. Like his grandmother, mother, and three of his four siblings, Hinojosa became a teacher; he has held several academic posts and has also been active in administration and consulting work. Although he prefers to write in Spanish, Hinojosa has also translated his own books and written others in English.

Hinojosa entered the literary scene with the 1973 *Estampas del valle y otras obras,* which was translated as *Sketches of the Valley and Other Works.* The four-part novel consists of loosely connected sketches, narratives, monologues, and dialogues, offering a composite picture of Chicano life in the fictitious Belken County town of Klail City, Texas. The first part of *Estampas* introduces Jehú Malacara, a nine-year-old boy who is left to live with exploitative relatives after the deaths of his parents. Hinojosa synthesizes the portrait of Jehú's life through comic and satiric sketches and narratives of incidents and characters surrounding him. The second section is a collection of pieces about a murder, presented through newspaper accounts, court documents, and testimonials from the defendant's relatives. A third segment, narrated by an omniscient storyteller, is a selection of sketches depicting people from various social groups in Klail City, while the fourth section introduces the series' other main character, Jehú's cousin Rafa Buenrostro. Also orphaned during childhood, Rafa narrates a succession of experiences and recollections of his life. Hinojosa later rewrote *Estampas del valle y otras obras* in English, publishing it as *The Valley* in 1983.

Hinojosa's aggregate portrait of the Spanish southwest continues in *Klail City y sus alrededores,* published in English as *Klail City.* Like its predecessor, *Klail City* is composed of interwoven narratives, conversations, and anecdotes illustrating the town's collective life spanning fifty years. Winner of the 1976 Premio Casa de las Américas, the book was cited for its "richness of imagery, the sensitive creation of dialogues, the collage-like structure based on a pattern of converging individual destinies, the masterful control of the temporal element and its testimonial value," according to Charles M. Tatum in *World Literature Today.* Introducing more than one hundred characters and developing further the portraits of Rafa and Jehú, *Klail City* prompts *Western American Literature* writer Lourdes Torres to praise Hinojosa for his "unusual talent for capturing the language and spirit of his subject matter."

Korean Love Songs from Klail City Death Trip and *Claros varones de Belken* are Hinojosa's third and fourth installments in the series. A novel comprised of several long poems originally written in English and published in 1978, *Korean Love Songs* presents protagonist Rafa Buenrostro's narration of his experiences as a soldier in the Korean War. In poems such as "Friendly Fire" and "Rafe," Hinojosa explores army life, grief, male friendships, discrimination, and the reality of death presented through dispassionate, often ironic descriptions of the atrocity of war. *Claros varones de Belken* (*Fair Gentlemen of Belken County*), released three years later, follows Jehú and Rafa as they narrate accounts of their experiences serving in the Korean War, attending the University of Texas at Austin, and begin-

ning careers as high school teachers in Klail City. The book also includes the narratives of two more major characters, writer P. Galindo and local historian Esteban Echevarría, who comment on their own and others' circumstances. Writing about *Fair Gentlemen of Belken County, World Literature Today* contributor Tatum comments that Hinojosa's "creative strength and major characteristic is his ability to render this fictional reality utilizing a collective voice deeply rooted in the Hispanic tradition of the Texas-Mexico border." Also expressing a favorable opinion of the book was *Los Angeles Times Book Review* writer Alejandro Morales, who concludes that "the scores of names and multiple narrators at first pose a challenge, but quickly the imagery, language and subtle folk humor of Belken County win the reader's favor."

Hinojosa continued the "Klail City Death Trip" series with *Mi querido Rafa.* Translated as *Dear Rafe,* the novel is divided into two parts and consists of letters and interviews. The first half of the work is written in epistolary style, containing only letters from Jehú—now a successful bank officer—to his cousin Rafa. Between the novel's two parts, however, Jehú suddenly leaves his important position at the Klail City First National Bank, and in the second section Galindo interviews twenty-one community members about possible reasons for Jehú's resignation. The two major characters are depicted through dialogue going on around and about them; the reader obtains a glimpse of Rafa's personality through Jehú's letters, and Jehú's life is sketched through the opinions of the townspeople. *San Francisco Review of Books* writer Arnold Williams compares the power of Hinojosa's fictional milieu, striking even in translation, to that of twentieth-century Jewish writer Isaac Bashevis Singer, noting that "Hinojosa is such a master of English that he captures the same intimacy and idiomatic word play in his re-creations."

After writing *Rites and Witnesses,* the sixth novel in the "Klail City Death Trip" series, Hinojosa turned to a conventional form of the novel with the 1985 *Partners in Crime,* a detective thriller about the murder of a Belken County district attorney and several Mexican nationals in a local bar. Detective squads from both sides of the border are called to investigate the case; clues lead to an established and powerful cocaine smuggling ring. Jehú and Rafa reappear in the novel as minor characters who nevertheless play important parts in the mystery's development. "Those who might mourn the ending of the ['Klail City Death Trip' series] and their narrative experimentation and look askance at Hinojosa's attempting such a predictable and recipe-oriented genre as the murder mystery need not worry," concludes Williams. "He can weave a social fabric that is interesting, surprising, realistic and still entertaining."

Hinojosa told *Contemporary Authors:* "I enjoy writing, of course, but I enjoy the re-writing even more: four or five rewritings are not uncommon. Once finished, though, it's on to something else. At this date, every work done in Spanish has also been done in English with the exception of *Claros varones de Belken,* although I did work quite closely on the idiomatic expressions which I found to be at the heart of the telling of the story.

"I usually don't read reviews; articles by learned scholars, however, are something else. They've devoted much time and thought to their work, and it is only fair I read them and take them seriously. The articles come from France, Germany, Spain, and so on, as well as from the United States. I find them not only interesting but, at times, revelatory. I don't know how much I am influenced by them, but I'm sure I am, as much as I am influenced by a lifetime of reading. Scholars do keep one on one's toes, but not, obviously, at their mercy. Writing has allowed me to meet writers as diverse as Julio Cortázar, Ishmael Reed, Elena Poniatowski and George Lamming.

"My goal is to set down in fiction the history of the Lower Rio Grande Valley, and with *Becky and Her Friends,* [which came] out in 1990, I am right on schedule. The Spanish version will also be out the same year. A German scholar, Wolfgang Karrer, from Osnabrueck University has a census of my characters; they number some one thousand. That makes me an Abraham of some sort.

"Personally and professionally, my life as a professor and as a writer inseparably combines vocation with avocation. My ability in both languages is most helpful, and thanks for this goes to my parents and to the place where I was raised."

In 1993, Hinojosa released *The Useless Servants.* This is a novel of the Korean War, told in the form of the journal of Rafe Buenestro, a Mexican American soldier. This novel exposes the negative treatment Mexican Americans and African Americans received from their fellow soldiers. *Publishers Weekly* says that in this book, "Hinojosa gives us a graphic picture of the unchanging face of war—raw, gritty and inhumane."

Further Reading

Bruce-Novoa, Juan, *Chicano Authors: Inquiry by Interview,* University of Texas Press, 1980.
Contemporary Authors, Volume 131, Gale, 1991.
Dictionary of Literary Biography, Volume 82: *Chicano Writers, First Series,* Gale, 1989.
Saldívar, José David, editor, *The Rolando Hinojosa Reader: Essays Historical and Critical,* Arte Público Press, 1985.
Hispania, September, 1986.
Los Angeles Times Book Review, April 12, 1987.
Publishers Weekly, November 28, 1986.
San Francisco Review of Books, spring, 1985, fall/winter, 1985.
Western American Literature, fall, 1988.
World Literature Today, summer, 1977, summer 1986. □

Sir Cyril Norman Hinshelwood

The English chemist Sir Cyril Norman Hinshelwood (1897-1967) was noted for his contributions to reaction kinetics.

Cyril Hinshelwood was born in London on June 19, 1897, the only child of an accountant who died in 1904. The boy was brought up by his mother. Hinshelwood won a scholarship to Oxford but was unable to accept it because of World War I. He became a chemist at an explosives factory at Queensferry, Scotland, and 2 years later he was appointed assistant chief laboratory chemist. In 1919 he entered Balliol College, Oxford, for the shortened postwar degree course. So sure was his grasp of chemical principles that his tutor, Sir Harold Hartley, recommended Hinshelwood for a fellowship at Balliol in 1920. A year later he was made a fellow of Trinity College, Oxford. He remained there until 1937, when he was named Dr. Lee's professor of chemistry at Oxford, a post he held until his retirement in 1964. He then became senior research fellow at Imperial College, London.

Hinshelwood's lifelong preoccupation with the energetics and rates of chemical reactions may be traced to his work of testing explosives at Queensferry. Early work included studies of the decomposition of solid potassium permanganate, reactions between gases on hot filaments, and reactions taking place in solution. Before long, however, he turned to the kinetics of homogeneous gas reactions. By studying the effects of pressure changes on these reactions, Hinshelwood inferred that in some circumstances molecules might gain the necessary energy to react (activation energy) by mutual collision, but in other circumstances deactivation might occur by this process.

Among the gas phase reactions studied at this time was the deceptively simple reaction between hydrogen and oxy-

gen to form water. By studying the way in which the rate of reaction was affected by temperature and pressure changes and by examining the conditions needed for explosion, Hinshelwood was led to propose a branching chain mechanism. By observing the effect of the wall surface, and especially the ability of nitric oxide to inhibit the reaction, he concluded that free radicals played a key role, postulating as active participants H, O, OH, and HO_2.

In the late 1930s Hinshelwood turned to a new field of activity. Recognizing that the growth of bacteria was essentially a complex of chemical reactions, he began to apply kinetic studies to the bacterial cell. He examined the effect of additives such as phosphorus and the alkali metals and concluded that bacteria could adapt to their new environment by a shift in the enzyme balance of their cells. He was able to systematize his results in terms of a "principle of total integration" and give them mathematical expression in his "network theorem."

Hinshelwood played an important part in the consolidation and organization of physical chemistry at Oxford for many years. He was a highly articulate scientist with deep insight into the philosophical implications of his subject, and his lectures were tinged with dry humor and delivered with great clarity. His international reputation was widened by his books. *The Kinetics of Chemical Change* (1926) was his masterpiece; the successive editions reveal the progressive sophistication that came to his views on his own special subject. *The Structure of Physical Chemistry* (1951) is a magisterial survey of the whole field from his particular viewpoint. In bacteriology, his early work, *The Kinetics of the Bacterial Cell* (1946), was followed by *Growth, Function and Regulation in Bacterial Cells* (1966).

Hinshelwood was knighted in 1948. From the Chemical Society he received the Longstaff and Faraday medals and from the Royal Society the Davy, Copley, Royal, and Leverhume medals. He became president of the Royal Society in 1955. He shared the Nobel Prize in chemistry and was admitted to the Order of Merit in 1956. He had the unique distinction of being simultaneously president of the Royal Society and of the Classical Association.

A man of many parts, Hinshelwood was a very accomplished linguist and had an expert knowledge of subjects as diverse as classical music, Chinese porcelain, and Persian carpets. He died in London on Oct. 9, 1967.

Further Reading

Biographical information on Hinshelwood is in Eduard Farber, *Nobel Prize Winners in Chemistry, 1901-1961* (rev. ed. 1963), and Nobel Foundation, *Chemistry: Including Presentation Speeches and Laureates' Biographies,* vol. 3 (1964). For background see Aaron J. Ihde, *The Development of Modern Chemistry* (1964). □

Susan Eloise Hinton

Often considered the most successful novelist for the junior high and high school audience, Hinton is credited with creating the genre of realistic young adult literature with the publication of her first book, *The Outsiders* (1967), at the age of seventeen.

Although not a prolific author, she is acclaimed for writing powerful and insightful fiction about adolescent males in hostile social environments. Her works are often acknowledged for their authenticity, candor, and appeal to young adults, especially teenage boys. Although her books include topical elements such as gang violence and drug abuse, Hinton focuses more on character and theme, an attribute praised for contributing to the universality of her works.

As a teenager in Tulsa, Oklahoma, S. E. Hinton enjoyed reading but often found her options limited: "A lot of adult literature was older than I was ready for. The kids' books were all Mary Jane-Goes-to-the-Prom junk. I wrote *The Outsiders* so I'd have something to read." Based on events that occurred in her high school in Tulsa, Oklahoma, the novel describes the rivalry between two gangs, the lower-middle-class greasers and the upper-class Socs (for Socials), a conflict that leads to the deaths of members of both gangs. Narrated by fourteen-year-old Ponyboy, a sensitive, orphaned greaser who tells the story in retrospect, *The Outsiders* explores the camaraderie, loyalty, and affection that lie behind the gang mystique while pointing out both the likenesses in the feelings of the opposing groups and the futility of gang violence; through his encounters with death, Ponyboy learns that he does not have to remain an outsider.

Initially regarded as controversial for its unflinching portrayal of disaffected youth, the novel is now recognized as a classic of juvenile literature as well as a unique accomplishment for so young a writer.

The Outsiders was a major success among teenagers, selling more than four million copies in the United States. The book's popularity enabled Hinton to attend the University of Tulsa, where in 1970 she earned an education degree and met her future husband, David Inhofe. However, being catapulted into fame and fortune at eighteen was not without problems; Hinton had a writer's block for several years. "I couldn't even write a letter. All these people were going, 'Oh, look at this teenage writer' and you think, God, they're expecting a masterpiece and I haven't got a masterpiece."

Eventually, however, Hinton produced a second novel, *That Was Then, This Is Now* (1971), a tale of two foster brothers, Bryon and Mark, who are moving apart; as one becomes more involved in school and girlfriends, the other moves deeper into a career of crime and drugs. In *Rumble Fish* (1975), Hinton continued exploring the themes of gang violence and growing up in the story of a disillusioned young man who, in a struggle to acquire a tough reputation, gradually loses everything meaningful to him. Hinton's next book, *Tex* (1979), which follows two brothers left in each other's care by their rambling father, likewise investigates how delinquent youths try to make it in a world shaped by protest, drugs, violence, and family disruption. *Taming the Star Runner* (1988) tells of a fifteen-year-old's self-discovery during a summer spent on his uncle's horse ranch.

In each of her books, Hinton depicts the survival and maturation of her adolescent male protagonists, tough yet tender lower-class boys who live in and around Tulsa and who grow by making difficult decisions. Using a prose style noted initially for its urgency but more recently for its more controlled, mature quality, Hinton addresses such themes as appearance versus reality, the need to be loved and to belong, the meaning of honor, and the limits of friendship. Underlying Hinton's works is her depiction of society as a claustrophobic and often fatal environment that contributes to the fear and hostility felt by her characters. Although she has been accused of sexism for inadequately developing several of the young women in her books, Hinton is often praised for the overall superiority of her characterizations and for her sensitivity toward the feelings and needs of the young. She has also written the screenplay for the feature film version of *Rumble Fish* with Francis Ford Coppola. In 1988, Hinton received the first Young Adult Services Division/ *School Library Journal* Author Award from the American Library Association.

Further Reading

Authors and Artists for Young Adults, Volume 2, Gale, 1989, pp. 65-76.
Children's Literature Review, Gale, Volume 3, 1978, Volume 23, 1991.
Contemporary Literary Criticism, Volume 30, Gale, 1984.
Daly, Jay, *Presenting S. E. Hinton,* Twayne, 1987.
American Film, April, 1983.
Book World, May 9, 1971.
Children's Book Review, December, 1971. □

Hipparchus

The Greek astronomer Hipparchus (active 162-126 B.C.) discovered the precession of the equinoxes, founded trigonometry, and compiled the first star catalog.

Born at Nicaea in Bithynia, Hipparchus studied astronomy, perhaps under Theodosius, and made some of his early observations in his native city. From at least 162 B.C. he was on the island of Rhodes, where he especially observed solstices, equinoxes, and lunar eclipses. His last recorded observation was made in 126 B.C. Hipparchus wrote on a variety of subjects connected with astronomy, but of his 14 works known once to have existed, only the commentary on Aratus's *Phaenomena* is extant. His astronomical work is known chiefly through the *Almagest* of Ptolemy and the writings of Strabo of Amisela.

Hipparchus seems to have initiated the study of plane trigonometry, devising for that purpose a table of chords of angles ranging from 0 to 180°. He also developed a method of solving spherical triangles. By means of his trigonometric calculations he was able to determine, with greater accuracy than ever before, right and oblique ascensions and declinations, as well as simultaneous risings or settings of stars at different terrestrial latitudes. He also applied his methods to the solution of the problem of determining planetary positions. In his later years he drew up an elaborate catalog of 850 or more fixed stars, giving for each its longitude and latitude and also the apparent brightness, based on a system of six magnitudes similar to that used today.

Precession of the Equinoxes

Hipparchus's greatest discovery was that of precession of the equinoxes, that is, the fact that the sun takes less time to return to the same solstitial or equinoctial point than it takes for the expiry of the sidereal year. He arrived at the discovery by a comparison of his own observations with those made earlier by Meton and Euctemon (432 B.C.) and Aristarchus (281 B.C.). He determined the annual amount of precession and from this obtained a nearly correct value for the duration of the tropical year (the period of the sun's rotation from equinox to equinox), which was too great by only 6 1/2 minutes.

Planetary, Solar, and Lunar Studies

In planetary theory Hipparchus was undoubtedly familiar with the work done by earlier astronomers, and he combined many of their observations with his own but was unsuccessful in formulating a planetary theory. However, he did explain that there are two inequalities for each planet, that the retrogradations of each are variable in extent, and that these phenomena can be represented by combining earlier hypotheses of eccentric circles and epicycles on concentric circles.

With respect to the moon and sun, Hipparchus was indebted to the Babylonians, but he improved upon earlier

Geographical Work

Hipparchus's work on geography was a criticism, in three books, of Eratosthenes. In his discussion of Eratosthenes's geography he is concerned with mathematical errors in determining the latitudes of, and distances between, places. He evidently desired to establish a coordinate system of parallels of longitude and latitude for determining geographical positions, such as he employed for fixing the positions of the fixed stars. The data at his disposal, however, especially those concerning terrestrial longitude, were not sufficient to carry out his scheme. Fundamental to this effort was his estimate, based on Eratosthenes's value for the circumference of the earth (252,000 stades), that 1° of either longitude or latitude on the earth's surface is equal to a distance of 700 stades.

Influence of Hipparchus

Hipparchus was a careful and cautious scientist who prepared the way for those who followed him by establishing a high standard of observational astronomy, by devising trigonometrical methods of solving problems in mathematical astronomy, and by collecting and criticizing the observational material of his predecessors, both Babylonian and Greek. Like many another, his greatest achievement was to make it possible for his successors to eclipse him and relegate his works to oblivion.

Further Reading

There is no comprehensive work on Hipparchus, but a good biography is in Henry Smith Williams, *The Great Astronomers* (1930). None of the discussions of his astronomical work in the standard histories of science is adequate. There is a brief discussion in J. L. E. Dreyer, *A History of Astronomy from Thales to Kepler* (rev. ed. 1953). A general survey of Hipparchus's life and an appreciation of his achievements, along with a detailed study of the fragments of his criticism of Eratosthenes, is in D. R. Dicks, ed., *The Geographical Fragments of Hipparchus* (1960). □

estimates of the size and distance of the two bodies. Though he himself observed lunar eclipses, he also employed the data on two sets of three eclipses of 383-382 and 201-200. On the basis of his examination of one of these two sets, Hipparchus determined the radius of the lunar epicycle, and on the basis of his examination of the other set, he determined the eccentricity of the lunar orbit. That these factors were equal was a fact about which Hipparchus was well aware. Evidently Hipparchus tried to account only for the inequality in lunar motion, which is due to the elliptical form of the moon's orbit. In discussing lunar latitude, he used data from the eclipse of 502, derived from cuneiform sources; he determined the inclination of the lunar orbit to the ecliptic to be 5°.

In devising a model to account for the inequity of solar motion, Hipparchus was more successful than with the planets and the moon. Brilliantly, by means only of estimates of the time between the vernal equinox and the summer solstice and of that between the summer solstice and the autumnal equinox, he proved that the apogee of the sun lies at Gemini 5;30° (5° 30′) and that the eccentricity of the solar orbit is 1/24 of the radius of the eccentric circle. His final work was the determination of the angular diameters and distances, in earth radii, of the sun and moon from the center of the earth. Though Ptolemy was able to improve on these parameters, the gross underestimation of the size of the solar system in antiquity could not be corrected before the 17th century.

Hippocrates

The ancient Greek physician Hippocrates (ca. 460-ca. 377 B.C.), the father of medicine, put a definitive stamp on the whole character of Greek medicine.

Only the barest outline of the biography of Hippocrates emerges from the ancient writings. He was born on the Aegean island of Cos, just off the Ionian coast near Halicarnassus. He is called Hippocrates Asclepiades, "descendant of (the doctor-god) Asclepios," but whether this descent was by family or merely by his espousing the medical profession is uncertain. His teachers in medicine are said to have been his father, Heracleides, and Herodicos of Selymbria. Hippocrates certainly was known in Athens, for Plato mentions him twice, on each occasion calling him Asclepiades. It is also clear that the height of his career was during the Peloponnesian War (431-404 B.C.).

The lack of knowledge concerning Hippocrates may seem strange in view of the great volume of writings attributed to him, the *Corpus Hippocraticum* (Hippocratic Corpus), the first known edition of which is from the time of the emperor Hadrian (reigned A.D. 117-138). It is clear, however, that this body of writings contains material of many different kinds and includes differences in standpoint toward medicine. This disparity was recognized even in ancient times, and Alexandrian scholars differed about the authentic Hippocrates, though none rejected every work.

Any notion of the nature of Hippocrates's medical procedure must be based on pre-Alexandrian texts, that is, on texts dating more closely to Hippocrates's lifetime and reflecting an untainted direct tradition. Two excellent sources are Plato's *Phaedrus* (270C-D) and Meno's account of Hippocrates in his history of medicine. There is sufficient evidence in these works to establish with certainty the main outlines of Hippocratic medicine.

In antiquity, some works in the Hippocratic Corpus were recognized as having been written by persons other than Hippocrates, but acceptance and rejection depended on a number of subjective stances. More modern scholarship has used as its touchstone the genuine doctrine of Hippocrates as found in Plato and Meno. This mode of investigation, while common to all scholars, has not produced general agreement. It is well to point out that neither

Plato nor Meno quotes word for word from Hippocrates's works; they seem in fact to summarize him in their own words, which of course have overtones from their own particular philosophy. So although there is a body of doctrine connected with Hippocrates, modern scholars have no inkling of his prose style, against which the Hippocratic Corpus could be tested.

Nowhere in the Hippocratic Corpus is the entire Hippocratic doctrine to be found. However, these numerous works are so multifarious that here and there parts of the doctrine come to light. It is worth noting that, since Plato and Meno discussed the work of Hippocrates, it is reasonable to assume that they had at their disposal medical books written by him. This makes the problem even more intriguing. Hippocrates's fame, though it was at such a height during his lifetime, still could not ensure the preservation of his works.

Hippocratic Corpus

The body of writing attributed to Hippocrates, the Hippocratic Corpus, is a collection of roughly 70 works that show no uniformity in teaching or in prose style. With a few exceptions the dates of these works range between 450 and 350 B.C.; they are the oldest surviving complete medical books. It would be unfair to allege deception as the motive behind attributing the entire collection to Hippocrates; nor was it the result of ignorance and carelessness, since Galen and those before him did not regard every work as genuine. A reasonable hypothesis holds that these works were gathered together to form the basis of the medical library of some school, probably at Alexandria.

An essential orientation to the Corpus is an appreciation of the audience for which the various works were intended. Some books are directed toward the physician, for example, the surgical treatises, *Prognostic, Airs Waters Places, Regimen in Acute Disease, Aphorisms* and *Epidemics i,* in which descriptions of symptoms employ sense data, though they surpass mere descriptions. There are books with complicated pharmacy mixtures, and equally complicated preparation and administration, aimed, no doubt, at the professional physician. Other books, however, are directed more at the layman, for example, *Regimen in Health, Regimen ii-iv,* and *Affections,* in which the introduction stresses the importance for the layman of understanding something of medical questions.

One must remember that in antiquity doctors wrote treatises for the educated public, who in turn discussed medical problems with their doctors. The aim of these books is not to advise on self-treatment or even first aid, and so to dispense with the need for a doctor; rather, it is to teach the layman how to judge a physician.

The Hippocratic Corpus also contains polemical works. The *Sacred Disease* attacks superstition, and *On Ancient Medicine* opposes the intrusion of speculative philosophy into medicine. The latter work also protests against "narrowing down the causes of death and disease." But there are indeed attempts to apply to medicine the speculative method of early Greek philosophy, as in *Regimen i* and *Nutrition.* Occasionally there is no carefully written treatise but a series of jottings—research material in notebook form: *Humors* and *Epidemics i-vii.*

Experimentation obviously played its role in the Hippocratic view of medicine, because the individual approach to disease as exemplified in the case histories of *Epidemics i,* though basic and undeveloped, is nothing more than experimentation. It is obvious, too, that first-hand experience, as opposed to theorizing, played a part, since in scattered references throughout the Corpus the botanical ingredients of remedies are described by taste and odor. There are also instances of very rudimentary laboratory-type experiments. The *Sacred Disease* describes dissections of animals, the results of which permitted analogies to the human body to be drawn. Further, in their attempts to describe the body, the Hippocratics made use of external observation only. In *On Ancient Medicine,* the internal organs are described as they can be seen or palpated externally. It is most unlikely that dissection of the human body was practiced in the 5th century.

In *Epidemics i* the patient's comfort is noted as a matter of concern to the physician, because he was given water when thirsty and cooled when feverish. E. A. Ackerknecht, in *A Short History of Medicine,* summed up: ''For better or worse Hippocrates observed sick people, not diseases.'' This attitude is a timely antidote to those who formerly insisted on the coldly scientific approach of the Hippocratic physician, who seemed to be so callous toward his patient, particularly in the blunt descriptions of the countenance before death in certain diseases, still known as *facies hippocratica.*

The above illustrations are meant to clarify the most fundamental concerns of the Hippocratic physician. Yet a too enthusiastic and uncritical attitude has been attached to the area of medical ethics also. Ludwig Edelstein commented in his important work on the oath (*The Hippocratic Oath,* 1943) that the high morality and ethics of this document were not true of the 5th century B.C. but were the result of the infusion of philosophical precepts (mainly Pythagorean) of the end of the 4th century B.C. and later. As a result, the ethic of the medical craftsman was renewed to conform with the various systems of philosophy. This was furthermore not an oath taken by all physicians, if in fact it was sworn by any doctor before the end of antiquity; its fame is more modern than that.

Further Reading

Several Hippocratic treatises are translated in the Loeb Classical Library, *Hippocrates* (4 vols., 1923-1931). The best treatment of Hippocratic problems is in Oswei Temkin and C. Lilian Temkin, eds., *Ancient Medicine: Selected Papers of Ludwig Edelstein* (1967). See also William A. Heidel, *Hippocratic Medicine: Its Spirit and Method* (1941). Background information is in G. E. Lloyd, *Early Greek Science: Thales to Aristotle* (1971). □

Hirohito

Hirohito (1901-1989) was the 124th emperor of Japan. He reigned during a period of internal turmoil, foreign expansion, international war, and national defeat, and presided over the transformation of the Japanese monarchy into a purely symbolic institution. As the occupant of Japan's throne for 63 years, he was the longest living monarch in modern history.

Childhood and Education

Hirohito was born on April 29, 1901. He was the first son of Crown Prince Yoshihito, who later became the Taisho emperor, and the grandson of Mutsuhito, the Meiji emperor. Following long-established custom, Hirohito was separated from his parents shortly after birth. He was cared for under the guardianship of a vice admiral in the imperial navy until November 1904, when he returned to the Akasaka Palace, his parents' official residence.

Even from early years, Hirohito was trained to act with the dignity, reserve, and sense of responsibility his future role would require. He grew into a shy and grave young boy. In April 1908 he was enrolled at the Gakushuin (Peers School) in a special class of 12 boys, among them two of his imperial cousins. The head of the school was Gen.

Maresuke Nogi, a celebrated soldier of the Russo-Japanese War. He took a personal interest in the education of the young prince and attempted to instill in him respect for the virtues of stoicism, hard work, and devotion to the nation.

Appointed Heir to Throne

Hirohito was appointed heir apparent on September 9, 1912, shortly after the death of his grandfather Mutsushito and the accession of his father Yoshihito to the throne. Hirohito lost his mentor when Nogi and his wife committed ritual suicide on the day of Mutsuhito's funeral. His education was continued under another military hero, Adm. Heihachiro Togo, who had won the victory over the Russian navy in 1905. But Hirohito never became as close to Togo as he had been to Nogi. In his studies he also had little patience with his tutor in history, who taught that the early myth of the founding of Japan by the sun-goddess was historical fact. Skeptical by nature and scientific in his interest, he found natural history more to his liking. Under the guidance of his natural-history tutor, who remained a lifelong mentor, he began to develop an interest in marine biology, a field in which he became an acknowledged expert.

Crown Prince and Regent

On February 4, 1918, Hirohito became engaged to Princess Nagako, daughter of Prince Kuniyoshi Kuninomiya. Aritomo Yamagata and others raised objections to the match on the grounds that Nagako was descended from the daimyos of Satsuma, who had a strain of color blindness. The defect, they said, would taint the imperial line. But the imperial wedding finally took place on January 26, 1924. The imperial couple later had five daughters, the first born in December 1926, and two sons, the first born in December 1933.

In March 1921 Hirohito, accompanied by a large retinue, set off for a tour of Europe. The event was unprecedented, for it was the first time a crown prince of Japan had visited abroad. Although Hirohito traveled in France, the Netherlands, and Italy, his visit to England made the deepest impression on him. He was attracted by the freedom and informality of the English royal family. On Hirohito's first day at Buckingham Palace, King George V paid him an unexpected breakfast visit in suspenders and carpet slippers, and Edward, Prince of Wales, played golf with him and accompanied him on a round of official gatherings.

On November 25, 1921, shortly after his return to Japan, Hirohito was appointed to serve as regent for his father, who had begun to show increasing signs of mental derangement. In December 1923 Hirohito escaped an attempt on his life by a young radical.

Emperor of a Restless Nation

Hirohito acceded to the throne on December 25, 1926, and his formal enthronement took place in accord with ancient rituals in November 1928. He took as his reign name Showa ("Enlightened Peace"), and he was formally known as Showa Tenno.

The choice of reign name proved highly ironic for, shortly after Hirohito became emperor, Japan's relations with the outside world began to deteriorate. In 1927 Japanese army officers arranged the assassination of Marshal Chang Tso-lin, warlord of Manchuria, in hopes of provoking a Japanese takeover of the area. The young emperor, angered at the event, urged Premier Giichi Tanaka to discover and punish the culprits. He was equally indignant in September 1931, when elements in the Japanese army engineered the occupation of southern Manchuria under their own initiative. Encouraged by advisers like Count Nobuaki Makino and Prince Kimmochi Saionji, the Emperor privately urged moderation and caution on the army as it continued to deepen Japan's military involvement on the Asian mainland.

The Manchurian incident ushered in a period of profound domestic unrest. Dissident young military officers, often with the covert encouragement of their superiors, allied with civilian right-wing radicals to plot a series of unsuccessful coups d'etat and a number of successful assassinations. They hoped to overthrow party cabinets in order to establish a military regime that could govern in the name of "direct imperial rule."

Hirohito, however, believed himself to be a thoroughly human monarch, bound by the constitution his grandfather had promulgated in 1889. He saw himself as an organ of state rather than a personal autocrat and believed that the leaders of government should be men of moderation and non-militaristic in outlook.

During the military insurrection of February 26, 1936, when elements of the First Division occupied large areas of downtown Tokyo and assassination bands murdered many leading public officials, the Emperor urged swift suppression and punishment of the mutinous soldiers and the assassins. The uprising was crushed, and a number of ranking generals who were thought to have encouraged the rebels were forced into retirement.

Road to War

The country nevertheless continued its drift toward war. In July 1937 hostilities with China broke out. During the late 1930s Hirohito's advisers in the palace bureaucracy had urged him to remain aloof from direct intervention in politics lest he compromise the position of the imperial family. The Emperor followed this advice, giving his consent to whatever policies the increasingly belligerent governments decided upon.

There is every evidence that the Emperor felt uneasy about the unfolding of events, particularly after 1940. He did not favor the alliance with Nazi Germany and Fascist Italy, but he made no effort to oppose it. Similarly, he had grown distrustful of the judgments of the military leaders who kept assuring him of a quick end to the war in China. But when the final decision on war with the United States was made on September 6, 1941, his opposition was confined to an oblique reference to one of his grandfather's poems, which expressed hope for peace.

During the war Hirohito refused to leave the imperial palace at Tokyo, even after air raids began to demolish the city and fires destroyed many buildings on the palace grounds. He wished to share the hardships of his subjects.

Japan Defeated

By the summer of 1945 it was clear to most informed public officials, including many military leaders, that defeat was inevitable. But the decision to surrender did not come until after atomic bombs were dropped on Hiroshima and Nagasaki. At a historic imperial conference on August 9, 1945, the Emperor made clear his determination to "endure the unendurable" and expressed his opinion in favor of surrendering to the Allies.

Following Japan's formal surrender in September 1945, there was much speculation about whether the Emperor would be punished as a war criminal. Hirohito himself frequently expressed his willingness to abdicate as a token of his responsibility for the war. But the American authorities, including Gen. Douglas MacArthur, decided that it would better serve the goals of domestic stability and internal reform of Japan to let him remain as ruler. On January 1, 1946, however, the Emperor once and for all gave up any claims to being a sacred monarch by issuing a rescript that denied his divinity as a descendant of the sun-goddess.

Emperor's Life as a Mortal

During the years of the occupation and afterward, every effort was made to "democratize" the throne by having the Emperor mingle with the people. At first, the Emperor was inept and ill at ease when he met his subjects. He won the nickname "Mr. Is-that-so?" because of his perfunctory comments on visits to factories and schools. Even though he was personally aloof and somewhat awkward in public, the Emperor nevertheless became a popular figure. Pictures of the imperial family and stories of their activities became steady grist for weekly magazine and newspaper copy.

A respected marine biologist with a number of books on that subject to his credit, the Emperor lived a modest, sober, and retiring life when not engaged in official functions. His son Crown Prince Akihito married a commoner in 1959, and the line of succession was assured through their son Prince Hiro. In 1972 Hirohito traveled to Europe and was met with hostile demonstrations. A 1975 trip to the United States resulted in a more friendly reception. Hirohito died on January 7, 1989, at the age of 87. Symbolic of his interest in science and in modernizing his country, Hirohito reportedly was buried with his microscope and a Mickey Mouse watch.

Further Reading

The most complete biography of Hirohito in English is by Leonard Mosley, *Hirohito, Emperor of Japan* (1966). A journalistic sketch of Hirohito was written during the war by Willard Price, entitled *Japan and the Son of Heaven* (1945). Reading on the troubled years of the 1930s is provided by Robert J. C. Butow, *Tojo and the Coming of the War* (1961), and James B. Crowley, *Japan's Quest for Autonomy: National Security and Foreign Policy* (1966). The Emperor's role in the surrender decision is related in Robert J. C. Butow, *Japan's Decision to Surrender* (1954).

In 1996, *Time* published two retrospective articles by Carl Posey about Hirohito's life: "The God-Emperor Who Became a Man" and "From Militarist to Beloved Monarch." *Time,* Oct. 21, 1996.

Additional Sources

Large, Stephen S. *Emperors of the Rising Sun: Three Biographies,* Kodansha International, 1997 [biographies of Hirohito, his father, and his grandfather]. □

Ando Hiroshige

The Japanese painter and printmaker Ando Hiroshige (1797-1858) is considered one of the six great masters of the Ukiyo-e school. He is most famous for his landscape prints, which render typically Japanese landscapes in their different moods in a very poetic manner.

Working during the closing decades of the Edo period, Hiroshige represents the last flowering of the Ukiyo-e school. After his death, the designs of the prints became ever more vulgar, the printing careless, and the colors garish. In fact, a few years before Hiroshige's death, Commodore Perry arrived with his famous "black ships" to break Japan's centuries-old seclusion, and the end of traditional Japanese art and culture was in sight.

Hiroshige was the son of a fire brigade chief in Edo (modern Tokyo). At the age of 14, he became a pupil of Utagawa Toyohiro, a well-known printmaker, and he also studied traditional Japanese painting. Hiroshige's early work, which consisted of actor and courtesan prints, was neither original nor particularly distinguished, and it was only when he turned to landscapes, after Hokusai's great success with his *Thirty-six Views of Mt. Fuji,* that Hiroshige found his own unique style and achieved a fame even greater than that of Hokusai. In 1831 Hiroshige produced his first important work, a set of 10 famous views of Edo. The next year he executed *Fifty-three Stages of the Tokaido Road,* which established him as the leading printmaker of the day. From that time on he continued to make a huge number of prints until his death.

Hiroshige's Landscapes

The subject of virtually all of Hiroshige's mature work was the Japanese landscape, which he portrayed in a lyrical manner with an emphasis upon the misty atmosphere, the picturesque old pines, the sea with its fishing boats, and the green or snow-covered mountains. No other Japanese artist has succeeded in expressing so well the feeling and appearance of Japan, nor has anyone portrayed it with more subtlety and poetry. Hiroshige depicted the landscapes, as well as the people traveling about the country or performing their daily tasks, with such care that they serve as a record of Japanese life of the mid-19th century. Whether he was

and 1858. The quality of this series is uneven, as much of his later work is, but the finest, such as *Rain Storm on the Ohashi Bridge* and *Kinryuzan Temple in Asakusa,* are among his most remarkable prints. Next to his landscapes, his best work is his bird and flower prints, called *Kacho* in Japan.

Further Reading

The best book in English on Hiroshige is Edward F. Strange, *The Colour-prints of Hiroshige* (1925). Yone Noguchi, *Hiroshige* (2 vols., 1934-1940), is a sensitive appraisal of the artist's work. See also Percy Neville Barnett, *Colour-prints of Hiroshige* (1937), and Basil William Robinson, *Hiroshige* (1963). □

Alger Hiss

A former U.S. State Department official, Alger Hiss (1904-1996) was indicted in 1948 and convicted in 1950 of having provided classified documents to an admitted Communist, Whittaker Chambers. Hiss became a controversial figure and his case helped precipitate McCarthyite politics during the early Cold War years.

Alger Hiss was born on November 11, 1904, in Baltimore, Maryland, of a genteel, long-established middle class Baltimore family. An exceptional student, confident and aristocratic in demeanor, Hiss attended Johns Hopkins University on scholarship. Compiling an outstanding record in the classroom and as a student leader, he graduated in 1926, earning a scholarship to Harvard Law School. Hiss's academic achievements included appointment to the law review staff, and he developed an intellectual and political friendship with Harvard law professor Felix Frankfurter. On Frankfurter's recommendation, in 1929 Hiss was appointed a clerk to Supreme Court Justice Oliver Wendell Holmes, Jr. Later that year, on December 11, he married Priscilla Fansler Hobson, whom he had met and courted while an undergraduate. Upon completion of his clerkship, Hiss accepted an appointment in 1930 with the Boston law firm of Choate, Hall & Stewart, leaving in 1932 to accept an appointment with the New York City law firm of Cotton, Franklin, Wright & Gordon.

Having moved leftward during law school under Frankfurter's influence and then his wife's socialist leanings, Hiss was further influenced by the political and economic crisis of the Great Depression to abandon in 1933 a promising career in corporate law for a position with the Legal Division of the Agricultural Adjustment Agency (AAA), headed by Jerome Frank. Associating with an able group of predominantly radical attorneys, in July 1934 Hiss was loaned by the Agriculture Department to assist the staff of the Senate Special Committee to Investigate the Munitions Industry, the so-called Nye Committee. An able investigator, Hiss became disenchanted with the committee's isola-

---

portraying the ancient capital of Kyoto or the new capital of Edo, the beauty of Lake Biwa, or the Tokaido or Kiso Kaido roads, the artist never tired of representing the varied aspects of his native land.

Of all the many sets of prints produced by Hiroshige, whose total output is estimated at more than 5,000, the finest is without question the *Fifty-three Stages of the Tokaido Road,* published in 1833 and reprinted innumerable times ever since. This highway, which linked Edo with Kyoto, was the main road of Japan and was used by officials, businessmen, pilgrims, and sightseers who enjoyed its magnificent scenery, for it was flanked by mountains on the north and the sea on the south. Hiroshige himself had traveled it as a member of an official party of the shogunate which had gone to Kyoto in 1832 to present the Emperor with a white horse. During this trip Hiroshige made many sketches, and upon his return he started the designs representing the wayside stations along the road. To the 53 stations he added a print showing the starting point of the journey at the Nihonbashi in Edo and another for the final destination at the Sanjo Ohashi in Kyoto.

Another set which is particularly fine is the *Eight Views of Lake Biwa* (1834), which gives expression to Hiroshige's sensitive feeling for the moods of nature during different seasons and under various atmospheric conditions. It is the kind of print which was so much admired by such impressionists as Claude Monet and James McNeill Whistler.

Of the works of Hiroshige's later period, by far the most outstanding is *Hundred Views of Edo,* dating between 1856

tionism and with the department following a purge of the Legal Division in a dispute over policy toward landowners.

In August 1935 Hiss accepted a position as a consultant with the Department of Justice and was assigned to the solicitor general's office headed by Stanley Reed. Hiss assisted in preparing the department's defense of the constitutionality of AAA's policy of imposing a processing tax on producers of commodities. His work helping prepare the department's response to an expected court challenge to the administration's reciprocal trade agreements policy rekindled Hiss's interest in international developments, and in September 1936 he accepted an appointment to the staff of Assistant Secretary of State for Economic Affairs Francis Sayre.

A Promising Career Cut Short

As a State Department employee, Hiss's career fortunes improved swiftly. With the outbreak of World War II, Hiss came to devote his time and talents to the task of formulating and developing the structure of a permanent postwar collective security organization, which became the United Nations. Hiss's expertise in the area of international organization resulted in his participation as a rather low-level functionary at the 1943 Dumbarton Oaks Conference as well as his selection as a member of the U.S. delegation to the Yalta Conference of February 1945. Subsequently he received an appointment to head the State Department's Office of Special Policy Planning and later to serve as executive-secretary in August 1945 of the San Francisco Conference at which the United Nations Charter was drafted and

approved. Hiss remained in the State Department until February 1947, when he accepted the office of president of the Carnegie Endowment for International Peace.

Hiss's promising career was abruptly shattered by events having their origins in the highly charged confrontation between congressional conservatives and the Truman administration during the early Cold War years. In dramatic and extensively publicized testimony before the House Committee on Un-American Activities (HUAC) on August 3, 1948, Whittaker Chambers, an admitted ex-Communist and at the time senior editor of *Time* magazine, identified Hiss as a member of a Communist cell which had operated in Washington, D.C., in the mid-1930s. Denying then that Hiss's activities included espionage, Chambers claimed instead that Hiss's role, as that of the other individuals whom he concurrently identified as Communists, was to promote Communist infiltration of the federal bureaucracy in order to advance Communist policy.

Demanding the right to appear before the HUAC, Hiss denied Chambers' charges of Communist membership (and further claim to close friendship) and challenged Chambers to repeat the charges without congressional immunity so that he could bring suit for libel. Chambers did so during an August 27, 1948, interview on "Meet the Press," and Hiss sued him for libel. In his congressional testimony, Chambers had repeated allegations he had made earlier about Hiss's pro-Communist activities, either to Assistant Secretary of State Adolf Berle in 1939 or to the FBI in 1942, 1945, and 1946. In these earlier interviews Chambers had also only accused Hiss of Communist membership and denied having any evidence which could support more serious allegations. In 1945 and 1946, moreover, the FBI had initiated an investigation of Hiss without any result. At the same time, conservatives in the Congress as early as 1946 were somehow privy to Chambers' then non-public accusations involving Hiss.

The Hiss-Chambers confrontation took a dramatic turn in November-December 1948. On December 2, 1948, Chambers turned over to the HUAC counsel 58 microfilm frames of State Department documents dated in 1938. Chambers claimed to have received the original documents from Hiss in the 1930s in his capacity as a courier for a Soviet espionage operation. Earlier, on November 17, 1948, during pre-trial hearings involving Hiss's libel suit, Chambers had produced copies of two other sets of documents, also dated in 1938, which he claimed had been given to him by Hiss: typewritten facsimilies of original State Department documents and handwritten summaries of others, in Hiss's handwriting.

Abruptly altering his earlier testimony, Chambers thereafter maintained that his relationship with Hiss involved espionage, adding that Hiss was one of the "most zealous" Communist spies operating in Washington during the 1930s. Based on this changed testimony and the documentary evidence, on December 15, 1948, a federal grand jury indicted Hiss on two counts of perjury: his denial of having given classified State Department documents to Chambers in 1938 and his denial of having met Chambers after 1937. While Hiss had only been indicted for perjury, his trial was publicly perceived as an espionage case—technically Hiss could not be indicted for espionage since the alleged activity occurred in 1938, in peacetime, and since there was no second witness to corroborate Chambers' allegations.

The Perjury Trials

Hiss's trial on the perjury charges began on May 31, 1949, in New York City and ended when the jury on July 7, 1949, was unable to reach the unanimity required for conviction (voting 8-4 for conviction). After a four-month delay, as Hiss's attorneys sought unsuccessfully to have the trial moved from New York, Hiss was retried in November 1949. In the second trial, the prosecution's strategy shifted to focus on the documents and not Chambers' credibility (Hiss's defense had capitalized effectively on the numerous changes in Chambers' testimony about his relationship with Hiss and his own activities as a Communist). This strategy succeeded, and on January 21, 1950, the jury convicted Hiss on both perjury counts. Sentenced to five years at the Lewisburg, Pennsylvania, federal penitentiary, Hiss was released in 1954, a scarred and controversial figure.

As with the Dreyfus Case of the 1890s in France, Hiss's indictment and conviction assumed major political significance during the Cold War years, a significance that transcended the specific issues brought out at the trial and had little bearing on the "espionage" importance of the documents Chambers had produced in 1948. The Hiss-Chambers confrontation had seemingly confirmed the existence of a serious internal security threat, thereby legitimizing the politics of exposure dramatically exploited by the House Committee on Un-American Activities and championed during the early 1950s by Sen. Joseph McCarthy. Because the Hiss-Chambers relationship had been uncovered by the HUAC over the opposition of the Truman administration, Hiss's conviction seemed to document the success of Communists in obtaining sensitive positions in the State Department and in shaping the by-then controversial policies of the Roosevelt and Truman administrations toward the Soviet Union at Yalta, Potsdam, and thereafter.

Throughout the trial, and extending after his release from prison, Hiss steadfastly affirmed his own innocence, claiming to have been the victim of unfair tactics and publicity. His various efforts at exoneration—whether unsuccessfully petitioning for a new trial in the 1950s or filing a *coram nobis* suit in the 1970s—proved unsuccessful. Hiss thought he may have achieved his vindication when in 1992, after the fall of the Soviet Union, Russian General Dimitri Volkogonov, who was in charge of intelligence archives, claimed there was no evidence that indicated Hiss was a spy. However, he later recanted his statement, saying he had misunderstood. Four years later, researchers found Soviet transmissions in U.S. intelligence documents that suggested an American, code-named "Ales," perhaps Hiss, had been spying on the United States during the time in question.

Hiss maintained his innocence up until his death on November 15, 1996, at the age of 92. Daniel Schorr of National Public Radio said in 1996, "We don't know to this day whether he was guilty."

Hiss's case, and the question of his innocence or guilt, continues to divide American intellectuals and activists. In a complex way, the Hiss-Chambers case at the time and currently encapsulates the division over McCarthyism and internal security policy which shaped the politics of Cold War America.

Hiss wrote two memoirs: *In the Court of Public Opinion* (1957) and *Recollections of a Life* (1988).

Further Reading

The literature on the Hiss case and on Hiss's career divides sharply along lines of his assumed innocence or guilt. See Athan Theoharis, "Unanswered Questions: Chambers, Nixon, the FBI, and the Hiss Case," in Athan Theoharis (editor), *Beyond the Hiss Case: The FBI, Congress, and the Cold War* (1982); "Alger Hiss, Perjurer," *The Detroit News* (November 20, 1996); Eric Breindel, "The Faithful Traitor," *National Review* (February 10, 1997); Evan Thomas, "An American Melodrama," *Newsweek* (November 25, 1996); William Buckley, "Alger Hiss Could Never Admit his Guilt," *Salt Lake Tribune* (December 13, 1996). Also see *The American Spectator* Online Update (November 19-25, 1996) at http://www.amspec.org/exclusives/update_archives.html. □

Alfred Hitchcock

Alfred Hitchcock (1899-1980), was a film director famous for skillfully wrought suspense thrillers. He was essentially concerned with depicting the tenuous relations between people and objects and rendering the terror inherent in commonplace realities.

Born into a working class family in London, Alfred Hitchcock attended St. Ignatius' College to prepare for the ministry. However, rebelling against his Catholic upbringing, he fled to the Bohemian seacoast in 1921. He soon involved himself in motion picture production, receiving valuable training with the British division of Famous Players Lasky. In 1923 he began writing scenarios for the Gainsborough Film Studios.

Hitchcock's first film, *The Lodger* (1925), an exciting treatment of the Jack the Ripper story, was followed by *Blackmail* (1930), the first British talking picture. Some think that Hitchcock's next films, *The Man Who Knew Too Much* (1934), and *The Thirty-Nine Steps* (1935), were responsible for the renaissance in British movie making during the early 1930s.

Fame Spread in Hollywood

In 1939 Hitchcock left England with his wife and daughter to settle in Hollywood. For the most part, his American films of the 1940s were expensively produced and stylishly entertaining. These included *Rebecca* (1940), based on a best-selling suspense novel; *Suspicion* (1941), about a woman who believes her husband is a murderer;

Shadow of a Doubt (1943), the tale of a small-town psychopath diabolically masquerading as a Good Samaritan; *Lifeboat* (1944), a heavy-handed study of survival on the open seas; and *Spellbound* (1945), a murder mystery about psychoanalysts. Less ambitious but more accomplished was *Notorious* (1946), praised for its rendering of place and atmosphere. Hitchcock's first decade in Hollywood ended with two interesting failures: *The Paradine Case* (1947) and *Rope* (1948).

Hitchcock Became Master of Suspense

Beginning with the bizarre *Strangers on a Train* (1951), Hitchcock directed a series of films that placed him among the great artists of modern cinema. His productions of the 1950s were stylistically freer than his earlier films and thematically more complex. His most significant films during that time were *I Confess* (1953), *Rear Window* (1954), *To Catch a Thief* (1955),*The Trouble with Harry* (1956), *The Man Who Knew Too Much* (1956), *Vertigo* (1958), and *North by Northwest* (1959).

Psycho (1960) was Hitchcock's most terrifying and controversial film, and made an entire generation of moviegoers nervous about taking a shower. *The Birds* (1963), *Marnie* (1964), and *Family Plot* (1976) were Hitchcock's final and less brilliant films. Hitchcock also expanded his directing career into American television, with a series that featured mini-thrillers (1955-1965). Because of failing health, he retired from directing after *Family Plot*. He was knighted in 1979 and died soon afterward in Los Angeles on April 29, 1980.

Hitchcock Renaissance in the 1990s

Hitchcock's films enjoyed newfound popularity in the 1990s. After a restored print of *Vertigo* was released in 1996 and became surprisingly successful, plans were made to re-release other films, such as *Strangers on a Train*. According to *Entertainment Weekly*, as of 1997 plans were underway to remake as many as half a dozen Hitchcock films with new casts, an idea that met with mixed responses from Hitchcock fans.

Further Reading

The finest critical study of Hitchcock's films is by the French critic and film maker François Truffaut, *Hitchcock* (1966; trans. 1967). Other valuable treatments are Robin Wood, *Hitchcock's Films* (1965; 2d ed. 1969), and George Perry, *The Films of Alfred Hitchcock* (1965). For analysis of Hitchcock's work from his silent films to the early 1960s see the relevant chapter in John Russell Taylor, *Cinema Eye, Cinema Ear: Some Key Film-makers of the Sixties* (1964).

Additional Sources

Nashawaty, Chris, "Deja View," *Entertainment Weekly,* Dec. 6, 1996.
Ryall, Tom, *Alfred Hitchcock and the British Cinema,* 2nd ed., Athlone, 1996. □

Gilbert Monell Hitchcock

Gilbert Monell Hitchcock (1859-1934), American newspaper publisher and U.S. senator from Nebraska, led the unsuccessful struggle in the Senate for United States membership in the League of Nations.

Gilbert M. Hitchcock was born in Omaha, Nebr., on Sept. 18, 1859. He was educated in the city's public schools and for 2 years attended the gymnasium (high school) in Baden-Baden, Germany. He received a law degree from the University of Michigan in 1881 and was admitted to the Nebraska bar. In 1885 Hitchcock and three associates founded the *Omaha Evening World*. In 1889 he purchased the *Morning Herald,* one of the most important Democratic newspapers in Nebraska, and consolidated it with the *Evening World* as the *Omaha World Herald.* From this solid financial and political base he launched his public career.

The Hitchcock family was traditionally Republican. But viewing the plight of western agriculture in the 1880s, Hitchcock aligned himself with the Democratic-Populist camp in Nebraska, whose leader was William Jennings Bryan. It was as a "Bryan man" that Hitchcock was elected in 1902 to the U.S. House of Representatives, where he served until elected senator in 1911.

In the Senate, Hitchcock showed considerable independence from the Woodrow Wilson administration. He opposed the Federal Reserve Act of 1913 and, in 1914, introduced a bill to embargo all arms to countries at war in Europe, a plan resisted vigorously by President Wilson. Germany's resumption of submarine warfare in 1917, and the publication of the Zimmermann telegram, brought Hitchcock to support of the administration. Reluctantly, he voted to declare war on Germany.

Hitchcock's greatest influence in the Senate began when he assumed chairmanship of the Foreign Relations Committee in April 1918. He was a reluctant internationalist, and it was only during World War I that he saw the necessity for some international agency to secure the peace. Yet, despite his conversion to advocacy of the League of Nations, Hitchcock's relations with President Wilson remained cool. The President ignored Hitchcock's suggestion that the modifications of the League's collective security provisions proposed by Republican senator Henry Cabot Lodge be incorporated into the Treaty of Versailles to make it more acceptable. Meanwhile, Democratic counter-proposals, acceptable to the President, had little general success. Though Hitchcock supported Wilson to the end, the League and the treaty were defeated.

Hitchcock was defeated for reelection in 1922 and in 1930. He served as chairman of the Democratic platform committee in 1932. He died in Washington, D.C., on Feb. 3, 1934.

Further Reading

There is no good biography of Hitchcock. Brief notes are available in the Congressional Directory for the years of his House and Senate careers. For Hitchcock's role in the peace negotiations see Thomas A. Bailey, *Woodrow Wilson and the Great Betrayal* (1945); John A. Garraty, *Henry Cabot Lodge* (1953); and Arthur S. Link, *Wilson the Diplomatist* (1957). □

Adolf Hitler

The German dictator Adolf Hitler (1889-1945) led the extreme nationalist and racist Nazi party and served as chancellor-president of Germany from 1933 to 1945. Probably the most effective and powerful demagogue of the 20th century, his leadership led to the extermination of approximately 6 million Jews.

Adolf Hitler and his National Socialist movement belong among the many irrationally nationalistic, racist, and fundamentally nihilist political mass movements that sprang from the ground of political, economic, and social desperation following World War I and the deeply upsetting economic dislocations of the interwar period. Taking their name from the first such movement to gain power—Mussolini's fascism in Italy (1922)—fascist-type movements reached the peak of their popular appeal and political power in the widespread panic and mass psychosis that spread to all levels of the traditional industrial and semi-industrial societies of Europe with the world de-

pression of the 1930s. Always deeply chauvinistic, antiliberal and antirational, and violently anti-Semitic, these movements varied in form from the outright atheistic and industrialist German national socialism to the lesser-known mystical-religious and peasant-oriented movements of eastern Europe.

Early Life

Adolf Hitler was born on April 20, 1889, in the small Austrian town of Braunau on the Inn River along the Bavarian-German border, son of an Austrian customs official of moderate means. His early youth in Linz on the Danube seems to have been under the repressive influence of an authoritarian and, after retirement in 1895, increasingly short-tempered and domineering father until the latter's death in 1903. After an initially fine performance in elementary school, Adolf soon became rebellious and began failing in the *Realschule* (college preparatory school). Following transfer to another school, he finally left formal education altogether in 1905 and, refusing to bow to the discipline of a regular job, began his long years of dilettante, aimless existence, reading, painting, wandering in the woods, and dreaming of becoming a famous artist. In 1907, when his mother died, he moved to Vienna in an attempt to enroll in the famed Academy of Fine Arts. His failure to gain admission that year and the next led him into a period of deep depression and seclusion from his friends. Wandering through the streets of Vienna, he lived on a modest orphan's pension and the money he could earn by painting and selling picture postcards. It was during this time of his vaga-

bond existence among the rootless, displaced elements of the old Hapsburg capital, that he first became fascinated by the immense potential of mass political manipulation. He was particularly impressed by the successes of the anti-Semitic, nationalist Christian-Socialist party of Vienna Mayor Karl Lueger and his efficient machine of propaganda and mass organization. Under Lueger's influence and that of former Catholic monk and race theorist Lanz von Liebenfels, Hitler first developed the fanatical anti-Semitism and racial mythology that were to remain central to his own "ideology" and that of the Nazi party.

In May 1913, apparently in an attempt to avoid induction into the Austrian military service after he had failed to register for conscription, Hitler slipped across the German border to Munich, only to be arrested and turned over to the Austrian police. He was able to persuade the authorities not to detain him for draft evasion and duly presented himself for the draft physical examination, which he failed to pass. He returned to Munich, and after the outbreak of World War I a year later, he volunteered for action in the German army. During the war he fought on Germany's Western front with distinction but gained no promotion beyond the rank of corporal. Injured twice, he won several awards for bravery, among them the highly respected Iron Cross First Class. Although isolated in his troop, he seems to have thoroughly enjoyed his success on the front and continued to look back fondly upon his war experience.

Early Nazi Years

The end of the war suddenly left Hitler without a place or goal and drove him to join the many disillusioned veterans who continued to fight in the streets of Germany. In the spring of 1919 he found employment as a political officer in the army in Munich with the help of an adventurer-soldier by the name of Ernst Roehm—later head of Hitler's storm troopers (SA). In this capacity Hitler attended a meeting of the so-called German Workers' party, a nationalist, anti-Semitic, and socialist group, in September 1919. He quickly distinguished himself as this party's most popular and impressive speaker and propagandist, helped to increase its membership dramatically to some 6,000 by 1921, and in April that year became Führer (leader) of the now-renamed National Socialist German Workers' party (NSDAP), the official name of the Nazi party.

The worsening economic conditions of the two following years, which included a runaway inflation that wiped out the savings of great numbers of middle-income citizens, massive unemployment, and finally foreign occupation of the economically crucial Ruhr Valley, contributed to the continued rapid growth of the party. By the end of 1923 Hitler could count on a following of some 56,000 members and many more sympathizers and regarded himself as a significant force in Bavarian and German politics. Inspired by Mussolini's "March on Rome," he hoped to use the crisis conditions accompanying the end of the Ruhr occupation in the fall of 1923 to stage his own coup against the Berlin government. For this purpose he staged the well-known Nazi Beer Hall Putsch of Nov. 8/9, 1923, by which he hoped—in coalition with right-wingers around World War I

general Erich Ludendorff—to force the conservative-nationalist Bavarian government of Gustav von Kahr to cooperate with him in a rightist "March on Berlin." The attempt failed, however. Hitler was tried for treason and given the rather mild sentence of a year's imprisonment in the old fort of Landsberg.

It was during this prison term that many of Hitler's basic ideas of political strategy and tactics matured. Here he outlined his major plans and beliefs in *Mein Kampf,* which he dictated to his loyal confidant Rudolf Hess. He planned the reorganization of his party, which had been outlawed and which, with the return of prosperity, had lost much of its appeal. After his release Hitler reconstituted the party around a group of loyal followers who were to remain the cadre of the Nazi movement and state. Progress was slow in the prosperous 1920s, however, and on the eve of the Depression, the NSDAP still was able to attract only some 2.5 percent of the electoral vote.

Rise to Power

With the outbreak of world depression, the fortunes of Hitler's movement rose rapidly. In the elections of September 1930 the Nazis polled almost 6.5 million votes and increased their parliamentary representation from 12 to 107. In the presidential elections of the spring of 1932, Hitler ran an impressive second to the popular World War I hero Field Marshal Paul von Hindenburg, and in July he outpolled all other parties with some 14 million votes and 230 seats in the Reichstag (parliament). Although the party lost 2 million of its voters in another election, in November 1932, President Hindenburg on Jan. 30, 1933, reluctantly called Hitler to the chancellorship to head a coalition government of Nazis, conservative German nationalists, and several prominent independents.

Consolidation of Power

The first 2 years in office were almost wholly dedicated to the consolidation of power. With several prominent Nazis in key positions (Hermann Göring, as minister of interior in Prussia, and Wilhelm Frick, as minister of interior of the central government, controlled the police forces) and his military ally Werner von Blomberg in the Defense Ministry, he quickly gained practical control. He persuaded the aging president and the Reichstag to invest him with emergency powers suspending the constitution in the so-called Enabling Act of Feb. 28, 1933. Under this act and with the help of a mysterious fire in the Reichstag building, he rapidly eliminated his political rivals and brought all levels of government and major political institutions under his control. By means of the Roehm purge of the summer of 1934 he assured himself of the loyalty of the army by the subordination of the Nazi storm troopers and the murder of its chief together with the liquidation of major rivals within the army. The death of President Hindenburg in August 1934 cleared the way for the abolition of the presidential title by plebiscite. Hitler became officially Führer of Germany and thereby head of state as well as commander in chief of the armed forces. Joseph Goebbels's extensive propaganda machine and Heinrich Himmler's police system simultaneously perfected totalitarian control of Germany, as demonstrated most impressively in the great Nazi mass rally of 1934 in Nuremberg, where millions marched in unison and saluted Hitler's theatrical appeals.

Preparation for War

Once internal control was assured, Hitler began mobilizing Germany's resources for military conquest and racial domination of the land masses of central and eastern Europe. He put Germany's 6 million unemployed to work on a vast rearmament and building program, coupled with a propaganda campaign to prepare the nation for war. Germany's mythical enemy, world Jewry—which was associated with all internal and external obstacles in the way of total power—was systematically and ruthlessly attacked in anti-Semitic mass propaganda, with economic sanctions, and in the end by the "final solution" of physical destruction of Jewish men, women, and children in Himmler's concentration camps.

Foreign relations were similarly directed toward preparation for war: the improvement of Germany's military position, the acquisition of strong allies or the establishment of convenient neutrals, and the division of Germany's enemies. Playing on the weaknesses of the Versailles Peace Treaty and the general fear of war, this policy was initially most successful in the face of appeasement-minded governments in England and France. After an unsuccessful coup attempt in Austria in 1934, Hitler gained Mussolini's alliance and dependence as a result of Italy's Ethiopian war in 1935, illegally marched into the Rhineland in 1936 (demilitarized at Versailles), and successfully intervened—in cooperation with Mussolini—in the Spanish Civil War. Under the popular banner of national self-determination, he annexed Austria and the German-speaking Sudetenland of Czechoslovakia with the concurrence of the West in 1938 (Munich Agreement), only to occupy all of Czechoslovakia early in 1939. Finally, through threats and promises of territory, he was able to gain the benevolent neutrality of the Soviet Union for the coming war (Molotov-Ribbentrop Pact, August 1939). Alliances with Italy (Pact of Steel) and Japan followed.

The War

On Sept. 1, 1939, Hitler began World War II—which he hoped would lead to his control of most of the Eurasian heartland—with the lightning invasion of Poland, which he immediately followed with the liquidation of Jews and the Polish intelligentsia, the enslavement of the local "subhuman" population, and the beginnings of a German colonization. Following the declaration of war by France and England, he temporarily turned his military machine west, where the lightning, mobile attacks of the German forces quickly triumphed. In April 1940 Denmark surrendered, and Norway was taken by an amphibious operation. In May-June the rapidly advancing tank forces defeated France and the Low Countries.

The major goal of Hitler's conquest lay in the East, however, and already in the middle of 1940 German war production was preparing for an eastern campaign. The Air

Battle of Britain, which Hitler had hoped would permit either German invasion or (this continued to be his dream) an alliance with "Germanic" England, was broken off, and Germany's naval operations collapsed for lack of reinforcements and matériel.

On June 22, 1941, the German army advanced on Russia in the so-called Operation Barbarossa, which Hitler regarded as Germany's final struggle for existence and "living space" (*Lebensraum*) and for the creation of the "new order" of German racial domination. After initial rapid advances, the German troops were stopped by the severe Russian winter, however, and failed to reach any of their three major goals: Leningrad, Moscow, and Stalingrad. The following year's advances were again slower than expected, and with the first major setback at Stalingrad (1943) the long retreat from Russia began. A year later, the Western Allies, too, started advancing on Germany.

German Defeat

With the waning fortunes of the German war effort, Hitler withdrew almost entirely from the public; his orders became increasingly erratic and pedantic; and recalling his earlier triumphs over the generals, he refused to listen to advice from his military counselors. He dreamed of miracle bombs and suspected treason everywhere. Under the slogan of "total victory or total ruin," the entire German nation from young boys to old men, often barely equipped or trained, was mobilized and sent to the front. After an unsuccessful assassination attempt by a group of former leading politicians and military men on July 20, 1944, the regime of terror further tightened.

In the last days of the Third Reich, with the Russian troops in the suburbs of Berlin, Hitler entered into a last stage of desperation in his underground bunker in Berlin. He ordered Germany destroyed since it was not worthy of him; he expelled his trusted lieutenants Himmler and Göring from the party; and made a last, theatrical appeal to the German nation. Adolf Hitler committed suicide on April 30, 1945, leaving the last bits of unconquered German territory to the administration of non-Nazi Adm. Karl Doenitz.

Further Reading

Hitler's own writings start with *Mein Kampf;* of its many translations, that of Ralph Mannheim (1943) is preferred. *Hitler's Secret Book* (1961), with an introduction by Telford Taylor, is a second book on foreign policy written by Hitler in 1928 but not published during the Nazi years. The most important book of speeches is Norman H. Baynes, ed., *The Speeches of Adolf Hitler* (2 vols., 1942). Records of Hitler's conversations are in Hermann Rauschning, *The Voice of Destruction* (1940); H. R. Trevor-Roper, ed., *Hitler's Secret Conversations* (1953); and François Genoud, ed., *The Testament of Adolf Hitler* (1961).
Of the numerous biographies of Hitler, Alan Bullock, *Hitler: A Study in Tyranny* (1952; rev. ed. 1962), is outstanding, and it is also the best general book on Nazi Germany. A shorter recent biography by a German historian is Helmut Heiber, *Adolf Hitler: A Short Biography* (1961). Konrad Heiden, *Der Fuehrer: Hitler's Rise to Power* (1944), is the classic biography written during the Nazi years, which contains important insights for the period up to 1934. The young Hitler was de-

scribed by friends and associates: Kurt G. W. Ludecke, *I Knew Hitler* (1937); Franz Jetzinger, *Hitler's Youth* (trans. 1958); and, the most recent and comprehensive, Bradley F. Smith, *Adolf Hitler: His Family, Childhood, and Youth* (1967). An account by an associate of Hitler in Munich after World War I is Ernst Hanfstaengel, *Unheard Witness* (1957).

A number of books deal with various aspects of Hitler's personality and his conduct of the war. James H. McRandle, *The Track of the Wolf: Essays on National Socialism and Its Leader, Adolf Hitler* (1965), and George H. Stein, ed., *Hitler* (1968), both deal with Hitler's character and the political consequences of his personality. See also Albert Speer, *Inside the Third Reich: Memoirs* (1970). Hitler's relationship with favored associates is examined in Joachim C. Fest, *The Face of the Third Reich: Portraits of the Nazi Leadership,* translated by Michael Bullock (1970). Hitler's conduct of the war generally is the subject of Felix Gilbert, ed., *Hitler Directs His War* (1951), and H. R. Trevor-Roper, ed., *Blitzkrieg to Defeat* (1964); and Hitler's invasion of Russia is related in Paul Carell, *Hitler Moves East, 1941-1943,* translated by E. Osers (1965), and Leonard Cooper, *Many Roads to Moscow: Three Historic Invasions* (1968). A Russian journalist's interpretation of the circumstances surrounding Hitler's death is Lev Aleksandrovich Bezymenskii, *The Death of Adolf Hitler: Unknown Documents from Soviet Archives* (1968).

Recommended for general historical background are Hannah Arendt, *The Origins of Totalitarianism* (1951; rev. ed. 1967); William L. Shirer, *The Rise and Fall of the Third Reich* (1960), highly readable and fair-minded if not always reliable in detail; Hajo Holborn, *A History of Modern Germany,* vol. 3 (1964); Ernst Nolte, *Three Faces of Fascism* (1965); Golo Mann, *The History of Germany since 1789* (1968); and Karl Dietrich Bracher, *The German Dictatorship: The Origins, Structure and Effects of National Socialism* (trans. 1970). □

John Henry Hobart

John Henry Hobart (1775-1830), American Episcopal bishop, was his denomination's leading statesman during the early decades of the 19th century.

John Henry Hobart was born on Sept. 14, 1775. His father, an enterprising ship captain, died the following year, and the serious, vigorously intelligent boy was raised by his mother, a member of an old Philadelphia family. After attending the Episcopal Academy, Hobart entered the College of Pennsylvania at the age of 13. Announcing his faith publicly 2 years later, he received confirmation. Hobart transferred to Princeton and obtained the highest baccalaureate honors in 1793. Rejecting a mercantile career after a short period in a Philadelphia countinghouse, he pursued ministerial studies while a tutor at Princeton. After further preparation under Bishop William White, he became a deacon in 1798.

Following brief tenures at parishes in New Jersey and on Long Island, Hobart was appointed assistant minister at Trinity Church, New York, in 1800. Even before his ordination to the priesthood in the same year, churchmen selected him for high posts in national and diocesan church councils. In 1811 a special convention elected him coadju-

tor to the infirm bishop of New York. Upon the bishop's death in 1816, Hobart assumed the chief office as well as rectorship of the wealthy and influential Trinity parish.

Hobart energetically and efficiently attacked the problems of identity facing a denomination associated in the public mind with aristocratic, Anglophile sentiments. On behalf of his extensive diocese, in 1826 alone, he traveled more than 3,000 miles. Pastoral work at Trinity and visitations to New Jersey and Connecticut during episcopal vacancies increased his burden. In addition, he labored for mission, Bible, and Sunday school causes and other benevolent ventures, and he took special interest in the Christianizing of the Oneida Indians. A founder of the General Theological Seminary (1819), he occupied the chair of pastoral theology and pulpit eloquence from 1822 to 1830.

Physically exhausted, Hobart toured Europe from 1823 to 1825. Upon returning home, he professed loyalty to his country in terms that excited British disapproval and American pleasure. Nevertheless, Hobart staunchly, often tactlessly, acclaimed the English heritage and American canonical distinctiveness of the Church. This sectarian approach distressed ecumenically minded Broad Churchmen, who hotly engaged him in pamphlet warfare.

Hobart was a prolific writer and an eloquent, impassioned preacher. Among his many works were *Feasts and Festivals* (1804), *Apology for Apostolic Order* (1807), and an edition of a popular family Bible (1818-1820). He died on Sept. 12, 1830.

Further Reading

A primary source is *The Correspondence of John Henry Hobart* (6 vols., 1911-1912). The only biographies of Hobart are John Frederick Schroeder, *Memorial of Bishop Hobart* (1831), and John McVickar, *Early Life and Professional Years of Bp. Hobart* (1838). More accessible and useful to the modern reader are such histories of religion in America as Clifton E. Olmstead, *History of Religion in the United States* (1960); H. Shelton Smith and others, *American Christianity* (2 vols., 1963); and Edwin S. Gaustad, *A Religious History of America* (1966). □

Thomas Hobbes

The English philosopher and political theorist Thomas Hobbes (1588-1679) was one of the central figures of British empiricism. His major work, "Leviathan," published in 1651, expressed his principle of materialism and his concept of a social contract forming the basis of society.

Born prematurely on April 5, 1588, when his mother heard of the impending invasion of the Spanish Armada, Thomas Hobbes later reported that "my mother gave birth to twins, myself and fear." His father was the vicar of Westport near Malmesbury in Gloucestershire. He abandoned his family to escape punishment for fighting with another clergyman "at the church door." Thereafter Thomas was raised and educated by an uncle. At local schools he became a proficient classicist, translating a Greek tragedy into Latin iambics by the time he was 14. From 1603 to 1608 he studied at Magdalen College, Oxford, where he was bored by the prevailing philosophy of Aristotelianism.

The 20-year-old future philosopher became a tutor to the Cavendish family. This virtually lifelong association with the successive earls of Devonshire provided him with an extensive private library, foreign travel, and introductions to influential people. Hobbes, however, was slow in developing his thought; his first work a translation of Thucydides's *History of the Peloponnesian* Wars, did not appear until 1629. Thucydides held that knowledge of the past was useful for determining correct action, and Hobbes said that he offered the translation during a period of civil unrest as a reminder that the ancients believed democracy to be the least effective form of government.

According to his own estimate the crucial intellectual event of Hobbes's life occurred when he was 40. While waiting for a friend he wandered into a library and chanced to find a copy of Euclid's geometry. Opening the book, he read a random proposition and exclaimed, "By God that is impossible!" Fascinated by the interconnections between axioms, postulates, and premises, he adopted the ideal of demonstrating certainty by way of deductive reasoning. His interest in mathematics is reflected in his second work, *A Short Treatise on First Principles,* which presents a mechanical interpretation of sensation, as well as in his brief stint as mathematics tutor to Charles II. His generally royalist sympathy as expressed in *The Elements of Law* (1640) caused Hobbes to leave England during the "Long Parliament." This was the first of many trips back and forth between England and the Continent during periods of civil strife since he was, in his own words, "the first of all that fled." For the rest of his long life Hobbes traveled extensively and published prolifically. In France he met René Descartes and the anti-Cartesian Pierre Gassendi. In 1640 he wrote one of the sets of objections to Descartes's *Meditations.*

Although born into the Elizabethan Age, Hobbes outlived all of the major 17th-century thinkers. He became a sort of English institution and continued writing, offering new translations of Homer in his 80s because he had "nothing else to do." When he was past 90, he became embroiled in controversies with the Royal Society. He invited friends to suggest appropriate epitaphs and favored one that read "this is the true philosopher's stone." He died on Dec. 4, 1679, at the age of 91.

His Philosophy

The diverse intellectual currents of the 17th century, which are generically called modern classical philosophy, began with a unanimous repudiation of the authorities of the past, especially Aristotle and the scholastic tradition. Descartes, who founded the rationalist tradition, and his contemporary Sir Francis Bacon, who is considered the originator of modern empiricism, both sought new methodologies for achieving scientific knowledge and a systematic conception of reality. Hobbes knew both of these thinkers, and his system encompassed the advantages of both rationalism and empiricism. As a logician, he believed too strongly in the power of deductive reasoning from definitions to share Bacon's exclusive enthusiasm for inductive generalizations from experience. Yet Hobbes was a more consistent empiricist and nominalist, and his attacks on the misuse of language exceed even those of Bacon. And unlike Descartes, Hobbes viewed reason as summation of consequences rather than an innate, originative source of new knowledge.

Psychology, as the mechanics of knowing, rather than epistemology is the source of Hobbes's singularity. He was fascinated by the problem of sense perception, and he extended Galileo's mechanical physics into an explanation of human cognition. The origin of all thought is sensation which consists of mental images produced by the pressure of motion of external objects. Thus Hobbes anticipates later thought by distinguishing between the external object and the internal image. These sense images are extended by the power of memory and imagination. Understanding and reason, which distinguish men from other animals, consist entirely in the ability to use speech.

Speech is the power to transform images into words or names. Words serve as the marks of remembrance, signification, conception, or self-expression. For example, to speak of a cause-and-effect relation is merely to impose names and define their connection. When two names are so joined that the definition of one contains the other, then the proposition is true. The implications of Hobbes's analysis are quite modern. First, there is an implicit distinction between objects and their appearance to man's senses. Consequently knowledge is discourse about appearances. Universals are merely names understood as class concepts, and they have no real status, for everything which appears "is individual and singular." Since "true and false are attributes of speech and not of things," scientific and philosophic thinking consists in using names correctly. Reason is calculation or "reckoning the consequences of general laws agreed upon for either marking or signifying." The power of the mind is the capacity to reduce consequences to general laws or theorems either by deducing consequences from principles or by inductively reasoning from particular perceptions to general principles. The privilege of mind is subject to unfortunate abuse because, in Hobbes's pithy phrase, men turn from summarizing the consequences of things "into a reckoning of the consequences of appellations," that is, using faulty definitions, inventing terms which stand for nothing, and assuming that universals are real.

The material and mechanical model of nature offered Hobbes a consistent analogy. Man is a conditioned part of nature, and reason is neither an innate faculty nor the summation of random experience but is acquired through slow cultivation and industry. Science is the cumulative knowledge of syllogistic reasoning which gradually reveals the dependence of one fact upon another. Such knowledge is conditionally valid and enables the mind to move progressively from abstract and simple to more particular and complex sciences: geometry, mechanics, physics, morals (the nature of mind and desire), politics.

Political Thought

Hobbes explains the connection between nature, man, and society through the law of inertia. A moving object continues to move until impeded by another force, and "trains of imagination" or speculation are abated only by logical demonstrations. So also man's liberty or desire to do what he wants is checked only by an equal and opposite need for security. A society or commonwealth "is but an artificial man" invented by man, and to understand polity one should merely read himself as part of nature.

Such a reading is cold comfort because presocial life is characterized by Hobbes, in a famous quotation, as "solitary, poor, nasty, brutish and short." The equality of human desire is matched by an economy of natural satisfactions. Men are addicted to power because its acquisition is the only guarantee of living well. Such men live in "a state of perpetual war" driven by competition and desire for the same goods. The important consequence of this view is man's natural right and liberty to seek self-preservation by any means. In this state of nature there is no value above self-interest because where there is no common, coercive power there is no law and no justice. But there is a second and derivative law of nature that men may surrender or transfer their individual will to the state. This "social contract" binds the individual to treat others as he expects to be treated by them. Only a constituted civil power commands sufficient force to compel everyone to fulfill this original compact by which men exchange liberty for security.

In Hobbes's view the sovereign power of a commonwealth is absolute and not subject to the laws and obligations of citizens. Obedience remains as long as the sovereign fulfills the social compact by protecting the rights of the individual. Consequently rebellion is unjust, by definition, but should the cause of revolution prevail, a new absolute sovereignty is created.

Further Reading

The standard edition is *The English Works of Thomas Hobbes,* edited by Sir William Molesworth (11 vols. 1839-1845). In addition see *The Elements of Law, Natural and Politic,* edited by Ferdinand Tönnies (1928); *Body, Mind and Citizen,* edited by Richard S. Peters (1962); and *Leviathan,* edited by Michael Oakeshott (1962).

There is a wealth of good secondary literature available. John Aubrey included a biography of his friend Hobbes in *Brief Lives,* edited by Oliver Lawson Dick (1950). Leo Strauss, *The Political Philosophy of Hobbes: Its Basis and Genesis* (trans. 1936); Leslie Stephen, *Hobbes* (1904); and Richard Peters, *Hobbes* (1956), are excellent studies.

Consult also John Larid, *Hobbes* (1934); Clarence DeWitt Thorpe, *The Aesthetic Theory of Thomas Hobbes* (1940); John Bowle, *Hobbes and His Critics: A Study in Seventeenth Century Constitutionalism* (1952); Samuel I. Mintz, *The Hunting of Leviathan: Seventeenth-century Reactions to the Materialism and Moral Philosophy of Thomas Hobbes* (1962); C. B. Macpherson, *The Political Theory of Possessive Individualism: Hobbes of Locke* (1962); J. W. N. Watkins, *Hobbes's System of Ideas: A Study in the Political Significance of Philo-*

sophical Theories (1965); and F. S. McNeilly, *The Anatomy of Leviathan* (1968). □

Oveta Culp Hobby

American government official and businesswoman Oveta Culp Hobby (1905-1995) held pioneering roles as the first head of both the Women's Army Corps (WACs) and the Department of Health, Education, and Welfare (HEW). In her leadership of the WACs, Hobby fought for the equal treatment of female soldiers, insisting that they be subject to the same rules and training as men and receive similar responsibilities. She received a number of honors for her life of public service, including the Distinguished Service Award and the George Catlett Marshall Medal for Public Service.

Oveta Culp Hobby was one of the most prominent women in American government in the 1940s and 1950s. During World War II, she became the original director of the Women's Army Corps, providing guidance in the creation of the first military group for women in the United States. In the 1950s, she was appointed by President Dwight D. Eisenhower to serve as secretary of the newly formed cabinet department of Health, Education, and Welfare. She was only the second woman in history to hold a U.S. cabinet post. After leaving government work, Hobby returned to a successful business career in which she headed a media corporation that included a newspaper and television stations. Throughout her career, Hobby was known for upholding her ideals on social issues while weathering difficulties with composure, dignity, and style. Her policies and example helped to win increased acceptance and respect for other women pursuing careers in the military, government, and business.

Hobby was born into a political family in Killeen, Texas, on January 19, 1905. Her father, Isaac William Culp, was a lawyer and state politician, and her mother, Emma Hoover Culp, was active in the women's suffrage movement. Hobby attended public schools in Killeen and received instruction from private tutors. Her education was also supplemented by her own enthusiastic reading on a variety of topics. The family interest in government and politics was inherited by Hobby, who was drawn to the subject even more after her father was elected to the Texas House of Representatives in 1919. During his first term in office, Hobby attended a year of classes at the Mary Hardin-Baylor College in Belton, Texas. With her father's reelection in 1921, Hobby moved to Austin with her father, beginning her own law studies by auditing courses at the University of Texas.

Advanced in Newspaper Career

Hobby became an expert on parliamentary procedure, and at the age of 20, began a lengthy term as parliamentarian for the state House of Representatives. She held the post from 1925 to 1931 and returned to the job from 1939 to 1941. She published a book on the subject in 1937 under the title *Mr. Chairman*. In 1929 she ran for a House seat herself, but was defeated by a Ku Klux Klan-supported candidate who accused her of being a "parliamentarian." This foray into the world of campaigning and elections did not suit Hobby; she never again ran for an elective post. Following her defeat, she changed the focus of her career and took a job in the circulation department of the *Houston Post*.

The president of the *Houston Post* was William Pettus Hobby, a friend of Hobby's father and a former governor of Texas. When Hobby met him, she was in her mid-20s and the businessman, in his 50s, had just suffered the death of his first wife. The two began a courtship that resulted in their marriage on February 23, 1931. Hobby continued working at the *Post,* beginning a syndicated column devoted to issues of parliamentary procedure. Over the coming years she took on increasing responsibility at the paper, advancing from research editor in 1931 to assistant editor in 1936 and executive vice president in 1938. She and her husband eventually purchased the newspaper and Hobby assumed the top management role, simultaneously serving as executive director of the radio station KPRC in Houston. During the 1930s the Hobbys also had two children, William Pettus Hobby Jr. in 1932 and Jessica Oveta Hobby in 1937.

Led Formation of WACs

Hobby returned to government activities in the summer of 1941 when she took an unpaid post as head of the recently formed women's division of the War Department Bureau of Public Relations. With the start of American involvement in World War II after the bombing of Pearl Harbor that December, she was approached by General George C. Marshall to help draw up plans for a women's branch of the Army. Shortly after the creation of the Women's Auxiliary Army Corps (WAACs) on May 12, 1942, Hobby was named its first director, receiving the military rank of colonel. In 1943, the force received full status in the army and its name was changed to the Women's Army Corps (WACs).

The new women's military force provided several challenges for Hobby. Her first task was to raise the required number of 12,200 volunteers and to recruit officer candidates. Having gathered an army, she then had to establish a role for it within the context of the male armed forces. Fighting the opinion that women should or could not endure the same regimen as men, Hobby insisted that her soldiers receive the standard Army training and be held to the same military traditions and discipline. She based her policies on research as well as her own opinions; in one instance she traveled to Great Britain with first lady Eleanor Roosevelt to study how women there participated in the war. Hobby struggled to win equal treatment for the WACs, defending her women even on the thorny issue of illegitimate pregnancy while in the service. Army officials stated that under such conditions, women should receive a dishonorable discharge and lose all pay and rights. But Hobby countered that such a policy would be an unfair double standard—male soldiers who had affairs resulting in pregnancy did not receive such treatment. The Army conceded her point and allowed pregnant soldiers to leave the forces with an honorable discharge.

Fought Prejudice against Female Soldiers

Not only did Hobby have to labor to win women assignments with Army commanders and resentful enlisted men, she played an important role in creating a positive image for the WACs. Rumors alleging that the ranks of female soldiers were filled with women of loose sexual morals and lesbians threatened to damage public support of the WACs as well as morale in the troops. As the top representative of the WACs, Hobby helped to diminish these ideas by her own example as an intelligent, dignified woman with a distinctive feminine style. Her traditionally elegant fashion sense, in fact, was one of her hallmarks; she frequently appeared at public occasions wearing white gloves and a hat. The billed cap that she wore while head of the WACs became popularly known as the "Hobby cap"and became part of the official WACs uniform.

Under Hobby's leadership, the WACs gained a solid foothold in the military. By the time of her retirement from the force in the summer of 1945, the number of female soldiers had grown to 200,000. In addition, the WACs had inspired the introduction of women into the other branches of the armed forces, resulting in the creation of the WAVES in the Navy, the SPARs in the Coast Guard, and the Women

Marines. For her work to establish the role of women in the army during wartime, Hobby was awarded the Distinguished Service Medal.

Named Secretary of HEW

Following her departure from the WACs, Hobby returned to Houston and resumed her duties at the *Post*. By 1952, she had become coeditor and publisher of the newspaper. Although traditionally she had backed Democratic politicians in her home state, during the post-war years she supported the Republican presidential candidacies of both Thomas Dewey in 1948 and Dwight D. Eisenhower in 1952. In the 1952 election she assisted in the Democrats for Eisenhower movement. When Eisenhower became president, Hobby's loyalty was rewarded; he appointed her to lead the Federal Security Agency. The agency was responsible for addressing issues that affected the health, education, and economic and social conditions of Americans. In 1953, at the recommendation of the Hoover Commission for the Organization of the Executive Branch of the Government, the agency received cabinet status and was reformed as the Department of Health, Education, and Welfare (HEW). Hobby remained at the helm of the department, becoming a cabinet secretary on April 11, 1953.

While Hobby distinguished herself a capable and forward-thinking member of the cabinet, her tenure there was filled with frustrations. One of her major proposals, to provide government support for lost-cost health insurance plans, was strongly opposed by both conservative legislators and the American Medical Association, and was defeated. After the polio vaccine developed by Jonas Salk became available, Hobby's department took on responsibility for insuring equitable distribution of inoculations for children across the nation. The effort became an organizational nightmare, however, as demand for the vaccine surpassed expectations and deliveries were delayed. In addition, one of the first batches of the vaccine was contaminated, resulting in several children contracting polio and a nationwide panic. Hobby worked to reassure the public that vaccinations were safe, but in the midst of the confusion her husband fell into ill health and she resigned her post to tend to him. She once again returned to Houston in July of 1955.

Honored for Public Service

Hobby managed her husband's businesses from their home until William Hobby's death in 1964. His companies were left to Hobby, who kept the businesses competitive by backing the use of the latest technologies at the *Post* and KPRC. She bought another television company, WLAC-TV of Nashville, Tennessee, in 1975. She also found time to serve on the boards of businesses and nonprofit organizations, including the Bank of Texas and the Corporation for Public Broadcasting. Her philanthropic activities included running the Hobby Foundation. Hobby occasionally was called to return to the service of the government, participating in the presidential commission on Selective Service and the Vietnam Health Education Task Force of HEW. For her lengthy history of public service, Hobby was awarded the George Catlett Marshall Medal for Public Service by the

Association of the United States Army in 1978, becoming the first woman so honored. Hobby died at the age of 90 on August 16, 1995.

Further Reading

Adams, Sherman, *Firsthand Report: The Story of the Eisenhower Administration,* Harper, 1961.

Crawford, Ann Fears, and Crystal Sasse Ragsdale, "Mrs. Secretary: Oveta Culp Hobby," *Women in Texas: Their Lives, Their Experiences, Their Accomplishments,* Eakin Press, 1982, pp. 249-59.

Eisenhower, Dwight D., *Mandate for Change, 1953-1956,* Doubleday, 1963.

Holm, Jeanne, *Women in the Military: An Unfinished Revolution,* Presidio Press, 1982.

Hurt, Harry III, "The Last of the Great Ladies," *Texas Monthly,* October 1978, pp. 143-48, 225-40.

Miles, Rufus E., Jr., *The Department of Health, Education, and Welfare,* Praeger, 1974. □

Leonard Trelawny Hobhouse

The English sociologist and philosopher Leonard Trelawny Hobhouse (1864-1929), one of the major theoreticians of liberalism in England before World War I, advocated a modified form of state socialism tempered by traditional liberal principles.

Born Sept. 8, 1864, at St. Ives, Cornwall, L.T. Hobhouse was the son of a prominent Anglican family. He entered Oxford in 1883 and later taught at Corpus Christi and Merton colleges until 1897. His many works in a variety of disciplines are unified by a commitment to the idea of social reform according to the criteria of morality and reason.

Hobhouse's first important work, *The Labour Movement* (1893), outlined his program to unite the forces of trade unionism with those of reform liberalism. The core of his program was the demand for collective control of industry and agriculture in order to secure efficiency and the equitable distribution of life's necessities. His next work, *The Theory of Knowledge* (1896), was a technical philosophical treatise opposing the philosophical idealism dominant at Oxford. He especially insisted upon the validity of rational knowledge, believing that to deny it meant denying the possibility of social reform.

In 1897 Hobhouse joined the staff of the *Manchester Guardian,* where he remained for the next 4 years, during which time he published *Mind in Evolution* (1901), recognized as one of the early classics of comparative psychology. Here he addressed himself to the claims of social Darwinists that social reform, by eliminating the struggle for existence, encouraged the survival of the unfit and thereby hindered the evolutionary advance of mankind. Hobhouse attempted to prove that, with man's discovery of science, random biological evolution had been replaced by directed, self-conscious development. Rational organization could now replace struggle as the means of preserving the species.

In 1902 Hobhouse moved to London, where he became actively involved in politics, serving as secretary of the Free Trade Union (1902-1905). In *Democracy and Reaction* (1904) he attacked the imperialist policies of the British government. In his most famous work, *Liberalism* (1911), he outlined his program for what he now called liberal socialism. This program attempted to harmonize the idea of collective control with that of individual liberty.

During this period Hobhouse began to devote himself primarily to sociology. He played an important role in establishing the Sociological Society and for a time served as editor of the *Sociological Review.* In *Morals in Evolution* (1906), perhaps his most impressive work, he attempted to classify the forms of human achievement, such as religion, morality, knowledge, and political institutions. He concluded that a general advance, though erratic and unequal, could be discerned in the forms of human creativity, and that mankind now possessed the ability to organize all of human life according to a rational system which would harmonize the claims and needs of individuals with those of society. Hobhouse became the first professor of sociology at the University of London, in 1907.

Hobhouse first opposed British involvement in World War I but eventually became a supporter of the war effort. In *The World in Conflict* (1915) and *Questions of War and Peace* (1916) he characterized the war as a civilizational struggle between the West, representing reason and morality, and Germany, representing violence and irrationality. In *The Metaphysical Theory of the State* (1918) he attacked Hegelianism, which he considered responsible for the German intellectual spirit. Nevertheless, throughout the war he argued for a negotiated rather than an imposed settlement with Germany and suggested a league of nations which might be transformed into a world state.

After the war Hobhouse served on a number of boards of trade and wrote *The Rational Good* (1921), *Elements of Social Justice* (1923), and *Social Development, Its Nature and Conditions* (1924). His work had some influence in the United States during the 1930s but remains largely unread today. His political views underwent a change after the war, and his disenchantment with large-scale government institutions led him to advocate a modified form of guild socialism. In the last years of his life, illness, his wife's death, and disillusionment with liberal bureaucracy resulted in his retirement from political activity, although he retained his professorship at the University of London until his death, at Alençon, France, on June 21, 1929.

Further Reading

The best secondary source on Hobhouse is J. A. Hobson and Morris Ginsberg, *L. T. Hobhouse: His Life and Work* (1931). Ginsberg also wrote a good, brief appraisal of Hobhouse's work in his introduction to Hobhouse's *Sociology and Philosophy* (1966). Hobhouse's sociological work is treated in Hugh Carter, *The Social Theories of L. T. Hobhouse* (1927), and in an essay in Harry Elmer Barnes, ed., *An Introduction to the History of Sociology* (1948).

Additional Sources

L. T. Hobhouse: his life and work, London: Routledge/Thoemmes Press, 1993. □

William Hobson

William Hobson (1793-1842) was a British naval commander and governor of New Zealand. He negotiated the Treaty of Waitangi with the Maori chiefs, which granted England sovereignty over New Zealand.

William Hobson was born at Waterford, Ireland, on Sept. 26, 1793. He entered the Royal Navy at the age of 9, became a midshipman in 1806, and rose to captain in 1834. He served at the North Sea, West Indies, North America, English Channel, and Mediterranean stations and in 1836 was posted to Australia, where he surveyed Port Phillip Bay, the northern part of which was named after him.

In 1837 Hobson was sent to investigate the situation in New Zealand, where tribal warfare was reported to be threatening the lives of British subjects. As a solution, he proposed the establishment within certain areas of a series of British enclaves, or "factories," on the model of those of the East India Company in India, but it came to nothing.

In 1839 Hobson was appointed British consul in New Zealand with authority to negotiate justly and fairly with the Maoris for recognition of British sovereignty over their territory. On Feb. 5, 1840, Hobson met with Maori chiefs at Waitangi, where they signed a treaty by which the chiefs ceded sovereignty to Britain in return for guarantees respecting their lands and possessions and their rights as British subjects. Three months later Hobson proclaimed British sovereignty over the whole of New Zealand and established the capital at Auckland in the center of the Maori population.

Hobson governed New Zealand as lieutenant governor under the jurisdiction of the governor of New South Wales, but in May 1841 New Zealand became a separate crown colony with Hobson as governor. In his short term of office he attempted to regulate land claims and as a result came into conflict with the New Zealand Company, which had been organized in 1839 by Edward Gibbon Wakefield and his followers and had claims to about 20 million acres. Hobson had virtually no military force to support him, and he experienced difficulty in reconciling the divergent interests of missionaries, traders, and Maoris. Moreover, he was not well served by the officials around him, and the expenses of his civil establishment were unnecessarily high. He himself was honest, religious, sociable, and well liked by the Maoris, who considered him a just man, but he was

dogged by failing health, which affected his grasp of the situation. He died at Auckland on Sept. 10, 1842.

Further Reading

Guy H. Scholefield, *Captain William Hobson, First Governor of New Zealand* (1934), is the standard biography. Important specialized studies are J. C. Beaglehole, *Captain Hobson and the New Zealand Company* (1928); T. Lindsay Buick, *The Treaty of Waitangi: How New Zealand Became a British Colony* (1933); James Rutherford, *The Treaty of Waitangi and the Acquisition of British Sovereignty in New Zealand, 1840* (1949); and A. H. McLintock, *Crown Colony Government in New Zealand* (1958). □

Ho Chi Minh

Ho Chi Minh (1890-1969) was the most famous Vietnamese revolutionary and statesman of his time. He was one of the shrewdest, most callous, dedicated, and self-abnegating leaders, a man apart in the international Communist movement.

The Democratic Republic of Vietnam, or North Vietnam, the little Asian country that held two leading Western powers—France and the United States—at bay after the end of World War II, was founded and proclaimed by Ho Chi Minh in 1945. In spite of his shrewdness, the frail, little Ho looked like an old peasant with a gaunt face, an expression of simplicity and gentleness, and nothing surprising except his amazingly lively eyes. His familiar garb consisted of a linen work suit and rubber sandals made of discarded tires.

Ho was born Nguyen That Thanh on May 19, 1890, in the village of Kim Lien, province of Nghe An, central Vietnam, into a family of scholar-revolutionaries, who had been successively dismissed from government service for anti-French activities. At the age of 9 Ho and his mother, who had been charged with stealing French weapons for the rebels, fled to Hue, the imperial city. His father, constantly persecuted by the French police, had left for Saigon. After a year in Hue, his mother died. Young Ho returned to Kim Lien to finish his schooling. At 17, upon receiving a minor degree, Ho journeyed to the South, where he spent a brief spell as an elementary school teacher.

At the news of the first Chinese revolution, which broke out in Wuchang, the fiercely patriotic Ho left for Saigon to discuss the situation with his father. It was then decided that Ho should go to Europe to study Western science and survey the conditions in France before embarking upon a revolutionary career. Unable to finance such a trip, Ho nevertheless managed to obtain a job as a messboy on a French liner.

Years in Europe

By the end of 1911 Ho began his seaman's life, which took him to the major ports of Africa, Europe, and America.

As World War I broke out, Ho bade farewell to the sea and landed in London, where he lived until 1917, taking on odd jobs to support himself. It was here that Ho cultivated contact with the Overseas Workers' Association, an anticolonialist and anti-imperialist organization of Chinese and Indian seamen.

In 1917 Ho departed for France. He settled in Paris, working successively as a cook, a gardener, and a photo retoucher. Ho spent half his time reading, writing, trying to gain French sympathy for Vietnam, and organizing the thousands of Vietnamese, who were either serving in the French army or working in factories. He also joined the French Socialist party and attended various political clubs.

Distressed by the Western powers' indifference toward the colonies both during and after the Versailles Conference in spite of the Fourteen Points of U.S. president Woodrow Wilson, Ho, whose only interest up to that time had been Vietnam's independence, began to drift toward Soviet Russia, the champion of the oppressed peoples. At its Tours Congress in 1920, the French Socialist party split on the colonial issue: one wing remaining indifferent to the problems of the colonies and another advocating their immediate emancipation in accordance with Lenin's program. Ho sided with the latter faction, which seceded from the parent organization and formed the French Communist party.

In 1921 Ho organized the Intercolonial Union, a group of exiles from the French colonies which was dedicated to the propagation of communism, and published two papers, one in French, *Le Paria,* and one in Vietnamese, the *Soul of*

Vietnam, which carried emotional articles denouncing the abuses of colonialism. His most important work, *French Colonialization on Trial,* was also written during this period.

In November-December 1922 Ho attended the Fourth Comintern Congress in Moscow. In October 1923 he was elected to the 10-man Executive Committee of the Peasants' International Congress. Late in 1923 Ho went to Moscow, where he absorbed the teachings of Marx and Lenin. Two years later he arrived in Canton as adviser to Soviet agent Mikhail Borodin, who was then adviser to the Chinese Nationalists.

Early Organizing Efforts

Passing for a nationalist, Ho brought the Vietnamese émigrés in Canton into a revolutionary society called Youth and organized Marxist training courses for his young fellow countrymen. The Youth members were the nucleus of what was to be the Indochinese Communist party. Those who refused to obey Ho's orders were severely punished; Ho would forward their names to the French police force, which was always eager to put them behind bars. Ho also set up the League of Oppressed Peoples of Asia, which was to become the South Seas Communist party.

In April 1927, as the Chinese Nationalists broke with their Soviet advisers, Ho had to flee to Moscow. Subsequently, he received a brief assignment to the Anti-Imperialist League in Berlin. In 1928, after attending the Congress against Imperialism in Brussels, Ho journeyed to Switzerland and Italy, then turned up in Siam to organize the Vietnamese settlers and direct the Communist activities in Malaya and the Dutch East Indies. Early in 1930 Ho went to Hong Kong, where on February 3 he founded the Indochinese Communist party.

A year later Ho was arrested by the Hong Kong authorities and found guilty of subversion. Thanks to a successful appeal financed by the Red Relief Association, Ho regained his freedom. He immediately left for Singapore, where he was again arrested and returned to Hong Kong. Ho obtained his release by agreeing to work for the British Intelligence Service. Back in Moscow in 1932, Ho underwent further indoctrination at the Lenin School, which trained high-ranking cadres for the Soviet Communist party. In 1936 Ho returned to China to take control of the Indochinese Communist party.

Return Home

In February 1941 Ho finally crossed the border into Vietnam and settled down in a secure hideout in a remote frontier jungle. With a view to bringing all resistance elements under his control, winning power, then eliminating all competitors and creating a Communist state, Ho founded an independence league called the Viet Minh, whose alleged program was to coordinate all nationalist activities in the struggle for independence. (At this time Ho adopted the name Ho Chih Minh—"Enlightened One.") While the Viet Minh included many nationalists, most of its leaders were seasoned Communists.

In August 1942 Ho went back to China to ask for Chinese military assistance in return for intelligence about the Japanese forces in Indochina. The Chinese Nationalists, who had broken with the Communists and been disturbed by the Viet Minh activities in both Vietnam and China, however, arrested and imprisoned Ho on the charge that he was a French spy. After 13 months in jail Ho offered to put his organization at the Chinese service in return for his freedom. The Chinese, who were in desperate need of intelligence reports on the Japanese, accepted the offer. Upon his release Ho was admitted to the Dong Minh Hoi, an organization of Vietnamese nationalists in China which the Chinese had set up with the hope of controlling the independence movement. Ho repeatedly offered to collaborate with the United States intelligence mission in China, hoping to be rewarded with American assistance.

The Statesman

As the war approached its end, Ho made preparations for a general armed uprising. Following Japan's surrender, the Viet Minh took over the country, ruthlessly eliminating their nationalist opponents. On Sept. 2, 1945, Ho proclaimed Vietnam's independence. In vain he sought Allied recognition. Faced with a French resolve to reoccupy Indochina and determined to stay in power at any cost, Ho acquiesced in France's demands in return for French recognition of his regime. The French, however, disregarded all their agreements with Ho. War broke out in December 1946.

Many nationalists, while aware of the Communist nature of Ho's government, nevertheless supported it against France. The war ended in July 1954 with a humiliating French defeat. An agreement, signed in Geneva in July 1954, partitioned Vietnam along the 17th parallel and provided for a general election to be held within 2 years to reunify the country. Because of mutual distrust, absence of neutral machinery to guarantee freedom of choice, and opposition of South Vietnam and the United States, the scheduled election never took place.

Ho, who had hoped that a larger population under his control, a Communist-supervised election in the North, and a more or less free election in the South would produce an outcome favorable to his regime, became greatly frustrated. He ordered guerrilla activities to be resumed in the South. Regular troops from the North infiltrated the South in increasing numbers. The United States, correspondingly, increased military assistance, sent combat troops into South Vietnam, and began a systematic bombing of North Vietnam.

Ho refused to negotiate a settlement, hoping that American public opinion, as French public opinion had done in 1954, would force the United States government to sue for peace. Apprehensive that his lifework might be destroyed and anxious to spare North Vietnam from further devastating air attacks, Ho finally agreed to send his representatives to peace talks in Paris. As the antiwar feeling mounted in the United States and other countries, Ho stalled, intent on obtaining from the conference table what he had failed to get on the battlefield. While the talks were dragging on, Ho died on Sept. 3, 1969, without realizing his dream of bringing all Vietnam under communism.

Further Reading

Of the several biographies of Ho Chi Minh, the most comprehensive, and critical is N. Khac Huyen, *Vision Accomplished?: The Enigma of Ho Chi Minh* (1971). A short and sympathetic biography is David Halberstam, *Ho* (1971). A short, quasi-official, and highly propagandistic biography was published by the government of North Vietnam: Tru'o'ng-Chinh, *President Ho-chi-Minh: Beloved Leader of the Vietnamese People* (1966). The following books contain enlightening chapters on Ho: Harold R. Isaacs, *No Peace for Asia* (1947); Frank N. Trager, ed., *Marxism in Southeast Asia: A Study of Four Countries* (1959); Bernard B. Fall, *The Two Viet-Nams: A Political and Military Analysis* (1963; rev. ed. 1964); Hoang-van-Chi, *From Colonialism to Communism: A Case History of North Vietnam* (1964); and Joseph Buttinger, *Vietnam: A Dragon Embattled* (2 vols., 1967). Recommended for general historical background are Ellen J. Hammer, *The Struggle for Indo-China* (1954); Donald Lancaster, *The Emancipation of French Indochina* (1961); Patrick J. Honey, ed., *North Vietnam Today: Profile of a Communist Satellite* (1962); Robert A. Scalapino, ed., *The Communist Revolution in Asia: Tactics, Goals, and Achievements* (1965; 2d ed. 1969); and Frank N. Trager, *Why Vietnam?* (1966). □

William Ernest Hocking

The American philosopher William Ernest Hocking (1873-1966) related idealism and pragmatism in an Absolute Idealism grounded in human experience.

William Ernest Hocking was born in Cleveland, Ohio, in 1873. After work as a surveyor, "printer's devil," map maker, and illustrator he entered Iowa State College of Agriculture and Mechanic Arts in 1894, intending to become an engineer. A chance reading of William James' *Principles of Psychology* determined him to go to Harvard to study with James. He spent four years—first as a teacher of business mathematics, then as a public school principal—before the funds were in hand to enter Harvard in the fall of 1899. He managed a trip to the Paris Exposition in 1900 by hiring on as a cattleman. He received his A.M. degree from Harvard the following year.

Hocking spent 1902-1903 studying in Germany at Göttingen, Berlin, and Heidelberg. He was the first American student to study with Edmund Husserl in Göttingen, which he did in the fall of 1902. He returned to Harvard to take his Ph.D. in 1904. In the fall of 1904 he became instructor in comparative religion at Andover Theological Seminary, following George Foot Moore, who had resigned from Andover to teach at Harvard. On June 28, 1905, he married Agnes O'Reilly, third daughter of John Boyle O'Reilly, a poet and leading Roman Catholic layman in Boston.

In 1906 Hocking joined the Philosophy Department of the University of California under George Howison. During this time he took part in the rebuilding of San Francisco after the great earthquake and subsequent fire. After two years at Berkeley he was called to Yale, where he served for the next

subtleties in the theory of knowledge, however, and his study with Josiah Royce at Harvard persuaded him that we can have a true idea of God. This truth is not established by some authority external to our experience, however, such as a church hierarchy, a tradition, or a transcendental form of knowing such as revelation. All these forms of religious knowledge are verified in the context of human experience. He did not believe in the pragmatist's positive principle that the truth of an idea can be determined by whether it works in our experience or not. He did believe, however, in a "negative pragmatism" which said that an idea which doesn't work can't be true. He was perhaps the last American practitioner of "philosophy in the grand manner." He believed that all of life was grist for the philosopher's mill. His major work was in the philosophy of religion, but his 22 published books include work on the philosophy of law and human rights; freedom of the press; world politics; a philosophical psychology of human nature; education; culture; morale and morality, and much more.

He is less well known today than his colleagues Royce and Whitehead, but his classic study of *The Meaning of God in Human Experience,* first published in 1912, went through 14 editions, and *The Coming World Civilization* (1956) which he described as "a conspectus of a life's thought" was still in print in the 1980s. He combined theoretical subtlety in philosophical reflection with concern for concrete issues of contemporary human life.

Further Reading

The Hocking *Festschrift, Philosophy, Religion and the Coming World Civilization* (1966) contains essays on Hocking's work by colleagues in various fields. The only book length study of Hocking's philosophy is Leroy S. Rouner, *Within Human Experience* (1969). For a collection of some of Hocking's shorter writings see John Howie and Leroy S. Rouner, *The Wisdom of William Ernest Hocking* (1978).

Additional Sources

Furse, Margaret Lewis, *Experience and certainty: William Ernest Hocking and philosophical mysticism,* Atlanta, Ga.: Scholars Press, 1988. □

six years as assistant professor of philosophy. *The Meaning of God in Human Experience,* Hocking's major work, was published in 1912. Two years later he was called to Harvard, where he eventually became Alford Professor of Natural Religion, Moral Philosophy and Civil Polity. In the summer of 1916 he enlisted with the Civilian Training Camp at Plattsburgh, New York, and in 1917 he went to England and France as a member of the first detachment of American military engineers to reach the front. In 1918 his appointment as inspector of "war issues" courses in army training camps in the northeastern United States led to the publication of his book on *Morale and Its Enemies.* He returned to Harvard after the war.

From 1930 to 1932 Hocking was largely occupied with the chairmanship of the Committee of Appraisal—a study of the foreign mission work of six Protestant Christian denominations in India, Burma, China, and Japan. The commission report, *Re-Thinking Missions,* produced a lively debate. Hocking went abroad again in 1936 to give the Hibbert Lectures at Oxford and Cambridge, later published as *Living Religions and a World Faith.* During 1936 and 1937 he was also Gifford Lecturer in Scotland. Those unpublished lectures were entitled "Fact and Destiny" and represented his mature metaphysics. After his retirement from Harvard he served several guest lectureships, notably at Dartmouth College and the University of Leiden, Holland.

Hocking's early interest in the philosophy of William James reflected his conviction that human experience is the fundamental context for all knowing, including knowledge of God. His graduate study with Husserl had presented new

David Hockney

In addition to his photographs and individual art shows, versatile artist David Hockney (born 1937) has also produced work as a painter, graphic artist, stage designer, and writer.

A self-taught artist, David Hockney is best known for his captivating photographs and individual art shows that display his work. Hockney has worked also as an independent painter, graphic artist, and stage designer. Hockney's reputation as a genuinely original and powerful artist is secure even though his work continues to push the boundaries of public perception and critical opinions. Although much of his work is considered "user-friendly'' and tasteful, thereby considered modernist, Hockney has the ability to shock. Hockney's uncanny ability to navigate the tides of public opinions and perceptions of him has provided him with a reputation that is not only accepting of criticism, but incorporates such criticism into future works. He has taught as an art instructor at a variety of schools, including the University of Iowa, the University of Colorado, the University of California at Los Angeles, and the University of California at Berkeley. Hockney was awarded an honorary degree in 1988 from the University of Aberdeen in Scotland. Although considered by some critics to be a lightweight, Hockney continues to prove his versatility through teaching and writing as well as his skill through painting to create works of an accomplished artist.

Introduction to Art

David Hockney was born in Bradford, Yorkshire, England on July 9, 1937. Hockney admired the likes of Picasso, Dufy, Matisse, and Fragonard. He tried to utilize their techniques in his "impressionistic" photographs which later lead to paintings. Hockney's parents, Kenneth and Laura Hockney, allowed their son early on to explore the world around him and have the freedom and mobility to interpret what he saw in way that pleased him. This freedom of expression enabled the young Hockney to not only gain admittance to the Bradford Grammar Art School Society, but he received his first recognition there as well. At eleven years of age, Hockney's work was characterized by happiness in images such as a wave cresting against the shore, a kiss, or a drop of water. The young Hockney believed that

life's simple pleasures were often not adequately imitated in art; that in the rush of people's existence they often failed to notice the simplicity and serenity of the world around them. Hockney believed he could reproduce these images through his art and thereby provide people with some of the pleasures they may have overlooked. Hockney felt his work would help people realize that play and its enjoyment in and of itself was serious work.

Formal Schooling and Influences

In addition to the Bradford Grammar School of Art, Hockney attended the Bradford College of Art between the years 1953 and 1957. He later attended the Royal College of Art in London, England, from 1959 until 1962. Even with the extensive formal training and education, Hockney's style was essentially acquired through self instruction. He was especially talented in the area of photography and learned his skill with constant practice and dedication beginning in 1962. Hockney's early exposure to art as well as the work he produced while training was considered to be largely conservative, thereby making it pleasurable to look at.

It is a widely held belief among those in the art world that Hockney's meeting with the modern artist Jacob Kramer in Leeds and the viewing of Alan Davie's exhibition in Wakfield in 1958 pushed Hockney towards the type of work that is considered avant-garde and identified him more with the pop artists of the late sixties. Alan Davie went on to hold a considerable influence over Hockney. This influence is dramatically represented by a series of abstract expressionists canvases that Hockney produced during his first year at the Royal College of the Arts.

That year, 1959, Hockney joined a small group of other young, experimental artists that included the likes of Peter Blake and Allen Jones. Another individual that tremendously affected Hockney and held considerable influence over the work produced by Hockney was American artist R. B. Kitaj. Kitaj's work was of commonplace scenes as well as contemporary people and events. Almost simplistic at first notice, Kitaj's work evolved into much more detail the more it was viewed. While Kitaj's work discreetly affected the British Pop Art movement, it profoundly affected Hockney. Hockney's keen awareness of the times around him is directly attributed, in many critic's opinions, to Kitaj.

Hockney developed the ability to take an ordinary scene and develop it through photographs and paint into something incredibly pleasing to view. The ability to develop such scenes immediately earned Hockney a place among contemporary artists of his time. Although not considered a master yet, his work was certainly begin to demonstrate the signs. A second American artist that influenced Hockney was Robert Rauschenberg. Rauschenberg's compositions also lead Hockney in becoming more aware of his surroundings and how such surroundings could be propelled into lasting art. These influences, along with Hockney's own indescribable tastes, allowed Hockney the rare privilege to experiment with his work, while still growing to become a serious artist.

Hockney's Arrival

David Hockney was able to combine his formidable knowledge relating to the history of art and its techniques with a very unusual insight or sensitivity to the contemporary visual currents. He was able to produce what the public wanted at the time, or more specifically, Hockney was able to create exactly what the art connoisseur thought he wanted. Regardless of the critics' interpretations, Hockney developed this keen sense and ability (along with his love of publicity, that at times has been considered flagrant opportunism by his challengers) into an art world marvel that has kept him on the forefront of the American and British art scenes.

Hockney arrived in the professional art world on the coattails of the 1960s and the world's fascination with Pop Art. Hockney was able to manipulate his innate skill as a photographer and his learned ability to paint and combined them into something that, while not new, took people by surprise. For example, Hockney would take two, sometimes more, photographs of the same image but from different vantage points, thereby changing the actual image only slightly. However, by combining the photos, Hockney created a distinct and well-integrated work. The idea of a photographic collage, while not new, provided Hockney with a new medium to capitalize on. Even though other artists such as Rejlander and Muybridge had done similar work to Hockney's, they had not attempted it on the same scale. Such ability earned Hockney the 1985 Infinity Award. This achievement is awarded to an artist in any media that utilizes photography.

Hockney's Ideas

For Hockney, the ability to capture ideas came easily. He possessed an insight that illuminated for him the hidden beauty in the person walking down the street or the poem written a hundred years ago. Hockney pulled ideas for art from everywhere. Some of his more significant sources, artists in their own right, included Paul Klee, Jean Dubuffet, and Francis Bacon. Hockney also admired William Blake. Blake's poetry provided Hockney with vivid imagery that he transferred with great success to canvas, but never showed publicly. Hockney did, however, produce and show several works based on the works of Walt Whitman. One such work, the 1961 etching *Myself and My Heroes,* depicted Hockney along with Whitman and Mahatma Gandhi. Quotations from Whitman are prevalent throughout Hockney's work. Hockney was able to use the words of Whitman to more clearly express the abstract and ambiguity in art. Such situations arose, according to Hockney, when a artist lacked skill or was confused.

Hockney drew ideas from fairy tales as well. Some of his more renowned work comes from his etchings of tales by the Brothers Grimm. His 1969 one-person show at the Kasmin featured etchings made up largely of six of the Grimm's tales. The completion of this particular work and show fulfilled a lifelong dream of Hockney's; he had even taken a boat trip on the Rhine from Mainz to Cologne so as to be able to capture the atmosphere and vividness of the tales.

Contemporary Hockney

By the early 1970s, Hockney had moved on to more realistic and conventional paintings. Increasingly inspired by Balthus, Edward Hopper, and Giorgio Morandi, Hockney's work became less and less influenced by literature. This move was well received by critics. While Hockney's work is physically larger than what he used to produce, his later work exemplified post-painterly abstraction in a combination with minimalism. Such a combination allowed Hockney to move even closer to a permanence within the art world. Hockney's work has been displayed internationally.

No longer does Hockney have to contend with accusations of not being a true artist. Hockney has not only proven his versatility in art but in other areas as well. He has published an extensive number of books and screenplays, worked as a set and costume stage designer, and has made numerous television and film appearances. Hockney has been awarded numerous honors, including the Guinness Award and the 1991 Praemium Imperiale from the Japan Art Association. Although Hockney was first identified with late Pop Art, he has transcended that label to become one of the few internationally known and lasting artists to come out of the 1960s.

Further Reading

Smith, Roberta, "From the Heart and Hand of David Hockney," in *New York Times,* April 3, 1996, p. B1.
Peppiatt, Michael, "Sunshine Superman," in *Town & Country Monthly,* April 1996, p. 43.
Glover, Michael, "David Hockney," in *ARTnews,* April 1996, p. 143.
Luckhardt, Urlich, and Melia, Paul, "A Drawing Retrospective," in *David Hockney,* Chronicle Books, 1996.
Webb, Peter, *Portrait of David Hockney,* Dutton, 1st American edition, 1988.
Livingstone, Marco, *David Hockney,* 1st American edition, Holt, Rinehart & Winston, 1981.
Knewstub, John, and Maurice Rothenstein, *Modern English Painters,* St. Martin's Press, 1952, 1974. □

Alan Lloyd Hodgkin

English physiologist Sir Alan Lloyd Hodgkin (born 1914) received the Nobel Prize for Physiology or Medicine (along with Andrew Huxley and Sir John Eccles) in 1963 for discovery of the chemical processes responsible for passage of impulses along individual nerve fibers.

Alan Hodgkin was born on Feb. 5, 1914, in Banbury, Oxfordshire, England. Educated at Trinity College, Cambridge, he began research on the mechanism of nerve conduction, a field in which a strong tradition had been built up at Cambridge by Keith Lucas, A. V. Hill, and Lord Adrian. Within a year he had obtained clear evidence that the "local circuit" mechanism did explain the spread of activity from each point to the next as an impulse travels along a nerve fiber. For this work he was elected to a fellowship of Trinity College in 1936.

Early Work

Hodgkin's first work was carried out on whole nerve trunks dissected from frogs, the classical material for investigations on nerve conduction. All his subsequent work on nerve tissue was done on isolated single fibers. By World War II he had published important papers on "subthreshold" potentials, that is, the electric events that lead up to the full-size nerve impulse, and on the electrical resistance of the protoplasm and surface membrane of the giant nerve fiber. He also issued, jointly with A. F. Huxley, a preliminary note on recording with an electrode actually inside a squid giant nerve fiber.

Hodgkin spent most of the war years developing airborne radar. He returned to Cambridge in 1945, holding college and university teaching appointments. From 1952 to 1969 he was a research professor of the Royal Society, and from 1970 a newly founded university professor of biophysics. He worked during this period at the Physiological Laboratory of Cambridge, as well as the Marine Biological Association at Plymouth in the autumn, when squid were available. He was awarded the Nobel Prize in physiology or medicine (with Andrew Huxley and Sir John Eccles) in 1963.

Later Work

Much of Hodgkin's later work was on muscle and had to do both with the relation of ions to the electrical changes and with the processes by which contraction is initiated within the fiber when an action potential passes along its surface membrane.

His publications include: *Conduction of the Nerve Impulse* (1964) and *Chance and Design* (1992).

Further Reading

There are very good accounts of Hodgkin's work in Bernard Katz, *Nerve, Muscle, and Synapse* (1966), and Hugh Davson, *A Textbook of General Physiology* (4th ed. 1970). There are sketches of his life and work in Sarah Regal Riedman and Elton T. Gustafson, *Portraits of Nobel Laureates in Medicine and Physiology* (1963), and in Theodore L. Sourkes, *Nobel Prize Winners in Medicine and Physiology, 1901-1965* (rev. ed. 1967). □

Dorothy Crowfoot Hodgkin

For her work with vitamin B-12, Dorothy Crowfoot Hodgkin (1910-1994) was awarded the Nobel Prize in chemistry.

Dorothy Crowfoot Hodgkin employed the technique of X-ray crystallography to determine the molecular structures of several large biochemical molecules. When she received the 1964 Nobel Prize in chemistry for her accomplishments, the committee cited her contribution to the determination of the structure of both penicillin and vitamin B_{12}.

Hodgkin was born in Egypt on May 12, 1910 to John and Grace (Hood) Crowfoot. She was the first of four daughters. Her mother, although not formally educated beyond finishing school, was an expert on Coptic textiles, and an excellent amateur botanist and nature artist. Hodgkin's father, a British archaeologist and scholar, worked for the Ministry of Education in Cairo at the time of her birth, and her family life was always characterized by world travel. When World War I broke out, Hodgkin and two younger sisters were sent to England for safety, where they were raised for a few years by a nanny and their paternal grandmother. Because of the war, their mother was unable to return to them until 1918, and at that time brought their new baby sister with her. Hodgkin's parents moved around the globe as her father's government career unfolded, and she saw them when they returned to Britain for only a few months every year. Occasionally during her youth she travelled to visit them in such far-flung places as Khartoum in the Sudan, and Palestine.

Hodgkin's interest in chemistry and crystals began early in her youth, and she was encouraged both by her parents as well as by their scientific acquaintances. While still a child, Hodgkin was influenced by a book that described how to grow crystals of alum and copper sulfate and

cal calculations on the distances and relative positions of the spots, the molecular structure of almost any crystalline material could theoretically be worked out. The more complicated the structure, however, the more elaborate and arduous the calculations. Techniques for the practical application of crystallography were few, and organic chemists accustomed to chemical methods of determining structure regarded it as a black art.

After she graduated from Oxford in 1932, Hodgkin's old friend A. F. Joseph steered her toward Cambridge University and the crystallographic work of J. D. Bernal. Bernal already had a reputation in the field, and researchers from many countries sent him crystals for analysis. Hodgkin's first job was as Bernal's assistant. Under his guidance, with the wealth of materials in his laboratory, the young student began demonstrating her particular talent for X-ray studies of large molecules such as sterols and vitamins. In 1934, Bernal took the first X-ray photograph of a protein crystal, pepsin, and Hodgkin did the subsequent analysis to obtain information about its molecular weight and structure. Proteins are much larger and more complicated than other biological molecules because they are polymers—long chains of repeating units—and they exercise their biochemical functions by folding over on themselves and assuming specific three-dimensional shapes. This was not well understood at the time, however, so Hodgkin's results began a new era; crystallography could establish not only the structural layout of atoms in a molecule, even a huge one, but also the overall molecular shape which contributed to biological activity.

In 1934, Hodgkin returned to Oxford as a teacher at Somerville College, continuing her doctoral work on sterols at the same time. (She obtained her doctorate in 1937). It was a difficult decision to move from Cambridge, but she needed the income and jobs were scarce. Somerville's crystallography and laboratory facilities were extremely primitive; one of the features of her lab at Oxford was a rickety circular staircase that she needed to climb several times a day to reach the only window with sufficient light for her polarizing microscope. This was made all the more difficult because Hodgkin suffered most of her adult life from a severe case of rheumatoid arthritis, which didn't respond well to treatment and badly crippled her hands and feet. Additionally, Oxford officially barred her from research meetings of the faculty chemistry club because she was a woman, a far cry from the intellectual comradery and support she had encountered in Bernal's laboratory. Fortunately, her talent and quiet perseverance quickly won over first the students and then the faculty members at Oxford. Sir Robert Robinson helped her get the money to buy better equipment, and the Rockefeller Foundation awarded her a series of small grants. She was asked to speak at the students' chemistry club meetings, which faculty members also began to attend. Graduate students began to sign on to do research with her as their advisor.

An early success for Hodgkin at Oxford was the elucidation of cholesterol iodide's molecular structure, which no less a luminary than W.H. Bragg singled out for praise. During World War II, Hodgkin and her graduate student

on X rays and crystals. Her parents then introduced her to the soil chemist A. F. Joseph and his colleagues, who gave her a tour of their laboratory and showed her how to pan for gold. Joseph later gave her a box of reagents and minerals which allowed her to set up a home laboratory. Hodgkin was initially educated at home and in a succession of small private schools, but at age eleven began attending the Sir John Leman School in Beccles, England, from which she graduated in 1928. After a period of intensive tutoring to prepare her for the entrance examinations, Hodgkin entered Somerville College for women at Oxford University. Her aunt, Dorothy Hood, paid the tuition to Oxford, and helped to support her financially. For a time, Hodgkin considered specializing in archaeology, but eventually settled on chemistry and crystallography.

Crystallography was a fledgling science at the time Hodgkin began, a combination of mathematics, physics, and chemistry. Max von Laue, William Henry Bragg and William Lawrence Bragg had essentially invented it in the early decades of the century (they had won Nobel Prizes in 1914 and 1915, respectively) when they discovered that the atoms in a crystal deflected X rays. The deflected X rays interacted or interfered with each other. If they *constructively* interfered with each other, a bright spot could be captured on photographic film. If they *destructively* interfered with each other, the brightness was cancelled. The pattern of the X-ray spots— *diffraction pattern* —bore a mathematical relationship to the positions of individual atoms in the crystal. Thus, by shining X rays through a crystal, capturing the pattern on film, and doing mathemati-

Barbara Low worked out the structure of penicillin, from some of the first crystals ever made of the vital new drug. Penicillin is not a particularly large molecule, but it has an unusual ring structure, at least four different forms, and crystallizes in different ways, making it a difficult crystallographic problem. Fortunately they were able to use one of the first IBM analog computers to help with the calculations.

In 1948, Hodgkin began work on the structure of vitamin B–12 the deficiency of which causes pernicious anemia. She obtained crystals of the material from Dr. Lester Smith of the Glaxo drug company, and worked with a graduate student, Jenny Glusker, an American team of crystallographers led by Kenneth Trueblood, and later with John White of Princeton University. Trueblood had access to state of the art computer equipment at the University of California at Los Angeles, and they sent results back and forth by mail and telegraph. Hodgkin and White were theoretically affiliated with competing pharmaceutical firms, but they ended up jointly publishing the structure of B–12 in 1957; it turned out to be a porphyrin, a type of molecule related to chlorophyll, but with a single atom of cobalt at the center.

After the war, Hodgkin helped form the International Union of Crystallography, causing Western governments some consternation in the process because she insisted on including crystallographers from behind the Iron Curtain. Always interested in the cause of world peace, Hodgkin signed on with several organizations that admitted Communist party members. Recognition of Hodgkin's work began to increase markedly, however, and whenever she had trouble getting an entry visa to the U.S. because of her affiliation with peace organizations, plenty of scientist friends were available to write letters on her behalf. A restriction on her U.S. visa was finally lifted in 1990 after the Soviet Union disbanded.

In 1947, she was inducted into the Royal Society, Britain's premiere scientific organization. Professor Hinshelwood assisted her efforts to get a dual university/college appointment with a better salary, and her chronic money problems were alleviated. Hodgkin still had to wait until 1957 for a full professorship, however, and it was not until 1958 that she was assigned an actual chemistry laboratory at Oxford. In 1960 she obtained the Wolfson Research Professorship, an endowed chair financed by the Royal Society, and in 1964 received the Nobel Prize in chemistry. One year later, she was awarded Britain's Order of Merit, only the second woman since Florence Nightingale to achieve that honor.

Hodgkin still wasn't done with her research, however. In 1969, after decades of work and waiting for computer technology to catch up with the complexity of the problem, she solved the structure of insulin. She employed some sophisticated techniques in the process, such as substituting atoms in the insulin molecule, and then comparing the altered crystal structure to the original. Protein crystallography was still an evolving field; in 1977 she said, in an interview with Peter Farago in the *Journal of Chemical Education*, "In the larger molecular structure, such as that of insulin, the way the peptide chains are folded within the molecule and interact with one another in the crystal is very suggestive in relation to the reactions of the molecules. We can often see that individual side chains have more than one conformation in the crystal, interacting with different positions of solvent molecules around them. We can begin to trace the movements of the atoms within the crystals."

In 1937, Dorothy Crowfoot married Thomas Hodgkin, the cousin of an old friend and teacher, Margery Fry, at Somerville College. He was an African Studies scholar and teacher, and, because of his travels and jobs in different parts of the world, they maintained separate residences until 1945 when he finally obtained a position teaching at Oxford. Despite this unusual arrangement, their marriage was a happy and successful one. Although initially worried that her work with X rays might jeopardize their ability to have children, the Hodgkins had three: Luke, born in 1938, Elizabeth, born in 1941, and Toby, born in 1946. The children all took up their parents scholarly, nomadic habits, and at the time of the Nobel Ceremony travelled to Stockholm from as far away as New Delhi and Zambia. Although Hodgkin officially retired in 1977, she continued to travel widely and expanded her lifelong activities on behalf of world peace, working with the Pugwash Conferences on Science and World Affairs. Hodgkin died of a stroke on July 29, 1994, in Shipston-on-Stour, England.

Further Reading

McGrayne, Sharon B., *Nobel Prize Women in Science,* Carol Publishing Group, 1993.
Opfell, Olga S., *The Lady Laureates,* Scarecrow Press, 1986.
Journal of Chemical Education, Volume 54, 1977, p. 214.
Nature, May 24, 1984, p. 309.
New Scientist, May 23, 1992, p. 36. □

Ferdinand Hodler

The Swiss painter Ferdinand Hodler (1853-1918), using stylized, awkwardly gesturing figures in conjunction with simplified color, overcame realistic and impressionist conventions and infused his works with an intellectual, symbolic content.

Ferdinand Hodler was born in Bern on March 14, 1853. His childhood was characterized by poverty, sickness, and death. His father died soon after Hodler's birth and his mother died when he was 13; nine of her children likewise died early. Hodler's first training as an artist was in the workshop of his stepfather; in 1867 he began to study with a local landscape painter. In search of better training, he went to Geneva in 1871, where he painted signs while learning French; until 1876 he studied under Barthélemy Menn, who introduced him to the works of Camille Corot, Eugène Delacroix, and J. A. D. Ingres. Hodler was greatly impressed by the paintings of Hans Holbein the Younger, and he studied the theories of Albrecht Dürer, Leonardo da Vinci, and Vitruvius in his search for answers to the artistic analysis of nature. Hodler's artistic formation formally ended in 1878, when he went to Madrid to study the work of Peter Paul Rubens and Diego Velázquez at the Prado Museum.

Hodler's paintings of the 1880s demonstrate a dichotomy of purpose. Although he worked in an impressionist or realistic manner, he sought to impart an intellectual or emotional content that transcended visible reality. In his *Prayer in the Canton Bern* (1880-1881) he carefully rendered peasants caught up in fervent prayer, simultaneously representing his own spiritual crises and his desire to flee industrialized modern society and find refuge in an innocent, ideal environment.

By 1886 Hodler had begun to paint in a sharply delineated, harsh style touched with rustic awkwardness and simplicity, as in the *Courageous Woman*. His paintings took on a more emotional quality as they represented moods of anger, despair, or yearning. *Night* (1889), completed after a serious psychological crisis, marked the final break with realism; it linked him with the symbolist movement then spreading throughout Europe. *Night,* with its enigmatic dreamlike scene, large format, monumental figures, tendency toward flatness, and repetition of similar colors and forms—a system of composition Hodler named "parallelism"—is characteristic of all Hodler's mature works.

These mystical, antirealistic paintings depicting an escape from the bourgeois cares of modern life gained Hodler first notoriety and then popularity. In 1900 he received a

Gold Medal at the Paris World's Fair, and in 1912 he was made an officer of the French Foreign Legion. In Germany he received commissions to create monumental patriotic murals, culminating in the *Jena Students Entering the 1813 War of Liberation* and the *Reformation Oath of Hanover on July 26, 1533* (1913-1914).

Hodler died on May 19, 1918, in Geneva. His formal vocabulary was too personal to act as a major influence, but his antirealistic attitude quickened the demise of naturalism and impressionism.

Further Reading

There is a short biography of Holder in Werner Haftmann, *Painting in the Twentieth Century* (trans., 2 vols., 1961; rev. ed. 1965). See also Peter Meyer, *Art in Switzerland: From the Earliest Times to the Present Day* (trans. 1946), and John Canaday, *Mainstreams of Modern Art* (1962).

Additional Sources

Hirsh, Sharon L., *Ferdinand Hodler,* New York: Braziller, 1982.
Selz, Peter Howard, *Ferdinand Hodler,* Berkeley, University Art Museum, 1972. □

Richard March Hoe

Richard March Hoe (1812-1886), American inventor and manufacturer, invented a high-speed printing press that helped revolutionize the newspaper industry in the United States.

Richard Hoe was born in New York City. After a common school education he went to work for his father, who manufactured printing presses. His father had begun experimenting with cylinder presses, and the younger Hoe carried on this work after his father retired in 1830. When Hoe finally perfected the single-cylinder press, it was capable of printing 2,000 pages (on one side) per hour. A cylinder press had been used to print the *London Times* as early as 1814, but Americans had been slow to adopt this method.

Hoe continued to improve his presses and was among the first to introduce a double-cylinder press, one cylinder of which carried the type and the other the paper to be printed. In 1847 he set up a press with five cylinders in Philadelphia. One cylinder carried the type, and the four others (each attended by a boy) fed sheets of paper against the first. This press was capable of making 8,000 impressions an hour.

The next major advance in printing appeared in 1865, when a press was invented that printed on a continuous roll of paper rather than on separate sheets. In 1871 Hoe began work on such a press and produced an improved model which could print (on both sides) 18,000 papers per hour. The addition of devices such as a machine to fold the newspapers (developed by a partner of Hoe) resulted in the modern high-speed printing press. Hoe's firm was the leading manufacturer of this equipment in the United States, and in the late 1860s he opened a branch factory in London.

Hoe's continually refined presses were of critical importance to the spread of news throughout expanding America during the 19th century. A literate and informed citizenry, capable of making its own political and economic choices, depended upon cheap and abundant news. The number of newspapers in the United States rose from 863 in 1830 to 3,725 in 1860. The Nov. 8, 1876, edition of the *New York Sun,* reporting the disputed presidential election between Rutherford B. Hayes and Samuel J. Tilden, ran to 220,000 copies. Such feats of rapid printing were possible only through the use of Hoe's steam-driven ''lightning'' presses.

Further Reading

There is no full-length biography of Hoe. His life and achievements must be gleaned from such histories of manufactures as J. Leander Bishop, *A History of American Manufactures from 1608 to 1860* (1861; 3d ed. 1868), and Victor S. Clark, *History of Manufactures in the United States* (1929). The standard history of newspapers in the United States is Frank Luther Mott, *American Journalism* (1941; rev. ed. 1962). For technical developments in printing see Merritt Way Haynes, *The Student's History of Printing* (1930). □

James R. Hoffa

Jimmy Hoffa's (1913-1975?) name will always be synonymous with the International Brotherhood of Teamsters, the largest union in the United States. Hoffa secured his place in union history with his zealous support of the Teamsters, which included conflicts with law enforcement and union leadership, dealings with organized crime leaders, criminal indictments, felony convictions, and, many speculate, his own murder.

J immy Hoffa is a name which will forever be associated with, and even synonymous with, the International Brotherhood of Teamsters, the largest union in the United States. From the 1930s Hoffa persevered through clashes with police, struggles with union members, fights for control of his union, known associations with organized crime, several indictments, a pair of felony convictions, banishment from union activity and even death to survive as a symbol of the Teamsters. Labor historians disagree about his relative value or disservice to the labor movement in America, but no one can question his legacy of power or his status as a legend.

Early Leadership

Hoffa's career in labor activity began as a teenager in the 1930s, when he engineered a strike on a Kroger grocery store loading dock in southwest Detroit. The strike was called the moment a huge trailer of fresh strawberries came

in. Management knew it wouldn't take the food long to spoil, and a new contract was reached in an hour. Within a year, Hoffa's ''Strawberry Boys'' joined Teamsters Local 674, and later merged with Truck Drivers Local 299. Hoffa demonstrated his clout when he transformed the local from a 40-member unit with $400 to its name to a 5,000-member unit with $50,000 in the bank.

Organized Crime Connections

In 1941 Hoffa entered a phase of his life which would remain with him until the end and would define a large part of his reputation when he formed his first alliance with organized crime. Involved in a turf fight with the Congress of Industrialized Organizations, he asked for help from some of Detroit's east side gangsters to roust his opposition. The east side crowd was happy to oblige, and drove the CIO local out of town. Contacts between Hoffa and the mob would continue for the rest of his life. Some of the activities Hoffa engaged in with organized crime are rumors, while others are known for sure, but his connection to mob figures were never a secret, nor did he try to keep them one.

Tough Times for Unions

The union movement was unpopular in many quarters in the pre- World War II United States, and Hoffa's early experiences with the truckers' union were trying. Company goons, labor goons, and the police all were physical threats, Hoffa's car was bombed, his office was smashed, and he was once arrested 18 times in a single day. ''When you went out on strike in those days, you got your head broken,'' he remembered to the *Detroit News*. "The cops would beat your brains out if you even got caught talking about unions." By the time he was 28, Hoffa was vice president and chief negotiator for the union. In one major negotiation he threatened to shut down one trucking company and leave others open, a ploy which won the union an unheard-of statewide contract.

Hoffa Elected Teamsters Vice President

In 1952 Hoffa won election as international vice president of the Teamsters under president Dave Beck, who was already under investigation by federal agencies. Hoffa centralized the administration and bargaining procedures of the union in the international union office and succeeded in creating the first national freight-hauling agreement.

In 1957 Beck was summoned before the U.S. Senate's McClellan Committee, where he took the Fifth Amendment approximately two hundred times. When Beck finished his testimony, he had little credibility left as the Teamsters leader. Hoffa moved in. The election to put Hoffa in the presidency was disputed, and the government publicly emphasized Hoffa's connections with organized- crime figures. Nevertheless, Hoffa held on to the presidency and avoided jail for almost a decade.

Hoffa's entrenchment in the Teamsters went hand-in-hand with the mob's entrenchment in the Teamsters. Several organized crime figures assumed positions in the union, and a phony Teamster local was reportedly set up in Detroit as a front for drug dealing. Rumors persisted that Hoffa had murder contracts out on John Kennedy and/or Robert Kennedy, and Hoffa's unconcealed satisfaction at the assassination of both brothers didn't dispel the rumors. He never hesitated to use force in the operations of his union, either: An economics professor who had a 90-day inside look at the Teamsters in the early 1960s wrote, quoted in the *Detroit News,* "As recently as 1962, I heard him order the beating of a man 3,000 miles away, and on another occasion, I heard him instruct his cadre on precisely how to ambush non-union truck drivers with gunfire . . . to frighten them, not to kill."

Criminal Activities

Hoffa faced a series of major felony trials in the 1960s. One factor which had worked in his favor at avoiding prosecution was that Attorney General Robert Kennedy and FBI director J. Edgar Hoover disliked each other too much to cooperate to prosecute him, but in 1962 he was tried for taking a million-dollar kickback for guaranteeing a company labor peace. He was acquitted, but on the last day of the trial he was accused of trying to bribe jurors. That charge brought Hoffa a conviction and an eight-year prison term in 1964, and two months later he suffered another conviction for mail fraud and misuse of a $20-million pension fund. The result was a 13-year combined sentence, which was commuted by President Richard Nixon in 1971 after Hoffa had served just under five years, during which he retained his presidency of the Teamsters.

One of the terms of Hoffa's commuted sentence was that he refrain from union activity, but he made no bones about wanting to regain the presidency of the Teamsters. He lost an appeal on the restriction before the U.S. Supreme Court in 1973, but still hoped to displace Frank Fitzsimmons, whom he had picked himself to serve as president upon his release from prison.

Mystery

That ambition reached its conclusion on the afternoon of July 30, 1975. Hoffa had apparently received an invitation to lunch at the Machus Red Fox restaurant in Southfield, Michigan. The mob had a good working relationship with Fitzsimmons at this time, and wanted to stop Hoffa from regaining control of the Teamsters. Hoffa presumably thought he was being invited to a meeting to work out an arrangement with the mob, but instead he may have been invited to his own murder. No one has ever been arrested in the Hoffa case, no body has ever been found, and no one has ever definitively solved the mystery, but this is the scenario which most parties, including the FBI, believe to be true: Anthony Provenzano, a mobster and New Jersey Teamsters boss, asked Hoffa to meet him for lunch to patch up their relationship, which had become strained while Hoffa was in prison. Anthony Giacalone had arranged the lunch, but neither he nor Provenzano showed up. Hoffa was picked up by several men in a maroon Mercury sedan, was murdered in Detroit and his body was disposed of at a mob-owned sanitation company in Hamtramck, Michigan. Hoffa was officially declared "presumed dead" in 1982.

Immortalized on Film

The Hoffa legend was immortalized in 1992 when director Danny DeVito put it on the big screen in the film *Hoffa*. The film, which admitted to taking some liberties with the truth, received mixed reviews, and some criticism was leveled at it for historical inaccuracies and an overly sympathetic, even apologetic portrayal of the title character by Jack Nicholson. In perhaps the perfect postscript to the Hoffa legend, Sean Wilentz, writing in the *New Republic,* blasted the film for having been conceived, originated, and outlined by organized crime figures.

Further Reading

Walter Sheridan, *The Fall and Rise of Jimmy Hoffa* (New York: Saturday Review Press, 1972).
Arthur A. Sloane, *Hoffa* (Cambridge: MIT Press, 1991). ☐

Abbie Hoffman

Writer and activist Abbie Hoffman (1936-1989) was best known for his anti-war protests as a leader of the Youth International Party in the 1960s.

Abbie Hoffman was born November 30, 1936, in Worcester, Massachusetts, and educated at Brandeis University (B.A., 1959) and the University of California, Berkeley (M.A., 1960). Like so many other activists of the 1960s, Hoffman was radicalized by participating in the civil rights movement. Among other activities, he founded a store—Liberty House—to sell products manufactured by co-operatives of poor people in Mississippi. In mid-decade he turned his attention to the war in Vietnam, which heated up just when Black Power was driving whites out of black freedom organizations. Hoffman's unique contribution, with Jerry Rubin, was to unite political activism with the emergent counter-culture. As a rule the two movements were antithetical, politics drawing young men and women into public affairs, the counter-culture attracting others to the private pleasures of rock music, drugs, indigency, and liberated sex.

Hoffman made activism glamorous, so to speak, by staging such media events as throwing money onto the floor of the New York Stock Exchange and wearing an American flag shirt on television. Hoffman's theory was that by ridiculing the symbols of authority one weakened its power as well. Deprived of legitimacy, Wall Street and Washington might wither away, or perhaps they would become so frail as to be easily overthrown. These hopes appear more unlikely in retrospect than they did at the time, when authority seemed discredited and many young people believed that the revolution was at hand.

Hoffman's Youth International Party, formed in 1968, was not so much an organization as a way of life. It enabled counter-culturists, known as hippies in their passive state, to express themselves politically without having to elect officers, pay dues, attend meetings, or perform any of the

tiresome work associated with real parties. The yippies, as Hoffman's followers were called, assembled at irregular intervals to hold Festivals of Life. These gatherings featured rock music, guerrilla theater, poetry reading, obscene language, and other activities meant to delight the young and aggravate the old.

Their most publicized effort took place at the Democratic National Convention of 1968. In cooperation with the National Mobilization to End the War in Vietnam some 2,500 yippies danced, sang, smoked marijuana, and advertised the virtues of their own candidate for president, a live pig named Pigasus. Poet Allen Ginsberg chanted mantras for peace. Hoffman inscribed dirty words on his forehead. All this inflamed Mayor Richard Daley of Chicago, whose police attacked the yippies with clubs and tear gas, then arrested many for having provoked uniformed officers to riot. The result was a famous trial when eight demonstration leaders—including Hoffman, Jerry Rubin, Tom Hayden of Students for a Democratic Society, and Bobby Seale of the Black Panthers—were indicted for conspiring to incite these riots. Most of the defendants abused and ridiculed Judge Julius Hoffman (no relation), destroying his composure. He had Seale bound and gagged, then declared a mistrial in Seale's case. The other seven were found guilty of various offenses, but as the trial had been a farce their convictions were not sustained.

This was the height of Hoffman's celebrity. With the war in Vietnam winding down and the turbulent 1960s giving way to quieter times Hoffman found himself at loose ends. On August 28, 1973, he was arrested for possession of a large quantity of cocaine. Claiming to have been framed, Hoffman jumped bail and went underground. The next seven years were busy and productive ones for Hoffman, whom the police could not seem to find even though he granted interviews to national magazines, served as travel editor of *Crawdaddy* magazine, and published two books and some 35 articles. In 1980 he surfaced and disclosed that he had been living for the previous four years in Thousand Islands, New York, under the name of Barry Freed. As environmental activist "Freed," minus the long hair and beard of his yippie days, he had appeared on local television and radio, been commended by the governor of New York, testified before a U.S. Senate subcommittee, and been appointed to a federal water resources commission. After serving a year in jail Hoffman returned to Thousand Islands where, as Barry Freed, he continued to campaign for the environment between engagements as a speaker on college campuses.

Hoffman's place in history will depend upon how much weight is given to his activities in the 1960s. Besides providing the young with a good deal of entertainment, Hoffman wrote extensively on behalf of social change. His *Revolution for the Hell of It* (1968) more or less seriously advocated transforming society by means of psychedelic drugs, rock bands, sexual freedom, communes, and the like. Similar themes informed many of his other books, which collectively sold over three million copies. He also figured in some of the most important events of the period. These included not only the Chicago demonstrations in 1968, but the earlier March on the Pentagon, October 21, 1967. At that event some 75,000 demonstrators gathered in Washington, many following Hoffman's lead in attempting to levitate the great military headquarters building. Whether Hoffman's efforts did anything to shorten the war is doubtful. The methods he employed, though they generated an immense volume of publicity, were short-lived, as were the theories he advocated in connection with them. Yet, whatever the lasting results, if any, of his stunts, Hoffman is likely to be remembered as one of the boldest and most imaginative spokesmen for the counter-culture in its days of glory.

Although there is some controversy concerning Hoffman's death in 1989, it seems certain that he killed himself with a lethal combination of 150 pheno-barbital pills and alcohol.

Further Reading

Among Hoffman's own books are: *Revolution for the Hell of It,* New York: Dial Press, Inc., (1968); (with Jerry Rubin and Ed Sanders),*Vote!* (1972); (with Anita Hoffman), *To America with Love: Letters from the Underground,* Stonehill Publishing, Inc., (1976); and *Square Dancing in the Ice Age* (1982). *Woodstock Nation: A Talk-Rock Album* New York: Random House (1969.) There are several biographies of Abbie Hoffman, in varying degrees of quality. Hoffman wrote his autobiography, *Soon to be a Major Motion Picture,* New York: Berkley Books, (1980), the year he surrendered to federal authorities.

Since Hoffman's death a great many books have appeared which explore the details of his life and his socio- political views and actions. There is even an Abbie Hoffman website on the Internet which contains reviews of his books and discussions of his life and political actions. There is also a copy of *Steal This Book,* New York: Private Editions, Inc., (1971), which may be down-loaded. The original volume was self-published, rocketed to the best seller list and sold more than one-quarter million copies at $1.95, the original volumes must all be in private hands as no copies seem to exist in libraries, and book dealers are asking $100.00 per copy if they have one.

Abbie Hoffman's place in history may be that of a political prankster; however, many current volumes are discussing him seriously as a political activist, for example, David DeLeon's *Leaders from the 1960s: A Biographical Sourcebook of American Activists,* Westport, Connecticut: Greenwood Press, (1994); Marty Jezer's *Abbie Hoffman: American Rebel,* New Brunswick, NJ: Rutgers University Press (1992); Jack Hoffman and Daniel Simon's *Run Run Run: The Lives of Abbie Hoffman,* New York: G.P. Putnam's Sons (1994); Theodore L. Becker and Anthony L. Dodson's *Live This Book: Abbie Hoffman's Philosophy for a Free and Green America,* Chicago: The Noble Press, Inc. (1991); and Jonah Ruskin's *For the Hell of It: The Life and Times of Abbie Hoffman,* University of California Press (1996). □

Ernst Theodor Amadeus Hoffmann

The German author, composer, and artist Ernst Theodor Amadeus Hoffmann (1776-1822) is known chiefly for his short stories and novels. His work **represents an extreme development of German romanticism toward the grotesque and the fantastic.**

On Jan. 24, 1776, E. T. A. Hoffmann was born in Königsberg, Prussia. He studied law at the University of Königsberg, and by 1800 he had become a court official with the Prussian government in Berlin. However, in 1802 he was forced to move to the Polish town of Plock, partly because he had drawn an uncomplimentary sketch of one of his superiors. He obtained an appointment to Warsaw in 1804 and there wrote music until 1806, when he lost his government position during Napoleon's occupation of Prussia.

During the next few years Hoffmann cultivated his talents as writer, artist, and composer. By 1808 he had become orchestra conductor for the theater in Bamberg. Here he began to write the first of his short stories. His first published collection was *Fantasiestücke in Callots Manier* (1814-1815; *Phantasies in the Fashion of Callot*), inspired by a French painter of grotesques. One of the best in this collection is *Der goldne Topf* ("The Golden Pot"), which tells of a law student torn between the love of a demonic "serpent-girl" and the daughter of a bureaucratic official. In the end the forces of the supernatural win out.

Hoffmann continued his career as musical director, moving to Dresden and in 1814 to Berlin, where he associated with other romantic writers, such as the poet Clemens Brentano. He was eventually reinstated as an official in the Prussian government, and in 1816 he became a judge with the superior court. He continued his literary activity, however, and in 1815-1816 published a horror novel, *Die Elixiere des Teufels* (*The Devil's Elixir*). This tale, inspired by the English Gothic novel, recounts in lurid detail a wicked monk's commerce with evil spirits. Another grotesque novel is *Lebens-Ansichten des Katers Murr* (1820-1822; *Views on Life of Tomcat Murr*).

Hoffmann continued to serve as judge until the year of his death, relatively unhampered by a capacity for alcohol that is thought to have been a source of some of his more striking literary inspirations. Hoffmann was the German romantic whose works were most enthusiastically read abroad. He died on June 25, 1822, in Berlin, of a spinal infection.

Further Reading

The best study in English of Hoffmann is Harvey W. Hewett-Thayer, *Hoffmann, Author of the Tales* (1948), which examines the relationship between his life and his writings. A brief, general discussion of the author is in L. A. Willoughby, *The Romantic Movement in Germany* (1930). Ralph Tymms, *German Romantic Literature* (1955), analyzes Hoffmann's writings as horror stories.

Additional Sources

Daemmrich, Horst S., *The shattered self; E. T. A. Hoffmann's tragic visit,* Detroit, Wayne State University, 1973.
Hoffmann, E. T. A., *Selected letters of E. T. A. Hoffmann,* Chicago: University of Chicago Press, 1977.

Kaiser, Gerhard R., *E.T.A. Hoffmann,* Stuttgart: J.B. Metzler, 1988.

Roters, Eberhard, *E.T.A. Hoffmann,* Berlin: Stapp, 1985.

Schafer, R. Murray, *E. T. A. Hoffmann and music,* Toronto; Buffalo: University of Toronto Press, 1975. □

Josef Hoffmann

Josef Hoffmann (1870-1956), Austrian architect and decorator, was a pioneer of European modernism and founder of the Wiener Werkstätte (Viennese Workshop).

Josef Franz Maria Hoffmann was born in Pirnitz (Brtnice), then in the Austro-Hungarian Empire, on December 15, 1870. He studied architecture at the trade school in Brünn. Following his graduation in 1891 he went to Würzburg for a year of practical experience and then entered the special architectural school of the Academy of Fine Arts in Vienna, where he studied until 1895, first under Carl von Hasenauer and then under Otto Wagner. Upon graduation he won the Rome Prize. Otto Wagner then employed him as a draftsman in his office for several years.

During his studies and early professional years Hoffmann assimilated the historicist architectural traditions of Vienna, as exemplified in the work of Hasenauer and Wagner (among others); Wagner's functionalistic theories; the stylistic experimentations of the European Art Nouveau; and the teachings of the English arts and crafts movement. Hoffmann's earliest independent works, such as the rooms of the second, third, and fourth exhibitions at the Vienna Secession that he designed in 1899 and the remodelling of the store Am Hof 3 in Vienna the same year, showed clearly the influence of Art Nouveau and of the English arts and crafts.

In 1899 Hoffmann became professor at the Kunstgewer-beschule (School of Applied Arts) in Vienna. His works of the following year, such as the rooms of the Kunstgewer-beschule at the Paris Exhibition, already showed a drastic change in his style from the flowing curvatures of the earlier works to a rectilinear simplicity of form and the tendency of superimposing rectangular elements and motifs; both of these would become Hoffmann's stylistic hallmarks. For this change Hoffmann was particularly indebted to the work of Charles Rennie Mackintosh, the Scottish master of Art Nouveau, who was highly regarded in Vienna.

Hoffmann's first important architectural commission was for a group of villas in the Hohe Warte near Vienna. These were designed in careful relation to each other so as to form a total composition. Moreover, their interior arrangement was expressed on the exterior and great emphasis was placed on color and texture. Yet one notices in them an increased simplicity of form; this became even more prominent in the works that Hoffmann exhibited at the 1902 *Kunstausstellung* in *Düsseldorf* .

Together with Kolo Moser, Hoffmann founded in 1903 the Wiener Werkstätte for the production of furniture and objects of the applied arts. In the same year he received the commission for the Purkersdorf Sanatorium, which was built in 1903 and 1904. This was a work of astonishing modernity and could be easily antedated by 25 years. It had plain white walls and ample, regularly placed windows almost devoid of surrounding frames. There were no cornices, and the roofs were completely flat. Hoffmann's *opus magnum,* the Palais Stoclet in Brussels, was designed in 1905 and built between 1905 and 1911. It was a large and luxurious mansion, asymmetrically composed and dominated by the stair-tower. The external walls were covered by a thin veneer of marble plaques contained within a decorative edging of gilded metal that defined the wall planes. Both the exterior and the lavishly appointed interior were characterized by a charm and playfulness that were Austrian in character; clearly Hoffmann's, however, was the pervasive effect of a relentless geometry of form inside and out. Both the Purkersdorf Sanatorium and the Palais Stoclet were entirely furnished by the Wiener Werkstätte.

Hoffmann did not develop his style further after the Palais Stoclet. Instead, he resorted to the Neoclassicism that became predominant all over Europe and in England after 1905. A notable work of the time was the Ast House in the Hohe Warte near Vienna, built in 1909-1911. This was also quite large and luxurious, although more massive and tectonic than the Palais Stoclet. The classicizing tendency in Hoffmann's work became more explicit in two later works, the Skyra-Primavesi House in the Hietzing suburb of Vienna and the Austrian Pavilion at the Cologne exhibition of the *Deutscher Werkbund* of 1914. In both Hoffmann articulated the exterior with broad, fluted pilasters; yet these elements of classical inspiration were used in a mannerist way that had little to do with their original structural and formal properties. For example, in the Austrian Pavilion the massive pilasters appeared to be supporting a cornice that was nothing more than a thin molding. Hoffmann's last great villa, the Knips House in Vienna of 1924-1925, was a compact block that emulated deliberately the *Biedermeier* architecture of its surroundings. Hoffmann became city architect of Vienna in 1920. The low-cost housing blocks that he designed in the mid-1920s in Vienna, such as the Klosehof and the Winarskyhof, retained in their simplicity and cleanliness of composition a good deal of the purist quality of his sanatorium at Purkersdorf. Hoffmann died in Vienna on May 7, 1956.

The Wiener Werkstätte that Hoffmann founded sought a new relation between formal beauty and functionalism and brought about a revival of the applied arts. The furniture and other objects that he designed for production at the Wiener Werkstätte exercised a great influence on the European taste for several decades. In their simplicity and formal expediency these prepared the way for the plainer surface articulation and purity of modernism.

Further Reading

The life and work of Josef Hoffmann are treated exhaustively in two recent monographs: Guiliano Gresleri, *Josef Hoffmann* (1985) and Eduard F. Sekler, *Josef Hoffmann. Das ar-*

chitektonische Werk: Monographie und Werkverzeichnis (Architectural Work: Treatises and Drawings) (1982). For a brief discussion of Hoffmann's contribution in the development of modern architecture and design see Henry-Russell Hitchcock, Architecture: Nineteenth and Twentieth Centuries (4th ed., 1977); Leonardo Benevolo, History of Modern Architecture, 2 vols. (1977); and Nikolaus Pevsner, Pioneers of Modern Design: from William Morris to Walter Gropius (2d ed., 1975).

Additional Sources

Hoffmann, Josef Franz Maria, Josef Hoffman, Wien: Edition Tusch, 1992.

Langseth-Christensen, Lillian, A design for living, New York, N.Y., U.S.A.: Viking, 1987.

Sekler, Eduard F. (Eduard Franz), Josef Hoffmann: the architectural work: monograph and catalogue of works, Princeton, N.J.: Princeton University Press, 1985. □

Paul Hofhaimer

The Austrian composer, organist, and teacher Paul Hofhaimer (1459-1537) was a great master of German song composition and one of the few Germanic organists widely known throughout Europe.

The father, brothers, son, and nephews of Paul Hofhaimer were all organists in Salzburg and Innsbruck. He received instruction from his father and from Jacob von Graz. Hofhaimer's first important position, that of chamber organist to Archduke Sigismund of Tirol at Innsbruck, was in 1480. He received an appointment for life, and in 1489, upon receipt of an offer from the Hungarian court, he was promoted to the position of director of the court chapel at Innsbruck. During the 1480s he met the composers Heinrich Isaac and Arnolt Schlick and fashioned a reputation as a teacher.

In 1490 the emperor Maximilian I took over the musical establishment. Apparently well satisfied with Hofhaimer's services, he ennobled the composer in 1515. During this period Hofhaimer apparently spent some time at other locations. He may have been at the court of the elector Frederick the Wise at Torgau with Isaac and Schlick.

Hofhaimer probably wrote most of his best songs between 1490 and 1510. The German song of this period was generally based on a familiar melody, such as a folk song or court song, which was kept largely unchanged in the tenor. The other parts wove contrapuntally around it. Unlike the songs written in the dominating Franco-Flemish style of the period, the German songs were in closed sections (often in the Bar form—AAB) rather than in continuous polyphony. With Hofhaimer's generation, progress was made toward equality of parts and strong interpart relation through the use of imitation. There is some melodic preeminence of the soprano part.

At Maximilian's death in 1519 Hofhaimer accepted the post of organist at the Cathedral of Salzburg and held it until at least 1524. He remained a resident of the city until his death. He became interested in the quantitative setting of Latin verse and began setting the Odes of Horace in this manner. After his death Ludwig Senfl completed these settings and published them as Harmoniae poeticae (1539). Only these pieces enjoyed any popularity after Hofhaimer's death.

Although Hofhaimer enjoyed a considerable reputation as an organist and teacher of organists, little of his organ music has survived. This may be due in part to a tradition of improvisation of organ music. Although his pupils have not been definitely identified, his doctrines were apparently widespread among German organ composers of the early 16th century, and elements of the style may have reached Italy. In music of this generation, ornamentation idiomatic to the instrument was applied to the melody, but not so copiously as to obscure the basically sound proportions of the piece. This restraint, which probably characterized Hofhaimer's music, generally disappeared later in the century under a welter of ornamentation.

Further Reading

The definitive work on Hofhaimer is in German. In English, Hofhaimer's music and that of his contemporaries are discussed in Gustave Reese, Music in the Renaissance (1954; rev. ed. 1959). □

August Wilhelm von Hofmann

The German chemist August Wilhelm von Hofmann (1818-1892) was one of the most influential organic chemists and teachers of the century.

August Wilhelm von Hofmann was born on April 8, 1818, in the small university town of Giessen. In 1836 he entered the University of Giessen, where he studied law, philosophy, and mathematics. However, in 1843 he turned to the study of chemistry. He received his doctorate summa cum laude with a thesis entitled Chemical Investigation of the Organic Bases in Coal Tar, a field in which he was destined to achieve worldwide fame.

In 1845, while holding a professorship at the University of Bonn, Hofmann derived analine from benzene and thus laid one of the foundations of the synthetic dye industry. He also worked out the problem of substituting atoms of chlorine for the hydrogen atoms of the aromatic compounds. This work won the coveted Gold Medal of the Parisian Société de Pharmacie and made Hofmann famous. He received and accepted an invitation from Queen Victoria in 1845 to transfer his scientific activities to London.

Working in England as researcher and teacher for 20 years, Hofmann trained a generation of brilliant chemists, including Frederick Abel, Warren de La Rue, E.C. Nicholson, Charles Mansfield, William H. Perkins, and Sir William

Crookes, and a host of future leaders of the German chemical industry such as Peter Griess, George Merck, C.A. Martius, and Jacob Vilhard. In 1865 Hofmann became professor of chemistry at the University of Berlin.

Honored by the leading scientific societies of Europe, Hofmann worked in a spacious new laboratory built by a grateful government. During this period his researches were directly related to the meteoric rise of the German dye and pharmaceutical industries, which with coal and iron were the foundations of the industrial supremacy of Wilhelmine Germany. Critical to this success was what became known as the Hofmann degradation process, the successive reduction of the length of a carbon chain through treating the amides of fatty acids with bromine and alkali. Indigo was produced industrially by precisely these steps. Another of Hofmann's industrially significant accomplishments was the production of formaldehyde by passing vapors of methyl alcohol over hot platinum.

Though most of Hofmann's 360 major papers grew out of his work with the derivatives of coal tar and the synthesis of related organic compounds, he also contributed to the chemistry of cadmium, antimony, phosphorus, and titanium. He discovered the quaternary ammonium salts and was thus led to classify all amines as formal derivatives of ammonia—an idea which was the foundation of the later "theory of types" of Charles F. Gerhardt.

Hofmann was married four times and was the father of 11 children. In 1868 he helped found the German Chemical Society and served as its president 14 times. Never spoiled by fame or fortune, he continued his teaching and writing until the very end, on May 2, 1892, in Berlin.

Further Reading

Eduard Farber, ed., *Great Chemists* (1961), contains a section on Hofmann. See also Archibold Clow, *The Chemical Revolution: A Contribution to Social Technology* (1952); Eduard Farber, *The Evolution of Chemistry: A History of Its Ideas, Methods, and Materials* (1952; 2d ed. 1969); and James R. Partington, *A History of Chemistry,* vol. 4 (1964). □

Hans Hofmann

The German-American painter Hans Hofmann (1880-1966) approached abstract painting through cubism and Fauvism. His teaching and painting were singularly influential for the development of American painting after 1945.

Born in Weissenburg, Germany, Hans Hofmann studied music and science before enrolling in 1898 at Moritz Heymann's Munich art school. Hofmann's early work was influenced by Wilhelm Leibl's impressionism and by French neoimpressionism. His pencil studies at this time also suggest an unusual preoccupation with the relationship of figures to their ground planes.

From 1904 to 1914 Hofmann, sponsored by a Berlin art collector, studied in Paris. He met many cubist and Fauve artists and was drawn particularly to Robert Delaunay's abstractions. When World War I began, Hofmann's patronage ended, and he returned to Munich.

Teaching in Munich

Because of a lung ailment, Hofmann was not drafted. He opened an art school in Munich in 1915, and for the next 15 years he articulated a philosophy of art based on Fauvism and cubism; in particular, he sought to redefine Paul Cézanne's two-dimensional picture plane in terms of light. Hofmann's concern with his students' development often took precedence over his own work. By the 1920s his reputation as a teacher was assured, and his school began to attract students from America, including Al Jensen, Louise Nevelson, and Carl Holty.

The political climate of postwar Germany made it increasingly difficult for Hofmann to maintain his school, and in 1930 he accepted an invitation to teach a session at the University of California. He returned to California the following summer, and in the fall he moved to New York City, where he joined the faculty of the Art Students League. In 1932 he opened his own art school in New York, with summer sessions at Provincetown, Mass.

Early Works

Although Hofmann virtually abandoned painting until the late 1930s, a few examples from his Munich period survive. His work from 1915 to 1930 suggests his increas-

ingly critical interpretation of cubism and Fauvism. In the mid-1920s a new interest in free-form motifs that seems to derive from Wassily Kandinsky appears. Although more relaxed, Hofmann's composition is never loose; the newly expressive forms are controlled by the planar integrity learned from Cézanne and synthetic cubism. *Apples* (1931) shows this approach.

Hofmann's essay, "Plastic Creation," in the *League* (1932-1933) is his first important statement made in America concerning the function of two-dimensional picture space. In it he articulated an academic approach that had far greater impact than his few paintings of the early 1930s. However, for Hofmann, the possibilities of painting always encompassed divergent approaches; the geometric and the curvilinear, the thickly impasted and the thinned surface were all concurrently viable throughout his career, although there were periods when one set of problems seemed to take precedence over another, such as in his 1941-1943 landscape studies.

Works of the 1940s

Hofmann's work beginning in the 1940s received great critical acclaim. In 1944 he exhibited at the influential Art of This Century Gallery in New York. Interest grew for works such as *Spring* (1940) and *Fantasia* (1943), which, in their innovative dripped and curvilinear forms spreading across the picture surface, substantiate the claim that Hofmann was a founder of automatism in American painting. In 1948 Hofmann was given a retrospective exhibition in Andover, Mass. At this time the publication of his selected writings provided explanations of the paintings and inspired a generation of younger American artists.

Although Hofmann continued to teach until 1958, he found more and more time for his painting and discovered new motifs in the work of younger painters. *Apparition* (1947) recalls Jackson Pollock, with its anthropomorphic shapes emerging from the scrambled background. At the same time, Hofmann could rethink Henri Matisse, as in *Liberation* (1947), in which the paint is thinned down and delicately contained within the outlines, or in *Magenta and Blue* (1949-1950), in which both color and relationship of figure to ground plane paraphrase Matisse.

Works of the 1950s and 1960s

Hofmann's reputation was firmly established by the 1955 and 1957 retrospective exhibitions given at Bennington College and the Whitney Museum. So too did his interests diversify and expand; technical virtuosity characterized his last decade. In his late 70s he retired from teaching to devote full time to painting. His message of "push and pull" against the picture plane is convincingly worked out in *The Gate* (1959), in which not only are the geometric shapes set in parallel planes but the palette knife and the brushstroke work to the same end. Comparing this painting with *The Conjurer* (1959), with its billowing forms and intense color range, again suggests the diversity and genius of Hofmann's art. *Agrigento* (1961), in the monumental simplicity of the monochromatic hue and the wide sweeping brushstroke, suggests that in spite of Hofmann's complex artistic theories

he was able to express a visual experience directly with a minimal amount of intellectualizing.

While Hofmann's success as a teacher can be judged by the success of his pupils, his own paintings and writings establish him as a major force in contemporary American painting. He died in New York.

Further Reading

Sam Hunter, *Hans Hofmann* (1963; 2d ed. 1964), is the most useful book for illustrations of Hofmann's work. Hunter includes many of the essays that originally appeared in Hofmann's own *Search for the Real, and Other Essays,* edited by Sara T. Weeks and Bartlett H. Hayes, Jr. (1948). A useful bibliography is in William Seitz, *Hans Hofmann: With Selected Writings by the Artist* (1963). For the most critical interpretation of Hofmann's work as painter and teacher, Harold Rosenberg's essays in *The Anxious Object* (1964; 2d ed. 1966) are indispensable. Equally perceptive is Clement Greenberg, *Hofmann* (1961). See also Frederick Wight, *Hans Hofmann* (1957).

Additional Sources

Goodman, Cynthia, *Hans Hofmann,* New York: Abbeville Press, 1986. □

Hugo von Hofmannsthal

The Austrian poet, dramatist, and essayist Hugo von Hofmannsthal (1874-1929) is best known for his opera librettos. He is also considered a master of German lyric poetry.

Hugo von Hofmannsthal was born in Vienna and spent most of his life there. He charmed the literary world at the age of 17. Hofmannsthal belonged to the circle of Jung-Wien poets, who were little affected by the naturalistic tendencies of their time. He was strongly influenced by the neoromantic movement and European symbolism.

Hofmannsthal's first period (1890-1899) began when the sensitive youth mingled with artists and men of letters in Vienna's famous Café Griensteidl. His first poems, critical essays, and lyrical playlets (two of which were professionally performed on the Berlin stage) appeared under the pseudonym Loris Melikow. The first of a dozen verse plays written in this period, *Gestern* (1891; *Yesterday*), shows him still a beginner, but with *Der Tod des Tizian* (1892; *Death of Titian*) and especially *Der Tor und der Tod* (1893; *Death and the Fool*), he reaches maturity as a master of German verse.

Hofmannsthal's middle phase (1900-1918) saw his greatest public success. In 1902, convinced that words had no meaning and that communication was impossible, he manifested this obsession in his famous literary credo *Brief des Lord Chandos*. His lyrical production ceased abruptly, and he turned instead to writing plays, opera, and even ballet. His most famous work from this period is *Jedermann*

Hofmannsthal: Studies in Commemoration (1963), which contains a useful bibliography on Hofmannsthal. Ronald Gray, *The German Tradition in Literature, 1871-1945* (1965), has a section on Hofmannsthal. ☐

Richard Hofstadter

American historian Richard Hofstadter (1916-1970) won two Pulitzer prizes in recognition of his leading role in reinterpreting United States history during the post-World War II period.

Richard Hofstadter was born on August 6, 1916, in Buffalo, New York. His father was a Jewish immigrant from Poland, his mother an American-born Protestant who died when her son was ten. Hofstadter received his undergraduate education at the University of Buffalo, graduating in 1937. He went on to do graduate work in history at Columbia University, completing his M.A. and Ph.D. in 1938 and 1942 respectively. After teaching for four years at the University of Maryland, he joined Columbia University's History Department in 1946 and remained on that faculty until his death in 1970. He was married twice, first (1936) to Felice Swados, with whom he had a son, and then (1947) to Beatrice Kevitt, with whom he had a daughter.

Hofstadter was a highly productive author of works on American political culture, a subject that allowed him to explore in depth both political history and the history of ideas. His first book, *Social Darwinism in American Thought, 1860-1915* (1944), was an analysis of how American thinkers attempted to adapt Darwinist ideas to their purposes between the Civil War and World War I. In his second book, *The American Political Tradition and the Men Who Made It* (1948), his focus shifted from intellectual to political history. The volume, which was made up of a series of essays on American political figures from the Founding Fathers to Franklin D. Roosevelt, sold very well and established his reputation as an able stylist and a skillful interpretative historian.

Hofstadter's iconoclastic bent was a trait for which he came to be widely admired. This was evident in the challenge he laid down to the prevailing view, one inherited from the so-called progressive historians of the early 20th century, that American party battles were based on a clear-cut, dualistic struggle between the "interests" and "the people"—that is, between a conservative elite's selfishness and the democratic aspirations of the general public. By contrast, Hofstadter argued that ideological cleavages had seldom been so sharply defined as the progressive thesis implied and that opportunism and expediency rather than idealism had generally motivated American political leaders of all stripes.

Between 1955 and 1965 Hofstadter's standing in scholarly circles continued to grow as he produced three significant books—*The Age of Reform: From Bryan to*

(1911; *Everyman*), based on a 15th-century English morality play and now produced every year at the Salzburg Festival. Other works from this phase are *Elektra* (1903), *Der Rosenkavalier* (1911), and *Ariadne auf Naxos* (1912), which were set to music by Richard Strauss. Thus began the close cooperation between Hofmannsthal and Strauss which was to last for 2 decades.

Hofmannsthal's last period (1919-1929) includes the delightful comedy *Der Schwierige* (1921; *The Difficult Gentleman*). But the collapse of the Hapsburg Empire in 1918 was for him a personal tragedy from which he never fully recovered. In a series of essays he spoke as an ardent interpreter and advocate of Austria and its cultural heritage.

To the Salzburg Festivals, which he confounded with Max Reinhardt, he dedicated *Das Salzburger Grosse Welttheater* (1922). Other works of this period are *Die Frau ohne Schatten* (1919; *The Woman without a Shadow*), which Strauss set to music, and, his last and most ambitious work, the tragedy *Der Turm* (1923; *The Tower*).

Hugo von Hofmannsthal lived with his wife and children in Rodaun, outside Vienna. He died there on July 15, 1929.

Further Reading

Austrian novelist Herman Broch wrote the best introduction to the work of Hofmannsthal available in English translation in Hofmannsthal's *Selected Prose* (1952). The Institute of Germanic Languages of the University of London, which had arranged a Hofmannsthal exhibition, published a collection of essays as volume 5 of its series, Frederick Norman, ed.,

F.D.R. (1955), *Anti-Intellectualism in American Life* (1964), and *The Paranoid Style in American Politics and Other Essays* (1965)—and won two Pulitzer prizes. The most important of his works from this period was *The Age of Reform,* a study of the liberal reform tradition from the 1890s to the 1930s. Most previous histories of the Populist and progressive reformers had been written from the reformers' perspective. Hofstadter was careful to acknowledge the positive achievements of the older liberals, but he went on to argue that a close examination of these supposedly idealistic reformers revealed a variety of traits, including tendencies toward nativism and jingoism, that were far from enlightened.

Hofstadter's emphasis on conservative and even retrogressive elements in the liberal reform tradition created something of a sensation in historical circles. Some critics, led by John Higham, suggested that Hofstadter and several other important postwar historians were homogenizing American history, downplaying the conflicts that had separated Americans and substituting a portrait that stressed a bland, middle-class consensus in national affairs. Other scholars, notably Norman Pollack, charged that Hofstadter's exposure of liberalism's supposed deficiencies served to discredit the progressive reform tradition and thus gave aid and comfort to the conservative causes and leaders that were flourishing in the 1950s. Although Hofstadter was certainly interested in describing what Americans had in common, he was not an unthinking defender of an American consensus on bourgeois values. Nor did he think of himself as a conservative simply because he criticized lib-

eralism. On the contrary, he argued that in spelling out liberalism's flaws he hoped to help American progressives put their house in order so that they could preserve the best of their tradition, which he said was his as well, against the attacks being made on it from every direction in the post-World War II period.

Hofstadter's worries about the illiberal mood that prevailed in postwar America were even more apparent in the two major books that followed *The Age of Reform.* In *Anti-Intellectualism in American Life* he presented a lengthy and at times tedious diatribe against the hostility he felt American popular culture had displayed toward urbane, cosmopolitan, and intellectually unorthodox views from colonial times into the 20th century. In *The Paranoid Style in American Politics* he examined the illiberality of a variety of American political movements after the 1890s, giving particular attention to the anti-Communist crusades of the McCarthy era and the militant conservatism of the Goldwater campaign in 1964. Once again, Hofstadter demonstrated his talent for advancing new historical perspectives by arguing that theories of political motivation that stressed rational sources of human conduct had to be supplemented by social scientific insights into the irrational and even unconscious origins of some political behavior.

In the few remaining years of his life Hofstadter continued to be an active publishing scholar. He produced a large volume, *The Progressive Historians* (1969), in which he discussed the careers and scholarly contributions of Frederick Jackson Turner, Vernon L. Parrington, and Charles A. Beard. *The Idea of a Party System,* Hofstadter's analysis of the virtues of the pragmatic and consensusoriented American party system, was published in 1969. He was beginning work on a projected three-volume study of American life (the unfinished first volume of which was published posthumously as *America in 1750: A Social Portrait* in 1971) at the time of his death from leukemia on October 24, 1970.

Hofstadter's achievement lay not in founding a school, something he made no attempt to do, but in challenging many of the established historical interpretations of his day. The gracefulness of his writing style and the boldness of his treatment of American ideas, reform movements, and political figures made him one of the most widely read and respected historians of the early postwar period.

Further Reading

The best introduction to Hofstadter's life and work is Stanley Elkins and Eric McKitrick, "Richard Hofstadter: A Progress," in *The Hofstadter Aegis: A Memorial,* edited by Stanley Elkins and Eric McKitrick (1974).

Additional Sources

Baker, Susan Stout, *Radical beginnings: Richard Hofstadter and the 1930s,* Westport, Conn.: Greenwood Press, 1985.

Cremin, Lawrence Arthur, *Richard Hofstadter (1916-1970); a biographical memoir,* Syracuse, N.Y. National Academy of Education 1972.

The Hofstadter aegis, a memorial, New York, Knopf; distributed by Random House 1974. □

William Hogarth

William Hogarth (1697-1764), the most original painter of his age in England, invented a new species of dramatic painting and is one of the great masters of satire in engraving and painting.

William Hogarth was born in St. Bartholomew's Close, London, on Nov. 10, 1697, the son of a classical scholar who conducted a private school. In his draft for an autobiography Hogarth wrote that he was exceptionally fond of shows and spectacles as a child and that he excelled in mimicry. He left school at his own request in 1713 and was apprenticed to the silver-plate engraver and dealer in plate Ellis Gamble.

Hogarth disliked the drudgery of his apprenticeship and especially copying the designs of others. His ambition to become a history painter was fired by seeing the late baroque paintings in process of execution by Sir James Thornhill at St. Paul's Cathedral and Greenwich Hospital. During his apprenticeship Hogarth invented a system of visual mnemonics, a linear shorthand that enabled him to reconstruct figures and scenes which had arrested his attention.

When his father died in 1718, "disappointed by great men's promises" to subscribe to a projected Latin dictionary, Hogarth's family supported itself by going into trade, his younger sisters setting up a dress shop and he himself going into business as a tradesman-engraver in 1720, the year his apprenticeship expired. His early commissioned work consisted largely of shop cards, ornamental and heraldic designs for silver plate, and illustrations for books.

In 1720 Hogarth joined the St. Martin's Lane Academy, the decisive step in his training as a painter. In 1724 he published his first independent print, *Masquerades and Operas, Burlington Gate,* an attack on English subservience to foreign art. During this period of intense activity as an engraver, he laid the foundation for his remarkable knowledge of prints, including reproductions of the Old Masters.

By 1728 Hogarth was ready to make his debut as a painter, and he quickly established a reputation as a master of the conversation piece. The following year he eloped with Jane Thornhill, the daughter of his boyhood hero Sir James Thornhill. The turning point in Hogarth's career (it is said to have effected the reconciliation with his irate father-in-law) was the success of the *Harlot's Progress* prints in 1732. The idea originated in a single picture, to which he was urged to add a companion, a typical rococo conceit, but other ideas multiplied until he had told the story of a prostitute's downfall in six stages. The original paintings were destroyed by fire in 1755.

There were precedents for narrative series on similar themes in Italy and the Netherlands, but Hogarth's invention is distinguished by its strict attention to the model of the English tragicomedy of manners. Publication of his second series in dramatic form, the *Rake's Progress,* was delayed until 1735 so that his rights could be protected by the Copyright Act of the same year, commonly known as Hogarth's Act. His dramatic trilogy concluded with *Marriage à la Mode,* published in 1745.

Encouraged by his friend Henry Fielding, Hogarth next turned to moral satires that burlesqued baroque grandmanner painting; that is, he chose epic models rather than dramatic ones. The masterpiece of this group is the four prints of *An Election Entertainment* (1755-1758). He was now an acknowledged leader of his profession, and he led the agitation against proposals to found a royal academy on the French model.

Hogarth's opposition to an academy is intelligible in the light of his earlier efforts to raise the status of British art and free its practitioners from dependence on aristocratic patronage. In the 1730s he had been active in a scheme for decorating the pleasure resort of Vauxhall Gardens with contemporary paintings and sculpture, and in 1745 he followed this up with an even more ambitious project for the presentation of works by living artists to the Foundling Hospital, the first donors being largely recruited from the St. Martin's Lane Academy, which he had revived in 1735. Hogarth believed that if artists united to exhibit their works and especially to sell prints made from their paintings they would be able to resist the influence of the connoisseurs, against whom he waged a lifelong war.

Hogarth threw himself with equal energy into moral and humanitarian causes as a governor of St. Bartholomew's Hospital and a foundation governor of the Foundling Hospital, frequently joining forces with Fielding, for example, in an anti-gin campaign. Hogarth was particularly concerned with the welfare of the young of the laboring and artisan classes, for whom he designed the series *Industry and Idleness* (1747), and with the prevention of cruelty, the theme of the *Four Stages of Cruelty* (1751). At the same time he never relinquished his ambitions to become a religious painter in the grand manner, executing more monumental pictures for churches and public institutions than any other English artist between Thornhill and Benjamin West.

His narrative satires gained Hogarth a Continental reputation. His income was adequate to support a town house, a country home at Chiswick, and six servants. In 1757 he obtained the highest honor open to his profession: the appointment as sergeant painter to the king. He was at work on his last print, the *Bathos,* a mock-rococo counterpart to Albrecht Dürer's *Melancolia,* when he was taken ill and died at Leicester Fields on Oct. 25, 1764.

Further Reading

Hogarth's autobiographical writings are published from the original manuscripts in the standard edition of his esthetic treatise, *The Analysis of Beauty,* edited by Joseph Burke (1955). Ronald Paulson, *Hogarth: His Life, Art, and Times* (2 vols., 1971), is the definitive modern biography, and Paulson's monumental *Hogarth's Graphic Works* (2 vols., 1965) is the definitive edition of his engravings. In Joseph Burke and Colin Caldwell, *Hogarth: The Complete Engravings* (1968), the emphasis is esthetic, and paintings and drawings are included for comparative purposes. The drawings and paintings are covered respectively in two illustrated catalogs: A. P. Oppé, ed., *The Drawings of William Hogarth* (1948), and R. B. Beckett, *Hogarth* (1949).

Additional Sources

Gaunt, William, *The world of William Hogarth,* London: J. Cape, 1978.
Gowing, Lawrence, *Hogarth,* London Tate Gallery 1971.
Hogarth, William, *The art of Hogarth,* London: Phaidon; New York: distributed by Praeger Publishers, 1975.
Jarrett, Derek, *The ingenious Mr. Hogarth,* London: M. Joseph, 1976.
Lichtenberg, Georg Christoph, *Lichtenberg's Commentaries on Hogarth's engravings,* London, Cresset P., 196.
Lindsay, Jack, *Hogarth: his art and his world,* New York: Taplinger Pub. Co., 1979, 1977.
Paulson, Ronald, *Hogarth,* New Brunswick: Rutgers University Press, 1991-c1993.
Paulson, Ronald, *Hogarth: his life, art, and times,* New Haven, published for the Paul Mellon Centre for Studies in British Art (London) by the Yale University Press, 1971.
Paulson, Ronald, *Hogarth: his life, art, and times,* New Haven, Yale University Press, 1974.
Rosenthal, Michael, *Hogarth,* London: Jupiter Books, 1980.
Webster, Mary, *Hogarth,* London: Studio Vista, 1979. □

Katsushika Hokusai

The Japanese painter and printmaker Katsushika Hokusai (1760-1849) is considered one of the six great Ukiyo-e masters and the founder of the school of landscape artists that dominated this form during its last phase.

While the Japanese wood block of the 18th century was dominated by the figure print, notably pictures of actors and courtesans, the prints of the early 19th century were largely devoted to landscapes and to scenes from the daily life of the common people. This development was due to the work of Hokusai, whose introduction of the landscape print was responsible for infusing Ukiyo-e, which had become decadent and stagnant at the end of the 18th century, with a new vitality.

Born of peasant stock in the Katsushika district on the outskirts of Edo (modern Tokyo), Hokusai never lost touch with the ordinary people of his native city. In his youth he was first adopted by a mirror maker and then apprenticed to a wood-block engraver and, later, to the proprietor of a lending library. His first teacher was Katsukawa Shunsho, an Ukiyo-e artist who was celebrated for his portrayals of Kabuki actors. Starting in 1778 Hokusai worked under Shunsho for 15 years, using the name Shunro for this period. At his teacher's death in 1792, he left his studio and studied the styles of the main schools of Japanese painting, such as Kano, Tosa, and Sotatsu-Korin, as well as Dutch engravings and Chinese painting. Hokusai's mature artistic style was not formed until middle age—in fact, the artist was fond of saying that he was born at the age of 50. However, once he had absorbed these various influences, he developed his own style and produced a huge body of work, much of it

highly original and of fine quality. Hokusai, who called himself the "old man mad with painting," died in his ninetieth year, in 1849.

Mature Work

Hokusai's mature work shows a marked inventiveness which is uniquely his own and reveals him as a true master. Speaking of his artistic development when he was 75, Hokusai said, "Since the age of 6 I had the habit of drawing forms of objects. Although from about 50 I have often published my pictorial works, before the seventieth year none is of much value. At the age of 73 I was able to fathom slightly the structure of birds, animals, insects, and fish, the growth of grass and trees. Thus perhaps at 80 my art may improve greatly; at 90 it may reach real depth, and at a 100 it may become divinely inspired. At 110 every dot and every stroke may be as if living. I hope all good men of great age will feel that what I have said is not absurd."

Hokusai varied his artistic personality frequently and used no less than 31 different names. His subjects included every genre from Kabuki actors and courtesans to landscapes and scenes from daily life. In addition, he illustrated novels, published his sketchbooks under the title of *Manga,* and produced guidebooks to famous places, books on how to paint, and erotica known as pillow books, one of which is called *The God of Intercourse with a Full Stomach.*

Artistic Style

Hokusai's style varied greatly from period to period and even from work to work. Not only did his painting differ from his sketches and wood blocks in being on the whole less inspired and more meticulous, but his prints also show a tremendous change in style. The most extreme contrast is that between his early, very conventional work produced while he was working in Shunsho's studio and his bold experiments with Western shading and perspective in a set of prints of 1798 which show the influence of Dutch engravings and the work of Shiba Kokan. Other works, notably his bird and flower paintings, reflect the influence of the Chinese bird and flower paintings of the Ming and Ch'ing periods.

Thirty-six Views of Mt. Fuji and Manga

The climax of Hokusai's career was no doubt achieved with his celebrated set of the *Thirty-six Views of Mt. Fuji,* which he produced some time between 1823 and 1831. This series, which actually has 46 prints since he added 10 when the set proved immensely popular, represents the genius of Hokusai at its very best. The most famous among the compositions are *Fuji on a Clear Day* and the *Great Wave at Kanagawa,* the former showing the red cone of Mt. Fuji, the sacred mountain of Japan, silhouetted against the white clouds and blue sky, and the latter, with Fuji in the distance, depicting a huge wave threatening to engulf fishermen in their open boats. Exhibiting a beautiful sense of pattern, first-rate drawing, and sensitive use of colors, these prints combine artistic excellence with interesting and typically Japanese subject matter. It is not surprising that Paul

Gauguin and Vincent Van Gogh admired Hokusai and were influenced by him.

Hokusai's other masterpiece is his *Manga,* a series of sketchbooks published in 15 volumes from 1814 to 1878. Painted in a loose and spontaneous manner, these drawings show Hokusai's amazing versatility with the brush and his keen observation of the world around him. No episode is too trivial, be it the comic appearance of old men, umbrellas in the rain, fat wrestlers in combat, the goddess Kannon riding on a carp, or the grotesque shape of the octopus. Among his other notable works are bird and flower prints, series of celebrated bridges and waterfalls, portrayals of spirits and ghosts, and a set of a hundred views of Mt. Fuji which he produced in his old age. All in all, it is estimated that Hokusai produced some 35,000 paintings, wash drawings, wood-block prints, and illustrated books during his long and immensely productive lifetime.

Further Reading

The best book on Hokusai in English is J. R. Hillier, *Hokusai* (1955). For the *Manga* see James A. Michener, ed., *The Hokusai Sketchbooks* (1958), and Theodore T. Bowie, *The Drawings of Hokusai* (1964). See also Muneshige Narazaki, *Hokusai: The Thirty-six Views of Mt. Fuji* (trans. 1968). □

Baron d'Holbach

Paul Henri Thiry, Baron d'Holbach (1723-1789), was a German-born French man of leisure, known as a conversationalist, host, scholar, secular moralist, and philosopher. He was celebrated for his freely spoken views on atheism, determinism, and materialism and for his contributions to Diderot's *Encyclopédie.*

Born in December 1723 in Edesheim not far from Karlsruhe in the Palatinate, Paul Henri Thiry was baptized a Roman Catholic. When he was 12 years old, his father took him to an ennobled and financially successful uncle, Franciscus Adam d'Holbach, a naturalized Frenchman living in Paris. From him the young Thiry received his upbringing, a fortune, and a new surname. After an early education in Paris, Paul Henri d'Holbach went in 1744 to the university at Leiden. By 1749 the young man had returned to France and become naturalized, and in 1753 he inherited his uncle's title and fortune.

At his town house in Paris and on his country estate at Grandval, D'Holbach entertained writers, philosophers, and other men of influence. His salon contributed much to the development and communication of 18th-century thought; but D'Holbach himself made a more direct contribution. This master of five languages wrote and studied continuously. In the 1750s he translated German scientific articles, and he contributed almost 400 such articles to Denis Diderot's *Encyclopédie.*

In 1761 began D'Holbach's written attacks on theologians and religious power. Under the name of his deceased friend N. A. Boulanger, D'Holbach published *Le Christianisme dévoilé,* a critical examination of Christianity. D'Holbach often resorted to pseudonyms or anonymity to protect himself from the conservative and repressive authorities. In the 1770s D'Holbach produced his positive substitutes for the religious and political dogmas he despised: *Système de la Nature* (1770), a secular ethics detailing the interrelation of ethics and government; *Le Bon sens* (1772; *Good Sense*), a very readable restatement of the radical ideas of the 1770 work; *Politique naturelle* (1773), a discussion of the moral influences exercised by government; and *Morale universelle* (1776), regarded by some as his ethical masterpiece.

D'Holbach taught that most of man's woes stemmed from religion. "Ignorance and fear," he claimed, "are the two hinges of all religion." He taught that morals were quite possible without religion: "Let . . . reason be cultivated . . . and there will be no need of opposing to the passions such a feeble barrier as the fear of the gods." D'Holbach, a provocative, freethinking iconoclast, died in January 1789.

Further Reading

S. G. Tallentyre (pseud. for Evelyn Beatrice Hall), *The Friends of Voltaire* (1907), contains an essay on D'Holbach, who also figures prominently in the essays on Diderot and Helvetius. Max Pearson Cushing, *Baron d'Holbach: A Study in Eighteenth Century Radicalism in France* (1914), is a short biography; W. H. Wickwar, *Baron d'Holbach: A Prelude to the French Revolution* (1935), connects D'Holbach with later events. A discussion of D'Holbach in relation to English and French materialism, sensationalism, and atheism is Virgil W. Topazio, *D'Holbach's Moral Philosophy: Its Background and Development* (1956). See also G. V. Plekhanov, *Essays in the History of Materialism* (trans. 1934).

Additional Sources

Svitak, Ivan, *The dialectic of common sense: the master thinkers,* Washington, D.C.: University Press of America, 1979. ☐

Hans Holbein the Younger

The German painter and graphic artist Hans Holbein the Younger (c. 1497-1543) combined consummate technical skill with a keen eye for realistic appearance and was the first portrait painter to achieve international fame.

Hans Holbein the Younger, born in Augsburg, was the son of a painter, Hans Holbein the Elder, and received his first artistic training from his father. Hans the Younger may have had early contacts with the Augsburg painter Hans Burgkmair the Elder. In 1515 Hans the Younger and his older brother, Ambrosius, went to Basel, where they were apprenticed to the Swiss painter Hans Herbster. Hans the Younger worked in Lucerne in 1517 and visited northern Italy in 1518-1519.

On Sept. 25, 1519, Holbein was enrolled in the painters' guild of Basel, and the following year he set up his own workshop, became a citizen of Basel, and married the widow Elsbeth Schmid, who bore him four children. He painted altarpieces, portraits, and murals and made designs for woodcuts, stained glass, and jewelry. Among his patrons was Erasmus of Rotterdam, who had settled in Basel in 1521. In 1524 Holbein visited France.

Holbein gave up his workshop in Basel in 1526 and went to England, armed with a letter of introduction from Erasmus to Sir Thomas More, who received him warmly. Holbein quickly achieved fame and financial success. In 1528 he returned to Basel, where he bought property and received commissions from the city council, Basel publishers, Erasmus, and others. However, with iconoclastic riots instigated by fanatic Protestants, Basel hardly offered the professional security that Holbein desired.

In 1532 Holbein returned to England and settled permanently in London, although he left his family in Basel, retained his Basel citizenship, and visited Basel in 1538. He was patronized especially by country gentlemen from Norfolk, German merchants from the Steel Yard in London, and King Henry VIII and his court. Holbein died in London between Oct. 7 and Nov. 29, 1543.

First Period: Basel (1515-1526)

With few exceptions, Holbein's work falls naturally into the four periods corresponding to his alternate residences in Basel and London. His earliest extant work is a tabletop with *trompe l'oeil* motifs (1515) painted for the Swiss standard-bearer Hans Baer. Other notable works of the first Basel period are a diptych of Burgomaster Jakob Meyer zum Hasen and his wife, Dorothea Kannengiesser (1516); a portrait of Bonifacius Amerbach (1519); an unsparingly realistic *Dead Christ* (1521); a *Madonna and Child Enthroned with Two Saints* (1522); several portraits of Erasmus, of which the one in Paris (1523 or shortly after), with its accurate observation of the scholar's concentrated attitude and frail person and its beautifully balanced composition, is particularly outstanding; and woodcuts, among which the series of the *Dance of Death* (ca. 1521-1525, though not published until 1538) represents one of the high points of the artist's graphic oeuvre.

Probably about 1520 Holbein painted an altarpiece, the *Last Supper,* now somewhat cut down, which is based on Leonardo da Vinci's famous painting, and four panels with eight scenes of the Passion of Christ (possibly the shutters of the *Last Supper* altarpiece), which contain further reminiscences of Italian painting, particularly Andrea Mantegna, the Lombard school, and Raphael, but with lighting effects that are characteristically northern. His two portraits of Magdalena Offenburg, as *Laïs of Corinth* and *Venus with Cupid* (1526), were evidently influenced by French portrait painting, although they reflect Leonardesque ideals and the *Laïs* extends her right hand in a manner reminiscent of that of Christ in Leonardo's *Last Supper.*

Second Period: England (1526-1528)

The preserved works of Holbein's second period consist exclusively of portraits, among them Sir Thomas More; Sir Henry Guildford and its pendant, Lady Mary Guildford; William Warham, Archbishop of Canterbury (two versions), all of 1527; and the very sensitive Niklaus Kratzer, shown with his astronomical instruments (1528). The lost portrait of Sir Thomas More and his family, known through Holbein's drawing of the whole composition, seven preliminary sketches for the heads, and several painted copies, is a pioneering work in group portraiture.

Third Period: Basel (1528-1532)

During this period Holbein continued his activity as a portrait painter, decorated the facade of a house, "zum Kaiserstuhl" (of which preparatory drawings exist), completed the decoration of the council chamber in the town hall (1530; fragments are preserved in Basel), and designed woodcuts for the Old Testament (1531, published 1538) and other books. The masterpiece among the portraits of this period is the *Artist's Family,* representing his wife and two of his children (1528/1529); it is a touching portrait painted with a dispassionate realism that conveys with utmost clarity the gloom and loneliness of the woman. The altarpiece *Madonna of Mercy with the Family of Jakob Meyer,* which Holbein had begun about 1526, before he left for England, was completed in 1528. It is a symmetrically organized picture with the figures closely contained in a pyramidal group in front of a shell-backed niche of Renaissance inspiration.

Fourth Period: England (1532-1543)

The last period of Holbein's life marks the culmination of his career as a portrait painter, with his subjects now mainly the wealthy German merchants in London and the King and his court. Characteristic examples are George Gisze (1532), a Danzig merchant shown in the surroundings of his business activity; Hermann Wedigh (1532), a merchant of Cologne; *The Ambassadors* (1533), a full-length double portrait, tightly organized and precise in the rendering of musical and astronomical instruments and an anamorphic skull; Robert Cheseman of Dormanswell (1533); Charles de Solier, Sieur de Morette (1534/1535); Henry VIII (1536; Lugano-Castagnola), the first of several portraits of the monarch shown in full regal splendor, and its pendant, Jane Seymour; Christina of Denmark, Duchess of Milan (1538), a full-length portrait; Edward VI as a child (1539); Anne of Cleves (1539/1540; Paris); and Sir William Butts (ca. 1543).

During this period Holbein learned the technique of portrait miniatures and produced important works of this kind, such as Anne of Cleves (1539/1540; London) and Mrs. Pemberton (ca. 1540). Other works of this final period include a project for a triumphal arch with Apollo and the Muses on Parnassus for the merchants of the Steel Yard on the occasion of the coronation procession of Anne Boleyn (1533); allegorical wall decorations in the guildhall of the Steel Yard (ca. 1533; lost); designs for goldsmith work and jewelry for Henry VIII (from ca. 1536 on); and the decoration of the privy chamber in Whitehall Palace (1537; destroyed by fire in 1698), for which a cartoon for the left side, showing Henry VII and Henry VIII, is preserved.

His Style

Holbein's art is characterized by superb technical skill, an unerring sense of composition and pattern, a sound grasp of three-dimensional form and space, and a sharp eye for realistic detail. His portraits are painted with a passion for objectivity, the outward appearance of his subjects directly reflecting their inner character or mood without the intrusion of the artist's attitude toward them. His drawings, frequently executed in black and colored chalks (following a practice he may have observed in France), bear testimony to this artistic temperament: they are precise and controlled, and the outline dominates as the expressive agent.

Holbein's development was gradual and appears to have been guided essentially by his successful search for objective precision. In the work of his second English period he concentrated more on clear contours and ornament and was less concerned with three-dimensional form and space, with the result that his last portraits are relatively flat and decorative, characteristics generally associated with 16th-century mannerism.

Further Reading

A concise biography and critical account of Holbein's work are in Paul Ganz, *The Paintings of Hans Holbein* (1st complete edition, 1950). See also Arthur B. Chamberlain, *Hans Holbein the Younger* (2 vols., 1913). Specialized studies include K. T. Parker, *The Drawings of Hans Holbein in the Collection of His Majesty the King at Windsor Castle* (1945), and James M. Clark, *The Dance of Death by Hans Holbein* (1947). □

Josiah Holbrook

Josiah Holbrook (1788-1854), American educator, founded the lyceum, a popular 19th-century lecture system for educating adults.

Josiah Holbrook was born into a prosperous farming family in Derby, Conn. At Yale College he developed an interest in chemistry and mineralogy under the direction of the noted scientist Benjamin Silliman. After graduation in 1810 Holbrook conducted a manual training school for the application of science to farming, and he also traveled throughout New England lecturing on geology.

In 1826 Holbrook published a proposal in the *American Journal of Education* for organizing the lyceum, a voluntary association of individuals seeking to improve their knowledge of natural science and other subjects and to advance the interest of public education. He organized his first lyceum in Millbury, Mass., in 1826. Within a short time neighboring towns followed this example, and by 1827 delegates from these lyceums formed the first country organization in Worcester, Mass.

Individual associations to investigate new knowledge existed prior to Holbrook's plan. He, however, envisioned a broad social institution that would join groups together for the organized advancement of knowledge. The lyceum would expand educational opportunity for adults by providing ''a system of mutual instruction.''

Holbrook used the profits of his successful Boston business, manufacturing equipment for use in educational establishments, to travel throughout America promoting the lyceum. He wrote instruction pamphlets and in 1832-1833 edited the *Family Lyceum*.

Holbrook hoped to organize the lyceum system into a national organization. His crusade expanded in the early 1840s as he sought to form an international lyceum. More formal means of education, however, steadily overshadowed such organization.

The town lyceum flourished, particularly in the Northeast and Midwest, up to the time of the Civil War. It served as a popular rostrum for men of letters, science, religion, and politics; provided a platform for the demonstration of scientific method and laboratory technique; and helped publicize America's need for more uniform educational improvements and better teacher training.

Holbrook had married Lucy Swift in 1815, and they had two sons. At the end of the 1840s he moved to Washington, D.C., where he continued to write about the benefits of the lyceum and to engage in geological expeditions. On an expedition in Virginia in June 1854, he drowned.

Further Reading

Holbrook's son Alfred provides information about his father in his *Reminiscences of the Happy Life of a Teacher* (1885). A comprehensive investigation of the lyceum movement and Holbrook's contribution is Carl Bode, *The American Lyceum: Town Meeting of the Mind* (1956). Also useful is Cecil B. Hayes, *The American Lyceum: Its History and Contribution to Education* (1932). □

Johann Christian Friedrich Hölderlin

The German poet Johann Christian Friedrich Hölderlin (1770-1843) sought to express a religious vision in which man would be reconciled to the world of nature and to all the forms through which God had revealed Himself.

Friedrich Hölderlin was born in Lauffen am Neckar on March 20, 1770. After his father's death the family moved to Nürtingen in Württemberg, where Hölderlin spent his childhood. In 1784 he went away to school at Denkendorf and later at Maulbronn. In 1788 he entered the Lutheran Seminary at Tübingen to prepare for the ministry. However, his attention soon turned to philosophy and poetry, and he became friends with the future

philosophers G. W. F. Hegel and F. W. J. von Schelling. He at first wrote verses in the style of local Swabian poets and the older poet Friedrich Gottlieb Klopstock. He later began a series of philosophical hymns under the influence of Friedrich von Schiller.

Hölderlin soon met Schiller himself, who helped him get a position as private tutor after leaving the seminary in 1794. After several months as tutor, he went to Jena, where he studied the philosophy of Johann Gottlieb Fichte and was introduced to the poet Johann Wolfgang von Goethe. Meanwhile, he continued to write poetry and worked on a novel, *Hyperion,* which he had begun while still in Tübingen.

In 1796 Hölderlin obtained his second position as tutor, with the family of the banker Gontard in Frankfurt am Main. He soon fell in love with Gontard's wife, Suzette, to whom, as ''Diotima,'' he addressed poems. He saw her as the personification of the ideals he had celebrated in his earlier poetry. However, their relationship was discovered, and he was forced to resign in 1798.

Hölderlin then moved to Homburg, near Frankfurt, where he devoted himself to literary work. His poetry began to show more spontaneity of feeling and a greater richness of natural detail. He also wrote theoretical essays on poetic form and three versions of an uncompleted tragedy, *Empedokles,* about a Greek philosopher and religious prophet who is rejected by society and by his gods and who decides to commit suicide by jumping into a volcano. In 1799 Hölderlin finished *Hyperion* . In its final form the novel tells of a young Greek who, inspired by the same

religious and philosophical ideals as Hölderlin himself, falls in love with a girl, Diotima, and later joins a Greek war of independence against the Turks. The revolt fails, and Diotima dies. In the end, Hyperion can only reconcile himself with the powers he feels are present in the natural world.

After leaving Homburg, Hölderlin lived for a while with friends in Stuttgart. About this time he perfected the style of his elegiac poetry. His most famous elegy, *Brot und Wein* (*Bread and Wine*), commemorates the religious happiness of the ancient Greek world and concludes with a decision for the poet to commit himself as a priest of Dionysus, who is here identified with Christ.

In 1801 Hölderlin began to develop his final religious vision in irregular hymns modeled after the Greek poet Pindar. One of the greatest of these, *Der Rhein,* turns from a meditation on the course of the Rhine to speculation on the reconciliation of mankind with all the gods ever worshiped.

In 1802 Hölderlin received his last appointment as tutor with a German family in Bordeaux, France. While there he suffered a mental illness and later returned home. After partial recovery he wrote the hymn *Patmos,* but for the next 2 years he suffered from occasional recurrences of insanity. After attempts at rehabilitation, Hölderlin was committed to an asylum and finally, in 1808, to the care of a carpenter in Tübingen. His condition remained virtually unchanged until his death on June 7, 1843.

Further Reading

The best study in English of Hölderlin is Ronald Peacock, *Hölderlin* (1938), which provides the literary and philosophical background necessary for an understanding of his poetry. Perhaps the best brief introduction to Hölderlin's poetry and thought is in Michael Hamburger, *Reason and Energy: Studies in German Literature* (1957). Walter Silz, *Early German Romanticism* (1929), considers Hölderlin's place in the German romantic movement. The question of Hölderlin's attitude toward Greek religion and culture is treated in E. M. Butler, *The Tyranny of Greece over Germany* (1935), and in Henry Hatfield, *Aesthetic Paganism in German Literature: From Winckelmann to the Death of Goethe* (1964).

Additional Sources

Constantine, David, *Hölderlin,* Oxford: Clarendon Press; New York: Oxford University Press, 1988.

George, Emery Edward, *Hölderlin and the golden chain of Homer: including an unknown source,* Lewiston: E. Mellen Press, 1992. □

Billie Holiday

Billie Holiday (1915-1959) was a jazz vocalist with perhaps the most emotional depth of any singer in jazz history.

B illie Holiday's life was tragic. Born into out-of-wedlock poverty, she rose to a position of artistic pre-eminence in the world of jazz, but her personal life was one of constant turmoil and struggle. She fought seemingly endless wars—with drug addiction, with narcotics agents' harassment, with racism, with self-serving lovers, and with human parasites in and out of the music business. Withal, her vocal artistry was joyously, bittersweetly transcendant. Many serious listeners consider her the greatest jazz vocalist ever.

She was born Eleanora Fagan on April 7, 1915, in Baltimore, Maryland. (The name ''Billie'' she later borrowed from one of her favorite movie actresses, Billie Dove.) At the time of Billie's birth, her mother, Sadie Fagan, was 13 years old, and her father, Clarence Holiday (later a jazz guitarist in Fletcher Henderson's band), was 15; they married each other three years later. As a child Billie ran errands for prostitutes in a nearby brothel, and as a reward they allowed her to listen to their Louis Armstrong and Bessie Smith records.

In 1928 she went to New York City with her mother, who secured work as a housemaid, but the 1929 depression soon left her mother unemployed. In 1932 Billie tried out for a job as a nightclub dancer, and when she was rejected, she spontaneously auditioned for a singing job and was hired. For the next few years she sang in a succession of Harlem clubs until her career received a boost from impresario John Hammond, who induced Benny Goodman to use her on a record in 1933. But it was through a series of superb recordings made between 1935 and 1939 that her international

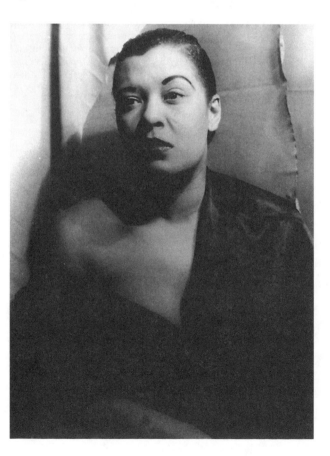

reputation was established; those performances are jazz classics not only for Billie's singing but also for the outstanding ensemble and solo work of the accompanying all-star groups led by pianist Teddy Wilson. During the late 1930s she was also a big band vocalist, first with Count Basie (1937) and then with Artie Shaw (1938).

Her relationship with Basie's star tenor saxophonist Lester Young is the stuff of legend: they were great musical collaborators and great friends for life (their lives, incidentally, followed a parallel disastrous course). He named her "Lady Day," and that title (or simply "Lady") became her jazz world sobriquet from the mid-1930s on; she in turn labeled him "Pres" (the "President of Tenor Saxophonists"). Their musical symbiosis, especially on the 1935-1939 small-group recordings, is one of the miracles of jazz; on "This Year's Kisses," "He's Funny That Way," "A Sailboat in the Moonlight," "Me, Myself and I," "Mean to Me," and a raft of other tunes tenor saxophone and voice interweave so sympathetically that they sound as if they're poured from the same bottle. After the late 1930s they rarely recorded together, but to the end remained soulmates. (They died the same year.) Billie's career reached its zenith in the very late 1930s. In 1938 she worked a long engagement at Cafe Society; the following year she joined Benny Goodman on a radio broadcast; she was regularly working the big New York theaters and the famous 52nd Street clubs, including Kelly's Stables and the Onyx Club—all in addition to her recording successes. Two songs of the period are noteworthy: the first, "Strange Fruit," with a haunting lyric by Lewis Allan to which Billie contributed the music, is a graphic depiction of a lynching; her record company, Columbia, considered it too inflammatory and refused to issue it, but it was finally released by a small record company (Commodore) in 1939 and, ironically, became a big money-maker because of the tune on the record's other side, "Fine and Mellow," a blues written by Billie. Another tune always associated with her was "Gloomy Sunday," which was expressive of such deep despair that it was for a time barred from the airwaves (the contention was that it was inducive to suicide).

By the mid-1940s Billie had been arrested many times for narcotics violations, and after one arrest in 1947, at her own request, was placed for a year and a day in a federal rehabilitation center at Alderson, West Virginia. Just ten days after being released she gave a concert at Carnegie Hall, but thenceforth was barred by New York City police licensing laws from working in any place that served liquor. The absence of a cabaret card in effect meant that she could never again appear in a New York nightclub.

Neither of her husbands—trumpeter Joe Guy (whom she divorced in the 1940s) nor Louis McKay (who survived her)—seemed able or inclined to save Billie from herself. By the 1950s alcohol and marijuana had taken a toll; her voice grew unnaturally deep and grainy and occasionally cracked during performance. Nevertheless, her singing was sustained by her highly individual style, the intimacy she projected, and her special way with a lyric. In 1954 she toured Europe to wide acclaim, and in 1958 she made a memorable appearance in the television special "The Sound of

Jazz," surrounded by an all-star ensemble which included the three reigning tenor saxophone kings, Coleman Hawkins, Ben Webster, and her beloved "Pres."

Billie made her final public appearance in a concert at the Phoenix Theatre, New York City, on May 25, 1959. She died in Metropolitan Hospital, New York City, on July 17, 1959, of "congestion of the lungs complicated by heart failure"; she had at the time of her death been under arrest in her hospital bed for over a month for illegal possession of drugs.

An elegiac poem written by Frank O'Hara, "The Day Lady Died" (1964), ends" . . . she whispered a song along the keyboard/ . . . and everyone and I stopped breathing"— lines that are evocative of the pindrop silence this extraordinary singer was able to command. Tall, sensually exotic, with a swatch of gardenias in her hair, she sang with her head tilted jauntily back and her fingers snapping to the beat; audiences unfailingly responded with hushed reverence.

Her early small-group recordings have been reissued in several boxed sets under the general title of "Billie Holiday: The Golden Years"; her best later work is to be found in "The First Verve Sessions" recorded in 1952 and 1954 with a Jazz at the Philharmonic group of all-stars that included trumpeter Charlie Shavers, tenor saxophonist Flip Phillips, pianist Oscar Peterson, and guitarist Barney Kessel.

Further Reading

Her autobiography, written in collaboration with William Dufty, *Lady Sings the Blues* (1956), is the most revealing work on her, but the 1973 movie version, bearing the same title, is sadly inaccurate. John Chilton's *Billie's Blues* (1975) is an excellent survey of her life and work in the recording years (that is, from 1933 to 1959). □

John Philip Holland

John Philip Holland (1840-1914) was an Irish-American inventor who succeeded in developing the submarine sufficiently to win it a place in the navies of the world.

John P. Holland was born in County Clare, Ireland, where, after going to school in his native town and in Limerick, he became a schoolteacher. In 1873 he emigrated to New York and the following year became a teacher in Paterson, N.J.

Holland had long been fascinated by the possibilities of the submarine. Attempts to build such boats had been made off and on since the 17th century, and in 1775 the American patriot David Bushnell had been the first to use a submarine to attack an enemy ship. In 1800 Robert Fulton built and tested the first all-metal submarine. Holland, a partisan of Irish independence, hoped to perfect the craft so that it could be used against the British navy. By 1870, after studying the failures of others, he was ready with plans for a craft of his own. He was without funds, however, and it was not until going to America that he was able to revive his plans.

In New Jersey, Holland found that the Fenian Society (a group of Irish republicans) was willing to support his experiments, and in 1878 he was able to launch his first boat, a 14-foot submarine. In 1881 he built a full-sized submarine, called the *Fenian Ram,* which contained many features of the modern submarine.

Holland knew that the submarine would have to win approval from the U.S. Navy before it could be perfected, and after 1888 he made frequent bids to build a ship for the U.S. government. After several were built without his direct supervision, in 1898 he was able to launch the *Holland,* a ship nearly 54 feet long and equipped with batteries for underwater cruising. It was purchased by the government in 1900, and six more were ordered. Holland built similar ships for the navies of Japan, Great Britain, and Russia but was unable to maintain control of his own company. Like many other inventors, he had to exchange control of the firm for working capital. His last years were spent in making aeronautical experiments and investigations.

Holland died on Aug. 12, 1914, within a few days of the outbreak of World War I, the war which proved the effectiveness of his weapon.

Further Reading

A good, full-length biography of Holland is Richard Knowles Morris, *John P. Holland, 1840-1914: Inventor of the Modern Submarine* (1966). The larger story may be followed in

Charles W. Rush and others, *The Complete Book of Submarines* (1958). □

Hanya Holm

Hanya Holm (born Johanna Eckert; 1893-1992) successfully moved from Germany to America, from modern dance to the Broadway musical in a unique rise to prominence.

Hanya Holm was born Johanna Eckert on March 3, 1893, in Worms, a small town near Frankfurt am Main in Germany. She spent her first 12 years of schooling at a Catholic convent. In those years she learned respect for knowledge and creative ability, a belief in perfectionism and discipline. At the age of 10 she studied piano, and after graduation from the convent she attended the famous music-oriented Dalcroze Institute.

Seeing a dance recital of Mary Wigman in 1921 became decisive for her life. She immediately joined Wigman's company and soon advanced to the position of chief instructor and co-director of the Mary Wigman Central Institute in Dresden. During the 1920s Holm danced many parts in Wigman's company, culminating in *Das Totenmal* (Death Monument) in 1930.

Holm was a petite person with fair skin and blonde hair. There was a distinct delicacy and an expressive lyricism in her dancing. She developed an impressive fleetness and strikingly quick footwork. What also distinguished Holm's dancing was her intimate relationship with music, which strongly motivated her. In 1929 she danced the princess in one of the early productions of Stravinsky's *L'Histoire du Soldat* (The Soldier's Tale), her first major solo part for which she did her own choreography. At that time she was not yet quite sure whether to become a dancer, choreographer, or teacher. Destiny decided for her when she became the head of the Mary Wigman School in New York.

In settling down in America in 1931, she did not immediately rush into creative work. During the first six years she traveled south, west, and north and lectured, taught, and demonstrated at more than 60 colleges and universities, creating real interest and helping tremendously to expand the scope of modern dance. She left bridgeheads at logistically important places which she soon secured with some of her best students who continued to teach and perpetuate Holm's concepts.

Her lecture-demonstrations, which explored the space and tension on which her teaching was based, were almost dreamlike in their lyric molding of space and mood. The distinctive movement of her students had a light and lyric air. Holm knew how to fuse her principles of the old world with the vitality, the energy, the swift spirit of the American dancers.

When she created for the concert stage, her dances were emotional responses to life. In 1937 she showed her

first major work, about which she said: "The idea of *Trend* grew upon me, it was not a sudden inspiration. The theme issued from life itself." In *New York Times* John Martin called it "a colossal theme . . . Miss Holm opens up a new vista for the production of great dance dramas."

At one point the small company she held together for a few years became a financial burden, and she had to dissolve it. Then for some time her major activity was teaching, but this changed in 1948 and changed her destiny completely. The lyricist John Latouche asked her to choreograph the third episode of his *Ballet Ballads: The Eccentricities of Davey Crockett*. It was an emphatic success, an event of great consequences. John Martin and another critic, Walter Terry, agreed that Holm "has done a magnificent job," that she had supplied the show with "witty and imaginative movement throughout."

Shortly thereafter Holm was acclaimed with even louder critical kudos when she choreographed *Kiss Me, Kate*. With this show she had become an established choreographer for Broadway musicals. John Martin summed up her accomplishments in January 1949, stating, "Nobody could have stepped more gracefully into a new field than Holm has done in her transition from the concert dance to show business."

Her most significant success came in 1956 with the musical *My Fair Lady*, based on George Bernard Shaw's *Pygmalion*, with such stars as Julie Andrews, Rex Harrison, and Stanley Holloway. It was the biggest hit Broadway had seen since *Oklahoma!*, and it turned out to be even bigger.

Everything in this show, and particularly in what Holm had to contribute, was flawless. *My Fair Lady* was called "a whale of a show" by the publication *Variety* and "sensational" by all the critics. One could feel Holm's hand in every effective entrance, in the grace with which the actors danced, or rather acted as if they danced. It was the overall pattern of motion which ran through the entire show.

In the final analysis it was theater that seemed to fascinate her. She ventured into directing plays and she staged a couple of operas. Her great success with the operatic musical *The Golden Apple* (1954) brought her to Hollywood, where she filmed *The Vagabond King*, based on the poet François Villon's life, for Paramount in 1956.

Holm had many firsts to her credit. Her *Metropolitan Daily*, a newspaper satire, was the first modern dance composition to be televised by the National Broadcasting Company (in 1939). The entire score of the choreography for *Kiss Me, Kate* was recorded in Labanotation and was the first choreographic work to be accepted for copyright at the Library of Congress in Washington.

She won a long list of honors, among them a Drama Critics' Award for *Kiss Me, Kate* and a Critics Circle Citation for *The Golden Apple* "as the best musical of the season" in 1954. She was nominated for a Tony for *My Fair Lady* in 1957 and received an honorary degree of Doctor of Fine Arts from Colorado College in 1960. Holm was still active as a teacher until her 92nd year, and before her failing eyesight forced her to retire she received the highly endowed Squibb Grant.

In 1990 the *Dance Magazine* Award was bestowed upon her for her unique contribution to dance in America, a vital force that brought new vision to the most ephemeral of all art forms. Holm died on November 3, 1992, in New York City.

Further Reading

Hanya Holm. The Biography of an Artist by Walter Sorell (1969, paperback edition 1979) was the best source for information on Holm's life and work. Hanya Holm published the following essays: "The Dance, the Artist-Teacher, and the Child," in *Progressive Education* (1935); "The German Dance in the American Scene," in *Modern Dance,* edited by Virginia Stewart and E. Weyhe (1935); "Mary Wigman," in *Dance Observer* (November 1935); "Dance on the Campus—Athletics or Art?" in *Dance Magazine* (February 1937); "Trend Grew Upon Me," in *Magazine of Art* (March 1938); and "The Mary Wigman I Know," in *The Dance Has Many Faces,* edited by Walter Sorell (1951; new revised edition, 1966). Her obituary appeared in the November 4, 1992 edition of the *New York Times.* □

Arthur Holmes

The English geologist Arthur Holmes (1890-1965) was a pioneer in geochronology, a gifted petrologist, and a lucid expositor of the physics and history of the earth's outer layers.

Arthur Holmes was born on Jan. 14, 1890, at Heb- burn-on-Tyne. At school he became interested in the age of the earth through reading Lord Kelvin's *Addresses*. Winning a scholarship to London's Imperial College, he graduated in geology and physics in 1911 and immediately began research on the radioactivity of rocks, guided by R. J. Strutt (later 4th Baron Rayleigh). Strutt's studies had revealed a source of heat within the earth, unsuspected when Kelvin made his estimate that not more than 40 million years had elapsed since the earth's crust had solidified from the molten state. Holmes shared with Strutt in overthrowing this conclusion, and he made successive advances toward establishing a new and much longer geological time scale, eventually showing the earth to be at least 4.5 billion years old.

Holmes's researches were twice interrupted by participation as geologist in commercial explorations, first in Mozambique (1911-1912), where he contracted tropical diseases which precluded military service in World War I, and in Burma (1921-1924); the latter expedition failed, and he had to sue for his pay on return to England.

Holmes was demonstrator in geology at the Imperial College from 1912 to 1921, where he wrote three books and published many scientific memoirs. From 1924 to 1943 he headed the geology department of Durham University, which gained international fame as a center of petrological research. He was regius professor of geology and mineralogy at the University of Edinburgh from 1943 until his retirement, in poor health, in 1956. While at Durham his wife died in 1938; in 1939 he married the distinguished petrologist Doris L. Reynolds, with whom he made important researches on the evolution of igneous rock.

Holmes's work touched nearly all aspects of geology except paleontology. His geological researches were widespread, concerning India, Mozambique, and elsewhere in Africa, besides his native Britain. His textbook *Principles of Physical Geology* (1944; 2d ed. 1965) is considered a classic. Though a man of quiet demeanor, whose main outside interest was music, he did not shrink from the controversies that have figured so notably in the history of his science. He was one of the earliest and most forceful supporters of the theory of continental drift and held that it must be produced by convection currents in the substratum of the crust. In his textbook Holmes gives some diagrams describing the formation of new ocean floor by rising materials—diagrams which are almost prophetic in their anticipation of later results. He died, after a prolonged illness, in London on Sept. 20, 1965.

Further Reading

Information on Arthur Holmes can be found in W. B. Harland, A. Gilbert Smith, and B. Wilcock, eds., *The Phanerozoic Time-Scale* (1964). □

John Haynes Holmes

John Haynes Holmes (1879-1964), American clergyman, was one of the foremost figures of the Social Gospel movement in 20th-century American Protestantism.

John Haynes Holmes was born in Philadelphia, Pa., on Nov. 29, 1879, the son of an unsuccessful but bookish businessman. Raised in Malden, Mass., young Holmes was educated at Harvard College and Harvard Divinity School, where he received his degree in 1904. That year he married Madeleine Baker. From 1904 to 1907 he served as minister to the Third Religious Society of Dorchester and then accepted the pastorate at New York's Unitarian Church of the Messiah. He served as president of the General Unitarian Conference and of the Free Religious Association in the years before World War I, but in 1919 he resigned his ministerial fellowship in the Unitarian Church. His congregation followed their independent minister, changing the name of their church to the Community Church of New York. Under Holmes's guidance the church became famous for its programs of civic education and social service.

Holmes said that his "passion" was "religion—liberal, or radical, religion," and he wrote widely on the need to transform traditional religious ideas and structures. The independent pastor was well known for his political and social activities. A pacifist, he refused to support the U.S.

government in World Wars I or II. When he later discovered the work of Mahatma Gandhi, he helped make the Indian leader known in the United States.

In 1906 Holmes was one of the founders of the National Association for the Advancement of Colored People (NAACP); he served as its vice president until the end of his life. He also helped establish the American Civil Liberties Union, and he actively participated in every major civil liberties controversy, notably as the leading clerical defender of Nicola Sacco and Bartolomeo Vanzetti in the famous 1927 trial. In New York City he served as chairman of the City Affairs Committee, a citizens' group combating political corruption.

An advocate of socialism, Holmes defended labor unions and social legislation. He traveled widely, including a trip to Palestine on behalf of American Zionists in 1929 and another to India in 1947 as a lecturer. On all these matters of public concern he wrote and lectured across the country. His writings also included a book of short stories, a play (produced in New York during the 1935-1936 season), and several poems and hymns. In 1949 he resigned his pastorate, but he continued to write and speak publicly until his death in 1964, at the age of 85.

Further Reading

The best source on Holmes is his own *I Speak for Myself: The Autobiography of John Haynes Holmes* (1959). A biographical study is in Carl H. Voss, *Rabbi and Minister: The Friendship of Stephen S. Wise and John Haynes Holmes* (1964).

Additional Sources

Voss, Carl Hermann, *Rabbi and minister: the friendship of Stephen S. Wise and John Haynes Holmes,* Buffalo, N.Y.: Prometheus Books, 1980. ☐

Oliver Wendell Holmes

Oliver Wendell Holmes (1809-1894), American physician and author, contributed to the advancement of medicine and wrote witty essays and popular poems.

Oliver Wendell Holmes was born in Cambridge, Mass., on Aug. 29, 1809, scion of a well-established New England family. Following his graduation from Harvard in 1829, he studied at the law school for a year (during which time he wrote the popular poem "Old Ironsides"). He gave up law in favor of a career in medicine. He rounded out his training at the Harvard Medical School with 2 years of study in Paris (1833-1835), where he learned new techniques and approaches in medicine, reflected in two important early papers, "Homeopathy, and Its Kindred Delusions" (1842) and "The Contagiousness of Puerperal Fever" (1843).

Holmes took his medical degree at Harvard in 1836. From 1838 to 1840 he served as professor of anatomy at Dartmouth College. In 1840 he married Amelia Lee Jackson and returned to general practice. He was appointed Parkman professor of anatomy and physiology at Harvard Medical School in 1847 and served as dean from 1847 to 1853. Holmes remained at Harvard until 1882 and established himself as an excellent lecturer and teacher.

Holmes's deterministic belief that man was the product of his heredity and environment provided the direction for his three pioneering, psychologically oriented "medicated" (as he termed them) novels: *Elsie Venner* (1861), *The Guardian Angel* (1867), and *A Mortal Antipathy* (1885).

Holmes held very definite opinions on a wide variety of subjects. He found the perfect outlet for expressing his ideas in the pages of the *Atlantic Monthly,* to which he contributed several series of chatty essays interspersed with light poetry. These were gathered in *The Autocrat of the Breakfast-Table* (1858), *The Professor at the Breakfast-Table* (1860), *The Poet at the Breakfast-Table* (1872), and *Over the Teacups* (1891). In addition to these and his volumes of verse, he also wrote biographies of John L. Motley (1879) and Ralph Waldo Emerson (1885). Among his best-known poems are "The Deacon's Masterpiece," "The Last Leaf," "The Chambered Nautilus," "My Aunt," "The Moral Bully," and "Brother Jonathan's Lament for Sister Caroline."

As scientist, teacher, lecturer, essayist, and writer of light verse, Holmes left his mark on his age, and many honors came to him both at home and abroad. He died on Oct. 7, 1894.

Further Reading

The Writings of Oliver Wendell Holmes (13 vols., 1891-1892) is standard. *The Complete Poetical Works of Oliver Wendell Holmes* (1895) is an excellent one-volume edition. The best biography is Eleanor M. Tilton, *Amiable Autocrat: A Biography of Dr. Oliver Wendell Holmes* (1947). A sound study is Mark A. De Wolfe Howe, *Holmes of the Breakfast-Table* (1939). Clarence P. Oberndorf offers a stimulating discussion and abridgments of Holmes's "medicated" novels in *The Psychiatric Novels of Oliver Wendell Holmes* (1943; 2d ed. 1946). □

Oliver Wendell Holmes Jr.

As a jurist and a legal writer, Oliver Wendell Holmes, Jr. (1841-1935), contributed mightily to the debate in the early 20th century concerning the role of law in a rapidly changing America.

The U.S. government is based on a document written in 1787, the Constitution, and an issue almost from the beginning of the new nation was the extent to which the demands of an ever-changing society could be encompassed within this structure. Few men played a more important role in this discourse than Oliver Wendell Holmes, Jr. Not only did he personally contribute to the debate, but he also served as a symbol to a generation of legal and political thinkers.

Oliver Wendell Holmes, Jr., was born in Boston, Mass., on March 8, 1841, into one of the city's most illustrious families. His father, Oliver Wendell Holmes, among the leading medical practitioners of his day, was also a writer and wit, famous to readers of the *Atlantic Monthly* as "the autocrat of the breakfast table." His family life brought young Oliver into contact with many of Boston's leading intellectuals, including Ralph Waldo Emerson, America's foremost essayist and lecturer during this period.

Harvard and the Civil War

Holmes entered Harvard College in 1857. There is little evidence that his college education was of great importance to him. Aside from the education he received simply by virtue of his family's ties, Holmes's greatest learning experience was his part in the Civil War. His participation in many battles resulted in three wounds, of which he was very proud. Thoughout the rest of his life he marked his wounds' anniversaries in letters to various correspondents. He left the military in July 1864.

The impact of the war on Holmes had less to do with the political issues over which it had been fought than with its demonstration of the importance of commitment to a higher cause. Holmes grew up in a world where many accepted beliefs were being challenged, and his response stressed the importance of devoting oneself to a cause even if it was incomprehensible. In his speech "The Soldier's Faith," he said: "I do not know what is true. I do not know the meaning of the universe. But in the midst of doubt, in the

collapse of creeds, there is one thing I do not doubt, . . . and that is that the faith is true and adorable which leads a soldier to throw away his life in obedience to a blindly accepted duty, in a cause which he little understands, in a plan of campaign of which he has no notion, under tactics of which he does not see the use."

Furthermore, the war confirmed Holmes's rejection of sentimentality and even humanitarianism. He regarded all of life as a battle, with victory going to the strongest. In this way he fully accepted the emphasis of his age on "survival of the fittest." Unlike many of his contemporaries, however, he pointed out that the strongest force in a society was its majority. When he became a judge, he used this argument to favor judicial acquiescence before majority rule.

Legal Career

After leaving the regiment Holmes attended Harvard Law School, from which he graduated in 1866. He was admitted to the Massachusetts bar the following year. After his first trip to England, he threw himself into his legal career, both as a practitioner and as a scholar. After experience in other firms, he helped found the firm of Shattuck, Holmes and Munroe, where he primarily practiced commercial law. The time that remained after practice he used for scholarly work.

Between 1870 and 1873 Holmes edited the *American Law Review*. Furthermore, 1873 saw the publication of the twelfth edition of Chancellor James Kent's classic *Commentaries on American Law,* which Holmes had brought up to date. Throughout the 1870s Holmes was also researching the questions he would consider in a set of lectures at the Lowell Institute in 1880. These, published the following year as *The Common Law,* brought him worldwide fame.

The first paragraph of *The Common Law* contains what is probably Holmes's most famous sentence: "The life of the law has not been logic: it has been experience." He goes on to argue that law is a series of responses to felt social problems, not simply a set of logical deductions from abstract theories. His book contributed to the awakening interest in the United States in "sociological jurisprudence," the interrelation between law and other social institutions.

Judicial Career

After less than a year as professor of law at Harvard Law School, Holmes became an associate justice of the Supreme Judicial Court of Massachusetts on Jan. 3, 1883. He was promoted to chief justice on Aug. 5, 1899. His reputation as a daring thinker grew during his tenure on the court, principally because of several opinions, some dissenting, in which he upheld the right of the state to engage in regulation of the economy and other social issues.

When Theodore Roosevelt became president in 1901, he was eager to appoint men to the Supreme Court who would uphold the new laws he himself wanted passed and who would confirm the changing conception of the role of government with which he was identified. Viewing Holmes as such a man, Roosevelt appointed him to the U.S. Supreme Court; Holmes took his seat on Dec. 8, 1902, at the relatively advanced age of 61. He served on the Court until Jan. 12, 1932.

Holmes's most important early opinions dealt with regulation of the national economy. He argued vigorously for wide latitude for the states in this and in other areas of social policy. His most famous opinion in the economic sphere is probably *Lochner v. New York;* he dissented when the Court struck down a New York law limiting the hours a baker could be made to work. He rejected the Court's social theorizing; for him the key question was not the correctness or incorrectness of economic theories but rather "the right of a majority to embody their opinions in law."

Holmes became even more famous after World War I because of his opinions regarding the regulation of freedom of speech. Though his reasoning was not always impeccable, he used his writing skills (probably the greatest of any Supreme Court justice in American history) to evoke a powerful sense of the importance of civil liberties. In *Schenck v. United States* (1919) he upheld the conviction of a man who had advocated draft resistance, but only after finding him a "clear and present danger" to the peace and order of society. He later dissented from other convictions of political dissidents whom he did not regard as presenting that threat.

In *Abrams v. United States* (1919) Holmes wrote his most passionate defense of free speech, arguing that only a "free trade in ideas" could guarantee the attainment of truth. He argued that "we should be eternally vigilant against attempts to check the expression of opinions that we loathe and believe to be fraught with death, unless they so immediately threaten immediate interference with the lawful and pressing purposes of the law that an immediate check is required to save the country."

Tall, erect, and handsome in his youth, Holmes had grown into an even more imposing man, with a splendid handlebar moustache and white hair. As an elderly judge, he was surrounded often by admiring younger men and was, by all accounts, a lively figure. In his old age he was increasingly admired by many of those who would lead the next political generation. He left the Court before it accepted his theories concerning its role in regulating the economy (as it did, indeed, accept them in the 1940s).

Holmes had married Fanny Dixwell on June 17, 1872. The marriage lasted until her death in 1929; they had no children. Holmes died on March 6, 1935.

Further Reading

A source for Holmes's own writings is Max Lerner, ed., *The Mind and Faith of Justice Holmes: His Speeches, Essays, Letters, and Judicial Opinions,* which also contains Lerner's important introduction to Holmes. Catherine Drinker Bowen, *Yankee from Olympus: Justice Holmes and His Family* (1944), is a popular biography that has had a great public impact. Mark DeWolfe Howe completed two volumes of the definitive scholarly biography before his death; *Justice Oliver Wendell Holmes: The Shaping Years, 1841-1870* (1957) and *The Proving Years, 1870-1882* (1963). Felix Frankfurter, *Mr. Justice Holmes and the Supreme Court* (1938; 2d ed. 1961), is a laudatory assessment of Holmes. For specific treatment of Holmes's judicial career see Samuel J. Konefsky, *The Legacy of Holmes and Brandeis: A Study in the Influence of Ideas* (1956). Recommended for general background are Eric F. Goldman, *Rendezvous with Destiny: A History of Modern American Reform* (1952; rev. ed. abr. 1956), and Arthur M. Schlesinger, Jr., *The Age of Roosevelt,* vol. 1 (1957). □

Gustav Holst

Gustav Holst (1874-1934) was one of the most important English composers of his time, even though little of his music continued to be played.

Gustav Holst's paternal great-grandfather was born in Sweden, but all his other forebears were English. For four generations they were professional musicians, his father being organist and choirmaster in Cheltenham. Gustav wrote compositions as soon as he was able to hold a pen and played various instruments as fast as they came his way. When he was 12, he was already studying Hector Berlioz's orchestration treatise.

Holst received his formal training at the Royal College of Music in London. When neuritis prevented his becoming a pianist, he took up the trombone, and for many years he supported himself by playing in opera and symphony orchestras, an excellent opportunity to become acquainted with a wide variety of music and to learn orchestration through practical experience. Beginning in 1903 he became a teacher at several London schools and, eventually, at the Royal College of Music. He knew Sanskrit and Hindu literature and composed several choral works and an opera based on Hindu epics.

During World War I Holst was sent to Salonika, Greece, and to Constantinople to organize musical activities among the British soldiers stationed there. In 1923 he conducted and lectured at the University of Michigan, and he lectured at Harvard in 1932.

Holst composed about 50 works. Because of the importance of choral singing in England, many of his compositions are for choir. The best known of these are *The Hymn of Jesus* (1917) and the *Ode to Death* (1922). He also wrote many songs and several operas, including *The Perfect Fool* (1923) and *At the Boar's Head* (1925).

Holst's most important piece, and the one that is most often played, is the orchestral suite *The Planets* (1914-1917). It is a large-scale, brilliantly orchestrated series of tone poems devoted to seven of the planets: Mars, Venus, Mercury, Jupiter, Saturn, Uranus, and Neptune. He uses polytonality and polyrhythms and treats the orchestra with great skill and freedom.

English composers of Holst's generation were at a disadvantage in that they wrote at a time when Igor Stravinsky began to dominate the international musical scene. In the late 1920s, when Stravinsky turned to neoclassic ideals, composers who wrote symphonic poems and folk-based choral pieces were considered old-fashioned. Holst was an honest, if unfashionable, composer, and he did not follow the musical fashions of his day. He was always true to his

background and convictions, and his music impresses by its sincerity and highly professional workmanship.

Further Reading

The best studies of Holst were written by his daughter, Imogen, who followed the family tradition of being a composer and critic. They are *Gustav Holst* (1938) and *The Music of Gustav Holst* (1951). Another study, by an English composer, is Edmund Rubbra, *Gustav Holst* (1947).

Additional Sources

Holst, Imogen, *Gustav Holst: a biography,* Oxford Oxfordshire; New York: Oxford University Press, 1988.

Holst, Imogen, *Holst,* London; Boston: Faber & Faber, 1981.

Short, Michael, *Gustav Holst: the man and his music,* Oxford; New York: Oxford University Press, 1990. □

Keith Jacka Holyoake

Keith Jacka Holyoake (1904-1983) was a New Zealand prime minister and leader of the National Party who subsequently became his country's governor general. An astute politician, he led his party to four successive electoral victories and presided over material prosperity and rising social expectations from 1960 to 1972.

The Right Honourable Sir Keith Jacka Holyoake was born near Pahiatua in the lower part of New Zealand's North Island on February 11, 1904. He was the third of seven children and descended from settlers who had migrated to New Zealand from England in 1842. Holyoake's father ran a small general store before eventually taking over a mixed hops, tobacco, fruit, and dairy farm at Riwaka near Motueka in the South Island.

At the age of 12, when his father became ill, Holyoake left school to help on the farm. His ex-schoolteacher mother continued to teach him at home in the evenings. Although he later in life joined the Presbyterian Church, Holyoake was raised in the Plymouth Brethren religion, and his social life as a child was very restricted.

As a young man "Kiwi Keith" Holyoake became much more involved with the wider community as a tennis and rugby football player and rugby administrator. He also served on the executive committees of various farming organizations, eventually becoming the president of the Nelson Province of the Farmer's Union (later known as Federated Farmers) and then that organization's New Zealand vice-president. In 1938 for a time he was acting dominion president of the Farmers' Union.

At the age of 28 Holyoake was elected to the House of Representatives in a 1932 by-election for the seat of Motueka, following the suicide of the member of Parliament from that district. Holyoake had contested the seat unsuccessfully as a coalition government supporter at a general election the previous year. Following the landslide Labour

Party victory of 1935 various antisocialist groups and parties formed the National Party, and Holyoake joined it. He held the Motueka seat until 1938 when, following extensive boundary changes and the influx into the electorate of hundreds of relief workers employed on public works, he lost to a Labour Party candidate.

For the next five years, 1938 to 1943, Holyoake returned to farming, first at Motueka. Following Ransom's retirement in 1943, Holyoake was selected unopposed as the National Party's candidate and was re-elected to Parliament as the representative for Pahiatua at the 1943 election. He held that seat until his retirement following his appointment as governor general in 1977.

Holyoake and his wife Norma (nee Ingram) had two sons and three daughters, and Holyoake always treasured the occasions he could escape from public life and spend time with his family on the farm or later at his holiday home on the western shore of Lake Taupo.

Rise of the National Party

When the National Party became the Government of New Zealand for the first time following the 1949 elections, Holyoake became deputy prime minister and minister of agriculture and marketing, negotiating minimum prices for wool in 1952, meat in 1955, and dairy produce in 1956. At the age of 53 he succeeded an ailing Sir Sidney Holland as prime minister three months before the 1957 election. Unable to establish himself sufficiently in the short time available, Holyoake and his party were defeated by the Labour

Party, which won the election with a working majority of one seat in Parliament. For the next three years Keith Holyoake effectively led the Opposition.

In 1960, after Holyoake had stumped the country criticizing the new Labour government's economic management and "the Black Budget" of 1958, the National Party swept back into office and Holyoake again became New Zealand's prime minister. He won four elections in succession and remained the country's leader for over 11 years. During that time he also held the foreign affairs portfolio and frequently travelled overseas to attend conferences and meet other world leaders.

A realistic tactician and pragmatic and effective manager of both cabinet and caucus, Holyoake created the public image of a government that was reluctant to intervene in the economy or in the affairs of the individual New Zealanders and that practiced cautious but liberal government by consensus. His 1963 election slogan "Steady Does It" summed up his approach to politics. Only the corrosive controversy of New Zealand's limited involvement in the Vietnam War in the mid-1960s divided the electorate seriously during that time.

Holyoake was not an innovator, but he presided over a period in New Zealand history during which there was considerable economic growth, material prosperity, and upward social mobility. It was also a time of considerable social and technological change during which the country only partially started to recognize that it had to become economically and diplomatically more self-reliant. The seeds of serious future conflicts over foreign affairs, defense, and race relations were being sown, though they did not become major issues until after Holyoake relinquished office.

In February 1972 Holyoake, who had been knighted in 1970, stepped down as prime minister and leader of the National Party. Only two New Zealand prime ministers had served longer—Richard John "King Dick" Seddon (1893-1906) and William Ferguson "Bill" Massey (1912-1925). Holyoake stayed in Parliament as an "elder statesman," and his experience and advice became essential to the National Party when it again tasted a bitter electoral defeat in November of that year. Within three years the National Party, under a new leader, Robert Muldoon, admirer of Holyoake, had won back the treasury benches, and in late 1975 Holyoake became minister of state in a new National Party government.

Becomes Governor-General

Tradition was broken in 1977 when the government appointed Holyoake as governor-general of New Zealand. Despite the controversy surrounding the nomination of an active politician as the queen's representative, Holyoake's three year term in the post passed without incident and he occupied the position with distinction and impartiality.

In 1980, shortly before retiring as governor-general, Holyoake became the only resident New Zealander ever to be honored by the queen as knight commander of the Order of the Garter. (Holyoake replaced the queen's uncle, Lord Mountbatten, who had been recently assassinated.) In addition to Knight of the Garter, Holyoake also could claim several other (lesser) honors.

Holyoake appeared somewhat aloof and sounded a little pompous in public. In fact he was a sensitive man who was remarkably modest about his role in New Zealand politics. Throughout his long public career—of over half a century and 16 election campaigns—Holyoake rarely if ever indulged in personality politics. He demanded and received from his National Party colleagues loyalty, "an ounce" of which, he frequently stated, was "better than a ton of cleverness." As prime minister Holyoake certainly earned for himself a place in New Zealand history as one of its greatest political figures. He died on December 8, 1983.

Further Reading

The only biography is by Ross A. Doughty, *The Holyoake Years* (1977). Keith Jacka Holyoake will be listed in the *New Zealand Dictionary of Biography* being prepared for publication during New Zealand's 150th anniversary in 1990. Holyoake is also discussed in two books by a successor as the National Party's leader, R. D. Muldoon: *The Rise and Fall of a Young Turk* (1974) and *Muldoon* (1977). See also B. S. Gustafson, *The New Zealand National Party: The First Fifty Years* (1986).

Additional Sources

Doughty, Ross Alexander, *The Holyoake years,* Fielding: R. Doughty, 1977. □

Jenny Holzer

An American Neo-Conceptualist artist, Jenny Holzer (born 1950) utilized the homogeneous rhetoric of modern information systems in order to address the politics of discourse. In 1989 she became the first female artist chosen to represent the United States at Italy's Venice Biennale.

Jenny Holzer was born July 29, 1950, in Gallipolis, Ohio, into a family of two generations of Ford auto dealers. She completed her undergraduate degree at Ohio University in Athens after attending Duke University and the University of Chicago. While enrolled in the Rhode Island School of Design, Holzer experimented with an abstract painting style influenced by the color field painters Mark Rothko and Morris Louis. In 1976 she moved to Manhattan, participating in the Whitney Museum's independent study program.

Language as Art

Holzer's conception of language as art, in which semantics developed into her aesthetic, began to emerge in New York. The Whitney program included an extensive reading list incorporating Western and Eastern literature and philosophy. Holzer felt the writings could be simplified to phrases everyone could understand. She called these summaries her "Truisms" (1978), which she printed anonymously in black italic script on white paper and wheat-pasted to building facades, signs, and telephone booths in lower Manhattan. Arranged in alphabetical order and comprised of short sentences, her "Truisms" inspired pedestrians to scribble messages on the posters and make verbal comments. Holzer would stand and listen to the dialogues invoked by her words.

The participatory effect and the underground format were vital components of Holzer's "Truisms" and of her second series, the "Inflammatory Essays," which laconically articulated Holzer's concerns and anxieties about contemporary society. Holzer printed the "Essays" in alphabetical order, first on small posters and then as a manuscript entitled *The Black Book* (1979). Until the late 1980s, Holzer refused to produce them in any non-underground formats because of their militant nature. Her declarative language assumed particular force and violence in the multiple viewpoints of the "Essays," ranging from extreme leftist to rightist.

Holzer initiated the "Living Series" in 1981, which she printed on aluminum and bronze plaques, the presentation format used by medical and government buildings. "Living" addressed the necessities of daily life: eating, breathing, sleeping, and human relationships. Her bland, short instructions were accompanied with paintings by the American artist Peter Nadin, whose portraits of men and women attached to metal posts further articulated the emptiness of both life and message in the information age.

Art and Technology

The medium of modern computer systems became an important component in Holzer's work in 1982, when nine of her "Truisms" flashed at forty-second intervals on the giant Spectacolor electronic signboard in Times Square. Sponsored by the Public Arts Fund program, the use of the L.E.D. (light emitting diode) machine allowed Holzer to reach a larger audience. By combining a knowledge of semantics with modern advertising technologies, Holzer established herself as a descendant of the conceptualist and pop art movements. She again utilized the electronic signboard with her "Survival Series" (1983-1985), in which she adopted a more personal and urgent stance. The realities of everyday living, the dangers, and the underlying horrors were major themes. Correlating with the immediacy of the messages, Holzer adopted a slightly less authoritarian voice. Her populist appropriation of contemporary "newsspeak" crossed the realm between visual art and poetry and carried a potent expressive force. Her attempt to make sense out of contemporary life within a technological framework also suggests the limitations of the information age, in which the world of advertising consumes everything, yet an underlying message no longer exists.

After the "Survival Series," Holzer's installations became more monumental in scale and more quasi-religious. Her "Under a Rock" exhibition combined the modern media of the communications industry, the electronic signboard, with marble benches printed in the block letters used in national cemeteries. The language measured angst and violence with the apathetic reportage of the most seasoned news personae: CRACK THE PELVIS SO SHE LIES

RIGHT, THIS IS A MISTAKE. WHEN SHE DIES YOU CANNOT REPEAT THE ACT, etc. The vivid juxtaposition between horrifying subject matter and the authoritarian voice, coupled with flashing diodes and cold marble, jars the spectator with its apparent paradox and brutal insistency. By utilizing the pronoun "she," Holzer allied the victimization with the female. The new urgency of the "voice" in Holzer's "Under a Rock" installation, first exhibited in 1986 at the Barbara Gladstone Gallery in New York, revealed a Holzer more overtly building images that suggest male power and control over women.

The birth of her first child in 1989 inspired Holzer's "Laments," perhaps the most personal and angst-ridden series she had done. The "Laments" address motherhood, violation, pain, torture, and death in the voices of "thirteen assorted dead people" (J. Holzer). The personae range in sex and age, yet a common insistency permeates their disembodied words. One passage suggests infanticide: IF THE PROCESS STARTS I WILL KILL THIS BABY A GOOD WAY. The contradictions inherent to the rhetoric, "to kill" but in "a good way," shape the negations and arbitrariness of contemporary linguistics. Holzer accessed the language structure and media of contemporary politics and advertising in order to reveal the tensions and male domination apparent in the contemporary linguistic system.

Virtual Art

The multimedia extravaganzas of Holzer's later installations, such as the 1989 Guggenheim exhibition, are exemplified by a 535-foot running electronic signboard spiraled around the core of Frank Lloyd Wright's architecture, flashing garish lights on the monumental stone benches arranged in a large circle on the floor below. In 1989 also, she became the first female artist chosen to represent the United States at the Venice Biennale, the international art world's premiere event. For the Biennale, Holzer designed posters, hats, and t-shirts to be sold in the streets of Venice, while her L.E.D. signboards and marble benches occupied the solemn and austere exhibition space. Her words were translated into multiple languages in order to communicate to an international audience. Despite the fact that she had won the prestigious Golden Lion award at the Biennale, Holzer also started to draw more negative reactions to her work. The size and expense of her exhibits, as well as her growing popularity in the art world, led some to accuse her of becoming elitist.

Holzer withdrew from the art world for a few years and then returned in 1993 with a fresh approach to her work and a new emphasis on the immaterial. In October of 1993 she partook in a virtual reality exhibit at the Guggenheim Museum. The following year she produced her next series, "Lustmord," which opened at the Barbara Gladstone Gallery in New York. The title is taken from a German word that means murder plus sexual pleasure. She was inspired by the violence of the war in Bosnia, formerly a republic of Yugoslavia. In 1996 she participated in the First Biennale of Florence. By accepting multivalent formats for her media-conscious verbal imagery, Holzer created a populist art of expressive and poetic force.

Further Reading

A number of important exhibition catalogs provide analysis and excellent color reproductions of Holzer's works. See especially Michael Auping's *Jenny Holzer: the Venice Installation* (1991) and Diane Waldman's *Jenny Holzer* (1989), the exhibition catalog for the Guggenheim Museum in New York. Earlier catalogs include the 1986 Cincinnati Contemporary Arts Center's *Jenny Holzer and Cindy Sherman: Personae;* the Israel Museum's *Jenny Holzer, Barbara Kruger* (Jerusalem, 1986); and the Knight Gallery's *Holzer. Kruger. Prince* (Charlotte, N.C., 1984-1985).

Additional Sources

Howell, John. "Jenny Holzer: The Message Is the Medium."*ARTnews* (Summer 1988): 122-127.
Schwartzman, Allan. "After Four Years, The Message is Murder." *New York Times,* 8 May 1994.
Snider, Ben. "Jenny Holzer: Multidisciplinary Dweeb." *Art and Design* 9 (Summer 1994): 17-19.
Taylor, Paul. "Jenny Holzer: I Wanted To Do A Portrait of Society." *Flash Art* 151 (March/April 1990): 116-119.
Teixeira, Kevin. "Jenny Holzer: Virtual Reality: An Emerging Medium." *Art and Design* 9 (Summer 1994): 9-15.
Turner, Jonathan. "Transporting Truisms." *ARTnews* (January 1997): 29.
Wei, Lilly. "Jenny Holzer." *Art in America* (September 1991): 126-127. □

George Caspar Homans

George Caspar Homans (1910-1989) an American sociologist, was a leading theorist in developing testable hypotheses and explanations about fundamental social processes in small groups.

George Homans was born August 11, 1910, in Boston, Massachusetts, the eldest child of Robert Homans, a lawyer and a fellow of Harvard Corporation, and of Abigail Adams Homans, a descendant of President John Adams. He married Nancy Parshall Cooper in 1941, and they had two children, Elizabeth Susan and Peter. Homans attended the prestigious St. Pauls preparatory school in Concord, New Hampshire, from 1923 to 1928 and graduated from Harvard University in English literature in 1932. Although he came from a long line of lawyers Homans opted to become a junior fellow in sociology at Harvard, 1934 to 1939, and then as professor of sociology when he was invited.

Homans taught at Harvard from 1939 to 1941, served four years as a naval officer during World War II, and then returned to Harvard where he was a faculty member from 1946 until 1970, when he retired. Homans was a fellow at the Center for Advanced Studies in the Behavioral Sciences, president of the American Sociological Association, and a member of the National Academy of Sciences.

English Villagers of the Thirteenth Century (1941) was the book that probably earned Homans tenure at Harvard. In his seminars he had been trained to look for relationships between variables. In this investigation the variables were two kinds of field systems (open and non-open); two settlement patterns (villages surrounded by farm lands and houses dispersed on individual family holdings); and two kinds of inheritance patterns (one in which the eldest son obtained all the family land and the other where all sons received an equal share). He discovered a high statistical correlation between these institutions: the open field system was associated with the village settlement pattern and inheritance by the eldest son. He later discovered that the two systems had different units of local government, different names for those units, differences in the peasant holdings, and different social classes among the peasants. These findings thrilled him because he had been trained to look for social systems, which are evidenced if the institutions of one are systematically interrelated and different from those of another. He ultimately found that the two social systems were part of the imported culture of two different sets of Germanic immigrants. This was a disappointment to Homans, however, because he never liked cultural explanations, even in graduate school.

A Text on Groups and Theory

Of Homans' books, the *Human Group* (1950) was the most popular, used by two generations of sociologists in courses on small groups and sociological theory. He composed it by hand at his summer house in Quebec, where he wrote easily, quickly, and with considerable charm. As an exercise in general theory, he showed how three classes of variables (interaction, sentiments, and activities) are mutually related in the behavior of group members (the internal system) but also in the relationship of the group to its physical and social environment (the external system). He presented accounts of five concrete field studies of groups by other investigators and showed how the data are appropriately classified under each of the variables in both the internal and external system and how the variables and systems relate to each other. An illustrative example of his propositions: the more frequently two persons in a group interact, the more apt they are to like one another.

Homans always believed in the folk adage that human nature is the same the world over and, hence, felt cross cultural generalizations should reflect that unity. For example, he was always fascinated by R. Firth's ethnography of Tikopia (in the Solomon Islands), a society where married couples lived with the husband's family and where the husband was given jural authority over his children. Firth noted that the relationships of children with the mother's brothers were extremely close, but with the father, distant and cool, and made the finding something of a puzzle. The explanation, suggested by A. R. Radcliffe-Brown, was that the jural authority of the father, since it involved punishment, inhibited emotional closeness. In contrast, the mother's brothers identified with their sister's children and tended, like her, to take a more nurturant role toward them. Consequently, they, too, had warm relationships with the children. On the other hand, among the Trobrianders (off New Guinea) married couples lived with the wife's family; her brothers were vested with the jural authority and, consequently, had strained relationships with the children. In contrast, the relationships with the father were nurturant and warm. Homans recognized that both societies, although their cultures were obviously different, evidenced the same behavioral generalization, namely that close and warm relations tend to occur on the side of the family away from the man who held jural authority over the children.

Homans was also pleased about this explanation because it provided an alternative to Freud's theory of the Oedipus complex, which explained the strained relations between boys and their fathers as the result of unconscious competition for the sexual favors of the mother. These cross cultural results tended to prove Freud's theory false because the mother's brothers were not rivals for the mother's sexual favors in either society, yet the relations were strained with the children in one and not in the other. Rather, the variation in warm versus strained relations with her children were explained by other variables (see *Marriage, Authority and Final Causes,* 1957).

From his graduate days Homans observed that sociologists all considered theory to be important but never defined what it was. He finally decided to adopt the view that a theory is an explanation by a "covering law." What sociologists try to explain are empirical propositions relating variables to one another, and Homans concluded that such generalizations are explained when they can be deduced under the specified conditions of their occurrence from more general propositions (covering laws). Homans further decided that for sociology the first approximation of covering laws were the reinforcement propositions of behavioral psychology, specifically those of his friends and colleagues B. F. Skinner and Richard Herrnstein which apply to the process by which a person learns actions and to the way he uses them afterwards (see *The Nature of Social Science,* 1967). Sociologists now tend to accept Homans' definition of theory, but are still hesitant about his suggestions for covering laws.

Theory of Stratification

Many feel Homans' best book was *Social Behavior: Its Elementary Forms* (1961, 1974), in which he described and explained small group behavior as an emergent social system of rewards, using as the explanatory logic Herrnstein's positive reinforcement propositions. Following this revised reasoning, for example, one would predict that the strained relations with the children in Tikopia and the Trobriands was not the result of the fathers' and the uncles' jural authority, but the use of punishment rather than rewards for disciplinary purposes. Considerable research has subsequently shown that the judicious use of rewards with children was actually more effective than the use of punishment, and that it builded rather than strained relations.

For sociology, perhaps the most important contribution in *Elementary Forms* was Homans' theory of stratification, which was stated in a series of scattered propositions and definitions. These included: The more valuable to other members of a group are the activities a person emits to them, the higher is the status they give him in return. The higher a person's status in a group, the greater his power is apt to be. The more members of a group a person is regularly able to influence, the greater is his power. The value of what a member receives by way of (monetary) rewards should be proportional to his status in the group. Distributive injustice occurs to the extent that the monetary rewards members receive are disproportional to their relative status in the group. The greater the distributive injustice in a group, the lower the productivity and morale of its members.

Homans' explanation of stratification may or may not be true empirically, but it was certainly interesting. He hypothesized that differences in status and power are natural, if not inevitable, but that distributive justice, the proportionality of relative status and monetary reward, may or may not occur. To the extent that it does not, he predicted the productivity and morale of group members naturally, inevitably would suffer. Homans' theory seemed to be an alternative to the Marxist formulation that stratification—that is, differences in monetary rewards—was the root cause of all social problems. Although Marx's theory can be criticized because it solves neither the free rider nor the exploitation problems for the low and high contributors respectively, it will be fascinating to see how the two sets of hypotheses fare in future research in sociology.

George Caspar Homans retired from his teaching position at Harvard University in 1980 to his home in Cambridge, from which he continued to write texts elucidating his social theories. He also published *The Witch Hazel, Poems of a Lifetime,* the year before his death. He died May 29, 1989 at Cambridge Hospital of congestive heart disease.

Further Reading

Homans' books included an *Introduction to Pareto: His Sociology,* with C. P. Curtis (1934); *English Villagers of the Thirteenth Century* (1941); *The Human Group* (1950); *Marriage, Authority and Final Causes,* with D. M. Schneider (1955); *Social Behavior: Its Elementary Forms* (1961, 1974); *Sentiments and Activities* (1962); *The Nature of Social Science* (1967); *Coming to My Senses: the Autobiography of a Sociologist* (1984).

Western Electric Researches printed a reprint series in the Social Sciences, one of which is *George C. Homans,* (1993 paperback); and some of Homans' books were re-printed in paperback after his death, notably *Anxiety and Ritual: The Theories of Malinowski and Radcliffe-Brown,* (1993); and *Social Behavior as Exchange* (1993 paperback); and *The Witch Hazel: Poems of a Lifetime* (1988) by George Caspar Homans which was only available in hardcover.

The *Boston Globe* (January 7, 1985) reviewed favorably Homans' *Coming to My Senses: The Autobiography of a Sociologist* (1984); and Edgar T. Driscoll, Jr., wrote Homans' obituary for the *Boston Globe,* May 31, 1989. ☐

Homer

Homer, the major figure in ancient Greek literature, has been universally acclaimed as the greatest poet of classical antiquity. The *Iliad* and the *Odyssey,* two long epic poems surviving in a surprisingly large number of manuscripts, are ascribed to him.

It is not possible to supply for Homer a biography in the accepted sense of a life history, since there is no authentic record of who he was, when and where he was born, how long he lived, or even if one and the same oral poet was responsible for the two long epic poems universally associated with his name. To be sure, a number of "lives" of Homer are extant from Greek times, but their authority is subject to such grave suspicion that they have been rejected as unfounded fabrications. In both the *Iliad* and *Odyssey* the personality of the poet remains wholly concealed, since he does not speak in the first person or otherwise refer to himself as the plot develops or the narrative proceeds.

Portrait of Homer

It is arguable that in one incident of the *Odyssey* the poet may be giving a glimpse of himself in the guise of a bard whom he calls Demodokos and whom he introduces to the court of the Phaeacian king, where the shipwrecked Odysseus is being generously entertained. This Demodokos (whose name may be rendered "favored of the people") is described as a "divine singer to whom the god gave delight of singing whatever his soul prompted him." He is introduced by a herald to the gathering of young and old and is called an "honored minstrel whom the Muse befriends— yet she gave him both good and bad, in that she conferred on him sweet song but deprived him of his eyesight." (In antiquity there was a persistent belief that Homer was blind.) Then the herald "placed for him a silver-studded chair in the midst of the feasters, propping it against a tall column. And from a hook above his head he hung the clear-

toned lyre [phorminx] that he might reach it with his hand; and beside him he set a fair table and a basket of food and a cup of wine, that he might drink withal." And after the company had "partaken of food and put aside their desire of meat and drink," then "the Muse stirred the bard to sing of the deeds of men, whose fame has reached wide heaven, to wit, the quarrel between Odysseus and Pelead Achilles, how they wrangled with violent words at a sacred banquet." When Demodokos finishes his heroic tale, Odysseus is made to remark how singers such as he "are held in honor and respect by all mankind; for the Muse herself has taught them." And again, addressing Demodokos, he says, "I praise thee beyond all mortals: either the Muse, God's daughter, has taught thee, or Apollo; for thou singest most fitly and aright the destiny of the Greeks, the deeds that they wrought and suffered, and the hardships they endured. Either thou thyself must have been present or heard it all from another."

This is the nearest and clearest approach to a picture of Homer in the act of reciting his poetry of heroic happenings. This passage from the *Odyssey* seems to have been responsible for the widespread modern idea that in the Homeric Age there were bards attached to the courts of local kings, who declaimed to the accompaniment of the lyre in great baronial halls—a complete misestimate of the poverty-stricken social conditions of the period.

Evidence from the Epics

This lack of any contemporary historical record of Homer's life leaves only what can be deduced from the poems themselves. On this task much ingenuity has been expended by modern scholars, often without acceptable result.

The setting of the *Iliad* is the plain of Troy and its immediate environment. Topographic details are set forth with such precision that it is not feasible to suppose that their reciter created them out of his imagination without personal acquaintance with the locality. To be sure, there is the apparent objection that not all the action of the poem can be made to fit the present-day terrain. This difficulty arises, however, only when it is assumed that the prehistorical fortified citadel which Heinrich Schliemann uncovered at a site known today as Hissarlik was the city of Priam described by the *Iliad*. But during the intervening centuries between the abandonment of Mycenaean Troy and its resettlement by Greeks of the classical period there could have been nothing to suggest to a visitor such as Homer that the meager traces of buried walls still visible to him could have marked the proud and great city about which local legend still recounted a protracted siege and sack. The plausible suggestion has been made that the ruins projecting at Hissarlik were locally identified as described in the *Iliad* as "the high tumbled wall of Herakles, that the Trojans under Pallas Athena built for him that he might escape the sea monster when it pursued him landward from the beaches." If this suggestion is accepted and the site of the storied city is moved farther inland, the congruence of local detail of gushing springs and running rivers will do much to convince the skeptic that the poet of the *Iliad* must have visited the Trojan plain and learned its topography from personal inspection.

Much the same conclusion results from a passage in the thirteenth chapter (or "book") of the *Iliad,* in which it is recounted how the sea-god Poseidon seated himself on the highest peak of the island of Samothrace "whence all Ida was visible and the city of Priam and the ships of the Achaeans." A map of the Aegean Sea will show that the direct line of sight between Samothrace and the Troad is blocked by the intervening island of Imbros, but the modern visitor to Troy discovers that the sharp 5,000-foot peak of Samothrace is visible over a notched shoulder of Imbros. Therefore when Homer put Poseidon "on the topmost peak of wooded Samos," he must have known that the god could have seen Troy because he himself had seen and remembered that from Troy one could see the peak of Samothrace.

In the *Odyssey* the situation is in many respects quite different. Although the poet demonstrably knew the western Greek island of Ithaca (where the second half of the epic is staged) as intimately as the poet of the *Iliad* knew the plain of Troy, the *Odyssey* elsewhere extends over many strange distant lands as Odysseus's homeward voyage from Troy to his native Ithaca is transformed into a weird sea-wandering from adventure to dreadful adventure—first to the land of the indolent Lotus-eaters, thence to the cave of the giant one-eyed Cyclops, thereafter to the island of Aiolos, king of the winds, and the harbor of the savage Laistrygones, and Circe's bewitched isle, to be followed by a visit to the underworld of dead souls, and finally past the fateful singing Sirens and between the sea beast Scylla and the vast whirlpool of Charybdis to the uttermost western land where the sun-god pastures his cattle.

Perhaps misled by the minute accuracy with which the Trojan plain is described in the *Iliad* and the island of Ithaca is pictured in the *Odyssey,* various modern commentators have attempted to impose the same topographic realism on Odysseus's astonishing voyage, selecting actual sites in the western Mediterranean for his adventures. But the true situation must be that the Homer of the *Odyssey* had never visited that part of the ancient world but had listened to the yarns of returning Ionian sailors such as explored the western seas during the 7th century B.C. and had fused these with ancient folktales that were the inheritance of all the Indo-European races.

Theory of Two Authors

That the author of the *Iliad* was not the same as the compiler of these fantastic tales in the *Odyssey* is arguable on several scores. The two epics belong to different literary types; the *Iliad* is essentially dramatic in its confrontation of opposing warriors who converse like the actors in Attic tragedy, while the *Odyssey* is cast as a novel narrated in more everyday human speech. In their physical structure, also, the two epics display an equally pronounced difference. The *Odyssey* is composed in six distinct cantos of four chapters ("books") each, whereas the *Iliad* moves unbrokenly forward with only one irrelevant episode in its tightly woven plot. Readers who examine psychological nuances see in the two works some distinctly different human responses and behavioral attitudes. For example, the *Iliad* voices admiration for the beauty and speed of horses, while the *Odyssey* shows no interest in these animals. The *Iliad* dismisses dogs as mere scavengers, while the poet of the *Odyssey* reveals a modern sentimental sympathy for Odysseus's faithful old hound, Argos.

But the most cogent argument for separating the two poems by assigning them to different authors is the archeological criterion of implied chronology. In the *Iliad* the Phoenicians are praised as skilled craftsmen working in metal and weavers of elaborate, much-prized garments. The shield which the metalworking god Hephaistos forges for Achilles in the *Iliad* seems inspired by the metal bowls with inlaid figures in action made by the Phoenicians and introduced by them into Greek and Etruscan commerce in the 8th century B.C. In contrast, in the *Odyssey* Greek sentiment toward the Phoenicians has undergone a drastic change. Although they are still regarded as clever craftsmen, in place of the *Iliad*'s laudatory *polydaidaloi* ("of manifold skills") the epithet is parodied into *polypaipaloi* ("of manifold scurvy tricksters"), reflecting the competitive penetration into Greek commerce by traders from Phoenician Carthage in the 7th century B.C. Other internal evidence indicates that the *Odyssey* was composed later than the *Iliad*.

Oral Composition

One thing, however, is certain: both epics were created without recourse to writing. Between the decline of Mycenaean and the emergence of classical Greek civilization—which is to say, from the late 12th to the mid-8th century B.C.—the inhabitants of the Greek lands had lost all knowledge of the syllabic script of their Mycenaean forebears and had not yet acquired from the easternmost shore of the Mediterranean that familiarity with Phoenician alphabetic writing from which classical Greek literacy (and in turn, Etruscan, Roman, and modern European literacy) derived. The same conclusion of illiterate composition may be reached from a critical inspection of the poems themselves. Among many races and in many different periods there has existed (and still exists sporadically) a form of purely oral and unwritten poetic speech, distinguishable from normal and printed literature by special traits that are readily recognizable and specifically distinctive. To this class the Homeric epics conform. Hence it would seem an inevitable inference that they must have been created either before the end of the 8th century B.C. or so shortly after that date that the use of alphabetic writing had not yet been developed sufficiently to record lengthy compositions. It is this illiterate environment that explains the absence of all contemporary historical record of the authors of the two great epics.

It is probable that Homer's name was applied to two distinct individuals differing in temperament and artistic accomplishment, born perhaps as much as a century apart, but practicing the same traditional craft of oral composition and recitation. Although each became known as "Homer," it may be (as one ancient source asserts) that *homros* was a dialectical Ionic word for a blind man and so came to be used generically of the old and often sightless wandering

reciters of heroic legends in the traditional meter of unrhymed dactylic hexameters. Thus there could have been many Homers. The two epics ascribed to Homer, however, have been as highly prized in modern as in ancient times for their marvelous vividness of expression, their keenness of personal characterization, their unflagging interest, whether in narration of action or in animated dramatic dialogue.

Other Works

Later Greek times credited Homer with the composition of a group of comparatively short "hymns" addressed to various gods, of which 23 have survived. On internal evidence, however, only one or two of these at most can be the work of the poet of the two great epics. The burlesque epic *The Battle of the Frogs and Mice* has been preserved but adds nothing to Homer's reputation. Several other epic poems of considerable length—the *Cypria,* the *Little Iliad,* the *Phocais,* the *Thebais,* the *Capture of Oichalia*—were widely ascribed to Homer in classical times. None of these has survived except in stray quoted verses. But even if they were preserved in full, it is highly doubtful whether modern scholarship would accept them as all by the same author. The simple truth seems to be that the name Homer was not so much that of a single individual as a personification for an entire school of poets flourishing on the west coast of Asia Minor during the period before the art of writing had been sufficiently developed by the Greeks to permit historical records to be compiled or literary compositions to be written down.

Further Reading

Excellent translations of Homer are Richmond Latimore's *Iliad* (1962) and *Odyssey* (1967) and Robert Fitzgerald's *Odyssey* (1961). The literature on Homer and his age is vast. A useful guide is John L. Myres, *Homer and His Critics,* edited by Dorothea Gray (1958). Since little is definitely known about the authorship of the Homeric poems, all studies on their origin are subject to controversy. Representing the view that, because of similarities, the *Iliad* and *Odyssey* were written by one man are the studies of Adam Scott, *The Unity of Homer* (1921) and *Homer and His Influence* (1930), which surveys what is known about Homer. Working from archeological evidence, Hilda Lockhart Lorimer, *Homer and the Monuments* (1950), concludes that the two poems were written by different men. Examining the poems in the tradition of oral literature, Rhys Carpenter, *Folk Tale, Fiction and Saga in the Homeric Epics* (1946), suggests that the poems began as oral literature; while Albert Bates Lord, *The Singer of Tales* (1960), contends that Homer was not an original writer but a singer of folktales. Homer's work is viewed as an aspect of the Greek genius in Gilbert Murray's classic study *The Rise of the Greek Epic* (1907).

Other useful studies include M. P. Nilsson, *Homer and Mycenae* (1933), a reconstruction of the historical background of the poems; S. E. Bassett, *The Poetry of Homer* (1938); Henry T. Wade-Gery, *The Poet of the Iliad* (1952); Cedric H. Whitman, *Homer and the Homeric Tradition* (1958); and Denys L. Page, *History and the Homeric Iliad* (1959), a detailed survey of the research on the *Iliad*. Cecil Maurice Bowra, *The Greek Experience* (1957), is recommended for background. □

Winslow Homer

Winslow Homer (1836-1910), a pioneer in naturalistic painting of the American scene, was the most versatile American artist of his period, with the widest range of subjects, styles, and mediums.

Of long New England ancestry, Winslow Homer was born in Boston on Feb. 24, 1836. Growing up in nearby Cambridge, he had an active outdoor boyhood that gave him a lifelong love of the country. From youth he was independent, and terse in speech, with a dry Yankee humor. He was almost entirely self-taught. About the age of 19 he was apprenticed to a Boston lithographer, but as soon as he became 21 he launched himself as an illustrator, especially for *Harper's Weekly* in New York.

Moving to New York in 1859, Homer free-lanced for *Harper's,* studied briefly at the National Academy of Design, and took a few private lessons in painting. During the Civil War he went to the Virginia front several times for *Harper's.* His illustrations of the 1860s and 1870s, notable for their realism, strong draftsmanship, and fine design, rank among the best graphic art of their time in America.

But an illustrator's career did not satisfy Homer. In 1862 he produced his first adult paintings. After the war he turned to the subject matter he always preferred, contemporary country life: summer resorts with their fashionable, comely young women; the simpler life of the farm; and the joys of childhood in the country. These early works, combining utter fidelity to the native scene with reserved idyllic poetry, form the most authentic and delightful pictorial record of rural America in the 1860s and 1870s.

From the first, Homer's work was based on direct observation of nature. Disregarding traditional styles, he put down his firsthand visual sensations of outdoor light and color. This fresh vision was combined with an instinctive feeling for decorative values and the sensuous qualities of color, line, and pigment. In these respects his work paralleled early French impressionism, but without any possible influence. Not until he was 30 did he go abroad, in late 1866, for 10 months in France, not studying but painting on his own. This experience had relatively little influence on his art.

In 1873 Homer took up a new medium, watercolor, which proved perfectly suited to his basically graphic style and which soon became as important to him as oil. Probably because of the modest success of his watercolors, after 1875 he gave up illustrating, except occasionally.

A decisive change in Homer's career came in 1881 and 1882, when he spent two seasons in England, near Tynemouth, a fishing port on the stormy North Sea. Working almost entirely in watercolor, he first began to picture the sea and the hardy men and women who made their living on it. These watercolors showed a new seriousness and depth of feeling and a great technical advance in atmospheric quality, deeper color, and rounder modeling.

In 1883 Homer left New York for good and settled in a lonely spot on the Maine coast, Prout's Neck. On the rocky shore he built a studio which was his home for the rest of his life. He lived alone, doing his own cooking and housework; he sometimes remained through the hard Maine winters. Always reticent about personal matters, Homer never divulged his reasons for this withdrawal from civilization. There had been an unhappy love affair some years before, and he had never married. But regardless of this, he had found the subjects that meant most to him. There was no element of defeat in his withdrawal; his letters to his family prove that his way of living was genuinely satisfying. "The life that I have chosen," he once wrote, "gives me my full hours of enjoyment for the balance of my life. The Sun will not rise, or set, without my notice, and thanks."

From this time Homer's art changed fundamentally. His themes now were the sea, the forest, the mountains, and the lives of sailors, fishermen, and hunters. His style became sure, powerful, and skilled, and within a few years he had attained full maturity. The first fruits of this growth were a series of marine paintings, including *Eight Bells* and *The Fog Warning,* which are pictorial classics of the sea.

The success of his sea paintings led Homer to embark on a new medium, etching. Seven of the eight plates he etched between 1884 and 1889 were based on these paintings and his English watercolors, but with changes that make them among the best designed of any of his works, and among the strongest 19th-century American prints. However, they failed to sell, and he abandoned etching after 1889.

As the years passed at Prout's Neck, Homer's dominant theme became the sea itself. It was the ocean at its stormiest that he loved. His marines take us right into the battlefront between sea and shore, making us feel the weight and movement of the wave, the solidity of the rock, the impact of their collision. In other moods they show us the radiance of dawn or sunset over the water. These marines are supreme expressions of the power, danger, and beauty of the sea.

Homer seldom discussed esthetic matters, and his few recorded statements express a straight naturalistic viewpoint. Although he once said; "When I have selected the thing carefully, I paint it exactly as it appears," his work itself gives ample evidence to the contrary. He simplified severely, concentrating on the large forms and movements. In his mature works, naturalism and decorative values achieved a synthesis; the balance of masses, the strong linear rhythms, and the robust earthy color harmonies were evidently the product of well-considered design.

Homer's purest artistic achievements, aside from his mature oils, were his later watercolors. Almost every year he and his elder brother Charles, both outdoor men, made camping visits to the northern woods—the Adirondacks and Quebec. Here Homer painted scores of watercolors which captured the unspoiled beauty of the wilderness with a vividness and force new in American painting. Their command of line and color and their unerring rightness of design present interesting parallels with the decorative values of Oriental art.

From the late 1890s Homer spent part of most winters in the Bahamas, Florida, or Bermuda. The West Indies revealed to him a new world of light and color. He romanticized the lives of blacks in the Bahamas in a series of superb watercolors that attained the highest brilliancy in all his work. These late watercolors, whether southern or northern, were the purest expressions of his visual delight in the external world. They contain the essence of his genius—the direct impact of nature on the artist's eye, recorded in all its purity by the hand of a master.

In old age Homer was generally considered the foremost painter living in America, and he received many honors. All his important oils were sold during his lifetime. None of this made any difference in the quantity or quality of his works or in his solitary way of living. He died at Prout's Neck on Sept. 29, 1910.

Homer was the greatest pictorial poet of outdoor life in 19th-century America. In his energy, his wide range, the pristine freshness of his vision, and his simple sensuous vitality, he expressed certain aspects of the American spirit as no preceding artist had.

Further Reading

Lloyd Goodrich, *Winslow Homer* (1944), based on Homer's letters, previously unpublished material, and a record of his works, is the most complete biography and critique. Albert Ten Eyck Gardner, *Winslow Homer: American Artist* (1961), presents interesting but questionable theories about Homer's relation to French and Japanese art. Philip C. Beam, *Winslow Homer at Prout's Neck* (1966), includes new, firsthand information on his life in Maine. James Thomas Flexner, *The World of Winslow Homer* (1966), places him in the context of American art of his period. Special aspects of his art are covered in Lloyd Goodrich, *The Graphic Art of Winslow Homer* (1968) and *Winslow Homer's America* (1969), and in Donelson F. Hoopes, *Winslow Homer Watercolors* (1969).

Additional Sources

Cikovsky, Nicolai, *Winslow Homer,* New York: Abrams, 1990.

Downes, William Howe, *The life and works of Winslow Homer,* New York, B. Franklin 1974; New York: Dover Publications, 1989.

Hendricks, Gordon, *The life and work of Winslow Homer,* New York: H. N. Abrams, 1979. □

Soichiro Honda

A maverick in a country not known for its willingness to accept nonconformists, Soichiro Honda (1906-1991) created an automobile giant despite the opposition of the Japanese government. One of his company's cars, the Accord, was a best-selling model in the American market.

The first son of blacksmith Gihei Honda and his wife Mika, Soichiro Honda was born on November 17, 1906, in rural Iwata-gun, Japan. In 1922 he graduated from the Futamata Senior Elementary School and began his career as an apprentice auto repairman for Arto Shokai, after which he established a branch shop for the firm in Hamamatsu. Honda also participated in auto races and became interested in cars and motorcycles. Soon he was experimenting with engines, and in 1928 he organized the Tohai Seiki Company to manufacture piston rings, some of which were sold to Toyota. During the 1930s it seemed his would become one of the hundreds of small shops that supplied the major companies in what still was a small domestic market.

Honda's business thrived during World War II, and after the war he tried to enter the personal motor business, a difficult task since the industry was virtually nonexistent. Realizing this, he designed and manufactured a small engine that could be attached to a bicycle to create a motorbike. The venture proved a great success. Encouraged, in 1948 he organized the Honda Motor Company. In the following year Honda manufactured a small motorcycle called the "Dream D" and prepared to enter the highly competitive (more than 20 firms at the time) Japanese market.

Once again Honda did well, also invading foreign markets effectively. This was made possible through his advertising campaign, in which he altered the image of motorcycling, then widely perceived as a rough way to travel for young males and identified with gangs. Hondas were advertised as a proper vehicle for middle-class individ-

uals of both sexes and all ages. Because of this, within a decade Honda was the leading motorcycle manufacturer in the world and had a larger share of the American motorcycle market than Toyota and Nissan (with its Datsun cars) had in automobiles.

Now Soichiro Honda attracted press attention, and, unlike most Japanese businessmen, he loved it. A small, individualistic, loquacious man, he was the antithesis of what westerners imagined Japanese tycoons to be. For example, he promoted executives on the basis of performance rather than age, an unusual practice at large Japanese firms. Honda continued racing autos and motorcycles, wore slacks and red shirts to work, and took pride in maintaining his independence from the Japanese business establishment. He was quite democratic in his approach. "I associate with anybody—rich, poor, it doesn't make a difference. I prefer to have the principle of egalitarianism rather than a class distinction of people," he told a reporter, and this could be seen in his free and easy way of living. Honda openly voiced his admiration of American business practices and way of life. In fact, there are few large Japanese companies more American in style than Honda.

Honda branched out into other industries in the late 1950s. In 1958 he brought out a successful electric generator, but, more important, considered entry into the automobile industry.

This was a time when the powerful Ministry of Trade and Industry (MITI) was trying to unite several small companies into a third large one to compete with Toyota and Nissan. MITI and the Department of Transportation tried to dissuade Honda from adding to the number of companies, but he persisted. The government and he were at odds ever thereafter. "Probably I would have been even more successful had we not had MITI," he said. "MITI was incapable of making automobiles, but I was."

He won MITI's grudging permission by coming out with a very low-priced small sportscar, the S 500, which was different from anything produced by the other companies. He followed it up with other sports models. His company was still very small. In 1966 Honda produced 3,000 cars, half of what Toyota was turning out in a week.

That year Honda tested the international market by sending its sportscar, the S 800, to Europe. It was not popular. This was followed by forays into the minicar market, which in Japan traditionally was for first car buyers, and experienced another relative failure. Meanwhile, research on new engines produced the compound vortex controlled combustion engine (CVCC), based on a dual combustion chamber, which produced significantly less pollution and greater fuel economy than any other than in production.

Honda sent his cars to America in 1970. The N 600 was far too small to attract many buyers, and the same was true of its successor, the AN 600. But its CVCC engine met all of the Environmental Protection Agency's requirements at a time when other cars had to use expensive and initially inefficient pollution control devices.

Honda introduced the Civic to the American market in 1972. It was smaller than all other Japanese models sold in the United States, but, at a time when gasoline prices were starting to rise, it got 39 miles per gallon (mpg) on the road and 27 mpg in city driving. It did better than the earlier Hondas, but in that year only 20,500 sedans were sold. However, the consistently improved model sold more units each year in the 1970s. In 1980 Honda sold 375,000 cars in the American market, almost three times as many as Subaru and twice as many as Mazda but behind Toyota and Nissan.

The reasons for this success were obvious. Honda combined high quality with efficiency and economy. But his small cars still appealed to a limited market.

Always a maverick in the Japanese industry, Honda was the first to accept the idea of manufacturing in the United States. Part of the reason was his perception of the coming market for automobiles. Honda felt that in time the Americans might clamp down on imports, so he wanted to make certain he had production facilities in the United States which would enable him to escape such restrictions. Then too, he knew there was no possibility of taking leadership of the Japanese auto industry from Toyota and Nissan, so the logical place to seek sales was in Europe and the Americas.

In the late 1970s and early 1980s Honda set out to transform his car into a major exporter and producer overseas. He planned to become a true multinational or transnational, highly unusual for a Japanese company at that time. Honda succeeded admirably. In 1979 it opened a plant near Columbus, Ohio, to produce motorcycles, and an auto plant followed soon after, prompting other Japanese companies to follow his lead. In the late 1970s Toyota and Nissan sold one-third of their cars to the United States, while Honda sold half of his in that market.

Honda Motors also enlarged the Civic to the point where it was approximately the same as the Toyota and Datsun and introduced successfully the larger Accord and sporty Prelude.

Soichiro Honda did not directly supervise these introductions or the development of overseas plants in the United States and Europe. He resigned in 1973, but stayed at the company as "supreme adviser." In 1988 he became the first Japanese carmaker to be inducted into the Automobile Hall of Fame. Honda died of liver failure August 5, 1991, in a Tokyo hospital.

Further Reading

There are two biographies of Soichiro Honda: Sol Sanders, *Honda: The Man and His Machine* (1975) and Tetsuo Sakiya, *Honda Motor: The Man, the Management, and the Machines* (1982). Also see Joel Kotkin, "Mr. Iacocca, Meet Mr. Honda," *Inc.* (November 1986); Lawrence M. Miller, "The Honda Way," *Executive Excellence* (March 1988); Ernest Raia, "The Americanization of Honda," *Purchasing* (March 22, 1990); and Gary S. Vasilash, "Honda Is World-Class in Ohio," *Production* (July 1988). For an overview of the Japanese automobile industry and its competition, see Robert Sobel, *Car Wars: The Battle for Global Supremacy* (1984). □

Erich Honecker

A German Communist Party leader, Erich Honecker (1912-1994) was instrumental in establishing a Communist government in East Germany after World War II (East Germany was reunited with West Germany in 1990). He became general secretary of the Communist Party in East Germany and head of the German Democratic Republic in 1971 until 1989.

Erich Honecker was born on August 25, 1912, to a working-class family in Neunkirchen, in the Saar province. He grew up in a strongly Communist milieu. His father was a militant coal miner who joined the Communist Party after it was founded in 1918. He spent his youth in Wiebelskirchen, which voted heavily for the Communists. Honecker joined the Communist Party's children's group in 1922 and its youth organization (KJVD) in 1926. His upbringing, youthful experiences, and early intellectual development convinced him that Communism was the solution to the troubles of the working class and that the Soviet Union (now Russia/The Commonwealth of Independent States) was the best friend of all Communist movements. Despite the imposition of a restrictive form of Communism upon Eastern Germany by the Soviet Union after 1945, Honecker never changed his mind about these two basic ideas. He gave his life to German communism.

Honecker finished high school in 1926. University study was out of the question for the son of a coal miner in those days, so he worked on a farm for two years. Returning to Wiebelskirchen, he became a roofer's apprentice. Honecker's most important work, however, was for the Communist Party, where his sober dedication and organizational skills were rewarded. In 1928 he became head of the local youth group. In 1930 the party offered him his only opportunity for formal study, at a party school in Moscow. By 1934 he was a member of the KJVD's central committee.

The Nazis outlawed the German Communist Party in 1933, but Honecker continued to fight against them. Because the Saar was separated from Germany by the Versailles Treaty of 1919, he could work there openly until a plebiscite in 1935 reunited it with Germany. When an acquaintance admired his courage in agitating against the Nazis despite certain reprisals after the plebiscite, Honecker replied it was simply his conviction, not any special courage. Forced to flee to France after the vote, he reentered Germany in the fall under a false passport to lead the illegal Communist youth organization in Berlin. The Gestapo arrested him in December 1935, and in 1937 he was sentenced to life imprisonment. He was freed by the Soviet Army in 1945.

After the war Honecker participated enthusiastically in building a new state in eastern Germany according to the Soviet model of socialism. He held leadership positions beginning in 1946 and was one of those responsible for turning the ideas of German communism into a state run by one party, the Socialist Unity Party (SED), in which the leaders determine and satisfy the interests of the populations as they see fit. In 1950 he became a member of the SED's Central Committee. A co-founder of the Free German Youth, he headed that organization from 1946 to 1955. He spent 1955 and 1956 studying security issues in Moscow, returning to play an increasingly important role within the party. By 1960 he was a full member of the Politburo, with responsibility for security and military questions. When Walter Ulbricht resigned in 1971, the party elected Honecker its general secretary, effectively making him head of state.

Honecker's policies bore both similarities and differences to those of Ulbricht. The SED still dominated the government and continued to forbid public criticism of its policies. In the most spectacular example of this, during 1976 and 1977 many artists who had protested the party's restrictions on artistic freedom lost their citizenship and were forced to emigrate to the West. The German Democratic Republic (GDR) also remained closely tied to the Soviet Union: 70 percent of the GDR's trade in 1980, for example, was with the U.S.S.R. and its socialist allies. Although Honecker mentioned the advantages of superpower negotiations perhaps more than the Soviet leadership wished, he supported the Soviet Union publicly on every issue.

Honecker's leadership differed in his emphasis on the material needs of the working class. Arguing that class differences still existed in the GDR, he began a program to improve the "well-being of people." In 1976 the SED increased the minimum wage and raised retirement benefits. In 1977 it shortened the working day for shift workers. Perhaps most important, in 1973 the party began a massive program to construct three million low-cost apartments.

During the 1970s détente between the United States and the Soviet Union provided a favorable climate for the improvement of relations between the German states. Honecker signed three treaties with the Federal Republic of Germany (FRG). The "Transit Agreement" and "Traffic Treaty" of 1972 facilitated trade and travel between the two countries. In the "Fundamentals Treaty" of 1973 the two countries agreed on the "inviolability of borders" and "respect for territorial integrity and sovereignty." Honecker achieved further recognition of the GDR's sovereign status through his position as signatory to the 1975 Helsinki accords. Trade with the West, and especially with the FRG, which these accords made possible, helped the East German economy and thus Honecker's program to improve citizens' well-being. The provisions which allowed freer travel were also widely popular in the GDR, especially because they allowed greater contact among family members separated by the border.

Further improvement in the relations between the GDR and FRG seemed unlikely. Honecker linked further concessions about travel with recognition of GDR citizenship, which the West German government refused. Tensions between the superpowers also reduced Honecker's freedom to make new overtures. After 1982 Helmut Kohl's new government in West Germany stressed anti-communism and German reunification rather than coexistence. Honecker appeared to want to retain good relations, but canceled a trip to the FRG in the fall of 1984 after hostile comments from conservative West German politicians, and, it was widely speculated, pressure from the Soviet Union.

Domestically, Honecker's greatest problems were economic. His campaign for economic improvement raised hopes in the GDR, but world-wide recessions made their fulfillment more difficult. Hopes for greater freedom to visit relatives in the West were threatened by stagnation in relations between the two governments. Honecker was expected to continue to seek rapprochement with the FRG, for diplomatic and economic reasons, but to pursue this only insofar as it could be reconciled with Soviet foreign policy. Not only was the GDR dependent upon the Soviet Union economically and militarily, but Erich Honecker remained loyal to the Soviet model of Communism.

Following the reunion of East and West Germany in 1990, Honecker was arrested on charges of treason and manslaughter and stayed in Moscow Hospital until 1991, when he sought asylum through the Chilean Embassy in Moscow. He was later charged with 13 counts of manslaughter for ordering the shooting of persons attempting to escape the German Democratic Republic, and was deported to Germany. Trial began in November, 1992, but was discontinued under controversy in January, 1993. Honecker was released and fled to Chile. He died there in exile at the age of 81 in May, 1994.

Further Reading

Honecker's autobiography, *From My Life* (Oxford 1980; Pergamon 1981), discusses all stages of his life. The last chapter contains an interview with a Western publisher. □

Arthur Honegger

Although Arthur Honegger (1892-1955) was a Swiss composer, he was identified with France because of his long residence in Paris. He was a middle-of-the-road 20th-century composer; as a result, some of his compositions were immediately popular.

Arthur Honegger was born in Le Havre, France, where his Swiss father was a coffee importer. The family was cultured and encouraged their son's interest in music by giving him violin and harmony lessons, studies that were continued at the Zurich Conservatory (1909-1911). In 1911 he commuted once a week from Le Havre to Paris to study violin at the conservatory and in 1913 became a full-time student.

This was an exciting time for a young musician to be in Paris, and Honegger plunged into the musical stream, attending the ballet and opera and becoming acquainted with the new works of Claude Debussy, Maurice Ravel, and Igor Stravinsky. Because of his study in Switzerland, his musical orientation had been German; Richard Wagner, Richard Strauss, and Max Reger had been his models, and he never really abandoned them even when he became influenced

by the newer French music. Darius Milhaud was his classmate at the conservatory and introduced him to a group of young composers; in 1920 they gave a joint concert of their works. The critic who reviewed the concert entitled his article "The Russian Five and the French Six," referring to the great school of Russian nationalistic composers and to Honegger and his friends—Milhaud, Francis Poulenc, Germaine Tailleferre, Louis Durey, and Georges Auric. The label stuck, and for the rest of their lives these composers never lived down the association, no matter how divergent their mature styles became. The term "Les Six" connoted an attitude that was antiromantic and which held that music should not take itself too seriously. "Down with Wagner. Down with Beethoven," they said. "Let's have music that is clever and gay, as simple as the music of the street."

Honegger never shared these views. On the contrary, he said: "My great model is J. S. Bach. I do not seek, as do some anti-impressionist composers, a return to harmonic simplicity. I find, on the contrary, that we should use the harmonic materials created by the school that preceded us, but in a different way, as the base for lines and rhythms. Bach availed himself of the elements of tonal harmony, as I want to avail myself of modern harmony. I am not a party to the cult of the Music Hall and the Street Fair, but on the contrary I am dedicated to chamber music and symphonic music in their most serious and austere aspects."

Honegger was fascinated by sports and machinery. Two of his early compositions, *Pacific 231* (1923), a vivid description of a powerful locomotive starting, accelerating, and stopping, and *Rugby* (1928), a description of a football game, were instantly popular. Another early work that brought him recognition was his oratorio *King David* (1923), a large-scale work for chorus, soloists, orchestra, and a narrator, who provides continuity between the musical numbers. Based on the biblical story of David, Honegger's score includes pseudo-Oriental orchestral pieces and Bach-style choruses, along with dissonant harmonies. The total effect is rich and brilliant. Other large-scale choral works include *Jeanne d'Arc aux bûcher* (1938; *Joan of Arc at the Stake*), which is sometimes staged in operatic manner, and *The Dance of Death* (1940). *Antigone* (1927) is an austere one-act opera. He also wrote chamber music and five symphonies, the fifth commissioned and first performed by the Boston Symphony in 1952.

Honegger stated his creed as a composer: "My desire and my endeavor have always been to write music which would be attractive to the large masses of listeners and which would, at the same time, be sufficiently devoid of banalities to interest music lovers." Certain of his compositions succeed in achieving this balance, and Honegger was one of the most successful composers of his generation.

Further Reading

There is no book-length study of Honegger in English, but a series of interviews with him has been translated as *I Am a Composer* (1966). Honegger is considered in these discussions of contemporary music: David Ewen, ed., *The New Book of Modern Composers* (1943; 3d rev. ed. 1964), and Ewen's own work, *The World of Twentieth-Century Music* (1968); Howard Hartog, ed., *European Music in the Twentieth Century*

(1957); Peter S. Hansen, *An Introduction to Twentieth Century Music* (1961); Joseph Machlis, *Introduction to Contemporary Music* (1961); and A. L. Bacharach, ed., *The Music Masters,* vol. 4 (1970). □

Honen

The Japanese Buddhist monk Honen (1133-1212) is considered the real founder of Japanese Amidism in the form of the Pure Land sect, or Jodoshu.

Honen was the son of an official of Mimasaka Province whose dying wish was that Honen become a monk. Honen began his studies at the great Tendai center on Mt. Hiei. Ordained, he withdrew to the outskirts of Kyoto to lead a solitary life of meditation and contemplation. Dissatisfied with religion as he had learned it, he wanted to break with traditional religious observance. It was only in 1175, when he was 43, that he began to teach his beliefs.

In 1198 Honen formalized his ideas in the *Senchakushu,* an abbreviated title which, rendered in full, means "Collection of Passages on the Original Vow of Amida, in Which the Nembutsu Is Chosen above All Other Ways of Achieving Rebirth." In this work, Honen made it clear that the *nembutsu,* or the calling of Amida's name for his aid, was superior to all other forms of religious practice. One was saved not through one's own efforts (*jiriki*) but through the compassionate mercy of another (*tariki*), that is, Amida. Traditional methods of salvation relied on severe personal disciplines that ultimately led to enlightenment; these he called the Path of Holiness (*shodo*) and the Path of the Pure Land (*jodo*), as the heaven over which Amida presided was called. To attain the Pure Land all that was necessary was the invocation of Amida's name and complete dependence on his mercy. It was felt that for most men the Path of Holiness was beyond their capacities and that hope for salvation thus lay in the second path, which was bound to be successful since it stood beyond personal jurisdiction.

This book was written for the edification of the premier, Fujiwara Kanezane; but when it came out, it provoked the harshest of criticisms from the monks of Mt. Hiei, who destroyed all the copies they could set their hands on. They felt that Honen was turning against Tendai teachings, and he was accused of moral laxity as well.

In 1207, as a result of a misunderstanding with the emperor Toba II, Honen was exiled to Tosa. He remained there only 10 months but was not permitted to return to the capital until 1211. He died in March 1212.

Further Reading

Excerpts of Honen's writings are in *The Buddhist Tradition in India, China, and Japan,* edited by William Theodore de Bary (1969). The most authoritative treatment in a Western language of Honen's life is Harper H. Coates and Ryugaku Ishizuka, *Honen the Buddhist Saint: His Life and Teaching* (1925). See also Mamine Ishii, *A Short Life of Honen* (1932). Alfred Bloom, *Shinran's Gospel of Pure Grace* (1965), contains pertinent material on Amidism.

Additional Sources

Honen the Buddhist saint, New York: Garland, 1981. □

Pieter de Hooch

The paintings of middle-class Dutch interiors by the Dutch artist Pieter de Hooch (1629-after 1684) are prized both for the vision of the serenity and order of the life they portray and for their qualities of abstract organization.

Born in Rotterdam in 1629, Pieter de Hooch, or Hoogh, was employed in 1653 as a "servant" and "painter" by a cloth merchant who had homes in both Delft and Leiden and who by 1655 owned 10 paintings by De Hooch. His early works were mainly crowded scenes of the activities of soldiers in their leisure time. In 1654 De Hooch was said to be living in his native city. That year he married a Delft girl, and the following year he was a member of the Delft guild.

De Hooch's best works were painted during his residence in Delft, roughly in the years between 1655 and 1662. They clearly belong to the Delft school, with marked resemblances to the mature works of Jan Vermeer. De Hooch's earliest dated pictures are from 1658, and they show him at the height of his powers. His mastery of elaborate spatial construction is exemplified in the *Card Players* (1658), where the rectangles of architectural details and furnishings form an abstract pattern in which figures are placed with an effect of the most satisfying equilibrium. The view from the interior to outside areas in this painting is the kind of problem in space representation that characterized De Hooch's works of his Delft period.

The interrelations between De Hooch and his great contemporary in Delft, Vermeer, are not fully understood. They obviously shared an interest in the representation of interior space with figures. De Hooch's style differs from Vermeer's in that his light and colors are warmer, his spatial constructions tend to be more complex, and his figures lack the monumental three-dimensionality of Vermeer's. The faces that De Hooch paints are particularly lacking in conviction; they are weak in both form and characterization.

In the 1660s and 1670s De Hooch lived and worked in Amsterdam. He gradually adopted a more upper-class orientation, with greater emphasis on the elaboration of decoration and costumes. From the later 1660s on his paintings were cold and dry and not above the level of achievement of his generally prosaic followers.

The latest date De Hooch inscribed on a painting was 1684. How long he lived after that and where he died are unknown.

Further Reading

The best study of De Hooch is in German. In English see C. H. Collins Baker, *Pieter de Hooch* (1925), and N. Maclaren, *The Dutch School* (National Gallery Catalogues; 1960).

Additional Sources

Sutton, Peter C., *Pieter de Hooch,* Ithaca, N.Y.: Cornell University Press, 1980. □

Sidney Hook

The philosopher Sidney Hook (1902-1989) was an exponent of classical American pragmatism. He brought the method of intelligence to bear on social issues, education, ethics, and philosophy itself.

Sidney Hook was born on December 20, 1902, to Issac and Jennie Hook. He studied at the City College of New York (BA) and at Columbia University (MA, Ph.D.). While at Columbia Hook studied with John Dewey. Without doubt Hook was the most distinguished of Dewey's students and one of the best exponents of classical American pragmatism. He lectured at universities throughout the United States and after 1927 taught in various capacities at New York University. Hook served as the head of the Department of Philosophy of New York University from 1948 to 1969, during which time he founded the New York University Institute of Philosophy.

Widely recognized for his contributions to philosophy, Hook received numerous honorary degrees and served as a president of the American Philosophical Association, East Division (1959-1960) and as a fellow of the American Academy of Arts and Sciences as well as of the National Academy of Education. Hook's insistence that philosophy address the affairs of life involved him in issues well beyond the confines of academic philosophy. For these contributions he also won distinction, receiving the Presidential Medal of Freedom in 1985. After 1973 he was a senior research fellow at the Hoover Institution, Stanford University, until his death in 1989.

Hook described his thought as pragmatic naturalism, experimentalism, or "the philosophy of pragmatism in the tradition of Charles Sanders Pierce and John Dewey." In essence, his philosophical approach amounts to the applying of the method of science, or experimentalism, to all domains of thought and life. This pragmatic method does not mean a rigid scientism denying all valuative dimensions of experience. In fact, Hook argued that warranted assertions can be made about matters of value as well as of fact. Accordingly, Hook stressed the importance of creative intelligence in thought and action. Such creative thought, however, must be informed and guided by a scientific method.

Hook argued, as William James did, that humans live in an "open universe" and thus play a creative role in the building of a social world and transforming the natural environment. Neither humanity nor its universe is closed, determined, or finished. Hook held this conviction to be crucial to an experimental view of the world, and it pitted him against all forms of determinism. He challenged the cogency of Marxist historical materialism, religious predestination, and forms of quietism. The demand placed on humans in an open universe, as Hook saw it, is to respond to concrete situations through informed thought and action. Of course, humans are not absolutely free; life takes place in relation to others and to the natural and social world. Nevertheless, there remains the capacity and demand for humans to act freely in their world.

The close relation of thought and action is another mark of Hook's thought, as it is of all forms of pragmatism. For Hook, ideas, whatever else they may be, were guides for action that were to be used in critical engagement with the affairs of life. They must be tested by their ability to inform further thought and action. This experimental testing of ideas against the demands and needs of experience is what Hook specifically meant by the scientific method. Not surprisingly, he saw experimentalism as the most adequate way to guide and test human thinking and doing in the quest to make a better world.

Hook applied his pragmatic naturalism to a wide array of philosophical and social issues. In his earliest work, *The Metaphysics of Pragmatism* (1927), he addressed fundamental issues in pragmatic philosophy itself. In his *The Quest of Being* (1961) he challenged many philosophical assumptions about the character of Being itself and the task of philosophy by bringing the pragmatic method to bear on the problems of ontology. Hook was also one of the first to introduce Marx to the American philosophical world. As early as 1933, in *Towards the Understanding of Karl Marx,* he explored the importance, relevance, and problems of Marxist thought. Social philosophy remained an abiding concern of his and was later voiced in *Marxism and Beyond* (1983) and *Out of Step: An Unquiet Life in the 20th Century* (1987). Hook was not, however, a Marxist thinker, since he rejected the theory of historical materialism and all determinist interpretations of it. He described himself as a social democrat. Besides these philosophical and social applications of his thought, Hook's writings covered such diverse topics as religion (*Religion in a Free Society,* 1967), education (*Education and the Taming of Power,* 1973), and constitutional problems (*Common Sense and the Fifth Amendment,* 1957). His list of publications is monumental, demonstrating the vitality and breadth of his thought.

Hook consistently claimed that philosophy is "the quest for wisdom." The philosopher's task is not to advocate specific policies or plans of action. Rather, the thinker is to employ the method of intelligence in order to define, clarify, and evaluate the social problems confronting us. Again, like Dewey, Hook understood philosophy as normative social criticism. As a normative discipline, it asks about truth and goodness; as social criticism, it explores the basic issues and problems of social existence. By rigorously practicing this idea of philosophy Hook made an enduring contribution to American thought and life. He made his home in Stanford, California, but was buried in South Wardston, Vermont, following his death on July 12, 1989.

Further Reading

For helpful works on Hook's thought see *Sidney Hook and the Contemporary World: Essays on the Pragmatic Intelligence* (1968) and also *Sidney Hook: Philosopher of Democracy and Humanism* (1983), both edited by Paul Kurtz. Hook's autobiography *Out of Step: An Unquiet Life in the 20th Century,* was published in 1987. ☐

Robert Hooke

The English physicist Robert Hooke (1635-1703) was one of the most ingenious and versatile experimenters of all time.

Robert Hooke, the son of a clergyman in Freshwater on the Isle of Wight, was born on July 18, 1635. He was too sickly for regular schooling until he was 13, when, left an orphan with a modest inheritance, he entered Westminster School. Later he earned his way as a chorister at Christ Church, Oxford, and attended Westminster College, graduating with his master's degree in 1663. Hooke remained at Oxford, where he became assistant to Robert Boyle. Together they conducted many experiments on the effects of reduced air pressure, using an air pump that had been designed and constructed by Hooke.

In 1662 Hooke became curator of the newly founded Royal Society, his duties being to produce three or four

significant experimental demonstrations for each weekly meeting of the society. He was ideally suited for such work, and his career thereafter was immensely active and fertile. He founded microscopic biology with his pioneering *Micrographia* (1665). He invented the first practical compound microscope, the spring balance wheel and anchor escapement mechanism, the universal joint, improved barometers, a screw-divided quadrant for astronomical measurements, a simple calculating machine, and a sounding device. He devised and performed numerous experiments to investigate the laws of gravity and suggested the inverse-square relationship for the decrease of gravity with distance. He proposed in rudimentary form a wave theory of light, a dynamical theory of heat, a theory of combustion, and even an evolutionary theory, all of which were accepted as scientific orthodoxy only in the 19th century. He made careful astronomical observations to try to prove the motion of the earth from stellar parallax, lectured on comets and earthquakes, and noted the relationship between a falling barometer and an approaching storm. After the great fire of London in 1666, he was engaged by the city in rebuilding projects and proved himself a skilled architect. For a time he also served as secretary and treasurer of the Royal Society.

Unfortunately, Hooke's many concurrent projects, and the necessary haste with which he did everything, meant that many of his ideas were never developed in depth. This led to several priority disputes, the most notable of which were with Isaac Newton. Hooke claimed that most of Newton's optical researches and his system of universal gravitation, which obeyed the inverse-square law, were in his own works. Hooke was no more belligerent or aggressive in pushing his claims than was common at the time, but Newton remained bitter. Hooke died in London on March 3, 1703, and during the 24 years after Hooke's death, when Newton was the dominant figure in the British scientific community, Hooke's reputation suffered. His true greatness was not generally recognized until the 20th century.

Further Reading

Most of Hooke's published writings are reprinted in Robert W. T. Gunther, *Early Science in Oxford* (15 vols., 1920-1945). The standard recent work on Hooke, rehabilitating his reputation after 2 centuries, is Margaret 'Espinasse, *Robert Hooke* (1956). A convenient short review of Hooke's life is in the *Scientific American*'s publication *Lives in Science* (1957). ☐

Richard Hooker

The English divine Richard Hooker (1554-1600) is best known for his "Ecclesiastical Polity," a work that provided a solid theological basis for the newly established Church of England.

Nothing is known of Richard Hooker's early life apart from his birth at Exeter in Devonshire. He went to Corpus Christi College, Oxford, about

1568. His appointment as deputy to the regius professor of Hebrew is one of the best-known events in his Oxford career; and a small pension of £4 a year was given Hooker by the mayor and Chamber of Exeter in 1582. It is likely that he left Oxford in 1584, when he was presented to the vicarage of Drayton Beauchamp. It is possible that he never resided there, because he was negotiating in London for the mastership of the Temple Church, which he got in 1585. In 1588 he married Joan Churchman; they later had two sons, who died in infancy, and four daughters.

While at Oxford, Hooker had been tutor to Edwin Sandys, who was to have a notable career as a statesman, become a director of the Virginia Company, and be knighted. Hooker sold the copyright in the eight books of his *Ecclesiastical Polity* to Sandys for about £50 plus a certain number of copies of the printed books; while, for his part, Sandys was to get the books printed. Only the first five appeared and at considerable cost to Sandys: the first four in 1593, the fifth book in 1597. Why the last three books were not published until the middle of the 17th century has caused much discussion among scholars, touching not least upon the genuineness of these volumes. In 1591 Hooker had accepted the living of Boscombe in Wiltshire, from which in 1595 he went to the living of Bishopsbourne, near Canterbury, where he died.

C. J. Sisson, perhaps the greatest modern Hooker scholar, stated: "In the long and crowded roll of great English men of letters there is no figure of greater significance than Hooker. . . . His own life's work is a monument of pure and splendid prose style and of lucid philosophic thought,

based on unsurpassed scholarship in the vast field of his theme."

Further Reading

Hooker's *Works* were published in three volumes in 1888. An early life of Hooker by Gauden, Bishop of Worcester, was so unsatisfactory that Archbishop Sheldon of Canterbury commissioned Izaak Walton to write a biography. This has been the standard life since its publication in 1665 and was included in the 1888 edition of Hooker's *Works*. C. J. Sisson, *The Judicious Marriage of Mr. Hooker* (1940), provided some important corrections. Modern studies of Hooker are F. J. Shirley, *Richard Hooker and Contemporary Political Ideas* (1949), and John S. Marshall, *Hooker and the Anglican Tradition* (1963).

Additional Sources

Archer, Stanley., *Richard Hooker,* Boston: Twayne, 1983. □

Thomas Hooker

Thomas Hooker (1586-1647), English-born Puritan theologian, was founder and spiritual leader of the Connecticut colony in New England.

Thomas Hooker was born in Leicestershire. After receiving a preparatory education, he attended Cambridge University, earning a bachelor of arts degree (1608) and a master of arts degree (1611). He remained as a fellow at the university until 1618, becoming a devout Puritan. In the 1620s Hooker served a congregation in Essex, where he became widely known for his excellent preaching. Because of his Puritan views, however, he attracted the attention of the Anglican authorities, who forced him to leave England. He eventually settled in Rotterdam, Holland, and here he received the call to the ministry of the Newtown (Cambridge) congregation in the American colony of Massachusetts.

Hooker was never happy in Newtown. His congregation was dissatisfied with its land; the religious challenges posed by Roger Williams and Anne Hutchinson were shaking the colony; and, most significantly, Hooker found himself incompatible with the leaders of Massachusetts. In 1636 the Newtown congregation received permission to emigrate, and Hooker led a majority of them to Connecticut.

The Hartford Church, under Hooker's pastorate, was exemplary for its lack of discord and controversy. Hooker was a humane and understanding clergyman. He made an outstanding contribution to the colony in a sermon in which he applied the principles of Congregationalism to political organization. Used as the basis for the Fundamental Orders, the sermon emphasized the election of public officials and the limitation of their power by the electorate. While Hooker's ideas seemed highly democratic, they were strictly qualified. His "people" were limited to full participating members of the Puritan church, and his emphasis on

Thomas Hooker (center, with staff)

the responsible use of power precluded unrestrained popular rule.

Hooker did not differ with orthodox New England Puritanism, although he practiced these beliefs with more humanity than his clerical colleagues. While living in Newtown, he had debated Roger Williams, and after moving to Connecticut, he returned to Massachusetts to serve on the court that tried Anne Hutchinson for heresy. His pamphlet "A Survey of the Summed of Church-Discipline," is an excellent explanation and defense of New England Congregationalism. Hooker retained his Hartford pastorate until his death on July 7, 1647.

Further Reading

The only book-length biography of Hooker is George L. Walker, *Thomas Hooker: Preacher, Founder, Democrat* (1891). A briefer biography is Warren W. Archibald, *Thomas Hooker* (1933). Background information is in Herbert L. Osgood, *The American Colonies in the Seventeenth Century* (3 vols., 1904-1907); Charles M. Andrews, *The Colonial Period of American History* (4 vols., 1934-1938); Albert E. Van Dusen, *Connecticut* (1961); and Mary Jeanne Anderson Jones, *Congregational Commonwealth: Connecticut, 1636-1662* (1968).

Additional Sources

Shuffelton, Frank, *Thomas Hooker, 1586-1647*, Princeton, N.J.: Princeton University Press, 1977. □

bell hooks

Social critic bell hooks (born 1952) is a prolific writer whose books analyze the function of race, as well as gender, in contemporary culture.

Writer, professor, and social critic, bell hooks is undeniably one of the most successful "crossover" academics of the late twentieth century. Her name, as well as the criticisms of racism and sexism that she has penned, are central to many current academic discussions, and they are also read widely outside of the educational arena. Her 1995 publication *Killing Rage: Ending Racism,* according to Ingrid Sischy in *Interview,* "unswervingly, unnervingly faces [the subject of racism], which is so often swept under the carpet and which is afloat in a big way. [hooks] shows racism as the minefield that it is."

Her other books, five of which were on the market before 1992, similarly analyze the function of race, as well as gender, in contemporary culture, taking as their subjects movies, television, advertising, political events, socioeconomic conditions—anything that reflects social inequality. In the introduction to *Black Looks,* which includes essays about Madonna, filmmaker Spike Lee, and the Anita Hill - Clarence Thomas hearings, hooks explained the fundamental political purpose of her cultural criticism: "It struck me that for black people, the pain of learning that we cannot control our images, how we see ourselves (if our vision is not decolonized), or how we are seen is so intense that it rends us. It rips and tears at the seams of our efforts to construct self and identify."

The essayist and teacher known to her readers as bell hooks was born Gloria Jean Watkins on September 25, 1952. The sense of community that would become so significant a note in hooks's work grew out of her early life in a black neighborhood in Hopkinsville, a small, segregated town in rural Kentucky. She recalled her neighborhood as a "world where folks were content to get by on a little, where Baba, mama's mother, made soap, dug fishing worms, set traps for rabbits, made butter and wine, sewed quilts, and wrung the necks of chickens." In the same essay, "Chitlin Circuit," hooks explained how the hardships created by racism could be turned by this community into a source of strength: "A very distinctive black culture was created in the agrarian South, by the experience of rural living, poverty, racial segregation, and resistance struggle, a culture we can cherish and learn from. It offers ways of knowing, habits of being, that can sustain us as a people."

Gloria was one of six siblings: five sisters and a baby brother. Her father worked as a janitor, and her mother, Rosa Bell Oldham Watkins, worked as a maid in the homes of white families, as did many of the black women in town. Although hooks—writing in the essay "Keeping Close to Home" from *Black Looks*—described her father as "an impressive example of diligence and hard work," she paid the most tribute to her mother's care; in "Homeplace" she explained, "Politically, our young mother, Rosa Bell, did

not allow the white supremacist culture of domination to completely shape and control her psyche and her familial relationships." The author further described how this role applied to mothers in black communities in general: "Black women resisted by making homes where all black people could strive to be subjects, not objects, where we could be affirmed in our minds and hearts despite poverty, hardship, and deprivation, where we could restore to ourselves the dignity denied us on the outside in the public world."

As a student at segregated public schools such as Booker T. Washington Elementary and Crispus Attucks High, hooks was taught by a dedicated group of teachers, mostly single black women, who helped to shape the self-esteem of children of color. But the late 1960s brought forced school integration to Kentucky. Looking back on her sophomore year of high school in "Chitlin Circuit," she recalled, "What I remember most about that time is a deep sense of loss. It hurt to leave behind memories, schools that were 'ours,' places we loved and cherished, places that honored us. It was one of the first great tragedies of growing up."

The neighborhood where she grew up provided young Gloria with the affirmation that fostered her resistance to racism, but it also provided her with the negative and positive experiences that would shape her feminism, which she discussed in the essay "Ain't I a Woman: Looking Back": "I cannot recall when I first heard the word 'feminist' or understood its meaning. I know that it was early [in my] childhood that I began to wonder about sex roles, that I began to see and feel that the experience of being 'made' female was

different from that of being 'made' male; perhaps I was so conscious of this because my brother was my constant companion. I use the word 'made' because it was obvious in our home that sex roles were socially constructed—that everyone could agree that very small children were pretty much alike, only different from one another physiologically; but that everyone enjoyed the process of turning us into little girls and little boys, little men and little women, with socially constructed differences."

Learned to "Talk Back"

Although Gloria was supposed to become a quiet, well-behaved young woman, she became instead a woman who "talked back." This phenomenon, for which hooks eventually named a volume of essays, actually refers to the development of a strong sense of self that allows black women to speak out against racism and sexism. In the introduction to *Talking Back: Thinking Feminist, Thinking Black,* a collection published in 1989, hooks emphasized the importance of this trait in her personality: "Folks who know me in real life and in the unreal life of books can bear witness to a courageous openness in speech that often marks me, becomes that which I am known by." In the essay of the same name, hooks noted the origin of this outspokenness: "I was always saying the wrong thing, asking the wrong questions. I could not confine my speech to the necessary corners and concerns of life."

Young Gloria's personality was a mix of this disobedient curiosity and a painful reserve; she explained, in retrospect, that "safety and sanity were to be sacrificed if I was to experience defiant speech. Though I risked them both, deep-seated fears and anxieties characterized my childhood days."

She wasn't, however, afraid of writing or of books; she used both to further develop her voice. In "'When I Was a Young Soldier': Coming to Voice," hooks explained that poetry—an element of particular importance in the growth of her voice—first captured her attention at church "with reading scripture with those awkward and funny little rhymes we would memorize and recite on Easter Sunday." By the time she was ten, she had begun writing her own poetry and soon developed a reputation for her ability to recite verse. She described the way poetry figured into her early life in "When I Was a Young Soldier": "Poetry was one literary expression that was absolutely respected in our working-class household. Nights when the lights would go out, when storms were raging, we would sit in the dim candlelight of our living room and have a talent show. I would recite poems: [William] Wordsworth, James Weldon Johnson, Langston Hughes, Elizabeth Barrett Browning, Emily Dickinson, Gwendolyn Brooks. Poetry by white writers was always there in schools and on family bookshelves in anthologies of 'great' works sold to us by door-to-door salesmen. . . . Poetry by black writers had to be searched for."

Although hooks has continued to write poetry and has published some, she gained notoriety as a writer of critical essays on systems of domination. In order to do this work, she found herself needing to develop a different voice, a different name. In an essay called "To Gloria, Who Is She: On Using a Pseudonym," hooks noted: "Gloria was to have been a sweet southern girl, quiet, obedient, pleasing. She was not to have that wild streak that characterized women on my mother's side."

She first used her pseudonym—her maternal great-grandmother's name—for a small book of poems; another woman in her community was named Gloria Watkins, and she wanted to avoid confusion. But a different purpose gradually developed, as she noted in "Talking Back": One of the many reasons I chose to write using the pseudonym . . . was to construct a writer-identity that would challenge and subdue all impulses leading me away from speech into silence." This writer-identity, represented by the pseudonym bell hooks, grew out of the reputation that the original bell hooks had in Gloria's community and, consequently, the sense of self that it could make for Gloria: "I was a young girl buying bubble gum at the corner store when I first really heard the full name bell hooks," she remembered in "Talking Back." "I had just talked back to a grown person. Even now I can recall the surprised look, the mocking tones that informed me I must be kin to bell hooks—a sharp-tongued woman, a woman who spoke her mind, a woman who was not afraid to talk back. I claimed this legacy of defiance, of will, of courage, affirming my link to female ancestors who were bold and daring in their speech."

Found Racism in Women's Studies

To a southern black girl from a working-class background who had never been on a city bus, who had never stepped on an escalator, who had never traveled by plane, leaving the comfortable confines of a small town Kentucky life to attend Stanford University was not just frightening, it was utterly painful. In "Keeping Close to Home: Class and Education," hooks described her difficult first journey out of Hopkinsville, which she made to begin her undergraduate education at Stanford, a white, ivy-league institution.

Accepting the scholarship that would take her to northern California, hooks gave up the affirmation of her black community but hoped to find a place that would affirm a woman's voice talking back. Initially, as she acknowledged in "Ain't I a Woman: Looking Back," she found some of the intellectual and political affirmation that she had anticipated: I eagerly responded to the fervor over contemporary feminist movement on campus. I took classes, went to meetings, to all-women's parties." But one of the significant weaknesses of that women's movement quickly became apparent to her: "It was in one of my first Women's Studies classes, taught by Tillie Olsen, that I noticed the complete absence of material by or any discussion about black women. I began to feel estranged and alienated from the huge group of white women who were celebrating the power of 'sisterhood.'"

That initial disillusionment would eventually fuel hooks's major contribution to mainstream feminism—her critique of its persistent racism. In "Feminism: a Transformational Politic," she translated that early experience in Women's Studies into broad political insight: "Within the feminist movement in the West, [there exists] the assump-

tion that resisting patriarchal domination is a more legitimate feminist action than resisting racism and other forms of domination." It became hooks's main work to change that assumption.

The unspoken racism she witnessed in the classroom reflected the racism embedded in the academy at large, where an institution run largely by middle-class, white men actively worked to limit the movement of the few people of color who were present. In "Black and Female: Reflections on Graduate School," hooks recalled the racism that began in her undergraduate education: "We were terrorized. As an undergraduate, I carefully avoided those professors who made it clear that the presence of any black students in their classes was not desired. . . . They communicated their message in subtle ways—forgetting to call your name when reading the roll, avoiding looking at you, pretending they do not hear you when you speak, and at times ignoring you altogether."

She encountered further obstacles when she pursued her study of literature later in graduate school. Several professors at the University of Southern California and the University of Wisconsin were determined to stop hooks—a black woman—from earning the graduate degree that she needed to become a university professor. Neither of these programs nor her final degree program at the University of California at Santa Cruz had black women on the faculty. Persisting against the racism, hooks completed her dissertation titled *Toni Morrison's Fiction: Keeping "A Hold on Life,"* in 1983. Although she would go on to teach African American literature, hooks only submitted this work for publication in the early 1990s. As early as 1981, however, she already had a major publication to her credit, *Ain't I a Woman: Black Women and Feminism.*

Wrote First Book at Nineteen

In the early 1970s, in order to combat the racism that permeated her world, hooks turned to the same strategy that had served her so well in childhood: talking back. She was experiencing, every day, as she recorded in *Ain't I a Woman,* "a social reality that differed from that of white men, white women, and even black men." She tried to find texts that would explain that difference and validate her recognition of the injustice. The impetus to write her own text finally came from a black male friend who was her lover at the time: "When I could not find sources, when I expressed mounting bitterness and rage, he encouraged me to write this book that I was searching for." In *Breaking Bread: Insurgent Black Intellectual Life,* she summarized the fundamental idea she needed to capture in that first book: "What I wanted so much to do . . . was to say there is a history that has produced this circumstance of devaluation. It is not something inherent in Black women that we don't feel good about ourselves, that we are self-hating. Rather it is an experience which is socially circumscribed, brought into being by historical mechanisms."

Despite the full-time studies she was pursuing at Stanford when she began *Ain't I a Woman* at the age of nineteen, hooks took a job as a telephone operator. Finding time for her writing was a challenge, but hooks also found that the job offered her something she didn't have in school at the time—a community of working-class, black women: "They provided support and affirmation of the project," she wrote, "the kind of support I had not found in a university setting. They were not concerned about my credentials, about my writing skills, about degrees. They, like me, wanted someone to say the kinds of things about our lives that would bring change or further understanding."

The author went through several drafts of the manuscript over the next six years before she had one that satisfied her. A large part of the process, as she reconstructed it in "'When I Was a Young Soldier': Coming to Voice," was once again about discovering a voice that was strong enough to talk back: "The initial completed manuscript was excessively long and very repetitious. Reading it critically, I saw that I was trying not only to address each different potential audience—black men, white women, white men, etc.—but that my words were written to explain, to placate, to appease. They contained the fear of speaking that often characterizes the way those in a lower position within a hierarchy address those in a higher position of authority. Those passages where I was speaking most directly to black women contained the voice I felt to be most truly mine—it was then that my voice was daring, courageous." It was at this moment that the persona of bell hooks truly rescued Gloria Watkins.

At first hooks had considerable trouble publishing her work: some publishers would release works on racism, and a number of feminist presses were printing anti-sexist books, but no one wanted to take a risk on a book that treated the two topics together. Eventually, hooks was directed to her future publisher, South End Press, while giving a talk at a feminist bookstore in San Francisco. Once published in 1981, *Ain't I a Woman* became central to discussions of racism and sexism. Eleven years later, *Publishers Weekly* ranked it among the "20 most influential women's books of the last 20 years." Much of the response, as hooks characterized it in "Talking Back," was shockingly negative: "The book was sharply and harshly criticized. While I had expected a climate of critical dialogue, I was not expecting a critical avalanche that had the power in its intensity to crush the spirit, to push one into silence."

Most of the criticism came from the academic community, both because hooks's form defied academic convention and because her subject matter pressed vulnerable points with established white feminists. The author explained in *Breaking Bread* that she received her most important feedback from her non-academic readers: "When *Ain't I a Woman* was first published I would get dozens of letters a week, where, say, a Black woman from a small town, out in the middle of nowhere, would tell me that she read my book at the public library and it transformed her life.

A Career in Higher Education

While *Ain't I a Woman* made bell hooks a vital name in feminist debate, Gloria Watkins continued her work. With a Ph.D. in English literature, she embarked on her teaching career. It was in her role as a teacher that hooks felt she was doing her most important work, as she explained in "On

Being Black at Yale: Education as the Practice of Freedom": "Fundamentally the purpose of my knowing was so I could serve those who did not know, so that I could learn and teach my own—education as the practice of freedom." She knew that for a people historically and legally deprived of the right to education, teaching was one of the most substantial forms of political resistance she could choose.

After holding various lectureships at Santa Cruz in the early 1980s, hooks left for Yale when she had the opportunity to teach in African American Studies, stating: "I would not have accepted a job solely in the English Department. I believed that I would find in African American Studies a place within the university wherein scholarship focusing on black people would be unequivocally deemed valuable—as necessary a part of the production of knowledge as all other work." In 1988, she joined the faculty at Oberlin College in Ohio, where she would teach in Women's Studies, a program that now offered the critique of racism that was absent during her undergraduate years.

Along with her teaching, hooks has continued to write and publish at a rate that is astonishing even for an academic. She published *Feminist Theory: From Margin to Center* while still lecturing at Santa Cruz in 1984 and followed it in 1989 with *Talking Back: Thinking Feminist, Thinking Black.* She then produced three books in three years: *Yearning: Race, Gender and Cultural Politics* in 1990; *Breaking Bread: Insurgent Black Intellectual Life,* which she wrote with Cornel West, in 1991; and *Black Looks: Race and Representation* in 1992. The following year saw the publication of *Sisters of the Yam: Black Women and Self-Recovery.* In addition, hooks's essays frequently appear in a publications that range from the *Journal of Feminist Studies in Religion* to *Essence.*

Taking a post with the City College of New York in 1995, hooks moved to the Henry Holt publishing company and came out with *Killing Rage: Ending Racism,* a book that calls for a more proactive approach to solving the problem of racism in America. When asked in *Interview* magazine why she chose this focus, hooks responded, "Wherever I went, I kept hearing people say, 'I will always be racist,' or 'This person will always be racist.' And I kept thinking, Why do so many people have bleak, passive responses to racism, where they just act as though it is some kind of illness that will never change, that will never go away. . . . I kept thinking how this passiveness really belies the history of resistance to racism in our culture. . . . When one looks at the history of African-Americans in our culture, it's amazing how much has been profoundly altered in people's lives, from the end of slavery to today." With her many critiques of America's societal problems, hooks has certainly proven her own commitment to play a role in bringing attention to all forms of prejudice.

It is clear that hooks intends to stick to the goal she once described in her essay "Talking Back": "Moving from silence into speech is for the oppressed, the colonized, the exploited, and those who stand and struggle side by side a gesture of defiance that heals, that makes new life and new growth possible. It is that act of speech, of 'talking back,' that is no mere gesture of empty words, that is the expression of our movement from object to subject—the liberated voice.''

Further Reading

hooks, bell, *Talking Back: Thinking Feminist, Thinking Black,* South End Press, 1989.

hooks, bell, *Yearning: Race, Gender and Cultural Politics,* South End Press, 1990.

hooks, bell, and Cornel West, *Breaking Bread: Insurgent Black Intellectual Life,* South End Press, 1991.

hooks, bell, *Black Looks: Race and Representation,* South End Press, 1992.

Essence, July 1992, p. 124; May 1995, p. 187.

Interview, October 1995, p. 122.

Publishers Weekly, June 15, 1992, p. 95; March 27, 1995, pp. 24-25. □

Benjamin Lawson Hooks

Attorney Benjamin Lawson Hooks (born 1925) was the executive director of the National Association for the Advancement of Colored People and served from 1972 to 1977 as the first African American commissioner of the Federal Communications Commission. He led the historic prayer vigil in Washington DC in 1979 against the Mott anti-busing amendment which was eventually defeated in Congress.

Benjamin Lawson Hooks, the fifth of seven children, was born in Memphis, Tennessee, in 1925 to Robert B. and Bessie Hooks. Hooks' family was relatively prosperous because, in 1907, his father and uncle established a successful photography business that was widely patronized by the Memphis African-American community. Because the society was so rigidly segregated along racial lines at that time, many establishments would not serve African Americans. Consequently, numerous African American-owned businesses were founded in the South to meet the needs of the African American populace. His grandmother, a musician who graduated from Berea College in Kentucky, was the second African American female college graduate in the nation. With such evidence of success and hard work as his personal examples, Hooks was encouraged to do well in his studies and prepare for higher education.

Following the Depression of 1929, changes occurred in the Hooks family's standard of living. With money so scarce during those years, African American clients could rarely afford the luxury of wedding pictures or family portraits, so business came to a virtual standstill. They were sad days indeed when the lights were turned out in the Hooks' home and when the bank foreclosed on the mortgage. Still, the family always had clothing and shelter, and no one ever went hungry. In the years after the Depression the family business revived and even several decades later, after his father's death, one of Hooks' brothers continued to maintain it. Perhaps because of the rigors of business life and social

prominence in the African American community, Hooks' parents were careful to see that all of their children were conscientious about their appearance, attitude, and academic performance. Hooks learned discipline from his parents' teaching and example.

After completing high school, Hooks decided to remain in Memphis to study pre-law at LeMoyne College. He successfully completed that program and then headed for Italy, where he served in the army during World War II guarding Italian prisoners of war. He felt humiliated that these prisoners were allowed to eat in restaurants that were off limits to him, and that in Memphis, they would have more rights than he. The experience deepened his resolve to do something about the bigotry in the South. When he returned to the United States, he continued his studies at Howard University. From there he went to Chicago where he attended DePaul University Law School—since no law school in the South would admit him. Although he could have established a law practice in Chicago when he graduated in 1948, he chose to return to Memphis to aid in the struggle for civil rights in the South. From 1949 to 1965 he practiced law in Memphis, as one of the few African American lawyers in town.. He recalled in *Jet* magazine ''At that time you were insulted by law clerks, excluded from white bar associations and when I was in court, I was lucky to be called 'Ben.' Usually it was just 'boy' [But] the judges were always fair. The discrimination of those days has changed and today, the South is ahead of the North in many respects of civil rights progress.''

In 1949, Hooks met a 24 year old teacher named Frances Dancy, whom he met at the Shelby County Fair. In 1952 they were married. Frances Hooks recalled in *Ebony* magazine that her husband was "good-looking, very quiet very intelligent. . .He loved to go around to churches and that type of thing, so I started going with him. He was really a good catch."

For years Hooks resisted the call to the gospel ministry. His father had little respect for organized religion, and Hooks had no urge to go against his father's wishes. However, in 1955 he began to preach, and in 1956 he was ordained a Baptist minister. He joined Reverend Martin Luther King's Southern Christian Leadership Conference. He pastored a church in Memphis and one in Detroit at the same time. Hooks, a man of many talents, was not content with his two chosen professions. His interest in business prompted him to become a bank director, the co-founder of a life insurance company, and the founder of an unsuccessful fried-chicken franchise. After several attempts to be elected to public office as a Republican candidate, his political ambitions were realized when he was appointed to serve as a criminal judge in Shelby County (Memphis) in 1965. He thus became the first African American criminal court judge in Tennessee history. The following year he was elected to the same position.

No matter how busy he was with his varied activities, Hooks always found time to take part in civil rights protests. He became a life member of the National Association for the Advancement of Colored People (NAACP) and served on the board of the Southern Christian Leadership Conference (SCLC). He was a pioneer in the NAACP-sponsored restaurant sit-ins and other boycotts that demonstrated the economic power as well as the anger of the African American community against the discrimination that was so pervasive at the time. In spite of his shyness he became a proficient orator whose combination of quick wit and homespun humor delighted audiences. He used this ability as the moderator of television shows called *Conversations in Black and White* and *Forty Percent Speak* (the percent of the African American population of Memphis) and as a panelist on the program *What Is Your Faith?*

Federal Communications Commissioner

Hooks was so often in the public eye that it is not surprising that Tennessee Senator Howard Baker submitted his name to President Richard M. Nixon for political appointment. While he was campaigning, Nixon had promised African American voters that he would see that they were treated fairly by the broadcast media. Thus, in 1972 when there was a vacancy on the seven-member board of the Federal Communications Commission (FCC), Hooks was named to fill it. Although Hooks was not the choice of the most articulate African American groups, including the Black Congressional Caucus, the great majority acquiesced gracefully to his appointment. Benjamin and Frances Hooks soon moved to Washington, D.C. Fortunately for Hooks, his wife matched him in energy, stamina and ambition. She often served as his assistant, secretary, advisor, and traveling companion, even though it meant that her own distin-

guished career as a teacher and guidance counselor was sacrificed. She told *Ebony* magazine, "He said he needed me to help him. Few husbands tell their wives that they need them after thirty years of marriage, so I gave it up and here I am. Right by his side."

The new position at the FCC gave Hooks a real opportunity to effectuate change in the roles of minorities in the entire broadcast industry. The FCC was responsible for granting licenses to television, radio, and cable television stations and for regulating long distance telephone, telegraph, and satellite communications systems. Hooks felt that his primary role was to bring a minority point of view to the commission. He stated that although he had been nominated by the president, he represented the interests of African Americans, the largest minority in the nation. Hooks was appalled to find that only three percent of those employed by the FCC were African American people, and they were generally in low-paying positions. He encouraged the commission to hire more African American workers at all levels. By the time that he left FCC, African Americans constituted about 11 percent of the employee population. Hooks made a concerted effort during his years as a commissioner to see that African Americans were fairly treated in news coverage and to urge public television stations to be more responsive to the needs of African American viewers by including historical and cultural programming directed toward them.

National Association for the Advancement of Colored People

After serving on the FCC for five years, Hooks was asked to be the executive director of the NAACP, the organization which had formed the vanguard of civil rights advocacy from the beginning of the 20th century. Roy Wilkins, who had held the director's position since 1955, was retiring, and the NAACP board of directors wanted an able leader to take his place. They unanimously agreed that Hooks was the man. He resigned from the commission and officially began his directorship on August 1, 1977.

When Hooks took over the organization, the NAACP was in financial straits and membership had dwindled from half a million to just over 200,000. Still the NAACP had local and regional offices throughout the country. He immediately directed his attention toward rebuilding the economic base of the association through a concentrated membership drive. He also advocated increased employment opportunities for minorities and the complete removal of United States businesses from South Africa. He told *Ebony* magazine "Black Americans are not defeated. . . .The civil rights movement is not dead. If anyone thinks we are going to stop agitating, they had better think again. If anyone thinks that we are going to stop litigating, they had better close the courts. If anyone thinks we are not going to demonstrate and protest . . . they had better roll up the sidewalks."

Hooks' tenure at the NAACP was fraught with bitter internal controversy. He was suspended by the chair of the NAACP's board, Margaret Bush Wilson, after she accused him of mismanagement. These charges were never proven.

In fact he was backed by a majority of 64 member board and continued his tenure until his retirement in 1992.

Throughout his career, Hooks has been a staunch advocate for self-help among the African American community. He urges wealthy and middle class African Americans to give time and resources to those who are less fortunate. "Its time today . . . to bring it out of the closet. No longer can we provide polite, explicable reasons why Black America cannot do more for itself" he told the 1990 NAACP convention as quoted by the *Chicago Tribune*. "I am calling for a moratorium on excuses. I challenge black America today— all of us—to set aside our alibis."

After his retirement, Hooks served as Pastor of Middle Baptist Church and president of the National Civil Rights Museum, both in Memphis. He also taught at Fisk University.

Further Reading

There is no full-length biography of Hooks. However, articles and biographical sketches are included in *Ebony Success Library* (1973); *Ebony* magazine (June 1975); *Jet* (December 1972); and *Broadcasting* (April 1972). See also Minnie Finch, *The NAACP, Its Fight for Justice* (1981) and Warren D. James, *NAACP, Triumphs of a Pressure Group, 1909-1980* (1980). □

Herbert Clark Hoover

Herbert Clark Hoover (1874-1964), thirty-first president of the United States, could not halt the severest economic depression in American history because his governmental theories prevented him from taking drastic steps.

On Aug. 10, 1874, Herbert Hoover was born at West Branch, Iowa, of Quaker ancestry. His father died when he was 6 and, after his mother's death less than 3 years later, he went to live with an uncle in Oregon. In 1891 he entered Stanford University, where he specialized in geology.

After graduating, Hoover worked as a mining engineer in the western United States, Australia, and China. In 1901 he became a junior partner in a London-based mining firm and 7 years later set up on his own. During these years he amassed a fortune estimated at $4 million. On Feb. 10, 1899, he married his college sweetheart, Lou Henry; they had two sons, Herbert, Jr., and Allan.

In London when World War I broke out, Hoover was asked to head the Belgian relief program. He was so successful that in May 1917 President Woodrow Wilson called him back to head the U.S. Food Administration. After the armistice he was placed in charge of the American Relief Administration, organized to feed war-ravaged Europe. When the congressional appropriation ran out, Hoover successfully appealed for private contributions to keep the work going.

Hoover was talked of as a possible 1920 presidential candidate by admirers in both parties. Although he publicly declared himself a Republican, the party's Old Guard disliked him because he was a late convert, and its isolationist wing disapproved of his advocacy of the League of Nations. Republican president Warren G. Harding, however, appointed him secretary of commerce, a post he held through the following administration of Calvin Coolidge.

Secretary of Commerce

During the 1920s Hoover set forth the basic philosophy that would guide him throughout his career. His central tenet was individualism, by which he meant equality of opportunity for each man to make the fullest possible use of his abilities. But he insisted that individualism be tempered by a sense of social responsibility and voluntary cooperation for the general good; he rejected old-fashioned free competition as wasteful. He believed that the government's function was to conserve natural resources, protect equality of opportunity, encourage business efficiency, promote scientific research, and build major public works.

Hoover transformed the Commerce Department into an effective instrument for implementing his philosophy. He fostered the growth of trade associations to bring improved efficiency and stability to industry, promoted American foreign trade, and expanded the Department's information and statistical services. He also set up a Division of Housing to encourage home building, built the Bureau of Standards into one of the country's leading scientific research institutions, and successfully pushed for stronger government regulation of the commercial aviation and radio industries.

Hoover's influence became increasingly important in all economic questions facing the Federal government. Believing that management and labor must cooperate for the good of all, he favored collective bargaining (though not the closed shop), worked behind the scenes to resolve labor disputes, and encouraged development of privately financed unemployment insurance. For relief to farmers he opposed government price-fixing of agricultural products, instead favoring increased Federal assistance to farm marketing cooperatives.

After Coolidge decided not to run again in 1928, Hoover was the popular choice of the party rank and file and won the Republican presidential nomination on the first ballot. In the election he defeated Democrat Alfred E. Smith by over 6 million votes, even breaking the "solid South."

Foreign Affairs

Hoover's record in foreign affairs was mixed. Immediately after his election he made a successful goodwill tour of Latin America, and throughout his term he actively worked for a good-neighbor policy south of the border. He was interested in promoting international disarmament, but the London Naval Conference of 1930 was only partly successful, and his efforts at the Geneva Disarmament Conference (which met in 1932 to secure abolition or reduction of offensive weapons) failed. His administration's worst mistake concerned the Japanese invasion and occupation of Manchuria in 1931. Secretary of State Henry Stimson was willing to impose economic sanctions against Japan, but Hoover, fearful of instigating a war, limited the American response to the ineffectual Stimson Nonrecognition Doctrine.

Domestic Policy

Domestically, Hoover expanded the national forests and parks, laid the groundwork for many of the later New Deal accomplishments in water-resource development, increased Federal highway spending, was instrumental in setting up the privately financed Research Committee on Social Trends, reorganized the Federal prison system, promoted the growth of civilian aviation, and even approved a bill which drastically limited the use of injunctions in labor disputes.

On the other hand, Hoover's opposition to government competition with business led him to veto a bill for government operation of the hydroelectric facilities at Muscle Shoals, Ala. And despite warnings from economists of its disastrous consequences for international trade and economic stability, he signed legislation which raised the average level of tariff duties from roughly 30 to about 59 percent. But what most damaged his reputation was the inadequacy of his response to the depression that followed the stock market crash of October-November 1929.

Voluntarism versus Federal Intervention

Although previous chief executives had taken the position that the business cycle would simply have to run its course, Hoover believed that the government could and should act to cushion economic shocks. When the Depression hit, he made repeated optimistic statements about the economy to bolster business confidence, had the Federal Reserve Board follow an "easy money" policy, and accelerated work on Federal projects. However, his major emphasis was on voluntary action rather than government intervention: he exhorted industry to maintain employment and wages, induced bankers to establish the National Credit Corporation to assist threatened banks, and relied upon the traditional agencies of private charity and local government to provide relief for the unemployed.

But this voluntarism was a failure. The business community lacked the discipline and sense of social responsibility for effective cooperation. Yet, despite increasing hardship in all sectors, Hoover was convinced that the country was basically sound. He held that the causes of the Depression lay outside the United States. To prevent the threatened breakdown of the German economy under the burden of reparations payments—which would have jeopardized millions of dollars of American loans—he arranged a one-year moratorium on payment both of reparations and inter-Allied war debts.

By late 1931 Hoover was driven to embrace more direct Federal intervention. He established the Reconstruction Finance Corporation to make emergency loans to financial institutions and certain corporations. He supported the Glass-Steagall Act, which liberalized the Federal Reserve System's credit requirements; and the Federal Home Loan Bank Act, to assist building and loan societies, savings banks, and insurance companies in expanding loans for residential construction. Hoover's program rested on the assumption that infusing additional credit into the economy would be enough to revive business activity. Still the economy continued its downward slide.

Nevertheless, Hoover stood firm against the massive public-works spending that Democrats and progressive Republicans increasingly demanded. He was adamantly against any direct Federal relief for the unemployed, not only for budgetary reasons, but because he was determined to preserve what he regarded as the fundamental American principles of individual and local responsibility.

Despite sharp Republican losses in the 1930 congressional elections, Hoover largely had his way. He successfully fought a proposal to strengthen the ineffective U.S. Employment Service. And the Relief and Construction Act (1932), which authorized loans of $1.5 billion to state and local agencies for self-liquidating public works and $300 million to the states for relief purposes, was watered down to meet his specifications. He suffered only two major legislative defeats: a proposed sales tax for balancing the budget and an overridden veto on the bill permitting veterans to borrow up to 50 percent of the face value of their bonus certificates.

"Bonus Army" Blunder

In his personal relations Hoover was affable and genial, a sensitive and humane idealist—qualities he was unable to project to the public. His sensitivity to criticism led to poor relations with the press, and his resistance to direct Federal relief made him appear callous to the suffering around him.

Perhaps Hoover's worst blunder was his handling of the ''bonus army.'' An estimated 17,000 former servicemen flocked to Washington in the spring of 1932 to demand that Congress authorize the immediate payment in full of their bonus certificates. When the Senate, under Hoover's prodding, defeated the measure, most returned to their homes. An attempt by Washington police to evict those remaining resulted in the death of two veterans and two policemen. Hoover then called out Federal troops on July 28, 1932—an action that made him even more unpopular.

New Deal Triumphs

In the 1932 campaign Hoover warned that the program of Democratic nominee Franklin D. Roosevelt threatened a ''radical departure'' from the American way of life. His efforts to cooperate with the president-elect came to naught, because Roosevelt and his ''Brain Trust'' correctly suspected that Hoover wanted to commit the new administration to a continuation of his own policies. When Hoover left office in March 1933, nearly the entire United States economy was paralyzed.

In the years that followed, Hoover remained politically active, attacking Roosevelt's New Deal policies, which he blamed for prolonging the Depression by destroying business confidence. Prior to Pearl Harbor, Hoover was a strong isolationist; after World War II he was a leading exponent of the ''Fortress America'' theory.

Elder Statesman

When Hoover left office, he was probably the most hated president in American history. Only the passage of time led to a fairer judgment. In 1947 President Harry S. Truman appointed him chairman of the Commission on Organization of the Executive Branch of the Government. In 1953 President Dwight Elsenhower appointed him to the same job. The work of these two Hoover commissions provided the basis for a major reorganization of the executive branch. When he died on Oct. 20, 1964, Hoover was widely respected as one of the nation's foremost elder statesmen.

Hoover did more than any previous chief executive to combat a depression, but the limitations of his political and social philosophy proved his undoing. Perhaps the most significant result of his experiment in voluntarism was that its failure prepared the public to accept the farreaching expansion of Federal authority under the New Deal.

Further Reading

Before his death Hoover completed his *Memoirs* (3 vols., 1951-1952), covering the years up to 1941. There is no adequate biography. Eugene Lyons, *Herbert Hoover: A Biography* (1964), is superficial and eulogistic. Harris Gaylord Warren, *Herbert Hoover and the Great Depression* (1959), and Albert U. Romansco, *The Poverty of Abundance: Hoover, the Nation, the Depression* (1965), are useful, but both suffer from lack of access to the Hoover papers. See also Harold Wolfe, *Herbert Hoover, Public Servant and Leader of the Loyal Opposition: A Study of his Life and Career* (1956). A discussion of foreign policy is Robert H. Ferrell, *American Diplomacy in the Great Depression: Hoover-Stimson Foreign Policy, 1929-1933* (1957). □

John Edgar Hoover

J. Edgar Hoover (1895-1972) was appointed assistant director of the Bureau of Investigation in 1921, and director in 1924; he was the popular (and then controversial) director of the U.S. Federal Bureau of Investigation from 1935 until his death in 1972, at age 77.

J. Edgar Hoover was born into a Scottish Presbyterian family of civil servants in Washington, D.C. on New Year's Day, 1895; his mother called him Edgar from the day he was born. He was a leader of the student cadet corps in high school, and a champion debater. He taught Sunday school at Old First Presbyterian Church. His life-long guiding principles were formed early: he was convinced that middle-class Protestant morality was at the core of American values, and he harbored a deep distrust of alien ideas and movements that called those values into question.

Working days and attending school at nights, Hoover earned his Bachelor of Law degree with honors from George Washington University in 1916. He excelled in mock court proceedings. In 1917 he earned a Master of Law degree and got a job with the Alien Enemy Bureau in the Department of Justice, administering the regulations governing the hundreds of thousands of German and Austro-Hungarian aliens interned or supervised by the department. In response to a series of bombings in the spring of 1919, supposedly carried out by radicals, Attorney General A. Mitchell Palmer decided to concentrate on aliens, since they could be deported summarily and wholesale, without due process, and in 1920 he put the 24-year-old Hoover in charge of the operation. Within a short period of time, Hoover had written briefs arguing that alien members of the new American Communist and Communist Labor parties were subject to deportation under the immigration laws; planned a raid on the headquarters of the Union of Russian Workers; and put Emma Goldman, Alexander Berkman, and 247 other ''radicals'' on a ship for the Soviet Union. A few days later, Hoover led a nationwide operation which arrested more than four thousand alien Communists.

While civil libertarians deplored the Justice Department's tactics and treatment of prisoners, Hoover had established his reputation as an organizational genius. In 1921, he was appointed assistant director of the Bureau of Investigation. Three years later, when the bureau had become known as ''the most corrupt and incompetent agency in Washington,'' Hoover was appointed Acting Director by a new Attorney General, Harlan Fiske Stone (later Associate Justice, then Chief Justice of the Supreme Court). Hoover took the job under the conditions that he would tolerate no

between 1932 and 1934 augmented that authority, and the FBI (so named in 1935) was in business, chasing down the likes of Machine Gun Kelly, Baby Face Nelson, Ma Barker and her sons, and John Dillinger.

Hoover was famous for his successes in public relations, legend-building and image-making his Bureau into a Hollywood extravaganza, firmly entrenched as a mainstay of popular culture through films, comic strips, books, and carefully orchestrated publicity campaigns. The FBI and its director became dear to the hearts of the American people and Hoover himself became a hero of almost mythic proportions. But during most of the 1930s, Hoover was relatively obscure, merely the head of just one of several investigatory agencies. In the art of public relations, Hoover was the beneficiary of Franklin Roosevelt's Attorney General Homer Cummings, who between 1933 and 1937 developed a massive, multi-front public relations campaign to make law enforcement a national movement wholly dependant on public support for its success in dealing with the gangsters of the Depression era. When Cummings suffered political decline, Hoover now head of the nation's only national law enforcement agency adopted many of his methods, always looking for new public enemies to protect the nation against. In the coming years, these were to include Nazi spies, Communists, Black Panthers, the New Left, and Martin Luther King, Jr. As for law enforcement, Hoover mostly abandoned it altogether after 1936.

After World War II Hoover took from the growing tension between the United States and the Soviet Union a mandate to prepare for domestic sabotage and subversion, and to round up Communists, siding with such anti-Communists as Richard M. Nixon and Senator Joseph R. McCarthy. He pursued the investigation of Alger Hiss that discredited the domestic security policies of the Truman Administration; he uncovered the alleged atom spy conspiracy of Klaus Fuchs, Harry Gold, and Julius and Ethel Rosenberg (who were subsequently executed as traitors); and his Bureau provided the evidence for the Smith Act convictions of the top leadership of the American Communist Party (later overturned by the U.S. Supreme Court).

During the late 1950s, Hoover developed a counterintelligence program (COINTELPRO) to covertly harass the remnants of the American Communist Party. In the 1960s he extended the program to harass and disrupt the Ku Klux Klan, the black militant movement and the antiwar movements, particularly targeting the Black Panthers and the Students for a Democratic Society. Now into his 70s, Hoover extended his defense of "Americanism" with public attacks on Martin Luther King, Jr., and two attorneys general Robert Kennedy and Ramsey Clark. His tactic in all cases included illegal wiretapping and microphone surveillance.

During all these years, Hoover managed to overlook organized crime. Robert Kennedy became a thorn in Hoover's side when he demonstrated otherwise as assistant counsel on the Kefauver committee's investigations into organized crime. Hoover ignored political corruption and white collar crime. Most of his work was political, in two senses of the word. First, he target individuals, groups, and movements which offended his moral sense. Second, he

political meddling and that he wanted sole control of merit promotions. Stone agreed. Almost immediately, the new director instituted new personnel policies; he fired agents he considered unqualified, abolished promotions based on seniority, introduced uniform performance appraisals, and laid out strict rules of conduct (including instructions that forbade the use of intoxicating beverages, on or off the job). He established new lines of authority (all regional officers were to report directly to Hoover) and did whatever he could to create power for his agency. At the time, for example, the Bureau had jurisdiction over little more than car-thefts. Agents were not allowed to carry firearms until 1934, and they did not have the power of arrest. Law enforcement was a state activity, not a federal one. Gradually, Hoover professionalized the organization and freed it from the taint of corruption. He was a pioneer in the areas of personnel training, the use of scientific laboratory techniques, accurate reporting, and filing large volumes of material. By 1926, state law enforcement agencies began contributing their fingerprint cards to the Bureau of Investigation. Early on, Hoover laid the foundation for a world-class crime fighting organization.

During this period, Hoover still maintained his card file of over 450,000 names of "radicals" and worked on building the bureau "his way, " but the agency slumbered through the violence of the Roaring Twenties. It took the Lindbergh kidnapping in 1932 to convince Congress that there was a need for national legislation authorizing the Federal government to act against crimes of violence on other than government reservations; companion legislation collected compromising information provided by his agents on all sorts of public officials. The fact that he had such information in his personal files or was merely thought to have such information was enough to sway congressional votes in favor of FBI appropriations requests and to keep presidents from removing him from office, even long after mandatory retirement age. The perception of "such information" worked both ways, however. It was long thought that Hoover denied the existence of organized crime because certain Mafia figures had photographs and other documentation of Hoover's alleged and widely-believed homosexuality. However, nothing could be proved, as after his death, Hoover's secretary obeyed instructions that all his personal files be burned.

J. Edgar Hoover died in May, 1972, still the Director of the FBI, and became the only civil servant to be honored with a state funeral. Post-Watergate investigations of the FBI's abuses of civil liberties under Hoover and recent releases of FBI files under the Freedom of Information Act (including files his secretary missed) have destroyed Hoover's reputation. Recent scholarly works have asserted that Anthony Summers book(1993), exposing Hoover's homosexuality, was based on slender and dubious evidence. Other works have also shown the FBI's ineffectiveness in pursuing organized-crime figures had little to do with Hoover's vulnerability, but rather from his lack of accountability, his use of illegal investigative techniques, and his obsessive focus on his own political agenda. J. Edgar Hoover's methods contributed substantially to a culture of lawlessness in the FBI itself. Within a few years of his death, public opinion about Hoover had shifted to the point that his name by itself conjured up the image of a government at war with the rights and liberties of its citizens.

Further Reading

Hoover's own writings *Masters of Deceit: The Story of Communism in America and How To Fight It* (1958) and *J. Edgar Hoover on Communism* (1969) were written for him by FBI publicists. The book that purports to expose Hoover's private life, Anthony Summers' *Official and Confidential: The Secret Life of J. Edgar Hoover* (1993), was not highly regarded even by Hoover's critics. Richard Gid Powers *G-Men: Hoover's FBI in American Popular Culture* (1983); Athan G. Theoharis and John Stuart Cox *The Boss J. Edgar Hoover and the Great American Inquisition* (1988); and Ronald Kessler *The FBI: Inside the World's Most Powerful Law Enforcement Agency* (1993) are useful works, as is the older "oral biography" by Ovid Demaris *The Director: An Oral Biography of J. Edgar Hoover*. Scholars will want to see three microfilm collections of documents edited by Athan Theoharis, *The J. Edgar Hoover Official and Confidential File* (1996); *FBI Wiretaps, Bugs, and Break-Ins: The National Security Electronic Surveillance Card File and the Surreptitious Entries File* (1996); and *The Louis Nichols Official and Confidential File and the Clyde Tolson Personal File* (1996). See also Alan Theoharis *J. Edgar Hoover, Sex, and Crime: An Historical Antidote* (1995); Alan Theoharis *From the Secret Files of J. Edgar Hoover* (1993); Richard Gid Powers, *Secrecy and Power: The Life of J. Edgar Hoover* (1993); Mark North, *Act of Treason: The Role of J. Edgar Hoover in the Assassination of President Kennedy* (1992); Curt Gentry *J. Edgar Hoover: The Man and His Secrets* (1992); Nelson Blackstock, *COINTELPRO: The FBI's Secret War on Political Freedom* (1988); Ward Churchill and James Vander Wall's two books, *The COINTELPRO Papers: Documents from the FBI's Secret Wars Against Dissent in the United States* (1990); and *Agents of Repression: The FBI's Secret War Against the American Indian Movement and the Black Panther Party* (1990). □

Bob Hope

In addition to his successes on radio, in movies, on television, and in live shows, Bob Hope (born 1903) has developed a reputation for his untiring efforts to entertain and boost the morale of American military personnel stationed all over the world and for the numerous appearances he has made in the name of various charities.

Bob Hope is perhaps the most widely known and loved stand-up comedian in America. On July 13, 1969, long before Hope reached his greatest fame, the *Milwaukee Journal* stated that Hope had "undoubtedly been the source of more news, and more newspaper feature stories than any other entertainer in modern history."

"Hopeless" Childhood

Born in Eltham, England on May 30, 1903, Leslie Townes Hope was one of seven surviving boys. By the age of four he was a skilled mimic and loved to sing and dance. In 1908 Hope's family moved from England to Cleveland, Ohio. Hope's father, Harry, was a hard-drinking stonemason whose income was irregular. For Hope, who looked and sounded British, the Americanization process was difficult. The Cleveland neighborhood in which he lived was tough, and the neighborhood kids made fun of him. They inverted his name, Leslie Hope, to create the nickname "Hopelessly." When he shortened his name to Les, they countered with another nickname, "Hopeless." Hope was a scrappy kid and to ward off the ridicule he fought easily and sometimes successfully, developing into a boxer of some skill.

As a youth Hope sold two-cent newspapers on the streets of Cleveland to supplement his family's income. On one occasion a gentleman in a long black limousine waited while Hope, who did not have change for a dime, rushed into a nearby store to get change. When he returned he received a lecture about the importance of keeping change in order to take advantage of all business opportunities. The man was oil magnate John D. Rockefeller, founder of Standard Oil Company.

As a teenager Hope once boasted that he would rather be an actor than hold an honest job, and he participated in all kinds of school and amateur training groups, specializing in dancing and in the one-liner jokes for which he ultimately became famous. He gained a great deal of experience in an act Hope formed with a comedian from Columbus, Ohio, named George Byrne. Adopting the name Lester, Hope went with Byrne to New York City in 1926. He and Byrne

performed in cities and towns outside New York City, and finally appeared in a New York City vaudeville production called "Sidewalks." They were fired within a month, however, because the show was a success and did not need the short dancing act that Hope and Byrne performed.

Vaudeville Comic

Hope got his first trial as a solo act at Chicago's Stratford Theatre in 1928. For this solo appearance he changed his name to Bob because he felt that would be "chummier" and look better on a theatre marquee. In solo appearances, Hope always made his audience feel at ease and comfortable with his self-deprecating humor. He worked desperately hard and succeeded but soon left the Stratford to tour midwestern cities.

From 1920 to 1937 Hope performed in all kinds of shows in vaudeville both on and off Broadway. Vaudeville was hard work for Hope. A typical show consisted of comedians running a patter of one-liners around various kinds of variety acts ranging from dancing dogs to sword-swallowers but featuring mainly dancing. Hope is considered a master of the one-liner. In later years Hope sometimes employed up to three joke writers at a time. One standard line when he boards an airplane is, "I knew it was an old plane when I found Lindbergh's lunch on the seat." He used a line in 1970 when he met with the English Royal Family: "I've never seen so much royalty. . . . It looks like a chess game . . . live!" In 1932, when fifteen million Americans suffered the joblessness of the Great Depression, Hope was earning a thousand dollars a week in his particular kind of

vaudeville act. But he was not satisfied. Hope was always ambitious and wanted to improve. He yearned, as he said, "to be the best," to be the outstanding comic in the business.

Hope and Crosby

Hope met actor and singer Bing Crosby in 1932. They liked each other immediately because their personalities and styles of acting fitted well, and they started performing together in song and dance routines. Hope met aspiring actress Delores Reade in 1933 and later married her. Already well established as a comedian by 1935, Hope that year joined the "Ziegfield Follies" and performed in cities outside New York; then on January 30, 1936, he opened in the "Follies" at New York City's Winter Garden Theatre, with such stars as Fanny Brice and Eve Arden. The "Ziegfield Follies" was a new vaudeville high for Hope. The show was the musical highlight of Broadway, consisting of dazzlingly beautiful girls and costumes, witty lines between the actors and actresses, and music by such great composers as Vernon Duke and Ira Gershwin. During his years in vaudeville, Hope was on the stage with such actors as Jimmy Durante, Ethel Merman, Edgar Bergen and Charlie McCarthy, Al Jolson, and many others.

Although Hope had acted in some short motion picture comedies as early as 1934, he began his feature-length movie career in Hollywood in 1938, with the Paramount film *The Big Broadcast of 1938* starring Hope, W.C. Fields, Martha Raye, Dorothy Lamour, and Shirley Ross. This was the beginning of an active career in film entertainment for Hope, who went on to appear in fifty-two movies; six of these comprise the *Road to . . .* series featuring Hope, Crosby, and Dorothy Lamour.

Hope has always been fiercely patriotic about his adopted country. On December 7, 1941, when Japanese attack planes bombed the American naval installation in Hawaii's Pearl Harbor, thereby provoking U.S. participation in the Second World War, Hope denounced the attack. On December 16, during a radio broadcast, Hope declared his patriotism and voiced optimism about the outcome of the war: "There is no need to tell a nation to keep smiling when it's never stopped. It is that ability to laugh the makes us the great people that we are . . . Americans!"

Performed for the Troops

One of Hope's former stand-ins who had joined the armed forces knew of Hope's reputation for charitable work and in 1942 asked the comedian to make an entertainment tour of Alaskan Army bases. Hope enlisted Frances Langford, Jerry Colonna, Tony Romany, and other performers to put together a variety show for the troops stationed there. That was the beginning of a commitment on Hope's part that has never ended. Every year, especially during the Christmas season, Hope has spearheaded a drive to present shows to American men and women in the armed forces. His service to American troops added to Hope's established reputation for activity in the name of numerous charities and benefits, including political, cultural, and humanitarian causes. In fact, at the Academy Awards on February 21,

1941, Hope was given an honorary award "to pay tribute . . . to a man who has devoted his time and energy to many causes. His unselfishness in playing countless benefits has earned him a unique position in a hectic community where his untiring efforts are deeply, profoundly appreciated." Hope also won honorary Oscars in 1940, 1944, 1952, and 1965.

Hope has long been many Americans' favorite comedian, from the average radio-listener and movie-goer to the rich and powerful. He often enjoyed a close relationship with the men serving as President of the United States. Since the administration of Franklin Roosevelt, Hope has appeared many times at the White House. President Jimmy Carter, in paying tribute to the man who had entertained America for so long, commented on Hope's role as White House guest: "I've been in office 489 days. . . . In three weeks more I'll have stayed in the White House as many times as Bob Hope has." Hope's seventy-fifth birthday party, held in the Washington Kennedy Center to honor the United Service Organization (USO), was attended by members of Congress and many of Hope's acting friends, including John Wayne, Elizabeth Taylor, and George Burns.

Another celebration was held at the Kennedy Center in 1983 when Hope turned eighty years old, this time hosted by President Ronald Reagan and his wife, Nancy. Again Hope's friends were present to honor the occasion, including models Cheryl Tiegs and Christie Brinkley. At the celebration Hope was still what *Time* magazine called "The All-American Wisecracker," and showed no signs of slowing down.

Hope can look back upon a life that has been full to the brim. One of his writers, Larry Klein, once said: "You know, if you had your life to live over again, you wouldn't have time to do it." Hope answered: "I wouldn't want to live it over again. It's been pretty exciting up to now. The encore might not be as much fun." Behind all Hope's humor is a serious core that directs his life, as evidenced by his efforts to help others less fortunate than himself. Some of his charitable activities involve golf benefits. A twelve stroke handicapper, Hope has played the game all his life, often joining presidents, Hollywood's greats, and golf's immortals on the links. Because of the benefits the game brings to charities, Hope agreed in 1964 to have the Palm Springs Classic golf tournament renamed The Bob Hope Desert Classic, and he has hosted it ever since. Hope's serious side was also apparent in the preface to his 1963 book *I Owe Russia $1200*, in which he wrote: "Yes, the conquest of space is within our grasp, but as we reach out we seem to have diminished the inward search. No significant breakthrough has yet been made in the art of human relations. So perhaps this is the precise moment in history for each of us to look into his heart and his conscience and determine in what way we may be responsible for our present dilemma."

Celebrated the First 90 Years

In May 1993, NBC celebrated Hope's 90th birthday with the three-hour special "Bob Hope: The First Ninety Years." The show, which won an Emmy, featured tributes from every living U.S. president at that time— Richard Nixon, Gerald Ford, Jimmy Carter, Ronald Reagan, George Bush, and Bill Clinton. By then, according to *TV Guide*, Hope had made more than 500 TV shows and 70 movies. Hope concluded his 60–year contract with NBC on November 23, 1996, when his final NBC TV special, *Laughing With the Presidents* was aired.

The Guinness Book of World Records called Hope the most honored entertainer in the world. By mid-1995, he had received more than 2,000 awards and citations, including 54 honorary doctorate degrees, *The Saturday Evening Post* reported. At age 92, he released a book, video, and two compact discs commemorating the 50th anniversary of the end of the Second World War. *The Saturday Evening Post* printed this excerpt from Hope's book: "I was there. I saw your sons and your husbands, your brothers and your sweethearts. I saw how they worked, played, fought, and lived. I saw some of them die. I saw more courage, more good humor in the face of discomfort, more love in an era of hate, and more devotion to duty than could exist under tyranny."

Further Reading

Faith, William Robert, *Bob Hope: A Life in Comedy,* Putnam, 1982.
Hope, Bob, *I Never Left Home,* Simon & Schuster, 1944.
Hope, Bob, *Have Tux, Will Travel: Bob Hope's Own Story,* Pocket Books, 1956.
Good Housekeeping, July 1982, pp. 107-130; December 1994, pp. 88+.
New York Times, January, 1985, p. 50.
The Saturday Evening Post, May/June 1995, pp. 16+.
Time, May 30, 1983.
TV Guide, May 21-27, 1983, pp. 14-16; May 8, 1993, p. 25
Los Angeles Times November 23, 1996, Sec: F, p: 1, col: 2. □

John Hope

African American educator, religious leader, and champion of racial equality, John Hope (1868-1936) early advocated liberal education for black youth and formed the first consortium of African American colleges in America.

John Hope was born in Augusta, Ga., on June 3, 1868. He finished the eighth grade, then worked in a restaurant. Encouraged to seek further schooling, in 1886 Hope enrolled in the Worcester Academy in Massachusetts. In 1890 he entered Brown University on a scholarship. Graduating in 1894, he was the commencement orator. That year Hope took a position at Roger Williams University in Nashville. He married Lugenia Burns in 1897; the couple had two sons.

Hope joined the faculty of Atlanta Baptist (now Morehouse) College in 1898. A master teacher, he deeply influenced the intellectual and moral growth of his students. He also had a strong impact on his peers. His writings were published in the *Occasional Papers of the American Negro Academy* and in other places. In 1906 he became the first black president of the college. As always, he stressed general culture, human dignity, and Christian principles.

Hope fought for racial equality in every way he could. In 1906 he joined W. E. B. Du Bois and others in the Niagara movement. He was the only college president (white or black) to participate in this protest meeting, which culminated in the founding of the National Association for the Advancement of Colored People (NAACP). In 1915 Hope was appointed to the NAACP advisory board.

Working to improve the living conditions of black people in Atlanta, Hope got Federal aid for slum clearance on Atlanta's West Side and secured funds for building model apartments for African Americans. During World War I, as special secretary for the YMCA in France, he devoted himself to the welfare of black soldiers there.

In 1929 Hope became president of Atlanta University, the first black institution in the South to offer graduate degrees. Under his leadership the university attained the highest regional accreditation rating a black institution could receive. Hope worked to affiliate Atlanta's six black colleges; three affiliated in 1929, and the others joined later.

Among his many honors, Hope was elected Phi Beta Kappa at Brown in 1919. He received the Harmon Award for distinguished service in education in 1929 and was awarded the doctor of laws degree by Bates College and Brown, Bucknell, Howard, and McMasters universities. He served as president of the National Association of Teachers in Colored Schools, the Georgia Commission for Work among Negro Boys, the Commission on Interracial Cooperation, and the Association for the Study of Negro Life and History. Among his other positions, he was a member of the Executive Committee of the New York Urban League and a delegate to the International Missionary Council.

Hope died on Feb. 20, 1936. He was awarded the Spingarn Medal posthumously for his outstanding services to African Americans.

Further Reading

The only full and complete biography of Hope is Ridgely Torrence, *The Story of John Hope* (1948), which is a thoroughly researched work. Clarence A. Bacote, *The Story of Atlanta University: A Century of Service, 1865-1965* (1969), contains a chapter dealing with Hope's administration. There is a sketch of Hope in Wilhelmena S. Robinson, *Historical Negro Biographies* (1967; 2d ed. 1968). □

Esek Hopkins

Esek Hopkins (1718-1802), first commander of the American Navy, was a Revolutionary patriot whose abilities were not equal to his important task.

Esek Hopkins, born in present-day Scituate, R.I., early turned to the sea for his livelihood. By the time of the American Revolution he was a veteran merchant captain who had sailed to almost every corner of the globe. His brother, Stephen Hopkins, served in the Continental Congress and was chairman of the Marine Committee, formed to supervise naval affairs. Consequently, Esek Hopkins's appointment as "commander in chief" of the infant navy was largely due to his brother's influence.

In January 1776 Congress instructed Esek Hopkins to raid British shipping along the coasts of Virginia and North Carolina. He decided instead to swoop down on New Providence in the Bahamas to capture guns and ammunition for the American Army. The undefended forts at the Nassau port were easy prey, and Hopkins's small fleet returned with badly needed military stores. This, however, was Hopkins's last triumph.

On his return voyage from the Bahamas, Hopkins missed an excellent chance to take the British *Glasgow*. Moreover, he angered southern congressmen by his failure to operate in the Chesapeake Bay and southward, and there were general complaints of his inactivity in late 1776 and early 1777. (In fairness to Hopkins, it should be noted that he found it impossible to enlist sailors because privateer captains were offering roughly twice the regular pay of Navy seamen.)

When H. M. S. *Diamond* ran aground on the Rhode Island coast and the sluggish Commodore Hopkins lost this excellent chance to destroy it, the officers of his own flagship petitioned the Marine Committee to remove him from office. Hopkins had already been indiscrete in criticizing both Congress and some of his subordinates. Therefore, it

was with no particular remorse that Congress in March 1777 suspended Hopkins and soon afterward dismissed him from the Navy.

Though a loyal officer, Hopkins was "an old-fashioned, salt horse sailor" who was probably too old and too set in his ways by the time of his appointment to adjust to his new duties as a fighting officer and administrator. From 1777 to 1786 Hopkins sat in the Rhode Island Legislature, and from 1782 until his death he served as a trustee of Rhode Island College.

Further Reading

The two biographies of Hopkins are inadequate and should be used with caution: Edward Field, *Esek Hopkins* (1898), and Charles H. Miller, *Admiral Number One: Some Incidents in the Life of Esek Hopkins, 1718-1802, First Admiral of the Continental Navy* (1962). A background study is Gardner Weld Allen, *A Naval History of the American Revolution* (2 vols., 1913). □

Sir Frederick Gowland Hopkins

The English biochemist Sir Frederick Gowland Hopkins (1861-1947) was the first to recognize the necessity for "accessory factors" in the diet, thereby initiating important work in vitamin research.

On June 20, 1861, F. Gowland Hopkins was born in Eastbourne, Sussex. He attended the City of London School at Enfield (1871-1875) but was forced to withdraw because of truancy caused by "sheer boredom," to use his own words. He then attended a private school.

Hopkins was apprenticed for 3 years to a consulting analytical chemist in London. At the age of 20 he entered the Royal School of Mines at South Kensington, where he took a course in chemistry, and after some analytical practice he studied at University College, London, for the associateship of the Institute of Chemistry. In 1883 he became assistant to Thomas Stevenson, Home Office analyst and lecturer on forensic medicine at Guy's Hospital. Meanwhile, Hopkins began to read for his degree from the University of London, and then in 1888 he began to study medicine at Guy's Hospital. In 1894 he graduated from the University of London in both science and medicine and became an assistant in the department of physiology at Guy's Hospital. In 1898 he joined the physiological department at Cambridge University as a lecturer in order to develop teaching and research in physiological chemistry. That year Hopkins married Jessie Anne Stevens; the marriage resulted in three children.

Hopkins's task at Cambridge, supplemented by tutorial work at Emmanuel College, left him little time for research. In 1910 Trinity College granted him a fellowship and appointed him praelector in physiological chemistry, a position with no formal obligations other than his own research.

During his last few years, Hopkins, who was the ablest analyst and medical specialist in England, suffered from a number of increasing disabilities, including loss of sight. His life's work had been "the exploration of the chemistry of intermediary metabolism, and the establishment of biochemistry as a separate discipline concerned with this active chemistry of the life process, and not merely with its fuels and end-products." When he died at Cambridge on May 16, 1947, he had already seen this aim accepted by scientists throughout the world. As the undisputed dean of English biochemistry, which he had established almost single-handedly, Hopkins was the recipient of many honorary degrees, honors, and prizes, including fellowship in the Royal Society (1906), knighthood (1925), the Copley Medal (1926), and the Nobel Prize in physiology or medicine (1929).

Butterfly Pigments

Hopkins's first mature research paper concerned the chemistry of the pigments of butterflies' wings. His first work on this topic appeared in 1889, but his complete research was not published until 1896 in *Philosophical Transactions of the Royal Society* as "Pigments of Pieridae." Hopkins showed that the opaque white substance in the wings of this butterfly was uric acid—an example of the use of a normal excretory product for purposes of ornamentation. His research on butterfly pigments led him to extend his work to uric acid problems in humans. In 1893 he published two papers describing a new method for determining uric acid in urine, which remained standard practice for many years. He published papers in 1898 and 1899 on the relation of uric acid excretion to diet, a reflection of the interest at that time in gout and its relation to uric acid formation.

Vitamin Research

Hopkins had not been long at Cambridge when he produced a piece of classic research that immediately brought him to the forefront of physiological chemists. While investigating the cause of failure of the Adamkiewicz color test (now called the glyoxylic test) for proteins, he found that the reaction was due not to acetic acid itself but to glyoxylic acid, an impurity. He then used his analytical skill to discover what substance in protein gave this purple color and consequently isolated the hypothetical amino acid tryptophan from the other amino acids present in protein digests. Rather than turning to another subject, Hopkins began feeding experiments with mice to ascertain the role of the newly discovered tryptophan in the diet. He found that although the tryptophan did not make the mice grow, it extended their life-span considerably. This experiment, one of the earliest (1907) demonstrating the importance of quality of diet, was one of the essential classic tests which brought this aspect of nutrition to the attention of the scientific world.

Hopkins's work on vitamins, summarized in his 1912 publication "The Importance of Accessory Food Factors in Normal Dietaries," is generally regarded as his masterpiece. Although other claimants for the honor exist, there is no doubt that Hopkins was the first to realize the full significance of the experimental facts about vitamins. His work had a far-reaching effect on nutritional research all over the world.

World War I interrupted Hopkins's research activities. His next major paper, "An Autoxidisable Constituent of the Cell," was published in 1921. An intervening lecture, "The Dynamic Side of Biochemistry," an address he gave as president of the Physiological Section of the British Association, is noteworthy in that in it Hopkins stated his outlook on chemical processes in living tissues. He pointed out that metabolic raw material is prepared so that it will be in the form of low-molecular-weight substances, and he underscored the importance of the new idea of endoenzymes as the universal agent of the cell. He also suggested greater use of the direct method of attack to separate from tissues additional examples of the simpler products of metabolic changes, regardless of the small amounts of these that were present.

Biological Oxidations

During the 1920s the study of biological oxidations was dominated by two rival theories which were apparently incompatible: one assumed a process due to activation of pairs of hydrogen atoms by tissue enzymes called dehydrogenases; and the other assumed a process brought about by an oxygen-activating catalyst which contains iron. Both of these processes are now known to be valid, and Hopkins, to some extent, succeeded in reconciling them. He isolated a substance which he called glutathione and showed that it could exist in two interconvertible forms: a reduced form and an oxidized form. He proposed that glutathione functioned as an oxygen-carrying catalyst (called by him a coenzyme), with the disulfide oxidized form acting as the hydrogen acceptor in being reduced and then passing on the hydrogen to oxygen during its spontaneous reoxidation. This proposal seems to have furnished the first hint that intermediate hydrogen transport might occur in living tissues, a now well-established fundamental fact in the field of biological oxidation.

True Measure of Importance

The true measure of Hopkins's importance lay not only in his own research but in the inspiration he provided to numerous biochemists who spread his teachings throughout the world. The number of his students elected to university chairs in biochemistry is particularly impressive. *Perspectives in Biochemistry,* published in 1937 in honor of his seventy-fifth birthday by a group of Hopkins's students, gives some idea of their productivity.

At the beginning of the 20th century, physiological chemistry and biochemistry were virtually a German monopoly. In England there were literally no biochemists and only a very few physiological chemists. At the time of Hopkins's retirement, British biochemists were the equal of any in the world.

Further Reading

Much useful information on Hopkins's life is in Joseph Needham and Ernest Baldwin, eds., *Hopkins and Biochemistry, 1861-1947* (1949). Detailed studies of Hopkins's life and work are the memoir by Sir Henry Dale in the Royal Society, *Obituary Notices of Fellows of the Royal Society,* vol. 6 (1948-1949); James Gerald Crowther, *British Scientists of the Twentieth Century* (1952); and Patrick Pringle, *Great Discoverers in Modern Science* (1955). □

Gerard Manley Hopkins

Although the English author and Jesuit Gerard Manley Hopkins (1844-1889) wrote no more than 40 mature poems, he is regarded as one of the major English poets.

Gerard Manley Hopkins was born at Stratford, Essex, on July 28, 1844, into a talented family which encouraged his artistic nature. In 1854 he entered Highgate School, where he distinguished himself as a gifted student and began to write Keatsian nature poetry. At the age of 19 he entered Balliol College, Oxford University. Hopkins's undergraduate letters, notebooks, and sketchbooks reveal his intelligence, sensitivity, and sensuous response to natural beauty. Yet he was physically delicate and revealed an ascetic tendency, a strongwilled desire to curb his passionate and egotistic spirit. At Highgate, for example, he once went a week without drinking any liquids, and at Oxford during Lent he allowed himself "no tea except if to keep me awake and then without sugar."

In 1864 Hopkins was deeply moved by his reading of John Henry Newman's *Apologia pro vita sua,* which carefully detailed the reasons for his conversion to Catholicism. On Oct. 21, 1866, Newman himself received Hopkins into the Roman Catholic Church. Once Hopkins became a Catholic, his need to control his sensuousness and individualism led him steadily toward the most ascetic mode of life he could choose. By January 1868 he had resolved to become a priest, and on September 7 he entered Manresa House, a Jesuit novitiate near London. For 2 years he was a novice at Manresa House. He then took his initial vows and began 3 years of study at Stonyhurst College. In 1874 he returned to Manresa House to teach classics. He then went to St. Beuno's College in North Wales for 3 years of theological studies. He was ordained a priest in 1877 and served for 4 years in parishes in London, Chesterfield, Oxford, Liverpool, and Glasgow. In 1882-1884 he taught Greek and Latin at Stonyhurst, and in January 1884 he was elected to the chair of Greek at University College, Dublin. He taught there until he died of typhoid fever, after a long period of ill health, on June 8, 1889.

"The Wreck of the Deutschland"

During the summer before Hopkins became a Jesuit novice, he burned all the poetry he had written at Highgate and Oxford and "resolved to write no more, as not belonging to my profession, unless it were by the wish of my

superiors." For 7 years (1868-1875) he kept this poetic silence. But on the night of Dec. 7, 1875, a German ship, the *Deutschland,* was wrecked by a storm in the mouth of the Thames River. Most of the passengers were lost, among them five Franciscan nuns who were religious exiles from Germany.

Hopkins was deeply moved by what he considered the martyrdom of the nuns, and when his rector casually expressed the thought that someone should write a poem about it, Hopkins felt relieved of his vow of silence and wrote "The Wreck of the Deutschland." The poem is too long and complex to summarize briefly, but it is essentially a justification of human suffering as God's only means of suppressing the human ego so that men may learn to love Him more than themselves.

The poem is thus conventional in theme. But it is radically innovative in technique, for it is the first poem which Hopkins wrote in what he called "sprung rhythm." Sprung rhythm basically consists of a set number of stressed syllables per line of poetry, but the number of unstressed syllables may vary considerably in each line. If few unstressed syllables are used, the line is heavily accentual, rugged, and slow. If many are used, the line moves quickly and lightly.

Hopkins chose sprung rhythm because he felt it most closely approximated the rhythm of natural speech but was also strongly musical. To heighten this musicality, he often used alliteration, assonance, and internal rhyme. He also made heavy use of elliptical compression, multiple meanings, ambiguous syntax, and paradox. He kept his diction simple and precise, but he borrowed words from Welsh and occasionally created his own. The end result is poetry which anticipates many of the characteristics of modern verse in its force, flexibility, and compression.

Nature Poetry

After "The Wreck of the Deutschland" Hopkins turned to shorter poetry, often written in the sonnet form. Yet he continued to experiment with sprung rhythm. As a result, many of these short lyrics exhibit a tension between the energy and force of the rhythm and the restriction of the form.

Many of the best of these lyrics express Hopkins's ecstatic joy in the beauty of nature. The journal which Hopkins kept from 1868 to 1875 reveals his constant effort to discern and reproduce the particular characteristics of a beautiful object or experience that distinguish it from any other. Hopkins called this individuality or "selfhood" of a thing "inscape" and designated the experience of perceiving inscape and thereby being joined more intimately with the object or experience as "instress."

The journal also shows that from his study of the *Spiritual Exercises* of St. Ignatius of Loyola and the philosophy of John Duns Scotus, Hopkins extended his earlier, purely sensuous view of natural beauty to a sacramental view of nature as a material symbol of God's perfect spiritual beauty. The realization of natural beauty thus becomes a religious experience in which a perceiver is instressed with the inscape of a beautiful thing and thus instressed with God, the creator of that beauty. Many of Hopkins's most beautiful nature poems, such as "Pied Beauty" and "Hurrahing in Harvest," describe precisely this experience. Others, like "God's Grandeur," express Hopkins's despair that man's corruption prevents him from seeing natural beauty as "news of God." His most famous poem, "The Windhover," records his realization of the inscape of Christ through the inscape of a hawk and poses his ecstatic joy in the beauty of both bird and Christ against his willing submission to the asceticism of routine religious duties.

Last Poems

During the last 5 years of his life several problems conspired to depress Hopkins's spirits and restrict his poetic inspiration. He disliked living in Dublin "at a third remove" from England and friends, his work load was extremely heavy, his eyesight began to fail, and his general health deteriorated rapidly. He felt confined in a "coffin of weakness and dejection." Moreover, as a devout Jesuit, he found himself in an artistic dilemma. He had decided never to publish his poetry, to subdue any egotism which would violate the humility required by his religious position. But Hopkins realized that any true poet requires an audience for criticism as well as encouragement. This conflict between his religious obligations and his poetic talent caused him to feel that he had failed both.

Hopkins found himself "time's eunuch," religiously sterile because removed from God's favor and poetically sterile because God is the religious poet's inspiration. In this "winter world" Hopkins's only solution was to make his religious sterility the subject matter of his seven "terrible sonnets . . . written in blood" in 1885. "To Seem the Stranger," "I Wake and Feel the Fell of Dark," "No Worst, There Is None"—poems which Hopkins said came to him "unbidden and against my will"—record his deep despair, feeling of separation from God, and sense of personal worthlessness.

During the last 2 years of his life Hopkins wrote only five additional poems. Two of them still voice despair, but three climb toward renewed hope for reunion with God. The triumphant poem "That Nature Is a Heraclitean Fire and of the Comfort of the Resurrection" explains Hopkins's dying words, "I am so happy."

Further Reading

Two good biographies of Hopkins are Eleanor Ruggles, *Gerard Manley Hopkins: A Life* (1944), and Jean Georges Ritz, *Robert Bridges and Gerard Hopkins, 1863-1889: A Literary Friendship* (1960). John Pick, *Gerard Manley Hopkins: Priest and Poet* (1942; 2d ed. 1966), offers additional insight from the Roman Catholic point of view. Excellent critical analysis of Hopkins's poetry is in *Gerard Manley Hopkins, by the Kenyon Critics* (1945); Wilhelmus Antonius Maria Peters, *Gerard Manley Hopkins: A Critical Essay towards the Understanding of His Poetry* (1948); and William H. Gardner, *Gerard Manley Hopkins, 1884-1889: A Study of Poetic Idiosyncrasy in Relation to Poetic Tradition* (2d ed., 2 vols., 1948-1949).

Additional Sources

Bergonzi, Bernard, *Gerard Manley Hopkins,* London: Macmillan, 1977.

Gerard Manley Hopkins (1844-1889): new essays on his life, writing, and place in English literature, Lewiston, N.Y.: E. Mellen Press, 1989.

Keating, John Edward, *Gerard Manley Hopkins,* Norwood, Pa.: Norwood Editions, 1977.

Kitchen, Paddy, *Gerard Manley Hopkins,* New York: Atheneum, 1979, 1978.

Martin, Robert Bernard, *Gerard Manley Hopkins: a very private life,* New York: Putnam, 1991.

Pick, John, *Gerard Manley Hopkins, priest and poet,* Westport, Conn.: Greenwood Press, 1978, 1966.

Roberts, Gerald, *Gerard Manley Hopkins: a literary life,* New York: St. Martin's Press, 1994.

Srinivasa Iyengar, K. R., *Gerard Manley Hopkins: the man and the poet,* Philadelphia: R. West, 1978.

Weiss, Theodore Russell, *Gerard Manley Hopkins, realist on Parnassus,* Philadelphia: R. West, 1978.

White, Norman, *Hopkins: a literary biography,* Oxford England: Clarendon Press; New York: Oxford University Press, 1992. □

Harry Lloyd Hopkins

Harry Lloyd Hopkins (1890-1946), American statesman, was a Federal relief administrator and personal confidant and emissary of President Roosevelt during World War II.

Harry Hopkins was born in Sioux City, Iowa, on Aug. 17, 1890, the son of a harness maker. He graduated from Grinnell College in 1912. His first job was in social work, and he became increasingly committed to this field. Hopkins was a strong partisan of New York governor Alfred E. Smith and of Franklin Roosevelt. In 1931 Hopkins became chairman of New York State's emergency relief administration. When Roosevelt became president, Hopkins was appointed to head the Civil Works Administration.

In May 1935 Hopkins became administrator of the Works Progress Administration (WPA). He was a determined foe of "the dole," insisting upon the principle that men should be given useful work to do, not subsidized in idleness. He showed remarkable administrative ability. Though he was compelled to attend to political considerations in appointing subordinates, the operations of his agency were carried out efficiently. In the course of his activities more than $8.5 billion was disbursed, and at the height of WPA more than 3 million people were on its rolls. Hopkins got highways, bridges, public buildings, and parks constructed and initiated important projects in conservation and public health. An important aspect of Hopkins's program was the employment of displaced musicians, artists, actors, and writers. An agency was established to resettle or provide loans for indigent farmers; a subordinate agency, the National Youth Administration, gave young people a

chance to earn money to pay for part of their education. A rural electrification program was also enacted. In all, some 15 million people benefited from the program.

In 1938 Hopkins was appointed secretary of commerce, but in this office he accomplished little. In May 1940, after his wife's death, Hopkins moved into the White House with his daughter. After the 1940 election he became interested in foreign affairs and acted as Roosevelt's emissary on trips to Great Britain and, later, to the Soviet Union. He won the complete confidence of Winston Churchill, who described him as "Lord Root of the Matter." During his first trip to the Soviet Union he procured useful information on conditions there through personal conversations with Premier Stalin.

Though racked by severe pain, and the victim of a wasting disease, Hopkins outlived Roosevelt. His last public service was a mission to Moscow at the request of President Harry S. Truman to prepare for the Potsdam Conference of 1945. Hopkins died in New York City on Jan. 29, 1946.

Further Reading

Robert E. Sherwood, *Roosevelt and Hopkins: An Intimate History* (1948; rev. ed. 1950), contains considerable biographical material on Hopkins. For the political background see Arthur Schlesinger, Jr., *The Age of Roosevelt* (3 vols., 1957-1960). ☐

Mark Hopkins

American educator Mark Hopkins (1802-1887) was president of Williams College and a defender of orthodox Protestant religious ideas.

Mark Hopkins was born in Stockbridge, Mass., on Feb. 4, 1802. He entered Williams College in 1822 and graduated 2 years later. After receiving a medical degree from the Berkshire Medical Institute, he alternated medical practice with teaching. In 1830 he became a professor at Williams, and in 1833 he was licensed to preach by the Congregational Church, an event that doubtless eased his election to the presidency of Williams in 1836.

Hopkins came to symbolize Williams College during his 36 years as president. Despite his administrative duties, he continued teaching moral philosophy, an admixture of various subjects connected by a theme of Christian piety and manliness. The course, a commonplace in American higher education of the day, was intended to give graduates a sound character as well as a disciplined mind. For generations of Williams students it was their most memorable experience at the college; it was the basis of Hopkins's fame.

Hopkins was not a sophisticated philosopher. He relied largely on a steadfast and uncritical acceptance of orthodox theology, tempered by common sense and humanity. By his own admission he was unacquainted with the scholarship of his day. He knew the Bible and he knew his students, and this he believed sufficient to achieve the college's purpose.

Although Hopkins's message was received with less enthusiasm as time passed, he was warmly regarded as a great teacher who had humor, compassion, and genuine affection for his pupils. His classes thrived on dispute, provoked by carefully formulated questions that almost invariably led students to the gentle conclusion admired by their professor. Hopkins's willingness to illustrate difficult points with diagrams and models, a novelty at this time, added to his popularity. However, the criticism leveled at the college for its slow response to educational changes after the Civil War led Hopkins to retire in 1872, "that it may not be asked why I do not resign."

Hopkins spent the remainder of his life lecturing, teaching, and writing. His books, generally collections of lectures and baccalaureate sermons, assert an undistinguished but elaborate system of harmony in man and nature under the sovereignty of God. He died at Williamstown on June 17, 1887. His marriage to Mary Hubbell of Williamstown in 1832 had produced 10 children, one of whom, Henry, eventually became president of Williams.

Further Reading

Frederick Rudolph, *Mark Hopkins and the Log: Williams College, 1836-1872* (1956), is a thoroughly documented, well-written analysis of Hopkins and the college within the context of American social and intellectual development. John H. Denison, *Mark Hopkins* (1935), is a somewhat laudatory study by

Hopkins's grandson. See also Estelle Lutta and Mary L. Allison, *Controversial Mark Hopkins* (1953). □

Samuel Hopkins

Samuel Hopkins (1721-1803), New England clergyman and theologian, was a disciple of Jonathan Edwards, whose work he attempted to systematize.

Samuel Hopkins was born on Sept. 17, 1721, in Waterbury, Conn. After a religious upbringing, he took a bachelor of arts degree at Yale College in 1741. This was a year of revival excitement in New England, following in the wake of the visit to America by revivalist George Whitefield. A sermon by Jonathan Edwards made such an impression on Hopkins that he resolved, though an utter stranger, to go to Edwards's Northampton home to live and study under his tutelage.

Hopkins spent 8 months in the Edwards household, the first of many such visits. In this manner, he came to know Jonathan Edwards's daily life, habits of study, and personal values perhaps better than anyone else of this generation. Fortunately, Hopkins left a valuable, short sketch of the great theologian.

During his lifetime Hopkins held two pastorates. The first was at a frontier settlement at Great Barrington, Mass. In 1769, after 25 years there, he was dismissed because the membership was dissatisfied with his preaching, which was evidently too abstract.

Hopkins's next pastorate, which lasted until his death, was in Newport, R.I. There his record was distinctly different. Beginning in 1770, Hopkins made his pulpit a center of protest against slavery. He succeeded in stirring up not only his church membership (among whom were many slaveholders) but also the larger community. He won press support, wrote numerous letters and articles, and agitated for organized political action. He also devised a plan for extensive missionary work in Africa and for colonizing black Americans there. His 1776 *Dialogue concerning the Slavery of the Africans* was perhaps his most outstanding printed contribution to this cause.

Better known and more influential in later times was Hopkins's *System of Doctrines* (2 vols., 1793), setting forth the New Divinity or Hopkinsianism, based on the ideas of Edwards. What Hopkins made of Edwards's imagination, perception, genius, and power may be criticized for its lacks, but he gave Edwards's ideas a chance to be known for another two generations. Hopkins died in Newport on Dec. 20, 1803.

Further Reading

Edwards A. Park, *Memoir of the Life and Character of Samuel Hopkins, D.D.* (1854), contains excerpts from Hopkins's *Autobiography* and *Diary*. A short biography of Hopkins and a selection from his writings are in Hilrie Shelton Smith and others, *American Christianity: An Historical Interpretation*

with Representative Documents, vol. 1 (1960). Stephen West, ed., *Sketches of the Life of the Late Rev. Samuel Hopkins* (1805), includes Hopkins's autobiography. A biography of Hopkins is in Franklin Bowditch Dexter, *Biographical Sketches of the Graduates of Yale College with Annals of the College History* (6 vols., 1885-1912). Joseph Haroutunian, *Piety versus Moralism: The Passing of the New England Theology* (1932), studies Hopkins's theology and writings in detail. □

Francis Hopkinson

Francis Hopkinson (1737-1791), the first native American composer, was also a literary satirist, jurist, and inventor.

Francis Hopkinson was born on Oct. 2, 1737, in Philadelphia. He studied at the academy there and then attended the recently opened College of Philadelphia (later University of Pennsylvania), graduating at 19. In 1759 he composed his first song, "My days have been so wondrous free." Hopkinson read law under the attorney general of the Pennsylvania province and was admitted to the bar in 1761. He was a member of an Indian treaty commission in 1765, the same year he translated the Dutch Psalter and opened a conveyance service in Philadelphia. Benjamin Franklin characterized the young dilettante as "very ingenious," of "good Morals & obliging Disposition." Hopkinson visited Franklin in London in 1766, vainly seeking royal preferment. Back home, he opened a dry-goods shop.

Hopkinson married Ann Borden, of Bordentown, N.J., on Sept. 1, 1768. In 1772 he was an organist at Christ Church in Philadelphia when England's prime minister Lord North appointed him customs collector for Newcastle, Del. Apparently dissatisfied with this position, he moved to Bordentown, resumed practicing law, and in 1774 rose to the governor's council. Also in 1774, he wrote *A Pretty Story,* a satirical anti-British nursery tale.

In 1776 Hopkinson was sent by New Jersey to the Continental Congress, which made him chairman of the naval board and, later, treasurer of loans. He was a signer of the Declaration of Independence. In 1778 he wrote his famous Revolutionary poem, *The Battle of the Kegs,* a jeering ballad commemorating a British "victory" over American mines on the Delaware River.

Hopkinson's *Temple of Minerva,* a gala "oratorical entertainment," was presented in 1781. His pro-Constitution satire, *The New Roof,* appeared in 1787. In 1788 he composed his charming book of music, *Seven Songs.* Also a scientist and inventor, he designed a floating lamp, a spring block to assist sailboats, and a better method of gassing ascension balloons. He is also said to have designed the American flag.

Hopkinson served as an Admiralty judge from 1779 to 1789, when President Washington appointed him a federal judge. He died in Philadelphia on May 9, 1791, survived by his wife and six children.

Further Reading

Hopkinson's *Miscellaneous Essays and Occasional Writings* (3 vols., 1792) is the basic collection of his literary production. Much of Hopkinson's most engaging writing is found in his correspondence, particularly to Jefferson. The best secondary source is George Everett Hastings, *The Life and Works of Francis Hopkinson* (1926). It provides a guide to the originals in the *Miscellaneous Essays* and contains manuscript and published articles not included therein. Benson J. Lossing reprinted the original version of *A Pretty Story,* retitled *The Old Farm and the New Farm: A Political Allegory* (1857). O. G. Sonneck, *Francis Hopkinson: The First American Poet-Composer* (1905), discusses Hopkinson's musical life. □

Edward Hopper

A pioneer in picturing the 20th-century American scene, Edward Hopper (1882-1967) was a realist whose portrayal of his native country was uncompromising, yet filled with deep emotional content.

Edward Hopper was born on July 22, 1882, in Nyack, N.Y. At 17 he entered a New York school for illustrators; then from 1900 he studied for about 6 years at the New York School of Art, mostly under Robert Henri, whose emphasis on contemporary life strongly influenced him. Between 1906 and 1910 Hopper made three long visits to Europe, spent mostly in France but also including

travel to other countries. In Paris he worked on his own, painting outdoor city scenes, and drawing Parisian types. After 1910 he never went abroad again.

Back home, from about 1908 Hopper began painting aspects of the native scene that few others attempted. In contrast to most former Henri students, he was interested less in the human element than in the physical features of the American city and country. But his pictures were too honest to be popular; they were rejected regularly by academic juries and failed to sell. Until he was over 40 he supported himself by commercial art and illustration, which he loathed; but he found time in summers to paint.

In 1915 Hopper took up etching, and in the 60-odd plates produced in the next 8 years, especially between 1919 and 1923, he first expressed in a mature style what he felt about the American scene. His prints presented everyday aspects of America with utter truthfulness, fresh direct vision, and an undertone of intense feeling. They were his first works to be admitted to the big exhibitions, to win prizes, and to attract attention from critics. With this recognition he began in the early 1920s to paint more and with a new assurance, at first in oil, then in watercolor. Thenceforth the two mediums were equally important in his work.

The 1920s brought great changes in Hopper's private life. In 1924 he married the painter Josephine Verstille Nivison, who had also studied under Henri. The couple spent winters in New York, on the top floor of an old house on Washington Square where Hopper had lived since 1913. He was now able to give up commercial work, and they

could spend whole summers in New England, particularly on the seacoast. In 1930 they built a house in South Truro on Cape Cod, where they lived almost half the year thenceforth, with occasional long automobile trips, including several to the Far West and Mexico. Both of them preferred a life of the utmost simplicity and frugality, devoted to painting and country living.

Hopper's subject matter can be divided into three main categories: the city, the small town, and the country. His city scenes were concerned not with the busy life of streets and crowds, but with the city itself as a physical organism, a huge complex of steel, stone, concrete, and glass. When one or two women do appear, they seem to embody the loneliness of so many city dwellers. Often his city interiors at night are seen through windows, from the standpoint of an outside spectator. Light plays an essential role: sunlight and shadow on the city's massive structures, and the varied night lights—streetlamps, store windows, lighted interiors. This interplay of lights of differing colors and intensities turns familiar scenes into pictorial dramas.

Hopper's portrayal of the American small town showed a full awareness of what to others might seem its ugly aspects: the stark New England houses and churches, the pretentious flamboyance of late-19th-century mansions, the unpainted tenements of run-down sections. But there was no overt satire; rather, a deep emotional attachment to his native environment in all its ugliness, banality, and beauty. It was his world; he accepted it, and in a basically affirmative spirit, built his art out of it. It was this combination of love and revealing truth that gave his portrait of contemporary America its depth and intensity.

In his landscapes Hopper broke with the academic idyllicism that focused on unspoiled nature and ignored the works of man. Those prominent features of the American landscape, the railroad and the automobile highway, were essential elements in his works. He liked the relation between the forms of nature and of manmade things—the straight lines of railway tracks; the sharp angles of farm buildings; the clean, functional shapes of lighthouses. Instead of impressionist softness, he liked to picture the clear air, strong sunlight, and high cool skies of the Northeast. His landscapes have a crystalline clarity and often a poignant sense of solitude and stillness.

Hopper's art owed much to his command of design. His paintings were never merely naturalistic renderings but consciously composed works of art. His design had certain marked characteristics. It was built largely on straight lines; the overall structure was usually horizontal, but the horizontals were countered by strong verticals, creating his typical angularity. His style showed no softening with the years; indeed, his later oils were even more uncompromising in their rectilinear construction and reveal interesting parallels with geometric abstraction.

After his breakthrough in the 1920s, Hopper received many honors and awards, and increasing admiration from both traditionalists and the avant-garde. He died in his Washington Square studio on May 15, 1967.

Further Reading

Lloyd Goodrich, *Edward Hopper* (1971), is a fully illustrated biographical and critical study. *Saõ Paulo 9* (1967), the catalog of the Biennial Exhibition held in Saõ Paulo, Brazil, that featured Hopper, contains essays on him by William C. Seitz and Goodrich. □

Grace Hopper

With the longest active military career, Rear Admiral Grace Hopper (1906-1992) was also known as "Amazing Grace" and "Grand Old Lady of Software." She played an instrumental role in the development of the COBOL computer programming language.

Grace Hopper, who rose through Navy ranks to become a rear admiral at age eighty-two, is best known for her contribution to the design and development of the COBOL programming language for business applications. Her professional life spanned the growth of modern computer science, from her work as a young Navy lieutenant programming an early calculating machine to her creation of sophisticated software for microcomputers. She was an influential force and a legendary figure in the development of programming languages. In 1991, President George Bush presented her with the National Medal of Technology "for her pioneering accomplishments" in the field of data processing.

Admiral Hopper was born Grace Brewster Murray on December 9, 1906, in New York City. She was the first child of Marry Campbell Van Horne Murray and Walter Fletcher Murray. Encouraged by her parents to develop her natural mechanical abilities, she disassembled and examined gadgets around the home, and she excelled at mathematics in school. Her grandfather had been a senior civil engineer for New York City who inspired her strong interest in geometry and mathematics.

At Vassar College, Hopper indulged her mathematical interests, and also took courses in physics and engineering. She graduated in 1928, then attended Yale, where she received a master's degree in 1930 and a doctorate in 1934. These were rare achievements, especially for a woman. As Robert Slater points out in *Portraits in Silicon,* U.S. doctorates in mathematics numbered only 1,279 between 1862 and 1934. Despite bleak prospects for female mathematicians in teaching beyond the high school level, Vassar College hired her first as an instructor, then as a professor of mathematics. Hopper taught at Vassar until the beginning of World War II. She lived with her husband, Vincent Foster Hopper, whom she had married in 1930. They were divorced in 1945 and had no children.

In 1943, Hopper joined the U.S. Naval Reserve, attending midshipman's school and obtaining a commission as a lieutenant in 1944. She was immediately assigned to the Bureau of Ships Computation Project at Harvard. The

project, directed by Howard Aiken, was her first introduction to Aiken's task, which was to devise a machine that would assist the Navy in making rapid, difficult computations for such projects as laying a mine field. In other words, Aiken was in the process of building and programming America's first programmable digital computer—the Mark I.

For Hopper, the experience was both disconcerting and instructive. Without any background in computing, she was handed a code book and asked to begin computations. With the help of two ensigns assigned to the project and a sudden plunge into the works of computer pioneer Charles Babbage, Hopper began a crash course on the current state of computation by way of what Aiken called "a computing engine."

The Mark I was the first digital computer to be programmed sequentially. Thus, Hopper experienced first-hand the complexities and frustration that have always been the hallmark of the programming field. The exacting code of machine language could be easily misread or incorrectly written. To reduce the number of programming errors, Hopper and her colleagues collected programs that were free of error and generated a catalogue of subroutines that could be used to develop new programs. By this time, the Mark II had been built. Aiken's team used the two computers side by side, effectively achieving an early instance of multiprocessing.

By the end of the war, Hopper had become enamored of Navy life, but her age —a mere forty years—precluded a transfer from the WAVES into the regular Navy. She re-

mained in the Navy Reserves and stayed on at the Harvard Computational Laboratory as a research fellow, where she continued her work on the Mark computer series. The problem of computer errors continued to plague the Mark team. One day, noticing that the computer had failed, Hopper and her colleagues discovered a moth in a faulty relay. The insect was removed and fixed to the page of a logbook as the "first actual bug found." The words "bug" and "debugging," now familiar terms in computer vocabulary, are attributed to Hopper. In 1949, she left Harvard to take up the position of senior mathematician in a start-up company, the Eckert-Mauchly Computer Corporation. Begun in 1946 by J. Presper Eckert and John Mauchly, the company had by 1949 developed the Binary Automatic Computer, or BINAC, and was in the process of introducing the first Universal Automatic Computer, or UNIVAC. The Eckert-Mauchly UNIVAC, which recorded information on high-speed magnetic tape rather than on punched cards, was an immediate success. The company was later bought by Sperry Corporation. Hopper stayed with the organization and in 1952 became the systems engineer and director of automatic programming for the UNIVAC Division of Sperry, a post she held until 1964.

Hopper's association with UNIVAC resulted in several important advances in the field of programming. Still aware of the constant problems caused by programming errors, Hopper developed an innovative program that would translate the programmer's language into machine language. This first compiler, called "A-O," allowed the programmer to write in a higher-level symbolic language, without having to worry about the tedious binary language of endless numbers that were needed to communicate with the machine itself.

One of the challenges Hopper had to meet in her work on the compiler was that of how to achieve "forward jumps" in a program that had yet to be written. In *Grace Hopper, Navy Admiral and Computer Pioneer*, Charlene Billings explains that Hopper used a strategy from her schooldays—the forward pass in basketball. Forbidden under the rules for women's basketball to dribble more than once, one teammate would routinely pass the basketball down the court to another, then run down the court herself and be in a position to receive the ball and make the basket. Hopper defined what she called a "neutral corner" as a little segment at the end of the computer memory which allowed her a safe space in which to "jump forward" from a given routine, and flag the operation with a message. As each routine was run, it scouted for messages and jumped back and forth, essentially running in a single pass.

During the early 1950s, Hopper began to write articles and deliver papers on her programming innovations. Her first publication, "A Manual of Operation for the Automatic Sequence Controlled Calculator," detailed her initial work on Mark I. "The Education of a Computer," offered in 1952 at a conference of the Association of Computing Machinery, outlined many ideas on software. An article appearing in a 1953 issue of *Computers and Automation*, "Compiling Routines," laid out principles of compiling. In addition to numerous articles and papers, Hopper published a book on computing entitled *Understanding Computers,* with Steven Mandrell.

Having demonstrated that computers are programmable and capable not only of doing arithmetic, but manipulating symbols as well, Hopper worked steadily to improve the design and effectiveness of programming languages. In 1957, she and her staff at UNIVAC created Flow-matic, the first program using English language words. Flow-matic was later incorporated into COBOL, and, according to Jean E. Sammet, constituted Hopper's most direct and vital contribution to COBOL.

The story of COBOL's development illustrated Hopper's wide-reaching influence in the field of programming. IBM had developed FORTRAN, the densely mathematical programming language best suited to scientists. But no comparable language existed for business, despite the clear advantages that computers offered in the area of information processing.

By 1959, it was obvious that a standard programming language was necessary for the business community. Flow-matic was an obvious prototype for a business programming language. At that time, however, IBM and Honeywell were developing their own competing programs. Without cooperative effort, the possibility of a standard language to be used throughout the business world was slim. Hopper, who campaigned for standardization of computers and programming throughout her life, arguing that the lack of standardization created vast inefficiency and waste, was disturbed by this prospect.

The problem was how to achieve a common business language without running afoul of anti-trust laws. In April 1959, a small group of academics and representatives of the computer industry, Hopper among them, met to discuss a standard programming language specifically tailored for the business community. They proposed contacting the Defense Department, which contracted heavily with the business industry, to coordinate a plan, and in May a larger group met with Charles Phillips. The result was the formation of several committees charged with overseeing the design and development of the language that would eventually be known as COBOL—an acronym for "Common Business Oriented Language ." Hopper served as a technical advisor to the Executive Committee.

The unique and far-ranging aspects of COBOL included its readability and its portability. Whereas IBM's FORTRAN used a highly condensed, mathematical code, COBOL used common English language words. COBOL was written for use on different computers and intended to be independent of any one computer company. Hopper championed the use of COBOL in her own work at Sperry, bringing to fruition a COBOL compiler concurrently with RCA in what was dubbed the "Computer Translating Race." Both companies successfully demonstrated their compilers in late 1960.

Hopper was elected a fellow of the Institute of Electrical and Electronics Engineers (IEEE) in 1962 and of the American Association for the Advancement of Science (AAAS) in 1963. She was awarded the Society of Women Engineers Achievement Award in 1964. She continued her work with Sperry, and in 1964 was appointed staff scientist of systems programming, in the UNIVAC Division.

While at Sperry, Hopper remained active in the Navy Reserves, retiring with great reluctance in 1966. But only seven months later, she was asked to direct the standardization of high level languages in the Navy. She returned to active duty in 1967 and was exempted from mandatory retirement at age of sixty-two. She served in the Navy until age seventy-one.

Although she continued to work at Sperry Corporation until 1971, her activities with the Navy brought her increasing recognition as a spokesperson for the usefulness of computers. In 1969, she was named "Man of the Year" by the Data Processing Management Association. In the next two decades, she would garner numerous awards and honorary degrees, including election as a fellow of the Association of Computer Programmers and Analysts (1972), election to membership in the National Academy of Engineering (1973), election as a distinguished fellow of the British Computer Society (1973), the Navy Meritorious Service Medal (1980), induction into the Engineering and Science Hall of Fame (1984), and the Navy Distinguished Service Medal (1986). She lectured widely and took on vested interests in the computer industry, pushing for greater standardization and compatibility in programming and hardware.

Hopper's years with the Navy brought steady promotions. She became captain on the retired list of the Naval Reserve in 1973 and commodore in 1983. In 1985 she earned the rank of rear admiral before retiring in 1986. But her professional life did not end there. She became a senior consultant for the Digital Equipment Corporation immediately after leaving the Navy and worked there until her death, on January 1, 1992. In its obituary, the *New York Times* noted that "[l]ike another Navy figure, Admiral Rickover, Admiral Hopper was known for her combative personality and her unorthodox approach." Unlike many of her colleagues in the early days of computers, Hopper believed in making computers and programming languages increasingly available and accessible to nonspecialists.

Further Reading

Billings, Charlene W., *Grace Hopper, Navy Admiral and Computer Pioneer,* Enslow, 1989.
Slater, Robert, *Portraits in Silicon,* MIT Press, 1987.
New York Times, January 3, 1992.
Sammet, Jean E., "Farewell to Grace Hopper—End of an Era!," in *Communications of the AMC,* April, 1992. □

Horace

Horace (65-8 B.C.), or Quintus Horatius Flaccus, was a Roman lyric poet, satirist, and literary critic. He is generally considered one of the greatest lyric poets of the world.

Horace's boast was to have been "the first to have brought over Aeolian song to Italian measures," that is, to have used the forms and themes of the great lyric poets of Greece in Latin. Although this is not technically correct (Catullus preceded him by a generation), it was nevertheless true that he was the first consistently to imitate and emulate the poets of the great classical age of the Greek lyric, that is, Alcaeus and Sappho, and to adapt the lyric form to patriotic and philosophical themes, rather than to the expression of feelings of love and other personal emotions. The almost total loss of the early lyric poetry of Greece has left Horace as the main transmitter of this tradition to poets of later ages, over whom his influence has been profound ever since his own time.

Horace was born on Dec. 8, 65 B.C., at Venusia (Venosa) on the borders of Lucania and Apulia. His father was a freedman, probably of old Italian stock, and had retired on his savings as an auctioneer's clerk to live on a small farm there. He had, however, high ambitions for Horace, who was apparently his only son, and took him to Rome, where he studied under the famous *grammaticus* Orbilius. Orbilius left Horace with the impression of numerous floggings and a deep distaste for Livius Andronicus and the early Latin poets. Horace's father himself served as his *paedagogus,* an office usually reserved for a slave, whose job it was to accompany a boy to and from school and in general to protect him from moral and physical dangers. Horace later paid tribute to his father for this care and attention, attributing whatever good there might have been in his character to the effects of this tutelage.

After his work with Orbilius, and presumably after advanced training under a *rhetor,* although this is never mentioned by Horace, he went to Athens for further study. As far as we know, his father did not accompany him, and he may have died before Horace's departure. At Athens, Horace studied Greek literature and philosophy and seems to have mingled on fairly easy terms with the other Roman students at what was then little more than a university town. The news of Caesar's assassination in 44 aroused great enthusiasm in the student colony there, who, filled with the romantic idealism of youth, saw in Brutus and Cassius the embodiment of the ideal of the tyrannicide, exemplified in the old Athenian heroes Harmodius and Aristogeiton, who were constant subjects for school exercises and were praised in the teachings of the philosophical schools.

Short Military Career

When Brutus himself visited Athens some 6 months later, Horace accepted his offer of a commission as a military tribune and found himself, along with fellow students like Cicero's son Marcus Tullius Cicero the Younger, an officer in Brutus's army. Horace saw some action and was at the Battle of Philippi in 42 B.C., which destroyed the army of the assassins. He says that he fled from the battle, leaving his shield behind: whether this is literally true or merely a literary convention intended to recall to the reader similar passages in the Greek lyric poets Archilochus and Alcaeus, and also perhaps designed to show that he was never a very significant figure in the resistance to Augustus, is a matter of dispute.

After the defeat at Philippi, Horace was a ruined man. His short military career was at an end; he was an officer of a defeated army and, technically at least, an enemy of the victorious Octavian (later Augustus), Mark Antony, and Lepidus. His father was apparently dead, and the estate which had come to Horace was confiscated to provide allotments for the soldiers of the victorious army on their demobilization. He was soon pardoned in the general amnesty granted by Octavian and then managed to obtain a position as a clerk in the treasury, which kept him from starvation. Whether he had written verse before, we do not know, but he now turned to writing verses in the hope of attaining recognition and patronage, and it is to this period that the earliest *Epodes* and *Satires,* full of the scenes and acquaintances of a rather bohemian life, belong.

Protégé of Maecenas

Horace was soon rewarded. Among the friends he made were the poets Varius and Virgil, who was then engaged in writing the *Eclogues.* Through them he secured, probably in 39 or 38 B.C., an introduction to Maecenas, the confidential adviser of Octavian, a generous patron of literature who was especially interested in obtaining the services of literary men for the glorification of the new regime. Horace was awkward and stammered, and Maecenas, as usual, kept his own counsel; Horace felt that he had failed in his efforts. Nine months later, however, Maecenas wrote to him, and he was admitted to the circle of Maecenas's friends. In 35 B.C. came Horace's first published work,

Book I of his *Satires;* a second book followed in 30 B.C.; and the *Epodes* were published, at Maecenas's suggestion, in 29 B.C.

Meanwhile, Horace was growing in Maecenas's favor and eventually in that of the future emperor Augustus. In 37 B.C. Horace accompanied Maecenas, along with Virgil and Varius, on a diplomatic mission to Brundisium (Brindisi), the discomforts and incidents of which are commemorated in one of the most famous satires of Book I. Sometime later, probably in 34 or 33 B.C., Maecenas presented him with a farm in the Sabine country, near Tibur (Tivoli), which not only provided him with a modest competence and independence and leisure to write but also was a major source of delight to him during the rest of his life.

Thereafter Horace led a life of comfort and retirement in the company of his books and good friends, including many of the most prominent men in Roman political and literary life, and the major events of his life were the publication of his various books: the first three books of his *Odes* in 23 B.C., by which time he was already recognized as being almost a poet laureate; the first book of his literary and philosophical *Epistles* in 20 B.C.; the frigid *Carmen saeculare*, composed under commission to be sung at Augustus's revival of the Secular Games in 17 B.C.; the second book of *Epistles*, published about 14 B.C.; and, at Augustus's express request, the fourth book of the *Odes*, published perhaps in 13 B.C. In the last years of his life, probably after the composition of the fourth book of the *Odes*, he wrote his *Ars poetica*. Horace died on Nov. 27, 8 B.C., only a few weeks after the death of his friend and patron Maecenas, who, on his deathbed, asked Augustus to remember Horace as he would himself.

Suetonius related that at one time Augustus had offered Horace the position of private secretary; but Horace, who had by then acquired a love of leisure and lazy habits totally unsuited to regular work (Suetonius says that Horace lay in bed until 10, which is even more indolent than it would be today, since the Romans were up by dawn), also had the tact, and confidence in the Emperor's good graces, to refuse without offending. He also says that Augustus once wrote complaining that Horace was not mentioning him and his regime's accomplishments enough (this would not necessarily have been considered immodest even for a private citizen at the time) and asking further references to him. This was probably not long before the writing of the *Carmen saeculare*, since Horace seems to have felt that his literary activity was finished with the publication of Book I of the *Epistles*, perhaps because of fears for his health: we do not know when Augustus offered him the private secretaryship.

Horace's Works

The *Satires*, Horace's first published works, although some of the *Epodes* seem to be earlier, were called by Horace himself *sermones* as well as *saturae*. This combination of terms is accurate in describing their nature. *Sermones* means "discourses" or "essays," with the emphasis on the conversational nature of these works. *Satura*, on the other hand, originally meant a mixture of some sort, a mingling of diverse elements. It had no original sense of

personal criticism or attack, nor does it in Horace; in his use of the term he is actually going back to an earlier form of *satura*, preceding his exemplar, Lucilius.

In the *Satires* of Horace, the friend of and apologist for Augustus, the faults and vices attacked are attacked in the abstract; the persons mentioned are types, not recognizable persons; and the geniality and humor with which such characters as the boorish host who makes every conceivable blunder in giving a dinner party or the bore who persists in offering his services and forcing his attentions on Horace cannot be compared to the loathing with which Juvenal pours his scorn on his victims.

Horace, in his *Satires*, is at his best and most typical in the anecdotal relation of his journey to Brundisium or in the satire in which his slave Davus takes advantage of the license of the Saturnalia to treat Horace to a pointed and detailed account of his faults. It might be said that Horace is throughout more interested in self-revelation and exploration than in the exposure of public vices and faults.

The *Epodes* (or "Iambs," as Horace called them, from the meter which predominates in the collection) have had the least influence of any of his works. They seem to be mainly inspired by Archilochus; part of them are satirical, in either the modern or the usual Horatian sense, while others treat various themes—an invitation to dinner, the delights of the country, politics—and are more characteristic of the *Odes*.

The Odes

It is generally considered that Horace's greatest achievement, and one of the greatest achievements of all poetry, was the first three books of the *Odes*. They are in many different meters and on many different themes, although some themes and types recur again and again—the pleasures of convivial drinking and conversation with friends; the joys (as distinct from the passions) of love (with a singularly unreal collection of girls); the shortness of life and the inevitability and finality of death; rather conventional hymns to the gods; and praises of the benefits and wisdom of Augustus's policies for the restoration of civil order and public morality, especially in the noble and stately first six odes of Book III, the "Roman Odes."

These "Roman Odes," if overpraised in the past, remain worthy of praise; they are not likely now, however, to attract the unqualified and unexamined assent to their assumptions they once received. The official *Carmen saeculare* and Book IV, largely official and national, are generally of less value: the additional nonofficial poems of Book IV, usually considered little more than filler, include, however, what many consider the greatest of all his poems, the magnificent *Odes* IV, 7, on the inevitability of death. Here, as in general, Horace's supreme achievement is the expression of ordinary thoughts and sentiments with perfection and finality: this is the true classical ideal, expressed by Alexander Pope as saying "what oft was thought, but ne'er so well expressed."

The *Epistles* of Book I are similar to the *Satires*, except that they are all written as letters, rather than as conversations and dramatizations of scenes. They are more reflective and philosophical in tone than the *Satires* and seem, as was indicated above, to have been meant as Horace's final statement, beyond which he did not intend to write more. In the last years of his life, however, he returned to the epistolary form to discuss his views on the nature of literature.

The second book of the *Epistles* consists of only two letters: the first, addressed to the Emperor, contains a sketch of the history of early Roman literature, which Horace prefers to the work of more recent writers, and an analysis of the inherent flaws of Romans which worked against the development of a great literature—coarseness of temperament, carelessness in composition, and the degenerate taste of readers; the second is largely autobiographical but also contains some remarks on the development of style, stressing the need for careful choice of diction and the essentiality of unremitting revision until perfect ease and aptness is obtained.

The *Ars poetica* (Art of Poetry), the last of Horace's works, is in form a letter to the Pisones, probably the sons of Lucius Calpurnius Piso, based on a lost Hellenistic treatise. It is divided into three parts, discussing, respectively, poetry in general, the form of the poem, and the poet. Throughout, suitability—of subject, of form and language to the subject, of thought and dialogue to the character—is stressed, and the poet is advised to read widely in the best models, to be meticulous in his composition, and to submit his work to the best criticism which he can obtain.

A very large part of the poem is concerned with the drama, and Horace's descriptions and precepts, hardened into unbreakable laws, had a great influence in and after the Renaissance, especially in setting the rigid rules which French classical drama imposed on itself. The poem as a whole, in fact, seems to the modern reader to suffer because it has been so often quoted and adapted, and its teachings so absorbed into the elements of criticism, that it must perforce seem hackneyed. Few works of literary criticism have ever had an influence approaching that of the *Ars poetica* or have contained such sound advice.

Further Reading

There have been several important books on Horace in English in recent years. Eduard Fraenkel, *Horace* (1957), provides the most masterly overall account of Horace's works. Sensitive attention to the lyric poems is given by L. P. Wilkinson, *Horace and His Lyric Poetry* (1945; 2d ed. 1951); N. E. Collinge, *The Structure of Horace's Odes* (1961); and Henry Steele Commager, Jr., *The Odes of Horace: A Critical Study* (1962). Two studies that deal with the *Satires* and *Epistles* are C. O. Brink, *Horace on Poetry* (1963), and Niall Rudd, *The Satires of Horace: A Study* (1966). See also Jacques Perret, *Horace* (1964); G. M. A. Grube, *The Greek and Roman Critics* (1965); and David West, *Reading Horace* (1967). Among the older works are W. Y. Sellar, *Roman Poets of the Augustan Age: Horace and the Elegiac Poets* (1892); John Francis D'Alton, *Horace and His Age: A Study in Historical Background* (1917); Grant Showerman, *Horace and His Influence* (1922); Tenney Frank, *Catullus and Horace: Two Poets in Their Environment* (1928), to be used with care; and J. W. H. Atkins, *Literary Criticism in Antiquity*, vol. 2 (1934).

Additional Sources

Lyne, R. O. A. M., *Horace: behind the public poetry*, New Haven: Yale University Press, 1995. □

Herman Harrell Horne

American philosopher and educator Herman Harrell Horne (1874-1946) was a leading spokesman for philosophical idealism in educational theory and practice during the first half of the 20th century. He advocated a spiritual and religious approach to education.

Herman Harrell Horne was born on November 22, 1874, in Clayton, North Carolina. His father was Hardee Horne, a farmer, and his mother was Ida Caroline Harrell Horne. Horne was educated in the public schools of Clayton and also at the Davis Military Academy in Winston-Salem, North Carolina. He attended the University of North Carolina in the early 1890s, receiving both the B.A. and the M.A. degrees in 1895. Shortly thereafter he attended Harvard University, where he received a second M.A. degree in 1897 and the Ph.D. degree in 1899. He did post-graduate work at the University of Berlin in 1906-1907.

Horne began his teaching career as an instructor in French at the University of North Carolina in 1894, a post he relinquished when he entered Harvard. Following the completion of the doctorate in 1899, Horne took a position as instructor in philosophy at Dartmouth College and quickly rose to the rank of full professor. While at Dartmouth part of his teaching responsibility was in the area of philosophy of education, and some of his students later became prominent educational leaders, such as Harry Woodburn Chase, later chancellor of New York University; Edmund Ezra Day, later president of Cornell University; and Frank Porter Graham, later president of the University of North Carolina. Horne's interest in philosophy of education prompted him to leave academic philosophy at Dartmouth in 1909 for the position of professor of history and philosophy of education at New York University, a post he held until his retirement in 1942. In addition to his regular academic posts, he also lectured at numerous other leading colleges, universities, and seminaries.

Horne was an advocate of that philosophical school of thought known as *idealism,* a school that dominated American philosophy from the mid-19th century well into the 20th. Although idealism fell from favor in more recent times, it exercised a decided influence on American schools and the theory of education and it continues to have moderate influence in religious education. Basically, idealism, as articulated by Horne in *Idealism in Education* (1910), holds to the centrality of the freedom of will, but it also recognizes that the individual is not an isolated entity; rather, the individual is a part of a larger whole.

In *The Philosophy of Education* (1927), Horne stated that "The part implies the whole, and the meaning of the part is that it suggests the nature of the whole." The meaning of the individual being educated, then, lies within the whole. Although our knowledge of the whole is incomplete, the whole partially manifests itself through its parts. For example, we know many things about the human mind and how it works, how good mental health is maintained, and what happens when mental illness afflicts us; however, we do not know as much as we would like to know. What we do have, however, helps us to study the mind and learn even more about health and illness. So it is with education: we may not know in every respect precisely how we can produce better people through education, but we have some partial knowledge, and we should put that knowledge to use. The ideal is spiritual and eternal, while human beings are caught up in a natural world of space and time; hence, the role of idealistic philosophy of education is to show how through education man may find himself as a part of eternal spiritual reality.

Horne argued that there were three main concepts to consider. First, the origin of man is God, the Ultimate Mind, and the distinguishing factor about the creation called man is the human mind. It is through the education of the mind by disciplined study that man perceives and orders the world about him and is able to contemplate God. Second, the nature of man is freedom, for man can choose and decide, although he may do this imperfectly or even badly. Thus, man can choose to be educated, to grow and develop in understanding and comprehension. However, he can also choose not to think. But if man does seek education and the full development of his mind, he becomes what he was intended to be—a thinking being who is capable of choosing and acting wisely. Third is man's destiny. Because no man is all he ever can be, but is in the process of developing, his education never ends. This continual seeking does not end with an individual's death, for it is passed from generation to generation. It extends beyond finite individual humans to the infinite human ideal for the whole human race. Man's destiny, then, is immortality, or to return to God and enter the realm that is spiritual and eternal.

As science, technology, and industrial development moved ahead, idealist philosophical explanations seemed to lose appeal as philosophies such as pragmatism offered more realistic and practical analyses. Horne rose to the challenge with one of his most popular books, *The Democratic Philosophy of Education* (1932, 1978), which was a critical appraisal of John Dewey's progressive educational ideas. Horne's book offered many cogent criticisms and refined analyses of Dewey's ideas and was a welcome addition to the literature of philosophy of education, but it did not stem the tide of philosophical change. Idealism continued to wane in both philosophy and the theory of education.

Horne's influence was, nonetheless, considerable. His popularity as a teacher and his many publications influenced several generations of classroom teachers and educational leaders in the nation's schools. During a teaching career in three different universities that spanned 48 years, Horne taught some 10,000 students and sponsored more than 50 doctoral candidates. He wrote numerous articles and published 26 books, some of which were translated into Chinese, Japanese, and Portuguese. In recognition of his many contributions, he was awarded honorary LL.D. degrees from Wake Forest College, Muhlenberg College, the University of North Carolina, and New York University. Herman Harrell Horne died on August 17, 1946.

Further Reading

Short biographical sketches of Herman Harrell Horne may be found in such works as *The National Cyclopedia of American Biography,* Volume 44 (1967), and the *Biographical Dictionary of American Educators,* Volume 2 (1978). The best brief statement of Horne's philosophy of education is his article "An Idealistic Philosophy of Education," in *The Forty-First Yearbook of the National Society for the Study of Education,* Part 1 (1942). Concise analyses of Horne's major publications are in John P. Wynne, *Theories of Education* (1963), and J. Donald Butler, *Four Philosophies and Their Practice in Education and Religion* (1957). □

Lena Horne

Lena Horne (born 1917) was one of the most popular Black entertainers of the 20th century. A woman of great beauty and commanding stage presence, she performed in nightclubs, concert halls, movies, and on radio and television.

Lena Horne was born in Brooklyn, New York, on June 30, 1917. Her father, Edwin "Teddy" Horne, a numbers game banker, left the household when Lena was three. Her mother, Edna, was an actress with a black theater troupe and traveled extensively. Horne was raised principally by her grandparents, Cora Calhoun and Edwin Horne. Even so, her early life was nomadic since her mother often took her on the road with her. They lived in various parts of the south before Horne was returned to her grandparents home in 1931. After they died, Horne lived with a friend of her mother's, Laura Rollock. Shortly thereafter, Edna married Miguel Rodriguez and Horne moved in with them.

From an early age, Horne had ambitions to be a performer—much against the wishes of her family who felt she should have higher aspirations. The Hornes were an established middle class family, with several members holding college degrees and distinguished positions in organizations such as the NAACP and the Urban League. Nonetheless, Horne pursued her own course and was hired at age 16 at Harlem's famed Cotton Club to dance in the chorus where she held her own against older and more experienced cast members. In 1934, though she had no previous singing experience, she was assigned a singing duet in the club with Avon Long (of "Porgy and Bess" fame). The success of the number inspired Lena to take voice lessons and also got a small role in an all-black Broadway show "Dance with Your Gods." In 1935 she became the featured singer with the Noble Sissle Society Orchestra, which performed at many first-rate hotel ballrooms and nightclubs, including the Cotton Club. She left Sissle in 1936 to perform as a "single" in a variety of New York clubs.

In 1937 Horne married minor politician Louis Jones, by whom she had a daughter and a son (they separated in 1940 and divorced in 1944). She gained some early stage experience in Lew Leslie's revues, "Blackbirds of 1939" and "Blackbirds of 1940," and crossed the racial barrier later in 1940 when she joined one of the great white swing bands, the Charlie Barnet Orchestra. But in that strained context she suffered the many indignities of racial prejudice, especially from hotels and restaurants catering exclusively to whites. She left Barnet in 1941, and her career received an immediate boost from impresario John Hammond, who got her a long engagement at the prestigious Cafe Society Downtown, a club in New York City that catered to intellectual and social activists, both black and white. It was at the Cafe Society that Horne learned about African American history, politics and culture and developed a new appreciation of her heritage. She rekindled her acquaintance with Paul Robeson, whom she had known as a child. In her autobiography, *In Person: Lena Horne* she stated that her conversations with Robeson made her realize "that we [African Americans] were going forward and that knowledge gave me a strength and a sense of unity. Yes, we were going forward and it was up to me to learn more about us and to join actively in our struggle." From that point onward, Horne became a significant voice in the struggle for equality and justice for African Americans in America.

In 1943, a long booking at the Savoy-Plaza Hotel brought her coverage in such national magazines as *LIFE* and, in conjunction with a number of movie appearances, established her as the highest-paid black entertainer in America. She was signed to a seven-year contract with MGM—the first African American woman since 1915 to sign a term contract with a film studio. "They didn't know what to do with me" she told Leonard Maltin of *Entertainment Tonight* regarding the studios dilemma, she wasn't dark enough in color to star with many of the African American actors of the day and her roles in white films were limited, since Hollywood wasn't ready to depict interracial relationships on screen.

Given these harsh limitations imposed on blacks in 1930s and 1940s Hollywood movies (they either played menials or performed song and/or dance numbers), Horne's film career is impressive. After singing roles in "Panama Hattie" (1942), "Harlem on Parade" (1942), "I Dood It" (1943), "Swing Fever" (1943), and "As Thousands Cheer" (1943), she was given a starring role as a seductress in an all-black allegory, "Cabin in the Sky" (1943), which also starred her idol, Ethel Waters (with whom she did not get along). There followed another major role in "Stormy Weather" (1943) and then some non-speaking roles in "Broadway Rhythm" (1944), "Two Girls and a Sailor" (1944), and a musical biography of Rodgers and Hart, "Words and Music" (1948). She refused to take on any roles that were demeaning to her as a woman of color. This alienated her from other black performers and caused an uproar among the black Hollywood "extras." Horne's daughter, in her book *The Hornes: An American Family*

called them "a stock company of stereotypes" who felt threatened by Horne's success. They accused her of being a tool of the NAACP. In her own defense Horne herself wrote in her own autobiography *Lena*, "I was only trying to see if I could avoid in my career some of the traps they had been forced into."

Despite her great fame, Horne continued to experience humiliating racial rebukes, and in the late 1940s she sued a number of restaurants and theaters for race discrimination and also became politically allied with Paul Robeson in the Progressive Citizens of America, a leftist group combating racism. While entertaining troops at Fort Reilly, Kansas during World War II, she saw German POW's seated in the front row and African American soldiers forced to sit behind them. Horne left the stage immediately, went to the local NAACP office and filed a complaint. MGM Studios pulled her off the tour, so she used her own money to travel and entertain the troops. She also assisted Eleanor Roosevelt in her quest for anti-lynching legislation. After the war, Horne worked on behalf of Japanese Americans who faced discrimination.

In 1947, shortly after performing at the London Casino, she married white bandleader Lennie Hayton, a marriage that was kept secret for three years because of racial pressures. Until his death in 1971, Hayton was also her pianist, arranger, conductor, and manager.

In 1950 Horne experienced great success at London's Palladium. However, upon her return to the United States, Horne became one of the many victims of the political blacklist. Because of her leftist sympathies and her racial militancy, she was denied work in radio, television, films, and recordings, though she continued to work the posh hotel and nightclub circuit. By the mid-1950s, the anti-left freeze had thawed somewhat and she made a movie appearance in "Meet Me in Las Vegas" (1956) and recorded for the first time in five years. In 1957 she drew record crowds to the Empire Room of the Waldorf-Astoria, and in 1958 and 1959 she starred in a Broadway musical, "Jamaica."

During the 1960's Horne was involved in the American Civil Rights movement. She participated in the March on Washington in 1963, performing at rallies in the South and elsewhere, and working on behalf of the National Council for Negro Women. During the same period, she was also very visible on television appearing on popular variety shows and in her own special *Lena in Concert* in 1969. In 1969 Horne also landed a straight acting role, starring opposite Richard Widmark in the movie "Death of a Gunfighter."

Lennie Hayton's death in 1971, which followed the deaths of Horne's father and her son, plunged her into a state of depression from which she emerged seemingly more resolute than ever. In 1973 and 1974 she toured England and the United States with Tony Bennett; in 1979, on a bill with composer Marvin Hamlisch at the Westbury (New York) Music Fair, Horne's performance inspired critic John S. Wilson to observe a change in her, "an intensity, sometimes warm and intimate, sometimes ominously commanding in every syllable that she projects." She also, for

the first time, shed her customary reserve, even permitting herself some patter between songs, and seemed to let the audience get emotionally closer to her.

In 1981 Horne had her greatest triumph, a Broadway show called "Lena Horne: The Lady and Her Music," which for 14 months was the talk of show business. It won a special Tony award, and the soundtrack won two Grammy awards. It became the standard against which all one-person shows are measured. In 1982 she took the production on a very successful cross-country tour. Horne wrote of the experience in *Ebony* magazine (1990) "as the most rewarding event in my entire career."

In the 1990's, Horne cut back on performing telling *Time*, "I went through this delayed reaction to the deaths . . . of my father and my son and my husband Lennie Hayton . . . For about nine years I went underground." She was drawn back from semi-retirement to do a tribute concert for a long-time friend, composer Billy Strayhorn at the JVC Jazz Festival "when I came back to do the concert . . . and it went over so well, everybody was saying 'You ought to keep singing.' So to shut them up, I did it," Horne told *Jet*. At age 76 she released her first album in a decade *We'll Be Together Again*. In 1997, on the occasion of her 80th birthday, Horne was honored at the JVC Jazz Festival, with a tribute concert and the Ella Award for Lifetime Achievement in Vocal Artistry.

Lena Horne was a woman of great beauty and majesty: the eyes sparkled vivaciously and the mouth curled with seething emotion. "She is one of the incomparable performers of our time," Richard Watts Jr. wrote of Horne in the *New York Post* in 1957. Her pride in her heritage, her refusal to compromise herself, and her innate elegance, grace and dignity made Horne a legendary figure, whose role as a catalyst in the elevation of the status of African Americans in the performing arts provide an enduring legacy.

Further Reading

An early biography is Helen Greenberg and Carlton Moss's *In Person, Lena Horne* (1950). A more recent work is *Lena: A Personal and Professional Biography of Lena Horne* (1984) by James Haskins with Kathleen Benson. The best sources, however, are Lena's autobiography, *Lena* (1965, paperback 1986) co-authored by Richard Schickel, and *The Hornes: An American Family* (1986) by Lena Horne's daughter Gail Lumet Buckley. □

Matina Souretis Horner

Scholar and administrator Matina Horner (born 1939) did early research into women's fear of success. She later became the youngest president of Radcliffe College during a period of redefining its relationship with Harvard University.

Matina Souretis Horner was born July 28, 1939, in Roxbury, Massachusetts, to Greek parents who decided to remain in the United States after World War II broke out in Europe. While attending Bryn Mawr College in Pennsylvania she became interested in experimental psychology and studied "need achievement" in Greek and Jewish subculture groups for her honors thesis. She obtained her BA degree *cum laude* in 1961. It was at Bryn Mawr that Matina Souretis met Joseph L. Horner, a future research physicist. The two were married in 1961 and in the autumn of that year both went to the University of Michigan for graduate studies. Matina Horner completed her Masters of Science degree in 1963 and earned her Ph.D. degree in 1968.

Horner possessed unusual intelligence and ambition. Even as a child in kindergarten she tutored other children in arithmetic and spelling. In 1960 she was a research assistant under a grant from the National Institute of Mental Health. At the University of Michigan, Horner served as research assistant in the Department of Psychology, held a teaching fellowship, and was a lecturer in the university's Department of Social Relations.

During Horner's early research into intelligence, motivation, and achievement she became aware that much of the research paid little attention to women's motivation toward achievement. She decided to concentrate her motivation research on that, and while her co-researchers concluded that high anxiety levels found in women they tested were caused by their fear of failure, Matina Horner reasoned that their anxiety might well have been caused by the possi-

bility of success instead. To verify her hypothesis Horner conducted a study of 90 female and 88 male students at the university in 1964. Males were asked to complete a story about John, a struggling male medical student, while females were to finish a similar story of Anne, a female student. Ninety percent of the men finished their story with John as happy, successful, and prosperous. However, 65 percent of the females saw Anne's future in negative terms. From their comments Horner concluded that women developed high anxiety levels because they could not reconcile their desire to excel with society's view that women who were very intelligent, independent, or ambitious were unfeminine. Horner's "fear of success" theory became a potent tool in the women's movement.

In 1969 Horner joined the faculty of Harvard University as a lecturer in the Department of Social Relations. The following year she was named assistant professor in that department's Personality and Development Wing. She was popular with Harvard and Radcliffe students, both at the undergraduate level and in graduate seminars.

Just three years after her appointment to the Harvard faculty Horner was selected by the Radcliffe board of trustees on May 15, 1972, to become the sixth and youngest president in its history, in which position she remained until 1989. She inherited the complex and continuing Radcliffe-Harvard relationship. When Radcliffe was started in 1879, its purpose was to offer women "equal access" to Harvard and its outstanding faculty. But only when World War II decimated the number of male students were Radcliffe women allowed into Harvard classes, and it was 1967 before women were permitted to use Harvard's undergraduate library. Men and women were allowed to have a joint commencement at Harvard first in 1970. When Mary Bunting, Horner's predecessor, resigned her post saying that there was not enough trust and not enough respect between the two colleges, the debate over whether Radcliffe College should be merged with Harvard was at its peak. Some believed that financial considerations would necessitate their merger, but Horner thought it important that Radcliffe retain its corporate independence in order to determine its own priorities.

Another problem facing Horner was the admission policy. Although Harvard had agreed to lower the percentage of men in its total student body from about 80 percent to 70 percent, it was still short of "equality." Some doubted that the young, soft-spoken Horner could gain any more concessions because of the fear that alumni donations would drop off if more women replaced men in Harvard's classes. Horner explained later that she listened to all the arguments and then said it was "interesting that all of the evidence seemed to indicate that Harvard alumni had only male children." It must have been an effective point since in 1975 it was declared that both Radcliffe and Harvard would no longer have limits on the number of women students who could be admitted.

Horner was also concerned that so few women were among Harvard's tenured faculty. To ameliorate the problem she used Radcliffe's independent status to encourage junior faculty women to publish by establishing the

Radcliffe biography series, a special book publishing program. In 1978 one of its first publications, entitled *Women of Crisis,* became a bestseller.

President Jimmy Carter in 1979 recognized Horner's special talents when he appointed her to the President's Commission for the National Agenda for the 1980s. The following year he asked her to serve as chairperson of the Task Force on the Quality of American Life.

Despite her many administrative duties at Radcliffe, Horner maintained direct contact with students by reserving time for weekly conferences with them and by teaching several classes. As a scholar, administrator, and mother of three children, Matina Horner became an important role model for many young American women who wished to combine the traditional feminine roles with a professional life.

Since her retirement as president of Radcliffe, she was named to the Boards of Directors of the Neiman Marcus Group and the Boston Edison Company; was executive vice-president of TIAA-CREF in New York; was on the Board of Trustees for Massachusetts General Hospital Institute of Health Professions (becoming chairman in 1995); received the Distinguished Bostonian Award in 1990, the Ellis Island Medal in 1990; and was an active member in NOW (National Organization for Women).

Further Reading

Biographical information for Matina Horner is available in the March 20 and May 29, 1972, issues of *Time.* Further data is in Barbara Rose's "Success: You Can Learn To Love It," *Vogue,* June 1973. A brief history of Radcliffe College and Horner's role in that institution may be found in "Fair Radcliffe at One Hundred," *Time,* March 19, 1979. In Kathleen Hirsch's "My Side: Matina Horner," *Working Woman,* January 1984, Horner reflected on advances for women and what the future may hold for them. □

Karen Danielsen Horney

The German-born American psychoanalyst Karen Danielsen Horney (1885-1952) was a pioneer of neo-Freudianism. She believed that every human being has an innate drive toward self-realization and that neurosis is essentially a process obstructing this healthy development.

Born in Hamburg on Sept. 16, 1885, Karen Horney received her medical and psychiatric education in Berlin. Her medical practice began in 1913, and then she taught in the Berlin Psychoanalytic Institute (1918-1932). She participated in many international congresses in which Sigmund Freud was the leading figure, but being influenced by the new currents of 20th-century science, she increasingly questioned some of Freud's ideas.

In 1932 Horney went to Chicago, Ill., where she served as associate director of the Chicago Psychoanalytic Institute

until 1934. Then she taught at the New York Psychoanalytic Institute until 1941, when she made her definitive move away from the Freudian group. She took the lead in founding the Association for the Advancement of Psychoanalysis; she was the founding dean (1941-1952) of the American Institute for Psychoanalysis and the founding editor (1941-1952) of the *American Journal of Psychoanalysis.*

In Europe Horney contributed to psychoanalysis in papers dealing mainly with the field of feminine psychology. She opposed Freud's idea that penis envy and the rejection of femininity were the basic factors in woman's psychology, that her wishes for a child and for a man were merely a conversion of her unsatisfied wish for a penis.

Between 1937 and 1951 Horney, a person of remarkable aliveness and dedication, was at the peak of her creative life. While practicing and teaching psycho-analysis, she wrote many articles and five books in which she presented the development of her psychoanalytic concepts.

In *The Neurotic Personality of Our Time* (1937) Horney expressed the view that neuroses are generated by cultural disturbances and conflicts which the person has experienced in accentuated form mainly in childhood, in which he did not receive love, guidance, respect, and opportunities for growth. She described the neurotic character structure as a dynamic process with basic anxiety, defenses against anxiety, conflict, and solutions to conflict as its essential elements.

In *New Ways in Psychoanalysis* (1939) Horney presented her major differences with Freud. While continuing to adhere to the fundamental importance of unconscious forces, inner conflicts, free association, dreams, the analytic relationship, and neurotic defenses in psychoanalysis, she rejected Freud's concepts of the role of instincts in health and emotional illness. She saw aggression and sexual problems as the result of neurotic development rather than its cause.

In *Self-analysis* (1942) Horney indicated the possibilities, limitations, and specific ways in which people can change through increasing self-awareness.

Horney focused on the central position of conflict and solutions to conflict in neurosis in *Our Inner Conflicts* (1945). She saw the neurotic child feeling helpless and isolated in a potentially hostile world, seeking a feeling of safety in compulsive moves toward, against, and away from others. Each of these moves came to constitute comprehensive philosophies of life and patterns of interpersonal relating. The conflict between these opposed moves she called the basic conflict and recognized that it required the individual to resort to means for restoring a sense of inner unity. These means she called the neurotic solutions.

Neurosis and Human Growth (1950) was Horney's definitive work, in which she placed her concept of healthy development in the foreground. She viewed the real self as the core of the individual, the source of inherent, constructive, evolutionary forces which under favorable circumstances grow and unfold in a dynamic process of self-realization. She presented "a morality of evolution," in which she viewed as moral all that enhances self-realization and as immoral all that hinders it. The most serious obstacle to healthy growth was the neurotic solution, which she called self-idealization, the attempt to see and to mold oneself into a glorified, idealized, illusory image with strivings for superiority, power, perfection, and vindictive triumph over others. This search for glory inevitably leads the individual to move away from himself (alienation) and against himself (self-hate). "At war with himself," his suffering increases, his relationships with others are further impaired, and the self-perpetuating neurotic cycle continues.

Horney died in New York on Dec. 4, 1952. She had helped to lay the groundwork for the Karen Horney Clinic, which was established in 1955.

Further Reading

Analytic and critical discussions of Karen Horney's ideas are in Ruth L. Munroe, *Schools of Psychoanalytic Thought: An Exposition, Critique, and Attempt at Integration* (1955); "The Holistic Approach" by Harold Kelman in Silvano Arieti, ed., *American Handbook of Psychiatry,* vol. 2 (1959); and "Karen Horney" by Jack L. Rubins in Alfred M. Freedman and Harold I. Kaplan, eds., *Comprehensive Textbook of Psychiatry* (1967). An important background study is Henri F. Ellenberger, *The Discovery of the Unconscious: The History and Evolution of Dynamic Psychiatry* (1970).

Additional Sources

Horney, Karen, *The adolescent diaries of Karen Horney,* New York: Basic Books, 1980.

Paris, Bernard J., *Karen Horney: a psychoanalyst's search for self-understanding,* New Haven: Yale University Press, 1994.

Quinn, Susan, *A mind of her own: the life of Karen Horney,* New York: Summit Books, 1987; Reading, Massachussetts: Addison-Wesley Publishing Co., 1988.

Rubins, Jack L., *Karen Horney: gentle rebel of psychoanalysis,* New York: Dial Press, 1978. □

Vladimir Horowitz

American pianist Vladimir Horowitz (1904-1989) was among the last performers in the 19th-century grand-virtuoso tradition. While his phenomenal technique sometimes overwhelmed the music, the power and energy of his playing were unsurpassed.

During his lifetime, Vladimir Horowitz was recognized as the greatest piano virtuoso of the 20th century. Michael Walsh noted in an 1986 report "At his peak Horowitz had it all, heightened and amplified by a daredevil recklessness that infused every performance with an exhilarating, unabashed theatricality.... [He was] this most extraordinary of artists." Vladimir Horowitz's birth occurred in 1904 in Russia. He began to study piano with his mother at around age three. Within a few years he was seriously studying the instrument and by his late teens had already composed several songs. Other members of the family were also musical, especially Horowitz's sister, Regina, who also became a concert pianist, and an uncle who

had studied composition with Scriabin and who arranged for Horowitz's concerts before the pianist left Russia.

Although Horowitz revealed talent at an early age, he was not considered a prodigy. He enrolled in the Kiev Conservatory in 1912, first studying with his mother's teacher, Vladimir Puchalsky, then Sergei Tarnowsky in 1915, and, finally, Felix Blumenfeld, a student of Anton Rubinstein, in 1919. Horowitz credited the last mentioned for his flat-fingered technique which resulted in a semistaccato attack and produced a brilliant tone. Blumenfeld was to be Horowitz's last teacher, although he would have occasional lessons with Cartot in France. Throughout his conservatory years Horowitz usually practiced less than four hours a day, and this rather inefficiently, at least from a technical standpoint, preferring to play through operatic literature rather than work at the progressive lessons and exercises familiar to most pianists. From the beginning his intention had been to pursue a dual career as composer-pianist in the tradition of Liszt and Rachmaninoff. The Bolshevik takeover of Kiev in 1920, however, put an end to this plan, forcing him to concentrate on concerts as an efficient means to deriving an income. In the 1920's Horowitz gave 100 performances and earned a reputation as an explosive pianist capable of breaking piano strings with his thundering style.

During this period Horowitz met the famous German pianist Arthur Schnabel, who advised him to leave Russia, and shortly thereafter, in 1923, he found the means to do so through Alexander Merovich, his first manager. Horowitz's first European tour, as arranged by Merovich, included per-

formances in Berlin and Paris; neither city accepted him without reservation. The rising anti-Semitism in Germany discouraged a Jewish musician who, moreover, did not play German music and who played in a romantic, high-flown style unacceptable to the German ideals of precision and strict adherence to the score. The French were as unreceptive to Horowitz's programming as the Germans, again preferring to hear music of their own composers.

Horowitz's New York debut took place on January 12, 1928, at Carnegie Hall, with Sir Thomas Beecham conducting the New York Philharmonic in the Tchaikovsky piano concerto. Although the passion and agility of Horowitz's playing amazed critics, the performance as a whole suffered from irreconcilable differences in interpretation and tempo between conductor and soloist.

A meeting with Rachmaninoff a few days before his New York debut marked the beginning of a friendship that would continue until Rachmaninoff's death in 1943. Equally important was his introduction to Toscanini in April 1932. In addition to the many fruitful collaborations that would take place between the two, Horowitz became further acquainted with Toscanini's daughter, whom he married in 1933.

The sensational qualities of Horowitz's playing soon established him at the forefront of the American concert scene. He found it increasingly difficult, however, to mediate between the public's and his manager's demands for brilliant showpieces and the more solid musicality of those around him, especially his father-in-law and mentor, Toscanini. This, along with the daily grind of a hectic concert schedule, a nervous constitution, and other personal problems, necessitated three extended absences from the stage and, partially, from recording. These occurred during the years 1936-1939, 1953-1965, and 1969-1973. Horowitz also became less interested in performing outside the United States, where he acquired citizenship in 1945. Between the years 1939 and 1986 he made only one tour of Europe, playing three London concerts in October 1951 and two recitals in Paris the following month. In 1986 he began a tour with a return to the Soviet Union—his first visit since leaving there 60 years before—for performances in Moscow and Leningrad in April. He then continued on to Hamburg, Berlin, and London.

Horowitz was undoubtedly one of the great pianists of the era and was compared to Franz Liszt in his total command of the instrument. He was most comfortable with Romantic works, especially Liszt and Rachmaninoff, and admitted a dislike for modern music that exploits the percussive, rather than lyrical, capabilities of the piano. Of the composers who can be admitted stylistically to the 20th century, Horowitz played only Debussy, Ravel, Scriabin, Prokofiev, and Barber. Acknowledging his affinity for their music, Prokofiev requested that Horowitz give the American premiers of his sonatas 6-8 (the *War Sonatas*), and Barber wrote the fourth movement fugue to his *Sonata, Op. 26* at the pianist's request for "something very flashy, but with content." In later years Horowitz tended away from these early moderns.

Among his many recordings, several deserve mention. Liszt's *Sonata in B Minor,* recorded in 1932 for RCA, shows Horowitz at the peak of his powers, especially in the clarity, evenness, and speed of his scale passages and octaves. A collaboration with Toscanini and the NBC Symphony Orchestra in a 1940 recording of Brahms' second piano concerto for RCA demonstrated the benefit of Horowitz's yielding control to the more solid formal instincts of the conductor. This recording also received praise for the comparatively life-like quality of the sound. Many consider Horowitz to be the foremost interpreter of Rachmaninoff, and especially of his third piano concerto. The first of Horowitz's three renditions of the work, a 1930 recording with Albert Coates and the London Symphony, is perhaps the preferred. Outside his usual repertory, Horowitz championed the works of two pre-Romantic composers, Muzio Clementi and Domenico Scarlatti, on two albums for RCA and Columbia, respectively.

Horowitz limited his teaching to only a few of the most talented prospects and later acknowledged only Byron Janis, Ronald Turini, and Gary Graffman as having studied with him. While Janis was typical in describing the difficulty of working with the strong personality of Horowitz, he ascribed his regard for pedaling according to varying acoustical situations to Horowitz's teaching. In 1995 and 1996, *The Private Collection I & II* were released based upon the private tapes owned by Horowitz.

Horowitz died of a heart attack on November 5, 1989 in New York City. "At his best," wrote Joah von Rhein in the *Chicago Tribune,* "Horowitz had a thunderous sonority and demonic daring that literally nobody in the world could match."

Further Reading

The most complete account of Horowitz's life is Glen Plaskin's *Horowitz* (1983). Thoroughly researched, meticulously documented, eminently readable, and impartial, it is a model of biographical writing. An abridged version of Chapter 10, describing Horowitz's introduction to the Toscanini family, appears in *Musical America* (March 1983). Shorter biographies are included in Harold Schonberg's *The Great Pianists* (1963) and in Wilson Lyle's *A Dictionary of Pianists* (1985). The May 5, 1986, issue of *Time* contains biographical material plus a description of his April 1986 return to Russia. The June 8, 1997 *Jerusalem Post* also had a fine feature on him, "The Fairy Tale Life of Vladimir Horowitz." □

Nicholas Horthy de Nagybánya

The Hungarian admiral and statesman Nicholas Horthy de Nagybánya (1868-1957) was regent of Hungary from 1920 to 1944. He led Hungary during a troubled period which began with a Communist revolution and ended with German and then Russian occupation.

By the Treaty of Trianon (June 4, 1920) Hungary lost 72 percent of its territory, 64 percent of its population, and most of its natural resources and markets. Hungary therefore hoped for treaty revision at the expense of its newly created neighbors, Czechoslovakia and Yugoslavia, and the much expanded state of Romania. Adm. Nicholas Horthy de Nagybánya, a convinced revisionist, believed that only friendship with England could effect the restoration of Hungary's prewar boundaries. But Hungary's economic subservience to Germany and the Reich's growing military strength brought Hungary within Germany's political sphere. The eventuality which Adm. Horthy feared most came to pass, for Hungary joined in World War II against England.

Nicholas Horthy de Nagybánya was born on June 18, 1868, in Kenderes of a Calvinist family of the middle gentry. He entered the Austro-Hungarian Naval Academy in 1882 and went on to serve uneventfully until 1908-1909, when he commanded the embassy yacht *Taurus* in Constantinople during the Young Turk revolutions of those years. In 1909 he was appointed naval aide-de-camp to Emperor Francis Joseph, a position which he held until 1914, acquiring the greatest respect for the aged emperor.

Horthy received command of the cruiser *Novara* in December 1914 and broke the Allied blockade during several actions in the Adriatic Sea. In May 1917 he commanded a squadron of three ships which conducted a successful action in the Straits of Otranto. In January 1918 he was named admiral and commander-in-chief of the Austro-Hungarian navy, in which position he had to surrender the fleet to the Yugoslav National Council on Oct. 31, 1918.

Regent of Hungary

Having returned to Hungary, Horthy became minister of war in the government Count Gyula Károlyi formed at Szeged to oppose Béla Kun's Bolshevik government in Budapest. He resigned in July 1919, though he retained command of the counterrevolutionary forces he had organized. Upon the Kun regime's collapse in August 1919, Horthy's forces began a "white terror" for which he was blamed by liberal elements. When the Romanian army, which had ejected the Kun regime, retired from Budapest, Horthy's forces entered the capital on Nov. 16, 1919. The parliament elected in January 1920 declared the restoration of the monarchy and, pending settlement of the status of the Hapsburg king Charles IV, elected Horthy regent of Hungary on May 1, 1920. Horthy then twice denied Charles his throne (March and October 1921), thereby offending conservative and legitimist elements. Simultaneously, the attempted restoration so frightened Czechoslovakia, Romania, and Yugoslavia that they concluded the Little Entente to oppose the restoration of the Hapsburg dynasty in Hungary and Hungarian revisionism.

Horthy was inactive in the period 1921-1931 because of his limited constitutional prerogatives and because of his confidence in his conservative prime minister, Count István Bethlen. Hungary's inability to export its agricultural surpluses, coupled with overborrowing during the 1920s, caused an economic crisis during the Depression, forcing the resignation of Count Bethlen and the appointment soon afterward of Gyula Gömbös, an admirer of Germany, to the premiership. Germany's willingness to absorb Hungary's agricultural exports and to support its revisionist claims caused Hungarian policy gradually to conform with Germany's. The rise of pro-German sentiment in the country and Germany's growing strength caused Horthy to assume a more active role in the country's affairs, and he received the power to prolong and prorogue Parliament in 1933 and the power to enjoy independence from parliamentary responsibility in 1937. Nevertheless, opposition from the Little Entente powers supported by France, combined with distrust of the Soviet Union and the indifference of England, led Hungary to a dependence on Germany and Fascist Italy.

Opposition to Germany

After the Anschluss of March 1938 united Nazi Germany and Austria politically, Horthy's policy consisted of opposing German influence in Hungary and attempting to retain the goodwill of the Western powers. This policy, however, was complicated by Hungary's acceptance of Czechoslovak and Romanian territories from Germany as a result of the Munich Agreement in 1938 and the Vienna Award in 1940. When Germany invaded the Soviet Union in June 1941, Hungary joined Germany and declared war on the Western Allies on Dec. 13, 1941.

Horthy resisted German economic and political demands during the war. He encouraged attempts to negotiate for peace with the Allies, but Hungary's geographic position made it difficult to break away from Germany. As the Eastern front reached the Hungarian border, German troops occupied the country in March 1944, but Horthy remained regent in order "to save what could be saved."

As Russian troops entered Hungary in September 1944, Horthy relinquished hope in the Western powers and dispatched a mission to Moscow to conclude a preliminary armistice. When he publicly pleaded for an armistice on Oct. 15, 1944, however, he was arrested by the Germans, forced to abdicate, and imprisoned in Germany. On May 4, 1945, Horthy was taken by American troops in the Tirol and imprisoned at Nuremberg. Finally it was decided not to try him, and so he was released on Jan. 2, 1946. Hungary was then Communist-controlled, and Nicholas Horthy de Nagybánya retired to Estoril, Portugal. He published his *Memoirs* in 1956 and died on Feb. 9, 1957.

Further Reading

Horthy wrote his *Memoirs* (trans. 1957). Also published were *The Confidential Papers of Admiral Horthy* (trans. 1965). For material on Horthy see Miklós Kállay, *Hungarian Premier: A Personal Account of a Nation's Struggle in the Second World War* (trans. 1954); Carlile Aylmer Macartney, *October Fifteenth: A History of Modern Hungary, 1929-1945* (2 vols., 1956-1957; 2d ed. 1961); and Denis Sinor, *History of Hungary* (1959). □

Hosea

Hosea (active 750-722 B.C.) was a prophet of the kingdom of Israel. He called on Israel to repent its sins of apostasy and warned of the judgment to come from God. His writings form the first of the Old Testament books of the Minor Prophets.

Hosea was the son of Beeri and apparently belonged to the upper classes. Judging from his elegant style, he was highly cultured. Hosea married Gomer, daughter of Diblaim, who bore him two sons, the older of whom he called Yezreel, meaning "God sows." This name may have been intended to signify the replanting of Israel back on its own soil after it had been dispersed in exile. The second son was called Lo Ami, meaning "not my people," to indicate God's rejection of Israel as His people because of its faithlessness. Hosea's daughter by Gomer was metaphorically named Lo-ruhamah, meaning "the unpitied one." Since Gomer after her marriage became an unfaithful "wife of harlotry," it is possible that Lo-ruhamah and perhaps her brothers were illegitimate children. Scholars have speculated whether the prophet's tragic marital experience was real or merely an allegory to stress the infidelity of Israel.

The prophet recalled God's affection for Israel, from the days of its infancy, when He taught it how to walk and led it through the perils of the desert to the Promised Land. But Israel's goodness is as evanescent "as a morning cloud and the dew that early passeth away"; it must therefore suffer dire punishment and divine wrath. Because it "sows the wind, it shall reap the whirlwind." Hosea, however, does not leave his people without hope; he conceives the God of Israel in the loftiest terms as a God of Love. Israel will yet repent and return to its God.

Hosea's times were confused. Economically a great change had taken place in the reign of Jeroboam II (785-745 B.C.). The cities had grown in wealth and fostered a small class of rich landowners, merchants, and creditors. However, the vast majority of the urban population was made up of poor artisans, craftsmen, and laborers who were frequently exploited or even enslaved by the rich. In the country indigent farmers were often compelled to sell their holdings to the rich and migrate to the cities. The upper classes were favored by the rulers and judges; they readily adopted the ways of their neighbors and worshiped their heathen gods in place of the God of Israel, who "demanded mercy and not sacrifice, and the knowledge of God rather than burnt offerings." For this reason Hosea denounced idolatry as the "spirit of harlotry," which leads to moral degeneration, sin, and corruption.

Politically, too, the times were turbulent. Tiglathpileser III threatened the Northern kingdom as well as other nations. Internally, vast dynastic changes were taking place, despite the external danger. In 2 decades, six kings—four of them regicides—ascended the throne of Israel. In this state of political chaos the rulers of Israel and Judea made alliances, at times with Assyria and at other times with its powerful rival, Egypt. Hosea ridicules the diplomacy of princes who do not know which way to turn and describes Ephraim "as a silly dove, without understanding." He saw the alliances as useless, for Ephraim must be punished for his vices and moral degeneracy; his sins shall be purged in exile. In 722 B.C. the Northern Kingdom of Israel came to an end and passed out of history.

The Book of Hosea consists of two sections. The first 3 chapters may be autobiographical. The subsequent 11 chapters deal with the religious and social collapse that called for God's punishment of His people. The book concludes with a plea to the people to return to God, who in His abiding love will be reconciled with them. The people that were "not loved" (Lo-ruhamah) would be loved once again, and "not my people" (Lo-ami) would be reunited with their God again, in a new spiritual betrothal.

Further Reading

The Book of Hosea has been annotated and commented upon in such works as Abraham Cohen, ed., *The Twelve Prophets: Hebrew Text, English Translation and Commentary* (1948), and George A. Buttrick, ed., *The Interpreter's Bible* (12 vols., 1951-1957). The chapter on Hosea in Abraham J. Heschel, *The Prophets* (1962), provides an understanding of the prophet and his times. □

Ho-shen

Ho-shen (1750-1799) was a high Manchu official in the government of the Ch'ing dynasty in China and a

close associate of Emperor Ch'ien-lung. Ho-shen's factionalism and corruption are generally considered among the major causes of the decline of the Ch'ing dynasty.

Ho-shen, the son of a Manchu military officer, received a rudimentary education in a government school and obtained the lowest examination degree in the Chinese civil service system. In 1772 he was designated an imperial bodyguard and stationed at one of the gates to the city of Peking.

A handsome and articulate young man, Ho-shen attracted the Emperor's attention and rapidly became the most powerful Ch'ing official and the closest confidant of the Emperor during the late 18th century. At one point he may have held as many as 20 posts concurrently. In 1780 Ho-shen's son was betrothed to Ch'ien-lung's youngest and favorite daughter. This marriage publically indicated Ch'ien-lung's great attraction for Ho-shen and increased the latter's influence over the imperial court.

By virtue of his exceptional relationship with the Emperor, Ho-shen was able to gain considerable factional leverage over political affairs and to accumulate enormous personal wealth. Throughout the central and provincial bureaucracy Ho-shen placed members of his family and close associates as his henchmen. In this fashion he managed to gain near-complete control over government finances and official appointments. By intimidation and corruption Ho-shen was reported to have accumulated some 80,000,000 taels of movable property (according to a contemporary British observer, this amounted to some £23,330,000 sterling). During the White Lotus Rebellion of the late 1790s Ho-shen diverted large sums designated for military expenditures to his own use, while reporting great "victories" to the Emperor.

Although several high officials protested about Ho-shen's devious activities to the Emperor, he continued to tolerate and even defend Ho-shen. The concept of loyalty, which originally permitted officials to criticize imperial policies and appointments in the name of higher principles, had gradually come to mean absolute obedience to imperial will. In the words of an earlier emperor in the Ch'ing dynasty, "Worthy men are the men of whom We approve, and you ought therefore to approve of them."

When Ch'ien-lung died in 1799, his successor, Chiach'ing, quickly arrested Ho-shen, "permitted" him to commit suicide, and confiscated Ho-shen's vast stores of wealth. In retrospect, Ho-shen was probably only one of several causes of the internal decay of the Ch'ing dynasty rather than the sole explanation. Nevertheless, he has become one of the most infamous villains in Chinese history.

Further Reading

The best treatment of Ho-shen's life and his relationship to the Emperor is David S. Nivison, "Ho-shen and His Accusers: Ideology and Political Behavior in the Eighteenth Century," in David S. Nivison and Arthur F. Wright, eds., *Confucianism in Action* (1959). A biography of Ho-shen is available in Arthur

Hummel, ed., *Eminent Chinese of the Ch'ing Period, 1644-1912* (2 vols., 1943-1944). A good background study is Edwin O. Reischauer and John K. Fairbank, *A History of East Asian Civilization*, vol. 1: *East Asia: The Great Tradition* (1960). □

Eugenio María de Hostos

Eugenio María de Hostos (1839-1903) was a major Puerto Rican social philosopher, educator, and writer. His lifelong mission was to create a Spanish West Indies Confederation.

Eugenio María de Hostos was born in Mayagüez on Jan. 11, 1839. He attended school in San Juan. At the age of 13 he went to Spain to study at the Institute of Bilbao and the University of Madrid. While studying law, he wrote newspaper and magazine articles on the need for autonomy for the Spanish West Indies. He joined the Spanish republicans because their leaders promised autonomy for Cuba and Puerto Rico; but when the republicans triumphed over the monarchy, he refused the post of deputy for Puerto Rico, feeling betrayed. In 1869 he left for New York, where he became managing editor of a Cuban revolutionary newspaper. He was already well known because of his sociopolitical novel, *La peregrinacion de Bayoán* (1863), as well as his articles.

From 1870 to 1874 Hostos sought aid for Puerto Rico and Cuba. He lived in Argentina and then, returning to New York, became involved in a mission to carry reinforcements to the Cubans, who were fighting for their independence. However, the expedition of which he was part sailed from Boston but never arrived in Cuba. Hostos next went to the Dominican Republic, where he edited *Las tres Antillas*. In 1877 he left for Venezuela, where he married Belinda Otilia de Ayala.

Returning to the Dominican Republic in 1879, Hostos became a teacher at Santo Domingo National University. During his 10 years there, he started the country's first normal school. He also wrote the Dominican laws for public education. His reputation as an educator was such that the government of Chile invited him to help reform its public educational system. He had just published his *Moral social* (1888), today considered one of his finest writings. While in Chile, Hostos gained that country's women the right to study at the university and to receive training in law and medicine.

When the Spanish-American War began in 1898, Hostos returned to Puerto Rico to work for both Puerto Rican and Cuban independence. He formed the League of Puerto Rican Patriots and led the commission that presented U.S. president William McKinley with a plan that would allow a Puerto Rican plebiscite to decide whether Puerto Rico should be annexed to the United States or become independent. The commission failed and no plebiscite was held.

Hostos left Puerto Rico in 1900, again disillusioned. He could not understand the United States desire for a Caribbean protective base for its future trade plans and its plans for Panama. He returned to Santo Domingo, at that government's invitation. He died there on Aug. 11, 1903.

Hostos's influence as an educator and social critic continues; his moral strength, passionate idealism, and personal magnetism are remembered to this day. His writings—over 50 titles—are still read throughout the Spanish-speaking world. His *Hamlet* (1873) ranks high among criticisms of the play. Commemorating the centennial of his birth, the government of Puerto Rico published the *Obras completas* of Hostos in 20 volumes.

Further Reading

The best essay in English on Hostos is ''Eugenio María de Hostos, A Public Servant of the Americas'' in Jose A. Balseiro, *The Americas Look at Each Other* (trans. 1969). Another essay on Hostos is in Jay N. Tuck and Norma Vergara, *Heroes of Puerto Rico* (1969). ☐

Harry Houdini

Harry Houdini (1874-1926)—The Great Houdini— is a name that will forever define the term ''escape artist.'' As the Budapest-born, American-bred performer would so often proclaim, ''No prison can hold me; no hand or leg irons or steel locks can shackle me. No ropes or chains can keep me from my freedom.''

No one before or since has so completely defined the art of escape as Harry Houdini, magician, actor, and stage personality. Old film footage and still photos recall Houdini as generations remember him— suspended upside-down high over the heads of the crowd, escaping from a straitjacket; plunging, manacled, into an icy river, only to reappear miraculously moments later; performing his signature Chinese Water Torture Cell illusion, in which audiences were invited to hold their breath along with Houdini as he made his escape from yet another watery coffin.

But there was a world of difference between what turn-of-the-century audiences saw, and what they *thought* they saw. Much of Houdini's escapes relied as much on myth and misdirection as they did on the magician's genuine physical and mental prowess. Likewise, Houdini made myth of his own life, elaborating details where he thought appropriate. Though in some documents Houdini claims to be born April 6, 1874, in Appleton, Wisconsin, this much is known: Erich Weiss, born March 24, 1874, in Budapest, Hungary, was the youngest of three sons of Rabbi Samuel and Cecilia (Steiner) Weiss (the couple also had a daughter, Gladys).

The Making of a Magician

To escape persecution and find a better life, the Weiss family immigrated to Appleton—''perhaps April 6 was the date Samuel Weiss arrived in Wisconsin,'' remarked Ruth Brandon in her *The Life and Many Deaths of Harry Houdini*. Other moves took the Weisses to Milwaukee and, eventually, New York. But the family remained poor. Completely devoted to his mother to the point of obsession, the young Erich sought ways to ease her hardscrabble life. At one point, he took to begging for coins in the street. True to his illusionist ways, he hid the coins around his hair and clothing, then presented himself to Cecilia with the command, ''Shake me, I'm magic.'' She did, and a flood of coins spilled out.

Magic was Erich's second obsession—indeed, ''the abounding takes of his childhood magical exploits carry the mythic fuzz Houdini liked to generate,'' as Brandon wrote. After serving as a young circus acrobat (Eric, Prince of the Air) the teenager focused his attention on locks and lockpicking. He financed his hobby by working as a necktie cutter—the garment trade being one of the few occupations open to Jews at that time.

So it was with great dismay from his parents that Erich announced he was giving up the tie business for show business. At age 17 he took the stage name Houdini, after the nineteenth century French magician Robert-Houdin. ''Harry'' was an accepted Americanized version of Erich. By age 20 Houdini had married Wilhelmina Beatrice Rahner (known as Bess); she became his partner onstage as well.

As "Mysterious Harry and La Petit Bessie," the Houdinis played dime museums, medicine shows, and music halls, eventually working their way up to small billing at larger theaters. At one point, the couple toured with a circus. When escape tricks and magic didn't pan out, the pair billed themselves as a comedy act, cribbing old jokes from magazines, as Brandon noted in her book.

Typically, during these early years, Harry would perform his famed "Hindoo Needle Trick," in which he appeared to swallow 40 needles, then drew them from his mouth, threaded together. Bess became a well-prompted "mentalist," performing mind-reading routines based on an alpha-numeric code known to her and Harry. In 1895, in Massachusetts, Houdini first conceived the notion of escaping not from his own handcuffs, but from those of the local police. These stunts brought free publicity, which eventually led to the Houdinis' crack at the big time—a booking in the Hopkins Theatre, a top Chicago vaudeville house.

Houdini the Headliner

American tours were followed by smash appearances in Europe. Of course, with success came imitators; after all, anyone could buy a version of the Hindoo Needle Trick (Houdini himself had purchased the illusion). But Houdini clones fell by the wayside as long as the original toured. Still, "he was always edgy with his contemporaries, and saw younger magicians only as rivals, ready to push him into obscurity," wrote Brandon.

So, ever seeking the bigger and better illusion, Houdini escaped from every combination of straitjackets, jails, coffins, handcuffs, and leg shackles. At each performance, he invited police officials onstage to examine him and his props for authenticity. But even this was a ruse, as Brandon wrote: "Houdini's skill as a magician, which meant he could palm, misdirect attention, and hide his [lockpicks] in unlikely places, came in useful here. A favoured hiding place was his thick, wiry hair. When he had to strip naked, he sometimes hid a small pick in the thick skin on the sole of a foot—not a spot that would ordinarily be searched."

But "something new was needed," said Brandon, "and on 5 January 1908, it appeared. It was a galvanized-iron can shaped like an extremely large milk can—large enough to hold a man: Houdini." As she went on to say, the can held 22 pails of water. Handcuffed, Houdini would immerse himself inside, but not before asking the audience to hold their breath along with him. "At the end of three minutes, by which time the audience's lungs were bursting . . . Houdini appeared, dripping but triumphant. The can was revealed, filled to the rim, all its locks intact."

In 1918, the film industry was still in its infancy. But Houdini was not; at age 44 he was uncertain how much longer he could leap from bridges and squirm from straitjackets. So in June of that year the performer made his move into film with a character called the Master Detective. In this series of stories the detective, named Quentin Locke, fought peril and saved damsels through great stunts, and of course, great escapes.

"The plots were ludicrous and the acting wooden," Brandon reported of Houdini's films. Still, they showcased Houdini the way his public wanted to see him. And, importantly, each magic routine or stunt was shown as "real," with no camera tricks or editing to enhance the Master Detective's mastery. Other films followed, with varying degrees of financial and critical success.

The Spirit World Beckoned

Houdini's varied career would take another turn. "After the death of his mother in 1913," as Steve and Patricia Hanson related in a *Los Angeles* magazine article, the illusionist "became obsessed with 'making contact with those who had gone beyond.'" This venture brought the performer into contact with another notable figure of turn-of-the-century pop culture—Sir Arthur Conan Doyle, the creator of Sherlock Holmes.

The association—and eventual bitter breakup—of Houdini and Doyle began as far back as 1908, when as a publicity stunt Houdini wrote a letter to "Holmes," asking for help in catching scalawags who were stealing his tricks. By 1920 the two had formed a friendship that seemed connected not only by their talent but by their tragedies—just as Houdini had lost his beloved mother, Doyle lived in grief over the death of his son, Kingsley, a casualty of World War I. Each man sought to explore spiritualism as a way of making possible contact.

But at one point the friendship began to unravel. Houdini was much more the skeptic than Doyle, and indeed made something of a second career from debunking fraudulent mystics. As the Hansons noted in *Los Angeles*, "Houdini thought that there was an irrational part of Doyle's psyche that desperately wanted to believe contact with the dead was possible. Doyle thought Houdini's campaign against spiritualism was a 'mania.' Thus the feud between the two quickly escalated."

The Passing of a Legend

No evidence of real contact with Houdini's mother was ever recorded. But the specter of his mother's death followed the illusionist until the occasion of his own passing. Even that event has since been clouded by the mythology that always seemed to accompany the magician. For instance, a feature film of Houdini's life, released in 1953, had him perishing in one of his own watery coffins during a performance. One magic expert collected seven different versions of the death.

In reality, the magician, while on tour in Montreal, was relaxing backstage where some college students met him. Always proud of his physique, Houdini had often challenged people to punch him with all their strength in the abdomen. He agreed to let one of the students take a punch. But—reclining on a couch at the moment of contact—Houdini had not yet prepared his muscles for the blows. An injury to the appendix (or perhaps, as Brandon has asserted, an aggravation of an existing appendix problem) left untreated for some days, turned into an attack of peritonitis that struck down Houdini during a performance in Detroit. Rushed to a hospital where the city's finest doctor attended him, Houdini lingered for a few days, then died in the arms of his wife at 1:26 p.m., October 31, 1926—Halloween day.

Even in death, Houdini knew how to create publicity. His widow made headlines in announcing a yearly seance on the anniversary of Houdini's passing to try and make contact with his spirit. The ritual went on for some ten years, and though Bess once asserted that contact was made, she later recanted her story. While no longer among the living, Houdini lives on in a collective cultural imagination. After a lifetime of embodying mythic attributes, Houdini has become a myth himself.

Further Reading

Brandon, Ruth, *The Life and Many Deaths of Harry Houdini,* Random House, 1993.
Los Angeles, April 1989, p. 94. □

Antoine Houdon

The portrait busts by the French sculptor Jean Antoine Houdon (1741-1828) are among the greatest of all time. His restrained yet graceful figures are classical with traces of the rococo style.

Jean Antoine Houdon was born on March 20, 1741, at Versailles, in the house of a rich nobleman for whom his father worked as caretaker; his mother's family were peasants and gardeners. In 1749 his father became caretaker of a newly established government art academy, where Houdon grew up. From the age of 15 he began to study under Michel Ange Slodtz, one of the finest sculptors in France. Later, when Houdon won a fellowship to the French Academy, his teachers included the painter Carle Vanloo and François Dandré Bardon, the historian of ancient Rome.

Years in Rome

In 1764 Houdon won a fellowship to the French Academy in Rome, where he studied until 1768. In this city with its abundant ancient ruins, where the French rococo style seemed remote and new evidence of Roman civilization was just then being uncovered in excavations, he set the main direction of his art.

Houdon also studied anatomy in Rome. Working under the direction of a surgeon, he learned the components of the body directly by dissecting corpses. The strong current of realism in Houdon's art is nowhere more apparent than in the anatomical statue called *L'Écorché,* or *The Flayed Man* (1767). There are endless copies. In his day no art school was complete without a bronze casting of this figure.

Houdon left one masterpiece in Rome, a colossal marble *St. Bruno* for the Carthusian monks of S. Maria degli Angeli (1767). The saint's eyes are closed, and his head is bent in prayer. But his motionless body stands straight, and straighter still hang the folds of his loose robe, like the fluting

of a Doric column, relieved only (but typically) by the gentle symmetrical arcs of cape, sleeves, and hood. This figure was Houdon's answer to the graceful, lightly swaying, rococo statue of the same saint that Slodtz had made for St. Peter's some 20 years before.

International Acclaim

Houdon returned to Paris in 1768. The sculpture he brought with him he exhibited at the Salon the following year. The critics liked his work, and his career seemed well launched, but the really big commissions, the ones for the King, somehow failed to arrive. Instead Houdon found his patrons among foreigners, the wealthy bourgeoisie, and the intellectuals.

Through the recommendations of the Encyclopedist Denis Diderot and the literary critic Baron Melchior von Grimm, both of whom admired his work, Houdon soon began to develop an international clientele. An introduction from Baron Grimm won Houdon a commission in 1771 to do a funeral monument for one of the dukes of Saxe-Gotha. In the years that followed, he made busts and medallions of almost all the members of the duke's family. Eventually his patronage extended across Europe, including (besides France) Italy, the Netherlands, Belgium, Switzerland, Germany, and Russia.

In 1778 Houdon joined the Masonic Lodge of the Nine Sisters in Paris. His fellow members included the writer Voltaire, the astronomer Lalande, the naturalist Lacépède, the Russian nobleman Count Stroganoff, and the American ambassador to France, Benjamin Franklin.

The large seated marble statue of Voltaire (1781) is Houdon's most famous work. The aged philosopher, draped in loose robes to disassociate him from any specific time or place, leans forward in his chair and turns as if about to speak. His withered fragile body seems to vibrate with life, as if the erosion of the flesh lets the spirit shine out brighter. Across the face a sardonic smile is breaking; deep shadows give the eyes extraordinary intensity. In almost all of Houdon's portraits the eyes seem to sparkle, and they look out at us with disconcerting intensity.

Frederick the Great bought two of Houdon's busts of his friend Voltaire. Stanislas Poniatowski, the last king of Poland, made a collection of plaster casts of Houdon's portraits of great men: Jean Jacques Rosseau, Alexander the Great, Molière, and Voltaire. Acting on the advice of Baron Grimm, Catherine the Great, Empress of Russia, acquired two of Houdon's most famous sculptures: a graceful marble statue, *Diana as Goddess of the Hunt* (1780), and a variant of Houdon's magnificent marble statue of Voltaire.

American Portraits

Houdon's first connections with America came through his friendship with Benjamin Franklin, of whom he executed a number of portraits. The most famous version (1778) shows an unpretentious old man, simply dressed, wrinkled and rather bald, but also contemplative, benevolent, and wise. Three years later, probably at the suggestion of Franklin, Houdon was asked to do a bust of John Paul Jones.

In 1781 the state of Virginia commissioned Houdon to do a bust of Lafayette to be given to the city of Paris in gratitude for Lafayette's help during the Revolutionary War. Four years later, when the state of Virginia wanted a commemorative statue of Washington, they called on Houdon again. This time it was Jefferson, then American ambassador to France, who handled the negotiations. In 1785 Houdon sailed for America—the first European sculptor to go there. He spent a fortnight at Mount Vernon, where he took a life mask of Washington and made a series of clay studies, and then returned to France. The marble statue, showing the general dressed as an 18th-century gentleman, stands in the Virginia State Capitol at Richmond. Other portraits Houdon made of famous Americans include busts of Jefferson (1789) and Robert Fulton (1803).

Waning Popularity

Houdon did not marry until 1786, when he was 45 years old. He had waited so long because he had taken on the responsibility of supporting many of his relatives, all of them poor. His marriage was not entirely a happy one, but from it came three daughters in whom he took unending pride. Their portraits exist in many versions: Sabine, age 4, for example, her serious child's face enframed by cascades of long, luxuriant curls; and Claudine, age 15 months, looking upward, wide-eyed and radiant.

The latter part of Houdon's life was not very happy. The Revolutionary period from 1789 to 1800 was especially difficult. Coming himself from a family that was extremely poor, Houdon was an enthusiastic supporter of the new government and its Declaration of the Rights of Man. But because of his associations with the old regime, he was suspected of being a counterrevolutionary. Besides, the new art dictator, Jacques Louis David, opposed him even to the point of having his studio searched. Inevitably Houdon was cut off from official patronage. One disappointment followed another as each successive commission eluded him. Worst of all was his failure to be asked to execute the memorial the government planned for Rousseau, whose writings had provided so much of the inspiration for the Revolution. Here being passed over was especially bitter, because Houdon alone possessed a death mask of the philosopher, which he had made immediately after Rousseau's death.

In 1800 the Napoleonic era dawned, but for Houdon there was little improvement. While 15 years earlier he had been thought of as the greatest sculptor in Europe, now he was considered out of date. Neoclassicism was all the rage. Houdon was still respected—he was one of the first artists to be made (in 1803) a cavalier of the newly created French Legion of Honor. But there was little demand for his art.

In 1814 he stopped working altogether. Two years later, when the new government finally offered him a commission to do a statue, he refused. In 1823 his wife died. He himself lived on for 5 more years, but only as a shell. Arterial sclerosis was causing progressive damage to his brain. In a touching passage Augustin Jal, who had known Houdon for a long time, described his last visit to the art exhibition held at the Louvre in 1827: "What is he doing here, this little old man, moving along quickly with short steps, dragging his feet? Let us greet him. He lifts his hat, showing us a head that is completely bald. He speaks but what he says is garbled. The mind that was once so strong is now weak. In this octogenarian child the body has survived but not the spirit." Death came the following year on July 15.

Further Reading

Charles Henry Hart and Edward Biddle, *Memoirs of the Life and Works of Jean Antoine Houdon* (1911), is useful for its illustrations, but the text, largely anecdotal, is incomplete and outdated. A special study is H. H. Arnason, *Sculpture by Houdon* (1964), with beautiful illustrations. For background see Michel Laclotte, ed., *French Art from 1350 to 1850* (1965). □

Godfrey Hounsfield

Sir Godfrey Hounsfield (born 1919) won the Nobel Prize for medicine for co-inventing the CAT-scan (computer assisted tomography).

Sir Godfrey Hounsfield pioneered a great leap forward in medical diagnosis: computerized axial tomography, popularly known as the "CAT scan." Ushering in a new and sometimes controversial era of medical technology, Hounsfield's device allowed a doctor to look inside a patient's body and examine a three-dimensional image far more detailed than a conventional X ray. The importance of this advance was recognized in 1979, the year Hounsfield received the Nobel Prize for physiology or medicine.

Godfrey Newbold Hounsfield was born August 28, 1919, in Newark, England, the youngest of five children of a steel-industry engineer turned farmer. Hounsfield's technical interests began when, to prevent boredom, he began figuring out how the machinery on his father's farm worked. From there he moved on to exploring electronics, and by his teens was building his own radio sets. He graduated from London's City and Guilds College in 1938 after studying radio communication. When World War II erupted, Hounsfield volunteered for the Royal Air Force, where he studied and later lectured on the new and vital technology of radar at the RAF's Cranwell Radar School. After the war he resumed his education, and received a degree in electrical and mechanical engineering from Faraday House Electrical Engineering College in 1951. Upon graduation, Hounsfield joined Thorn EMI (Electrical and Musical Industries) Ltd., an employer he has remained with his entire professional life.

At Thorn EMI, Hounsfield worked on improving radar systems and then on computers. In 1959, a design team led by Hounsfield finished production of Britain's first large all-transistor computer, the EMIDEC 1100. Hounsfield moved on to work on high-capacity computer memory devices, and was granted a British patent in 1967 titled "Magnetic Films for Information Storage."

Hounsfield's work in this period included the problem of enabling computers to recognize patterns, thus allowing them to "read" letters and numbers. In 1967, during a long walk through the British countryside, Hounsfield's knowledge of computers, pattern recognition, and radar technology all came together in his mind. He envisioned a medical diagnostic system in which an X-ray machine would image thin "slices" through the patient's body and a computer would process the slices into an accurate representation which would display the tissues, organs, and other structures in much greater detail than a single X ray could produce. Computers available in 1967 were not sophisticated enough to make such a machine practical, but Hounsfield continued to refine his idea and began working on a prototype scanner. He enlisted two radiologists, James Ambrose and Louis Kreel, who assisted him with their practical knowledge of radiology and also provided tissue samples and test animals for scans. The project attracted support from the British Department of Health and Social Services, and in 1971 a test machine was installed at Atkinson Morely's Hospital in Wimbledon. It was highly successful, and the first production model followed a year later. These original scanners were designed for imaging the brain, and were hailed by neurosurgeons as a great advance. Before the CAT scanner, doctors wanting a detailed brain X ray had to help their equipment see through the skull by such dangerous techniques as pumping chemicals or air into the brain. As head of EMI's Medical Systems section, Hounsfield continued to improve the device, working to lower the radiation exposure required, sharpen the images produced, and develop larger models which could image any part of the body, not just the head. This "whole body scanner" went on the market in 1975.

CAT scanners generated some resistance because of their expense: even the earliest models cost over $300,000, and improved versions several times as much. Despite this, the machines were so useful they quickly became standard equipment at larger hospitals around the world. Hounsfield argued that, properly used, the scanners actually reduced medical costs by eliminating exploratory surgery and other invasive diagnostic procedures. The scanner won Hounsfield and his company more than thirty awards, including the MacRobert Award, Britain's highest honor for engineering. In 1979, Hounsfield's collection of scientific tributes was topped off with the Nobel Prize. That year's Nobel was shared with Allan M. Cormack, an American nuclear physicist who had separately developed the equations involved in reconstructing an image via computer. A surprising feature of the selection was that neither man had a degree in medicine or biology, or a doctorate in any field. Asked what he would do with the large monetary award which came with the Nobel selection, Hounsfield replied he wanted to build a laboratory in his home. In an interview with Robert Walgate of the British journal *Nature* after the Nobel announcement, Hounsfield commented, "I've always searched for original ideas; I am absolutely opposed to doing something someone else has done."

Hounsfield moved on to positions as chief staff scientist and then senior staff scientist for Thorn EMI. He continued to improve the CAT scanner, working to develop a version which could take an accurate "snapshot" of the heart between beats. He has also contributed to the next step in diagnostic technology, nuclear magnetic resonance imaging. In 1986, he became a consultant to Thorn EMI's Central Research Laboratories in Middlesex, near his longtime home in Twickenham.

Further Reading

Engineers and Inventors, Harper, 1986, pp. 85–86.

Di Chiro, Giovanni, with Rodney A. Brooks, "The 1979 Nobel Prize in Physiology or Medicine," in *Science,* November 30, 1979, pp. 1060–1062.

"Nobel Prizes," in *Physics Today,* December, 1979, pp. 17–20.

"Nobel Prizes: Emphasis on Applications," in *Science News,* October 20, 1979, p. 261.

"Scanning for a Nobel Prize," in *New Scientist,* October 18, 1979, pp. 64–165.

Seligmann, Jean, "The Year of the CAT," in *Newsweek,* October 22, 1979, pp. 75–76.

"Triumph of the Odd Couple," in *Time,* October 22, 1979, p. 80.

Walgate, Robert, "35th Prize for Inventor of EMI X-ray Scanner," in *Nature,* October 18, 1979, pp. 512–513. □

Felix Houphouët-Boigny

Felix Houphouët-Boigny (1905-1993), president of the Ivory Coast, was one of the first leaders of a successful nationalist movement in the French West African Federation. His policy was based on cooperation with France and moderation in domestic affairs.

Felix Houphouët was born in October 1905 in the village of Yamoussokro to an important Baoule family on the Ivory Coast. In 1946 he added Boigny to his family name. Houphouët attended schools at Bingerville and in 1918 entered medical school at Dakar. He qualified as a medical assistant in 1925 and practiced medicine in the Ivory Coast for more than 15 years, also becoming a successful planter.

In 1940 Houphouët was selected chief of his district. His first political activity was in reaction to the Vichy regime's policies which discriminated against African planters. In 1944, he helped organize the Syndicat Agricole Africain. It was the only large organization to protest against favoritism for Europeans at the expense of African producers. By 1945, the organization had branches throughout the country and served as the base for the Parti Démocratique de la Côte d'Ivoire (PDCI), the first effective party in the Ivory Coast, whose leadership was greatly influenced by Marxism.

Interterritorial Party

Houphouët was elected in 1945 to the French Constituent Assembly. Disappointed over the restrictions on colonies contained in the second constitution of the Fourth Republic, he met with other African deputies at Bamako in October 1946 to form a new inter-territorial party, the Rassemblement Démocratique African (RDA), and he was elected president. In November 1946 Houphouët was elected to the French National Assembly. The RDA and its Ivory Coast base, the PDCI, were supported by the Metropolitan Communist party. In the latter 1940s the RDA organized strikes and boycotts of European imports.

Government reaction, particularly in the Ivory Coast, was severe. Hundreds were arrested, and in January 1950 one police action resulted in the death of 13 Africans. Control of a much-weakened RDA thus fell to Houphouët, who had parliamentary immunity from arrest. Houphouët decided that continued cooperation with the French Communists was a dead end, and he broke irrevocably with them in late 1950. The elections to the National Assembly in 1951 were the low point for the RDA, when it won only three seats.

The five years before the National Assembly elections of January 1956 was a period of rebuilding for the RDA, which had initiated its new policy of close cooperation with France. The elections vindicated Houphouët's decision, since the RDA won nine seats. Houphouët became mayor of Abidjan and later in the year was appointed a minister in the French government. In this influential position he was largely responsible for drafting the *loi cadre* of 1956, which devolved more authority to the territorial assemblies. The RDA dominated the 1957 elections for these assemblies in all but a few segments of the federation, and the PDCI had almost no opposition in the Ivory Coast.

Failure of Federation

The issue of federation or autonomous development divided the RDA. Some of its leaders agreed with Senegal's Léopold Senghor that the future of West Africa lay in a continued large federation. Houphouët, whose rich Ivory Coast provided a large portion of the federation's budget, wanted political evolvement to take place on the territorial level. The De Gaulle referendum of 1958 concerning association with the revised community was the turning point for French Africa and the RDA.

Guinea, the only territory to vote no, was given immediate independence. In early 1959, attempts to create a strong Mali Federation threatened Houphouët's plans. Bringing economic pressure to bear upon Upper Volta (Burkina Faso) and Dahomey (Benin), he caused their defection from Mali and later associated them and the Ivory Coast with the weak Conseil de l'Entente. These events lessened the RDA's influence in the federation, and Houphouët decided to concentrate upon the PDCI and the Ivory Coast. He resigned as a minister in the French government in April 1959.

De Gaulle's decision to grant independence to the Mali Federation within the French community so angered Houphouët that he demanded independence for the Ivory Coast. French acquiescence to requests for independence ended any chance for a meaningful federation. The Ivory Coast became independent in August 1960, and in November Houphouët was elected president. The legislature, chosen from a single list, were all PDCI members.

Pan-African Leader

Houphouët had a great impact upon pan-Africanism. In 1960 he proposed a meeting of French African leaders to help end the Algerian War, and in October 1960 representatives of 12 states met at Brazzaville. These states soon became known for their pro-Western ideas of gradualism and their opposition to the Ghana-dominated Casablanca powers. Houphouët's opposition to immediate political federation became the attitude not only of the Brazzaville powers but also of other states which were not members of the Brazzaville group.

Houphouët's control of the PDCI and the Ivory Coast did not lessen after independence. There were no serious challenges to his leadership, and the country's prosperity minimized unrest. In foreign affairs he continued to support moves toward greater economic cooperation between states such as the Organization Common Africaine et Malagache (OCAM). While opposing any political unification which would submerge the sovereignty of the Ivory Coast, Houphouët supported the Organization for African Unity (OAU) created in 1963.

The cornerstone of Houphouët's policy was close cooperation with France. His attitudes disturbed the radical bloc, and both Kwame Nkrumah and Sekou Touré accused him continuously of advancing neo-imperialism. Houphouët responded by organizing opposition against the expansionist dreams of Ghana and the leftist regime in Guinea. He was instrumental in denying Nkrumah a much-needed triumph during the 1965 OAU meeting at Accra.

After Nkrumah's overthrow Houphouët was ready to call for French military aid against Guinea's threat to restore the Ghanaian leader by force. Houphouët braved the opposition of other states during the Nigerian civil war and recognized Biafra, thus alienating temporarily the victorious military leaders of Nigeria. Houphouët's policies, however they are criticized by some African leaders, have given the Ivory Coast, since its independence, one of the most stable governments in Africa.

The Legacy

While in office, Houphouët built the world's largest basilica in the jungle near his home village, Yamoussoukro, at a cost of approximately $300-million. He convinced Pope John Paul II to appear and bless the marble and glass cathedral with the gold dome.

At the outset of the 1980s, commodity prices of cocoa and coffee plummeted. Economic strife caused a public outcry that resulted in demands for Houphouët-Boigny's resignation. He fled to France where he spent most of his time.

Through most of his time in office, however, the Ivorians were happy with their one-party system, believing it a fair exchange for a time of prosperity. In 1990, pro-democracy protesters forced multi-party elections. Houphouët won with more than 90% of the vote.

Suffering with prostate cancer, Houphouët had arranged for his life support systems to be turned off at dawn on December 7, 1993—the 33rd anniversary of independence from France—the Ivory Coast's National Day. When Houphouët died, he had been president of the Ivory Coast since its 1960 independence, his 33 year reign the longest of any African leader. While he was officially 88 years old at death, many believed he was actually much older than that.

Further Reading

No biographies of Houphouët-Boigny are available in English. An understanding of the man and his policies can be gained only by reading a number of general works that deal with various aspects of modern West African politics and the Ivory Coast. For general background see Ruth Schachter Morgenthau, *Political Parties in French-speaking West Africa* (1964), and John Charles Hatch, *A History of Postwar Africa* (1965). A fine detailed review of politics is Edwin Munger's "The Ivory Coast" in his *African Field Reports, 1952-1961* (1961), and in Aristide R. Zolberg, *One-party Government in the Ivory Coast* (1964; rev. ed. 1969). See also Ronald Segal, *Political Africa: A Who's Who of Personalities and Parties* (1961).

Much of the information updating the life of Houphouët-Boigny comes from the Web site of the *Electric Library*. These include a transcript of *All Things Considered* from December 7, 1993, *Los Angeles Times,* January 1, 1995, *Time International,* November 6, 1995. □

Edward Mandell House

Edward Mandell House (1858-1938), American diplomat, was President Wilson's most intimate counselor for several years.

E dward M. House was born on July 26, 1858, in Houston, Tex., the son of a prosperous planter and exporter. Edward was educated in England and at Cornell University. After 10 years of managing his inherited properties, he sold them and lived comfortably off the interest and other investments for the rest of his life.

Though outwardly self-effacing, House was driven to become influential. "I have been thought without ambition," he noted autobiographically. "That . . . is not quite true. My ambition has been so great that it has never seemed to me worthwhile to strive to satisfy it." In truth, he did try to satisfy it by counseling men of power and by writing a political novel, *Philip Dru, Administrator* (1911), under a pseudonym. *Philip Dru* was the story of a man who became dictator of the United States, imposed an enlightened reform program upon the country, and then voluntarily relinquished his power. The hero of the novel, House admitted, "was all that he himself would like to be but was not."

House became the close adviser of a string of Texas politicians. Four times between 1892 and 1902 he successfully managed the campaigns of Texas gubernatorial candidates. In the first of these, he acquired the honorary title "Colonel," which he kept throughout life.

House supported Woodrow Wilson's successful bid for the presidency in 1912. The key to his relationship with Wilson was his penetrating insight into the President's char-

acter and personality. Further, his own views coincided with Wilson's on most substantive issues—House was a conservative progressive in domestic policy and an internationalist in foreign policy—and it seems fair to conclude that he served as much as a confidant and representative of the President as a true counselor. Moreover, he smoothed Wilson's relations with congressional leaders and with the Allied powers both before and after American entry into World War I.

During 1915 and 1916 House performed the fruitless task of sounding out the British, French, and Germans on ending the war through mediation. He concluded that the United States should expand its armed forces, and he may have influenced Wilson's decision to come out for "preparedness" in 1915. When the United States entered the war, House became chief of the American mission to London and Paris, serving as the President's spokesman. He also took charge of the preparations for the Paris Peace Conference and drew up a preliminary draft of the League of Nations Covenant. House's most striking success was in persuading the Allies to accept Wilson's Fourteen Points program as the basis for peace shortly before the armistice.

As one of the five members of the United States peace commission in Paris, House continued to consult intimately with the President. He evidently persuaded the President to be conciliatory toward the British and French; yet Wilson was already beginning to turn against House. After June 1919 House and Wilson never saw each other again; nor did the President respond to House's urgent recommenda-

tion to compromise with the Republican moderates during the Senate fight over ratification of the League of Nations.

House continued to play a behind-the-scenes role in Democratic politics until his death in New York City on March 28, 1938, but his influence was negligible. His wife and two daughters survived him.

Further Reading

For House's own story, Charles Seymour, ed., *The Intimate Papers of Colonel House* (4 vols., 1926-1928), is indispensable. House lacks a full-scale biography, but a perceptive work is Alexander L. George and Juliette L. George, *Woodrow Wilson and Colonel House: A Personality Study* (1956). See also Rupert Norval Richardson, *Colonel Edward M. House*, vol. 1: *The Texas Years* (1964). The interested reader should also consult the many works of the Wilson scholar Arthur S. Link, including *Woodrow Wilson* (1963). □

Alfred Edward Housman

The English poet and classical scholar Alfred Edward Housman (1859-1936) is known for the simplicity of his form and language, the narrow range of his subject matter, and the attitude of traditional stoicism which his poems present.

The eldest of seven children, A. E. Housman was born in Fockbury, Worcestershire. He entered St. John's College, Oxford, in 1877, where, after a distinguished start, and despite apparent brilliance as a classical scholar, he failed to gain his honors degree. This failure was, apparently, such a disgrace for Housman as to cause his withdrawal both from academic life and from his family to take up a post in the civil service in London. It was but one of a series of disappointments which strongly affected an acutely sensitive nature. The death of his mother when he was 12 years old disturbed him so profoundly, according to his sister, that death thereafter became an obsession with him; the death of his father in 1894 was another deeply felt loss; and the abrupt dissolution, in 1887, of his one deep, youthful friendship (with Moses Jackson) ensured his settling into a somewhat solitary, if not quite reclusive, pattern of life.

Housman's written works of Greek and Latin criticism are marked by devastating wit at the expense of professional colleagues, and those who knew him well found him a charming conversationalist. But his poetry is of a type which, like scholarship itself, emanates from a man meditative and alone.

It was a surprise to both his personal and professional acquaintances when Housman's first volume of poems, *A Shropshire Lad* (1896), appeared. He had taken up residence in London upon entering the civil service in 1882 and had resumed the classical studies which he had begun at Oxford. The reviews and articles on Greek and (primarily) Latin authors which he began to publish at this time were of

guage. The very clarity and perfection of his lyrics have led some critics, like Edith Sitwell, to find them simply "bare and threadbare." But to Housman's admirers his poems represent, in a manner replete with irony and paradox, the complex emotional responses of man to a world of transience, where the only certitude is that one which is least desired—the certitude of death itself.

Further Reading

The seeming transparency of Housman's verse and a suspicion that his own personality and life may be the clues to deeper meanings have led to more critical and biographical studies than his output might warrant. In addition to the memoirs by Laurence Housman, *My Brother, A. E. Housman: Personal Recollections, together with Thirty Hitherto Unpublished Poems* (1938), and by his sister, Katherine Elizabeth Symons, *Memories of A. E. Housman* (1936), biographies include George L. Watson, *A. E. Housman: A Divided Life* (1957), and Norman Marlow, *A. E. Housman, Scholar and Poet* (1958). Tom Burns Haber provides a readable yet scholarly introduction to the poetry in *A. E. Housman* (1967). A study both broad and detailed is Bobby J. Leggett, *Housman's Land of Lost Content: A Critical Study of A Shropshire Lad* (1970).

Additional Sources

Bryn Mawr College Library, *The name and nature of A.E. Housman: from the collection of Seymour Adelma,* Bryn Mawr, Pa.: Bryn Mawr College Library; New York, N.Y.: Pierpont Morgan Library, 1986.

Clemens, Cyril, *An evening with A. E. Housman,* Folcroft, Pa.: Folcroft Library Editions, 1977.

Graves, Richard Perceval, *A. E. Housman, the scholar-poet,* New York: Scribner, 1980, 1979.

Housman, Laurence, *Alfred Edward Housman's "De amicitia,"* London: Little Rabbit Book Co., 1976.

Jebb, Keith, *A.E. Housman,* Bridgend, Mid Glamorgan: Seren Books; Chester Springs, PA: U.S. Distributor, Dufour Editions, 1992.

Naiditch, P. G., *A.E. Housman at University College, London: the election of 1892,* Leiden; New York: E.J. Brill, 1988.

Naiditch, P. G., *Problems in the life and writings of A. E. Housman,* Beverly Hills, CA: Krown & Spellmam, 1995.

Page, Norman, *A.E. Housman, a critical biography,* New York: Schocken Books, 1983.

Withers, Percy, *A buried life: personal recollections of A. E. Housman,* Philadelphia: R. West, 1976. □

such recognizably high quality that in 1892 he was elected to the chair of Latin at London University, where he remained until 1911. But although he was a prolific critic and editor of classical texts, he had given no indication of what he later called the "continuous excitement" under which, in 1895, he wrote a majority of the poems which appeared in his first volume.

The poems of *A Shropshire Lad,* in form brief pastoral lyrics of perfect simplicity, detail an obsession with the transience of the human experience. Ostensibly written by a naive rustic, and handling subjects appropriate to the rural setting of village society, they lament the loss of friends, the inevitability of death, the vanity of all human aspiration.

In 1911 Housman took the chair of Latin at Cambridge, where, as a fellow of Trinity College, he became a regular and popular lecturer in the classics and continued his editions of Latin authors and his essays on textual criticism until the time of his death. In 1922 he published a new volume of 41 lyrics, under the title *Last Poems,* most of which date from 1895 to 1910; one further collection, *More Poems,* was published after his death by the poet's brother in 1936.

In 1933, a year after his appointment to the Leslie Stephen lectureship at Cambridge, Housman delivered his lecture "The Name and Nature of Poetry," in which he affirms that the purpose of poetry is "to transfuse motion" and that its value is not in "the thing said but a way of saying it." Such are the criteria by which Housman's own poetry should be judged, and by such criteria he is recognized among the most consummate lyricists in the English lan-

Bernardo Alberto Houssay

The Argentine physiologist Bernardo Alberto Houssay (1887-1971) is noted for his research in endocrinology, particularly on the activity of the hypophysis.

B
ernardo Alberto Houssay was born in Buenos Aires on April 10, 1887. His father, Alberto Houssay, was a French-born lawyer and philosopher. Young Bernardo was a prodigy: by the age of 9 he had completed secondary school and was a mere 13 when he received his bachelor's degree. He then entered the Buenos Aires Col-

lege of Medical Sciences, specializing in pharmacology, a concentration which was to be reflected in many of his research papers over the next 60 years. In 1904 he completed these studies and began medical training.

Houssay graduated with honors in 1911, presenting for his thesis an elaborate study of the pituitary body. These early studies marked Houssay as a laboratory researcher rather than as a practitioner of medicine. He was named professor of physiology in the Faculty of Veterinary Medicine and Agronomy of Buenos Aires, and in 1919 he was appointed to the first full professorship in the Buenos Aires School of Medicine. Under Houssay's direction the Institute for Physiology was established, where for over two full generations he labored on a frontier of biology. Following clues observed in his early student years, he tracked down the elusive hormonal and enzymatic systems that regulate the body's metabolism.

In 1947 Houssay received the Nobel Prize. In his acceptance speech he described how observations on the hypophysis, or pituitary body, made during his student days, had led him to his lifelong research program. "The production and consumption of glucose and hence the sugar level are controlled by a functional endocrine equilibrium. The endocrine glands are ductless glands secreting hormones into the bloodstream. This mechanism acts on the liver—the organ which produces and stores glucose—and on the tissues which are the consumers of glucose, by means of hormones which play a part in the chemical processes of

carbohydrate metabolism. . . . I was attracted to the study of the hypophysis because the microscopic picture showed that glandular activity, and its lesions, was accompanied by serious organic disturbances such as acromegaly, dwarfism, etc."

Houssay had been expelled from his university post in 1943 during Juan Perón's regime but continued his research with private support. He was reinstated after Perón's overthrow in 1955. Houssay died in Buenos Aires on Sept. 21, 1971.

Houssay published over 1,000 research papers. Perhaps his life is best told, not by listing his prizes, honorary degrees, memberships in scientific academies, and other plaudits, but in listing the topics which his work has benefited. These include pituitary anatomy and physiology, diabetes and the role of insulin, hormone biochemistry, the pancreas, general endocrinology, the renal glands and adrenalin, the thyroid and its secretions, hematology and immunology, cardiology, human metabolism and problems of nutrition, snake venom, the venom of spiders and other insects, respiratory functions, hypertension from a biochemical point of view, biology of the sexual functions, comparative physiology, and the physiological action of curare.

Further Reading

A short biography of Houssay and his Nobel lecture are in Nobel Foundation, *Physiology or Medicine: Nobel Lectures, Including Presentation Speeches and Laureates' Biographies* (3 vols., 1964-1967). The technical problems of carbohydrate metabolism which led to Houssay's Nobel Prize are analyzed in Herman M. Kalckar, comp., *Biological Phosphorylations: Development of Concepts* (1969). Further insights and additional references may be found in Philip Handler, comp., *Biology and the Future of Man* (1970). □

Bernardo Alberto Houssay (forefront, in white)

Charles Hamilton Houston

While with the NAACP, Houston (1895-1950) teamed with the American Fund for Public Service to direct a program of legal action and education aimed at the elimination of segregation.

Charles Hamilton Houston, a groundbreaking lawyer and educator, is credited with having recognized in the 1930s that the incipient black civil rights movement would achieve its greatest and most lasting successes in the courtroom. Endowed with a legal mind celebrated for its precision, Houston believed that the U.S. Congress and state legislatures, mired in the politics of race and beholden to constituencies that might be reluctant to disavow institutional discrimination against blacks, were more likely to frustrate the advances sought by civil rights leaders. In Houston's eyes, the courts, as ostensibly apolitical forums, would be more responsive to sound, analytical, legal arguments elucidating the nature and consequences of Jim Crow laws—which enforced discrimination against blacks after the Civil War—and state-sanctioned segregation.

Whether plotting strategy for the National Association for the Advancement of Colored People (NAACP), arguing cases before the U.S. Supreme Court, or retooling a second-rate law school into a first class institution that churned out generations of brilliant black lawyers, Houston helped focus politicians and courts in the United States on the patently unconstitutional foundation of racial inequality. Although he labored quietly and without self-promotion, his famous students and more flamboyant colleagues were always quick to point out that he effectively laid the groundwork for many of the century's milestone court decisions that progressively undid the knot of legal discrimination in the United States.

Unlike the more prominent civil rights leaders of the 20th century, Charles Hamilton Houston did not experience abject poverty or suffer the injurious tentacles of blatant discrimination as a child. He was born on September 3, 1895, in Washington, D.C., the only child of William, a lawyer, educator, and future assistant U.S. attorney general, and Mary, a public school teacher who abandoned her career for hairdressing and sewing in order to provide additional money for the family. The Houstons revered education, surrounding young Charles with books and encouraging his prodigious intellect. Legend had it that Houston's grandfather, a Kentucky slave, constantly provoked the ire of his illiterate master by reading books that had been smuggled onto the plantation. Largely insulated from the ways in which society denigrated blacks—including inadequate housing, lower wages for doing the same work as whites, and racial violence—Charles Hous-

ton attended what was arguably the best all-black high school in the country, from which he graduated as class valedictorian in 1911.

Excelled in School, Became Activist-Dean

Houston enrolled at Amherst College in Massachusetts, where he was elected to Phi Beta Kappa and was one of six valedictorians in 1915. Determined to be a lawyer like his father, Houston taught English for a couple of years back in Washington in order to save enough money to attend Harvard Law School. With an ever-sharpening analytical eye, Houston saw his choice of career validated when, while teaching, he came to see that blacks had not advanced meaningfully in the past 20 years and were becoming increasingly victimized by segregation in the public and private sectors.

After serving in the army during World War I, Houston entered Harvard Law School, where his intellectual zeal and worldly curiosity found a home. Author Richard Kluger wrote in his 1976 book *Simple Justice: The History of Brown v. Board of Education and Black America's Struggle for Equality,* "From the start, it was evident that [Houston] had a mind ideally contoured for a career at law. He relished the kind of abstract thinking needed to shape the building blocks of the law. He had a clarity of thought and grace of phraseology, a retentive brain, a doggedness for research, and a drive within him that few of his colleagues could match or understand."

After his first year, Houston was elected to the *Harvard Law Review,* a prestigious scholastic honor, and discovered a legal mentor in the eminent professor and future Supreme Court Justice Felix Frankfurter. Graduating with honors, Houston decided to obtain his doctorate degree in juridical science under Frankfurter, who taught his student not only the finer points of constitutional law but also the need to incorporate the lessons of history, economics, and sociology into a comprehensive, legalistic world view. These teachings, in combination with his own growing awareness of the second-class citizenship forced on blacks, forged in Houston the conviction of a social activist and the strategic thinking of a lawyer who understood the power of law to effect social change.

Returning from a one-year fellowship at the University of Madrid in Spain, Houston practiced law with his father, an experience that exposed him to the minutiae of case preparation and provided courtroom opportunities for him to exercise his blossoming forensic talents. In 1929 Houston was appointed vice-dean at the Howard University School of Law, a black institution that, despite glaring weaknesses, had produced nearly all the distinguished black lawyers in the country for two generations after the Civil War. Recognizing the need for blacks to thoroughly understand constitutional law with an eye toward dismantling the legal basis of segregation, and for black students to have higher education institutions on a par with those available only to whites, Houston set about reconstituting the law school. He shut down the night school, from which his father had graduated, toughened admissions standards, improved the library and curriculum, and purged from the faculty those he believed were not tapping the intellectual potential of the next generation's black lawyers and leaders.

By 1935, although there was still only one black lawyer for every 10,000 blacks in the country, Houston was optimistic. August Meier and Elliot Rudwick, writing in the *Journal of American History* in 1976, quoted Houston as saying at an NAACP convention, "The most hopeful sign about our legal defense is the ever-increasing number of young Negro lawyers, competent, conscientious, and courageous, who are anxious to pit themselves (without fee) against the forces of reaction and injustice. . . . The time is soon coming when the Negro will be able to rely on his own lawyers to give him every legal protection in every court."

Pursued Civil Rights as a Teacher and Lawyer

It was not only as an administrator that Houston advanced his cause. As a professor, he was empowered to directly shape the future of black law. His principal goal was to elucidate for his students—the future fighters for racial justice—the stark differences between the laws governing whites in American society and those governing blacks. In his book *Black Profiles,* George R. Metcalf wrote that Houston "called it making 'social engineers.' He had become dean in 1929 with but one purpose: to make Howard, which was then second rate, a 'West Point of Negro leadership' so that Negroes could gain equality by fighting segregation in the courts."

Of the students who braved Houston's intense mock court proceedings and military-style cerebral drillings, none would more successfully carry the torch that Houston had lit than Thurgood Marshall, who would ultimately be appointed to the Supreme Court. "First off, you thought he was a mean so-and-so," Marshall was quoted as saying in *Simple Justice.* "He used to tell us that doctors could bury their mistakes but lawyers couldn't. And he'd drive home to us that we would be competing not only with white lawyers but really well-trained white lawyers, so there just wasn't any point crying in our beer about being Negroes. . . . He made it clear to all of us that when we were done, we were expected to go out and do something with our lives."

In 1934 Houston was retained by the NAACP, then the dominant civil rights organ of the century, to chip away at segregation by leading a legal action campaign against racially biased funding of public education and discrimination in public transportation. One of his first cases, in which his legal artfulness was fully displayed, involved a black man from Maryland who wished to attend the University of Maryland Law School, the same school that years earlier had denied Thurgood Marshall admission on the grounds that he was black. Houston operated on the 1896 Plessy v. Ferguson Supreme Court decision, which validated separate but equal public education. University officials had told Donald Murray that because he was black he would not be admitted, but that he was qualified to attend Princess Anne Academy, a lackluster, all-black institution that was an extension of the university. Houston and Marshall set out to prove that Princess Anne Academy, without a law school or any other graduate programs, did not provide an education on a par with the University of Maryland, and therefore, the state had violated *Plessy.*

Houston and Marshall were victorious, not only in getting Murray into the University, but in showing that states that wanted to sustain separate but equal education had to face the onerous and expensive task of making black institutions qualitatively equal to white institutions. The courts, it became clear, were going to carefully scrutinize the allegedly equal education in states hiding behind *Plessy.* Segregation took on an impractical quality to those who tried to defend it on moral grounds. In subsequent pioneering cases, Houston would further lead the attack on segregated education by using the testimony of psychologists and social scientists who claimed that black children suffered enormous and lasting mental anguish as a result of segregation in public schools and the societal ostracism of blacks.

Argued Against Discrimination Before Supreme Court

Houston's first case before the U.S. Supreme Court involved a black man named Jess Hollins who had been convicted of rape in Oklahoma by an all-white jury and sentenced to death. Brandishing arguments he had used before in lower courts, Houston claimed that because blacks historically had been denied jury placements in Sapulpa, Oklahoma, only on the basis of their race, black defendants could maintain that they had been denied due process under the law. The Supreme Court, citing one of its recent decisions, concurred. Houston became the first black to successfully represent the NAACP before the highest court in the land.

During his tenure at the NAACP, Houston was praised not only for his legalistic virtuosity but for his prescience in picking cases that would collectively help erode segregation in the country. In his second major Supreme Court victory, he succeeded in guaranteeing that an all-white firemen labor union fairly represent in collective bargaining black firemen excluded from the union. Houston also persuaded the court that racially restricted covenants on real estate—such as deeds prohibiting blacks from occupying a house—were unconstitutional. In 1945 he argued and won a case involving a black woman from Baltimore who, on the basis of her skin color, had been denied entry into a training class operated by a public library and funded by tax-payer dollars.

Always trying to expand the scope and appeal of the NAACP, Houston suggested the establishment of satellite offices on college campuses and advised the association's officials to attend conferences of religious leaders as a way of better accessing black communities. As a native Washingtonian with many political contacts, he was also expected to comment on the racial consequences of legislation that was being considered by Congress, where he frequently testified before legislative committees. In 1944 Houston was appointed to the Fair Employment Practices Committee, created to enforce integration in private industries, but quit 20 months later, decrying what he viewed as a transparent commitment to racial equality on the part of the administration of President Harry S. Truman.

Houston died in 1950, four years before his star pupil, Marshall, succeeded in arguing before the Supreme Court that the separate but equal defense of segregated education was unconstitutional. The precedent set in *Brown v. Board of Education* was the culmination of decades of legal challenges, many of which had been masterminded and implemented by Houston. Although his name never would be as widely known as others in the civil rights community, many lawyers and activists who worked with him, including Marshall, have never strayed from their belief that Charles Hamilton Houston was one of the early, unsung heroes of the assault on segregation. Richard Kluger quoted Howard University Professor Charles Thompson in *Simple Justice* as saying, ''[Houston] got less honor and remuneration than almost anyone else involved in this fight. He was a philanthropist without money.''

Further Reading

Auerbach, Jerold, *Unequal Justice,* Oxford University Press, 1976.
Bardolph, Richard, *The Negro Vanguard,* Vintage Books, 1959.
Franklin, John Hope, and August Meier, editors, *Black Leaders of the Twentieth Century,* University of Illinois Press, 1982.
Kluger, Richard, *Simple Justice: The History of Brown v. Board of Education and Black America's Struggle for Equality,* Knopf, 1976.
Metcalf, George R., *Black Profiles,* McGraw-Hill, 1970.
Segal, Geraldine, *In Any Fight Some Fall,* Mercury Press, 1975.
Journal of American History, March 1976.
Additional information for this profile was obtained from papers housed at Howard University, Washington, D.C. □

Samuel Houston

Samuel Houston (1793-1863), American statesman and soldier, was the person most responsible for bringing Texas into the Union.

Sam Houston's life was controversial and colorful. It exemplified the opportunities that existed on the American frontier: he rose from humble origins to become governor of two states and to represent both in Congress.

Houston was born on March 2, 1793, in Rockbridge County, Va. Following the death of his father, he and his mother moved to Blount County, Tenn., in 1807. Houston received less than a year and a half of formal education. In 1809, when farming and clerking proved distasteful to him, he ran away to live with the Cherokee Indians for 3 years. The Cherokee called him ''The Raven.'' In 1812 he established a subscription school, where he also taught for a year.

Soldier and Lawyer

During the War of 1812 Houston enlisted as a private and rose to the rank of second lieutenant. He was severely wounded during the Battle of Horseshoe Bend, and Gen. Andrew Jackson, commander in the engagement, commended him for his coolness and courage. After the war

Houston applied for a commission in the Regular Army and was assigned to Jackson's command at Nashville, where he also served as subagent to the Cherokee. Resigning his commission in 1818, he studied law and was quickly admitted to the bar. He established his practice at Lebanon, Tenn.

Entering politics in 1819 as a Jacksonian Democrat, Houston proved a colorful and magnetic orator and was elected attorney general of Tennessee. Two years later he was named major general of the Tennessee militia. In 1823 he was elected to Congress and reelected in 1825. He was elected governor of Tennessee in 1827 and probably would have been reelected in 1829 had not personal tragedy interfered. In January 1829 he had married Eliza Allen, but in April she left him. In response, Houston resigned his governorship and went to live with the Cherokee in the western part of Arkansas Territory.

Establishing himself near Ft. Gibson (in present Oklahoma), Houston opened a trading post and took a Cherokee wife, Tiana Rogers. Twice he represented the Cherokee in dealings with the Federal government. On the second trip, in 1832, Ohio representative William Stanbery charged him with misdealings with the Indians; enraged, Houston beat the congressman with a cane. Houston was tried by the House of Representatives, which issued a reprimand.

Career in Texas

In late 1832 President Andrew Jackson sent Houston to deliver peace medals to tribes of western Indians and to negotiate with them. After fulfilling this obligation, he de-

cided to cast his lot with Texas, at this time a Mexican province, because of the land available there at reasonable prices. He established a law practice at Nacogdoches.

Houston was elected a delegate to the Convention of 1833, which advocated separate statehood for Texas within the Mexican Republic. He aligned himself with the militant faction of Texans, and when the revolution began in October 1835, he was elected commander in chief of the army. However, the volunteers refused to follow his lead during the winter of 1835/1836, and he spent his time with the Cherokee. Again, in 1836, he was named commander in chief of the Texan forces, this time by the convention that met to declare Texas independent.

Houston rallied a small army, drilled it briefly, then led it into battle. On April 21, 1836, he met the force commanded by Mexican president Antonio López de Santa Ana at San Jacinto. Houston's 783 men fought an estimated 1,500 Mexicans. The battle lasted 18 minutes and was a decisive defeat for the Mexicans. Santa Ana was later captured.

In 1836 Houston was elected the first president of the Republic of Texas. During his 2-year term he followed a conservative policy, seeking annexation to the United States, peace with the Indians and with Mexico, and minimum government spending. He served as president again from 1841 to 1844. His chosen successor, Dr. Anson Jones, concluded the annexation of Texas to the United States in 1845, and Houston became one of the state's first senators.

National Politics

Houston served Texas as a senator from 1845 to 1859. He was the only Southern Democrat to vote for the Compromise of 1850 and against the Kansas-Nebraska Act of 1854. Also, he frequently spoke for Indian rights. In 1859, fearing the drift toward Southern secession from the Union, he returned to Texas to campaign for the governorship. Despite charges of cowardice and treason, he was elected. He opposed secession and was able to force a statewide vote on the issue. When the vote favored secession, Houston refused President Abraham Lincoln's offer of troops to help him retain office. In March 1861 Houston was deposed from office for failure to take the oath of allegiance to the Confederacy.

Houston had remarried in 1840, following a Texas divorce. His third wife, Margaret Lea of Alabama, bore him eight children. They maintained a home at Huntsville, Tex., and there Houston died on July 26, 1863, having seen most of his predictions about the disaster of secession borne out. Proud to the point of being vain, Houston in later years had signed his first name with an "I" instead of an "S," so that his signature read "I am Houston."

Further Reading

Most of the known writings of Houston are contained, with adequate footnotes and introduction, in *The Writings of Sam Houston,* edited by Amelia Williams and Eugene C. Barker (8 vols., 1938-1943). A thorough and factual biography of Houston is Llerena Friend, *Sam Houston* (1954). Marquis James,

The Raven: A Biography of Sam Houston (1929), is slightly more readable but very romanticized. □

Carl I. Hovland

The American psychologist Carl I. Hovland (1912-1961) was one of the pioneers in research on the effects of social communication on attitudes, beliefs, and concepts.

Carl I. Hovland was born in Chicago, Ill. He attended Northwestern University and completed his graduate studies at Yale University, receiving his doctorate in 1936. He then joined the faculty at Yale, where he remained throughout his entire career.

During the late 1930s and early 1940s Hovland made major contributions to several areas of human experimental psychology, such as the efficiency of different methods of rote learning. From his close association with Clark L. Hull and other psychologists working at the Yale Institute of Human Relations, Hovland developed a comprehensive view of the behavioral sciences that led him to extend the analytic experimental approach of research on human learning to underdeveloped areas of research in the human sciences.

Hovland's first opportunity to work intensively in the underdeveloped area of social psychology arose during World War II, when he took a leave of absence from Yale for over 3 years to serve as a senior psychologist in the War Department. His main role was to conduct experiments on the effectiveness of training and information programs that were intended to influence the motivation of men in the American armed forces. He assembled a group of six psychology graduate students who worked with him on these studies for several years. One of the most widely cited of the pioneering experiments on opinion change by Hovland and his group involved testing the effects of a one-sided versus a two-sided presentation of a controversial issue. The results contradicted contentions of totalitarian propagandists, who claimed that a communication that presents only one side of the issue will generally be more successful than one that mentions the opposing side of the argument. These wartime studies were reported in *Experiments on Mass Communication* (1949), written jointly by Hovland, A. A. Lumsdaine, and F. D. Sheffield.

After the war Hovland returned to Yale University, where he recruited several members of his wartime research team, with whom he continued to study the factors that influence the effectiveness of social communications. Among Hovland's best-known studies are those elucidating the influence of the communicator's prestige and the ways that prestige effects disappear with the passage of time. For example, Hovland and his collaborators showed that when a persuasive message is presented by an untrustworthy source, it tends to be discounted by the audience, so that immediately after exposure there is little or no attitude change; but then, after several weeks, the source is no longer associated with the issue in the minds of the audience and positive attitude changes appear. This delayed, or "sleeper," effect was shown to vanish, as predicted, if the unacceptable communicator was "reinstated" several weeks later by reminding the audience about who had presented the earlier persuasive material.

For 15 years Hovland and his group systematically investigated different ways of presenting arguments, personality factors, and judgmental processes that enter into attitude change. While pursuing his own research, Hovland continually encouraged his associates on the Yale project to select other problems in line with their own research interests. The work of Hovland's program was described in *Communication and Persuasion* (1953) by Hovland, Irving L. Janis, and Harold Kelly.

In the last decade of his life Hovland's research on verbal concepts and judgment led him into an intensive analysis of concept formation. Once again he played a pioneering role in developing a new field of research— computer simulation of human thought processes.

Further Reading

A summary of the research developments and theoretical ideas that have grown out of Hovland's pioneering projects is presented in a comprehensive chapter by Irving L. Janis and M. Brewster Smith in Herbert C. Kelman, ed., *International Behavior* (1965). Hovland's work is also discussed in Arthur R. Cohen, *Attitude Change and Social Influence* (1964). □

Oliver Otis Howard

Oliver Otis Howard (1830-1909), a general on the Union side in the American Civil War, was commissioner of the Freedmen's Bureau and helped establish an educational system for Southern African Americans.

Oliver Otis Howard was born on Nov. 8, 1830, on a farm in Leeds Township, Maine. He graduated from Bowdoin College in 1850 and entered the U.S. Military Academy at West Point. After graduating fourth in his class in 1854, he held minor Army appointments before returning to West Point as an instructor of mathematics.

At the outbreak of the Civil War, Howard became colonel of the 3d Maine Regiment. He held important commands in the Army of the Potomac and participated in most of the major battles in the eastern theater. He lost his right arm at the Battle of Fair Oaks, Va., in 1862. A devout Congregationalist, he earned the sobriquet of "the Christian Soldier." He commanded a Union Army corps at Chancellorsville and at Gettysburg and fought with the Army of the Tennessee, which captured Atlanta. By 1864 he had risen to brigadier general in the Regular Army. In July 1864 he took command of the Army of the Tennessee and led part of Gen. William T. Sherman's troops on the march through Georgia.

Howard's sympathetic interest in African Americans led president Andrew Johnson to appoint his commissioner of the Freedmen's Bureau in May 1865. Though one generation of American historians charged the Bureau with fostering racial discord in the South and exploiting the misery of the defeated Confederates, it is now believed that the Bureau followed a moderate course, often adopting the planters' viewpoint in contract disputes with freed slaves, and helped facilitate the return of confiscated lands to their former Confederate owners. The Bureau's most constructive achievement was its partnership with Northern missionary societies in establishing more than a thousand schools for freed slaves, out of which evolved public schools for African Americans and the network of Southern African American colleges. The foremost African American college, Howard University, was named after the commissioner, who served as its president from 1869 to 1874.

Howard returned to Army life in 1874. He commanded expeditions against Indians in the West in 1877 and 1878. He was superintendent of West Point from 1880 to 1882. From 1886 until his retirement in 1894, he commanded the prestigious Division of the East. Howard wrote 10 books, several dealing with his work among Native and African Americans. He died on Oct. 26, 1909.

Further Reading

The *Autobiography of Oliver Otis Howard* (2 vols., 1907) is a basic source. A sympathetic modern biography is John A. Carpenter, *Sword and Olive Branch: Oliver Otis Howard* (1964). See also George R. Bentley, *A History of the*

Freedmen's Bureau (1955), which treats Howard impartially. William McFeely, *Yankee Stepfather: General O. O. Howard and the Freedmen* (1968), is critical of Howard.

Additional Sources

Famous Indian chiefs I have known, Lincoln: University of Nebraska Press, 1989.

Weland, Gerald, *O.O. Howard, Union general,* Jefferson, N.C.: McFarland & Co., 1995.

Weland, Gerald, *Of vision and valor: General Oliver O. Howard, a biography,* Canton, Ohio: Daring Pub. Group, 1991. ☐

Edgar Watson Howe

Edgar Watson Howe (1853-1937), American author and editor, wrote realistic regional and romantic novels and coined widely circulated aphorisms.

Edgar Howe was born on May 3, 1853, in Wabash County, Ind. He acquired much of his education while learning and practicing the printer's trade, and he eventually became a journalist.

Howe was editor and proprietor of the *Atchison* (Kans.) *Daily Globe* (1877-1911) when he wrote his first and most famous novel, *The Story of a Country Town* (1883). Harshly realistic, it portrayed, in a rather colorless but easygoing style, the hopeless lives of men and women in two midwestern prairie towns. Unable to place his novel with any publishing house, Howe ran it off in his own printshop. It was a great success. It was praised by such prominent contemporary writers as William Dean Howells and Mark Twain, and years later it was rediscovered and hailed as a classic. Later Howe turned from realism to romance in *The Mystery of the Locks* (1885) and *The Moonlight Boy* (1886), which were less successful.

A character in Howe's first novel observes, "A man with a brain large enough to understand mankind, is always wretched, and ashamed of himself." This shrewd and disillusioned comment was typical of Howe, who was known as "the Sage of Potato Hill." He won fame as a commonsense coiner of curdled aphorisms. His domestic life may well have helped sour him; in 1873 he married Clara L. Frank, but his home life was "wretchedly unhappy." In 1901 he was divorced and never remarried. *E. W. Howe's Monthly,* which he edited between 1911 and 1937, contained many of his bitter observations. Books in which these were collected include *Country Town Sayings* (1911), *The Blessings of Business* (1918), *Ventures in Common Sense* (1919), and *The Anthology of Another Town* (1920). Howe's two sons became successful journalists, and his daughter became a successful novelist. One of Howe's great admirers was H. L. Mencken, himself skilled in creating cynical aphorisms. Howe died in Atchison on Oct. 3, 1937.

Further Reading

Howe's autobiographical account is *Plain People* (1929). Calder M. Pickett, *Ed Howe: Country Town Philosopher* (1969), is

the first book-length biography. Lars Ahnebrink, *The Beginnings of Naturalism in American Fiction* (1950), relates Howe's writings to developments in the latter part of the 19th century. An interesting critical analysis of *The Story of a Country Town* (1883) is in Jay Martin, *Harvests of Change* (1967).

Additional Sources

Howe, E. W. (Edgar Watson), *Plain People,* St. Clair Shores, Mich.: Scholarly Press, 1974. ☐

Elias Howe

Elias Howe (1819-1867), American inventor, is credited with designing the first workable sewing machine, an invention which revolutionized garment and shoe manufacture.

Elias Howe was born in Spencer, Mass., where his father operated a gristmill and sawmill. In 1835 Elias was apprenticed to a manufacturer of cotton machinery in Lowell, Mass. Two years later he worked briefly in a machine shop in Cambridge, then apprenticed himself in Boston to a maker of watches and scientific instruments.

While working in this shop, Howe is said to have overheard the owner discussing the need for, and problems involved in making, a sewing machine. By 1844 Howe himself began trying to build a workable model. Even though he had acquired a family, he quit his job and, with financial support from his father, worked full-time on the invention. Later he was able to take in a partner, who provided more capital.

Howe had a sewing machine working as early as April 1845, and in September 1846 he obtained a U.S. patent for his second machine. One key to his success was the placement of the eye of the needle near the point, rather than at the opposite end as in a regular needle. Howe sent his brother to England to seek a market and there sold his third machine to a manufacturer of corsets, umbrellas, and shoes. This manufacturer saw the possibilities the sewing machine would have if it could be redesigned to sew leather for shoes. He asked Howe to come to England to work on the problem. The two soon quarreled, however, and Howe was forced to pawn his model and the patent papers to raise enough money to return home.

Upon his return Howe discovered that several manufacturers were developing a market in America for sewing machines. This appeared to infringe his patent. In a lawsuit that lasted from 1849 to 1854, he finally vindicated his claims to originality and priority and was able to extract a license fee for each machine produced by his rivals. At the height of his prosperity Howe received as much as $4,000 a week in royalties.

Howe's new wealth was but one measure of the success of the sewing machine. Within the decade of the 1850s it became a major trade item. In 1860 some 110,000 sewing

machines were manufactured. In turn, there was a rise in the number of ready-to-wear garments. The sewing machine was applied to shoemaking with the same results.

Further Reading

There is no full biography of Howe. Facts on him must be gleaned from biographical collections and histories of technology. Egon Larson (pseudonym for Egon Lehrburger), *Men Who Shaped the Future: Stories of Invention and Discovery* (1954), has a profile of Howe. James Parton, *History of the Sewing Machine* (1872), discusses Howe and his major achievement. Frederick J. Allen, *The Shoe Industry* (1916), may be consulted for the application of sewing machines to shoe manufacture. See also Eric J. Hobsbawn, *The Age of Revolution, 1789-1848* (1962). □

Florence Rosenfeld Howe

American author, publisher, literary scholar, and historian, Florence Howe (born 1929) was a nationally recognized leader of the contemporary feminist movement.

Florence Howe was born in Brooklyn, New York, on March 17, 1929, to Samuel and Frances Stilly Rosenfeld. Her father, a taxi driver, and mother, a book-keeper, instilled a love of learning in Florence. Frances Rosenfeld encouraged her daughter to pursue a teaching career.

In 1943 Howe was one of the five young women from Brooklyn, and the only one of non-middle-class background, to win a city-wide exam to attend exclusive Hunter College High School. In 1946, at age 16, Howe entered Hunter College. She was elected to Phi Beta Kappa in 1949. The literature faculty, dean of students, and college president encouraged Howe to take graduate courses in literature and become a college professor. After receiving a BA in English in 1950, Howe attended Smith College and earned a MA in English in 1951. She continued graduate work at the University of Wisconsin in art history and literature until 1954.

Howe's academic education, however, left the role of women in society unquestioned. Her transformation into a widely acclaimed scholar and feminist leader is discussed in many of her writings, which are often autobiographical. It paralleled the civil rights, anti-war, and women's movements of the 1960s.

By 1960, after teaching at Hofstra University and Queens College in New York, Howe was an assistant professor of English at Goucher College in Maryland. She taught writing and literature at the private women's college, but it was her work teaching underprivileged Afro-American female students in a Mississippi Freedom School in summer 1964 that led to a reappraisal of her education and the education that young women, white and black, were receiving.

Howe analyzed women's education and discovered it had harmful cultural and political effects. She concluded that its lack of concern with women as contributors to the professional and political arenas had detrimentally influenced women and society. The upbringing of young women compared to that of young men became a major theme of her numerous essays, many of which were reprinted in textbooks on education, politics, and literature.

Howe's book *Myths of Coeducation, Selected Essays, 1964-1984* (1984) includes her first major essay, "Mississippi Freedom Schools: the Politics of Education." Written in 1964, published in *Harvard Educational Review* in 1965, and reprinted in textbooks, it describes the events that turned her into an activist and made her connect the issues of race, education, and politics. Another essay, "Myths of Coeducation," written in 1978, discusses how women's education "functions within the patriarchal limits of the society in which it exists."

Howe's dedication to feminism was based on wanting "knowledge that is accurate and honest, which omits no essentials—like the history of half the human race in making a judgment about an age and civilization." Of equal concern was her desire to help shape the lives and opportunities of both men and women. She stated, "What you learn in school is not a joking matter. It forms an invisible network of belief—interfaced by the networks of church and family and now the media—that may blind us or may free us to see." She called for men and women to become reformers, to question the underlying assumptions forming their lives and work, and to become freer as individuals and thus contribute to a freer civilization.

To implement her beliefs, Howe helped found The Feminist Press in late 1970. Her goal was to provide texts for teaching about women. The Feminist Press published books and educational materials to help change the "content and focus" of all levels of classroom education. These materials included modern women's studies, rediscovered feminist literary classics, and curriculum guides. The Feminist Press publishes *Women's Studies Quarterly* and *AFFILIA Journal of Women and Social Work,* both pioneering feminist journals.

President of The Feminist Press from its founding, Howe also edited the *Women's Studies Quarterly* from 1972 to 1982. She was elected president of the Modern Language Association in 1973, where she held other important positions. Between 1964 and the mid-1980s she wrote essays and authored or edited 13 books and monographs. She received an honorary doctorate of humane letters from New England College in 1977 and an honorary doctorate of humane letters from Skidmore College in 1979. During November and December 1977 Howe was in India on a Fulbright award; in May 1980 and again in April 1985 she was a U.S. delegate to UNESCO World Conferences on Teaching and Research about Women. She received fellowships from the National Endowment for the Humanities, the Ford Foundation, a Mellon Fellowship, and a U.S.I.S. (Department of State) travel and lecture grant to Japan, India, and West Germany. Additional grants for writing and directing projects published by The Feminist Press acknowledge her valuable contributions to women's studies.

Howe lived in New York City where she successfully pursued goals established in the 1960s. She also lectured on college campuses across the country and for national organizations, and remained on the staff at State University of New York (SUNY) as professor of humanities in 1987. She was an U.S. Department of State grantee in 1983 and 1993.

Her publications include co-editing (with Marsha Saxton) *With Wings: An Anthology of Literature By and About Disabled Women* (1987); *Traditions and the Talents of Women* (1991); and *No More Masks* (1993).

Further Reading

The best sources on Florence Howe's career and philosophy are her own writings. She is included in *American Women Writers, A Critical Reference Guide from Colonial Times to the Present* (1980), Vol. 2: *Who's Who of American Women 1985-1986* and in *Contemporary Authors,* Vol. 109 (1983). Several *New York Times* articles from the 1970s give insight to her impact and approach. These include: "Language Unit Elects Women's Liberation Leader," by Will Lissner (Dec. 31, 1970) and "New View of Women and Power," by Judy Klemesrud (July 11, 1975). □

Sir Geoffrey Howe

British Foreign Secretary Geoffrey Howe (born 1926) was one of Britain's most important political leaders through the 1980s.

Sir (Richard Edward) Geoffrey Howe was the chancellor of the Exchequer, entrusted with the key job of directing economic policy, in the Conservative government of Prime Minister Margaret Thatcher which took office in 1979. In 1983, after Thatcher won re-election, Howe became foreign secretary. Called the "patient Fabian of Thatcherism" by one writer, Howe was less outspoken than the prime minister, but he was closely identified with her vigorously right-wing policies, especially in economics.

Geoffrey Howe was born in Port Talbot, Glamorgan, Wales, on December 20, 1926, the son of B. Edward Howe and E. F. (Thomson) Howe. His father was a solicitor who served as a court clerk and coroner and his mother was a justice for community affairs. Although his parents were of English ancestry, Howe often talked of his identification with his native Wales. He received his early schooling at local schools and in England before attending the prestigious Winchester College from 1939 to 1945. Then, with World War II just ending, he joined the army and was sent to East Africa as a lieutenant in the Royal Signals. After he was discharged in 1948 he entered Cambridge University on a scholarship. At Cambridge he was active in political

affairs and in 1951 became chairman of the university Conservative Association. He decided to follow in his father's footsteps and become a lawyer and was admitted to the bar, Middle Temple, in 1952.

Howe pursued an active career in the law in the 1950s and 1960s and in 1965 was appointed queen's counsel. His service was rewarded with a knighthood in 1970. His hopes of winning election to parliament were frustrated at first, with two defeats in Aberavon at the hands of Labour Party candidates in 1955 and 1959. He finally won election to the House of Commons in 1964 from Bebington, but lost his seat two years later. He returned to the House of Commons in 1970 from Reigate and, representing first this district and then after 1974 East Surrey, was a member into the mid-1980s.

Within the Conservative Party, Howe joined with other younger intellectuals to start the Bow Group, which he chaired in 1955. Here, and in the group's journal *Crossbow,* which he edited from 1960 to 1962, he worked to revive the party and provide it with new policies which fit the times. As reformers, this group was often described as on the left wing of the party, but their proposals were in fact quite moderate. Occasionally, Howe did emerge as an outspoken critic of the establishment. In 1969, for instance, when he chaired a committee investigating the abuse of mental patients at a hospital near Cardiff, he had to overcome official opposition to release his report.

In the Conservative government of Edward Heath, which took office in 1970, Howe became solicitor general and played an important role in drafting the controversial Industrial Relations Act of 1971. The grandson of a trade union leader, Howe nevertheless shared the Conservative conviction that excessive trade union power and lack of labor discipline had weakened Britain's economy, and the act, which was eventually rejected, was designed to help correct the situation. Howe went on to become Minister for Trade and Consumer Affairs from 1972 until the Heath government fell in 1974.

Howe was one of those in the running for head of the Conservative Party when Heath was ousted from leadership in 1975. He quickly allied himself with Margaret Thatcher, who became the party leader, and became the opposition spokesman on the economy, the shadow chancellor. Like Thatcher, Howe advocated a sharply conservative course in industrial and economic policy which stressed encouraging initiative in the private sector and a sharp reduction in public sector spending. Conservative victory in the 1979 general elections elevated Margaret Thatcher to prime minister and gave Howe the chance to put his ideas into practice. Within weeks of the election, Howe produced his first budget as chancellor, a bold document which set the course for Thatcherism.

This course, which in broad outline resembled that which the Reagan administration introduced in the United States a year later, involved sharp cuts in government spending, especially in the field of social welfare; lowering income taxes in favor of indirect taxes; and strong efforts to curb inflation. In the face of sharply rising unemployment and bitter opposition to his policies even from within his own party, Howe refused to modify his monetarism. His next budget continued to stress cuts in government spending and increased incentives for businessmen.

Thatcher led the Conservatives to victory again in the 1983 general elections over a divided opposition following Britain's victory in the Falklands war with Argentina. Howe was rewarded for this loyalty with the position of foreign secretary. In that post, he was generally supportive of the United States and assertive with Britain's partners in the European Economic Community (EEC). On issues such as price supports for agricultural products and the contributions which Britain is obligated to make to the EEC budget, Howe took a tough line.

During a major Cabinet reshuffle in 1989, Howe was moved from the foreign office to lead the House of Commons. However, he insisted on keeping an official country residence, with the title of deputy Prime Minister.

While Howe was not a charismatic leader, he was thought to be well placed to succeed Margaret Thatcher at the head of his party if she were to leave office. Instead, John Major took the helm; Major was replaced by Labour Party head Tony Blair in 1997. Married (in 1953 to Elspeth Rosamund Morton Shand), Howe was the father of three children.

Further Reading

In 1994, Howe published his insightful *Conflict of Loyalty.* While there is no biography of Howe available, he figures prominently in general works such as Peter Riddell, *The Thatcher Government* (1983) and Alan Sked and Chris Cook, *Post-War Britain, A Political History* (1984). □

Gordie Howe

Former professional hockey player Gordie Howe (born 1928) earned the distinction of the most durable player of all time, playing 26 seasons spanning five decades in the National Hockey League, and during that time was one of the game's most prolific scorers.

When Gordie Howe broke the National Hockey League (NHL) scoring record of Maurice "Rocket" Richard, the debate among hockey buffs was whether Richard or Howe was the best player of all time. Years later when Wayne Gretzky broke Howe's record, the debate was renewed, this time Gretzky versus Howe. Gretzky himself declared to Hal Quinn of *Maclean's* that Howe "is the best hockey player there ever was." Howe, for his part, told Jay Greenberg of *Sports Illustrated,* "If you want to tell me [Gretzky's] the greatest player of all time, I have no argument at all."

Howe was born in Floral, Saskatchewan on March 31, 1928. He was the fifth of nine children. At three months of age, his family moved to nearby Saskatoon where his father was a mechanic, laborer, and construction worker. The family was poor as many of their neighbors were during the Great Depression. Once when a neighbor was selling some used belongings to get some cash, Howe gained his first pair of skates. "She had a sack of stuff my mother bought for 50 cents," Howe recalled, reported Larry Batson in his book *Gordie Howe.* "I dug into it and found some secondhand skates. I grabbed a pair for myself. They were so big I had to wear a couple extra pairs of socks." He was then about five years old.

Devoted to Hockey

Howe immersed himself in hockey, playing day in and day out throughout the year, using a puck, tennis ball, or even clumps of dirt. He was a big boy but was initially clumsy. He did not make it the first time he tried out for a local midget team. By the time he was 12 years old, however, Howe had developed into an excellent skater.

During the summers, Howe worked with his father at construction sites. He described it as "throwing concrete," noted Batson. The heavy work helped give him the exceptional strength that he would use to develop one of the fastest shots in hockey. At the age of 15, Howe was a 6-foot 200-pounder, very big at that time for a hockey player.

Pro Tryouts

Howe had already caught the eye of the professional scouts and, when he was 15, the New York Rangers invited him to a tryout camp. The camp director, though, was unimpressed. "You're too awkward, son," he remarked to

Howe, reported Batson. "You'll never make the major leagues." Despite this rejection, the next year Howe landed a tryout with the Detroit Red Wings. Jack Adams, coach and general manager of the team, was definitely impressed by young Howe and signed him to a contract.

There was just one snag in the contract negotiations with Howe. Adams recalled, as Roy MacSkimming wrote in *Saturday Night,* "He looked at [the contract] but didn't sign it. So I asked him what was wrong, wasn't it enough money? He just looked at me and said 'I'm not sure I want to sign with your organization, Mr. Adams. You don't keep your word. You promised me a windbreaker and you never gave it to me.' You can imagine how quickly I got that windbreaker."

Howe, then 17 years old, was assigned to the Red Wings' minor-league farm team in Omaha, Nebraska. He had an excellent season and the next year was given a shot at making the major-league club. He made the Red Wings and in his first game gave a glimpse of what was to come. "Gordon Howe is the squad's baby, 18 years old," Paul Chandler wrote about the contest, as E.M. Swift of *Sports Illustrated* related. "But he was one of Detroit's most valuable men last night. In his first major league game, he scored a goal, skated tirelessly and had perfect poise. The goal came in the second period, and he literally powered his way through the players from the blue line to the goalmouth."

Production Line

It was in 1947 that new Red Wings' coach Tommy Ivan put together the Production Line, a forward line consisting of Howe, Ted Lindsay, and Sid Abel. According to Mac-Skimming, it was "the most successful, exciting, and dominant attacking line of its era." The three had an "instinctive rapport."

It took Howe three seasons to "mature" as a professional, wrote William Barry Furlong of the *New York Times.* He scored a total of 35 goals those first three years "or as many goals as he scored in his fourth year alone." From that point on, Howe was a consistent scorer. "Beginning in 1949-50," Swift noted, "Gordie Howe started a string in which for 20 consecutive years—two solid decades—he finished among the top five scorers of the NHL."

A Serious Accident

In 1950, though, Howe's career almost came to an abrupt end. In the first playoff game against the Toronto Maple Leafs, Howe collided with Toronto's Ted Kennedy and flew head first into the sideboards. His skull was fractured and he suffered a concussion. He also had his cheekbone and nose broken. In the hospital, surgeons had to operate to relieve the pressure on his brain. He was in critical condition for days.

The next season Howe came back. The question was, would he still have the same fire and aggressiveness that he had before? Howe responded by playing in every game and by leading the NHL in goals, assists, and total points that season.

League Leader

Leading the league in scoring became a regular occurrence for Howe. He won the scoring title six times. He was selected the NHL's Most Valuable Player six times. Howe's emergence as a star also led to his team's emergence as a consistent winner. From 1949 to 1955, the Detroit Red Wings won the league title seven straight times and were Stanley Cup playoff champions four times.

In 1951, Howe met Colleen Joffa at a bowling alley where the players liked to hang out. Afterwards, reported Batson, the owner asked her, "How did you like meeting a celebrity?" "Who's a celebrity?" she answered. She had never heard of Howe. However, she did see and hear from him quite often after that, and in 1953, the two were married. They would eventually have four children: Martin, Mark, Cathy, and Murray. The boys soon became involved in youth hockey.

Religious Hockey

Throughout his career, Howe was a proponent of "what he called 'religious hockey': it's better to give than to receive," wrote Trent Frayne of *Maclean's*. He was a feared figure on the ice. "Due to his sharp elbows and quick stick, foes considered him sneaky-mean and steered clear of even accidental altercations," Joe LaPointe of *Sport* magazine noted. "Howe is everything you'd expect the ideal athlete to be," an opposing player said to Furlong. "He's soft-spoken, deprecating and thoughtful. He's also the most vicious, cruel and mean man I've ever met in a hockey game." But another hockey great, Bobby Hull of the Chicago Black hawks, defended Howe. Hull asserted, wrote Jim Vipond in his book *Gordie Howe Number 9*, "Howe is not the demon some people say. If you want to play hockey, he'll play. He just wants to play hockey, but if guys want to fool around they always come out second best."

With the flying elbows and flying pucks of hockey, and no helmets during this time, facial cuts and stitches were a very normal hazard of the game. Howe estimated that he had received 300 stitches in his face, Furlong reported. "I had 50 stitches in my face one year—that was a bad year," Howe said. "I had only 10 stitches taken last year—that was a good year."

Joined His Sons

Howe surpassed Maurice Richard's scoring record in 1963. By the time he retired from the Red Wings in 1971, at the age of 43, he had the records for goals, assists, and total points. He also had the record for most games played. He accepted a job in the team's front office. But, in 1973, when the Houston Aeros of the new World Hockey Association (WHA) signed his sons Marty and Mark, Howe asked about joining them. Playing on the same professional team as his sons had been a dream. He got himself back into shape and returned triumphantly, scoring 100 points, winning the league's Most Valuable Player award, and leading his team to the WHA championship.

Howe continued to play in the WHA through 1977. He moved to the Hartford Whalers and when that club was merged into the NHL in 1978, he was back for a second tour of duty in his old league. Howe's autobiography, *And . . . Howe!: An Authorized Autobiography* was published in 1995. He continued to make special appearances playing in charity games well into the 1990s.

Asked once why he kept playing, Furlong wrote, Howe remarked, "Well, the hours are good and the pay is excellent." And of his incredibly long career, he told Swift, "One of my goals was longevity: I guess I've pretty much got the lock on that." In September of 1997, at the age of 69, Howe announced he would play one game, the October 3 season opener, with the International Hockey League's Detroit Vipers. This would make him the only professional hockey player to play in six consecutive decades.

Further Reading

Batson, Larry, *Gordie Howe,* Amecus Street, 1974.
Vipond, Jim, *Gordie Howe Number 9,* Follett Publishing Company, 1968.
Maclean's, October 23, 1989, p. 62.
Maclean's, March 21, 1994, p. 49.
Furlong, William Barry, *The New York Times Encyclopedia of Sports,* Arno Press, 1979, pp. 165-167.
Saturday Night, November, pp. 62-68, 96.
Sport, May 1989, p. 60.
Sports Illustrated, October 23, 1989, pp. 50-53. □

Joseph Howe

Joseph Howe (1804-1873) was a Canadian journalist, reformer, and politician who led the fight for "responsible government" in Nova Scotia, opposed confederation with Canada, and eventually came to terms with the federal union of British North America.

Born in Halifax, Nova Scotia, on Dec. 13, 1804, Joseph Howe was of a loyalist family connected with printing. Howe himself went into journalism at an early age, becoming the editor of the *Novascotian* in 1828. His extensive knowledge of his native province gained from continuous traveling, his engaging personality, his argumentative powers, and his clear and lively prose made him a political commentator of great force.

Howe soon took up the reform cause against the group of merchants and officials who dominated the governing circle of the colony. A celebrated libel trial, in which he conducted his own defense and won acquittal, led him to intervene directly in politics. In 1836 he was elected to the House of Assembly and thereafter began, in the legislature and through his newspaper, a determined agitation for "responsible government." This campaign reached a peak of intensity after 1843, when Howe resigned from a coalition ministry to carry out a savage attack on the lieutenant governor, Lord Falkland.

sweeping victory in the 1867 elections, when 36 anticonfederates were returned in the 38 seats allotted to Nova Scotia in the Dominion Parliament.

Later, realizing that further opposition was useless, Howe bent his efforts to secure "better terms" for Nova Scotia in the federation agreement. In 1869 negotiations with the Ottawa government produced a higher annual subsidy for Nova Scotia, and Howe entered the Cabinet of John Alexander Macdonald, first as president of the council, then as secretary of state. Howe's service in Ottawa was not satisfying to him, and in 1873 he returned to his native province as lieutenant governor. He died on June 1, three weeks after taking office.

Howe was the best-loved Nova Scotian of his day and is still a legend in the Atlantic province. He was a consummate writer and speaker, and his advocacy of popular rights won him the affectionate title of "tribune of the people" among his countrymen.

Further Reading

Selections from Howe's writings, with an introductory essay, are in *Joseph Howe: Voice of Nova Scotia,* edited by J. Murray Beck (1964). Also important is *The Speeches and Public Letters of Joseph Howe,* edited by Joseph Andrew Chisholm (2 vols., 1909). A short biography is William Lawson Grant, *The Tribune of Nova Scotia: A Chronicle of Joseph Howe* (1915). A modern life is James A. Roy, *Joseph Howe: A Study in Achievement and Frustration* (1935). See also J. W. Longley, *Joseph Howe* (1904; rev. ed. 1926).

Additional Sources

Beck, J. Murray (James Murray), *Joseph Howe,* Kingston: McGill-Queen's University Press, 1982-c1983.
Hill, Kay, *Joe Howe: the man who was Nova Scotia,* Toronto: McClelland and Stewart, 1980.
Percy, H. R., *Joseph Howe,* Don Mills, Ont.: Fitzhenry & Whiteside, 1976. □

Julia Ward Howe

Julia Ward Howe (1819-1910), American author and reformer, wrote the words for "The Battle Hymn of the Republic."

Julia Ward, the daughter of a noted banker, was born in New York City on May 27, 1819, and was privately educated there. Rejecting a life of cultivated leisure, she married Samuel Gridley Howe, a physician, reformer, and pioneer teacher of the blind. They lived in Boston and edited the *Commonwealth,* an antislavery paper. Howe's first book, a collection of poems, was published in 1854; thereafter she wrote many volumes of verse, travel sketches, and essays. None was so popular as her patriotic song, "The Battle Hymn of the Republic," which she composed in a tent one night after visiting military camps. Because of this song she became one of the best-known and most widely honored women in America.

In the elections of 1847 the liberal forces won a majority in the legislature, and a new governor, Sir John Harvey, on Feb. 2, 1848, installed a ministry committed to responsible government. Howe did not head this ministry but filled the position of provincial secretary from 1848 to 1854. The ministry was the first to operate under the principle of cabinet government in any colony of the British Empire, preceding the Baldwin-Lafontaine government in Canada by 5 weeks.

Howe's period in office was an active one of railroad building in Nova Scotia, which he aided when he became chairman of the government railway board in 1854. The period was also one of denominational bitterness in Nova Scotian politics, and Howe lost some support when he criticized the loyalty of Irish Roman Catholics in the province. In 1856 Howe was reelected after a short period out of the Assembly and served in opposition from 1857 to 1860. In 1860, Howe again became provincial secretary, then premier after August 1861, and remained in office until his government was defeated in 1863.

Toward Confederation

During the negotiations with Canada over confederation Howe was on imperial service as commissioner to ensure that the fisheries clauses of the Reciprocity Treaty of 1854 were being observed. He entered the lists against the confederation project in 1865, criticizing the terms, although not the principle, of federation with Canada. He led the anticonfederate forces in an unsuccessful mission to Great Britain in 1867 to forestall the project and won a

Though Howe was an ardent unionist in the Civil War, other conflicts repelled her. As a Francophile, she was horrified by the Franco-Prussian War, and she became president of the American Branch of the Woman's International Peace Association in 1871. It failed, as women were not yet ready for such work.

Howe did better at interesting them in more domestic concerns. She helped found the New England Woman's Club in 1868. That same year she organized the New England Woman Suffrage Association and later the American Woman Suffrage Association. The latter was a product of the conflict within the suffrage movement over strategy and principles. New York feminists, led by Susan B. Anthony and Elizabeth Cady Stanton, wanted the cause to embrace many social and political issues, from the marriage question to labor unions. More conservative Boston feminists, such as Mrs. Howe and Lucy Stone, focused on woman's rights alone. They encouraged men to join, whereas the New Yorkers believed that men compromised their efforts. For over 20 years these differences divided the movement into two organizations: the American Woman Suffrage Association and the Stanton-Anthony National Woman Suffrage Association. After the National came around to the American's point of view, they united in 1890 as the National American Woman Suffrage Association. Thus, Howe's cautious strategy was adopted, though it would take another 30 years to get woman suffrage.

Howe died on Oct. 17, 1910. She is remembered chiefly for "The Battle Hymn," in some ways the least of her accomplishments. Yet there is justice in this. She wrote it to

help free the slaves; later it became the anthem of the woman suffrage movement. Even later it was used by civil rights workers. In 1968, when Senator Robert Kennedy's funeral train carried his body from New York to Washington, "The Battle Hymn" was sung as a dirge by mourners.

Further Reading

Julia Ward Howe's memoir, *Reminiscences, 1819-1899* (1899), is useful. The standard biography is Laura E. Richards and Maud Howe Elliott, *Julia Ward Howe* (2 vols., 1915). See also Louise Hall Tharp, *Three Saints and a Sinner: Julia Ward Howe, Louisa, Annie, and Sam Ward* (1956).

Additional Sources

Clifford, Deborah Pickman, *Mine eyes have seen the glory: a biography of Julia Ward Howe,* Boston: Little, Brown, 1979.

Grant, Mary Hetherington, *Private woman, public person: an account of the life of Julia Ward Howe from 1819-1868,* Brooklyn, N.Y.: Carlson Pub., 1994.

Richards, Laura Elizabeth Howe, *Julia Ward Howe, 1819-1910,* Atlanta, Ga.: Cherokee Pub. Co., 1990. □

Richard Howe

The British admiral Richard Howe, Earl Howe (1726-1799), commanded England's naval forces during the early years of the American Revolution and won the "First of June" victory over the French in 1794.

Richard Howe was born on March 8, 1726, in London. He entered the British navy at the age of 13 and saw service in the South Atlantic and the West Indies. By 1745 he had received his first command. In June 1755 he captured a French vessel off the mouth of the St. Lawrence River, thus firing the first formal exchange of the French and Indian War. On the death of his older brother in 1758, he became Viscount Howe in the Irish peerage. He served on the Admiralty Board and as treasurer of the navy. On the eve of the American Revolution, in 1775, he was advanced to the rank of vice admiral.

Howe and his younger brother, Gen. William Howe, played important parts in the American Revolution. They had a difficult mission: they were to crush the rebels militarily but also negotiate restoration of peace. The British armies, under William Howe, were generally successful in the summer and fall of 1776, but they failed to crush the colonial army. And the colonists, having declared independence in 1776, refused to negotiate on terms that implied willingness to submit to British control.

In 1776 and 1777 Richard Howe's fleet was limited to transporting and supplying the army under his brother's command. The admiral's only notable contribution came in August 1778, when his forces roughed up several French vessels, thus helping prevent a cooperative Franco-American attack on the British forces at Newport, R.I.

Frustrated by continuing American resistance, irked by criticism at home, and feeling he had not received adequate

support, Richard Howe resigned his command in October 1778. In the succeeding months a pamphlet war over the American Revolution was waged in England, culminating in an inconclusive parliamentary investigation. Meanwhile, Howe refused to serve under the existing ministry.

In 1782 Howe was granted a new command, promoted in rank, and made a British peer—Viscount Howe of Langar. These signs of confidence were justified by his relief of Gibraltar in October in the face of superior French numbers. From 1783 to 1788 he served as first lord of the Admiralty. He was created Earl Howe in 1788.

In 1793, after the start of the French Revolutionary Wars, Howe was put in command of the Channel fleet. The following year, when a French fleet attempted to prevent him from intercepting a convoy of provisions headed toward Brest from the United States, there occurred the series of high-sea engagements off Ushant collectively known as the "Battle of the Glorious First of June." The British victory, though not total, was great and caught the imagination of the public.

Howe helped negotiate a settlement in a naval mutiny at Spithead in 1797. He died on Aug. 5, 1799, in London.

Further Reading

The most thorough study of Howe in America is Troyer S. Anderson, *The Command of the Howe Brothers during the American Revolution* (1936). Most of the family papers were destroyed by fire. □

Samuel Gridley Howe

Samuel Gridley Howe (1801-1876), American physician and reformer, was a pioneer in educating the blind and a militant abolitionist.

Samuel Gridley Howe was born in Boston on Nov. 10, 1801. After studying at Brown, he received his medical degree from Harvard in 1824. He then set out for Greece to participate in the War for Independence against the Turks. He gave valorous service there, both as a soldier and surgeon, and stayed for 6 years, distributing American relief shipments and assisting Greek efforts to repair and improve the nation.

On a brief trip back to America, Howe published *Historical Sketch of the Greek Revolution* (1828). When he returned home again in 1831, he was hired by the state of Massachusetts to start a school for the blind. By 1832 he had opened a school in his home with six pupils. He got financial help from private philanthropists as well as from states surrounding Massachusetts.

By April 1833 Howe had established in Boston the New England Institution for the Education of the Blind. He taught that the blind should be treated with confidence rather than pity. He developed new and simpler devices for instructing blind children and innovated in finding inexpensive ways to print in raised letters. Howe himself authored textbooks on grammar, spelling, and geography. His annual reports on the work of the institution influenced other states to follow his example. His success with Laura Bridgeman, who was both blind and deaf, helped prove that persons with such challenges were not mentally inferior.

Howe joined many other reform movements. He advocated better public schools, better treatment of the insane, and reforms in the prisons. He was chairman of a group of Bostonians who opposed the Fugitive Slave Law by arming themselves to protect African American fugitives. He ran unsuccessfully for Congress as an antislavery candidate and was among those zealous New Englanders who worked to keep Kansas from permitting slavery and supported John Brown's raid on Harpers Ferry in 1859. During the Civil War and Reconstruction he served on national commissions and various agencies concerned with the conduct of the war and aid to freed slaves.

In 1843 Howe had married Julia Ward, who, during the Civil War, wrote the words for "The Battle Hymn of the Republic." Howe died on Jan. 9, 1876.

Further Reading

For a reliable scholarly biography of Howe see Harold Schwartz, *Samuel Gridley Howe: Social Reformer, 1801-1876* (1956). A more colorful story is Louise Hall Tharp, *Three Saints and a Sinner: Julia Ward Howe, Louisa, Annie, and Sam Ward* (1956), which tells of Julia Ward Howe's family. James M. McPherson, *The Struggle for Equality* (1964), is both scholarly and spirited in its interpretation of the abolitionist movement during the Civil War and Reconstruction. □

William Howe

William Howe, 5th Viscount Howe (1729-1814), was British army commander-in-chief in America during the early years of the Revolution.

William Howe was born on Aug. 10, 1729, the younger brother of the future admiral Richard Howe. After attending Eton, he entered the army at the age of 17. For the next 30 years he rose steadily in rank. He distinguished himself in the Canadian campaign of the French and Indian War. Serving under Gen. James Wolfe at the siege of Quebec in 1759, Howe in the succeeding year commanded the attack on Montreal. In 1762 he participated in the siege of Spanish-held Havana, Cuba. When the war was over, he had a brilliant record. He also enjoyed important family connections at court and by 1772 had been advanced to major general.

Commander in Chief in America

Howe also held political office. In 1758 he had been elected to a seat in the House of Commons. While he did not take an active role in Parliament debate, he made clear his opposition to the Foreign Ministry's American policy and declared that he would refuse to accept a command in the Colonies. Yet Howe did go to America in May 1775, explaining that "he was ordered, and could not refuse." His command of the British forces in the Battle of Bunker Hill displayed personal valor and a considerably greater degree of energy and decision than he would show later. By October, Howe had been given a local rank of full general and made commander-in-chief of the British army in the Colonies. Considerable controversy has always surrounded the roles played by William and Richard Howe during the Revolution, because in addition to commanding the military they were supposed to negotiate peace with the Americans.

Howe was forced to evacuate Boston in March 1776; he moved his troops by sea to New York. His invasion of Long Island and Manhattan included a series of tactical successes. But the long delays and ineffective pursuits that followed, though they mauled the American forces, left Gen. George Washington's retreating army intact.

British overconfidence, the dilatory movements of Gen. Howe, and the failure of Gen. Charles Cornwallis to catch the retreating Washington all contributed to a surprising turn of events at the end of 1776. Howe had left scattered forces occupying central New Jersey as far as the Delaware River. In a surprise attack on December 6, 1776, the Americans routed a garrison at Trenton, and then 8 days later triumphed in a full-scale battle at Princeton. Gen. Howe had lost another chance to destroy Washington, and 1776 ended on a note of rebel victory.

Again, in 1777, Howe's strategic failures resulted in reverses for the British. The grand British strategy that year involved a two-pronged attack against the Americans. First, Gen. John Burgoyne would move down from Canada into

New York to interrupt colonial communications, recruit Tory allies, and prepare for a later invasion of rebel strongholds. Second, Howe would move overland to engage the Continental Army in a contest for the American capital, Philadelphia. But Howe changed his mind, decided to bring his invading forces by water, wasted time maneuvering in New Jersey, and then spent nearly all of August at sea. Consequently, Howe's land movement toward Philadelphia did not begin until the end of August. A series of engagements—including British victories at Brandywine and Paoli—saw the British safely into the American capital. And American efforts to oust them were repulsed in early October.

Meanwhile, Howe was confronted with the decisive defeat of Gen. Burgoyne's troops at Saratoga. Burgoyne had earlier assured Howe of his ability to care for himself; and as a result, when he was besieged, there were no British forces near enough or large enough to rescue him. While the capture of Philadelphia did not really shake the Revolutionary cause, the defeat at Saratoga truly injured the British. It also made possible the Franco-American alliance of 1778.

Return to England

In October 1777, the month of Burgoyne's surrender, Howe offered his resignation. He then tried unsuccessfully to lure Washington into a general engagement. While Howe's army wintered in relative comfort in Philadelphia, Washington's men barely survived their encampment at Valley Forge. Howe finally received word that his resignation had been accepted and left Philadelphia in May 1778.

Back in England, Howe became involved in an inconclusive debate on the conduct of the war and published a defense, claiming that all his actions had been determined by military necessity, not by any desire to appease the colonists.

Howe went on to hold a variety of important military positions. He became a full general in 1793. When the wars of the French Revolution began, he held important commands in the north and then in the east of England. In 1799, on the death of his brother, Richard, he succeeded to the Irish title of viscount. Failing health forced him to retire from active office in 1803. He died in Plymouth on July 12, 1814.

Further Reading

Useful for information on Howe are Troyer S. Anderson, *The Command of the Howe Brothers during the American Revolution* (1936), and Piers Mackesy, *The War for America, 1775-1783* (1964). ☐

William Dean Howells

William Dean Howells (1837-1920), American writer and editor, was an influential critic and an important novelist of the late 19th century.

William Dean Howells's career spanned a period of radical change in American literature; as novelist, critic, and editor, he contributed greatly to those changes. An advocate of honesty and social responsibility in literature, he led the struggle against escapist fantasy and for realistic and morally and politically committed fiction.

Howells was born March 1, 1837, at Martin's Ferry, Ohio. His father was a country printer and journalist who displayed the best American frontier traits—independence, self-reliance, and conscience. William spent scarcely a year in the classroom, but his father's offices afforded a thorough and meaningful education. In *Years of My Youth* (1916) Howells recalled his earliest training: "I could set type very well, and at ten years and onward till journalism became my university, the printing office was mainly my school."

When William was 3 the family moved to Hamilton—the delightful book *A Boy's Town* (1890) records experiences there. The family moved to Dayton when he was 11 and, after a memorable year in a log cabin, to Columbus when he was 13. Two years later the elder Howells became editor of the *Ashtabula Sentinel*. During these years young Howells taught himself German, French, Spanish, and some Latin; he became conversant with great poets, especially Shakespeare, and grew to love such prose masterpieces as *Don Quixote*. By 1857, when he returned to Columbus to work as a political reporter, Howells had acquired a truly liberal education.

Author and Propagandist

Howells inherited his father's strong abolitionist convictions. These are reflected in the narrative poem "The Pilot's Story," a pathetic account of a slave girl's suicide, which was one of several of Howells's poems published by the *Atlantic Monthly* in 1860. More important, he wrote an official campaign biography supporting the Republican candidates in the 1860 election. The *Lives and Speeches of Abraham Lincoln and Hannibal Hamlin* may have helped elect Lincoln and change the history of America; it unquestionably changed Howells's personal history.

Though Howells saw many friends marching off to fight in the Civil War, he had little interest in joining them. He had applied for a diplomatic appointment and was finally given Venice. The months before his departure were important; traveling east, he met some of America's most important writers: James Russell Lowell, Nathaniel Hawthorne, and Ralph Waldo Emerson in Massachusetts; Walt Whitman in New York. Returning to Columbus, he met Elinor Mead, a young woman who was visiting her cousin, Rutherford B. Hayes. They were married in 1862 and sustained a happy relationship for 48 years.

Howells's Italian experiences, together with his discovery of the comedies of the 18th-century dramatist Carlo Goldoni, turned him from poetry to prose, from romance to realism, and from provincial to cosmopolitan subjects. Some of his best fiction would treat Americans in Italy, but the first fruits of his foreign residence were travel sketches, published in American periodicals, and a graceful volume of impressions, *Venetian Life* (1866), which went through a score of editions in his lifetime.

Career as Editor

Howells returned to America with his wife and infant daughter in 1865. He accepted an editorial post on the *Nation* in New York, but his ambition was to live in Boston and work on the *Atlantic Monthly*. In January 1866 the offer came, and Howells's 14-year association with the country's most respected magazine began. He served as assistant editor until 1871 and as editor in chief to 1881. His literary judgments soon dominated the *Atlantic,* which he transformed from a regional to a national magazine. He published the work of talented local-color writers from every part of the country: Sarah Orne Jewett, Edward Eggleston, Bret Harte, and many more. He featured works of fellow pioneers of the new realism and important writings of two of his closest friends, Henry James and Mark Twain. Neither of those giants could abide the other's writings; Howells could admire, help, and learn from both. Both writers had reason to be grateful for the enthusiastic reviews. Howells published in the *Atlantic:* James because his difficult prose might otherwise have attracted no audience at all, Twain because his humorous tales might have appealed only to the uncultivated if they had not borne the imprimatur of the *Atlantic.*

Howells's relation with Twain has given rise to some controversy; hostile critics claimed that he censored or bowdlerized the works of his exuberant friend. In fact, Howells was a remarkably helpful editor and critic for Twain, as he was for many lesser writers. An honorary master of arts degree from Harvard University (1867) and an appointment there as university lecturer (1869-1871) were recognition of Howells's self-taught attainments. He was later offered professorships at Johns Hopkins University and at Harvard but was not attracted to the academic life.

Career as Novelist

In 1871 Howells published his first novel, *Their Wedding Journey*. The book follows Basil and Isabel March on their honeymoon trip from Boston to Quebec. Basil is Howells only slightly disguised; Isabel is Mrs. Howells. These two characters appear again and again in Howells's fiction, usually at some distance from the center of the action. Throughout his career, Howells treated his characters with a gentle irony that at once humanizes them and calls attention to their weaknesses. Howells was honest with everyone, most of all with himself.

The novels Howells published in the next 10 years were consistently good but, with the exception of *The Undiscovered Country* (1880), they are low-key and perhaps a little drab. In these years he was reading and praising European realists, especially the Russian novelist Ivan Turgenev, who confirmed many ideas Howells had already come to: for example, that character counts for more than action in fiction, and that dialogue, not exposition, should carry the burden of a novel. These ideas were revealed in Howells's first major novel, *A Modern Instance* (1882), the tragic story of an impossible marriage that ends in divorce. This was the first compassionate treatment in American fiction of the problems of a divorced woman.

In 1881 Howells resigned his editorship of the *Atlantic* and in 1882 took his wife and three children to Europe for a year. Of the novels of the 1880s *The Rise of Silas Lapham* (1885) is the most famous. In this story of a self-made man who tries to buy social position in Boston for his country-bred family, Howells broadened his scope to include characters of a variety of backgrounds and classes. In *The Minister's Charge* (1887) Howells for the first time introduced the concept of "complicity"—the responsibility everyone shares for each individual's deeds. While he was writing the book in 1886, a bomb exploded during a political meeting in Chicago's Haymarket. There were casualties, and a group of anarchists was charged—falsely, it appeared—with murder. Howells was shocked and took a leading part in a national campaign for justice for the unpopular anarchists, but justice was denied.

Howells's awareness of social and class injustice and of each man's complicity in such injustice was strengthened by his reading of another Russian novelist, Leo Tolstoy, whose influence is apparent in the structure of *A Hazard of New Fortunes* (1890). In this book the Marches (like the Howellses) have moved to New York; a newly rich family is seeking social acceptance; a journalist is seeking a magazine that will give him editorial freedom; and class is trying to speak to class, region to region, generation to generation. The novel is compassionate, humane, and tragic. Other social problems also engaged Howells's attention. In the impressive novella *An Imperative Duty* (1892), he argued eloquently against racism at a moment when his readers were turning rapidly toward white supremacist doctrines. He presented his ideas of a good society, essentially socialistic and libertarian, in the long tale *A Traveler from Altruria* (1894).

Literary Critic

In 1886 Howells had begun the regular review column, "Editor's Study," in *Harper's*. He moved this column from one magazine to another during the 1890s, returning to *Harper's* in 1900. His reviews consistently recognized the best in contemporary literature. He was the first critic of note to praise Stephen Crane and the only important critic to review Emily Dickinson's poems with real appreciation. The principles of his literary judgments are set out in *Criticism and Fiction* (1891), a work of enduring importance. *My Literary Passions* (1895), *Heroines of Fiction* (1901), and *My Mark Twain* (1910) are other critical works of interest.

Every conceivable honor came to Howells (known as "the Dean") in the last 20 years of his life—honorary doctorates, the first presidency of the American Academy of Arts and Letters, and the most practical of prizes, a library edition of his own writings (1911). In 1916 he published *The Leatherwood God*, a powerful analysis of religious frenzy on the early American frontier, and in 1920 *The Vacation of the Kelwyns*, a "summer idyll" rich in wisdom, humor, and sadness. The book is in every way Howells's, but the title was the publisher's, for the novelist had died in New York City on May 11, 1920, before its publication.

Further Reading

The literary situation in Howells's America is well delineated in his *Literary Friends and Acquaintance* (1900). Among his other memoirs are *My Year in a Log Cabin* (1893) and *Impressions and Experiences* (1896). Edwin H. Cady's *The Road to Realism* (1956) and *The Realist at War* (1958) together constitute the best biography of Howells. Kenneth S. Lynn, *William Dean Howells: An American Life* (1971), is another excellent choice. Clara M. Kirk and Rudolf Kirk, *William Dean Howells* (1962), is an impressive shorter study combining biography and criticism. Van Wyck Brook, *Howells: His Life and World* (1959), is impressionistic but valuable. Kermit Vanderbilt, *The Achievement of William Dean Howells* (1968), reinterprets the major novels convincingly. Howells is placed in the context of his time in Larzer Ziff's excellent *The American 1890s* (1966).

Additional Sources

Alexander, William Raymond Hall, *William Dean Howells, the realist as humanist,* New York, N.Y.: B. Franklin, 1981.

Cady, Edwin Harrison, *The realist at war: the mature years, 1885-1920, of William Dean Howells,* Westport, Conn.: Greenwood Press, 1986.

Cady, Edwin Harrison, *The road to realism: the early years, 1837-1885, of William Dean Howells,* Westport, Conn.: Greenwood Press, 1986, 1956.

Cady, Edwin Harrison, *Young Howells & John Brown: episodes in a radical education,* Columbus: Ohio State University Press, 1985.

Cook, Don Lewis, *William Dean Howells: the Kittery years,* Kittery Point, Me.: William Dean Howells Memorial Committee, 1991.

Crowley, John William, *The black heart's truth: the early career of W.D. Howells,* Chapel Hill: University of North Carolina, 1985.

Howells, William Dean, *Years of my youth, and three essays,* Bloomington, Indiana University Press, 1975.

The mask of fiction: essays on W.D. Howells, Amherst: University of Massachusetts Press, 1989.

Olsen, Rodney D., *Dancing in chains: the youth of William Dean Howells,* New York: New York University Press, 1991. □

William White Howells

William White Howells (born 1908) was an American anthropologist specializing in human evolution and variation. A major focus of his researches was the anthropology of Oceania.

William White Howells was born on November 27, 1908, in New York City, the son of the architect John Mead Howells (1868-1959) and the grandson of William Dean Howells (1837-1920), the literary critic, novelist, and close friend and adviser of Samuel Clements (Mark Twain). After attending St. Paul's School in Concord, New Hampshire, he entered Harvard University, where he studied anthropology under Earnest Albert Hooton (1877-1954), and in 1934 he received the Ph.D.

degree in physical anthropology for his dissertation. *The Peopling of Melanesia as indicated by cranial evidence from the Bismarck Archipelago.*

Following a period as a research associate at the American Museum of Natural History in New York (1934-1939), Howells was appointed assistant professor in the then Department of Sociology and Anthropology at the University of Wisconsin (Madison). In 1943 he was commissioned a lieutenant in the U.S. Navy and assigned to Naval Intelligence (Far East Division) in Washington, D.C. He returned to Wisconsin in 1946 as an associate professor and was made a full professor of anthropology there in 1948. He left Wisconsin in 1954, upon succeeding Hooton as professor of anthropology at Harvard University. After 1974 he was anthropologist emeritus at Harvard.

A particular characteristic of academic anthropology in America is the blending of its biological, social, and archaeological elements into a uniquely holistic science. While its practitioners receive this all-encompassing view of the discipline in their training, the vast majority, inevitably, succumb to specialization; few aspire successfully to dominate the entire field. Howells, however, distinguished himself by writing critically acclaimed texts in the three sub-areas of anthropology, and as such he was justly regarded as outstanding both as a general anthropologist and as a physical anthropologist.

While at Wisconsin Howells produced three of his most successful and influential books, namely *Mankind So Far* (1944), *The Heathens* (1948), and *Back of History* (1954), which reflect the breadth of his anthropological knowledge and interests. During the same period he became involved in the affairs of national organizations such as the American Association of Physical Anthropologists (AAPA), as well as the American Anthropological Association (AAA) and Section H of the American Association for the Advancement of Science. Between 1939 and 1943 he served as secretary-treasurer of the AAPA, and from 1949 to 1954 as editor of its publication, the *American Journal of Physical Anthropology.* In 1951 he was elected president of the AAA. He also played an active role in the affairs of the Division of Anthropology and Psychology of the National Research Council and was later a member of the first advisory panel for anthropology (Division of Biological and Medical Sciences) of the National Science Foundation.

It is possible to identify two major research foci within the wide range of Howells' anthropological interests: the anthropology of Oceania and general human evolution. With regard to the first, Howells, after his student years, gathered large amounts of metrical data on cranial series from Oceania as well as other regions of the world in an effort to shed light on the question of the origin and variation of Pacific populations. Between 1966 and 1972 he participated in the Harvard Solomon Islands Project and was responsible for conducting an intensive study of the medical and biological variation of several native communities, such as Lau Lagoon and Baegu. Drawing on the results of his own researches and those of other workers in physical anthropology, as well as the discoveries of recent archaeological and linguistic investigations, he published in 1973 a major synthesis of the prehistory of the Pacific region: *The Pacific Islanders.* His later work involved multivariate analysis of cranial series in studies of the origins of the Chinese (1983) and the Japanese and Polynesians (1981).

As these and related studies indicate, Howells throughout his career gave critical attention to the improvement of methods applied to the study of both skeletal and living populations. Drawing attention to the need for more reliable analytical techniques in anthropometry, he began with the demonstration in the early 1950s of how factorial analysis may be applied to anthropometric data to specify parameters of components making up the human physique. Later in the decade he applied this approach to the problem of variation in cranial morphology and showed that "10 measurements account for virtually all of the correlation in the cranial vault proper." Shortly thereafter he turned to multivariate analysis and embarked on a long-range program of research to determine racial affiliation of human crania and their respective ranges of variation. This work culminated with the publication of his book *Cranial Variation in Man* (1973).

Since then, he has published *Skull Shapes and the Map* (1989); *Getting Here: The Story of Human Evolution* (1993); and *Who's Who in Skulls* (1995). He received the Charles R. Darwin Lifetime Achievement award in 1992.

Intimately interwoven with the above studies was Howells' ongoing interest in the topic of general human evolution. Here he focused on the question of the origins of anatomically modern (a.m.) humans, and in particular on the issue of whether all living populations had a single origin (in the late Pleistocene), or whether they evolved in many different regions from local archaic populations. In contrast to the views of such workers as Franz Weidenreich (1873-1948) and Carleton Coon (1904-1981), who argued for an essentially polycentric origin for a.m. *Homo sapiens* (1976), Howells contended that the variation of recent people is primarily the result of dispersion from a common source. In taking this position, he was critical of the idea of a polytypic Neanderthal stage as the antecedent to modern humans. While acknowledging the possibility of some admixture between Neanderthals and essentially a.m. *Homo sapiens* populations of the Upper Paleolithic (as indicated by the presence of Neanderthaloid features among the Skhul skeletons) Howells considered this admixture as modest—if at all. The presence of such traits at Skhul have been taken by some workers as evidence of direct descent from Neanderthals or of hybridization with Neanderthals. Commenting on this, Howells wrote: "Though it is entirely likely that Neanderthal genes survive, general aspects of facial and cranial shape fail completely to sustain either idea. In fact, multivariate analysis of measurements makes a strong distinction between Neanderthals and modern crania." (*Evolution of the Genus Homo,* 1973)

Howells received a number of prestigious awards, including the Wenner-Gren Viking Medal in physical anthropology (1955), the AAA Distinguished Service Award (1978), and the Société d'Anthropologie de Paris Broca Prix du Centennaire (1980). He also received honorary doctorates.

Further Reading

Although there is no biographical study of William Howells, some background information (including a bibliography covering the period 1934-1975) can be found in the introduction to a festschrift marking his retirement from Harvard, written by colleagues and former students, entitled "The Measure of a Man: William White Howells." This volume was published in 1976 under the title *The Measure of Man: Methodologies in Biological Anthropology,* edited by Eugene Giles and Jonathan S. Friedlaender. A brief evaluation of Howells' osteometric work can be found in T. D. Stewart, *Essentials of Forensic Anthropology* (1979); see also F. Spencer (editor), *A History of American Physical Anthropology, 1930-1980* (1982). References to Howells' paleoanthropological studies can also be found in this latter work and in F. H. Smith and F. Spencer (editors), *The Origin of Modern Humans* (1984). □